This is the third and final volume of Anthony Emery's magisterial survey, *Greater Medieval Houses of England and Wales, 1300–1500*. The late middle ages was the first great era of house building in England and Wales. The many surviving residences were often a consequence of social aspiration and financial good fortune, but frequently also a reflection of political, economic, and regional circumstances. Together, these houses stand as a vital mirror of everyday life during the two centuries before the Tudors.

Across the three volumes Emery has examined afresh and reassessed nearly 700 houses, the first comprehensive review of the subject for 150 years. Covered are the full range of leading homes, from royal and episcopal palaces to smaller manor houses and more modest residences, as well as relevant community buildings such as academic colleges, monastic granges, and secular colleges of canons.

This third volume surveys southern England and is divided into three regions, each of which is given a separate historical and architectural introduction. Included throughout the volume are thematic essays prompted by key buildings, addressing subjects as varied as household lodgings, the defence of southern England during the Hundred Years' War, and medieval furnishings. The text is complemented throughout by a wide range of plans and diagrams and a wealth of photographs showing the present condition of almost every house discussed.

For the general and academic reader alike, nearly every page offers fresh insights into both well-known and lesser-known houses, including many never before described. The richness of the subject and the author's probing analysis of early houses across the country make this volume – and the series – an essential source for anyone interested in the history, architecture, and culture of medieval England and Wales.

GREATER MEDIEVAL
HOUSES OF
ENGLAND AND WALES
1300–1500

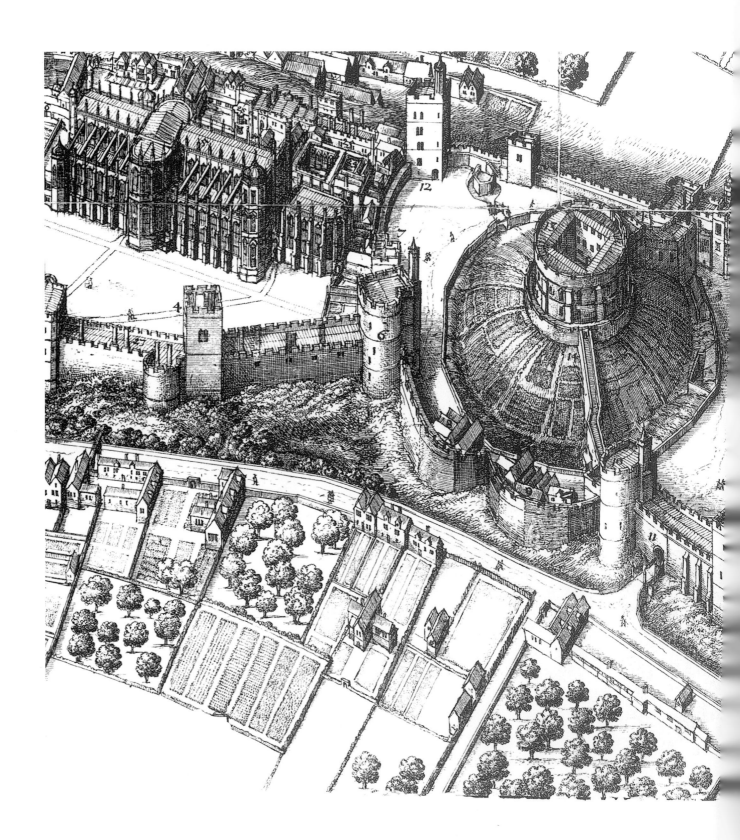

GREATER
MEDIEVAL
HOUSES OF
ENGLAND
AND WALES

1300–1500

Volume III

SOUTHERN ENGLAND

ANTHONY EMERY

CAMBRIDGE
UNIVERSITY PRESS

CAMBRIDGE UNIVERSITY PRESS
Cambridge, New York, Melbourne, Madrid, Cape Town, Singapore, São Paulo

Cambridge University Press
The Edinburgh Building, Cambridge, CB2 2RU, UK

Published in the United States of America by Cambridge University Press, New York

www.cambridge.org
Information on this title: www.cambridge.org/9780521581325

First published 2006

Printed in the United Kingdom at the University Press, Cambridge

A catalogue record for this publication is available from the British Library

Library of Congress Cataloguing in Publication data

ISBN-13   978-0-521-58132-5 hardback
ISBN-10   0-521-58132-X hardback

Frontispiece Windsor Castle: Upper Ward by Wenceslas Hollar (*c.*1659)

To John

CONTENTS

ACKNOWLEDGEMENTS

NEITHER this nor the previous volumes on medieval houses could have been written without the wholehearted co-operation and support of their owners and occupiers, who have been extremely generous in allowing me to explore occupied and unoccupied rooms, open cupboards, climb into their roofs, and discuss the changes and problems many of them face in maintaining their properties today. Most owners have most generously given me total freedom of access, while only three custodians – those of Shirburn Castle, Creslow Manor House and Bratton Court – have refused internal access. Even so, their houses were of sufficient importance to warrant inclusion after external documentary, and photographic examination. The properties in south-east England were visited in 1988–9 with revision in 2002–3, while the remainder were assessed between 1998 and 2004. In order to respect individual privacy, no owners have been identified, but without their unstinting co-operation this volume would not have been possible.

The text has benefited considerably from the input made by Steven Brindle (Windsor Castle), Nicholas Cooper (Shute), Jeffrey Cushman (Lustleigh Old Hall), Nicholas Deas (Kingston Seymour Manor House), Mark Girouard (Wardour Castle), John Goodall (Shirburn Castle), Mansell Jagger and the late Nicholas Moore (South Charford Manor), Barry Jones (Greys Court), Peter E. Leach (Ightham Mote), Patric Morrissey (Forde Abbey), Sarah Pearson (Nettlestead Place), Dorothy Presswell (Powderham Castle), Nigel Thomas (Cotehele), and John Winstone (Clevedon Court, Tickenham Court). Several owners have also added considerably to the quality of the text on their residences by comments and suggestions, including Lord Camoys, Lord Saye and Sele, Alaister Cobb, Robert Floyd, Geoffrey Gilbert, and Gerald Yorke. I am particularly grateful to Jayne Semple, who contributed the entry on Old Soar Manor, to Professor Norman Pounds for his advice, and to Dr Charles Coulson for allowing me to use his lists of licences to crenellate. None of the above is responsible for the errors that remain.

The illustrations have been drawn from a wide range of sources with the majority of photographs taken by myself. I have also prepared all the maps, plans, and diagrams except for the two plans of Berkeley Castle. Caren Knight gallantly transcribed my typed, rewritten, and overwritten manuscripts to produce an excellent clean text for the publishers.

My family and friends across the region provided a spread of hospitality which made travelling much more pleasurable, but my greatest debt is to John Feldman. A volume on this scale takes several years of research, writing, and cross-referencing. The three volumes have spanned a total of eighteen years and their completion would not have been possible without the support, quiet encouragement, chauffeuring, and balanced environment conducive to seeing the project through to completion. If the raw material has been made available by the generosity of house owners, then any textual quality has been essentially based on John's unfailing enthusiasm and ability to bolster the author's energy levels as the scale of the trilogy unfurled. Without his support, this volume would have been a distant prospect.

ABBREVIATIONS

Antiq. Jour.   *Antiquaries Journal*
Arch. Cant.   *Archaeologia Cantiana*
Arch. Hist.   *Architectural History*
Arch. Jour.   *Archaeological Journal*
Berks. Arch. Jour.   *Berkshire Archaeological Journal*
Berks., Bucks. and Oxon. Arch. Jour.   *Berkshire, Buckinghamshire*
     and Oxfordshire Archaeological Journal
Bod. Lib.   Bodleian Library, Oxford
Brit. Lib.   British Library, London
Brit. Mus.   British Museum, London
Bull. Inst. Hist. Res.   *Bulletin of the Institute of Historical Research*
Cal. Charter Rolls   *Calendar of Charter Rolls*
Cal. Inq. Misc.   *Calendar of Inquisitions Miscellaneous*
Cal. Inq. P.M.   *Calendar of Inquisitions Post Mortem*
Cal. Pat. Rolls   *Calendar of Patent Rolls*
Com. Peer.   *The Complete Peerage* ed. G. E. Cockayne *et al.*
     (1910–59)
Cornish Arch.   *Cornish Archaeology*
Croydon Nat. Hist. and Sc. Soc.   *Croydon Natural History and*
     Scientific Society
Devon Arch. Soc.   *Devon Archaeological Society*
Eng. Hist. Rev.   *English History Review*
Eng. Med. Arch.   *English Medieval Architects* by J. Harvey (2nd
     edn 1984)
Eng. Med. House   *The English Medieval House* by M. Wood (1965)
Greater Med. Houses   *Greater Medieval Houses of England and Wales*
     by A. Emery, I (1996), II (2000)
HKW   *The History of the King's Works* ed. H. M. Colvin *et al.*, I
     and II (1963), III and IV (1982)
Itinerary   *Itinerary* by John Leland, ed. L. T. Smith, 5 vols. (1901)
Jour. Brit. Arch. Assoc.   *Journal of the British Archaeological*
     Association
Jour. Inst. Cornish Studies   *Journal of the Institute of Cornish*
     Studies
Jour. Roy. Inst. Cornwall   *Journal of the Royal Institute of Cornwall*
Jour. Soc. Arch. Hist.   *Journal of the Society of Architectural History*
London Arch.   *London Archaeologist*
Med. Arch.   *Medieval Archaeology*
NMRC   National Monuments Record Centre, Swindon
Northampton Archit. & Arch. Soc.   *Northampton Architectural and*
     Archaeological Society
Nott. Med. Studies   *Nottingham Medieval Studies*
Oxford Hist. Soc.   *Oxford Historical Society*
PRO   Public Record Office, Richmond
Proc. Devon Arch. Soc.   *Proceedings of the Devon Archaeological*
     Society

Proc. Devon Arch. Exploration Soc. *Proceedings of the Devon Archaeological Exploration Society*

Proc. Dorset N. H. and A. S. C. *Proceedings of the Dorset Natural History and Archaeological Society*

Proc. Hampshire F. C. and A. Soc. *Proceedings of the Hampshire Field Club and Archaeological Society*

Proc. Somerset Arch. and N. H. Soc. *Proceedings of the Somerset Archaeological and Natural History Society*

RAI Royal Archaeological Institute

RCAHM Royal Commission on the Ancient and Historical Monuments of Wales

RCHM Royal Commission on the Historical Monuments of England

Rec. of Bucks. *Records of Buckinghamshire*

Somerset Rec. Soc. *Somerset Record Society*

South Midlands Arch. *South Midlands Archaeology*

Surrey Arch. Coll. *Surrey Archaeological Collections*

Sussex Arch. Coll. *Sussex Archaeological Collections*

Trans. Anc. Mon. Soc. *Transactions of the Ancient Monuments Society*

Trans. Bristol & Glos. Arch. Soc. *Transactions of the Bristol and Gloucestershire Archaeological Society*

Trans. Devon. Assoc. *Transactions of the Devonshire Association*

Trans. Essex Arch. Soc. *Transactions of the Essex Archaeological Society*

Trans. London & Middx Arch. Soc. *Transactions of the London and Middlesex Archaeological Society*

Trans. Newbury Dist. F. C. *Transactions of the Newbury and District Field Club*

Trans. Roy. Hist. Soc. *Transactions of the Royal Historical Society*

V & A Victoria and Albert Museum, London

VCH Victoria County History

Vern. Arch. *Vernacular Architecture*

WCAS Winchester College Archaeological Society

Wilts. Arch. and N. H. Mag. *Wiltshire Archaeological and Natural History Magazine*

INTRODUCTION

N O new cathedrals were built in England or Wales after 1250, and few monasteries were established between that time and their dissolution 300 years later. The castles of Edward I in North Wales were almost the last fortresses to be erected in this country before the advent of Henry VIII's coastal forts and blockhouses. A considerable number of churches were extended or rebuilt during the later middle ages but they conformed in plan and liturgical function to those of an earlier age. On the other hand, houses had begun to take a recognisable form during the twelfth and thirteenth centuries which reached fulfilment as a prism of society during the following two centuries. They reflected the spread of wealth, the rise of new families, social differentiation, and the organisation and growth of household institutions. Out of the one and a half thousand medieval houses that have survived in England and Wales, nearly 700 are described in these three volumes.[1] They stand as testimony to the first great age of domestic architecture, for that was not an achievement of the Tudors but a development of Plantaganet society between 1300 and 1500. It is these houses that lie at the heart of architectural and related institutional development during the later middle ages.

The crown, the aristocracy, and the gentry of medieval England were the movers and shakers of society. What they did, and how they did it, at national, regional, and local levels affected the government, the economy, the welfare, and the social justice or injustice of the country at all levels of society. It also determined the character, taste, and standards of society, and their homes are the visible witness to those standards.

Innovations in house design and layout occurred in residences of the ruling class. The crown and the aristocracy had the financial means and the need to encourage the necessary developments. Changes were gradual rather than dramatic, but once a technical improvement or social enhancement had been achieved, it was usually swiftly followed by people of the same social scale. Furthermore, there was considerable mobility of craftsmen throughout the later middle ages, capable of adapting or modifying recent technical developments or the greater residential scale demanded by a client. There was therefore a fairly rapid 'trickle down' effect from high-status buildings. Leading members of society were able to call upon the services of architectural practioners who not only served regionally distinguished patrons but might well carry out royal commissions. During the late fourteenth century, the master-mason John Lewyn was as important in the north of England as William Wynford in the south-west or Henry Yevele in south-east England. Such people travelled considerable distances to give their advice or submit designs for a new project. Consequently, stylistic developments and architectural innovations

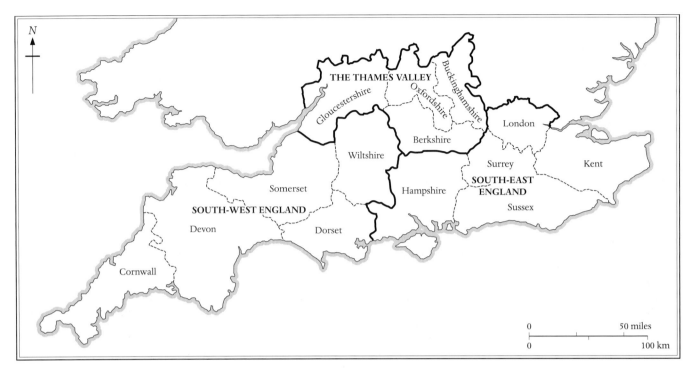

FIGURE I The region covered in volume III

spread rapidly, contrary to the commonly held assumption that the further houses lay from the metropolis, the more old-fashioned they became. Enough contracts survive to show that kings, magnates, leading prelates, and élite gentry had a very clear idea of what they wanted in the way of building requirements and laid down precise parameters. Palace-fortresses and large houses were not built from off-the-peg designs but were a reflection of the personal lifestyle and individual needs of the patron.

The consequences were threefold. The houses of England and Wales display very considerable individuality. They follow the basic components of residential planning – hall, chamber, and services – but with variety and character. They made a visual and symbolic statement befitting the owner's rank, with their form and planning determined by military or defensive factors, social status, domestic comfort, ceremonial setting, circulation patterns, and the need for privacy. Yet no two houses are alike, even when built for the same patron or by the same master-mason.

These houses reveal something of the career, taste, and financial resources of the owner. The availability of funds helped to determine the scale and quality of the residence and the standard of decoration and content. A house can also indicate the size of the patron's patrimony, his political and social standing, and the scope of his household. It is a living organism expressing his needs and habits as well as those of his descendants, for most houses are subject to the changes and modifications of later generations. In distinguishing those changes, you also see the aspirations and culture of later periods – whether of the fifteenth, seventeenth, or nineteenth century – as well as those of the originator. More precisely, houses reflect the temper, the fears, and the ebullience of the years when they were constructed or modified.

A house is essentially the framework to provide living space, so that, apart from its form, the use made of that space is a primary function of the building. This flows from an understanding of the organisation of a household, how the occupants lived, and how the demands for greater privacy were met through the planning function. Churches were built for contemplation, prayer, and ceremony – an envelope for reflecting on the infinite wisdom and wonders of God. Greater houses were built to induce awe, to declare status, and to accommodate the owner's family and his household. Neither were built for the contemplation of architectural historians. Houses were living units, sometimes with decorative features and increasingly so as the middle ages progressed. Earlier historians have been prone to concentrate on architectural analysis and detailing in preference to working from the residence's initial function and purpose, so that my approach has embraced different tenets:

- House development did not occur in a vacuum but as a consequence of political, social, economic, and financial factors. Hence the historical introductions and the references to the contemporary milieu in many individual house assessments.

- Domestic architecture was not a single stream of technical development, emanating from some central but unspecified source. It was a series of eddies – with regional centres – which interrelated and spread to a greater or lesser extent. They were most obvious in Durham, Winchester, and London during the later fourteenth century and in Exeter, Shrewsbury, and Cheshire in the later fifteenth century. These volumes have been divided on a regional basis to help point up some of these local movements.

- Across this movement was a contrary one based on personal relationships and the networking of friends. The royal court, parliament, and private households were obvious channels of intercommunication where senior churchmen, leading nobles, and courtiers could discuss their building plans and influence each other, as the royal court did during the mid-fourteenth century, or the friends of Ralph, Lord Cromwell and succeeding treasurers of England in the mid-fifteenth century. The same interrelationship can be seen between the greater and lesser gentry as they served local administrative interests. Hence the thematic essays on tower-houses, lodging ranges, and trophy houses.

- Houses were the framework accommodating the household, the family, and their support staff, of different social rank under the same roof. The major concern of architectural historians with architectural detailing has obscured the fundamental purpose of medieval house development – social distinction, greater privacy, and more elaborate lifestyles. Some of the essays embrace these considerations, including those on licences to crenellate, secular art, and the impact of the Hundred Years' War on English houses.

- We have usually lost the immediate environment of any medieval residence. In recent years, the study of monastic establishments has turned from the church and claustral buildings to those of the outer court. This has yet to extend to the greater houses where the buildings and enclosure were frequently timber-framed and modest. But the larger picture extends to the adjacent landscape, though post-medieval developments, changing taste, and fashion have replaced or destroyed the gardens and parklands that were frequently an adjunct to such properties. Within the last few years, landscaping and setting have been given more weight, particularly in castle studies, while the archaeological examination of early gardens has become a specialist discipline. But we still need to try and establish why a patron chose a particular location or how he modified it to meet his particular needs. Why did John Holand, earl of Huntingdon, build Dartington Hall so far from the royal court, and to what extent did he develop the previous house or landscape the grounds close to his residence?

- If houses are the means to protect the family unit, then they need to be considered in the broader context of comparable residential institutions – contemporary educational foundations, secular colleges of priests, monastic granges and lodgings – with their comparable structural and functional components.

Like most disciplines, that of architectural history never stands still. That is what makes it so fascinating. Studies like this are simply snapshots of appreciation and understanding at a particular time. They will undoubtedly be challenged or confirmed, though there is a danger when the most recent critical appraisal is automatically considered to be the most reliable one. On the one hand, studies change with fashion, personal enthusiasm, or tendentious views (as with military architecture). On the other hand, new documentary sources are uncovered, greater academic precision is applied, technological developments are harnessed, and reassessments made leading to new perspectives (and prejudices). Examples have arisen during the course of preparing this trilogy. In volume I, my view that Markenfield Hall was a single build of c.1310 was queried by a correspondent who pointed out that there are some architectural features that suggest the incorporation of a thirteenth-century structure. I agree with him.[2] Since volume II was published, the dendrochronology analysis of Baddesley Clinton has brought some much-needed precision to this essentially Tudor house with only a small standing part credited to 1458–9.[3] While I was preparing volume III, an even more radical review was made of Acton Court,

highlighting how the interpretation of an apparently straightforward house can totally change. Within a few years, a house attributed to the early seventeenth century, and essentially considered to be of one build with some jaded classical detail,[4] proved to be a complex medieval site with a sequence of standing structures initiated for a visit by Henry VIII and Anne Boleyn in 1535 and developed piecemeal during the mid-sixteenth century rather than to a pre-ordained plan. The new ranges were innovatory, structurally and decoratively, and were the precursor of the Elizabethan style. Yet the site retained several medieval buildings to create a vital link bridging the formative years of post-medieval architecture.[5] None of this is likely to have been appreciated had Acton Court continued to remain in occupation. At how many other houses would such a revealing study be possible if family use did not inhibit such thorough examination? And in this particular instance, the proposed 'redevelopment' programme by a developer in 1984 included pulling down the internal partition with the rarest wall paintings (at that stage unknown), multi-room division, new windows, no site excavation, and the construction of four private houses within the immediate grounds. I have no doubt that some of the other houses in this volume will similarly reveal a more complex development history during the next century or so.

As in the previous volumes, secular cathedral closes, town houses, and vernacular properties have not been covered as they warrant separate study, while the opening and closing dates of the later middle ages have been generously interpreted. The three regions of southern England embrace the pre-1974 county boundaries, with the property assessments prefaced by short historical and architectural introductions. Relevant houses serve as an introduction to the essays covering broader aspects of domestic architecture. Thornbury Castle introduces one on household lodgings, the defences added to Amberley Castle and Halnaker House lead to a consideration of the impact of the Hundred Years' War on English houses, while the wall paintings at Cothay and Fiddleford Manor initiate a discussion on medieval secular art. Regional bibliographies are selective while those listed under a property are limited to publications which contribute to our knowledge of that building.

Visiting a substantial body of houses over an eighteen-year period has been a joy, but it has not been without some limitations. In his introduction to *Castles* in 1926, Sir Charles Oman told intending visitors that they must not attempt to present themselves at a property as the resident owner might be giving a garden party, holding a political meeting, or offering lunch to his tenants.[6] I have never experienced any of these activities taking place. Owners are often at business, frequently in London, helping with farm or estate maintenance, or organising the opening of the house to the public. Their wives are either driving the children to or from school, maintaining the garden, or cooking for visitors. Permanent staff are rare: part-time staff are precious and few in number. Some houses have been converted into hotels, schools, or holiday homes, while others are in multi-occupation. Even so, I have been overwhelmed by the house standards maintained and the love given to so many properties. The great majority I have visited are still inhabited, with rooms in regular use, beds made and slept in, and kitchens adapted with modern facilities. In more than a handful of properties, I have finished my visit with a headache after losing count of the number of rooms examined and making notes on the extent and sometimes contradictory nature of the surviving evidence. For you are privileged to see areas where visitors rarely penetrate, examine roofs, and scour cellars (nearly all post-medieval though Hunsdon was a welcome exception) in the hope of finding earlier structures.

There are few pleasures greater than privacy and I have been most privileged to intrude on it. The amount of time I have been able to spend examining a property therefore depended entirely on the wishes of the owner. I have had to cover a number of houses in less than an hour, walking behind the owner while scribbling at a rate of knots as we move through an environment never before seen by an architectural historian. Usually owners have been most generous with their time, and at some of the largest properties I have been allowed to stay for days. There have been occasional restrictions. I have not taken interior photographs. The exceptions have been few and with permission. Owners are equally cautious about the preparation of floor plans. Some ask that they should not be published, while others only allow a skeleton outline. Occasionally, one or two rooms have been excluded from a visit, for security has become of paramount importance since the 1970s.

Owners and architectural historians see houses in a different light from each other, but there are also other approaches. The engravings of the Buck brothers encouraged the appreciation of the ruinous and Gothick disorder in place of the symmetry and formality of earlier topographical studies, while J. M. Turner's perception of our architectural heritage was steeped in the contagious spirit of Romanticism. Whereas I see Trecarrell Manor as a never completed courtyard residence of *c.*1500–10, with the granite hall and freestanding chapel with their retaining roofs bearing comparison with those at Cotehele, John Piper saw Trecarrell Manor as 'farm buildings with medieval remains, perfect in rare and once common relationship of old and new. Medieval doorheads, mouldings, and other

fragments here and there . . . lying in grass and nettles. The whole well-placed among old trees in a dip, approached only by remote flower-starred lanes of East Cornwall. The ruins of hall of manor house . . . of exquisite colour, greys, pale, stained with yellow litchen. Interior used as a store, drying place, etc., earth floor, good beamed ceiling. Darkness penetrated by lights from open door, cracks and crevices. Windows largely blocked with slate slabs. Chapel across the yard. Stone floor, traceried window intact without glass. Spreading ash tree with twisting bole at corner. Muddy roads, washing hanging out!'[7] All these are valid approaches to a subject that can be inspiring, frustrating, puzzling, and quirky. It can bring discoveries as well as disappointments, but most of it is a journey of adventure and fun, as I hope the following pages will gradually reveal.

NOTES

1 In addition to the 700 houses noted in detail, a further 350 are briefly described in the text. The earlier centuries were covered by Margaret Wood in her two *Archaeological Journal* studies in 1935 and 1950 listing thirty-nine Norman and seventy thirteenth-century houses. As a consequence of more recent research, these numbers should be increased by at least 20–25 per cent. The balance is essentially made up of medieval town houses. Fragmentary and excavated evidence is excluded from this total.
2 Since confirmed in *Med. Arch.* 47 (2003) 292.
3 N. Alcock and R. A. Messon, *Antiq. Jour.* 85 (2005), which corrects *Greater Med. Houses*, II (2000) 359–61.
4 N. Burton, *Arch. Jour.* 134 (1973) 329.
5 K. Rodwell and R. Bell, *Acton Court* (2004).
6 (1926) v.
7 July 1943, quoted and illustrated in R. Ingrams and J. Piper, *Piper's Places* (1983) 96–7.

Part I
THE THAMES VALLEY

1

THE THAMES VALLEY:
HISTORICAL BACKGROUND

GLOUCESTERSHIRE

T H E River Thames and its tributaries have determined the land-scape of Berkshire, Buckinghamshire, and Oxfordshire but the river barely affects Gloucestershire. Its birth there is indistinct and the nascent water barely achieves scale before it has left the county a little beyond Lechlade. The River Severn and the Cotswold hills are the primary features of Gloucestershire, determining three contrasting landscapes. The Vale of Gloucester is spanned by the Severn and its tidal estuary. The latter is flanked by the Forest of Dean towards the Welsh border and the Vale of Berkeley (a continuation of its sister vale) to the foot of the south Cotswolds. This range of hills extends the length of the county and initiates its most lovable characteristics. Beyond the Cotswold escarpment lies a broad, gently sloping limestone plateau dipping towards the distant Thames valley.

Each of these distinctive landscapes determines its building materials, population, and economic prosperity. The Forest of Dean was little populated and therefore lacks major medieval houses. In contrast, the Severn was a leading trade route, frequently subject to flooding but serving a rich pastoral region. The Cotswolds were exposed, windswept, and thinly inhabited, as some parts still are, but the hills provided some of the most profitable sheep runs in England.

Arable farming was the main source of livelihood in the early middle ages but the sheep runs developed in size between the twelfth and fourteenth centuries to become the dominating resource of the region. The lay subsidy of 1334 reveals that the income-generating resources of Gloucestershire positioned the county as eighth in England even though it had a relatively low population.[1] Bristol, near the mouth of the Severn estuary was the leading export centre for the region. By the mid-fourteenth century, it had become the second most wealthy town in the country.

The limestone hills were a primary source of high-quality build-ing stone and roof tiling, with a coloration that ranges from deep cream to pale tobacco tones that has endeared it to generations of church, house, and village builders. It was used for all high-quality houses throughout the middle ages. The low plateau of the Forest of Dean contains three series of rocks, a deep red sandstone suit-able for building, coal measures, and limestone with iron ore deposits which provided the livelihood of Forest occupants until the twentieth century. The clay soils of the Vale and the lack of building stone encouraged the use of timber framing, particularly for houses lower down the social scale. The prior of Llanthony used it for his country houses at Prestbury (fourteenth century) and

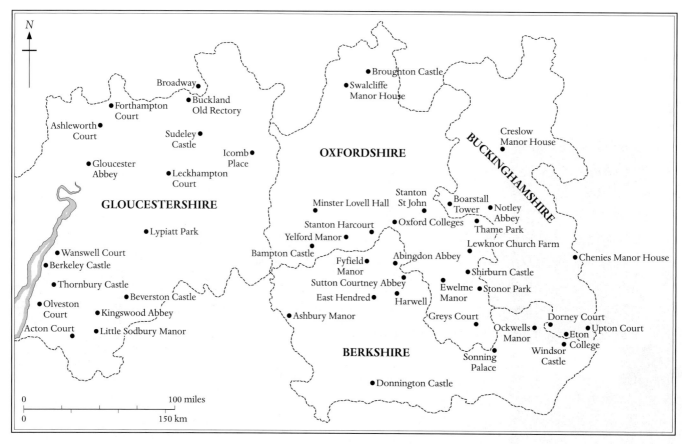

FIGURE 2 The Thames valley: residences described in the text

Brockworth (1534–9), both timber-framed above a stone ground floor, as was Manor Farm at Frampton on Severn (early fifteenth-century rear wing). Total timber framing as at Ashleworth Manor was not socially acceptable before the early sixteenth century. Like Worcestershire, Gloucestershire is still a rural county, and like its northern neighbour it was dominated throughout the middle ages by ecclesiastical institutions.

There were fifteen monasteries in the county excluding short-lived or minor foundations, six of them among the largest and most wealthy in the country. The older-established Benedictine order led with its foundations at Gloucester, Tewkesbury, and Winchcombe, but the three twelfth-century Augustinian foundations at Bristol, Cirencester, and Llanthony were almost as wealthy. Their manors dominated the region, with just over a third of the county in the hands of the church, though much of the territorial wealth of Tewkesbury lay south of the Thames rather than in Gloucestershire. The Cistercian foundations at Flaxley, Kingswood, and Hailes were less important than their sister houses in northern England.

Tewkesbury and Bristol abbeys also enjoyed the benefit of being adopted by the two leading families – the Despensers made the former their mausoleum from the early 1320s, while the lords of Berkeley, who had founded St Augustine's, Bristol, maintained their patronage throughout the thirteenth and fourteenth centuries but particularly during the vital years of rebuilding from 1298 to about 1330. Gloucester was not so fortunate initially, but its acceptance of the body of the murdered Edward II at the close of 1327 transformed its finances through royal donations and privileges. In all three cases, the building consequences were among the most innovative for the period in Europe.

The Berkeley family dominated lay society in the county. It might be thought that the Clare earls of Gloucester would be more powerful but they held relatively few estates in the region. The majority lay in East Anglia, Kent, and Glamorgan, and after the death of the last male heir at Bannockburn (1314) they were divided between three co-heiresses with the Gloucestershire estates going to the Despenser family. They lived at Hanley Castle in Worcestershire from the early fourteenth to the late fifteenth century and now acquired the important lordship and manor of Tewkesbury 7 miles away, where Edmund Despenser (d.1375) built a house destroyed in 1471.[2] Permanent occupation by the Berkeleys made them the foremost family in the region before the advent of the Beauforts in the eighteenth century. This long-living house eschewed national politics in favour of local supremacy, except in the fourteenth century when the two aspects were in tandem. The Berkeleys also had several collateral branches to maintain their influence more widely than would otherwise have been possible.

There were few other major families. Giffard of Brimpsfield came to prominence under John Giffard (d.1299), a follower of the earl of Gloucester with cousins who held prominent positions

PLATE I Berkeley Castle: hall range

as archbishop of York (d.1279) and bishop of Worcester (d.1302). However, the capture and execution of his son John (d.1322) as a rebel supporter of the earl of Lancaster brought the direct line to an end. The Giffards were the only family to establish a baronial *caput* on the inhospitable Cotswolds. The younger branch of the family that settled in the region at this time did so at Leckhampton Court at the foot of the escarpment facing the Vale, where virtually all the other leading families settled. This included the earls of Stafford who had held the manor of Thornbury since 1348. It was only after Edward Stafford, 3rd duke of Buckingham chose to make that manor house his principal seat and redeveloped it as a magnificent palace-fortress from 1507 onwards that the spotlight of national politics fleetingly illuminated this corner of Gloucestershire.

During the first part of the fourteenth century, about half the manors in the county were held by the gentry.[3] Of this broad social group of knights and esquires, the number of resident members of substance has been estimated as about fifty in the 1340s with about thirty of knighthood status, apparently reducing to about half that estimated number by 1400.[4] They included the four collateral branches of the house of Berkeley at Beverston, Coberley, Dursley, and Uley and lesser families such as de la Mare of Cherington,

Denys of Syston, and Poyntz of Iron Acton. The foundations at Acton Court nearby represent one of the few fourteenth-century gentry houses to survive, together with the hall and services range of Giffard at Leckhampton Court. They and the courtyard walls of the Berkeleys at Coberley and the Willingtons at Yate make up less than a tenth of the gentry houses known to have existed at that time.[5]

It is often forgotten that knights were a broadly based class of society, variously and vaguely defined, with a diverse span of incomes that fluctuated between generations depending on the number of manors they held and the range of additional financial resources they mustered. In 1316, some knights and esquires in Gloucestershire lived on the resources of a single manor (Sir John Giffard of Leckhampton) but the average was about four manors (John Berkeley of Dursley). Holders of six to eight manors were less frequent (Theobald Russel of Dyrham with six manors in other counties), while ten to thirteen manors were rare (Sir John Willington of Yate with eight manors in other counties).[6]

More houses survive from the fifteenth century, including the spectacular residence of the last Lord Sudeley, the Blaket family at Icomb, Sir Maurice Denys at Olveston, followed by the expansion of Acton Court by Sir Nicholas Poyntz during the 1530s. Poyntz was one of the local gentry families which rose on the tide of Tudor politics and prosperity to mix with those newly risen from yeoman stock or successful immigrant courtiers. Together, their industry and resources transformed the landowning pattern of Gloucestershire and its houses.[7]

Until the early fourteenth century, wool from the Cotswolds was not significant, but its exploitation by monastic and lay families from the fourteenth to the sixteenth century brought about an era of sustained expansion and economic prosperity. For the monasteries, it offset the decline in lay interest and property bequests that many houses suffered during the last two centuries of their life. Their granges spanned the Cotswolds as their abbatial houses did the Vale. In 1276, Kingswood had eight granges producing wool sales of 40 sacks per annum during the second half of the thirteenth century. With a sack equalling 364 lb, this implied a flock of at least 8,000 sheep.[8] In the following century, Winchcombe had a similar annual output.[9] The granges are mainly identified today by their barns, as at Siddington (1245–7 Cirencester), Calcot (c.1300 Kingswood), Frocester (c.1300 Gloucester), Stanway (c.1370 Tewkesbury), and Farmcote (c.1500 Hailes)[10] but the houses at Ashleworth, Brockworth, Forthampton, and Prinknash are still occupied, though the last three have been extended by later generations.[11]

Sheep farming consolidated and enhanced the predominant position of the Berkeleys and was a major factor in the redevelopment of their houses as well as Berkeley and Beverston castles during the first half of the fourteenth century. It brought similar benefits to a broad span of 'gentle' families as well as those lower down the social scale, but it was exploitation from a distance by families living in the Vale and on the west flank of the Cotswolds rather than on the hills. The anomaly of this era of rebuilding from the late fourteenth to the mid-sixteenth century was that though many parishes rebuilt their churches on the grandest scale and many small households and townspeople benefited from redeveloping their homes in stone, the more substantial landowners preferred the softness of the Vale to the high, windswept hills.[12]

There are few gentry houses before Richard II's reign but their numbers swell rapidly towards the Tudor period. Of the forty-seven resident gentry families in the fourteenth century, two-thirds lived in the Vale.[13] At least twenty-three houses in south Gloucestershire retain part of their late medieval roof structures, a further twenty have features suggesting medieval origins, and a further seven have reused medieval timbers.[14] These fifty homes are admittedly at the vernacular rather than the gentry level but they again reflect the wealth of the region and its residential distribution pattern. As in Wiltshire and Somerset, it is not the absence of later industrialisation that might otherwise have destroyed such homes but the prosperity of the region that accounts for the existence of such a substantial number of houses today of late medieval origin. Even after cloth making supplanted wool growing under the Tudors and Stuarts, the centres of profitability did not move far, only from the Cotswold hills to the valleys round Stroud, and to the Wiltshire towns of Bradford-on-Avon and Trowbridge a little further south.

OXFORDSHIRE

Unlike Gloucestershire, none of the three counties of the central Thames valley makes a natural unit, physically or administratively. More than its neighbours, the county of Oxford straddles the Midlands and southern England, with the River Thames acting as much as a physical division as the administrative boundaries mark its territorial limits. In contrast, the Thames forms a well-defined and long-standing administrative division between Berkshire and Buckinghamshire at variance with its geographical impact as a primary traffic artery serving the whole region.

None of the counties has a distinctive personality. They are physically modest, rural, and long dominated by the county town, though that has always been modest in the case of Buckinghamshire. Oxfordshire is bounded by the Cotswolds to the west, the Berkshire Downs to the south, and the Chilterns to the south-east. The meadows and pastureland of the Thames and its tributaries are the primary characteristics of the region. However, the transfer of the lowland Vale of Whitehorse immediately south of the Thames from Berkshire to Oxfordshire in 1974 was one of the few sensible local government and boundary changes made at that time. Berkshire and Buckinghamshire are also defined by the tributaries that drain into the ever-widening Thames, and by the low chalk hills to the south. The former created two broad clay lowlands – the Vale of Aylesbury to the north-east crossed by the Thame and the Ray, and the Vale of Whitehorse to the south with the Ock as its most important tributary. The chalk downs sweep south-westwards, with the Thames gap at Goring separating the beech-clothed Chiltern Hills of south Buckinghamshire and Oxfordshire from the open, bare downs of Berkshire. South of these downs is the Kennet valley, the major routeway from the Thames at Reading to Bath and the west followed in turn by road, canal, railway, and motorway to the point north of Newbury where Swindon's presence forced the concrete ribbon to cross the downs.

Oxfordshire has been well endowed with good-quality building stone. The Cotswold limestone in the west runs into iron ore deposits to the north-east, creating a distinctive belt of golden brown stone in the area around Banbury and nearby Northamptonshire. Oxford and the university in the central clay vale were fortunate in the ready availability of ragstone from the low hills west of Oxford with better-quality stone initially from Taynton, followed by Wheatley from the late thirteenth century, Upton-by-Burford during the fourteenth century, and Headington before the close of that century. It was the combination of high-quality building stone, a well-organised quarry industry, and river transport availability that made it suitable not only for prestigious building at Oxford and mansions such as Blenheim Palace, but also further afield at Windsor Castle, St Paul's Cathedral, and Westminster.[15] To the south-west, the flint of the Chilterns is far less practical, as Greys Court demonstrates, making the area among the earliest to take advantage of the virtues of brick at Stonor Park (1416–17) and Ewelme (1430s).

Except for the modest acres of the Wychwood Forest between the Evenlode and Windrush valleys, there is little trace today of the royal forests that extended across the centre of Oxfordshire. They were essentially in three groups, with much open countryside and fields between the more dense woodland. Wychwood in the west extended from Burford to Woodstock, Shotover lay east of Oxford, centred on Beckley, with Stowood immediately north of it and continuing to the forest of Bernwood in Buckinghamshire.[16] Henry I had built a royal hunting lodge at Woodstock, much favoured by his successors, King John built another further west at Langley, and Edward III rebuilt the earlier lodge at Beckley. There was also a

PLATE 2 Broadway, Abbot's Grange: from the east

separate tract of woodland covering much of the Chiltern Hills, with a line of medieval parks centred on the major houses at Thame, Shirburn, Ewelme, Stonor, Greys Court, and Watlington Castle. These, together with the royal residences, were the two major concentrations of private parks. They reached a development peak during the second half of the thirteenth century,[17] with that established by Lord Lovel in 1442 for his mansion at Minster Lovell among the last of the medieval creations.

Considering the region's accessibility and intense cultivation, it is interrupted by surprisingly few large towns, though Oxford and Wallingford both suffered from economic misfortune throughout the later middle ages. People in the south-west and near Henley looked towards London as the outlet for their goods and produce, while those in the north-west and at Banbury found accessible markets in the south Midlands and the Cotswolds. It is in this latter part of the county that the combination of the wool trade and intensive farming practices resulted in the line of splendid churches from Adderbury and Bloxham to Chipping Norton, Burford, Witney, and Bampton. The royal castles guarding the strategic river crossings at Oxford and Wallingford made them significant during the mid-twelfth-century struggles between Stephen and Matilda and again during the reign of King John, but Oxfordshire otherwise played little part in national affairs until the outbreak of Civil War in 1642.

As with Gloucestershire, the largest landowner in the county was the church. The estates of the bishop of Lincoln were important long after the see had been moved from Dorchester to Lincoln four years after the Conquest. The bishop's substantial holding, centred on Banbury, Dorchester, and Thame, was not far less than that of the bishop of Winchester with his estates at Witney (with an early palace there) and in the north-west. Not surprisingly, the monastic houses were in the vanguard of sheep farming,[18] with Osney as the pre-eminent monastic landowner, together with Thame and Dorchester. And of course, the Oxford colleges were fundamentally religious foundations with an ever-growing body of local estates.

Until the mid-fourteenth century, secular holdings had been modest, with no dominant magnate or gentry leader. But the growth of estate sales, particularly after the Black Death, and the increasingly popular practice by monastic houses of leasing their land rather than farming it directly, encouraged the prosperity of several local families. The Stonors, for instance, initially built up their estate by gradually purchasing one manor after another. By 1300, their holding comprised at least a dozen tenements varying from 10 to 40 acres, scattered across the parishes of Stonor, Watlington, Pyrton, Pishill, and Bix.[19] From such modest beginnings, the family developed their landholding and standing in society with a house that reflected the financial acumen of Sir John Stonor (d.1361) as much as his appointment as Chief Justice of

Common Pleas. Sir Edmund Chelrey (d.1372) similarly built up an estate centred on his manor house at Childrey, near Wantage (formerly in Berkshire). He also came from a family of slender means but became a lawyer in the 1340s, and a local administrator, and was appointed to the King's Bench in 1371.[20] In the fifteenth century, Richard Quatremains (d.1473), a customs official in London, became a justice of the peace, a knight of the shire, and sheriff of Oxfordshire.[21] Living near Thame, he founded the chapel at Rycote and the almshouses at Thame. Similar gentry evidence can be seen in the brasses of the Dormer and Quatremains families at Thame, that to Thomas Chaucer (d.1434) at Ewelme, and the chapel at North Leigh built by Elizabeth Wilcote in about 1440 in memory of her husband.

The shire's landscape is still reflected in the agricultural pattern of today – sheep to the west, open farmland and some woodland in the centre, pasture and more dense woodland towards the Chilterns. Equally telling are the considerable number of villages that were deserted from the mid-fourteenth century onwards,[22] one of the more heavily affected areas in England, and the seventy or so moated sites established in the clay vales. Though the forests have been fragmented and frequently cleared, much post-medieval parkland has been created out of them to form the ornamental settings for the stone mansions at Cornbury (1666–77), Blenheim (1705), and Ditchley (1720), though those at Bletchingdon (1782) and Kirtlington (1742) were created out of farmland.[23]

BERKSHIRE AND BUCKINGHAMSHIRE

Berkshire and Buckinghamshire were essentially pastoral counties, with the two vales practising mixed farming and the downs supporting extensive sheep runs. Many of the large flocks were owned by the abbeys of Abingdon, Notley, and Reading, but they were increasingly outnumbered by those of minor gentry families like the Stonors who took advantage of the leasing of monastic demesne lands during the later middle ages. Their wool served the cloth towns of Abingdon, Newbury, and Reading, but there were no comparable centres in Buckinghamshire apart from the market centre at Aylesbury.

Buckinghamshire was (and still is) one of the most secluded of the home counties close to the metropolis, and its low-density population was scattered across the region as far as the infertile Chilterns. Berkshire was not much more densely populated except in the Vale of Whitehorse which enjoyed a buoyant economy arising from its agrarian prosperity and the migration of cloth making from Oxford and Abingdon to villages such as East Hendred and Steventon in the fourteenth century, and developing high productivity levels in the later fifteenth and early sixteenth centuries.

The light sandy soils of south-east Berkshire severely restricted economic growth, while the several thousands of acres covered by the royal forest of Windsor inhibited settlement. The situation changed to some extent with extensive disafforestation after 1227, with evidence of occupational growth for about a century until stunted by the Black Death.[24] Recovery to the same level was not achieved before the early sixteenth century. Disafforestation was also responsible for the parallel development of deer parks, which similarly declined in number and extent after the mid-fourteenth century.[25] Over forty have been identified in Berkshire (and more than fifty in Buckinghamshire), principally established in east Berkshire and the Kennet valley between 1200 and 1350. The

PLATE 3 East Hendred, Hendred House: rear frontage with chapel

crown was the leading holder with twelve, followed by the six belonging to two bishops and four monasteries. Most of the remaining parks were held by local landowners, for the six magnate holdings were those of the absentee earls of Pembroke, Leicester, and Salisbury.[26]

Considering the long-standing presence and ever-developing magnificence of the royal castle at Windsor, the region was surprisingly lacking in magnate presence. The middle Thames valley was dominated by the pivotal position of the royal castles at Wallingford and Reading. There was a royal manor at Princes Risborough throughout the middle ages, while the earl of Norfolk had a house of some importance at Hampstead Marshall which came into the king's hands between 1345 and 1361.[27] Some of the most wealthy and active centres were the monasteries at Abingdon, Reading, Missenden, and Thame. Their hospitality, particularly at the first two, was often stretched to the limit. Their estate houses could be large as at Cumnor, while their granges differed little in scale and layout from gentry houses as Charney Bassett and Sutton Courtenay still show, though the latter was only developed to its present scale after the abbey had given it up in the 1280s. This is demonstrated even more forcefully at Bisham, the Thames-side preceptory built by the Knights Templars in c.1260, taken over by the earl of Salisbury in 1338 who added a chamber block to the earlier hall to increase the accommodation for himself and his family.[28] Even then, the magnate's house was considerably smaller than that of his ecclesiastical equivalent, the bishop of Salisbury, at Sonning.

Sonning has long since been pulled down but has been excavated, while Hampstead Marshall has entirely passed into history. As early as Edward I's reign, it had a great gate, two courts, and a hall, chapel, and cloister to which Edward III may have added a second hall.[29] Other houses that have vanished include those of Sir Thomas Sackville at Fawley (fourteenth century) and the Besils at Besselsleigh (early fifteenth century), and the moated and brick remains at Southcote near Reading (late fifteenth century). The only evidence of the home of the de la Beche family of Aldworth is the moated site 400 yards south of the church holding the impressive collection of tombs to seven knights and two ladies, all dating from the early to mid-fourteenth century. Nor is there any standing evidence of the four houses crenellated by Sir John Moleyns in the early 1330s at Stoke Poges, Ditton nearby, Weston Turville, and Aston Mullins.[30] At the height of his switchback career, Sir John was the wealthiest man in Buckinghamshire but he was also an opportunist who paid dearly for crossing both king and queen.[31]

The houses that have survived are those of the lesser gentry. Those from the first half of the fourteenth century are medium sized – Creslow, Fyfield, and Upton Court, Slough – with a number held by gentry with only one or two manors such as Richard Brounz at Harwell. His success in local service contributed to the rebuilding of Bayliol's Manor, just as that of Richard Abberbury in royal service helped him to build and then extend his hilltop house at Donnington in the 1380s. The reduced demand for new seats during the first half of the fifteenth century was offset by the increase in the size of existing estates through the acquisition of smaller ones.

The new wave of courtiers who prospered under Henry VI's inept rule was led in this region by John Noreys, whose spacious and forward-looking timber and brick mansion at Ockwells in the 1450s made the subsequent brick houses at Chenies and Dorney Court look parochial. Though a staunch Lancastrian supporter, Noreys' career did not suffer from the accession of a Yorkist monarch. But the Dissolution of the Monasteries nearly eighty years later brought an influx of new estate owners. Out of the thirty-eight gentry families in seventeenth-century Berkshire, only seven had been established in the county before 1500 and not one of their houses has survived subsequent rebuilding.[32] Nor did Berkshire experience that spate of later-generation prodigy houses that are the true architectural and landscape glory of Buckinghamshire.[33]

NOTES

1 H. C. Darby (ed.), *A New Historical Geography of England* (1973) 141, 191; R. E. Glasscock, *The Lay Subsidy of 1334* (1975) xxvii.

2 The present house at Tewkesbury Park, a mile south-west of the town, is late eighteenth century. For Hanley, A. Emery, *Greater Med. Houses*, II (2000) 396 n.2.

3 N. Saul, *Knights and Esquires: The Gloucestershire Gentry in the Fourteenth Century* (1981) 5.

4 *Ibid.* 32–5. This work modifies the early fourteenth-century figure of ninety given by R. H. Hilton, *A Medieval Society* (1966) 53.

5 Saul, *Knights and Esquires* 268–9.

6 *Ibid.* 226–7, with figures showing that out of forty-eight knights and esquires in 1316, 25 per cent held only one manor, 46 per cent held two to four manors, 16 per cent held five or six manors, and 13 per cent held between seven and fifteen manors. Of the fourteen holders that make up the last two groups, only one person, Sir John Bures of Boddington, held the majority of his ten manors in Gloucestershire.

7 N. Kingsley, *The Country Houses of Gloucester*, I (1989) 2–6.

8 E. S. Lindley, *Trans. Bristol and Glos. Arch. Soc.* 73 (1954) 115–91.

9 G. Haigh, *History of Winchcombe Abbey* (1947).

10 Barns are similarly the primary evidence of granges in the Vale as at Hartpury (fourteenth century, Gloucester) and Dymock (sixteenth century, Flaxley), with Ashleworth (1490s) as the outstanding exception where the house stands nearby. The barn of 1342 at Winterbourne Court is a rare example built for secular landowners, the Bradestons, with another secular example of *c.*1400 at Southam.

11 The grange of Kingswood Abbey at Bagstone Court Farm, Wickwar, retains a fourteenth-century open hall and end chamber with solar above. *Med. Arch.* 26 (1982) 170–1 and 27 (1983) 165.

12 To take one example over a period of two centuries, the Tames developed from graziers near Northleach to wool merchants and then clothiers of considerable wealth. They purchased the manor of Fairford, rebuilt the church except for its tower (*c.*1490–1510) and built a substantial house nearby where Sir Edmund Tame (d.1534), knighted on the Field of the Cloth of Gold, entertained Henry VIII. Sir Edmund also purchased Rendcomb manor near Cirencester and rebuilt the church there, a simplified version of Fairford. Neither Fairford Place nor his house at Rendcomb survives.

13 Saul, *Knights and Esquires* 268–9.

14 L. J. Hall, *The Rural Houses of North Avon and South Gloucestershire 1400–1720* (1983) 87.

15 W. J. Arkell, *Oxford Stone* (1947); E. M. Jope in *Wheatley Records 956–1956*, ed. W. O. Hassall (1956) 17–26.

16 B. Schumer, *The Evolution of Wychwood to 1400* (1984); E. Roberts, 'The boundaries and woodlands of Shotover Forest circa 1298', *Oxoniensia* 28 (1963) 68–73; J. M. Steane, 'Bernwood Forest', *Agricultural Jour.* 9 (1985) 39–55.

17 J. Bond in *The Archaeology of the Oxford Region*, ed. G. Briggs *et al.* (1986) 153 points out that these parks, unlike the landscaped grounds of eighteenth-century mansions, were often some distance from the relevant mansion. That at Watlington was 2 miles from the castle, Shirburn Park was 1½ miles from the castle, while the bishop of Winchester's park was just over a mile west of his palace at Witney.

18 Sheep farming is recorded in the region during the twelfth century, with cloth centres at Witney, Burford and Chipping Norton, and fulling mills at Cleveley (near Enstone) in 1185, Thame in 1197, and Brightwell in 1208.

19 F. Emery, *The Oxfordshire Landscape* (1974) 97.

20 P. J. Jefferies, 'Social mobility in the 14th century. The example of the Chelreys of Berkshire', *Oxoniensia* 41 (1976) 324–36.

21 J. T. Driver, 'Richard Quatremains: a 15th century squire and knight of the shire for Oxfordshire', *Oxoniensia* 51 (1986) 87–103.

22 About 110 sites have been identified so far, modestly adding to the one hundred or so listed by K. J. Allison, M. W. Beresford, and J. G. Hurst, *The Deserted Villages of Oxfordshire* (1965). Also J. Bond in *The Archaeology of the Oxford Region*, ed. G. Briggs *et al.* (1986) 140–3. Forty such sites have been identified in the Vale of Whitehorse.

23 F. Woodward, *Oxfordshire Parks* (1982) 28–9. Other contemporary grand houses include Heythrop (1706), Shotover (1714), Rousham (1738), Thame (1745), and Nuneham Courtenay (1756).

24 S. Ford, *East Berkshire Archaeological Survey* (1987) 102–4.

25 *Ibid.* 104–5.

26 J. M. Hatherley and L. M. Cantor, *Berks. Arch. Jour.* 70 (1979–80) 67–80.

27 *HKW*, II (1964) 955–6.

28 This establishment's development is extraordinary. It began as a Templar preceptory from 1139 to 1312. It was transformed into an Augustinian priory in 1337 but was taken over by the earl of Salisbury a year later for his personal use. He built a new priory for the monks a little distance away that became a Benedictine abbey in 1537. The Templars' vaulted porch, unaisled ground-floor hall, and offices and chamber wing were indistinguishable from those of a contemporary secular residence. The withdrawing chamber added by William, earl of Salisbury (d.1344) at the upper end of the hall was built above a narrow undercroft and cloister passage. The latter was part of a quadrangle of lodgings pulled down in *c.*1560 when the withdrawing chamber was ceiled and divided. 'Travels and life of Sir Thomas Hoby', *Camden Miscellany* 10 (1880) 18. Also VCH, *Berkshire*, III (1923), E. T. Long, *Country Life* (April 1941), J. Fletcher and C. A. Hewett, *Med. Arch.* 18 (1969) 220–4.

29 *HKW*, II (1964) 955–6.

30 The present house of 1813–17 at Ditton stands within a moated site, with evidence of brickwork from the 1511–16 or early seventeenth-century rebuilding, incorporated in the early nineteenth-century gate-house. M. Levy, *Country Life* (January 1990).

31 Beginning as a clerk in chancery in the 1320s, he made a propitious

marriage to the wealthy daughter and heir of Sir John Maudit, and became an intimate of Edward III after helping him to capture Roger Mortimer at Nottingham Castle (1330). Appointed treasurer of the royal chamber and steward of its manors, Sir John was showered with grants, knighted in 1339, and appointed justice of the peace for Buckinghamshire in 1340. However, he sought to capitalise on the king's financial difficulties in 1339–40, and swiftly paid the price after the king's return to England in late 1340 with the confiscation of all his estates. A temporary respite failed to restrain him from feathering his own nest again, this time as steward of the queen's lands, so that this bully and brigand spent the last three years of his life in prison until his death in 1360. N. Fryde, 'A medieval robber baron: Sir John Molyns of Stoke Poges', in F. F. Hunnisett and J. B. Posts (eds.), *Medieval Legal Records* (1978) 198–221. Also *Com. Peer.*, IX (1936) 36–7; G. R. Elvey, *Rec. of Bucks.* 19 pt 2 (1972) 194–8.

32 J. Dils (ed.), *An Historical Atlas of Berkshire* (1998) 58–9. The families were Clarke (Ardington), Darrell (Kintbury), Feteplace (Childrey), Hyde (Kingston Lisle), Moore (Fawley), Sambourne (Moulsford), and Vachell (Coley).

33 This sequence of houses began quietly with Chequers (1565), Gayhurst (1597), and Hartwell (*c.*1610) but it developed spectacularly at Chicheley (1719), West Wycombe (1750s), and Stowe (1770s), culminating in Cliveden (1849) and the enclave of Rothschild mansions at Mentmore (1850), Waddesdon (1877), and Halton (1881).

2

THE THAMES VALLEY:
ARCHITECTURAL INTRODUCTION

CASTLES

THREE royal castles guarded the central Thames valley, Windsor, Wallingford, and Oxford, though this last was founded by a leading baron with the Conqueror's consent and came into royal hands during the twelfth century. Wallingford and Oxford were prominent in the war between Stephen and Matilda, and while Oxford had fallen into disrepair by the early fourteenth century, Wallingford was maintained for residential purposes for a further century. To the west, the Severn estuary was guarded by the royal fortresses at Bristol, Gloucester, and St Briavels. Bristol fell into decay during the fifteenth century and Gloucester from the close of that era, but though St Briavels lapsed from its primary purpose as an administrative centre for the royal forest of Dean, it was maintained for its court and prison function until the mid-nineteenth century.[1]

The region shows a broad span of private castles, chronologically, tenurially, and structurally, with three of them retaining substantive evidence. Those of modest defensive capacity such as Ascott d'Oilly, Stratton Audley, and Deddington had been abandoned before the close of the fourteenth century. The stronghold of the Giffards at Brimpsfield was destroyed on the orders of Edward II in 1322[2] to join the earlier abandoned earthworks and adulterine sites scattered across the region. Nor does anything survive of Banbury Castle, first erected by bishop Alexander of Lincoln in about 1130 as the administrative centre of the bishop's extensive estates in the area. It was almost entirely rebuilt during the early fourteenth century in concentric form with drum towers and a massive gateway and so maintained until the Civil War.[3]

Berkeley Castle retains the motte and bailey initiated by William FitzOsbern, earl of Hereford after 1067, with the motte enclosed by a shell keep in 1153–6 with a soil-raised interior. Most of the slightly later curtain wall was swamped by the early to mid-fourteenth-century residential development mentioned below. The early thirteenth-century castle at Beverston was similarly expanded a century later with residential additions by the Berkeley family. The 1340s tower was an early example of a solar tower linked to a first-floor hall, while the slightly later second-phase work was an independent residential suite. The Beverston tower is a fine example of the complex internal planning beloved of the mid and late fourteenth century, similarly exhibited in the south-west at Nunney and Wardour castles. The entirely new castle built at Bampton by Aymer de Valence, earl of Pembroke in about 1315 was very different in form and scale. Four times the size of Maxstoke Castle and surrounded by a broad moat and water courses, it is an early example of the totally rectangular plan with round corner towers and opposing central gatehouses. In contrast with Aymer's fortress at Goodrich, no more survives than the lower half of the west gatehouse, flanked by a lodging block and a 30 foot stretch of curtain wall.

PALACE-FORTRESSES

The mid to late Saxon and early Norman complex at Old Windsor was identified by excavation in 1953–8, but no halls were uncovered and our appreciation of the site is enigmatic.[4] It seems to have been abandoned by the crown by the early twelfth century in favour of the defensive and pleasurable attractions of the castle founded by William the Conqueror 2 miles upstream. This change was spurred by Henry I's rebuilding of the motte and bailey structure in wood between 1107 and 1110, with the name of the 'old' settlement transferring with the court to the 'new' Windsor. The castle was rebuilt in stone between the mid-twelfth and mid-thirteenth centuries, with Henry II responsible for the stone curtain enclosing the upper ward punctuated by square towers, and Henry III for that enclosing the lower ward with rounded towers. The castle's present form had been fixed before Henry III's death, with his successors remodelling the contained enclosure, principally the royal apartments of the upper ward under Edward III and the college of St George under Edward IV. Despite all subsequent changes, Windsor Castle still holds to the triple complex of fortification, palace, and college – a medieval power-house of several hundred inhabitants that still functions in most respects little differently from its role over 500 years ago.

Edward III's fundamental redevelopment of the royal apartment between 1352 and about 1370 was the outstanding royal project of the mid or later fourteenth century, whether considered by the scale of the work force, the cost incurred, or its architectural significance in disseminating the newly developed Perpendicular style. The work was the matrix for the extensive building projects of the master-mason and one of the clerks of work – William Wynford and William Wykeham – but it was equally significant in the development of palace-fortresses, and in the historical psyche of the country. Only limited site evidence of this activity survives today, but its importance has been more appreciated since the discoveries made in the aftermath of the fire of 1992 confirming that Edward III made the castle one of the pre-eminent buildings of the later middle ages in a development programme of European significance.

The sequence of apartments initiated at Berkeley Castle by Thomas, Lord Berkeley in 1326–7 and continuing until the mid-1340s anticipated many of the key features of Edward III's work. Lord Berkeley erected an imposing new hall, a substantial kitchen and associated group of service rooms, a large private chapel next to the hall, a spectacular sequence of first-floor family apartments, and a two-storeyed lodging range. The whole was enclosed within the castle's earlier curtain wall, and though confined within a less spacious bailey than at Windsor the project was on the grandest scale for a magnate.[5] In addition, the workmanship and architectural detailing reflected the distinctive Bristol version of the flamboyant Decorated style just as Windsor trumpeted the early Perpendicular form. A similar programme was being undertaken at the same time by another leading magnate at Warwick Castle. This movement of converting a fortress into a major residence without inhibiting its defensive capability had been initiated at Goodrich at

PLATE 4 Greys' Court: Great Tower from the east

the beginning of the century, but Berkeley was its first full expression. Palace-fortress conversion was only practised at the highest level of society, but the royal programme prompted Gaunt as well as several northern magnates to follow suit during the later years of the fourteenth century.[6]

Gloucestershire also enjoys two similar-scale projects from the mid-fifteenth and early sixteenth centuries respectively. As they were new residences rather than fortress conversions, their military aspects were honoured more in form than in substance. Much of Sudeley Castle (c.1441–58) has been lost or absorbed through late sixteenth-century rebuilding or nineteenth-century restoration but its vast scale, with a double-courtyard plan that had the great hall at the furthest end of the inner court, bears more than a passing resemblance to Lord Cromwell's contemporary palace-mansion at Wingfield. Just as that residence moved up the social scale when it was purchased by the earl of Shrewsbury, so Sir Ralph Boteler's castle at Sudeley was equally elevated through its acquisition by Richard, duke of Gloucester. Even so, he replaced the family apartments with a semi-royal suite (c.1469–78), which testifies to the scale, taste, and splendour of contemporary court work.

The same applies a generation later to the duke of Buckingham's jewel at Thornbury, an even more imposing palace-fortress developed between 1507 and the duke's execution in 1521. Following the same double-courtyard plan as Sudeley, with the family apartments filling one side of the inner court that terminated in the great hall, Thornbury bristles with military elements in comparison with Sudeley or any other early Tudor mansion. The mixture of fortress and residential features was audacious, as witness the juxtaposition of the self-proclaiming gatehouse frontage with the duke's lavishly fenestrated apartment range. His huge windows would be outstanding in any context, but like those of Edward IV's time at Sudeley, those of Henry VIII's reign at Thornbury are supreme.

These three palace-fortresses are the only residences in Gloucestershire of sufficient size and with owners of sufficient social standing to need extended ranges of lodgings. Those enclosing the outer court at Thornbury are particularly well preserved, particularly as the Sudeley ranges were reconstructed in c.1572. A small late fifteenth-century lodging unit was built next to the gatehouse at Berkeley Castle but there is little doubt that further accommodation was erected in the outer court for the large household of the Berkeleys at their *caput*. But over and above their architectural importance, these three residences are also of political and social significance. Berkeley's redevelopment was primarily a consequence of sheep farming profitability, Sudeley reflected loyal service to the crown, while Thornbury was a statement of ducal hubris.

DEFENDABLE HOUSES

There were more lightly fortified houses across the region than stone castles, and there is more evidence of them. There were at least seventeen defendable houses in Gloucestershire but except for Sudeley and Thornbury – and they were exceptional in every way – the sites were only modestly fortified. All but four were in the Vale, equally distributed between the fourteenth and fifteenth centuries. The majority were the homes of lesser gentry such as the Poyntz of Iron Acton (from mid-fourteenth century), Thorpe at Wanswell (mid-fifteenth century), and Denys at Olveston (later fifteenth century). Defence was limited to a moat, an enclosure, a gateway as at Icomb Place, Yate Court, and Olveston, or a turret as at Court Farm, Almondsbury.

In comparison with such minor remains, Broughton Castle stands as one of the most important medieval houses of central England. Its defensive capacity was always modest – an impressive moat, a small gatehouse, and an embattled enclosure wall – and its significance lies in the extent and quality of the residential range of the family apartments, all the more important because they were undertaken by a family of no more than local standing. At least six medieval phases can be identified, centred round two vaulted undercrofts at right angles to each other. All expansion has developed round this L-shaped core of later thirteenth-century date, beginning with a ground-floor corridor enclosure and room between 1295 and 1315 with first-floor ante-chamber above. This enlargement was associated with a replacement hall that is the basis for the present Elizabethan structure. Very shortly afterwards, a three-storeyed bedchamber block was added, allowing the earlier bedchamber to be converted into a chapel rising through two storeys, one of the finest and best-preserved domestic chapels in the country. Within a few years, the ground-floor corridors had been embellished with vaulting so that the house now had a substantial group of family apartments with large-scale windows and work-

manship of high architectural quality. An imposing flight of chapel stairs and an unusual loggia were added by bishop Wykeham of Winchester after he had purchased the manor in about 1380, but the major conversion of this residence occurred from 1540 onwards when the earlier plan was reversed and the house was remodelled as an Elizabethan mansion.

The appellation 'castle' to Broughton is a Victorian one that was, rightly, never bestowed on Greys Court. Its plan is not easily identifiable, for the four flint-built towers that survive are isolated units in an area of considerable size that lacks the gatehouse and retains only fragments of its curtain walls and residential block. The licence to crenellate obtained by Lord Grey in 1346 was for the development of his earlier house, as was that sought for Broughton in 1406, but Lord Lisle's licence of 1377 for Shirburn Castle applied to an entirely new structure. Stone-built and moat-surrounded, it was a precursor of Bodiam Castle in its quadrangular form with round corner towers, single central entry, and range-enclosed courtyard. As at Broughton Castle, post-medieval development has been contained within the original walls, but the early eighteenth-century remodelling was drastic and overwhelming.

Twelve licences to crenellate were granted to Oxfordshire landowners and gentry between 1316 and 1377 – eight for houses that no longer exist, and four covering the castles at Bampton and Shirburn, Greys Court, and Camoys Court at Chiselhampton. This last is even more of a domestic residence than the 'castle' at Broughton, for although moated it shows no evidence of defensive structures.[7] Camoys Court is yet another example where the line between defensive and unprotected houses is too blurred to be meaningful.

The gatehouses at Boarstall and Donnington, both protecting strongly ditched enclosures, are high-quality examples of a military form modified to domestic circumstances. Boarstall (1312) may never have been more extensive: a low-lying and therefore well-moated enclosure (like Bampton Castle) but with no more than a palisaded surround. Donnington (1386), though high on a spur overlooking the Kennet valley, was well protected by a towered enclosure. Grove Farm, Ashley Green, was never licensed but retains a strongly banked and ditched outer enclosure with a water-filled inner moat protecting the base of two polygonal gatehouse towers and part of the curtain. The small flint-built residential unit is of late medieval date, uncertain purpose, and drastic restoration in 1961.[8] The house fortified by Sir John Moleyns at Weston Turville was in the castle bailey of the Turville family, as had been that of William Beauchamp at Castlethorpe in 1282,[9] but moats are the only evidence at the three other licensed sites in Berkshire and Buckinghamshire.

ROYAL HOUSES

At the opening of the fourteenth century, the crown held two houses in Buckinghamshire and three in Oxfordshire. The hunting lodge at Brill serving Bernwood Forest ceased to be royal property at the beginning of our period, while the moated house at Princes Risborough, west of the church, declined in importance after the death of the Black Prince though there was continuous site occupation until the sixteenth century.[10] The house at Beaumont, outside the walls of Oxford, was abandoned by Edward I and given to the Carthusian order for priory conversion, and was demolished at the Reformation. The house at Beckley north-east of Oxford, initiated by the earl of Cornwall in the mid-thirteenth century, was rebuilt by Edward III in 1375–6 and well maintained to 1441, though only the triple moats remain.[11] Edward III also developed a complex of manor houses and lodges belonging to the castle and forest of Windsor. Easthampton and Wychemere were manor houses, Foliejohn and Collingridge were lodges, though nothing survives at any of the sites.[12]

The same applies to the third royal Oxfordshire property, Woodstock, the most important crown residence with Clarendon Palace away from the Westminster/Windsor area. It lay on the north bank of the river running through the 1,000 acre park,[13] close to Vanburgh's later bridge across Lancelot Brown's lake. The additions made by successive monarchs to Henry I's 'favourite seat of retirement and privacy' converted the timber-framed hunting lodge into a building of some size and splendour. In particular, Henry III's extensive work programme encompassed rebuilding the twelfth-century aisled hall in stone, the development of separate apartments roofed with Cotswold stone for the king and queen, the addition of several chapels including a round one and a vaulted one for the queen, and extensive wall paintings in the royal apartments. Later work included a new apartment for the queen (1354), and a tower by the entrance to the king's chamber (1439–41), which was not completed until after Edward IV's accession.[14] Major repairs and partial rebuilding were undertaken during Henry VII's reign, including reroofing the two aisled halls and reconstructing the great gateway (1494–1503). The property was kept in good order until the early seventeenth century, and was only stripped of furniture after a survey of the palace and park had been made in 1650. This and earlier documentation show that the royal country retreat at Woodstock was built round two courtyards, with the hall and several lodging ranges facing the large gatehouse, and the royal apartments encircling the smaller second courtyard. A drawing of the manor in 1714 shows a tightly packed group of buttressed buildings with a prominent two-storeyed oriel, and an embattled tower above the roofline that was probably the gatehouse, all ruthlessly swept away at the duchess of Marlborough's insistence in 1723.[15]

MAGNATE AND GENTRY HOUSES

More than many regions, the greater houses of the Thames valley can be considered in three ways. They display the three primary building sources of the later middle ages – stone, timber, and brick – and can be considered on the basis of these materials. They display a range of house forms extending from fortified to non-defensive, and from open aisled hall with cross wings to single- and double-courtyard houses. They can also be considered under the status of their builders, with magnate development at Minster Lovell, Ewelme, and Sonning, a broad range of greater and lesser gentry dwellings, and a substantial number of monastic residences and high-quality lodgings. No single approach is satisfactory, but in reviewing under building materials, it should be remembered that few houses survive of single-period build. Upton Court (c.1325), Minster Lovell Hall (1430s), Ashleworth Court (early fifteenth century), Ockwells (c.1455–65), and Yelford Manor (c.1498) are the prime exceptions. Some houses show that one of the wings (the upper at Sonning Palace, the lower at Bayliol's Manor, Harwell) pre-dates the hall that was rebuilt during the fourteenth century (Sonning Palace, Sutton Courtenay 'Abbey') or the later fifteenth century (Hendred House). The initial plan therefore is not always

easy to determine, for what we see today is the culmination of a house's development. An initial T-plan of hall and cross wing survives at Ashbury Manor and Ashleworth Court and may be suspected at many other properties,[16] but the majority in the region today are H-shaped with only a handful of single build.

Two Oxfordshire houses encapsulate the problems of material and form. Stonor Park is a complex structure of almost continuous development by a single family over an 800 year period. This house of accretion begins with a mid to late thirteenth-century stone hall of two aisles with a cross wing at the lower end. Prudent financial stewardship by the Stonors enabled them to enlarge their residence in the mid-fourteenth century with a timber-framed hall with cross wings. As it superseded but did not obliterate the earlier hall, Stonor Park is rare in retaining the two succeeding cores of the house, though built in different materials. Continuous use and post-medieval alterations mean that less can be seen of the later than the earlier hall, but this is not the case at Lewknor Church Farm. This contemporary timber-framed hall similarly has a spere truss as at Stonor Park, but its 30 foot wide span was so inherently weak that the central truss had to be supported on aisle posts inserted *after* construction. It is not known whether this hall was free-standing or had an attached offices and chamber block, for all site occupation has been abandoned in favour of farm activity, with the hall now used as a barn.

Stone

Gloucestershire and Oxfordshire are primarily stone counties, with some timber framing in the Vale (Ashleworth Manor, early sixteenth century) and brick first occurring in Oxfordshire at Stonor Park in 1416–17.

Gloucestershire amply demonstrates that there was no standard medieval house plan. The twelfth-century abbot's living quarters at Gloucester were towered, and the bishop of Hereford's moated house at Prestbury had a thirteenth-century aisled hall with a detached solar at its lower end,[17] whereas the bishop of Worcester's house at Bishop's Cleeve of c.1280 was L-shaped, with the solar wing projecting from the upper end of the hall and services range.[18] Hall and services with chamber over was adopted by Sir John Giffard at Leckhampton Court (1315–20), Daneway (1315), Buckland Old Rectory (fourteenth century), and possibly Lypiatt Park (late fourteenth century). The Bishop's Cleeve plan of hall with lower end block and an upper cross wing was adopted at Ashleworth Court (early fifteenth century) and Buckland Old Rectory as rebuilt in c.1470, while the alternative H-form was chosen at Wanswell Court (c.1450–60). Ashleworth Court and Wanswell Court had ground-floor parlours with fireplaces, regrettably removed at Wanswell which had less-altered interiors than any other house in the county before the earl of Berkeley's deprivations in the 1920s. Icomb Place (later fifteenth century) aped the form displayed on a much grander scale at Sudeley Castle, but with the hall in the central cross range of this small double-courtyard house.

The halls at Leckhampton Court (1315–20) and that at Forthampton Court (by early fifteenth century) have been much abused but are still open to the roof, as are the better-preserved mid to late fifteenth-century structures at Wanswell Court, Little Sodbury Manor, Buckland Old Rectory, and Icomb Place. That at Ashleworth Court has been floored and ceiled but is otherwise well preserved while that at Berkeley Castle is in a class of its own. Roofs are fairly plain, usually supported on arch-braced collar trusses, though Buckland has a central hammer truss of the 1470s. The hall at Berkeley had two louvres to clear the smoke from the central hearth whereas the later halls at Wanswell and Little Sodbury had wall fireplaces. There are porches at Little Sodbury and Wanswell (until 1929), contemporary glass in the hall windows at Buckland, and a stair lobby opening off the upper end of the hall at Ashleworth Court and at Little Sodbury Manor in one of the two opposing bays.

Berkeley Castle retains its splendid chapel, and there are smaller but still complete examples at Forthampton Court (with a retained panel painting) and two finely detailed examples in the tower added by the 3rd Lord Berkeley at Beverston Castle. The chapels are free-standing at Lypiatt Park and Sudeley Castle though close to the house. Some of the outbuildings also survive at Lypiatt Park, an early Tudor garden layout at Thornbury Castle, and rare painted cloth hangings, admittedly of late seventeenth-century date but following a medieval form, at Owlpen Manor.

Initially, the house form in Oxfordshire was as varied as that further west. The mid-thirteenth-century prebendal house at Thame began as a first-floor timber-framed hall with stone solar and chapel projections.[19] Excavations at Harding's Field, Chalgrave, revealed that this moated residence of the Barentin family included a stone aisled hall of c.1250–60 by Sir Drew Barentin (d.1264) and an early fourteenth-century cross wing.[20] The popularity of the H-shaped plan of hall and cross wing has a long history in Oxfordshire, beginning with Swalcliffe Manor House. Only the cross wings survive of this mid to late thirteenth-century residence, the lower one with its original screens passage doorways, and the upper one with its vaulted undercroft.[21] The hall between them was rebuilt by bishop Wykeham of Winchester after he had purchased the property in 1381. The same plan had been adopted at Stonor Park (mid-fourteenth century) and at the close of the fifteenth century at Yelford Manor.[22] Oxfordshire is usually considered a stone county but Yelford is another example of a timber-framed structure, in this case built entirely of elm. Though it now lacks most of its original detailing, it retains its early form and internal volumes to an uncommon degree.

Apart from Swalcliffe rectory manor, all these houses were gentry owned – lower gentry in the case of Yelford and the earlier-mentioned Lewknor, higher gentry at Stonor where the family were poised at the close of the fifteenth century to take a higher social position that, in the event, was never realised. That was not so with the Harcourts, who had vacated their old family home at Stanton Harcourt by 1688 and used much of its stonework for the foundations of the mansion they built at Nuneham Courtenay to celebrate their elevation to an earldom. Stanton Harcourt had been an early example of a double-courtyard house, which, not surprisingly, is little evident today. Even so, the beautifully landscaped garden serves as a setting for the isolated remains retained for tenant occupation – the late fourteenth-century kitchen, the mid-fifteenth-century chapel and tower, and the mid-sixteenth-century entry range. The kitchen is one of the most important to survive, with a striking octagonal roof structure, still smoke blackened through current use. The chapel adjoined the family apartments, whereas it had been detached initially at Stonor (early fourteenth century) and was so left at Rycote (c.1449) enabling this fine chapel to survive when the moated mansion was burnt in 1745.

This is not the only one of several greater houses of fifteenth-century Oxfordshire to have fared badly. Nothing survives of the Fettiplace mansion of c.1490 at Swinbrook, pulled down without record in 1805 after the last member of the family died without heirs. The toy castle at Hanwell (1498–1520s) was abandoned in the late eighteenth century and reduced to a brick corner tower and part of the south range.[23] Minster Lovell Hall was similarly abandoned in the mid-eighteenth century but the ruins are more extensive and almost entirely of one period, the 1430s. Built round three sides of a quadrangle with an enclosing wall towards the River Windrush, this mansion has a particularly tall hall with high windows, a central hearth, and an exceptionally fine vaulted porch. Next to this was an unusually sited self-contained suite with the chapel above linked to the solar range in its usual position at the upper end of the hall. The only subsequent addition was made a generation or two later, a four-storeyed tower with a lodging suite and prospect room at the top like that at Stanton Harcourt. The house that developed into one of even higher status was Ewelme Manor, acquired through marriage by the de la Poles, earls of Suffolk, from the Chaucer family. The mansion has been all but destroyed but the one undistinguished fragment that remains conceals part of a two-storeyed lodging range of independent rooms at both levels. It may have been the work of Thomas Chaucer, the poet's son, and more significantly a wealthy wool merchant and royal councillor. However, it is the almshouse, school, and rebuilt church that are Suffolk's outstanding survivals at Ewelme, still fulfilling their original function to create a glorious picture in stone and brick.

It is arguable whether the outstanding survival from the close of our period was more secular than monastic in origin, though the question had become academic within a generation. The abbot's lodging is the primary survival of the abbey at Thame, and a glorious one, extending for 105 feet from one side of the subsequent Palladian mansion. This two-storeyed range, interrupted by bay window and turret projections, terminates in a three-storeyed tower. Superficially all of one period in a golden-coloured stone, this lodging range was developed in three phases, two of the mid to late fifteenth century with the tower and projections added between 1510 and 1520. Internally, a sequence of high-status apartments was developed, some of them sumptuously decorated shortly after 1530 to give a spectacular final flourish to the broad span of early domestic architecture that enriches this area.

Timber

Buckinghamshire and Berkshire are both poor in good-quality building stone. Neither the limestone of north Buckinghamshire, part of the great belt that sweeps from Lincolnshire to Dorset, nor the chalk of the Chilterns was good building material. The primary stone houses are Creslow Manor House to the east and the manors at Ashbury and Childrey near Wantage to the west.[24] Flint was used in conjunction with stone at Bisham and with timber at Fyfield Manor and Sutton Courtenay 'Abbey', but timber was the primary source for a wide range of houses throughout the period.

Upton Court near Slough is a fine timber-framed example of about 1320–5, probably built by Merton Priory as an administrative centre but otherwise indistinguishable from a contemporary gentry house. Restoration in 1986–90 has displayed its plan and form with great clarity. Even so, it stands on the cusp of several developments of that period. The lower block is in line with the

PLATE 5 Sutton Courtenay 'Abbey': from the east

central hall, but the contemporary upper block was built as a cross wing, a practice that became common at both ends as the century progressed. The hall was of aisled form but with a central truss that avoided the clutter of aisle posts. This was achieved by a highly unusual hammer-beam structure of experimental form. Finally, the approach to the first-floor solar in the cross wing was by an external stair – a late example when such stairs were increasingly internal. Two contemporary houses nearby, Denham Court and Savay Farm near Denham, also have aisled halls, with the latter retaining its cross wings, but York Farm, West Hagbourne (1284–5) is the earliest timber-framed aisled hall to survive in the Vale of Whitehorse.[25]

Aisled halls were of box-frame construction but the use of base crucks avoided the need for aisle posts. In houses of base-cruck construction, the inward-curving timbers or blades rise from the ground and are joined at the head by a tie beam or collar carrying the upper members of the roof to create a broad open area.[26] It has been estimated that nearly 120 examples survive, widely distributed south of the Humber, Trent, and Mersey, but not beyond the Welsh borderland, east of the Fens, or south of the Thames estuary.[27] They were built between the mid to late thirteenth and the late fourteenth centuries to roof high-status and manorial buildings until superseded by arch-braced and hammer-beam roofs. Among such houses (described in volume II) are Tabley Old Hall (Cheshire), Coningsby Old Rectory (Lincolnshire), West Bromwich Manor House (Staffordshire), Mancetter Manor House (Warwickshire), and Eaton Hall (Herefordshire).

The form was adopted in Buckinghamshire at Creslow Manor House (early fourteenth century), Huntercombe Manor (mid-fourteenth century), and Long Crendon Manor (probably late fourteenth century) but barely thereafter. Long Crendon Manor has been altered out of all recognition[28] whereas the lavishly provided stone-built cross wing added at Creslow was modelled on the recently completed family apartments at Broughton Castle.

Considerably more is known of these structures in Berkshire, through the extensive research carried out between about 1960 and 1990 on the many late medieval and sub-medieval timber-framed houses in the Vale of Whitehorse. Several parishes such as East Hendred, Harwell, Long Wittenham, and Steventon retain up to a dozen examples each, indicative of the area's economic prosperity

at that time. Initially, studies were limited to cruck cottages, in tune with social studies at the time,[29] but it was not long before it was necessary to extend the work to the greater houses in the region.[30] Helped by proximity to the Department of Forestry at Oxford University and the nearby Research Laboratory for Archaeology, this work pioneered the development and use of dendrochronology in the dating and interpretation of framed buildings. It quickly established that many timber buildings were far earlier than had been previously considered, and that complex construction techniques were being practised in lowland England by the early thirteenth century. This research, including an important paper on crown-post roofs,[31] ran parallel with the broad-based studies into cruck construction, the seminal papers of J. T. Smith, and the carpentry analysis and chronology proposed by Cecil Hewett in Essex. The work in the Vale of Whitehorse culminated in the extended survey, detailed analysis, and reinterpretation of the larger medieval houses by Christopher Currie published in 1992.[32]

Sutton Courtenay 'Abbey', one of the earliest high-status houses in the Vale, is also one of the most striking. It began as a timber-framed hall and lower cross-wing house, probably built in c.1290 by the Courtenay family after they had won back their right to a rectorial holding from Abingdon Abbey. The stone-built upper cross wing may have earlier origins, but it is probably contemporary with the hall. This is of base-cruck form, again creating an uncluttered open area, but the extended sweep and weight of the roof proved so heavy that the low timber walls had to be strengthened in c.1330–40 by stone encasement. The majority of the other base-cruck halls in the Vale were developed before the Black Death, including the much altered hall of the Brounz family at Sutton Courtenay Manor House (mid-fourteenth century) and the hall of South Moreton Manor, built by Sir Thomas Sandervill in c.1340.[33] In 1372–3 Richard Brounz, who subsequently became a shire member of parliament and sheriff, replaced the earlier hall at Bayliol's Manor, Harwell, with one of base-cruck form, and also added an upper cross wing to the earlier house.

Well before the fifteenth century, the alternative way of clearing away hall aisle posts and arcades through the development of tie-, collar-, and hammer-beam trusses in association with side purlins and wind braces had become popular for high-status buildings. The lack of late fourteenth- and early fifteenth-century houses in the region makes it difficult to clarify the transition, but Ockwells Manor (c.1455–65) is one of the most striking box-framed houses with such a hall. The hall of Sir John Noreys' house is spanned by arch-braced collars with side purlins and a line of wind braces, contributing to a house of considerable elegance, while the late fifteenth-century hall at East Hendred was enhanced with a central hammer-beam truss.[34] But it is all too easy to become bogged down in the techniques of timber framing when the significance of a major house such as Ockwells lies in other aspects. Following the extensive use of brick in the construction of the royal collegiate foundation at Eton (1440–9), brick was used extensively in association with framing, as Sir John Noreys did at Ockwells, followed by the Kestwold family at Dorney Court. But whereas Dorney is essentially an early twentieth-century evocation of Ockwells, the latter is one of the best-preserved and least-altered houses of mid-fifteenth-century England. Delightful in colour and texture, it is an unequivocal statement of a courtier's success and affluence. This house is important because of its marked individuality and forward-looking internal layout, with the usual services block replaced by a paired lodging with chamber above. The kitchen and services were moved away from the polite rooms to the further side of a small courtyard which was lined with an internal corridor to facilitate food movement and improved access to the first-floor rooms. In addition, Ockwells retains some of the stunning stained glass that has always furnished the great hall, a complete serving hatch, and many of the forecourt buildings that have so often been swept away by later generations as at Dorney Court.

By the close of the fifteenth century, courtyard development was becoming popular, as at Wytham 'Abbey' under the Harcourts, and was percolating down the social scale. Additional ranges were added between the mid-fifteenth and mid-sixteenth centuries to convert the H-shaped 'Abbey' at Sutton Courtenay into a quadrangular residence, while similar expansions were made to the granges at Cumnor (fifteenth century) and Steventon (mid-sixteenth century). Some of the larger houses extended their accommodation with lodging ranges for their household staff as at Ewelme Manor, but similar ranges are evident, roofed at Abingdon Abbey (mid-fifteenth century), still occupied at Chenies (c.1526), and identified after destruction in 1920–30 at Wooburn D'Eyncourt.[35]

Considerable emphasis has been placed on the pivotal role of the hall, but the close of the fifteenth century marks a reduction in this position by restricting it to a ground-floor chamber to allow the important withdrawing chamber to be sited over it. Ashbury Manor is a particularly early and explicit example of about 1490 of a practice that had been developing rapidly in the south-west since the middle of the century and was to become widespread within the next fifty years. Ashbury Manor exhibits this movement because it is essentially a stone-built Somerset house in a Berkshire landscape. It was a development of Glastonbury Abbey on long-held monastic land, and stands remarkably complete with retained original fittings, enhanced by harmonious internal modifications immediately after the Reformation. It is also one of the few late houses in the district that does not incorporate earlier site antecedents.

Apart from the hall, the Thames valley region exhibits a greater number and broader range of domestic chapels than in any other part of the country. The four-bay chapel at Hendred House, East Hendred, has been in continuous Catholic use since 1256, while domestication has not damaged the mid-thirteenth-century chapel at the Prebendal House, Thame, or the late thirteenth-century chapel off the first-floor chamber at Charney Bassett Manor House. The early fourteenth-century example at Broughton Castle is as fine as any in an English house, though it would have been close run if the earl of Berkeley had not role-reversed that at Berkeley Castle in the 1920s. The vaulted and finely decorated mid-fourteenth-century chapel in Beverston Castle is superior to the domestic survivals close to the post-medieval replacement houses at Widmere near Marlow, Chelmscote Manor (licensed in 1343), and Liscombe Park. The chapels at Stanton Harcourt and Rycote, though similarly sited, are superior fifteenth-century examples but pall in comparison with the several collegiate examples at Oxford.

Brick

The use of brick first occurs in the region for the chapel tower of Stonor Park in 1416–17, and was followed by its adoption at Ewelme for the manor, almshouse, and school. The almshouse, founded by the earl of Suffolk in 1437, was directly informed by

PLATE 6 Dorney Court: hall with reinstated bay window

Eton College. It broke with the earlier tradition of a large dormitory for the inmates by housing them in individual dwellings grouped round a small cloistered quadrangle. Like the contemporary school built next to it, both structures still maintain their original function 600 years later.

The extensive use of brick at Henry VI's collegiate foundation between 1441 and 1449 (but not the chapel) helped to make it a fashionable material. It informed the development of Ockwells Manor, Dorney Court, and the Hospital of the Guild of the Holy Cross at Abingdon (1440s), all in association with timber framing. Eton College is also important for the early use of diaper patterning, the combination of brick with stone for doors, windows, and in this case buttresses, and the very early use of cuspless windows. Though brick was the sole building material at Chenies Manor House, it was used in association with stone dressings at Southcote Manor, near Reading. Here the thirteenth-century dwelling on the moated platform was replaced by a brick-built house during the second half of the fifteenth century by Walter Sambourne or his son Drew. The house was demolished in 1926 leaving only a freestone 'tower' of uncertain purpose and the moated enclosure.[36]

Henry VII's treasurer chose brick for Hanwell House (recently upgraded to 'Castle') that he initiated in north Oxfordshire in 1498, but only two mock-military ranges survive. Brick was also used in the mid-Tudor expansion of Rycote, Beckley Park, and Stonor Park when it was transformed into a grand mansion, but apart from its use in 1514 for chimneys at Thornbury Castle, Gloucestershire eschewed brick before the seventeenth century as high-quality building stone was so readily available.

ECCLESIASTICAL HOUSES

Until the Reformation, most of Gloucestershire was part of the diocese of Worcester with the Forest of Dean and the area west of the Severn within the jurisdiction of Hereford. Oxfordshire and Buckinghamshire were part of the vast diocese of Lincoln, while Berkshire was under the bishop of Salisbury. The episcopal houses at Cumnor (Salisbury), Dorchester (Lincoln), and Withington (Worcester) are non-existent. Those at Prestbury (Hereford) and more importantly at Sonning (Salisbury) and Witney (Winchester) have been excavated, but little of the late thirteenth-century house at Bishop's Cleeve (Worcester) survived the drastic remodelling of the 1660s.

There was a wide spread of monastic foundations from the estuary of the Severn to that of the Thames. Some of their magnificent churches are still in use (Gloucester, Tewkesbury, Dorchester, St Frideswide, Oxford), some have only fragmentary evidence that hardly bespeaks their wealth and standing (Hailes, Abingdon, Reading), and some are now abandoned or grass-covered sites (Winchcombe, Cirencester, Eynsham, Godstow). Little of the region was remote, nurturing future ruins on the scale of Tintern or Cleeve. It was extensively crossed by travellers throughout the middle ages. Osney acted as a bank for many Oxford people while Bruern had a high reputation for the quality of its wool. Several towns were dominated by Benedictine and Augustinian foundations and some still are through their churches, while it was the country houses and the secular character of some abbatial lodgings that ensured their survival after the Dissolution.

The twelfth- and fourteenth-century abbatial lodging at Gloucester continued in domestic use until the twentieth century as the abbey became one of Henry VIII's 'new foundations'. The embellishment of the abbot's guest chamber at Flaxley Abbey for Edward III in c.1355 made it the core of the present mid-sixteenth- and late eighteenth-century house. The country houses at Prinknash (1520–5 for the last abbot of Gloucester) and Brockworth Court (1534–9 for the abbot of Llanthony) were similarly enveloped in post-medieval developments, but the former retains two fine first-floor rooms (one with an oriel), and the latter retains some contemporary wall paintings in the attic. Far finer are the three country houses for the abbots of Pershore, St Augustine's, Bristol, and Tewkesbury. Pershore's house of c.1330 at Broadway retains its open hall and residential cross wing with chapel block in fine condition. The even more complete early fifteenth-century Court at Ashleworth has the added attraction of a nearby tithe barn, church, and green of rare charm. The most imposing but altered residence is Forthampton Court near Tewkesbury with a large-scale if heavily renovated early fifteenth-century hall, chamber block, and chapel.

The two other substantive lodgings are within a short distance of each other, either side of the River Thames and equidistant from Thame. The high-quality domestic accommodation built at both Thame Park and Notley Abbey was developed in the mid-fifteenth century and extended in the early sixteenth century. Both residences, almost self-contained, were built on a lavish scale, and embellished at the close of their life with exquisite panelling and early Renaissance decoration by craftsmen who also worked a few miles away for one of Henry VIII's leading civil servants, Sir John Daunce, at Nether Winchendon House. In 1780, the high-quality panelling from the Notley lodging and in 1851 a fine roof with some original colouring from the abbey buildings were removed to crown and furnish an early Tudor chamber block attached to the mid-Tudor Weston Manor in Oxfordshire. The line between secular and ecclesiastical patronage had already become blurred by the mid-fifteenth century and had become indistinguishable within seventy years, as visits to this intriguing circlet of houses confirm.[37]

Other secular elements of a monastic environment are modest. The monastic colleges at Oxford occupied a distinctive position in the university, of which the fifteenth-century work at the Benedictine foundation (now Worcester College) and the Cistercian establishment are the most significant survivals. Other monastic buildings include the corridor-lined lodging range and a plain gatehouse at Abingdon, part of the abbey's thirteenth-century grange at Charney Bassett, considerably less of that of c.1300 at Dean Court, and hardly anything of the important mid-fourteenth-century grange at Cumnor.[38] The gatehouse at Reading Abbey was rebuilt by George Gilbert Scott in 1861 and looks it, so that the more decorative but little-touched one at Kingswood is the most pleasing entry survival in the region. It is a fitting contrast to the more secular fourteenth-century version prefacing Standish Court, originally a country house of Gloucester Abbey. Finally, the Shaven Crown at Shipton-under-Wychwood is a particularly complete fifteenth-century house in form and fenestration, originating as a hospice for the monks of Bruern Abbey nearby and now a hostelry welcoming architectural historians among its many travellers.

COLLEGIATE FOUNDATIONS

The college buildings of Oxford have been described as 'a living museum of Perpendicular development'[39] and its succeeding forms can be clearly traced in the space of a short walk in the city. Early structures were haphazard in layout and growth, as at Merton College (c.1266–1311), showing little concern for student accommodation. It was only with the creation of Merton's Mob Quad by the addition of the library range in 1371–8 to the earlier courtyard buildings that a formal plan was developed, and this was through the close partnership between client and architect. That proved to be the keynote to the radical concept of New College almost immediately afterwards, with its provision of good-quality accommodation for students as well as fellows.

The college buildings of the late middle ages are significant not only because they stand in less altered condition than most residences of this period, but because they reflect the stylistic leadership of the court and of the magnates and prelates of the realm.[40] It was the patronage of the Winchester bishops Wykeham (New), Waynflete (Magdalen), and Fox (Corpus Christi), and leading officials such as the chancellor (Merton), the treasurer of England (Exeter), as well as the monarch (co-founder of All Souls) and a royal consort (Queen's), that ensured that the design and construction would be of the highest standards, particularly as colleges were houses of religion as well as of education. Colleges, therefore, had to embody facilities for both activities. A chapel was essential for the round of religious services with facilities for protecting its vessels and valuables as well as the muniments of the college. Study rooms were needed for fellows (and later for students) as well as a library, and a dining room for communal meals and corporate life, together with the necessary kitchen and offices. Sanitary needs had to be met, and an accounting and audit room, special rooms for the college head, and a lodge for the porter were also essential. All these facilities can be identified in the great foundations that have survived, for the medieval colleges can be grouped into those that were 'grand' in scale as New College was, followed by All Souls, Magdalen, and Christ Church, and those that were 'smaller' like Queen's, Balliol, and Lincoln. New College (1379–c.1406) not only provided the matrix for collegiate layout for several centuries but was the foundation that introduced the Perpendicular style to Oxford. Chapel and hall are in line in a con-

PLATE 7   Oxford, New College: front quadrangle

tinuous range, with the first-floor hall windows suitably more modest and thereby defining the relative importance of their interiors and function. The T-shaped chapel, following the Merton precedent, never developed a nave, while the remaining three ranges contained rooms for study and sleeping by students as well as fellows, a library, and the rooms of a watchful warden above the first of Oxford's gate-towers. This symmetrically closed quadrangular plan was surrounded by high walls to ensure peaceful study rather than protection against civil commotion. The basic college layout was completed in little more than six years (1379–86), a remarkably speedy and sophisticated achievement on a scale hitherto unknown for any comparable building for students or secular canons.

All Souls (1438–43) and Magdalen (1474–90 with slightly later tower) followed the overall pattern, but with greater emphasis given to the street frontage and a more imposing gateway. Whereas Merton and New College were withdrawn from the city, All Souls and Magdalen were more outward-facing. All Souls was also on a smaller scale but its front quadrangle gives the closest impression of the proportions and chapel domination intended by its founder through retaining unheightened enclosing ranges.

The reaction to the 'superfluous curiosity' of ornament and decoration that was among the instructions to Thomas Elkyn in 1439

when completing the south side of the Divinity School is well known. The architectural watchword was now austerity – the preference for gridiron tracery as at All Souls, Balliol College library (c.1431–80), and Merton College chapel tower (1448–51).

A more exuberant style developed during Edward IV's reign, identifiable at Magdalen where the mixture of gridiron tracery in the chapel west front contrasts with the invention of the founder's tower, including the introduction of oriel windows, the bay window in the hall, and the first embattled parapet in Oxford crowning the fellows' lodgings. Gateways became more prominent as at St John's and Merton, while window tracery became less austere, particularly in the patterning of large window heads.

The final phase of late Gothic is marked by the more austere character of Henry VIII's reign in the grandest of all Oxford colleges. Christ Church under Cardinal Wolsey (1525–9) united quadrangle and cloister as at Magdalen, erected the most imposing of gateways and halls, and worked on a scale such that his quadrangle has been likened to a piazza.[41]

In their rectangular planning, communal occupation, and spiritual purpose, colleges were analogous with some monastic foundations, and more particularly with colleges of secular priests, but with greater emphasis given to scale, high-quality workmanship, and specialist residential accommodation. Nor were they markedly different from leading magnate houses in their adoption of a common quadrangular layout, prefaced by a commanding gate-tower. The dining halls were similar in form and function to those of a larger secular household, though the collegiate halls are often in a better-preserved early condition. Many kitchens and offices hold to their original purpose, while college heads were soon demanding less confining accommodation than above the entry gate. In this, they were only following the trend of improved-quality accommodation for secular as well as monastic heads. Lodging ranges were adapted for their educational function through corner studies in each heated living room. College chapels were larger than in most secular households, and though the cloister and integrated quadrangle design developed at Magdalen was repeated only at Christ Church, the precedent had lain at Eton College (1440s) and Herstmonceux Castle (c.1438–49).

We look to the major colleges for architectural innovation and design development rather than the financially restricted smaller foundations. New College set the standard by using the best talent of the time, the master-mason William Wynford who had worked under Wykeham at Windsor Castle, and the master-carpenter Hugh Herland. Both worked closely with the king's master-mason, Henry Yevele, in their advice on other projects for Wykeham, and in concert at Winchester College. William Humberville, another former mason from Windsor Castle, and Wallingford Castle, had been in charge of the library at Merton College (1370s). In the mid-fifteenth century, Richard Chevynton and John Branche were the master-mason and master-carpenter at All Souls, while William Orchard who was responsible for Magdalen College had such an extensive practice that he did not need to be in the orbit of royal works.

In these major projects of the late middle ages, in many respects similar to mansions such as Dartington Hall, Wingfield Manor, or Sudeley Castle, the colleges of Oxford with their equivalents at Cambridge are without parallel in university architecture in Europe. The university and college buildings in France, Spain, Portugal, and Italy are almost always later in date, and despite many individual glories, do not form a comparable medieval *corpus*.

In 1440, Henry VI established 'The King's College of our Lady of Eton' when he was only eighteen years old. His foundation owed nothing to Oxford's collegiate development but much to Wykeham's college at Winchester. Eton's role as a college of secular priests was initially more important than that of the school, while the church was intended to be a leading pilgrimage centre. The school survived and expanded: the church's purpose changed. Not so with that developed nearly forty years later within the royal castle overlooking Eton. In 1475 Edward IV refounded the college established by his predecessor at Windsor in 1348 and initiated the spectacular and continuing foundation of cathedral-like proportions.

MOATED SITES

Interest in moated sites of the region has declined since the 1980s though the subject warrants more detailed study, particularly as the region suffers in comparison with the more extensive research input for the central Midlands. About eighty sites have been identified in Gloucestershire,[42] seventy in Oxfordshire,[43] nearly sixty in Berkshire,[44] and 170 in Buckinghamshire. Those in Gloucestershire are mainly in the Severn valley north of Gloucester, but they extend across the length of the clay lowland of the Thames to the Chiltern

scarp, turning northwards across Buckinghamshire towards the Ouse valley. There are fewer than might be expected in the Vale of Berkeley and on cleared sites in Wychwood and Shotover forests. It seems that the majority belong to sites of manorial rank rather than resulting from colonisation of forest land or waste. Some reveal housing evidence as at Bradwell Bury, the site of the Barry manor,[45] or Harding's Field, one of the three moated manorial sites at Chalgrove identifying the extended development of a domestic and farm site between the late twelfth and the late fifteenth centuries.[46] A fourteenth-century manorial site at Leckhampton was excavated in 1933 with gatehouse and bridge evidence,[47] while some sites support post-medieval houses on the earlier platforms as at Beckley Park and Wightfield Manor near Deerhurst, purchased by Sir John Cassey (d.1400) in 1382 to become the principal seat of the family until 1574 with a house rebuilt in the 1540s.[48] Otherwise their chronology and morphology follow the pattern of neighbouring regions, including moats round hunting lodges of which eleven have been identified in east Berkshire in or near deer parks.[49] A considerable number of monastic sites were also moated, such as Abingdon Abbey and Otley Grange in Oxfordshire, and Steventon Priory and Cholsey Grange in Berkshire. Quadrilateral enclosures are most common but with more subsidiary enclosures than are usually recognised. The three concentric moats at Beckley Park reflect different periods of occupation, of decreasing depth from the inner moat, with the less continuous outer moat dug in 1376 when the royal lodge was being rebuilt.[50] The deliberate incompleteness of many enclosures points to their being for status rather than for defensive purpose.[51]

NOTES
1 *HKW*, II (1964) 577–81, 651–6, 772–5, 821–3, 850–2. For St Briavels with its hall and solar block of 1209–11 and gatehouse of 1292–3, D. Verey and A. Brooks, *Gloucestershire*, II (2002) 657–60.
2 But the crown granted out the Giffards' fortress at Carreg Cennan in South Wales.
3 K. A. Rodwell, *Oxoniensia* 41 (1976) 90–147.
4 *Med. Arch.* 2 (1958) 183–5.
5 Berkeley is another fortress like Kenilworth, Framlingham, and Saltwood where extensive water defences, now drained, may well have been modified during this period for landscape purposes.
6 A. Emery, *Greater Med. Houses*, I (1996) 15–17.
7 Only the two-storeyed upper cross wing with garderobe projection survives of the house built by Sir Richard Louches in 1318. It is flanked on one side by a seventeenth-century farmhouse on the site of the hall, and on the other by a nineteenth-century extension. The solar was raised over a low ground-floor room, both chambers with two-light end windows (upper one blocked) with trefoil ogee lights and head circle. The three-bay upper room retains a wagon roof with king-post trusses. *VCH, Oxfordshire*, VII (1962) 7.
8 RCHM, *Buckinghamshire* (1912) 16–17.
9 P. St. J. Yeoman, *Rec. of Bucks.* 28 (1986) 169–81; 37 (1995) 79–99.
10 It was held by the crown from the thirteenth century until 1628, but excavations in 1955 failed to find the hall although they identified the associated residential block, probably two-storeyed, with low flint and chalk walls supporting chalk, mud, and straw walls above, and a thatched roof. The ground-floor room with fireplace and garderobe had decorated paving tiles made at Penn. The kitchen was a wooden building on low walls, with an attached services unit. E. H. Pavry and G. M. Krocker, *Rec. of Bucks.* 16 pt 3 (1957–8) 131–78.
11 VCH, *Oxfordshire*, V (1957) 56–62; *HKW*, II (1964) 898–900. King John had ordered a timber hunting lodge to be built at Finmere Park in 1207

and there was one of stone and timber at Cornbury by 1337. F. Woodward, *Oxfordshire Parks* (1982) 8–9.

12 The moated manor house of Easthampstead had already been acquired from the bishop of Bath and Wells in 1320, but Edward III added Wychemere and Foliejohn in 1359 and probably Collingridge. Edward spent over £500 between 1353 and 1361 on improving the moated house at Easthampstead and it was retained in royal hands throughout the later middle ages. Small repairs were carried out at Foliejohn and Wychemere but the latter was pulled down in 1395. The stone tower built for the foresters at Collingridge in 1379–80 must have been similar to that still standing near Thetford. *HKW*, II (1963) 247, 903, 925–7, 939–40, 1020–1.

13 It was enclosed not by wood paling but by stone walls, frequently repaired during the thirteenth century. The park at Beckley was stone walled by 1296–7 and that at Middleton Stoney by 1328. F. Woodward, *Oxfordshire Parks* (1982) 6–7.

14 *HKW*, II (1964) 1009–17; VCH, *Oxfordshire*, XII (1990) 431–9.

15 Brit. Lib. K. Top. XXXV 28 e; *HKW*, IV pt 2 (1982) 349–55; *Blenheim: Landscape for a Palace*, ed. J. Bond and K. Tiller (1987). The site of the royal manor is marked by a small monument. Excavation is unlikely to reveal much, as the site was thoroughly flattened in the eighteenth century.

16 Fyfield Manor (*c.*1335–40) has lost its upper wing, so that the present T-shape may not be original. Even so, the first-floor chamber above the services was of high quality.

17 *Trans. Bristol and Glos. Arch. Soc.* 75 (1956) 5–34.

18 Though the house retains its three services doors and solar roof, it was wholeheartedly remodelled for the bishop of Gloucester in 1667, and again for company offices in 1999.

19 This moated house was established after Thame church became a prebend of Lincoln in 1234. After the Reformation, the hall was converted into a barn, and it was pulled down in the eighteenth century except for its south gabled wall with its large fifteenth-century window. For some time, there have been plans to reinstate this link building with a purchased medieval roof. The chapel has been little touched but the solar was extended in the fourteenth century when the fireplace and crown-post roof were inserted. A ground-floor hall with extended windows was built in the fifteenth century, now divided and much reordered, with end offices and kitchen block. *South Midlands Arch.* 21 (1991) 93.

20 A chapel of *c.*1370 was also identified during the excavations. *South Midlands Arch.* 13 (1983) 117–20. The late thirteenth-century south block at Cogges Manor Farm may have begun as a chapel but became the hall. T. Rowley and M. Steiner (eds.), *Cogges Manor Farm, Witney* (1996) 143–7.

21 The county retains a considerable number of lesser fourteenth-century hall and chamber houses, particularly in the Banbury region, such as Priory Farm, Balscott, Manor Farm, Cottisford, and Park House, Hurley, detailed in R. B. Wood-Jones, *Traditional Domestic Architecture in the Banbury Region* (1963).

22 Grange Farm, Balscott (*c.*1500) maintains the richness of the Banbury region, and there are lesser fifteenth-century halls at Great Milton Manor House, North Aston Manor House, and Haseley Court, all now subdivided. This last had become the Barentin residence by 1485 in place of their earlier house at Chalgrove.

23 VCH, *Oxfordshire*, IX (1969) 113–16.

24 Childrey was the home of the Rampayn family to 1329 and the Fettiplace family from 1480 to 1806 (though vacated in favour of Swinbrook in the seventeenth century). The late fifteenth-century hall with mural fireplace, uncusped lights, oriel, and arch-braced collar-beam trusses, was pulled down in 1824 except for the porch and service doorways. C. R. J. Currie, *Oxoniensia* 57 (1992) 108.

25 *Ibid.* 125–32.

26 N. W. Alcock and M. W. Barley, *Antiq. Jour.* 52 (1972) 132–68.

27 N. W. Alcock (ed.), *Cruck Construction* (1981) 12.

28 Long Crendon Manor, not a manor house at all but a dwelling of the FitzPerys, was converted by Philip Tilden between 1918 and 1922 into a thoroughly unhistorical but highly picturesque mélange. He did not destroy anything that was original but he rebuilt, extended, and heightened (in the artistic sense) 'a mere farm of four or five bedrooms . . . into a house of five sitting rooms and twenty bedrooms'. Philip Tilden, *True Remembrances* (1954) 60–7. The fifteenth-century stone gateway from the street was originally stone vaulted and has lost its upper floor. The much better preserved two-storey gatehouse to Missenden Abbey was built in *c.*1406–10. *Vern. Arch.* 24 (1993) 54–5. The base-cruck form was also used in the destroyed two-bay hall of the D'Eyncourt family at Wooburn D'Eyncourt, and for three minor Buckinghamshire halls at Old Manor House, Thornborough, Old Bakery, Denham, and The Brills, Weston Turville. J. C. Trench and P. Fernley, *Rec. of Bucks.* 23 (1981) 39–50; RCHM, *Buckinghamshire* I (1912) 323–4.

29 J. M. Fletcher in *Scientific Methods in Medieval Archaeology*, ed. R. Berger (1970) 141–57; C. R. J. Currie and J. M. Fletcher, *Med. Arch.* 16 (1972) 136–42.

30 J. M. Fletcher, *Oxoniensia* 33 (1968) 71–88; J. M. Fletcher and C. R. J. Currie, *Arch. Jour.* 136 (1979) 173–92.

31 J. M. Fletcher and P. S. Spokes, *Med. Arch.* 8 (1964) 152–83. This has been supplemented by several paragraphs on such roofs in *Med. Arch.* 27 (1983) 132–3.

32 *Oxoniensia* 57 (1992) 81–244.

33 *Ibid.* 175–81. The chamber block added at about this time at Bisham Abbey by William, earl of Salisbury was of base-cruck construction.

34 The hammer-beam form also occurs at the de Grey manor house at Bletchley, dendro dated to *c.*1475, now reduced to Rectory Cottages. A. J. Adams and P. N. Jarvis, *Rec. of Bucks.* 30 (1988) 1–15.

35 The range was at least 50 feet long, possibly added in the early sixteenth century. Trench and Fernley, *Rec. of Bucks.* 23 (1981) 39–50.

36 Since 1926, the 'tower' has been reduced to a stump. A swiftly conducted excavation in 1976 prior to redevelopment revealed little of significance, C. F. Slade, *Berks. Arch. Jour.* 69 (1977–8) 49–59. Also E. W. Dormer, *Berks., Bucks. and Oxon. Arch. Jour.* 10 (1905) 9–15; VCH, *Berkshire*, III (1923) 366.

37 Other monasteries in the region that proved readily adaptable to house conversion included Missenden (Bucks.), Bisham, Hurley, and Sandleford (Berks.), Bruern, Clattercote, and Wroxton (Oxon.), Bristol, Deerhurst, Flaxley, and Hailes (Glos.).

38 Some of the stone barns in the region enhanced a grange's security as well as providing food storage facilities. The high-quality stone survivals, together with those in Gloucestershire, Worcestershire, and Wiltshire, form a group continuing the tradition established by such well-known aisled structures as the vast one at Cholsey (*c.*1200? Reading) pulled down in 1815, and that at Great Coxwell (*c.*1300–10 Beaulieu). They include those at Enstone erected by Winchcombe Abbey in 1382, Swalcliffe by New College, Oxford in 1402–6, Upper Heyford only a little later by the same college, and that at Adderbury of two building periods, converted into stables in 1877. The barns of the middle Thames valley and the Vale of Whitehorse were more often timber-framed such as the base-cruck barn at Lockton's Farmhouse, Harwell (*c.*1325). For the barns in Gloucestershire see page 13, note 10.

39 J. H. Harvey in *The History of the University of Oxford*, II, ed. J. L. Catto and T. A. R. Evans (1992) 747.

40 *Ibid.* 751.

41 R. H. C. Davis, *Oxoniensia* 11–12 (1946–7) 83.

42 F. A. Aberg (ed.), *Medieval Moated Sites* (1978) 2–3.

43 J. Bond in *The Archaeology of the Oxford Region*, ed. J. M. Steane (1986) 150.

44 Twenty-six in the Vale of Whitehorse and about thirty in east Berkshire

with a further ten possible sites. S. Ford, *East Berkshire Archaeological Survey* (1987) 106–8.

45 R. A. Croft and D. C. Mynard, *The Medieval Landscape of Milton Keynes* (1984) 16–17. Several others in the region seem to be of more modest character, like Caldecotte, excavated in 1978–9 with little trace of any substantial buildings, *ibid.*

46 *Med. Arch.* 22 (1978) 181; 23 (1979) 270–1.

47 *Trans. Bristol and Glos. Arch. Soc.* 60 (1933) 235–48; *Med. Arch.* 19 (1975) 75.

48 Verey and Brooks, *Gloucestershire*, II (2001) 148–9.

49 Ford, *East Berkshire Archaeological Survey* 106–8.

50 *Med. Arch.* 17 (1973) 175.

51 Bond in *The Archaeology of the Oxford Region*, ed. Steane, 151.

3

HOUSEHOLD EXPANSION, CHAMBERS AND LODGINGS

GREATER HOUSEHOLDS

THE élite households of medieval England were limited to the upper echelons of society, and they were distinguished and clarified by that rapid movement in social mobility that marked the 150 years between the beginning of the Hundred Years' War and the accession of the Tudor dynasty. As discussed in volume II,[1] the gradual definition of the aristocracy from the relatively loose terms used in 1300 and the subsequent expansion of its lower ranks were essentially determined by financial standing.

By the close of the fourteenth century, the number of hereditary peers regularly summoned to parliament had stabilised at about eighty holders. Though new ranks were created such as marquess (1385) and viscount (1440), the number held fairly constant at between eighty to ninety families until the close of that century. To this number should be added the forty leading bishops and high-income ecclesiastics deeply involved in the political life of late medieval England. Landowners with an annual income of more than £40 were expected to take up knighthood, though knights banneret were an enigmatic group who gradually disappeared after the first quarter of the fifteenth century. They were paid a daily rate twice that of a knight, but it was not a hereditary rank, so that holders moved either upwards into the peerage or downwards to the knightly class. The demands of the crown on the battlefield and the growing complexity of administration during the fourteenth century helped to clarify the status of knights as well as the lower one of esquires. It has been estimated that there were about a thousand knights towards the close of the fourteenth century, but this number had fallen by about half by 1500.[2] It was these three élite groups, broadly reducing from nearly 1100 to 700 people between the mid-fourteenth and the early sixteenth century who sought to establish substantial houses and fill them with a household reflecting their 'estate' – their rank, their public standing, and their generosity.

The first half of the fourteenth century marked a gradual reduction in the number of meaningful houses held by the leaders of society.[3] Edward I inherited twenty houses from his father, and though this number rose to twenty-five early in Edward III's reign, it had fallen to seventeen houses by the close of the century, twelve under Henry VI, and ten with the advent of Henry VII. The same movement applied to many of the bishops. The bishop of Hereford held at least thirteen houses in the early fourteenth century, but the decision was made in 1356 to limit them to seven. In 1450, the bishop of Lichfield was granted permission by the pope to abandon all his residences except his castle at Eccleshall, his palaces at Lichfield and Coventry, and three other houses. The remainder were to be abandoned and their materials used to repair those that remained in the bishop's hands.

The practice of concentrating one's resources on a few properties equally applied to the aristocracy. At the beginning of the fourteenth century, Aymer de Valence, earl of Pembroke, had castles at Haverfordwest, Pembroke, Goodrich, and Sutton Valence (Kent), and residences at Moreton Valence (Gloucestershire), Newton Valence (Hampshire), Inkberrow (Worcestershire), and Hertingfordbury (Hertfordshire), and he built a new house at Bampton in Oxfordshire. Yet we have records of him visiting Bampton only twice, in 1307 and 1312, and hardly at all for travelling to Pembroke or Haverfordwest.[4] The limitation of long periods of occupation to two or three houses is one of the key changes in residential development during the fourteenth century. It arose because the practice of peripatetic travelling to use up the crops and resources of an estate was no longer efficient or necessary.[5] There was also the realisation that all those resources needed to be husbanded so that they could be lavished on a handful of properties to achieve the necessary scale of magnificence. Higher living standards also made it financially prohibitive to bring the houses of earlier generations up to date.[6] The consequence was that households became much more settled from the second quarter of the fourteenth century and almost universally so by Richard II's reign. Instead of moving between properties once or twice a month, settlement in a single house from four to eight months at a time and only between two or three properties became the norm.[7] A London house, though, became increasingly essential for any courtier.

Having shorn themselves of their peripheral properties for all practical purposes, crown and aristocracy concentrated their resources on those that mattered, expanding and improving the comfort of those they favoured. And in so doing, they also helped to build up their spheres of influence – their 'locality'. John of Gaunt spent much of his time at Leicester and Kenilworth castles in the Midlands, and to a lesser extent at Tutbury and Higham Ferrers not far away. He enjoyed visiting Pontefract Castle in the centre of his northern estates, and expanded Hertford Castle at the heart of his south-eastern interests, though he never visited or spent money on Pevensey Castle or any of his residences in Wales. In the mid-fifteenth century, Richard, duke of York, had extensive estates on the Welsh border, centred on Wigmore and Ludlow castles, and further centres of locality in Northamptonshire based on Fotheringhay Castle, in Yorkshire centred on Sandal Castle, in East Anglia from the long-established castles at Clare and Stamford, and in the pale in Ireland with Trim Castle at its heart.

For many families, the reduction in houses had been offset by a contrary trend. Children, particularly those of leading families, often spent their formative years in the household of a superior, but as soon as they were married they would be granted a subsidiary house for their own establishment.[8] A network of family-related residences therefore gradually spread across a region such as those of the Courtenays in Devon during the mid-fourteenth century, the Beauchamp family in the Midlands, and the Nevilles and Percys throughout northern England a little later. And just as each leading magnate had his 'locality', so did each rank below, with the more important controlling several residences like the Clifford family holding four castles in the Eden valley as well as Skipton Castle. The Berkeley family dominated Gloucestershire from their *caput* at

Berkeley, supported by relations in the castles at Beverston and Dursley, the defensive houses at Coberley and Yate, and the manor house at Wotton-under-Edge. Most knights had to be satisfied with one or two good-quality houses but they shared the same outlook, aspirations, and values in life as a magnate, and emulated those of higher rank in their standards of living, the form of their household, and the scale of their houses.

Architectural and academic historians often forget that a house is essentially an envelope to contain a household, whether a magnificent one or that of a modest family. Furthermore, we know considerably more about the form and development of the medieval house than we do about the household that occupied it. The organisation of the royal household has long been a fruitful field of research but the crown has always been an exceptional case in scale and in the wealth of documentation.[9] Otherwise the examination of households has been limited to a handful of studies on single families, or to the quagmire of the causes and effects of bastard feudalism on high society. It is only within the last few years that historians have focussed their attention on the size, membership, finances, and work practices of the household, essentially through the work of Kate Mertes,[10] Christopher Woolgar,[11] and Christopher Dyer.[12] Even so, only a limited number of household accounts, ordinances, and other documents have been pressed into use so far. As some of the evidence is conflicting, considerable further research and debate is necessary before we have a clear picture of this vital aspect of medieval society.

The nucleus family of husband, wife, and children was characteristic of English society from at least the fourteenth century and probably far earlier than that.[13] Relations did not usually live under the same roof, though widows and in-laws sometimes did in élite families.[14] The staff and servants of a house made up its household, and it was the size, splendour, and hospitality of that household that indicated a lord's standing in society. Such a household expressed a person's 'lordship', and in so doing made a political statement. The scale and magnificence of a leading household made an equally important social statement in which display and ceremony contributed even more than hospitality and charity. In concentrating on the households of magnates, bishops, and knights, it is not intended to minimise those of the lesser gentry but to indicate the standards and scale achieved using the more extensive sources available for élite households.

A household was essentially made up of two groups – the staff and domestic servants *permanently* working for the lord and his family, and the people retained by the lord but only *periodically* attached to him. A lord's household was a very hierarchical organisation with clearly defined departments, responsibilities, and status rules. The permanent household of a leading magnate was divided into three levels of rank, headed by three senior officers. The steward was the general manager of a household in charge of its discipline, conduct, and day-to-day running. The treasurer was responsible for its financial administration, overseeing its income and more particularly its expenditure, and preparing regular accounts.[15] The most important households would also have a chamberlain, responsible for the staff of a lord's private or personal chambers, and this position became more significant from the mid-fourteenth century onwards as private apartments became increasingly extensive and important. The treasurer might be a clerk, but laymen were increasingly employed, particularly as senior officers increasingly provided a lord with advice and counsel. Chamberlains were frequently privileged associates of a lord and would sometimes be a knight such as Sir Robert Swillington (1376–83) in John of Gaunt's household, Sir William Oldhall in that of the duke of York (c.1448–60), or Sir William Knivet who served the duke of Buckingham from about 1514.

Beneath these three senior officials came a second group who dealt with the more routine aspects of a household's welfare. Though there might be a kitchen clerk who handled all food accounts, responsibility for the running of the kitchen and all food preparation in the adjoining offices lay with the chief cook. He was one of the highest-paid employees in a household. Under him would be several 'departments', including the pantler responsible for bread and table linen, the butler responsible for ale, beer, and wine, and the person overseeing the scullery, saucery, and pastry making.[16] (For kitchens, see pages 161–2.)

For more personal service, a lord would have a secretary responsible for his letters, business correspondence, and legal papers. The wardrober was responsible for the lord's clothes, jewels, furniture, furnishings, candles, and spices, and there would be a varied number of personal or chamber servants in attendance on the lord and his wife. The chaplain ordered the religious life of a house, for every one had a private chapel, even that of an esquire. The chaplain might help with the education of the children of a household,[17] and he would be assisted in his duties in larger residences by a number of clerks. Finally, the marshall accounted for the lord's stables, hunting, and falconry, and by his quasi-military role he could take charge of discipline in the hall of the largest household.

The third stratum in a residence consisted of the domestic staff – valets, grooms, pages, and servants – employed to ensure the smooth running of the household, cater for its needs, and provide the comforts and lifestyle that the lord and his family demanded. In larger households, each function or office would have its own grooms and pages, under the responsibility of a valet or supervisor so that there would be grooms, pages, and a valet for the larder, the washhouse, the bakery, and the poultry, as well as for the hall, the lord's private chambers, the chapel, and the guests' chambers. As households grew from the mid-fourteenth century onwards, they would worship in the lower chapel, possibly eat and sleep in their own hall, and be employed to help create that atmosphere of goodwill and service that made life as comfortable as possible for the lord and his family.

Just as the household of a leading magnate tended to mirror that of the king, the world of a knight would reflect that of a magnate. Scaling down would inevitably mean simplifying the structure. The steward would serve as the treasurer, the chaplain would also be the lord's secretary, a valet would be in charge of the stables, and the grooms and pages would share a broad range of duties between them. Yet each household, whether that of minor gentry or a leading magnate, reflected the fourfold division of personal service, religious duties, food preparation, and hospitality. During the fifteenth century, duties in a large household became increasingly fragmented and formalised, with individual responsibility for carving, cup-bearing, handing round ewers, and acting as physicians for health-care reflecting the increasing elaboration and rituals of domestic life.[18] Standards also tended to be more formal

and exacting as the century progressed, reflecting the increase in house size, intimacy, and luxury.

It can be seen that a household covered a wide social spectrum. The majority of staff would be drawn from the locality, but the more senior members, particularly in the fifteenth century, would be esquires or gentlemen, hopeful of advancement through serving those in a household of higher standing.[19] For those working in such an environment, it could be a centre of patronage and a source of political, social, or financial well-being. Employment was relatively stable at all levels, with food, shelter, and clothing provided free, and a salary scaled to the employee's position. Sleeping conditions were crowded and privacy was limited, but there were the off-setting benefits of gifts, tips, and perhaps promotion.

A household was almost entirely a male society throughout our period. The only women were washerwomen, a nurse for the householder's children, and the serving ladies of the lord's wife. This partly arose from a household's political role and the need to support its head at times of war, partly through economic considerations, and partly because the exclusion of women was considered necessary for the maintenance of decorum and status whether the lord was absent or at home.[20] This situation started to change among the lower ranks of a household during the later fifteenth century,[21] but throughout our period, wives and children were expected to live outside or away from the employer's residence.

All the members of the lord's household identified so far were expected to live within the curtilage of his house and to be ready to attend him at all times. They were given a household title and were listed on the household wage account. The other part of his household consisted of those members who were only employed periodically. They were his retainers and councillors, closer to the lord in social standing than nearly all other members of his entourage. They were essentially knights and esquires who took the lord's livery and wore it with pride, for livery wearing was standard.[22] This practice of retaining developed during the fourteenth century as local offices were increasingly granted to local men, and this, in turn, enhanced their importance to a nearby magnate. The principal way of securing their support was to grant them a retainer, so that the practice of retaining or even employing members of the gentry on a more permanent basis became a significant development during the later years of the century. Most magnates had a score of knights and esquires in their retinues, but dukes and earls could have fifty or more. John of Gaunt was exceptional in having 200 or so retainers during the early 1380s. 'Indentured' retainers, despite the extensive literature about them, seem to have been unusual.[23]

Specially favoured retainers might be chosen to be among a magnate's councillors. They would be available to advise him on a broad range of personal matters such as the running of his business affairs, his political attitudes, and his private life, and their names frequently occur in records as executors or trustees. They might include the leading officers of his household, but were essentially neighbouring landowners, politically influential knights, and lawyers. Thus Sir Thomas Hungerford, member of parliament for Wiltshire and Somerset, had initially acted as steward to the bishop of Salisbury, but John of Gaunt appointed him steward of all his lordships south of the Trent in 1375 and he held that position until 1393. He was too important to be a household steward, for he was a great estate agent and political persuader, wealthy enough to remodel and expand his residence at Farleigh Hungerford, and just the sort of person Gaunt needed to advise him over the troubled waters of Richard II's rule.[24] His contemporary Sir Hugh Cheyne (d.1404) of Cheyney Longville Castle similarly advised the earls of March. If the senior officers and favoured retainers helped to make up the equivalent of a board of directors, supporting the lord in his role as chairman or chief executive of a business company, some high-ranking councillors, particularly those with political clout, would serve as the equivalent of executive directors.[25] What is surprising is the number of lawyers retained by a lord. There were at least nine on the Black Prince's council in the 1350s and the earl of Devon retained fourteen in 1384–5. Most of these would only work to specific requests, but most large households had at least one permanent lawyer charged with safeguarding the lord's rights and interests.

Councillors were particularly valuable in guiding a magnate during periods of political uncertainty such as the middle years of the fifteenth century, but their worth was equally important during a minority in safeguarding an heir's interests, or during the absence of the lord on military service at home or abroad. And the rewards for such service could be substantial – bequests in a will, fees for good service, gifts and patronage from people hoping that a good word would be put in for them in seeking a magnate's approbation.

Most important of all was the magnificence of a household for this was the most visible and outward sign of a lord's largesse. Status was all-important in late medieval England and all staff played a part in demonstrating this. Their numbers and their dress advertised a lord's magnificence, particularly those making up his entourage when he rode to parliament or to a tournament, or visited a neighbour. By observing a luxurious house, spectacularly furnished, with a generous table and a well-filled stable, a visitor would identify his host's standing with his peers, his neighbours, and his tenants. Outward show rather than personal ability was all-important in late medieval society, for conspicuous expenditure and conspicuous display were regarded not so much as virtues but as the essential fabric of a magnate's way of life.

If a magnate's landholding was the principal source of his wealth, his lifestyle was his prime area of expenditure, and one that was frequently monitored and checked. There is considerable evidence that most leaders took a detailed interest in the running of their estates. Ralph, Lord Cromwell as much as the Ferrers family of Baddesley Clinton regularly checked his accounts, be they household, building, or estate returns. Richard Beauchamp, earl of Warwick, 'retained full and active control in the administration of his great landed inheritance . . . even if he was overseas'.[26]

Analysis of the accounts that have survived shows that nearly half a lord's income was spent on maintaining his household, whether it was the Black Prince, Lord Berkeley, or the Stonor family.[27] The largest item was food and drink, its scale determined by the size of the household and the extent of a lord's entertaining and hospitality. Some of this seems conspicuously extravagant, like the meal served at the enthronement of archbishop Neville in 1466 or the vast amounts of food consumed in the household of the 5th earl of Northumberland as described in volume I.[28] But when these are considered in institutional terms, the quantities are modest.[29] Diets were reasonably varied from produce obtained locally, supplemented with ale from malt and barley, and the produce of the

demesne manors and rents in kind. Next to food was cloth and clothing (a particularly conspicuous yardstick of status as the sumptuary legislation shows), followed by candles, wax, and fuel. Luxury goods such as wine, spices, and silk fabrics depended on income availability but would be supplemented by gifts. Staff salaries, unlike the present day, were relatively modest.[30]

The medieval household not only became numerically larger and with a greater division of duties as the fourteenth and fifteenth centuries developed, but it varied continuously in size and content. Councillors and friends would come and go, estate staff would make periodic visits, knights and esquires would be in attendance for limited periods, while records show that some of the permanent members of the household would be given leave of absence, occasionally for extended periods. Some households had to accommodate the lord's mother who might be a wealthy widow who wanted her own staff. In 1436, thirteen of the fifty-two peerages at that time were held jointly between male heirs and widows.[31] And if the lord was away on military service, then the residential household would be smaller as he would have taken some of his staff to cater for his personal needs and to serve as part of his retinue. It is therefore extremely difficult to give a precise indication of a household's size, for the snapshot offered by one record can be at variance with that of another only a few years later. As today, it would also depend on such vital factors as the fluctuations in income, the range of his interests, the extravagance or frugality of his wife, the age and marriage prospects of their children, and the number of maintained residences.

Because of the extended time-span, the varied range of financial resources available to a broad band of society, and the fragmentary nature of the documentation, it is all too easy to draw dubious conclusions from the limited information currently available. The household of the 3rd Lord Berkeley (1326–61) included twelve knights and twenty-four esquires,[32] while Edward Courtenay, earl of Devon had a complement of eight knights including five members of his own family, forty-one esquires, fourteen lawyers, and sixty-one servants in 1384–5.[33] William, Lord Hastings in the most fully documented fifteenth-century household had ninety permanent retainers.[34] In 1442, Humphrey Stafford, 1st duke of Buckingham, one of the three wealthiest persons at the time, had eighty-three retainers of whom a significant number were lawyers and counsel, while the 3rd duke of Buckingham had a household of between 300 and 400 between 1511 and 1514.[35] All these can be related to still-standing properties, and though the last confirms the almost royal scale of Buckingham's domestic and political base at Thornbury Castle, numbers by themselves and the broader conclusions drawn from them are not too meaningful. Holding to averages across a range of fourteenth-century families, it has been estimated that the household of an earl was usually between fifty and a hundred permanent staff. A baron would have between thirty and fifty staff, a banneret between twenty and forty, and knights and esquires between ten and thirty full-time staff.[36] To these numbers should be added the periodic visits of knights and esquires to earls and barons, as well as friends and guests of all rank, some of whom would bring their own servants.

There is considerable evidence for the view that the households grew in scale at all levels during the fifteenth century.[37] However, Christopher Woolgar has made some calculations based on food consumption which suggest that the largest households occurred in

PLATE 8 Thornbury Castle: engraving from the south by S. and N. Buck (1732)

the first half of the fourteenth century, and that they decreased in size during the late fourteenth and fifteenth centuries, with some growth towards the close of the century.[38] Even so, household numbers suggest a widespread pattern of increase during the century, partly arising from the weakness of royal authority, but partly to meet the culture of greater luxury and display. It was in response to swollen household numbers that ordinances were written in an attempt to control and regulate them, such as the household regulations of Edward IV, and those for George, duke of Clarence, the 3rd duke of Buckingham, and the 5th earl of Northumberland.[39] The Black Book of Edward IV's household for instance, written in c.1471–2, suggests that the size of a household should be 240 for a duke, 200 for a marquis, 140 for an earl, eighty for a viscount, forty for a baron, twenty-four for a banneret, sixteen for a knight, and ten for an esquire. This is an ideal which in reality was less at the upper levels but more at the lower. Nevertheless, it highlights the increase in size and indicates the relative scale thought appropriate to a person's station.[40] And should it be thought that only the greater households had substantial staff numbers, esquires such as Robert Waterton of Mexborough had a household of forty staff in 1419–20, William Vredale of Wickham had one of thirty-five staff in 1478–9, while Robert Melton, a Suffolk yeoman farmer, had a household of seventeen from 1499 to 1508.[41]

To emphasise this last point, not only did the nobility and gentry share the same attitudes, lifestyle, and aspirations, but there was little distinction between their homes as well. It is not immediately apparent standing in front of Bolton Castle in Yorkshire and Bodiam Castle in Sussex which was built by a knight and which one by a magnate and officer of state. Nor is there any obvious differentiation in the size and character of the magnate's manor at Wingfield in Derbyshire and the knight's house nearby, Haddon Hall. The impressive fortified house at Brinsop Court in Herefordshire was

built by a local squire, while the far more modest house not far away at Cheyney Longville was developed by a wealthy knight and long-standing member of parliament. Lord Cromwell's mansion at Wingfield was eagerly acquired by the earl of Shrewsbury, a higher-ranking magnate, with virtually no addition or alterations whatsoever. Sudeley Castle in Gloucestershire was built by a parvenu lord, but Edward IV's brother was happy to take it over and enlarge the house as his principal residence in the south before ascending the throne in 1483.[42]

CHAMBER EXPANSION

These social and cultural changes substantially impacted on the organisation and layout of the greater medieval houses. They did not, however, affect the form and focal position of the hall and its service rooms. The structural changes that occurred such as the removal of aisle posts, the elaboration of roofs, and the insertion of bay windows lighting the dais, were essentially intended to impress visitors of all ranks and standing. The principal cultural change was that the hall tended to become more of a ceremonial apartment – used for feasting, entertainment, formal receptions, and hospitality. The only development in service rooms was an increase in their number and specialisation to meet this demand.

The prime structural developments during the later middle ages occurred in the growth of private chambers and apartments, and in intriguingly different ways. The status of an apartment depended on several factors, succinctly analysed by Graham Fairclough.[43] The most important was its position in the house in relation to the hall. If it was beyond the screens and cross passage at the lower end of the hall, that is close to the offices and kitchen, it was usually of relatively low status. If it was beyond the dais and high table in the hall, it would be of high status. Furthermore, ground-floor rooms were of lesser standing than first- or upper-floor rooms. In some of the largest houses in the later middle ages, the hall was elevated to a first-floor position as at Windsor, Llawhaden, and Wardour castles and Wingfield Manor. Size and form had always been essential factors in determining a room's importance but it was now marked by the size and number of its windows, the scale of its entry, and the form of its roof, remembering that the upper rooms of a two-storeyed house were nearly always open to the roof structure. As the benefits of privacy became increasingly appreciated, a room's position in relation to other comparable apartments became increasingly significant. Privacy meant controlling access, and that was much easier as the common practice was for rooms to be approached one from another. Corridor access throughout our period only occurred in very limited circumstances. The extent of a room's facilities was significant. They were, in order of importance, a fireplace, a separate lavatory, a closet for clothes, and a wall cupboard. Occasionally there would be a wall drain for washing as at Dacre Castle or Battel Hall. A room's decorative qualities also contributed to its standing, particularly an elaborate and decorated roof structure which is often the primary survival when the chamber it served has been totally altered. Equally indicative are the architectural embellishment of the doorway and the windows, the inclusion of painted glass (or even glass at all), elaborate scenes or designs painted on plastered walls, and at the close of our period, the inclusion of decorative woodwork. Finally, the status of a room depended on whether it was shared or not, or whether it was part of a suite. Suites were usually of two rooms, with the larger outer chamber with fireplace and garderobe serving as a withdrawing chamber, and the smaller inner chamber lacking such facilities used primarily as a bedchamber.

These factors translated into house development in a number of ways during the later middle ages. The first was a substantial increase in chamber accommodation, and more specifically in the accommodation for the owner of the house and his family. There were comparatively few chambers (or little privacy) in twelfth- and early thirteenth-century houses, but the documentary evidence for the royal houses at Westminster, Clarendon, and Woodstock reveals the increasing number of rooms demanded by Henry III and Edward I and their queens. An examination of two major fourteenth-century residences, Goodrich Castle and Bolton Castle, reveals the scale of the development within two or three generations. Externally, Goodrich (c.1280–1300) rising from its rock-hewn moat is as impressive and as formidable as any built by Edward I in North Wales. Internally, as much care was taken with the residential accommodation as with its military capacity. Furthermore, the accommodation of halls and associated chamber blocks, offices, and chapels was carefully interlocked, pentice linked, and integrated with the defensive frontages so that their function was in no way endangered. Goodrich Castle is also particularly important because it initiated the movement when residential planning became as important as defensive arrangements, a movement stimulated by the mid-century redevelopments at Berkeley and Windsor castles. By the time Lord Scrope built Bolton Castle (1376–96) the frowning exterior concealed a veritable warren of halls and chambers, skilfully interlocking but ensuring individual privacy and scaled by size and appointments to the rank of the occupier.

Bolton Castle makes it clear that chambers were increasingly assigned to individuals. They were not, however, used for a single purpose as most of our rooms are today, but were multi-functional. They could be a withdrawing room, a bedroom, a dressing and

PLATE 9 Sudeley Castle: windows of private apartments of Richard, duke of Gloucester

ablution room, and equally used for taking meals and receiving guests. Most important, though, was that chambers were usually of single social status. A lord's chamber was strictly out of bounds to all but him and those honoured few he cared to admit.

Chambers increased in the number and quality of their appointments. The number of garderobes and fireplaces at both Goodrich Castle and Haddon Hall shows that comfort was becoming increasingly important, and this began to apply to rooms used not only by the owner but by his guests, senior members of his household, and even some of his staff. Furnishings improved and decorative features helped to enhance a chamber, as discussed in the last essay in this volume, pp. 468–82. What is quite clear is that by concentrating on fewer residences than in the early middle ages, it was possible for a major householder to expand the number of good-quality rooms in his house, and to furnish them appropriately with comfortable facilities and luxurious materials.

The increase in the number of chambers and the growth of household numbers inevitably meant an increase in the size of a house. The development of courtyard houses brought discipline to residential layouts. By the beginning of the fourteenth century, it was the primary shape for most high-status residences, and by the close of the century the courtyard was nearly always rectangular. The Neville family rebuilt their castles at Brancepeth (c.1360–80) and Raby (c.1367–90) on the plan of towers and apartments irregularly grouped around courtyards. Within a few years, the family had adopted a more formal quadrangular plan at Sheriff Hutton Castle (1382–1402), as the Percy family did at Wressle Castle (1390s) not far away.

A quadrangular courtyard enabled ranges to be built against its outer walls providing a line of lower- (ground-floor) and higher-status (upper-floor) accommodation as at Maxstoke and Penrith castles. But whereas initially such ranges were simply built against the walls, they quickly became integrated with the walls during the second half of the fourteenth century to create enclosing ranges round a central court, as at Bolton and Wressle castles. Towards the later fifteenth century, expansion might come up against site restrictions, forcing an owner to develop additional higher-status rooms above the services at the lower end of the hall as at Ightham Mote and Cotehele.

PLATE 10 Thornbury Castle: windows of private suites of the duke and duchess of Buckingham

A single courtyard was adequate for most households; two courtyards became desirable in the larger ones. Fortresses had often been built with an outer and inner courtyard for defensive reasons and to provide lines of protection, but the form did not develop in residential architecture until the later thirteenth century. It can be seen in some of the largest episcopal palaces in London such as Winchester House and Lambeth Palace, but one of the earliest purely country houses to adopt the double-courtyard plan was Dartington Hall during the 1390s. The form had become the norm for high-status houses by the second quarter of the fifteenth century as at Caister Castle, Wingfield Manor, and Haddon Hall. The two courtyards were nearly always separated by the hall, facilitating the distinction of an outer court for services, and an inner court for the private apartments of the householder. The outer court was more open to the world and had greater public access. The inner court encouraged privacy, and the development of secondary or inner chambers and even suites, and gave greater control over access.

THE DEVELOPMENT OF LODGINGS

Guests were an extremely important factor in any household, particularly from the mid-fourteenth century onwards when there is a

great deal of information about visitors to great houses, their length of stay, and the costs involved. The late fourteenth-century poem *Sir Gawain and the Green Knight* brilliantly depicts Gawain's cordial reception at the castle of Sir Bertilak, and though it may be idealised, it encapsulates the principles to be accorded to all guests irrespective of their rank. Some analysis of household accounts shows that visitors – from magnates to workmen – in some bishops' households accounted for between 20 per cent and 30 per cent of those present at meal times, while they were between 44 per cent and 50 per cent of those present in the duke of Buckingham's household at Thornbury Castle.[44] Short- and long-stay guests would be accompanied by servants who also had to be housed and fed.

Two new types of accommodation were conceived to meet the increasing numbers and status of household staff and provide generous hospitality facilities. One was the development of lodging accommodation from the mid-fourteenth to the mid-sixteenth century. The other was the introduction of residential tower-houses from the second quarter of the fifteenth century to the closing years of that era. As the latter was discussed in volume II,[45] the origin and different types of household lodgings are considered in the remainder of this chapter.

In its fully developed form, a secular lodging usually consisted of a room, about 20 feet square, with its own entry, window, fireplace, and garderobe. They rarely existed as singletons but in a group, usually a minimum of four lodgings – two at ground level and two above approached by an external or internal stair. Lodgings lay outside the immediate area of the family apartments and would be described today as 'bed-sitters'. However, such units did not suddenly appear fully formed.

References to chambers for senior staff and guests frequently occur in thirteenth-century records, particularly those for royal palaces.[46] They may have been large undivided rooms, rather like small dormitories. So far, no such survivals have been clearly identified, though this is surely only a matter of time. That might have been the purpose of the two rooms, one above the other, between the services and the earlier keep at Berkeley Castle (second quarter of the fourteenth century) now displayed as a dining room with picture gallery above. A similar lodging existed next to the gatehouse at the archiepiscopal palace at Charing where the principal lodging wing consisted of two communal rooms at the upper level and two below, if the scale of the two garderobe projections is taken into account.[47] The ground floor could have held as many as twenty-five staff, with fewer above if those rooms were occupied by more senior people. Attributed to *c*.1340, this accommodation may represent an early form before the rapid development stage of the mid-century.

One of the themes of these volumes has been the close relationship during the later middle ages between large-scale houses and analogous buildings. This is particularly relevant to the development of secular lodgings. The retinue of the king, a magnate, or a church-leader was of sufficient scale to be considered a community of people, and in planning accommodation for them it was natural to look at existing institutions that had already faced comparable accommodation needs. They would, in turn, be affected by the fully developed secular form.[48]

There were three such communities – educational, ecclesiastical, and charitable. Their organisation within a single residence and their multiplication was a feature of the later middle ages. Nearly all the educational establishments were founded by the crown and élite leaders of lay and ecclesiastical society, the same strata who needed to enhance and extend their own accommodation facilities. The ecclesiastical communities, including the vicars choral or subsidiary clerics of a cathedral, the secular canons serving a large parish church, and even extending to the Carthusian order where monks lived a self-contained existence, were brought together under a corporate umbrella. The charitable institutions – hospitals and almshouses – are less important in the antecedents of lodging ranges than in their reaction to them.

Architecturally, educational colleges are the most significant of these community establishments for their ranges prefigure comparable secular examples. The north range (1304–7) and the east range (1308–11) enclosing two sides of Mob Quad at Merton College, Oxford, are the earliest college rooms at either Oxford or Cambridge. They were two-storeyed with a room each side of the small entry lobby holding a steep stair to the upper rooms, initially open to the roof. The internal layout is difficult to make out today as the windows have been remodelled and the internal partitions and ceilings reflect post-medieval changes, but it has been established that each heated room included four partitioned study closets for occupation by four fellows.[49] Between 1352 and 1377, two-storey lodging ranges were being developed round three sides of the quadrangle at Corpus Christi College, Cambridge, but with students, four to a room, occupying the ground floor with the more senior fellows at the upper level. A relatively complete collegiate lodging of 1376–7 at King's Hall has been incorporated in Trinity College, Cambridge.[50]

The organisation of the priests serving collegiate churches into college-like premises occurred during the first half of the fourteenth century.[51] Until then, chantry priests had lived locally but communal living brought greater discipline as at Ottery St Mary (1339), St Stephen's, Westminster (1348), and St George's, Windsor (1348). Some of the college buildings erected by Sir John Cobham at Cobham (c.1370), the earl of Arundel at Arundel (1380), and archbishop Courtenay at Maidstone (1395) still stand, grouped round a quadrangle as in the larger academic foundations, with gateway, dining hall, and lodgings.

The earliest standing college of vicars choral is that at Lincoln, started in c.1270 with completion in c.1380. The gradually developed quadrangular form of this Vicars' Close included a two-storey residential range of apparently individual lodgings on the south side dominated by massive garderobe stacks.[52] Re-examination of this much-altered structure of c.1300–9 shows that it initially consisted of a hall with offices, and a group of six similar chambers at the west end. There were three on each floor furnished with a fireplace, garderobe, and at least two (possibly four) windows. The upper floor was more probably accessed by a newel rather than a straight stair.

The famous close at Wells of c.1340 is made up of two parallel accommodation ranges on either side of the street, but they are a line of individual two-storey and self-contained houses. Though some monastic dormitories came to resemble the upper floor of a lodging range, the division into separate cubicles was a relatively late and independent development arising from the growth in privacy.

Just as the organisation of specialist ecclesiastical communities helped to transform parish churches, architecturally and constitutionally during the later middle ages, so the organisation and hierarchial development of a magnate's household led to a comparable secular development. From the early fourteenth century, their houses were increasingly formalised round a court, as were those of comparable educational communities. In both instances, the construction of lodging ranges was a contributing factor, but if educational and some ecclesiastical communities influenced the development of secular houses, the form – once conceived – swiftly developed in secular hands.

It might be anticipated that the earliest structure specially designed to provide a sequence of rooms for household officials would be in a royal palace and it is possible that the crown led this movement as it did in other fields. In 1975, the flint foundations of a lodging range, 300 feet by 16 feet, were uncovered at King's Langley Palace. Probably built initially as a timber-framed structure on flintstone foundations, and ascribed to 1308–10, it consisted of eight rooms with the fireplaces subsequently inserted in some rooms in c.1370.[53] There is a fifty-year gap before any comparable royal work was undertaken but it was possibly preceded in the late 1350s by a two-storey lodging range at the Black Prince's palace at Kennington known as the squires' chamber, though the evidence is documentary, not structural or excavated.[54]

Among the earliest ranges of retinue lodgings identified so far are those lining two sides of the rectangular courtyard at Maxstoke Castle, built by William, earl of Huntingdon between 1342 and 1346. Both ranges are ruined but the outer walls survive with post sockets showing that the timber-framed lodgings on the south side of the court consisted of four rooms for retainers at the upper level with stores and services below. The north range was of a higher standard with three paired lodgings, heated and garderobe provided, at the upper level with a fourth one below and three single lodgings.[55]

The crown soon consolidated this initiative in spectacular form. After completion of the royal apartments on the north side of the upper ward at Windsor Castle, the east and south sides of the ward were lined with ranges of two-storeyed lodgings between c.1365 and 1377. The rooms were generously scaled with the upper lodgings reached by a straight internal stair. Though separated by six four-storey towers which provided further accommodation, it is possible there were up to twenty lodgings in the east range and considerably more in the longer south range, with the upper rooms, marked by larger windows, occupied by more senior staff. Hollar's engravings of the upper ward show that both ranges were regularly configured, a practice adopted shortly afterwards by bishop Wykeham at New College, Oxford and Winchester College. However, Wyatville's remodelling of Windsor's upper ward (1824–30) virtually destroyed most of the fourteenth-century work in favour of his corridors and replacement suites of royal apartments.

The Windsor development can be sensed a generation later in the semi-royal development by Richard II's half-brother at Dartington Hall. During the last decade of the fourteenth century, John Holand, earl of Huntingdon, erected two-storeyed ranges of lodgings filling both sides of the 250 foot long outer court. Eschewing the single-minded uniformity of Windsor, the east range (c.1390–5) has two-centred doorway heads, external entries, and stone rear garderobes, whereas the west range (c.1395–1400) adopted four-centred doorway heads and wood-encased rear garderobes, and retains the projecting porches with external stairs to the

PLATE 11 Dartington Hall: engraving from the east by S. and N. Buck (1734)

upper rooms. The east range was made up of fourteen pairs of lodgings, while the west range consisted of ten pairs, with the two next to the hall considerably larger and probably for communal use by junior staff. On the basis of two staff per lodging and about eight in each communal room, then the two ranges could accommodate up to 108 staff. The Dartington plan was swiftly reflected locally by the 3rd earl of Devon's four-room unit next to the chapel at Okehampton Castle and by Sir Philip Courtenay's short range at Powderham Castle (1392–1406) where the upper floor has since been converted into a chapel.

Turning to northern England, some of the rooms against the courtyard walls at the mid-fourteenth-century quadrangular castles such as Chillingham and Ford may have been dormitory-type rooms, but subsequent redevelopments have obliterated their initial function. The irregular-shaped palace-fortress of the Neville family at Raby, developed piecemeal between c.1367 and 1388, would certainly have had lodging accommodation, particularly as the two-tiered hall range on one side of the kitchen court (complementing the much larger one for this powerful family astride the main court) may well have been used by greater and lesser household officials. But though the castle retains several single and paired lodgings, post-medieval remodelling and the landscaping of the outer ward have cleared any evidence of early lodging ranges. This is not the case, however, with the next generation of the Neville family at their stronghold at Middleham. Between c.1400 and 1430 Ralph, Lord Neville and his son Richard Neville, earl of Salisbury, shortly after his succession built three such ranges round the court that encircled the Norman keep. Though ruined, the changes in their form reflected stop–start construction. There were external stairs to the upper rooms on the south and west sides but internal stairs to the lodgings on the later north side. All units were heated and garderobe provided, with single and paired lodgings in the south and north ranges, individual lodgings on the west side. Middleham Castle provided up to twenty-four mainly single-room lodgings with the paired rooms among the earliest of this form.

Tiered accommodation developed concurrently with horizontal planning. Among the earliest was the three-storeyed gatehouse to the Bishop's Palace at Wells, erected in the early 1340s by bishop Ralph to hold seven lodgings, probably for his household officials. Equally quick off the mark was Thomas Beauchamp, earl of Warwick, with his imposing frontal towers at Warwick Castle, the three-tiered lodgings in Caesar's Tower of the 1340s and the slightly later Guy's Tower where the first four high-standard lodgings were identical. The north quickly followed, initially by Sir William Aldeburgh with two similar but far more modest tiered units at Harewood Castle (1366–c.1388). Lord Scrope adopted the same principle in the entrance range at Bolton Castle (c.1378–96) with two lodgings over the entry and three pairs to the side of it, all off a central stair. A similar tiered pattern was adopted by John Lord Lovel, filling two sides of his hexagonal castle at Wardour (c.1393) with paired as well as single lodgings, though few of them survived the Civil War bombardment.

In little more than a single mid-century generation, the need for substantial household and retinue lodgings had developed in three ways from a dormitory-type unit – as a four-room unit, as an extended range of many units, and as tiered lodgings. As might be expected, all such lodgings were initially crown or magnate led (ecclesiastical as well as secular), though the form had begun to trickle down the social scale as at Powderham, at the enigmatic but early range at Burwell, possibly influenced by Cambridge colleges, and at Farleigh Hungerford Castle.[56]

The fifteenth century brought refinements and modest improvements rather than fundamental changes to the fully developed form. The rooms at Ewelme Manor (possibly c.1420–30), though heated, lacked individual garderobes, pointing to median social status. There were also two communal end rooms as at Dartington Hall, but the structure is notable for the external gallery approach to the upper rooms, repeated in the range 243 feet long at Bishop's Waltham Palace (1438–43). The richly embellished upper lodgings round part of the earl of Pembroke's Fountain Court (1465–9) at Raglan Castle were approached by a grand stair, while internal corridor access occurs at Gainsborough Old Hall (1479–85).

35

Legend:
- ✕ Dormitory
- ● Unit: two pairs of lodgings on two floors
- ■ Range: two-storeyed line of lodgings
- ▲ Tiered: lodgings on three or more floors
- (d) Destroyed

N

Edlington Castle (d)

Askerton Castle

Bolton Castle ▲

Middleham Castle

Sheriff Hutton Castle (d)

Harewood Castle ▲

Leconfield Manor (d)

Cawood Castle

Wressle Castle (d)

Howden Manor (d)

Gainsborough Old Hall

Haddon Hall ■▲

Tattershall Castle

Ince Manor

Wingfield Manor ■▲✕

Holme Pierrepoint Hall

Codnor Castle

Ashby de la Zouch Castle ●

Lichfield Palace (d)

Apethorpe Hall

Caister Castle ▲

Pooley Hall

Fotheringhay Castle (d)

Maxstoke Castle

Warwick Castle ▲

Giffords Hall

Burwell

Compton Wynyates

Hedingham Castle (d)

Broughton Castle

Ampthill Castle (d)

Llawhaden Castle

Raglan Castle

Minster Lovell Hall

King's Langley Palace (d)

Sudeley Castle

Ewelme Manor

Ockwells

South Wraxall Manor

Eltham Palace (d)

Thornbury Castle

Windsor Castle

Knole

Wells Palace ▲

✕ Farleigh Hungerford Castle (d)

Croydon Palace

Charing Palace ●✕

Dunster Castle ▲

Wardour Castle ▲

Bishop's Waltham Palace ■✕

Herstmonceux Castle (d)

Cothay Manor ✕

Brympton d'Evercy

Amberley Castle ●

Oakhampton Castle ●

Shute (d)

Cotehele ■✕

Powderham Castle

Dartington Hall

Old Newnham ●

0   100 miles

0   150 km

FIGURE 3 Late medieval houses: lodging units and ranges

PLATE 12 Haddon Hall: lower court, west lodging range

PLATE 13 Winchester, Hospital of St Cross: west lodging range

Ralph, Lord Cromwell's mansion at Wingfield (*c*.1440–56) is a summation of the hierarchial standards appropriate to the household of a leading magnate. The outer court included two-storeyed, unheated, stone-built dormitories with a shared central garderobe, and a more superior range opposite, possibly timber-framed to the courtyard, with wall fireplaces and garderobes. There were three lodgings on both floors of the cross range, either side of the central gateway, not all identical. The twelve lodgings in the three-storeyed west range of the inner court were of superior standard – the lowest heated but with no windows to the field. Those above, approached from two projecting octagonal stairs, had opposing windows, fireplaces and garderobes in a bold stack and closet pattern. This was the precursor to the even more complex internal layout of four suites of two rooms and one of four rooms in the west range at Gainsborough Old Hall for Sir Thomas Burgh (1479–85). But Wingfield Manor went one step further with a tier of four large-scale, well-lit, comfortable lodgings in a commanding tower-house appropriate to guests or officials of the highest rank.

Lodging ranges were now as much a part of the lifestyle of the higher gentry as of magnates, with mid-century examples by John Sydenham at Brympton d'Evercy, Sir William Fiennes at Broughton Castle, and Sir Ralph Boteler at Sudeley Castle, by Sir Henry Vernon at Haddon Hall later in the century, and by Sir William Pierrepont at Holme Pierrepont Hall early in the sixteenth century.[57] The facilities developed by Sir William Vernon to accommodate his household and guests are as varied and as generously scaled as those at Wingfield Manor. They have the advantage of still being roofed, little altered externally or internally, and in part still occupied by the duke of Rutland's staff.[58]

We do not know to what extent such lodgings were limited to permanent household staff, periodic retainers, guests, or visitors. There was probably considerable flexibility depending on the circumstances and standing of the lord, and that was liable to change from generation to generation. The lodgings built by archbishop Bourchier lining the east side of the outer court at Croydon Palace (1454–86) were built to a higher standard than those he developed on the west side. A survey of the earl of Northumberland's house at Leconfield in 1537 makes it clear that the upper lodgings of a two-storey galleried range were for gentlemen attending the earl and the lower lodgings were for yeomen servants.[59] A leading household

official would warrant a single room where he could work and sleep – a combined bed-sitting room and office. He would expect a separate entry for privacy, and a fireplace and garderobe for his comfort. Less senior staff might enjoy the same amenities but would expect to share, at least two or more to a room. Junior staff would be in dormitory-like accommodation which would need to be heated and provided with a communal garderobe. Windows would be unglazed but shuttered and walls probably plastered. Furniture would be spartan, a bed with possibly a truckle bed underneath, a table, a stool, and a washbowl. Guests would be allocated accommodation appropriate to their rank, but family guests and visitors of high standing would expect a spacious self-contained lodging and possibly one with an outer and an inner chamber. They would be accompanied by their own servants and grooms who would also need to be housed,[60] possibly the senior servants in rooms like the low ground-floor lodgings in the west range at Wingfield Manor, close to their masters above. Dormitory-type accommodation can also be seen above the bakehouse and brewhouse at Bishop's Waltham Palace (1439–43).

The early sixteenth century opened with the impressive ranges lining the outer court at Thornbury Castle (1507–21) and the similarly positioned ranges at Hampton Court (1514–*c*.22) with its forty two-roomed guest lodgings round the Base Court. Both residences aroused the ire of the king, who took them both for his own use. Fifty years later, three sides of the outer court at Sudeley Castle were almost entirely rebuilt by Lord Chandos (1570–2) at the same time that Sir Humphrey Stafford was developing lodging ranges at Kirby Hall (1570–5). Both followed the same plan of courtyard entrances to paired lodgings with guest chambers above and a long gallery. Although the ranges were more sophisticated, they differed little in planning terms (apart from the gallery) from those of Edward III two centuries earlier for his courtiers and household officials at Windsor.

There was a reciprocal development in other community institutions. Until the late sixteenth century, collegiate lodgings at Oxford and Cambridge continued to be two-storeyed, of one room thickness (except the upper floor at Magdalen College, Oxford) and usually filling at least two sides of the quadrangular layout. But following the royal precedent, bishop Wykeham introduced the social concept at New College of providing ground-floor lodgings for those of lower status (students) with the upper rooms (with garderobes) for those of higher standing (fellows). The accommodation would be for three or four occupants at ground-floor level and two or three above, though his ground-floor communal rooms at Winchester College could take up to thirteen scholars.

The radical improvement in the layout of secular colleges of priests is reflected in Thomas de la Warr's foundation of 1421 in Manchester (now Chetham's). The rooms, cloister approached, were grouped round a small quadrangle, at two levels: eight lodgings with individual entries, some with garderobes, at ground level and eight further individual lodgings above. Bishop Stanbury's equally well-preserved college of 1472–5 at Hereford Cathedral held twenty-seven two-roomed houses. The almshouse at Ewelme, established by the earl of Suffolk in 1437, marked the development of individual lodgings round a small court in place of the community accommodation hitherto.[61] Even more impressive was bishop Beaufort's regeneration of the Hospital of St Cross at Winchester, matching the quality and scale of the Norman church and the late fourteenth-century hall.[62] The brethren's ranges of *c.*1445 were made up of forty units. They were two rooms thick, not an outer and inner chamber as in a paired lodging, but with a large courtyard-facing room with fireplace and two smaller rooms at the rear, one with the garderobe projection that served both floors as at Dartington Hall.[63]

NOTES

1 *Greater Med. Houses* II (2000) 485–8.
2 *Ibid.*
3 K. Mertes, *The English Noble Household 1250–1600* (1988) 11–15.
4 J. R. S. Phillips, *Aymer de Valence, earl of Pembroke* (1972) 323–35.
5 Bishops and their households were the principal exception. They continued to be mobile throughout the later middle ages to fulfil their diocesan responsibilities.
6 In the case of the crown, this reduction in property numbers was also a consequence of the centralisation of government at Westminster by the mid-fourteenth century.
7 Mertes, *The English Noble Household* 185; C. M. Woolgar, *The Great Household in Late Medieval England* (1999) 46–7.
8 Even lower down the social scale, married children increasingly moved away from the manor after 1350. Z. Razi, 'The myth of the immutable English family', *Past and Present* 140 (1993) 8, 23.
9 T. F. Tout, *Chapters in Medieval Administrative History* (1930); A. R. Myers, *The Household of Edward IV* (1959); C. Given-Wilson, *The Royal Household and the King's Affinity 1360–1413* (1986); D. A. L. Morgan in *The English Court, from the War of the Roses to the Civil War*, ed. D. Starkey (1987) 25–70; R. A. Griffiths in *Princes, Patronage, and the Nobility: The Court at the Beginning of the Modern Age c.1450–1650*, ed. R. G. Asch and A. M. Birke (1991) 41–67.
10 Mertes, *The English Noble Household*, though the majority of material refers to the period from about 1340 to 1540.
11 Woolgar, *The Great Household in Late Medieval England*; *Household Accounts from Medieval England*, ed. C. M. Woolgar (1992–3).
12 *Standards of Living in the Later Middle Ages: Social Change in England c.1200–1520* (1989).
13 P. Fleming, *Family and Household in Medieval England* (2001) 1–2.
14 *Ibid.* 77; L. Stone, *The Family, Sex and Marriage in England 1500–1800* (1977) 23–5.
15 The treasurer might be assisted by a comptroller or deputy treasurer.
16 For household provisioning and the preparation of food and drink Woolgar, *The Great Household in Late Medieval England*, 111–65.
17 From the mid-fourteenth century, sons of gentry were often educated in grammar schools. N. Orme, *From Childhood to Chivalry: The Education of the English Kings and Aristocracy: 1066–1530* (1984) 85.
18 For a household's daily and seasonal routine, Woolgar, *The Great Household in Late Medieval England* 84–96.
19 Those who maintained London houses, essentially the episcopacy and leading barons, often had Londoners looking after their country residences. Mertes, *The English Noble Household* 61.
20 This situation also applied to establishments headed by women. In 1290, fewer than 10 per cent of Eleanor of Castile's household were women. Woolgar, *The Great Household in Late Medieval England* 8, 34–5.
21 P. W. Fleming, 'Household servants of the Yorkist and early Tudor gentry' in *Early Tudor England*, ed. D. Williams (1989) 19–36.
22 Woolgar, *The Great Household in Late Medieval England* 9, 172–5.
23 M. Jones and S. Walker, 'Private indentures for life service in peace and war, 1278–1476', *Camden Miscellany* 32 (1994) 1–190.
24 J. S. Roskell, *The Commons and Their Speakers in English Parliaments: 1376–1523* (1965).
25 There is some evidence that household officials became more influential and active members of a lord's council during the later fifteenth century. Mertes, *The English Noble Household* 129–32.
26 A. Emery, *Arch. Jour.* 142 (1985), 281; Mertes, *The English Noble Household* 25; C. D. Ross, *The Estates and Finances of Richard Beauchamp, Earl of Warwick* (1956), 13–14.
27 In an analysis of the average annual income and household expenditure of fifty-five families, Kate Mertes, *The English Noble Household* 216–17, calculated that the latter was between 45 and 46 per cent of the former, irrespective of the size of the household.
28 A. Emery, *Greater Med. Houses*, I (1996) 292–4.
29 Mertes, *The English Noble Household* 102–8.
30 From the summary figures given by Kate Mertes, *The English Noble Household* 216–17, the proportions of household expenditure incurred where there were fifty or more staff, was food 56 per cent, clothing 19 per cent, and wages 11 per cent. For households of fewer than fifty people, the figures were food 85 per cent, clothing 5 per cent and wages 7 per cent.
31 It has been estimated that two-thirds of nobles and gentry left widows, half of whom lived up to sixteen years after their husband's death. P. Fleming, *Family and Household in Medieval England* (2001) 83–4.
32 J. Smyth, *Lives of the Berkeleys*, I (1883) 304.
33 M. Cherry, *Southern History*, 1 (1979) 72.
34 W. H. Dunham, *Lord Hastings' Indentured Retainers 1461–83* (1955) 27–8.
35 C. Rawcliffe, *The Staffords, Earls of Stafford and Dukes of Buckingham* (1979) 73–4, 88–9.
36 C. Given-Wilson, *The English Nobility in the Late Middle Ages* (1987) 90.
37 *Ibid.* 89–90; C. D. Ross, *The Estates and Finances of Richard Beauchamp* (1956) 20–2; Mertes, *The English Noble Household* Appendix C, 218; J. M. W. Bean, *From Lord to Patron* (1989).
38 Woolgar, *The Great Household in Late Medieval England* 11–15.
39 J. Nichols (ed.), *A Collection of Ordinances and Regulations* (1790).
40 A. R. Myers (ed.), *The Household of Edward IV* (1959).
41 Mertes, *The English Noble Household* 207, 214; Lady Kerrison and L. T. Smith (eds.), *A Commonplace Book of the Fifteenth Century* (1886).
42 The wider ramifications of a household such as the way in which it helped a lord to exercise his authority and patronage at a local, regional, or national level, its stimulation of the local economy, and its role as an organised substitute for the family are considered further by Mertes, *The English Noble Household* and Woolgar, *The Great Household in Late Medieval England*. Households gradually began to shrink in size under the early Tudors as power moved more and more to the royal court.
43 *Antiquity* 66 (1992) 348–66.
44 Woolgar, *The Great Household in Late Medieval England* 21–4.
45 *Greater Med. Houses*, II (2000) 349–55.

46 *HKW*, II (1963) 914, 916 (Clarendon), 935 (Eltham), 1013 (Woodstock).
47 S. Pearson, *Arch. Cant.* 121 (2001) 335.
48 W. A. Pantin, *Med. Arch.* 3 (1959) 216–58.
49 *Ibid.* 244–6. There were no garderobes.
50 Emery, *Greater Med. Houses*, II (2000) 66–8.
51 A. H. Thompson, *The English Clergy and Their Organisation in the Later Middle Ages* (1947); A. H. Thompson, 'Notes on colleges of secular canons in England', *Arch. Jour.* 74 (1917) 139–239; G. H. Cook, *English Collegiate Churches of the Middle Ages* (1959).
52 The most recent and detailed analysis is S. Jones *et al.*, *The Survey of Ancient Houses in Lincoln*, II (1987) 40–64 and *Vicars Choral at English Cathedrals*, ed. R. Hall and D. Stocker (2005) 76–97.
53 D. S. Neal, *Med. Arch.* 21 (1977) 124–65.
54 G. J. Dawson, *The Black Prince's Palace at Kennington, Surrey* (1976) 58.
55 For descriptions of these and all other lodgings mentioned hereafter, see the individual house entries in these volumes.
56 It is possible that the ranges built by Sir Thomas Hungerford round three sides of the First Court (c.1375–85), now reduced to foundation level, were dormitory-type accommodation.
57 The brick-built range of the much-abused Hall at Holme Pierrepont, two lodgings on both floors either side of the gateway, was stripped of its 1810–applied plaster in 1975 when the garderobe- and fireplace-provided rooms were reopened and an upper lodging exposed to its wind-braced roof of *c.*1509. *Vern. Arch.* 21 (1990) 37–9; M. Binney, *Country Life* (September 1979).
58 The ruined lodging range at Ince Manor, a fortified grange of St Werburgh's Abbey, Chester, attributed to *c.*1400, was roofed and floored for occupation in 2003. The mid-fourteenth-century hall was repaired and reroofed at the same time.
59 *Greater Med. Houses*, I (1996) 362.
60 Woolgar, *The Great Household in Late Medieval England* 21–6.
61 W. H. Godfrey, *The English Almshouse* (1950); B. Howson, *Houses of Noble Poverty* (1993); J. A. A. Goodall, *God's House at Ewelme* (2001).
62 R. M. Clay, *The Medieval Hospitals of England* (1909); E. Prescott, *The English Medieval Hospital 1050–1640* (1992).
63 For the development of lodgings at inns, see W. A. Pantin in *Studies in Building History*, ed. E. M. Jope (1961) 166–91; *Vern. Arch.* 31 (2000) 81–3.

4

THE THAMES VALLEY:
BIBLIOGRAPHY

GLOUCESTERSHIRE has been exceedingly well served by its early historians. The 860 pages by the landowner and lawyer Sir Robert Atkyns, *The Ancient and Present State of Glostershire* (1712), are stunningly interlaced with seventy-three plates prepared by Johannes Kip between 1700 and 1710. They are almost all of country houses, and where they can be checked with existing buildings or other sources Kip's bird's-eye views prove to be extremely accurate. Samuel Lysons, *A Collection of Gloucestershire Antiquities* (1803), has even more plates of almost equal interest. Samuel Rudder, *A New History of Gloucestershire* (1779), has a number of country house plates engraved by Bonner, while Thomas Rudge, *The History of the County of Gloucester* (1803), 2 volumes, an update of Atkyns, completes this quartet of outstanding county histories.

For the landscape and its historical development, see H. P. R. Finberg, *The Making of the English Landscape: Gloucestershire* (1975), B. S. Smith and E. Ralph, *A History of Bristol and Gloucestershire* (3rd ed. 1996), and C. and A. M. Hadfield (eds.), *The Cotswolds: A New Study* (1973). For the leading families, see J. Johnson, *The Gloucestershire Gentry* (1989) and the more specialist N. Saul, *Knights and Esquires: The Gloucestershire Gentry in the Fourteenth Century* (1981).

The *Transactions of the Bristol and Gloucestershire Archaeological Society* have been published since 1876, but medieval houses have not been well served in this county in comparison with medieval churches. J. and H. S. Storer and J. N. Brewer, *Delineations of Gloucestershire, Being Views of the Principal Seats of Nobility and Gentry* (1825–7), is self-explanatory. The late twentieth-century version is in three volumes by Nicholas Kingsley, *The Country Houses of Gloucestershire* (1989–2001). Unfortunately volume I (1989) omits some of the most fascinating properties as its coverage to 1660 starts with the Tudors at 1500. Berkeley and Sudeley castles, in particular, badly need the detailed analysis so far limited to one residence, *Acton Court: The Evolution of an Early Tudor Courtier's House* by K. Rodwell and R. Bell (2004). Otherwise the articles in *Country Life* are often the only reliable source, even for some major houses. For smaller houses, L. J. Hall, *The Rural Houses of North Avon and South Gloucestershire 1400–1720* (1983), points up the contrasts with the greater houses in the region. The two volumes on *Gloucestershire* by David Verey (1970) in *The Buildings of England* series did not maintain Pevsner's high standards because of the author's routine eye, though this has been eradicated in the much-improved revised edition by Alan Brooks, I *The Cotswolds* (1992), II *The Vale and Forest of Dean* (2002), both with separate multi-introductions. Verey also contributed an essay on the Perpendicular style in the Cotswolds in *Essays in Bristol and Gloucestershire History*, ed. P. McGrath and J. Cannor (1976).

The *Victoria History of the County of Gloucester* is continuing slowly but majestically, with ten volumes published to date. Summer Meetings of the Royal Archaeological Institute have been based at Gloucester, 78 (1921), Cheltenham, 122 (1965) and Cirencester, 145 (1988) with useful programme notes including some covered in sorties from Bath, 87 (1930) and Bristol, 134 (1977).

There are no indispensable early histories of Oxfordshire. The earliest is Robert Plot, *The Natural History of Oxfordshire* (1677). Its interest is natural resources, not history, and only the first volume of John Dunkin's projected county history was published, *The History and Antiquities of the Hundreds of Bullingdon and Ploughley* (1823). In the same year, J. Skelton published his *Engraved Illustrations of the Principal Antiquities of Oxfordshire*. The only survey, therefore, is J. Meade Falkner's popular *History of Oxfordshire* (1899), supplemented by the detailed early and mid-nineteenth-century architectural drawings of J. and J. C. Buckler. For all literature, see E. H. Cordeaux and D. H. Merry, *A Bibliography of Printed Works Relating to Oxfordshire* (1955) and the smaller *Oxfordshire: A Handbook for Students of Local History*, ed. D. M. Barratt and D. G. Vaisey (1977). The most detailed coverage of the county is in the volumes published to date of the Victoria County History, supplemented by the volumes of the Oxfordshire Record Society since 1919 for documents relating to the history of the shire, and the volumes of Oxford History Society since 1884 for historical records relating to the university and city of Oxford. The Oxfordshire Archaeological and History Society was founded in 1839, with its *Proceedings* ceasing in 1900. They have been replaced since 1936 by *Oxoniensia*, a more valuable journal than many for the history and architecture of a region as well as its archaeology. The *Journal of Banbury History Society* has covered that locality since 1960.

During the later twentieth century, the county was served by F. Emery, *The Oxfordshire Landscape* (1974) and by A. F. Martin and R. W. Steel, *The Oxford Region: A Scientific and Historical Survey* (1954), but the chapter by W. G. Hoskins and E. M. Jope has been superseded by that by J. Bond in *The Archaeology of the Oxford Region*, ed. J. C. Steane (1986) 135–59. Similarly, E. T. Long's overview of medieval domestic architecture in *Oxfordshire Arch. Soc. Reports* 84 (1938) 45–56 and 85 (1939) 97–105 has been superseded by J. Sherwood and N. Pevsner, *Buildings of England: Oxfordshire* (1974), J. C. Pilling, *Oxfordshire Houses* (1993) aptly subtitled 'A guide to local traditions', and the Summer programmes of the Royal Archaeological Institute for 1910 and 1978. Specialist historical studies include A. Ballard, *The Black Death on the Manors of Witney* (1916), P. Harvey, *A Medieval Oxfordshire Village: Cuxham 1240–1400* (1965), R. B. Wood-Jones, *Traditional Domestic Architecture of the Banbury Region* (1963), and the valuable booklet by F. Woodward, *Oxfordshire Parks* (1982). A detailed study on Oxfordshire manorial sites, co-ordinated by Dr J. Blair, was planned in 1986. That section covering the Vale of Whitehorse was published in *Oxoniensia* in 1992. An overview of medieval discoveries in the county and city between 1975 and 2000 by John Steane was published in *Oxoniensia* 66 (2001) 1–12.

The University of Oxford has been covered exhaustively ever since Anthony Wood assembled an invaluable collection of material, brought together in editions by J. Peshall (1773), J. Gutch (1786–96), and A. Clark (1889). Thomas Hearne's collections were edited by C. E. Doble, H. E. Salter *et al.* in eleven volumes between 1884 and 1918, while the important drawings of the colleges by John Bereblock (1566) and David Loggan (1675) have been frequently reproduced in architectural studies on the colleges. All books prior to 1968 are listed in E. H. Cordeaux and D. H. Merry, *A Bibliography of Printed Works Relating to the University of Oxford* (1968). The three key volumes surveying all the colleges are Aymer Vallance's extensively illustrated and personal assessment, *The Old Colleges of Oxford* (1912), RCHM, *An Inventory of the Historical Monuments of the City of Oxford* (1939), and VCH, *Oxfordshire*, III (1954) which details the sites and historical development of the individual colleges as well as their architectural story. Among more recent popular books are M. Jebb, *The Colleges of Oxford* (1992), J. Prest (ed.), *The Illustrated History of Oxford University* (1993), and G. Tyack, *Oxford: An Architectural Guide* (1998). Specialist studies include W. J. Arkell, *Oxford Stone* (1947) and W. F. Oakeshott (ed.), *Oxford Stone Restored* (1974), and papers by R. H. C. Davies, 'The chronology of Perpendicular architecture in Oxford', *Oxoniensia* 11–12 (1946–7) 75–89; E. A. Gee on Oxford masons 1370–1530, *Arch. Jour.* 109 (1952) 54–131 and Oxford carpenters 1370–1530, *Oxoniensia* 17–18 (1952–3) 112–84, and a stimulating essay by H. S. Goodhart-Rendal, 'Oxford buildings criticized' in the same volume, 200–15; and J. Harvey, 'Architecture in Oxford 1350–1500' in J. Catto and R. Evans (eds.), *History of the University of Oxford*, II (1992) 747–68. This seven-volume comprehensive *History* is superseding G. E. Mallet, *A History of the University of Oxford* (1924–7).

Neither Buckinghamshire nor Berkshire has been well served by early studies. The best for Buckinghamshire is G. Lipscomb, *The History and Antiquities of the County of Buckinghamshire* (1831–47). However, both counties have benefited from completed surveys by the Victoria County History. That for the *County of Buckingham* is in four volumes (1905–28) with a separate index. The shire has also been surveyed by the Royal Commission on Historical Monuments, *Buckinghamshire*, I, South (1912), II, North (1913). N. Pevsner, *Buildings of England: Buckinghamshire* (1960) was vastly extended and rewritten by E. Williamson and G. K. Brandwood for the second edition (1994). Other relevant works include M. Reed, *The Buckinghamshire Landscape* (1979) and *A History of Buckinghamshire* (1992) and the recent papers in *Records of Buckinghamshire*, the journal of the architectural and archaeological society for the county, established in 1847 with the first volume issued in 1854.

The four volumes of the Victoria County History for the *County of Berkshire* were published between 1906 and 1924 but the last two volumes had been completed by 1914 with publication delayed by the First World War. J. Dils, *An Historical Atlas of Berkshire* (1998) covers the county before the drastic boundary changes of 1974. As with several other historical atlases, the choice of subjects is eclectic, not comprehensive. Specialist works include R. Faith, 'Berkshire: fourteenth and fifteenth centuries' in P. D. A. Harvey (ed.), *The Peasant Land Market in Medieval England* (1984), but the medieval aristocracy and gentry of Berkshire (and Buckinghamshire) have yet to find their recorder.

The *Berkshire Archaeological Transactions*, first published in 1878, became the *Journal* in 1889 and the *Berkshire, Buckinghamshire and Oxfordshire Archaeological Journal* from 1895 until 1931 when it reverted to its former *Journal* title in recognition of its long-held concern with the one county. The *Transactions of the Newbury District Field Club* have concentrated on west Berkshire since 1870.

Some of the recent archaeological surveys published under the auspices of the Berkshire Archaeological Committee touch on the medieval period, including G. G. Astill, *Historic Towns in Berkshire* (1978), J. Richards, *The Berkshire Downs* (1978), S. Ford, *East Berkshire* (1987) and S. J. Lobb and P. G. Rose, *The Lower Kennet Valley* (1996). The principal overview of medieval domestic architecture in the county is in three articles by E. T. Long, *Berks. Arch. Jour.* 44 (1940) 39–47, 101–13, and 45 (1941) 28–36. They are supplemented by N. Pevsner, *The Buildings of England: Berkshire* (1966) and by the series of papers since about 1960 on timber-framed buildings in the Vale of Whitehorse, detailed in the architectural introduction to the region.

5

THE THAMES VALLEY: SURVEY

ABINGDON ABBEY, Berkshire and monastic granges

At the time of the Dissolution, Abingdon Abbey was the sixth wealthiest Benedictine monastery in England and one of the most high-profile communities in the region. The scanty monastic remains have some relevance to contemporary residential work, while its granges are even more pertinent to our purpose.

The site is now almost completely covered by the borough offices, houses, and gardens of Abingdon town, so that only the abbey gateway[1] and a line of domestic buildings of the monastic base court survive. The latter consist of the bakehouse and granary (twelfth century with mid-fifteenth-century roof), the two-storeyed exchequer (c.1260) and a residential range (mid-fifteenth century) now used as a dwelling, a theatre, and an empty area respectively. For our purposes, the residential range is of considerable value for comparison with contemporary secular ranges. Over 70 feet long, this two-storeyed range is stone-built towards the mill-stream and river Thames, but timber- and brick-built towards the abbey court, the upper part open-framed. It is now curtailed by about 25 feet at the east end, and with the lower half of the inner wall stone rebuilt after 1820 (possibly during the 1895 restoration), but the brick noggin between the studs is original, as are the first-floor windows towards the river of paired cinquefoil lights, transomed, under square heads, dating the range between the mid and late fifteenth century.

The significance of the range lies not in its drastically modified ground floor, possibly used for storage initially, but in the layout of the upper floor. The original approach has been lost, but it led to a corridor 4 feet wide with continuous unglazed windows towards the court that ran the length of the range and accessed the line of rooms. All partitions have been torn down leaving a single open area and a line of corridor posts, but the mortices on the underside of the tie beams identify the former partition positions separating the two large central rooms from the three smaller rooms at each end. The range is now divided into ten bays (formerly twelve). Beginning at the exchequer end, the first rooms of a single bay each were followed by a three-bay room with central fireplace (now moved below) and two flanking windows. The further three-bay room retains its central fireplace with replacement Elizabethan lintel, and one of the two flanking windows. Only one of the three further single-bay rooms survives plus a rebuilt end wall. The rooms were open to the roof of braced tie beams with collars and wind braces, with crossed braces spanning the corridor. The roof was not elaborate but the tie beams were cambered rather than flat within the two larger chambers and some of the partitioning infill survives within the roof space. Whether this floor was intended for

PLATE 14 Abingdon Abbey: corridor-lined lodging range

GRANGES IN THE VALE OF WHITEHORSE

The leading Benedictine houses, in particular, were richly endowed with extensive estates. By the mid-fourteenth century, Abingdon held about seventy, mainly in two groups centred on the meadowland south of the Thames and the claylands of the Vale of Whitehorse, with a second block on the Berkshire Downs as far as the Kennet valley.[4] About twenty-eight of these estates were key demesne manors, principally in the Vale, about half of them with a substantial domestic range, and others with a significant complex of farm buildings. Both are exemplified in five granges in the region, four of them belonging to Abingdon.[5] Charney Bassett Manor House retains the thirteenth-century solar and chapel wing of the grange, now attached to an early nineteenth-century Tudor-style replacement hall and slightly later offices block.[6] The well-documented residential range at Cumnor Place was regrettably pulled down in 1810, while Dean Court was excavated in the mid-1970s and mid-1980s. The origins of two wings of Culham Manor House lay in a grange of Abingdon, while that at Steventon was the farm of an alien priory, granted to Westminster Abbey in 1399.

The architectural and archaeological examination of monastic granges is still in its infancy, and the parallels with secular architecture have hardly begun. Those in Berkshire are an ideal starting point for they are among some of the best examples in England. Dean Court, for instance, was one of the most extensive in the country, but its importance lies not only in its size but that there were two successive granges on different sites. Developed in the north of Cumnor parish[7] and excavated in two phases in 1975–6 and 1984–5, Dean Court was a late twelfth-century property of the abbey, with a group of early thirteenth-century stone buildings including a modest house, larger barn and cowshed. This early grange was abandoned when a new one was established in the valley bottom towards the close of the century, moat surrounded, and developed with a stone hall and solar (1280–1320), chapel, barn, stables, dovecote, boundary wall, and fishponds. The reasons for moving are uncertain, but the later grange was far more spacious in layout and domestic facilities than the previous one. It was leased out from the later fourteenth century and continued to be farmed until the late twentieth century. The solar block still forms part of the 1620 farmhouse, while the excavation confirmed the markedly secular character of the buildings on this ecclesiastical site.[8]

This was even more evident at Cumnor, near Oxford. The grange at this valuable estate was rebuilt in the mid-fourteenth century as a country residence for the abbot and a sanitorium for the monks of Abingdon Abbey. The residential range initially consisted of a central hall with end blocks, and windows similar to those inserted at about the same time in the hall and solar at Sutton Courtenay 'Abbey'. The hall, 44 feet by 22 feet and better proportioned than the earlier hall at Sutton Courtenay, had been fitted before the Dissolution with a stone fireplace with the arms of one of the abbots. The solar above a low ground-floor chamber was lit by a striking end-wall transomed window with ogee-traceried head. The chamber above the offices at the lower end of the hall was newel approached. During the fifteenth century, the house was expanded on the east side by ranges on three sides of a small court, one with a chapel, and each was interrupted by access approaches from the main road, churchyard, and garden respectively.[9]

The house was chosen by the last abbot of Abingdon as his dwell-

guests or abbey staff is unclear, but the layout of corridor-lined rooms was comparable with those prefacing the prior's lodging at Wenlock Priory (c.1430), the inner court at Ockwells Manor (c.1455–65), the east range (mid-1460s) and west range (c.1479) at Gainsborough Old Hall, and in its present undivided layout with the balconied north range (early 1460s) at Tretower Court.

Abingdon Abbey was among the largest landholders in Berkshire and held properties in several neighbouring shires. The abbey chronicler records that it was a veritable centre of civilisation during the later middle ages, though it was more notably a centre of controversy throughout most of the fourteenth century over the monastery's right to the town market. Major riots broke out over this dispute in 1327, causing damage estimated at £10,000, and though the abbey's domination was restored, there was perpetual friction during the extended rule of abbot Hanney (1361–1401).[2] For Langland, writing in about 1377, this abbot of Abingdon symbolised all that was wrong with the church and promptly prophesied the fall of the great abbeys.[3] These disputes subsided in the next century, and although there was initially a period of mismanagement, stability and modest economic prosperity based on wool were achieved during the last hundred years before the Dissolution.

PLATE 15 Cumnor Place: engraving by N. Whittock (1830)

ing and it remained little modified until the early nineteenth century, though part of it had become ruinous. Because of its unaltered condition, it is one of the most missed of nineteenth-century domestic demolitions, particularly as it had valuable parallels with the development of Sutton Courtenay 'Abbey'.[10] Destroyed by the earl of Abingdon in 1810, some of its stonework was incorporated in Wytham church, 2 miles distant, during its rebuilding by the earl in 1811–12.[11] Five two-light windows were reused, one as the chancel window, and three lighting the south side of the nave. These are all of Decorated character with flowing traceried heads, but the fifth window on the north side of the nave with cinquefoil lights and quatrefoil head is fifteenth century. The corbels supporting the nave roof came from the hall, even though its roof was still in reasonable condition at the time of demolition, while the churchyard gateway with a two-centred head may have been the hall entrance, and the late fifteenth-century embattled entry was that from the garden.

Steventon Priory was established as a grange of the abbey of Bec in Normandy, but with the advent of the Hundred Years' War the property was unable to pay its regular subsidy to the alien motherhouse. The abbey therefore leased the grange to Sir Hugh Calveley

in 1379 and sold it to him six years later.[12] It was given to Westminster Abbey in the last year of the century who leased it out for nearly 450 years.[13] Renamed Manor Farm and leased to absentee gentry who sublet to yeoman farmers, the property was divided into two habitations in 1843, amended to three in the 1950s.

The house lies at the church end of the raised causeway between the village green and the parish church. This grange was a small establishment under a prior, sub-prior, and seneschal and developed its quadrangular plan in stages as at Sutton Courtenay 'Abbey'. At Steventon, the hall and a short west wing of offices with prior's chamber above had been erected by 1324.[14] This modest house was extended northwards (towards the street) in 1443–4 by an L-shaped block to provide more generous residential accommodation.[15] The services may have been moved to the east wing at this point. Within a generation, the hall had been replaced by the present one, creating a house round three and a half sides of a small courtyard. The gap was closed in 1462–3 by Richard Doo (d.1476) at a cost of £13 11s. 5d.[16] to create the present street façade of three different building periods, immediately obvious by the contrasting framing techniques. Therein lies part of this house's interest, together with the survival of its hall, open to the roof.

The two-bay hall, 20 feet by 19 feet, stands at the rear of the property. This small chamber was made more imposing by its steeply pitched roof, 40 feet high to the roof ridge, though the stack built against its upper wall in the late sixteenth century substantially reduces these proportions. The two bays with original framed end walls are separated by a false hammer-beam truss with open trefoil lights between the beams and posts,[17] and the roof is stabilised by two lines of wind braces. The room was lit by timber-framed windows in the upper half of the walling, with one of four lights open to the courtyard and a blocked one opposite. The entry door from the west wing has a four-centred head with decorated spandrels, and the prior's chamber above projects slightly into the hall.

The two-phased parlour range extended in 1443–4 retains similar doorways with traceried spandrels but with mullioned bay windows and decorative gables added in the early seventeenth century. The substantial east wing, modified at the same time as the hall, is close studded with brick infill. The ground floor held a new kitchen, replacing a lost detached one, offices, and a new screens passage. Though the roofs are spanned by the original tie-beam trusses, the interiors throughout the property have been modified through continuous occupation. This applies even more so at Culham where the L-shaped core of Steventon survives on a larger scale. Timber-framed above a ground-floor stone base, the kitchen was in the better-preserved fifteenth-century west wing with original oak-block stair and king-post roof. The hall in the immediate half of the range at right angle was refaced, floored, and thoroughly remodelled in 1610 though the roof wall plate was retained.[18]

MONASTIC GRANGES IN ENGLAND AND WALES

Although Abingdon Abbey was a Benedictine foundation, the great majority of granges were established by the Cistercians as part of their pursuit of the austere in location and building and an economy of self-sufficiency. They pioneered the monastic farm, dividing their properties from their earliest days in the twelfth century into easily manageable agricultural units. To achieve this, it was necessary to provide accommodation, cover for the equipment and stock, and protection for the produce. Cistercian establishments were usually isolated, while those of other orders were not far from the mother church, as was the case with those of Abingdon or Glastonbury Abbey.

A grange was the focus of monastic estate management, but the word is not a very satisfactory term. Derived from contemporary Cistercian usage, it can refer to an entire monastic estate, to the group of domestic and agricultural buildings at its centre, or more recently to the great barn that has often survived when most of the other buildings have gone. Because of their continuing agricultural purpose, a number of medieval granges still fulfil their purpose as working farms as at Grange Hall, Westmorland, or Meare in Somerset.

Initially, the prime need was for a small dwelling from which the estate could be run. Such buildings would be modest and sometimes built of wood. Greater prosperity during the late twelfth and thirteenth centuries and the priority completion of the mother house freed funds for rebuilding or enhancing a grange's residential accommodation. Very often, a basic domestic unit for eating and sleeping with separate kitchen would be replaced by a hall with end unit, either offices with chamber above as at Steventon, or a solar

block as at Dean Court. Subsequently, a second chamber, a kitchen, or a chapel might be added, while the barn and agricultural buildings such as granary, byre, or dovecote would be extended or reconstructed.

The houses at Swanborough (Lewes Abbey) and Minster (St Augustine's, Canterbury) are among the few to survive from the twelfth century, both reflecting the plan of a small manor house with hall, chamber, and chapel, and subject to substantial updating at the beginning of the fifteenth century. Charney Bassett dates from the thirteenth century, but the majority of houses are of the following period, with obvious parallels to domestic architecture. The early fourteenth-century grange at Haversham in Buckinghamshire (Lavendon Abbey) retains a slightly foreshortened two-bay hall, now 24 feet by 19 feet, with screens passage, two-light window, and fine central king-post truss. Though the lower cross wing is a seventeenth-century rebuild, there is nothing to distinguish this property from a small Northamptonshire stone manor house, not even the square dovecote that stood near the cross wing until the late 1950s.[19] This symbiosis is even more obvious in the larger granges built by the Benedictines at Broadway, Meare, and Cumnor. These fourteenth-century houses are also a reflection of their growing popularity as rest centres for the monks, or as country retreats for the abbot or prior. A small gatehouse prefaces the domestic quarters at Hawkshead Hall (Furness Abbey), while another stands near the river approach to the grange of Shaftesbury Abbey at Bradford-on-Avon. Here a second large barn has been traced, contemporary with and at right angles to the famous early fourteenth-century great barn and opposite a rare granary of the same period to close the yard of a planned complex.[20] Bradford also retains its chapel, an oratory as in a private house rather than a free-standing structure like those at Salmestone in Kent and Wykeham Hall in Lincolnshire. Some of these communities were given rudimentary protection such as the banks and ditches at Monknash in Glamorganshire, but they were essentially to keep out animals rather than human intruders, though occasionally local circumstances warranted a tower as at Wolsty (Hulme Cultram Abbey) in Cumberland.[21]

Unlike monasteries, granges were not built to a standard plan. They reflected the terrain, estate size, and agrarian function of the area. They all needed a range of agricultural buildings and usually a dwelling, but the early structures that have survived have frequently been modified by post-medieval developments so that the earthworks of a property can give a better idea of a grange's layout than the remains of the buildings as at Monknash. Excavations help to flesh out the visual evidence as at Dean Court, the home grange next to Waltham Abbey, and the preceptory of the Knights Templars at South Witham where a complete farm layout of the thirteenth century was revealed.[22] All three sites exhibited a group of domestic buildings as in a manor house, but with a greater number of agricultural units including kilns, corn-drying ovens, barns, vehicle sheds, dovecotes, fishponds, and mills, haphazardly positioned round one or more yards. The larger sites, particularly during the later middle ages, tended to separate the domestic and agricultural functions between two or more courtyards. This is particularly clear at Tisbury (Shaftesbury Abbey) where the two courts are prefaced by separate gatehouses.

Of the agricultural buildings, the most useful and substantial has naturally tended to survive above all others. Barns were expensive

PLATE 16 Steventon Priory: street frontage

as well as structurally forceful, usually intended for storing grain brought from associated estates rather than local produce. But though the huge size of these roofed and often still functioning structures has long aroused admiration, dendrochronology has dramatically altered their dating since the 1970s to reveal a broad span extending from the barley and wheat barns at Temple Cressing (c.1200–40 and 1257–80, a Knights Templar grange) and Great Coxwell (shortly after 1300, Beaulieu) to Middle Littleton (c.1315 Evesham), Bredon (c.1345–50 Worcester), Enstone (c.1382 Winchcombe) and a number of fifteenth-century structures that include Swalcliffe (1402–6 New College, Oxford) and Bretforton (mid and late fifteenth century, Evesham). Not only had the structural developments of the earlier period been completed by about 1350, but later barns tended to be smaller than their predecessors.[23] It is because their structural similarities to domestic architecture can be underestimated that the most important have been noted during the regional coverage of these volumes.

Granges fulfilled several purposes. Many were estate centres rather than home farms. Others were stopping places for itinerant monks, rest or retirement houses for the monks of the mother house, or served as a country residence for the head of the community. It was probably to meet this need that a large chapel, such as that at Wykeham was built in the early fourteenth century. But standing and excavated evidence is now being complemented by topographical surveys such as those for Abingdon and Evesham abbeys, enabling a more coherent picture to be built up of a monastery's estate and practices over several centuries.[24]

The number of granges held by a foundation depended on a range of factors that include the size and financial standing of the mother house, its location, and the extent of its estate holding. By the fourteenth century, Furness Abbey held twenty-six granges, mainly in Cumbria, Margam owned about the same number spread across Glamorganshire, while the small foundation of Stoneleigh in Warwickshire held eight in that region at the close of the century.[25] Permanent staffing levels obviously depended on the size and location of an estate, but the number tended to be modest. During the mid-thirteenth century, there were between ten and twenty permanent staff on the lowland granges of Kingswood Abbey, seventeen at Wellingborough grange (Croyland Abbey) in 1290, and sixteen

at Great Coxwell (Beaulieu Abbey) half a century later.[26] Temporary staff were recruited as necessary, for the running of Cistercian properties by lay brethren after their initial development is no longer accepted.[27]

The development of monastic estates reached its peak at the close of the twelfth century and had come to a halt by the early fourteenth century. Even so, they tended to remain relatively immune from confiscation, subdivision, or transfer through failure in the male line as often occurred with lay properties. Yet the problems of staff recruitment, inadequate capital investment, and debts were beginning to be felt before the close of the thirteenth century, exacerbated by climatic problems and economic contraction during the early fourteenth century. The leasing of the more distant or less prosperous properties was the obvious solution. After the Black Death, staff shortages and the rising costs of hired labour, combined with too few men choosing the life of conversi, made the organisation and practice of demesne farming increasingly unprofitable. Leasing became widespread, often with the choicest properties subject to short leases, with one or two retained as the home farm, or for use as an occasional residence or retreat. The latter applied to both Tisbury 8 miles north-east of the mother house at Shaftesbury, and Broadway 11 miles south-east of Pershore Abbey where the farmland was sublet but the residence retained for the sole use of the head of the house. The consequence was that the grange system barely survived into the late middle ages. The properties became increasingly secular in character, particularly through residential additions and agricultural units to meet changing farm practices. The process was completed by the suppression of all religious houses during the late 1530s. But whereas a monastery's function and purpose ceased forthwith, granges retained a substantial element of continuity. Their agricultural and domestic buildings were often retained intact, even after the demesne lands had been partitioned among several Tudor claimants, hungry for land.

NOTES
1 Abingdon's dramatic baroque county hall of 1678–82 is a vivid contrast to the very conventional abbey gateway opposite, rebuilt in the 1450s under abbot Asshenden. Two-storeyed with vaulted central entry and side passage, the right-hand passage is a mid-nineteenth-century conversion of the porter's lodge made after the gateway had been converted from gaol to borough office use. For a detailed plan of the monastic layout, Med. Arch. 34 (1990) 206. The abbey was moat enclosed.
2 VCH, Berkshire, II (1907) 51–62. Hanney was impeached in 1368. G. Lambrick, Eng. Hist. Rev. 82 (1967) 250–76.
3 W. W. Skeat, Piers the Plowman (1886) B, book X, 332; N. Coghill, Medium Aevum 4 (1935) 83.
4 C. J. Bond, 'The reconstruction of the medieval landscape: the estates of Abingdon Abbey', Landscape History 1 (1979) 59–75.
5 Fragmentary or uncertain evidence survives at Appleford, Goosey, and Shippon, but nothing at Barton, Blewbury, Fitzharris, Garford, Northcourt, Shellingford, or Uffington. Barns remain at Northcourt, Shippon, and Tadmarton. C. J. Bond, 'Reconstruction' 64–8.
6 M. E. Wood, Thirteenth Century Domestic Architecture in England (1950) 8–10; C. R. J. Currie, Oxoniensia 57 (1992) 163–7.
7 The abbey held five granges in the parish at Botley, Dean Court, Synford, Wootton, and Cumnor itself.
8 T. Allen, Oxoniensia 59 (1994) 219–447.
9 For the description before demolition, Gentleman's Magazine 91 (1821) 2, 201–5. The east front was engraved by N. Whittock, Microcosm of Oxford (1830). Samuel Lysons made some sketches and a rough plan of

the site, *Magna Britannia* (1813) I, pt 2, 213. The site is now the garden of a twentieth-century house, west of Cumnor churchyard. A report on this property has been promised by Dr E. Impey.

10 They shared the same plan of hall and offices block in line and projecting solar block, contemporary fenestration when the timber-framed house at Sutton was stone-clad, and the certain knowledge that the hall windows at Cumnor were under mini gables. The quadrangular expansion plan was also common to both houses.

11 The earl had virtually rebuilt his nearby residence, Wytham 'Abbey', in 1809–10. Sir Richard Harcourt had acquired this property in about 1480 and he or his son initiated the present double-courtyard house. The three-storeyed gatehouse, with four-centred outer arch, diagonal buttresses, and three-sided oriels lighting the two upper floors, is the principal survival of this time, together with traces of contemporary work in the flanking ranges. VCH, *Berkshire* IV (1924) 427–8.

12 J. Fletcher suggested that this soldier of fortune, now about sixty years old and retired, may have also been responsible for widening the nave of Steventon church and reroofing the nave and chancel. *Trans. Newbury Dist. Field Club* 12, no. 1 (1970) 75–85.

13 Currie, *Oxoniensia* 57 (1992) 181–95.

14 *Ibid.* 182.

15 *Vern. Arch.* 33 (2002) 84–5; 35 (2004) 100.

16 Currie, *Oxoniensia* 57 (1992) 183. Doo's brass survives in the church. For some of the other timber-framed houses in Steventon, S. E. Rigold, *Trans. Newbury Dist. Field Club* 10, no. 4 (1958) 4–13.

17 A similar late fifteenth-century truss occurs at Hendred House, East Hendred.

18 G. Nares, *Country Life* (July 1950); VCH, *Oxfordshire*, VII (1962) 29.

19 P. Woodfield, *Northamptonshire Archaeology* 16 (1981) 173–4; E. Mercer, *English Vernacular Houses* (1975) 139.

20 *Med. Arch.* 28 (1984) 246–7.

21 C. Platt, *The Monastic Grange in Medieval England* (1969) 30–1.

22 P. J. Huggins, *Trans. Essex Arch. Soc.* 4 (1972) 30–127; P. Mayes, *Med. Arch.* 11 (1967) 274–5. Excavations at Badby grange in Northamptonshire and Ernsford in Warwickshire revealed domestic complexes comparable to manorial establishments, while the Templar manor at Bisham was simply taken over and extended by the earl of Salisbury as a house for himself.

23 J. H. Le Patourel in *The Agrarian History of England and Wales*, III: *1350–1500*, ed. E. Miller (1991) 867.

24 Note 4 above and C. J. Bond, *Vale of Evesham Research Papers* 4 (1973) 1–62.

25 A. Emery, *Greater Med. Houses*, I (1996) 209; RCAHM, *Glamorgan*, III pt 2 (1982) 245–306; Platt, *The Monastic Grange* 81.

26 V. R. Perkins, *Brist. & Glos. Arch. Soc.* 22 (1899) 179–256; Platt, *The Monastic Grange* 79–80.

27 Platt, *The Monastic Grange* 81–93.

J. Stevenson (ed.), *Chronicon Monasterii de Abingdon* (1858)
VCH, *Berkshire*, IV (1924) 430–2
A. E. Preston, *St Nicholas, Abingdon, and Other Papers* (1929)
A. C. Baker and W. H. Godfrey, *Abingdon Abbey* (1949)
M. Cox, *The Story of Abingdon* I (1986), II (1989)

The economic aspects of monastic estate management are covered in a number of single-house studies including M. Morgan, *The English Lands of the Abbey of Bec* (1946), B. Harvey, *Westminster Abbey and Its Estates in the Middle Ages* (1977), and R. B. Dobson, *Durham Priory: 1400–1450* (1973). C. Platt, *The Monastic Grange in Medieval England* (1969) established the current historical and architectural basis for the subject, superseding earlier studies such as R. A. Donkin, 'The Cistercian grange in England in the 12th and 13th centuries', *Studia*

Monastica 6 (1964) 95–144. Platt's work has not yet been followed up though there are brief surveys on late medieval farm buildings by J. H. Le Patourel in *The Agrarian History of England and Wales*, II, *1042–1350* (1988), ed. H. E. Hallam, 888–98, and III, *1350–1500* (1991), ed. E. Miller, 865–85. Despite individual studies such as H. Williams, *The Cistercians in the Early Middle Ages* (1998) and the beautifully produced volume by W. Horn and E. Born, *The Barns of the Abbey of Beaulieu* (1965), a detailed architectural analysis of the monastic grange is still awaited.

ACTON COURT, Gloucestershire

Acton Court is a classic example of how a well-known house, essentially considered to be sixteenth century, proves to be a highly complex site with a development span of more than four centuries retaining structural and decorative work of national importance. Site excavation, building analysis, structural consolidation, and garden archaeology between 1986 and 1996 are responsible for our reappraisal of this manor house of the Poyntz family.

Acton Court was the principal seat of the Gloucestershire branch of the Poyntz family from 1343 to 1680. It subsequently declined to farm status, with the house gradually falling into a neglected condition for most of the twentieth century until vacated by the farmer in 1984. The house is L-shaped, representing the east range and half of the north range of a larger quadrangular courtyard residence, originally moated, developed in stages, and with the medieval house crossing much of the site.

The earliest foundations can be attributed by excavated finds to the twelfth or early thirteenth century and were possibly an industrial building or the outbuilding of the earliest residence, which may have lain north-east of the present Court. The house was moated from an early date, with its position quickly revealed during preliminary excavations, but it was only a late excavation in 1997 that revealed evidence of a co-eval outer moat. The inner moat was given a stone revetment in the mid-fourteenth century when the advent of the Poyntz family led to a major construction campaign. The buildings erected within the inner curtilage included a gatehouse or porch leading directly into the screens passage of the hall on its left, which was flanked by a narrow chamber block at either end. There were further residential structures of uncertain purpose built at an oblique angle north of the hall.

Occupied continuously from the second half of the fourteenth century, the gatehouse was rebuilt during the early fifteenth century (presumably replacing an earlier structure) and was repaired in 1469. That there was a major refitting of the house towards the close of the fifteenth century was evidenced by the quality of the excavated finds, including glazed floor tiles of Malvern type, part of a sculptured fireplace of *c.*1480–1520, imported glass and pottery, and an elaborate small window built into the east range during the eighteenth century. Whether this refurbishment occurred in 1486 when Sir Robert Poyntz and his house were host to Henry VII is not known, but what is clear is that the Poyntz family enjoyed an extremely high standard at Acton Court during the late middle ages. Much of this site work has been left open for visitors.

The detailed study of the standing structure revealed its outstanding importance through several building phases within the relatively short timescale of 1534 to 1575. The two ranges were

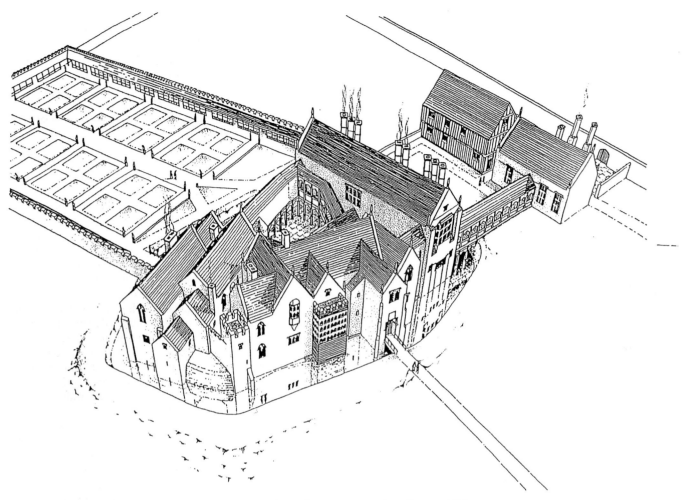

PLATE 17 Acton Court: reconstruction of house *c*.1535

erected on a different alignment from the medieval structures, though some of the earlier buildings continued in use. The east range of the L-shaped house was constructed by Sir Nicholas Poyntz (d.1556) in 1534 for a visit by Henry VIII and Anne Boleyn in the following year. This tall, oblong, two-storeyed range consisted of a single reception area at ground-floor level, plastered throughout in a single sweep, with three state apartments above of great size and height (presence, withdrawing, and privy chambers), lit by vast windows including one at either end of the range and two in the east front. The parallel with the rooms of the ducal suite at Thornbury Castle twenty years earlier is immediate. Other innovations included laying the sandstone walls in loam rather than mortar, and omitting any masonry cross walls to support the range. A few years after the royal visit, the ground floor was divided into a central entrance flanked by lodgings, one with a reused three-light, late medieval window. But the inserted partition walls did not overcome the range's instability. Ambition had outstripped technological capability, for the building's great height and overlarge windows made it unsafe. The windows had to be reduced in size in about 1700 and the walls were buttress-supported during the eighteenth and nineteenth centuries.

The north and lost west ranges were erected in the late 1540s,

with use being made of a roof of late fifteenth-century date brought from elsewhere (probably Kingswood Abbey given to Sir Nicholas in 1538) to cover the long gallery of the north range, though without the wind braces that had been an essential part of its original construction. The stair turret in the courtyard angle, seemingly contemporary with the north range, was added in about 1575. The excavations also revealed two totally unexpected factors affecting our interpretation of the standing buildings on this side of the site. What one imagines would have been an open court between the north range and the two wings in a balanced Tudor design was divided in two by a cross wall to create a small entrance court approached through the retained medieval gateway and hall. Furthermore, the other half of this enclosed area retained a further medieval building cutting diagonally across the inner angle, destroying its symmetry still further. This building must have been of some essential purpose such as a chapel or chamber block, which Poyntz felt unable to give up or replace.

Acton Court reveals architectural and painted classical details of considerable importance. That in the east range of *c*.1535 may be compared with contemporary work in the Loire valley, while the inscriptions and paintings in the north range of *c*.1550 are contemporary with work at Lacock Abbey, Broughton Castle, and the circle of the duke of Somerset. In addition to its newly revealed role in the vanguard of classical decoration in England, Acton also marks a stage in the development of early Tudor garden design. In clearing the approach court south of the house, a polyhedral sundial was found, attributable to the king's astronomer and dated 1520. This was probably the focus of a major Renaissance garden for Sir Robert Poyntz (c.1520), which lay north of the house, aligned on the medieval residence and not on the north range of c.1550. It was then that the south or approach court, influenced by nearby Thornbury Castle, was bounded by the crenellated and towered wall in antique style. At the same time, the inner moat, cleared for the royal visit in 1535, was filled. Finds excavated at most sites usually date from the period prior to its destruction (in this case, the late seventeenth century) but a very considerable number of those recovered at Acton Court date from this short fifteen-year period. They are of particularly high quality and among some of the finest artefacts ever recovered from this period. One final discovery awaited the excavators working on the east of the house. Instead of finding a garden layout as had been anticipated, the footings were revealed of a large range of stables and lodgings, linked to the main house by wooden corridors, indicating that Acton Court was a multi-courtyard residence.

This Gloucestershire house not only reflects the standing and lineage of Sir Nicholas Poyntz, but incorporates one of the few palace-like structures to survive from the early Tudor period and reveals his response to his rapidly improving circumstances. Although the Poyntz family was essentially of local importance during the late middle ages, they clearly enjoyed a high level of luxury. With the rise of Sir Nicholas in favour at the court of Henry VIII and the honour of a royal visit, most of the older buildings were replaced with ranges reflecting the latest architectural, technological, and decorative developments. Yet the shape of the Tudor house was determined by the plan of the medieval moat, while several uncomfortably positioned medieval buildings were retained as a deliberate reminder of his family's antiquity. Unfortunately Sir Nicholas' sudden downfall from royal favour in the early 1550s and that of his patron, the duke of Somerset, meant that he was unable to develop Acton Court any further.

The medieval entrance range, the Tudor west range, and half of the north range were demolished after 1680 when the house was reduced to farm status. It continued to be so used until 1984, smothered with ivy, and in a state of worrying decay. Yet it was precisely these circumstances, the almost total absence of Georgian and Victorian alterations, and the possibility of stripping out the farmhouse interior of inserted floors, partitions, ceilings, stairs, and cupboards that have enabled its complex history to be recovered in such detail.

K. Rodwell and R. Bell, *Acton Court* (2004)

ASHBURY MANOR, Berkshire

Ashbury lies at the foot of the Berkshire Downs, immediately below the slopes traversed by the ancient Ridgeway and facing the pasturelands of the Vale of Whitehorse. It is still a small agricultural community, a world apart from Swindon less than 7 miles away. Superficially, the Manor looks a single-period structure of advanced late fifteenth-century design with a ground-floor hall and withdrawing chamber above to the left of the entry porch, and the offices and kitchen under bedchambers to the right of the porch.

The house seems to have retained this fundamental plan throughout more than five centuries of occupation. This is true, but only as a result of at least five building phases.

Its present form was initiated by the abbey of Glastonbury using two contrasting types of stonework, probably in the 1480s. The western half is of that date, but the eastern half is later, marked by unvaried stonework and a lower roofline. Its buttressed façade can be dated by the uncusped Tudor window to the mid-sixteenth century, but the storeyed structure behind is a nineteenth-century rebuilding, maintaining the earlier room usage.

The property is rectangular in plan with a short contemporary wing at the rear angle, and interest almost entirely centres on the left-hand half. The ground floor was built of coursed chalk rubble, but the upper walling was constructed of better-quality and larger blocks of a lighter, cream-coloured chalk stone. The porch, which is not bonded to the main structure, reverses these materials and separates them with a string course not maintained across the body of the range. These two phases are reflected in the form of the outer and inner arches, both four-centred but the former with a continuous shallow-moulded arch while the main entrance has hollow moulding and quatrefoil spandrels set in a square frame. Following these two phases, another is identified by the datestone in the upper brick face of the porch inserted by T. White in 1697. Below this is an enigmatic second date with an oddly shaped second numeral which has been conjectured to be Mr White's misinterpretation of an earlier datestone of 1488,[1] a not unreasonable suggestion for the initial development of the house. To this close sequence of work c.1488, c.1495, and c.1545 as well as that of 1697 and the nineteenth century, all unified by the stone slate roof, the restoration of 1957 should be added – mainly windows copying the late medieval form.

The façade left of the porch is interrupted by two attractively stepped buttresses with a diagonal one at the corner, dividing the structure into three bays with two-light windows at ground- and first-floor level. All dressed stonework is built of the better-quality chalk stone. The lower windows are transomed, with the upper cinquefoil lights under an ogee head, set in a moulded square-headed frame without a label. The upper lights, lacking the transom, are a little smaller. The west end wall is original, with internal flues, but has a 1957 ground-floor window and door, the latter replacing an early window.[2] The rear (north) wall retains the cross-passage entrance with the same hollow moulding as the opposing entrance, but the stone chimney stack is an early addition, while the adjacent brickwork and window are nineteenth century.

The lower two-storey rear wing maintains the pattern of two building materials and the two-light window form (copied in the recent insertions), plus loops to the west and single trefoil lights to the east and north. Despite the fall in ground level, this projection is not buttress supported.

The frontage right of the porch was formerly triple buttressed as shown on the elevation of the house at the bottom of a pictorial map of the land held by the tenant farmer, T. White, in about 1700.[3] Only one buttress survives, though the line of those removed can be traced in the stonework. The elevation also shows two small square ground-floor windows in the position of the present larger ones and the uncusped two-light window at first-floor level.[4] The rear wall, set back 6 inches from the line of the earlier structure, is far less well built in the cream-coloured stone.

The entry doors open into the cross passage of the ground-floor hall, though the original screen has been replaced by a nineteenth-

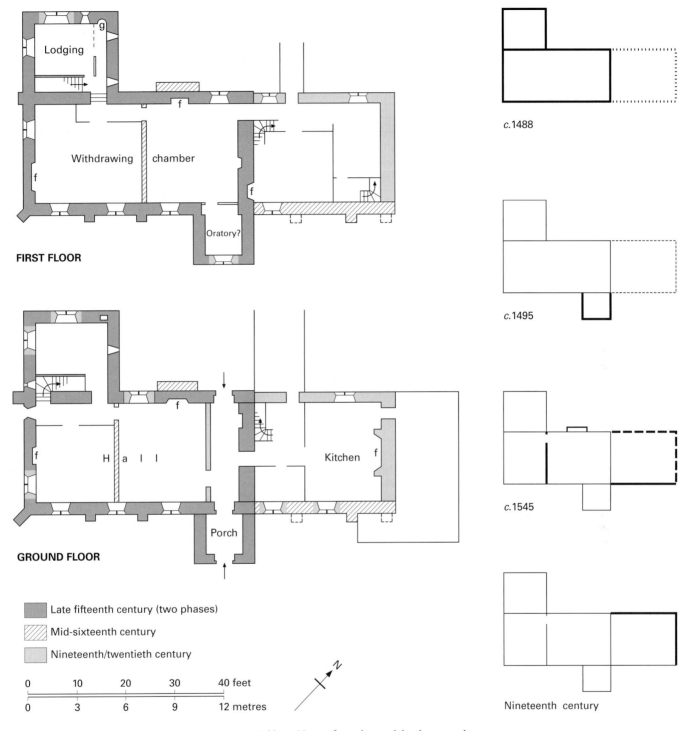

First Floor labels: Lodging, g, f, Withdrawing | chamber, f, f, Oratory?, **FIRST FLOOR**

Ground Floor labels: f, f, H a l l, Kitchen, f, Porch, **GROUND FLOOR**

Legend:
Late fifteenth century (two phases)
Mid-sixteenth century
Nineteenth/twentieth century

0 10 20 30 40 feet
0 3 6 9 12 metres

N

Development phases: c.1488, c.1495, c.1545, Nineteenth century

FIGURE 4 Ashbury Manor: floor plans and development phases

century wall cutting across the first ceiling timber. The original screen may have been like that at Wortham Manor on the line of the first cross beam. The four-bay form of the hall, 40 feet by 20 feet, was emphasised by the three south-facing windows,[5] and the rectangular pattern of moulded cross beams with three well-carved central bosses with leaf surrounds lapping into the angles. The hall was divided into two rooms in the mid-sixteenth century by a well-made post and wood panel partition astride the second window. It was at this time that the north stack and fireplace (1957 replacement) were added. The inner room was partially panelled in the early seventeenth century but the end-wall fireplace (1957 replacement) may be in the original position warming the hall, as that immediately above heated the withdrawing chamber.

The ground floor of the north wing is essentially a single room,

15 feet square excluding the intruding stair housing. The plainness of the cross beams and joists and the single loop (until the twentieth century) emphasise this room's utilitarian character. The stair from the upper end of the hall is more stylish, lit by a trefoil light at the lower level and a loop at the landing. The stone steps are in first-class condition because wooden steps had long covered them, although these have recently been removed. They access a half-landing, marked by twin doorways to a lodging, with the wooden ceiling rib coved over the remaining steps to the top of the stair. The landing doorways with four-centred heads access a bedchamber and garderobe respectively. The bedchamber is separated from the stair by a plain post and wood panel partition, but the garderobe division was replaced by a wider one in 1957 appropriate to a bathroom. The wooden garderobe seat discovered at that time and taken away by Dr Pantin was inadvertently burnt a few years later.

The great chamber followed the same plan as the hall below with three south-facing windows, but with a further window in the opposing wall above the rear entry. It was heated by the broad end-wall fireplace with four-centred head, three lines of moulding and base stops, cut in a single block of stone. The chamber was initially open to a highly elaborate roof structure, basically divided into four bays by arch-braced collar trusses with reverse-curved upper struts. Each bay was subdivided by higher intermediate trusses springing from small wall shafts. There were two tiers of cusped and counterchanged wind braces with an uppermost line of cusped braces shaped as two quatrefoils to a bay (only one survives). This is a Somerset roof in a Berkshire environment. Like the hall, this richly decorated and comfortable apartment was divided by a post and panel partition in the mid-sixteenth century when the second fireplace was added with its effete chamfer.[6] The west room was ceiled at wall-plate level but the east chamber was ceiled at a higher level to enable an embellished coving to be inserted round each side of the newly created room, covered with sub-medieval Flamboyant-style decoration of encircled S-shaped character. The original truss in line with this partition had to be replaced with a tie beam with upright posts to allow for the added coving.

The porch room, 10 feet square, was separated from the withdrawing chamber by a three-bay screen. The lower half is panelled below a line of open trefoiled lights with ogee heads and quatrefoil spandrels continuing above the four-centred doorway. The room was formerly open to a modest version of the adjacent main roof. The two bays were spanned by braced collar trusses with higher mid-arches, quatrefoil spandrels, and a quatrefoil frieze. It is possible that this room was an oratory but it has no features to confirm this apart from the screen. The walling that might have held an altar or piscina was rebuilt in 1697.

A particularly substantial stone wall has always separated the two parts of Ashbury Manor. The offices half is of markedly utilitarian character with low ceilings, crudely shaped beams, and Georgian-style windows. The offices, initially flanking a central passage, have been replaced, but the end kitchen (now a dining room) retains a small fireplace set in the original larger stack. There are two bedrooms above, one with a mid-Tudor window, and both with roof trusses of extremely basic form.

The manor of Ashbury had been held by the abbey of Glastonbury since late Saxon times. A thirteenth-century survey notes that abbot Robert (1261–74) built an inner gate and lodging, and added a kitchen and offices to the house, and a dovecote.[7] The house proved an extremely convenient lodging for the abbots on

PLATE 18 Ashbury Manor: entry frontage

their journeys to and from London, and though the farm was leased out by the fifteenth century, the house with its inner court and 2 acre garden was retained by the abbot as a country residence.[8] A terrier of 1519 also confirms that the house had become a welcome resting stage for scholar monks travelling between Glastonbury and their academic lodging at Gloucester College, Oxford.[9]

All earlier structures were swept away in the late fifteenth century when the house was redeveloped in a sequence of closely related phases spanning the years between monastic and secular ownership. The agricultural buildings that line the approach to the house mark the position of the outer court where the tenant farmer lived in 1519. The inner court area is now lawn, but a comparable twin-court approach with gates survives at Place Farm, Tisbury. The body of the manor house consisted of the ground-floor hall with withdrawing chamber above and a small lodging reserved for the abbot or a leading official. There is little doubt that the house was built by Somerset craftsmen employed on the abbey estates. The windows, in particular, are very similar to those in the George Inn, Glastonbury, built by abbot Selwood (1457–93) as pilgrim accommodation.[10] The Berkshire rebuilding may be reasonably attributed to him. Such a house could not function without the appropriate kitchen and offices and they were possibly in a timber-framed extension initially, particularly as Ashbury lay in a well-wooded part of central England. The property not only is a compact one, but is an early and clear example of the growing preference in smaller houses for a one-storey hall with chamber over rather than a hall open to the roof. This form was already becoming popular in the south-west[11] and in East Anglia during the last quarter of the century[12] though it did not spread to the south-east before Henry VIII's reign.

Ashbury Manor was acquired by Sir William Essex four years after the dissolution of the abbey's estates in 1539. Several alterations were immediately put in hand to adapt the property as a home for Essex's eldest son. The two building stone form was abandoned in favour of the lighter-coloured stone throughout. The kitchen and offices were replaced by a buttressed, storeyed extension. The hall and withdrawing chamber were divided, and the north chimney stack was added to serve the newly created rooms. There is very little to distinguish between these late medieval and sub-medieval phases. The style of the roof trusses of the added porch differs little from that of the slightly earlier principal chamber. The form of the mid-sixteenth-century room divisions is close to that of the late fifteenth-century stair partition. The triple-buttressed character of the kitchen extension mirrors the buttresses of the hall block, while the decorative coving of the partitioned upper chamber maintains the style of an earlier age, though without a trace of the cusping that had characterised the windows, screen, and wind braces. Ashbury Manor was an outlier – a striking late medieval stone house from Somerset in a region of timber-framed houses. The new owner was anxious to maintain its earlier character rather than introduce fashionable classical decoration or vernacular-type additions.

It was probably in the early nineteenth century that the kitchen and offices block was rebuilt behind the retained façade, with the new roof positioned above the line of the earlier one but maintaining its lower level to the body of the range.[13] Even so, this house retains its initial compactness, its little-altered state, and a great deal of its original character. This is all the more surprising in a property that is still the heart of a working farm. Though the present holding is not dissimilar in size to the 796 acres farmed by the abbey of Glastonbury in the thirteenth century,[14] it is essentially an arable one rather than supporting the extensive sheep runs that made the manor profitable during the late middle ages.

NOTES

1 Wood (1963) 8; Oswald (1966) 976. The porch upper window is a 1957 replacement.
2 Shown in the watercolour of 1818 by J. C. Buckler, Bodleian Library, illustrated in Oswald (1966) 975.
3 This map is held in the house.
4 The drawing of c.1700 confirms that the Gothic-style doorway below the mid-Tudor window, depicted in J. C. Buckler's watercolour of 1818, was a Georgian insertion.
5 There is no structural evidence that the nineteenth-century opposing window is in the position of a taller original one.
6 A further fireplace was inserted in the central wall after the corridor added before c.1700 had shut off this mid-Tudor one.
7 VCH, IV (1924) 505; Oswald (1966) 975.
8 Two deep gullies behind the house, formed by springs at the foot of the Downs, afforded some protection on the north side. One of the gullies was filled in the 1970s when the garden was extended.
9 VCH, IV, (1924) 506. Six of the students at the college in 1336 came from this abbey, R. A. Devereux and D. N. Griffiths, *Worcester College, Oxford* (1969 edn) 4.
10 M. Wood, *The English Medieval House* (1965) 360.
11 See page 460. Also W. A. Pantin, *Med. Arch.* I (1957) 118–46. Ashbury is among the houses mentioned in his survey, together with a plan and section, 144–6. Pantin and Wood considered the entire property to be of the late fifteenth century, including the offices wing and upper-chamber division. Their assessment was followed by Oswald, and more recently by C. R. J. Currie who was unable to see the house, *Oxoniensia* 57 (1992) 102.
12 A. Emery, *Greater Med. Houses*, II (2000) 25.
13 'rebuilt in comparatively modern times', VCH, IV (1924) 503.
14 VCH, IV (1924) 505–6.

VCH, *Berkshire*, IV (1924) 503–6
M. Wood, *Trans. Newbury Dist. Field Club* 2 no. 3 (1963) 5–18
A. Oswald, *Country Life* (October 1966)

ASHLEWORTH COURT, Gloucestershire

The grouping of church, house and tithe barn facing Ashleworth's untrimmed green is a classic composition, backed by the west meadows of the River Severn. The Court is a splendid survival,

PLATE 19 Ashleworth Court: west frontage

53

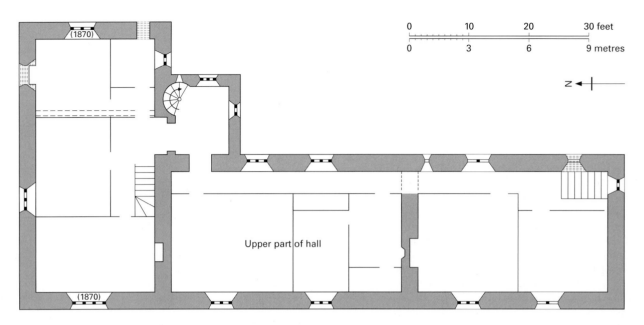

FIRST FLOOR

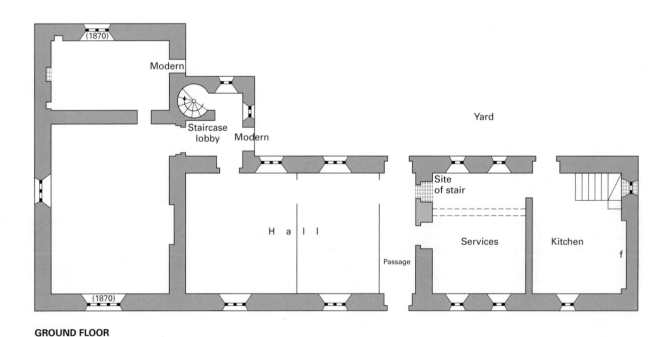

GROUND FLOOR

FIGURE 5 Ashleworth Court: floor plans

hardly spoilt by any major alterations. An upper floor was inserted in the open hall in the late sixteenth or early seventeenth century and a considerable number of internal partitions (mainly at first-floor level) were added in 1870 and the early twentieth century. None of this work has impaired the basic character of the house, which looks externally much as it did when it was erected.

Built to a classic plan of a central hall with two-storeyed end blocks, the house was spaciously planned with the services and kitchen in line at the lower end and the two upper chambers at right angles in a partial projection. The house is a hybrid of the hall and cross-wing form resulting in an elongated L-shape with the hall and lower block under a single roof ridge.

Totally unbuttressed, the principal frontage has a flat-chested appearance emphasised by the non-projection of the upper block and lack of a hall porch. The house is built of local Blue Lias stone, which weathers badly, and was formerly thatched until this was replaced with roof tiles in the late nineteenth century; the chimneys were replaced at the same time. The staircase lobby in the rear angle rose higher before truncation in the late sixteenth century.

The hall entry with its two-centred head and decorated square hood stops opens directly into the cross passage, with the screen replaced in the late sixteenth century by a timber-framed and brick-filled partition. The hall, 37 feet by 18 feet, is a magnificent four-bay apartment lit by a pair of two-light transomed windows in both side walls, with trefoil heads, lobed quatrefoil, and square hood stops. Two sills were lowered to provide more light when the hall was floored and partitioned. The roof is spanned by arch-braced collar trusses with embattled wall plates, and three tiers of curved wind braces. There is no wall fireplace evidence.

The projecting lobby at the upper end of the hall accesses both floors of the upper residential block. The ground-floor parlour with a nineteenth-century replacement fireplace retains its close-beamed ceiling. The rough-hewn condition of the beams contrasts with the equally close-set but finely chamfered beams in the ground-floor hall of Ashleworth Manor nearby.[1] The end windows at both ground- and first-floor level are restorations or renewals of 1870 in keeping with the original work. The much smaller inner chamber has two wall cupboards but no other original features.

The newel-approached upper floor was initially to the same plan, but the partition has been removed though the slots remain for the vertical members in the collar beam. The principal retiring room, formerly open to the roof, was of three bays with arch-braced collar beams with wind braces and embattled wall plate as in the hall. The single-bay room lacks wind braces and formerly possessed an outside door. It is more likely to have led to a garderobe than the usual attribution of an external entry to a court room.

Two doors in the cross passage accessed the services and kitchen passage. Some projecting stones in the ceiling and a narrow light above mark the site of the stair to the upper floor. The kitchen at the far end of the house, closely beamed like the parlour, has door access to a rear yard. An immense stone fireplace fills most of the end wall. The upper area, presumably divided into two rooms as below, was lit by paired lights under rectangular hood moulds.

The manor of Ashleworth was given by the Berkeley family to Bristol Abbey in the mid-twelfth century and held by them throughout the middle ages. It was one of the abbey's richest manors, most of which were located in south Gloucestershire and north Somerset. Though the Court is all of one build, its date is unclear. The form of the hall windows could be as early as those at the Abbot's Grange, Broadway (c.1330) or as late as the Tattershall tower-house (1440s), while the contemporary hall doorways are more fourteenth than fifteenth century. However, the inclusion of a heated parlour and a solar stair projection as at Wanswell Court (1450–60) suggests a date nearer the mid-fifteenth century. It is usual to attribute the construction of this house to c.1460[2] under abbot Walter Newbury (1428–73) on the evidence of one of the two stone corbels at the top of the newel stair representing a crowned head with the letter 'h' on his surcoat, taken to be Henry VI, but the corbels are not *in situ*. Leaving aside Newbury's deposition between 1451 and 1456, construction during the second quarter of

the century is suggested here until documentation or dendrochronology brings greater precision. Of very considerable size for a rectorial manor, the house was possibly constructed shortly after the estate had been let out on a lay tenancy basis rather than being the work of the abbey.[3] With its pristine plan, unitary construction, and almost intact condition, Ashleworth Court has few peers as an example of a fifteenth-century manor house.

NOTES
1 The contrast between the Court and Ashleworth Manor (only so-called since 1937) half a mile away could not be greater. The Manor is timber-framed throughout to an E-shaped plan with two-storey porch and single-storey hall. The left-hand wing is a mid-nineteenth-century rebuild, probably on the site of a comparable cross wing. The right-hand rear wing was added at the same time, making the house H-shaped. As at the Court, the thatched roof has been replaced by tiles. The heavily beamed hall, 24 feet by 18 feet, has an end-wall fireplace with four-centred but bastardised head. The beamed parlour in the cross wing retains the jamb of its original fireplace behind the present Victorian one but little more of the early roof survives than a single row of wind braces. The house is usually credited to abbot Newbury of Bristol (d.1473) but no supporting documentary evidence has been traced. The attribution rests on the fleur-de-lis and wheat sheaves on the stops of the entry doorway and the vine and rose in its spandrels similarly found on the abbot's tomb. They could have been a Victorian enhancement, for the house is mid-sixteenth century.
2 M. Wood, *The English Medieval House* (1965) 355; D. Verey and A. Brooks, *Gloucestershire*, II (2002) 155. Newbury was responsible for the abbey's central tower and the reconstruction of the transepts as well as the remodelling of the church at Ashleworth.
3 For early sixteenth-century tenants, C. Platt, *The Monastic Grange in Medieval England* (1969) 188. According to the Berkeley recorder, Smyth, the tithe barn of ten bays with queen-post trusses was erected by abbot Newland (1481–1515). Newland also initiated the transept vaulting at St Augustine's Abbey and a replacement nave. He also rebuilt the cloisters, added the upper part of the gatehouse with its oriel windows above the late Norman entry gate (drastically restored in 1888), and rebuilt the prior's lodging. *Bristol Cathedral*, ed. J. Rogan (2000) 34.

D. Verey, *Arch. Jour.* 122 (1965) 238

BAMPTON CASTLE, Oxfordshire

The royal manor of Bampton was granted by Henry III to William Valence, earl of Pembroke in 1248 and passed to his son Aymer in 1296. Bampton Castle was built by Aymer Valence, earl of Pembroke, under a licence to crenellate awarded in May 1315.[1] It could not have formed a greater contrast to the Herefordshire castle that Valence's father had built at Goodrich. The latter was rock-hewn, tower-encircled, compact, and internally complex: Bampton was low-lying, grandiosely scaled, and internally spacious.

Parts of the west gatehouse and curtain wall survive, fortuitously supplemented by a sketch of 1664 of the entire west front in its completed state by Anthony Wood.[2] The castle plan was simple, a 350 foot square described by Wood at the time of his drawing as built with 'a round Tower at each corner, which was ascended to by stone-steps: And for spedier conveyances up to the said wall there were besides these 4 Towers, a larg and high Gatehouse (Tower like) on the West and East sides (some say on every side) of which this here represented was the west tower.'[3] Their extent makes it likely that the north and south frontages were interrupted by mid towers. Most of the castle had been demolished before the close of the following century, leaving no further visual or documentary evidence of its form.

The site was surrounded by an extremely wide moat with an even larger quadrangular enclosure to the north, ditch enclosed.[4] The whole is visible to the eye, with the moat drained on two sides and reduced to a sluggish watercourse on the south and east sides. Most of the castle enclosure is covered by post-medieval farm buildings,[5] but the farmhouse is made up of three original stone structures – the lower half of the west gatehouse, a stretch of curtain wall to the south, and part of a two-storeyed chamber block to the north. All three structures are contemporary, with detailing entirely consistent with the second decade of the fourteenth century.

The castle, called Ham Court since the seventeenth century, is entered from the south so that the early buildings are approached from the rear prefaced by a dominant Victorian extension. Their early form becomes more obvious from the garden. The centre of the farmhouse is the lower half of the west gatehouse, with the upper floor reduced to a pitched attic. The entry passage has been blocked at both ends and floored at mid-level. The Victorian extension of about 1870 has been built against the south curtain which has never been reduced in height or suffered from inserted windows, and though the balancing wall to the north has gone, single-storey outhouses rise from its footings to the chamber block immediately behind it.

The gatehouse projects 12 feet from the curtain, with two pairs of corner buttresses and a blocked arrow slit on the south side and less obvious evidence of one on the north. The outer arch survives behind the ivy, with two late seventeenth- or early eighteenth-century mullioned windows in the entry infill. The same form occurs in the rear face though the entry arch is visible. The two-bay passage is now divided into two rooms at both levels but the internal faces of the entry arches are in mint condition, those to the front with single chamfer and those to the rear with triple chamfer. Opposing two-centred doorways access the stone newel and lodging range. The upper rooms are dominated by the pristine octopartite vaulting with single-chamfered ribs and badly worn central bosses in each bay. The broad stairs in the polygonal turret continue to the upper floor, which was replaced by an attic in the late seventeenth or early eighteenth century. Wood's drawing shows that the lost chamber was lit to the front by a two-light transomed window with shaped head, no doubt a larger version of that lighting the upper room of the adjacent block. A drawing of 1821 by J. C. Buckler shows that this upper chamber had a fireplace with a chimney head decorated with a ball-flower frieze.[6]

The lodging block is only just over 10 feet wide internally and stood in line with the rear face of the gatehouse. It was set back 3 feet from the inner face of the curtain rather than built against it. The ground floor reflects the modifications of about 1700, but the upper floor is a high-quality chamber retaining a fine two-light transomed window with ogee shaped trefoil heads and a quatrefoil below the two-centred hood. It accords extremely well with the licence of 1315, as does the fireplace with double-corbel-supported stone lintel and hood. The room was entered from the north end, now lost, so that a forced entry has been made from the gatehouse.

Thirty feet of embattled curtain wall stands 33 feet high. Wood's scale drawing of 1664 shows that the curtain, extending about 160

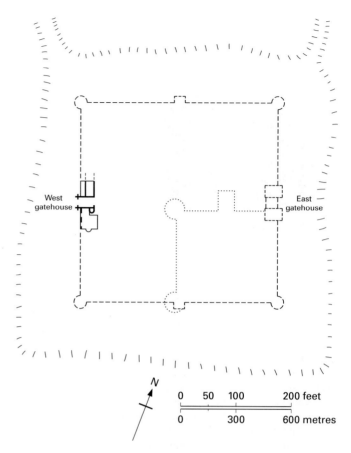

FIGURE 6 Bampton Castle: suggested plan (modified from Blair) with comparative area of Maxstoke Castle marked in south-east quarter

feet either side of the gatehouse, was interrupted midway by a corbelled-out turret, buttress supported, and terminated in three-storeyed round towers. There was a line of elongated cross slits at the lower level and smaller cross slits in alternate merlons. Two of these lower cross slits survive in broad semi-circular embrasures 7 feet deep, visible internally by opening farmhouse cupboards. Two of the merlons are also original, confirming the accuracy of Wood's drawing.

The importance of Bampton Castle lies even more in its planning than in the evidence of good-quality workmanship. Valence adopted the quadrangular plan of regular form that became a standard pattern for fortified houses and those that aspired to that form for nearly two centuries. Many of the key elements had been adopted in the inner ward of Caerphilly Castle (c.1268–72), but the slightly larger and more regular inner ward of Beaumaris Castle (1295–c.1298) was a closer model for Bampton. Though Bampton lacks Beaumaris' concentric outer wall, both castles were developed on entirely new and level sites, were constructed on low-lying ground that facilitated broad watercourses, and followed a rectangular plan of imposing symmetry with opposing central gatehouses, high curtain walls, rounded angle towers and mid towers in the two other fronts. But Valence's court was three times larger than that at Beaumaris and four times the size of that at Maxstoke Castle, one of several residences that followed Bampton's form.[7] But there were other differences too. Bampton was externally formidable, unbro-

PLATE 20 Bampton Castle: engraving of gatehouse and curtain wall from Parker (1853)

ken by windows (apart from the gatehouse) if the west front reflects the pattern for the other frontages. Whereas later quadrangular castles were built with their perimeter ranges against the outer curtain, those at Bampton were set back to allow immediate access to the defensive embrasures that are likely to have been repeated on all sides. Nor was an opposing gatehouse or even a second entry repeated at Maxstoke, Shirburn, Bolton, Wressle, or Lumley castles, though it was adopted at Bodiam. And though we are not clear whether the west or the lost east gatehouse was the principal entry at Bampton, the small scale of the existing gatehouse as well as an inner arch that was more complex than the outer one suggests that it may have been primarily approached from the courtyard side and was therefore the rear gate to the castle.

The tight residential planning imposed by site restrictions at Goodrich did not apply at Bampton, where a residential complex of greater spread was possible. High standards and quality workmanship are evidenced in the gate-passage vaulting, in the broad steps of the newel and in the chamber fireplace, but the vast internal area is likely to have been divided into more than one court. Like Goodrich Castle, Bampton could well mark an early stage by one of the key figures of Edward II's court in this country's movement from fortress to palace-mansion.

The castle was strategically sited midway between Valence's block of properties in Gloucestershire and Herefordshire centred on Goodrich Castle, his major group of estates in eastern England and Kent, and the seat of government in London.[8] Goodrich's development was determined by the still unsettled border conditions whereas Bampton was on the edge of a flourishing market town and meadows of the Thames plain, with the river 2 miles south. The castle was externally strong and internally spacious. Was it simply the comfortable *caput* of Valence's Midland estates[9] or was it a private stronghold developed as a potential refuge during the political uncertainties of Edward II's rule, like the 2nd earl of Lancaster's contemporary castle at Dunstanburgh (1313–22)? The Oxfordshire and Northumbrian castles have vast courts in common, while the castle under construction by the young Gilbert Clare at the same time at Llangibby (*c.*1310–14) has one of the largest single enclosures in England and Wales.[10] Some thirteenth-century castle courtyards were almost as large as at Pembroke (mid-

thirteenth century) and Denbigh (1282–95), with the terrain determining their irregular shape, but the only subsequent court of comparable size and similarly capable of holding a substantial force was the outer court of Thornbury Castle built by the provocative and ill-advised duke of Buckingham (*c.*1510–21).[11]

Aymer is known to have visited Bampton Castle in 1307 and 1312, and probably did so in 1321 when he participated in a tournament at Witney nearby.[12] He left no record of his intentions and the property was of little interest to his successors, the Talbots, later earls of Shrewsbury. Like Beaumaris and Llangibby, Bampton was possibly never completed and, like Llangibby, quickly became a white elephant after the death of its builder in 1324.[13] There are no grounds to believe that Aymer was hedging his political bets when he sought the licence to crenellate in 1315, even though he had lost his pre-eminent advisory role to the crown as Warwick and Lancaster gained in importance (autumn 1314 to April 1316).[14] It is arguable whether Aymer Valence was responsible for leading a 'middle party' of magnates and prelates between Edward II and the duke of Lancaster from 1317 to 1321, but he was always in favour of moderation and negotiation rather than provocation. As Goodrich Castle was too far from government to be a power-base, Bampton seems to have been intended for this role. Aymer also had a substantial retinue, as befitted a leading magnate, and Bampton was capable of housing them on a generous scale. Apart from his permanent household members, he had between fifteen and twenty retainers at any one time from a pool of between forty and fifty supporters. This increased to eighty-one when he went on campaigns against the Scots in 1314 and was well over a hundred in his 1315 and 1322 campaigns.[15] He also needed a suitable retinue befitting his position when he went on embassies to France. Yet despite its scale, Bampton Castle was essentially residential rather than a fortress enclosure.[16]

NOTES

1 *Cal. Pat. Rolls: 1313–17*, 278. Aymer's father built a house close to the present site in *c.*1256 when he purchased oak and beams for a new hall. VCH, XIII (1996) 23. It was visited by his wife in August 1296. C. M. Woolgar, *The Great Household in Late Medieval England* (1999) 49.

2 Bod. Lib., Wood MS EI, f.12. Blair (1988) fig. 5 and VCH, XIII (1996) 24.

3 Bod. Lib., Wood MS EI, f.12. Blair (1988) fig. 5 and VCH, XIII (1996), 24.

4 It is described briefly in VCH, *Oxfordshire*, II (1907) 331. Dr Blair suggests it may have contained gardens and orchards, or was even the curtilage of the earlier royal manor before it was granted by Henry III to Valence's father. Blair (1988) 6.

5 A cruck barn of sub-medieval date stands on the north side of the site. For its position and a reconstruction of the castle plan, *Med. Arch.* 32 (1988) 269.

6 Brit. Lib. Add. MS 36372 f.118 and verso.

7 Bampton 335 feet by 335 feet; Beaumaris 194 feet by 175 feet; Maxstoke 175 feet by 153 feet.

8 For Joan Valence's itinerary between the estates in 1296–97, Woolgar, *The Great Household in Late Medieval England* 48–9.

9 VCH, XIII (1996) 24.

10 Dunstanburgh, determined by the headland area, was approximately 570/660 feet by 600/730 feet; Llangibby 540 feet by 270 feet. The purpose behind Llangibby seems to have been precautionary against Welsh attacks, not Edward II whom Clare warmly supported before his death at Bannockburn.

11 Pembroke 330 feet by 300 feet; Denbigh 310 feet by 290 feet; Thornbury 275 feet by 275 feet. The large area at Greys Court, 350 feet by 220 feet, was developed in stages. For large-scale domestic courts, see page 125.

12 Blair (1988) 1; J. R. S. Phillips, *Aymer de Valence* (1972) 35, 215. It is arguable that part of the castle had been completed when he visited his wife there in June 1312 whilst conveying Piers Gaveston to Wallingford Castle. Leaving his prisoner unguarded at Deddington enabled the earl of Warwick to seize Gaveston and execute him nine days later.

13 Severe financial difficulties from 1317 after his unexpected capture and ransom in France would have curtailed any further building activity. He died in debt. After Aymer's death, his young widow founded Pembroke College, Cambridge and was responsible for remodelling Denny Abbey where she lived from the 1330s to 1377. A. Emery, *Greater Med. Houses*, II (2000) 60, 80–3.

14 Phillips, *Aymer de Valence* 71–99.

15 *Ibid.* 252–61, 295–311.

16 Several items of the Valence family have survived. The Valence casket (V & A) made in sheet metal but enamel decorated was probably a jewel casket made for William or his son Aymer. The lid of a nautilus-shaped cup (All Souls College, Oxford) was possibly made in Paris in *c*.1300 for Aymer's wife and enamelled with her arms. A horse harness pendant (Brit. Mus.) with the enamelled arms of the family also pre-dates 1324. *The Age of Chivalry*, ed. J. Alexander and P. Binski (1987) 259, 357–8.

J. Blair, *Bampton Castle*, Bampton Research Paper 1 (1988)
VCH, *Oxfordshire*, XIII (1996) 23–5

BERKELEY CASTLE, Gloucestershire and the house of Berkeley

For Leland, Berkeley Castle was 'no great thinge'. Certainly, it is the antithesis of town-dominating fortresses such as Richmond, Ludlow, or even Cardigan, so that many travellers might well agree with their Tudor predecessor in seeing little of interest behind the church and the screen of trees. As at Warwick, it is necessary to cross the river to see the castle's dominating face, or in the case of Berkeley to cross the marshy meadows of the Little Avon river. Even so, the fourteenth-century developments which transformed both fortresses reflected the contrasting attitudes of the Beauchamp and Berkeley families. The domestic rebuilding at Warwick was secondary to its military development, whereas the concentration of the less political Berkeleys was essentially on residential enhancements within the earlier buttressed curtilage. This is emphasised by the absence of an inner gatehouse. Since the fourteenth century, access has always been through the door and portcullis-protected passage[1] piercing the inner enclosure as in a fortified house.

On entering the castle courtyard, the visitor faces a unified development extending round three sides from the shell keep of *c*.1153–6 to the early Tudor gatehouse extension marked by the change to three storeys using blocks of Cotswold stone. Built in a unified programme against the three-quarter circular Norman curtain of *c*.1180, this two-storeyed development in local tufa limestone ranging from red and purple to grey and brown tones with ashlar dressings is one of the most impressive domestic survivals from the first part of the fourteenth century, unfolding like a cardboard cut-out model encompassing staff quarters, offices, and kitchen serving the great hall in the centre preparatory to the extended residential range on the right-hand side. Continuous occupation has meant

that the interiors have been subject to more radical changes than are apparent externally. The plan is complete but not the detailing. Only the kitchen, hall, chapel, and 'cellars' retain their early character, for the remainder is a reflection of early nineteenth-century pastiche and early twentieth-century medievalising.

The last earl of Berkeley (1916–42) expended a fortune between 1920 and 1930 on restoring the state and private apartments to their earlier form, richly furnished, and supplemented by imported architectural features from England and France as Randolph Hearst was similarly doing at St Donat's Castle. The work was financed by the earl's sale of Berkeley Square and other Mayfair holdings for nearly £2 million.[2] He acted as his own architect and archaeologist and was not prepared to brook criticism, though the work was completed to extremely high standards and created a sequence of evocative and lavishly furnished apartments. The ground plan by Turner and Parker (1858) and combined ground- and first-floor plan by G. T. Clark (1876) helped Patrick Faulkner to establish the castle's medieval plan (1965) prior to the changes highlighted by comparing Marklove, *Views of Berkeley Castle* (1840) with the photographic record in *Country Life* (1932).

The hall and kitchen are single-storeyed but a deep-corbelled battlemented parapet maintains a common height with the remainder of the range.[3] The hall is its heart, sited like its forerunner almost opposite the entrance but emphasised by a recessed frontage with a line of close-set windows. The two-storeyed porch is characterised by a feature that is the signature of all the early fourteenth-century work at Berkeley, half-octagonal headed openings, here marking both outer and inner entrances (pl. 1). They are plain, like the vault of the porch (head corbels and stops excepted), though the heart-shaped side window suggests that more elaborate forms will follow.

They do so in the screens passage where the three service doorways, the central one to the kitchen passage higher than its colleagues, are enhanced by multi-foiled inner arches, the Berkeleys' other signature of this period. The early Tudor screen with Elizabethan painted decoration is a 1925 importation from Caefn Mably, Pembrokeshire, replacing one long destroyed. Never partitioned or floored, the hall continues to impress today by its scale, as it was purposed to do in the fourteenth century. The remains of the late Norman hall were not fully disclosed until 1922–3 when its three window embrasures in the outer wall and that of the two-storeyed end block were revealed. Its early fourteenth-century successor combined the two units in a single wider apartment, 62 feet by 32 feet and 32½ feet high.

The four courtyard-facing windows of the hall, the upper lights with trefoiled heads and the lower with scalloped shouldered heads, are enhanced with half-octagonal cusped rear arches.[4] Separated externally by mini triangular buttresses, they have low window seats facing imported medieval French frames in the embrasures opposite. A four-light traceried window illuminates the lower end of the hall as at Clevedon Court (*c*.1320). The contemporary eight-bay roof is ceiled at the head of the braced collar trusses to create a double-pitched roof with a third line of wind braces.[5] The mid-fifteenth-century wall fireplace is a 1925 insertion brought from the hall of Wanswell Court to replace an early nineteenth-century Gothick mantelpiece. The added stack to a formerly sixteenth-century hearth here replaced the central hearth with its two louvres, shown in Buck's 1732 engraving and restored in 1925.

Access from the hall dais to the residential range is by a 1925

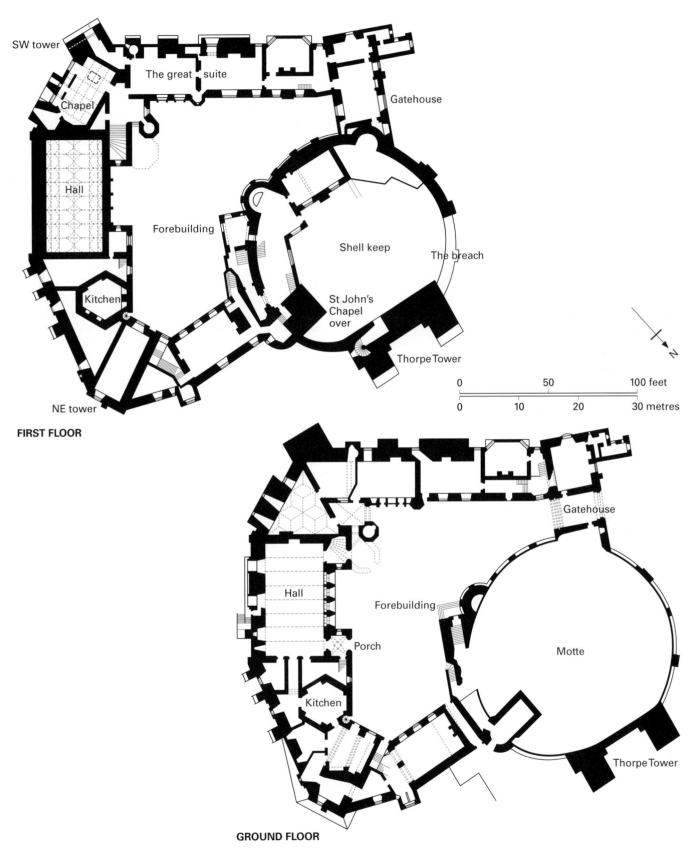

FIRST FLOOR

SW tower

The great suite

Chapel

Gatehouse

Hall

Forebuilding

Shell keep

The breach

Kitchen

St John's Chapel over

Thorpe Tower

N

0		50		100 feet
0	10	20		30 metres

NE tower

GROUND FLOOR

Hall

Forebuilding

Gatehouse

Porch

Motte

Kitchen

Thorpe Tower

FIGURE 7 Berkeley Castle: floor plans

PLATE 21 Berkeley Castle: engraving from south-east by S. and N. Buck (1732)

replacement Berkeley arch. It opened into a stair bay, presumably rectangular to balance the entry porch but rebuilt in 1637 when the present stair was inserted. It was extended in 1925 with a half-octagonal outer porch embellished with French elements.[6] In its early form, the stair would have risen to a rectangular ante-chamber above the ground-floor lobby, possibly with a ribbed ceiling. This was the prelude to the three first-floor family apartments, the chapel at the angle, and the great or outer chamber followed by the inner chamber filling the remainder of the courtyard range. The moulded jamb of the chapel doorway was revealed in 1923 with the opposing end-wall entry to the great chamber repositioned in the nineteenth century.[7] The forward newel turret which dominated the courtyard until 1925 gave immediate access to the ante-chamber and private apartments.

The fourteenth-century private chapel is one of the most gloriously preserved in England. The last earl of Berkeley, already having a chapel sufficient for his needs in the keep, unnecessarily converted this one in 1922 into a morning room or 'solar' by reversing the entry to the opposite end of the room, inserting a fifteenth-century French doorway, fireplace and overmantel, and removing the outstanding private pew to the adjacent room.[8] Despite these solecisms, the individuality of the chapel survives: 39 feet by 23 feet with an apsed east end, the chapel is lit at both ends by a generous window in the outer wall with twin trefoil lights and quatrefoil head backed by a multi-cusped rear arch. Between them, a passage 3 feet wide was created in the thickness of the 14 foot deep wall, spanned by curved shouldered openings, with the inner wall little more than a screen with foliated open windows and doorway. The tie beams of the low-pitched five-bay roof and shallow-apsed end bay are carried on short triple columns supported on head corbels of marked individuality.

The braces are enhanced with blind trefoil decoration with contra braces in line with the walls. The braces and ribs retain early painted decoration with an inscription added by John Trevisa, the chaplain of the castle (1379–1402). The text is that of a thirteenth-century Anglo-French manuscript of the Apocalypse, the only surviving example of such an extended medieval Bible translation on a ceiling in France or England. It continues above the ceiling panels. Similar inscriptions were traceable on the walls of the south passage and, according to Trevisa's translation of Higden's *Polychronicon* (1387), inscriptions in Latin and French formerly covered the chapel walls.[9] The piscina with ogee head between the door and window, shown in early *Country Life* photographs, was removed in 1922. The narrow chaplain's room off the apse, created within thickened walling, retains incised decoration on its plaster walls.

The gallery at the opposite end of the chapel, now in the next room, is an extremely rare survival. It is usually stated that this pew, of Tudor date, had been brought to the castle after the Reformation from Longridge Hospital in Berkeley, founded by the family in the twelfth century and pulled down in 1586.[10] It would have been rather overwhelming for such a location, could well be fourteenth-as much as fifteenth-century work, and is more likely to have been an integral fitting of this impressive private chapel than in the Hospital. The pew is 7 feet deep, carried on a single frontal beam with carved spandrels, with the projecting central bay, supported on two pillars. The raised frontage is divided into two, the lower part of solid panels with blind trefoil decoration, and the upper part with an open screen (central bay mullions restored in 1922) surmounted by an embattled cresting.

The two private apartments of the Berkeley lord are fourteenth century in their rectangular shaping but too heavily modified in

PLATE 22 Berkeley Castle: interior of chapel

Tudor and Georgian times to give much indication of their early character. The 1800s remodelling was particularly thorough, including replacement windows to the courtyard (original rear arches) and one in each room through the 12 foot thick curtain, as Kip's engraving of 1712 shows. The purpose of the early twentieth-century work was to restore a medieval character to the rooms as a background for the magnificent parcel gilt furniture and tapestries. It included revealing the stone walls and post medieval roofs, and inserting replacement mid-fifteenth-century fireplaces in the outer walls, from Wanswell Court in the outer chamber (great drawing room) and probably from this source in the inner chamber (small drawing room).[11] Intercommunication between the two rooms was by the charming open-sided turret lobby spanning the courtyard end of the partition wall, with a garderobe in the opposite corner.

The post-medieval changes to the ground-floor porch and hall stair, and the devaluation of the ground-floor rooms of the south range have concealed their original function. The open-vaulted porch entered alongside the range gave access in two directions, to the vaulted chamber below the chapel and to the apartment below the great chamber. The roughly triangular-shaped corner room has long served as a beer cellar, but such a function would never originally have been sited in this superior position almost on the same level as the hall. Lit by lancets pierced through the buttressed outer wall, it is enhanced by an ingeniously groined and vaulted ceiling. A trefoil-headed doorway in the west wall opens into a small ribbed and vaulted room, 5 feet lower and between 8 and 10 feet wide. It is ill lit by a replacement lobby window and is now used as a wine cellar. The large vaulted chamber served a superior function, perhaps a staff room as a vice in the outer corner of the wine cellar intercommunicated with the family suite above.

The two ground-floor chambers in the south range mirrored the apartments above. Now corridor lined and fitted as a modern kitchen and offices, their position and size indicate that they were originally a suite of lesser family apartments.

The planning of the medieval kitchen and offices was conditioned by the curved shape of the outer curtain, with service rooms either side of the single-storey kitchen positioned in the courtyard angle. Even so, the facilities ran for 50 feet from the hall porch (80 feet to the field) in a more extended sequence than any other contemporary survival. The first section retains early windows and parapet to the courtyard but the remainder is an early nineteenth-century remodelling. Only the entry doorways survive to the kitchen passage, subsequently absorbed into the buttery. The kitchen, an irregular-sided hexagon approximately 21 feet in diameter, is a fine survival, open to the roof, with the three longer sides filled with broad hearths and internal stacks with flanking lights in the upper walling.[12] This pivotal centre has been subject to several late medieval renewals, including the fireplace lintels, windows, and roof structure attributed by Smyth to the close of the fifteenth century.[13] There was no courtyard access for it was approached only from the kitchen passage and the bakehouse. This last was the largest of the irregular-shaped offices, spanned by two massive low vaulting ribs with further wall hearths, ovens, and entry to the courtyard well passage.

The range filling the north side of the courtyard, now a dining room display with picture gallery above, may have been a staff hall with communal lodgings above. The present through-passage at the side of the keep is a mid-nineteenth-century insertion replacing a cross passage within the staff hall marked by the courtyard and opposing entries converted into windows. The head of the courtyard doorway and the machicolation above the outer entry survive and a postern bridge in line with the doorways was recovered by excavation in the 1930s.[14] This rear entry, well sited for services and goods, is similar to the Tudor facility at Ightham Mote. The two fourteenth-century triangular-headed arches on square piers spanning the upper end screened the stair to the staff lodging above and a pair of garderobes in the opposing turret.

DEVELOPMENT ASSESSMENT

Among the outstanding facets of the early fourteenth-century residential development of Berkeley Castle are the quality and scale of the accommodation facilities for household staff as much as for family.[15] Not until the rebuilding of the domestic accommodation at Kenilworth Castle later in the century was there such extensive work within a castle courtyard. The kitchen was supported by a substantial number of offices and service rooms, and the staff by their own hall and accommodation above. The family enjoyed a sequence of private apartments at ground- and first-floor level, and probably the lodging above the services next to the screens. The whole was centred on a hall of impressive scale and character. The decorative qualities of this work are equally striking, using masons who had been employed on the rebuilding of St Augustine's Abbey, Bristol.

The remodelling of the castle followed in the wake of one of the most brilliant and contrasting displays of English architectural inventiveness when the choir, aisles, and lady chapel of three abbey churches in the lower Severn region were rebuilt in turn, at Bristol (1298–c.1325), Tewkesbury (1322–c.1344), and Gloucester (1331–51). Berkeley's use of masons from the Bristol lodge is not surprising. The family had founded St Augustine's Abbey, which had become their mausoleum, and they were financially supporting the new work under abbots Barry (1294–1306) and Knowle (1306–32). The castle's redevelopment also reflects the planning

clarity, block form, and spaciousness of the Bristol choir, not often found in a domestic context.[16] Berkeley eschewed ball-flower decoration which was spattering the region further north, as in the nave south aisle at Gloucester abbey (1319–29) before supplanted there by the Perpendicular style, while the castle was sparing in its use of the ogee form and flowing tracery adopted for the choir at Tewkesbury (c.1325–40).

The years from about 1310 to 1320 may not be unreasonable for the commencement of this building activity by Thomas, 1st Lord Berkeley, who spent the later years of his long life at Berkeley when not on the battlefield, but Smyth only refers to Thomas' responsibility for gatehouse building in 1313.[17] The five years between 1321 and 1326 can be eliminated because of the imprisonment of Maurice, 2nd Lord (d.1326) and his son. The first years of Thomas, 3rd Lord Berkeley are most likely for initiating the major rebuilding programme, arising from his marriage to Roger Mortimer's young daughter in 1320 and his growing prosperity through estate enhancement and improved agricultural husbandry (see below). His work, encompassing both service and family apartments, was centred on the chapel and the hall. Both have distinctive architectural features. The inner cusping of the chapel windows is close to the shaping of the hall windows at Caerphilly Castle of c.1326 for Hugh Despenser the Younger. The semi-octagonal head of the hall and cross-passage doorways, the so-called Berkeley arch, also distinguishes the Berkeley tombs in St Augustine's Abbey, Bristol (now the cathedral) erected during the 1330s. Lord Berkeley's responsibility has never been in doubt, confirming Smyth's statements to that effect. Furthermore, it is not unlikely that the rebuilding of the hall and apartments at Caerphilly Castle, particularly the scale of the unaisled hall, may have spurred Lord Berkeley to undertake his own plans.

Richard K. Morris has added some flesh to these bones. The combination of carved foils with delicate ogee arches like those in the chapel windows occurs in the Berkeley chapel at Bristol (1320s), Wells Cathedral presbytery (after 1326), and Bristol Cathedral presbytery high vault (late 1330s/early 1340s), giving a twenty-year span.[18] The roll and undercut chamfer moulding of the chapel windows is repeated in the broken pulpitum of Tintern Abbey (c.1330?), Wells Cathedral clerestory (1330s), and the south transept aisle windows of St Mary Redcliffe, Bristol (1340s).[19] The timber ribs of the chapel ceiling are identical in form to those of the main vault of Bristol Cathedral (1330–45) and the eastern arm of Ottery St Mary (after 1337).[20] It is therefore likely that the chapel was begun in 1327 when, as Smyth noted, Thomas III 'In the first year of King Edward III . . . and the year following somewhat built, but more beautified his castle of Berkeley',[21] and that it was completed during the 1330s.[22] The work is likely to be by William Joy, who was responsible for the major work at Wells Cathedral triforium (after 1329), Bristol Cathedral east arm (1330–45), St Mary Redcliffe south porch (c.1340), and the front of Exeter Cathedral (1346–7).[23]

The great hall seems to have been the work of a different and slightly later master-mason, influenced by the earlier idea of Joy.[24] In particular, the distinctive Berkeley arches with more simple chamfer mouldings than those in Bristol Cathedral more readily compare with those at St David's and more particularly in the cathedral pulpitum screen and the palace hall porch (probably 1340s).[25] Morris attributes the castle hall to the 1340s with the same master

PLATE 23 Berkeley Castle: hall interior

responsible for the Pembrokeshire and Gloucestershire work.[26] This is supported by the form of the lierne vault of the quadrangular hall porch which has an affinity with those spanning the transepts at Ottery St Mary and St Mary Redcliffe of the 1340s.[27] This attribution coincides with Smyth's documentary reference to 'newe worke at the castle in 18th–19th year of Edward III [1344–5] which is that part without the keepe on the northeast next the little parke and next to the great kitchen, the roofe wherof Henry VII brought from Wootton as tradition tells us'.[28]

It is remarkable that although the Berkeleys were the leading Whig family in eighteenth-century Gloucestershire, they never seriously attempted to remodel the castle interior, while irregular occupation in the nineteenth century inhibited the Victorianisation that afflicted Alnwick, Arundel, and Cardiff castles. Consequently Berkeley Castle stands alongside Haddon Hall as one of the supreme residential survivals of the fourteenth century. It provides an uncluttered and little-altered example of domestic planning at the upper level of society, particularly important when as much sur-

vives of the household and staff quarters as of the family apartments. The French additions of the last earl can irritate in this English context and some of his changes were autocratic, but without his financial resources and historically sympathetic approach by an enquiring mind, Berkeley Castle would not stand today in such splendid condition.

THE BERKELEY FAMILY

The house of Berkeley is as colourful as any in the English peerage, with a more than ample share of eccentrics and cads. Their activities have ranged from the battlefield and royal murder to scientific exploration and diplomacy – from vicious feuds and the last private battle on English soil to an infamous case of bastardy spanning most of the nineteenth century. They are one of the longest-living families in English history, were responsible for the longest case of litigation in English law (1417–1609), have been the outstanding county name for centuries and continue to occupy the castle of their ancestors.

During the fourteenth century, the Berkeley family attained regional rather than local influence and power, comparable to that of some of the greatest families. Yet unlike the houses of Mortimer, Neville, or Stafford, they were never granted an earldom at that time and the likelihood of achieving this slipped away between the early fifteenth century and the Tudors. That we know so much about this family is due to the extensive archive still held in the castle[29] and the survey built up from that material in 1618 by John Smyth of Nibley, the Berkeley's steward, who used documents that no longer survive.

After the Conquest the lordship and castle were held by a Berkeley until the time of Stephen when they were given by Henry II to the Bristol merchant Robert FitzHarding for his financial support. FitzHarding subsequently married into the Berkeley family and adopted their name. The barony by writ begins with Thomas, 1st Lord Berkeley (d.1321) who inherited in 1295 and spent much of his adult life until after Bannockburn fighting the Welsh, Scots, and French. His son Maurice (d.1326) spent his last adult years in prison so that it was left to Thomas, 3rd Lord Berkeley (d.1361) to continue expanding the patrimony when he was not fighting in the Scottish and French wars. Maurice (d.1368) died at a relatively early age, as a result, it is said, of war wounds. Thomas, 5th Lord Berkeley (d.1417) enjoyed a long tenure and was a noted patron of the arts, particularly authors and illuminators.[30] James, 6th Lord Berkeley (d.1463), his 23-year-old nephew and male heir, kept a low profile during an extended period of high politics to defend his inheritance against the claims and assaults of the daughter of the 5th Lord and her co-heirs after her death in 1422. These claims were stifled in 1470 by the death of Viscount Lisle and many of his supporters in an armed feud with William, 7th Lord Berkeley (d.1492) at Nibley Green. William restored the family's depleted lands by acquiring half the vast Mowbray inheritance through the reversion rights of his mother and the associated title of earl of Nottingham (1483). To disinherit his brother and successors, this vituperative person settled virtually all the family estates on Henry VII and his heirs male and received a marquisate in return (1489). When the royal male line failed in 1553, all the outstanding alienated estates were returned to the family.

Throughout the fourteenth century, the Berkeley lords were intent on building up their two groups of estates centred on the Hundred of Berkeley and the outskirts of Bristol by expanding elsewhere in Gloucestershire and into neighbouring Wiltshire and Somerset. The most successful was Thomas, 3rd Lord who inherited a relatively rich holding of thirty-three manors which he extended in 1330 by purchasing Beverston on the Cotswolds, with two further manors to the north and six in nearby Wiltshire. He added three manors to his estates near Salisbury and four close to the Somerset border. Within thirty years, he had added nineteen manors and twenty-eight lesser areas to the family holdings, mainly adjoining the larger properties, drained and enclosed land at Slimbridge,[31] and with his second marriage to a rich widow in 1347 consolidated his hold on the Tortworth area south-east of Berkeley. Similarly, his grandson's marriage to the heiress of the Lisle estates added about two dozen of their manors spread across seven counties to the Berkeley holding in 1382.

There was a triple purpose to this policy – to increase the family resources and support a retinue of size and magnificence, to make provision for younger sons who could further the Berkeley influence without breaking up the estate, and to capitalise on the region's rich agricultural resources through astute estate management, progressive husbandry, and domestic efficiency. South Gloucestershire and north Wiltshire were particularly well placed to benefit from extensive sheep runs, the dominant economic resource of late medieval England. In 1327, about 90 per cent of the Berkeleys' demesne was arable; forty years later this had fallen to 65 per cent with the remainder taken up by pasture.[32] This was the motive prompting Thomas' purchase of Beverston with its stock of 1,500 sheep, a further 1,500 wethers in 1344,[33] and pasture holdings round the mouth of the Wye in the 1340s and 1350s. The rise in his annual income from £425 in 1328 to £659 in 1335, and then £977 in 1345 to £1,150 in 1347 was reflected in his enhanced lifestyle which marked the zenith of Berkeley fortunes in the middle ages.[34] Yet land acquisition and economic development were matched by accounting stringency. Smyth cites documents confirming that the Berkeleys were as assiduous in checking their financial records in the fourteenth century as the duke of Buckingham was with his at Tudor Thornbury.[35]

The Berkeley records reflect the size and multi-dimensional activity of the household. Under the 1st Lord (d.1321), the household consisted of '200 persons and upwards, milites, armigeri, valeti, garciones et pagetti, knights, esquires, yeomen, groomes, and pages beside husbandmen . . . and others of lower condition'.[36] Under the 3rd Lord (d.1361) Smyth estimated that at least 300 mouths of the standing house were fed each day.[37] 'All the knights robes were of cloth of ray, and of bastard scarlet, furred with the best miniver. And the habit of the lord himself was therto sorted. The robes of an esquire were of fine broad ray colour cloth, fured with a courser sort of miniver. And so were the clerks of the chapel and men of office . . . The livery of the gartion and underservants were all of them of cloth and fured with coney, lambskin and budge, each a degree under other.'[38] A retinue of this size demonstrated a lord's standing, his reputation, dignity, and 'presence', not only when he travelled between his estates or to London, but when he was entertaining distinguished guests. The Berkeley retinues were among the largest but they were by no means the most ostentatious. What they did do more clearly than anything else was underline the Berkeleys' pre-eminence in the region. Smyth noted that the 3rd Lord's retinue included twelve knights and twenty-four esquires while Saul established that the majority of knights were local men, with the remainder drawn from Somerset and other nearby counties where there were Berkeley interests.[39] Under the daughter of the 5th Lord (d.1417) who had married Richard Beauchamp, earl of Warwick, the household account book for 1420–1 creates a vivid picture of a great medieval household and its progress from Berkeley to the countess' various family estates, mainly in the Midlands. They include such details as the household stores and stock, with wine and ale making up the largest purchases at Berkeley. In one year, 3,000 gallons of wine were purchased and 19,000 of ale were consumed, though Dr Ross concluded that the household was one of ordered domestic efficiency.[40]

Berkeley Castle illustrates better than most medieval houses the axis of progression from humble to grand, and from public to private – from hall (both public and grand) to family suite (both grand and private). Furthermore a residence on this scale received and disgorged a spectrum of society from royal guests to family friends and local landowners. Equally both outer and inner courts encompassed pages, grooms, servants, and hangers-on, who spread the word about the plenitude of the family and the Berkeleys' 'good lordship'. Their castle is one of those rare examples where the standing buildings and the documentary evidence combine to reflect the plenitude and patronage of the lord more vividly than in most county communities in fourteenth-century England.

Berkeley influence was extended by four related branches of the family. The original line had moved to Dursley and flourished there until 1403.[41] A branch of the founder had long been established at Coberley near Birdlip.[42] The second son of Maurice, 2nd Lord founded the Berkeleys of Uley (and Stoke Giffard) while John, the younger son of the 3rd Lord, established the Beverston line. The 3rd Lord sought to protect the patrimony from partition between co-heiresses or other alienation by entailing the estate in 1349 solely on his heirs male, while the 5th Lord spent most of his life fighting to prevent such an occurrence.[43] A similar campaign was rerun against the crown during the first half of the sixteenth century.

Roger Berkeley who had initiated the development of Berkeley Castle also founded the Augustinian priory of Leonard Stanley before his death in 1131. His son of the same name established Dursley Castle before the mid-twelfth century, while Robert FitzHarding founded St Augustine's Abbey, Bristol in 1141. It served as their mausoleum until the fifteenth century as much as Tewkesbury Abbey did for the Despensers.[44] Kingswood Abbey near their house at Wootton-under-Edge, founded by William Berkeley in c.1170, benefited substantially from his successors after the Black Death had impoverished the monastery, though the surviving gatehouse was the result of an improving economy under the first Tudor. In the 1520s, Maurice, 9th Lord paid for rebuilding the church of Greyfriars, Gloucester, though there had been numerous bequests over the previous three centuries since its foundation by the family (c.1231) as well as to churches on their properties.[45]

During the second quarter of the fourteenth century, the 3rd Lord had houses at Bedminster, Bradley Wendora, and Portbury, built one at Awre (1327), had lodges at Newpark (1328) and Over (1346), spent £100 repairing that at Wootton-under-Edge (1346) 'and in other years the like', and purchased Beverston Castle and remodelled it, as well as consolidating the family seat at Berkeley.[46] 'In the course of his whole life, I seldom observed [Thomas, 3rd Lord] to continue one whole year together at any one of his houses but having many furnished, he easily moved without removing.'[47] Yate was purchased by Maurice, 8th Lord after his brother had settled all the Berkeley holdings on the crown. It was occupied by his son and grandson and retains some sections of the earlier moated structures.[48] The partly embattled wall that encloses two sides of the churchyard at Coberley screened the courtyard immediately in front of the fifteenth-century house shown by Kip before its destruction in 1790. The present farmhouse was part of the outer court and there was a third court south of the house.[49] The castle at Beverston still stands but that of younger members of the main line at Bradley Court, Wootton-under-Edge was rebuilt by them in 1559.[50] The house of the Uley and Stoke Giffard branch at Stoke Park just north of Bristol was similarly rebuilt in the later sixteenth century and again in 1750–64, shortly before it passed to the Beaufort family.[51] It was only with their advent that Berkeley ceased to be the pre-eminent lay magnate in the county.

NOTES

1 The inner archway portcullis groove was noted by Clark (1884) 230–1.
2 H. P. R. Finberg, *Gloucestershire Studies* (1957) 145. The magnitude of this transformation is described by James Miller in *Country Life* (December 2004).
3 'Most of the cross loops [in the castle] have wandered from their right places, and most of the crenellations refashioned by amateur masons.' Baddeley (1926) 156–7.
4 This feature also occurs in the north Somerset halls at Meare Manor (1322–35) and the Treasurer's House, Martock (c.1330).
5 The earl of Berkeley reinstated the wind braces after removing the early nineteenth-century additions. R. Cooke, *West Country Houses* (1957) 16. The hall roof had been repaired or releaded in c.1497. Berkeley (1938) 185.
6 Until then, the stair had been lit by an early seventeenth-century square-framed window.
7 Faulkner (1965) 200.
8 During his work, the earl found evidence of a floor 2 feet below the present one which he considered to be the chancel of a mid-thirteenth century chapel, 18 feet by 11 feet, running north to south. Berkeley (1927) 185. Hussey noted the discovery of a newel stair and Norman window in the north-east corner of the chapel ((1932) 672) and a Norman arch in the west wall to a base 2 feet below the present floor level which he assessed as an earlier solar block ((1932) 673).
9 E. W. Tristram, *English Wall Painting of the Fourteenth Century* (1955) 140. For Trevisa, D. C. Fowler, *Trans. Bristol and Glos. Arch. Soc.* 89 (1971) 99–108.
10 Baddeley (1926) 175–9, Hussey (1932) 699, but see Faulkner (1965) 200. The added arms are those of Henry VII. Turner and Parker (1859) 178, show the gallery's pre-1922 position.
11 This second fireplace was found in a cottage in the village appropriate to this position. Hussey (1932) 699. Yet it was clearly not *in situ* and may be the one from the parlour at Wanswell Court described as 'broken and mutilated' in 1859 (Turner and Parker (1859) 268) but still 'handsome' in 1881–2 (*Trans. Bristol and Glos. Arch. Soc.* 6 (1881) 319). It was subsequently removed. It is of the same period as the hall fireplace from Wanswell with the similar unusual feature of splayed jambs, fragmentary by 1922 but repaired by the earl.
12 Baddeley ((1926) 140) was convinced that the kitchen was a reused Norman mural tower but its position and form rule out such a possibility.
13 J. Smyth, *The Lives of the Berkeleys*, ed. J. Maclean, I (1883) 309. Baddeley ((1926) 162) added that it suffered from fire in 1603 and was drastically restored in 1604–7.
14 Berkeley (1938) 314–15. Other fourteenth-century defensive work included rebuilding the north turret of the shell keep as a much larger and higher tower (Thorpe Tower) in 1342 at a cost of £108 3s. 1¼d. Smyth, I (1883) 308–9. Its domination is well shown in Knyff's landscape views of c.1676 held in the castle. J. Harris, *The Artist and the Country House* (1979) 64–5. The three-storeyed gateway to the inner court had also been rebuilt with a larger porter's lodge (believed by the earl to have been used for stabling at some time: Berkeley (1938) 325) and two sets of lodgings, the larger outer room above the entry passage with a projecting garderobe turret off the smaller west-facing room. The gatehouse 'builte of newe in 1313', Smyth, I (1883) 168, was that with polygonal end towers excavated by the earl immediately to the rear of the present outer gateway ascribed to c.1360: (1938) 308–9. Thomas

(d.1417) enlarged the ditch round part of the shell keep by taking part of the churchyard in return for any annual rent of 6s. 8d. Smyth, II, (1883) 12.

15 The apartments in the early Tudor block and gatehouse are still used by the family. The interiors are as much 1920s as the inserted corbelled gallery on the inner face of the gateway, the side entrance, most of the windows, and the internal staircase to the family rooms.

16 J. Bony considers the choir of Bristol reveals an architect accustomed to working on domestic architecture: *The English Decorated Style* (1979) 36.

17 Smyth, I (1883) 168.

18 S. A. Harrison, Richard K. Morris and D. M. Robinson, *Antiq. Jour.* 78 (1998) 235–6.

19 *Ibid.* 228–9.

20 *Ibid.* 226.

21 Smyth, I (1883) 308. The spur for this work was 'the marriage of his only sister, and the receiving thither his own wife . . . and against the cominge of the Queene mother and her minion the Ld. Mortimer this lords father-in-lawe', *ibid.*

22 Richard K. Morris also notes that the beautifully moulded but now damaged chapel door incorporates sunk wave mouldings which have their origins in similar forms in the presbytery arches at Wells Cathedral (1326–40). *Bristol in the Middle Ages*, ed. L. Keen (1997) 50.

23 Harrison *et al.*, *Antiq. Jour.* 78 (1998) 226–7, 247.

24 *Ibid.* 227–8, 244.

25 Morris in *Bristol in the Middle Ages*, ed. Keen, 49; R. Turner, *Antiq. Jour.* 80 (2000) 166.

26 Harrison *et al.* (1998) 243–4.

27 *Ibid.* 227, with Berkeley lacking any cusping as it was secular work.

28 Smyth, I (1883) 309. A detailed architectural study of Berkeley Castle is badly needed. In its absence, some major modifications are noted after the erection of the last structure, the early Tudor lodging block between the gatehouse and the south range. The principal stair to the reception rooms was rebuilt in 1637, the breach in the keep wall was made good after the Civil War, and the 'metely strong' outer ward that Leland saw had been pulled down before the close of the century. The stables were rebuilt in 1763 and the two-storeyed house at the foot of Thorpe Tower was probably erected at this time. Further work in a Gothick style was carried out in 1805–7, including the Georgian block inside the keep (replaced by the earl's extension in the 1920s), the fireplace and hall additions, and the frontages of the south range and staff hall opposite.

29 Wells-Furby (2004).

30 V. J. Scattergood and J. W. Sherborne (eds.), *English Court Culture in the Later Middle Ages* (1983) 173.

31 H. P. R. Finberg, *The Gloucestershire Landscape* (1975) 79.

32 C. Given-Wilson, *The English Nobility in the Late Middle Ages* (1987), 125 with a map of the Berkeley estates, xiv–xv. N. Saul, *Knights and Esquires* (1981) 62–9.

33 Saul, *Knights and Esquires* 250. 'In some of his manors he had flocks of 1500 sheep, [and] in some from 1000 to 400 and in none under 300. At Beverston in the 7th of Edward III [1333] he had 5775 sheep'. Smyth, I (1883) 302.

34 Smyth, I (1883) 306. The same record shows that Thomas was living well beyond his means, with expenditure on food and household expenses reaching £1,308 in 1346. D. Dyer, *Standards of Living in the Later Middle Ages* (1989), 56, 70.

35 Smyth, I (1883) 156.

36 *Ibid.* 166.

37 *Ibid.* 308–9.

38 *Ibid.* 305.

39 *Ibid.* 304; Saul, *Knights and Esquires* 72–5.

40 C. D. Ross, *Trans. Bristol and Glos. Arch. Soc.* 90 (1952) 81–105.

41 Sir Henry Barkly, *Trans. Bristol and Glos. Arch. Soc.* 8 (1883–4) 193–220; 9 (1884–5) 227–76.

42 *Ibid.* 17 (1892–3) 96–125. Further afield, the Berkeleys of Wymondham, Leicestershire were descended from the second son of Thomas (d.1321), and the Berkeleys of Shropshire from the third son of Maurice (d.1326).

43 For this famous Berkeley lawsuit, Smyth, II (1883) 41–76; J. H. Cooke, *Trans. Bristol and Glos. Arch. Soc.* 3 (1878–9) 305–24; R. A. Griffiths, *The Reign of King Henry VI* (1981) 572–4. James was the son of Sir James Berkeley of Raglan Castle, the younger brother of the 5th Lord Berkeley.

44 Apart from their support in the redevelopment of St Augustine's Abbey at the beginning of the century, the family contributed substantially to the lady chapel window of *c.*1360 with the arms of Thomas, 3rd Lord and his relatives. The early fourteenth-century south chapel and ante-room became the Berkeley chapel in 1337 as a result of the 3rd Lord's establishment of a chantry foundation. The abbey church contains several of their tombs, contributing to one of the longest runs of a late medieval family. The others are in the churches at St Mary Redcliffe, Berkeley (3rd and 6th Lords), and Wootton-under-Edge (5th Lord), with those of the collateral branches at Coberley church and the Stoke Giffard branch at St Mark's Chapel, Bristol.

45 N. Saul, *Trans. Bristol and Glos. Arch. Soc.* 98 (1980) 101, 105, 107. In the mid-fourteenth century, they included the churches at Upper Cam, Coberley, and Synde.

46 Smyth, I (1883) 301, 308–9.

47 *Ibid.* 308–9.

48 See page 132.

49 R. Atkyns, *Gloucestershire* (1712) 376–7; VCH, *Gloucestershire*, VII (1981) 176–7. The Coberley Berkeleys added the south chapel to the church in *c.*1330 and the fifteenth-century tower with buttresses carrying their arms. The outer arch cusping of the church south door is a Bristol/Berkeley motif. Their home at Coberley passed by inheritance in the mid-fifteenth century to the Brydges family, later of Sudeley Castle.

50 N. Kingsley, *The Country Houses of Gloucestershire*, I (1989) 64–5. The grammar school at Wootton-under-Edge founded by the second wife of the 3rd Lord for a master and two poor boys in 1384 still flourishes. Smyth, I (1883) 346–7.

51 N. Kingsley, *The Country Houses of Gloucestershire*, I (1989) 9, 176–8. The massive rampart on which the eighteenth-century house still stands, overdramatised in Kip's engraving of *c.*1700, probably has its origins in a defensive structure, retained by the Elizabethan builders.

Berkeley Castle

T. H. Turner and J. H. Parker, *Some Account of Domestic Architecture in England*, III pt 2 (1859) 253–6

G. T. Clark, *Trans. Bristol and Glos. Arch. Soc.* 1 (1876) 115–37; reprinted in *Medieval Military Architecture*, I (1884) 228–39

St Clair Baddeley, *Trans. Bristol and Glos. Arch. Soc.* 48 (1926) 133–79

Earl of Berkeley, *Trans. Bristol and Glos. Arch. Soc.* 49 (1927) 183–93, a critical riposte and correction to Baddeley's article

C. Hussey, *Country Life* (June 1932)

Earl of Berkeley, *Trans. Bristol and Glos. Arch. Soc.* 60 (1938) 308–39 for his excavations at the castle

P. Faulkner, *Arch. Jour.* 122 (1965) 197–200

Berkeley family

John Smyth, *Lives of the Berkeleys, Lords of the Honour, Castle and Manor of Berkeley in the County of Gloucester from 1066 to 1618 with a description of the Hundred of Berkeley and its inhabitants*, ed. Sir John Maclean, 3 vols. (1883–5)

G. E. C., *The Complete Peerage*, II (1912) 118–47

H. P. R. Finberg, *Gloucestershire Studies* (1957) 145–59.

W. J. Smith, *Trans. Bristol and Glos. Arch. Soc.* 70 (1951) 64–80 and 71 (1952) 101–21 for the period 1248 to 1361

B. Wells-Furby (ed.), *A Catalogue of the Medieval Muniments at Berkeley Castle* (2004)

BEVERSTON CASTLE, Gloucestershire

The thirteenth-century defensive features of Beverston Castle 2 miles west of Tetbury are formidable enough to justify its castle nomenclature, but its non-strategic position on the high but flat Cotswold uplands shows that the moat, gatehouse, and towers are more truly those of a fortified house. Today, an attractive seventeenth-century manor house occupies the site of the earlier hall so that the mixture of medieval ruins and a broad-windowed house combined with the jumble of Cotswold roofs and a well-maintained garden create a highly picturesque ensemble.

The origins of the castle lie in the work of Maurice Gaunt (d.1230), who built it without crown authority but subsequently validated by a licence to crenellate in 1229.[1] When the castle was purchased a hundred years later in 1330 by Thomas, 3rd Lord Berkeley (d.1361), it consisted of a single courtyard of rhomboid shape defended by several circular or half-circular towers and gatehouse of ovoid form protected by a drawbridge and a portcullis.[2] Most of the south side of the small courtyard was enclosed by a first-floor hall range with a residential wing at right angles to it. When the hall was replaced by the two-storeyed Jacobean house, the thirteenth-century upper-end wall was retained with its ground-floor window with semi-circular rear arch, evidence of internal wall arcading in the hall above (shaft and capital), and a roofline immediately below the later oratory window. Much more survives of the contemporary west wing with its two ground-floor vaulted rooms and single chamber above, now used as bedrooms. A third storey was unlikely at this stage.

Lord Berkeley began his redevelopment by removing the west

and south-west circular towers to replace them with a dominating rectangular residential tower next to the hall range and a short link joining up with the earlier west wing. The existence of earlier buildings meant that this work, apparently three-storeyed externally, was multi-levelled internally. Standing to parapet level and little altered since its construction, the only replacements are some late sixteenth-century mullioned and transomed windows and a contemporary newel stair in an unbonded half-octagonal projection at the angle where the tower touched the upper end of the hall. It is this stair opening from the still-occupied house that gives access to a structure which, though empty, has the distinction of never losing its roof or foregoing its frittered stonework, vacant windows, uneven floors, and bats.

Basically, the tower has a single room on each floor, with two rooms in the adjacent wing at the lower and a single room at three upper levels, all linked by a plethora of stairs. The ground floor was originally approached from the hall undercroft, but a trefoil window was converted in post-medieval times into an outer doorway. The room is vaulted, and retains a fine trefoil light and a fireplace in the south-west corner.

The first floor was approached by a still-surviving door from the former hall opening into a narrow stepped passage. This floor was entirely filled by the chapel, one of the finest of such survivals in any castle. It is divided into two parts. The body of the chapel has a fine tierceron vault with carved bosses at the rib intersections, an ogee-headed trefoil light in the south wall, and a late sixteenth-century replacement window at the west end. The sanctuary at a slightly higher level has a ribbed barrel vault and is distinguished by the double sedilia and piscina with crocketed ogee canopies separated by elegant pinnacles.[3] The piscina across the corner has a trefoil head and a credence shelf, while the three-light east window with cinquefoil heads (an early example) retains some of its trefoiled kite-shaped tracery which can be seen more completely in the chancel of the nearby church.

From the chapel passage, steps lead at a lower half-level to an

PLATE 24 Beverston Castle: engraving from the north by S. and N. Buck (1732)

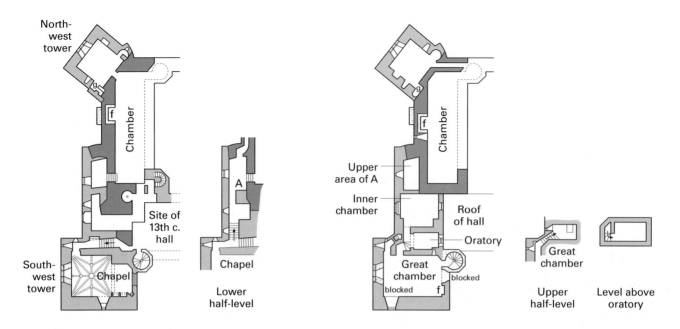

FIRST FLOOR   **SECOND FLOOR**

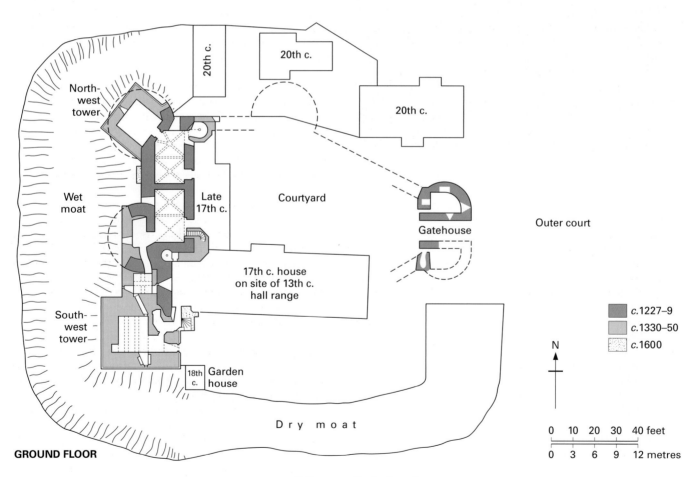

GROUND FLOOR

FIGURE 8 Beverston Castle: floor plans

PLATE 25 Beverston Castle: great tower

ante-chamber and room in the projecting wing, apparently with a blocked fireplace beneath a window in the west wall.

Direct access from the hall via the newel stair bypassed the chapel but gave immediate entry to the great chamber on the second floor of the tower. It is lit today by a large square-headed sixteenth-century window in the west wall but there were formerly traceried windows in the east and south walls, now blocked. The roof is a relatively modern replacement.

Several rooms lay north of the great chamber, needless to say at differing levels, to make the second floor a private suite for the castle's owner. At a higher level lay Berkeley's inner chamber and oratory, with the latter reached first through a broken-down west wall. This little-touched room retains its canopied piscina, a pair of twin diagonal squints opening into the residential chamber on each side, and a large circular (possibly rose) east window immediately above the earlier hall roof, now blocked by a later square opening. The inner chamber is rather featureless, with replacement windows. The tiny room beneath part of the oratory is said to have been a well chamber though it may have been used for storing valuables, while the narrow room above the oratory was probably for the chaplain.

Berkeley's tower has affinities with contemporary solar towers such as that at South Kyme (mid-fourteenth century) in its relationship to a first-floor hall and its residential purpose at all levels. It is an early example of that enthusiasm for interlocking levels and multiple chambers popular in the later fourteenth century, while its decorative qualities are a fitting adjunct to the sophisticated earlier work at Berkeley Castle. But whereas that nearby residence has been continuously occupied and thoroughly restored, the Beverston tower and associated wing were abandoned in the mid-seventeenth century and have remained untouched.

In a second phase, Berkeley modified the west wing to create an independent suite, probably for honoured guests. The wing was heightened by a second floor with a contemporary window inserted in the outer wall and courtyard-facing stair turrets added at either end. The earlier circular north-west tower was replaced by a square one, set diagonally, to provide comfortable retiring chambers at first- and second-floor levels with garderobes and a fireplace, linked by a minute newel stair.[4] The tower is ruined, the courtyard wall reduced and the uppermost floor partially open to the sky but the plan is clear. The first-floor chamber, possibly partitioned, was accessed from the upper end of the hall. The courtyard stair opposite the retiring chamber led to the uppermost suite, where the large outer chamber was independent of the tower chamber. The two fireplaces in the body of the range are sixteenth century.

The castle's remodelling is dated by Smyth, chronicler of the Berkeley family, to 1348–9.[5] It is built in a distinctive style favoured in south-west England between about 1320 and 1350 (as at Wells and Exeter cathedrals and Ottery St Mary collegiate church) and more particularly comparable to the work in the prime Bristol churches of the 1330s and 1340s such as the east arm of St Augustine's Abbey (c.1330–45) and the south porch of St Mary Redcliffe (c.1340). The ornate sedilia in the chapel can be compared particularly with the lady chapel reredos in St Augustine's Abbey (now the cathedral) and the lady chapel screen at Ottery St Mary.[6] The ascription to the years 1348 and 1349 given by Smyth may point towards the conclusion of this work, or rather to the second phase of a project that had been initiated some years earlier during the 1330s.

Leland records that the work was funded by the 'spoyles that he wan yn France' for he was told by Sir William, the collateral great-grandson, that Berkeley 'was taken prisoner in Fraunce, and after recovering his losses with Frenche prisoners and at the Batail of Poyters buildid after the castell of Beverstane thoroughly, a pile at that tyme very preaty'.[7] Not only is this historically questionable[8] but it is more likely that rebuilding was resourced by Berkeley's progressive husbandry on this estate in particular. The large sheep runs of the high Cotswolds made the Beverston property highly attractive to the 3rd Lord, particularly as he was in the forefront of those changing from an arable to a pastoral economy. It became one of the primary centres of his sheep-rearing activities,[9] helped to treble his annual income,[10] and almost certainly prompted and probably funded the castle's remodelling.

The result was to make the castle the equivalent of an eighteenth-century country villa centred on an agriculturally prosperous estate. By updating the earlier fortified house, Berkeley not only provided personal comfort for himself in a powerful but non-military tower reflecting his elegance and wealth, but also provided generous independent accommodation for his guests. The moated outer court, barely traceable today but marked by a late fourteenth- or early fifteenth-century barn,[11] probably always fulfilled a farming function.

Berkeley granted Beverston to John, the younger son of his second marriage, who established the prominent gentry line of Berkeley of Beverston until the castle was sold in 1597. It was subject to some updating but was besieged and captured by the parliamentarians in 1644, then abandoned in part shortly afterwards, with the Jacobean house subject to further repairs after a fire of 1691 and continuous occupation ever since.

NOTES

1 *Cal. Pat. Rolls: 1225–32*, 260.
2 J. Smyth, *Lives of the Berkeleys. . .* ed. Sir John Maclean, I (1883) 326.
3 For a cross-section of both chapel and oratory above, T. H. Turner and J. H. Parker, *Some Account of Domestic Architecture in England*, III (1859) 183.
4 The earlier thirteenth-century tower form can be established externally in the use of rubble walling and its shaping where it joins the later dressed stonework.
5 *Lives of the Berkeleys*, ed. Maclean, I, 309. 'In 22 and 23 years of that kinge, hee much re-edified his castle of Beverston where he spent many months in the yeare, especially after it was become the joynture of his second wife and entailed upon her children.'
6 S. Harrison *et al.*, *Antiq. Jour.* 78 (1998) 223, 232–3. The authors include a valuable discussion on the work of Thomas, 3rd Lord Berkeley at Beverston and Berkeley castles in the stylistic context of a major architectural lodge in south-west England under the innovative master William Joy, 177–268.
7 *Itinerary*, IV, 132–3. This dating attribution was followed by Joan Evans, *English Art 1307–1461* (1949) 120 and D. Verey and A. Brooks, *The Buildings of England: Gloucestershire*, I (1999 edn) 65, 165.
8 It was Berkeley's son who was taken prisoner at the battle of Poitiers, and he was only ransomed with difficulty. First noted by Elizabeth Hodges in *Some Ancient English Homes* (1895), this was more academically considered by K. B. McFarlane, *The Nobility of Later Medieval England* (1973) 22 note 1, who did not entirely rule out ransoms achieved before the 1356 battle, by either Berkeley or his son.
9 C. Given-Wilson, *The English Nobility in the Late Middle Ages* (1987) 125–6.
10 Smyth, *Lives of the Berkeleys*, ed. Maclean, I, 306.
11 Described and illustrated in E. Mercer, *English Vernacular Houses* (1975) 157, 106.

A. H. Thompson, *Arch. Jour.* 87 (1930) 453–5
C. Hussey, *Country Life* (February 1944)
P. A. Faulkner, *Arch. Jour.* 122 (1965) 201–2
N. Pounds, *Arch. Jour.* suppl. 145 (1988) 48–51

BOARSTALL TOWER, Oxfordshire

This is the gatehouse to a residence crenellated under licence by John Handlo in 1312,[1] close to Bernwood Forest and the royal manor of Brill. Handlo had acquired the property by marrying the last of the FitzNigels in 1299 and it is possible that the 3 acre platform was already in existence. The east arm of the wet moat was infilled when the gardens were formalised in the early eighteenth century, while the large courtyard house on its south side was pulled down in 1778. An equally major change was the loss of the village of Boarstall, destroyed during the Civil War, leaving only the house and

the now rebuilt church alone on the broad clay Vale of Aylesbury.[2]

The gatehouse is a striking three-storeyed structure with bold hexagonal turrets at each corner of the rectangular block. The slimmer rear turrets hold newels and rise above the roof, as did those facing the approach (see blocked loops below south-east battlements). They were reduced in the early seventeenth century when the gatehouse was totally refenestrated with handsome square-headed, mullioned, and transomed windows, and canted bays to the front and sides. The roof was raised by 28 inches and balustraded to create a viewing platform. The property is as much like a Jacobean hunting box as a fourteenth-century gatehouse.

Built of local rubble limestone with ashlar dressings, the body of the gatehouse is original, as are the gargoyles and cross-shaped arrow loops at several levels. The seventeenth-century balustrade was raised directly over the original crenellated parapet, encasing its embrasures. The entrance, partly masked by the supports to the bay window above, may have been buttressed and was portcullis protected.[3] There was a drawbridge, raised by a central chain[4] to fit under the lip of the string course above the entry with its depressed segmental head. It opened into the central passage with a room on either side. The east partition wall was removed in 1926 when the property was rehabilitated and entries forced through to the rear newels. The mezzanine floor repeats the same plan while the uppermost floor is a single chamber, magnificently windowed and heightened with a roof of *c*.1615.

The internal medieval features that survived the Jacobean remodelling are limited. All doorways with two-centred heads to the closets and from the stairs to the upper rooms are original. Only two single lights with trefoil heads at the top of the south-east turret escaped the remodelling programme but some of the Jacobean windows reused the earlier splays. No garderobe evidence has been found but the rough ceiling joists in the porter's lodge have been dendro dated to a felling date of 1312/13.[5] The modest changes made in the late fifteenth/early sixteenth century included new courtyard doorways to the newels, the moulded frame to the first-floor chamber entry, and the finely shaped fireplace to that apartment.

This was a spacious gatehouse with ground-floor staff rooms, generous and multi-lit frontal closets at all levels, and an important top-floor lodging, probably originally divided into two with a larger heated outer chamber and a smaller inner chamber. It would have been approached from the south-east stair, slightly wider than its fellow and opening via an original wooden doorway instead of the stone form used elsewhere. This gatehouse was more for show than for defence. No evidence was found of an enclosing curtain wall or corner towers during a geophysical survey in 1998, and they are absent from the illustration of 1444 (see below). The site was probably always palisaded and was still so enclosed during the Civil War.[6] The tower frontage was embellished with ashlar banding while the pair of newels rather than a single one points up its residential purpose. It should be compared with the slightly later gatehouse at the Bishop's Palace, Wells, in form and function.

This moated manor house is depicted in two important documents. The Boarstall Cartulary was prepared for Edmund Rede, lord of the manor, in 1444. It includes a coloured picture depicting the village, the nearby open fields and woods, and the stand-alone gatehouse with a notional representation of the manor house to its rear.[7] The other is a superbly detailed engraving of 1695 by Michael

PLATE 26 Boarstall Tower: gatehouse from the north-east

Burghers giving a bird's-eye view of the property. It shows that the house originated with a hall and entry porch almost facing the gateway and developed into a substantial courtyard residence with a services yard to the east, surrounded at that time by formal gardens.[8]

NOTES

1 *Cal. Pat. Rolls: 1307–13*, 493.
2 S. Porter, *Rec. of Bucks.* 26 (1984) 86–91.
3 The grooves have been infilled but the RCHM is quite clear about their existence in 1912: I (1912) 57.
4 Responsible for the grooves in the window sill above.
5 *Vern. Arch.* 30 (1999) 99.
6 *Symonds' Diary*, Camden Soc. 74 (1940) 231.
7 *The Boarstall Cartulary*, ed. H. E. Salter and A. H. Cooke (1930). The volume is held in Bucks. County Record Office, Aylesbury. The map and a 1970 aerial view to the same scale and position are reproduced in M. W. Beresford and J. K. St Joseph, *Medieval England* (1979 edn) 110–13. See also R. A. Skelton and P. D. A. Harvey (eds.), *Local Maps and Plans from Medieval England* (1984) 211–19, and P. D. A. Harvey in *Medieval Villages*, ed. D. Hook (1985) 33–45, for a consideration of the cartulary and later documentary evidence.
8 Engraved for W. Kennett, *Parochial Antiquities Attempted in the History of Ambrosden, Burcester* (1695). Reproduced in J. Harris, *The Artist and the Country House* (1979) 105.

RCHM, *Buckinghamshire*, I (1912) 57–9
The National Trust, *Boarstall Tower: Guide* (1989)

BROADWAY, ABBOT'S GRANGE, Worcestershire[1]

'The Abbot of Peareshore was onely Lord of the Manor, but also had here a farme famous for the greatness.'[2] Thomas Habington's comment of 1586 still holds good for the abbot's house at Broadway.

Close to the parish church at the Evesham end of this show village, the house was rescued by the American artist Frank Millet and his wife towards the close of the nineteenth century. They were responsible for the two Jacobeathan-style wings of 1907 and 1933 that create the open west court. Though Abbot's Grange is a three-period house, each phase is self-contained. The fourteenth-century hall and upper cross wing with chapel extension fill the east side of the court. The early seventeenth-century block abuts its upper end. The site of the services and kitchen is covered by the 1907 family wing while that of 1933 touches the Jacobean block (pl. 2). The house is built of Cotswold stone throughout, with Cotswold tiled roofs. There is no documentary evidence to identify the first construction period, but it is a single-phase structure which can be attributed on architectural grounds to the years close to 1320–30.

The hall, 26 feet by 20 feet, is open to the roof. The cross-passage entries were not porch protected. That to the east (facing the village) retains its single-chamfer jambs with a remade two-centred head. That to the west, now blocked, was remodelled with a square head in the early seventeenth century at the same time that a floor was inserted in the hall. This apartment is entered from the 1907 wing via a wide Jacobean archway, probably replacing a smaller one like the two to its side with bold ogee-decorated heads. Nothing survives of the services cross wing, now covered by the panelled dining room and staircase hall, but the three doorways suggest two service rooms and a stair to the chamber above. Traces were found of such a spiral stair in 1907[3] while a drawing by Blore of *c*.1820 shows a square building north-east of the hall that may have been the kitchen.[4]

The hall is lit by four windows, all of different character. Those to the west are of two lights, transomed, with ogee-shaped trefoil heads. That by the entry has upper cusps which the larger window lacks though it is set in a square hollow-chamfered frame. Both were restored by Millet, based on retained features. The two opposite windows follow a similar but less ornate form, with that next to the chapel wing obliquely angled because of the chapel wing and the only one to retain its original tracery. The different size and

PLATE 27 Broadway, Abbot's Grange: from the west

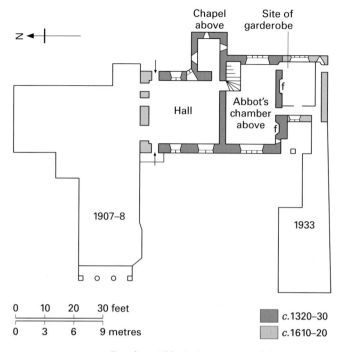

Chapel above   Site of garderobe

Hall   Abbot's chamber above

1907–8   1933

0 10 20 30 feet
0 3 6 9 metres

■ c.1320–30
▨ c.1610–20

FIGURE 9 Broadway, Abbot's Grange: ground plan

character of these windows is unusual, though there is no reason to doubt the accuracy of their restoration.[5]

The two-bay roof is spanned by arch-braced collars with upper collars to heavily moulded purlins, close-set rafters, and a single line of wind braces. The ogee moulding of the central truss that ceases about 6 feet from the ground appears to have been continued in stone to the floor but has been hacked away.[6] The end-wall fireplace is a 1913 insertion, for the hall would have been heated originally by a central hearth. The two doorways in the south-east angle open to the chapel and solar wings, the latter repeating the ogee-headed form.

The one unusual feature of this house is that the stone stair to the solar cross wing serves both ground and upper floors. Though the steps were remade by Millet, they follow the original form, including the divergence to solar and chapel. The ground-floor chamber retains a single two-centred light in one corner but both end windows and the fireplace are seventeenth-century replacements of original features. The upper chamber is partitioned by an open Victorian screen to create a corridor to the Jacobean room beyond. Ignoring this, the abbot's withdrawing chamber is little touched, with a fine west window set in a hollow-chamfered frame internally, of two transomed trefoiled lights with a reticulated head. The lower lights were shuttered; the upper lights were glazed. The two-light east window is more modest. The two-bay roof is similar to that in the hall, repeating the arch-braced trusses rising from low-set wall posts with a single line of wind braces. The fireplace jambs, double brackets, and stone hood are a rebuild but apparently follow the original evidence to the undisturbed corbel-supported chimney stack.[7] The two-centred doorway to the Jacobean block initially accessed a timber-framed garderobe projection.[8]

The ground floor of the chapel wing, approached by an early seventeenth-century entry, retains its three original window splays though one has been enlarged.[9] The room above does not show any

altar (the window sill?), piscina, or sedilia evidence but its claim to be a chapel is not unreasonable.[10] The east end is lit by two single trefoil lights in the side walls, and a two-light east window with reticulated head similar to but less elaborate than that in the abbot's chamber. The circular window looking into the hall shows evidence of lost cusped running tracery. The moulded wall plates and plain double-raftered roof are original.

Pershore Abbey held major sheep pastures on the hills above Broadway, for the manor was the most profitable of the abbey's possessions at the time of the Dissolution and accounted for a quarter of its income. This well-preserved country house of the abbey, a particularly fine example of a single-phase structure, is attributable to abbot William Herwynton (c.1307–40) with the outside possibility that it may have been by abbot Thomas Pyriton (1340–9). Note the subtle design emphasis at two key points – the west window of the abbot's chamber, and the chapel east window compared with its neighbour serving the abbot's chamber.

NOTES

1 The houses of Worcestershire were covered in volume II, but Broadway is geographically and architecturally part of the Cotswolds and should be considered with comparable buildings in Gloucestershire.
2 *A Survey of Worcestershire*, ed. J. Amphlett, II (1899).
3 VCH, IV (1924) 35.
4 Brit. Lib., Add. MS 42108, 15/16. Substantial stone foundations including the south corner of a building were traced west of the hall in 1991 at the same time as a geophysical survey was made of the earthworks surrounding the grange. *Med. Arch.* 35 (1991) 163–4.
5 Millet was advised by William Morris, who had recommended the house to him.
6 VCH, IV (1924) 35.
7 Tipping (1911) 58.
8 The narrow ground-floor doorway immediately below in heavily disturbed stonework may have served a similar purpose. The jamb of an entry arch against the south face of the replacement extension is early seventeenth century, not original work *pace* Tipping and Pevsner, *Worcestershire* (1968) 103.
9 The 'oriel-like chamber' of M. Wood is unconvincing: *The English Medieval House* (1965) 103.
10 A similarly positioned chapel had been built a few years earlier at Evesham Abbey. According to the abbey's chronicler, abbot Brokehampton (1282–1316) built 'a magnificent abbot's hall, the walls of which were completed in stone, and above it he constructed a wooden roof of wonderful workmanship, covered with lead, and made a vaulted porch at the entrance of the said hall, and above it a reception room, similarly roofed with lead. He added a kitchen to this hall, finely finished throughout in stone. He built a pantry by the abbot's kitchen, and also the abbot's chamber, painted with the story of Joseph, together with a small chapel adjacent to it. He constructed a strong vault beneath this chamber where the wine cellar now is'. *The Chronicle of Evesham Abbey*, ed. D. C. Cox (1964) 50–1.

H. A. Tipping, *Country Life* (January 1911)
VCH, *Worcestershire*, IV (1924) 34–6

BROUGHTON CASTLE, Oxfordshire

Broughton Castle is one of the medieval jewels of central and southern England, even though it was initiated by a family of no more than local importance. Seen across the sparkling water of the moat and the verdant lawns that enclose the house on three sides, the vast windows and multiple gables of the castle suggest that it is essentially an Elizabethan mansion with evidence of its medieval origins towards the east end. In fact, it was never a castle,[1] is medieval throughout, and has achieved its present state through at least eleven building stages – six medieval, two Elizabethan, one mid-Georgian, and the restorations of the 1860s and 1980s. Not surprisingly, the architectural story of the house has not yet been fully unravelled, mainly because of the idiosyncratic development of the medieval apartments which are as spectacular in execution as they are intriguing in layout.

OUTER COURT, c.1250–1500

The house and church stand immediately west of the Sor Brook, with an approach that immediately reveals the three defensive elements of the site and their order of importance – moat, gateway, and embattled enclosing wall. The width of the brook-fed moat varies between about 50 feet where it was crossed by two bridges and about 130 feet where it widens on the north side into a small ornamental lake. It is one of the most impressive moats in England and encloses an equally imposing rectangular platform of between 3 and 4 acres. The embattled wall divides the area into two, with the house and courts to the front and rear filling only half the site, but there was evidence early in the twentieth century of a watercourse immediately under the battlemented wall dividing the area into two courts.[2]

The two-storeyed gatehouse is relatively modest, mainly late fourteenth century in its present form but at least fifty years earlier in origin. It consists of no more than a through-passage with chamber above, and an embattled parapet initialled W S from the repairs of 1655. The entry was protected by a drawbridge[3] and an outer and inner pair of doors with the former dated 1617. There was no portcullis. The lower walling and mid-arch were incorporated from an early fourteenth-century entrance with cross loops similar to those in the garderobe turret at the south-east corner of the house. The outer and inner arches with their depressed heads,

stair turret, and upper storey (originally two floors) are a rebuilding later in the century, with generous two-light windows of that date.

The enclosing wall is a late feature. Too low to be described as a curtain wall and protecting only half the platform, the wall extends for about 70 feet before its reduction to a garden wall. Standing 10 feet high to the broad wall-walk with the embattled parapet adding a further 4 feet, it is little more than a decorative enclosure similar to the brick garden wall of the 1470s at Buckden Palace. Buck's engraving of the castle in 1729 shows that it continued southwards, linked up with the four-centred arch that stands as a garden feature close to the south arm of the moat, and continued along the east side to the surviving lodging range. This east wall was interrupted by two features in line with the wall, though projecting internally: a secondary entry with room over and a two-storeyed embattled turret. Neither was a significant defence, and the entry was characterised by an arch that Buck shows was similar to the gatehouse entry.

Only the two-storeyed lodging range survives of the forecourt buildings, filling most of the north side. The upper floor retains a line of narrow slits to the forecourt, fireplace evidence, and two decorative mid-fifteenth-century windows overlooking the moat of twin cinquefoil lights with traceried heads. The range was used for lodgings above ground-floor stables. There is no documentary evidence of further structures in the forecourt or service court, though they must certainly have existed. Stone bases of unknown date have been noted during trenching at the north-east and west ends of the house, but the removal of all service buildings and other traces of the hugger-mugger of life creates a sylvan picture which is certainly false to the house's late medieval character.

HOUSE DEVELOPMENT, c.1250–1330

Built of local golden-brown limestone, Broughton Castle was as extended in its late medieval state as the present structure, marked by diagonal buttresses at both ends. The house has always been in line, for unlike most properties on this scale it has never needed projecting wings. In plan, the house has always centred on the great

PLATE 28 Broughton Castle: engraving from the north-east by S. and N. Buck (1729)

hall, with the kitchen and offices originally at the lower end and the family rooms at the upper. This plan was present from the first, but it was developed and expanded between the second half of the thirteenth and the second half of the fifteenth centuries in a sequence of phases. Their identification lies essentially in a consideration of the architectural evidence, with the caution that all roofs are post-medieval, and that the Victorian restoration by George Gilbert Scott Jnr. was an extremely sensitive one. The documentary evidence is also scanty before the mid-nineteenth century. Only two medieval references directly relate to the building, a licence granted in 1331 to allow divine service to be celebrated in the chapel,[4] and a licence to crenellate granted in 1406.[5] Neither sits comfortably with the surviving structures.

Today, the *hall* is essentially an Elizabethan four-bay chamber, 54½ feet by 28¾ feet, with large rectangular windows in both side walls, two forecourt bays, and a decorative plaster ceiling. Nothing is as it seems. The hall was originally a three-bay structure, about 40 feet by 28¾ feet internally, with entry at the lower (west) end, not at the upper (east) end as at present. The left-hand outer jamb and hood of the south cross-passage door survive, though the evidence for the principal entry from the forecourt was lost when the Elizabethan bay window was inserted. At that time, the outer walls were totally refenestrated. However, the Elizabethan entry and staircase projection at the upper end did not entirely destroy earlier window evidence and unblocking has revealed opposing tall windows in this end bay with depressed heads and roll-moulded splays of late fourteenth-century date. The early hall, open to the roof, was generously scaled and is still so, despite the ceiling inserted in the mid-sixteenth century, with simulated Elizabethan plasterwork of the 1760s.

The early hall was increased to the present size during the third quarter of the fifteenth century by taking in the original two-storeyed *offices and chamber block*. That had been made up of a central passage flanked by the buttery and pantry, with a residential chamber above. The evidence can be read in the present end wall, which was the outer wall of the block facing on to an offices yard. At ground level, the nearly central door opened to the passage of an independent kitchen, flanked by a hatch on one side and a door on the other from the yard. The blocked openings above from south to north are a fourteenth-century barred doorway, a tall recess of unknown date and purpose, a barred fifteenth-century doorway, and an internally approached fourteenth-century doorway. The barred openings suggest the first-floor chamber was externally approached across two centuries, though this would be surprising even by the fourteenth century when internal access from the screens was common, particularly in a residence of this scale. The alternative is that the barred approach was from the upper room of a double block of which all trace was destroyed in the post-medieval rebuilding. The chamber above the offices was lit by a cusped window in the south wall that survives in part, and there would have been a similar one in the lost north wall. The first-floor north door is likely to have opened on to a garderobe.

The buttressed outer walls at the west end of the house are part of the enclosure wall of the *kitchen and offices* yard, but all evidence of the internal buildings was destroyed when the west end of the house was totally remodelled during the later sixteenth century. Some drainage evidence survives in the cellar below the Gothick library.

PLATE 29 Broughton Castle: engraving of vaulted south corridor from Parker (1853)

Of the two fourteenth-century-style doorways at the upper end of the hall giving entry to the *family apartments*, only that next to the sixteenth-century stair is original. The other, by the present forecourt entry, is a late nineteenth-century insertion by Scott.[6] The contrast between the simple chamfered doorway and the elaborate vaulted corridors that it reveals is one of the many surprises that Broughton Castle offers. Turning to the left, the corridor immediately behind the dais wall accesses the room below the great chamber. This is the core of the house and its earliest structure.

The principal *undercroft* is an extended room, 38 feet by 15 feet, with three bays of quadripartite vaulting with single-chamfered ribs springing from moulded corbels. The square-headed fireplace lintel is a mid-fifteenth-century insertion, as is the stylish south doorway. Parker's plan of 1853 and his drawing of the corridor show that it was matched by two taller openings in the same wall of eighteenth-century form, made at the same time that the Gothick windows were inserted. The plain character of the vaulting ribs and the corbel mouldings indicates construction during the second half

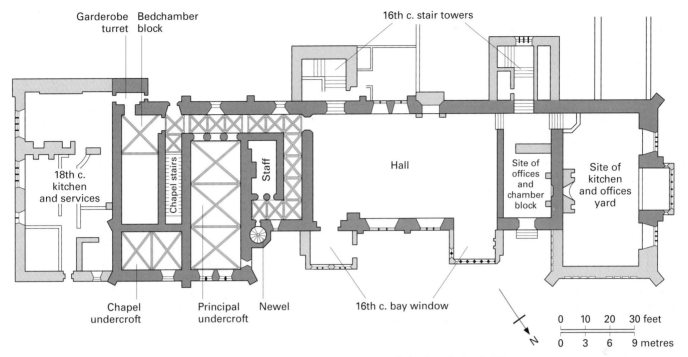

FIGURE 10 Broughton Castle: annotated ground plan from Parker (1853)

of the thirteenth century. The same construction occurs in the adjacent room at right angles below the chapel. This second undercroft consists of two bays of quadripartite vaulting springing from similar moulded corbels, though the two mid corbels are carved with oak and hawthorn leaves. This room could only be approached externally until its use as a kitchen in the twentieth century necessitated a forced link between the two undercrofts and the conversion of the east window into a doorway.

The corridors almost encircle a narrow internal room next to the larger undercroft. The passage entry and adjacent window (blocked) are original, as the vaulting seems to be,[7] but the second entry, fireplace, and recesses are relatively recent. The purpose of this room is not immediately clear but its position opposite the newel stair to the family rooms above indicates staff usage. It may have been for a porter guarding access to those rooms or more likely for junior staff attendant on the family and within close call of their needs.

The 6 foot wide *corridors* are a highly individual feature of the house. Lit by replacement Gothick windows of mid-eighteenth-century date, these corridors encircle the staff room and undercroft to lead to the newel turret on the north side, and a flight of steps to the first-floor chapel on the east side. The south and short east corridors are spanned by chamfered cross arches helping to support the rooms above, but all four corridors are divided into two (north), four (west), seven (south), and one (east) bays of quadripartite vaulting. There are no ceiling bosses and the springers are of darker stone than the ribs, which are of triple-roll form. There are two types of corbels: the majority are carved with animals, faces, and foliage, but two or three are smaller moulded corbels, possibly reused. The vaulting does not rise over the chapel stair, which has a crude barrel vault. Four deductions may be made. The corridors were an integral part of the development of the hall, with their outer

walls in common. Secondly, they were contemporary with the expansion of the family apartments, with doorways of similar form (single-chamfered jambs, two-centred head, single hood mould) to the newel, undercroft, staff room, and hall dais. Thirdly, the elaborate vaulting is an addition, cutting across the line of the cross arches. Fourthly, the vaulting stops against the cross arch at the foot of the chapel stair, which in turn blocks a large window in the right-hand wall. The stair is a subsequent development inserted in what had previously been a narrow room, approached from the short east corridor. The likely dates for these three phases of construction identified so far will be considered below.

The far end of the south corridor opens into a single-bay vaulted room of the bedchamber block repeating the plain chamfered ribs and foliated corbels, with the jamb of an east window (within a cupboard). Forced openings in the side walls access the twentieth-century staircase hall (north) and the garderobe drain (south) serving the bedchambers above. Though the vaulting is of the earlier form, the absence of angle buttresses to this block, the cessation of the moulded plinth, and its projection 2 feet further than the chapel block indicate that it was an addition.

The newel (with added stone hand-rail) in the polygonal turret in the north angle was the original approach to the *first-floor family rooms* – ante-room, great chamber, chapel, and bedchamber with garderobe projection. The newel approach to the ante-chamber has long been blocked, so that it can only be approached today from the door that always led to the great chamber. This heated room, backing on to the hall dais wall, has been divided into a bedroom of entirely modern character and a panelled ante-room. It was lit in each end wall by a two-light trefoiled window with cusped circular head, but that overlooking the forecourt has been replaced by a Gothick window.

The heated great chamber, an impressive 45 feet by 15 feet, has

PLATE 30 Broughton Castle: engraving of chapel east window from Parker (1853)

head and hacked pinnacles. The east window glass is made up of three fourteenth-century shields and sixteenth-century armorial glass in a stained glass setting created in 1994. The squints, gated newel opening, and balcony door are insertions, as is the flight of steps from the ground-floor corridor, made when the chapel became more public in the late fourteenth century rather than being the family chapel solely approached from the great chamber.

From the south-east corner of the great chamber, a door opened into a bedchamber, originally similar in area to the chapel, with projecting garderobe turret with large cross slits (one remade) in its outer faces. The room has since been divided into a stair lobby and the extended bedroom has been united with the garderobe.

The newel shows signs of extension to the *second floor*, internally by a change in stonework and externally by a truncated canopied head of two shafts and capitals flanking a (renewed) trefoiled light. As there was no ante-chamber at this level, the stair originally opened directly into the room above the great chamber, though it does so today by some forced steps. This privy chamber is now partitioned into two bedrooms; the principal one (Queen Anne Room) is an Elizabethan state chamber with window, ceiling, and room-height fireplace and mantel of that period. There was no access from this privy chamber to any chapel balcony, only an unglazed window facing the altar, but it was the approach (now via a bedroom with early sixteenth-century window heads) to the privy bedchamber in the south-east angle, again with garderobe provision in the projecting turret. Though currently divided into a bathroom and landing, this room enjoys its original fenestration: two windows with twin cinquefoil lights with five-lobed circular head. The garderobe closet also retains its shouldered entry and large cross slits in the three outer walls.

BUILDING RESPONSIBILITY, *c.*1250–1330

In a particularly complex and unorthodox house, its development so far should be summarised with an indication of responsibility from the limited recorded history. The manor was held by John Broughton in 1242–3.[10] In 1301, a John Broughton, either his son or his grandson and referred to here as John Broughton 2, was granted free warren at Broughton.[11] He fought overseas and against the Scots, was knighted by Edward I, and died in 1315.[12] He was succeeded by his son, John Broughton 3, who was still alive in 1346.[13]

The vaulted undercrofts of the L-shaped chamber block were erected during the second half of the thirteenth century, possibly during the last quarter. Vaulted undercrofts beneath first-floor residential chambers were common in high-quality homes. Boothby Pagnell Manor, Little Wenham Hall, and Penshurst Place immediately come to mind, as do those at Drayton House, Southwick Hall, and Swalcliffe Manor House closer to Broughton. It is now known that Boothby Pagnell and Little Wenham Hall were associated with a probably contemporary hall, possibly timber-framed, and this may have been the case at Broughton Castle, with the hall initially next to the chamber block with the two undercrofts supporting a great chamber and bedchamber[14] (see page 78).

With the rise in the family fortunes under John Broughton 2, the earlier house was substantially enlarged in two phases. The hall was rebuilt as a three-bay structure, now separated from the earlier chamber block by a ground-floor staff room and encircling corridor, with a turret stair approach to the upper floor. While the hall would have been an imposing one on the same scale as Clevedon

been similarly divided into two rooms, a withdrawing room and a study, again of entirely modern character with no visible early evidence apart from the moulded jambs of the south window[8] and the chapel doorway.

The fourteenth-century *chapel* is one of the most beautiful private chapels to have survived. It is small but lofty, 17½ feet by 10¾ feet, rising through two storeys to a low-pitched timber roof, a Scott replacement following the original form. It is lit by an east window of three cinquefoil lights below tri-lobed heads to the side and a central head of three five-lobed circles.[9] The north window of two cinquefoil lights and cusped circular head is a Scott replacement, closely based on original evidence. The chapel retains its original floor tiles, bracket-supported altar slab, and piscina with cinquefoil

Court (40 feet by 26 feet) and Haddon Hall (42 feet by 27 feet), the corridors are an early example of restricting circulation, rare in a gentry house, but marking a stage in the desire for greater privacy. This part of the property can still be readily divorced from the remainder of the house 700 years later. This highly unusual plan seems to have been a local development. Whichford Castle, 7 miles south-west of Broughton, was a fortified house which had a narrow passage between the hall and the upper residential block. Excavations in the 1950s showed that it was not later than the early fourteenth century, when the property was abandoned. Swalcliffe Manor House, only 2 miles from Broughton, similarly retains a mid to late thirteenth-century vaulted undercroft beneath the solar with a vaulted passage parallel with the north wall.

The expansion of the family apartments was a second phase undertaken during the opening years of the fourteenth century. A three-storeyed bedchamber block with associated garderobe turret was added at the south-east angle of the chamber block, this time lacking the buttress support or the moulded plinth of the earlier work.[15] This enabled the former bedchamber to be developed as a chapel rising through two storeys. At the same time, the turret stair was heightened to provide access to a more private second-floor chamber and the second-floor bedroom.[16] Three-storeyed chamber blocks were not common at this time, but the form was being adopted by leading magnates as at Acton Burnell Castle (c.1284–94), and at Ludlow Castle (c.1290–5) at the lower end of that hall, but duplicated between 1308 and 1328 at the upper end of that same hall. These additional structures at Broughton are linked by the very similar window forms in the chapel, first-floor ante-chamber, and second-floor bedchamber. All these apartments offer the same large Rayonnant windows, a display which would have been even more impressive when seen in association with those in the hall.[17] They follow the form first seen locally at Merton College chapel (1290–4), so this work was probably not initiated before about 1295, and would have been completed before the regional diffusion of the ogee form after about 1310.[18] Like the plain doorways in the family apartments, these windows reflect the early formality of the Decorated style rather than the inventiveness and exuberance of the 1320s and 1330s. Though built by a knight of no more than local significance, the alliances on Sir John's tomb show that he was related to many regionally important families. He ensured that his building programme was no less than that of the best of his peers and that it was a 'fair manor place' 200 years before Leland said so.[19]

His son added the corridor vaulting. This is a secular example of the dramatisation of space, the domestic equivalent of the compartmentalising of a narrow aisle and the tight mesh of multiple division developed at St Augustine's Abbey, Bristol (1298–c.1330). Such a display of inventiveness is usually seen in an ecclesiastical context, but this miniature secular example similarly offers 'the novel means . . . of stressing the longitudinal continuity of the interior'.[20] As the corbels are orthodox rather than ebullient and the roll-moulded ribs are not dissimilar to those lining the jambs of the chapel east window, this addition was made in the 1320s, certainly before 1327 when John Broughton 3 had already come of age.[21]

HOUSE DEVELOPMENT, c.1375–1600

No building activity can be ascribed to Sir Thomas Broughton, who died without heirs before 1377, leading to complex negotiations

PLATE 31 Broughton Castle: engraving of south front from Parker (1853)

that resulted in William Wykeham, bishop of Winchester, purchasing the manor of Broughton early in Richard II's reign.[22] Although there was an episcopal manor at Adderbury East, the bishop purchased Broughton to have a property in the area more befitting his position and not too far distant from overseeing his collegiate foundation at Oxford, initiated in 1379. Such an enthusiastic builder did not leave Broughton alone but enhanced it as an occasional dwelling for himself with a most unusual structure, a loggia. He raised a double arcade between the two end walls of the chapel and bedchamber projections, rising through two floors. The retained area, virtually 19 feet square, was left open towards the moat but was vaulted in two bays. Vaulting rather than a timber ceiling was chosen for aesthetic reasons and to support a belvedere opening from the second-floor bedchamber. Concurrent with this work, the window in the east-facing ground-floor room was blocked, and Wykeham inserted a straight flight of stairs to what had hitherto been a family chapel but now warranted a more imposing approach befitting a grandee bishop. Additional chapel accommodation was also achieved by an inserted balcony, approached from the head of these steps by a short mural stair and newel.

The loggia survived for nearly a century, but during the later fifteenth century the vaulting was taken down and replaced by a lower flat ceiling, leaving only the springers as evidence. The arcade was infilled, a mid floor was inserted (since removed), approached from a door made at the head of the chapel stair and lit by the plain square-headed windows shown in Buck's engraving.[23] The area is now the staircase hall of the private apartments with a 1970 free-standing concrete spiral stair. The belvedere above was also enclosed in the later fifteenth century when a central fireplace flanked by two highly individual windows was inserted in the outer wall. This room became part of a suite with the adjacent bedchamber, lit by windows of four upper trefoil lights and two larger cinquefoil lights below, set in a square frame of convex jambs.

The house remained little altered until the 1540s, when the

GROUND FLOOR   **FIRST FLOOR**   **SECOND FLOOR**
                                                    East end

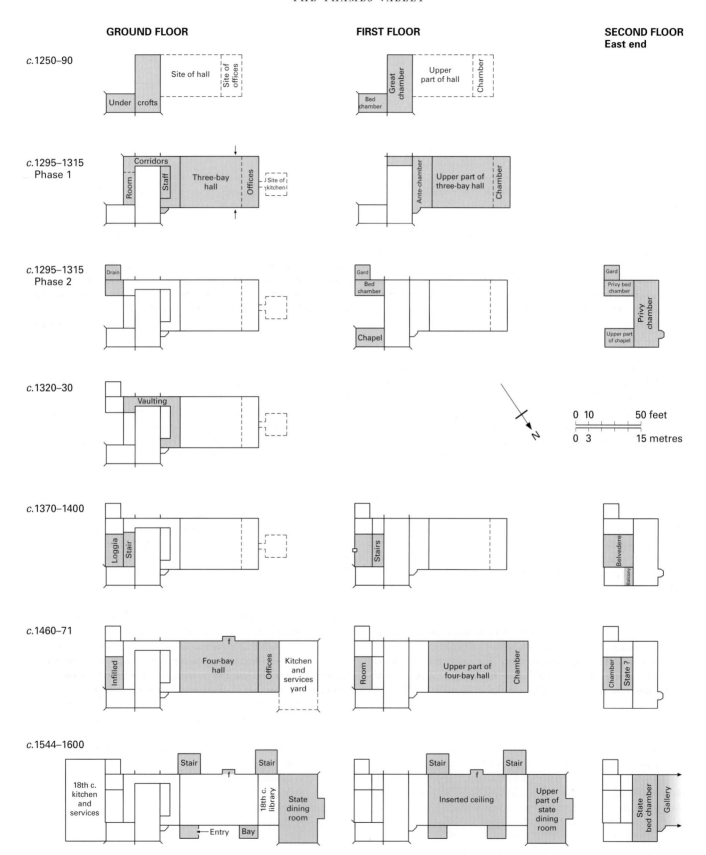

FIGURE 11 Broughton Castle: primary development phases 1250–1600

process began of converting it into an Elizabethan mansion with the earlier plan reversed. The kitchen and offices were replaced by new reception rooms and the hall was remodelled, but the medieval family apartments were left relatively untouched. The work can be divided into two main phases. In the first, the hall was completely remodelled through the removal of its roof and the insertion of a low ceiling to allow two floors to be created above. Externally, the double-storeyed bay windows were added facing the forecourt, with a first-floor oriel between them to impart a fashionable symmetrical character to the entrance front, surmounted by a gabled roof-line. To the rear, imposing gabled staircase projections were added and a central chimney to the hall. Internally, the reshaped hall was given new windows, a fireplace, staircase doorways, and a new entry at the former dais end.

The medieval west end of the house was totally transformed in the second phase. The kitchen and offices had possibly already been transferred to the south side of the house, but all earlier structures were stripped out to allow two state rooms to be created within the shell, one on each floor. The ground-floor chamber was intended as a dining room, elaborately wainscoted and plaster ceiled, while the withdrawing chamber above has an equally elaborate ceiling.

DEVELOPMENT SUMMARY

Broughton Castle is one of the largest and best-preserved houses of medieval England. The work is of outstanding quality, marked individuality, and considerable complexity, heightened by equally significant alterations and additions of the Elizabethan era. Bringing the architectural and limited documentary evidence together, the development of this fortified house over a span of five centuries can be summarised. The choice of site and the creation of the broad platform, spectacularly moated, is not later than the middle of the thirteenth century when it is known that John Broughton 1 held the manor. There is no documentary evidence to indicate when the present house was begun, but the two undercrofts date from the second half of the century and this reasonably applies to the two family rooms above. The early house was enlarged by a replacement three-bay hall and associated offices block towards the last years of the century by John Broughton 2, separated by corridors from the family apartments. In a second phase during the first years of the fourteenth century, he improved the extent and quality of his accommodation by remodelling the earlier family apartments, raising a second-floor privy chamber, and building a three-storeyed bedroom block with garderobe turret. This allowed him to convert the earlier first-floor bedchamber into a chapel. By this phase, Broughton, already a substantial house, had become a very stylish one, heralded by a gatehouse. His son, John Broughton 3, heightened the approach to the family apartments during the 1320s with corridor vaulting.

The property appealed to bishop Wykeham of Winchester, who purchased the manor shortly after 1377. He added to its character by creating the loggia with its second floor belvedere, and a more imposing approach to the private chapel. The hall was updated with new fenestration, while the gatehouse was similarly modernised by masons who worked for Wykeham at Winchester and Oxford.[24] Two years before the bishop's death in 1404, the manor had passed to his nephew, Sir Thomas Wykeham, who was granted licence to crenellate his property in 1406. It is tempting to attribute the low embattled wall to this phase but it is more likely to be co-eval with

the lodging range sixty years later. There was probably some type of enclosing wall well before the fifteenth century for the present length is more ornamental than formidable. The licence may have been precautionary or for status reasons.

Upon Sir Thomas' death in 1443, the estate passed to his son, followed by his granddaughter, Margaret, who married Sir William Fiennes, 2nd Lord Saye and Sele, in 1451. Fiennes succeeded to Broughton in right of his wife in 1457 and died in 1471 at the battle of Barnet fighting for Edward IV. Fiennes' father had built Herstmonceux Castle and it was during the 1460s that Sir William updated part of Broughton Castle. He enlarged the hall by incorporating the offices and chamber block in it, and built new offices and kitchen further west. Because of the scale of this work, a new hall roof was also likely. At the same time, he added further rooms to the private apartments by infilling the bishop's loggia, inserting a mid floor in the newly created space, and making a new room over the loggia. A new door and fireplace were inserted in the larger ground-floor undercroft, and a two-storeyed lodging range was erected next to the gateway. Where it survives, this work is marked by elaborate mouldings and window heads.

Some years after his coming of age in 1541, Richard Fiennes, 6th Lord Saye and Sele (d.1573) initiated the transformation of this fortified house into an Elizabethan mansion, completed by his son by about 1599. The late medieval hall was converted by about 1554 into a three-storeyed central range with frontal bays and rear stair towers accessing the second-floor long gallery which was twice as wide as it is today. The west end of the house was totally remodelled to create two state chambers for dining, with parlour above. A state bedchamber was created out of the medieval privy chamber, the only part of the earlier family rooms touched in the sixteenth century. Some of this work shows the influence of the contemporary Fontainebleau style, but the two western chambers were in the late Elizabethan style. The result was that the now lowered hall served as a reception room and the approach to the state dining chamber. The new east stair led to the broad long gallery, with the state bedchamber at one end and the state parlour at the other with descent by the new west stair. By this transformation, Broughton Castle developed its present form of an Elizabethan mansion with a suite of impractical state apartments, and a close-knit group of medieval rooms at the east end.

All subsequent modifications have been modest and have left the earlier fabric undisturbed. The most important was the low, battlemented eastern service block added in the eighteenth century, and the remodelling of several principal rooms in the fashionable Gothick taste of the late 1760s, including the ground-floor library and narrowing the long gallery for bedrooms. This work, like that undertaken at all key building periods, was funded by property sales.[25] This pattern culminated in the sale of all contents in 1837 to meet the extravagances of the 14th Lord Saye and Sele, but prudent husbandry since then has regenerated the castle so that it stands in better condition, internally and externally, than at any time over the last 400 years.

NOTES
1 Broughton House prior to its Victorian embellishment.
2 Tipping (1930) 54.
3 The small wheels were not part of the raising mechanism but were used in association with a belt for opening the gates.

4 Bod. Lib., MS Top. Oxon, C 394, p. 197.

5 *Cal. Pat. Rolls: 1405–08*, 161.

6 See the important plan in Turner and Parker (1853) opp. 262.

7 It is not shown on Turner and Parker's plan, suggesting Scott insertion, but their text refers to a 'groined room of small size' adjoining the newel staircase, 262.

8 Turner and Parker's 1853 illustration of this front shows the window restored to its early form, identical with that lighting the ante-chamber, opp. 261, 265.

9 *Ibid.* opp. 79.

10 *Book of Fees*, 824.

11 *Cal. Charter Rolls: 1300–26*, 1.

12 He is buried in the nearby church which was redeveloped by him.

13 *Feudal Aids*, IV, 178.

14 It would be feasible to stretch the construction of these undercrofts to the close of the century, as commentators have done prior to Slade (1978) 142, but the family were clearly living at Broughton much earlier in the century and my gut feeling is that the present chamber block was the core of their residence.

15 The single-vaulted bay of the ground-floor area is similar to those of the undercrofts, but the external evidence makes it clear that it is part of the added structure.

16 Without the second floor, access to the upper bedchamber has to be ascribed to the inserted second-floor stair and its return, *vide* Slade (1978) 148 who recognised clumsiness, sudden reversal in planning sophistication, and obvious contrivance.

17 A similar display was adopted at Markenfield Hall, Yorkshire (*c*.1310–15).

18 The ogee form occurs before 1312 on St Edburga's shrine at Bicester Priory, now in Stanton Harcourt church. It is also present in the chancel side window of St Mary's church, Broughton, and the tower west door where it is used in association with ball-flower decoration. The only evidence of the ogee form at the castle is the chapel piscina head, a late insertion possibly related to the oratory licence of 1331.

19 *Itinerary*, II, 14. See Creslow Manor House for a similar group of family apartments of *c*.1330, probably modelled on those at Broughton.

20 J. Bony, *The English Decorated Style* (1979) 51.

21 As an indication of the architectural problems still to be resolved at this fascinating house, it has been suggested to me that though the corridor ribs are medieval, the vaulting construction is not. Elizabethan make-up or Civil War repairs have been suggested.

22 Slade (1978) 149. Wykeham also purchased other manors in the area as part of his endowment of New College, Oxford, including Swalcliffe and Adderbury where the college was responsible for rebuilding the chancel (1408–19).

23 Confirmed by further work in 1995, *Med. Arch.* 40 (1996) 277, though the opinion that there was always a chamber above the vaulting is open to doubt.

24 Slade (1978) 151, where their marks are reproduced. The gateway was more domestic than the contemporary three-storeyed gatehouse at Michelham Priory.

25 The Knole and Hever estate (mid-fifteenth century), land in Hampshire and Somerset (mid-sixteenth century), Lincolnshire (mid-seventeenth and mid-nineteenth centuries), Kent (mid-eighteenth century).

T. H. Turner and J. H. Parker, *Some Account of Domestic Architecture in England*, II (1853) 261–7

W. H. St J. Hope, *Arch. Jour.* 67 (1910) 382–6

H. A. Tipping, *Country Life* (January 1930)

VCH, *Oxfordshire*, IX (1969) 87–91

M. Binney, *Country Life* (December 1976)

H. G. Slade, *Arch. Jour.* 135 (1978) 138–94

BUCKLAND OLD RECTORY, Gloucestershire

This small hall house, attractively situated below the Cotswold escarpment near Broadway, offers a four-phase development. The central hall rising the height of the building is flanked by two-storeyed end blocks in line, but though the hall was built during the third quarter of the fifteenth century, the lower block is earlier. It was a timber-framed structure with an outside staircase on the west side leading to a first-floor chamber. The gable-end wall survives completely to form the lower-end wall of the fifteenth-century hall. The jetty at first-floor level confirms that it was an exterior wall, built of hornbeam with each member numbered for erection. Probably fourteenth century, this building was subsequently faced with stone to blend in with the remainder of the house.

During the late fifteenth century, the hall and north residential block was added to the earlier house and the outside staircase was enclosed. The residential block was rebuilt in 1630 and the timber-framed unit was extended at the same time. Some further offices were added in 1849 and again in 1993.

Mid-nineteenth-century modifications including roof dormers have made the entrance frontage too bland but the rear elevations show the late medieval character of the house more clearly. It is also well shown in a drawing by Buckler of *c*.1805. The outer jamb of a now destroyed porch survives on this side, but there is no evidence of a matching porch on the present entry side. The opposing doors open into a cross passage created within the fourteenth-century house area, with the timber-framed end wall doubling as a screen with central hall entry.

The impressive two-bay hall is open to a roof, divided centrally by an unbuttressed hammer-beam truss with angels bearing shields on the beam-ends. The upper end wall was rebuilt in 1630 but the side walls are original, pierced by a pair of tall two-light transomed windows. Those in the west wall are original, with trefoil heads, and retain much of their contemporary stained glass. One light has the rising sun of Edward IV and the other the rebus of William Grafton and the arms of Gloucester Abbey. Both windows are decorated with birds, apparently woodcocks, in various attitudes holding scrolls inscribed *In Nomine Jesu*. The lights in the east-facing windows were replaced in the early seventeenth century. All four windows have shutters, not the original ones, but following an original feature. There is no trace of any central hearth, fireplace, or

PLATE 32 Buckland Old Rectory: from the south-east

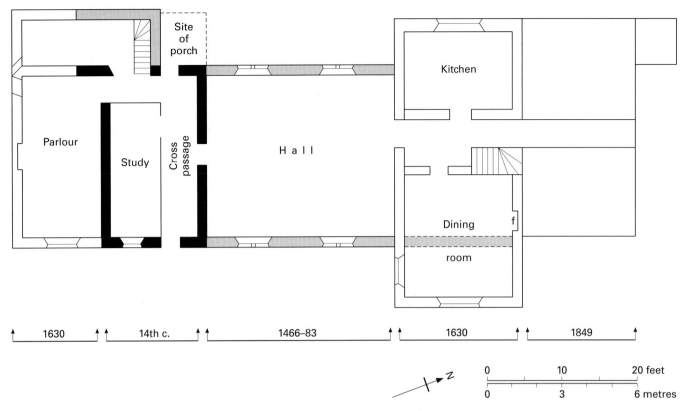

FIGURE 12 Buckland Old Rectory: ground plan

louvre in the restored roof with its heavily moulded wall plates and two tiers of wind braces.

The late fifteenth-century residential block was replaced by the projecting one in 1630, but the foundations of its west wall in line with that of the hall were discovered in 1972 beneath the dining room floor. Traces of an earlier, possibly late fifteenth-century fireplace were also identified.

The staircase on the south-west side was roofed separately. It encloses the original outer stair and probably garderobes at ground- and first-floor level, lit by slits, now blocked but still traceable. The present staircase is seventeenth century but the original well-worn stone steps remain underneath. The upper chamber retains its early roof above the seventeenth-century ceiling. The kitchen was a separate building, long since destroyed.

The late fifteenth-century rebuilding of Buckland occurred during the rectorship of William Grafton (1466–1510) whose name and rebus occur in the hall windows.[1] As one of the lights also has the sun in splendour, construction can be limited to the years of Edward IV's reign between 1466 and 1483. But was this residence intended for the rector? It has always been assumed so but the village always was a small one and the rectory is a very large and pretentious house for the parish priest. The hall has a hammer-beam truss which is not only structurally unnecessary for such a small room but is likely to have been inserted for swank. Was the house built by the Abbey of Gloucester who held the living, and subsequently let out to the rector? It ceased to be so used only towards the close of the twentieth century. In any case, Buckland is essentially a small manor house built on quite a grand scale.

NOTES
1 Illustrated in *Trans. Bristol and Glos. Arch. Soc.* 45 (1923) pl. 19.

W. Bazeley, *Trans. Bristol and Glos. Arch. Soc.* 9 (1884–5) 103–24

CHENIES MANOR HOUSE, Buckinghamshire

The Cheyne family held the manor between the late twelfth and early sixteenth centuries. The earliest residential evidence is stone-built, an isolated undercroft, possibly of *c.*1300, roofed by a series of chamfered transverse ribs with evidence of end doorways. There is also a 164 feet deep well (under an early nineteenth-century well-house), constructed before 1400 on the evidence of excavated material.[1]

Of inverted L-shape and brick built, the occupied manor house was developed in two phases. The short north wing consisting of the so-called hall and stair tower is early sixteenth century, while the extended east wing was added in the 1550s by the Russell family who owned the property until 1957. The later brickwork is slightly deeper and warmer in colour than that employed slightly earlier. Leland recorded that 'the olde house of the Cheyneis is so translated by my Lorde Russel . . . that little or nothing of it yn a maner remaynith ontranslatid and a great deale of the house is even newly set up made of brick and tymber'.[2]

The south end of the earlier core has been absorbed by the extended east wing built by the Russell family. This leaves a short block on two planes with angle pinnacles and finials, separated by a

81

prominent three-storeyed octagonal stair turret. The right-hand bay and turret with two original ground-floor windows with square hood moulds is the only surviving early work. It is a fine regional example of brickwork in a high-status house, and incorporates some diapering. The structure is attributed on architectural grounds to the 1520s, probably after the Russell family acquired the property in 1525–6.

Both frontages are marked by Blore's crow-stepped gables of 1829–30 while most of the windows on the west side are copies made at the same time. There are few original features internally apart from the cut-brick hand-rail (overpainted) to the stair, comparable to those at Faulkbourne and Oxburgh Hall. The initial plan is unclear. The stone-flagged parlour in the lower north end of the wing is said to have been the hall with a central hearth, open to the roof. This is a structure of alternating diagonally braced trusses and queen posts, now concealed above the first-floor plaster ceiling, but the size and position of the room do not fit comfortably with its supposed purpose. On the other hand, the timbers are soot covered and a huge six-chimney stack was inserted when the area was floored by 1535 (dated stack).

The 140 foot long east wing with its splendid line of chimney stacks was added by Sir John Russell, later 1st earl of Bedford (d.1555) in c.1552[3] when Chenies Manor was extended into a double-courtyard house. This two-storeyed range of lodgings (with unbroken attic) consists of a row of interconnecting chambers at both levels, linked to the west wing by a narrow gallery and at the further end by a staircase pulled down by Blore. To the rear are six (formerly seven) bold projections, crow-stepped gabled and chimney surmounted, holding fireplaces, closets and garderobes, separated midway by a taller stair turret. This is an important range of sub-medieval lodgings and the most rewarding architectural feature of the house. The north side of the courtyard was bounded by a mainly timber-framed range, pulled down in the eighteenth century, and the courtyard was formerly enclosed by a low brick gatelodge. There were further Tudor buildings west of the house including a ruined one, part of Russell's 'fair logginges . . . new erected in the garden'.[4]

NOTES
1 Haslam (1982).
2 *Itinerary*, I, 105. The Russells moved to Moor Park, Rickmansworth by 1608 and to Woburn Abbey in the 1630s.
3 *Vern. Arch.* 35 (2004) 96.
4 *Ibid.*

RCHM, *Buckinghamshire*, I (1912) 90–1
G. S. Thompson, *Two Centuries of Family History* (1930)
R. Haslam, *Country Life* (October 1982)

CRESLOW MANOR HOUSE, Buckinghamshire

This exceptionally interesting but heavily altered house 5 miles north of Aylesbury can be dated on architectural grounds to c.1325–40. It was built by John Stretley, an under-tenant of the earls of Salisbury who held the manor in dispute with the crown between acquiring it in 1312 and settlement in 1324 in the latter's favour.[1] Stretley subsequently held the property unfettered until his death

in 1346.[2] Built of rubble limestone, Creslow Manor formerly consisted of a hall with three-storeyed solar wing at right angles to it with contemporary chamber and tower projections, and an offices wing at the lower end of the hall. The house was altered in the early seventeenth century while the offices wing, depicted in drawings of c.1820, was pulled down shortly afterwards at the same time that the end bay of the hall was removed.

The hall, initially of four but now of three bays, is still essentially single-storeyed with attic windows added in the steeply pitched roof during the early seventeenth century[3] when the hall was remodelled with an inserted floor, partitions, and a tall stair tower with a contemporary stair and crow-stepped gable. Further changes were made during the mid-nineteenth and mid-twentieth centuries so that this apartment has become suburban with its early character limited to one small window and the sooted roof structure. The former is a stone circular opening with quatrefoil tracery at ground level in the dais bay. The latter (visible from the cross-wing attic) consists of base crucks to cambered tie beams with moulded arched braces and braced collars, intermediate upper trusses repeating the braced collars, and two lines of curved wind braces.

The three-storeyed upper cross wing is taller than the hall, with seventeenth-century stepped gables at both ends. Below the eastern third of this cross wing is a small undercroft, 14 feet square and 9 feet high, with a high-quality tierceron star vault, well-carved bosses, a single light, and a projecting external entry.

The ground floor consists of two stone-divided rooms with a fifteenth-century intercommunicating doorway, one room with an original window, and the other with a raised floor over the undercroft and two replacement rectangular windows.

The first and second floors were remodelled in the early seventeenth century. The first-floor great chamber was partitioned into two and refurbished with moulded ceilings and chimneypiece, though it is said to retain an original single light with tracery in the return wall facing the hall. The second floor was converted into a long gallery with a plaster ceiling and enlarged windows.

The three-storeyed tower projects from the south-west corner of the solar wing, with an octagonal stair turret at the junction serving all floors and rising above roof level. The tower is built of roughly coursed stone blocks with slit windows and a parapet supported on a fourteenth-century corbel table, enriched with ball-flower decoration and gargoyles. A drawing of c.1860 in the Bodleian Library[5] shows the tower with a crenellated parapet rather than the present plain unbroken one. The ground-floor room is approached by an arched doorway and retains a lancet in each face (one converted into a door) but two facing the approach. The first floor retains original moulded ceiling beams and a fine window of two trefoil lights under a Flamboyant head with label and stops externally and a rear arch springing from slender pillars internally. The remaining windows were replaced in the seventeenth century and the fireplace a little later. The uppermost room repeats the evidence of a two-light window (blocked) and the replacement windows, but holds its fourteenth-century fireplace lintel with Decorated head and jambs. The stone newel continues to the roof.

The two-storey extension projecting from the south-east corner of the cross wing faces the tower, with a twentieth-century ground-floor infill between. It retains its fourteenth-century internal doorways opening from the cross wing.

The parish church immediately north-west of the house is of

PLATE 33 Creslow Manor House: from the north-west

limestone rubble. 41 feet long, the walls hold a twelfth-century doorway, two thirteenth-century windows, and several of the fifteenth century. They were blocked in Stuart times when the chapel was floored and the fifteenth-century roof was given a timber east gable.[6]

Creslow Manor House is a particularly important survival that is currently barred to architectural historians who contaminate privacy. Even without inspection, it is clear that this was a major H-shaped house with base-cruck hall and a far larger upper cross wing than was usual at the time. The tower was not defensive but served as a contemporary chamber extension to each floor, with the more important upper rooms heated. This structure, in combination with the second extension and cross wing, closely resembles the near-contemporary family apartments at Broughton Castle, 25 miles to the north-west, similarly built by a family of no more than local importance. The three vaulted ground-floor rooms at Broughton are replaced by unvaulted ones at Creslow, though they are associated with the independent vaulted undercroft of otherwise unclear purpose.[7] The great chamber, 47 feet by 17 feet, was slightly larger than that at Broughton, similarly divided today into two rooms with early features limited to a window and an internal doorway. The tower room would have been a bedchamber, and it is possible that the second extension followed the Broughton pattern as a chapel. The second floor repeated the Broughton plan of linked privy chamber and inner chamber. Though the Broughtons developed their family wing over a span of at least forty years with completion by about 1320, that at Creslow seems to have been a single-phase project undertaken shortly afterwards, with work completed during the years close to 1330–5.

NOTES
1 VCH, III (1925) 337. The manor passed out of crown hands in 1673.
2 Stretley settled the manor on his widow for life, with remainder to her son and his five brothers.
3 c.1610, RCHM, II (1913) 95; c.1646–47, VCH, III (1925) 335 and *Northampton Archit. and Arch. Soc. Reports and Papers* 43 (1935–6) 13.
4 RCHM, II (1913) 95.
5 Copy in NMRC, Swindon.

6 The church is now used for storage, while the former village close to the house has been reduced to earthworks.
7 The brief note in T. H. Turner and J. H. Parker, *Some Account of Domestic Architecture in England*, II (1853) 269 refers to 'two wings or towers of stone, one of which has been destroyed, the other remains tolerably perfect, with the ground rooms vaulted as usual'. Despite the initial error, it is possible that some ground-floor vaulting has been destroyed since the 1850s.

RCHM, *Buckinghamshire*, II (1913) 94–8
VCH, *Buckinghamshire*, III (1925) 335–6
N. Pevsner and E. Williamson, *The Buildings of England: Buckinghamshire* (1994) 261–2

DONNINGTON CASTLE, Berkshire

Is this late fourteenth-century residence, constructed by one of Richard II's three guardians, a fortress or a fortified house? Dominating the broad valley between the Lambourn and Hampshire downs and the road from London to Bristol, the manor of Donnington had been held by the Abberbury family since the late thirteenth century. There is no evidence of an earlier structure before the present one, which was built in two stages. The present walls 2–3 feet high are the lower courses of the curtilage of a small courtyard house. They are prefaced by an almost complete gatehouse which is now the principal feature of the site.

The semi-rectangular courtyard residence with its prow-shaped west end is approximately 120 feet by 80 feet externally. Built of flint with sandstone dressings, it has four small round towers at the corners and two rectangular side towers, but no projection at the point of the prow. Ranges were built against the walls, with some footings of internal walls on the east side, but the remaining ranges round the cobbled courtyard were probably timber-framed. Hearths, the base of at least one stair tower (north-west) and the chute of the garderobe tower (north) can be traced, together with the residential character of the apartments of the east range with its inner face common with the added gatehouse.

The centrally positioned entrance, thrust forward of the earlier building, is a three-storeyed block with frontal drum towers rising a further stage. That to the south held the stair and its companion held garderobes, necessitating a straightened side to allow for drainage shafts. The gatehouse was protected by a barbican with short side walls, a drawbridge across the ditch,[1] a well-set-back entrance with double doors, and a portcullis. The entrance passage was vaulted in two bays, and there was a large single room on both upper floors with square-headed fireplaces. The battlements are in good condition.

The young Richard Abberbury did not succeed to the family lands until the early 1360s.[2] He was a scion of Berkshire and north Oxfordshire gentry who had pursued a successful administrative career earlier in the century before the family suffered an eclipse through minorities and early deaths. Richard restored the family fortunes through war service, initially under Henry, duke of Lancaster in Brittany and Normandy in 1356, followed by service under the Black Prince in Aquitaine in 1366 and in Aquitaine and Castile in 1368–71. Though he was never a member of the prince's inner circle,[3] he was for a brief time steward of his son's lands and then tutor to the young Richard II. It was at this point that the financial rewards became substantial, helped by serving the new king in a diplomatic capacity and as chamberlain to the king's first wife (1383–6).[4] During the subsequent problematical times at court, he kept out of the way by busying himself with judicial duties in Oxfordshire and Berkshire, though he was among those expelled from court by the Lords Appellant early in 1388. He subsequently resumed his diplomatic career and extended his family holding.[5] Abberbury chose to make Donnington his *caput honoris*, founded the almshouses for twelve poor men and a master in the village in 1393,[6] and died six years later.

In June 1386, Abberbury was granted a licence to 'build anew and fortify with stone and lime and crenellate a certain castle on his land at Donyngton'[7] and the gatehouse is ascribed to this period.[8] This is not certain. The licence could equally have applied to the towered and crenellated courtyard house as much as to the gatehouse, for there was little time difference between the two structures. In planning terms, the house follows the same form as that at Shirburn Castle (1377–*c*.1382), particularly before Abberbury replaced the modest entrance with the present gatehouse. The plan also superficially resembles Bodiam Castle (1385–*c*.1390) where the mid towers were repeated. The gatehouse similarly has affinities with the double-towered entrance added by Courtenay to his earlier castle at Saltwood (1380s). That the Donnington gatehouse was an addition against the east face of the earlier house, with its still extant but lower battlemented head, is made clear by the building lines at the angles, the cramped window hoods, and the unusually sited portcullis position slotted between the two faces and therefore at the rear of the entry passage. Structurally, both phases were built of the same materials, with the gatehouse maintaining the modest batter that runs round the outer walls of the courtyard house and towers, and the string courses at first-floor level. Common straight-headed fireplaces and square window hoods, as well as cinquefoil lights in the house, indicate that there were few years between the two phases.

The detailing of the gatehouse demonstrated the owner's standing and refinement. The drum towers were designed to taper upwards and were given the appearance of being five-storeyed through the slight set-backs emphasised by projecting string courses. Above the small rectangular first-floor window was a larger one of two trefoil lights with a quatrefoil head. The first two string courses rose decoratively over these windows as labels and were extended across the outer face of the courtyard house. The second and third courses were ornamented with gargoyles. The entry was framed with handsome mouldings, the side walls of the passageway were chequered in flint and stone, and the central panels of its vaulting were decorated with trefoiled lobes. The two upper floors were comfortable apartments and extended the earlier quarters in the adjacent courtyard range.

Donnington's position is outstanding, commanding western Berkshire where the road from London to Bristol crosses that from Oxford to Southampton. The steep slopes of the spur on which the castle stands make it particularly difficult to attack, as was proved in the famous nineteen-month siege during the Civil War (1644–6). Though Sir Richard's licence was for a replacement house, the site does not seem to have been fortified before his time.[9] Nor do events nearly 300 years later necessarily dictate its original character. The choice may have been determined initially by the 'fair prospect' noted by Camden and equally applicable today,

PLATE 34 Donnington Castle: gatehouse from the south-east

emphasised by the 'windows in all sides, very lightsome'.[10] Though the walls are 4½ feet thick, the towers are no more than turrets and that to the south-west has extremely thin walling. The entry was simply a passage in the east wall (as at Shirburn), while the decision not to protect the head of the prow-shaped west face undermined any serious defensive intent. Appearance was all, and like Shirburn, Donnington made a statement by a returning soldier from France.[11] The gatehouse is rather different. Like that at Saltwood Castle, it combines an external seriousness of purpose with internal comfort – in this case, an extension of the apartments of the adjacent eastern range. But whereas the Kent gatehouse was in reaction to the anticipated invasion from France during the 1370s and 1380s, Donnington is similar to the gatehouse-towers at Bothal (1343), Hylton (1390s), and Bywell (*c*.1418) in Northumbria – a combined imposing entrance and comfortable residence. In addition, it was a much more obvious advertisement of Sir Richard's hard-earned prosperity.

In just over a century, the Abberburys had risen from the ranks of the free peasantry to the position of friend and advisor of kings and princes. As a consequence, Donnington was converted in quick succession from a crenellated house into a gated house that made a clarion statement of Sir Richard's personal achievement to society throughout the region.

NOTES

1 Replaced by a bridge in 1568 preparatory to Elizabeth I's visit.
2 S. Walker, 'Sir Richard Abberbury and his kinsmen: the rise and fall of a gentry family', *Nott. Med. Studies* 34 (1990) 118.
3 *Ibid.* 120.
4 At the same time, Sir Richard's son served under Gaunt in Portugal in 1386–8 and became his chamberlain. After Henry IV's usurpation, the fortunes of the family quickly declined, *ibid.* 132–4.
5 *Ibid.* 124.
6 Refounded by the duchess of Suffolk in the 1430s and by the earl of Nottingham in 1602, and rebuilt in 1822. In 1415, Sir Richard's son had sold the manor to Thomas Chaucer of Ewelme, whose only daughter became duchess of Suffolk through her third marriage.
7 *Cal. Pat. Rolls: 1385–9*, 156.
8 Wood (1964) 2, 3; C. Platt, *The Castle in Medieval England and Wales* (1982) 118–19.
9 Before then, the nearest castle had been at Hamstead Marshall, 3 miles south-west, where three mottes survive, close together.
10 *Britannia* (1586). By Camden's day, such windows may well have been enlargements. Not surprisingly, it was this part of the castle that suffered most severely from Parliamentary guns during the Civil War siege, Godwin (1872).
11 When I first visited the castle in 1947, the gatehouse was still occupied by a First World War veteran.

H. Godwin, *Archaeologia*, 44 pt 2 (1872) 459–79
VCH, *Berkshire*, IV (1924) 91–4
M. Wood, *Donnington Castle: Handbook* (1964)

PLATE 35 Dorney Court: hall interior

DORNEY COURT, Buckinghamshire, and local framed houses

Between the early eighteenth and early twentieth centuries, Dorney Court was a house of Georgian character concealing a Tudor, timber-framed structure. At the beginning of the twentieth century, the three-storeyed Georgian-pedimented east frontage, built of stock brick, was pulled down, at the same time that all casement windows and walls in the south-east and north-west frontages were remodelled. All three faces were replaced by multi-gabled, timber-framed and red brick façades with Tudor-style windows, decorative barge boards, and the considerable use of old materials. At the same time, the hall was embellished with a bay window, and the plaster-covered offices range was stripped and renewed in harmony with the other façades (pl. 6). Only the eighteenth-century dining and kitchen ranges in a cottage vernacular style were left untouched.

Christopher Hussey enthused over this transformation in 1924 in a manner that would be decried today. The word 'fakery' slips all too easily from the lips of many architectural historians. Yet the Georgian remodelling was entirely alien to the house's internal character, an ill-fitting and cheaply made dress dictated solely by fashion. The restoration was sympathetic in its choice of materials and proportions, even if it betrays a character equally as much of its time as the mid-Tudor period it was seeking to evoke.

Dorney Court stands 3 miles west of Windsor on a slight rise on the flood plain of the River Thames. Very roughly Z-shaped, the house was developed during at least five phases – late fifteenth century, early to mid-sixteenth century, 1733, 1867 (both drainpipe dates), and *c.*1905–10. The property was formerly much larger, for garden activity has revealed evidence of brick courtyard ranges to

the south and north, with the latter enclosed by a turreted wall and the gatehouse that formed the original approach to the house.[1] Both courts were pulled down by the early eighteenth century when the entrance was moved to the middle of the residential wing and prefaced with a seven-bay classical frontage. Not surprisingly, the hall lost its prime position, whereas it still dominates the frontage at Ockwells, the model for the house's rehabilitation in *c.*1905–10 and obviously so from the garden side of the hall.

The house was originally a timber-framed structure with brick noggin infill and this was repeated in the most recent stage of its development. The phases in between used brick only. The hall, 38 feet by 23 feet and open to the roof, retains its original volume and has regained its early character and atmosphere. The cross-passage doorways survive with four-centred heads, that to the south with leaf-decorated spandrels. Any porch was subsumed in the late nineteenth-century lobby, while the opposing door opens into a corridor range added in 1867 against the north wall of the hall. This conceals any early window evidence, for those on the south side are entirely reasonable reinstatements, made in *c.*1905–10 with a continuous line of upper lights in the second and third bays and a full-height dais bay window *à la Ockwells*.[2] Other replacements at that time included the late fifteenth-century fireplace with a stone lintel

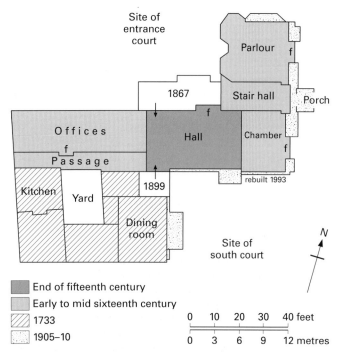

Site of
entrance
court

Parlour f

1867

Stair hall

Porch

f

Offices

f

Hall

Chamber

f

Passage

1899

rebuilt 1993

Kitchen

Yard

Dining
room

Site of
south court

N

█ End of fifteenth century

░ Early to mid sixteenth century

▨ 1733

▦ 1905–10

0   10   20   30   40 feet

0   3   6   9   12 metres

FIGURE 13 Dorney Court: site plan

of low four-centred head with spandrels of quatrefoil-enclosed shields, the seventeenth-century screen with gallery over, and the linenfold panelling that originated in the abbot's quarters of Faversham Abbey. This last partly covers the original end walls with broadly spaced vertical posts. The roof is divided into four bays, spanned by arch-braced collar trusses with a single line of curved wind braces. The roof was ceiled above the collars in the early sixteenth century, concealing the crown posts above. An original door with plain four-centred head opens from the dais to the residential wing, and there has never been more than a single door to the offices. It is probable that the hall was built before the close of the fifteenth century.

Much of the two-storeyed wing beyond the dais seems a generation later, though both rooms on each floor have been subject to several phases of remodelling including the creation of a central entrance and staircase hall in the early 1730s. The original chimney stacks with diapered faces and stone fireplaces on both floors have survived all later modifications while Hussey identified the position of the bay windows as 'authoritative'. Subsequent additions include the two mid-sixteenth-century polygonal bays in the parlour, initially fully glazed, and the early twentieth-century frontage with its imported features.

The house retains its early layout of kitchen and offices, with the passage-approached kitchen on the further side of a small courtyard as at Ockwells. The core of these two ranges is probably late fifteenth century, heavily modified in the early to mid-sixteenth century and so marked on the plan.

Dorney Court follows in the footsteps of Sir John Noreys' house (c.1455–65) but lacks its documentation. The manor of Dorney was held during the late fifteenth century by John Scott who was in possession of the house in 1490 and may have been responsible for its initial development. The property passed through a succession of

families during the next half-century, beginning with Richard Restwold (d.1505) and then Thomas Lytton to whom he had sold the reversion. Lytton may have expanded the property before selling it in 1513 to Richard Hill who was lord of Dorney in 1530. Seven years later, the property was purchased by Sir William Garrard, later lord mayor of London, whose early seventeenth-century successor married a Palmer, the present owners of the house. Despite the many changes, Dorney Court retains some of its early layout and character, though far less so than Ockwells or Hendred House, East Hendred. On the other hand, it is an instructive example of successive changes of taste, particularly that art historical yearning for the style of an earlier age, either late medieval or romantic Tudor.[3] Dorney Court is also the best preserved of the late medieval gentry-type houses in Buckinghamshire of timber-frame construction with brick infill.

Three such houses retain evidence of their fourteenth-century origins, two of them in the pretty village of Denham, still not overwhelmed by the suburban tentacles of Outer London. Denham Court was the manor of Denham. It is primarily a late seventeenth- to nineteenth-century residence, but it encases the frame of a two-bay aisled hall with part of a cranked tie-beam truss with arch braces at the services end. It was built well before 1350 when it was among the properties leased out by the abbots of Westminster. Savay Farm, a sub-manor of Denham by the Durdents family, retains considerably more evidence of its original hall and cross-wing plan. The aisled hall, 36 feet by 34½ feet, has lost its west aisle (though not its posts) but retains the arcaded east aisle. The apartment has been devalued through division and flooring in the mid-sixteenth century. The cross passage holds evidence of its service doors and access to the chamber over the services. The upper cross wing with an oversailing first floor was added in the late fourteenth century. It has an early Tudor end extension, made at the same time that the services wing was replaced.[4] Both houses were moated, but there is no such evidence at Huntercombe Manor, Burnham, probably developed by the Huntercombe family during the mid-fourteenth century. The two-bay hall is of base-cruck construction, still open to its roof with a central cambered tie beam supported on large arch braces. The offices wing retains evidence of the buttery, passage, and kitchen, the last with an unsophisticated roof. Huntercombe Manor, though, is far more significant for the internal character of its upper wing, remodelled and staircase enlarged in Carolean style in about 1670.[5]

Ignoring county boundaries, six high-status late medieval houses co-exist within a 6 mile radius of Slough, three of monastic development – Upton (q.v.), Denham, Huntercombe – and three of secular origin – Savay, Dorney, Ockwells (q.v.). All are timber-framed with brick or plaster infill, of hall and cross-wing plan, with a development span across a 150 year period. They extend from the modest two-bay aisled form at Denham Court and Savay Farm, via the three techniques for dispensing with arcade posts using base crucks as at Huntercombe, a hammer-beam truss as at Upton, and braced collar trusses with side purlins and wind braces as at Ockwells and Dorney Court. The expansion of cross wings was helped by jetties from the mid-fourteenth century onwards as at Upton Court and Savay Farm, by the extension of these wings on a substantial scale for high-status rooms as at Ockwells and Dorney Court, and by their development round service courtyards at the same houses to facilitate generous hospitality.

NOTES

1 The two crude crayon drawings in the house showing these extensions are unreliable, as are their sources, two mid-eighteenth-century miniatures in the Palmers' pedigree book.

2 Two windows filled with early stained glass had been removed in 1840 when the hall was 'improved'.

3 C. Aslet, *The Last Country Houses* (1982) 155–81, though the influence of the work at Ockwells and Dorney Court, disseminated by word of mouth as well as through the pages of *Country Life*, is not mentioned.

4 RCHM, I (1912) 116–18.

5 *Ibid*. 78. A. Oswald, *Country Life* (June 1949). The hall was altered during Charles II's reign when its walls were raised and brick faced (subsequently stucco covered), the central crown post was removed, and the roof was ceiled at collar level.

RCHM, *Buckinghamshire*, III (1925) 221–3
C. Hussey, *Country Life* (July/August 1926)

EAST HENDRED, HENDRED HOUSE, Berkshire

The restoration of the volume and character of the hall of this manor house through the removal of the inserted floor in 1971 has substantially increased its architectural and aesthetic value. Hendred House stands foursquare to the open approach from near the centre of this compact nucleated village. It is a hall and cross-wing house with an immediate clarity of plan. The central hall is flanked by narrow projecting cross-wings with a low eighteenth-century forward projection to the right (single storey with attic), and a much larger early nineteenth-century projection to the left (two storeys with attic). The whole house is rendered, completely concealing its timber-framing but winningly colour-washed in pale lemon with white woodwork.[1] It might be anticipated that the cross wings are similarly modest in their rear projection. This is true of

the offices, but the solar wing is in line with a mid-thirteenth-century chapel, clunch built with ashlar dressings but now rendered and coloured to match the remainder of the property. The mid-nineteenth-century wing, almost a mini house in itself, equals the length of the chapel to create a three-sided courtyard, open to the garden on the fourth side (pl. 3).

The Turberville family held the manor from about 1150 to 1308, marked by Sir John Turberville's receipt of papal authority in May 1256 to build a chapel and appoint a chaplain. The property passed to William Arches through his first marriage and was held by that family from 1323 until it passed to the present holders, the Eyston family, in 1453. The manor of Arches was one of six recorded in the relatively wealthy village of East Hendred[2] but it is the only one to have retained its leading house, essentially rebuilt in the late fifteenth century. In addition to the two late extensions, the house was thoroughly refenestrated in the eighteenth century, with casements under later rectangular hoods, and the front door was centred. Barge boards were added to the cross wings in the early nineteenth century and the roofs were covered with clay tiles.

The entry was correctly removed to its present cross-passage position in 1971, though no evidence of the earlier doorway was recovered. The opposing one is also a relatively modern replacement. The hall, 32 feet by 22 feet, is divided into four short bays, once more open to the roof though retaining the nineteenth-century stair against the upper end wall and galleried landing round two sides of the apartment. The first and third trusses are arch-braced intermediate collars, moulded with hollow chambers. The second truss is a false hammer beam with solid braces, a fine central feature when viewed from the dais. There are two lines of wind braces, four-centred with modest chamfers. Though the entrance wall has a line of ground-floor sash windows and two upper casements, two timber windows (externally blocked) have been uncovered in the opposite upper wall, divided into four lights with plain

PLATE 36 East Hendred, Hendred House: entry frontage

four-centred heads.[3] The roof timbers were sooted when revealed in 1971, but the open hearth must have had a short life for a mural fireplace was inserted in the east wall close to about 1500 with moulded four-centred head and panelled frieze of quatrefoil roundels.[4] The absence of any medieval documentation concerning the house (excluding the chapel), the lack of decorative detailing, and dendro analysis limitations have inhibited close dating this apartment so far.[5] The hammer-beam truss could be mid-fourteenth century on analogy with that at Upton Court, but there is no evidence that the truss at Hendred House was an insertion. The proportions of the hall, the line of upper windows, and the roof structure point to the fifteenth century and more particularly to the mid to later years, the work of John Eyston (d.1492), the first of that family.

The northern lower cross wing was thoroughly remodelled when the early nineteenth-century extension was added against it. This unit with its four-centred ogival wind braces has been dendro dated to c.1535–6.[6] Nor does the broader upper cross wing retain much early internal character through its eighteenth-century remodelling. The ground floor is at a lower level than the hall, possibly reflecting that the predecessor (see below) was used for storage. The present single room has recently been created out of two, with windows of the form common throughout the house. The two bedrooms are ceiled, but the four-bay roof structure above is unsophisticated – the timbers are rough, with thin purlins, crude collar braces and cranked wind braces. The structure has been attributed by analogy to the early fourteenth century,[7] with dendro evidence of timber felling in 1335–6 and 1375–1407.[8]

The single-storey chapel, in line with this wing and its roof ridge, is linked internally with it for there is no stone west wall, merely a partition. Clearly, the chapel originally abutted an early timber-framed chamber block, subsequently replaced by the present cross wing. The chapel is a substantial one, comparable with the much later chapel at Rycote and one of the three in this country to have retained unbroken Catholic use.[9] It has diagonal end buttresses, central mini buttresses, and renewed opposing west porches. It was originally lit by opposing lancets in broad splays[10] with the east window replaced in the mid-fourteenth century by a larger one with twin lights and reticulated tracery. The south-facing windows in fourteenth-century style are late Victorian replacements of earlier insertions with timber mullions, made when the chapel was restored and reroofed,[11] and the tabernacle overdecorated. The sedilia opposite is original. The balconied west end was separated in the later middle ages by a lath and plaster partition to create an upper room for the chaplain. Part of a straight-headed, four-light window (blocked externally) survives in a north-facing cupboard, with the broad splays retaining traces of wall painting (Virgin Mary on the west side) and timber mullions with sliding-shutter evidence. The fireplace opposite has a four-centred head. This room was opened up to become part of the chapel in the nineteenth century.

NOTES

1 A few elements of the hall framing have been left exposed at the rear.
2 VCH, IV (1924) 296–300.
3 Mr Eyston tells me that identical windows remain covered up in the front wall and both cross wings.
4 The fireplace was recovered from a house in the village in the 1860s and inserted against the staircase in the hall. During the restoration a

hundred years later, it was found to fit perfectly the blocked-up opening discovered in the third bay.
5 *Vern. Arch.* 33 (2002) 83.
6 *Vern. Arch.* 32 (2001) 77–8.
7 Currie (1992) 117, revising his attribution to the late fourteenth century in *Med. Arch.* 19 (1975) 249.
8 *Vern. Arch.* 33 (2002) 83.
9 The others are at Hazlewood Castle and Stonor Park. Recent refurbishment has helped to overcome its 'singularly dull and disappointing interior' occasioned through looting by William of Orange's soldiers in 1688 and the Victorian restoration. E. T. Long, *Berks. Arch. Jour.* 44 (1940) 107–8.
10 Incised pilgrim crosses and other graffiti have recently been discovered on one of them.
11 The line of the former plaster ceiling is marked on the west wall.

VCH, *Berkshire*, IV (1924) 295
C. R. J. Currie, *Oxoniensia* 57 (1992) 114–18

ETON COLLEGE, Buckinghamshire

CONCEPT AND DEVELOPMENT

The original layout of Eton College is not as immediately obvious as that of Winchester or New College, Oxford. This arises from the very particular purpose of this royal foundation which enshrined three objectives – education, religion, and charity. It was not only a school for boys, but a college of secular priests, and an almshouse for poor men. Education was an integral element of Henry VI's concept, and is the immediate response to the name 'Eton'. Yet this was not its founder's primary purpose. Religion was its cornerstone, and it was this religious intent which determined the pivotal role of the chapel. Not only was this building meant to be amongst the largest in England, but it went through three modifications in quick succession, each one increasing the size, before it attained its present impressive but truncated scale. The same purpose determined the provision for chaplains, the elaborate services, and the many relics and gifts bestowed on the foundation. Furthermore, Henry preferred not to put his faith in the prayers of monks but turned to poor bedesmen, and the prayers of men of learning. As well as being a centre of pilgrimage, Eton was a vast chantry to pray and sing masses for the souls of the king and his family and all other college benefactors. The education aspect was intended not as a separate end in itself, but as a means to an end, and that again meant the church. It was a school for training scholars who would help spread theology, propagate the faith, and put their wisdom and learning at the service of the state.

Henry's intentions not only affected the architectural character of the 'The King's College of Our Lady of Eton beside Windsor' but account for the overwhelming size of the chapel in the first court, and the relegation of the hall and kitchen to the second court. Furthermore, the initial staffing levels of the college as well as its architectural form were substantially amended by the founder in a wildly ambitious scheme which had a major effect on the present structure. To appreciate the constitutional and architectural form of Eton, therefore, it is prudent to remember that although the religious foundation and the school may be considered as separate architectural elements, they were joined in a common purpose.

Eton College was established by Henry VI when he was only

eighteen years old. It was symbolic that it was his first act upon attaining his majority in September 1440. His intention was to surpass Wykeham's foundation at Winchester which he had visited in 1440, and just as Winchester had its counterpart at Oxford, so Henry created a sister foundation in 1441 at Cambridge, formally linked two years later. Although less was built at King's College than at Eton, both foundations represent the king's personal involvement as well as his patronage. This was both beneficial and disadvantageous. Henry's caring interest meant a generous flow of funds, but it also led to major building changes during the course of construction.

The king's initial intention (11 October 1440) was to create a college of secular priests with the addition of a small school and almshouse. It would consist of a provost, ten fellows who were priests, four clerks, six choristers, a schoolmaster, twenty-four indigent scholars aged between eight and twelve who would receive free education, and twenty-four poor and infirm men. The foundation was, therefore, quite different in intent from Wykeham's foundation at Winchester but was in tune with more recent establishments such as that by the duke of York at Fotheringhay (1415) or archbishop Chichele at Higham Ferrers (1422). It was a religious centre with a nave and a choir for parish and college respectively, supporting a community of priests, an educational foundation, and an almshouse. It was underpinned by lavish grants of land, a huge collection of ornaments and holy relics, and the rare papal privilege of indulgences to all penitents who visited Eton on the Feast of the Assumption. The scheme was intended to make Eton the most important place of pilgrimage in England.[1]

It was not long before Henry modified his intentions. In 1442 William Waynflete, headmaster of Winchester College, was installed as provost of Eton. A year later, the educational side of Henry's foundation was developed and extended. The number of scholars was increased to seventy (as at Winchester), the choristers to sixteen, and the clerks to ten. Ten chaplains and an usher were added to the complement, while the bedesmen were reduced to thirteen. At the same time, the educational link with the king's establishment at Cambridge was formalised.

Five years later, Henry drastically extended the architectural design of his foundation. The chapel was to be pulled down and rebuilt on a cathedral-like scale with a nave almost as large as any in England.[2] It is likely that the newly built hall filling one side of the second court was to be rebuilt,[3] at the same time that the court was to be made three times as large, with a towered entrance on the north side giving access to a new outer court containing the college offices and almshouses. There was to be a vaulted cloister on the site of the present School Yard (like those at Winchester and New College) with a bell tower 140 feet high on the west side. There were to be no rooms above or adjoining this cloister. As at Winchester and New College (and again perhaps through Waynflete's influence), it was to be an environment for contemplation, study, and burial.[4]

This revised scheme was an astonishing concept for any English monarch. Not surprisingly in this instance, ambition outstripped financial resources. Only one element of this grandiose scheme was carried out. The chapel that had been built during the previous eight years was pulled down and the present structure commenced to dimensions laid down in a further document known as 'The King's Avyse', probably drawn up early in 1449. Only the chancel

PLATE 37 Eton College: School Yard

of his enormous church was constructed, now the body of the chapel that stands today. Work continued throughout the 1450s, but at a slower pace than during the previous decade because of the king's financial and mental difficulties.

All building activity ceased with Henry's deposition in 1461 and the advent of a new dynasty. Two years later, Edward IV obtained a papal bull for the abolition of the college and transferred all its lands and relics to St George's Chapel in Windsor Castle. Possibly through the advocacy of bishop Waynflete, the young king was persuaded from dissolving the foundation and restored sufficient endowment to enable it to survive. This process began in 1469, with work resuming on the unfinished chapel, and was extended after Henry VI's mysterious death in 1471. Even so, the reduced income made it essential to curtail the founder's cherished ambitions, primarily by jettisoning the nave, reducing the number of priests and abandoning the almshouse for poor men. The concept of a college of secular priests, as well as a school, survived. What also survives, architecturally, is essentially Henry VI's work. In his will of 1448, Henry speaks of the foundation of his two royal colleges at Eton and Cambridge as 'the prymer notable work' of his reign. They still are, with much more evidence of royal intention at the former than the latter. For Henry wanted his foundations to be his monument, not leadership on the battlefield in France. He cared deeply about his projects and showed a determination, purpose, and enthusiasm for them which he never felt or expressed for politics.

BUILDING HISTORY

Educationally, the college was based on Wykeham's precedent at Winchester and New College, Oxford, with the latter becoming the predominant influence in Henry's revised scheme. But while the Wykehamist concept continued to dominate college design at Oxford with the hall and chapel in line as the principal courtyard feature, the Henrician concept placed much greater emphasis on the chapel and made this the dominant feature, with the domestic and residential quarters relegated to a second court. Hence the chapel virtually overwhelms the first court, with the scholars taught and accommodated in the brick range opposite. The provost, fellows, and conducts (chaplains) were housed round the second court, with one side filled by the unobtrusive first-floor hall.

Work began on site in July 1441 with the royal laying of the foundation stone of a chapel that was just slightly larger than the chapel at Winchester – royal one-upmanship. There were large deliveries of bricks in 1442, and over one million bricks were delivered in 1443. But we have few details about the work carried out, nor do we know the exact nature of the original plan. Work probably began at once on the chapel and the school buildings opposite. By the autumn of 1443, the school was nearing completion, for Thomas Beckington gave a banquet in the new buildings on the north side of School Yard before the ground-floor chamber had been divided.

With the stabilisation of the foundation's membership in 1443, a contract was signed that November for the carpentry associated with the buildings round the second court – the hall, ten chambers, and seven towers and turrets. The buildings round Cloister Court with its three angle towers and four garderobe turrets were erected during the next few years. The north, east, and south sides were under construction in 1443; the west side (towards School Yard) was still incomplete in 1448 when it was estimated that only £40 was necessary for making the housing closing the quadrant. The hall was in use by 1449, though the windows had not yet been glazed. Towards the end of Henry's reign, the Cloister Court is alluded to as a completed building, so presumably the west range had been built by then. At the peak of construction nearly 150 workmen had been employed.[5]

In 1448, all work on the chapel ceased in favour of the king's more ambitious scheme. The present structure was initiated and progressed slowly during the next twelve years, with the east window erected by 1460. But the nave and aisles for parish use were never built, nor were any of the original collegiate buildings pulled down to make way for the more grandiose elements of Henry's 1449 scheme. Even so, most of the college had been erected within the first ten years of its foundation. It was only because of Henry VI's subsequent plans for the chapel that the whole project was not completed before his deposition in 1461.

After Edward IV decided against annexing the college to St George's at Windsor, work restarted with the chapel, roofed in wood rather than stone between 1469 and 1475. Plans for the nave were abandoned and the west end was completed by a much more modest ante-chapel on the Oxford model between 1479 and 1482 by bishop Waynflete, Henry's executor and now patron of the building. The paintings in the chapel, also financed by Waynflete, were executed between 1477 and 1487 in place of the stall canopies originally proposed.

Provost Lupton (1504–35) made a number of modifications. He altered the kitchen in 1507, added a side chapel in 1515, refenestrated Lower School, and rebuilt the range separating the two courts in 1517–20, marking this activity with the imposing gateway that bears his name.

No further work was undertaken until School Yard was enclosed on the street side by Upper School in 1670, rebuilt in 1694.[6] The brewhouse was added in 1714, and a new wing for the provost was erected north of Cloister Court in 1765–6.[7]

SCHOOL YARD

Henry VI's intention that his foundation should be primarily a religious rather than an educational foundation has determined the form of the first and larger of the two courts. The entrance to School Yard from the street is markedly undemonstrative compared with contemporary colleges at Oxford or Cambridge. It is through an arch in the middle of the west range or Upper School. The high wall with centrally positioned wooden gates which originally closed the court was replaced in c.1670 by a two-storeyed range, rebuilt in a similar style in 1689–94.

Seventy boys had been admitted by 1447. To teach them there was a *magister informator*, still the formal title of the headmaster. They were taught and housed in the originally detached brick range filling the north side of School Yard. The boys were taught in a single ground-floor schoolroom (Lower School) and slept in the large single dormitory above (Long Chamber). The headmaster worked and slept at the street end, while the master in college (originally the usher), was accommodated at the other end.

The two façades of the two-storeyed battlemented school range are quite different. That facing School Yard is a long flat frontage running the length of the quadrangle. It is broken only at ground level by irregularly positioned doors and occasional two-light windows with hood moulds, but with a larger number of windows, more regularly spaced, lighting the first-floor dormitory. The façade is plain as befitted its purpose.[8] There is evidence that the school was originally designed with a cloister-walk facing School Yard. A course of lead is visible in a set-back just below the first-floor window sills, and in 1876 the foundations of a brick wall were discovered 10 feet from the outer wall. Whether it was the first element of a cloister-walk or simply a pentice giving protection to scholars and fellows between Cloister Court and School Yard is not clear. It seems to have been removed in 1504 by provost Lupton who was also responsible for altering many of the existing windows in Lower School.[9]

The north façade towards Weston's Yard is much more varied. It is built on a stone base, is buttressed, and has a stone string course marking the two floors (as against a brick rebate in School Yard). It is broken by two projecting stair turrets of three storeys, with a third diagonally at the west end for the headmaster. The ground floor is filled with close-set windows, much larger than those on the opposite side. They are still of two lights, but transomed and with sills closer to the ground. There is considerable evidence of diapered brickwork.

Internally, the rooms have been modified. Lower School was divided by two rows of posts in c.1630, but is still used for teaching purposes. Long Chamber, 172 feet by 27 feet, originally extended almost the length of the range. It served as the dormitory for all seventy scholars until 1716 when the number was reduced to fifty-two.[10] In 1967, Long Chamber was gutted and a new interior inserted in the old shell to provide individual rooms for the senior members of the seventy king's scholars.

The chapel, totally built of stone, is the revised version initiated in 1449 and developed until 1461. It was designed to be a pilgrimage centre as much as a collegiate church, with fourteen services a day, and a flock of pilgrims attracted each August by the indulgences and relics given by Henry before his dethronement. The building is entirely out of proportion with the remainder of the college, and would have been even more so had the original intention of the founder been carried out. It was erected on a site artificially raised by 13 feet to avoid flooding from the Thames, and it is possible that this (as much as royal dithering) was the cause of the abandonment of the initial work in 1448. Henry also took the opportunity to

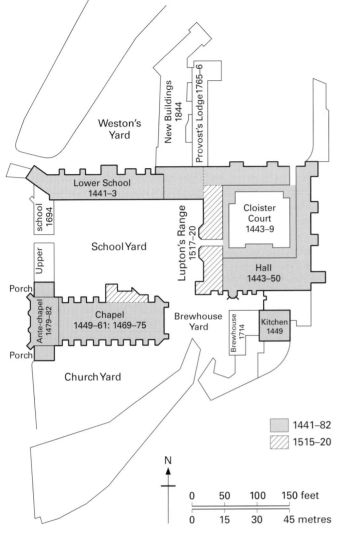

FIGURE 14 Eton College: site plan

ings below. Until the refashioning of the chapel in 1699, Waynflete's pulpitum separating the collegiate body from the parish church stood half-way down the building.[12] The form of the original roof is not known, though medieval timbers, panels, and beams were found when the 1670 roof was replaced in 1957 by the present stone fan vault hung from steel trusses.

The monochrome paintings in the former parish half of the chapel took ten years from 1477 to 1487.[13] Although the names of two of the painters are known, Gilbert (1485–6) and William Baker (1486–7) who were clearly English, the style of the paintings seems more Flemish than English. Extending for nearly 70 feet and filling both walls to the window sill moulding, the paintings were in two tiers, each 6 feet high, separated by a 2 foot border. Each tier was divided into eight panels containing scenes separated by prophets in niches in the upper tier and saints in the lower. Unfortunately, the upper tier has been virtually destroyed, mainly in 1847 when they were scraped off except for a small section on the south side. The scheme was apparently designed to give the impression of aisles on either side once it was recognised that Henry VI's original plans had been abandoned. Hence, the division of the individual scenes by pillars, and the use of perspective and depth, a characteristic particularly obvious on the north side. The paintings on the north side depict miracles of the Virgin Mary in a series of individual scenes with a few figures in generous settings. The less satisfactory south side relates a popular medieval story about a mythical empress in a continuous narrative crowded with figures. From a historical point of view, they are also important for illustrating contemporary costume, and a contemporary bedroom (north side).

The paintings use linseed oil applied directly to the stonework, for although the walls were originally intended to be plastered this was not done. The paintings are in grisaille with touches of colour, and give the effect of an unbroken source of light from the west. Different designers worked on the north and south sides with several artists working on each, while Andrew Martindale has suggested that a pause may have occurred between the north wall (c.1480) and the south wall (c.1486) arising from the shortage of funds, and explaining the change in style.[14] These paintings are the finest examples of fifteenth-century work to survive in England and because of their scale they are without peer outside Italy. Those at Winchester are similar in subject but later in date and inferior in quality. Whether the work was under the direction of a Flemish master, or by an Englishman who had first-hand knowledge of contemporary Flemish art, has not yet been determined.

The east side of School Yard is filled with Lupton's range and gateway, built by Henry Redman between 1517 and 1520 after working at Hampton Court. The dominating four-storeyed gateway with its commanding stone oriel (and lead cupolas of 1776) must have replaced a simpler entry linking the two courts. Redman continued the use of brick, and designed elements which had not substantially changed in seventy years. The principal first-floor chamber over the vaulted passage (election chamber) was probably intended to be Lupton's withdrawing chamber, associated with his rooms to the right. These terminate in the three-storeyed rectangular sluice tower in front of the hall. The sluice in the basement regulated the flow of water into the sewers running under the main buildings. The range to the left with its paired windows of the first-floor library has been rebuilt, except for that part facing Cloister Court.

ensure that the rebuilding was without any of the fussy mouldings of which he disapproved. This was a further reason for pulling the first structure down, for the present arch surmounting the east window is made up of earlier work with mouldings on the inner face in a more elaborate style than elsewhere in the present building.[11]

The chapel was built as a free-standing structure, and remained so until Upper School was built in 1670. The nave that was planned and never built was replaced by an ante-chapel in 1476–83, paid for by Waynflete at the same time that he was building a similar structure under the same mason, William Orchard, at Magdalen College, Oxford. The ante-chapel has a single window at either end above the porches, and three five-light windows towards the street. Henry VI's eight chapel bays are filled with tall five-light transomed windows above a span of blank walling, separated by deep-stepped buttresses. The nine-light east window is flanked by polygonal turrets at the corners of the building. Internally, the wall shafts in the eastern half of the chapel reach to the ground, whereas those in the western half cease at the window sill to allow for the wall paint-

CLOISTER COURT

Three of the ranges round this relatively small court, constructed between 1443 and 1449, were brick-built with stone dressings, and were originally two-storeyed. The hall on the fourth side was stone-built. As the court accommodated the provost, fellows, and conducts of the college, the standard of accommodation was substantially higher than for the boys in School Yard, with separate lodgings, stair turrets, corridors, and garderobe turrets. Subsequent modifications include Lupton's partially rebuilt west range, the second storey added to the north and east ranges for additional accommodation in 1759–62, and the cloister arcade and gallery built in classical form in front of the hall in 1725–9 to create a wider corridor supporting a new college library above. Nevertheless, the original design is clear.

The ground floor has an open arcade of six stone arches with continuous moulding on each side. The arches are separated by buttresses rising to the original battlement level (as on the west range). The buttresses terminate abruptly and Loggan's engraving of 1685 shows this form on the east side before the further storey was added. The lodging entries are in pairs round three sides of the cloister, with adjacent pairs of windows. The door heads terminate in diamond stops.

In each angle is a narrow projecting stair turret giving access to the first floor. This was corridor-lined on three sides, including one on the site of the early eighteenth-century library. Whether Lupton destroyed a corridor on the fourth side when he built his early sixteenth-century library is not known. Each corridor bay was filled with a four-light straight-headed window, again of simple design. The pattern is varied on the west side where Lupton inserted paired windows to light his library. Individual lodgings opened from the corridor. There are two former garderobe towers in the outer face on the east and north sides respectively. These three-storeyed

PLATE 38 Eton College: Cloister Court

façades facing the provost's and fellows' gardens respectively are now filled with Georgian sashed windows.[15]

The west range was altered by provost Lupton, beginning with some demolition work in 1516. The angle turrets and the cloister arcade and brickwork up to the sills of the first-floor windows were retained, including the part that became Lupton's Gateway with large windows rather than an oriel. The upper floor was rebuilt as a library with roundels of stained glass in the top of the twelve windows identifying the subject matter of the books in the adjacent bays. One of the western windows has the date 1524. The library, of course, was for the use of the fellows and had nothing to do with the boys. The first library seems to have been in the eastern cloister in 1445 but was moved from there by the close of the century to the vestry. The books only stayed for twenty-five years in Lupton's new library, for in 1547 the room was taken over by the provost as his dining room. The screen is attributed to that year, though the roof was apparently reconstructed in 1691.

The raised hall can be best appreciated from Brewhouse Yard, where the buttressed ragstone façade, surmounted by eighteenth-century brickwork above the line of windows (1728), is broken by the traceried bay window at the upper end. This side also shows that the hall was not finished in accordance with the original design of 1443. The stonework terminated below its intended height, the buttresses were cut short, the windows were truncated and finished in brick, while the oriel window is arched with timber internally whereas stone was clearly intended. The reasons for this by 1450, ten years before Henry's deposition, are not known but it may have been to avoid unnecessary expenditure through demolition and rebuilding, or possibly the need to concentrate all available funds and workmen on the urgent task of rebuilding the chapel.[16]

Because of flooding from the nearby River Thames, the hall was raised above an undercroft 12 feet high. It was originally ceiled with wood, but this was replaced with brick vaulting in 1690. The hall is reached by a wide flight of steps, much damaged in 1691, leading to the screens passage with the usual three doors. The hall was where the priests, headmaster, and scholars dined each day. Apart from the stone-panelled bay window and the highly unusual number of three fireplaces (none had a chimney when discovered in 1858 and they had been supplanted by a louvre), the interior essentially dates from 1858 – panelling, dais, stained glass, floor tiles, and screen – with a replacement roof in 1970.

The offices include a buttery, with its hatch still in use, a door now leading to the screens gallery, and a third door to a flight of stairs linking the hall with the ground-floor kitchen. The detached kitchen was under construction in 1449, and in 1451 the clerk of works went to Kent to choose paving for the floor.[17] The present octagonal roof and lantern were rebuilt by Lupton in 1507.[18] The kitchen was built above arches under which a brook formerly flowed, diverted from the main channel under the sluice tower. The kitchen is square in plan, with the upper octagonal part terminating in a lantern. Part of the lower walls (south-west) are of stone, but brick was used elsewhere (north-west and north). Two sides are filled with hearths with gigantic relieving arches. The centre of the room is filled with stoves, stainless steel tables, and the paraphernalia of modern cooking facilities, for the room is still in daily use.

The irregular back yard, Brewhouse Yard, gives the best view of the hall, and access to its undercroft. The brewhouse was erected in 1714. Both areas are now used for exhibitions.[19]

PLATE 39 Eton College, Cloister Court: first-floor east corridor showing fifteenth-century work (1966)

OVERVIEW

Eton College lies in the same relation to Windsor Castle as Lord Cromwell's foundation does to Tattershall Castle or the duke of York's establishment to Fotheringhay Castle. Eton College was built of brick, except for the chapel, hall, and part of the kitchen which were in stone. Robert Westerley, the king's master-mason, was in charge until 1448 when he was succeeded by John Smyth until 1453 followed by Simon Clerk up to 1461. Robert Whetely was the chief carpenter throughout the college's development.[20] The college is profoundly important for domestic studies because it gave a further royal *imprimatur* to the use of brick as a fashionable building material. Henry V had used it at Sheen (1414–22), work concluded by the king's council for the young Henry VI (1429–39), but Henry's own use of this material made it acceptable for buildings of more profound intent – educational and religious establishments – as well as domestic residences. It immediately influenced the development of contemporary buildings as diverse as Queens' College, Cambridge, Herstmonceux Castle, Ewelme almshouse and school, and Ockwells Manor. Furthermore, John Goodall has pointed out that the college buildings introduced diaper patterning, with a variety of designs including those of

diamond and cross form, possibly through employing foreign craftsmen.[21] The combination of brick and stone exploited in Cloister Court demonstrated the aesthetic harmony of these two materials. Though brick was capable of being highly decorative, as the Rye House gatehouse amply demonstrates (1443), the windows at Eton are of uncusped form. They are among the earliest examples in the country of a type which quickly became popular, as at Caister Castle (1432–45), Queens' College, Cambridge (1448–9), and particularly Tattershall church (1475–82) built for bishop Waynflete by John Cooper who had served his apprenticeship at Eton during the 1440s.

The layout of Cloister Court is exactly as in a major secular residence. It displays differentiated accommodation standards as well as a hall and kitchen that retain their original character and function to the present day. Moreover, the Court can be closely paralleled with that at Herstmonceux Castle (*c*.1438–49). It mirrored Eton's embattled parapet and small towers projecting above the rear of the ranges, as well as the cloister-walk with glazed gallery above. This raises the question as to which was the precursor with the possibility that this lay with the castle. On a broader field, the construction of the college also spurred the building activities of several of the king's ministers and court favourites involved in the organisation and administration of the foundation, including Thomas Beckington, Henry VI's secretary who was created bishop of Bath and Wells in the college (1443), William Alnwick, bishop of Lincoln who was the first Visitor to the colleges at Eton and King's, William Waynflete, the second provost until appointed bishop of Winchester, and William earl of Suffolk who superintended the work on the king's behalf. Through them and their association with the development of Eton, the college exerted a powerful influence on the mainstream of English domestic architecture for the next two or three generations.

NOTES

1 J. Saltmarsh, *King Henry VI and The Royal Foundations* (1972); K. Selway, 'The role of Eton College and King's College in the polity of the Lancastrian monarchy', DPhil, University of Oxford (1993).

2 Plans of the proposed and built structures are given in *HKW*, I (1963) 286. For a summary of the problems, Goodall (2002) 252. For the projected extent of this further enlargement, see the plaque in Keate's Lane opposite the west end of the ante-chapel.

3 Goodall (2002), 252–3.

4 The fragment of a plan closely related to this grandiose project was discovered in 1989, Society of Antiquaries, London, MS 252. It seems to be a draft proposal for the royal design, datable to the late 1440s and therefore the earliest known English architectural drawing, J. Goodall, *Country Life* (15 November 2001).

5 Willis and Clark (1886) 380–441; *HKW*, I (1963) 283; Knoop and Jones (1937) 77.

6 For an early view of the college, little altered since its construction, see David Loggan's engraving of 1685 in his *Cantabrigia Illustrata*.

7 On the renovation of these and the other buildings, J. D. R. McConnel, *Eton Repointed: The New Structures of an Ancient Foundation* (1970).

8 The oriel window at the east end is a nineteenth-century addition.

9 Hussey (1940) 4–5; Goodall (2002) 254.

10 Mid-sixteenth-century records show that two or three scholars slept in a bed.

11 H. M. Colvin, *Rec. of Bucks.* 17 pt 2 (1962) 105–6. For a representation of mass being celebrated in the unfinished chapel, see the almost contemporary drawing in Higden's *Polychronicon*, Eton College Library.

12 Martindale (1971) 189–93.

13 M. R. James and E. W. Tristram, 'The wall-paintings in Eton College Chapel and in the Lady Chapel of Winchester Cathedral', *Walpole Society* 17 (1928–9) 1–43; A. Martindale in *England and the Low Countries in the Late Middle Ages*, ed. C. Barron and N. Saul (1995) 133–52 where the previous starting date of *c*.1478–9 is amended.

14 Martindale, *England and the Low Countries* 148–9.

15 The rooms round Cloister Court are occupied today by the provost, vice-provost, headmaster, bursar, and administrative offices of the school.

16 Goodall (2002) 252–3. Henry's 'will' also specified that the hall should have a second bay window on the north side of the dais and an entry porch with a tower over it.

17 Hussey (1940) 34.

18 *Ibid*.

19 For essays on the silver, manuscripts, books, tapestries, furniture, etc. held by the college, *Treasures of Eton*, ed. J. McConnell (1976).

20 J. Harvey, *Eng. Med. Arch.* (1984) 331, 277, 56, 331. For building materials and organisation *HKW*, I (1963) 280–4.

21 Goodall (2002) 254–6.

R. Willis and J. W. Clark, *The Architectural History of the University of Cambridge and the Colleges of Cambridge and Eton* (1886)

H. C. Maxwell Lyte, *A History of Eton College* (1889, 4th edn 1911)

RCHM, *Buckinghamshire*, I (1912) 142–51

C. Hussey, *Eton College* (1922, 3rd edn 1940, rev. edn 1952)

D. Knoop and G. P. Jones, 'The building of Eton College 1442–1460', *Ars Quatuor Coronatorum* 46 (1937) 70–114

H. M. Colvin *et al.* (eds.), *History of the King's Works*, I (1963) 279–92

A. H. R. Martindale, 'The early history of the choir of Eton College Chapel', *Archaeologia* 103 (1971) 179–98

J. A. A. Goodall, 'Henry VI's court and the construction of Eton College', in *Windsor: Medieval Archaeology, Art and Architecture in the Thames Valley*, ed. L. Keen and E. Scarff (2002) 247–63

EWELME MANOR, Oxfordshire

The mid-fifteenth-century church, almshouse, and school tiered above the stream that runs through the village of Ewelme present one of the most striking and attractive compositions in Oxfordshire. They are also a splendid memorial to the duke and duchess of Suffolk, whereas their manor house to the south-west has been reduced to an isolated Georgian-looking brick house set back from the village street. Standing next to open fields, it looks for all the world like a small early nineteenth-century farmhouse, two-storeyed with a central porch and large sash windows. Only the angle buttresses at one end hint at its earlier origins. It is one third of a lodging range of the manor, fortunately drawn by Samuel Buck in 1729 before its partial destruction, depicting its early form and character. This is supplemented by a drawing of 1821 by J. C. Buckler illustrating the range reduced in size but before the late Georgian make-over that it displays today.[1]

This 150 foot long range was a two-storeyed structure made up of a series of independent rooms at each level, each with its own entry door, window, and rear-wall fireplace. The upper rooms were reached from a gallery marked in Buck's engraving by the line of sockets for the floor and roof joists. The first of the pair of doors at the east end was for the stairs to the gallery, and there was a change in internal plan at the west end, marked by a larger ground-floor entry with a superior window above and another in the end wall. It is this end of the range with its different planning pattern that forms the basis of the present residence.[2]

The house frontage 50 feet long and side walls 20 feet deep are basically the same as those shown by Buck, with the core of brick walling in common, the stepped buttresses, and the steep pitch of the roof. Some further features can be made out in the brickwork, including the outline of the window above the large entry door (which has been completely brick infilled), and the position of the first-floor end window. It is also possible to identify the position of some of the upper entry doors with a little imagination. The east end of the range is marked in the garden by a single line of bricks.

Internally, the two floors of the house are entirely late Georgian in layout, but the original roof survives in the attic in first-class condition. The five and a half bays are divided by a partition separating the first three from the remainder. Each of these 8 foot wide bays is divided by a braced collar truss with upper collar, enhanced by two lines of sharply curved wind braces, unusually built in pairs to spring from intermediate couples as well as the main truss. All members are hollow chamfered to enhance a sturdy but pleasing structure of clearly superior form. The remaining two and a half bays are more simple, with only a single line of more gently arched wind braces, one pair per bay. The last one was truncated by a brick wall when the remainder of the range was pulled down.

Leland's record of Ewelme Manor in 1542 was that 'the base court of it is fair, and is buildid of brike and tymbre. The inner part of the house is sette with in a fair mote, and is buildid richely of brike and stone. The haul of it is fair and hath great barres of iren overthurt it instead of crosse beames. The parler by is exceeding fair and lightsum: and so be al the lodginges there. The commune saying is that Duk John made about the beginning of King Henry the vij. tymes most of the goodly buildinges withyn the mote.'[3]

Bringing the existing illustrative and documentary evidence together, it looks as though the range with its stepped gables at both ends was a freestanding structure within the base court. However, the lack of buttresses at the east end suggests that it adjoined the two-storey brick gatehouse range, described in the valuation of 1612, and was the range of brick building 'where in the Honour Court is monethlie kept'.[4] Buck shows a watercourse beyond the right-hand end of the range, probably part of the moat which has disappeared at this point. The ground floor consisted of six identical self-contained chambers of two-bay form, 17 feet by 16 internally, with a narrow stair lobby at the east end and a two-bay hall at the opposite end. The upper floor was made up of five identical chambers, gallery entered, with a single bay giving access to the end hall of narrower bays but larger windows. This end hall and lobby were the equivalent in size to two lodgings, with the otherwise dark lobby possibly lit from the rear.[5] All upper rooms were open to the roof but their superior status is also marked by windows with two-centred heads rather than the square form below, and the larger windows in the end hall with its more decorative roof. The hexagonal turret shown by Buck to the rear of the north-east buttress is in the apposite position for a garderobe projection serving both halls, though its shape is unusual for such a purpose. The scale of the lower hall doorway suggests it may have opened into a through passage, but this rear projection would have prevented this. In all, the range consisted of eleven individual lodgings and two halls, all heated,[6]

PLATE 40 Ewelme Manor: engraving from the south-east by S. and N. Buck (1729)

with the 5 foot wide gallery shed-roofed and column supported to give the two-storey appearance described in the 1612 inventory.[7]

The parallel with the west lodging range at Dartington Hall (c.1390–1400) is immediate, repeating the two-storey line of chambers and halls. The Devon lodgings were rather larger, following the door, window, and rear fireplace pattern but with bigger windows. While the gallery approach to the upper rooms at Ewelme might be considered a planning improvement to the individual staircases at Dartington, the lack of individual garderobe facilities was certainly not. In both cases, occupation by senior household staff or possibly guests is most likely.

The manor of Ewelme had been held by Sir John Burghersh (d.1391) before it passed to his younger daughter, Maud, who had married Thomas Chaucer, aspiring courtier and son of the poet Geoffrey Chaucer. His marriage as well as his career can only be explained if he had the personal support of the king. He had probably served under John of Gaunt, and was constable of Wallingford Castle in 1399, chief butler (1402–13), seven times member of parliament, and speaker of the House of Commons in 1414. Chaucer was a wealthy wool merchant and royal councillor (1423) who consolidated his standing in the region by arranging the marriage of his daughter Alice to the earl of Salisbury (1424), and on the earl's death four years later at the siege of Orléans, this ennobled widow made an equal match with William de la Pole, earl of Suffolk (1430). 'For love of her and the commodite of her landes, [the earl] fell much to dwelle yn Oxfordshir and Barkshir wher his wifes landes lay'.[8] Providing a centre for cultured company, William and Alice were responsible for rebuilding the church, establishing the almshouse, and founding the school, and 'translatid and encreasid the manor place of Ewelme'.[9] Sir Thomas Chaucer probably initiated the rebuilding of the church before his death in 1435, with its further development coinciding with Suffolk's rise to all-powerful political leadership. Created duke of Suffolk in 1448, his increasing unpopularity came to a head in a

wave of hatred and his murder at sea (1450). Ewelme Manor was forfeited to the crown after the execution of John, duke of Suffolk in 1513, but despite occasional royal occupation, the house was in ruin by 1612 and became a much-used source for building material thereafter.[10]

It has been suggested that the range was part of William and Alice's improvements to the estate after 1430[11] and, more particularly, in the years after 1444 onwards when William was made a marquis.[12] There is little doubt that a substantial house had existed here since Thomas Chaucer's time and probably well before. Though it is likely that the property was enhanced by William and Alice, it is pushing the modest evidence too far to claim total rebuilding.[13] Enhancement and refurbishing to create awe-inspiring interiors was certainly commensurate with their position and ambition. Though the lack of window cusping has parallels with projects such as the Cloister Court at Eton College (1440s), the use of two-centred heads and hoods moulds throughout the range (except for the ground-floor windows) compared with the more pronounced four-centred form and rectangular hoods for the smaller windows in their firmly accredited almshouse buildings of 1437–42[14] may indicate that the range was a development of the previous generation. This is not at variance with Thomas Chaucer's own high standing, with construction possible during the 1420s commensurate with the enhancement of his own household. It would make the lodgings an early example of brickwork in the region, though the material had already been used in large quantities in 1416–17 at Stonor Park nearby. Until resolved by dendrochronology, attribution of this intriguing range rests between the years from c.1420 to c.1450.

The church, almshouse, and school were not conceived as a unified scheme but developed over a period of twenty years to cover the spiritual, educational, and ageing needs of the manor where Alice Chaucer was born (c.1404) and lived with her second husband. This outstanding group of buildings is linked physically

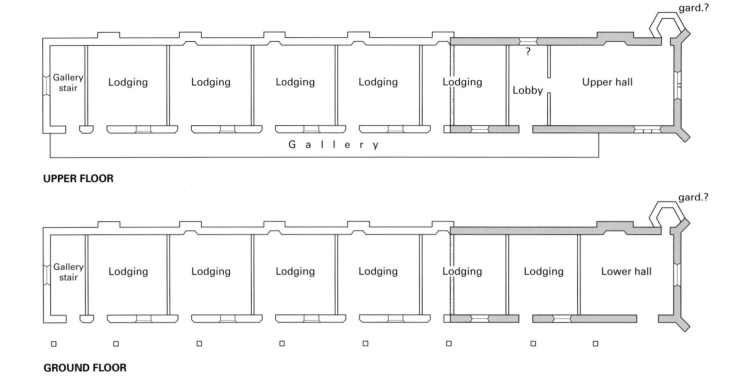

UPPER FLOOR

GROUND FLOOR

FIGURE 15 Ewelme Manor: lodging range, floor plans

and metaphorically on the valley slope to form a magnificent display of mid-fifteenth-century benevolence and architectural unity which was formerly matched by the spectacular mansion of this family. The standing buildings were developed in sequence, beginning with the expansion of the church before 1435 followed by William and Alice's remodelling and embellishment of it between 1437 and 1450. The almshouse was licensed and initiated in 1437 and probably completed by about 1442, followed by the school, which was functioning before 1455.

The almshouse statutes of 1448–50 provided for thirteen men under the care of two resident priests, the master, and the grammar school teacher. The structure is of flint and brick externally, and timber-framed with brick noggin towards the central court. Leaving the manor house range to one side, the use of brick here was probably a consequence of the earl of Suffolk's origins in Hull, the early centre of brick manufacture in this country; brick was used at this time at Eton College where the earl was an overseer and patron. More importantly, this almshouse exhibits an innovatory plan. In a complete break with the tradition of a large dormitory, separate dwellings were provided for the inmates round a small quadrangle. The plan is reminiscent of Carthusian practice such as the charterhouse founded by the earl of Suffolk's grandfather at Hull in 1370, but it equally reflects the growing practice of individual lodgings in corporate buildings such as secular colleges of priests, and more pertinently, household lodgings such as those at the manor house nearby.

The principal entrance is through a tall, diagonally buttressed porch on the north side with stepped brick gable head, enhanced with an inset arch with blind trefoiled tracery. There is a second approach on the east side where a covered passage from the church leads down steps to the almshouse at a lower level. Both approaches bring visitors to the small court with a lean-to arcade with decorative gabled entry in the middle of each walk.[15] Each lodging consisted of a single room with fireplace, but the higher level towards the church enabled the east side to be two-storeyed, with the upper floor holding the muniment room and the master's lodging. The common hall was on the upper floor. The short projection on the west side was a much later two-seater garderobe for the community. Mid-nineteenth-century modifications included the insertion of a stair in each lodging to the gable-lit bedroom created in the roof, the enhancement of the decorative woodwork, and the replacement of the thatched roof with tiles. The 1970 renovation created six flats in place of the thirteen lodgings and many new windows, and involved the removal of several chimney stacks.

The school, first mentioned in the statutes of 1448–50,[16] is likely to have been the last of the three buildings developed by the Suffolks. It is entirely brick-built on a flint base, has more ornate features than the almshouse, and was probably not finished until several years after the earl's murder.[17] The school is essentially a two-storeyed block with stepped angle buttresses, but advantage was taken of its position at the foot of the slope to create a striking street frontage. The principal face of mellow brickwork is interrupted by two prominent chimney breasts with tall stacks, separating several windows of two cusped lights with pierced spandrels under square hoods terminating in armorial stops. Those on the south and west sides are original; those on the east side are replacements. A lower porch projects from the north end, with contemporary traceried doors brought from the church. There is a single room at each level, linked by an altered spiral stair at the side of the porch, with the room above the entry serving the grammar master's successor. Both schoolrooms are warmed by fireplaces, with the upper room covered by an arch-braced roof of six bays with three rows of wind braces and rectangular framing in the end walls. As a design, the school is striking: to today's children, the building is 'lovely'. Between the almshouse and the school is the contemporary two-storeyed master's house, drastically expanded in Georgian times.

The relevance of the almshouse and school to domestic architecture is not peripheral. Apart from the deliberate choice of different building materials – stone, flint, and some brick for the church; flint, brick, and timber-framing for the almshouse; brick in an enhanced decorative manner for the school – the secular buildings are indicative of the growing desire for privacy at the lower social level. This ensemble stands virtually unaltered, still serves its original purpose, and above all is a rare example of mid-fifteenth-century charitable and educational patronage that was all too often destroyed by the Reformation to give us a distorted picture of late medieval England.

NOTES

1 Brit. Lib., Add. MS 36373 f.21.
2 The kitchen wing to the rear, not shown in Buckler's drawing, was presumably added when the house was remodelled in c.1830.
3 *Itinerary*, I, 113.
4 The survey of the manor made by John Thorpe and Richard Stevens estimating the value of the property for the Exchequer in 1612 itemised the base-court ranges. The principal house was organised round an inner courtyard with named rooms. Inventory transcribed by Goodall (2001) 293–5.
5 The roof structure makes the existence of this division clear.
6 To be precise, Buck shows that the first upper chamber had a louvre, but all the other twelve rooms had chimneys which are carefully depicted in his engraving.
7 *HKW*, II pt 2 (1982) 91–2; Goodall (2001) 294.
8 *Itinerary*, I, 112; E. A. Greening Lamborn, *Oxoniensia* 5 (1940) 78–93.
9 *Itinerary*, I, 112. Also N. Wilkins in *English Court Culture in the Later Middle Ages*, ed. J. V. Scattergood and J. W. Sherborne (1983) 198.
10 Goodall (2001) 293–5; *HKW*, IV, pt 2 (1982) 92.
11 Airs (1978) 280. The plan on page 277 is at variance with the text.
12 Goodall (2001) 12–13.
13 *Ibid*., 18–20.
14 The two-centred brick form of the almshouse porch entry (1445–50) is quite different with its inset trefoil cusping, forming a composition markedly Flemish in character. Goodall (2001) 99–100.
15 The arcaded walk and decorative gable heads should be compared with those at Ockwells Manor (c.1455–65).
16 The statutes refer to the duty of the schoolmaster 'to teche and informe Chylder in the faculte of gramer'.
17 Goodall (2001) 28–31.

M. Airs, *Arch. Jour.* 135 (1978) 276–80
J. A. A. Goodall, *God's House at Ewelme* (2001)

FORTHAMPTON COURT, Gloucestershire

Forthampton Court was a major country house of the abbots of Tewkesbury who owned the manor from the early twelfth to the mid-sixteenth century. In 1541, it was given to the last abbot, John Wakeham (d.1549), who was appointed the first bishop of Gloucester. The property was subsequently held by the crown and was granted to Robert Cecil at the beginning of the early seventeenth century. It passed through a sequence of families until it came to the Yorkes in 1762.

The Court is a rambling multi-period house, which makes it difficult to disentangle the late medieval core from the substantial additions of 1647, and of 1788 by Anthony Keck, and the individual but sympathetic work of 1889–92 by Philip Webb. The hall and first-floor chapel are immediately obvious, but it is possible to identify further medieval work by tracing the lower courses of freestone walling with its angle buttresses, and to use early nineteenth-century house plans to identify internal walls of similar thickness. This reveals a substantial two-storeyed block linked by the chapel to a corner of the hall with a short timber-framed wing to the north-west.

The plan is unorthodox. It consisted of the hall with its upper end close to the present entrance lobby of 1958–60. A door at this end would lead to a staircase, approximately on the site of the present open one of 1891 by Philip Webb, leading to the upper floor of the residential block containing the private apartments of the abbot.[1] The three chambers beyond the chapel may well have been his great chamber (with projecting inner room) and privy chamber. The block at the lower end of the hall is contemporary and was presumably used for services.

The hall has been subject to so many alterations that it conveys the form rather than the detail of a medieval apartment. It was used

PLATE 41 Forthampton Court: hall interior

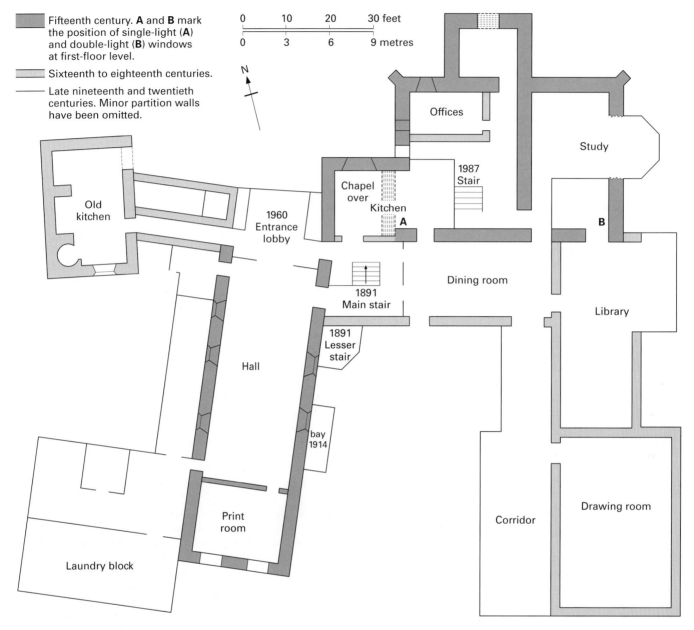

Fifteenth century. **A** and **B** mark the position of single-light (**A**) and double-light (**B**) windows at first-floor level.

Sixteenth to eighteenth centuries.

Late nineteenth and twentieth centuries. Minor partition walls have been omitted.

0   10   20   30 feet
0   3   6   9 metres

N

Old kitchen

1960 Entrance lobby

Chapel over Kitchen

Offices

1987 Stair

Study

A

B

Dining room

Library

1891 Main stair

1891 Lesser stair

Hall

bay 1914

Print room

Laundry block

Corridor

Drawing room

FIGURE 16 Forthampton Court: ground plan

as a barn in the seventeenth century, divided into two floors and many rooms in the eighteenth century, with roof repaired by Webb in 1889, and the whole drastically restored by Maurice Chesterton in 1913. Only the roof clearly betrays its medieval origin. The room lacks any original entrances, windows, or fireplace. The upper end wall has been removed, the walls are badly patched, and the approach to the private apartments has been destroyed.

The hall, 53½ feet by 21 feet, would have been windowed on both sides originally. According to an early nineteenth-century plan, there were at least three windows on the north and two on the south, but only the jambs of one window and its glass rebate survive and that is at the upper end of the hall at a curious half-level. What was its purpose, and why was it built above a ground-floor projection

almost totally removed in 1914? There is no architectural evidence for the bay window created by Chesterton in that same year which was necessary to provide light in an otherwise over-dark apartment. The fireplace built by Philip Webb in 1891 was based on evidence of fragments of moulding found in situ, now kept in the study.

The hall is divided into five bays. The roof is spanned by arch-braced collar beams, formerly supported on corbels which have been destroyed except for one, conventionally decorated with a shield-holding angel. Moulded wall plates, double purlins, and two tiers of wind braces survive while the two horizontal timbers in the central bay may indicate a smoke outlet, subsequently replaced by the fireplace.

The wall at the lower end of the hall is too thin to have been an external one and there is little doubt that the studding is original. However, this end has been subject to fire at some time which not only affected the wall (substantially repaired in 1914) but also severely damaged the lower-end block (now the print room). Its walls are of the same thickness as the hall and probably represent original work, perhaps the buttery and pantry. It is likely that the entrance to the screens would have been on the site of the bay window, with the principal entrance opposite for the house was initially approached from the west, not the north as at present.

The approach to the upper residential block has been destroyed and there are no original ground-floor features except a doorframe and fireplace. On the first-floor, two blocked windows survive serving the two principal rooms. They are of one and two lights, marked A and B on the plan. Rather surprisingly, the first-floor chapel in the angle between this block and the hall survives complete: 16 feet long, it is lit by two windows with traceried heads, the larger of three lights in the east wall and the second of two lights facing north. Neither the entrance wall, altar, piscina, nor aumbrey remains. The roof of two bays is a modest version of that above the hall but with a single line of ogee wind braces.[2]

The present kitchen, built in the mid-sixteenth century, lies at the opposite end of the hall to the original one. Originally detached, it has been encased in brick, but retains its original hearth in the north wall.[3]

In the absence of any documentation, dating depends entirely on the architectural evidence. The occurrence of four-centred forms in the hall window, and roof braces, suggests the fifteenth rather than the fourteenth century. The chapel windows are no later than the middle of the century while the trefoil lights and vertical bars in the heads suggest early in the century. In that case, Forthampton was probably built for abbot Thomas Parker (1389–1421) or William Bristow (1421–42).

The size of the great hall calls for further comment. Assuming that the present proportions are the original ones, it was a particularly large apartment for an abbot's country house. Because Tewkesbury Abbey was only 2 miles away, the house was probably used for entertaining and therefore intended to vie with comparable episcopal halls. But the apartment is curiously narrow for its length. Nearly all halls in the later fourteenth and early fifteenth centuries were more than 30 feet wide. Yet that at Forthampton was only 21 feet wide. Was it formerly of three-bay length instead of five, with the upper two bays separated from the hall by a destroyed wall to form a withdrawing chamber? Even the roof timbers here were so heavily restored by Webb in 1891 that any confirmatory evidence has been eradicated.

Forthampton is an excellent example of a house irregularly extended and developed throughout its history. Yet it is also one with a particularly warm personality, helped considerably by the additions of Philip Webb, the modifications of the twentieth century, and the broad-ranging collection of the Yorke family.

NOTES
1 VCH, VIII (1968) 202 suggests that the timber-framed building to the north-west is likely to have contained the principal apartments. However, this part of the Court is probably sixteenth century. The VCH also suggests that the buttressed block opening from the chapel was an early sixteenth-century addition.
2 The very fine panel painting here of c.1370 of Edward the Confessor and St John the Baptist is believed never to have left the house since its incep-

tion or the abbey's dissolution. This helps to explain its remarkably fresh condition. E. W. Tristram, *Burlington Magazine* 83 (1943) 160–5; J. Alexander and P. Binski (eds.), *Age of Chivalry Catalogue* (1987) 214–15.
3 After he was appointed first bishop of Gloucester, John Wakeham made improvements to the house, apparently with stone taken from demolishing Tewkesbury's lady chapel. Hence the stumps of roof bosses in the outer walls of the residential block and the effigy of William de la Zouche (d.1335) in the house grounds.

VCH, *Gloucestershire*, VIII (1968) 199–202
C. Aslet, *Country Life* (September/October 1979)

FYFIELD MANOR, Berkshire

Fyfield Manor looks like an unhappy conjunction of two houses. The porch and abutting cross wing of a substantial fourteenth-century timber-framed house are overwhelmed by the three-storeyed Elizabethan stone block in the position of the earlier hall. The loss of the upper cross wing emphasises the disparity.

The porch is of two storeys – a stone ground floor separated by a low-pitched lip from the timber-framed upper chamber, now roughcast covered. The outer and inner two-centred entrance arches are of continuous double-wave moulding, the upper half of the inner arch enriched with ball-flower decoration.[1] The contemporary wooden window above, of two ogee lights, central quatrefoil, and blank shields in the spandrels, was inserted here from the adjacent cross wing by James Parker, the geologist son of the antiquarian John Parker, when he restored the house in 1868.[2]

The cross wing, timber-framed above a limestone rubble ground floor, stands in line with the porch and dominates it. Two conjoined arches in the centre of the cross-passage wall, again with continuous double-wave moulding, accessed the services. It is usually considered that the larger chamber, 25 feet by 17 feet, with a domestic hearth and an enlarged replacement window, was the kitchen, with the smaller room used for services. A third contemporary arch at the far end of the cross passage now opens into a passage but was formerly the approach to the first-floor chamber. This upper room, now reached from the added Victorian stair, is of three bays with a late Elizabethan fireplace and contemporary window below a fourteenth-century gable window. The three-bay roof is its principal original feature with heavy braced tie beams supporting queen posts and a single row of large cusped wind braces.

The late sixteenth-century block incorporates the lower walling of the earlier hall, 35 feet by 25 feet, when it was divided into two rooms and the walls heightened to create two further storeys and a gabled and stone-slate roof line. Two doorways at right angles to each other in the north-east angle of the ground-floor dining room indicate the long-established pattern of ground- and first-floor access to a now lost residential wing. The curved external walling suggests there was initially a spiral stair here, but the present broad doorways are of late fifteenth- or early sixteenth-century character with convex moulding and low four-centred heads.[3] They and the much finer late fifteenth-century doorway inserted in the north-west angle to an extension of the lower cross wing point to early Tudor modifications, possibly when the property was held by the four-times married Lady Katharine Gordon (d.1537).

The porch and cross-passage arches are of c.1330–40 and there is every reason for believing that the cross wing with its impressive

PLATE 42 Fyfield Manor, south front

upper chamber is contemporary. The manor of Fyfield was held by Richard Fyfield in the late twelfth century and passed to Sir John Golafre (d.1363) through his marriage to Elizabeth Fyfield in about 1335.[4] He was responsible for building the present hall and impressive service wing immediately afterwards. Golafre was also responsible for the chancel of the nearby church, rebuilt after a fire in 1893.[5] It holds a terrifying *memento mori* monument of a descendant who died in 1442. This Sir John Golafre founded a chantry in the church in 1442 and provided the money to build and maintain the chantry priest's house and almshouse for five bedesmen, completed two years after his death.

This Fyfield almshouse, a T-shaped structure, consists of a rubble-built hall, screens passage, offices, and kitchen in line, with a timber-framed parlour cross wing at the upper (west) end. The hall is open to an arch-braced roof with the tall framed window lighting its upper bay reinstated in 1963. A door in the timber-framed partition at the upper end of the hall opens to the parlour lobby and the stone newel to the solar above. A pair of doors in the partition at the lower end of the hall access the buttery and pantry, with a further screens door to the chamber over. A door from the pantry led to the kitchen beyond. The chantry priest occupied the solar, and the bedesmen the room over the services, but the almshouse now offers hospitality as the White Hart Inn.

This structure did not fundamentally differ in its layout from the manor house built by a Golafre predecessor a century earlier, except for the position of the kitchen. Yet the manor kitchen may have served as the precedent, sited beyond the pantry, opening from it (as a corner door still does), until replaced by the present late medieval three-bay extension. The kitchen may then have been transferred to the south-west extension with its smoke-blackened timbers.[6]

NOTES

1 The opposing cross-passage doorway is early Tudor, opening into a Victorian stair lobby.
2 Marcon (1919) 372. For a photograph of the house frontage before this restoration, *Berks., Bucks., and Oxon. Arch. Jour.* 23 (1917) pl. 1, opp. 110.
3 Currie (1992) 121 points out that the head of the east-facing door incorporates a two-centred head suggesting a date of *c.*1300 for this residential wing, but the evidence is too slight for such precision.
4 VCH, IV (1924) 346.
5 C. E. Keyser, *Berks., Bucks. and Oxon. Arch. Jour.* 23 (1917) 2–8, 86–8.
6 Reported by Currie (1992) 124.

A. Marcon, *Country Life* (April 1919)
VCH, *Berkshire*, IV (1924) 345–6
C. R. J. Currie, *Oxoniensia* 57 (1992) 120–4

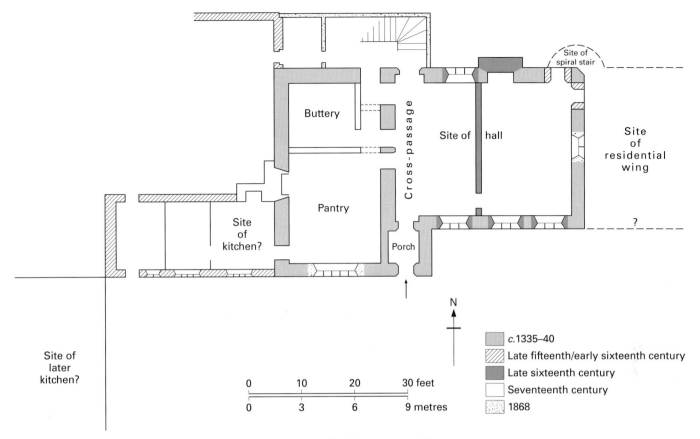

FIGURE 17 Fyfield Manor: ground plan

GLOUCESTER ABBEY and regional abbatial lodgings

The cluster of major monastic foundations in the lower Severn valley were among the wealthiest in England. Their churches survive at Tewkesbury, Gloucester, and Bristol and some of the monastic buildings at Gloucester, but Flaxley, Hailes, and Kingswood have been reduced to site fragments while Winchcombe and Cirencester lack even that benefit. Since the Bristol riots of 1831 when the bishop's palace was burnt down,[1] only Gloucester retains its early abbatial lodging. The surviving range at Tewkesbury may have served the same function as did that at Flaxley. In addition to these three lodgings, seven monastic country houses survive, though none of them of major extent outside Forthampton Court (q.v.).

Abbot John Thoky (1306–28) of Gloucester was an exemplar of the fourteenth-century practice of erecting enhanced accommodation for himself, vacating his Norman house in favour of a new and quieter site for his lodgings north of the Little Cloister. The chapel was built by abbot Horton (1351–77), the apartment was extended during the fifteenth century, while abbot Parker (1514–39) created the first-floor gallery on the north side linking the hall to the private rooms at the east end.[2] This lodging served as the bishop's palace from 1541 until damaged in 1856, when wholesale rebuilding by Ewan Christian rather than rehabilitation was the preferred option for a residence that has been occupied since 1955 by the King's

School. Only an outer wall of the medieval lodging survives, utilised for a first-floor gallery and serving as a forecourt boundary in front of Christian's house since 1861.

The abbot's Norman house was promptly taken over by the priors of Gloucester Abbey for their own use in about 1316 and extended not long afterwards. Built in line with the west front of the abbey church facing the great or outer court (now College Green), this remarkably early house was a two-part residence – a barrel-vaulted chapel of c.1130 above the abbey's outer parlour, and a taller three-storeyed block of services, camera, and upper chamber with corner garderobe projection (destroyed after 1809).[3] During the fourteenth century, the priors continued to occupy this Norman towered residence but removed whatever building lay to the north-west to erect a two-storeyed block at right angles, linked to the earlier house by a stair turret at their junction. The Norman work is ashlar-faced; the fourteenth-century extension has been rock-faced since its mid-Victorian restoration by Thomas Fulljames.

The early form of this fourteenth-century extension is unclear. It may have begun life as a first-floor hall open to the roof above a ground-floor room, 18 inches lower than today.[4] During the fifteenth century, the upper floor was partitioned into two chambers. The earlier roof was hidden when the south (Laud) chamber was ceiled and panelled in c.1600 but the original trusses survive, terminating in corbel-supported hexagonal shafts with moulded capitals and bases and braced ends poking below the ceiling. The visible

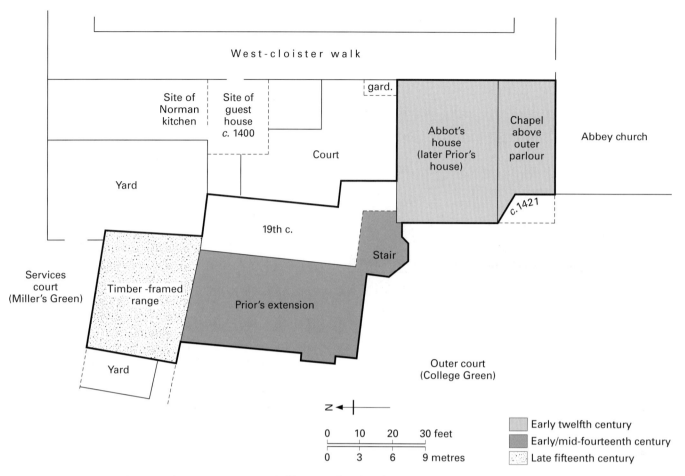

FIGURE 18 Gloucester, Prior's Lodging: site plan

elements are similar to those supporting the mid-fifteenth-century roof at Wanswell Court, while the low pitched roof in the adjacent (Henry) room is a little later in that century.[5] The rough carpentry of its four tie beams is relieved by mottled paintwork attributed to the late sixteenth century.

This embattled block was attached on its north side to a thirteenth-century stone building, originally part of the almoner's range but subsequently converted into the great hall. In the late fifteenth century, this building was cut down, reduced in height and the lower side walls utilised to support a timber-framed upper floor creating a gallery, subsequently curtailed at the west end. This structure is concealed from College Green by its twentieth-century brick entry but the stone ground and timber-framing of the upper floor and end walls dominate Miller's Green, the former services court.[6]

The prior's lodging was occupied between 1541 and 1940 by the dean of the cathedral. Among the many alterations for this occupant was the integration of the timber-framed range with the remainder of the dean's house, though the unbroken party wall confirms that it had never previously formed any part of it. This has distorted the plan of the lodgings more than the room partitions and stair enlargements. This activity culminated in the drastic restoration of 1863–70 when all windows were recut, the corridor range added, and the stair remodelled with a visually intrusive spirelet so that the complex lost most of its remaining medieval character.[7]

Throughout this era, the house continued to function in association with the three-storeyed Norman house and chapel in what was always an awkwardly shaped residence. Since 1948, the two parts have been separated. The Norman block is used for diocesan administration and the conjoined late medieval buildings serve public functions as a refectory and kitchen with reception rooms above. Even so, this house can show nearly 900 years of unbroken house occupation by abbots, priors, deans, and diocese.

The remaining abbatial lodgings in Gloucestershire are small beer. That between the precinct gatehouse and the west front of Tewkesbury abbey is a two-storeyed range which may have been the abbot's lodging or the community's guest house (now the vicarage). Buck's engraving shows that the building was in bad condition by 1732 with the late fifteenth-century street frontage standing to roof level but the remainder close to ruin until its rehabilitation in 1790 when the brick frontage was erected on the south side. The ground-floor hall and a major upper room with oriel suggest that the range is likely to have been for the head of the monastery. The hall has fifteenth-century cusped windows and close-studded partition walls with three doors at the screens end. The oriel carries the initials of abbot Beoly (1509–31) with three shields, a damaged inscription, and a pendant vaulted ceiling internally but frontage renewal and internal changes have deprived this building of its early residential value.

The abbatial chamber at Flaxley fares little better at a site in a

PLATE 43 Gloucester, Prior's Lodging: from College Green

combe on the edge of the Forest of Dean less than 2 miles from the River Severn. Most of the monastic buildings were torn down by Sir William Kingston shortly after 1540 so that nothing survived of this Cistercian foundation by the time of Kip apart from the west claustral range and projecting reredorter, partly rewindowed in Charles II's reign.[8] A fire in 1777 led to the reduction of half the range, the remodelling of the remainder, and the south extension by Anthony Keck in a pseudo-Gothic style, handsomely refurbished by Oliver Messel in 1960–2.

The twelfth-century vaulted undercroft, possibly the lay brothers' refectory, has been restored but any evidence of the abbot's quarters above was supplanted in the late seventeenth century by a line of bedrooms, leaving his reception chamber as the sole survival. The ground floor of the projecting wing consisted of two tunnel-vaulted chambers[9] serving the reredorter above until it was appropriated by the abbot in the mid-fourteenth century. The reason for this was that the crown had long favoured Flaxley as a base for hunting in the Forest of Dean, and this apartment was created in c.1355 for Edward III's personal use. Only the garderobe chute opposite the group of four twelfth-century narrow lights shown in Kip's engraving of 1712 remains from its early ablution use, for the traceried windows and fireplace are imaginative reconstructions of 1913 and the entrance was remade in 1960 when the opposite doorway was inserted. The fourteenth-century roof is the prime survival, crowning a chamber 40 feet by 16 feet by 25 feet. The three and a half bays are spanned by braced collar trusses on embattled corbels with intermediate mini trusses terminating at purlin bosses. There are two rows of cusped wind braces and an embattled wall plate. This quite grand chamber reflects royal as much as abbatial dignity, though interest at Flaxley lies as much in its post-medieval developments and interiors.[10]

None of the country houses of the abbots of Gloucester was far from the city. They include three that no longer exist at Over, built

by abbot Staunton in c.1337, Highnam, and the Vineyard west of Gloucester,[11] and standing evidence at Prinknash and Standish. Once more serving a community of Benedictine monks, Prinknash commands extensive views over the Severn valley. The abbot of Gloucester had erected a hunting lodge here in the mid-fourteenth century which may be incorporated in the south wing[12] of the present substantial house, developed and internally marked with the rebus of abbot Parker (1514–39). This H-shaped building with two late nineteenth-century upper-arm extensions, first mentioned as an abbatial residence in 1526[13] was erected during the preceding ten years. The central hall block with its uncusped windows, concave mouldings, and square hoods was floored by Sir John Bridgeman in c.1630. The ground-floor rooms south of the hall were used for services, with the abbot's withdrawing chamber above retaining its fan-vaulted oriel. Death duties in 1927 forced the sale of much heraldic glass and its transfer to Gloucester cathedral cloisters[14] but the contemporary angel glass in the chapel is still *in situ*. The eastern arm of the south wing is also early sixteenth century and the only part of the house to retain its early two-storeyed form, for the remainder, altered in every succeeding century, now looks the epitome of a Cotswold vernacular gabled house of the Elizabethan period.

Forthampton Court was the major country house of the abbots of Tewkesbury, last used by abbot John Wakeman (1531–49) who became the first bishop of Gloucester. A much smaller house, Mythe Tower, a mile north-west of Tewkesbury also seems to have been abbey property for Wakeman leased it to his brother in 1534. The squat, three-storeyed fifteenth-century tower was not defensive and was probably associated with an attached residential wing, but the present one is seventeenth century, as are the windows in the tower. The rubble walls were heavily cut back in the nineteenth century.[15]

Mythe Tower is a very different structure from the prior of Llanthony's house at Prestbury near Cheltenham which repeats the stone ground floor and close timber-framed upper section of the semi-domestic range that is the sole survivor of the mother house next to Gloucester docks. The prior's dwelling at Prestbury immediately west of the church retains a four-bay fourteenth-century hall, now floored, stone cased, and with most of the arch-braced collar-beam trusses cut back. The two-storeyed north wing retains one original and one recut first-floor window with cinquefoil ogee heads.[16] Another house of Llanthony, Brockworth Court, now swept up in the suburbs of Gloucester, was built by the last prior, Richard Hart (1534–9). It repeats the stone and timber-framed form but with the withdrawing chamber positioned above rather than beyond the ground-floor hall. The arch-braced collar trusses and roofs of the upper rooms are complete, and part of a wall painting survives in the withdrawing chamber with the initials of prior Hart, a Tudor rose, and the pomegranate badge of Catherine of Aragon.[17]

NOTES

1 The location of the abbot's lodging at St Augustine's is not certain for it is by no means clear that it was taken over by the bishop. His property may originally have been the infirmary but it was heavily rebuilt under bishop Butler (1738–50) and abandoned after its destruction in 1831. *Bristol Cathedral*, ed. J. Rogers (2000) 50–1. The last remains were demolished without adequate recording in the 1960s.

2 VCH, *Gloucestershire*, IV (1988) 283; Welander (1991) 150, 309–10, 410. The gallery windows and oriel overlooking Pitt Street are probably a legacy of abbot Parker (1514–39).

3 The Norman gable survives with shallow panels and chevron decoration. The façade below was remodelled in *c*.1200 in three contrasting-shaped openings, filled with Victorian tracery at ground- and first-floor levels and mid-fourteenth-century tracery above. The adjacent chapel and outer parlour were shortened and set back when the abbey's west front was rebuilt by abbot Morwent (1421–37) and the joining wall to the house awkwardly splayed. The chapel window is inaccurate nineteenth-century work.

4 W. H. St John Hope thought that this guest hall may have been built by abbot Horton (1351–77); W. Bazeley, *Records of Gloucester Cathedral*, I (1882) 90–130.

5 VCH, *Gloucestershire*, IV (1988) 282 favours a late fifteenth- or early sixteenth-century date for this roof. The embattled parapet dates from this reroofing. Oswald (1962).

6 The function of this range is difficult to establish since the curtailment of its west and presumably entrance end. The open-braced collar trusses are rough, not helped by the indifferent quality of the almost straight-sided wind braces. The problem is compounded by what is now the central truss which either is a crude replacement or was always intended to be a room division. The mortice holes on its underside suggest such a use or reuse but the third truss is also poorly finished and its line interrupted by one of the oriel windows (reinstated in 1962). Whether this was an uninterrupted hall or a divided area, architectural pathfinding had stopped at the church and cloister doors after the fourteenth century.

7 The stair retains its fifteenth-century embattled stone lantern, supported on a shaped corbel.

8 The probable layout is described in *Trans. Bristol and Glos. Arch. Soc.* 6 (1881–2) 280–3.

9 Now boiler rooms. Keck concealed their function with pastiche blind windows and wall rendering, and balanced the frontage with a matching wing at the north end.

10 The Cistercian abbey at Hailes followed the same post-Dissolution pattern as Flaxley, with the destruction of all but the west claustral range which had been similarly taken over by the abbot by the fifteenth century. Kip's engraving of 1712 shows a two-storeyed tower-like block at its south end, a fashionable domestic remodelling undertaken towards the last quarter of the fifteenth century when the cloister was rebuilt. Lyson's view of 1794 depicts the ruined embattled unit before the last of the range was pulled down. Kip also shows a projection at the opposite end of the range, similar in appearance, reredorter position, and possibly function to that at Flaxley. J. Coad, *Hailes Abbey: Official Handbook* (1985 edn) 7. The Prior's House at Deerhurst is a post-Dissolution residence on the site of the chapter-house and east cloister, incorporating earlier elements.

11 Leland, *Itinerary*, V 158. It was granted as a country house to the first bishop of Gloucester.

12 Bazeley (1890) 6.

13 *Abbot Parker's Register*, ed. W. Bazeley, *Records of Gloucester Cathedral* (1882–3), I, 328. Standish Court, built for the abbots of Gloucester, is similarly H-shaped with a central hall, but as the house has been subject to even more drastic alterations than Prinknash its ruined gatehouse is a more instructive survival (see page 111).

14 Welander (1991) 292–3. The Prinknash Room in the City Art Museum, St Louis, is made up of several hundred feet of panelling and one of the two magnificent chimney pieces of *c*.1630 sold at this time; Kingsley (1989) 148–52.

15 J. Grenville, *Southern History* 9 (1987) 19–33; VCH, *Gloucestershire*, VIII (1968) 135–6. The Elizabethan house, Hatherop Castle near Fairford, rebuilt in 1850–6, incorporated a low three-storeyed tower, possibly of late medieval origins when the manor belonged to Lacock Abbey. Illustrated in Kingsley (1989) 105.

16 The bishop of Hereford also had a country house at Prestbury, useful when travelling to and from London. For its excavation, H. E. O'Neil, *Trans. Bristol and Glos. Arch. Soc.* 75 (1956) 5–34.

17 *Med. Arch.* 23 (1979) 274.

W. Bazeley, *The History of Prinknash Park* (1890)
VCH, *Gloucestershire*, II (1907) 1–108
A. Oswald, 'Old Deanery, Gloucester', *Country Life* (April 1951; December 1962)
J. Lees-Milne, 'Flaxley Abbey', *Country Life* (March/April 1973)
B. Watkins, *The Story of Flaxley Abbey* (1985)
N. Kingsley, *The Country Houses of Gloucestershire*, I (1989)
D. Welander, *The History, Art and Architecture of Gloucester Cathedral* (1991)

GREYS COURT, Oxfordshire

The layout of this defendable house is not immediately apparent. The towers that form part of its curtilage have been subsumed into the landscaped gardens surrounding the mid-Elizabethan dwelling that stands on one side of the sward filling much of the former courtyard. Four towers remain, two octagonal shaped and two square shaped. The former are at either end of the present approach frontage; the latter are near each other towards the north-east corner of the site, with one diagonally positioned to improve its defensive capability. This substantial courtyard house was roughly quadrangular but the sites of the north and south frontages are now entirely open landscapes facing the parkland and Rother valley respectively.

The manor of Rotherfield was in the hands of the Grey family between the late eleventh and early fifteenth centuries, with documentary evidence of the family resident here during the late thirteenth century.[1] Sir John Grey was a long-serving soldier, councillor, and steward of the royal household (1350–6) who died in 1359. As 2nd Lord Grey of Rotherfield from 1338, he obtained a licence to crenellate his house in 1346[2] but was followed by a line of short-lived successors with the hereditary barony merging in 1408 with that of Deincourt upon the death without heirs of Joan Grey. The difference between the almost miniature octagonal towers and the more aggressive square towers at Greys Court suggests two phases of construction, with the square towers as the earlier (pl. 4).

The earlier structures are flint-built with some tile banding, and dressed stone for windows and doorways. The probably dry moat has been filled and replaced in part by a ha-ha. The two square towers, a roofed one of four storeys and a ruined one of two storeys, stand free of the buildings that formerly abutted them. With walls 5 feet thick, the larger tower ('Great Tower') has angled buttresses to the field and a rebuilt embattled parapet. The single room on each floor, 12½ feet by 11 feet internally, is fenestrated with loops to the lower and single lights to the upper room. Two-centred headed doorways give access to the ground and first floors, both with garderobe recesses. The two upper rooms were reached from an internal stair (replaced). The second square tower (North-East Tower) stands 50 feet northwards. Of comparable form, the ground and first floors had broader window splays indicative of superior rooms, and part of the ground-floor garderobe seat. The curtain wall between the two towers was originally about 25 feet high but has been capped for most of its length at about 15 feet. A two-storey range was built against it with an inserted sixteenth-century doorway and brick fireplace at ground level, but with a line of original loops above.

The much repaired east curtain continues southwards towards the South-East Tower. This and the similar octagonal south-west tower ('The Keep') are 17 feet in diameter externally, three-storeyed, pyramid-capped, and still inhabited though attached to much-altered dwellings. The South-East Tower retains its original loops in each outer face (at least one at ground level with an *œillet*) and a tall first-floor internal doorway with two-centred head.

In addition to these four towers, two sides of the forecourt lawn are lined with domestic buildings. The stone-lined well 200 feet deep within the 1586 wheel-house (donkey driven between the late sixteenth and early twentieth centuries) suggests the site always extended over an area almost as large as the present one. The kitchen at the rear of the Elizabethan house retains a large brick hearth and a brick doorway with two-centred head. This was part of a timber and brick range that formerly extended a further 55 feet southwards, dendro dated to 1450–1. On the opposite side of the courtyard are the so-called Cromwellian stables, probably a lodging range, dendro dated to 1578, abutting a low brick wall that is earlier.

These disparate elements essentially fall into three groups – the medieval structures of the Grey residence, the mid-fifteenth-century range of the Lovel family, and the sequence of Elizabethan developments of Sir Francis Knollys after the property had become a gentleman's residence. English Heritage conducted a building recording project at Greys Court in 2002–3, and after examination of the evidence with Barry Jones of English Heritage, it is clear that the standing medieval structures reveal several construction phases between the twelfth and mid-sixteenth centuries.

The early development of Greys Court has to be read entirely on the east side of the site, for of the four towers that at the south-west angle is a red herring. It is a brick and render structure, dendro dated to 1587, and erected by Knollys to match the retained South-East Tower at the opposite end of the south approach.

Phase 1. The earliest surviving structure is the lower part of the inner face of the 'Great Tower' where the walling consists of alternate courses of knapped flint and tiled bands. This was the end wall of a chamber 18 feet wide with shadow evidence above the wall patterning of a timber roof truss of arch-braced collar and higher collar. The truss shaping is more clear in 1950 photographs held by the NMRC than today, though the plaster infill between the trusses is still apparent. The roof was probably a fourteenth- or fifteenth-century structure but the end wall of a quite grand chamber is earlier. Banded walling was used as early as the mid-twelfth century (east hall at Wolvesey Palace) and even the late eleventh century (great tower hall at Chepstow Castle). A twelfth-century date is possible, though the earliest documentary evidence for a house is the late thirteenth century.

Phase 2. The curtain wall extending southwards from within the 'Great Tower' to A on the plan is built of random flint with occasional bands of reused tiles. It was formerly higher (to 30 feet) but the upper level has been rebuilt and the central section thinned. The walling lacks datable features but its height makes it the earliest defensive addition, attributable to the years between the late thirteenth and mid-fourteenth centuries.

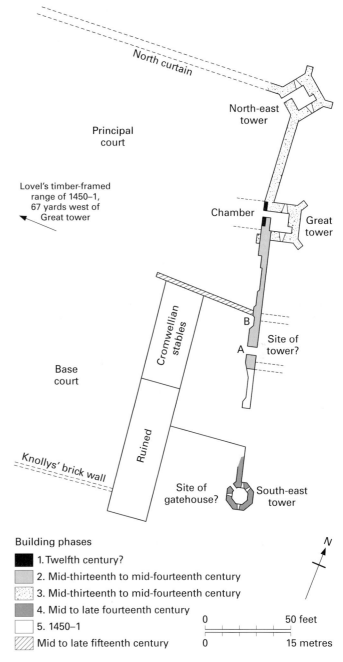

FIGURE 19 Greys Court: ground plan

Phase 3. The 'Great Tower' was built against part of the phase 2 wall, covering putlog holes in its face. The ground- and first-floor doorways were punched through the phase 1 walling to give access to the added tower. The North-East Tower and linking curtain wall are coeval, making a prestige statement about the house's development. Square or rectangular mural towers were a development of the late twelfth century (Windsor, Dover, Framlingham) and early thirteenth century (Ludlow) until replaced by rounded towers from the 1220s onwards (Beeston, Bolingbroke). The form continued to be popular in the north throughout the fourteenth century (Bolton,

Lumley, Brancepeth), and returned to greater favour in central and southern England in the mid-fifteenth century (Tutbury, Sudeley, Kirby Muxloe). The blocked doorway or possibly recess marked B on the plan has a near-triangular head which suggests the later thirteenth or early fourteenth century but the broader phasing of the mid-fourteenth century to the death of the 3rd Lord Grey in 1375 is preferred, possibly but not necessarily associated with the licence to crenellate of December 1346.

The quite grand ground-floor doorway at A with its taller rear arch suggests the approach to a now lost tower built against the curtain during this phase. The opening at B looks like the inner face of a loop but it is more likely to be a doorway. It is possible that the tower was not as large as suggested on the plan and that this doorway was a postern. The matter remains open but as the doorway at B is blocked with bricks matching the Tudor brickwork elsewhere at the Court, it is probable that this tower was pulled down in the sixteenth century.

Greys Court is such an extensive site that it is not unlikely that it always consisted of at least two courts, a principal court and a base court. The principal court extended for at least 180 feet westwards from the North-East Tower. It would have included the hall and family rooms, although their location is unclear. The base court incorporated the well and was probably still wood palisaded during the second-phase stone enclosure, but it is an open question when this court was rebuilt in stone.

Phase 4 (or 2A?) The octagonal South-East Tower retains several early to mid-fourteenth century features. It is larger than the octagonal turrets of the contemporary gatehouse at Maxstoke Castle built by William Clinton, Grey's custodian during his personal dispute with Sir William de la Zouche in 1332.[3] Octagonal towers were characteristic of the mid-fourteenth century as at Wells Palace precinct (1340), Maxstoke Castle (1342–6), and Stafford Castle keep (1348), and though the Greys Court tower is not as markedly tall as those serving the Maxstoke entry, it would have been more imposing when it carried its original top. It is possible, but by no means certain, that it may have been one half of a gatehouse entrance.

The site lacks such a structure but aerial photographs indicate that the approach to the house lay from the east, north of the present carriage drive. Among the improvements to the house by the Grey family during the early to mid-fourteenth century, the construction of a gatehouse should be numbered. It may have been at the south-east angle to create an approach position like that at Barnwell Castle. Stylistic elements suggest association with phase 2 while its form is more common in the middle of the fourteenth century. The problem is not helped by the tower's dissociation from the remainder of the medieval evidence so that its position within the house's chronology is uncertain. The construction of a small tower at A could also be part of this particular phase.

Phase 5. Dendro analysis has dated the kitchen area at the rear of the house to 1450–1 and confirmed that it was part of a jettied timber-framed range extending southwards. Its construction, again parallel with the late fifteenth-century jettied timber range at Maxstoke, can be attributed to the Lovel family of Titchmarsh and Minster Lovell. They held the property after Alice, the elder of the Deincourt heiresses, married William Lovel (d.1455) in 1422 and this extended range, almost 100 feet long, was for services and lodging units. It betokens increasing comfort in a house that was forfeited by Francis Lovel for rebellion in 1485. The position of this timber-framed structure in relation to the well points to the possibility of a third smaller service court by the mid-fifteenth century.

Phase 6. The character of the truncated brick wall abutting the Elizabethan 'stables' favours the mid to late fifteenth century. It has a low crenellated parapet and a doorway in it closely resembles a mid-fifteenth-century one at Ewelme. This brick wall was part of a passageway separating the two principal courts while enhancing the approach to the upper one.

Only one side stands of this large-scale quadrangular residence developed over an extended time-scale that lacks early documentary confirmation. It has lost the towers that would have marked its north-west and south-west angles, the associated curtain walls, and initial gateway evidence. Even so, much of the value of Greys Court lies in tracing the development of an early fortified residence of probable double-courtyard plan over an extended period. By the close of Edward III's reign, it proffered an east-facing parade approach made up of an octagonal tower (possibly a gateway element), a tower (lost), the Great Tower (standing), and the North-East Tower (standing). This was especially noted by Leland in 1542 who recorded: 'There appere enteringe into the maner place on the righte hand 3 or 4 very olde towers of stone, a manifest token that it was sume tyme a castle. There is a very large courte builyd about with tymbar and spacyd [infilled] with brike; but this is of a latter worke.'[4]

The early domestic apartments must have lain on the east and north sides of the upper courtyard, for no structural evidence prior to the mid-fifteenth century has been identified on the west side where the majority of post-medieval developments lay. All early domestic buildings were pulled down during the later sixteenth century as part of the redevelopment of the house. In 1503, Robert Knollys was at least the third of several tenants with his son holding the property under letters patent in 1518. The strongly Protestant Sir Francis Knollys (d.1596) had tactfully gone abroad during Mary's reign, but immediately upon his return after the accession of Elizabeth I, he had commenced the major building project in a series of developments from 1559 that totally transformed the character of Greys Court over the next thirty years. He demolished many of the medieval buildings but there is strong evidence that the multi-courtyard plan was retained at this stage, for Napier's *History of Ewelme and Swyncombe*[5] shows the house in its late seventeenth-century state after some of Sir Francis' work had been demolished. By that time, it consisted of a large quadrangle spanned by two low gated walls of Tudor date in line with the octagonal towers and the north end of Knollys' house respectively,[6] with a new south-facing outer court. Except for the loss of these brick walls and the changes brought about by eighteenth-century landscaping, the appearance of Greys Court is not radically dissimilar 300 years later.

NOTES
1 Sir Robert Grey (d.1295) complained in 1290 that deer had been taken from his park at Rotherfield, while the inquisition post mortem of 1295 identifies the existence of a house. His grandson was born there ten years later. *Com. Peer.*, VI (1926) 144–5.
2 *Cal. Pat. Rolls: 1345–48*, 514. The licence also covered his dwelling place at Sculcoates in the East Riding of Yorkshire. The licence was renewed in February 1348.

3 *Com. Peer.*, VI (1926) 145–6.

4 *Itinerary*, V, 72.

5 Published in 1858. The illustration of the Court is a lithoprint copied from an undated drawing.

6 Their position shows when the grass is parched as in 1955 and 1976. For a resistivity survey of the site, *South Midlands Archaeology* 14 (1984) 70 and English Heritage (2004). The two courts at Brancepeth Castle were similarly united into one vast area by post-medieval development.

C. Hussey, *Country Life* (June 1944)

The National Trust, *Greys Court: Guide Book* (1986)

English Heritage, *Greys Court: Historic Building Report*, ed. B. Jones (2004) and *Vern. Arch.* 35 (2004) 99

HARWELL, BAYLIOL'S MANOR, Berkshire

This timber-framed house, set back from the centre of Harwell, seems merely to be one of the larger properties in a village retaining an extensive number of framed dwellings. They have been subject to a considerable volume of research,[1] but Bayliol's Manor stands out as the house of an estate purchased by Richard Brounz in 1355. Brounz enjoyed a trajectory career. Initially one of ten freeholders in Harwell, he was chosen to be one of the two knights of the shire to represent Berkshire in most of the parliaments between 1379 and 1390, and held the office of sheriff of Berkshire and Oxfordshire in 1381–2. He died in about 1392. His house has been known under several names, reflecting its changes of ownership: Bayliol's Manor when it was held by that family during the thirteenth century, Brunce's Court from the early fourteenth to the early fifteenth century, and Middle Farm after it had been settled

on Magdalen College, Oxford, in 1484 until its sale in 1946. The property reverted to its earliest name in the late 1980s.

Bayliol's Manor is a hall and cross-wing house with the wings in line to the front but with rear projections. It is not the largest hall and cross-wing house in the region. Hendred House, East Hendred, 2 miles west, is considerably larger, but in contrast with that manor house the framework at Bayliol's Manor is displayed with a clarity too often obscured by internal divisions and occupational modifications.

The exterior is not immediately prepossessing. All the windows are nineteenth-century casements, and while much of the frontal timberwork was refaced in the early twentieth century, part of the south wing is an earlier rebuild. At the rear, the opposing walls of the cross-wing projection have been enclosed by single-storey extensions with the clay tile roofs sweeping over them from the ridges. However, the front porch commands immediate attention.

There are two single-storey porches, the original one in line with the cross passage and an early twentieth-century addition at the other end of the hall, best removed. Like the hall and upper cross wing, the contemporary porch stands on a low stone still. The outer arch has a two-centred ogee head, while the frame of the pitched roof is multi-cusped. The opposing cross-passage entries have single-chamfered two-centred heads, but the front entry retains its original door with lines of studs.

In 1589 (dated bracket), a floor was inserted in the hall and a substantial chimney stack built at its lower end with its rear face now forming the right-hand side of the cross passage. A corridor was also inserted at ground level, not repeated above so that the two cross wings are still not linked at first-floor level. Originally 31 feet by 23 feet, the hall was divided into two bays by a handsomely

PLATE 44 Harwell, Bayliol's Manor: from the rear

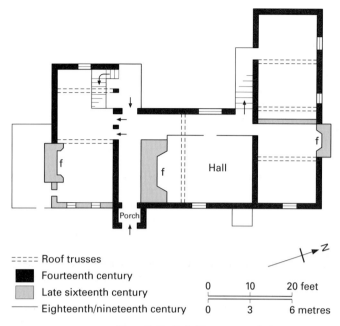

- - - - - Roof trusses
■ Fourteenth century
▨ Late sixteenth century
— Eighteenth/nineteenth century

0   10   20 feet
0   3   6 metres

FIGURE 20 Harwell, Bayliol's Manor: ground plan

exposed central cruck truss of braced tie beam with plain braced crown post. The wind braces and, more surprisingly, the massive double wall plates are markedly plain, particularly as the added member on top of the tie beam was crenellated towards the dais.[2] Smoke-blackened timbers indicate an open hearth.

The four-bay upper cross wing is now divided into three rooms in line at ground- and first-floor level with exposed posts and braces, bold but plain as elsewhere in this house. The upper rooms are ceiled but the roof structure has been little touched and stands unpainted in comparison with the framing elsewhere. The upper floor was divided into a large three-bay chamber, open to the tie-beam and crown-post roof, with a single end bay forming an inner chamber.[3] The original ground-floor layout is not clear.

Two adjacent doors with two-centred heads and single chamfers give access to the lower cross wing. This is earlier than the remainder of the house and has been subject to several drastic changes. The only medieval ground-floor evidence is these doorways, oddly sited towards the rear of the cross passage with one narrower than the other, inserted when the hall was added. Whatever was here beforehand became the services, though the present kitchen is late sixteenth century, when the stack was added, the ceiling raised, and the east end rebuilt.[4] The upper floor of two and a half bays suggests a narrow stair bay, still partly filled by the modern stair,[5] opening into a substantial chamber. The area is now divided into two bedrooms with exposed tie-beam trusses with plain crown posts, both braced four ways but one with two straight and two downward-curved braces. None of the beams is chamfered.

For much of the middle ages, Harwell consisted of two manors held by the bishop of Winchester and the earl of Cornwall. The earls held the honour of Wallingford and used its castle so that the prosperous village of Harwell was a potential source for royal servants such as John Harewell, one of the Black Prince's closest advisors, and Richard Brounz. No medieval documentation has survived for this property but dendrochronology has identified two con-

struction periods. The timbers of the south wing were felled in 1323–4, and those of the hall and contemporary upper cross wing were felled between 1367 and 1371.[6] The south wing was always 15 feet wide and apparently two-storeyed rather than a hall unit, so that its attachment to an earlier hall, possibly as a solar wing, may be assumed. Sir Richard Brounz replaced this earlier hall with a more generous one and an upper wing in about 1372–3 as befitted his improving position and standing, while the south wing was downgraded to service use, though still with a high-quality chamber above. There is a growing body of evidence for this practice elsewhere in lowland England during the fourteenth century.[7] Incidentally, the difference in building periods is also reflected in the different cusping of the rear barge boards and the narrower scantlings of the timbers in the earlier wing.

Bayliol's Manor reflects the rising status of its gentry owner during the third quarter of the fourteenth century, though the house's expansion was spacious rather than sophisticated. Whereas single-storey church porches are common, the survival of a single-storey domestic one is comparatively rare. The property also retains a later-fourteenth-century outhouse, east of the south wing, and an early fifteenth-century cruck barn at the corner with Grove Road.

NOTES

1 J. M. Fletcher, *Oxoniensia* 26 (1961–2) 207–14; J. M. Fletcher, *Berks. Arch. Jour.* 62 (1965–6) 45–69; C. R. J. Currie, *Oxoniensia* 57 (1992) 136–62.
2 Currie (1992) 151 suggests it was probably the remains of a later smoke hood with vertical studs. He also notes that the double tie of the base cruck is the last known example of this type of construction in a domestic context.
3 Currie (1992) 151 hazards that it may be the oratory that was granted to Richard Brounz and his wife in 1389. Wiltshire Record Office, *Reg. Waltham*, f.95 v.
4 This, of course, has destroyed any evidence of whether this wing originally projected forward or not.
5 The infill between the posts was removed at the same time (as shown on the ground plan).
6 Currie (1992) 151.
7 E.g. Tiptofts Manor and Little Chesterford Manor, Essex.

J. M. Fletcher, *Berks. Arch. Jour.* 62 (1965–66) 47–56
C. R. J. Currie, *Oxoniensia* 57 (1992) 143–51

ICOMB PLACE, Gloucestershire

The village of Church Icomb lies on the sheltered slopes of the Cotswolds overlooking the upper Evenlode valley with Icomb Place on the edge of the combe to the south-west which gives the house its name. It was probably built on the site of an earlier moated house[1] and it is a good example of a later fifteenth-century gentleman's residence with pretensions to style and scale.

Except for the hall, Icomb Place is a two-storeyed quadrangular house lacking any forecourt enclosure evidence. The fine ashlar gateway, slightly forward and to one side of the frontage, is the only part of the house to retain embattled evidence. The broad four-centred entry arch, flanked by shallow buttresses, is closed by modern double doors replacing the original ones which existed in 1869.[2] The ogee four-light window above with scraped multi-traceried head and a rear arch with open spandrels, retains the square-headed label that characterises all the plainer windows of this frontage remade in the early sixteenth century. The ground floor formerly consisted of two medium-sized rooms and a porter's lodge immediately right of the passage. The upper floor retains two original fireplaces with bold external stacks at mid level rising well above the eaves. The roof trusses, comparable to those in the hall[3] but not necessarily of the same date, survive above the present bedroom ceilings.

The gateway opens into an intimate, irregular-shaped court, no longer paved since 1956 when it was grassed in the interests of dryness. The hall lies opposite, filling the south side. Lacking any porch, the screens entry is a deeply moulded four-centred arch with tracery and shields in the spandrels, and a more simple opposing entrance to the south court. The hall, 44 feet by 20 feet, is lit by two windows of transomed twin lights towards the north and one to the south. The graceless horse-collar tracery is a stripped-down version of the original cusped form in the solar range. The fireplace is a seventeenth-century replacement brought from the lower solar. The hall is divided into five bays by braced collar-beam trusses sunk into the side walls, with three lines of wind braces, one with the regional characteristic of a counter curve (e.g. Frocester barn).

A doorway in the north-east corner,[4] originally larger, opens into the lower solar or parlour with its replacement fireplace. This handsome room retains a six-light window towards the north court with cinquefoil heads and a line of cusped ovoids above. Nearby is the lower half of the bay window which is the dominant feature of the courtyard with its carved label and buttress stops. Unfortunately, the bay was truncated when the solar block was foreshortened by 6 feet (except for its north-west corner) to enable the north range to be extended. This suggests that the entrance range may initially have been little more than a gateway in a curtain wall.

A newel stair, formerly accessing the roof, leads from the lower to the upper solar or withdrawing chamber. It repeats the fine features and proportions observed below, except that the courtyard window was of three lights until its enlargement in c.1900. The barrel-shaped roof with close rafters was reopened in the 1970s when the room was converted into a chapel. This was the use described by Royce in 1869, but apart from its domestic character and relation to the hall, the orientation is inappropriate. The stoup in the north-facing closet is a late Victorian insertion.

The fact that the primary reception rooms were on the cheerless north-west side of the house was not a worry before the twentieth century when the occupants preferred the warmer south-east range. Consequently the withdrawing room and smoking rooms with their low bay windows were created within the former kitchen and service areas. Only the evidence of the arches in the cross passage and a service hatch[5] testify to the former layout and use.

The smoking room is the one unit of the south court to survive. The remainder was pulled down in 1884 after the house had been 'rescued' by Simpson-Hayward from two centuries of farmhouse status. Victorian photographs show that this south court possessed a late sixteenth- or early seventeenth-century character, but the siting of the hall suggests it may have been an element of the late medieval plan.

Icomb Place was attributed by Royce to Sir John Blaket (d.1430) whose tomb lies in the nearby church, but there is no confirming documentary evidence. His son's will of 1444 notes 'the manor house at Iccumbe with hall, chambers, bakehouse and kitchen' but this may refer to the earlier residence.[6] The double-courtyard plan suggests that the house followed in the wake of Sudeley Castle (c.1441–58) 12 miles west. The form and decoration of the solar windows are later fifteenth century while the internal form of that

PLATE 45 Icomb Place: entry range

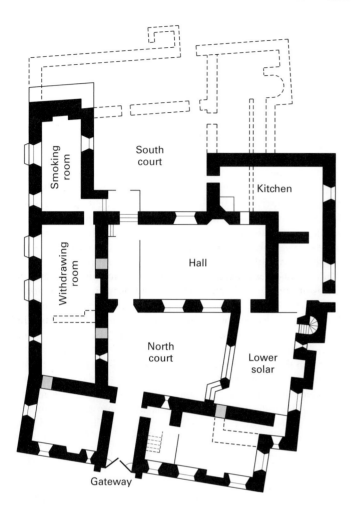

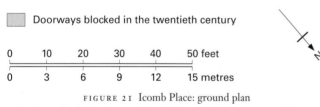

Doorways blocked in the twentieth century

0   10   20   30   40   50 feet

0   3   6   9   12   15 metres

FIGURE 21   Icomb Place: ground plan

above the entrance gate emulates a ground-floor window in the east range at Sudeley Castle (1470s). The hall has scale, and the double residential block with its common bay window shows panache. The gateway attempts to emulate more pretentious houses, as does the existence of a second court.

It seems that Icomb Place reflects several development phases. The outer wall of the hall cutting across the splay of the first-floor window of the solar range is indicative of earlier walling. Not only is the hall out of proportion to the rest of the house but its upper end cuts into the line of the solar range. And that range is not to its rear but to one side of its high end. Icomb Place therefore seems to have its origins in a modest courtyard house, possibly early fifteenth century, aggrandised later in the century when the larger hall was created, the solar range remodelled, and the entrance range formed. This last was remodelled in the early sixteenth century, the south court may have been remodelled or extended in c.1600, while the

graceless hall windows are probably contemporary with the nave windows of St Mary's, Warwick of 1698–1704.

The Blaket family had held Icomb since the 1340s but when Sir John's son, Edmund Blaket, died in 1444, the estate passed to his sister Anne and her husband Ralph Baskerville (d.c.1480) and their daughter until the coming of James Whitney of Hereford late in the fifteenth century. His family sold the estate in 1654, but when this was partitioned forty years later, the house followed a path of neglect until its purchase by Simpson-Hayward in 1881. Excessive tidying and alterations by him and his successors have left a stripped-down house interior.

NOTES

1 The moat evidence does not share any conformity with the present building.
2 Royce (1869–70) 102. Cooke (1957) 31 has an illustration also confirming the existence of the embattled parapet and window below.
3 Royce (1882–3) for longitudinal section, pl. 24, fig. 3.
4 That in the north-west corner is a twentieth-century insertion.
5 Noted by Royce (1882–3) 187. The Jacobean replacement hall screen was moved into the body of the hall by Hayward and taken out fifty years later.
6 Royce (1882) 179.

D. Royce, *Reports of the Association of Archaeological Societies* 10 (1869–70) 101–8
D. Royce, *Trans. Bristol and Glos. Arch. Soc.* 7 (1882–3) 172–90
T. Garner and A. Stratton, *The Domestic Architecture of England During the Tudor Period*, I (1911) 30–1
VCH, *Worcestershire*, III (1913) 412–15
R. Cooke, *West Country Houses* (1957) 31–3
N. Kingsley, *The Country Houses of Gloucestershire*, I (1989) 111–13.

KINGSWOOD ABBEY and Gloucestershire gatehouses

The gateways at Kingswood and other monastic houses are included in this volume for comparison with those of nearby secular residences. Kingswood was a Cistercian house founded by William Berkeley in c.1170 after monks from Tintern had tried to settle at Hazleton and Tetbury. It became a large and important monastery during the thirteenth century as a result of its sheep holding. It suffered in the Black Death but recovery was aided by the Berkeleys and sub-leasing its granges during the fifteenth century. It was dissolved in 1538, with clearance proving so wholesale (but helping with the construction of the hunting lodge at Newark Park in c.1550 by the Poyntz family) that the site of the church and claustral buildings are not even known.[1]

The single survival is the richly decorated mid-fifteenth-century gateway astride the village street with flanking lodges. Only the front portion of the central gateway survives, for the rear bay has been pulled down and the upper part board-faced. The central passage with foot entrance retains its richly bossed lierne vault. The two-light cinquefoil-headed window above lights a room with a plain braced collar and two rows of wind braces.

The prime interest of the Kingswood gatehouse lies in its embellishment and treatment like a fifteenth-century Flemish painting of the Annunciation. The façade is decorated with flanking niches (one almost destroyed), a shield-carrying angel, pinnacled but-

PLATE 46 Kingswood Abbey: gatehouse

secular survivals covering a broader time-span. The fourteenth-century gatehouse at Quenington originally served a property of the Knights Hospitallers though it is now the entry to a nineteenth-century house.[2] The origin of this tall two-storeyed gateway is possibly thirteenth century (postern doorway) but the principal chamfered archway with four-centred head is a fifteenth-century replacement. Above is an image niche with cinquefoil arch, finial, and pinnacles fronting the upper room with quatrefoil-enriched roof trusses.[3]

The fourteenth-century ruined gatehouse at Standish Court guards an immaculately maintained house of 1548 and later, replacing that built for the abbot of Gloucester.[4] Formerly two-storeyed but lacking its upper floor, the still imposing entry passage, front buttressed, was divided into vehicular and foot entry (two-centred heads) to front and rear, as well as dividing the central cross wall as at Tewkesbury. The porter's lodge on the right-hand side was a substantial room with passage window.

The mid-fifteenth-century gatehouses at Icomb Place and at Olveston and Court Farm, Lower Almondsbury, are described separately. The early Tudor one at Down Ampney near Fairford was burnt in 1961 and demolished two years later. It was a development of the entry to Kingswood Abbey with its crocketed entrance gable and flanking lodges, separated here by tall embattled turrets forward of the entrance. It was built in 1537 as the entrance to the home of a younger branch of the Hungerfords of Farleigh Hungerford Castle.[5]

NOTES

1 E. S. Lindley, *Trans. Bristol and Glos. Arch. Soc.* 73 (1954) 115–91 with supplements in the following two volumes. Lindley suggested that the abbey lay between the mill leat and the stream north of the gatehouse, *ibid.* 176. The gatehouse roof has been dendro dated to 1441–66. *Vern. Arch.* 34 (2003) 105–6.
2 *Trans. Bristol and Glos. Arch. Soc.* 93 (1975) 136–41. The medieval barn and dovecote also remain.
3 The twin-entranced gatehouse to Cirencester Abbey, all that stands of that foundation, is late twelfth century but is an early version of that to the preceptory at Quenington.
4 VCH, *Gloucestershire*, X (1972) 234.
5 T. Garner and A. Stratton, *The Domestic Architecture of England during the Tudor Period* (1911) 102, pl. 138. J. A. Henderson, *Down Ampney and the Families of Hungerford and Eliot 1374–1929* (1974). The much-altered four-bay hall, 39 feet by 24 feet, with embellished queen-post trusses and reversed access, accords more with the Henrician date it used to carry than with the mid to late fifteenth-century date sometimes accorded it.

LECKHAMPTON COURT, Gloucestershire

This substantial U-shaped house was developed by a branch of the Giffard family of Brimpsfield. Their thirteenth-century castle, like those at Berkeley and Beverston sited next to the church, was destroyed by Edward II in 1322 for the family's support of the baronial cause. Its owner, Sir John Giffard, was captured and hanged.[1] A younger branch of the family had acquired the manor of Leckhampton 4 miles northwards early in the fourteenth century and erected the earliest part of the Court in *c.*1315–25. The openness of the hall range built by Sir John Giffard (d.1330) could not have formed a greater contrast with the keep and towered enclosure of the family's abandoned fortress at Brimpsfield on the hills above.

tresses, and gable ridge crockets. They serve to heighten the imagery including the Manueline-like mullion of the central window carved with a lily in a vase, the head of God above, and the dove in the right-hand niche which formerly held, with its opposing one, statues of the Virgin Mary and the Archangel Gabriel. The gable apex still retains the Crucifixion.

The two-storeyed lodgings, with pinnacled buttresses and square-headed windows missing their cinquefoil lights, were separately roofed. The lodging to the right is no more than a façade but the left-hand one is still occupied.

The gatehouse at Llanthony Priory, Gloucester (1494–1500) was embellished with the coats of arms of builders and patrons, but as less than half its frontage stands, the late fifteenth-century gatehouse of Tewkesbury Abbey, more obviously utilitarian in design than Kingswood, forms an instructive contrast. It is two-storeyed but box-like, and the broad ground-floor passage of the Tewkesbury gatehouse was divided by a cross wall with vehicular and foot entries into two vaulted halves. There was again a single upper chamber but much of the late fifteenth-century detailing dates from the capable 1849 restoration.

These three monastic gatehouses should be compared with several

PLATE 47 Leckhampton Court: hall and services range from the south-east

Leckhampton Court remained in the possession of the Giffards until 1486, when it passed by marriage to John Norwood (d.1509) who built the timber-framed south wing. His son extended an early residential range on the north side to create a wing of comparable length. An improvement in Norwood prosperity in c.1570 through marriage to the daughter of Lord Beauchamp of Madresfield led to internal improvements and the south-east extension where a doorway is dated 1582, but the Court subsequently suffered from a series of misfortunes. Kip shows its standing in 1712 but a fire twenty years later destroyed the majority of the north wing, which was curiously replaced by a three-and-a-half-storeyed Georgian house abutting the hall, leaving the end of the wing as a detached residence. It is in this form that the Court is shown in Lyson's *Antiquities* (1803). The Georgian house was pulled down in 1848, the Georgian inserted floor in the hall was removed, and the bay window added at its upper end. The detached north block was united with the hall by an infill by H. A. Prothero in 1894–1905, well modelled externally but financially stringent within. The Court was used as a hospital during the First World War, then suffered from intermittent tenancies, occupation by German prisoners of war in 1941–5, use as a boarding school in 1957–69, and subsequent vandalism. Conversion into a hospice in 1979–82 had to be drastic but it brought renewed life to a building which had partly collapsed.

Built and roofed with Leckhampton stone from the hill immediately behind the house, the Court stands on the lower slopes of the Cotswold scarp immediately above a band of unstable clay. The frontage still faces farmland along the foot of the hills, with its back to the visible expansion of Cheltenham. The architectural development of the Court is written more boldly on the exterior than the interior of the house as a result of the many domestic changes made during the last hundred years – not least in adapting it as a hospice.

The early fourteenth-century hall, chamber block, and services were built in line under a continuous roof ridge. The residential wing on the left-hand side of the court overlapping the upper end of the hall is in two sections of 1894–1905 and c.1510–15 respectively. The staff wing on the right-hand side of c.1490 beyond the line of the hall range has rear additions of 1848. The ends of the wings show that enclosure of the courtyard was always by a wall and not by a gatehouse range.

The two-storeyed entry is a mid to later fifteenth-century addition with quatrefoil stops to the outer hood and a late sixteenth-century frontal window above. The diagonal buttresses, four-centred doorheads, and side openings to the beamed porch and upper chamber reflect the form of the porch at Little Sodbury Manor, though surmounted at Leckhampton by an embattled parapet.[2] The cross-passage doorways were replaced at the same time to their present plain four-centred form.

The outer walls of the hall and service range are early fourteenth century but the hall, 33 feet by 25 feet, is the only apartment to retain evidence of its initial character. Both side walls are lit by twin transomed trefoiled lights with quatrefoil head, three on the west and two on the east, lacking window seats. The end bay of similar window form is an 1848 viewing insertion while the two north

112

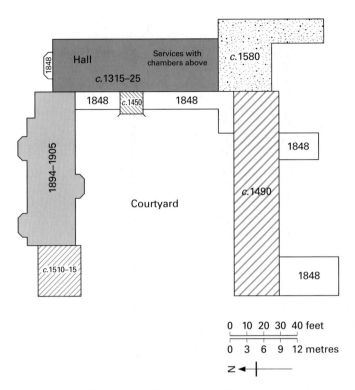

FIGURE 22 Leckhampton Court: site plan (limited measurement)

windows are 1979 rebuilds arising from roof collapse. The new almost parabolic roof did not attempt to follow the preceding traditional form of unclear date – thought to be fourteenth century[3] but more probably nineteenth century.[4]

There is no evidence of a residential block beyond the upper end wall of the hall, this being precluded by falling ground,[5] but an added wing on the site of the Georgian house and the late Victorian replacement is likely. The conversion of a window rather than an original doorway in the north-west angle of the hall suggests that such a wing may have been a later fourteenth- or fifteenth-century addition replacing the family chambers above the services.

Only the outer walls and end stack survive of the services and chamber end of the hall range. The stack indicates that the ground-floor offices were followed by the kitchen, with an outer and an inner chamber above for family use. Part of a doorhead east of the stack may have been a garderobe entry. The two pseudo-fourteenth-century windows in the east side are mid-nineteenth century; those to the courtyard are late sixteenth-century replacements. Even so, the standing remains at Leckhampton hardly do justice to the quality of Giffard's house, particularly if the vaulted chancel and tower of the church in the grounds of the house, reasonably attributable to Sir John, are taken as a yardstick of his work.[6]

The staff and services south wing has a buttressed stone ground floor and close timber-framed upper floor similar to the late fifteenth-century courtyard range at Llanthony Priory, Gloucester. It is broken by three eighteenth-century window frames cutting through both floors, replacing earlier openings – rectangular ones in stone and unframed windows above between the vertical post and central rail. The rear façade was stone-faced in the eighteenth

century, with the west end remodelled in the nineteenth century to match that of the opposing wing. Apart from the upper framing of two partition walls and a bay with wind braces (as in the early Tudor unit opposite), the interior was completely remodelled as bedrooms in 1980–2.

The family wing was extended in c.1510–15 by a two-storeyed buttressed unit with uncusped windows under square hoods with diamond-shaped stops. The courtyard doorway is a window conversion but the principal chamber was the upper one, formerly open to the roof of collar-braced trusses (one original). Well lit on three sides including an oriel in the north wall, the corbelled chimney stack serving a forward lintel is surmounted by two contrasting brick chimneys, one of twisted moulds.

NOTES
1 J. N. Langston, *Trans. Bristol and Glos. Arch. Soc.* 65 (1944) 105–28; A. Dodd and P. Moss, *Glevensis* 25 (1991) 34–7. In 1283 Sir John Giffard, a leading supporter of the earl of Gloucester and the most prominent member of the family, founded Gloucester Hall at Oxford to encourage the monks of St Peter's Abbey to study there. The monastic lodgings are now part of Worcester College.
2 The hall range parapet is mid-nineteenth century.
3 N. Kingsley, *The Country Houses of Gloucestershire*, I (1989) 123.
4 D. Verey and N. Pevsner, *The Buildings of England: Gloucestershire*, II (1970) 285.
5 The Georgian clasping of the north-east angle, one block incised 1794, probably made good a destroyed east court wall.
6 Sir John Giffard is also credited with building the south chapel but the table tomb formerly here was poked into a rear corner of the church and the effigies of Sir John and his wife transposed when the nave was rebuilt in 1866–8. A pertinent parallel with Leckhampton's original hall and chamber form is the more humble Daneway House at Sapperton, 10 miles south. This much-altered and extended 45 foot rectangular block, dendro dated to 1315, retains its hall (now floored) with an arch-braced collar-beam roof, and services unit with chamber over. The oratory that Henry Clifford obtained permission to erect may have been above the added porch, marked by a possible stair entry from the ogee trefoil-arched doorway next to the hall entry. This house has a complex development that extends to the present day. D. Verey and A. Brooks, *The Buildings of England: Gloucestershire*, I (1999) 593–4; T. Garner and A. Stratton, *The Domestic Architecture of England During the Tudor Period*, II (1911) 178–80; C. Hussey, *Country Life* (January 1952); VCH, *Gloucestershire*, II (1976) 17; W. Rodwell, *Trans. Bristol and Glos. Arch. Soc.* 118 (2000) 11–12.

E. Andred and E. Brewin, *Leckhampton through the Ages* (1979)

LEWKNOR CHURCH FARM, Oxfordshire

Immediately south-west of the church, a weather-boarded barn, 50 feet by 32 feet, encases the frame of a medieval timber-framed hall. Crude framing on a brick base, planking, and a hipped roof have replaced the west end and side walls of the earlier house so that there is no door or window evidence – only the timber trusses that supported the roof, and part of the east end wall.

The hall was of two and a half bays, separated by two cambered tie-beam trusses. The whole of the first or west-facing bay is filled to its plain wall-plate level by a steel grain store that conceals all structural evidence. The upper half of the end wall is a nineteenth-century remake, as is this end of the roof structure, so that only half

PLATE 48 Lewknor Church Farm: hall interior

the roof bay retains its wind braces. It is probable that this was originally never more than a half bay, about 9 feet deep, at the lower end of the hall, particularly as the first truss is a spere truss. The cambered tie beam is supported on two square posts, the central span double braced, while the 6 foot wide aisles have trefoil-shaped braces of embryonic ogee form. Above are queen posts with wide braces to the collar and purlins, and side braces against the roof tiles to the end of the tie beam. Above is a second collar with multicusped braces and cusped wind braces to the clasped purlins. The aisles of this spere truss retain their upper infill support.

The second bay, 15 feet deep, is separated from the third bay by a much-altered truss. Originally, it was a massive tie beam, supported by arch braces from the side walls with the same superstructure as the spere truss. However, an inherent weakness in this 30 foot span necessitated the insertion of aisle posts, replicating the form of those used in the spere truss, with the braces reused to support the narrowed central span. It is possible that the arch braces were originally cusped on the inner edge, hacked away during their reuse but leaving mutilated mortices.

The third bay, 20 feet deep, has an end wall that was clearly meant to be appreciated. It is divided into three registers to the later hipped gable. The lowest consisted of four panels, recently replaced by concrete blocks but with slight evidence that it was braced.[1] The second is divided by struts into four equal panels with cusped braces repeating the ogee head. The highest level has a simple braced central panel.

Lewknor Church Farm is a two-and-a-half-bay hall, approximately 42 feet by 29 feet internally, with a remodelled central truss and spere truss division. It was clearly an impressive and richly ornamented structure, though it now lacks all fenestration or entry evidence. The hall may have been free-standing or with an associated block at the lower end, but destruction makes this unclear. It is a late structure, comparable in span to the hall of Stokesay Castle. It is attributable to the second quarter of the fourteenth century on analogy with raised aisle structures in Essex and the rudimentary ogee-nipped heads, until dendrochronology identifies a more precise date.[2] The house was not manorial. From its position close to the church, it may have been a rectorial property of Abingdon Abbey until acquired by All Souls College in 1440.[3] It is more likely, however, that it was the home of the Lewknor family who were established in the parish between the twelfth and later fourteenth centuries. John Lewknor (d.c.1360) represented the county in parliament between 1332 and 1354, and was responsible for rebuilding the east end of the church between 1320 and 1340.[4] Despite its much-mauled condition, the hall was a substantial and impressive one, but as the farm and outbuildings are all post-medieval, evidence of the house's scale and enclosure is absent. The lack of any fireplace insertion suggests the hall was abandoned before the close of the fifteenth century, possibly after the Lewknors died out, allowing it to be downgraded.

NOTES

1 Morrey and Smith (1973) 343.
2 The period between 1325 and 1360 is also suggested by J. M. Fletcher on a comparative basis with other nearby fourteenth-century halls: (1974) 250. Dendrochronology has proved inconclusive so far. *Vern. Arch.* 21 (1990) 47, 49.
3 H. L. Turner, *Oxoniensia* 37 (1972) 187–91.
4 VCH, *Oxfordshire*, VIII (1964) 101–2; Fletcher (1974) 250–1.

M. C. J. Morrey and J. T. Smith, *Oxoniensia* 38 (1973) 339–45
J. M. Fletcher, *Oxoniensia* 39 (1974) 247–53
E. Mercer, *English Vernacular Houses* (1975) 194

LITTLE SODBURY MANOR, Gloucestershire

The unorthodox plan and development of Little Sodbury Manor has been determined by its steep siting on the Cotswold escarpment, but lightning and fire in 1556, storms in 1703, and nineteenth-century neglect have taken their toll. The result is a mélange of several building periods in roughcast Cotswold stone round an impressive fifteenth-century hall, perched on a narrow platform of land below the crest of the hills. It was subject to an extended restoration by Harold Brakspear in 1913–15 for Lord Grosvenor and between 1919 and 1926 for Baron de Tuyll incorporating early material Brakspear found on the site.

The sharp fall in ground level meant that the early approach to the house lay at the south end of the upper terrace. The gateway there was destroyed in the 1630s but its foundations survive beneath the grass. Because the present approach is from the north directly into the 1703 wing, it is necessary to walk round the west end of the house to the garden front to reach the former entrance court and house approach.

The two-storeyed porch with four-centred entrance arch is supported by diagonal buttresses with decorated offsets. Rising ground within the porch necessitated a flight of steps to the hall doorway. The decorative squints here, and in the room above, looking towards the gateway site were covered when the two-storeyed south range was added in the early sixteenth century. The room over the porch has a two-light cinquefoil window above the entrance and a roof modestly reflecting that of the hall.

The screens passage, unusually 10 feet broad, is as wide as the porch. The two arches with depressed four-centred heads formerly giving access to the offices may be associated with the added south range rather than the earlier hall. The lower end of that apartment

PLATE 49 Little Sodbury Manor: garden front

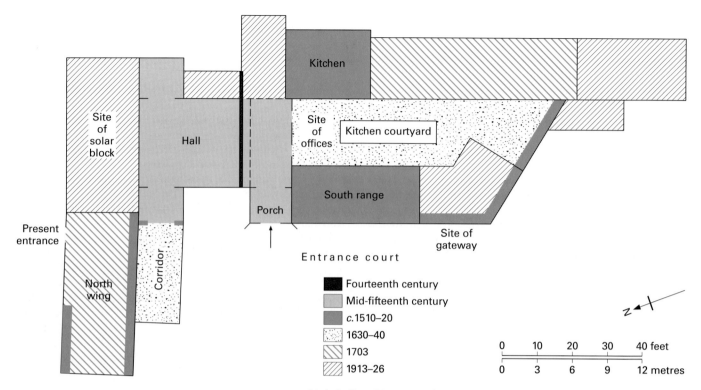

FIGURE 23 Little Sodbury Manor: site plan

is filled with a towering wall of close-set studding divided into five tiers. As at Buckland Rectory, use was made of the projecting outer wall of an earlier, possibly fourteenth-century, timber-framed house. The screen is made up of panels with blind traceried heads, but although it is said that the section near the porch has always been there, this is doubtful.

The hall is divided into four bays spanned by arch-braced collar beams carried on stone corbels decorated with angels holding blank shields. The steep pitch of the roof necessitated four tiers of wind braces. Its lofty upper reaches were lit by two windows in the further end gable with cusped heads. In contrast, the paired lights in the upper side walls are plain, and are probably early sixteenth-century replacements set within steep four-centred rear arches. There were probably no lower windows in the west wall, for the present ones are 1919 copies replacing 1703 insertions.

The present fireplace is a 1914 insertion, for old photographs show that it was previously in the middle of the upper end wall. Equally drastic has been the eradication of the two bays at the upper end of the hall, leaving only their entry arches. That towards the west originally provided the principal light at the upper end of the hall, but it was destroyed in the early sixteenth century to serve as an approach to an extension to the solar block. The east bay, almost abutting the hillside, enclosed the stair to the solar until the early nineteenth century. The wall of the chamber above was pierced by a spy hole in the shape of a mask, allowing people to look into the hall unperceived as at Great Chalfield Manor. This bay was reconstructed by Brakspear reusing an elaborately decorated window found in the rockery. It serves as a lobby to cloakrooms and the stair leading to his externally hung corridor ingeniously linking the north and south ends of the house without having to traverse the

hall. The hacked courses below the base stops of the entry arches were a consequence of lowering the hall floor in 1703.

The north wing was remodelled in 1703 and possibly the adjacent solar block was abandoned at that time or not long afterwards. It was pulled down in the early nineteenth century and reconstructed by Brakspear in 1919. He incorporated a number of very attractive fifteenth-century windows with multi-cusped heads here and in other parts of the house, including the east oriel, kitchen, and offices at the south end of the house. They betoken rooms of considerable splendour and probably originated in the solar apartments of this manor.

Because of the earlier timber-framed structure, the lower chamber block was three-storeyed under a common roof ridge with the hall. The ground-floor offices were altered during the building of the early sixteenth-century south range. The single rooms on the first and second floor retain no pre-Reformation features outside the first-floor oriel and the single roof bay with its three tiers of wind braces. The approach to these rooms may have been from a staircase on the site of the present one of c.1635 built by Edward Stephens, high sheriff of the county.

The kitchen projected east of the services instead of in line with them. It retains the original fireplace (oak lintel replaced) in the south wall with an oven at the side. The two wooden arches with flattened heads opposite were formerly the original kitchen entrance and a hatch, though when the latter was blocked, the doorway was converted into a hatch and the present entrance inserted. The window is a 1919 make-up from recovered fragments.

There is little documentation for the early history of this dramatically sited house overlooking the Vale of Berkeley and the Severn estuary. Three late medieval building phases can be established.

The retained part of the timber-framed house is possibly fourteenth century. The hall and destroyed solar block were characterised by steeply pitched four-centred arches and highly ornate decorative windows of the second quarter of the fifteenth century as at the Divinity School, Oxford (*c*.1430–9), while the plan of porch, hall, and opposing bays was adopted at a number of nearby houses including South Wraxall Manor (*c*.1460–90), Great Chalfield Manor (*c*.1478–85), Bewley Court (later fifteenth century), and Hazelbury Manor (late fifteenth century). Construction during the third quarter of the fifteenth century is likely for this work by a member of the Stanshawe family who had acquired the manor early in that century.

In 1472, Elizabeth Foster of Little Sodbury Manor married John Walsh of Olveston Court. Their son, Sir John (d.1547), who inherited the property in 1504, remodelled the house in *c*.1510–20, characterised by plain lights and depressed four-centred arches. A popular courtier, he added the south range, rebuilt the kitchen with its upper room, remodelled the hall windows and west bay, and extended the north wing. The Walsh line continued to occupy the house until 1608 when it was purchased by Thomas Stephens. His son Edward inserted the stair tower south of the hall during the 1630s at the same time as he updated some of the rooms nearby. The two-storeyed wing north of the hall with its fine fenestration was rebuilt in *c*.1703. This and the Brakspear extension of 1913–15 on the site of the solar block provide the house with an attractive suite of family rooms.

H. A. Tipping, *English Homes*, Pds 1 and 2, II (1937) 105–12
R. Cooke, *West Country Houses* (1967 edn) 34–7

LYPIATT PARK, Gloucestershire

Commandingly sited on the crest of the Cotswolds overlooking Stancombe valley, Lypiatt Park, formerly the manor house of Over Lypiatt, was first recorded in 1324 when it was the home of the Mansel family until the year before Sir Philip Mansel's death in 1396. His father Sir William may well have been responsible for the original house, but it was replaced by that of the Wye family at the beginning of the sixteenth century. Theirs was a double-courtyard house separated by the great hall flanked by the residential block and services block under a common roof ridge, not unlike the early fourteenth-century hall and services range at Leckhampton Court. Only the walls of the extended hall range at Lypiatt seem to have been incorporated in Sir Jeffry Wyatville's remodelling of the house in 1809–15 for Sir Paul Wathen. Wyatville was typically wholesale in his impressive Gothick castellated style. The hall has always remained open to the roof but the apartment is essentially Regency in character, as are the reception rooms, some whitewashed to set off Lynn Chadwick's sculptures. In 1876, Thomas Henry Wyatt added a more correct but dreary south-west wing in a half-hearted Tudor style.

The more interesting medieval elements to survive are supplementary to the house – the independent chapel and two agricultural outbuildings. Sir Philip Mansel was granted a licence for a private chapel in 1362 and the present two-cell structure in a corner of the outer court probably dates from that time. The side windows in both nave and chancel are early Tudor but the four-light tracer-

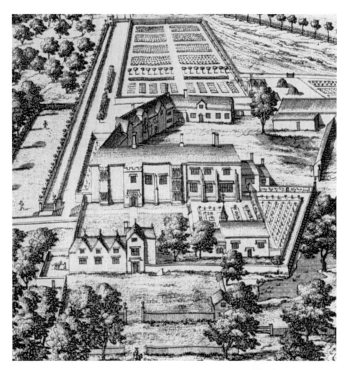

PLATE 50 Lypiatt Park: engraving from the south by Johannes Kip (*c*.1700)

ied windows at the east and west ends, the latter with the family's arms on the head stops, are earlier. The corridor linking the chapel to the house is a pretty Wyatville addition.

The fourteenth-century granary is a well-preserved two-storeyed buttressed structure above a low base with external steps to the first floor and a contemporary grain chute terminating in a spout shaped like a bull's head. The floor is supported on an externally projecting stone ledge to carry the weight of the grain and deter rats. Kip's view of the early Tudor house in *c*.1700 shows that the granary and the contemporary dovecote nearby were among a considerable number of outbuildings beyond the courtyard curtilage and of a kind all too often swept away in a continuing domestic context.

R. Cooke, *West Country Houses* (1967 edn) 29–30
VCH, *Gloucestershire*, II (1976) 111–13

MINSTER LOVELL HALL, Oxfordshire

The principal approach to this early to mid-fifteenth-century mansion of the Lovel family is unclear. The Hall lies next to the church at the end of a lane from the village and this is the approach used today. A less clear one is the path from Witney across the replacement footbridge on medieval stone abutments spanning the River Windrush 300 yards south-east of the house. This leads to a passageway next to the stables and a cobbled path to the hall, but the entry was a particularly modest one, whereas that from the village led through the area now occupied by Manor Farm to the vaulted hall porch. Perhaps this was used by visitors and guests, with their horses being taken by staff to the river entrance and the adjacent stables.

PLATE 51 Minster Lovell Hall: engraving from the north by S. and N. Buck (1729)

Footings of the earlier house of the Lovels were exposed during site excavations in 1937–9 and have been left, to make the courtyard layout a confusing one through their lack of differentiation. All earlier work was swept away by William 7th Lord Lovel (d.1455) and replaced by the present structure between about 1431 and 1440. His son (d.1465) rather than his grandson (d.1487) added a residential tower, but there were no major additions after the property was forfeited to the crown in 1485 or after its purchase by Sir Edward Coke in 1602. Thomas Coke, later 1st earl of Leicester, spent his honeymoon here in 1721 and considered residing permanently at Minster Lovell.[1] Buck's valuable engraving of 1729 shows the house in its occupied state, but Coke initiated the development of Holkham Hall five years later, permanently moved to Norfolk, and abandoned his Oxfordshire property. The Hall was dismantled in about 1747 and became a quarry for building material,[2] but the ruins have changed little since that time.

The mansion was built round three sides of a quadrangle, with the fourth side open to the river until a low buttressed wall was added to hold back winter flooding. Local Cotswold limestone was used throughout, with many of the walls retaining putlog holes. The hall and line of residential apartments stand to roof height, as does the added tower, but the two wings of lodgings and offices facing each other have been reduced to foundation level (fig. 24).

The garden of Manor Farm necessitates an approach today through the churchyard to the decorative cobbled path of uncertain date leading to the hall porch.[3] It is part of the residential range built in front of the hall that introduces the only variant to the normal fifteenth-century house plan that Minster Lovell otherwise displays. Instead of the usual porch tower projecting from the hall face, this porch is at one end of the ground floor, as an integral part of a two-storeyed range with a major apartment at each level. Entry is by a two-centred outer arch with wave and hollow moulding, repeated on the inner face. There were no outer doors. The deep, two-bay passage with stone side benches was quadripartite vaulted with oakleaf and rose bosses. Walls and vault were formerly plastered and there was a pair of doors framed by the inner arch with

bold roll mouldings. The latter is characteristic of the first half of the fifteenth century but wave moulding is a common West of England feature of the late fourteenth century. Lacking the moulded plinth used throughout the remainder of the north range, this outer arch was probably reused from the earlier house.

The walls of the hall, 50 feet by 26 feet, stand to eaves height, creating an apartment 40 feet tall with the gables reaching considerably higher. The relationship of height to length and width is disproportionate to our eyes, emphasised by the practice at the time of limiting the windows to the upper walling, to allow for wall hangings below, but reduced still further here on the north side by the abutting residential block. Most light comes from the two tall square-headed transomed and mullioned windows in the south wall with four-centred rear arch and evidence of cinquefoiled lights. Only a limited amount of light came from the two opposing windows, one of which is still complete though lacking the armorial glazing of the Lovels and associated families that formerly filled all the hall windows.

The walls retain much of their plasterwork but the form of the four-bay roof supported on the continuous moulded corbel is not known. The central hearth was never replaced by a mural fireplace, while Buck's engraving confirms that there was no louvre, only small gable-end chimneys. Cross draughts high in the roof helped the smoke to escape through them and the three square openings in the gable ends. The cross-passage bay at the lower end has a single central entry with double doors opening into the kitchen passage, with a stair entry nearby to the chamber over the services. There is no evidence that the entry to the south court was porch protected, for the passageway here, reduced to footings, is a sixteenth-century addition. The unbroken dais wall is flanked by identical doorways, relatively small in contrast with those at the lower end as befitted the approach to the private apartments.

There were two such groups of apartments, only united at first-floor level. The south door opened into a square stair projection with angled passage to the ground-floor parlour. Its fireplace was originally in the wall common with the hall dais but it was moved to the opposite side in the sixteenth century, retaining the earlier lintel with quatrefoil spandrels. The principal window was in the lost south wall with a slit window in the north-west corner. There was no link between the parlour and the smaller north-facing room.

The main stair ascended to a vaulted lobby and angled passage to the first-floor withdrawing or great chamber, nearly 50 feet by 20 feet, extending over both ground-floor rooms. This important chamber was lit by two-light, mullioned and transomed end-wall windows, that to the north shown by Buck. His engraving also includes the chimney to the fireplace that retains no more today than jamb evidence. This chamber was the pivot to the more private rooms – the chapel lobby to the north, a mural stair to a secure room over the lobby vault (Lovel's treasury), and the family's more privy chambers to the west.

The north door from the hall dais opens into a poorly lit lobby with three-way access – to a west room reduced to foundation level, to a newel at the north-west corner, similarly reduced, and to a fine apartment separated from the lobby by a stone screen. The north-facing wall was filled by three windows set in broad splays to the floor, with rear arches rising to piered quatrefoil spandrels in four-centred heads. The rectangular window frames have lost their heads, but Buck shows that they were of two traceried lights. The end wall is solid, common with the vaulted porch, but the south side had a large fireplace, now bereft of all dressed stonework. Though the newel led to the chapel above (and to a post-Reformation two-storeyed range shown by Buck but leaving no ground evidence), these two larger and smaller ground-floor rooms, lobby separated, were a self-contained suite for a person of quality.

The upper floor, also lobby separated, opened into a five-bay room which extended over the ground-floor porch. Little remains other than its inner wall (common with the hall) and moulded roof corbels. Again, Buck's engraving shows its four windows of three traceried lights and similar east window, all with two-centred heads as against the square heads common elsewhere. Its east-facing position, the distinctive window form, and the shallow scar of the fireplace inserted later point to its use as a chapel before becoming residential at a later stage in the Hall's occupation. The principal entrance, however, was always from the withdrawing chamber into the lobby or ante-chapel.

The north-west range, similarly two-storeyed, has two low ground-floor rooms and a particularly tall upper floor. The lower rooms are without character beyond a simple splayed opening and corner fireplace to the inner room. The upper floor was almost identical in proportions to the withdrawing chamber but the thickness of the ground-floor division and the function of private apartments at this time suggest that it was probably divided into a larger outer and smaller inner chamber.[4] The key survival is the splendid transomed end window with its pair of upper and lower cinque-foiled lights with quatrefoil heads. With its flying rear arch, concave jambs, window seats, and external hood with head stops, this window confirms Buck's evidence that rich fenestration was characteristic of Lovel's mansion.

Little survives of the two-storeyed courtyard wings beyond their foundations. The west wing was divided into five ground-floor rooms, the first two with doorways, the first three with fireplaces, and the last room with end garderobe drain. Of the upper rooms, possibly lodgings or guest accommodation, only the end gable survives with square-headed two-light window.

Early foundations run across the west wing, as they do confusingly across the east wing, particularly at the south end. The broad kitchen passage opening from the lower end of the hall was flanked by timber-partitioned services, one with a double wall cupboard. The chamber above was a major one with a five-light transomed end window (Buck). The passage turned a right angle to the cobbled kitchen with its well and massive hearth in the thickened outer wall. Further south was the river entry and cobbled through-passage, flanked by the stables with two rows of stalls on either side of the central alley.

The Lovel family had held the manor of Minster Lovell since the twelfth century, with documentary and structural evidence of a much-loved house here. They also had a large fortified house in Titchmarsh in Northamptonshire during the thirteenth and early fourteenth centuries but this had fallen into disrepair. Rather than remodel the family home at Minster Lovell, John 5th Lord Lovel had erected an entirely new residence at Wardour in Wiltshire (c.1393). William 7th Lord Lovel did not enter into his inheritance until the death of his grandmother in 1423, a year after his marriage to the heiress of the Deincourt and Grey of Rotherfield baronies, three years after he had successfully claimed Lord Burnell's estates, and fifty years after his grandfather had married the Holand heiress. William served in France during the 1420s but not after 1431. He obtained a licence to impark land close to his manor of Minster Lovell in 1440 and to hold it as free chase under his own rather than the king's forest officers two years later.[5] Reconstruction between about 1431 and 1440 is most probable, by a person who, despite his very considerable wealth, kept a low profile throughout the years leading to the outbreak of the Wars of the Roses in the same year that he died.

Lord Lovel's financial resources were the equal of those of Lord Cromwell,[6] but while the latter was remodelling Tattershall Castle and building Wingfield Manor in addition to his other less expensive projects, Lovel's contemporary activity was far more modest in scale. It was also conventional in layout, particularly in contrast with his grandfather's development at Wardour. The foundation evidence from the earlier manor house still standing in 1423[7] suggests that Lovel followed its layout, with the kitchen and services facing a two-storeyed residential wing as it had at Stanton Harcourt fifty years earlier. The awkward proportions of the hall show the influence of the similarly scaled hall at Wardour Castle, here sited at ground level reusing the previous entry. A ground-floor chapel like that at Rycote was eschewed in favour of a more old-fashioned first-floor one opening from the withdrawing chamber, like that at Broughton Castle a century earlier. The private apartments were two- rather than three-storeyed, with relatively low ground-floor rooms.[8] Buck's engraving as well as the surviving evidence show that the house was generously windowed and richly traceried, for the site had no pretensions to defence or protection. It was simply a comfortably furnished country house, still memorably close to the River Windrush in its field- and tree-framed setting.

The only addition was the four-storeyed tower overlapping the south-west corner of the west wing and almost touching the edge of the river. It was a combined garderobe and lodging tower with prospect room, standing to roof level on the west side and partially so to the north and south. It was built in better-quality stone than the adjoining west wing and was richly decorated with traceried windows and gargoyles at roof level and supporting the newel turret. The ground floor was divided into two garderobe closets

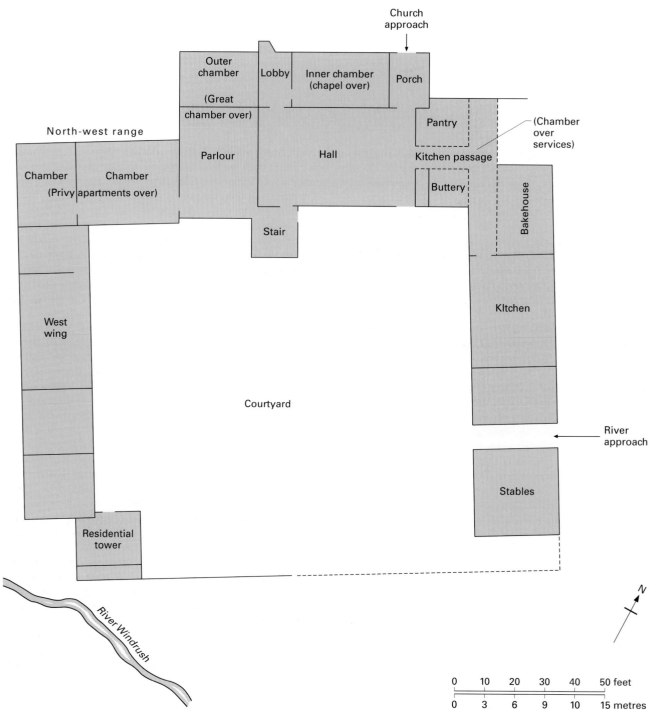

FIGURE 24 Minster Lovell Hall: site plan

served by a pit against the end wall, flushed by the river. An external stair rose to the first floor, retaining a single light and splay evidence of a south-facing window. The two principal rooms above were reached from the first-floor landing by the newel that terminates in an octagonal head above roof level. The second-floor room was fairly low, with a drain and south-facing window, while the uppermost room retains part of a larger south-facing oriel with stopped hood. The ground floor of the High Tower at Wingfield Manor (1440s) was similarly planned for garderobe purposes with the first floor approached from the adjacent wing, and the uppermost room, as in the 1460s tower at Stanton Harcourt, designed to command wide views.

PLATE 52 Minster Lovell Hall: south-west tower

There is little difference between the character of this secondary structure and the earlier windows, plain chapel parapet and gargoyles, so that it is more likely to be the work of John 8th Lord Lovel who died in 1465 than of his successor, Francis 9th Lord Lovel. Francis did not enter into his inheritance until 1478 when he was twenty-two years old, already one of the closest friends and a most loyal supporter of Richard, duke of Gloucester. As a ward of Richard Neville, earl of Warwick, he was brought up with Richard at Middleham Castle, served with Richard in the north, and became chamberlain of the household shortly after Richard's accession to the throne. Gloucester had extended the private apartments at Sudeley Castle, 20 miles away, between *c.*1469 and 1478 so that the usual attribution of the south-west tower to the young Lovel at his family home cannot be entirely dismissed. Though Francis escaped from the battlefield at Bosworth, he failed to do so at Stoke two years later and never saw Minster Lovell again.[9]

NOTES
1 He was created Baron Lovel of Minster Lovell in 1728.
2 The massive fifteenth-century door and fireplace with quatrefoil spandrels in Manor Farm was transferred from the Hall at about this time.
3 The farm has a similar cobbled path.
4 The projection immediately south of the entry probably held garderobes. Buck's engraving shows a surprising absence of windows on the north side of this range, perhaps to ensure privacy from the churchyard.

5 Taylor (1997 edn) 18.
6 R. L. Storey, *The End of the House of Lancaster* (1966) 23.
7 Taylor (1997 edn) 18.
8 The church was also totally rebuilt by Lovel on earlier foundations.
9 For the apocryphal story concerning the discovery of a skeleton two and a half centuries later, Taylor (1997 edn) 19.

A. J. Taylor, *Minster Lovell Hall: Handbook* (1939 and many subsequent editions)

NOTLEY ABBEY, Buckinghamshire

The principal survival of the monasteries at Notley and nearby Thame is their late medieval abbatial lodgings, sharing a common development and stylistic enhancement pattern almost indistinguishable from that of fashionable contemporary society. Notley's domestic range stands in the lee of Long Crendon and at the end of a tree-lined approach and crossing over the River Thame. This Augustinian house, founded before 1162, became one of the wealthier monasteries in the region. The abbey church was excavated in 1937[1] and two sides of the thirteenth-century cloister garth survive as a barn and the domestic offices range of the present house. The main residence is L-shaped, two-storeyed throughout, built of rubble stone with some dressed work. It has been continuously inhabited and has not suffered major structural loss, though it had devolved to farmhouse status by about 1730 until regenerated in about 1890. The tactful restoration gave it a sympathetic late medieval character by replacing the many Georgian casement windows with those of early Tudor form.

The west claustral range, 82 feet long, probably the cellarer's domain with guest accommodation above, has been so thoroughly adapted for twentieth-century kitchen, offices, and bedrooms that interest focuses entirely on the late medieval north-west building. It was developed in two phases, a mid-fifteenth-century structure at right angles to the earlier west range, and an early sixteenth-century cross wing with a slightly higher roof and a stair turret at the north-west angle.

The ground floor of the fifteenth-century unit consists of two unequal-sized rooms (now dining and withdrawing), as it did originally, but the present division is comparatively recent and has reversed the rooms' proportions. The original division is marked by an external buttress, while the roof structure confirms that the block was of five bays, with the outer room of three and the inner room of two bays. The same plan was followed at first-floor level where the chambers were open to the roof. They are lit at both levels by identical windows of paired cinquefoil lights, well moulded internally and externally, with four small trefoil lights in line above under square hoods. However, this striking fenestration is a rearrangement of *c.*1890. Late nineteenth-century photographs show only the two windows to the right of the buttress in their present position, with a blocked second one at first-floor level further to the right and another one opposite it on the north side of the block. Though these last two have been resited to the left of the buttress to create the present regular pattern, there is no doubt that these windows are genuine and pertinent to this block.

It consisted of a hall 35 feet long and an inner chamber 20 feet long at both levels. The ground-floor approach from the claustral

PLATE 53 Notley Abbey: east frontage

range was by a fifteenth-century doorway with continuous moulded jambs and two-centred head (now blocked).[2] The larger room had a ground-floor fireplace in the middle bay, now eliminated. The chamfered ceiling beams in both rooms are markedly plain. The upper floor has been ceiled and divided into bedrooms and a north-facing corridor, with all windows on this side uncusped lights of c.1890. Originally the larger outer chamber was open to a fine three-bay roof spanned by collar-beam trusses supporting V struts filled with open quatrefoil tracery, now badly damaged. The two-bay inner chamber was spanned off-centre by a collar-beam truss supported by curved moulded braces but minus any decorative quatrefoil between the struts. The two chambers are separated by a tie-beam truss to support a partition, with the plaster infill to the roof ridge decorated with sprigs of flowers. Both chambers have moulded wall plates and a single line of wind braces. In the absence of smoke-blackened timbers, a mural fireplace to the upper hall using the same stack as below may be assumed, but the inner chamber fireplace survives. Both hall and chamber were lit by the earlier-mentioned windows – the hall with two facing south and one in the north wall, and the inner chamber with one identical with that reinstated next to the fireplace. The markedly low ground-floor rooms are likely to have been the abbot's kitchen and offices, conveniently next to the cellarer's range, with the upper rooms occupied by the abbot.[3] Their approach has not been traced, but it may have been in the end wall, rebuilt when the north cloister range was pulled down.

The abbot's accommodation proved inadequate, and it was extended in the early sixteenth century by a wing almost at right angles to the earlier block. It consisted at both levels of a single room and short projection at the south-west angle, linked by a newel in the hexagonal turret at the north-west angle. The wing was raised on a continuous low plinth and supported by end buttresses, diagonal to the south, with no evidence of a building break between the projection and the body of the wing. The ground-floor north window of paired transomed lights with uncusped four-centred heads under a square hood is original,[4] and was the pattern for all the window replacements of c.1890. The stair turret with light slits, two string courses, and an embattled head is in excellent state, and is unusual in having its own external entry.

The ground floor of the cross wing is an imposing one, particularly as it is now approached through a forced doorway from the preceding low-ceiled rooms, whereas it was originally entered from the newel lobby. This spacious chamber, with its original north window, has a high ceiling, well-moulded beams, and a striking fireplace 9 feet wide. The wooden lintel and jambs are a copy of those in the room above, while the low fireplace in the projection was a doorway at the beginning of the twentieth century.[5] The newel steps are broad, and though the entry to the lower room has been walled up, that serving the room above has not. The upper chamber retains its stone jambs to the wooden lintel, with a garderobe to the side with its shaft integral with the chimney stack. The roof of tie-beam trusses with queen-post-supported collar and wind braces is utilitarian and undecorated, and was probably never visible.

This extension was a two-unit lodging at both levels, interlinked,

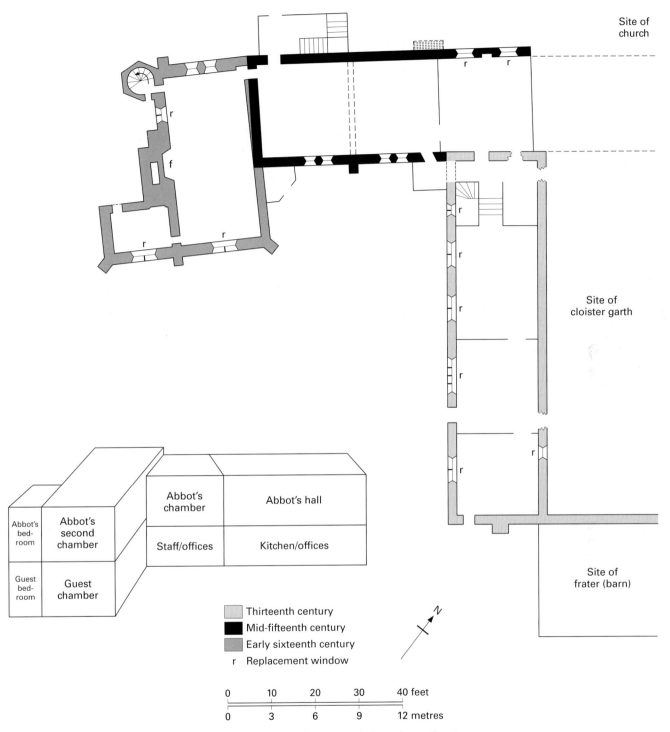

Site of church

r r

r

Site of cloister garth

r

r

r

r

r

r

Abbot's chamber

Abbot's hall

Abbot's bed-room

Abbot's second chamber

Staff/offices

Kitchen/offices

Guest bed-room

Guest chamber

Site of frater (barn)

Thirteenth century

Mid-fifteenth century

Early sixteenth century

r   Replacement window

N

0	10	20	30	40 feet
0	3	6	9	12 metres

FIGURE 25 Notley Abbey: ground plan and room function

but its occupation pattern is conjectural. Because of the height of the ground-floor room, the chamber above was at a higher level than the earlier rooms used by the abbot so that the present forced passage and steps between them would have had to be made at that time. The abbot now enjoyed a grand suite of rooms – hall, chamber, second chamber, and bedchamber – while the ground-floor lodging,

with its independent entry from the newel lobby, would have been reserved for special guests. It was probably this added first-floor chamber that was enhanced in about 1530 with the exquisite panelling made for the last abbot, Richard Rydge (1529–39) and bearing his name in the wooden cornice. In about 1780, the five tiers of linenfold panelling 12 feet high and the elaborately carved cornice were moved to Weston Manor, 12 miles away, where they now line the great hall.[6]

This mid-fifteenth-century development and early sixteenth-century expansion of the abbot's lodging closely parallels that at the Cistercian abbey at Thame, 3 miles to the south. Similarly two-storeyed but slightly smaller in scale, Notley retains the roof structures that Thame has lost, whereas Thame retains the contemporary panelling and cornice that have been taken from Notley. The cornice design with its heads in medallions, mermaids, urns, arabesques, and acanthus scrolls is very similar to that at Thame. It is evidence of the close ties between these two foundations where the last abbot, Robert King (1530–9), was similarly enhancing his lodgings with comparable internal decoration of outstanding quality. About twenty years earlier, his predecessor John Warren (1509–29) had extended and enhanced the lodgings at Thame at about the same time they were being extended at Notley. Both residences point to the highest standards of comfort and scale, no different by this time from those of secular society. Less than 3 miles away, the same craftsmen also worked at Nether Winchendon House, a residence long owned by Notley Abbey and leased in 1527 to one of Henry VIII's privy councillors, Sir John Daunce (d.1545).[7] The ground-floor parlour in the extension he built was lined during the early 1530s with linenfold panelling surmounted by a delicately carved cornice with early Renaissance decoration repeated on the underside of the intersecting cross beams and comparable with the work at Thame. Ecclesiastical and secular patronage had become indistinguishable, but who was the initiator in this closely related circle of early Renaissance craftsmanship in the Buckinghamshire/Oxfordshire area, church or state?

NOTES

1 Pantin (1941) 25–34. Earlier cloister excavations in 1932–3 recorded by C. Hohler, *Rec. of Berks.* 12 and 13 (1939–40).

2 All other doorways throughout the range, internal and external, are post-medieval.

3 The *camera abbatis* is mentioned in a visitation of 1447. A. H. Thompson, *Visitations (1436–49)* (1918) 256.

4 See page 183 n.5.

5 See RCHM (1912) 245, plan and comment. The shaft access from the ground-floor hearth is a mid-twentieth-century forced entry.

6 Weston Manor is a mid-sixteenth-century house developed round a moated medieval house of Osney Abbey and used by their bailiffs from the thirteenth century to 1539. Though the low north and west wings round a small court to the rear of the Tudor house retain some medieval evidence, the principal structure is the early sixteenth-century hall, 42 feet by 19 feet, in the south range. It may have been used as the court room of the manor but the mid position and height of the projecting stair turret suggest that it was more probably created from a two-storeyed chamber block. Today, this room is embellished with the early sixteenth-century panelling from the abbot's house at Notley and a fifteenth-century roof from one of its claustral ranges. This fine five-bay structure has arch-braced collar trusses with two rows of wind braces, moulded wall plates, and traces of blue, green, and deep red colouring. It was initially moved from the abbey to Great Chesterton in the eighteenth century until transferred to Weston in 1851 and positioned on Victorian corbels. H. Carr, *Country Life* (August 1928); VCH, *Oxfordshire*, VI (1959) 347.

7 The timber frame of the fifteenth-century hall survives within the post-medieval stone-clad and brick-built residence. The house retains the lease of 1527 between Daunce and John Marston, abbot of Notley, and also holds a near-contemporary tapestry of Henry VIII flanked by Lord

Russell and archbishop Cranmer, with a particularly fine border of early Renaissance decoration. A. Oswald, *Country Life* (April–May 1960).

VCH, *Buckinghamshire*, IV (1927) 36–7
RCHM, *Buckinghamshire (South)* (1912) 244–6
W. A. Pantin, *Oxoniensia* 6 (1941) 22–43

OCKWELLS MANOR, Berkshire

The court of Henry VI at Windsor Castle and the construction of Eton College influenced the development of Ockwells Manor, 7 miles distant. Well over 500 years later, a motorway and the spread of suburban housing from Maidenhead to within a field's distance have deprived the property of its long-held isolation, although it still faces a rural landscape.

DEVELOPMENT

The manor was acquired by the Lancashire family of Noreys in 1268 when it was granted to Richard Noreys, cook to Queen Eleanor.[1] It passed in 1422 to Sir William Noreys, the younger son of Sir Henry Noreys of Speke near Liverpool, the chosen centre of the family's extensive and continuously expanding landholding in south-west Lancashire and west Cheshire. William served as sheriff of Berkshire under Henry V and was an esquire of the body to Henry VI during his infancy. The manor of Ockwells passed to his son John in about 1446,[2] who had entered royal service by 1429 as an usher of the chamber.[3] Grants, custodies, and benefits flowed towards him during the 1430s and 1440s.[4] He rose to the key household positions of master of the royal wardrobe (first recorded in 1447) and treasurer of the queen's chamber (1446–52). He built up a substantial landholding in Oxfordshire and Berkshire, was sheriff in those and several other counties between 1437 and 1448, and was a member of parliament on seven occasions between 1439 and 1453.[5] Though a long-standing and dependable household figure and a staunch Lancastrian, he seems to have retained his position as master of the wardrobe under Edward IV.

John Noreys married three times. By 1437 he was married to Alice Merbrooke of Yattendon near Reading, who brought him that manor which served as Noreys' principal residence for much of his life, crenellated under licence in 1448 and where he rebuilt the church.[6] His second wife was Eleanor Clitherow, a Kentish heiress whose fortune helped to pay for Ockwells Manor, while his third wife was Margaret Chedworth who married Noreys in September 1459. Within four months of Noreys' death in September 1466, Margaret had married that zealous Yorkist the duke of Norfolk (d.1485), but she retained Ockwells until her own death ten years later.[7]

Initially John Noreys owned a house at Windsor to be close to the royal court he served,[8] but he initiated the construction of Ockwells during the last decade of Henry VI's reign. The armorial glass in the hall includes the arms of his first and second wives, but not those of his third, and those of Henry VI and his queen but not those of Edward IV. It is unlikely that the arms of the house of Lancaster would have been displayed so prominently after the deposition of Henry VI, particularly as Noreys owed his knighthood to his Yorkist successor. Other arms limit the construction of the hall to a date after 1451 when Richard Beauchamp, one of Noreys'

PLATE 54 Ockwells Manor: entrance front from the outer court

associates, was appointed bishop of Salisbury and before 1459 when Noreys remarried for the third time. In his will of April 1465, Noreys made a bequest of £40 to 'the full bilding and making uppe of the Chapell with the Chambres ajoyning with'n my manoir of Okholt in the p'issh of Bray aforesaid not yet finisshed, x1 pounds'.[9] Construction of the house was therefore initiated during the early 1450s, and it was essentially built by 1459, with the final work nearing completion by 1465, eighteen months before Noreys' death.

The highly important hall glass is entirely a display of the builder's patrons, friends, and associates. Apart from the arms of Henry VI and Queen Margaret, there are those of the queen's chamberlain (Lord Wenlock), her keeper of the wardrobe (Richard Bulstrode), the dukes of Somerset (d.1455), Suffolk (d.1450), and Warwick (d.1446), the earl of Wiltshire (d.1461), Sir Richard Nanfan (d.1447), and more locally John Purye of Bray, another household official, and Sir William Lacon, the chief justice, buried in Bray church. Just as Ralph, Lord Cromwell, was the centre of a building programme involving his circle of friends, so Noreys was influenced by his patrons and associates, including the work of the king at Eton College, the Beauchamp family at Warwick, Elmley, Hanley, and Cardiff castles, as well as their extensions of Warwick collegiate church, Lord Wenlock at Someries, and Sir Richard Nanfan who initiated the development of Birtsmorton Court. Noreys' display could not be a more ostentatious demonstration of political partisanship[10] (see plate 201).

No evidence has been found of any earlier house before the present one, which stands complete, as do some of the contemporary outbuildings round two sides of the outer court. Quadrangular shaped round its own smaller inner court, Ockwells Manor stands two storeys high except for the hall (and originally the kitchen) which is open to the roof. The entrance façade is nearly symmetrical, with the hall block in the centre, flanked by a residential range at each end. The kitchen and service rooms were in an unusual position filling the fourth side of the inner court.

In 1583, the Noreys family sold the property to William Day, provost of Eton, whose son rebuilt the north side of the inner court to accommodate a new staircase. The house was rescued from its dilapidated farmhouse state by Sir Stephen Leach in 1889 who initiated the restoration, completed at the beginning of the twentieth century by Sir Edward Barry (d.1949).[11] Their thorough programme under Fairfax Wade made good the original fabric, but no record was kept of their work so that the house is now seen through a late Victorian 'bloom'. Few basic changes were made, but the staircase was moved and a large window inserted to light it. The hall windows were left alone, but all the others in the outer façade were reconstructed and enhanced with elaborately decorated lights. Those in the other fronts were totally renewed, and the openings round the inner court were glazed. Two elaborate sixteenth-century fireplaces were brought in, while Barry also added a wing of offices and staff quarters at the north-west angle.

FORECOURT

The manor house stands on one side of a grassed forecourt which may have originally been divided, physically as well as functionally, for the outer part is devoted to estate facilities (base court) and the inner part to domestic buildings (outer court).[12] Today, it is among the larger forecourts of its period in England. Approximately 220 feet by 140 feet towards the lower end, it is smaller than the north court of Dartington Hall (1388–99) and the contemporary institutional quadrangles planned though not built by Henry VI at Eton College and King's College, Cambridge, but larger than the outer court of Lord Cromwell's Wingfield Manor (1440–c.1456).[13] It was exceeded by only a handful of quadrangles during the close of the middle ages such as Thornbury Castle and the outer court of Eltham Palace which did not take its final shape until the early Tudor period.[14]

The forecourt is entered through an open archway abutting the house end of the stable block. This was the original approach from Windsor, and though it lacks door evidence, the entry was presumably closed initially. It was no more defensive than the chambered lich-gate (1448) to Bray church or that to Long Compton church in Warwickshire. The stable block is a single storey, timber-framed with brick infilling, whereas the gateway upper storey is plaster-filled between the posts. The first-floor room with its apparently original courtyard-facing oriel of eight cusped lights[15] was reached from the adjacent range, but since the destruction of the latter in the eighteenth century, the room has been deprived of any point of entry.

The east side of the court is closed by a box-frame and brick-built barn of eight bays, 120 feet long, with two prominent wagon entrances facing the house. Beyond its north end is a brick dovecote, supported by four added stepped buttresses with stone facings. There is no reason to doubt that these outer buildings are contemporary with the house.[16] They provided the essential support for the estate of a large household, including stabling, straw, hay, wagon storage, and winter food provision.

That part of the court closer to the house is flanked by two ruined brick walls marking the position of former ranges. That on the left has four-centred doorways at each end, separating irregularly spaced windows. The arms and animals in the spandrels of the doorway next to the house are claimed to be the arms of Noreys and his first wife, with the supporters of his second wife.[17] It is immediately followed

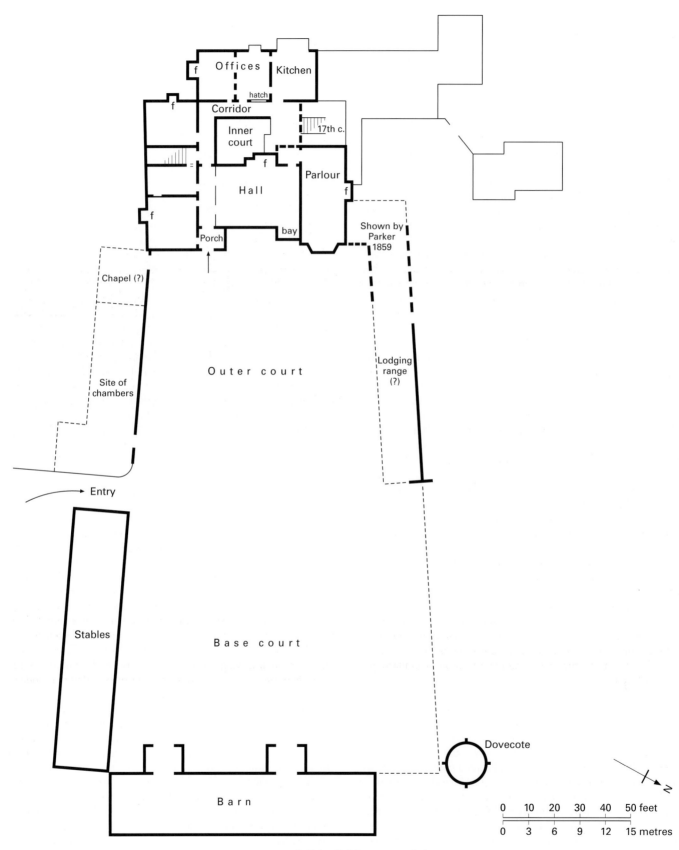

FIGURE 26 Ockwells Manor: ground plan

by a four-light window with a low sill and a prominent chalk stone which may mark an internal division of a room 20 feet long. All but one of the windows in the remainder (and greater part) of the range are blocked, but the stub of brick walling in the south garden, 30 feet from the range entry, hints at an L-shaped building. Said to have been destroyed by fire in 1720,[18] this range is the only one to use dressed stone and a diamond pattern of dark brick headers. These features point to a slightly later date of construction, while its east-facing position next to the house gives credence to its attribution as the chapel and group of chambers mentioned in Noreys' will of 1465.

The right-hand wall is equally impassive. Of single-storey height and at a slight obtuse angle to the house, it is interrupted by five slits in wide embrasures under wooden lintels, 10 feet apart. It has been suggested these were arrow slits in a curtain wall protecting the approach from Maidenhead,[19] but it is more likely that it was the outer wall of a courtyard range. Nash and Parker show part of such a structure on this side of the court, two-storeyed and timber-framed, linked by a narrow gabled block to the house.[20] It had been truncated by 1859, but the standing brick wall may be part of its outer face, a remnant of a staff or household lodging range, similar to those lining the outer court at Wingfield Manor. Furthermore, this and the opposing ranges slightly taper towards the entrance front of the house, creating a theatrical approach as the similarly positioned ranges do more forcefully at Lord Cromwell's Derbyshire mansion.

HOUSE

The house is a box-frame structure, laid on a brick sill, with brick noggin externally, and plaster infill between the timber studs internally. Despite its late Victorian elaboration, the entrance façade was always intended to be a show front. It is not entirely symmetrical in design, for the outer gables at each end of the central hall block are slightly higher and larger than the inner gables above the porch and hall bay window, while the two-storeyed porch projects more prominently than the bay window, just as the left-hand range does compared with that to the right.

The façade's embellishment lies in four planes – brick noggin, window heads, gable heads, and barge boards. The brick infill is patterned in four designs, created by setting the lines of bricks at different angles between the timber supports. This is most obvious in the central bays of the hall and the side wall of the porch. Suspicion that this may be late Victorian elaboration is allayed to some extent by its depiction at first-floor level in Parker's illustration of 1859, and by the increasing identification of similarly patterned contemporary work.[21]

Apart from the hall with its plain two-centred lights, each window is of wide proportions with different patterns of ingeniously shaped heads. These are insertions by Barry. Comparison with Joseph Nash's illustration of this frontage in 1838 shows that only the hall windows survive unaltered. All the others were two- or three-light openings of Elizabethan date, except for that serving the first-floor solar where the three lights have the four-centred heads of the hall oriel.[22] Fred Crossley noted that the oriel windows in the end gables were reconstructed from sufficient indications, but were reproductions with problematical tracery.[23] The three shields and motto on the underside of the porch oriel is again Barry elaboration. Garner and Stratton noted that the foundations of the

PLATE 55 Ockwells Manor: engraving of hall interior by Joseph Nash (1838–48)

bay window to the withdrawing room under the solar existed below ground and the mortise holes where the main timbers had been removed gave clear indications of the missing parts. In their opinion, the rebuilding of this bay had been carried out with much skill and commendable conservatism.[24]

The gable heads are filled with blind panelling and the ornate barge boards, not surprisingly damaged in places, are also original. While the two on the left differ slightly from those on the right, Nash shows them in existence in 1838, as do Turner and Parker with one illustrated in detail.[25] Reference has already been made to the lost gabled range to the right of the residential block and in line with it (though lacking its barge board by 1859). The entrance front, therefore, was less elaborate and more extended than today, and though Barry's work was intended to enhance the façade, it over-gilds the lily. The other three façades are plain. Their brickwork is regularly laid and the windows are all Barry replacements.

The hall is entered from the storeyed porch with its small upper chamber. The spandrels of the depressed four-centred outer arch have dragons and oak leaves, and those of the similar inner arch have a griffin and an antelope. The entry door is original, but there is a secondary door facing the open framework on the north side of the porch. The hall is of four bays, 41¾ feet by 24 feet. The screens passage fills half the first bay, with an original door at the further end opening into the inner court corridor. The screen, in part original, is a plain structure of strong vertical studs with a mid-rail and two broad openings into the body of the hall. It has a few panels with cinquefoil heads near the entry doors, and a low battlemented cornice.

The hall is lit by windows with plain four-centred lights in the upper half of the second and the east side of the third bay, with the fireplace filling most of the opposite wall. The projecting square window of the fourth bay with two tiers of six lights and three more in the upper return opens from the dais under a four-centred arch.[26] The fireplace is a well-proportioned stone structure, 8 feet wide and almost as tall, with a pillar on either side and space for an oblong panel or painted frieze above the head of the four-centred opening. The lower half of the walls is covered with seventeenth-century panelling, but the timber framing and plaster infill above are exposed. The open roof, 36 feet from floor to apex, is a braced collar-beam structure with simple mouldings and a single line of curved wind braces.

The hall essentially survives in its original condition, a relatively plain but well-proportioned structure. The one elaborate feature is the almost complete and rare display of contemporary armorial glass in the windows towards the forecourt. Eight out of the nine upper lights in the bay and the ten lights in the two adjacent windows are filled with a brilliantly coloured display of arms and helms against quarries painted with the badge of three distaffs tied by a gold ribbon, thought to be the badge of the royal wardrobe which had been under Noreys' control.[27] If so, he was simply emulating Ralph, Lord Cromwell's practice of displaying the Treasurer's purse at Tattershall Castle and Wingfield Manor. Each light is banded with diagonal stripes of white glass with the mottoes *dieu et mon droit* and *humble et loial* enriching the two royal arms and the words *ffeyth fully serve* about the rest. Noreys' dedication to the Lancastrian cause could not be clearer, while the quality is so capable that it could have been the work of the king's glazier, John Prudde.[28] The arms are no longer in their original order as they were removed to Taplow Court early in the nineteenth century until the restoration of the house by Barry warranted their return.

The original approach to the family residential unit has been superseded by the seventeenth-century staircase, moved by Barry from the courtyard, but direct corridor access towards the kitchen at this point would have been unlikely. The ground-floor parlour, 35½ feet by 16½ feet, is divided into three bays, with ceiling beams of the plainest character. The fireplace is mid-sixteenth century, the panelling early seventeenth, and the ten-light bay window a Barry re-creation on the original foundations.[29] The chamber above is of similar proportions (now with end lobby and bathroom) with a comparable fireplace to that below and a queen post roof.

The rooms at the lower end of the hall do not follow the conventional plan. Two adjacent contemporary doorways open from the screens passage into differently proportioned rooms. The larger one is also approached from a door in the porch (a feature repeated at Ufton Court) and has a fireplace which the second room lacks. As there is evidence of a door in the partition wall, Noreys planned a two-roomed lodging in this position with its own independent entrance, possibly for a special member of his family. There is a single large room above.

The small inner court was originally surrounded on three sides by a double-storeyed cloister with a continuous row of unglazed wooden windows with plain four-centred heads at both ground- and first-floor level.[30] The north side was modified in the seven-

PLATE 56 Ockwells Manor: hatch to buttery

teenth century, and the fourth side is taken up by the hall chimney stack and rear wall. The ground-floor corridor accessed the offices and kitchen. The pantry and buttery were formerly separated by a stud and panel partition, since removed to create a single room, but the impressive servery hatch survives with its fall-front shelf towards the corridor, original hinges, and unglazed window above.[31] The kitchen, formerly open to the roof and with a large hearth in its outer wall and two wells nearby, has been completely modernised. Leach and Barry's alterations thoroughly modified this part of the house when they converted the three service rooms and the large chamber separating them from the subsidiary staircase to residential use, and inserted the two elaborate fireplaces dated 1601 and 1673.[32] For a family with cooking ability in their blood, the facilities at Ockwells are elaborate and well planned. Food prepared in a kitchen well away from the rest of the household would have been passed to the servery, carried down the two unglazed corridors to the screens passage, and thence through the hall towards the dais table.

The first-floor rooms can be approached from the original subsidiary staircase on the south side of the house. They essentially follow the plan of the rooms below, and have not been greatly altered from their initial condition through adaptation to modern living purposes. They benefited from the independent corridor access, although the area next to the bedroom above the parlour may have been an outer chamber. None of the fireplaces is of consequence, while all the rooms are open to braced collar-beam roofs with king- or queen-post supports and single lines of wind braces.

OVERVIEW

Ockwells Manor is a pristine example of a mid-fifteenth-century home of a well-to-do knight with close courtly connections, little altered in materials, plan, elevation, or occupation. It is enhanced by survival of some of the associated outbuildings, and the remains of a chapel and lodging range. Though not as imposing as contemporary magnate-built double-courtyard mansions such as Sudeley Castle and Wingfield Manor, Ockwells can be compared in overall layout with Great Chalfield Manor (1478–85). They both have an outer court with chapel, stables, barn, and arched entrance, a symmetrical façade, a slightly unusual disposition of generously proportioned rooms, and a small inner court with arcaded passages.

Ockwells takes pleasure in the use of its building materials. Pevsner described it as 'the most refined and most sophisticated timber-framed mansion in England',[33] although his assessment included the Victorian embellished windows. Nevertheless, Ockwells is restrained in comparison with framed houses of the Weald, and positively subtle judged against work in the Welsh borderland and Cheshire.[34] Ockwells has been compared by John Harris with Cresswells (or Philiberds) Manor in Berkshire, a destroyed timber-framed residence nearby with some similarities, though the framing of the timbered gables and the large windows look sixteenth rather than mid-fifteenth century.[35] The primary influence was undoubtedly the school buildings at Eton College (1441–9), not only through links of patronage but also through the predominant use of brick and possibly the employment of the same craftsmen, initially for in-filling between the timbers, but more extensively for the ranges round the outer court. The College was equally influential in the use of glazed windows without decorative cusping, and the decision to build a double-storeyed cloister with unglazed windows round the inner court.

Decoration was primarily concentrated on the entrance façade. Superficially symmetrical, the frontage is inventive and welcoming. In proportions, tones, and harmony of materials, this façade is an aesthetic pleasure. In contrast, the lack of internal ornamentation is striking. This particularly applies to the hall screen and roof, the plain four-centred window heads (where not Victorianised), and the roofs of the principal upper rooms. On the other hand, the dazzling armorial glass in the hall suggests that the plainness of the building may have been deliberate to offset the richness of its furnishings.[36] This splendid example of the glazier's art, proudly displaying Noreys' badge of office just as Lord Cromwell did, creates a sumptuous effect that also points up what has been lost in other houses through centuries of destruction.

Internally, the Manor was (and is) a spacious, airy residence which was not so much unconventional as advanced and highly practical in its planning. The offices and kitchen were moved some distance from the polite rooms, and a paired lodging was created at the lower end of the hall pointing towards the preference by later generations for a second parlour in this position. Noreys' near contemporary Thomas Tropnell built a comfortable parlour below the screens at Great Chalfield Manor, a further example of the desire for privacy initiating new design concepts at this period. The size of the first-floor rooms is noteworthy, while the highly practical internal corridors at ground- and first-floor levels are a reflection of the cloister practice adopted at the highest level, including Herstmonceux Castle, Eton College, and Tattershall Castle,[37] to bring order, shelter, and privacy to the household. Far less altered than most contemporary houses, Ockwells Manor is a prime example of a mid-century residence, designed to impress Noreys' courtly friends and to be a convivial centre to entertain them, and an unequivocal statement of his success and affluence.

NOTES

1 *Cal. Pat. Rolls: 1266–72*, 190.

2 VCH, III (1923) 103.

3 J. C. Wedgwood, *History of Parliament: 1439–1509* (1936) 637.

4 *Ibid.* 637–9.

5 R. A. Griffiths, *The Reign of King Henry VI* (1981) 340–1. He is mentioned as 'The Conduite' among the courtiers listed in the political song 'On the Popular Discontent at the Disasters in France' written in *c.*1449. T. Wright, *Political Poems and Songs*, II (1861) 222.

6 *Cal. Charter Rolls: 1427–1516*, 100. Silk (1989) 20 for his responsibility for the church. She also draws attention to the roof's design similarity with that over the hall at Ockwells.

7 *The Com. Peer.*, IX (1936) 612.

8 Griffiths, *The Reign of King Henry VI*, 303. In 1443, John Noreys had received a hundred marks for the repair of Windsor Castle and the lodge in Windsor park, *Cal. Pat. Rolls: 1441–46*, 151.

9 D. Lysons, *Magna Britannia*, I pt 2 (1813) 449, 247.

10 The display is interrupted by the arms and crests of a Mortimer, possibly the Chirk Castle branch of this Yorkist family. This suggests that partisanship had not become totally entrenched when the window glass was designed and made. Later fifteenth-century displays of family alliances have also survived at Cotehele House (Sir Piers Edgcumbe) and at Athelhampton Hall (Sir William Martyn). That at Adlington Hall is a display of arms on the canopy over the hall dais.

11 For the later history of the manor, VCH, III (1923) 103–4; Andrews (1918) 19–28. For the restoration, Tipping (1937) 163–88; N. Carew, *The Connoisseur Year Book* (1953) 20–6.

12 There was a similar base court with barn and stables at Kimbolton Castle, and also at Compton Wynyates, lost in both cases. A. Emery, *Greater Med. Houses*, II (2000) 264, 381.

13 Dartington Hall, 265 feet by 164 feet towards the lower end; Wingfield Manor, 195 feet by 155 feet.

14 Thornbury Castle, 315 feet by 245 feet; Eltham Palace, 319 feet by 263 feet.

15 A modest four-light window faces the countryside.

16 Though Yattendon Manor was replaced in the eighteenth century, the mid-fifteenth-century barn in its grounds was contemporary with the house crenellated in 1448.

17 VCH, III (1923) 96.

18 Carew (1953) 20.

19 C. Hussey in Tipping (1937) 166.

20 J. Nash, *The Mansions of England in the Olden Time* (1838) pl. 77; T. H. Turner and J. H. Parker, *Some Account of Domestic Architecture in England*, III pt 2 (1859) opp. 278.

21 Ewelme almshouse *c.*1437–42; Hertford Castle gateway 1462–3.

22 Nash, *The Mansions of England in the Olden Time* (1838) pl. 77.

23 *Timber Buildings in England* (1951) 151.

24 T. Garner and A. Stratton, *The Domestic Architecture of England During the Tudor Period*, I (1911) 46.

25 *Some Account of Domestic Architecture in England*, III pt 2, opp. 278. Alec Clifton Taylor believed them to be late nineteenth-century work, but he confused their dating with that of the windows, *The Pattern of English Building* (1962) 42.

26 The position of the dais is indicated by the change in floor level to the bay window and replacement door opposite.

27 Tipping (1937) 179.

28 Prudde was responsible for the glass at Eton Chapel in 1445–6, *HKW*, I (1963) 284. For armorial details, E. Green, *Archaeologia* 56 (1899) 323–36, summarised in Carew (1953) 21–3.

29 An oddly sited four-centred arch immediately below ceiling level at the lower end of the room suggests there may have been a further window position.

30 Nash, *The Mansions of England in the Olden Time* pl. 79. These and the hall windows are the only early ones left in the house.

31 There is a similarly positioned hatch at Ufton Court, Ufton Nervet. This mainly sixteenth-century timber-framed house of elongated E-shape retains the screens passage, offices, and kitchen of its late fifteenth-century predecessor. As the offices now hold an Elizabethan stair and the kitchen has an inserted floor and blocked stack, the serving hatch is the most interesting early survival in this house. VCH, III (1923) 437–43.

32 The plans in Garner and Stratton, *The Domestic Architecture of England* (1911) 45 and VCH, III (1923 though prepared before the 1914–18 War) show considerable discrepancy in their layout of this part of the house.

33 *The Buildings of England: Berkshire* (1966) 187.

34 Compare, for instance, with the elaborate character of Speke Hall, developed by the Noreys family during the 1530s and 1540s.

35 *The Artist and the Country House* (1979) 43, 58, pl. VIII. Also VCH, III (1923).

36 Christopher Hussey, repeated by Joan Evans and Geoffrey Webb, was keen to point out the exploitation of the special properties of timber in the hall through its proportions, but the aesthetic role of the master-carpenter can be overplayed when the roof structure and screen prove so plain. Tipping (1937) 171–3; *English Art: 1307–1461* (1949) 134; *Architecture in Britain: The Middle Ages* (1956) 163.

37 The open cloister at Tattershall Castle linked the hall with Cromwell's tower-house (probably early to mid-1440s). One of the earliest glazed double corridors was that at the prior's lodging, Wenlock Priory, dendro dated to 1424–7.

H. C. Andrews, *Berks., Bucks. and Oxon. Arch. Jour.* 24 (1918) 19–28
VCH, *Berkshire*, III (1923) 93–6, 103–4
H. A. Tipping, *English Homes*, Pds 1 and 2, II *1066–1558* (1937) 163–88
N. Carew, *The Connoisseur Year Book* (1953) 20–6
C. Silk, 'The lifestyle of the gentry in the later middle ages, with special reference to John Noreys of Ockwells Manor, Berkshire', University of Southampton BA dissertation (1989)

OLVESTON COURT and Gloucestershire fortified houses

This lightly fortified manor house, 5 miles south-west of Thornbury, came into the possession of the south Gloucestershire family of Denys through the marriage of Sir William Denys to Margaret Corbett of Olveston in 1378. His son similarly acquired Dyrham Park through marriage in 1416, adding to a portfolio which already included houses not far away at Alvestone and Siston. Sir Maurice Denys, who seems to have been a Yorkist supporter, improved Dyrham by adding 'a new courte' to the previous 'meane howse there'.[1] In 1472, Olveston Court was acquired by John Walshe whose family held it until 1600. John Walshe (d.1498) married Elizabeth Foster of Little Sodbury Manor and their son moved there in 1511 in preference to the Court. By the close of the sixteenth century Olveston had entered a period of neglect, and it was in ruins by 1712 when Atkyns wrote his history of the county. The remains are not all that different today.

Although the present approach to Olveston Court is from the village, originally it lay in the opposite direction, with a visitor cresting a low rise to look down on the moated manor house. The visitor would then wend his or her way towards the embattled frontage and gateway, like the similar approach to the grander fortified houses at Nunney and Wardour. The crenellated enclosing wall and relatively tall but simple gateway are the main survivals of a site that has lost the principal house. The rubble-built wall extends 330 feet

PLATE 57 Olveston Court: gatehouse and south frontage

west of the gateway, water-protected since 1992, and interrupted towards the west by a postern of dressed stone with holes above the blocked entry for drawbridge chains. At its far end, the wall turns north for 30 feet until broken away; its eastwards continuation was incorporated in the farmhouse next to the gateway. The Court lay on the west side of this entry.

The two-storeyed gateway with tall central carriage and blocked pedestrian side entry has a small porter's lodge and a pristine newel to the rear behind an early oak door. The undivided upper chamber was lit by a twin light above the rear entrance and a single one to the front with a stone oriel over the foot entry. This had been removed to Bristol but a wooden replacement was created in 1994, supported on the massive corbel which had survived. This three-bay lodging retains its collar-beam trusses and cusped wind braces (now concealed), end-wall fireplace (formerly with hood), and garderobe retaining a wooden seat at the opposite end. This last is valuable because it discharges into a drain that runs parallel for the length of the outer wall, cleaned out by a spur from the nearby mill-leat: the Denys family appreciated cleanliness. The four-centred entrance arch and square hood moulds above the windows suggest a date in the last third of the fifteenth century, possibly the work of Sir Maurice Denys.

The two isolated stone buildings within the enceinte have been used for farm purposes for more than two centuries, obscuring their original function. They were contemporary with the gatehouse. Building 1, about 54 feet long internally, retains its five-bay roof with three rows of purlins and two rows of wind braces. It had long been used as a barn and may always have been one, but was con-

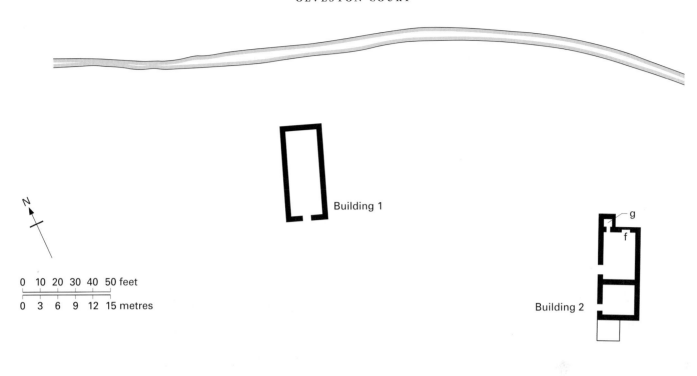

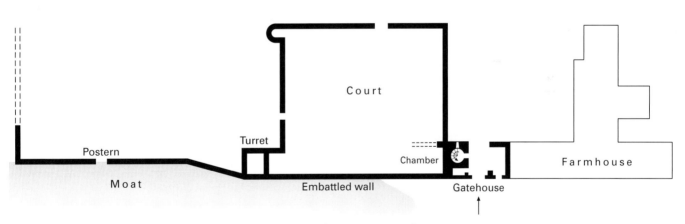

FIGURE 27 Olveston Court: site plan

verted in 1977–8 to domestic use. Building 2, about 5 feet longer internally, was a two-storeyed structure, again of five bays. The single upper room was furnished with an end-wall fireplace and garderobe projection. Its roof is plain, not arch-braced collar trusses, while the windows were unglazed, with closure by an iron grille.

The court area is enigmatic, with evidence of a two-storeyed turret with fireplaces and building foundations on the inside of the curtain wall to its west. Sloping cobbles in front of the north wall helped with roof drainage, while the present owner has found frag-

ments of two types of late medieval decorated floor tiles. The present farmhouse, reconstructed in 1973, incorporates two or three late fifteenth-century doorways and early beams, while site walking and an earthworks survey in 1977 revealed further isolated buildings on a particularly large site.[2]

The gatehouse and enclosing wall are evidence of a large and substantial defendable property. The scattered siting of the internal buildings presupposes development over a period of time and the earthworks survey and documentary evidence of a manor house here from the early fourteenth century confirm this.[3] Most of the standing work is later fifteenth century, lower down the social scale than, say Wanwell Court, though time has not been kind to the Denys family home. The area was large but lacked compactness. It has all but lost the primary residence (until excavated) though it retains some of the lesser structures so often swept away through post-medieval occupation and the division of the site since 1988 between four ownerships.

Olveston Court is one of a small group of fortified manors on the clay soils north of Bristol, mainly the homes of lesser Gloucestershire gentry as at Acton Court, Almondsbury Court Farm, and Yate Court – the last an important medieval house that served as the base of the Berkeley family during their early Tudor exile from Berkeley Castle. Sir John Wyllington had obtained a licence to crenellate his house at Yate in 1299 and his family held the property for almost a century before it passed through a succession of husbands of heiresses until its sale to the Berkeley family early in the sixteenth century. In 1548, a survey stated that the courtyard, 220 feet by 150 feet, was surrounded by a crenellated wall fronted by a moat 30 feet wide. The gatehouse on the south side retained its portcullis but the drawbridge had been replaced by a causeway. The hall was 40 feet by 24 feet, with two four-light windows and a central hearth. The moat, some of the 20 foot high wall, part of the hall block, and a tower remain. The present stone farmhouse, much altered through ongoing occupation, incorporates a hall and parlour block attributable to Maurice Berkeley (d.1523), but the fourteenth-century two-storeyed gatehouse was demolished in about 1930 for reuse in the restoration of Berkeley Castle.[4]

The foundations of the early fifteenth-century gatehouse at Acton Court have been recovered (q.v.) while the entrance range of Court Farm, Almondsbury, a manor of St Augustine's, Bristol, 7 miles westwards, is a near contemporary of Olveston Court. The gatehouse at Court Farm is less elaborate than that at Olveston, with a side room, unheated chamber above with external stair, and end lodging. It is attributable to abbot Newbury (1428–73) and, according to Smyth, before his deposition between 1451 and 1456. The added wing and chamber over the gate were added about fifty years later by abbot Newland (1481–1515).[5] The site was moated and retains the foundations of a polygonal tower at the end of a devalued range, converted into a house in 1985.

The other late medieval fortified houses in Gloucestershire can be grouped into three areas. Listing them can quickly become a catalogue for few of them still stand, but more existed than might be expected in a region that was not defensive after the wars of Stephen.

In the north, Icomb is a late survivor but not Boddington (licensed 1334) or Stanley Pontlarge (licensed 1391). Boddington was described by Leland as 'a fair maner place and a parke' and by Brayley and Britton as a house 'in the first style of building after castles were no longer necessary',[6] but except for two medieval shields with the arms of the earls of Gloucester and Tewkesbury Abbey the present house is an 1842 rebuilding. Even the ogee-headed light in a square frame illustrated in 1849[7] has gone from the house at Stanley Pontlarge ascribed to John Rous who had obtained a pardon in 1391 for crenellating this home just as he had done ten years earlier at Ragley Castle, 17 miles northwards. Equally lost is the important fortified house at Kempsford west of Lechlade defending an important crossing over the infant Thames. It had passed through marriage in 1297 to the earl of Lancaster,

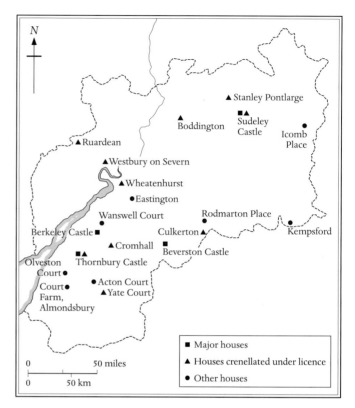

FIGURE 28 Gloucestershire: late medieval fortified houses

with his son granting it to his new collegiate foundation at Leicester in 1351. Anything that survived was destroyed by Sir Thomas Thynne (d.1639) when he built the mansion demolished in the late eighteenth century.

In the Forest of Dean, Turner and Parker recorded a few standing fragments at Ruardean (licensed 1311)[8] but that at Westbury on Severn (licensed 1330) had been replaced by early Tudor times.[9]

In the Vale, Wheatenhurst (licensed 1347) may be represented by the hall and residential core of the present Whitminster House,[10] Wanswell still stands (q.v.), but the house within the moated site west of the church at Eastington was pulled down in about 1578 to make way for a compact Elizabethan house demolished two centuries later. The moat was spanned by a drawbridge, and the medieval house with its hall, great chamber, and chapel was encircled by an embattled wall broken by a gatehouse.[11] Rodmarton was similarly moat provided but we know more about this house from the engraving in Grose's *Antiquities* of 1785 before its destruction a few years later. Built round three sides of a courtyard like Leckhampton Court, the body of the house had four substantial hall-like windows with at least one cross wing. Grose stated that it had a first-floor hall with an external stair, though this is unlikely by its accredited early fifteenth-century date.[12]

NOTES

1 Leland, *Itinerary*, V, 94, 99. Leland adds that Sir Maurice's grandson (d.1533) 'builded a nother courte of late yeres', but none of these late fifteenth- and early sixteenth-century extensions to the earlier house at Dyrham survived William Blathwayt's total rebuilding of the property between 1692 and 1704.

2 P. Ellis, *Trans. Bristol and Glos. Arch. Soc.* 101 (1984) 185–7. See also report on Olveston Court for English Heritage (1998) by R. Shoesmith.

3 *Cal. Inq. P.M. Gloucestershire* 5, 201. In 1310, Sir Walter Gloucester was given custody of the Court because its heir, Robert Crok, was only nine years old. The Court, known at that time as Crocker's Court, included a hall.

4 K. A. Rodwell, *Trans. Bristol and Glos. Arch. Soc.* 109 (1991) 179–93. See also *Trans. Bristol and Glos. Arch. Soc.* 21 (1898) 8–12 (description), 22–3 (inventory), 25–31 (Berkeley occupation). The Court was badly damaged during the Civil War, but the inventory of 1548–9 enables the room layout to be established.

5 E. S. Lindley, *Trans. Bristol and Glos. Arch. Soc.* 85 (1966) 156–63. Also *Trans. Bristol and Glos. Arch. Soc.* 21 (1898) 8–12, 22–4.

6 *Itinerary*, IV, 133; *Beauties of England and Wales*, V, 704.

7 *Arch. Jour.* 6 (1849) 41.

8 *Trans. Bristol and Glos. Arch. Soc.* 3 (1859) 261.

9 VCH, *Gloucestershire*, X (1972) 86–8.

10 *Ibid.* 297; D. Verey and A. Brooks, *The Buildings of England: Gloucestershire*, II (2002) 805.

11 VCH, *Gloucestershire*, X (1972) 128–9.

12 VCH, *Gloucestershire*, IX (1976) 236–7.

OXFORD, MERTON COLLEGE and the early development of the University

The origins of teaching at Oxford, recorded during the twelfth century, developed more formally in the thirteenth with the establishment of separate faculties during the first decade, a chancellor in 1214, student hostels by the middle of the century, and academic colleges shortly afterwards. The founding of residential colleges during the second half of the thirteenth century brought greater cohesion to groups of graduate teachers, enabled them to further their education for higher degrees, gave them financial stability and independence as members of an institution endowed with land and rents, and ensured that the founders and other benefactors benefited from the regular practice of masses said for their souls. Architecturally similar to colleges of secular canons (see volume II, 134–7), it was their academic purpose which ensured their survival at the Reformation when all other religious foundations were suppressed.

Three colleges were founded in quick succession in this prosperous town. Statutes were issued establishing Merton in 1263–4, University College in 1280, and Balliol in 1282, even though the founders' intentions at the last two had been declared in 1249 and 1255 respectively. As no standing evidence earlier than the seventeenth century survives at University College or before the fifteenth at Balliol, Merton enjoys the earliest collegiate buildings in Oxford.

Except for John Balliol, a nobleman who established a fund for supporting sixteen poor scholars as a penance for kidnapping the bishop of Durham in 1255, all thirteen pre-Reformation colleges at Oxford were ecclesiastical foundations. Founders varied from beneficed clerk and rector to archbishop and cardinal, initiated by the three colleges mentioned above of thirteenth-century origin. Four colleges were established in the following century, Exeter (1314), Oriel (1326), The Queen's (1340), and New College (1379). They were followed in the fifteenth century by Lincoln (1427), All Souls (1438), and Magdalen (1458) and by a further three before the Reformation, Brasenose (1509), Corpus Christi (1517), and Christ Church (1525). Apart from Henry VI's associa-

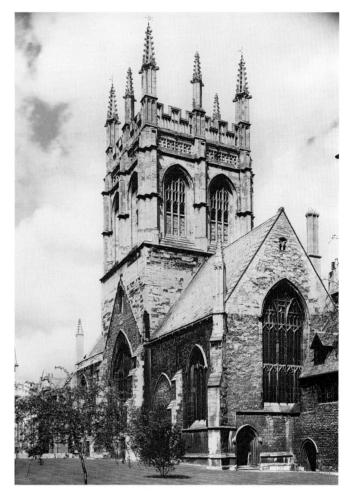

PLATE 58 Oxford, Merton College: chapel exterior

tion with archbishop Chichele's foundation at All Souls, three years before his own foundation of King's at Cambridge, only one other layman was associated with these projects – the lawyer Sir Richard Sutton, as co-founder of Brasenose with bishop Smyth of Lincoln.

Excluding the three Tudor foundations, seven colleges are relevant to this study, with four of them major examples of their era – Merton for the late thirteenth century, New for the late fourteenth, All Souls for the mid-fifteenth, and Magdalen for the later fifteenth century. All four foundations were for between about thirty and seventy members, but it is all too easy to forget from their post-medieval expansion that most of the other colleges were initially very small communities – Balliol, Queen's and Exeter were for sixteen scholars, while Oriel was for ten, Lincoln for seven, and University for four.[1] Their more limited endowments and modest numbers were reflected in the scale of their buildings. To these should be added a group of post-Reformation institutions which made use of earlier monastic colleges which had occupied a distinctive position in the medieval university. The other essential residential components of the university were the *hospicia* (lodgings) and *aulae* (halls) of student accommodation. As colleges were initially founded for scholars, students had to find their own lodgings in the town. As at Cambridge, they were leased to graduate teachers who

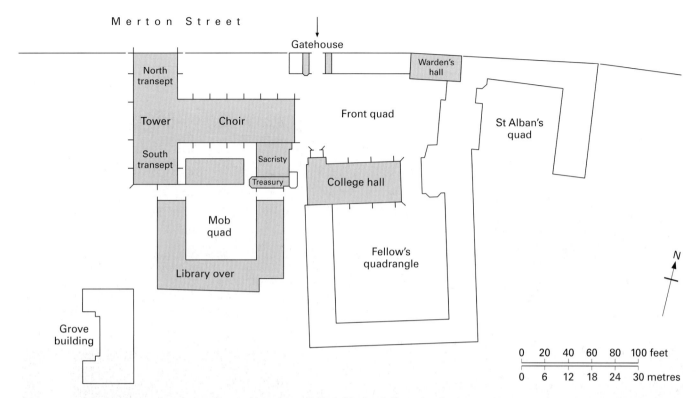

Merton Street

Gatehouse

North transept

Tower

Choir

South transept

Sacristy

Treasury

Warden's hall

Front quad

St Alban's quad

College hall

Mob quad

Library over

Fellow's quadrangle

Grove building

N

| 0 | 20 | 40 | 60 | 80 | 100 feet |

| 0 | 6 | 12 | 18 | 24 | 30 metres |

FIGURE 29 Oxford, Merton College: site plan

sub-let the rooms to students. From a high of about a hundred such hostels and halls in the fourteenth century, nearly seventy have been identified by the mid-fifteenth century, varying in size as hotels do today from the very small to quadrangular establishments (St Alban Hall). Though William Wykeham's college set a precedent in housing students as well as scholars, student lodgings continued to exist until the sixteenth century. For unclear reasons, their numbers swiftly fell from fifty-two in 1500 to eighteen in 1513, and eight in 1537.[2] There is more standing evidence of such halls at Oxford than at Cambridge, including part of a purpose-built one of *c*.1320–4 known as Tackley's Inn,[3] Beam Hall (late fifteenth century) opposite Merton College, and St Mary Hall (fifteenth century) incorporated in Oriel College in the nineteenth century. Architecturally, they were essentially town houses, sometimes with a row of shops fronting the street (Tackley's Inn, St Mary Hall), but only one is known to have had a library (Hart Hall) and one a chapel (New Inn Hall).

Unlike Peterhouse at Cambridge, a very considerable amount of late thirteenth-century work survives at the earliest standing foundation in Oxford. The approach to Merton College reveals the scale of the chapel, while two early halls are immediately apparent standing in Front Quad. Furthermore, the internal link between college hall and chapel is Mob Quad, the most complete fourteenth-century quadrangle prior to New College. Merton was initiated by the royal clerk, Walter Merton (d.1277) in 1262 after his early career success. Chancellor to Henry III (1261–3) and Edward I (1272–4) and appointed bishop of Rochester in 1274, the scale of Walter's patronage is apparent from the outset, though his initial licence was for allowing two manors to be used to support clerks

'studying at a university'. Oxford is only named in the statutes drawn up between June 1263 and September 1264 which established his foundation, supported by further grants and land purchases including the college site between 1266 and 1268. The final statutes of 1274 transformed Walter's establishment for secular clergy into a self-governing residential community of about forty fellows with about twenty-five undergraduates living in the town. The fellows were to teach the liberal arts, while studying themselves for a higher degree in medicine, law, and particularly theology. Merton's generous endowments provided the resources to build on a liberal scale,[4] and though there was no architectural precedent for an academic establishment, the founder's detailed regulations for his community imply the building of a hall, chapel, library, scholars' accommodation, and separate lodgings for the warden. Building therefore developed relatively swiftly, if piecemeal, at an establishment referred to as a *collegium* as early as 1280.[5]

Standing in the cobbled Front Quad, the modest character of Warden's Hall in the north-west angle forms a dramatic contrast with College Hall filling most of the south side. Warden's Hall is rubble faced as against the golden dressed stone of College Hall. The former stands at ground level; the latter is raised above an undercroft. The one is a two-bay hall; the other is of four bays. Yet though these are contemporary structures, most of College Hall is a nineteenth-century display while much of Warden's Hall is original, though mercilessly restored. Reasonably attributed to about 1285 and occupation by the warden,[6] this small hall, 28 feet by 21 feet, has two twin-light windows to the quadrangle, both with triple-cusped spherical heads, with that lighting the upper end of the hall extended by transomed lights to within 3 feet of the

PLATE 59 Oxford, Merton College: Mob Quad

ground. The tall entry arch with two-centred head opened directly into the hall, now with a Victorian mid floor but with the exposed two-bay roof of braced tie beams with queen posts supporting collar beams and crown posts. The cross wing at the lower end was always two-storeyed with a tall twin-light window to the street lighting the first-floor chamber. This and the remainder of the street frontage was refaced and overelaborated by Blore in the 1830s to harmonise with his refronting of the late sixteenth-century gatehouse range.

College Hall was always on a generous scale, 78 feet by 27 feet. Built during the last quarter of the thirteenth century,[7] the line of single lights to the undercroft and the transomed twin lights with trefoiled heads and internal seats to each bay shown by Loggan (1675) fell victim to Scott's virtual rebuilding of 1872–4. Though his fenestration followed the original form, the buttressed, embattled, and dressed frontages facing Front and Fellows' quadrangles are his work, as are the internal fittings and roof. Of the original structure, only the undercroft[8] and the end walls survive, with that

at the lower end defining its early character. The two-storeyed entrance porch is a rebuilding of 1579 with an inner entrance that retains its late thirteenth-century massive four-plank door covered with contemporary scroll work. Loggan shows two louvres, one for the hall and one for the kitchen which always seems to have been sited at the south-west angle.

The chapel, developed in stages over one and a half centuries, was never in axis with the hall. The choir and east piers were erected in 1290–4, the remaining crossing piers in 1330–5 preparatory to the building of the nave and aisles. This never took place. The south transept was constructed in 1367–8, the north transept in 1419–25, and the tower in 1448–51. As the nave was never built, the resulting T-shaped structure became the norm for Oxford colleges until the eighteenth century. The choir was of the noblest and most lavish design. Each of the seven bays was lit from both sides by tall triple-light windows, with the east end virtually filled with a seven-light window and a luxuriant head contrasting with the more controlled spherical tracery of the side windows. All heads retain contemporary glass, but whereas the lights of the east window have fifteenth-century panels and heraldic shields brought from elsewhere in the college, the side windows are filled with contemporary grisaille and painted glass of saints flanked by representations of the donor, Henry Mamesfeld (d.1328), a college fellow. The painted chapel ceiling is a Butterfield structure of 1850 hiding the original trussed rafter roof. The transepts are displays of Perpendicular work: three-light windows in both transepts with larger end windows and one filling the western arch after the nave project had been shelved. The roofs are again mid-nineteenth century but the stately tower of 1448–51 fittingly concludes the sequence of medieval buildings at Merton.

Before that had occurred, the fourth important medieval development had been completed, a quadrangle of scholars' rooms, enhanced by the treasury and the earliest purpose-built library in England. At first, the scholars occupied existing houses on the site and others in Merton Street (as the college initially made use of the old church of St John the Baptist for its services), but early in the new century, the first of a range of purpose-built chambers was erected. Positioned south of the chapel choir but not in line or linked with College Hall or the chapel entrance, Mob Quad[9] was built in stages, like the chapel, as funds allowed, and developed its quadrangular shape almost by accident. The first structure was the treasury, begun before 1288 and completed by 1291.[10] The north range in front of the choir followed in 1304–7, succeeded by the east range in about 1308–11, and the sacristy between the treasury and choir in 1311–12. There was a gap until the west and south ranges were built in 1373–8 with funds from the former bursar, bishop Rede of Chichester. All ranges are two-storeyed with those on the east and north side built for scholars and those on the west and south sides with similarly purposed ground-floor rooms and the library above.

The ranges display a variety of windows. The most obvious and earliest to survive are the close-set line of single windows to the first-floor library with trefoil heads to the field and contemporary cinquefoil heads to the quadrangle. There are occasional single fourteenth-century lights in the other ranges, but the majority are single and twin lights under rectangular hoods with uncusped or square heads of sixteenth-century date. The walls are rubble-built, and if the inserted dormers and stone bay windows at roof level are ignored, this quadrangle is one of the finest medieval courts to survive in central England. It is also the earliest formal quadrangle in Oxford, but by accretion and not design. It is also singular in that it is almost entirely residential for it does not include the components of hall or chapel that made up all other medieval quadrangles at Oxford and Cambridge. If this had been a monastic foundation, it would have been integrated with the chapel, and at this date probably cloistered too.

The north-east unit of entry passage and treasury, both quadripartite vaulted, is surmounted by the muniment room with shouldered lights, tiled floor, and an unusually steep-pitched stone roof for fire protection, carried on transverse stone arches. The doorways to the sets differ but are original, with two-centred heads and moulded hoods. Though they are the entries to the earliest college rooms in Oxford or Cambridge, all internal layouts were remodelled in the seventeenth century and later, leaving only the main timber ceiling beams untouched. Dr W. A. Pantin reasonably conjectured that the relatively short north and east ranges were both

divided by a single central entry lobby and steep stair with a chamber on each side, 22 feet by 17 feet, with three small study cubicles against the end walls and a fourth under the stairs, all lit by partly identifiable narrow windows.[11] Thus the north range held a maximum of eight scholars at each level, and slightly fewer in the east range as the treasury precluded end-wall windows.

The warden visited Salisbury, Sherborne, and Winchester, and with the master-mason, William Humbervylle, examined the library of the Blackfriars in London before beginning work on that at Merton.[12] The bays on each side of this first-floor library had cusped single lights but the end bay of the south range has cinquefoil twin lights suggesting that it was originally partitioned from the remainder. The junction of the two ranges is also marked by a larger transomed two-light window. All lights were originally shuttered and protected by waxed cloth, but they are now filled with painted glass, one window as early as the fifteenth century. The floor is original, with the middle filled with medieval tiles laid in 1623 but replacing earlier tiles damaged by braziers used to heat the room. Coldness explains the ceiling introduced as early as 1502 below the original trussed rafter structure. The present library fittings were introduced between 1589 and 1623 when the bay roof windows were inserted, though some of the fourteenth-century benches were retained.[13]

The street range and three-storeyed entry are undistinguished. The gateway was developed between 1416 and 1465, supported with a licence to crenellate granted in 1418[14] but with the majority of the work undertaken in Edward IV's reign.[15] It is typical of Oxford college gateways, lacking the flamboyance of those at Cambridge, though Blore did his best in 1836–8 by overelaborating the entrance arch, the canopy heads and the central windows, and adding corner turrets.[16] Only the St John the Baptist tympanum of 1464–5 immediately above the entry is original (and lowered by Blore). The courtyard rubble face and window frames are more in accord with the gateway's early condition, as are the entry doors and two-bay tierceron vaulted passage. The axis of this gateway facing the hall porch was not an original element of Merton's development, for the gateway replaced a tenement known as Herptut's house that had occupied the site since before 1267.

Not only is Merton the first college in England with substantial evidence of its early form, but the chapel and College Hall testify to its founder's determination that his establishment should be on the grandest scale. From the domestic point of view, there is the fortuitous survival of a contemporary small-scale Warden's Hall (with lower-end chamber block) opposite the ghost of the much larger College Hall – a private hall as against one for communal dining and lectures. In addition, Merton enjoys one of the least-altered courtyards of fourteenth-century England. Still occupied and retaining its original vaulted treasury and muniment tower, this quadrangle was independent of hall and chapel in a building that until then had been made up of disparate units. Three of the prime components of any college – hall, chapel, and warden's lodging – existed from the first at Merton, irregularly grouped round Front Quad. A quarter of a century later, Mob Quad was initiated, and though developed by accretion rather than by design, it is the first college quadrangle that is regular in shape and scale. It was without compare in educational endowment and architectural magnificence until the establishment of Wykeham's twin foundations towards the close of the fourteenth century.

NOTES

1 Queen's could only afford two or three fellows in the fourteenth century, and few more in the fifteenth, while there were still only three fellows and the master at University College during the early fifteenth century, though the number had increased to nine by the close of the century. VCH, III (1954) 132, 64.

2 A. B. Emden in *Medieval Learning and Literature: Essays Presented to R. W. Hunt*, ed. J. Alexander and M. Gibson (1976) 355. Among the reasons for the decline were their impermanent character, disciplinary control, the lack of security of tenure, and the expansion of secular college facilities. New College, for instance, was the first to ceil the upper chambers to create attic rooms (known as cocklofts) for undergraduates in 1539, with the practice becoming common before the close of the century.

3 The hall for dining and lectures at 107 High Street retains its fourteenth-century window and early sixteenth-century roof, but the chamber block where students lived five to a room has been pulled down and the fronting shops that supplemented the student income have been rebuilt. W. A. Pantin, *Oxoniensia* 7 (1942) 80–92 and J. Munby, *Oxoniensia* 43 (1978) 123–69. For academic halls, W. A. Pantin in *Oxford Studies Presented to Daniel Callus* (1964), and A. B. Cobban in *The History of the University of Oxford*, II, ed. J. Catto and T. Evans (1992) 624–33.

4 In marked contrast with the modest property held by Balliol and University colleges. The latter could only support four scholars.

5 Cambridge's Peterhouse (1284) was deliberately modelled on Walter Merton's Oxford establishment.

6 A Merton record mentions an *aula custodis* in 1282 and a *parva aula* in 1285 in contrast to the great hall of the college, *magna aula*. VCH, III (1954) 98. Oxford college heads are given a range of names including dean (Christ Church), master (Balliol, University), president (Magdalen, St John's), principal (Brasenose, Hertford), provost (Oriel, Worcester), rector (Exeter, Lincoln), and warden (All Souls, Merton). For the roof of Warden's Hall, M. R. Bismanis, *The Medieval English Domestic Timber Roof* (1987) 101,105.

7 The hall is first mentioned in a document of 1277 and again in 1282, and was glazed in 1291. Its kitchen is mentioned in 1288. Warden's Hall had a separate kitchen from at least 1296; VCH, III (1954) 99–102 where a summary is given of the extensive college building accounts that begin in 1287.

8 Vaulted in the early nineteenth century.

9 So called since the late eighteenth century. It had previously been known as Bachelors' Quad – the name for junior fellows – and from the late seventeenth century as Little Quad. Butterfield's proposal to destroy Mob Quad in 1864 in favour of his own design was only averted on the objections led by the sub-warden.

10 Bott (1993) 16–18.

11 W. A. Pantin, *Med. Arch.* 3 (1959) 244–6. The ground-floor scholar rooms in the west and south ranges were converted to a student library in the nineteenth century.

12 The college accounts refer to a library at Merton forty years before this new undertaking. VCH, III (1959) 101.

13 A thirteenth-century oak chest with replacement lid is kept here.

14 The licence of 14 April 1418 is preserved among the college muniments. It was never enrolled by the royal clerks. P. S. Allen and H. W. Garrod, *Merton Muniments* (1928) viii, xvb.

15 Bott (1993) 5–6.

16 A. J. Bott and J. R. L. Highfield, *Oxoniensia* 58 (1993) 233–40. For 'before' and 'after' illustrations, Vallance (1912) 21.

A. Vallance, *The Old Colleges of Oxford* (1912) 18–25
RCHM, *City of Oxford* (1939) 76–84
VCH, *Oxfordshire*, III (1954) 95–106
R. L. Highfield, *The Early Rolls of Merton College* (1964)
A. Bott, *Merton College: A Short History of the Buildings* (1993)

OXFORD, NEW COLLEGE and the fourteenth-century foundations

William Wykeham's twin collegiate foundations at Oxford and Winchester were as revolutionary in concept as they were spectacular in execution. Their educational importance and architectural majesty have long been appreciated, but their significance in the development of late medieval domestic architecture has been less fully recognised. Just as Edward III's redevelopment of the residential apartments of Windsor Castle was the primary building project of the third quarter of the fourteenth century, so it was father to two magnificent sons who, in turn, created a broader progeny in the following era.

Four colleges were founded in Oxford during the fourteenth century, all by ecclesiastics. Exeter (1314) was established by bishop Stapledon of Exeter, Oriel (1324) by Adam Brome, rector of St Mary's church nearby, The Queen's (1341) by Robert Eglesfield, Queen Philippa's chaplain, and New College (1379) by the bishop of Winchester. The first three were modest in scale, limited to only a handful of students, with financial restrictions confining building to piecemeal development round an open space. We have some documentation and the pictorial evidence of Bereblock (1566) and Loggan (1675) but no structural remains. Chapels were erected at Exeter (1321–6), Queen's (c.1373–82), Oriel (1372–9), and University College (by 1399). Following Merton's precept in the 1370s, libraries were built at Exeter (1383), Queen's (c.1392), and University College (by 1391).[1] Though the chapel east window at Queen's was in the late Decorated style, the hall was in the early Perpendicular style (1398–1402), a late work by William Wynford who also provided the necessary building stone. But it is the bishop of Winchester's co-foundations at Oxford and Winchester that provide a far more immediate appreciation of Wynford's design qualities, workmanship, and building capabilities.

William Wykeham's twin establishments cannot be considered apart, even though New College was initiated three years before that at Winchester. Wykeham's concern was to conceive education as a single span, aimed at countering 'the fewness of the clergy arising from pestilence, wars, and other miseries of the world', and helping poor students to become 'men of Great learning, fruitful to the church of God and to the king and realm'. Winchester College sourced their childhood years, while New College provided the advanced learning they needed for their first degree from the age of sixteen, with the facility to prepare, if they wished, for the more advanced master's degree and doctorate. The curriculum was less theologically determined than hitherto, with greater emphasis on the liberal arts. The statutes laid down that the students were to live within the same premises as the fellows instead of leading a separate life in hostels in the town, and that senior members should give tuition to their juniors in college. New College was the prototype of the present college organisation and university tutorial system, a truly educational community with learning pursued in common rather than as a residence for fellows.[2]

Wykeham's architectural vision matched his educational concept, with foundations developed on an unprecedented scale, to consistent and innovative plans, and in a form that introduced the fully fledged Perpendicular style to Oxford as it did to Winchester. Most of the buildings survive, not radically altered by later generations, and still used for their original purpose. At both establishments, the principal units were logically and formally grouped round a quadrangle entered through a towered gateway. This gave the building presence and appropriately sited accommodation for the warden overseeing the college's welfare. The hall and chapel were built back-to-back to fill one side of the quadrangle, with a tower for valuables nearby, and the courtyard closed by accommodation ranges. The importance of the library for higher learning at New College was stressed by its position opposite the entrance gateway. All these units had previously existed in the six earlier foundations at Oxford, with those at Merton grouped round two courts. What was totally new was bringing these functions together in a coherent plan, with less essential buildings such as the kitchen, offices, and cloister built in arms, out of immediate sight. What was equally radical was providing accommodation for students and fellows in the same ranges, not separated into dormitories for the more junior and chambers for the more senior students. 'Nothing is more evident than the close dependence of all the buildings of the college on the purpose which they served, and their relation to the manner of life enjoined on the society which used them'.[3] The further importance of Wykeham's concept was ensuring that it was so generously resourced that it was completed in his lifetime, a factor significantly contributing to New College (and Winchester) setting the pattern for subsequent academic foundations, and its gradual adoption at Oxford by those of earlier date. The one development that did not find universal favour was the cloister for the burial of fellows and the associated bell tower that tolled their passing. Canterbury College of c.1364–97 had been the earliest establishment in Oxford to adopt the Perpendicular form (see page 151), but as none of its buildings exists, New College is the earliest one to display the newly honed style, as Winchester College is in Hampshire. And its use on such a large scale by a leading entrepreneur in two buildings of innovatory plan and purpose naturally impacted on major domestic buildings in central and southern England.

Born in 1324 of humble parents in the Hampshire village of Wickham, William's early career was as an efficient building administrator as much as cleric. Initially employed by the constable of Winchester Castle and probably by the royal treasurer, bishop Edington of Winchester, his recommendation to Edward III by the bishop resulted in his appointment in 1356 as surveyor of the king's works. His immediate task was to co-ordinate the reconstruction of the domestic apartments at Windsor Castle currently in progress (1356–61). Ordained priest in 1362, his administrative and aesthetic talents brought him the king's high favour, the reward of a wealthy bishopric within five years, and his appointment as chancellor (1367–71). Wykeham was as assiduous in diocesan as in royal and official affairs, but he was equally adept at amassing a fortune through plurality. The political storm of 1376–7 whipped up by Gaunt enveloped Wykeham on charges of embezzlement and the loss of his estates, but disgrace was avoided by the accession of Richard II and a less recriminatory government. Though reappointed chancellor in 1389–91, his interests no longer lay in politics but in husbanding the resources of his office to fund his twin educational foundations and the rebuilding of his cathedral church from 1394 onwards. Physically tall, highly capable, politically astute, devotionable and charitable but coolly prudent, Wykeham died in 1404 at the age of eighty.[4]

WYKEHAM'S BUILDINGS

The site chosen by Wykeham for his college at Oxford lay in an area of tenements blighted and abandoned since the Black Death. Its position between the north-east angle of the bastioned city walls and a dog-legged public lane which long formed the college perimeter made the college virtually invisible to the outside world, as it still is. Wykeham began purchasing land for his establishment in 1369, held a quarter of the site by the close of 1370, acquired the remaining thirty-six plots over the next few years, issued a foundation charter in November 1379, and laid the foundation stone in March 1380 for his college of a warden and seventy scholars, with ten priests, three lay clerks, and sixteen choristers.

The quadrangle with hall, chapel, library, and lodgings was ready for occupation in April 1386 and the chapel was dedicated in December 1387, though its furnishing was not completed for twenty or more years. Building activity between 1387 and 1394 was transferred to the construction of Winchester College, followed by the nave of Winchester cathedral. Land, however, had been purchased in Oxford for the college cloister in 1388–9, with construction in hand between about 1390 and its consecration in 1400. The associated bell tower was erected between 1396 and 1403, and the warden's barn was in progress in 1402. These last three structures are the first building references in the college accounts, for there is no specific documentation for the earlier structures. One rare manuscript survival, though, is the pictorial frontispiece to a collection of Latin pieces in praise of the founder written by the warden, Thomas Chaundler, between 1461 and 1465. This bird's-eye view gives a detailed representation of the college as well as its members within eighty years of occupation, and is an extremely valuable antecedent to the engraving by David Loggan of 1675, just before a sequence of major alterations were made to some of the college buildings.[5]

In contrast with the early buildings at Merton, the approach to New College could not be more self-effacing – a narrow lane between the blank walls of the cloister and the warden's barn. The constricted gateway, three-storeyed with a plain parapet, was as innovatory as its occupation by the warden, a practice still followed by all his successors to the present day. The entry face has been little altered, with its broad four-centred archway with continuous hollow chamfers (as at Winchester College), two-light windows (first floor) and renewed single-light windows (second floor) either side the central canopied niche with its statue of the Virgin, flanked by the kneeling founder and the angel Gabriel. The inner face is similarly patterned, as are both faces of the middle gate at Winchester. The original two-leaf doors open into a three-bay passage with simple octapartite vaulting and south porter's lodge, originally larger, with its windows in both outer walls and towards the passage.

On entering Front Quad, the scale of Wykeham's concept is immediately apparent. The chapel and hall fill the north side under a common parapet and pinnacled roof line with the similarly buttressed muniment tower and south transept of the ante-chapel acting as end stops, binding the whole composition together. There was a subsidiary exit opposite the towered gateway, with the founder's library above. The remainder of the quadrangle was filled with two-storeyed lodging ranges, initially without a parapet (vide Chaundler). The dominant role of the hall and chapel would have

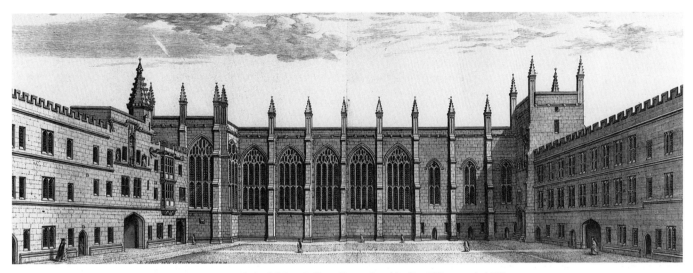

PLATE 60 Oxford, New College: Front Quad by David Loggan (c.1670)

been more pronounced before the ranges on three sides of the quadrangle were raised by an additional storey in 1674, subsequently topped by an embattled parapet, and with all windows sashed in 1718. The further storey, modified windows, and smooth-textured stonework have given these ranges a rather forbidding appearance at odds with their original character, and they diminish the status of the gate-tower.[6] Chapel and hall are unified by the rhythm of pinnacled bay buttresses, a corbelled string course, and common roof line, but the scale of the chapel windows, virtually filling each bay compared with the narrower and lower windows of the hall, makes it clear that the secular was subservient to the religious as the heart of college life. Window position and size identify function throughout the building, but this frontage also brilliantly demonstrates the difference between the fenestration of ecclesiastical and secular buildings in late fourteenth-century England.

The hall is raised above a lower storey that originally consisted of four rooms – one for some fellows, and the remainder for the chaplains and choristers. Though some of the doors and windows survive, these rooms were swept away in 1722 in favour of a vaulted area that has since been used for storage and an end passageway. The steep flight of steps to the hall rises through a two-centred arch with single hollow chamfer to a lierne-vaulted lobby. The three-light trefoiled window holds fragments of late fourteenth-century armorial glass moved from the hall windows in 1865. A broad doorway with four-centred arch in a square head opens into the hall. This particularly tall four-bay apartment is lit from both sides by transomed windows of two cinquefoil lights instead of the four lights chosen for the chapel, with quatrefoil heads, moulded rear arches dying into the splays, and window seats. The hall is 79 feet by 32½ feet internally and 50 feet high, and the screen and panelling were inserted in 1533–5. The tie-beam roof was designed by Scott in 1865–6, modelled fairly closely on the original structure found after James Wyatt's eighteenth-century roof and plaster ceiling had been removed. The walls are unplastered, and though they were covered in 1453 with hangings of painted cloth brought from London, their present

plainness and the dense Victorian stained glass give the hall an austere character.[7]

The taller of the three central doorways to the offices in the lower end wall opens on to a steep flight of steps to the ground-floor kitchen. The smaller doorways with chamfered rather than the moulded jambs of the kitchen approach are wood-surrounded, with the early sixteenth-century spandrels carved with a rare demonstration of purpose – boys carrying blackjacks of beer and baskets of bread. The rooms retain their original function of buttery (north) and pantry (south) with ground-floor staff quarters either side the kitchen steps. A spiral stair from the buttery accesses the contemporary beer cellar filling the area next to the city wall. The low quadripartite vault springs from a central octagonal pier.

The late fourteenth-century kitchen projects from the end of the range and beyond the main quadrangle to minimise disturbance and fire risk. Still in everyday use, the original central hearth was replaced by two wall hearths in the sixteenth century, blocking some of the original square-headed windows. The original three-bay room of braced collars with two lines of wind braces retained its vaned octagonal louvre (shown in the Bereblock view of 1566) until the eighteenth century.

The chapel differs fundamentally from any attributable precedent, for that at Merton was still intended to be a cruciform church, while Wykeham's concept was T-shaped from the first.[8] The five bays of the choir are filled with four cinquefoiled and transomed windows with vertical traceried heads spanned by a reticulated Y. Because of the hall dais immediately behind, the usual east window was replaced by a reredos from floor to roof, with serried ranks of figures in canopied niches. The present structure is a Gilbert Scott remodelling in stone of James Wyatt's plaster restoration of 1789–93, based on the badly mutilated evidence of stone statues set in ultramarine blue niches with gilded canopies and pedestals.[9] Scott similarly sought to reinstate the original form of the roof destroyed by Wyatt. He insisted on a hammer-beam and arch-braced structure, a higher-pitched roof than originally, and in so doing distorted the founder's original design, externally as well as internally. A lower-pitched hammer-beam roof with braced collars

PLATE 61 Oxford, New College: hall interior

as at All Souls chapel rather than a Westminster Hall-type braced arch is most likely, with the original line marked by the curvature of the fourth tier of the reredos, minus Scott's added band.[10] The twenty-eight alternate king and bishop roof corbels, the sixty-two finely detailed misericords, and the central doors of the rood screen are original, but the organ gallery, the opposing sedilia, and most of the three lines of stalls replacing the original single one are work of 1877–81. The ante-chapel is more compact than the Merton development, with two-bay transepts, tall elegant aisle pillars, and no crossing tower. The form is referred to as the chapel 'nave' in the founder's statutes. The windows are similar in design to those of the choir, filled with late fourteenth-century glass except for the larger west window which is eighteenth century, as are those throughout the choir.[11] Apart from being used for services and devotions, the founder's statutes laid down that the ante-chapel could be used for disputations, business meetings, law suits, and elections.

The cloister stands as a detached unit, 17 feet west of the chapel and not visible from the quadrangle. It is linked to it by an untidy entrance with one of several doorways in the college with a two-centred head, and a narrow passage that masks its lack of integration with the ante-chapel. The concept of a cloister garth with

roofed walks was a novel concept in college planning, subsequently repeated at All Souls and Magdalen and planned at King's College, Cambridge, but it bears all the marks of an after-thought. The walks of twelve bays (east to west) and eight bays (north to south) are lined with unglazed windows of three cinquefoil lights under a broad traceried head in almost continuous line, separated by no more than the buttresses to the garth. The walks were covered with simple wagon roofs. This cloister, intended for processions, burials and perhaps study, is now little used except as a repository for memorial tablets. The four-stage bell tower, built in the absence of a chapel crossing tower, purposely projects outside the city wall because it replaces a bastion which Wykeham was allowed to remove. It has minimal openings except for the bell-chamber stage. The embattled parapet was originally the only one in the college which otherwise adopted plain parapets.

Architecturally, the four-storeyed muniment tower counterbalances the chapel south transept. Parts of the ground and first floor form the hall entry with three external niches and statues similar to those above the main gateway. The other half of the ground floor is a room with a two-bay quadripartite vault springing from sculptured corbels, barred square-headed windows, and a con-

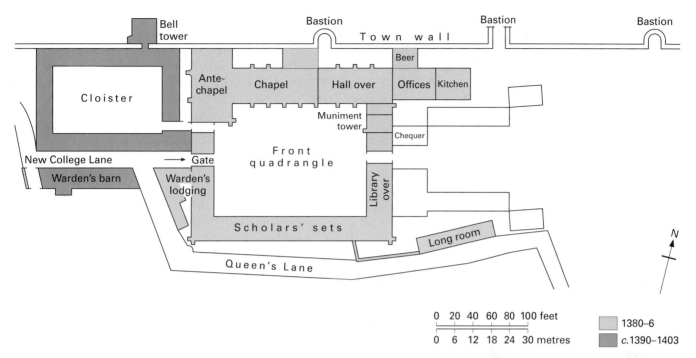

temporary tiled floor. The same forms of vault, flooring, and windows with original shutters occur on the first floor, opening from the hall lobby, and are repeated in the two larger upper rooms reached from a spiral stair initially opening from the screens passage. These four rooms, securely protected by original iron-plated doors, have barely changed since their construction over 600 years ago. The ground floor was used for vessels of modest value, the first floor was for charters, deeds, account rolls, and the college seal, the second for the gold and silver objects used on feast days in hall, the college statutes, and sums of money, while the uppermost room held the chapel vestments, plate, and ornaments. Three of the founder's great oak chests used for archive storage and built *in situ* have survived in rooms continuing to serve their original function.

The east and south ranges retain their initial pattern of entries, and window positions of either one or two lights. The latter were square-headed with moulded reveals but all heads have been cut back and hold sashed frames inserted in 1718. The ground floor of the east range consisted of the library entry and the beamed bursary, a room designated by the founder for the college's domestic and business transactions. It is followed by a quadripartite vaulted passage with outer rebate for doors, and a chamber for fellows. The line of deep-set windows above mark the founder's library, with another line of windows on the further side. The nine-bay library, with stone party walls for fire protection, was refitted in 1780 and converted to senior common room use in 1952. Work at that time revealed three original windows in the east wall, blocked when a small law library was built in *c*.1480[12] over a short ground-floor addition to the bursary made in 1449. The early window form is shown externally by a 1950 copy inserted next to the muniment tower. The deep-set, twin-transomed lights with trefoiled head were larger than those in the lodgings which lacked transoms and the broad window seat. The upper lights were glazed, those below

shuttered but with glass set in removable frames as part of the original design. Books were stored in lectern-shaped desks between the windows, like those later installed in Duke Humphrey's library, while the centre of the library over the ground-floor passage was tiled rather than boarded, possibly for a brazier. A small section of medieval ceiling survives over the original stair.

The south range, together with the adjoining chamber at each level on the east and west sides, served as the living quarters for the seventy scholars. Each doorway gave access to a tiny lobby with flanking doors and a straight flight of stairs to the upper sets. Each set consisted of a large heated chamber with a two-light trefoiled window to the quadrangle, and a tall capped chimney to the rear (*vide* Chaundler). This was the combined living and bed chamber with partitioned study cubicles at both ends of the room, one for each fellow, with a single light. The ground-floor rooms have four cubicles per chamber, and the upper rooms enjoyed three to a chamber. This gave a pattern of a large window and a pair of single lights, with every second pair of lights separated by the entry doorway. At the upper level, the internal stair enabled the lights over the doorway to be brought closer together and the larger window repositioned, though the furthest lights of each set were aligned exactly.[13] This gave a flexible rhythm to the range as the very different fenestration did to the opposite range. There were twenty sets, eleven at ground- and nine at first-floor level, for there was a single set beneath the upper ends of the library and the hall. Four junior fellows lived in each of the ground-floor rooms (three below the library) and three more senior fellows to an upper chamber, making the disposition of forty-three junior and twenty-seven senior members of the society. Windows were probably shuttered rather than glazed and the beds in the middle of the rooms were stored one under the other when not in use, as was certainly the case at Magdalen. The lower chambers had earth floors until 1534 and

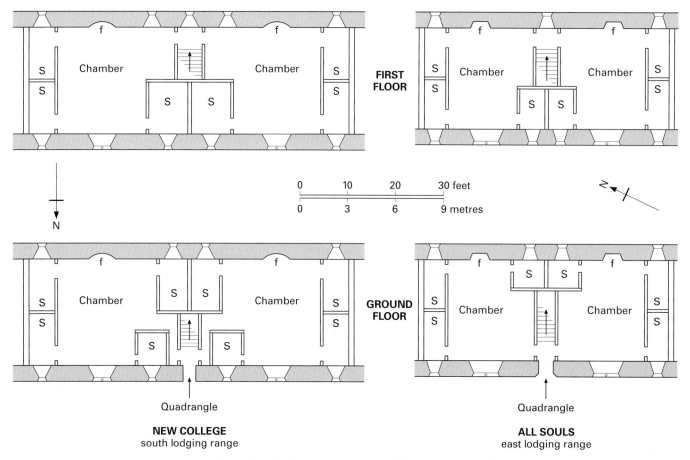

FIGURE 31 Oxford, New College (south range) and All Souls (east range): floor plans

the upper rooms were open to the roof. Chambers may well have been decorated on the basis of their names (e.g. the Rose and Vine, the Baptist's Head, and the Crane's Dart) and there is the fragmentary evidence of a medieval fresco of wild roses behind the panelling in a room on number 2 staircase. Most of the chambers were remodelled and refenestrated in 1718–20, but some of the original partitions survive and a stair on number 1 is on the original lines.

To the rear of the south range is the so-called 'long room': a detached two-storey block that was, and is still, used for the college garderobes. Unlike comparable secular examples, garderobes were not an integral part of the college sets, but the latter were soon linked to the communal garderobe (if not originally) by an L-shaped covered passage shown in Loggan. The line of garderobes on the upper floor was approached by an outside staircase at the west end (now a window to what has become the junior common room) with five loop lights and an open tie-beam roof. The ground floor was the cesspit, periodically cleaned, but cleared away in 1880 and refurbished with lavatories served by running water.

The initial layout of the warden's lodging can be recovered from the sequence of modifications made by holders of the office since the mid-sixteenth century.[14] A narrow stair from the quadrangle opened on to a generous landing and ante-room over the original porter's lodge south of the gateway. The warden's lofty hall over the gate-passage, heated and well windowed,[15] was initially furnished with pewter dishes and flagons (kept in the ground floor of the

muniment tower), but by the late fifteenth century, silver-gilt vessels were also being used, including the beautifully preserved warden's grace-cup of c.1480, and the warden's salt of c.1490. An outside stair from the ante-room accessed the single-storey kitchen and office, sited across a tiny court in the detached angled block fronting Queen's Lane. The warden's private rooms were approached from his hall. His study or privy chamber lay immediately to the north, formerly with an oriel to the quadrangle highlighting the importance of the college head.[16] A narrow oratory lay beyond, with a loop light into the ante-chapel and an original west-facing window. The added room with garderobe opening off the study may have been a guest room, for the warden's own bedchamber was the second floor of the gate-tower, initially approached by a spiral stair. He also had the use of the ground-floor chamber below his study, entered from the cloister passage. It may have been his beer cellar, but it has been occupied for well over a century by the college porter (pl. 7).

The barn on the other side of the lane was divided in four units – passage entry, storage for produce from the college estates, stabling for the warden's six horses with hayloft above, and a two-storeyed lodging for his grooms with a visitor's room above – hence its original two-light shuttered window.[17] Later changes have included a more imposing entry stair (1675), the creation of a first-floor dining room out of a scholars set to the south (1684), infilling the triangular kitchen court, and converting the barn to residential use served by a bridge across the Lane (1676). Even so, the lodging and associated barn was an independent residence, comparable to that of an abbot or prior, strategically sited for carrying out his duties to the college, its guests, and its properties. No other foundation retains such clear evidence of the form and volume of its head's original lodgings, was so copied,[18] or has a longer record of occupation by the head of college.

ASSESSMENT

William Wykeham was absorbed by beauty in architecture and in art. Wycliffe referred to the preferment that could be obtained in the church by a clerk 'wise in building castles' but this ecclesiastical grandee used his talents to reconstruct his cathedral nave, build two large-scale educational foundations, and furnish them with the finest gifts that he could bestow.[19] Post-medieval changes have not fundamentally altered Wykeham's purpose or achievement and therein lies its relevance and importance for both collegiate and domestic architecture. He was erecting a group of buildings to accommodate a multi-layered society under a single head. The significance of New College rests not only on its sheer size and the scale of its buildings to house seventy scholars as against Merton's forty and Oriel's ten, but on their logical organisation, the extent of their survival, and the standard of workmanship involved. The walls are relatively thin, with the wide tall windows of the principal range separated by pinnacled buttresses to take the thrust from the weight of the roof. Tracery was restrained to allow greater concentration on the stained glass. A large chapel choir was built to serve the needs of the sizeable college body that worshipped in it, but as the chapel was not parochial, side altars and a disputation area were best served by building an ante-chapel. The windows in the muniment tower were necessarily arrow-slits for protection, while those in the library were large and closely spaced to maximise light availability. The reredos panels that have survived post-medieval mutilation are of better quality than the sculpture over the gateway and the muniment tower, but the design and technical accomplishment of the stained glass is outstanding by any standards.

It has often been pointed out that Wykeham's foundation was the prototype followed by many subsequent colleges at both Oxford and Cambridge. The most obvious successors were the archiepiscopal foundations of All Souls and Magdalen, and Henry VI's twin foundations at Eton and King's, Cambridge, but in broader terms, New College was the model for the fully developed quadrangle plan, the building of the hall and chapel in line, the introduction of the T-shaped chapel, the entrance tower with warden's lodgings over, and to a limited extent a cloister and bell-tower. New College also scores a first through incorporating a library into a college plan, introducing junior as well as senior fellows' rooms in two-storeyed lodgings, and the use at Oxford of dressed stone for most of the college façades.

Less attention though has been paid to the college's influence on domestic planning, particularly in conjunction with its sister foundation at Winchester. Wykeham created a quadrangle that does not differ greatly in concept or execution from that of a major secular household, for the cloister and bell-tower do not impinge on the scene. Though the lodging ranges have been remodelled internally, their two-storeyed form of individual heated chambers, severally occupied, had rarely been seen before on such an extensive scale outside those overseen by Wykeham at Windsor Castle. The rooms

for a house's administration, muniments, and valuables were sometimes tiered in a tower (e.g. Ashby de la Zouch Castle, Bolton Castle, Minster Lovell Hall) but those at New College are particularly valuable as examples of little-changed interiors. The hall is similarly little altered, totally interchangeable with one in a domestic environment, and originally with decorative quarries and armorial glass. Naturally, the chapel dominates at New College rather than the hall, and as a consequence their roof designs are a reversal of those likely in a high-status residence. The warden's lodging is a miniature version of that in a major household, comparable with those of a monastic head. It is a self-contained unit, but otherwise the size of the college, the formal layout, the accommodation standards, and the domestic facilities are analogous to those of a private mansion.

L. G. Wickham-Legg was the first person to draw attention to the close links between Edward III's mid-century residential redevelopment of the upper court of Windsor Castle and New College, Oxford,[20] but recent work at Windsor has shown that the parallels were even more marked. The towered castle enclosure and the bastioned city walls dictated the elongated rectangular shape of both structures. The back-to-back first-floor hall and chapel range is the key unit common to both structures, but the chapel and muniment tower and projections at the college are a reflection of the earlier gate-towers at each end of the castle range. Furthermore, they incorporated the entrances to the religious and secular centres of the college, with the latter almost of fortress character, and internally separating the housing of ecclesiastical plate from that for lay use. The two-storeyed lodging ranges enclosing two sides of the castle quadrangle with the more important officials on the upper floor was the architectural and functional precept for those at Oxford, and similarly sited in relation to the domestic range. The strictly regular quadrangular form followed century-old fortress precedent, just as the cloister and bell-tower followed long-established monastic practice. The colleges of secular priests at Cobham and a decade later at Arundel had brought some of these elements together in the 1370s and 1380s, but these modest establishments failed to match the scale and vision of Wykeham's concept. At the same time that New College is a summation of secular development of the last quarter of the century, it became the source and spur for domestic architecture during the next century.

Wykeham built a domestic residence that was large in scale, formal in design, and swift in completion. It was also a building that balanced architectural dignity with practical convenience. Apart from Windsor Castle, several other palace-fortresses had shown similar planning regularity as at Bolton and Wressle castles. What Wykeham's community foundation demonstrated was its application to a more domestic hierarchical environment with a formality that many magnate households such as Holand at Dartington Hall were still seeking. But outside that Devon example, there are hardly any contemporary exemplars on a comparable scale. A raised hall was a sign of status in major episcopal and magnate households, supervised at Windsor, experienced by the bishop at Southwark and Wolvesey palaces, repeated at Winchester College, and adopted under Wykeham's aegis at the Hospital of St Cross a mile away. The kitchen and offices at Oxford are standard but the lodgings show an advancement over those at Dartington Hall in their elimination of separate entries in favour of a single one to each group of four units. On the other hand, it was nearly a century before collegiate lodgings adopted the common domestic practice of associated garderobe provision. The college entry is badly sited architecturally, for it is too close to the hall and chapel frontage to make an impression. This would have been obviated had it been placed in the middle of the south range, and at the same time it would have created a more balanced quadrangular design. These major flaws probably arose from site limitations that were corrected in the building of the feeder school at Winchester. Two courts were built there to allow for additional facilities and an improved layout befitting the multi-layered society that occupied it. The gate-towers were better positioned and gave improved presence facing the hall and chapel, which were again built back-to-back. The muniment tower, cloister, and bell tower were repeated and the window tracery was almost identical. Garderobes were now made an integral part of the upper-floor chambers for fellows, while the sculptural quality was markedly higher at Winchester than at Oxford. The lack of any post-Reformation added storey round the principal court at Winchester also means that it has retained the original proportions that the Oxford foundation has lost. It was this improved development in Hampshire that most influenced domestic architecture in the following century, but it was the Oxford college that was the vital precedent.

It is clear that Wykeham had built up a team of craftsmen who were continuously employed by him throughout Richard II's reign and possibly as early as the 1360s.[21] The same names recur in the documentation while the stylistic similarities are immediate in what was virtually a private version of the office of the king's works. The college statutes and Wykeham's will reinforce the standing evidence that he was responsible for the overall concept, distinctive form, and precise character of New College. William Wynford was most probably the master-mason responsible for interpreting and executing Wykeham's vision, as he did at Winchester College and cathedral and had done earlier under Wykeham's charge at Windsor Castle.[22] Hugh Herland was the other key figure responsible for designing the roofs of both colleges,[23] together with Simon Membury as clerk of works. All three are depicted in the east window at Winchester College chapel. More pertinently, Wynford and Herland dined several times with the fellows in the hall of New College after the completion of the main ranges, together with the royal master-mason Henry Yevele, whose advice may well have been sought by the bishop.[24] Equally important to their success was that Wykeham maintained the financial resources to ensure the completion of his projects within his lifetime. This group of patron, master-mason, and master-carpenter brought fresh life to secular architecture, working in a plain but powerful linear style with rich mouldings and relatively austere window tracery.

Their success was emulated at the two outstanding fifteenth-century foundations at Oxford, both by Winchester associates working within affordable limits. Overreaching prevented similar achievement by Henry VI at Eton and Cambridge, and by Wolsey at Cardinal College. Less obvious but equally significant was this group's influence in southern England on domestic architecture, consolidating the precept of the royal apartments and lodgings at Windsor Castle by demonstrating the attributes of the new style on a similar heroic scale but in a more domestic context. Outside Dartington Hall, Wykeham's twin foundations are the primary secular residences to survive from the late fourteenth century. Because of limited building activity over the next thirty years, their influence was not felt for a generation or two, until the revival of domestic work during the second quarter of the fifteenth century encouraged patrons to look at Wykeham's foundations as worthy exemplars. Their influence on the equally structured, functionally organised, and stylishly built mansions developed at Wingfield, Herstmonceux, Sudeley, and Knole was as much a consequence of Wykeham's collegiate foundations as those of Henry VI.

NOTES

1 Vallance (1912) 11–12, 25–6, 28, 30–1.
2 Wykeham's radical plan is one reason given for the college being dubbed 'New'. Another is that the official title of St Mary's College of Winchester in Oxford was likely to be confused with the college already dedicated to St Mary at Oriel. For the educational innovation of Wykeham's foundation, A. B. Cobban in *The History of the University of Oxford*, II, ed. J. Catto and T. Evans (1992) 581–99.
3 Smith (1952) 28, who also details the prescribed lifestyle followed in the medieval buildings, 21–60.
4 W. Haytor, *William of Wykeham, Patron of the Arts* (1970).
5 The Chaundler Manuscript ed. M. R. James (1906); D. Loggan, *Oxonia Illustra* (1675). The Chaundler view forms the frontispiece to Smith (1952) and is included in VCH, III (1954) opp. 148, and *New College, Oxford* (1979) pls. 2, 3. These last two works also identify the construction dates, see (1954) 146 and (1979) 152–6. See also F. W. Steer, *The Archives of New College, Oxford: A Catalogue* (1974).
6 The college was built of Headington hardstone, with local rubble for the little-seen rear walls, and freestone from Taynton and Burford for dressed work. The results have been distorted by the extensive use of ashlar replacement in the nineteenth and twentieth centuries, cloister and bell-tower excepted.
7 The portrait of the founder in the middle of the dais is a copy of that by Samson Strong in the chapel, painted in 1596. It depicts New College to his left and Winchester college to his right. There are further copies at Winchester.
8 The development of Merton was still being realised during the first half of the fifteenth century with the overambitious concept not abandoned until the early sixteenth century. The suggestion on slender architectural grounds that Wykeham intended to build a nave is doubtful enough, partly because it would delay completion in his lifetime. In any case, the idea was swiftly rejected as the construction of the cloister proves. The T-shaped plan set a pattern followed by seven other Oxford colleges.
9 Fragments from the life of the Virgin over the high altar have been assembled on a wall of the chapel's song room.
10 G. Jackson-Stops prefers a low-pitched tie-beam structure for the chapel, not dissimilar to the adjoining hall roof. Buxton and Williams (1979) 171. The essays in this sixth-centenary volume give the most detailed assessment to date of the history, architecture, and possessions of the college.
11 C. Woodforde, *The Stained Glass of New College, Oxford* (1951). Most of the original glass from the central west window is in the south choir aisle of York Minster, but that removed from the choir in the eighteenth century seems to have been lost, except for a fragment at Bradford Peverell, Dorset. The founder's glass at Winchester College suffered a similar fate in the nineteenth century.
12 Some cinquefoiled window tracery and shutters, two book cupboards, and the medieval roof survive, hidden behind later panelling and the plaster ceiling.
13 VCH, III (1954) 151, 153 for plans and window elevations.
14 M. Girouard, *Country Life*, 5 April 1962.
15 In addition to the two dais windows overlooking the college approach, there are two side windows, blocked by later buildings.
16 Shown in the drawings by Chaundler and Loggan, and needlessly destroyed by Wyatt.

17 This end unit was never a brewhouse. A latrine was installed for visitors' use in the mid-fifteenth century, and the paddock for the warden's horses was converted into his garden in the late seventeenth century. An outrider is still appointed each year to accompany the warden when he makes his annual tour of the college estates.

18 Lincoln (c.1430), Exeter (1432), Magdalen (c.1475), Brasenose (1509), Corpus Christi (1517), and Wadham (1610). The position was never adopted at Cambridge.

19 The college no longer holds the secular plate given by its founder but has retained several artefacts associated with Wykeham including his jewelled mitre and leather case, embroidered gloves, a jewel in the form of a crowned M, two rings, a girdle of enamels, a silver gilt spoon, and his pastoral staff. The staff, one of the most spectacular examples of mid to late fourteenth-century goldsmith's art in England, is covered with silver gilt decoration over a wooden core. It is made up of a shaft, a highly decorated architectural knop, and a crozier head decorated with translucent enamels. Charles Oman in Buxton and Williams (1979) 293–9; *The Age of Chivalry*, ed. J. Alexander and P. Binski (1987) 471–3.

20 *Jour. Brit. Arch. Assoc.* 3 (1938) 83–95.

21 Jackson-Stops in Buxton and Williams (1979) 152.

22 J. H. Harvey, *Eng. Med. Arch.* (1984) 353–4. The construction clumsiness of the cloister suggests the work of a junior master-mason rather than Wynford who is not mentioned in the cloister accounts.

23 *Ibid.* 138–9. The same master glass painter, Thomas of Oxford, worked at both colleges, as did the same misericord craftsmen.

24 *Ibid.* 364; Jackson-Stops in Buxton and Williams (1979) 158–60. The sons of Wynford and Herland were among the earliest scholars at New College.

H. Rashdall and R. S. Rait, *History of New College* (1901)
A. Vallance, *The Old Colleges of Oxford* (1912) 33–41
RCHM, *City of Oxford* (1939) 84–91
A. H. Smith, *New College Oxford and Its Buildings* (1952)
VCH, *Oxfordshire*, III (1954) 144–62
J. Buxton and P. Williams (eds.), *New College, Oxford* (1979)

OXFORD, MAGDALEN COLLEGE and the
fifteenth-century foundations

Compared with the five new colleges founded in Cambridge during the fifteenth century, only three were established in Oxford, all founded by high-ranking churchmen. Lincoln was a modest foundation by bishop Fleming of Lincoln in 1427 whereas All Souls and Magdalen were resourced by episcopal grandees. All Souls was realised by archbishop Chichele of Canterbury in 1438 and Magdalen by bishop Waynflete of Winchester in 1458, though building did not begin until nine years later. During this century, considerable work was also undertaken at several earlier foundations, including Balliol, Exeter, Merton, and University College.[1] The university also erected an important academic building,[2] while contemporary developments at the monastic establishments will be considered separately.

ALL SOULS

Architecturally, the palm goes to All Souls and Magdalen, with the former reflecting a development position midway between New College in 1389 and Magdalen in 1458. Archbishop Chichele had been educated at New College so that Wykeham's foundation influenced the development of All Souls in size, form, and establish-

ment. Initially co-founded with Henry VI at Chichele's request until the monarch's own projects took wing, All Souls was planned to educate secular clergy and ecclesiastical lawyers. Intended to hold a warden and forty fellows (nearly half the number of those at New College), All Souls is the only medieval college to have maintained its original concept of an entirely graduate society. It was also a chantry, as well as an educational foundation, praying in particular for 'the Souls of All the Faithfully Departed' who had drunk 'the cup of bitter death' on the battlefield in the wars with France.[3] Generously endowed and prominently sited next to St Mary's church, the heart of university life at the time, the T-shaped chapel with its eight altars (six in the ante-chapel) was purposely made the dominant feature of the college, and there was also a funerary cloister. Under the direction of the master-mason Richard Chevynton, work was swiftly completed in a five-year period between the initiation of the High Street frontage in February 1438, the consecration of the chapel in September 1442, and the completion of the hall and kitchen in 1443.[4] Building stone came from Headington, with Cotswold stone from near Burford for all dressed work, and timber from Beckley, Shotover, and near Marlow. Chichele had spent nearly £4,200 on the college shortly before his death in 1443 but fitting out continued for at least the next four years. The earliest illustration of the college is the bird's-eye view, drawn between 1594 and 1606 before the destruction of the cloister, hall, kitchen, and offices.[5]

The front quadrangle survives in its original state, heralded by an extended High Street frontage and four-storeyed gate-tower. The two first-floor statues of the co-founders in canopied niches are 1939 copies, allowing the well-carved originals to be preserved in the chapel undercroft. Though the two-storeyed street frontage was ruthlessly refaced and the windows were overembellished in 1826–7 when the post-medieval extensions further east were similarly made decorous, this mid-fifteenth-century street façade with its entry tower one floor higher than usual is All Souls' contribution to the development of the classic Oxford college plan.

Front Quad is one of the least-altered late medieval quadrangles in England. The lodging ranges round three sides of the quadrangle have never been raised by a third storey or a high-pitched roof interrupted by dormer windows, so that this relatively narrow quadrangle still 'breathes'. It also means that the chapel filling the north side opposite the entrance continues to dominate the college as the founder always intended and shows to better effect than at New College. The embattled parapets of c.1510 and the later removal of the cusped window heads do not disturb the harmony or the architectural value of this quadrangle.

The gate-tower has a single modern figure over the inner entry and twin-light windows. The function of the room immediately over the two-bay lierne-vaulted entry passage is not known, but the two above were the muniment room and treasury, all approached from the projecting stair turret. The two uppermost rooms retain their original doors and window shutters.

The line of eight original close-set twin lights at first-floor level in the east range marks the old library, always separately approached. It was the most significant part of the college for the founder after the chapel. It was remodelled in 1598 and again in 1750. Between the entrances to the library and hall was the ground-floor bursary, with the remainder of the quadrangle filled with lodgings approached by doorways with four-centred heads set in square

PLATE 62 Oxford, All Souls: Front Quad towards chapel

frames and steep stairs on original lines to the upper rooms. The Merton and New College plan of a single heated chamber with twin-light window and several study cubicles lit by single windows was repeated here, though with a slightly larger chamber and three rather than four unheated cubicles[6] (fig. 31). Most of their windows were converted into twin lights and sashed in the eighteenth century and their interiors have been completely altered. The ground-floor bursary and first-floor library restricted the chambers on the east side to three, while those in the corners of the quadrangle differed in their facilities, including those of the warden in the south-east corner.[7]

The chapel entry and that formerly to the hall in the north-west and north-east angles have the earliest fan vaults in Oxford. The chapel follows the form initiated at New College but site limitations meant that the hall could not follow the Wykeham model in line with the chapel, but had to be built northwards from its east end with its quadripartite vaulted buttery cellar positioned below the altar.[8] The ante-chapel was also forced to follow the curve of Catte Street, giving it an irregular shape. The balance of the area behind the chapel was taken up by the cloister with glazed windows to the

alleys, erected between about 1494 and 1510 and destroyed 200 years later. It was replaced by Hawksmoor's North Quadrangle and Codrington Library with a new hall in place of the old one in 1730–4.

The five-bay buttressed and pinnacled choir and aisled ante-chapel essentially stand as designed by Chevynton, with three-light cinquefoiled and transomed windows filling the upper walling with the mullions carried to window heads that are flatter than those at New College. Apart from the heavy replacement Caroline screen, remodelled by Thornhill in 1713, the chapel retains more original work than at New College or Magdalen. The roof, though low pitched, is of hammer-beam form by John Branche, with the braced beams supported on carved stone corbels and carrying angel ends. The architectural framework of the reredos by John Massyngham is also original, with evidence of its gold, blue, and vermilion colouring, and red and dark green still visible. The statues are replacements of the 1870s under Sir George Gilbert Scott's direction to make up for those destroyed at the Reformation.[9] The sedilia, stalls, misericords, and two rows of tiles are mid-fifteenth century, as is the stained glass of the hierarchy of saints in the four east windows by John Glasier (*c*.1442) in the ante-chapel. In 1462, there were six altars here, each one screened. The glass in the two lights flanking the seven-light west window and above the north door has been brought from the Old Library and is therefore more secular in character, with representations of bishops and the kings of England from Constantine to Henry V.[10]

MAGDALEN COLLEGE

Bishop Waynflete of Winchester (1447–86) emulated his predecessor in the see of Winchester not only by becoming the chancellor of England (1456) but also by founding a college at Oxford that rivalled New College in scale, organisation, and architectural realisation; lavishly endowed for forty fellows, thirty scholars, four priests, eight clerks, and sixteen choristers.[11] Waynflete also matched his predecessor's ambition in founding Magdalen School next to the college, though it differed from Wykeham's school at Winchester in being a free grammar school.[12] Built a hundred years after Wykeham's foundation, Magdalen College has the same components and integrated plan and is massed to similar effect, though with some telling differences – cloister-walks round the main quadrangle, a spectacular bell tower, and no funerary cloister. Magdalen was also the first college to be totally embattled – until then, this feature had been limited to gate-towers – and it enjoys the luxury of more spacious grounds than any other college through its ownership of the water-meadows of the River Cherwell. Magdalen and New College are also comparable in the extent of their original buildings, but Magdalen lacks the texture and warm stone that enhances so many Oxford colleges. The street frontage is a dull twentieth-century refacing, the cloister quadrangle was clothed in synthetic stone in 1936–46, while several communal areas of the college are internally drab.

As the college was developed outside the city, Waynflete's first step between 1467 and 1473 was to suppress the Hospital of St John the Evangelist that had occupied part of the land since the thirteenth century and enclose the site with an embattled precinct wall that still lines part of Longwall Street. If Waynflete's probable education at New College and his mastership of Winchester (1429–42) were key influences on the founder, so was his tenure as provost of Eton from 1443, but it was holding one of the richest sees in England and the chancellorship that made it possible for him to realise his long-held plans on the grandest scale. Work on the residential buildings at Magdalen, initiated in 1474 and mainly completed by 1480, was under the direction of the master-mason William Orchard, who had worked at Eton College and the Oxford Divinity School. With a role comparable to that of William Wynford at New College, Orchard similarly used stone from Headington less than 2 miles away, with better-quality stone from Taynton and Wheatley for carved detail. Most of the timber came from Shotover and Wychwood. Work began with the chapel and hall in line on the south side of the quadrangle. The west range was mainly taken up with the entry tower, the muniment tower, and the library, while the north and east cloister ranges were essentially accommodation lodgings. The chapel was finished in 1480, the muniment tower by 1488, and the south cloister-walk was added in front of the hall and chapel in 1490. As the president almost immediately outgrew his rooms in the Founder's Tower, a new frontal lodging wing was built between 1485 and 1488, replaced on the same site in 1886–8. The detached bell tower, erected slowly

between 1492 and 1509 for financial reasons, was absorbed by the High Street range not long afterwards that now forms the principal street frontage of the college[13] and created the triangular-shaped chaplain's quadrangle to the rear. Though he followed the century-long precedent of college planning, Orchard was less austere than his forebears at New College or All Souls. The entry gateway was highly elaborated with two-storeyed oriel windows in both faces, the chapel and hall windows were pointed rather than four-centred, and the hall dais was embellished with an oriel window.

The original approach to the college was from a path further west than at present that turned through an entry at right angles into an open forecourt (now St John's Quadrangle) flanked by the since-replaced grammar school on the left and an obscure academic hall, Magdalen Hall, on the right that was certainly in existence by 1487.[14] The early sixteenth-century street range and present end-entry create an oblique approach to the college that disguises the majesty of Waynflete's foundation, as does the disconnected placement of the nineteenth-century buildings round St John's Quadrangle. The Founder's Tower, the original entrance to the college, is a four-storeyed gateway that was grander than anything previously built in Oxford and a splendid example of the architectural exuberance of Edward IV's reign. The buttressed, embattled, and pinnacled façade is highly decorated with a four-centred west entry prefaced by a flying arch, set in a multi-leaved cusped design that extends to a blind panelled frame above, a two-storeyed oriel window flanked by four canopied niches holding statues of bishop Waynflete, Edward IV, and two saints, and a three-light uppermost window. The entry passage (permanently closed by the original doors except for ceremonies) has an elaborate lierne vault, while the inner face of the gate-tower is almost as striking as the outer one, similar in design but modified in detail. The president's rooms were initially over the entrance as at New College and All Souls, with ready access to the library and muniment room. The first-floor chamber (state drawing room) retains its oriel windows at both ends, fireplace, and beamed ceiling, with further rooms today for the president in Bodley and Garner's adjoining frontal wing.[15] The president's timber-framed oratory on the south-west corner of the cloister roof was swept away in 1830.

This grand entrance, quite unlike that at New College, was balanced by a three-storeyed projection with newel stair to the north and a short two-storeyed library block to the south, both enhanced by first-floor oriels. The south block abuts the four-square muniment tower, a three-storeyed structure that held the college archives as at New College, but here with a ground-floor vaulted vestibule with decorative bosses that has always served as the chapel approach and has been the principal approach to the cloistered quadrangle since the mid-sixteenth century.[16] The structure is almost as plain as the west front of the ante-chapel in line with it, though that is enriched by a decorated west door with another flying arch. The massing and differing heights of the components that contribute to this college frontage, topped with embattled parapets and crocketed finials, create a rhythm that makes it one of the most attractive concepts of the late fifteenth century.

The quadrangle was larger than that at All Souls and with windows that the founder declared were to be as good as those of that foundation or better. The design was no doubt influenced by Orchard's work at Eton. It similarly consisted of ground-floor covered walkways, timber ceiled, with an outer rim of chambers and

PLATE 63 Oxford, Magdalen College: Founder's Tower, chapel and hall from Great Quadrangle

an upper floor of rooms extending the width of the range, except on the south side where the hall and chapel rose behind the single-storey cloister-walk. This cloistered quadrangle is the only pivotal one in an Oxford college and is admired by many critics for its unity and harmonious character. The bays, ten on the north and south sides, eight on the east and west, are separated by low buttresses surmounted by figures and beasts added in 1509, subsequently coloured. The cloister windows are of three open lights with multi-cusped tracery to a four-centred head (east and west walks largely original). The upper-floor windows are of the uncusped two-light form under square heads so popular at the time. Some of the ground-floor rooms off the west range retain doorways with four-centred heads and glazed windows towards the cloister-walk, while the upper floor is divided into two unequal portions. The north part is the old library with windows of two cinquefoiled lights and a 1609 roof above the eighteenth-century plaster ceiling. The south part beyond the Founder's Tower continues the president's rooms with five oriels, three towards the quadrangle and two facing the college entry. The other ranges have suffered a sequence of vicissitudes during the sixteenth and late eighteenth centuries, culminating in

the factional destruction of the north range in 1822. It was rebuilt within two years, followed by the east range in 1825–6.

The five-bay hall, 73 feet by 29½ feet, stands at first-floor level over chapel vestries (now senior common rooms). Marginally smaller in scale internally than New College hall, it has twin-light cinquefoiled and transomed windows with panelled heads that are similarly smaller in scale than those of the chapel. The dais oriel lighting the high table was an innovatory feature (with sixteenth-century armorial shields). The roof was not spectacular, braced tie beams on carved stone corbels (retained) supporting a shallow pitched roof, copied in 1902 from early sources and the smoke silhouettes on the end walls, to replace Wyatt's plaster ceiling of 1790. With its early sixteenth-century linenfold panelling to windowsill level, the oak screen of 1605, tables, benches, floorboards, and roof, this hall has a dominant 'fumed oak' character. The broader and taller of the four doorways at the service end gave access to the ground-floor kitchen, the reused late thirteenth- and early fourteenth-century building of the Hospital of St John with a sixteenth-century tie-beam roof.

The chapel is a disappointment. T-shaped as at Merton and All

Souls, chapel and ante-chapel retain their three-light transomed windows and the slender piers in the ante-chapel, but the whole has been altered too many times to retain any value of its early character. Some late fifteenth-century stalls line the perimeter of the ante-chapel, but all the other features are of 1790–6 (Wyatt's plaster vault in place of the original timber roof) or 1829–35 (Cottingham's statued reredos, stalls, stone partition screen) with seventeenth- and mid-nineteenth-century stained glass. Even the founder's chantry tomb was not spared, for Cottingham agreed that part of it should be 'donated' to Theale church. All is dour and joyless, a reflection of the relatively recent medievalising tastes that mirrored the form but not the spirit of that age.

Fortunately, the college's late medieval character ends on a high note. Begun by an unknown mason six years after Waynflete's death, Magdalen's 125 feet high bell tower makes that at New College look parochial. Still singularly well positioned to announce the college to all who approach Oxford from London, this beautifully proportioned tower has polygonal angle buttresses, with a plain side to the college but a single twin-light window at each stage in the other faces. This throws into greater relief the exuberant fifth stage that is the crowning glory of the college. The tall traceried windows are in pairs, separated by mini buttresses, leading the eye to a fizzing architectural crown of enriched string courses, traceried panels, pierced parapets, and crocketed pinnacles. It is regrettable that the slightly later street range at its base is so determinedly second rate and that the tower was not left freestanding.

OTHER COLLEGES

The remaining fifteenth-century collegiate buildings are of minor interest, by less well-endowed colleges expanding as financial resources allowed. Bishop Fleming died four years after founding *Lincoln College* in 1427 and before much work had been accomplished. Part of the street range with its towered entry, rector's lodging, and muniment room above is attributed to him, but it was fifty years before the quadrangle was completed for the college was nearly extinguished twice before bishop Rotherham put it on a sound financial and regulatory basis. By 1437 John Forest, an elderly friend of the founder and dean of Wells, had completed the street range, erected the north range with its first-floor chapel and library, and filled much of the east side with a buttery and hall. Money from the executors of bishop Beckington of Wells initiated the rector's lodging south of the hall (1465–70), and the quadrangle was closed by a south range built at the expense of bishop Rotherham of Lincoln (1478–9) to provide chambers for extra graduates.

The dour street frontage shown by Loggan was refenestrated in 1816–19. The quadrangle is much smaller than at New College, for the establishment was initially for a rector and only seven graduates dedicated to promoting religious orthodoxy at a time when the reforming views of John Wycliffe were appealing to many members of the academic community as they had initially done to Fleming when he was at Oxford. The ranges are still two-storeyed with a ground-floor hall rather than a raised one, befitting the college's modest scale. But while the bones of the quadrangle are medieval, the chapel was replaced in 1631 and sash windows and refacing have transformed its flesh, now creeper clad. The four-bay hall and kitchen retain more visible evidence of their origins through their roofs, both with braced collar trusses, wind braces, and the hall with

a pretty original polygonal louvre. The college did not expand beyond this quadrangle until the early seventeenth century and it differs little in scale and layout from that of a contemporary country house, though Lincoln lacks vividness.

Several of the smaller fourteenth-century foundations developed their sites during the following century so that they began to resemble their more well-endowed neighbours rather than academic halls, but in all cases the process was slow, as at Lincoln. *University College* built a chapel in *c*.1395–8, a hall and kitchen range in 1448–9, and a gateway in *c*.1472–3, all swept away in the comprehensive mid-seventeenth-century rebuilding, as was the fifteenth-century work at *Oriel College* a few years earlier.[17] The gateway of Exeter College warrants little more than a footnote, while much of the extensive rebuilding scheme at Balliol has been replaced by mid-Victorian historicism.[18]

The gateway of 1432 at *Exeter College* is not the current seventeenth-century entrance from Turl Street but the isolated gate-tower in the north-east corner of the front quad to the rear of the totally alien mid-Victorian chapel. Originally approached from a vanished lane and now an adjunct to the rector's lodging of 1857, the three-storeyed tower is more slender than its contemporaries at All Souls and Merton, with a modest two-bay vaulted passage, a single room on the upper floors, and the single- and twin-light cinquefoil windows ubiquitous to the period. In this most poorly endowed of the medieval colleges, Palmer's Tower is no different from any domestic gateway of the period.

Like Front Quad of Lincoln, that of *Balliol College* was developed piecemeal during the fifteenth century after it had acquired more land next to its Broad Street site. The quadrangle was smaller than that at All Souls and Magdalen, with the first-floor library opposite the present entry and more dominant than the adjacent chapel. The sequence of ranges was initiated at the close of the fourteenth century by the east range. After a gap of about twenty years, the ground-floor hall was built opposite (1412–23), followed by the library range to the north, begun in 1431 but extended by four bays in 1477–83 to house the 181 manuscript volumes donated by bishop Gray of Ely which makes it one of the most important private medieval collections in England. The master's lodge in the south-west corner was built slowly (1454–78), while the south range was erected in about 1495. The east and south ranges were rebuilt by Waterhouse in 1867–8 and the replacement chapel of 1520–9 was superseded by Butterfield's parti-coloured structure of 1856–7.

The value of Balliol lies in the differing fifteenth-century windows of the three surviving medieval units – hall, library, and master's lodge – though even here, the windows of the hall and master's lodge were extensively restored by Wyatt in 1794. The interiors have been too drastically remodelled to be of value to the medievalist so that interest rests entirely on the outer walls.[19] The buttressed ground-floor hall was initially lit by three large twin-light cinquefoiled and transomed windows to the quadrangle and three similar windows to the west, with the south end bay serving as a screens passage opening into an end buttery below the master's lodging. The courtyard face is enlivened by attractively carved figures to the two-centred hoods and at string course level. The clean vertical lines and uncluttered tracery of these windows were old fashioned for the time – twenty years later than the similar form at Westminster Hall. Facing towards the library range built two generations later, the ground floor was lit by utilitarian trefoiled lights under square hoods (now mid-nineteenth century) but the more important upper floor has a close succession of eleven paired cinquefoil lights, transomed, and with panelled heads under flattened four-centred hoods. In the south-west corner, the master's lodge retains a large first-floor oriel of Yorkist exuberance with the arms of bishop Gray (d.1479). Supported on three combined corbels and mini fan vaults, it has much elaborate but repetitive decoration, faithfully renewed by Waterhouse in 1867–8.

NOTES

1 For these and all other lost early buildings, see particularly Vallance (1912) who considered that all work after the glories of medieval and Tudor architecture was degrading and in savage taste.

2 St Mary's church had long been the university's official meeting place used for convocation, the chancellor's court, and disputations. It was supplemented in the 1320s by the first purpose-built university building, *Congregation House*, a two-storeyed secular structure on the north side of St Mary's church but independent of it, funded by bishop Cobham of Worcester to house his collection of books on the upper floor as the nucleus of a university library. The quadripartite-vaulted ground floor was used as the university's treasury and muniment room. Both floors were initially one bay longer than at present, while the library was refenestrated in the late fifteenth century to give it the character of a single-storey building. In 1423, funds were being solicited for a purpose-built lecture room for the study of theology in place of some of the rented rooms concentrated in the area immediately north of St Mary's church. Built on a grand scale befitting its study subject, the *'Divinity School'* was a single-storey hall initiated by 1427 and soon placed under the direction of Robert Winchcombe. The five-bay interior was flooded with light from large cinquefoiled windows under low-pitched heads as at the contemporary prior's lodging at Wenlock Priory. The effect is of a screen of windows rather than a wall, originally glass-filled with the coats of arms of benefactors, separated by huge panelled buttresses for an intended stone vault. This richly decorated structure was prefaced by an intricately carved west door in a panelled façade, porch protected. Work ground to a halt in 1440 for lack of funds. Elaborate mouldings had to be abandoned, as the plainer south wall buttresses and window reveals show under the replacement mason, Thomas Elkyn. The bequest of his books by Humphrey, duke of Gloucester in 1444 transformed the situation, for the decision was made not to accommodate them with bishop Cobham's books but to build a special library over the incomplete Divinity School. Congregation House and more particularly Fromond's Chantry at Winchester College (1431–5) were the precedent for this arrangement, increasing the influence of this important Hampshire foundation on Oxford planning. The duke's funding enabled a low-pitched roof to be erected over the library in 1458. Twenty years later, Thomas Kemp, bishop of London gave a thousand marks to complete the building. William Orchard's stunning vault over the Divinity School (1480–3) with its 455 carved stone bosses is one of the architectural *tours de force* of fifteenth-century England. A consequence was that the library roof of 1458 was raised wholesale by 5 feet in 1485–6 with new longer arch braces and wall posts on the original corbels: *Vern. Arch.* 30 (1999) 102. The library was also aptly matched in building expansion and content richness under Sir Thomas Bodley (1598–1602), followed by the Arts (1610–12) and Selden (1634–40) extensions at each end and the School Quadrangle of teaching rooms (1613–24) that replaced the School of Arts erected in *c*.1439 by Thomas Hokenorton, abbot of Osney. W. St J. Hope, *Arch. Jour.* 71 (1914) 217–60; RCHM (1939) 1–9, 136; J. N. L. Myres, *Archaeologia* 101 (1967) 151–68; S. Gillam, *The Divinity School and Duke Humphrey's Library at Oxford* (1988).

3 Chichele had founded a college for secular canons at Higham Ferrers in 1422.

4 For the extensive accounts detailing the workmen, materials, and building progress, Jacob (1933) 121–35.

5 *Typus Collegi*, College archives. Reproduced in Vallance (1912) 44–5 and VCH, III (1954) opp. 173.

6 Original floor plans in VCH, III (1954) 189.

7 Additional land to the east of the High Street frontage was purchased in 1472 where a more private and larger warden's residence was built, developed further in 1553.

8 The four-bay hall, shown in the *Typus*, was almost 60 feet by 30 feet with a high-pitched, probably hammer-beam roof. The buttery separated it from the kitchen to the east with its central south-facing stack, large flanking windows, and conical roof.

9 For some fragments of the canopied niches and other parts of the reredos discovered in 1983, N. Doggett, *Oxoniensia* 44 (1985) 277–87.

10 F. E. Hutchinson, *Medieval Glass at All Souls College* (1949). Since 1549, this chapel has been the only long-established one in Oxford without an organ – unnecessary for worship by such a select society.

11 Funding came from suppressed religious foundations such as the hospitals at Brackley and Romsey and the priories at Selbourne and Sele, and from estates administered by Waynflete, particularly those of Sir John Fastolf of Caister Castle. Under the presidential rule of Richard Mayew (1480–1506), the organisation of further benefactions made the college the wealthiest in Oxford. It was Mayhew's appointment that initiated the formalisation of the college's statutes, now known from a notarial copy of 1487.

12 Waynflete followed Wykeham's precept of building the school after the college. Erected in 1480–7, the earliest remains are of 1614, though the school moved to new premises the other side of Magdalen Bridge in 1894. Two years before his death Waynflete had also built and endowed a free school at his birthplace in Lincolnshire.

13 The street range incorporates the thirteenth-century chapel of the Hospital of St John. This is not apparent from the High Street but is identifiable by its rubble wall towards the Chaplain's Quadrangle inside the college. For details of the building programme, VCH, III (1954) 202–6.

14 It seems to have originated in a hall founded by Waynflete in 1448. In 1822, Magdalen Hall was moved to the site of the first Hertford College. For the approach in 1675, see Loggan's engraving of the college.

15 D. Watkin, *Country Life* (February 2000). For the dating of chests held in the Muniment Tower, including two from the fourteenth century, *Vern. Arch.* 31 (2000) 95–6.

16 Window with inserted fragments of fifteenth-century stained glass; the two upper rooms with early glazed floor tiles.

17 For the medieval buildings at Oriel, VCH, III (1954) 126–7.

18 For the north transept (1419–25), chapel tower (1448–52), and gateway (*c*.1465) of the more wealthy Merton College, see page 135–6. The decorative crossing tower with its large traceried windows, openwork parapet, and crocketed pinnacles is in marked contrast with the austerity of New College's bell tower fifty years earlier and a foretaste of that at Magdalen fifty years later.

19 The hall has an inserted floor by Salvin as part of its mid-nineteenth-century library conversion. The library was totally altered by Wyatt, who embattled the quadrangle ranges, and the lodge is virtually a Waterhouse rebuilding.

All Souls College

A. Vallance, *The Old Colleges of Oxford* (1912) 44–9

E. F. Jacob, 'The Building of All Souls College 1438–1443' in *Historical Essays in Honour of James Tait*, ed. J. G. Edwards, V. H. Galbraith, and E. F. Jacob (1933) 121–35

RCHM, *City of Oxford* (1939) 15–19

VCH, *Oxfordshire*, III (1954) 173–93

Balliol College
H. W. C. Davis, *Balliol College* (1899)
A. Vallance, *The Old Colleges of Oxford* (1912) 14–17
RCHM, *City of Oxford* (1939) 20–3
VCH, *Oxfordshire*, III (1954) 82–9
J. Jones, *Balliol College: A History 1263–1939* (1988)

Exeter College
A. Vallance, *The Old Colleges of Oxford* (1912) 25–8
RCHM, *City of Oxford* (1939) 54–7

Lincoln College
A. Vallance, *The Old Colleges of Oxford* (1912) 41–3
RCHM, *City of Oxford* (1939) 63–8
VCH, *Oxfordshire*, III (1954) 163–73
V. H. H. Green, *Lincoln College* (n.d. [c.1975])

Magdalen College
H. A. Wilson, *Magdalen College* (1899)
A. Vallance, *The Old Colleges of Oxford* (1912) 49–61
RCHM, *City of Oxford* (1939) 69–76
VCH, *Oxfordshire*, III (1954) 193–207

University College
A. Vallance, *The Old Colleges of Oxford* (1912) 11–14
RCHM, *City of Oxford* (1939) 114–18
VCH, *Oxfordshire*, III (1954) 61–4, 71–3

OXFORD, WORCESTER COLLEGE and monastic academic foundations

Between the late thirteenth and early sixteenth centuries, several monastic establishments built residences for the benefit of monks studying at Oxford. Though their buildings conformed to a great extent to the standard college plan (with one exception), they occupied a distinctive position in the medieval university. There were five such foundations, developed by different orders or provinces, where their members could study in common in a disciplined environment.[1] After the Reformation, three were refounded as secular colleges and retain some of their fifteenth-century buildings. Canterbury College was lost in the development of Christ Church,[2] and St Mary's College reverted to the function of a private house in 1580.[3]

Monastic foundation		Incorporated in
Gloucester College 1293–8	Benedictine–southern province	Worcester College
Durham College c.1286	Benedictine–northern province	Trinity College
Canterbury College 1363	Benedictine–south-east province	Christ Church
St Mary's College 1435	Augustinian canons	Frewin Hall
St Bernard's College 1437	Cistercian	St John's College

St Bernard's College was founded by archbishop Chichele in 1437 and incorporated in *St John's College* in 1557. Most of Front Quad dates from this initial development, helped by annual contributions from Cistercian abbeys, though the construction dragged on for well over a hundred years.[4] It differs little from any other college of the period. The hall, kitchen, and chapel were built in line on the north side of the quad, with completion by about 1517, though the usual position of the hall and kitchen were reversed, with the hall tightly positioned in the north-west corner with a room above (possibly an oratory), while the larger kitchen closer to the chapel was open to the roof. The hall's disproportionate size suggests this may have been a temporary measure pending a larger hall projecting north of the quadrangle as at All Souls.[5] Not surprisingly the kitchen with its contemporary collar-beam roof became the college hall in c.1557 while the end buttery is above a little-altered four-bay vaulted cellar of c.1494.

The south range was also commenced in 1438, setting the pattern for the other two-storeyed residential ranges with four-centred doorway heads, plain as befitted a Cistercian establishment, and single or double lights under square hoods (now with sashed frames and an embattled parapet of 1617). The gate-tower and street range on the west side were probably built between 1480 and 1490.[6] The gate-tower was three-storeyed and centrally positioned in a two-storeyed range as was usual by this date. It retains its multi-pillared four-centred entry with projecting doorframe, a canted oriel flanked by statues in niches above, and a two-bay vaulted entry passage with original traceried doors. The chambers north of the gate-tower had only one study cubicle, presumably for senior members, while those student chambers south of it had two such cubicles, with the remains of one in room 29. The east range of chambers and library (part of the president's lodging since 1555) was not completed until roofed shortly after the Dissolution, creating a pleasant quadrangle with no obvious sign of its extended timeframe. It is the most complete of the monastic colleges in Oxford, larger than the contemporary quadrangle at Balliol next door, and the only foundation to have retained part of its forecourt.

In comparison with St John's, *Trinity College* retains only the shadow of its predecessor. Durham College was a cell of Durham Priory just as Canterbury College was a cell of Christ Church, Canterbury. They were the only two monastic houses to found their own university establishments. All the other Benedictine houses had to share premises at Gloucester College. Durham had sent monks to Oxford since the late 1280s, but the foundation of a regular college was not financially possible until the legacies made by bishop Hatfield (1381) and bishop Skirlaw (1405–8). The hall was probably the first structure built, followed by the gateway in 1397, the chapel in 1405–9 at a cost of over £135, and the two remaining ranges that make up the small quadrangle between 1409 and 1425.[7] The college was suppressed in 1544 but the buildings were taken over eleven years later as the basis of the newly established and quickly occupied Trinity College. The hall and chapel at right angles to each other are late seventeenth-century replacements followed by the north range of lodgings in 1728, all built on the foundations of the early buildings shown by Loggan (1675). Only the east range of 1417–21 survives, with its first-floor library at the south end built at a cost of £42. Its plain paired first-floor lights towards the quad now lack their cusps, but those overlooking

PLATE 64 Oxford, Worcester College: south range

the garden are cinquefoil transomed lights with several panels of contemporary stained glass of evangelists and coats of arms.

In many ways, *Gloucester College* is the most interesting of these monastic foundations, with a highly individual plan. Since the general chapter of 1247, the Benedictine order had encouraged study and education as part of its efforts to return to the stricter interpretation of the rule of its founder. To further this aim, it was decided in 1277 to found a house of study at Oxford. With the encouragement of Gloucester Abbey, Sir John Giffard of Brimpsfield purchased a site *extra muros Oxoniae* in 1283 as a house for thirteen monks of that abbey, although control was transferred to Malmesbury Abbey after Giffard had been buried there in 1299.[8] At the same time, eligibility was extended to all Benedictine houses throughout the province of Canterbury, and from 1336 to those of the province of York. It was laid down, however, that student monks were not to be dispersed round the town, but to study together in groups of not less than ten.[9]

Thirty-eight out of sixty-five Benedictine monasteries used Gloucester College at various times. Some just sent students, but others built their own lodgings to create the most unusual of the late medieval college plans at Oxford. The foundation was made up of a series of units owned by individual monasteries with a hall (fourteenth century), library (1421), and chapel (*c.*1420–4) in common, grouped round a small court. From this extended a number of ranges, built piecemeal, of which nearly half have survived in three separate blocks. Loggan's view of 1675 shows the fully developed foundation before the hall and chapel court was replaced by the present hall, chapel, and library block in the eighteenth century. The south range of two-storeyed *camerae* or lodgings survive complete, but only the walls of the shorter ranges of similar *camerae* to the south-east and north-east. They were all built during the fifteenth century and incorporated in Gloucester Hall in 1560, refounded as *Worcester College* in 1714.

The important south range is a line of stepped, weatherbeaten fifteenth-century lodgings, two-storeyed but independent of each

other rather than a unified range like that at Ewelme Manor. They form a striking contrast with the taller eighteenth-century ranges on the other two sides of the quadrangle, sited on higher ground, and built of dressed stone in Palladian style. They also serve as a reminder that most of the college buildings were more humble than those of New College, All Souls, or Magdalen.

Numbered 7 to 12, each lodging is virtually complete and in an impressive state of preservation. They were built one after the other, marked by building lines and slightly different roof levels of stone tiles. The little-touched frontages retain their original entries and windows, though the latter now lack the cusps of their early lights. There is little difference in construction, for all doorways have four-centred heads under square hoods, though with differing spandrel decoration and stops to the two end lodgings (7 and 8). The arms of Malmesbury are over stair 12, those of Norwich or St Augustine's, Canterbury are over stair 11, and those of Pershore or Eynsham Abbey over stair 7. All windows have square frames, many with shaped jambs with those of 9 in slight bays rising through both floors and those of 8 of three cinquefoiled lights in a unified frame with blind panelling between the windows. The rear is more varied and imposing as a result of the end projections, the multiplicity of dormers to inserted attic rooms, and the white-painted early nineteenth-century wooden cinquefoil lights and barge boards. The rooms were heated but the interiors have been totally modified except for their ceiling beams, and a first-floor wagon roof with moulded ribs at the east end.

The walls of the two further lodging ranges stand, but post-medieval alterations have curtailed their structural value in favour of the documentary evidence. Those round Pump Quadrangle south-east of the Georgian hall were raised a storey and refenestrated in the eighteenth century. Only a single trefoil light remains, and the entries to 14 and 15 on the south side and 16 on the east. The lodgings of Bury St Edmunds and Glastonbury Abbey were here, plus the early kitchen in the west extension, now converted into rooms. The north-east group of *camerae* stand behind the Georgian chapel with a street-facing blank wall and single ground-floor lights towards the fellows' garden. The range has been remodelled internally as the senior common room and stair 3 (Abingdon Abbey) of the classical north range. Loggan shows two blocks projecting from this extended range, that of Worcester Cathedral Priory on the site of the classical loggia, and of St Albans Abbey in the middle of the replacement north range.

NOTES

1 Bishop Fox intended to establish a college for eight monks of Winchester cathedral priory, but it was abandoned after 1513 in favour of the secular Corpus Christi College of 1517.

2 Loggan's view of Christ Church shows the hall of Canterbury College with its early Perpendicular windows (1364–78) and the chapel and two sides of the quadrangle built by prior Chillenden of Canterbury (1379–97). W. A. Pantin, *Oxford. Hist. Soc.* 6 (1947).

3 Hardly any of the college buildings survive. The lower half of the front wall of the fifteenth-century gateway with its four-centred entrance, small windows, and one side of the two-bay vaulted passage stands as the entry to Frewin Hall, a hall of residence of Brasenose College. The remains are the ground floor of a conventional gate-tower, opening into an early sixteenth-century cloistered quadrangle – one of three in medieval Oxford. The chapel hammer-beam roof of *c.*1515–20 was moved to Brasenose College. J. Blair, *Oxoniensia* 43 (1978) 48–99.

4 Colvin, *Oxoniensia* 24 (1959) 37–48.
5 *Ibid.* 42.
6 R. H. C. Davis, *Oxoniensia* 11–12 (1946–7) 87. VCH, III (1954) 259. The third storey was added to the street range in the late sixteenth century, but the attic rooms round the quadrangle are only lit by dormers facing away from the quadrangle.
7 R. B. Dobson, *Durham Priory: 1400–1450* (1973) 348–59.
8 Giffard had been granted the castles of Llandovery (1282), Carreg Cennen (1283), and Dynevor (1290), and was responsible with his son (d.1322) for the present substantial structure at Carreg Cennen.
9 For the college's history, Pantin (1946–7) 65–74.

St John's College
A. Vallance, *The Old Colleges of Oxford* (1912) 77–83
W. H. Stevenson and H. E. Salter, *The Early History of St John's College* (1939)
RCHM, *City of Oxford* (1939) 103–8
VCH, *Oxfordshire*, III (1954) 251–64
H. M. Colvin, *Oxoniensia* 24 (1959) 37–48

Trinity College
A. Vallance, *The Old Colleges of Oxford* (1912) 73–77
RCHM, *City of Oxford* (1939) 108–14
VCH, *Oxfordshire*, III (1954) 238–9
M. Maclagan, *Trinity College: 1555–1955* (1955)

Worcester College
A. Vallance, *The Old Colleges of Oxford* (1912) 92–5
RCHM, *City of Oxford* (1939) 123–5
W. A. Pantin, *Oxoniensia* 11–12 (1946–7) 65–74
R. A. Devereux and D. N. Griffiths, *Worcester College* (1951)
VCH, *Oxfordshire*, III (1954) 302–7
H. Wansbrough and A. M. Crosby (eds.), *Benedictines in Oxford* (1997)

Monastic colleges
J. Blair, *Arch. Jour.* 135 (1978) 263–5
R. B. Dobson, *The History of the University of Oxford*, II, ed. J. I. Catto and T. A. R. Evans (1992) 539–79

SHIRBURN CASTLE, Oxfordshire

Shirburn Castle has a well-deserved reputation for being barred to all students of architecture. This practice is currently maintained by the present members of the Macclesfield family who are following the precept of their forebears.[1] Consequently, the castle has never been studied in detail. No floor plans, elevations, description, or dating analysis have been published[2] so that the castle poses several questions for the medievalist that need to be addressed.[3]

It is usually considered that the property has been fully occupied since its construction during the later fourteenth century, but this is probably not so. The Lisle family only came into the manor of East Shirburn in the mid-fourteenth century, but after East and West Shirburn manors had been united in about 1361, Warin, 2nd Lord Lisle (1361–82) took the opportunity to build a new house on the site of West Shirburn manor, and the earlier property was allowed to decay.[4] Lisle spent much of his adulthood fighting in France, initially with Henry, earl of Lancaster in 1359, and subsequently with John, duke of Lancaster in 1369, 1372, and 1378. As the family estates were centred on Kingston Lisle in Berkshire, Warin was appointed a commissioner of peace for Berkshire in 1364 and was summoned to parliament from 1369 onwards. Lisle was

granted a licence to crenellate his residence at Shirburn in March 1377[5] and is held responsible for the present structure. He died five years later at the age of fifty-two, when the castle passed initially to his daughter and heir who married Lord Berkeley, and then to her daughter who married Richard, earl of Warwick (1399). The castle was in the earl's hands in 1418 when minor alterations were made to it and in the following year.[6]

The property was subsequently occupied by several families, with the longest tenure held by the Chamberlain family between the close of the fifteenth and the mid-seventeenth century when they held the castle for the king throughout the Civil War. It is likely that it was damaged but not totally ruined during an attack in 1644 for the house was assessed at thirty-two hearths in 1665.[7] Even so, partial rather than total occupation of a habitable but dilapidated building is most likely, for the reconstruction undertaken by Thomas Parker, 1st earl of Macclesfield after he purchased the property in 1716 was fundamental. As it entailed rebuilding more than three-quarters of the castle, the clearance of decayed ranges and unstable walls by this time is more likely than the wholesale destruction of perfectly sound structures and their total replacement in a building programme that mirrored the earlier form. What stands today at Shirburn is essentially an early eighteenth-century interpretation of the medieval castle, following its original plan.

The property stands on a chamfered stone and brick plinth, square-shaped under the round towers, but the castle is a mixture of dressed stone, rubble masonry, and brickwork. The gate-tower is of dressed chalk and limestone, the south-west tower of rubble masonry and dressed stone, and the south-east tower of masonry with added brickwork. The hideous grey rendering which has completely covered the castle since the early nineteenth century is falling away to reveal the materials behind it. This amalgam and the rough-cast facing give the castle what has been generously described as an 'unkempt beauty of texture'.[8] Stripped to its basics, the castle was probably built entirely in limestone with most of the brick casing added in the eighteenth century while the rubble on the western towers is also facing material only.

Shirburn follows a plan common to many castles of the mid to late fourteenth century, quadrangular with two-storeyed ranges enclosing a central courtyard, and three-storeyed towers at each corner. It rises directly from the spring-fed moat which broadens into a lake on the north side. The square gate-tower is in the middle of the west range, but the angle towers are round rather than the square form preferred in northern England (Bolton, Lumley, Sheriff Hutton, Wressle). The tower heads are marked by two string courses, one supporting the embattled parapet. It is claimed that there were originally three drawbridges on the east, west and south sides[9] but it is more likely that there were two, the main entrance and possibly a postern opposite. The present working drawbridge to the former is a Regency *jeu d'esprit* with contemporary footbridges serving the other two ranges.

Without examination, it is impossible to determine how much of the original structure survived the Macclesfield reconstruction during the 1720s. The flat-fronted gate-tower is relatively complete, and though drastically altered above ground level, arrow loops can be traced either side of the uppermost window. This three-storeyed gate-house is an interesting variation on the more common projecting form and stands to its original height. The

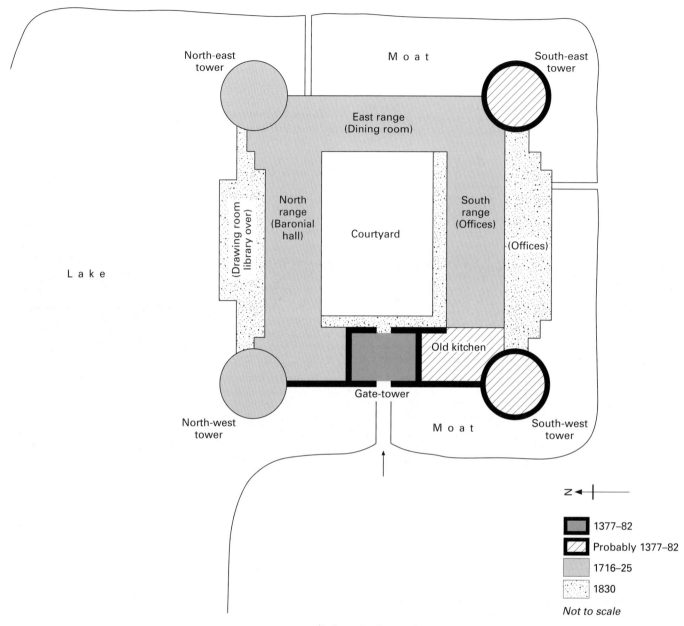

FIGURE 32 Shirburn Castle: site plan

plain, double-chamfered, four-centred entrance was protected by a portcullis and double doors[10] but not necessarily by a rising draw-bridge.[11] It has a broad vaulted entry with moulded ribs rising uninterrupted from corner columns and with plugged (now open) holes instead of bosses.[12] The lower part of the west range is probably contemporary for there is a porter's squint, while an internal photograph taken at the beginning of the twentieth century in the 'comparatively unaltered old kitchen'[13] shows a late fourteenth-century doorway with moulded two-centred head set in a moulded square frame opening into a tall room.[14] However, it is unlikely to be the medieval kitchen for it shows no evidence of service doorways while there is a suspended doorway of fourteenth-century character near the ground-floor entry. This indicates that the range was always two-storeyed and gives us the scale of the rooms. The

range was refenestrated in the early eighteenth century when the third storey was added, reducing the impact and proportions of the gate-house. Masonry evidence in the lower stages of the south-west tower seems to be original, as does that in the south-east tower. The masonry below the sill level of the east front is also early, but nothing else is in the east, north, or south ranges.[15] A low line of rooms, added in front of the north wall in the early eighteenth century, was replaced in 1830 by a two-storeyed projection of drawing room with library over. There was a similar addition for offices and bedrooms on the south side and courtyard corridors on the south and west sides.

The original internal layout of the castle is not known. One of the corner towers was referred to as 'the lord's tower' in 1418–19 when repair work was carried out,[16] but there is no further docu-

PLATE 65 Shirburn Castle: from the north-west

mentary evidence for pre-Georgian building work. It is possible that the hall lay opposite the gatehouse with the further end of its screen passage opening on to a postern as at Bodiam Castle. The 'lord's tower' may have been the north-east tower with its two side projections towards the lake for the stair and garderobes.[17] Most of the apartments were courtyard lit, with the outer-facing walls marked by loopholes[18] and small openings rather than the present regular pattern of large windows, though Bodiam shows that such a pattern was possible. An inventory of 1539 refers to the hall, the chamber over the parlour (presumably at the upper end of the hall) and an inner chamber there, a great chamber at the lower end of the hall, and rooms for the chamberlain, butler, priest, and cook, as well as various offices and outhouses.[19]

In 1716, Thomas Parker, lord chief justice, lord chancellor in 1718, and 1st earl of Macclesfield in 1721, paid £7,000 for the castle and grounds.[20] He spent a prodigious sum lavishly redeveloping the castle between 1716 and 1725 when he was imprisoned in the Tower of London for massive corruption. He retained the earlier castle shape but new-built the three-storeyed ranges on the south, east and north sides, reconstructed the two north-facing corner towers, and remodelled the west range with an added third storey. Large round-headed windows without keystones were inserted throughout the castle at all levels, overlooking the moat. Macclesfield was following the same road as Vanburgh in a range at Kimbolton

Castle (1707–10), but Shirburn Castle was the first major Georgian essay in a revived Norman castellated style.[21] Further additions were made to the north and south fronts in 1830 as well as extensive internal alterations and refenestration on three sides with segmental-headed sash windows. The early Georgian and Regency interiors are dominant,[22] but until the castle has been subject to a sympathetic examination and analysis, the extent of any further retained medieval structure and its internal layout is unknown.

It is often claimed that Shirburn is the first brick-built castle in England and the earliest use of this material in Oxfordshire. This is not so. The early use of brick for fortifications rests on the fourteenth-century towered circuit at Kingston upon Hull and the brick extensions to the gatehouse at Thornton Abbey (1380s). The earliest certain use of brick for castellated residences does not occur until the second quarter of the fifteenth century at Caister (1432–c.1445), Herstmonceux (c.1438–49), and Tattershall (mid-1440s). These structures were following the example set by Henry V at Sheen (1414–22) and his immediate circle such as Bedford at Fulbroke Castle (c.1420–35) and the royal councillors who completed Sheen for the young Henry VI (1429–39). There may be some fifteenth-century brickwork at Shirburn but the doorway in the gatehouse passage is more likely to be Tudor. Externally, the brick casing of the house is eighteenth century so that Shirburn can be excluded from the incunabula of this material in the Thames valley.

If any part of the castle dates from the 1370s, it is the stone gate-tower with its entrance displaying fashionable open holes in its stone vaulting. This decorative feature seems to have connotations with the royal masons for an early example occurs in the vault of the Bloody Tower (1360–2) at the Tower of London. It was quickly picked up and repeated not only in the gatehouses at St Albans (1362–5), Holt Castle (1367–88), and Worcester Abbey (1368–9) as well as at Bodiam Castle (c.1385–c.1390) but also in the entrance to the Abbot's House at Westminster Abbey (1370–9). In the latter case, the openings are plugged with plain discs of stone, often referred to as 'murder-holes', though this feature was essentially intended to heighten the importance of the entrance. Part of the west range at Shirburn also incorporates original stonework, as do the south-west and south-east towers confirming the overall shape of Lisle's residence.

Is Shirburn the work of a well-heeled property-owning husband of two successive heiresses, or the work of a battle-scarred warrior? It seems to have had less of a martial air than the castle by Lisle's contemporary, Sir Edward Dalyngrigge at Bodiam. But both are similar in respect of their rectangular shape, broad moat enclosure, central gateway, round angle towers, and residential ranges round each side of the central court. Bodiam has two mid towers, and a postern tower opposite the gateway which may have been repeated at Shirburn. Lisle's castle is no smaller than Bodiam but has a square gate-tower that is closer to Dalyngrigge's vaulted and ceiling-pierced postern tower with its single portcullis chase than to his formidable twin-towered gate-house. It is possible but unlikely that the present entry was Lisle's postern tower, and that the gate-house on the east side has been totally destroyed. In any case, the parallel between the two castles is heightened by the combined use of drum and square-planned towers, and possibly by a differentiation between external and internal decorative treatment.[23] If Shirburn anticipated the form of Bodiam by a few years, this furthers the debate between external militant ostentation and internal domesticity which has excited the minds of many scholars so far as the Sussex structure is concerned.

Are their strictures equally relevant to Lisle's castle as to that of Dalyngrigge? Shirburn was described by Leland as a 'strong pile or castlelet'[24] and the gate-tower certainly follows Bodiam in being portcullis and 'murder-hole' protected. However, rebuilding and rough-castfacing have so totally modified the castle's early character that the possible provision of gun ports, first noted in the Quarr Abbey precinct wall of 1365 and increasingly common from the late 1370s[25] rests on further examination. It will also be necessary to consider the landscaping and development of the pleasure grounds during the early 1720s to clarify whether there was originally an outer court, a barbican, or even a contemporary example of landscaping, for the choice of a site with natural springs makes the waterscape parallel with Bodiam pertinent.

Shirburn was a stone-built castle of the late 1370s of which the gatehouse survives, a reasonable amount of the west range, the lower stages of two corner towers, and possibly some ground-level walling internally. It is this ghost of its early form that determined the shape of the present eighteenth-century mansion. It was also the precedent to the castle built a few years later at Bodiam, but to what extent Shirburn was a demonstration of the imagery and symbolism of fortification as against the technology of defence is an open question, though the evidence points to the former. Further research

will also determine to what extent the castle reflects Lord Lisle's war service, financial circumstances, and personal aspirations, as well as his castle's association with domestic, collegiate, and castle building in the south of England.

NOTES
1 The list extends from Lord Torrington in 1785 to Nikolaus Pevsner, the architectural staff of *Country Life*, and the Department of the Environment recorders 200 years later. Although the 7th earl of Macclesfield was a vice-president of the Victoria County History during the early 1960s, the author of the Shirburn entry in volume VIII was not permitted to examine the castle's interior. However, the earl's offer to lend him a book on the subject from his library, written by his forebear, was taken up after the author had driven the vice-president back home from a committee meeting. The castle's interior had to be appraised during the few minutes it took them to reach the first-floor library, and return to the entrance.
2 The three plans held by the NMRC, Swindon, are for internal alterations to a tower in 1873. Not surprisingly, Shirburn has been ignored by all writers on castles except for the summaries of ownership by Sir James Mackenzie, *The Castles of England*, I (1897) 163–5 and Sir Charles Oman, *Castles* (1926) 46–9. My sketch plan is simply to help identify features noted in the text and is not to scale.
3 Some of the problems leading to the present decayed state of this occupied house were detailed in *The Times*, 9 June and 25 July 2003, following a High Court case in July 2003. The 9th earl was evicted in 2004.
4 VCH, VIII (1964) 179, 184–5.
5 *Cal. Pat. Rolls: 1374–77*, 434. For Lisle, *Com. Peer.*, VIII (1932) 51–3.
6 VCH, VIII (1964) 179.
7 *Ibid.* 179, 182, and 190 for maintained occupation, the attack of 1644, surrender to parliamentary forces in 1646, and estate difficulties thereafter.
8 Mowl and Earnshaw (1981) 289.
9 VCH, VIII (1964) 179.
10 Made of 'solid oak studded with heavy square-headed nails, and when the many coats of paint were removed in 1854, several bullets were found flattened in the wood'. W. Money, *Jour. Brit. Arch. Assoc.* 1 (1895) 290.
11 The parallels between Bodiam and Shirburn castles are noted later, but despite the existence of a drawbridge recess at Bodiam, there is no counterbalance pit, nor, with the portcullis, could there have been a system of chains to lift the bridge.
12 Illustrated by F. Mackenzie in Skelton's *Illustrations of the Antiquities of Oxfordshire* (1823) Pirton Hundred, pl. 2.
13 VCH, VIII (1964) 180.
14 NMRC, C 45/1541.
15 Mowl and Earnshaw correcting VCH, VIII (1964) 179–81 through an examination from the castle's grounds.
16 VCH, VIII (1964) 179.
17 Shown in the exterior engraving in Skelton's *Antiquities of Oxfordshire* (1823) Pirton Hundred, pl. 1.
18 *Ibid.* shows two cross loops that survived the early eighteenth-century remodelling.
19 VCH, VIII (1964) 179.
20 Mowl and Earnshaw (1981) 292 correcting VCH, VIII (1964) 179.
21 Shirburn Castle predates Vanbrugh Castle, Blackheath, by a year or two. For the origins and development of this style, T. Mowl, 'The Norman revival in British architecture 1790–1870', PhD thesis, University of Oxford (1981).
22 *Country Life* (July 1911) 176–8 for a description of the two libraries, and NMRC for some early twentieth-century internal photographs. *Country Life* (January 1900) has a brief article on the gardens.
23 Dr Goodall has drawn my attention to the difference between the larger external windows at Bodiam (hall, chapel, and withdrawing chambers)

which are uncusped and the more decorative internal-facing windows – a mannered architectural contrast between a forbidding exterior and a more relaxed and ornate interior. The surviving evidence at Shirburn would suggest the same kind of treatment – the moulded doorway in the west range strikes exactly the same contrast with the rugged detailing of the main entrance gate.

24 *Itinerary*, I, 115.

25 D. F. Renn, *Arch. Jour.* 125 (1968) 301–3; J. F. Kenyon, *Arch. Jour.* 138 (1981) 205–12.

Frances, Countess of Macclesfield, *Scattered Notices of Shirburn Castle* (1887)

W. Money, *Jour. Brit. Arch. Assoc.* 1 (1895) 289–95

VCH, *Oxfordshire*, VIII (1964) 179–81

T. Mowl and B. Earnshaw, 'The origins of the 18th century neo-medievalism in a Georgian Norman castle', *Jour. Soc. Arch. Hist.* 40 (1981) 289–94

SONNING PALACE, Berkshire

All that is visible today of the bishop of Salisbury's residence at Sonning is part of the brick wall surrounding its outer court. It now encloses the cemetery extension south of the parish church,[1] with the remainder of the site in the grounds of Holme Park.

The palace stood on the south side of the River Thames, enclosed by a ditch still traceable on the west side at the beginning of the nineteenth century. The bishop had a residence here long before the Norman Conquest, but the recovered structures spanned at least four building phases – the thirteenth century, the fourteenth century and two phases near the middle and at the close of the fifteenth century. Leland described it as a 'fair olde house of stone . . . and therby is a fair park',[2] but the palace was demolished shortly after the property passed out of the bishop's hands in 1574. A late seventeenth-century house built south of the kitchen site was pulled down in 1760.[3]

The palace was excavated in 1912–14 under unsatisfactory conditions. The work had to be completed quickly and the site reinstated before the First World War broke out. As the foundations proved to be buried between 4 and 10 feet deep, the task became essentially one of wall chasing to obtain the ground plan. The report published in 1916–17 is particularly inadequate.[4]

The residence expanded round an inner court, with the larger outer court rebuilt at the end of the fifteenth century during the last phase of site development. Decorated stonework of the twelfth century, reused in the following century, marked an early stage in the palace's history, but the earliest structure recovered was a first-floor chamber block of the thirteenth century backing on to the dais wall of the later hall. It was a two-room vaulted structure with a garderobe pit at one end and a south extension at the other. The excavators assumed that it was an externally approached first-floor hall above a ground-floor kitchen and services. It is more probable that the building was an entirely residential block to a timber-framed hall on the site of the later stone-built one. This is supported by what seemed to be an east-facing chapel added during the fourteenth century as an extension to the bishop's apartments. Harold Brakspear thought that it was likely to be a ground-floor chapel with a balcony pew opening from the upper end of the private apartments, though a two-storey structure cannot be ruled out.

The bishop was granted a licence to crenellate his residence at Sonning in August 1337[5] and its substantial expansion during the fourteenth century was attributed to about this time. A stone-built hall was constructed, 74 feet by 36 feet, with a cross passage and evidence of three entries to the services, though this south wall had been completely destroyed. The offices were extensive, running in two directions – eastwards with chambers above (for guests?) filling one side of the inner court, and southwards separated by a yard and covered way from the semi-detached kitchen. The yard was flanked by a narrow dormitory-like room with a multi-use garderobe pit at its south end. The kitchen, 35 feet square, had walls 5½ feet thick built of flint and chalk rubble with flint and chalk chequer facing work. The two fireplaces were in the wall furthest from the entrance with a scullery alongside.

In the mid-fifteenth century, the hall was partially rebuilt with a new buttressed façade towards the outer court, entry porch and bay window lighting a new dais wall. The new work was built of rough flint and chalk rubble walls, faced with cut flint and finely wrought stonework. The porch, 12½ feet square, was embellished with decorative double buttresses at the outer corners which could have been pedestals supporting armorial beasts or intended for pinnacles. The recovered stonework showed that this porch was a highly decorated one. The entry was vaulted, with the inner doorway set in a delicately moulded frame.

The hall was divided into five bays with the 6 foot deep dais gable wall built in front of the thirteenth-century residential range. The apartment was spanned by a new roof of unknown form. The hearth in the middle of the hall was 7 feet square with a stone kerb and tiles set on edge. The 11 foot wide dais was covered with square unpatterned green tiles. It was lit by the west-facing bay window, square in shape, with its own internal newel to an upper room as at Nevill Holt and Fawsley Hall. Finally, a new stair was constructed opening from the dais to serve the bishop's private apartments. All this work was tentatively attributed by the excavators to bishop Beauchamp (1450–81). During the first part of his tenure, he rebuilt the hall and porch at his palace at Salisbury,[6] and in 1473 he was appointed master and surveyor of the king's works at the chapel of St George, Windsor, and 'divers other works'. Apart from his responsibility for the first stage of St George's Chapel (*c.*1477–83), he oversaw the building of the lodgings of the vicars choral round the Horseshoe Cloister (1478–81).[7]

The earlier private apartments were expanded towards the close of the fifteenth century by a new range filling the east side of the inner court and closing this formerly open site. The walls were built of flint with brick, and were stuccoed externally. The plan of the three ground-floor rooms may have been followed on the upper floor, approached from a gallery in continuation of the stair from the hall. The range would have been like those at Southwell Palace, with the ground floor occupied by personal staff serving the bishop on the upper floor. The first of his rooms had an extension, perhaps for a pew overlooking the chapel altar. The second chamber was enhanced with a buttress-supported oriel window, and the third was an inner bedchamber. By this time, the inner court was surrounded by a covered walk.

The other work of this last phase was the rebuilding of the outer court in brick. A rather splendid towered gatehouse was raised, with a central passage 11 feet wide flanked on each side by a porter's lodge. The frontal corner turrets were solid, but the rear turrets

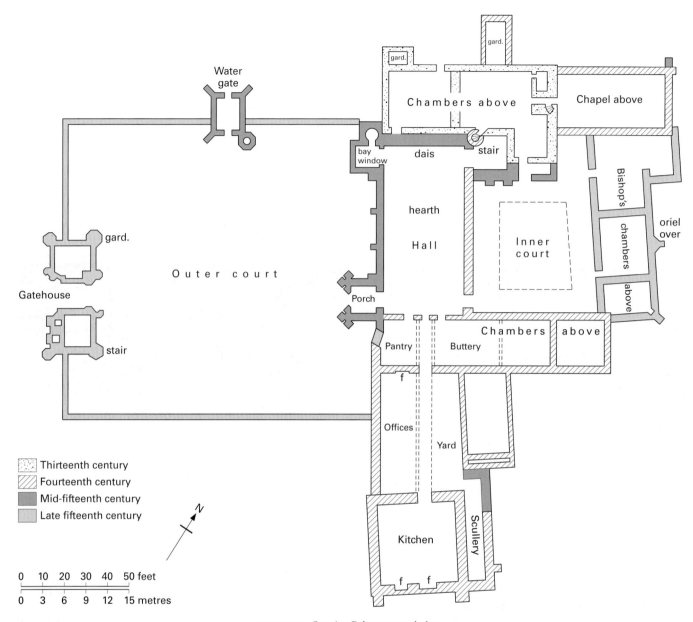

FIGURE 33 Sonning Palace: ground plan

held a garderobe and newel stair respectively. The gatehouse was aligned on the hall porch and was probably three storeyed if the two separate garderobe chutes to the front are any guide. The 10 foot high enclosing wall respected the slightly earlier and more simple water gate, flint built with diagonal corner buttresses and rear stair turret.

Apart from the cemetery extension, the site is still green field, with the recovered artefacts, particularly the larger number of floor tiles, held by Reading Museum Services.

NOTES

1 The Tudor-style entry arch was erected in 1948.
2 *Itinerary*, I, 109.

3 For the history of the site, E. W. Dormer, *Berks. Arch. Jour.* 38 (1934) 177–83.
4 Excavation notes by C. E. Keyser in Keyser and Brakspear (1916–17) 2–8; descriptive account by H. Brakspear, in *ibid.* 9–21.
5 *Cal. Pat. Rolls: 1334–38*, 498. This was granted at the same time as licences were issued for five episcopal sites in Wiltshire, two in Dorset, and one for the bishop's house in Fleet Street, London. The licences were repeated in July 1377, *ibid. 1377–81*, 9.
6 RCHM *Salisbury: The Close* (1993) 54.
7 *HKW*, II (1963) 884–7. The excavators considered that details of the Sonning hall resembled the form of those at St George's Chapel.

C. E. Keyser and H. Brakspear, *Berks., Bucks. and Oxon. Arch. Jour.* 22 (1916–17) 2–21

STANTON HARCOURT MANOR, Oxfordshire

The significance of Stanton Harcourt Manor lies in the existence of a ground plan of this early example of a double-courtyard house, prepared not long before the property was all but destroyed in the mid-eighteenth century, and the survival of a little-touched late fourteenth-century kitchen. The manor has been held by the Harcourt family since the late twelfth century, but the present manor house was developed from the close of the fourteenth century. It was occupied by the family until 1688 when they moved to Cokethorpe, 3 miles away, and was subsequently a primary source for the foundations of the house they initiated in 1756 at Nuneham Courtenay.[1] An offices range was retained for farm purposes, and the entrance and stable block was adapted as a dower house in 1868 and became the family home again only after the sale of Nuneham Courtenay in 1948.

A carefully drawn plan of the manor house and park of Stanton Harcourt, made by Joseph Wright on 15 April 1726, shows the double courtyard layout.[2] The outer court consisted of no more than a gateway and walled enclosure. The hall range with stair projection, twin parlours, and chapel with tower above separated the two courts, with the kitchen and offices on the west side of the second court and the family quarters opposite. A pentice linked the hall cross passage with the offices and service quarters on the south side of the second court. A resistivity survey carried out under current ownership has confirmed the accuracy of Wright's plan. The layout was unusual in that family and staff quarters faced each other in what was increasingly becoming the more private part of a residence from the later fourteenth century onwards. The failure to separate these two functions suggests that the house was developed before the close of the century, probably by Sir Thomas Harcourt who entered the property at an early age, married Maud Grey (d.1394) and lived until 1417. He was the first Harcourt to become involved in local administration and was a knight of the shire in 1376. Nor was the house subject to major modification by later generations, for the Harcourts never rose above élite gentry status until Queen Anne's reign.

The house lacked defensive capability.[3] The moat, still visible on the south side, was primarily for drainage purposes, while the embattled precinct wall simply linked minor perimeter ranges. When Sir Robert Harcourt was warned of an impending attack by 200 Stafford supporters in May 1450 seeking revenge for his killing Sir Humphrey Stafford's eldest son, he fled the manor house for the safety of the church tower. Sir Robert was besieged there for six hours until his assailants abandoned their task after failing to burn down the tower.[4] Only three structures survived Georgian quarrying – the entrance, the kitchen with part of the offices range, and the chapel with tower above – all now standing within an attractive modern garden setting, enclosed by a moat on the south side and retaining part of the rebuilt embattled wall towards the churchyard.

The two-storeyed entrance and stable block was a rebuilding of Henry VIII's reign, datable by the arms of Harcourt and Darell either side the entry arch to the years before Sir Simon Harcourt's death in 1547. The passageway was closed and extended at the rear in 1868, with an east wing added in 1953 to make the residence more suitable for current occupation.

The kitchen is the earliest building to stand, one of the most

PLATE 66 Stanton Harcourt Manor: chapel tower

spectacular medieval survivals so commonly replaced in contemporary domestic residences; 26 feet square internally and rising 53 feet to the apex of the roof, it is built of local rubble limestone with dressed work for the embattled parapet and newel head. The octagonal stone tiled roof is crowned by a Harcourt lion finial. The work area was lit by two twin-light windows with boldly shaped trefoiled heads under square hoods in the east wall and by three linked windows of similar form in the west wall. Internally, the roof is supported on stone squinches across the angles, enabling an octagonal structure to be erected. Eight wooden blades spring from stone corbels to the apex, spanned by stone arches supporting two tiers of wooden louvres and a cone of rafters. The arches are wood faced with quatrefoil pierced spandrels, and the purlins are strengthened by three diminishing rows of wind braces.

The fireplaces were not the usual hearth, hood, and flue. The hearth was simply built against the south wall and divided by low stone screens to form two fireplaces. The smoke and heat from the room collected in the cone of the roof and was extracted by opening some of the louvres at the base of the roof, depending on the direction of the wind. A newel in the north-west corner allows a person to walk round the allure behind the battlemented parapet opening the appropriate number of louvres, now replaced by glass windows.[5] As I have seen, when fires are lit in the hearths, only one or two windows need to be opened to allow the smoke to escape. Opening too many creates draughts, filling the room with clouds of smoke.

There are three ovens in arched recesses in the north wall, now

PLATE 67 Stanton Harcourt Manor: engraving of kitchen from the
north-west from Parker (1853)

PLATE 68 Stanton Harcourt Manor: kitchen interior

minus their chimneys, a cupboard, and a tall hatch opening on to
the pentice. The well towards the west wall has been filled. This
kitchen has been ascribed to the fourteenth century[6] and to the fifteenth century,[7] with dates ranging from the particular[8] to the all-
embracing.[9] The four-centred doorway heads and rear arches as
well as the trefoiled lights point to the last quarter of the fourteenth
century, but only dendrochronology will determine whether the
roof is a contemporary structure or a rebuilding of 1485.[10] The
erection of an octagonal-type roof above a rectangular stone carcase
had been adopted for the kitchen of the Bishop's Palace, Chichester
in about 1300, and for that at Raby Castle in about 1370. There is
no internal or external evidence that the upper walling or the
squinches are a rebuilding, while the floor-to-roof newel as well as
the form of the spandrels and ribbing suggest that the structure is
contemporary work.

Nothing survives of the hall, the great and little parlours that
opened out of it, or the large wing extending southwards[11] but the
principal apartments were extended in the mid-fifteenth century by
a two storeyed chapel block with a 54 foot high tower above the
chancel. Nave and chancel are fenestrated with opposing single and
double cinquefoil lights under square moulded hoods, deeply
recessed internally and externally. An Elizabethan doorway opens
into the two-bay nave with a wooden ceiling, described in 1818 as
decorated with gold stars on a blue ground with red and gold
mouldings.[12] A wide four-centred arch divides the nave from the
single-bay chancel. The latter has a fan-vaulted stone roof supported on head and angel corbels with a formerly painted wooden
central plug with leaf boss. The three-light east window with traceried head was formerly enriched with quarterings of the
Harcourts.

Above the nave is a single room with fireplace and original low-
pitched panelled roof. The west entry, opening from the great
chamber behind the hall, has been converted into a window. An
unglazed opening above the chancel arch, now blocked, enabled the

family to partake in services through the opening so that staff worshipped in the nave while the Harcourts prayed from above. The
importance of the chapel lies in its scale and no-expense-spared lavishness, despite the close proximity of the parish church.

There was a single room on each of the three floors of the tower.
Approached from the projecting newel by the chancel arch, two
rooms (one heated, one not) formed a lodging for the priest like that
in the tower of Rycote chapel (1449). The top floor is a heated prospect room with two windows on the north side instead of the single
windows in the other outer walls and on the floors below.[13] Similar
rooms can be found at Wingfield Manor and at Minster Lovell Hall.

Chapel and tower were erected during the first reign of Edward
IV on the evidence of the arms of Sir Robert Harcourt (d.1470) who
had long been involved in Oxfordshire politics, and those of his
wife, Margaret, daughter of Sir John Byron.[14] The shields on either
side of the chancel arch are now blank. Chapel and tower were
probably designed by William Orchard, who seems to have added
the Harcourt aisle in the parish church. Orchard worked extensively in and around Oxford, particularly at Magdalen College, and
the aisle piers are identical in section with those of the college ante-
chapel, initiated when Sir Robert was high steward of the university (1446–70).[15]

Both chapel and kitchen at Stanton Harcourt are in regular use,
though the kitchen is used to seat visitors today rather than to
prepare food for them. Alexander Pope likened its interior to
Vulcan's forge, and there are still occasions when it can be totally
smoke filled, as the blackened roof testifies. Kitchens were usually
detached structures to limit fire risks, and though frequently
timber-framed, this facilitated rebuilding, six times at Weoley
Castle between 1200 and 1260.[16] Not surprisingly, few framed
structures have survived, and where this is so it is because they were
stone clad at a later date (Martholme, early sixteenth century). A
considerable number of medieval stone kitchens exist, either in line
with the hall, or at right angles to the cross passage, with those in
fortresses heavily site-restricted. These last are usually ruined, but
a number survive in little-altered condition among the greater
houses.[17]

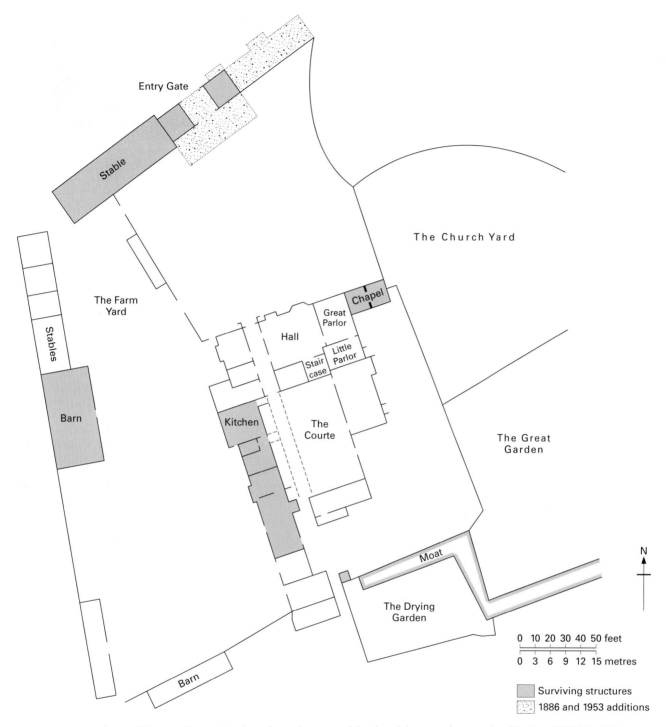

FIGURE 34 Stanton Harcourt Manor: site plan redrawn from part of the plan of the manor house and park by Joseph Wright, 1726

Some idea of their furnishing can be drawn from a range of sources. Inventories list the permanent equipment used of some value. Such inventories were usually more detailed for a monastic than a secular household, occasioned by the arrival of a new obedientiary. Account rolls identify utilitarian or disposable items as well as the repairs to existing equipment by itinerant workmen such as rehooping barrels, repairing bronze vessels, or sharpening knives. Recipe books show how all these items were used in a noble or well-to-do household, with later receipts often identifying the utensils required.[18] Throughout the medieval period, bronze was used for vessels in which food was cooked such as hanging pots, cauldrons, pans, and mortars.[19] Iron was used for hearth and fire equipment such as spits, tripods, hooks, knives, rakes, and shovels.[20] Wood was the common material for food preparation and storage, including cupboards, vats, trays, sieves, and trenchers.[21] Pewter was preferred for dishes, plates, and spoons, though no mention of domestic pewterware has been found before the 1290s.[22] Pottery vessels are a frequent artefact of site excavations. They were used initially in the preparation of food and for cooking, often using the double-boiling method where the pot was placed within a larger bronze vessel. Soot marks and residue analysis can identify what the pots have been used for, but by the close of the middle ages, pottery kitchenware had changed from cooking to storage.[23] Manuscript illustrations provide many scenes of kitchen and fireside cooking, while excavations provide a wealth of artefacts to substantiate the narrative, documentary, and pictorial sources.[24]

In general terms, kitchen equipment changed little throughout the middle ages but there was no set pattern of items to be found in a major household, anymore than there is today. It depended more on the size of the establishment, the regularity or infrequency of the owner's visits, and the extent of his entertaining. Even so, the existence of a large stone kitchen suggests that keeping open house and a fine table was an integral part of the builder's philosophy. If the scale of his hall reflected his power and status, the extent of his hospitality, the quality of his table, and the pageantry of presentation constituted an equally important component of his lifestyle. The kitchen was a key element in that function. Nor should kitchens be considered in isolation. Whereas preparation and cooking might occur together in a minor household, the kitchen was solely used for cooking in all great houses. Ancillary functions such as storage and the preparation of different foods were carried out in offices nearby. There is a line of such offices at Stanton Harcourt immediately south of the kitchen. The presence of several windows of one or two cinquefoil lights suggests that the range was rebuilt in the fifteenth century, possibly as a result of more extensive hospitality by the Harcourts. It was so drastically remodelled in the eighteenth century that it is not possible to determine how the rooms were used, assuming that their functions never changed even though diet and social habits altered during the middle ages. Presumably, staff occupied the rooms over the ground-floor offices where they regularly worked.

NOTES

1 *Com. Peer.*, VI (1926) 298 n. (c).

2 Preserved in the present house. It should be compared with the inventory of the house made on the death of Sir Philip Harcourt in 1688. Bod. Lib. Harcourt Papers; Hussey (1941) 674–6.

3 The licence to crenellate granted in October 1327 to John Wyard for his house at Stanton Harcourt applied to an unknown site, *Cal. Pat. Rolls: 1327–30*, 179; VCH, XII (1990) 279.

4 R. L. Storey, *The End of the House of Lancaster* (1966) 57–8.

5 The wooden louvres are shown in Parker (1859) opp. 151 which gives a clearer idea of the roof's character than the present smoke-smothered structure.

6 Hussey (1941) 677; R. B. Wood-Jones, *Traditional Domestic Architecture of the Banbury Region* (1963) 27 n.1.

7 H. M. Colvin in *Medieval England*, ed. A. L. Poole (1958) 44–5; J. Bunby in *English Medieval Industries*, ed. J. Blair and N. Ramsey (1991) 393; VCH, XII (1990) 277.

8 For *c.*1470, J. A. Gotch, *The Growth of the English House* (1909) 60; 1461–83, M. Wood, *The English Mediaeval House* (1965) 251.

9 'of the fourteenth and fifteenth centuries', N. Cooper, *Arch. Jour.* 135 (1978) 304.

10 J. Sherwood and N. Pevsner, *Oxfordshire* (1974) 782, recording Lord Harcourt's view.

11 By the seventeenth century, the south wing included a large ground-floor chamber with bedrooms above. VCH, XII (1990) 276.

12 The similar decorated ceiling at Rycote chapel was created in the seventeenth century with the stars cut from playing cards. The moated medieval house at Rycote was acquired by the Quatremayne family through marriage in 1415, and it was Richard Quatremayne and his wife who built the chapel, consecrated in 1449 as a chantry foundation for three priests. The house, probably rebuilt by Sir John Williams in about 1535, was burnt out in 1745 and pulled down in 1800 except for part of the stable range, reinhabited in 1920, when some thirteenth-century stonework fragments of the earlier house were dug up. The chapel stands alone, entirely of one build and unaltered. It consists of an uninterrupted nave and chancel under a continuous wagon roof, divided by pinnacled buttresses into five bays with generous two-light windows under steeply pitched heads. The elaborate north entrance was the approach to the mansion: the two doors in the north-east corner were possibly to the long-lost collegiate buildings. The stately buttressed and battlemented tower at the west end is divided into three stages; the second of these, with a fireplace, was the priest's room. The interior with its contemporary pews and tiled floor is notable for its sumptuous seventeenth-century fittings, dominated by two great pews flanking the chancel. VCH, *Oxfordshire*, VII (1962); J. Salmon, *Rycote Chapel: Handbook* (1969).

13 The present lights are enlarged sixteenth-century replacements in a room panelled in the late seventeenth century, and used by Alexander Pope in 1717–18 to compose his translation of the *Iliad*.

14 VCH, XII (1990) 275; Parker (1859) 276.

15 J. H. Harvey, *Eng. Med. Arch.* (1984) 222–3. Sir Robert was murdered by Sir Humphrey Stafford's bastard son in retaliation for the lack of success twenty years earlier. The tomb of Sir Robert and his wife inaugurated the Harcourt aisle.

16 A. Oswald, *Med. Arch.* 6–7 (1962–3) 109–34, though the purpose of the building changed in about 1230.

17 M. Wood, *The English Mediaeval House* (1965) 247–56.

18 B. A. Henisch, *Fast and Feast: Food in Medieval Society* (1976); J. M. Thurgood, 'The diet and domestic households of the English lay nobility, 1263–1531', MPhil thesis, University of London (1982).

19 A. R. Goodhall in *Medieval Industry*, ed. D. W. Crossley (1981) 63–71. This source also covers other kitchen items as do some of the chapters in *English Medieval Industries*, ed. J. Blair and N. Ramsay (1991).

20 J. S. Lindsay, *Iron and Brass Implements of the English House* (2nd edn 1970).

21 C. A. Morris, 'Anglo-Saxon and medieval woodworking crafts', PhD thesis, University of Cambridge (1984).

22 J. Hatcher and T. C. Barker, *A History of British Pewter* (1974); R. F. Homer in *English Medieval Industries*, ed. J. Blair and N. Ramsay (1991) 66–80.

23 M. R. McCarthy and C. M. Brooks, *Medieval Pottery in Britain, AD 900–1600* (1988). S. Moorhouse, 'Documentary evidence for the range and uses of medieval pottery and its archaeological implications', PhD thesis, University College, Cardiff (1991).

24 G. Egan, *The Medieval Household: Daily Living 1150–1450* (1997); *London Museum Medieval Catalogue 1940*, ed. J. B. Ward-Perkins (1993).

T. H. Turner and J. H. Parker, *Some Account of Domestic Architecture In England*, III pt 2 (1859) 276–7

J. A. Gotch, *The Growth of the English House* (1909) 63–5

C. Hussey, *Country Life* (October 1941) 628, 674

VCH, *Oxfordshire*, XII (1990) 274–8

STANTON ST JOHN MANOR, Oxfordshire

Immediately north of the church of Stanton St John, this manor house looks primarily like a small seventeenth-century farmhouse of irregular shape, with clay tile roofs and casement windows. This impression is heightened by the high-walled foregarden, shaped by the curve of the road, with two farm buildings against the perimeter wall – the buttress-supported stone stables dendro dated to 1646/7, and the thatched cart shed, erected in 1801 reusing timbers of 1349. Externally, only the tall two-light gable end window points to the house's earlier origins, and possibly to the fact that the St John of Lageham family who had long held the manor enjoyed baronial status for half a century after 1299. By 1992, the property had become a run-down tenanted farm but new ownership combined with fundamental rehabilitation and dendrochronology analysis has transformed the interpretation of this residence.

The manor house, two-storeyed throughout, is built of local Headington stone. Not surprisingly, occupational changes are writ large on a structure which has been extended as well as reduced in scale. To anticipate the conclusion, what survives is the chamber block to a lost hall, with two near-contemporary extensions creating a Z-shaped structure developed during the first decade of the fourteenth century.

The east range has always been the core of the house. The entrance with two-centred head is a 1996 rebuild of an original doorway of which the rear arch remained. It opens into one half of the ground-floor area, now used as the entrance hall, with evidence of an early end-wall window. The large inserted fireplace is dendro dated to 1599 when the area became the farmhouse kitchen. The other half of the range, now used as a dining room, similarly holds an inserted hearth in the north wall. The ceiling joists in both rooms are rough and unchamfered, seemingly seventeenth or eighteenth century but dendro dated to 1303 and 1305.[1] The stone party wall between the two rooms is original, with the left-hand jamb of a wide off-centre doorway, though the right-hand jamb seems to be a rebuild. The second room may have had a separate entry in the south wall or merely a window as today. What is unusual is the depressed head of a wide arch (with plaster-covered relieving arch) above the inserted fireplace and opposite the window that shows signs of having been made into a comparable arched opening. Although suggesting conversion to an open passageway, this would have been a late or sub-medieval development, though pre-dating the fireplace and stack added at the close of the sixteenth century.

The upper floor is a single chamber, 34 feet by 16 feet, once more open to the roof. It is dominated by its south window of two transomed lights with plain Y tracery, window seats, and a simple external hood. The splays of a similar window at the opposite end were recovered in 1996. Nearby in the south wall is the internal shaping of a wide doorway, now with a casement window, followed by a single light of c.1600, a more recent window, and the jambs of a doorway to the cross wing. The north wall, rebuilt in about 1600 when the two chimney stacks were added, retains one of the two fireplaces with four-centred head of that time following room division. To its left is the springer of a north-west doorway and its lower jambs externally. The roof was rebuilt in the mid-nineteenth century, supported on three queen-post trusses using seventeenth-century beams.

The east range was a two-storeyed residential block, constructed

PLATE 69 Stanton St John Manor: from the south (1957)

in about 1308–10 with the principal chamber on the upper floor. It would have been attached to a hall, most probably abutting its south-east corner and linked to it by an internal stair to the first-floor doorway within the broad recess now lightly infilled with a casement window. Such an entry at the lower end of the chamber is matched by the doorway at its upper end leading to the cross wing. An alternative position for the hall would be north of the range, accessed from the north-west doorway with that in the broad recess serving a garderobe, but the hall would then lie at the furthest point from the approach to the house. Early nineteenth-century estate maps also indicate a substantial structure in the south-east position, no longer shown on those from 1856. There may well have been a garderobe to the north-west and possibly a central fireplace in the north wall, but rebuilding at this level has destroyed any such evidence.[2]

The two extensions are less informative for the medievalist. The cross range with a south-wall string course stands at a slight angle to the east range and is therefore possibly a secondary phase. Both floors were single chambers, approached from contemporary doorways in the east range – evidenced by a relieving arch at ground level and jambs at the upper level – with the floor joists dendro dated within the span of 1290 to 1322 even if there are no comparable architectural features outside the lower part of a first-floor light. The range was remodelled in about 1475 when the roof was replaced, the moulded cross beam added, and possibly the end-wall fireplaces inserted, the lower one with recovered evidence of a moulded jamb. The depressed rear arches of opposing ground-floor windows, one a little south of the present window, were found in 1996 behind the seventeenth-century panelling.

The narrower west range, apparently of mid-seventeenth-century character, retains floor joists of 1299–1331 so that it is a component of the original development. The solid party wall and external entry (blocked) suggest that it may have been a single lodging at ground level while the short projection at the north-west corner, now reduced since the mid-twentieth century to a single storey, may have been a garderobe.

The St John family had held the manor of Stanton since the early twelfth century but they only became prominent during the second half of the thirteenth century. Sir Roger St John was a leading supporter of the baronial reformers under Henry III until killed at the

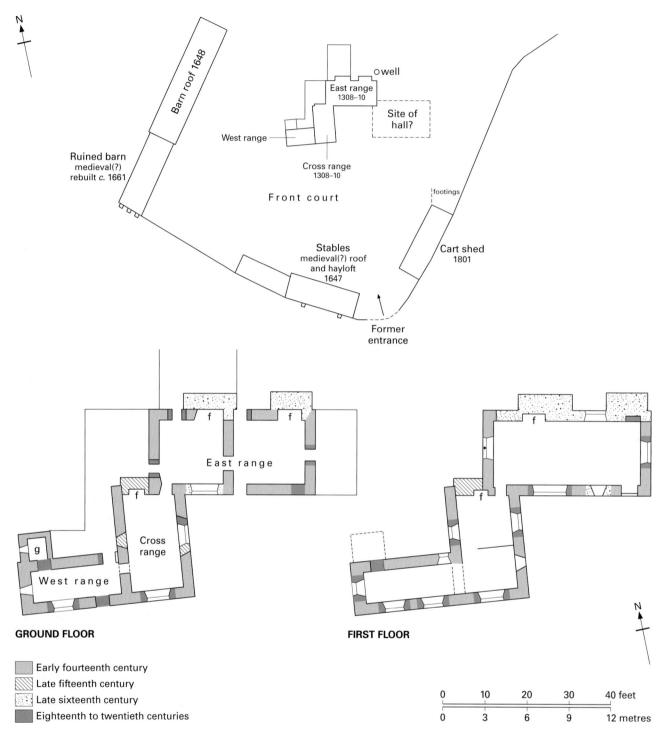

FIGURE 35 Stanton St John Manor: site and floor plans

battle of Evesham (1265). Three years earlier, he had rebuilt the family home at Lageham in Surrey.[3] His son, Sir John St John was a career soldier who supported Edward I in his Welsh campaigns of 1276–7 and 1282–3, commanded the field in Gascony in 1294–7, and frequently fought in Scotland between 1299 and his death in 1316. Initially a knight of the royal household, he was ennobled in 1299, and though he added a high-quality tiled floor to the family home, he preferred to develop the family holding 3 miles north-east of Oxford. His career was the peak of this family's achievement, for Lord St John's great-grandson died without heirs in the mid-fourteenth century, the properties passed into female hands, and the title became extinguished.[4]

The manor house at Stanton St John is a development of the first decade of the fourteenth century. Part of the buttressed wall enclosing the site is medieval but the entry directly opposite the church between the later stables and cart shed had to be infilled in 1996 for safety's sake and a new approach made further west. The forecourt probably included a timber-framed hall abutting the south-east angle of the standing east range, its presence possibly indicated by a line of parched grass in dry conditions.[5] The east range was a two-storey residential block, surprisingly old-fashioned in its window tracery and lack of decorative detailing, particularly compared with the contemporary chancel windows of the nearby church. The cross range and its extension, the latter possibly with a garderobe, were chambers of increasing privacy at the upper level, with a ground-floor lodging at the west end. No contemporary fireplaces or stairs have survived, though any internal link between the two floors would have been limited to the upper end of the hall. Some changes were undertaken to the cross range in the mid-1470s which may have extended to the ground floor of the east range, but more fundamental alterations to this irregular group of buildings were carried out in about 1600, including the upper division of the east range when much of its north wall was rebuilt. The hall, possibly in truncated form, seems to have survived until the mid-nineteenth century, not long before the property was subject to further modifications.

NOTES
1 *Vern. Arch.* 29 (1998) 114–16.
2 Traces of a central burnt area carried on the party wall below were found in 1994 but as they were totally lacking in context, a louvred hearth should not be assumed.
3 Lageham was a moiety of the manor of Walkhampstead in Surrey, now Godstone. The homestead of the St John family is marked by an extensive moated site enclosing a 5½ acre platform, now lacking the house crenellated under licence in 1262, *Cal. Pat. Rolls: 1258–66*, 199; L. Ketteringham, *Surrey Arch. Coll.* 75 (1984) 235–49.
4 *Com. Peer.*, II (1949) 340–51.
5 Stone footings and a drain immediately north of the cart shed of 1801 may be the remains of a service range extending from the lower end of this hall.

STONOR PARK, Oxfordshire

Stonor Park, held by the same family for over 800 years, is a complex house that has been aptly described as an architectural nightmare.[1] It also forms the background to one of the most important collections of private correspondence of the later middle ages, illuminating many of the social and domestic characteristics of the property during the reign of Edward IV. Hidden in a fold of the Chilterns 5 miles from Henley, Stonor Park 'standithe clyminge on an hille'.[2] Beautifully sited on one side of a beech-encircled combe, this unusually elongated two-storeyed mansion with its regularised red-brick façade of sixteen bays with central porch and end wings appears to be of symmetrical form and to date from the sixteenth to the eighteenth centuries. However, an aerial view reveals a series of roofs and valleys and several tiny courtyards, while an internal examination quickly loses the visitor in a warren of rooms, passages, and medieval features. The development of the house was initially unravelled by Dr Pantin and Dr Sturdy in 1964,[3] but their work has

been subject to some modification in the light of subsequent discoveries.

The house has been occupied continuously by the Stonor family since they were first recorded living here in 1204.[4] The family were comparatively well off under Sir Richard Stonor (1273–1314), who held sixteen manors in four counties, but it was his son, Sir John, who quietly developed the fortunes of the family by expanding his initial holding of nine manors to twenty-two in eight counties by the time of his death in 1354.[5] Justice of the common pleas in 1320 and chief justice for nearly twenty-five years, Sir John Stonor was described by the prior of Christ Church, Canterbury, as 'prudent, well-known, and beloved amongst the great'.[6] His immediate successors continued to hold a range of local offices throughout the later middle ages and were associated with several important neighbouring families and houses. They included the Lisles of Shirburn Castle through the marriage of Sir Edmund (d.1382),[7] Thomas Chaucer of Ewelme who bought the wardship and marriage rights of Thomas Stonor (d.1431) in 1403, the de la Poles of Ewelme through the marriage of Thomas Stonor (d.1474) to the duke of Suffolk's daughter, Jeanne, and their children's marriages to the Harcourts of Stanton Harcourt. These advantageous relationships and the extensive sheep flocks they built up on the Cotswolds and Chilterns greatly strengthened the family's financial resources, supplemented under Sir William (d.1494) by the beneficial wardships and stewardships he held. The Stonors managed to avoid embroilment in the Wars of the Roses except for the short-lived set-back after Sir William joined Buckingham in his rebellion against Richard III. Thrice married, the last to a wealthy niece of Warwick the Kingmaker, Sir William could look back during the early 1490s upon the rise of his family from gentry to substantial landholders of standing and now to a social position at court.

THIRTEENTH CENTURY
The core of the house is the 'old' hall, a thirteenth-century structure attributed by Pantin and Sturdy to c.1280–1300, but now considered to be a little earlier.[8] It was originally divided into two aisles by a central line of stone pillars and chamfered two-centred arches. These still remain, with one aisle subsequently partitioned into two rooms and a passage (possibly in the sixteenth century), covered by a mid to late fifteenth-century roof of queen posts above the principal truss.[9] The other aisle was destroyed at an unknown date and left open to the sky until roofed in the 1970s. The bases of the five round pillars start 4 feet above the present ground level, which suggests substantial floor lowering.

One end of the hall, like the whole of the north side of the house, is built against the rising ground of the hillside. It is therefore probable that the cross wing of ground-floor offices with chamber above was necessarily built at the lower rather than the upper end of the hall, though it may have been secondary work. On the other hand, it has to be questioned whether the hall was not initially the lower part of a chamber block, for halls were usually arcaded either side the room, not centrally divided.

FOURTEENTH CENTURY
The chapel was originally a detached building south of the house with flint walls, and stone window and door frames. It is little altered externally, but the interior was totally Gothicised in 1757 and 1790, although the medieval roof of c.1500 survives above the

PLATE 70 Stonor Park: 'old' hall

plasterwork.[10] Its building date is conjectural. The present structure was developed during the early fourteenth century, first recorded in 1331, and enlarged in 1349 when Sir John Stonor obtained a licence to build a dwelling for six chantry priests,[11] but a recent examination suggests that the foundations may be twelfth century.[12]

The development of the chaplain's wing joining the chapel with the earlier hall range is unclear. It may have occurred after 1349 and the construction of the 'new' hall (see below) with the old hall and cross wing allocated to the chaplains who occupied this new linking wing.[13] However, an indenture of 1421 by Thomas Stonor (1394–1431) implies that the mid-fourteenth-century foundation had been for three priests only and that it had not been put into effect, possibly on account of the Black Death.[14] If the chantry did not come into effect until 1431, then a wing for chantry priests is unlikely to have been built until the mid-fifteenth century. The front of it was refaced in brick in the sixteenth century, but the rear shows mainly flint walling which is typical of the medieval work at Stonor. The wing may be mid-fourteenth-century work and I have shown it as such on the diagram, but there is no decorative detail and the later date cannot be excluded.[15] As the wing is now a sequence of post-medieval rooms and passages on both floors, its original occupational purpose and internal layout is unclear.

The most substantial mid-fourteenth-century development was the construction of an entirely new hall with cross wings to the west of the earlier one which was relegated to an angle of the house as subsequently occurred at Amberley Castle. The new hall was a timber-framed structure of two bays with a screens passage approached through a two-storeyed porch. There was possibly an opposing porch (by the later main staircase), but the rising ground would have rendered it valueless.[16] Brick may have been used rather than plaster infilling between the timbers, for although the south wall has been replaced, the brickwork on the north side and at the east end is particularly early. Very little of this hall has survived later alterations. The front porch was brick cased and raised by one storey during the sixteenth century. A new screens passage was created in 1757 when the hall was divided into two floors, with the

ground floor further partitioned into a dining room and colonnaded drawing room in 1834. The large north-facing windows, made in 1771 and filled with stained glass of 1669 from the chapel, are in the position of the earlier work, leaving the low end bay of the roof as the principal remnant of this mid-fourteenth-century phase. Part of the spere truss separating the screens passage from the hall has been revealed in a room two floors above, with decorative ogee tracery in its apex. The head of a timber pillar and a severed brace also survive, but the remainder of the roof is a mid-eighteenth- and early nineteenth-century structure.

Timber-framed cross wings were erected at each end of the hall, now encased in the body of the house. The upper cross wing of ground-floor parlour with great chamber above was so heavily modified in post-medieval times that no early evidence is visible, though the original scissor truss roof survives, though hidden.[17] The ground floor of the lower cross wing was the usual kitchen passage and flanking offices, now the family kitchen and dining room. The area above should have been a withdrawing chamber but it seems to have been divided into three units to judge from partition evidence in the roof,[18] though this may be the result of later alterations. The scissor truss and two-way braced arch are original, but post-Reformation alterations have obliterated all earlier occupational evidence.

It is probable there was a detached kitchen on the site of the later one (now a children's room), and I see no evidence why the present walls should not delineate it. Again, the area has been subsequently divided into two floors.

Although the mid-century expansion of the previous modest house is not in doubt, the evidence is skeletonic and characterless. All the rooms are devoid of any visible contemporary features – even the kitchen lacks an early fireplace – while the overall layout is disjointed. Some glazed floor tiles of late medieval date have been found, several of four-tile design. Displayed in the rear passage, they probably came from the chapel during its restoration in 1959–60 when the floor of 1349 was uncovered.[19] However, the most significant aspect of this development phase was the construction of a timber-framed hall, used by Sir Edmund Stonor (1361–82) to entertain and impress three justices and their trains in 1378 as they travelled round the country.[20] The late twentieth-century repair and maintenance programme revealed that the house was far more extensively timber-framed than is now visible.

FIFTEENTH CENTURY

In 1416–17, the newly married Thomas Stonor (1394–1431) paid £40 for 200,000 bricks made at Nettlebed, and used Flemish brickworkers to lay them.[21] Four structures might be ascribed to this period but only one can be with certainty. The chapel tower, an unusually slender structure, was erected by the brickworkers for £13 13s. 4. This work is important for it is the earliest dated example of this material to have survived in south-east England. Brick was used by Henry V for his palace at Sheen (1414–22), encouraging its use as a fashionable material. But the work at Stonor is also important for identifying the employment of 'Flemynggs' and as the earliest recorded example of diaper design, on one face of the tower.

The other brick structures that may date from this time or possibly later in the century include the brick casing of the free-standing kitchen. Though this was considered early sixteenth-century work in 1964, the south-facing gable end was stripped in

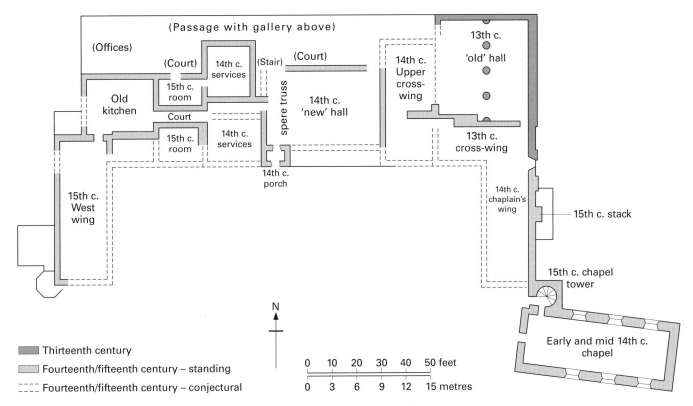

FIGURE 36 Stonor Park: ground plan

1970 to reveal a virtuoso display of decorative and moulded fifteenth-century brickwork within the timber framing. Two chimney stacks also date from this period, one against the east wall of the chaplain's wing, and one in the roof above the fourteenth-century offices and chamber cross wing.

During this century, this lower cross wing and independent kitchen were linked with a timber-framed and brick gabled structure. It was in this state that the house was subject to the inventory made after Thomas Stonor's death in 1474 (see below). Four years later, some rebuilding was undertaken in stone by the wealthy Sir William Stonor (1474–94).[22] This was possibly the west wing abutting the kitchen, attributed by the VCH to the 1530s, though the use of flint and rubble for the west wall (revealed in the 1970s) points to Sir William's time. The east wall was timber-framed, originally with an overhang, but this was altered when the brick facing was added by the Tudors. The size of the rooms in this wing suggests they were used by the family (as they still are) and that its odd position close to the kitchen was occasioned by the restrictions imposed elsewhere by rising ground.

SIXTEENTH CENTURY

A period of short-lived successions, a protracted lawsuit with the Fortescue family of Devon over the ownership of Stonor, and the long minority of Sir Walter Stonor (d.1550) meant that he did not recover his 'poore house' until 1534. It was not in good shape until 'augmentyd and strengthed' by Sir Walter.[23] The alterations to the solar cross wing and the addition of the forecourt gateway, lodges, and walls, as well as the west wing and kitchen encasement, have been attributed to him.[24] The most substantial Tudor remodelling,

however, has been credited to his grandson, Sir Francis Stonor (1564–1625), justice of the peace and sheriff of Oxfordshire and Buckinghamshire in 1592 and 1622. He tried to bring order to this straggling medieval house by creating a symmetrical front through infilling its irregularities, refacing the timber parts with brick, adding the gables and mullioned windows and heightening the porch. At the same time, he added a new range at the rear of the house of ground-floor passage with gallery above, and though built against the slope of the hill, it linked the lower cross wing with the old hall.[25]

Current thinking is that the west wing is late fifteenth-century work, and that the brick frontage of the house was part of Sir Walter's enlargement. It was he who was responsible for the sculptures by the front door after the Fortescue lawsuit. It is also more likely that this work was carried out before the burden of Recusancy fines had started to fall on the family which drained it of financial resources between the third quarter of the sixteenth century and the mid-eighteenth century. Though Leland recorded between c.1535 and 1540 that the house 'hathe 2 courtes buyldyd with tymber, brike and flynte',[26] the timberwork was probably concealed during the 1560s rather than towards the close of the century.

EIGHTEENTH AND NINETEENTH CENTURIES

Stonor Park is a fascinating complex of considerable size, in which the quite extensive early structures have been so swamped by later alterations that it has become a palimpsest of the medieval house. A painting of 1690 in the house reveals its unaltered form between the late sixteenth and mid-eighteenth centuries, for no building was undertaken during the Recusancy and little money was available for

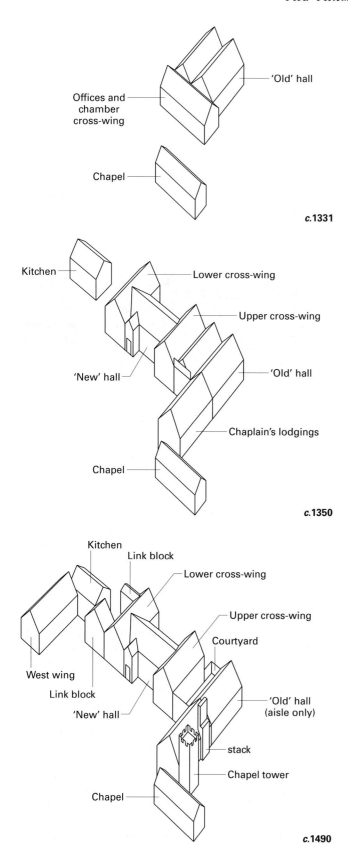

Offices and chamber cross-wing
'Old' hall
Chapel

*c.*1331

Kitchen
Lower cross-wing
Upper cross-wing
'New' hall
'Old' hall
Chaplain's lodgings
Chapel

*c.*1350

Kitchen
Link block
Lower cross-wing
Upper cross-wing
Courtyard
West wing
Link block
'New' hall
'Old' hall (aisle only)
stack
Chapel tower
Chapel

*c.*1490

FIGURE 37 Stonor Park: early development phases (modified from VCH)

modest improvements or even maintenance. It was not until the ferocious Catholic laws were relaxed that alterations could be envisaged, and then they proved extensive. Thomas Stonor (1724–72) began by refenestrating the façade with sash windows and those of Venetian character in the porch. The Elizabethan gables were replaced by a hipped roof with dormers, while the Tudor gateway and forecourt wall were pulled down. Between 1753 and 1760, the fourteenth-century hall was redecorated, screened, and vaulted in the fashionable Gothick style, the east wing was partly rebuilt, the gallery was refenestrated, and a Gothick vault was inserted in the chapel. A new staircase with ironwork balustrade was added in 1796–1800, when the chapel was also given a new gallery, altar rails, and painted glass windows. The final phase of development took place in 1834, when the hall was divided lengthways into two rooms, and the fireplaces moved to the middle of the inserted wall.

Though the architectural development of this house is academically fascinating, not the least important step in its history has been its retention and preservation by Lord and Lady Camoys since 1975 – a heroic task summarised by Jeremy Musson in April 2001.

The park is of considerable age, though now of eighteenth-century planting and layout with long-established herds of fallow deer. There are references to John Parker of Assendon, keeper of the fishery and warren in 1395, and 'le pale' surrounding the park.[27] Leland also referred to the 'fayre parke, and a waren of connes, and fayre woods',[28] while its deer are mentioned in several of the family papers, for the abundant game in the park not only supplemented the large amounts of food consumed in the house, but made useful presents to friends in London.[29]

THE STONOR PAPERS

Except for the Paston Letters, the Stonor papers are the most important collection of private correspondence of the late middle ages. About sixty papers cover the 100 years from about 1360, but nearly 300 relate to the years between 1460 and 1483, an underused resource of family life under Edward IV that adds flesh to the bones of this house.[30] They reveal there was always a plentiful table at Stonor Park, a necessity as the household included not only the Stonor family and their children, but the four young Fenn children, distantly related and in Sir William Stonor's care during the late 1470s, as well as several other wards.[31] Food was provided chiefly from the estate or the neighbourhood, and from nearby towns such as Reading and Henley.[32] More unusual items and delicacies, in particular fish and wine, were brought by barge from London to Henley over a period of four or five days.[33]

The house was particularly well stocked at Christmas time and for funerals.[34] In 1481, Sir William Stonor and his third bride, Lady Anne Neville, were entertained at Christmas by players from Gloucester and from Leighton Buzzard.[35] Three years earlier, Sir William had entertained the chancellor, bishop Rotherham of Lincoln, at Stonor Park. The preparations had included the importation of a butt of Greek wine, three pipes and a hogshead of red wine and claret, and much fish as well as additional glassware and bowls.[36] Overindulgence sometimes necessitated prescriptions, including those given by a London doctor brought to Stonor to attend the ailing and short-lived second Lady Stonor (d.1481). They were made up by a nearby apothecary and included a laxative.[37]

The Stonors maintained a good wardrobe. In 1478, Sir William had a half gown of black puke lined with green velvet, protected

PLATE 71 Stonor Park: from the south

when not in use by a sheet.[38] In the following year, Dame Elizabeth, who had a considerable fondness for clothes, bought 38 yards of green sarsenet (fine silk) at five shillings a yard which, she was assured, would last her own lifetime and that of her child's after her.[39] The servants were given kersey, usually russet coloured, some of it woven from home-grown wool by a weaver at Watlington.[40] In 1478, the family shoemaker made six pairs of boots, two pairs of wooden pattens, and 126 pairs of shoes for the family and their staff including fifty-five pairs for the children and twenty-five for Chowne in the stable.[41] Servant problems, though, were just as common in the fifteenth century as they are today, 'for servants be not so delygent as þei were wonto bee'. This particular letter of about 1470 from Jeanne Stonor to her husband in London carries a postscript reminding him to bring home some 'gentian, rhubarb, baize caps, pots, cheverel-laces, an ounce of flat silk, laces, and treacle'.[42]

Household accounts were rendered to the head of the family in the hall of the house,[43] which was furnished in about 1474 with hangings of black say (a quality cloth), a pair of 'coburnes' (irons for the spit), and a 'fire-fork'.[44] These are part of an inventory which, though not dated, seems to have been drawn up after the death of Thomas Stonor as it refers to his wife, Jeanne.[45] The little chamber next to the parlour was hung with purple and green striped material. Three chambers were hung with red and green striped cloth, and one of them had bed hangings of the same material. The chamber at the nether end of the hall was hung with grey worsted and had a bed in it, while the bed in the parlour with its two pairs of blankets, pair of sheets, and red coverlet with green chapelettes worked on it was perhaps the principal bedroom in the house. There was also a feather bed in this room on loan from Jeanne Stonor, and a green coverlet with spots and ostrich feathers worked on it. Only three

chairs are recorded in this inventory, two plain and one turned. Six cushions are itemised. The buttery had a basin and jug of brass and similar items of tin, a brass chaffing dish, cloths, several towels and table cloths, a trencher knife, and various brass canisters and leather pots.[46] The kitchen was furnished with three spits, several pots, and two hanging racks for them, and there were the usual pans, pewter vessels for the table, a stone morter, knives, and an axe. A vat, nine barrels, a tub, and two sifters were noted in the bakehouse. Items in no specified place included two silver gilt cups and covers, a great engraved silver bowl, five jacks, two halbards, three head-pieces, and a boar spear.

All these items were considered to be the permanent furnishings of the house – the 'standorerdus' or immovables – not the personal items of family members, such as bed linen or clothes.[47] The furnishings of the chapel, therefore, are more extensive and ranged from three sets of vestments, two copes, various altar cloths, hangings, and frontals, to an alabaster figure of the Trinity, a silver chalice, a silver gilt crucifix, a pair of silver cruets, and five books. There was also an alabaster retable with 'storyus of þe passyon of owr lord, þe wych Tabutle Mastres Jeanne Stonor has yeft unto þe chapelle of Stonor with many oþer þynges þereto belongyng'.

NOTES
1 J. Sherwood and N. Pevsner, *The Buildings of England: Oxfordshire* (1974) 792.
2 *Itinerary*, V (1910) 72.
3 VCH, VIII (1964) 144–7.
4 *Pipe Roll: 1204*, 111.
5 By exchange such as those with Dorchester Abbey in 1316–17, by inheritance from his mother in Gloucestershire, and through purchase during the middle years of his life, including an important manor in south Devon.

6 Kingsford (1919) I, ix.

7 On his death, Sir Edmund's estates were valued at £346 a year, Stonor (1951) 112.

8 They suggested that the house was probably built after 1280 when Sir Richard Stonor (1250–1314) married his second wife, Margaret Harnhull, a daughter of a Gloucestershire knight (VCH, VIII (1964) 142, 154), but his father Richard Stonor (1225–73) is just as likely to have been responsible for the hall.

9 *South Midlands Archaeology* 25 (1995) 68.

10 VCH, VIII (1964) 176.

11 *Cal. Pat. Rolls: 1348–50*, 290. The consecration in this year was a consequence of this expansion.

12 It is one of the three chapels in England that has maintained continuous Catholic worship since its construction. The others are at East Hendred (Berkshire) and Hazlewood Castle (Yorkshire), but in neither case has the chapel been in unbroken single-family ownership. For private chapels of the nobility and gentry, N. Orme, 'Church and chapel in medieval England', *Trans. Roy. Hist. Soc.* 6 (1996) 75–102.

13 VCH, VIII (1964) 145.

14 *Ibid.* 142 n.77.

15 The almost contemporary range for chantry priests at Farleigh Hungerford Castle is much better preserved.

16 Lady Elizabeth Stonor's account book for 1478–9 refers to a payment to the smith for making a lock for the porch chamber, suggesting there was only one such room, Kingsford (1919) II, 72.

17 VCH, VIII (1964) 145. The ground floor is used as the formal dining room, cloakroom, and passageway; the barrel-vaulted library spans the length of the upper floor.

18 *Ibid.* 145.

19 *Ibid.* 176.

20 Kingsford (1919) I, 13–14.

21 *Ibid.* I, 29–30.

22 *Ibid.* II, 168. He also made a new garden in 1480, *ibid.* 98–9.

23 *Itinerary*, V (1910) 72.

24 VCH, VIII (1964) 147.

25 *Ibid.* 147.

26 *Itinerary*, V (1910) 72.

27 *Cal. Close Rolls: 1392–96*, 342.

28 *Itinerary*, V (1910) 72.

29 Kingsford (1919) II, 106,110.

30 The letters are almost all in English and are a mixture of business, legal and personal correspondence, and household accounts. Though they lack the political interest of the Paston letters, the fortunes of both families were laid by successful lawyers. But whereas the Pastons had a struggle to retain their holdings and rank during the third quarter of the fifteenth century, the Stonors were country gentlemen who maintained their stock through good marriages and economic exploitation. They saw little military service, and tried to keep out of national politics. The family papers were seized and kept with the public records either through Sir William Stonor's attainder in 1483 or because of the extremely protracted lawsuit that began in 1500 over the betrothal of Sir William's heir to Sir John Fortescue's daughter.

31 Kingsford (1919) II, 74.

32 *Ibid.* I, 151–2, II, 272–3.

33 *Ibid.* II, 4–5, 45–6, 46.

34 *Ibid.* I, 143–4; II, 72–3, 95; and Stonor (1951) 151–2, 174.

35 Kingsford (1919) II, 139–40.

36 *Ibid.* II, 45–6.

37 *Ibid.* II, 107–8. An urgent journey to or from the capital 40 miles away could be completed on horseback within a long day, II, 10–11.

38 *Ibid.* II, 60–1.

39 *Ibid.* II, 90–1.

40 *Ibid.* I, 153–4, 101.

41 *Ibid.* II, 74.

42 *Ibid.* I, 109–10.

43 *Ibid.* I, 151–2.

44 Two generations earlier, Sir Ralph Stonor (d.1394) had sold the hall hangings from his house in Westminster to Henry, earl of Derby, who used them for his mobile 'hall' which accompanied him on his journeys to Prussia and the Holy Land in 1390–3. Stonor (1951) 109.

45 Kingsford (1919) I, 145–7. It is given in full in Stonor (1951) 133–7.

46 An inventory eight years later shows that the number of items in the buttery had increased. Kingsford (1919) II, 141.

47 A year later, for instance, Edmund Stonor, Sir William's younger brother, made a will bequeathing his bedding, a feather bed, a pair of blankets, a pair of sheets, a coverlet, a bolster, and a pillow to his brother, and also his own psalter. He bequeathed his great rug to Power, his russet gown lined with horse fleece to Thomas Wood, and his gown furred with shanks to John Matthew, *ibid.* II, 186–7.

C. L. Kingsford (ed.), *The Stonor Letters and Papers: 1290–1483*, 2 vols. (1919)

C. Hussey, *Country Life* (October 1950)

R. J. Stonor, *Stonor* (1951)

VCH, *Oxfordshire*, VIII (1964) 142–7, 154–5, 175–6

J. Musson and J. Goodall, *Country Life* (April 2001)

SUDELEY CASTLE, Gloucestershire

The ownership of Sudeley Castle has been held by five important families after the estate passed in 1417 to Ralph Boteler (d.1473) as brother and heir of the sixth holder of the lapsed barony of Sudeley. Ralph held it until 1469 when the property was sold to Edward IV who granted it to his brother, Richard duke of Gloucester. It reverted to the crown nine years later in exchange for Richmond Castle as part of the duke's enhancement of his already large Yorkshire holding. The crown retained Sudeley (except for a short interval) until 1547 when it was given to Lord Admiral Seymour who married Catherine Parr, Henry VIII's widow. Seymour's occupation lasted no more than seven years, for confiscation arising from his treason resulted in the estate being granted to Sir John Bridges, subsequently created Baron Chandos of Sudeley (d.1557). Sale by the Chandos family in 1810 enabled the Dent family to acquire the castle in 1837 and they have held it until the present day.

Sudeley castle was built in four phases – by Ralph, Baron Boteler in the mid-fifteenth century, Richard duke of Gloucester a little later in the century, Baron Chandos in the later sixteenth century, and partial restoration by the Dent family during the mid-nineteenth century. The post-medieval work will only be noticed where it affects the earlier buildings but it should be noted that the Victorian rehabilitation has obscured much of the castle's architectural development.

As at Wingfield Manor, nothing survives of any structures prior to the mid-fifteenth century. Leland noted that the previous manor lay in Sudeley Park, where its site could be seen in his day. It seems to have been to the east of the present garden terraces.[1] Boteler planned to build a double courtyard house from the first. Part of his outer court and a section of his inner court survive, though the principal ruins of the second court are those of his successor. Boteler was also responsible for the independent chapel and barn. All building work was carried out in ashlar blocks of local honey-coloured

PLATE 72 Sudeley Castle: engraving from the south-west by S. and N. Buck (1732)

Cotswold stone, with rebuilding by the Dent family distinguished by a deeper yellow material.

OUTER COURT

Boteler's storeyed gatehouse was initially protected by a moat and guarded by a drawbridge. Only the drawbridge rebate survives above the wide entrance arch with its slight chamfered mouldings and peaked four-centred head. This gateway was modest and, despite the embattled parapet, utterly domestic. The right-hand chamber flanking the central passage was the porter's lodge, with a shelf opening into the passageway. The entrance doors and passage ceiling are Victorian. The single upper room is lit by two projecting oriels of late sixteenth-century date.

The ranges on three sides of the outer court were almost entirely rebuilt by Edmund, 2nd Lord Chandos in about 1572 (datestone on south-west turret) incorporating Boteler's gateway and at least part of a contemporary outer wall on the north side (blocked first-floor opening at end of range). The form of Boteler's outer court is not certain. The outer wall may have been little more than a curtain wall but it is more likely to have been part of a range of lodgings and perhaps offices lining the sides of the court as befitted a leading courtier magnate.

Chandos' two-storeyed ranges of 1572 were designed as lodgings of paired rooms with their own entrances from the courtyard. These and the large squared windows lighting both ground- and first-floor rooms are the prominent feature of his work today. The upper floor also held the principal guest suite and a long gallery, approached from staircases in the angle of the court.[2]

The cross range separating the two courts is now a low corridor of 1889. It replaces the stub walls of a similar range, possibly built in 1614, the date above one of the doorways. The Victorian corridor gives no idea of the size and design of the medieval structure on its site. Only the wall ends and vaulting corbels of a ground-floor chamber built against the Garderobe Tower give an indication of what was formerly here and this will be considered later.

What do survive are the towers at either end of the range. The Garderobe Tower has been heavily restored and shows little evidence of its original form. It is of two periods on the garden (east) side but mid-fifteenth century on the west, even though the first-floor doorways have different heads, one two-centred and one four-centred. Half the ground floor is a loggia and the remainder dates from 1572. The tower is divided by a cross wall at first-floor level with the two rooms originally approached separately from the cross range. The rooms may have been garderobes but they are very large for such a purpose (compared with those in the Dungeon Tower), while the elaborate oriel inserted in the late fifteenth century suggests that they were small private chambers.

The Portmare Tower at the west end of the cross range is enveloped on two sides by buildings of 1857 and 1887 but survives untouched on the north and west sides. This tall, slender, five-storey tower has no original features internally, but its outer face shows that it consisted of a private chamber at each of the four upper floors lit by narrow vertical single lights on the three outer faces. Their position on the south side shows that a range was always intended in this position. The gunport at ground-floor level suggests an adjacent subsidiary entrance into the outer court. This tower is spartan in its design.

THE INDEPENDENT UNITS

One of the two independent units marks a change in Boteler's style. The fine but ruined mid-fifteenth-century manorial barn is divided into two parts, the barn of nine bays and a two-storeyed residential unit in the last three bays. Each bay is marked by tall slit openings. The residential unit, with its own entrance, was separated from the storage bays by a (destroyed) wooden partition wall.

The large detached chapel was erected outside the moat of the castle with a pentice from its south side linking it to the main building. Only the shell of this attractive private chapel survived the damage of the Civil War and subsequent neglect. All interior work, including the tomb of Catherine Parr (d.1548), was erected under

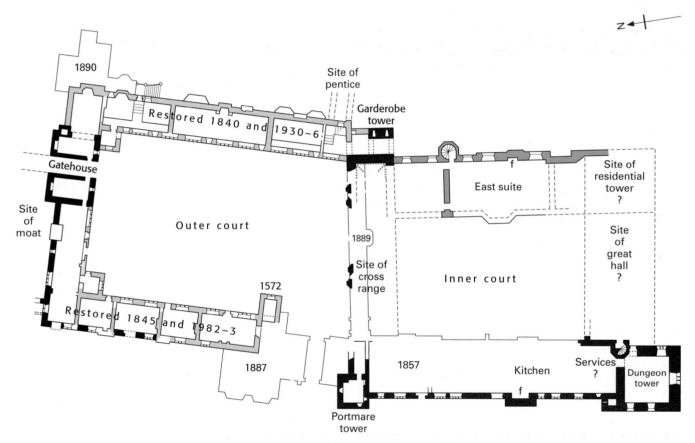

FIGURE 38 Sudeley Castle: ground plan

the supervision of Sir George Gilbert Scott (1859–63) and is markedly Victorian.

Boteler's secular work is spare. The Portmare Tower, for instance, is particularly so. His work is also marked by simple mouldings and a lack of ornament. In comparison, his chapel is considerably richer, with pinnacled buttresses, ornate window heads, bold gargoyles, battlemented parapet, and finely carved stops to the hood moulds. This work closely resembles the contemporary aisles at Winchcombe parish church to which Boteler contributed.[3]

INNER COURT

The west range from the Portmare Tower to the Dungeon Tower was taken up by the kitchen and presumably some offices and services. The kitchen can still be identified by its great stack, now with a Victorian archway forced through its base. However, by the early nineteenth century, only the lower part of the outer wall survived and apart from this, the range is entirely work of 1857. Buck's engraving of 1732 illustrates the structure before its total ruination and shows a range divided internally with different window levels. The north end seems to have been two storeyed,

PLATE 73 Sudeley Castle: Dungeon Tower

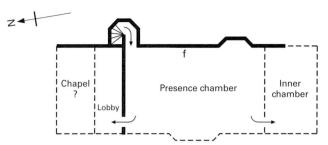

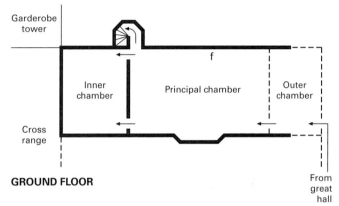

FIGURE 39 Sudeley Castle: east suite layout

with a tall window rising through both floors. The southern end, interrupted by the kitchen which may have risen through two storeys, has a low ground floor with inserted or replacement Tudor windows above.

The three-storeyed *Dungeon Tower* is considerably larger than the two cross-range towers. The ground and first floors have been restored but the second floor is still ruined. The large single apartment at each level was approached from the destroyed south range. The staircase gave access (now blocked) at a half landing to the first-floor apartments in the west range. There was a garderobe turret in the north-west angle entirely lacking windows (but with a door at its base), projecting as a turret above the roofline. Emma Dent stated that she examined three unlit chambers below ground level in this tower in the late nineteenth century, since sealed. The windows at all levels look as though they are of 1572, but their stonework seems integral with the walls and therefore could be a century earlier, though all doorway arches are four-centred. There are no original features internally, but the more angular moulding of the ground-floor doorway as against the convex form of the gatehouse entry suggests that the tower was secondary to the outer courtyard. It was certainly built to provide high-quality residential accommodation and may well have been matched by a comparable

tower at the further end of the south range reflecting the developing taste for impressive towered lodgings.

Nothing survives of the south range and the site is grassed. The entrance to the Dungeon Tower and its staircase show that the range and tower were contemporary.

The east range is by far the richest part of the castle, albeit ruined, but dominated by the incredible elaborate outer wall to full height as is one of the cross walls. The foundations of the inner wall have also been recovered. This range was a suite of three apartments at ground- and first-floor level; both similar in plan, but the position of the doorways, fireplaces, and oriel indicates that the two floors worked in reverse directions. It is probable that it replaced Boteler's more conventional residential range.

The middle of the ground-floor suite was marked by the principal chamber, with a central bay window in the courtyard wall and a fireplace with a low lintel and three ornate windows in the outer wall. Hardly anything remains of the southernmost chamber, which would have been about 24 feet square (the cross wall, now destroyed, is shown in Buck's engraving). The upper cross wall of the large middle chamber retains twin doors giving access to the north chamber built up against the Garderobe Tower and cross range. This north chamber has two four-light windows in the outer wall.

A wide staircase in the half-octagonal turret at the upper end of the principal chamber accessed the first-floor suite. The large presence chamber was even more ornate than that on the floor below. It rose through two storeys (and above the level of the adjacent roof to the north) and was lit at its lower end by a magnificent nine-light window (two blind) filling the upper part of the cross wall. The outer wall was on a royal scale with its two floor-to-roof windows of twelve and fifteen lights respectively, the later within a fan-vaulted oriel. Between are two windows of four lights in the upper walling and they, like the larger windows, have elegant moulded mullions, two transoms, cinquefoil heads, panelled reveals, and an embattled base string course. The richly decorated fireplace is immediately above that on the ground floor. The roof was supported on slender wall shafts rising from angel corbels at the side of the windows (pl. 9).

Hardly anything survives of the southernmost room except part of a window. The chamber to the north had two quite different types of windows, with a fireplace to the side of one of them almost burning anyone coming through the adjacent door. Was this room divided by a partition creating a chapel to the north, lit by the three-light east window with an altar filling the blank walling underneath?

RALPH BOTELER

Born in 1396, Ralph Boteler inherited the Sudeley estate in 1417. He spent much of his youth in the 1420s and 1430s fighting in France and was granted lands there in 1420–1.[4] He was held in high esteem by the Regent, the duke of Bedford, and appointed a councillor of the infant Henry VI in 1423. In 1430, Sir Ralph became a member of the nine-year-old king's bodyguard and sailed with him to Calais in that year. At the time of Bedford's death in 1435, Boteler was his chief chamberlain and councillor. He remained in France and, though becoming a member of the King's Council of France and Normandy under the duke of York in 1440, he returned to England permanently shortly after July 1441.

Honours and appointments followed in rapid succession – chief butler of the household in 1435 (until 1458), knight of the garter in 1440, chamberlain to the king in 1441 (until 1447), and Baron Sudeley immediately after his return from France in 1441 with an annuity of 200 marks to support the honour. This was the first creation by the king rather than his advisors, and indicative of Boteler's personal qualities of loyalty and industry as declared in the grant.[5] It was also a signal act of patronage for it was the first royal creation by patent of this dignity in tail male outside a short-lived one of 1387 (Beauchamp of Holt Castle).

Baron Sudeley was a loyal courtier, a leading councillor, and a royal favourite throughout the next twenty years. He owed his advancement as much to the all-powerful Suffolk as to the crown, forming part of that inner circle determining royal patronage and politics which included other leading house builders such as Ralph Lord Cromwell, James Lord Say and Sele, and John Lord Stourton. Sudeley replaced Cromwell as treasurer of England in July 1443 and held the post until December 1446. He was appointed steward of the household two months later. After Suffolk's death in 1450, Sudeley continued to be a courtier magnate, councillor, and close member of the king's inner group as steward of the household until 1457, though he had to contend with the abrasive duke of York whose politics were such anathema to him.

Sudeley's fortunes were intimately bound up with those of Henry VI, and when the king was deposed in 1461, the aged baron retired to his castle, bereft of offices and influence. From Leland onwards, Sudeley's unyielding Lancastrian sympathies are believed to have enabled the Yorkist Edward IV to force the sale of the castle to the crown in 1469. This is doubtful, for Sudeley had been exempted from attending council or holding office in 1462 on the grounds of age and infirmity, and did not pose a threat to Edward when he was

PLATE 74 Sudeley Castle: east range of inner court

seventy-three years old and retired from politics.[6] The fact that he had no heirs is a far more likely explanation for the sale.[7]

Benefiting from early advantages,[8] Boteler was an opportunist with abilities and loyalty recognised in turn by Henry V, Bedford, Henry VI, and Suffolk. Nearly twenty years of military, diplomatic, and council experience in northern France fitted him for the role of leading councillor at home for the next two decades. He was an effective negotiator, as in his dealings with France in 1442, 1446, and 1449, and financially astute, leaving the Treasury in 1446 with a balance of £60,000. Yet he was so entrenched in his lifetime's support for the house of Lancaster that, despite his age, he took the opportunity afforded by Edward IV's flight in 1470–1 to raise Lancastrian support for Henry VI's readeption by parading the king through the streets of London before his cause was finally quashed by Edward's victories at Barnet and Tewkesbury.

DATING AND DESIGN

Leland states that Boteler built the castle *a fundamentis*, and that when it was built, it had the prize for all the buildings in those days.[9] The architectural evidence bears out the first part of the statement, and the second is indicative of its size and splendour under Boteler. Leland also noted that the castle was said to have been built with spoils acquired in the French wars and that a tower called Portmare was named after the ransom Boteler received from capturing this French fighter.[10] In a later part of his *Itinerary*, Leland notes that Boteler built the castle in the time of Henry VI and Edward IV.[11]

Boteler's financial resources were very substantial. Apart from his inherited wealth and that acquired through marriage to a wealthy widow, twenty years' service and landholding in France is likely to have made a marked contribution to his resources, substantially enhanced by an equally long tenure of crown offices and a range of subsidiary appointments.

Historically, a date for the castle not long after Boteler's return to England and elevation to the peerage in 1441 is likely, and this is supported by the record that the mason Robert Janyns, working on the new bell tower at Merton College, Oxford, travelled to Sudeley in 1448 to hire a mason.[12] Architecturally, Winchcombe parish church was built by the abbot of the adjacent abbey, William Winchcombe (1458–68), with financial support from Boteler, which helps to date the chapel to the same period. Even more important is the general pardon Boteler sought in May 1458 in the atmosphere of a possible Yorkist triumph for his good services to Henry V and the king in France, Normandy, and England from his youth onwards, and a pardon for crenellating without licence his manors of Sudeley and The More in Hertfordshire.[13] The construction of this large double-courtyard residence may be attributed to the years between 1441 and 1458, with the chapel as secondary work of the early 1460s.

The key structure missing today is the great hall. Its siting is unclear but it is more likely to have been in the absent south range as suggested by Faulkner[14] than in the cross range as marked by Walter Godfrey on his plan of the castle.[15] The remains of the vaulted chamber at the east end of the cross range show that it was only 18 feet wide internally. Although it might have been possible to fill the remainder of that range with a hall, it would have been impossibly squashed.

A position on the far side of the second court had recently been established by Boteler's friend Lord Cromwell at Wingfield Manor, approached through a gateway in the middle of his cross range and was adopted seventy years later at Thornbury Castle. A similar plan at Sudeley is quite possible, particularly in view of the narrowness of the cross range and the kitchen position. The siting of that service unit in the middle of the west range is not obviously suited to either of the proposed positions for the great hall. Yet Edward IV's kitchen at Eltham Palace was similarly built at right angles to the hall and separated from it. A comparable position at Sudeley enabled the services to be placed in line towards the angle common with the lower end of the hall filling the south range. The Dungeon Tower was a major lodging unit and probably matched by an even more privileged one at the upper end of the hall.

The impressive richness of the east suite is a subsequent development. Its ornateness and magnificence suggests the crown rather than Boteler's more astringent residential style, so that the attribution to Richard, earl of Gloucester during his ownership between November 1469 and 1478 is plausible. Edward IV had granted Sudeley to his sixteen-year-old brother as a reward for his support against Warwick the Kingmaker, to act as a counterpoise to his extensive block of Worcestershire and Warwickshire estates, and to keep an eye on Clarence.[16] The grandiose development of Sudeley can be explained by Gloucester's plan to make it a power-base until his southern holdings became peripheral to his north-eastern 'empire' nearly a decade later. But once on the throne, Richard III renewed his interest in Sudeley Castle. He appointed John Huddlestone constable of the castle,[17] the son of a staunch Yorkist supporter from Cumbria, Sir John Huddlestone of Millom Castle. In the following year, mid-1484 to mid-1485, Richard authorised repairs to the castle.[18]

This palace-like suite is unmatched by other work of the period. It would be an appropriate adjunct to Edward IV's standing hall at Eltham (1475–83) and, in the absence of the royal domestic additions at Nottingham, Fotheringhay, and Dover castles, the Sudeley suite testifies to the scale, taste, and splendour of Court work. Walling has virtually become a skeleton framework for a sequence of windows which would have been matched to a great extent on the courtyard side. Windows glazed with round beralls (beryls) as in the hall,[19] stained glass, tapestries, and ornate ceilings would have complemented the sun-lit apartments. Magnificently sited today in a Gloucestershire garden, this refined range is a declaration of wealth and status in no way inferior to contemporary work in France such as Loches and Angers. Possibly influenced by Burgundian grandeur and more particularly by the palaces of Ghent and Bruges seen by Richard in exile in 1470–1, the Sudeley range was a comparable setting for elaborate etiquette and ceremonial. Very fortunately, the Victorians did not attempt to rebuild this structure.

It has been suggested that the west range was also built by Gloucester rather than Boteler.[20] The high position of the windows in the Portmare Tower overlooking this range, the lack of decoration in the Dungeon Tower, the financial resources available to Boteler, his courtier magnate position, and Leland's claim of his vast expenditure suggest that the west range was part of his development. It was Gloucester, though, who inserted the richer windows at its north end.

Sudeley Castle is an object lesson in architectural style during the mid-fifteenth century. As the house of a devout royal supporter, it reflected the plain character favoured by Henry VI during the second half of his reign, but progressed to the more richly decorated form of the 1460s, and the exuberant outburst of the 1470s. This mirrored the crown's improved prosperity and a Court style favouring cinquefoil cusping, super mullions, bay windows and extended windows, flat four-centred arches, and decorative enrichment.

The reason for the two courtyards being askew is not clear, but they are integral to Boteler's double mansion concept. As at Wingfield Manor, the outer courtyard was very much subsidiary to the inner court with its two smaller and two larger and taller towers on the far side of the court creating a progressive elevation. These two larger residential towers flanking the great hall were positioned at the furthest point from the outer gate. The layout of an outer court of lodgings, a gatehouse-approached inner court culminating in an opposing hall range with great end towers would also make Sudeley a precursor of Hampton Court and Nonsuch Palace. Furthermore, the ruined residential range on the east side of the second court is as close to contemporary royal work as exists today.

NOTES

1 *Itinerary*, II, 56; *Country Life* (November 1940).

2 These ranges should be compared with contemporary work at Kirby Hall, Northants: Faulkner (1965) 190. Internally, all work is mid to late nineteenth century, remodelled during the twentieth century.

3 *Itinerary*, II, 55: 'The parishioners had gathered a £200 and beganne the body of the church; but that summe being not able to performe so costly a worke, Rafe Boteler, Lord Sudeley helped them and finished the worke.' Leland's description of Winchcombe and Sudeley reflects his extended visit there.

4 *Com. Peer.*, XII (1957) 420.

5 *Cal. Pat. Rolls: 1441–46*, 2, 51. J. E. Powell and K. Wallis, *The House of Lords in the Middle Ages* (1968) 469–71.

6 *Itinerary*, II, 56. G.E.C. *Com. Peer.*, XII (1957) 421 points out that the form of exemption differs from that granted to his father in 1398. Furthermore,

Edward's hostility towards Sudeley is weakened by this exemption and a general pardon for trespasses and debts in 1468. *Cal. Pat. Rolls: 1467–71*, 50. During his life, Boteler had also held a range of lesser (and financially rewarding) offices such as constable of Kenilworth and subsequently Conway castles between 1433 and 1461, chamberlain of South Wales, keeper of the Channel Isles, steward and surveyor of Wychwood Forest, keeper of the manor of Woodstock etc., *ibid*. 421 note f.

7 In 1419, Boteler had married the widow of Sir John Hende from whom he acquired estates in Essex and London. She died in 1462. In the following year, when Boteler was sixty-seven years old, he married the widow of Lord Lovel. His son had married the daughter of the 1st earl of Shrewsbury in 1448–9 but he died before his father.

8 His mother was governess to the infant Henry VI and he was related to the Beauchamp family.

9 *Itinerary*, II, 55.

10 *Ibid.* 56; V, 221 repeats that the castle was built *ex spoliis nobilium Gallico captorum*.

11 *Ibid.* V, 154.

12 J. E. Rogers, *History of Agriculture and Prices*, III (1866–92) 720.

13 *Cal. Pat. Rolls: 1452–61*, 422.

14 *Arch. Jour.* 122 (1965) 190.

15 Prepared in the early 1930s when he was remodelling the family rooms. It has been published in all guidebooks since 1950.

16 R. Horrox, *Richard III* (1989) 33.

17 R. Horrox and P. W. Hammond, *British Library, Harleian Manuscript 433*, I (1979) 153.

18 *Ibid.* II (1980) 227. Christopher Wilson's view that Jasper Tudor (d.1495) may have been responsible for this substantial development after Henry VII had granted the castle to his uncle in 1485 is speculative: *Gothic Art for England: 1400–1547* (2003) 284–5. Jasper had just married into the Stafford properties and was almost certainly responsible for developing Thornbury Castle during these years instead. See page 188 n. 9 and R. S. Thomas, 'The political career, estates, and "connections" of Jasper Tudor', PhD thesis, University College, Swansea (1971) 265–76.

19 Leland, *Itinerary*, II, 56; V, 155.

20 *Arch. Jour.* 122 (1965) 190.

E. Dent, *Annals of Winchcombe and Sudeley* (1877)

M. Dent-Brocklehurst, *Trans. Bristol and Glos. Arch. Soc.* 33 (1910) 6–11

A. Oswald, *Country Life* (November/December 1940)

M. Dent-Brocklehurst, *Sudeley Castle Guidebook* (c.1950) with plan by Walter Godfrey

P. A. Faulkner, *Arch. Jour.* 122 (1965) 189–90

R. Kretschmer, 'Ralph Botiller, Lord Sudeley', BA thesis, Keele University (1973)

M. Hall, *Country Life* (April 1990)

SUTTON COURTENAY 'ABBEY', Berkshire

The village of Sutton Courtenay has three substantial medieval houses near its well-tended greens.

• Norman Hall, originally part of the manor of Sutton, developed from a chapel of *c*.1200 (formerly thought to be a hall), now attached to an essentially seventeenth-century house.

• The 'Abbey', initially a rectorial holding, developed from a late thirteenth-century core into a compact quadrangular stone and timber-framed house.

• The Manor House, the dwelling of an early fourteenth-century subsidiary manor of Sutton (Brunce's Court), held by the Brounz family from at least 1303 to about 1459.[1]

The ascription 'abbey' to the second of these houses arises from its early ownership under Abingdon Abbey. It was a rectorial holding from the late eleventh century, but after an extended legal wrangle in 1284, it passed into the hands of the Courtenay family who had held the manor of Sutton since the mid-twelfth century.[2] Whether any of the existing structure pre-dates this change in ownership is arguable, but the property was developed in several stages between the close of the thirteenth and the sixteenth centuries.

The approach to the house is enticing. The west front seems to have the rare character of a little-touched mid-fourteenth-century residence, retaining its single-storey embattled hall flanked by two-storeyed cross wings with striking contemporary fenestration. All is not as it seems. The hall and lower cross wing were timber-framed, not stone-built, much of the fenestration has been reorchestrated, most of the remaining plaster-covered ranges are timber-framed above a stone ground floor, and the whole house is now covered with sweeping clay-tiled roofs (pl. 5).

There are two development problems. The first concerns the date of the north range beyond the upper end of the hall. On the basis of stone walls 3 feet thick, roof timbers, and some tiny lancets, it has been claimed as the earliest structure, an independent thirteenth-century hall and offices block under ecclesiastical ownership. The second concerns the original form of the present hall, an apparently mid-fourteenth-century stone structure with complex stylistic and structural problems.

There is no evidence that the hall entry was porch protected. The opposing cross-passage doorways are plain, a continuous chamfered two-centred arch with hood mould. That towards the courtyard is unrestored: all but the base of the principal entry is a nineteenth-century renewal. The late Victorian screen opens into the imposing hall, unusual for never suffering from partitioning or an inserted floor. This apartment, 40½ feet by 24 feet, is lit on the west side by two floor-length late Victorian windows replacing two transomed windows with flowing tracery similar to that nearby lighting the solar. Turner and Parker show them with heads under mini-gabled roofs, though the text makes it clear that the illustration was an imaginative reconstruction which has confused writers for over a hundred years.[3] Their plan, though inaccurate in some respects, shows there were similarly large windows in the opposite wall.[4] The present fifteenth-century lights were inserted during the late Victorian alterations to the hall. Parker also illustrates an unusual shuttered square opening under the window at the upper end of the hall. Now lost, the frame was filled with a quatrefoil of four cusped mouchettes.[5]

The two-and-a-half-bay roof of unusual character has been subject to considerable renovation, with many timbers replaced in 1960. The central truss is supported on moulded braces rising from low-set corbels to form a massive arch spanning the middle of the hall. The cambered collar beam carries a crown-post structure with four-way struts to the collar purlin and the braces of the trussed rafter roof. The rafters are close-set and were modified to their present form when the low side walls were raised and embattled by the close of the nineteenth century. The upper-end truss has two principals embedded in the dais wall, corbel supported. The lower truss marking the cross passage was of spere form, again shown in the Parker illustration with evidence of an early screen.[6] From the two spere posts, curved braces making a two-centred arch rose to the collar beam supporting the crown-post and trussed-rafter roof.

PLATE 75 Sutton Courtenay 'Abbey': hall interior

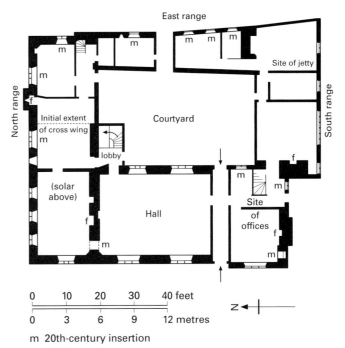

FIGURE 40 Sutton Courtenay 'Abbey': ground plan

The faces of the spere posts towards the body of the hall have moulded capitals supporting braces to the purlins.[7]

The structure marks a development stage from an aisled hall to one totally cleared of posts and consequently created a hall of broad span in relation to its length and height. The character of the roof and the absence of the ogee form in the spere capitals suggest a date between c.1290 and 1320, with the former as most likely. The scale of this hall is notable, so large that its construction by the first of the Courtenays is quite possible, rather than by any ecclesiastical tenant.[8] However, the roof proved extremely heavy and began to spread, necessitating remedial action. In about 1330–40, additional support was given by casing the timber walls with stone at the same time that the windows were brought up-to-date. Surprisingly, none of the trusses was buttressed, either initially or after cladding.

The doorway to the upper cross wing has been stripped out and partly brick rebuilt, leaving only an inner chamfer. The timber-framed lobby may be original, now with a modern replacement stair. The ground floor of this upper wing is a room with a wall cupboard, moulded single cross beam, two windows of trefoiled lights and two with cinquefoiled lights. Though there is evidence that the wing was always on an imposing scale, smaller windows might have been expected in a room in this position. The transomed windows with well-moulded trefoiled heads seemingly date the wing to the late thirteenth century, but they are very grand, possibly moved from the hall in c.1330–40, though one of them is certainly a late Victorian addition.[9] The cinquefoil-light windows are fifteenth-century insertions.

The lobby stair rises to a plain chamfered doorway with two-centred head, now opening into the middle of the north range. Only stripping away the plaster will tell whether it was originally a doorway or not, or whether it has been repositioned, but it is further evidence that the range is late thirteenth century and always extended beyond the line of the hall. This half of the upper floor, now divided into a bedroom, short corridor, and solar, may originally have been one large room or subdivided into an outer and an inner chamber.[10] All rooms on this floor have been ceiled since the mid-nineteenth century. The solar is dominated by two handsome Decorated windows, both transomed with that in the gable wall under a two-centred rear arch and hood mould. Above the two ogee lights is a Flamboyant head composed of central trefoiled lobe and outer mouchettes. The form, similar to the former hall windows, is repeated in the second window but with the head necessarily curtailed by the lower walling, more obvious before the ceiling was inserted.[11] However the rear arch lower than the window head points to it being an insertion. The adjacent bedroom has the reveals of a similar window, not noted (or visible?) by Parker. He also observed that the lintel of the solar fireplace was supported on corbels of ball-flower and twisted stem design,[12] whereas one of the present corbels is a musician, probably fifteenth century, late Victorian inserted.

The remainder of the upper floor of this range is partitioned into a sitting room and a bedroom. The former has exposed framed partition walls, one with a four-centred doorway, and a fireplace with square-headed lintel of late medieval form. Just as the range reflects two building phases, so does the roof. The east end had fallen into such a bad state by 1982 that most of it had to be rebuilt using rescued timbers. The western half retains three unequal bays of a crown-post roof with four-way struts to the trussed-rafter roof, extending over the two rooms with the Decorated windows. It seems to be late thirteenth century[13] but it may even be earlier because of its primitive character.[14] The timbers are unbelievably rough hewn, with no decorative evidence. Their markedly inferior character raises the question whether this roof could ever have been open to the high-quality room(s) below or whether it is a replacement roof copying its predecessor, occasioned by severe racking. This might have occurred when the north range with its equally rough ground-floor timbers was added in the fifteenth century to the earlier cross wing. Timber-framed towards the courtyard, it made use of an existing north wall and would explain why there is no stone gable or supporting wall between the two parts of the range.

The lower cross wing, apparently stone-built in the nineteenth century, is largely timber-framed. It is basically contemporary with the hall, but the roof is post-medieval, while later internal alterations have eradicated any evidence of the former offices or the original character of the chamber above.

The late medieval south range was initially shorter. The jetty that stopped short of the tall corner room, and which became internal when the east range was extended, was removed in 1982. The three ground-floor rooms and the bedrooms have been thoroughly refenestrated in Gothick character. They are likely to have started as offices with staff rooms above, possibly added in the sixteenth century.

As with the north range, the jettied upper floor of the east range is more telling than the ground floor with its 1980s central passage separating the stone base to the north from the framed walling to the south. From the north, the first floor retains an original door-frame with four-centred head, a square timber-framed window with wooden mullions, and a central room with exposed tie beam, wind braces, and post and panel partitioning. A sixteenth-century date is likely. The room open to the roof at the south-east corner was an added kitchen or bakehouse.

The development of Sutton Courtenay 'Abbey' occurred in four key phases. It was probably initiated by the Courtenay family rather than by an ecclesiastical tenant shortly after it passed out of the hands of Abingdon Abbey in 1284. This would have been the work of Sir Hugh Courtenay (d.1292) rather than his son Hugh, who did homage for his lands in 1297, was summoned to parliament as Lord Courtenay in 1299, became earl of Devon in 1335, and died in 1340 (q.v. Tiverton Castle). The work included the quasi-aisled timber-framed hall, with a contemporary stone upper cross wing that projected at the rear, and a timber-framed lower cross wing in line with the hall. In about 1330–40, the hall was modified, stone-faced, and rewindowed as was the solar wing. The latter was extended by the north range in the mid to late fifteenth century, followed by the east range and the linking south range not long after.[15] The result is one of the most attractive medium-sized courtyard houses in central England. In 1461, Thomas Courtenay 6th earl of Devon and a die-hard Lancastrian, was convicted of treason and his lands were confiscated. Henry VII gave the manor to the dean and chapter of St George's Chapel, Windsor Castle, who still hold the living. The house was leased to secular tenants, subject to alterations at the end of the nineteenth century and hard times thereafter, until restored by a charitable organisation in the 1980s.

NOTES
1 J. M. Fletcher, *Sutton Courtenay: Personalities and Places* (1984) unravelled the long-established historiographical confusion of these properties.

Also C. R. J. Currie, *Oxoniensia* 57 (1992) 208–12. The core of the manor house is a mid-fourteenth-century timber-framed hall at right angles to a considerably earlier two-storeyed stone block. The hall retains three arch-braced cruck trusses, but it has been curtailed and floored, and the house so heavily altered, not least in the early twentieth century, that its architectural value is limited. C. Hussey, *Country Life* (May 1931); C. R. J. Currie, *Oxoniensia* 57 (1992) 214–22; J. Musson, *The English Manor House* (1999) 52–8.
2 A. E. Preston, *Berks., Bucks. and Oxon. Arch. Jour.* 25 (1919–20) 23–38, 94–113.
3 Turner and Parker (1853) opp. 272 and 273, note o. The drawing by C. Jewitt opp. 32 shows their truncation to transom level by 1840.
4 *Ibid.* opp. 272 and 32.
5 *Ibid.* 273.
6 *Ibid.* opp. 32.
7 The high crossbars associated with the speres are also shown, while the beams in the form of a St Andrew cross spanning this narrow bay survive *in situ*. Measured drawings given by J. M. Fletcher and P. S. Spokes, *Med. Arch.* 8 (1964) 175, who noted that the form of the spere truss resembled late thirteenth-century work, though the roof was probably a little later. Subsequent work on crown-post roofs suggested a general revision towards the 1290s. *Med. Arch.* 27 (1983) 133.
8 The view preferred by Currie (1992) 233.
9 See plan in Parker (1853) opp. 272.
10 *Ibid.* 274 suggests the former, a room 35 feet by 17 feet.
11 Illustrated by Turner and Parker (1853) opp. 87. Incidentally, this view suggests there was a garderobe off the north-west angle of this room.
12 *Ibid.* 274.
13 Currie (1992) 233 states that it was designed by the same carpenter as the hall roof. Also Fletcher and Spokes, *Med. Arch.* 8 (1964) 174, though they seem to have relied on Jewitt's illustration in Parker which is highly flattering to its condition. They attributed the windows to *c.*1300.
14 This is the opinion of the English Heritage inspector who saw a vestigial capital, identified as that shown at the head of the crown post in Turner and Parker, opp. 87. Despite the considerable dendrochronology research in north Berkshire, the house has not yet been subject to any such examination.
15 Currie proposes a more complex development, suggesting that the north range was an early to mid-thirteenth-century stone building, facing north, centred on a putative cross passage almost in the middle of the present range to the hall. This was subsequently converted into the solar block and reroofed; see (1992) 238–9.

T. H. Turner and J. H. Parker, *Some Account of Domestic Architecture in England*, II (1853) 32, 174, 272–4
VCH, *Berkshire*, IV (1924) 371–3
C. R. J. Currie, *Oxoniensia* 57 (1992) 222–40

SWALCLIFFE MANOR HOUSE, Oxfordshire

This is a rectorial house, not the house of the manor of Swalcliffe which lay on the site of Swalcliffe Park, now an eighteenth- and nineteenth-century building. Built of the ferruginous limestone which is so characteristic of the area, with stone slates, it follows the H-shaped plan of a central hall separating the two-storeyed lower and upper chamber blocks. The house was built during the mid-thirteenth century, with the hall remodelled in the late fourteenth century and a floor inserted towards the close of the sixteenth century.

The hall and cross passage may retain the core of early stone walls but the present buttressed form reflects the late fourteenth-century

PLATE 76 Swalcliffe Manor House: from the south

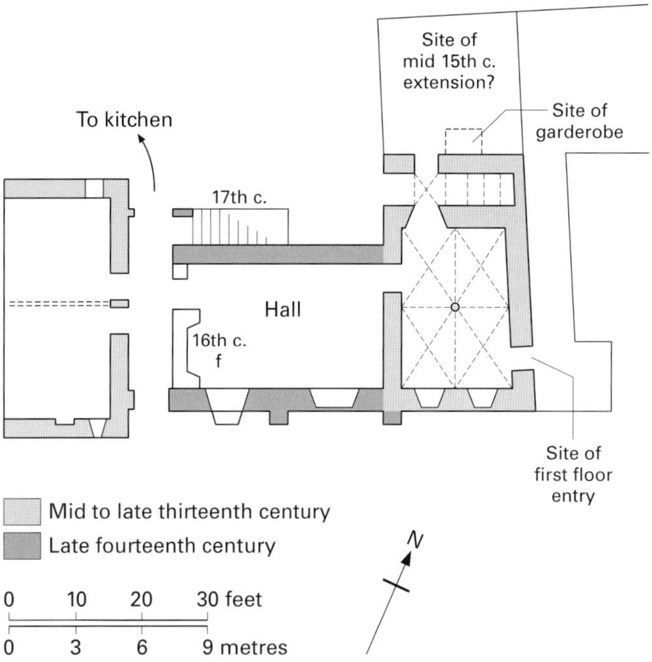

FIGURE 41 Swalcliffe Manor House: ground plan

(figure labels) Site of mid 15th c. extension? · Site of garderobe · To kitchen · 17th c. · Hall · 16th c. f · Site of first floor entry

Mid to late thirteenth century
Late fourteenth century

0 10 20 30 feet
0 3 6 9 metres

N

remodelling.[1] Both cross-passage entries, without porch protection, are identical with chamfered jambs and two-centred head with hollow orders in two planes, and a hood with face stops (missing on the north side). Approximately 39 feet by 20 feet, this formerly three-bay hall is fenestrated on the east side only, with a blank wall opposite supporting a roughly built staircase against its outer face. It is likely that there were initially two opposing windows but they were infilled when the floor was inserted and the stone fireplace wall added, backing on to the cross passage. The lower splays of the two fourteenth-century windows survive to nineteenth-century frames, cut back except for one which retains its polygonal rear arch moulding (as in the hall dais window at Broughton Castle). The two upper rooms and broad corridor betray no pre-Reformation work, nor does the roof rebuilt in the late sixteenth century.

The cross-passage wall common to the offices and chamber block is in good condition, with conjoined mid-thirteenth-century doorways in the centre of the wall with two-centred heads, labels, and inserted stops. The buttery and pantry have been converted into a single room of recent character, retaining a single lancet with moulded head and plain stops overlooking the front approach. The remainder of the block was thoroughly remodelled and partially rebuilt in the early nineteenth century. There is no evidence of the approach to the upper floor, though it was probably by external stair as in the case of the upper block, while the kitchen would have lain beyond the further cross-passage doorway.

The upper chamber block retains more of its original character. The ground floor consists of a vaulted chamber, approached from the upper end of the hall, with central pillar and four bays of quadripartite vaulting. The room has been badly treated, with all wall shafts replaced with corbel supports in the corners and roughly built columns in the middle of each side. The two thirteenth-century style windows are similarly crude replacements of earlier

openings. The vaulted ribs are single-chamfered, creating a vaulted undercroft similar in form to those at Broughton Castle, 2 miles away. There are no bosses. A 5 foot wide opening in the west wall with acute head and base stops opens into a 3 foot wide corridor, parallel with the end wall, spanned by chamfered cross arches and intersecting ribs astride the small entry lobby. It might be assumed that this was a stair approach, except there is no rise in the ground level, the stair lay elsewhere, and the form replicates the ground-floor passages at Broughton Castle.

The upper chamber is divided into bedrooms, corridors, and offices, but it retains two doorways, though no early window evidence and a roof of uncertain date.[2] The principal doorway is the entry from an outer stair in the north-east corner with concave jambs, two-centred head, and plain hood. It is now approached from its inner face into a room built against the wall. The plainer doorway in the middle of the west wall with higher rear arch opened into a now displaced garderobe.

This house was a substantial one, of common plan with two office doorways, vaulted undercroft, and solar doorways of mid to late thirteenth-century form with no obvious difference between the forms.[3] The narrow ground-floor passage with its basic vaulting betrays the influence of the Broughtons' grander house nearby, attributed to the close of the century, but its function at Swalcliffe is unclear. The hall was remodelled after bishop Wykeham of Winchester had given the property to New College, Oxford in 1381 as part of the endowment for his foundation, and the college held it until the later twentieth century. The carpenter John Jylkes was employed by the college to work on the hall and stables in 1397–8[4] and the hall windows may be associated with that work. The warden and some fellows of New College visited Swalcliffe four times in 1403–4 to supervise further reorganisation of the grange, and a great gate was added seven years later when farm buildings were

179

being developed round a courtyard.[5] John Jylkes was again working on the chambers and a chapel at Swalcliffe in 1432–3.[6] In 1444–5, a subsequent college carpenter, John Wiltshire, bought timber for the south chamber, and in 1448–9, built a chamber at the west end of the great chamber.[7]

NOTES

1 Though there are building lines between the hall and end blocks, an initial timber-framed hall as suggested by Wood (1950) 59 is unlikely in such a predominantly stone area. Wood's text is followed by Wood-Jones (1963) 27 and VCH, X (1972) 238.
2 M. R. Bismanis, *The Medieval English Domestic Timber Roof* (1987) 131, 133.
3 It is possible to construct a scenario of a mid-thirteenth-century lower block with hall, subsequently extended by a late thirteenth-century upper block, but the form of the solar doorways is against that.
4 J. Harvey, *Eng. Med. Arch.* (2nd edn 1984) 165.
5 VCH, X (1972) 238. The ten-bay buttressed barn immediately west of the manor is the finest, architecturally, in the county. With two gabled porches and a cruck-truss roof, it was erected by New College in 1402–6. J. T. Munby and J. M. Steane, *Oxoniensia* 60 (1995) 333–78. A seven-bay lesser barn, converted to housing in 1990, was also part of this rectorial farm complex.
6 J. Harvey, *Eng. Med. Arch.* (2nd edn 1984) 165.
7 *Ibid.* 335–6. It was probably on the site of the seventeenth-century extension that was used as a kitchen until 1996.

M. Wood, *Thirteenth-Century Domestic Architecture in England, Arch. Jour.* 105, Supplement (1950) 59
R. Wood-Jones, *Traditional Domestic Architecture of the Banbury Region* (1963) 25–8
VCH, *Oxfordshire*, X (1972) 237–8

THAME PARK, Oxfordshire

The Palladian mansion built in about 1745 by William Smith of Warwick for 6th Viscount Wenman (d.1760) incorporated two ranges of Thame Abbey. They are two-storeyed, stretching eastwards from the rear of the mansion which towers above them, with the fourth side of the rear court left open. One range was used for offices and staff quarters in an extension to the eighteenth-century house kitchen. The former abbot's lodgings in the other wing of sun-facing rooms was remodelled internally for Georgian occupation. The contrast between the commanding west frontage of the mansion and the elongated late medieval south range, between Georgian restraint and Gothic informality in the same parkland setting, is one of the dramatic contrasts in English architecture. It is as striking as that between King's College chapel and the Senate House at Cambridge, but the contrast also highlights the continuity of English country life under two totally different leaders of society.

The Cistercian abbey of Thame, founded by bishop Alexander of Lincoln in about 1139, was a large one, though the site has never been properly excavated. The church lay north of the mansion house. It was consecrated in 1145, and served an abbey that was reported in the early sixteenth century to be the same size as that at Furness. A superficial examination by William Twopenny in about 1840 revealed fourteen nave piers, to give an estimated size of 230 feet by 70 feet with a 45 feet lady chapel at the east end.[1] The surviving north wing looks like part of a cloister range with recently

revealed later twelfth-century arcaded bays and a contemporary roof to the upper area.[2] However, it is by no means certain that the open area between the two ranges was part of the cloister garth, for the north range seems to have been an independent wing and the abbot's lodging is without the slightest claustral evidence.[3]

This splendid residential unit from the close of the middle ages is one of the largest and most ornate of monastic lodgings, but its significance also lies in the high quality of its internal decoration. This work is by Robert King, who became the last abbot of Thame in 1530 and was appointed the first bishop of Oxford shortly after the abbey's dissolution in 1539. Some of the building work has been attributed to him, but the development of the range is more complex and was undertaken in three or four stages, clarified in 1998 when the interior plaster was stripped back to the bare walls.

The range is 105 feet long with a multi-windowed south-facing frontage and blank rear wall. It terminates in a three-storey tower built in front of the south-east corner. The roof has two mismatched steep pitches, rising to about the same height as the embattled tower. The frontage is interrupted midway by a two-storeyed bay window either side a newel turret, with the slight change in roof pitch marking the internal division of the range into a greater and lesser room at both levels. The highly attractive irregular façade with its bold terminal is enhanced by the use of warm-toned local limestone, giving it a unity which belies its development. Furthermore, the roof is entirely a post-medieval replacement, as is most of the flooring, while the windows were subject to an extensive but careful restoration in about 1920.

Whatever existed on the site before the fifteenth century was pulled down and the range built anew without recourse to earlier materials or decorative work. It was developed in two parts, marked by a shorter western half about 19 feet wide internally, and a longer eastern half about 23 feet wide. The north wall has been heavily rebuilt,[4] with the eastern part thinned by at least a foot internally, but the opposing wall stands 3 feet forward of the remainder, with the newel concealing this difference in the south building line. The west end abuts the later mansion and has been incorporated in it, while most of the north wall facing the twelfth-century range was blind until the Palladian doorcase and windows were inserted. However, a ground-floor doorway 5 feet wide survives towards the south-east corner of the range, with hollow-chamfered jambs, four-centred head with blind quatrefoil spandrels, and a square hood. This was the principal entry to the eastern ground floor, redundant when the three-storeyed tower was added against it but still capable of being used in reverse as the entry to the ground-floor tower room. As it is of later-fifteenth century date, the two-part range and the added tower betray a three-phase development.

Whatever fenestration existed was replaced in the early sixteenth century with windows of uncusped lights with blank spandrels under square hoods. They are of a form unlikely to be earlier than the years close to 1500[5] and are apparently common throughout the range. The two–three–two lights of both bays are separated by mini buttresses with modified windows below and original above with plain internal jambs. The second bay is more ornate, with a decorative frieze at the head of the lower window, pinnacled heads to the mini buttresses, and the royal coat of arms with supporters under a crown between the two string courses separating the upper from the lower window. The polygonal newel turret has a single mid string course and tiny lights to the stair. Later changes to this front-

PLATE 77 Thame Park: from the south-west (1904)

age include replacing some of the ground-floor windows in the late sixteenth century with square-headed mullioned lights, and subsequently lowering the first window and bay almost to the ground.[6] At the same time, two mid-eighteenth-century garden doorways were inserted under earlier windows, with that towards the tower reduced from three to two lights. The tower repeats the four-light windows at first- and second-floor level but the west face has a shallow two-storeyed oriel of one–three–one lights, with the royal coat of arms under the lower window with a rose on each side.

The added tower and higher newel, not bonded to the wall and with curtailed string courses, almost crush the very similar windows in the body of the range. And while the tower is an obvious late development, examination of the bay windows and central newel reveals that they are also additions with features in common with the tower. The latter has a single plinth, and the bays and newel have a double plinth which is not continued along the body of the range. They have the same gargoyle heads and embattled parapet as the tower and higher newel, while the range lacks both. Internally, the stripped walls confirmed that the bays and newel were not bonded to the range and revealed cracks where they are

pulling away from the wall, particularly at first-floor level. The thinness of the newel stonework is also apparent, with poor-quality construction allowing daylight between the stones (1998). When the bays were inserted, it was necessary to strengthen the now weakened wall with an added buttress. The windows in this wing, therefore, are of two phases – those in the body of the range, and those of the added tower and bays – but the modest differences, only apparent internally, indicate that the phases were close together.

Internally, the first ground-floor room, 40 feet long, was divided in the mid-eighteenth century by a screen into a lobby and main room at the same time that William Smith blocked an early door and an inserted window in the west end wall. The body of the room with its eighteenth-century ceiling and fireplace is flanked by a revealed early Tudor doorway and the jamb of a large late sixteenth-century window.

The second room, 61 feet long, has an essentially eighteenth-century brick north wall with doorcase, fireplace, window insertions, and replacement ceiling beams. The newel entry has double hollow jambs, the south-facing lights have squared jambs, and the two end windows are entirely 1995 renewals.

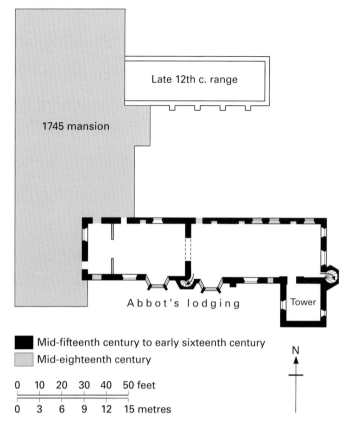

Late 12th c. range

1745 mansion

A b b o t ' s   l o d g i n g   Tower

■ Mid-fifteenth century to early sixteenth century

▨ Mid-eighteenth century

N

0   10   20   30   40   50 feet

0   3   6   9   12   15 metres

FIGURE 42 Thame Park: abbot's lodging, ground plan

The first of the upper rooms has been converted into a library with a nineteenth-century fireplace and Jacobean-style panelling, and mid-twentieth-century bookcases. The boarded ceiling is original, divided into three parts by two cross beams with a central rose and leaf boss. Each part is crossed by narrow ribs to create a repeated diamond pattern with shields at the intersections. The first part by the entry is a Georgian copy, but the other two are early sixteenth-century work added by Robertus King, whose name is spelt out in the middle of the decorative plaster frieze of vine trails and ornament along the north wall.[7] The west wall of this room stands on the line of the Gothick division below, cutting off the end section which was subsumed into the mansion in the eighteenth century and has recently been converted into a bathroom.

The stone partition of the second chamber retains the line of the original lower-pitched roof below the added gable head which supports the present late sixteenth-century structure. This enabled attic rooms to be created, lit by a contemporary window in the roughly treated end wall, with forced entries from the tower newel into this and the attic floor.[8] None of the original trusses remains, though some wind braces were reused. The north wall retains evidence of eighteenth-century brick windows, but an original fireplace survives in the end wall with a high mantel and a blank shield at each end of the low four-centred fireplace head. The two- and four-light windows in the south wall have modest roll-moulded jambs.

The tower ground floor is approached from the rear side of the 5 feet wide later fifteenth-century doorway with its decorated front

facing into a room with original chamfered cross beams. The first-floor room, 17 feet by 16 feet, is the well-known early Tudor chamber with plain-chamfered doorway, fireplace, and a second doorway hidden behind the panelling to a lost garderobe, marked externally by the abruptly cut string course. The room is lit by the five-light oriel and four-light south window. The awkward approach by two steps from the body of the range is again indicative of the tower's late development.

However, the glory of this chamber is the sequence of decoration, beginning with the untouched linenfold panelling which encircles the room, with the newel entry protected by one of the earliest surviving internal porches in England. Above the panelling is a line of oblong panels with roundels enclosing heads, except on the fireplace wall where they are of heraldic form, all surrounded by early Renaissance filigree patterns of arabesques, mermaids, and scrolls. The more narrow frieze above of cherubs and leaves has the initials RK for Robertus King.[9] The two cross beams spanning the damaged ribbed ceiling are also plaster-embellished. All this decoration, originally coloured and gilded, is now painted white against a sea-blue background. It is workmanship of the highest quality.[10]

The broad newel continues to the second-floor chamber which repeats the fenestration and fireplace position of the room below, but with an external cross loop in place of the garderobe. The two cross beams have applied wooden moulding, but this plain plastered room is otherwise bare. The newel rises a stage further above the low-pitched roof.

In sum, the body of the range is of two builds of the second half and close of the fifteenth century, and was almost certainly purposed for residential use. The ornate 5 foot wide doorway could be as late as the early sixteenth century (though I have reservations about this) contemporary with the refenestration of the range after about 1500 when windows with uncusped lights and roll-moulded internal jambs were inserted. Shortly afterwards, the tower was added against the range, at the same time as the resplendent bay windows and central newel were inserted, all lit by windows with concave internal jambs.[11] This work is probably of between 1510 and the early 1520s, attributable to abbot John Warren (1509–29), whose expensive and florid lifestyle called down the wrath of bishop Longland of Lincoln who sought to curtail it.[12] These last additions show no sign of any early Renaissance decoration such as embellished abbot Vyntoner's oriel window of 1527 at St Osyth Priory. Such work is confined to the first-floor interiors created for the last abbot, Robert King, after his appointment in 1530, and who surrendered the abbey nine years later to his brother's brother-in-law. Subsequent alterations included raising the roof in the late sixteenth century when attics were inserted, mid-eighteenth-century internal remodelling, a major restoration in 1920, and a further one during the last years of the twentieth century.

The original layout of this range is entirely speculative. It might be presumed on the decorative evidence that the abbot's apartments lay entirely at first-floor level, but there is no wall, ceiling, or roof evidence to suggest the layout at either level outside the single stone division. If the abbot's hall was open to the roof, then it can only have been at the upper level and in the eastern part of the range, but there is no kitchen or oratory evidence, nor is the point of entry obvious at either level. The ground floor may have been used for guests, and if the upper floor was limited to the abbot, its approach was possibly from a stair outside the line of the north wall close to the revealed ground-floor Tudor doorway. This would open into a private dining room (the Robert King ceiled chamber) with the offices through the entry in the west wall to the area that has been converted into a bathroom. The second chamber was almost certainly divided into the abbot's privy and inner chamber, with the newel and more elaborate bay window with the royal coat of arms serving the first. The inner room benefitted from the end-wall fireplace and three-light window with immediate access to the abbot's study and retiring room above. What is indisputable is that these lodgings point to the highest standards of domestic comfort, with the study displaying as much concern for excluding draughts by an internal porch as for showing off the abbot's personal heraldry alongside that of important local families, as in a leading secular household.

Like Battle Abbey, Forde Abbey, Wenlock Priory, and Whatton Priory, Thame Park retains one of the best-preserved and relatively complete examples of a late lodging of a monastic head, even if we are not clear about its precise internal layout. Developed during Yorkist and early Tudor rule, it follows the pattern of many such houses in adding a tower to the earlier facilities as at Newstead, Hailes Abbey, and Norton Priory. But equally distinctive are the further bays and newel which help to create an enfilade of high-status apartments of considerable architectural presence, irrespective of the two sumptuously decorated early Renaissance interiors. Abbots and priors were leading an increasingly secular life, little different in property ownership, estate management, and domestic lifestyle from that of any lay patron. Such heads were rivalling courtiers and magnates in the magnificence of their apartments, so that the Thame Park frontage parallels the grander contemporary one by the duke of Buckingham at Thornbury Castle. But Thame is also important because while the structural additions were backward-looking – a late fling of Gothic forms – the internal decoration was extremely progressive, as much as in any comparable secular survival.

NOTES

1 VCH, VII (1962) 169.

2 *South Midlands Archaeology* 17 (1987) 72–5; *Vern. Arch.* 24 (1993) 41–2.

3 Viscount Wenman pulled down several low, straggling buildings, remnants of the abbey, before erecting his new mansion at right angles to the abbot's lodging. The new mansion is very similar to that built at the same time for Sir John Dashwood, Wenman's second cousin, at Kirtlington.

4 Not so extensively as shown on the plan in VCH, VII (1962) 168. There is no building line in the middle of its outer face, cleaned and repointed in 1985 when the 1939 corridor against it was removed.

5 Uncusped lights were first used at Eton College (1440s) and Ockwells Manor (1450s) and later in the century at Great Chalfield Manor (1478–85) and Hatfield Palace (1479–86). The form became popular in central England during the early years of the new century, as at Horham Hall (*c*.1502–20), Pooley Hall (*c*.1509), and Fawsley Hall (*c*.1510). The form was used in combination with cusped lights at Thornbury Castle (*c*.1510–21) and Forde Abbey (*c*.1521–8).

6 Also the matching window near the tower until about 1920.

7 The frieze is similar to work formerly at Notley Abbey, 3 miles away, where the name of the last abbot Richard Rydge (1529–39) occurs in similar lettering in the woodwork. It has been transferred to Weston Manor, Oxfordshire, see page 124 n. 6.

8 The roof over the first-floor chamber was raised in the mid-eighteenth century using a brick infill between the two pitches, and heightening part of the south-facing wall.

9 F. G. Lee, *The History . . . of Thame* (1883) and H. A. Tipping, *Country Life* (July 1909), repeated in Tipping (1924) interpreted the damaged K as an R for Robertus Reonensis, titular bishop of Rheon, a very doubtful attribution. For the interpretation of the coat of arms, Godfrey (1929) 64–8.

10 Similar workmanship occurs at Nether Winchendon House, a timber-framed house initially owned by Notley Abbey until 1527 when it was leased to Sir John Daunce (d.1543), who remodelled it. The parlour has linenfold panelling below a plaster frieze of early Renaissance decoration, very similar to that at Thame in style and date. Royal craftsmen have been suggested for the work at Nether Winchendon.

11 The square internal jambs of the windows in both ground-floor rooms and the first of the upper rooms are twentieth-century restorations. For those of 1920, see *The Architectural Review* 51 (Jan. 1922) 17–19.

12 The bishop complained to the head of the Cistercian order in England in 1525 about the laxity, immense debts, and ruined buildings at Thame, while abbot Warren lived in expensive style. The replies to the charges were evasive and insincere. VCH, *Oxfordshire*, II (1907) 84–5.

F. G. Lee, *Building News* (1888) 455–7

H. A. Tipping, *English Homes* Period 2, I (1924) 253–60

W. H. Godfrey, *Arch. Jour.* 86 (1929) 59–68

A. Oswald, *Country Life* (Nov. 1957)

VCH, *Oxfordshire*, VII (1962) 168–170

THORNBURY CASTLE, Gloucestershire

The Stafford family rose above their west Midland prosperity during Edward III's reign with their acquisition of Thornbury as part of the extensive Audley inheritance of 1343. The hall and chapel on the site were retained when Edward, 3rd duke of Buckingham began extensive repairs to the earlier buildings in 1507–8 prior to developing a large double-courtyard castle.[1] He obtained a licence to crenellate his new mansion in July 1510:[2] the principal gateway is dated 1511 and the south range chimneys 1514. Work temporarily ceased in 1519 to meet Buckingham's more pressing financial needs arising from a royal visit to Penshurst, his daughter's wedding, and his display at the Field of the Cloth of Gold. The duke spent the next year and a half at Thornbury in a huff from courtier politics[3] but building recommenced early in 1521 with the purpose of completing the gatehouse range and the remainder of the outer court.[4] All activity ceased immediately with the duke's execution in May of that year. A survey was made immediately after the castle's confiscation[5] but the incomplete castle was capable of occupation by Mary Tudor during the years of her childhood and by Henry VIII and Anne Boleyn in 1535. The property was returned to the Stafford family in 1554 but it became too expensive to maintain, as the survey of 1583 reveals,[6] and decay set in. Thornbury Castle is a classic example of the palace-fortress concept, spanning the divide between the more military-like castle at Raglan half a century earlier with the open palace style maturing under Henry VIII.

THE BUILDINGS

As at Kirby Muxloe, the castle's development was caught at the stage it had reached by the owner's execution and it was little touched thereafter. Partial destruction of the inner courtyard has since taken place, while the outer court stands in ruined abandonment. One gate-tower and the southern part of the principal entrance range

PLATE 78 Thornbury Castle: entrance frontage

were roofed and rehabilitated in the 1720s, the great south-west tower in 1809–11, and the many-windowed south range was sensitively restored by Salvin in 1854–5.[7] The occupiable portion of the castle has been used as a hotel since 1966.

The outer court, 315 feet by 245 feet, covers nearly 2½ acres. In plan, two-storeyed ranges of lodgings and stables were erected round three sides of the rectangle, with the entrance frontage to the inner court filling the fourth. Two ranges remain in ruin, with projecting stair and garderobe turrets, a portcullis-protected gateway in the middle of the north side, and gun ports in the north-west bastion (pl. 85). The grassed south side on the site of the great stable is currently used as the approach to the castle.

Access to the inner court, 120 feet by 110 feet, was through the west range with its dominating six towers. It was only partly completed. The polygonal south-west tower with machicolated parapet was fully finished together with the intermediate turret. The towered entrance gate and north end of the range did not progress above their present levels. The gateway was left without its proposed entrance vaulting and first-floor oriel, while the north-west end lacks the imposing corner tower planned. There were cross loops at ground level and two-light cinquefoil windows above. The steward occupied the upper rooms immediately south of the gate, with supplementary rooms for the duchess' staff below and porters' rooms north of the passageway.

The north range held the larders, bakehouse, and boiling house with lodgings above, terminating in the great kitchen and privy kitchen. The range had been completed by 1521 but only partially stands, for it has been the most robbed of all the courtyard stone structures.

The east range opposite the entrance contained the great hall and chamber block, 'all of the old building and of an homely fashion', with the chapel to the rear.[8] The hall and chamber block above the services were certainly timber-framed, and it was presumably intended to replace them with more splendid structures until the plan was aborted by the duke's sudden demise. A range north of the

great hall, linked to Buckingham's private apartments and overlooking its own garden, was probably used as guest chambers, in all likelihood built by Jasper Tudor between 1485 and 1495 when he died at Thornbury.[9] All the remains on this side of the court had been pulled down by 1732 when the standing stone ruins were engraved by Buck (pl. 8). The hall foundations were recovered by excavation in 1982.

The south range, roofed in 1514, was 'fully fynished with curious workes and stately loggings' which so impressed the commissioners in 1521. Tall, but only two storeys high though retaining its original embattled parapet, this 150 foot frontage is dominated by three full-height bay windows to differing plans, made more voluptuous at the upper stage. Each bay was elaborated with strong vertical lines, many cusped lights and a bevy of panes – the cinquefoil bay holding 720 panes of curved glass[10] (pl. 10). This range contained the parallel apartments of the duke and duchess, with those of the duchess on the ground floor and the duke's suite above to a more enriched standard. In both cases, the suites consisted of three large chambers in the body of the range with their bedchambers in the south-west tower. The duke's suite was supplemented by a lobby or antechamber before his great chamber at the head of the stair from the hall dais, and a privy or jewel chamber. The 1521 survey shows that the two floors above the bedchambers in the south-west tower were used for private and estate papers rather than accommodation.[11]

GARDENS AND PARK

The walled privy garden (the 'proper gardeyn' in the 1521 survey) between the south range and the churchyard is a rare early Tudor survival. The enclosure embattled on three sides had a ground-floor loggia and a 'goodly galery' at first-floor level built of 'tymbre covered with slate'. The gallery could be approached from rooms at either end of the duke's private apartments and had windows in the west wall and oriels in the south wall. A now destroyed extension led to a pew by the north chancel window in the adjacent parish church. It was inspired by the timber loggia and framed upper

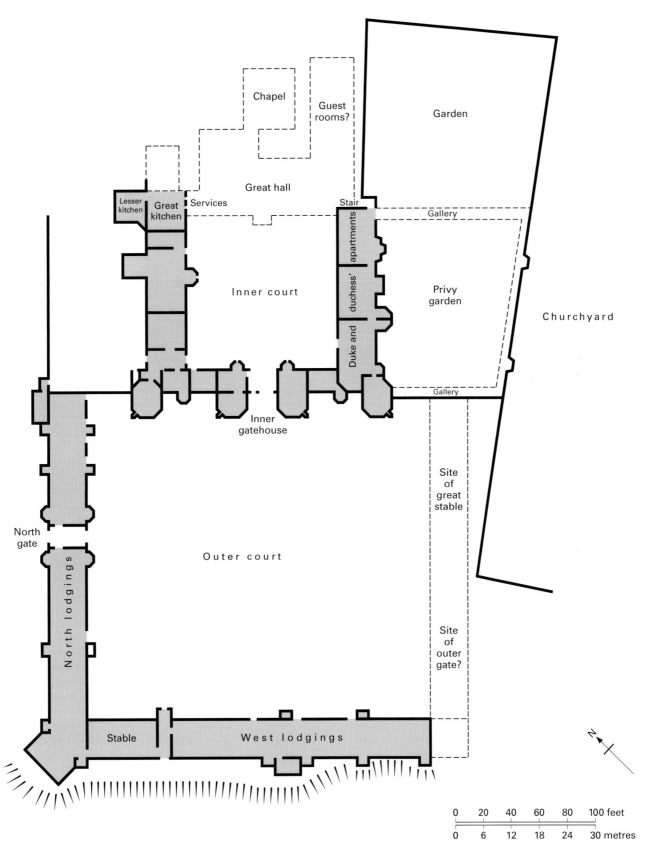

Chapel

Guest rooms?

Garden

Great hall

Lesser kitchen

Great kitchen

Services

Stair

Gallery

apartments

Inner court

duchess'

Privy garden

Churchyard

Duke and

Inner gatehouse

Gallery

North gate

Site of great stable

North lodgings

Outer court

Site of outer gate?

Stable

West lodgings

0	20	40	60	80	100 feet
0	6	12	18	24	30 metres

FIGURE 43 Thornbury Castle: site plan

gallery at Richmond Palace built for Henry VII in 1502 (rebuilt 1506) which similarly backed on to the walls round the privy garden with private apartments access. Excavations in 1992 revealed that Tudor garden features still survive 3 feet below the present surface and it is likely that traces of this loggia and gallery would also be found.

There was a much larger 'goodly gardeyn to walke ynn' (1583 survey) east of the privy garden. The orchard north of the hall and chapel had covered alleys to protect people from the sun or the rain, planted with hazel and whitethorn bushes. Attempts in the 1970s to grow vines within the castle grounds, as in early Tudor times, proved a failure.

Buckingham's crenellation licence also permitted him to enclose a park of 1,000 acres, supplemented in 1517 by a second licence for a further 500 acres. To achieve his 'fayre parke hard by the castle', 4 miles in circumference and stocked with 700 deer, he had no compunction in refusing to compensate any dispossessed tenants.[12]

POLITICAL SIGNIFICANCE

Though he had recently been appointed virtual ruler of Wales for life by Richard III, the family's Lancastrian sympathies encouraged Henry, 2nd duke of Buckingham to join a plot in favour of Henry Tudor, prompting swift execution for his disloyalty (1483). Two years later, Henry VII restored the family estates and titles to the duke's seven-year-old son, who subsequently earned high favour with Henry VIII during the first ten years of his reign. However, his high-born descent encouraged an already haughty and wealthy magnate to regard himself as a possible successor to the king, who sought to expunge any such notion.[13] He was summoned to London to answer trumped-up charges by discontented staff, including his chancellor and confessor, and was summarily executed. In any case, the duke had been declining in the king's favour for the past two years while Wolsey had quietly encouraged his extravagant lifestyle and conspicuous display at the Field of the Cloth of Gold to the dual end of irritating the king and increasing his debts that had brought work to a halt on the castle.[14]

Edward had developed Thornbury rather than his castles at Brecon and Newport in south-east Wales, Stafford and Maxstoke in the west Midlands, or Tonbridge and his manor houses at Penshurst, or Writtle near London because his Gloucestershire estate was poised midway between two key areas of his patrimony in Wales and the Midlands.[15] The River Severn did not unduly hinder communication. The castle's outer gate faced its broad waters 2 miles away, and a linking canal, possibly using the creek from the Severn to Thornbury mentioned by Leland, seems to have been contemplated and begun.[16] Nor was Thornbury a difficult journey from London, and the manor had become an agriculturally rich one. Thornbury Castle was intended and built to a size which enabled it to be Stafford's prime estate and administrative centre and a potential power-base. It was designed as a visual expression of his patronage, and provided sufficient accommodation for a household which numbered over 500 personal and support staff, retainers, and servants and therefore became the focus of a large social community. It was also the spectacular residence for his family and their guests and a retreat from court factions.

Buckingham's decision at the close of 1520 to seek royal permission to raise an armed bodyguard so that he could visit his Welsh lordships, no matter how realistic and financially necessary, was

extremely ill-judged and was refused. It had fostered the suspicion at court that he was intent on fomenting rebellious activities as his father had done. That Thornbury Castle could now accommodate such a factious force in lodging ranges greater in extent than almost anywhere else exacerbated the threat that his pride, wealth, and territorial power seemingly posed to the established order, and he paid the penalty.

ARCHITECTURAL SIGNIFICANCE

Had Thornbury Castle been completed, it would have been one of the largest and finest palaces in a period notable for their proliferation. Even in its present state, the remains are of outstanding national importance, for Thornbury is as much an expression of Buckingham's character and aspirations as the palaces of Henry VIII or those of Wolsey. Thornbury is usually compared with the latter before its royal enhancement (1515–26) but it may be more validly compared with a number of earlier residences.

Buckingham's work was much influenced by contemporary royal palaces, particularly Richmond (1497–1501). The towered entrance frontage reflected the river frontages at Richmond and Greenwich (1500–1) which had incorporated massive fifteenth-century tower-houses in the royal work.[17] The siting of the duke's residential range above that of the duchess had similarly been adopted at Richmond (but not Bridewell 1510–23) and by Edward IV at Nottingham Castle (1463–78). The two-tiered galleries enclosing the perimeter of the privy garden also reflected a form initiated at Richmond with direct access at both levels from the private apartments. These aspects suggest that Thornbury was among the most up-to-date residences in the country, but other elements show that it was more backward-looking, for Buckingham was unable to give up a century-old aristocratic tradition of fortress-like residences with an exemplar not far from Gloucestershire. In its conception and development, Thornbury is as much a regularised Raglan Castle (c.1455–69) as an open-windowed Henrician palace.

The surveyors who visited the castle after Buckingham's execution could not decide whether Thornbury was a castle or a manor house and used both terms. Later writers are equally divided over its military significance. Simpson, Stone, Platt, and Hawkyard[18] rate it more highly than McFarlane, Girouard, Thompson, and Cathcart-King.[19] It was fortress-like externally with a low but defendable base court, large enough to be an assembly ground, with bastions, gun ports, and moated protection on the two approach sides. An array of six towers dominated the entry range to the inner court – two corner bastions, two intermediate towers, and twin gateway towers. Rising one storey above the remainder of the range, the four principal towers were crowned with embattled machicolated parapets owing much to those at Raglan Castle. The effect was heightened by a windowless ground floor throughout the range except for crosslet loops, two gun ports by the entrance, and a portcullis.[20] Thornbury was not a fortress but it was capable of being a defendable residence.

The domesticated south front which belies this fortress-like statement could not be seen in the approach from the west and was partly concealed by the privy garden wall and church to the east. This many-windowed range is an architectural tour-de-force and a classic of its time, with windows surpassing contemporary work at Windsor Castle and the apsidal bays of Henry VII's chapel at

PLATE 79 Thornbury Castle: garden frontage

Westminster Abbey. Yet in its domestic planning, Thornbury was following the long-established pattern of horizontal unitary occupation, directly accessed from the courtyard or from protruding stair turrets, and with the status of the occupant determining chamber size and facilities such as fireplaces and garderobes. Thornbury had not developed far from the accommodation standards at Raglan and Sudeley castles half a century earlier, though it followed the latter's more regularised double courtyard plan.

The castle displays a progressive approach and elevation development from the low outer gate to the taller ranges of the inner court with the hall sited on its far side. Similar practices had been adopted in the mid-fifteenth-century palace-mansions at Wingfield and Sudeley. This effect was heightened at Thornbury by the employment of contrasting building materials. A coarse local stone with ashlar dressings was used for the outer court while Cotswold stone of exceptionally fine quality was chosen for the inner court. The family apartments were distinguished further by contrasting brick chimneys, while the earlier hall, service and chamber block, and chapel were timber-framed. Enlargement or replacement was probably Buckingham's long-term intention, but not necessarily in Cotswold stone. The roofs were covered with Devon slates.

Like the lodgings at Wingfield, those at Thornbury reflected dif-

fering levels of society. The two lodging ranges round the outer court were two-storeyed above a low basement used for storage and cesspit clearance access. Those of the highest standard (and the best preserved) were east of the north gate. The five lodgings, approximately 20 feet square, were well windowed, with individual or paired stair access, fireplace, and garderobe. Those west of the gate were much larger, two rooms on each floor without fireplaces. A stable at the angle separated the north range from the larger communal lodgings on the west front, poorly built and more ruined.

As at Fotheringhay, Tattershall, and Warkworth, Buckingham planned to found a college of priests next to the church at Thornbury. He obtained such a licence in 1514 but though his chapel held the twenty-two stalls numbered in his foundation, it is likely that a separate establishment was intended but never begun.

Buckingham was out of step with the political tune of the time, for he failed to appreciate that the crown was as intent on curbing the power of the aristocracy as it was on preventing it from playing any significant role in affairs of state. Thornbury Castle was similarly out of key, a transitional building with private apartments and gardens no less splendid than those of the crown, but the remainder of the castle looked to a past that the duke was neither willing nor able to forego.

187

A SOCIAL AND ADMINISTRATIVE CENTRE

Thornbury Castle provided the backcloth to Buckingham's position in society. The scrolled inscription above the inner gate proclaimed his standing; supported by the ducal motto, garter enclosed arms, and his emblems. His own apartments were encrusted with emblematic carvings and reliefs across doorway jambs, chimney pieces, and window splays, as well as spandrels and dripstones. The glazed windows were probably and the floor tiles were certainly embellished with mottoes and badges,[21] while the range was surmounted by gargoyles and elaborately moulded chimneys. His rooms are known to have been tapestry hung. The castle was meant to be as impressive as his table, his personal display, and his love of ceremony.

Details about the household Buckingham maintained rival those given in the contemporary household books of the 5th earl of Northumberland,[22] for historians increasingly appreciate that the household state that such aristocrats kept was not senseless extravagance but an accepted and necessary state of social standing and visual display if they were to maintain the respect and reputation deemed appropriate to their position.

Buckingham kept house on the grandest scale: 519 persons were present at his epiphany feast in January 1508 and 400 sat down to supper on the same day. Leading guests brought their own guests to enjoy the sumptuous feast. Trumpeters, minstrels, waits, and players added to the festivities, when 521 quarts of ale were consumed, and vast amounts of beef as well as fresh poultry and game. Yet this feast day took place in the old manor house at Thornbury and not in the present spectacular edifice. Such extravagance might look to us as baronial excess but as K. B. McFarlane pointed out, the total cost was just over £13 by a host whose net landed income was £4,906 in 1521.[23] Furthermore, Buckingham was fastidious in supervising his accounts, kept a close check on the financial performance of his officials, assiduously practised efficient estate management, and exploited all available sources of revenue.[24]

Nine household books survive for the 3rd duke of Buckingham recording a wealth of household details.[25] In 1508–9, 150 staff were resident at the personal service of the duke, 130 at a point between 1511 and 1514, and 148 in 1521. Eighty-six were assigned to the duchess in the 1511–14 record.[26] In 1517 there were forty-six personal attendants, including three gentlemen ushers and five valet ushers who guarded Buckingham's privacy and controlled those admitted to his presence. The duchess had four personal servants, and their son a schoolmaster, master valet, chamberer, and groom responsible for his robes.[27]

This permanent household was supplemented by Buckingham's travelling household of liveried retainers, though they seem to have been fewer in number than those of the first and second dukes even though Edmund's immediate entourage was larger.[28] In addition, there were servants, occasional staff employed for special events, builders, musicians, and other casual labour which enhanced the membership of Buckingham's household to about 500 people.[29]

Yet Thornbury was also developed because the duke turned away from the peripatetic lifestyle of his father and grandfather in favour of a more settled existence.[30] Thornbury was to be the pivot of his broad spread of estates, an administrative and financial centre enabling him to use officials and agents to carry out his business rather than maintain an itinerant diary to do it himself. Consequently, the developing tendency for a larger household and greater specialisation among officials, developing in the royal and the largest magnate households, culminated at Thornbury in a building which enabled this to be achieved.

NOTES

1 Hawkyard (1977) 51.
2 *Letters & Papers Henry VIII*, 1, 172.
3 Rawcliffe (1978) 42 and 137–43 for a financial analysis of this period.
4 *Ibid.* 137; Hawkyard (1977) 53.
5 *Letters & Papers Henry VIII*, 3, pt. 1, 506.
6 W. A. Caffell, *Society for Thornbury Folk Bulletin* 8 (1990) 63–75; J. J. Burke, *Visitations of Seats and Arms*, II, 1 (1854) 144–7.
7 J. Allibone, *Anthony Salvin* (1987) 180.
8 The hall with porch and central hearth had been erected by 1360; the chamber block was demolished and re-erected in a modified form in 1399, and the chapel built in 1453. Hawkyard (1977) 52 draws attention, as does W. D. Simpson (*Antiq. Jour.* 26 (1946) 168), to the similarly sited chapel at Cowdray (*c.*1520–30). For the most detailed analysis of the castle's internal planning, see Hawkyard (1969) 187–235.
9 Called the earl of Bedford's lodging in the 1583 survey, the range may be attributed to Jasper, Katherine Woodville's step-father, after his reinstalment as earl of Pembroke in 1485 shortly after he had been created duke of Bedford.
10 This frontage was famously engraved by A. and A. W. Pugin, *Examples of Gothic Architecture*, II (1838) 28–38. Also the drawing in A. Garner and T. Stratton, *The Domestic Architecture of England During the Tudor Period*, I (1911) pl. 28.
11 Hawkyard (1977) 56. The interiors are almost entirely by Salvin with Tudor-style doorways, dark panelling, heavy ceilings, and Willement painted glass.
12 Rawcliffe (1978) 64.
13 He was descended from Edward III's sixth son, Thomas of Woodstock, and his mother, Katherine Woodville, was the sister of Edward IV's queen. He was considered as a possible heir to the throne as early as 1499 when Henry VII was ill, with such gossip continuing in courtier circles well into Henry VIII's reign.
14 For Buckingham's finances, Rawcliffe (1978) 126–43; T. B. Pugh, *The Marcher Lordships of South Wales 1415–1536* (1963) 241–61; K. B. McFarlane, *The Nobility of Later Medieval England* (1973) 207–12. The entertainment he laid on for the king and court at Penshurst in 1519 was particularly lavish, while his attacks on the cardinal's foreign policy exacerbated their mutual dislike.
15 Maxstoke had been well maintained during his minority but in due course Buckingham reroofed the hall at Brecon, and repaired the castles at Newport and Tonbridge and his manor at Penshurst. Writtle and Kimbolton Castle fell into disrepair but he extended Bletchingley Manor at the turn of the century to be a convenient stopping place near London.
16 *Itinerary*, II, 64; V, 100.
17 S. Thurley, *The Royal Palaces of Tudor England* (1993) 27–36.
18 W. D. Simpson, *Antiq. Jour.* 26 (1946) 165–70; L. Stone, *The Crisis of the Aristocracy 1558–1641* (1965) 253–4; C. Platt, *The Castle in Medieval England and Wales* (1982) 179–82; Hawkyard (1977) 57. The 1510 licence to crenellate granted permission to build a fortalice or castle, though the earlier manor was not defensibly sited.
19 McFarlane, *The Nobility of Later Medieval England* 209; M. Girouard, *Life in the English Country House* (1978) 69; M. W. Thompson, *The Decline of the Castle* (1987) 63. The castle is not listed in D. J. Cathcart-King, *Castellarium Anglicanum* (1983).
20 Reconstructions of this frontage in R. Cooke, *West Country Houses* (1957) 48; N. Kingsley, *Country Houses of Gloucestershire*, I (1989) 188. Cooke usefully includes Buck and Lysons' engravings, 46–9. The drawings by Edward Blore are held in Brit. Lib., Add. MS 42023 f.106.

21 Some are retained on site: others are held in the V & A Museum and Gloucester Museum. Also J. Wight, *Medieval Floor Tiles* (1975) 148–50.

22 A. Emery, *Greater Med. Houses*, I (1996) 292–4.

23 Rawcliffe (1978) 133. Also McFarlane, *The Nobility of Later Medieval England* 4. Buckingham's journal is held in the Staffordshire Record Office. Extracts by J. Gage, *Archaeologia* 25 (1834) 311–41.

24 McFarlane, *The Nobility of Later Medieval England* 50–2, 223–7; Rawcliffe (1978) 56–65, 89.

25 K. Mertes, *The English Noble Household 1250–1600* (1988) 210.

26 Rawcliffe (1978) 88.

27 Mertes, *The English Noble Household* 45.

28 Rawcliffe (1978) 101.

29 Mertes, *The English Noble Household* 210.

30 Rawcliffe (1978) 86–7.

R. Ellis, *The History of Thornbury Castle* (1839)

J. M. Langton, *Trans. Bristol and Glos. Arch. Soc.* 72 (1953) 79–104

A. D. Hawkyard, 'Some late medieval fortified manor houses', MA thesis, University of Keele (1969) 187–235

A. D. Hawkyard, *Trans. Bristol and Glos. Arch. Soc.* 95 (1977) 51–8

C. Rawcliffe, *The Staffords, Earls of Stafford and Dukes of Buckingham 1394–1521* (1978)

UPTON COURT, Buckinghamshire

Slough and despond are bedfellows, but the Bunyanesque gloom of Slough has been lifted for architectural historians by the revelatory restoration of an early fourteenth-century house on its outskirts. The Norman church at Upton, hitherto the sole reason for venturing to Slough,[1] has been joined since 1990 by the house immediately south-west of it on the road from Datchet.

Upton Court is a timber-framed open-hall house with colour-washed plaster infill. It consists of a two-storey upper cross wing, and an aisled-hall range encompassing the services at its lower end with the steeply pitched tiled roof sweeping to within 8 feet of the ground. Dendro dated to the early 1320s,[2] the house seems to have been built as an administrative centre by Merton Priory, the holders of the manor of Upton from the twelfth century to the Dissolution. It is only the form of the roof over the services that differentiated it from several contemporary houses in the region.[3] The jettied upper cross wing was altered in the late sixteenth and early seventeenth centuries, but the substantial insertions made by later generations (floors, dormers, and central stack) were removed between 1986 and 1990 so that the house has virtually regained its original plan, internal character, and function.

The hall range stands on a flint base with its frame built of widely spaced posts. Opposing cross-passage doorways, lightly chamfered with two-centred heads (west original, east restored) open into the hall, 40¼ feet by 28½ feet. The east (front) entrance was formerly porch-protected, possibly always so. The 6 feet wide cross passage retains the two centrally positioned doors to the services. The plainer and narrower door at the west end to the stair serving the chamber above has been blocked. On the other side is a spere truss with the posts supporting a deeply braced cambered tie beam with braced crown post and upper collar. Further braces extend from the posts to the arcade plate, and the lower part of the truss has reinstated infill to the outer wall of screen-like character.

With the cross passage filling half a bay, the body of the hall is divided into two almost equal bays with 6 feet wide aisles, a central truss, and close-set rafters. Replacement windows throughout the body of the hall were among the many post-medieval changes, but mortices and shutter grooves on the underside of the wall plates revealed that there was originally a pair of windows in each bay. Two-light glazed replacements have been inserted. Part of the clay-tiled hearth was found beneath the central truss, now covered by a floor trapdoor. There was no louvre, for the smoke escaped through openings in the apex of the end walls.

The central truss is highly unusual. It is of hammer-beam form, with the beams tenoned into the wall posts instead of continuing through to act as cantilevers supporting the rafters. This suggests that the original aisle posts were taken down within a generation of the house's construction to facilitate freedom of movement and spatial development with a truss that was still in an experimental stage during the mid-fourteenth century. The inserted example in the hall at Tiptofts immediately springs to mind. However, the Upton Court truss is more complex. The hammer beams are very thin, barely capable of supporting the weight of the main truss. Instead, the tie beam was doubled[4] and the wall posts, found to be truncated at wall plate-level, seem to have continued outside the roof line to support a braced extension of the lower tie beam. This highly unusual structural protrusion was concealed by using it to form one side of a dormer window on each side of the roof. That such dormers existed was revealed by the absence of original rafters at these points and the existence of mortices for the parallel support to the dormer frame.[5] These two dormers had the benefit of enhancing the light capacity of the upper-end bay, and displaying an ingenious architectural solution, decorated (on the dais side only) with a carved quatrefoil on the solid hammer-beam brace. For structural reasons, this truss is likely to be original to the development of the house.[6]

The two adjacent doors in the north-west corner of the dais opened into the ground floor of the upper cross wing, and an external stair to the chamber above. The stair, almost certainly covered and possibly enclosed, was replaced in the early seventeenth century by one within an octagonal turret added outside the north-east corner of the cross wing. The outside stair was taken down and the original upper entry with two-centred head was sealed so that it now opens into space.

The frame of the upper cross wing is original, contemporary with the hall range, and with an identical crown post to its central truss. Though the outer faces of the curved braces are exposed, their barely weathered condition and slight recess from the wall line suggest they were originally plaster covered and not visible to the outside world. The wing was subject to several changes in the late sixteenth and early seventeenth centuries. A brick chimney stack was initially added, with fireplaces at both levels with low four-centred heads.[7] In a second phase, the ground floor was enhanced with an oriel and side windows in the east-facing wall, now brought forward 2 feet in line with the original jetty above. The stair turret was erected to serve both floors, the upper chamber was lit by two oriels (one reinstated) and a plaster ceiling was inserted at tie-beam level of which half survives.

The buttery and pantry below the cross passage, separated by the original wattle and daub partition, retain some of their ceiling beams, though the two rooms (and the chamber above) had been heavily modified long before the 1990 restoration. The rafters show

PLATE 80 Upton Court: from the east

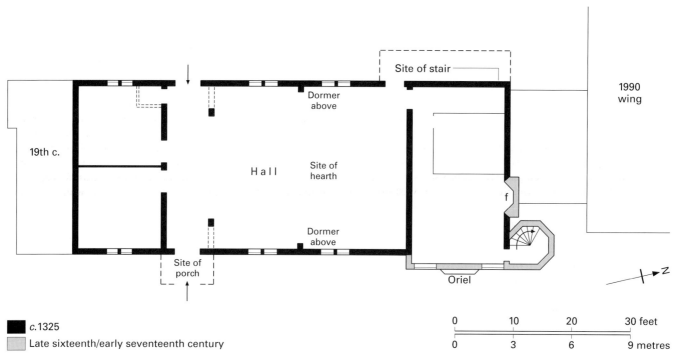

FIGURE 44 Upton Court: ground plan

190

that the roof was not a gabled cross wing but one at right angles to the line of the range, falling from a mid truss to the head of a low extension. This is the only part of the house where the restorers were unable to determine the original extent and roof shape. There was modest structural evidence suggestive of an additional bay (the present nineteenth-century extension has been retained) with either a hipped roof or a half-hipped roof (the preferred form rebuilt) with a window lighting the upper chamber.[8] The value of this room was restricted by its attic-like character with limited headroom. The kitchen would have been a detached building.

The value of Upton Court lies in it being a house of a single period at the close of Edward II's reign, handsomely restored to its original condition except for the porch and external solar stair. This private restoration included replacement windows, doors, iron-work, and all the necessary timber framing which was fitted into the original mortices. Modern usage permits the aisled hall to be left entirely open so that the house joins that select few that are close to their original state. More rare is that its current use as administrative offices prevents museum sterility.

NOTES

1 Since the 1960s, Slough has also completely absorbed the village and church at Langley Marish with its remarkable chapel and library of 1613–31 by Sir John Kedermister.
2 Felling dates of 1319–20, *Vern. Arch.* (1988) 46.
3 Page 86.
4 A double tie beam occurs, for instance, at West Bromwich Manor House (*c.*1273).
5 The large curved braces between the hammer beams and posts close to the roof slope were inserted at a later date, probably after the dormers had been removed. Thornes and Fradgley (1988) 215–16.
6 There are two other hammer beam trusses in Buckinghamshire: one at Bletchley, possibly a court house, and a modest one in Aylesbury.
7 The decorated overmantel and the painted walls are additions of 1989–90.
8 Thornes and Fradgley (1988) 211–14.

J. C. Trench, *Berks. Arch. Jour.* 70 (1983) 81–5
R. Thornes and N. Fradgley, *Arch. Jour.* 145 (1988) 211–21

WANSWELL COURT, Gloucestershire

This mid-fifteenth-century house stands on the north side of an extended rectangular platform, approximately 80 yards by 60 yards, with east and west bridges replacing earlier crossings. Since 1953, they span a dry moat which formerly widened on the west side into a large pool. It was for an earlier dwelling on the site that Philip Leicester, husband of Isabel Wanswell, obtained a licence in 1256 from the abbot and convent of St Augustine's, Bristol, to erect a chapel within his manor house of Wanswell for the accommodation of his family and guests, except at the principal feasts when they had to go to Berkeley church a mile away.[1]

John Thorpe (d.1441), a burgess of Bristol, acquired Wanswell through marriage in 1402. He and his successors became feudal tenants of the Berkeleys and gave their name to the mid-fourteenth-century tower of the castle's shell keep, probably during the turbulent decades of the fifteenth century when the castle's ownership was in dispute and Thorpe was charged with holding it for the

PLATE 81 Wanswell Court: from the south

family.[2] John Thorpe was succeeded by his son, who purchased several adjoining properties in 1456 and was probably responsible for building the present house at Wanswell. He died in 1469, with successive members of the family continuing to occupy the court until 1672 when it was sold to Daniel Lysons of Gloucester. Colonel Berkeley acquired the property from this family of Gloucestershire antiquarians in 1818 and it has been held since 1952 by the trustees of Ernest Cook.

The Court is in two contrasting sections, the low-roofed hall and end wings under a common roof ridge, and the three-storeyed double-pile addition almost overwhelming the earlier structure. It is remarkable that this work was never replaced or remodelled by the later Thorpes but retains the low form more frequently associated with Welsh gentry hall houses than those of the west Midlands. No courtyard or enclosure structures survive.

Built of limestone ashlar blocks on a low plinth, the hall is flanked by narrow storeyed wings, only 3½ feet forward under a single sweeping roof of Cotswold slates interrupted by the hall chimney stack after the removal of the porch and solar gables. The two-storeyed porch[3] was stripped away by the earl of Berkeley in 1929 for reuse at Berkeley Castle and the door surround patched with rubble sandstone.

The simple entry with two-centred head and unbroken moulding opens into an almost square hall, 25 feet by 22 feet and 30 feet to the roof pitch. The end walls were of stone to the 11 foot high cross rails, embattled at the upper end and plain at the lower, surmounted by timber-framed partitions, roughly renewed at the upper end. Two doorways remain to the lower wing and a slightly wider cross-passage doorway, all with four-centred heads and chamfered jambs. There is no evidence of a screen, which may have been of modest or movable form.

The hall is lit on the south side by two twin-light transomed windows under square hoods. They differ in detail, for the smaller has trefoil lights and the larger one illuminating the upper end has cinquefoil lights, rectangular stops, moulded outer jambs, and window seats. The substitute fireplace between them replaces the fine specimen with broad moulded arch falling to splayed jambs, surmounted by a mantel of blind trefoil panels and embellished ledge, transferred to the hall of Berkeley Castle in 1926 but illustrated *in situ* in Lysons' *Collections of Gloucestershire Antiquities* (1803).

The high-pitched three-bay roof is spanned by collar trusses with moulded braces supported on short hexagonal pillars with capitals

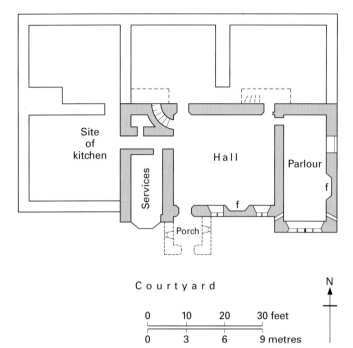

FIGURE 45 Wanswell Court: ground plan

is not external as might be expected but an internal doorway, while the complete absence of hall windows in the north wall is equally indicative of some sort of structure on this side. The present north-east unit seems to be early sixteenth century, with a first-floor fireplace with running vine ornament removed to the great drawing room of Berkeley Castle.[8] The scale and quality of this fireplace matches the others. It could well be later fifteenth century, and was not necessarily *in situ* before its removal from the Court.

Wanswell repeats the earlier craftsmanship noticed at Berkeley Castle of enriched stonework but plain woodwork, particularly in the roofs. Despite the depredations (though fortuitously neighbourhood retained), Wanswell Court is a relatively complete gentry house of *c.*1450–60, still in open countryside. The stonework detailing is of a remarkably high standard, with the removed fireplaces in no way inferior to the castle enfilade they now grace.

NOTES

1 Licence held with the Berkeley Castle muniments.
2 Cooke (1881–2) 315.
3 Illustrated in Turner and Parker (1859) 267. It was not reinstated at Berkeley but divided up for reuse.
4 Three steel girders, wood cased, were inserted for stability in 1991 when the house was regenerated after two and a half centuries of farm occupation.
5 Illustrated in Turner and Parker (1859) 269.
6 See Berkeley Castle, note 11.
7 It was believed in the nineteenth century that the area above the parlour ceiling was open to the hall roof. Turner and Parker (1859) 78 and Cooke (1881–2), though the illustrations in Turner and Parker opp. 78 and Lysons show its original form.
8 Cooke (1881–2) 318; Oswald (1954). When it was removed the back was found to be part of a life-size representation of a bishop or abbot, indicative of a grave reused, C. Hussey, *Country Life* (18 June 1932).

T. H. Turner and J. H. Parker, *Some Account of Domestic Architecture in England*, III pt 2 (1859) 266–9

J. H. Cooke, *Trans. Bristol and Glos. Arch. Soc.* (1881–2) 310–23

A. Oswald, *Country Life* (September 1954)

WINDSOR CASTLE, Berkshire

Though the borough of Windsor is the urban centre at the base of the castle, much of the latter is like a further enclosed hillside town at the foot of a grand mansion – the lower end church-dominated and busy with people and movement, the residence at the upper end stately and seemingly silent. About 500 people live or work within this highly active precinct that still reflects its threefold medieval structure and purpose – the fortifications that determined its shape, the college of St George filling the lower ward, and the royal apartments of the monarch ranged round the upper ward.

SOURCES

Our appreciation of the castle rests on the integration of four diverse sources. There is the substantial body of documentation. The majority of it was transcribed by Sir William St John Hope and published in his magisterial volumes in 1913,[1] but it has been revised and augmented by further research included in the volumes of the *History of the King's Works*.[2] All this documentary material has been checked, corrected, and expanded by Stephen Priestly prepar-

and bases on stone corbels of a man and woman. Similar in form to the roof above part of the Prior's House at Gloucester Abbey, the corbels and pillars on the north side have been replaced by crudely inserted columns to the floor.[4] The two lines of purlins and three rows of wind braces are surprisingly plain.

Adjacent doorways in the upper corner of the hall gave direct access to the parlour wing and to the upper floor via a destroyed stair, though its shaping, trefoil spyhole, and head ridge survive. Both cross wings were less than 12 feet wide. The courtyard-facing parlour wall is filled by a pair of twin cinquefoil lights in line under a single hood with head stops[5] flanked by squints, one towards the east bridge (blocked) and one towards the porch in the form of a miniature version of the smaller of the hall windows. The dominating feature of this comfortable room was the handsome fireplace with multi-cusped jambs and lintel, here in 1881 but probably that now in the small drawing room at Berkeley Castle.[6] The upper chamber retains a plain fireplace but the end window has long been destroyed. Presumably it was gable-enclosed to match the porch, probably similar in design to the parlour lights, and supported on the two visible relieving arches. The open roof of a single bay continued the hall form, now ceiled and inaccessible.[7]

The lower wing was made up of services, kitchen passage, and stair entry. The services area has lost its hall doorway, the passage retains both end entries to a free-standing kitchen on the site of the double-pile extension, and the stone newel stair is complete to its landing. This and the stair to the upper wing terminated on landings outside the line of the north wall, now destroyed except for the base of the lower landing and the line of both roof covers. It is likely that the landings, timber enclosed, ran parallel with the wall to provide entry to the upper chambers. This unusual feature is matched by two more factors which suggest that the north side of Wanswell Court was not necessarily open. The cross-passage entry atory to the report by Brian Kerr and Steven Brindle for English Heritage.[3]

Not surprisingly, this royal palace-fortress has an extended pictorial record as far back as a pen drawing made in about 1450 in a manuscript history of England,[4] a valuable bird's-eye view by John Norden in *c.*1607,[5] and the primary evidence of Wenceslas Hollar, who made a number of detailed drawings in the late 1650s for Elias Ashmole's *History and Institutions of the Order of the Garter* (1672) showing the castle immediately before the extensive changes by Charles II.[6] This pictorial resource became far more extensive in the eighteenth and early nineteenth centuries, particularly through the work of Thomas and Paul Sandby[7] and William Pyne.[8]

The third source is the surviving structure that has withstood not only destruction, rebuilding, and fire but phases of drastic alterations and additions. This is supplemented by the final source, the analysis and deductions from excavations, hitherto extremely limited but fruitful where they have been allowed.

The two-volume survey *Windsor Castle: An Architectural History* (with a separate box of coloured plans) by Sir William St John Hope in 1913 was one of the peaks of late Victorian and Edwardian architectural studies. It was extremely thorough for its time, combining an examination of the documentation and illustrative material with a detailed analysis of the existing buildings and their phased development. However, Hope was a medievalist and he was far less interested in the work of Wyatt, Wyatville, and their successors which totally transformed the residential and visual character of the upper-ward buildings. Even so, Hope's study has proved a sound basis for nearly a hundred years, modestly supplemented by a brief architectural essay on William Wykeham's work by Wickham Legg,[9] an illustrated historical account by Sir Owen Morshead,[10] and a brief social one by Mark Girouard.[11]

Two disasters have altered our perception of the castle's development. In 1988, the Round Tower was discovered to be unstable, necessitating underpinning and strengthening and therefore archaeological excavation and architectural recording. In November 1992, part of the state apartments and some of the semi-state rooms from St George's Hall to Chester Tower were totally gutted by fire. Roofs, ceilings, floors, and wall linings suffered extremely badly, but the stability of the outer walls was not put at risk. The fire revealed hitherto unsuspected architectural evidence, facilitated a detailed fabric survey of the devastated rooms, and allowed the excavation of the Kitchen Court to be carried out, prior to the reconstruction of the royal apartments by 1997 with some internal remodelling to enhance their usefulness. The complex technical and environmental work of restoration has been the subject of a separate illustrated record,[12] but the discoveries arising from this work have also enabled English Heritage to undertake a new architectural assessment of the castle's development. Initial reviews were published in 1997[13] and in 2002,[14] pending the more detailed monograph, re-examining and supplementing the original sources, incorporating the recent archaeological and structural research, and reassessing the castle's development in the light of current scholarship. This project covers the whole castle until the last quarter of the fourteenth century and the royal apartments until the close of the twentieth century, but excludes the college of St George.[15]

Despite the extremely rich documentary, pictorial, and archaeological record, there are major limitations to our understanding of Edward III's development of the royal apartments. They were very heavily rebuilt, first under Hugh May between 1670 and 1685, and then under Sir Jeffry Wyatville between 1824 and 1840. May's neo-Norman exteriors deliberately contrasted with a sequence of elaborate baroque interiors, just as Wyatville's martial cloak was uncompromisingly at variance with the sequence of lavishly furnished Régence interiors. Continual reference will be made to May's and Wyatville's activities which so drastically modified or eliminated the medieval structures. The fire of 1992 and the subsequent examination were confined to less than half of the state apartments. The remainder has not yet been subject to a detailed analysis, and until that can be achieved our understanding of the historical and architectural development of the residence must be a partial one. This last area includes the monarch's apartments, which are necessarily subject to some restrictions. Even so, initial studies are already fundamentally illuminating the planning, functional design, and influence of the major work undertaken at this fortress by Henry III and Edward III respectively.[16]

EARLY DEVELOPMENT

The castle, first mentioned in Domesday Book, was established by William the Conqueror on a chalk bluff commanding the River Thames. It consisted of a timber defence on a man-made motte, ditch surrounded, with the lower ward probably a generation later than the timber-palisaded upper ward. The castle was adopted as a royal residence from about 1110 onwards and has remained so to the present day.

Between 1165 and 1179, Henry II undertook a raft of building projects. The most important was his replacement of the upper ward defences with a stone wall punctured by projecting rectangular towers, evident today only as low-level masonry and part of the King's Gate, his approach to the upper ward.[17] Henry also remodelled some of the earlier residential accommodation, and built a precursor of the present shell keep on the chalk motte.

After the castle was subject to an unsuccessful three-month siege by a French army in 1216, the lower ward defences, possibly already masonry-built on the north side, were completed with a stone curtain broken by rounded towers and a new gatehouse (1224–30).[18] It was almost certainly at this time that the embryonic middle ward became a substantive one, with a new south wall with massive towers at each end, the present Henry III and Edward III Towers.[19] The castle's circuit and hourglass form was now permanently established.

Documents suggest that Henry II rebuilt 'the king's houses', a hall, chapel, and some domestic apartments in the upper ward, and was responsible for the great hall next to the still evident residential block in the lower ward. From an early stage, the royal apartments may have been grouped round a quadrangle, but we are only on firm ground with the accommodation developed by Henry III on the north side of the upper ward between about 1240 and 1263. These were initially intended for the queen and the royal children, for the king's own apartments in the lower ward were being extended with two new chambers and a chapel, separated by a cloistered court (the present Dean's Cloister). However, the distinction between the status of the two wards was about to change.

By the close of Henry III's reign, the royal lodgings of the upper ward had been developed as two parallel ranges, one against the north curtain and one facing the ward, separated by short ranges to create at least two internal courtyards (fig. 46).[20] The principal one, a cloister walk, was used as a spicerie or herb garden, now covered by the Waterloo Chamber (1830). The royal hall lay on its east side, a ground-floor structure open to the roof.[21] Whether the blocked doorway with moulded jambs and the two ground-floor window embrasures date from this time or earlier is an open question. A range of two-storeyed apartments with a low-pitched roof was built on the south side of this court. The documents suggest it may have included a chapel, while the structural evidence points to a first floor division (now the western half of St George's Hall)[22] with a narrower extension at the east end. The ground-floor undercroft here, five vaulted bays to central columns, is often ascribed to this period (Steward's Hall).[23] The remaining sides of the court and the later ranges round the west court have never been stripped for architectural analysis, so that the inclusion of thirteenth-century work is not yet known. However, a contemporary doorway revealed in the south-west corner of the present kitchen indicates that it has always been sited here.

EDWARD III'S PROGRAMME

Building activity at Windsor during the fifty years between the death of Henry III and the accession of Edward III was primarily for maintenance and repair. Edward's own work began comparatively modestly, spurred by the growing cult of chivalry. At a tournament held at Windsor in January 1344, the thirty-two-year-old king announced the foundation of the Order of the Round Table. The chronicler, Adam Murimuth, recorded that work on 'a most noble house' to accommodate its meetings was in progress that summer, 'sparing neither labour nor expense',[24] but the project was abandoned soon afterwards and has left no visible trace. Four years later, Edward established the Order of the Garter at Windsor for a considerably smaller number of knights. He centred it upon Henry III's chapel and hall in the lower ward, to be served by a dean (warden), twelve canons, and thirteen vicars, and set about renovating the chapel and adding a chapter-house, treasury, vestry, canons' and clergy lodgings, and a warden's lodge. Because of the plague of 1348–9, work was not begun until 1350, with completion seven years later, celebrated by a great feast in April 1358.

The splendour of this occasion was in harmony with recent political events, for the war with France had swung decisively in England's favour with the dramatic success at the battle of Poitiers and the capture of the French king (1356). The seismic expansion of Edward's building programme at Windsor reflected the euphoria of a monarch now seen to be of European standing. So far, work on the royal lodgings in the upper ward had been limited to repairs. The wholesale rebuilding of these apartments between 1357 and 1377 cost £44,000, the most expensive secular building project in England throughout the middle ages. In addition, a further £6,500 was incurred between 1350 and 1357 on remodelling the keep and establishing the college in the lower ward, with just over £500 on the aborted Round Table building.[25]

The residential development of the upper ward extended across three phases, initiated by remodelling the Round Tower between 1353 and 1357 to provide a temporary royal lodging before work was put in hand on the much larger project of rebuilding the upper ward accommodation. The second phase began with the reconstruction of the inner gatehouse (the misnamed Norman Gate) in 1358, a defensive-looking but ceremonial entrance, and proceeded

clockwise round the ward to the south-west corner. The construction of the royal apartments serving both king and queen[26] was undertaken in a surprisingly short time, with the majority of work completed between 1357 and 1363, followed by the finishing trades including plastering, paving, glass, and furnishings between 1363 and 1365. Recently discovered building accounts are giving a much clearer picture of the way that England was scoured for workmen during this period, as well as the employment of master craftsmen with links to contemporary and later building projects.[27] The appointment of a keeper of the upper ward in October 1365 suggests that the royal lodgings were ready for occupation. The third phase was the development of an extended line of lodging ranges round the east and south sides of the upper ward from 1364 onwards. Though the detailed accounts cease at the end of 1368, the total expenditure incurred shows a marked falling off after 1370 until the king's death seven years later.

Round Tower

Not long after the construction of the palisaded motte, its summit was surmounted by a defensive enclosure wall which began to slip soon afterwards, necessitating buttress support on the south and south-west sides. It seems to have been replaced during the minority of Henry III with the present shell keep inside the line of the first wall; excavation in 1989 revealed evidence of a contemporary hall, chamber stair, and kitchen against its inner face on the site of their fourteenth-century successors. The interior of the keep was totally rebuilt as a self-contained house in four years, with laths purchased in 1354, timber felled in 1355, new stone foundations laid in 1356–7,[28] and reused timbers from abandoned work of the 1340s, possibly from the Round Table building.[29] The structure, initiated by the royal surveyor Robert Burnham, and completed after October 1356 by William Wykeham, is a unique residential survival. Though the shell keeps at Durham and Fotheringhay were similarly rebuilt in the aftermath of that at Windsor, none of their internal structures has survived (see frontispiece).

Edward III's portcullis-protected entry opened into a small central court enclosed by four timber-framed ranges abutting the inside of the shell keep – the single-storey kitchen and hall on the north and west sides, and two-storeyed residential ranges on the south and east sides (fig. 46). These ranges remained little touched until about 1670 when their window tracery was altered and the plaster infill of the courtyard framing was replaced with brick. During the eighteenth century, two-storeyed corridors were erected against the courtyard faces of the ranges to facilitate circulation. In 1830–1, Wyatville doubled the thickness of Henry II's shell wall internally so that he could raise it twice as high. This was simply to create a visual climax to the castle, for no structures were erected behind it. The huge additional weight of this theatrical gesture proved too much for the man-made motte. Radical structural engineering was essential to relieve the crumbling foundations. A ring-beam girdle resting on steel columns plunging to the base of the motte was inserted in 1990–2 to stabilise the earlier structure and allow new offices and a steel roof to be built behind Wyatville's stage scenery.

Despite all these changes, the framework of the Edwardian ranges round the central court has survived, as well as doorways with two-centred heads and the frames of some of the cusped and transomed courtyard windows. The stone ground-floor window

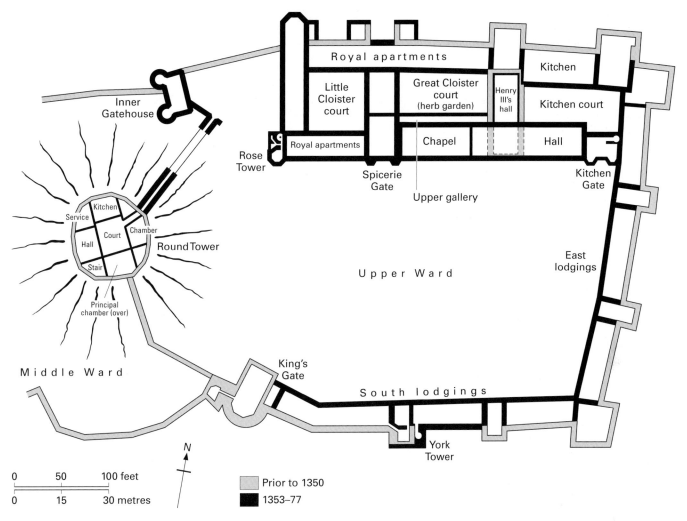

FIGURE 46 Windsor Castle: site plan of the Round Tower and the primary Upper Ward structures of Edward III

frames inserted in the outer wall have always been retained, though those above were renewed or inserted by Wyatville. The hall entry opposite that to the keep had been replaced, but the adjacent services doorway survives behind hinged panelling. The four-bay hall, originally with cusped and transomed courtyard-facing windows, has an inserted floor of 1830. It was originally open to the exposed low-pitched roof spanned by braced tie-beam and king-post trusses, with evidence of a louvre serving a central hearth. The door was traced to the stair approach to the principal chamber beyond the upper end of the hall, positioned in the corner created by the chamber block at right angles to it. The principal chamber was at first-floor level, more highly decorated than the other rooms, with recovered evidence of later pargetted wall finishes. It is not clear what purpose was served by the ground-floor room with its courtyard-facing arcade (with later heads) which continued along the further storeyed range of unknown occupational use. Partition walls here, as elsewhere in the building, are nineteenth or early twentieth century.[30] The kitchen filling the north side between the keep and hall entrances benefited from a central smoke bay and a serving hatch.

Fragments of painted glass, including some of heraldic character,

were found during the excavations of 1989 as well as a quantity of decorated floor tiles from Penn. Their high quality and the house's construction immediately before the redevelopment of the royal apartments indicate that this self-contained unit was built as temporary accommodation for Edward III and Queen Philippa. It was subsequently used as a high-status lodging, and became the residence of the constable of the castle between the later seventeenth and early twentieth centuries, when it was converted into the castle's muniment rooms holding the royal archives.

The fore building was rebuilt in the later fourteenth century, while the magnificent covered stone stair to the keep, lit by cinque-foil windows, was erected in 1439–40 by John Cantelow.[31] The roof has been reconstructed, and though many of the supporting corbels are genuine, they have been reset in the Bath stone used by Wyatville. Edward III's doorway at the head of the steps was similarly refaced in the same material.

Royal apartments

Edward III ruthlessly remodelled and expanded the earlier royal house on the north side of the upper ward. By building his ceremonial as well as some of his private apartments above a line of ground-

PLATE 82 Windsor Castle: the Great Undercroft

floor undercrofts, he created a palace in the form which has dictated all subsequent development. Hollar's 1658 view of the castle provides the most important evidence for the plan and character of Edward's palace-complex before May's redevelopment of a major part of it shortly afterwards (see frontispiece). The two-storeyed ranges were built round three courts in line – the Little Cloister (later Royal or Brick Court), the Great or King's Cloister (later Horn Court), and the Kitchen Court. All three courts have since been covered over, but the main apartments were disposed round the Little and Great Cloisters, with one line of apartments against Henry II's north curtain wall, and a second parallel range holding the ceremonial and some private apartments facing the body of the ward. This south frontage was the principal one, with a small corner tower (Rose Tower) near the motte, the Spicerie or primary gateway positioned almost opposite Henry II's gatehouse to the upper ward, and the Kitchen gateway towards the east (fig. 47). The exterior walls were faced in hard-wearing Bagshot Heath stone over

a chalk or clunch rubble core, with quality ashlar for the two entry gates and the Rose Tower. Internal walls were lined in dressed stone from Reigate and the quarries at Taynton.

Not surprisingly, several centuries of alterations, rebuilding, and infilling have left only five structures from Edward's three-courtyard complex – the Great Undercroft below the royal hall and chapel, the Armoury Undercroft below some of the king's apartments, the Rose or royal privy tower, the kitchen, and a short arcaded walk opposite. Except for the royal privy tower, all five structures are limited to ground level. Attention will be drawn to the revealed evidence for two or three first-floor apartments, but our picture of Edward's residence is necessarily incomplete and will be subject to modification as more evidence comes to light in the future.

Ground Floor

The first part of the courtyard frontage and fenestration is essentially by James Wyatt, who worked at Windsor from 1796 to 1804.

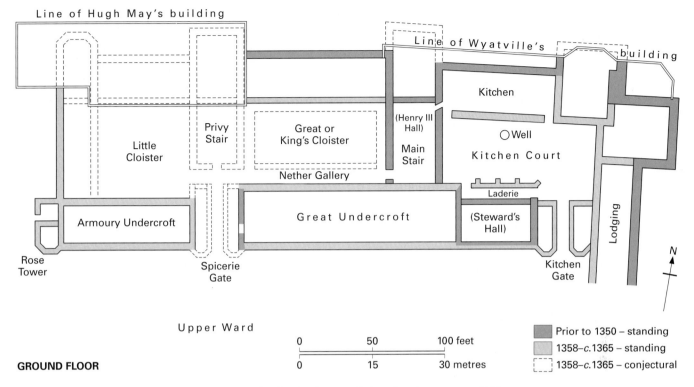

Line of Hugh May's building

Line of Wyatville's building

Little Cloister

Privy Stair

Great or King's Cloister

Nether Gallery

(Henry III Hall)

Main Stair

Kitchen

○Well

Kitchen Court

Laderie

Armoury Undercroft

Great Undercroft

(Steward's Hall)

Lodging

Rose Tower

Spicerie Gate

Kitchen Gate

N

Upper Ward

0   50   100 feet

0   15   30 metres

GROUND FLOOR

Prior to 1350 – standing
1358–c.1365 – standing
1358–c.1365 – conjectural

FIGURE 47 Windsor Castle: ground plan of royal apartments c.1365

Wyatville's State Entrance of 1827 stands forward of the Spicerie Gateway (1357–8), a structure which no longer exists, so that Hollar's engraving is the essential guide to its form. It was three-storeyed with the entry passage vaulted and portcullis protected. It did not lead into a courtyard as might be expected but to the privy stair, the private stair to the royal lodgings, with lateral entrances to the courtyard either side. This gateway was the key approach to Edward's palace but it was almost destroyed by Wyatville, while Salvin's alterations within this area ensured that no medieval evidence was retained. The remainder of the frontage is by Wyatville, with windows copying his father's work.

To the right of the State Entrance is the Great Undercroft, the most imposing of the three vaulted undercrofts to have survived and the one which gives an idea of the scale of Edward III's hall and chapel immediately above (now St George's Hall). Approximately 193 feet by 31 feet internally, this undercroft is divided into thirteen bays (including a half bay at the east end) by a central line of octagonal pillars with swollen bases and plain-moulded capitals. Plain-chamfered ribs spring from high-set half pillars in the side walls to create quadripartite vaults (1362–3). There are no decorative bosses in an apartment of plain but monumental character. The west entrance is original, though altered, but the direct courtyard access shown by Hollar in the eighth bay from the west has been lost. The courtyard-facing wall was virtually rebuilt by Hugh May in the 1670s, who created the present fenestration pattern to match the thirteen-bay rhythm he had imposed on the medieval eighteen bays above. The original fenestration seems to have been a single tre-foiled light in alternate bays, of which some splays can be made out. There was a line of high-set windows in the western half of the

opposite wall, but an abutting structure precluded any in the six bays further east. The present lights in this north wall are nineteenth century but several of the wide splays are original, set in high sills, some cut away. The seventh bay retains the cinquefoil head of a two-light window of fifteenth-century date.[32] The original flagstone floor lies 3 feet below the present wooden one, while the raised level towards the east marks a seventeenth-century inserted wine cellar.

The Great Undercroft opens into the more narrow one attributed to Henry III (Steward's Hall, mentioned above), though Christopher Wilson has argued that it was part of a short-lived early scheme of Edward III.[33] The second-bay fireplace with decorated splays, a broad lintel with the quatrefoil-enclosed badge of Edward IV, and an elaborate frieze was inserted during his reign.

To the left of the Spicerie Gateway is the Armoury Undercroft, adapted by Wyatville and Salvin as their approach to the state apartments. This eight-bay undercroft, similar to that under the hall and chapel, was also quadripartite vaulted in 1362–3. Wyatt was responsible for replacing the ward-facing wall, but the central line of columns, similar to those of the Great Undercroft, seem to be genuine. Divisions have been inserted into them at some time with brick infill, but these were removed and cement-filled in the nineteenth century. The form of the vaulting ribs and lack of bosses reflect the plain character of the larger undercroft, but the ribs and vaulting here were scraped by Wyatville as part of his entrance hall conversion. The two western bays have been cut off (now cloakrooms), but there was never any link between this vaulted chamber and the adjacent Rose Tower.

The Kitchen Gateway (now the Guests' or Equerries' Entrance)

197

is a second entry point in the south frontage. Built in 1362–3, its façade was identical with that of the main entrance but it was only half as deep. It was replaced by Wyatville's indulgent entry. The 1992 fire revealed more of this structure than had been previously known, including a well-preserved west turret chamber with fireplace, and the canted shape of the chamber on the other side of the broad gate-passage. This entrance was portcullis protected, with the position of the great doors still marked by pintles. The scar of the outer arch identifies its site before it was taken out as part of Wyatville's development. The scar of the removed inner arch similarly marks the side walls in front of Blore's Kitchen Cloister archway of 1841–2. Doorways with two-centred heads at the far end of the gate-passage opened into the guardrooms, with evidence of an independently approached newel stair to the first floor. The present floor level is higher than originally, leading now to the infilled Kitchen Court. The scale and purpose of this defensive-looking gateway, apparently serving only the kitchen and offices, warrants further consideration (see below).

Immediately north of Steward's Hall stands the Larderie Passage, a four-bay arcaded walk, 7 feet wide, originally open to the Kitchen Court. Each bay has a quadripartite vault with thin hollow-chamfered ribs and a double rose boss. The walk was developed in several stages, beginning with the north wall of the earlier undercroft.[34] The arcade was erected in the mid-fourteenth century, and though it might be expected that the buttresses were integral, they abut the arcade instead of bonding with it and project either side the shaped jambs of the arcade arches. Clearly the arcade and added buttresses were intended to support the extension of the hall above, broader than Henry III's undercroft. The vault was an addition of 1362–3 with ribs of a different character from Edward's work elsewhere.

The recovery of Edward III's kitchen after the 1992 fire has been a revelation. It is now the finest medieval room in the upper ward as well as the oldest and least changed kitchen in Europe. The walls and roof-base of this majestic and still-used apartment essentially date from the mid-fourteenth century. Internally 80 feet by 30 feet and rising through two floors, it was constructed against Henry II's north curtain. The lower part was thickened to hold three hearths with low-pitched heads, two still in use and the third converted into a doorway. The hearths in the lower part of the opposite wall are later sixteenth-century insertions (brick repaired a century later), while the ends of the kitchen were filled by Wyatville in 1828 to contain additional grates and ranges.[35] That at the east end blocked the original broad kitchen entry, a continuous moulded arch, visible externally from the Kitchen Court. The wall surfaces are Wyatville, as are the high windows in the south wall replacing those set in seventeenth-century brick splays and much altered fourteenth-century openings. This exterior face of the kitchen has been left exposed by building the adjacent corridor of the 1995 Kitchen Court buildings a few feet away from it.[36] Apart from the fire-stained walls, the line of the original external string course can be traced, cut away by Wyatville except for a small section at the east end.

The kitchen roof and lantern are a rare survival. Dividing the kitchen into five full bays and two end half-bays, the four trusses spring from lower wall plates which have been dendro dated to after 1337.[37] The position of these spring points and the corbels seem to be original and may well complement the documentary evidence for lathing and plastering this ceiling in 1362–3. The roof was

PLATE 83 Windsor Castle: Kitchen interior

reconstructed following the original design in 1489–90, with the present low-pitched tie beams with sweeping braces and king posts of that time.[38] The cusping is a Wyatville embellishment in softwood. The renewed plaster coving is enigmatic. It is unlikely to have been medieval, for exposed framing would be probable, but it might be eighteenth-century work, subsequently painted to represent stonework as shown in James Stephanoff's watercolour of c.1819 for Pyne's Royal Residences.[39] The earliest drawing of the castle of about 1450 shows an elongated lantern lighting and ventilating the kitchen, similar to the present one, now reconstructed after the 1992 fire.[40]

The excavation of the Kitchen Court proved more rewarding than that of the much abused kitchen floor, for it revealed the original well chamber.[41] The 9½ foot wide well, 130 feet deep to the water table, was lined with greensand masonry, probably surmounted by cross beams and winding equipment. It was covered with a brick dome by Hugh May, and infilled by Wyatville, who subsequently inserted a crudely built shaft. Presumably the ground-floor rooms in the towers flanking the kitchen and any under the hall approach were for services, but there is no structural confirmation. We know their names from the accounts – the bakehouse, the larderye (for meat), the salting house, and the pasterye – while the scanty evidence indicates they were not generously housed.

First floor

The first-floor hall and chapel, the heart of the royal apartments, were built in line, back-to-back with the chapel next to the Spicerie Gateway and the hall further east (fig. 48). The courtyard frontage had a line of identical windows with no obvious division, buttress support, or wall thickening between the two apartments. Nor was there any structural division in the undercroft, so that the first-floor partition had to be timber-framed, not stone-built. Its position can be determined by reading the bay configuration shown in Hollar's

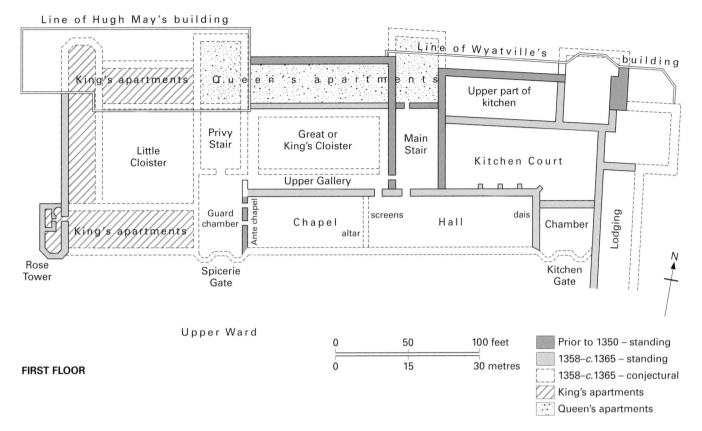

FIGURE 48 Windsor Castle: first-floor plan of royal apartments *c*.1365

engravings, making it clear that the chapel surmounted seven bays of the undercroft and the hall was over the remaining eleven bays with the dais at the east end and the low end of the hall next to the chapel altar end.[42] In 1680–5 Hugh May virtually rebuilt the two apartments, including most of the exterior elevation, and heightened the north wall in brick to support his new roof. His work and Verio's mural paintings were almost entirely destroyed in turn by Wyatville when he combined the two apartments in 1829–30 to create St George's Hall,[43] almost entirely reconstructed in 1996.

In 1993, the west end of the chapel was stripped of its plasterwork to reveal a palimpsest of its development. The lower part of the wall was thirteenth century, heightened in the fourteenth century to take a steeply pitched roof. The chapel was approached from the room over the Spicerie Gate through a tall arched entry towards its northeast corner with a fourteenth-century inset arch, its moulded head cut back (visible from the gallery staircase of St George's Hall). Its north rather than central position suggests it was the approach to an upper or privy pew extending over the large but lost central entry to the chapel proper. Hollar's drawings of the chapel interior show the fittings and panelled ceiling inserted by Elizabeth I, not its original character which included a painted wooden (not stone) reredos similar in character to that filling the end wall of the chapel at New College, Oxford (*c*.1380).

The form of the great hall can be best read from Hollar's engraving of *c*.1668 showing Charles II holding a Garter feast. Each of the eleven bays of this 108 feet long hall was marked by a tall courtyard-facing window and spanned by great arched trusses. The windows,

of two-transomed, trefoil lights with quatrefoil head, rose to the embattled wall plate. Unusually, there were no windows in the north wall, possible because of the main stair and kitchen activities, or perhaps for the display of wall paintings or expensive tapestries. The head of the dais wall was filled with three lines of repetitive blank panelling, in either stone or wood. The roof collar trusses were supported by great arching braces that sprang from small corbels, embellished with Perpendicular tracery of open trefoil lights to the trusses. This roof had a much steeper pitch than its predecessor of unclear date, but it was subsequently reduced by May, followed by one at a slightly higher level by Wyatville.[44]

It is probable that this hall was built in two closely related phases. Though the Larderie Passage arcade against the earlier Steward's Hall is mid-fourteenth century, the line of added buttresses against it points to essential secondary work necessary for supporting the massive weight of the hall roof, now extended from a modest six bays to one of eleven bays. It is not unlikely that the larger and smaller louvres shown in Norden's bird's-eye view, with the smaller one close to the dais, reflect this extension.

The approach to the hall was via the main stair in the cross range between the Great Cloister and the Kitchen Court. The hall entry for diners was not in the end bay as was usual, but partially along the length of the hall to give room for service preparation in the two end bays. The upper end of the hall abutted the first floor of the Kitchen Gateway. It is not known whether the door to this room from the hall dais, shown by Hollar and in eighteenth-century survey plans, was original or inserted later for convenience. As the

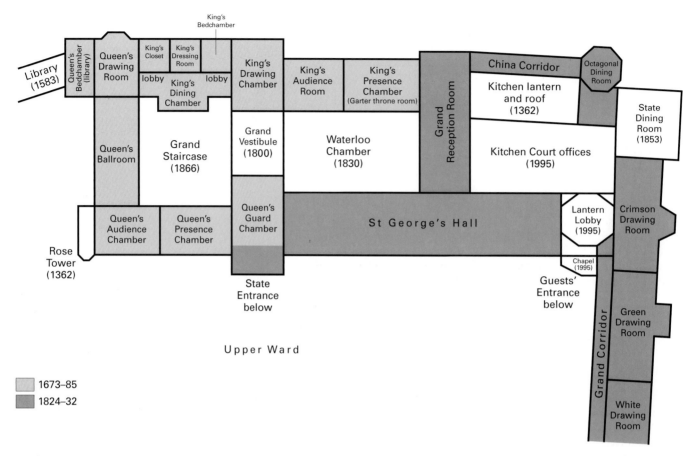

FIGURE 49 Windsor Castle: first-floor plan of state apartments today

king's apartments lay elsewhere, there was no need for the usual private approach to and from the dais. On the other hand, the route for food from the kitchen to the low end of the hall was a particularly long one. Crossing the Kitchen Court and using the spiral stair in the Kitchen Gateway to serve the king or his dais guests personally would shortcircuit this. The garderobe points to the room over the gate initially as an ante-room as much as a residential one, though it may have become this later. An entry jamb of this garderobe[45] has been left exposed in Giles Downes' Lantern Lobby of 1996, while part of the newel is concealed by the silver-gilt buffet plate display there.

The royal apartments were ranged round two courtyards – the Great or King's Cloister and the Little Cloister. The former was filled by Wyatville in 1830 to create the Waterloo Chamber; the latter by Salvin in 1866 to create the Grand Staircase. Before then, Hugh May had erected his Star Building in 1670, overriding the line of the early curtain wall and completely destroying the western half of the north range, and virtually rebuilding the three ranges to the south leaving only the Rose Tower and the Armoury Undercroft (fig. 49). As his work was erected over a cyclopean basement, all medieval foundation evidence was destroyed. Nor has it been possible to explore the architectural development of this half of the state apartments as the 1992 fire afforded to the eastern half. Our current knowledge of the medieval private rooms is therefore still very patchy.

Before considering the most extensive early survival, the Rose Tower, medieval work has been identified so far in several current state apartments. It is known that early stone masonry exists behind the panelling of the Waterloo Chamber, though its character and date have not been determined. Furthermore, low-pitched tie-beam trusses with king posts of late medieval date survive above the later ceilings of the King's Audience Room (1677–8) and the Garter Throne Room (1830).[46] Hugh May's redevelopment of the curtain range north of the Brick Court was total, extending to basement level. The outer wall of the western range facing the motte and Round Tower may well be fourteenth century, refenestrated by May (1670s) with heads to the windows in the Queen's Ballroom added by Wyatt. The outer wall of the south range facing the upper ward may similarly retain its medieval core above ground level. The windows are by Wyatt set in May's embrasures, but possibly reflecting the original fenestration position shown in Hollar's bird's-eye view.[47] The two 1675 rooms, Queen's Audience Chamber and Queen's Presence Chamber, are over an undercroft 80 feet by 30 feet ('Armoury' Undercroft), undivided as the first-floor chamber probably was originally. A door in the west end corner opened on to the stair serving the royal chambers in the angle tower.

The other first-floor apartment of which we have any evidence is now incorporated in the Grand Reception Room, a wholehearted creation of 1830.[48] The position of the wall that originally divided this medieval room from the former tower to the north was identified after the 1992 fire by a partition at ground level and a wall scar above. A large fourteenth-century door with a three-centred arch was found behind the panelling in the south-west corner accessing the upper gallery to the royal apartments, though the majority of the gilded panelling could not be stripped for fear of damaging it. Originally the upper half of Henry III's hall, it was floored by Edward III to create the main stair to his new hall, chapel, and suites of private apartments. Refenestrated and reroofed by Edward IV in 1478, the room was torn down and extended into the north tower by Hugh May in c.1674–80 to create the King's Guard Chamber when two huge windows, a fireplace, and the external galleting were inserted in the retained medieval wall (visible since 1995 from the Kitchen Court corridor).

The three-storeyed Rose Tower is an extremely fortuitous survival, spared by all later builders and restorers (1362–3). Its form, internal plan, and standard of decoration indicate it was an integral part of the royal lodgings. It consists of a single chamber on each floor, with a lobby prefacing separate garderobe and wardrobe, linked by a newel that rose from ground to roof. The exterior of the tower is Wyatville-faced, covering the original masonry, with recut windows following the original form. The attic floor and turret were added by Wyatville in c.1830 for aesthetic effect.

The courtyard entrance with two-centred head and simple chamfer is original, retaining its door pintle. It opens into an altered lobby with a similar inner door nearby, but the precise layout at this point is unclear. A chicane approach to the newel might be expected for security, though this is fouled by the present ceiling. The closet next to the lobby was presumably a garderobe for those using the ground-floor chamber. This semi-octagonal room with Wyatt windows in place of the earlier loops has a most striking vaulted ceiling. From the corners of the room, eight main ribs and alternate sub-ribs from higher corbels (Wyatt replacements) converge upon the central keystone.[49] The central boss is a well-carved rose that has helped to give the tower its name. There is no contemporary fireplace evidence and the walls and doorways are now covered with Roman cement. This unheated chamber, next to the private entrance and with one of the highest-quality vaults in the castle, would probably have been used by the crown's personal bodyguard.

The stone newel, overlain with less steep timber steps, leads to the cross-vaulted lobby of the royal suite. Two angled doorways with two-centred heads access a garderobe and wardrobe, each lancet-lit, with the hollow-moulded outer arch of a (blocked) doorway opposite from the private apartments (now Queen's Audience Chamber). The fourth doorway, outward opening, is the approach to the royal chamber. This particularly tall room is lit by two transomed and trefoiled lights in two faces, and a single transomed and trefoiled light in the third side facing towards the upper end of the ward. Externally, these windows have a blind sexfoil above the lights under a bold hood mould. With their finely moulded internal jambs, they are among the few windows in the castle with retained medieval tracery. The present thin-ribbed ceiling, inserted during Edward IV's reign, conceals the window heads, but above it is the original vaulted ceiling identical with that seen in the chamber below. The low fireplace is eighteenth century, but it is probable that it replaces an original one.

The second-floor chamber repeats the first-floor plan with lobby, independent garderobe, and closet with retained trefoiled light, prefacing a room 10 feet high. This privy chamber with its two-light windows, smaller than those below, plain replacement ceiling, and eighteenth-century replacement fireplace is lined with eighteenth-century ovolo panelling. However, the chamber walls are covered with painted decoration of Edward III's time that extends round the door arch and lobby walls. On a small-scale squared background, green mandola-shaped lozenges are painted, each one enclosing a rose set in a flowery border. Though covered by panelling, this is the only royal domestic chamber with original painted decoration to survive from the middle ages and it can be dated from the accounts to 1365–6.[50] The lobby is also one of the few areas in the castle to retain medieval floor tiles, covered at present by the Victorian floor.

The Rose Tower is part of the royal lodging with its own highly privileged courtyard entrance, guard-protected at ground level, with a high-quality chamber on each of the two floors above. They were both provided with separate garderobes and wardrobes, with first floor access from the line of royal apartments overlooking the castle ward. The second floor chamber, covered from floor to ceiling with brilliant painted decoration, was positioned above the roof level of the adjacent ranges (see Hollar's engraving: frontispiece), giving uninterrupted views across the castle so that it was almost a belvedere.

The records give a tantalising glimpse of the two sequences of royal apartments, and it may be possible to pinpoint their position within the complex. The king's suite of nine rooms, listed in the furniture inventory of 1365, had a first, second, third, and fourth chamber, one called 'La Rose', a painted chamber, and a great chamber, closet, and private chapel. The queen had a first and second chamber, the latter with an oratory, a chamber with mirrors, and a 'daunsyng' chamber.[51] Both suites were prefaced by an outer room, the guard chamber. It is known that there was a vault below the king's chamber for which John Martyn was paid £40, so that by eliminating the vaults below the chapel and hall, the existing vault between the Spicerie Gate and the Rose Tower must have been that under the king's great chamber. The wall paintings in the Rose Tower help to identify the 'painted chamber' so that the sequence of apartments occupied by the king begin with the south-facing 'great chamber' over the present 'Armoury' undercroft, include the Rose Tower, and continue the length of the west range and part of the north range. The queen's less spacious apartments lay entirely within the north range. Their position and function have been pinpointed with unflinching certainty by Christopher Wilson.[52] Under the Tudors, there was some change in their disposition[53] which became more significant under Elizabeth I, leading to a total reversal under the Stuarts, with those of the king in line against the north curtain wall, and those of the queen starting on the first floor of the Spicerie Gateway and continuing along the south and west ranges. This layout persisted through Hugh May's total rebuilding to the present day (fig. 49).

Lodging ranges

Henry II's towered curtilage helped to determine the form of the lodging ranges round two sides of the upper ward (fig. 46). Some, possibly all of his late twelfth-century towers were open-backed, as the Chester Tower certainly was until the rear wall was added in the thirteenth century. The 1992 fire also revealed the foundations of a contemporary narrow range built against the curtain or at least its north-east segment. This was replaced from the mid-1360s by a broader two-storeyed lodging range erected against the length of the east and south curtain walls of the ward from the Prince of Wales Tower to the King's Gate (mainly 1824) where some characterless late medieval masonry has been revealed.

The fire exposed the inner wall of the lodging range immediately south of the Prince of Wales Tower overlooking the Kitchen Court. The lower clunch-faced wall, visible from Blore's Kitchen Cloister, revealed two ground-floor doorways, while the upper face was marked by the evidence of large two-light transomed windows, almost certainly with traceried heads.[54] Their scale and embrasure shape were revealed behind the panelling of the Crimson Drawing Room (1820) and have been left exposed behind hinged panelling in the State Dining Room (1853). The only fireplace evidence was of that inserted in the ground floor of the Chester Tower (otherwise rebuilt by Wyatville), for no stacks or chimneys are shown in Norden's or Hollar's views. A roof scar was traced against the Prince of Wales Tower, while the late seventeenth-century floor of the Grand Reception Room contains a large number of reused common rafters of mid-fourteenth-century date.[55] Their jointing allows a reconstruction of their widths which suggests they probably came from the roofs of these lodgings after May had remodelled them in the 1670s.

No evidence was found of external stairs to the upper rooms such as those serving the lodging ranges at Dartington Hall (c.1390–1400) and none are indicated in Hollar's drawing of the upper ward from the Round Tower which shows paired doors in each length of the range between the towers.[56] Either one door accessed the lower rooms and one a stair to the upper rooms, or the smaller doors are later insertions with the taller doors opening into lobbies with flanking entries to the lower rooms and a straight stair opposite to the upper floor, i.e. the layout at New College, Oxford. The size of the upper windows, not much smaller than those of the hall and chapel frontage, shows that these rooms were most generously scaled, more so than the term 'lodging range' usually implies. This reflects the high status of this accommodation, presumably for the many guests, courtiers, senior officials, and members of the household in a rigorously hierarchical society. Hollar's views and that of Norden show that the scale was maintained consistently throughout the length of these ranges, and that the outer walls remained unpierced[57] (see frontispiece).

These stone-built ranges, initiated on both sides of the ward between 1364 and 1366, were probably completed not long after 1370. They seem to have stood about 23 feet high to the base of the embattled parapet, with rooms 23¼ feet deep. The lower lodgings were about 9 feet high internally, with the more important rooms at the upper level generously windowed to the courtyard but unheated, with low-pitched roofs, king-post trusses, and close-set chamfered rafters.[58] Unlike the north-facing wall and towers of the royal lodgings, the outer faces of these ranges were virtually unbroken, for the east and south sides of the castle were still held to be potentially vulnerable.

Hugh May rebuilt the outer curtain wall in brick and remodelled the ranges and towers as far as the York Tower, with his round-headed windows, prominently visible in Kip's and Knyff's engravings from the south of 1711.[59] Wyatt made the present windows, while Wyatville added the attic storey and the courtyard corridors, and thoroughly recast both ranges as a new sequence of semi-state and personal family apartments which continue to be so used to the present day.[60] The 1992 fire has shown that far more medieval fabric survives in the north-east angle of the castle than had previously been suspected. The same probably applies to the remainder of the east and most of the south lodging ranges.

DESIGN VOCABULARY

The royal apartments are significant in representing the first secular residence in the fully developed Perpendicular style (fig. 50). There is a cohesive drive behind this harmonious structure, reflected in the extended courtyard frontage with its imposing line of first-floor windows above a barely pierced ground floor, common moulding lines, and a uniform embattled parapet with a high-pitched roof marking the hall and chapel and a lower one over the king's first apartment.[61] It is interrupted by three projections – two gatehouses and an end-stop tower – seeking though not achieving a balanced façade. The two embattled gateways (and to some extent that built by Edward at the entrance to the ward) with their line of machicolations between the turrets, portcullis, heavy gates, and probably modest fenestration (fronting portcullis mechanism) gave the appearance of military architecture. Here it was used for aesthetic and status effect only two generations after the meaningful gatehouses of the North Wales fortresses. Two omissions are surprising. One is the complete absence of buttresses. This applied to the gatehouses as well as to the frontage length. The consequence was an almost unbroken ground floor and sharply pitched roofs to ensure stability. All other roofs round the ward were low-pitched. Buttresses would have helped to create a pattern of light and shade, particularly necessary with such an extended façade. This was not helped by the second omission, the lack of decoration in the form of window heads, blind panelling, emblematic carvings, or parapet supports. This is particularly noticeable in comparison with the ornate decoration applied to the Aerary porch of 1353–5 in the Lower Ward.

The line of identical tall windows above modest ground-floor openings was repeated throughout the lodging ranges, similarly creating a linear contrast between the horizontal line of these decoratively embattled ranges with their low roofs, and the vertical accents of the upper-floor windows and probably deliberately raised towers behind. The turret added to the earlier York Tower, for instance, was work of 1367–8.[62] The consequence was an austere design throughout the inner court of the castle, an impression of monumentality barely relieved by any lead spirelets over stair turrets or colourful banners.

Internally, ground-floor rooms were plain, almost utilitarian, with two-centred doorways, undecorated jambs, and trefoiled lights. The trefoil was ubiquitous throughout the complex, common even to the window heads of hall and chapel. The more elaborate windows and delicately moulded jambs of the Rose Tower were the only exception, highlighting its high-status occupation. Roofs outside the ceremonial apartments were simple – low-pitched with tie-beam and king-post trusses. Architectural features in the private apartments such as door arches and fireplace lintels in greensand suggest this darker stone was deliberately used to add tonal qualities to the pared-down design. Where there was scope for decorative detailing, such as above the hall dais, the repetitiveness of blind panelling occurs.

Design simplicity was offset by the richness of the furnishings. Marble flooring and stained glass with borders was ordered in abun-

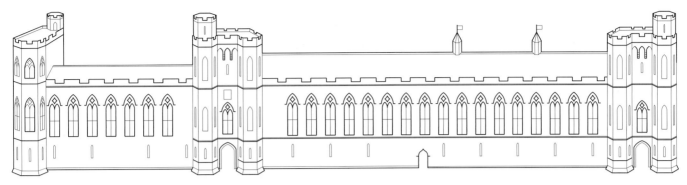

FIGURE 50 Windsor Castle: reconstruction of upper-ward frontage *c*.1365

dance in 1363–5, as well as more individual items such as mirrors, and four figures of the evangelists for the Queen's Chamber.[63] Some of the royal apartments had elaborate doors, wainscoting, and timbered ceilings, the latter often coloured with yellow ochre. Evidence of glazed floor tiling survives in two rooms in the Norman Gate and the second-floor lobby of the Rose Tower. Internal walls were probably limewashed, not plastered, though they would be covered with tapestries or hangings. The discovery of the repetitive painted decoration over the walls of the uppermost room and lobby in the Rose Tower is only matched by the contemporary fragments from St Stephen's Chapel, Westminster, but the scheme is secular, *in situ*, and complete.

CONSTRUCTION AND FUNDING LIMITATIONS

The development of the royal apartments at Windsor Castle under Edward III is of outstanding significance – historically, architecturally, and artistically. It reflects his triumphalist position as monarch and the prestige of the crown as leading a nation of European standing. Initially, Edward's work was prompted by the cult of chivalry. Though the Order of the Round Table which he initiated in his early thirties proved a false step, as did the structure to house its members, the collegiate buildings of the Order of St George survive in the lower ward to the present day.

His sumptuous building project during the later years of his reign was of European significance. It was affected and determined by two major events. Bubonic plague, and its lethal variants pneumonic and septicaemic plague, swiftly spread across England and Wales between about August 1348 and September 1349. There were further visitations in 1361–2, 1369 and 1375, with more sporadic outbreaks thereafter, but its impact was overwhelming. The mortality rate across the total population was not less than a third, trade was temporarily dislocated, and there was an immediate if short-lived food shortage, though some of the long-term consequences only developed towards the closing years of Edward's reign. More immediately damaging was the acute scarcity of skilled labour, compounding and accelerating the movement for rising wages and the mobility of labour that had developed twenty years or so before the plague. The extended campaign for rebuilding Windsor Castle over a period of about twenty years from 1354 could only be achieved by coercing masons and carpenters from across the country, creating a scarcity for other people's projects until the 1370s.[64] Their names and places of origin, listed at the end of the monthly account rolls, reveal the widespread coverage forced on the king's sheriffs to achieve and maintain the necessary build-

ing teams. In 1360, the sheriffs of thirteen counties were ordered to send 568 masons to Windsor, and in 1361 a total of 1,360 masons were sought from seventeen sheriffs.[65] The number employed was far fewer than the number sought, with some remaining for only a few months, but it was during these key stages of building that William Wykeham's abilities came to the fore. As surveyor of the king's works at Windsor, he was responsible for ordering materials, engaging workmen, paying their wages, and imprisoning malefactors during the critical early years of construction (1356–61). His successors, William Moulsoe (1361–5) and Adam Hartington (1365–77), were the beneficiaries of Wykeham's prodigious efficiency in extremely difficult circumstances.

The costly alliances that had marked the early years of the war against France had created severe financial difficulties for the king in 1340–1, but Edward's reputation had soared with victory in the field at Crécy and the establishment of a permanent bridgehead through taking Calais.[66] Edward was now seen as a monarch of European stature, capable of humbling the French, and the decision to rebuild Windsor was taken in that light. Yet it was the subsequent victory at Poitiers in 1357 and the capture of the French king that confirmed the superiority of the English crown and stimulated a wave of nationalism that was apparently consolidated by the Treaty of Brétigny in 1360. Edward III personified the country's pride and confidence at all levels of society in defeating the national enemy.

Against this background, the foreground becomes clearer. The wars had stimulated a national hegemony. It was only appropriate that the monarch should have an up-to-date palace befitting his status. The Palace of Westminster was central but old-fashioned, while Windsor was not too far distant – in the same relation to the capital as the Palace of Versailles was to Paris in a later age. The castle was the most spacious of all residences in royal hands, so it could take the form of a palace-fortress, with the power and character of a formidable defensive enclosure, cloaking the multi-windowed heart of a palatial residence. The Order of the Garter had consolidated Edward's relationship with his most trusted companions in arms, and was a distinctive if inexpensive form of patronage. The rebuilding of the castle was a broader affirmation of pride and confidence in the monarchy at a time when it 'enjoyed a degree of popularity unparalleled in the history of the Plantaganet dynasty'.[67] It was also an opportunity to give substantive employment at a time of sudden demographic change, and unlike many of his successors, Edward's building extravagance never attracted criticism.

Money, however, was always a problem for Edward. The French king's ransom of £500,000, payable in seven annual instalments, and the £66,666 of King David of Scotland, together with the lesser sums from other nobles, literally provided a war-chest to fund this costly project, just as the grant of the Gascon town, castle, and mint of Bergerac to Henry, duke of Lancaster in 1347 had enabled him to build his palace of the Savoy in London. Edward's funding was essentially private, with little recourse to government funds and potential opprobrium. But ransoms were rarely paid in full[68] and there was an uneasy peace with France between 1360 and 1369 when comparable replenishment was barely available. To help contain costs, the decision was taken to eschew adventitious ornamentation. Design simplicity and uniformity was the keynote. It applied externally to the courtyard façade, fenestration, and embatlement of the royal apartments and the two extended lodging ranges. It applied internally to all dressed stonework and roof structures with the exception of the hall and chapel, though even these were hardly lavish. The practice not only would have considerable financial benefits but would help to overcome the ongoing difficulties of limited skilled craftsmen. It would also hasten completion, in marked contrast with the unstructured and turgid alteration and development of the apartments under Henry III (1233–63). Architectural uniformity, minimalist decoration, and plain roofs all played their part in achieving the twin goals of cost efficiency and speedy completion – the same targets behind the restoration programme of 1992–7.[69] The design was driven by the singleness of purpose that is popularly attributed to William Wykeham, following the ascription by the continuator of Ranulph Higden's *Polychronicon*.[70] But apart from the much greater design responsibility of the master-mason, John Sponlee, together with William Wynford from 1361, and William Herland as the master-carpenter throughout,[71] it is not unlikely that the fundamental strictures of architectural style were made by the king.

PLANNING AND FUNCTION

Henry III and Edward III were among the leading royal builders of the middle ages, but whereas Henry incurred over £42,000 in rebuilding Westminster Abbey and less than a quarter of that updating his palace nearby, Edward's expenditure on the chapel of St George at Windsor was even more proportionally modest than on his extravagant remaking of the upper ward. This was a reflection not only of their respective character and priorities, but of Edward's closer attunement to the mood of the country. Windsor Castle was literally and metaphorically a flagship site. One of the consequences was that it became a benchmark in the movement from meaningful to decorative fortification. Edward I's sequence of castles in north and central Wales had an overwhelmingly military purpose. They were intended to overawe and hold down a restive populace. The same attitude applied to the next generation, including the keep built by the belligerent Lord Somery at Dudley Castle (*c*.1310) and to a lesser extent the formidable towered frontage of Warwick Castle (*c*.1340–70). In contrast, Edward's defensive gatehouse, the so-called Norman Gate, was almost theatrical in narrowing a visitor's progress from the middle to the upper ward, as well as being furnished with the trappings of defence, under the menacing presence of the towered motte. Both inner gateways were multi-storeyed, and embellished with defensive features, machicolations, and portcullises, but faced with a smooth freestone rather than the rough heathstone used elsewhere. They were essentially grand porch entries to residential courts, with the battlements encircling

all the ranges round the ward clearly symbolic and decorative. This would have been recognised and appreciated by contemporary visitors. The multi-polygonal-towered castle at Caernarvon, built by Edward's grandfather and the birthplace of his father, was possibly a structural and symbiotic precursor of Windsor, but the defensive features adopted were already common currency. It was the architectural equivalent of the crossover from bloody tournaments to chivalric encounters and was both contemporary with and complementary to that movement.

The plan of the new royal apartments was not limited by the earlier site layout and was totally different from that of any contemporary mansion. The towered curtain wall, the courtyards, and the kitchen position were retained, but there was a total separation between ground- and first-floor functions, with all the primary apartments at the upper level. It was inappropriate that the monarch should participate in the growing popularity of the ground-floor hall such as that built earlier at the castle, and more recently those at Caerphilly Castle, Mayfield Palace, and Penshurst Place. Henry III's hall was swept away in favour of a ceremonial apartment raised over an undercroft. The prominence of the chapel was a reflection of the scale of that recently completed by the king at his Palace of Westminster. But whereas that was two-storeyed in emulation of the Sainte Chapelle of the French king in Paris and Saint-Germain-en-Laye, the Windsor chapel was ground-breaking in its siting, back-to-back with the great hall. The interlocking character of these two inaugural state apartments and their close association with the Garter is clear.[72] What is only just being comprehended is the further function of these apartments for other ceremonies and high-status activities.

If the architectural decoration and roof structures of both state and private apartments were relatively plain, walls and roofs could be embellished with a wealth of colour and applied decoration. A glimpse of such overall patterning can still be seen in the uppermost room of the Rose Tower, but records also refer to the timber ceilings of the various chambers, wainscoting, and stained glass windows as well as decorative floor tiles and mirrors. The painted and gilded fragments of 1340–63 that have survived from St Stephen's Chapel, Westminster, with their numerous figures, dense patterning, and illusionistic devices hint at what has probably been lost, for Decorated and Perpendicular structures were essentially settings for decoration and imagery.[73] Tables, benches, desks, trestles, screens, cupboards, and iron utensils were supplied to the royal apartments between November 1363 and April 1365.[74] Unfortunately, we have no record of the plate, hangings, and jewels that sumptuously befitted and dramatically furnished the royal apartments and contributed to the backcloth of lavish hospitality and deliberate splendour that was a hallmark of Edward's reign.

The scale of the approach to the royal residence impressed the medieval visitor as much as it does 700 years later. Channelled through the new ceremonial gate (Norman Gate), the visitor would enter the massively scaled upper ward to be faced by dramatic façades of uniform design on all sides except the approach which was itself closed by the great motte of an earlier age. Crossing the multi-populated courtyard, he entered through an imposing porch-like gateway, opening by the sixteenth century into a two-storeyed cross wing on the site of the present Grand Vestibule, and almost certainly so considerably earlier to separate the two cloistered courts. It held the private stair leading to the king's apartments. The scale and spaciousness of the king's and queen's apartments (an early example of the more familiar early Tudor concept) would have amazed contemporaries. Those of Edward I at Conwy Castle were an extended sequence, but the king's apartments at Windsor eighty years later were a dramatic spatial parade of nine chambers, prefaced by a guard chamber and increasingly private in purpose until the royal bedchamber was reached. The delightful angle tower with its privy stair, painted chamber, and belvedere[75] was a deliberately positioned *bonne bouche* before the more intimate line of rooms. The sequence not only reflected the increase in household staff and royal protocol but was a reflection of the king's majesty at the apex of society. The queen had a similar if shorter line of apartments terminating in the royal bedchamber, back to back with that of the king.

A less privileged visitor would pass through the Great Cloister, like the Little Cloister a timber-framed structure, two-storeyed, and possibly glazed at both levels as it was a royal residence.[76] It led to the foot of the second cross range that had been Henry III's hall but was now the ceremonial stair to the grand new hall. As there is a touch of the theatre about Edward's work, it is likely that the first-floor approach was anticipatory and imposing, just as Edward II had created in his solar tower at Knaresborough Castle (1307)[77] and as Gaunt was to preface his hall at Kenilworth (1376–7). It may well have been a long straight flight of steps such as that seen to good effect added by Wykeham to the earlier chapel at Broughton Castle (c.1380) but the concept did not originate at Windsor. The late thirteenth-century approach to the chapter-house at Wells Cathedral or to the bishop's two halls at St David's Palace (c.1330–40) are earlier examples, though the Windsor stair was innovative in serving as the all-embracing approach to hall, chapel, and royal apartments, and from the kitchen.

Edward's ceremonial hall showed up that at Westminster to be an old-fashioned ground-floor aisled structure. The visceral impact on the visitor would be enhanced by the breathtaking richness and scale of the adjacent chapel. Neither of the royal suites was in the usual domestic position beyond the high end of the hall, emphasising the latter's pre-eminent ceremonial function but also facilitating a response to the need for the royal apartments to be more private and comfortable. If the visitor cared to see the new kitchen, he would be impressed by its scale as he would by the number of subsidiary offices. Even the number and extent of the lodgings round two sides of the ward would be beyond belief – extended ranges of upper rooms for leading guests, courtiers, and officials, with ground-floor rooms for the staff attendant on them.

The impact of remodelling the Round Tower at Windsor was limited. The revitalisation of the shell keep at Alnwick Castle by the 2nd Lord Percy (d.1352) had preceded that at Windsor, and there is little doubt that it created the incentive for the similar redevelopment of those not far away at Durham Castle by bishop Hatfield (between 1345 and 1381) and at Warkworth Castle by the 1st earl of Northumberland in the 1390s. Yet the rebuilding of the shell keep at Fotheringhay Castle by Edward III's youngest son shortly after 1377 is attributable to his father's precept.

EDWARD III'S LEGACY

The redevelopment of the palace-complex at Windsor reverberated for decades. It made a political, symbolic, and aesthetic statement for secular architecture through consolidating the development of

the proto-Perpendicular style, introducing new planning concepts, and initiating the structured contrast between external rectilinear formality and internal exuberance. If Edward III created a 'Windsor style', it was one of chivalric splendour, the contrast between external discipline and internal richness.

Windsor confirmed the quadrangle as the basis of multi-purpose occupation in a secular environment. The cloister had long been the centre of monastic establishments; just as courtyards had been for site-dictated fortresses. It was the concentric form of defence which had determined the quadrangular form at Caerphilly, Harlech, and Beaumaris castles, though its value was being appreciated in fortified houses, such as Maxstoke. The quadrangle in older castles such as Ludlow and Berkeley had hitherto been additive, whereas the Windsor complex was the consequence of a single unified and speedily achieved scheme. It was swiftly adopted across the country – in the south at Winchester College, Bodiam Castle, and Cobham College, in the Midlands at New College, Oxford, Drayton House, and Kimbolton Castle, and in the north at Bolton, Lumley, and Wressle castles. It became the paradigm for large-scale residences for the next 300 years.

William Wykeham, rewarded with the bishopric of Winchester for his services to the king, used the financial resources of this wealthy see to establish his colleges at Oxford and Winchester that disseminated the Windsor style, particularly through using the same master-mason, William Wynford. Newly cleared sites enable the courtyards at New College, Oxford, and Winchester College to be regular, with lodgings round at least two sides following earlier collegiate precedents such as Corpus Christi, Cambridge. As was usual, the upper lodgings (for fellows) were more generous than those below (for students), but several Windsor innovations were repeated. Wykeham's two colleges were the first to be approached by a dominant three-storeyed entry gateway, have regularised courtyard frontages, hall and chapel built back-to-back, and the kitchen and offices sited outside the courtyard enclosure. Even the concept of a cloister, and more particularly a belfry which Wykeham had overseen at Windsor in 1359–61,[78] was introduced at Winchester and New College, with the fifteenth-century Oxford foundations of All Souls and Magdalen repeating this particular feature. Yet there were some differences between the royal and episcopal projects. Wykeham's hall and chapel ranges were buttressed, their upper ends (dais and altar) were built either side the dividing wall, and the pivotal role of the chapel was signalled by its larger windows.

The Windsor complex renewed the status and importance of the first-floor hall, initially at Kenilworth, Bolton, and Raby castles and subsequently at leading academic foundations including Eton College and Christ Church, Oxford, and at particularly magnificent residences such as Wingfield Manor and Hampton Court. Windsor encouraged the development of the palace-fortresses at Bolton, Lumley, Raby, Sheriff Hutton, and Wressle, built by magnates who considered themselves and acted as mini-rulers of northern England. The remodelling and expansion of Kenilworth Castle by Edward's third son was more rightly prompted by his claim to a regalian title. Apart from Raby, which was developed round an earlier site, the northern fortresses were more compact than the royal exemplar, but followed the same principles of rectangular enclosure with a clear division between ground-floor services, the separation of public and private apartments above, the development of private chambers of increasing privacy, and the contrast between imposing but severe exteriors and an internal sequence of lavish first-floor apartments. Bolton Castle may have followed the same extended approach to its great hall as at Windsor, diagonally positioned across the courtyard from the gatehouse, and accessed through an extended passage and stair of increasing splendour.[79] The principal apartments of the tower-house at Warkworth were similarly approached. Windsor was also the exemplar for the marked uniformity of their façades, the balanced frontage at Kenilworth, and the elongated lodging ranges at Dartington Hall, Hampton Court Palace, and Kirby Hall. What is missing is the essential complement to all these stone envelopes, for the paucity of artefacts and never-ending changes in taste have deprived even the roofed buildings of their rich furnishings and showy interiors. Documentary evidence and manuscript illustrations are no substitute for the almost total loss of contemporary artistic production.

Cultural and artistic influences did not cease because England and France were at war. The main stimulus of the Flamboyant style in France came from across the Channel during the 1360s and 1370s. By that time, the Decorated style in England had been abandoned, whereas its vocabulary was taken up and developed to create a distinctive movement across France and beyond. Rather earlier, the rebuilding of Windsor Castle had made its own impact on French royal works. Philip of Valois had immediately imitated Edward's establishment of a Round Table as a centre of chivalric excellence in France in 1344, but it was John II who initiated a generation of royal projects based on the English model. Immediately after returning from his three years' English custody in 1361, he promptly set about building a massive residential tower-house at Vincennes. He built the first three floors before he had to honour a breakdown in the chivalric code by returning to England where he died. His son, Charles V, immediately completed the structure between 1364 and 1370. Like Windsor, the Vincennes tower-house was externally defensive but internally residential, with delicate vaulting, refined carving, and suites of apartments in vertical mode. Under Charles V, Vincennes became the king's favourite abode and it was completed as a symbol of royal prestige and power with a symmetrically towered and moated circuit (1370–80) that almost mirrored the much earlier ward enclosure at Windsor, adopted similar rectangular flat-topped towers, and deliberately surpassed it in size (15 acres to Windsor's 13). The vast courtyard included the earlier *manoir*, several *hôtels* for senior officials, and a large chapel initiated in 1379 to create, like Windsor, the equivalent of a miniature city.

Charles V also followed the English precedent by transforming the Louvre (1364–71). The work was not as wholesale as that at Windsor for the earlier massive stone keep was retained, but new living quarters were built round the courtyard, approached by a magnificent pillar-supported stair.[80] More fundamental was the work of Charles' younger brother, John duc de Berry, who immediately initiated the rebuilding of the castle at Saumur in 1367 after returning from seven years in England as a hostage. Though he adopted the Flamboyant rather than the English linear style, the formidable defensive quadrangular enclosure, completed in about 1380, concealed magnificently appointed courtyard ranges of first-floor apartments. It also followed the Windsor practice of an independent hall with the family apartments beyond its lower end. This range no longer survives, nor its courtyard stair approach.

LATE MEDIEVAL MODIFICATIONS

The royal apartments were little touched for nearly three centuries. During the closing years of the middle ages, the most important work was the construction of the magnificent replacement chapel of St George in the lower ward from 1477 onwards under Edward IV, slowly completed by the first two Tudor monarchs.[81] All three kings were also responsible for some minor changes to the royal apartments. Edward IV remodelled the Great Chamber with a line of upper windows and roof in 1477–8. Henry VII added a tower-like wing of personal apartments extending from the north-west corner of the palace complex (1499–1501). Consisting of a bedchamber, inner chamber, and closet, now entirely altered to serve as the lower end of the Royal Library, its most conspicuous features are the multi-faceted oriels on both sides, similar to those subsequently built at Thornbury Castle and Henry VII's Chapel, Westminster Abbey. Henry also rebuilt the roof over the kitchen in 1489. Henry VIII erected a timber precursor of the north terrace as well as an architecturally conservative replacement of the early thirteenth-century main gatehouse to the lower ward in 1513–16, while his daughter refitted the chapel (1570–1) and added a gallery range in 1582–4, now the upper end of the Royal Library.[82] Despite small-scale additions, fabric repairs, and internal alterations, Windsor Castle stood essentially unaltered for 300 years from the death of Edward III until the reign of Charles II. Even so, Edward's work established the matrix for all later modifications and rebuilding within the upper ward up to and including the twentieth century. What the visitor sees today is an exhilarating display of English baroque and a glorious exhibition of Regency romanticism, but its core is the pre-eminent chivalric palace-fortress of fourteenth-century England.

NOTES
1 *Windsor Castle*: I *Documentary History*; II *Architectural Description*.
2 Ed. H. M. Colvin, 6 vols. (1963–82).
3 *A History of Windsor Castle* (forthcoming).
4 Ranulph Higden, *Polychronicon*. Eton College Library, MS 213 fol.Xv. It belonged to John Blacman, one of the first fellows of Eton.
5 Brit. Lib., Harleian MS 3749.
6 The pre-eighteenth-century illustrations are most readily accessible in Hope's volumes, though their accuracy, particularly Norden's, must not be taken for granted. For a review of these sources and the value of Tudor heraldic accounts, C. Wilson in Keen and Scarff (2002) 17–19.
7 A. P. Oppé, *The Drawings of Paul and Thomas Sandby in the Collection of His Majesty the King at Windsor* (1947); J. Roberts, *Views of Windsor* (1995).
8 *History of the Royal Residences* (1819).
9 'Windsor Castle, New College, Oxford, and Winchester College: a study in the development of planning by William of Wykeham', *Jour. Brit. Arch. Assoc.* 3 (1938) 83–95.
10 *Windsor Castle* (1951, 2nd edn 1957).
11 *Windsor: The Most Romantic Castle* (1993).
12 A. Nicolson, *Restoration: The Rebuilding of Windsor Castle* (1997).
13 S. Brindle and B. Kerr, *Windsor Revealed: New Light on the History of the Castle* (1997). Also *Med. Arch.* 40 (1996) 244–5.
14 S. Brindle, 'Windsor Castle: the 1992 fire, the restoration, archaeology and history', in *Windsor: Medieval Archaeology, Art and Architecture of the Thames Valley*, ed. L. Keen and E. Scarff (2002) 110–24.
15 The buildings of the lower ward are being surveyed by T. Tatton-Brown. The description of the Deanery in *Arch. Jour.* 78 (1998) 345–90 has been followed by the important 'Constructional sequence and topography of the chapel and college buildings at St George's', in *St George's Chapel, Windsor, in the Late Middle Ages*, ed. C. Richmond and E. Scarff (2001)

3–38; and *St. George's Chapel, Windsor in the Fourteenth Century*, ed. N. Saul (2005).

16 C. Wilson, 'The royal lodgings of Edward III at Windsor Castle: form, function, representation'; V. Jansen, 'Henry III's Windsor: castle-building and residences'. Both in Keen and Scarff (2002) 15–94, 95–109.

17 The right-hand jamb of the entrance arch, the portcullis slot, and the gate position survive from his time.

18 The Curfew Tower has the most complete early medieval interior in the castle. Its apsidal ground-floor chamber has five deep embrasures and a great rib vault while the upper void is filled with the timber bell-frame of 1478–9.

19 Though remodelled by Edward III, this tower is a century earlier, with its tall ground-floor chamber terminating in a high-quality rib-vaulted apse of early thirteenth-century date.

20 Jansen in Keen and Scarff (2002) 95–109.

21 The great hall of the castle always lay in the lower ward until destroyed in 1473–4 to make way for St George's Chapel.

22 Identified in the west wall elevation, Brindle and Kerr (1997) 35, and by the reference to a first-floor fireplace further east, *ibid.* 36.

23 It has recently been argued to be part of a short-lived scheme of the late 1350s, *Med. Arch.* 40 (1996) 245, and Wilson in Keen and Scarff (2002) 30–33. The windows are by Wyatville.

24 *Adae Murimuth Continuatio Chronicarum*, ed. E. M. Thompson (1889) 155–6, 231–2. The royal accounts show that the building was circular and mainly of stone, supervised by the mason William Ramsey and the master-carpenter William Hurley. *HKW*, II (1963) 870–2.

25 *HKW*, II (1963) 881.

26 The clear separation of the royal apartments under Henry III between those of the Queen in the upper ward and those of the King in the lower ward ceased after a fire in the latter in 1295, when Edward I moved back to the upper ward. For their separation during Edward III's reign, Wilson in Keen and Scarff (2002) 73–5.

27 They included Robert Skyllington and Henry Spencer who subsequently worked for Gaunt at Kenilworth Castle. Brindle in Keen and Scarff (2002) 118–19.

28 Hope (1913) I, 153–4; *HKW*, II, 876.

29 *Vern. Arch.* 21 (1990) 46–8; 26 (1995) 60–1.

30 Evidence of some fourteenth-century room divisions was found in the form of stone footings or posts enclosed in later partition walls.

31 The chemise encircling the base of the Round Tower may date from this time. Hope (1913) II, 545.

32 The adjacent springers are the stubs of Wyatville's now destroyed lobby walls. The arches further east are Hugh May insertions.

33 Wilson in Keen and Scarff (2002) 30–3.

34 The trefoiled light in this wall is a fourteenth-century insertion. For a cross-section of the complex at this point from the upper ward to the north terrace, Nicolson, *Restoration* 156.

35 It is ironic that the earlier side hearths have been brought back into use while the Wyatville additions have not.

36 Fabric elevation of external face, Brindle and Kerr (1997) 27. See also Nicolson, *Restoration* 153–61.

37 *Vern. Arch.* 28 (1997) 139, 147.

38 *Ibid.* The documentary evidence of a plumber, mason, and carpenter at work in that year probably refers to this roof. *HKW*, III (1975) 306. It was built by John Squyer who roofed Henry VII's wing, and the choir of St George's Chapel.

39 The photograph in Nicolson, *Restoration* 132 illustrates the roof closer to its medieval character before the plaster coving was restored. Also Brindle in Keen and Scarff (2002) 114–15.

40 Brindle and Kerr (1997) 14–17, 26–7.

41 *Ibid.* 24–5; Brindle in Keen and Scarff (2002) 115.

42 Hope sited the dais at the east end against the chapel, and the screens next to the kitchen gate: (1913) II, 569.

43 He retained but refaced the medieval buttressed wall facing the Kitchen Court. Wilson in Keen and Scarff (2002) 36–7.

44 Photogrammetric elevation of west end, Nicolson, *Restoration* 115; Wilson in Keen and Scarff (2002) 36–7. Although undoubtedly impressive, Wyatville's hall, as he recognised, was too badly proportioned to overcome its similarity to a railway carriage. Vastly improved after the 1992 fire, it would have been valuable to have signalled the two-room division and inserted a more steeply pitched roof. For the difficulties, Nicolson, *Restoration* 77, 212–17.

45 Its chute and ground-floor pit were traced in 1994.

46 The exterior wall of the King's Dining Room (1670s), now part of the Grand Staircase, may incorporate some medieval work.

47 The wall above these windows was heightened by Wyatville to match his St George's Hall.

48 Photogrammetric survey of east wall, Nicolson, *Restoration* 112.

49 Similar to the ground-floor vaults of 1362–3 in the inner ward gate-house.

50 Hope (1913) I, 197.

51 *Ibid.* 190.

52 Wilson in Keen and Scarff (2002) 21.

53 *HKW*, III pt 1 (1975) 316–17 follows Hope, whose suggested medieval room layout was never convincing.

54 Fabric elevation, Brindle and Kerr (1997) 18–19.

55 *Med. Arch.* 40 (1996) 244.

56 Hope (1913) I, pl. 31.

57 *Ibid.* pls. 4 and 32.

58 The ragstone lodging range of six dwellings on the south side of the lower ward, now occupied by military knights, was built in 1359–60 for the clerks of the chapel. It was altered in 1557–8 when the range was doubled in length, and was subject to a wholehearted refitting by Blore in 1840.

59 *Britannia Illustrata*.

60 According to Hope, 'none of the ground floor rooms exhibit anything of antiquarian interest' (II, 560), while the upper rooms seem to be entirely of Wyatville's day, as amended by subsequent generations (*ibid.* 572–5). Charles II's state apartments have not been occupied since the royal family vacated them early in the nineteenth century in favour of Wyatville's more comfortable accommodation.

61 It is assumed that this was an original structure and not a late fifteenth- or sixteenth-century replacement of a higher-pitched roof.

62 Hope (1913) II, 576.

63 *Ibid.* I, 189–90; *HKW*, II (1963) 877–9.

64 Continuator of Ranulph Higden's *Polychronicon*, ed. J. R. Lumby (1886) 184.

65 D. Knoop and G. P. Jones, 'The impressment of masons for Windsor Castle 1360–63', *Economic History* 3 (1934–7) 350–61.

66 The Order of the Garter was established in the flush of these victories.

67 W. M. Ormrod, *The Reign of Edward III* (1990) 39. Edward's popularity, of course, had worn dangerously thin by the closing years of his reign through indolence and reliance on court sycophants.

68 Edward received less than half the French king's ransom while the Scots refused to pay David II's ransom between 1360 and 1366.

69 Nicolson, *Restoration* 250–70.

70 'In about . . . 1359 . . . William Wikham, clerk, caused many excellent buildings in the castle of Windsor to be thrown down and others more beautiful and sumptuous to be set up . . . He counselled [the King] to build . . . in the form in which it appears today to the beholder', ed. J. R. Lumby (1886) 359.

71 J. Harvey, *Eng. Med. Arch.* (1984) 280–1, 352, 142. See also note 27 above.

72 The association and splendour is still maintained by the sovereign and the Garter knights on 16 June each year.

73 N. Coldstream, *The Decorated Style* (1994) 59.

74 The furniture inventory of *c.*1365 is proving invaluable in identifying the likely layout of the royal apartments.

75 Wilson in Keen and Scarff (2002) 64–7 draws attention to the upper ward towers as viewing platforms and, less convincingly, to the Rose Tower as a prototype dining bay window off the hall.

76 Gaunt may have built a timber-framed cloister at Hertford Castle (*c.*1380) but that at Ockwells Manor (1450s) reflected contemporary developments at Eton College, not at Windsor nearly a century earlier.

77 P. Dixon, *Château Gaillard* 14 (1990) 121–39.

78 This three-storeyed belfry has been converted into the Governor's Tower.

79 The hall approach at Raby Castle (*c.*1367–77) from the Neville Gateway may have been similar, but the evidence was destroyed by Austin and Johnson in 1864 when they inserted their grand staircase. There seems to have been a vaulted approach at hall level. A. Emery, *Greater Med. Houses*, I (1996) 127.

80 For an important contribution to this aspect of Windsor, M. Whiteley, 'The courts of Edward III of England and Charles V of France: a comparison of their architectural setting and ceremonial functions', in *Fourteenth Century England*, ed. N. Saul (2000) 153–66.

81 In the lower ward, the Vicars Choral were provided with a new hall in 1415, now the Chapter Library. The chimneypiece is an early Tudor replacement, but the tie beams are original. The Horseshoe Cloister nearby was built for the vicars in 1478–81 when their accommodation was supplanted by the new chapel. Timber-framed with brick noggin and ogee-shaped braces, the fronts of these twenty-one two-storeyed houses face the open cloister, each one with the newel close to the entry door, but the hand of George Gilbert Scott (1871) lies heavy.

82 *HKW*, III pt 1 (1975) 302–27.

Sir William St John Hope, *Windsor Castle* (1913)

Sir Owen Morshead, *Windsor Castle* (1951)

H. M. Colvin *et al.* (eds.), *History of the King's Works*, 6 vols. (1963–82)

S. Brindle and B. Kerr, *Windsor Revealed* (1997)

L. Keen and E. Scarff, *Windsor: Medieval Archaeology, Art and Architecture of the Thames Valley* (2002), including papers on the castle by Grenville Astill, 1–14; Christopher Wilson, 15–94; Virginia Jansen, 95–109; Steven Brindle, 110–24

S. Brindle, S. Priestley and B. Kerr, *A History of Windsor Castle* (forthcoming)

YELFORD MANOR, Oxfordshire

The present lane through the secluded village of Yelford necessitates rear access to the manor, but the show front was originally approached from a bridleway close to the contemporary church across the surviving arm of the spring-fed moat.[1] The house is unusual because it is entirely timber-framed in a region noted for stone houses including Stanton Harcourt Manor House, Minster Lovell Hall, and Cokethorpe Park nearby. It is of box-frame construction to the classic plan of a central hall, initially open to the roof, with two-storeyed upper and lower cross wings. The H-shaped plan of the house is not obvious from the front which is almost flat except for the jettied upper floor of the wings. The rear shape is also disguised by a sixteenth-century stair projection in the centre, a truncated solar wing, and a low eighteenth-century extension.

Elm was used throughout the house, brought from the woods that densely surrounded the settlement until decimated by Dutch elm disease in the 1970s.[2] The close-set timbers, lath and plaster infilled, are set on a low stone base and support a Cotswold slate roof. The hall and cross wings are not tied together structurally, but there was no time lag between the stages of construction, with many common carpenters' marks throughout the house. The property was built at the close of the fifteenth century by a junior branch of the Hastings family who had held the manor since at least the early thirteenth century. Construction was by John Hastings (d.1542) after he had settled at Yelford in the 1490s,[3] with dendro dating in 2001 giving a felling date for the hall timbers of 1499 and a year later for those of the cross wings.[4] A floor was inserted in the hall during the sixteenth century when the two-storeyed bay window and rear staircase were added. Subsequent changes have been minimal. The property became a farmhouse during the late seventeenth century, and was subsequently divided into three cottages that had sunk into an appalling state of repair by the mid-twentieth century. The house would have fallen into ruin except for the effort of the Babbington Smiths after 1952. Subsequent improvements in the 1980s have built on their rescue work[5] so that the house has regained most of its original character externally, and its early volumes internally.

The hall entry is not prefaced by a porch and is marked externally by the sixteenth-century additions made when the hall was floored: the oriel immediately above with moulded timbers and the multi-sided bay window, both with individual gables. The remaining windows are eighteenth century (or later), as are those in the cross wings. The ends of the solar jetty have been cut off for an unknown reason, and the side and rear walls of the wing have been rebuilt in stone, possibly in the late sixteenth or early seventeenth century. The offices wing also has a stone stack, and retains external evidence of a first-floor timber-framed garderobe towards the north-east corner.

Internally, the hall, 31 feet by 18½ feet, was divided into two and a half bays. The two full bays were open to the roof and the 7 foot wide half bay was developed as a cross passage between the opposing entry doors with a narrow room above. The plain post and panel screen is original except for the remade central entry. The replacement of the flagged floor in the hall in 1952 revealed twelfth-century pottery and an associated hearth, but all earlier site structures were destroyed when the present house was erected.[6] The central hearth was retained initially in the new hall, creating a small deposit of soot on the roof timbers. Sixteenth-century division into two floors created the opportunity to insert new windows, including the bay lighting the dais end of the hall, and to add fireplaces at both levels served by a common stack. The ground-floor fireplace is a 1950s replacement, while that in the room above has been blocked but retains its original moulded mantel and the capitals of the support columns. They are of a form common in the fifteenth and early sixteenth centuries rather than later. Two original features of the hall have survived the inserted floor and ceiling – the corbels that supported a shallow canopy above the high table, and the central cross beam astride the hall of slightly arched form with a small central nip.[7]

Both cross wings were originally three-bayed, jettied to the front and projecting only to the rear. The offices wing has a single entry from the cross passage with moulded jambs, a square head, and high stops. There is evidence next to it of a hatch above a stone sill. The present fireplace is a 1980s replacement in a stack that may be original if the upper fireplace is any guide. This suggests that the ground floor was primarily a kitchen, with associated offices. There is some evidence that a stair rose from the cross passage to the landing

PLATE 84 Yelford Manor: from the south-west

above before the present stair was inserted. The residential room above the kitchen was never open to the roof. It is spanned by a heavy cross beam with a single line of plain wind braces as elsewhere in the house.

The truncation of the solar wing has reduced its architectural though not its visual value. The small ground-floor parlour repeats the single cross beam of the opposing wing, was panelled in the seventeenth century, and has a 1950s fireplace.

The very limited amount of roof soot and the character of the inserted features suggest that the alterations to Yelford Manor occurred earlier rather than later in the sixteenth or early seventeenth century.[8] The four-centred doorcase between the stair and gallery landing has the spandrel initials I H, which may identify John Hastings (1542–85) or his grandson (1610–29), but could also refer to late work by the house's initiator. The manor was sold by the Hastings family to their kinsman, Speaker Lenthall, in 1651. The Lenthall family held the property for virtually three centuries, but because they lived at Burford Priory and later at Bessels Leigh, the house was let to tenants. As it was not subject to extensive Georgian or Victorian alterations, it has been possible to bring the property back to its early form with a clear demonstration of the early to mid-Tudor modifications.

Yelford Manor lacks the decorative panache of some timber-framed houses in nearby regions, though it may have been more elaborate than seems at first sight. The replacement solar window has not destroyed the support timbers of an earlier oriel,[9] while the original barge boards may have been more decorative than their later replacements. The house lacks original windows[10] and most of its fireplace evidence, and the arch-braced roofs are plain, but it is rare to see naturally coloured timbers, uncluttered rooms, and such little modification to a gentry house of this period in the middle Thames valley. A map of 1625 shows that it was prefaced at that time by a central gateway and flanking ranges on the north and south sides of the forecourt, but all such evidence has long since disappeared.[11]

NOTES

1 The full extent of the moat has not been traced. There is no evidence that it was defensive; rather it was for drainage in a particularly wet and floodable area.

2 Oak rather than elm struts were inserted in the early 1950s to arrest the movement that was threatening to bring the house down.

3 VCH, XIII (1996) 208.

4 *Vern. Arch.* 33 (2002) 85.

5 *South Midlands Archaeology* 14 (1984) 76–7.

6 Yelford suffered heavily from depopulation between 1327 when there were sixteen taxpayers and 1523 when the manor house was the only taxable household. VCH, XIII (1996) 207–8.

7 The south end of this truss had to be supported by a roughly shaped blade to counteract the tilt occasioned by the inserted upper fireplace under it. The blade was book-enveloped at the time of Jennifer Sherwood's suggestion that it was a cruck truss, J. Sherwood and N. Pevsner, *The Buildings of England: Oxfordshire* (1974) 869.

8 As favoured by VCH, XIII (1996) 209.

9 It seems to be shown in a drawing of 1825, primarily of the church, by J. C. Buckler: Bod. Lib., MS Top. Oxon. a69 no.643. This shows the house when it was plaster-covered. It is possible that the ground-floor window was also of oriel form, VCH, XIII (1996) 209.

10 Most of those in the church, built immediately after the manor house had been constructed, are uncusped arched twin lights under square hoods with end stops.

11 Illustrated in VCH, XIII (1996) pl. 39.

VCH, *Oxfordshire*, XIII (1996) 205–10

APPENDIX 1
THE THAMES VALLEY CASTLES: RESIDENTIAL ADDITIONS

*c.*1310–45	Berkeley, Glos.	Hall, apartments	see text
*c.*1330–50	Beverston, Glos.	Residential towers	see text
1353–7	Windsor, Berks.	Keep remodelled	St John Hope, *Windsor Castle* (1913) and S. Brindle, S. Priestly, and B. Kerr, *A History of Windsor Castle* (forthcoming)
1357–63	Windsor, Berks.	Royal apartments rebuilt	*ibid.*
1364–*c.*1370	Windsor, Berks.	Lodging ranges round two sides of upper ward	*ibid.*

PLATE 85 Thornbury Castle, outer court: north lodging range

APPENDIX 2

THE THAMES VALLEY: RESIDENTIAL LICENCES TO CRENELLATE

STANDING			DESTROYED		
1299	Yate (Court), Glos.	Sir John Wilington			
			1304	Haversham, Bucks.	James Plaunche
			1311	Cromhall, Glos.	Sir William Wauton
				Ruardean, Glos.	Alexander Bicknor (tower fragment)
1312	Boarstall, Bucks.	John Handlo			
1315	Bampton, Oxon.	Aymer Valence, earl of Pembroke			
			1317	Cassington, Oxon.	William, Lord Montagu
1318	Chiselhampton (Camoys Court), Oxon.	Sir Richard Louches	1318	Culverton, Glos.	Henry Wilington
			1327	Stanton Harcourt, Oxon.	John Wyard
			1329	Drayton, Oxon.	Robert Ardern
			1330	Wykham (Park), Oxon.	Robert Ardern
				Westbury, Glos.	Robert Sapy
			1331	Stoke Poges, Bucks.	John Moleyns
				Ditton, Bucks.	John Moleyns
			1334	Stoke Poges, Bucks.	John Moleyns (repeat)
				Ditton, Bucks.	John Moleyns (repeat)
				Weston Turnville, Bucks.	John Moleyns and wife
				Boddington, Glos.	Sir John Bures and wife
			1336	Aston Mullins, Bucks.	John Moleyns
			1337	Sonning, Berks.	Robert, bp of Salisbury
			1338	Aldworth, Berks.	Nicholas de la Beche
				Beaumys, Berks.	Nicholas de la Beche
				Watlington, Oxon.	Nicholas de la Beche
1346	Rotherfield Greys (Greys Court), Oxon.	John, Lord Grey			
			1347	Kingham, Oxon.	Gilbert Chastelyn
				Wheatenhurst (Whitminster), Glos.	Humphrey Bohun, earl of Hereford
1348	Rotherfield Greys (Greys Court), Oxon.	John, Lord Grey (repeat)			
			1356	Newnham Murren, Oxon.	Richard English
			1360	Great Holcombe, Oxon.	Richard English

STANDING			DESTROYED		
1377	Shirburn, Oxon.	Warin, Lord Lisle	1377	Sonning, Berks.	Ralph, bp of Salisbury (repeat)
1386	Donnington, Berks.	Sir Richard Abberbury	1391	Stanley Pontlarge, Glos.	John Rous
1406	Broughton, Oxon.	Sir Thomas Wykeham	1446	Thatcham Chamberhouse, Berks.	John Pury
			1448	Yattendon, Berks.	John Noreys
1458	Sudeley, Glos.	Sir Ralph Boteler (pardon)			
1510	Thornbury Castle, Glos.	Edward, duke of Buckingham	1510	Hanstead Hall, Bucks.	Robert Drury

Part II
LONDON AND SOUTH-EAST ENGLAND

6

LONDON: AN INTRODUCTION

BY the Norman Conquest, London was the primary centre of England's trade and industry, and subsequently became that of royal government. It developed into one of the leading cities of medieval Europe and its buildings were among the most distinguished in the country. Yet five centuries later, Elizabethan illustrations show that the city was still essentially confined within the much repaired Roman walls, with two or three suburbs immediately outside them, several religious foundations a little further away, and a scattering of dwellings lining the approach roads before quickly thinning to the fields of the countryside.

As with Paris, a never-ending sequence of demolition, rebuilding, and expansion has left little evidence of the medieval city, though we have a very considerable idea of what it was like. The same applies to the immediate suburbs, Southwark, Holborn, and Westminster. We know considerably less about the Strand and Charing, the area between the largest city in England and the centre of government, where many palaces and mansions were erected by those who needed to be close to the crown or to the seat of government.

The fire of 1666 and three centuries of commercial development have devastated medieval London and neighbouring Westminster, but it is not always appreciated that the inexorable expansion of the metropolis between the eighteenth and twentieth centuries also destroyed the less well-documented medieval buildings within a 15 mile radius of the city. Nothing remains of the early villages that used to edge the capital such as Kensington, Shoreditch, or Clapham, and little of those further afield at Kingston, Richmond, Greenwich, Harrow, and Uxbridge. A small number of heavily restored parish churches survive but no leading monasteries or mansions remain in an area which contained several market towns and over 300 villages or settlements serving the capital with agri-cultural produce or manufactured goods. There was also an unknown number of manor houses, barely served by the recovered evidence of properties such as Brook House, Hackney, or the moated houses at Headstone and Low Hall Manor, Walthamstow. For the visitor, the region within a 10 mile radius from the banks of the London Thames is a medieval waste that does not abate until a circle of survivals is reached that encompasses Waltham Abbey, Hampton Court, and Croydon and Eltham palaces.

Though town houses are not included in these three volumes, the scale, considerable number, and political significance of those in London and its suburbs in lay and ecclesiastical ownership warrant an exception. Medieval London was crowded with the town houses of the royal family, magnates, and bishops, supplemented by those of the leading monasteries and merchant-princes. Most of these res-idences were known to contemporaries as inns, though we tend to misapply the word 'palace' to those occupied by the summit of society. The changing use of this word was discussed in volume II,

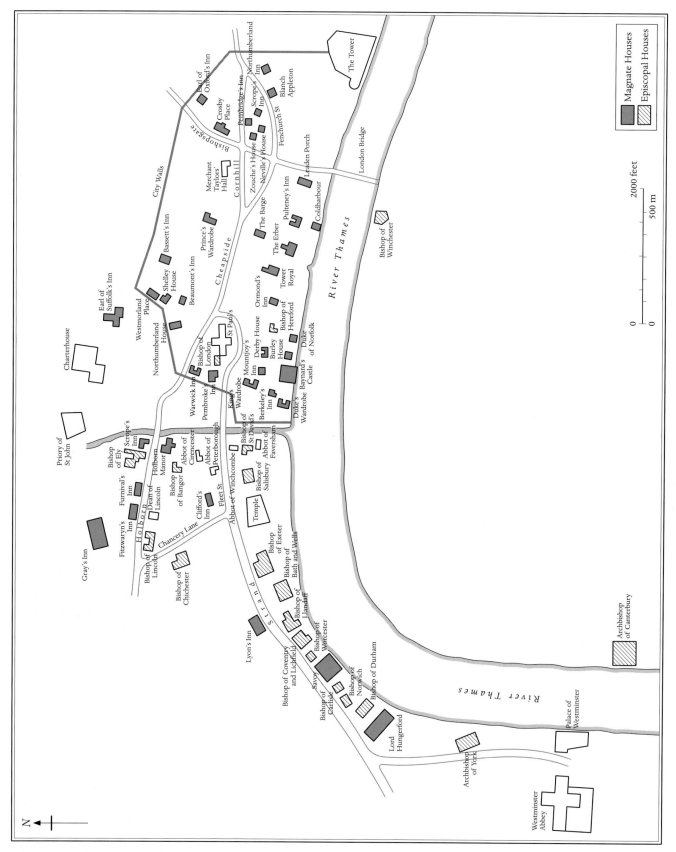

FIGURE 51 London houses in the late middle ages

N

Magnate Houses
Episcopal Houses

2000 feet

500 m

The Tower

River Thames

London Bridge

Northumberland Inn
Scrope's Inn
Blanch Appleton
Pembridge's Inn
Fenchurch St
Earl of Oxford's Inn
Crosby Place
Zouche's House
Neville's House
Leaden Porch
Bishopsgate
Merchant Taylors' Hall
Cornhill
The Barge
Pulteney's Inn
Coldharbour
Bassett's Inn
Prince's Wardrobe
The Erber
Bishop of Winchester
Cheapside
Ormond's
Tower Royal
Shelley House
Beaumont's Inn
Bishop of Hereford
Westmorland Place
Derby House
Burley House
Duke of Norfolk
Earl of Suffolk's Inn
Bishop of London
St Paul's
Mountjoy's Inn
Baynard's Castle
Northumberland House
Berkeley's Inn
Duke's Wardrobe
Charterhouse
Warwick Inn
King's Wardrobe
Pembroke's Inn
Priory of St John
Scrope's Inn
Bishop of St David's
Bishop of Ely
Abbot of Faversham
Holborn
Holborn Manor
Abbot of Cirencester
Abbot of Peterborough
Furnival's Inn
Dean of Lincoln
Bishop of Bangor
Fleet St
Fitzwaryn's Inn
Clifford's Inn
Abbot of Winchcombe
Temple
Bishop of Salisbury
Gray's Inn
Bishop of Lincoln
Chancery Lane
Bishop of Chichester
Bishop of Exeter
Bishop of Bath and Wells
Strand
Bishop of Llandaff
Lyon's Inn
Savoy
Bishop of Worcester
Bishop of Coventry and Lichfield
Bishop of Carlisle
Bishop of Norwich
Bishop of Durham
Lord Hungerford
River Thames
Archbishop of York
Archbishop of Canterbury
Palace of Westminster
Westminster Abbey
City Walls

for it applied to only a single property in London before the fifteenth century, the royal residence at Westminster. Yet the houses of the upper élite were of a scale and distinction to warrant this tautological extension.[1] Not one magnate residence survives, but part of the palace of Westminster does and much of that of the archbishop of Canterbury. Two or three halls, a chapel, and some undercrofts constitute virtually the sum of such buildings today, but pictorial evidence and archaeological research show that these hundred or so metropolitan houses differed little in scale, layout, or appointment from their sister houses and palaces in the country. They are the corollary of those addressed throughout this and the two other volumes on the greater houses of late medieval England and Wales.

Apart from the scale of the chapel, there was little difference architecturally between those in lay and those in ecclesiastical ownership. This is highlighted by the ease of movement of ownership between social groups. Simon de Montfort occupied the bishop of Durham's palace in 1258, while John of Gaunt used that of the bishop of Ely until his death after the sacking of the Savoy eighteen years earlier. The bishop of London's residence was often lent out to royalty during the fifteenth century, while Queen Joan of Navarre held the earl of Northumberland's house after its forfeiture to the crown in 1403. The mid-fourteenth-century house built by that leading merchant Sir John Pulteney known as Pulteney's Inn or the Manor of the Rose subsequently became the home of the Black Prince, the earl of Arundel, and the earl of Suffolk. His second house, Coldharbour, was granted to the prince of Wales in 1410 and became the home of Lady Margaret Beaufort, Henry VII's mother. Similarly, Sir John Crosby's mid-fifteenth-century mansion in Bishopsgate became a semi-royal court under Richard, duke of Gloucester and was an early home of Catherine of Aragon. Early guild and livery companies and legal inns of court began taking over such courtyard residences for their communal use, and retained that character when premises were purpose-built by later generations.

A late-twelfth-century traveller riding from Westminster to the City would pass from the abbey and court precincts through open countryside a little distance from the banks of the tidal River Thames. Passing through the settlement at Charing and along the rutted Strand way, he would reach the city boundary close to the Temple precinct before crossing the River Fleet to enter the city through Lud Gate. The Roman turreted walls still demarcated the city enclosure on the north side of the river, criss-crossed by an irregular pattern of broad and narrower streets, an abundance of stone churches, some monastic establishments, and a hotch-potch of mainly timber-framed shops and houses, with the skyline dominated at one end by St Paul's Cathedral and at the other by the Tower of London. The suburb of Holborn lay to the north-west, stretching towards St Giles in the Field, while Southwark lay south of London Bridge, the only one spanning a river that was almost half as wide again as today before its Victorian embankment. There were still some open green spaces within the city, but beyond the turreted walls only an occasional monastic foundation interrupted the fields and farms of the open countryside.

With the expansion of London as England's commercial and entrepreneurial capital during the thirteenth century, and the development of Westminster as the political, judicial, and financial centre of the realm between the mid-thirteenth and mid-fourteenth centuries, a permanent abode nearby became essential for the upper élite. Far more archaeological and documentary research has been undertaken on episcopal than on lay residences and this may well have distorted our view of their relative importance and scale. Bishops, of course, were as intimately involved in the government of medieval England as the baronage and we know when most of their properties were established. Canterbury and Winchester led the way before 1200, swiftly followed by virtually all fellow bishops within the next hundred years.[2] Furthermore, most of these residences were not within the city but lined the north bank of the Thames towards Westminster, with the archbishop of York positioned as close to the seat of government as Canterbury was on the opposite river bank. We know less about the development of magnate houses and their physical form, for the majority were within the city, only used when necessary for business purposes or attending Westminster, and because some of the leading families leased properties rather than purchased land for residential developments. There were no aristocratic mansions near the Tower or on the south side of the river. The majority lay on the west side of the city, with some of the most important close to the river. Ecclesiastical pre-emption left little room for secular expansion along the Strand, but two of the largest houses during the later middle ages were those of the duke of Lancaster and Lord Hungerford.

Merchant capitalists followed suit within the city from the early fourteenth century, while the first phase of company halls and corporate buildings for lawyers developed from modest roots during the fifteenth century. In the mid-1170s, William FitzStephen had written of his native city as a prelude to his life of St Thomas Becket: 'Almost all the bishops and abbots and magnates of England are, as it were, citizens and burgesses of the city of London; they have there their own splendid houses where they dwell, where they lay out great sums, when they answer the king's summons to the city for royal councils, the archbishop's for ecclesiastical gatherings, or the call of their own affairs.'[3] This had barely changed 300 years later, though the houses had now spread from the city along the riverside to Westminster.

Whether called palace, inn, place, wardrobe,[4] or house, the components of these leading residences were the same as those in the country – entry gate, courtyard, hall, suite of private chambers, chapel, kitchen, and offices. They also tended to be laid out in the same way, with courtyard and hall as the axis of the house and halls of sufficient scale to impress all visitors. Lambeth Palace hall was used for councils, convocation, and consecration banquets, with the most lavish occurring in 1367 when William Wykeham was appointed bishop of Winchester. Henry IV used Ely Place during the summer of 1409, while Winchester House was the scene of the wedding feast in 1426 of James I of Scotland and Joan Beaufort, cardinal Beaufort's niece. The bishop of Ely's house in Holborn virtually touched the countryside, enabling the bishop to enjoy a large orchard and 14 acres of pasture as well as an enclosed garden. There was little difference in scale or setting between this and the duke of Lancaster's palace at the Savoy, or the Inn of the bishop of Bath and Wells, Lambeth Palace, or Winchester House.[5]

Documentary research on Winchester House illustrates what can also be discerned at Ely Place, the Savoy, and Westminster Palace. From the early fourteenth century onwards, these late medieval palaces were planned to provide an increasing sequence of limited access and privacy to the head of the establishment. Initially this might take the form of a secular tower, intended not for defence but as a tier of increasingly private rooms like the south tower at Stokesay

Castle. This form was soon abandoned in favour of the double-courtyard plan restricting access from the relatively public outer court with stables and offices, to more limited access for staff and retainers, leading to the private quarters of the king, magnate, or bishop. The hall might be sited midway between these functions as at Ely Place, Lambeth, and Westminster, or close to the river as at Winchester House with its outer and inner gatehouses. In either case, traversing a sequence of rooms of increasingly restricted access, the *sine qua non* of Tudor palaces, had become a well-established practice in the largest households during the fifteenth century.

The outstanding differences between many of these mansions and those in the country lay in two aspects: an imposing river façade (the Savoy and Winchester House were particularly impressive), and access to the river for leading figures of state. Three successive wharves are associated with the bishop of Winchester's palace: a timber one of *c*.1200, replaced in *c*.1354, and succeeded by one in stone during the fifteenth century. The first was as much for commercial activity as for politics and household needs, but the latter gradually predominated. The wharf next to Sir John Fastolf's house may have been necessary for his extensive commercial interests, but the riverside towers at Baynard Castle (*c*.1428), Lambeth Palace (1435), York Place (1465–76), and Bridewell Palace (1515–23) were as much for provisions, building materials, and heavy goods as for household and visitor access.

In an area continuously subject to occupational expansion and burgeoning commercial pressures, it is not surprising that so few residences have survived.[6] Quite a number have been revealed by excavation since the 1950s, including Kennington Palace, Winchester House in Southwark, Neville's Inn and Warwick Inn in the City, and the Inn of the Bishop of Bath and Wells in the Strand. Single ownership and continuous occupation has ensured that the abbatial lodging at Westminster stands complete, the royal complex within the Tower of London exists in part, while Lambeth Palace is the exemplar of *rus in urbe*. Otherwise it is a case either of key components surviving – the halls at Westminster, Barnard Inn, and Guildhall, the two-storey chapel at Ely Place, and the gatehouse and chapel at Lambeth Palace – or of some lesser elements such as the Jewel Tower and the undercroft of St Stephen's chapel at Westminster, or part of the hall of Winchester House. By the fifteenth century, wealthy entrepreneurs were seeking to emulate the aristocracy with courtyard houses of which there is considerable documentary evidence (building contracts, house surveys, panoramas[7]), but only Crosby Hall survives on its relocated site. Five houses passed to livery companies during the fourteenth century, including that owned by Edward III's tent maker which was acquired by the Merchant Taylors Company,[8] but such institutions grew considerably in number during the fifteenth and early sixteenth centuries to become a key link with élite houses.[9] There were in the region of at least forty-five lay and nearly fifty ecclesiastical mansions in late medieval London, with the great majority of them adopting the courtyard plan. Their almost total eradication between the mid-sixteenth and eighteenth centuries is one of the outstanding losses of medieval England, far greater than that of Old St Paul's on the grounds of scale and number, their architectural quality and individuality, and their intimate involvement in the politics of late medieval England.

All these houses were built of stone, but this material could only be afforded by the most wealthy, usually brought from Kent or Surrey, and little enough of this had survived by the beginning of the nineteenth century. The majority of domestic structures were timber-framed and thatched, far more capable of being burnt, pulled down, and rebuilt. A handful of stone undercrofts still exist (and more were found during nineteenth-century redevelopments but not preserved), providing secure and dry storage facilities under timbered structures. The widespread introduction of brick towards the close of the fifteenth century was the primary development of the early Tudor period. Initially used for undercroft vaults and load-bearing walls, its preference by the crown as a fashionable material as at Bridewell Palace (1515–23) meant its speedy adoption by aristocracy, merchants, and institutions.

The Reformation was followed by a tidal wave of secular expansion throughout London and its suburbs. Most of the episcopal palaces along the Strand were taken over by the nobility, while many of the monastic inns needed little or no modification for lay occupation. The crown's disposal of the monasteries and their urban properties led to dramatic landholding and investment changes. So far as the monastic precincts were concerned, some like Charterhouse and Bermondsey Abbey became large-scale mansions, while others within the city walls were converted into multiple occupation as at St Bartholomew's Priory and Holy Trinity Priory, Aldgate. The wholesale redistribution of monastic properties resulting in some bizarre town houses as well as secularised mansions and houses, combined with the influx of migrants from the countryside and abroad, and the growth of the legal profession and trade companies, fundamentally changed the face and character of the medieval capital.

NOTES

1 It is reasonable to consider Westminster, the Tower, and Kennington as royal palaces, Lambeth, Winchester House, Ely Place, and some of the Inns lining the Strand as ecclesiastical palaces, and the Savoy as the sole representative of a magnate's metropolitan palace, though this is mainly through the lack of research to date. Sheen, Greenwich, and Eltham were country palaces. Rotherhithe was a country house.

2 Exeter was the last in 1310. Apart from the houses of the two archbishops and eighteen bishops, at least twenty-two abbots and six priors had houses in medieval London.

3 John Stow, *Survey of London*, ed. C. L. Kingsford (1908).

4 Three substantial houses were taken over by the Black Prince, Edward III, and duke Humphrey of Gloucester. Named Prince's, King's, and Duke's Wardrobe respectively, they were primarily storehouses for the owner's goods, including tapestries, but were used for household and estate administration and as occasional residences.

5 At the opening of the thirteenth century, the bishop of Winchester's manor was even larger than that of Ely. It embraced a 16 acre field, 30 acres of meadow, and several smaller plots as well as the kitchen, privy, and great gardens within the palace enclosure. Information from C. Phillpotts.

6 The only evidence for many of them lies in surviving place-names such as Durham House Street for the bishop of Durham's house, Salisbury Square for that of the bishop of Salisbury, Suffolk Lane for the home of the dukes of Suffolk, and Warwick Square for the courtyard house of the Beauchamp family and Warwick the Kingmaker.

7 J. Schofield in *Medieval Art, Architecture and Archaeology in London*, ed. L. Grant (1990) 16–28.

8 This property retains the ghost of the medieval hall and its detached kitchen, rebuilt in the fifteenth century and still in use.

9 There were twenty-five livery companies by the close of the fifteenth century and sixty by 1533.

LONDON: BIBLIOGRAPHY

T H E earliest historical resources for London reveal considerable evidence of the medieval city before the progressive rebuilding after the fire of 1666. For Wyngaerde's panorama of 1543 and the Agas map of the 1560s, P. Glanville, *London in Maps* (1972). The major edition of John Stow's *A Survey of London* of 1603 is by C. L. Kingsford, (2 vols., 1908). For the engravings by Hollar of the 1630s, A. M. Hind, *Wenceslaus Hollar and His Views of London* (1922). H. T. Riley (ed.), *Memorials of London Life in the XIII, XIV, and XV Centuries: 1276–1419* (1868), includes many extracts from the extensive city records, subsequently summarised by P. E. Jones and R. Smith, *A Guide to the Records in the Corporation of London Records Office and the Guildhall Library Muniment Room* (1981).

Extensive research on London houses has been published by John Schofield in *The Building of London from the Conquest to the Great Fire* (1984) and his well-illustrated and detailed *Medieval London Houses* (1995). See also C. Thomas, *The Archaeology of Medieval London* (2002); and C. Barron, *London in the Later Middle Ages* (2004). Valuable earlier studies include E. Beresford Chancellor, *The Private Palaces of London* (1908), C. L. Kingsford, 'Historical notes on medieval London houses', *London Record Society* 10 (1916) 14–144; 11 (1917) 28–81; 12 (1920) 1–66, and his reports in *Archaeologia* 71 (1921) 17–54; 72 (1922) 243–77; 73 (1923) 1–54; 74 (1924) 137–58. There are also the volumes of the *Survey of London* (1900 and ongoing); RCHM, *London* (5 vols., 1924–30); and N. Pevsner, *The Buildings of England: London*, 2nd edn, 6 vols. (1998 – in progress). M. Lobel (ed.), *The British Atlas of Historical Towns*, vol. III, *The City of London* (1989), is a most valuable resource for the late medieval period.

Recent studies on the immediate suburbs include K. McDonnell, *Medieval London Suburbs* (1978); A.G. Rosser, 'Medieval Westminster: the vill and the urban community 1200–1540', PhD thesis, University of London (1984) and *Trans. Roy. Hist. Soc.* 24 (1984) 99–112; and M. Carlin, *Medieval Southwark* (1996). The Strand area between the city and Westminster still awaits an appraisal.

Between 1889 and 1965, much of outer London was within the county of Middlesex. The VCH volumes covered the area within the boundaries of the London County Council rather than being limited to the administrative county of Middlesex. Eleven volumes have been published since 1911, with three planned covering Westminster and Chelsea. See also RCHM, *Middlesex* (1937), one of the earliest volumes of N. Pevsner, *The Buildings of England: Middlesex* (1951), and J. Symonds, *Middlesex* (1954).

The annual *Transactions* of the London and Middlesex Archaeological Society, founded in 1855, cover the whole of the Greater London area. So does the quarterly magazine *London*

Archaeologist, published by the Association of that name since 1970 to provide news of excavations, fieldwork, and ongoing projects. The Centre for Metropolitan History was established in 1988 as a research centre within the Institute of Historical Research at Senate House, University of London. In addition to its own academic publications, it is closely involved in *The London Journal* and the London Record Society.

BARNARD INN and London corporate institutions

The well-endowed and nodal position of London had helped it to become the premier port of England by the mid-fourteenth century, supplanting Boston in wool exports by 1306, ousting foreign interests in the wine trade by 1330, and taking over merchant banking after the ruination of the Italians by Edward III's early campaigns against France. Nor is there much evidence of the decay or retrenchment in trade that affected most other English towns during the fifteenth century. Also, the royal palace at Westminster had become the centre of government and law administration by the mid-fourteenth century. At the same time that specialist craftsmen and trading merchants were beginning to establish trade and craft guilds to protect their interests and control their communities, lawyers and law students were similarly organising themselves into associations. In neither case did they initially build special meeting places; they simply took leases or purchased substantial houses or inns where they could meet, administer their rules, and dine in common.

Initially the craft guilds used the houses of prominent members or hostelries for their meetings, but they soon preferred to acquire their own properties. Only four craft guilds – the Goldsmiths, Cordwainers, Merchant Taylors, and Saddlers – had their own premises by 1400, but this had risen to twenty-eight companies by 1485 and thirty-eight companies by 1520. The process was nearly always the same. A prominent member would bequeath his house to the guild, or it would purchase suitable premises, nearly always a courtyard house, which could be adapted and expanded for their purposes. The Goldsmiths bought a house in Foster Lane as early as 1339 and developed it nearly twenty-five years later so that it contained a hall, kitchen, pantry, buttery, and two chambers.[1] The Merchant Taylors similarly acquired the house of John Yakeslee, the king's tent-maker, in 1349 and expanded it. In 1425, the Grocers' Company acquired the Inn of Lord FitzWalter and rebuilt the hall two years later, and in 1432 the Fishmongers' Company took over a mid-fourteenth-century house owned by a succession of mayors including Sir William Walworth (d.1385) who had added a tower to the property.[2] In 1505, the Bakers similarly acquired a fifteenth-century merchant's house and converted it for use as their company hall.[3]

Previous domestic form and occupation determined the character of purpose-built Company halls. This usually meant not only a courtyard layout[4] but the primary elements of a substantial residence – a hall for feasting and ceremony with end dais, kitchen and domestic offices, together with a retiring chamber for the warden of the craft, rooms for court, financial, and estate purposes, and a

PLATE 86 London, Barnard Inn: hall interior John Crowther (1885)

garden providing a quiet haven from the noise and stench of the streets. A chapel was the only notable omission, whereas communal feasting helped to extend the life of the open hall long after it had been abandoned in domestic circumstances. Only one early fragment survives of these corporate properties, the Merchant Taylors' hall and kitchen in Threadneedle Street where the walls of the mid-fourteenth-century hall may be those from when it was a private house. The great kitchen was a rebuilding of 1425–33 with its roof modelled on that at Kennington Palace, while the surviving oriel (the opposite one has been destroyed) opening off the hall dais was added a generation later.[5] The post-Reformation buildings of many other city companies were similarly developed on medieval residential sites.

Concurrent with this development was that of legal inns of court which, like the collegiate foundations at Oxford and Cambridge,

started as communities of like-minded professionals – in this case, aspiring lawyers. Once the royal chancellor's household had settled in the tolerably open countryside between the Strand and Holborn (later Chancery Lane), students swiftly organised themselves nearby into groups in town houses or inns. It is unclear whether these early premises were simply communal lodgings or included a teaching element. The first Inns of Chancery were in Holborn, beginning with Thavy's Inn at the close of the fourteenth century, followed by Furnival's Inn, Staple Inn, and Barnard's Inn by 1430. Further south were the Inns of Court – Lincoln's Inn, Gray's Inn, Inner and Middle Temple – to which the Inns of Chancery were eventually subordinated. Both groups began acquiring existing town houses rather than building their own premises, such as the house of the Grey family which began by leasing out rooms to lawyers during the second half of the fourteenth century and was known as Gray's Inn by 1397.[6] The house occupied by Sir William Furnival between 1382 and his death six years later was purchased by the Inn of Chancery that had taken the same name by 1408,[7] while Lincoln's Inn was initially established in the thirteenth-century house of the bishop of Chichester.[8] The societies of the Temple, as the name implies, took over the vacated buildings of the Knights Templars.

It was because the executors of John Macworth, dean of Lincoln and Henry V's chancellor, had sold his town house in Holborn by 1435 to the Inn of Chancery founded by Lionel Barnard that the dean's hall has survived. Rebuilt by the dean in the early fifteenth century, this three-bay stone-built apartment, 33 feet by 22½ feet, is still used as a dining hall by the staff of a business corporation. Though thoroughly scraped during successive restorations, it retains an uncouth timber roof of tie-beam trusses supported by massive arched braces springing from replacement corbels. More importantly, this hall retains its probable original octagonal louvre with simple trefoil openings in each side.[9]

The earliest purpose-built legal premises are those of Lincoln's Inn. Dissatisfied with the limitations of the bishop of Chichester's house, the society erected a new four-bay hall in 1489–92, modelled on the latest style by being brick-built above an undercroft, with opposing bay windows lighting the dais, and an open collar-beam truss roof with fashionable S-shaped wind braces. (The hall was extended by a further bay at the lower end in 1623.) The brick gate-house, added in 1518–19, is a smaller version of archbishop Morton's gateway at Lambeth Palace, and was followed two years later by a four-storey range of chambers with polygonal stair turrets at the corners, since rebuilt.[10] The development of legal establishments adopting the same scale and layout as the educational foundations at Oxford and Cambridge was gathering pace, though the domestic origins of these London foundations are more clearly identifiable.

NOTES

1 Schofield (1995) 184.
2 *Ibid.* 223, 208, 219.
3 S. Thrupp, *A Short History of the Worshipful Company of Bakers of London* (1933) 162.
4 The Brewers' hall had a *tresaunce* or cloister in the fifteenth century. M. Ball, *The Worshipful Company of Brewers* (1977) 46–9.
5 C. M. Clode (ed.), *Memorials of the Guild of Merchant Taylors* (1875); H. L. Hopkinson, *A History of the Site of Merchant Taylors' Hall in the City of London* (1913); RCHM, *London*, IV (1929) 34–7; Schofield (1995) 223–5.
6 The hall was rebuilt in brick in 1556–60 and the chapel a little later.
7 Early nineteenth-century drawings on this totally rebuilt site suggest that the hall was a fifteenth-century structure. Schofield (1995) 192.
8 It had acquired the name Lincoln's Inn by the mid-fifteenth century. Fragments of a thirteenth-century doorway have been reset in the hall of 1489–92.
9 RCHM, *London*, IV (1929) 159. The louvre is currently inaccessible. The date of the hall is based on its architectural form rather than any precise data. Schofield (1995) 190.
10 RCHM, *London*, II (1925) 45; Schofield (1995) 170–1.

G. Unwin, *The Gilds and Companies of London* (1908)
I. G. Doolittle, *The City of London and Its Livery Companies* (1982)
J. Schofield, *Medieval London Houses* (1995)
J. K. Melling, *Discovering London's Guilds and Liveries* (6th edn 2003)

CROSBY PLACE and London merchants' houses

Merchant-princes were not a late medieval phenomenon, but the scale of their houses became so. The 'castle' built by the wool merchant Laurence of Ludlow at Stokesay (*c.*1284–90) was one of the earliest, while Sir John Pulteney's country house at Penshurst (*c.*1341) was the equal of any in the city. Pulteney, mayor in 1336, was notable for the loans he advanced to Edward III but nothing survives of either of his two London properties. Pulteney's Inn, later known as the Manor of the Rose, was his principal residence, developed in the late 1330s with a crenellated range (possibly the hall) and a four-storey tower at its upper end erected under a licence of 1341. The property was subsequently held by a number of distinguished magnates including the Black Prince, the earl of Arundel (1385–97), Edmund, duke of York, the dukes of Suffolk (1439–1504), and Edward, duke of Buckingham (1506–21). This was a mansion on the grandest scale, but though a late thirteenth/early fourteenth-century two-bay vaulted undercroft, narrow vaulted passage, and two small chambers in line were discovered in 1894, they were ruthlessly destroyed.[1]

In 1334, Pulteney purchased a second house of thirteenth-century date closer to the river. It came to be known as Coldharbour, but declined in standing during the late fourteenth century and was used for commercial premises after 1408.[2] To the considerable confusion of later historians, the name Coldharbour was acquired by the house immediately eastwards purchased by Alice Perrers, Edward III's mistress, in the 1370s and rebuilt by her. Initially known as 'la Tour', it was numbered among the most desirable houses in the city, occupied after 1410 by the prince of Wales, the dukes of Exeter, Henry VII's mother, and the Talbot earls of Shrewsbury throughout the sixteenth century. By the late fifteenth century, this courtyard property of more than forty rooms included a great hall with great chamber over, a little hall with great chamber over, offices to both halls, several large private chambers, a chapel, street and waterside gates, and gardens.[3]

The mercer Sir Richard Whittington (d.1423), three times mayor of London, advanced loans to Richard II and his two successors, but there is no trace of his home in College Hill or his plutocratic benefactions to the city – his library at the Greyfriars (1411), his public lavatory flushed by the tide with sixty-four seats for men and sixty-four for women, the rebuilding of Newgate prison, or the almshouse he established next to his college (Whittington College) attached to the church of St Michael Paternoster that he had rebuilt in 1409.[4] Whittington, who had been born into a prosperous family in Gloucestershire, was also more typical of London merchants in preferring to live in London or its suburbs throughout their lives rather than retire to the country as Pulteney had done.

It is possible that the origins of the fourteenth-century hall of the Merchant Taylors lie in the substantial house that this group of tailors and linen drapers purchased from John Yakeslee, the king's tent maker, in 1347. Subsequent alterations, additions, fire in 1666, and bomb damage in 1941–4 have stripped the early walls of any meaningful character so that their dating is problematical. The side walls of the five-bay hall are no later than 1375, when the Company built a ground-floor chapel above a vaulted undercroft at the lower end of the hall. Of uncertain date, the undercroft may also be a relic

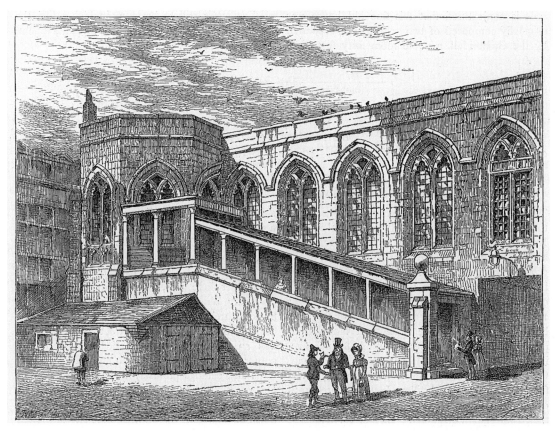

PLATE 87 London, Crosby Place: engraving of hall from the inner court (1790)

of this property when it functioned as a private house.[5] For its subsequent Company use, see page 222.

CROSBY PLACE

Sir John Crosby's fortune in the grocery trade can be readily appreciated. Like a pliant mistress, the hall of Crosby Place has been enjoyed, neglected, and cast aside until relocation has enabled her to shine again in a far more honourable environment. In the mid-1460s, John Crosby, an extremely wealthy merchant, alderman, sometime Warden of the Grocers' Company, and member of parliament for the City, decided to enlarge the already substantial house he held on lease from the nearby Benedictine nunnery of St Helen. In June 1466, he obtained a fresh lease on the property, together with a lease on six adjacent tenements in Bishopsgate Street and three in Priory Close. He retained one wing of the earlier house to form the southern range of his enlarged dwelling, now approached through a passage in place of the last of the street-facing tenements. Work had begun shortly after the new leases had been granted, was in hand in 1468,[6] and was completed 'at great and notable cost' according to Crosby's will, well before his death in 1475.

Progress had been interrupted in 1471 when the change in political fortunes led to Henry VI's brief reinstatement, the re-adoption of Edward IV, and the siege of London by the Bastard of Falconbridge. As a fierce Yorkist supporter and sheriff of London in 1471, Crosby had driven off the Bastard's attack on London Bridge and was knighted by Edward IV. The king subsequently employed Crosby on diplomatic missions to the dukes of Burgundy and Brittany. Nothing survives of his religious, public, and charitable donations and bequests to the city, but he and his first wife lie in the altar tomb in the south transept of St Helen's church, and his lavishly designed hall now stands nearly 5 miles away, close to the River Thames at Cheyne Walk.

Crosby Place lay along the line of Bishopsgate 'builded of stone and timber . . . and the highest at that time in London', according to Stow.[7] The newly built entrance from the street opened into the outer court with the hall entry opposite, and its imposing façade dominated by a great bay window. The north-facing, two-storeyed residential range at right angles to the hall was similarly stone-built, raised on a low brick-vaulted undercroft, and boasted its own semi-octagonal bay window lighting the ground-floor parlour and the great chamber above. Both chambers had fireplaces. The flat ceiling of the parlour was decorated with cusps, as were the panels of the great chamber above, eight panels to a bay, separated by at least eleven arched principals.[8] It is clear that Crosby's private rooms were no less lavish than his hall, and there were four further rooms to the rear, two on each floor, separated by a vestibule and a square stair turret accessing the upper floor. The earlier house on the south side of the outer court was retained, but modified by Crosby. He kept the vaulted undercroft but shortened the two-storey range above it.[9] The hall cross passage opened not into Crosby's newly built rear court but into the range on its north side. Crosby's additions were orderly and regular in contrast with the earlier house, extending some distance to the south as revealed by the vaults found

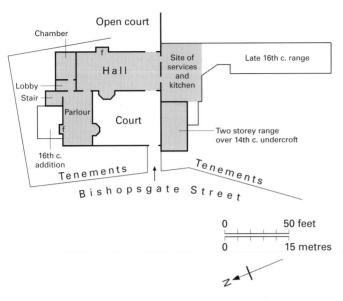

FIGURE 52 Crosby Place, Bishopsgate: site plan

in the early nineteenth century.[10] The whole, like so many contemporary London mansions, was set off by a generous garden bounded by Crosby's rear court and the earlier property.

For two centuries, Crosby Place symbolised the financial, political, and diplomatic success of a merchant-prince, and was a leading venue in the city. It was of sufficient scale and dignity to be tenanted by the king's brother and his household, and was the base where Richard, duke of Gloucester engineered the citizens to offer him the crown of England in 1483.[11] It was leased to the mayors of London in 1501 and 1505, and accommodated Catherine of Aragon and her retinue on her arrival in England to marry Henry VII's eldest son, prince Arthur in 1501. This 'large and sumptuous dwelling' (Stow) passed through a succession of wealthy owners, from Sir Thomas More (1523–4) and his son-in-law William Roper (1547–50), to the Elizabethan merchant-adventurer William Bond, and Mary, dowager countess of Pembroke (1609–15). The property survived the fire of London in 1666 but fell victim to a fire ten years later which destroyed the south range. The remainder, abandoned for residential purposes, was divided into tenements, accommodated by inserting a mid floor in the hall, and subsequently a further one immediately under the elaborate roof in 1778.[12]

By the early twentieth century, the remains of the mansion were in a poor state. The rear court had been pulled down shortly after the fire of 1666 to become Crosby Square. The parlour and chamber bay window had been utilised in the eighteenth century as a staircase for an adjoining house, while a stone doorway still enhances the dairy in the grounds of Fawley Court in Buckinghamshire. The north wing lost its woodwork in 1819 with a 'highly enriched panelled ceiling of oak with its corbels, spandrils, pendants etc. painted and gilt'[13] to be utilised in the church of 1853–4 on Brownsea Island, Dorset.[14] Plans in 1831 to pull down the remainder of the house and sell the site as a vacant building lot enraged public opinion. A new lease was secured, the residential wing was restored, and the much abused hall was cleared so that it regained some of its early character until it was purchased by a bank in 1906 for demolition and site redevelopment.

Outraged public opinion had no effect on government, city, or council indifference, but private efforts secured the hall's removal and re-erection in 1909–10, appropriately on the garden of Sir Thomas More's house in Chelsea. The survival of one of the finest halls of its age is nothing short of incredible.[15] A residential wing for university occupation was added by Walter Godfrey in 1925–7, and was reutilised in the redevelopment of the site in 1996–2003 as a private Tudor-style house for Christopher Moran. Sir John Crosby's fifteenth-century hall once again forms one side of a quadrangular courtyard residence.[16]

Standing on a low brick undercroft, the hall is 69 feet by 27 feet and 40 feet high. The ashlar stone walls were originally rubble-filled but this was replaced with brick after its relocation in 1910. The side walls are original but the end walls are Godfrey's rebuilds of lost walls. The inner faces were always plastered.

The original character of the hall entrance is not known, as it was destroyed by the early nineteenth century in favour of a through carriageway. The present entry is by Godfrey (1910). As at Eltham Palace hall (1475–83), the windows are in pairs filling the upper half of the walls to allow wall hangings or tapestries to hang below. Sir John Crosby traded in luxury textiles, particularly silk from his warehouse just off Poultry, so that the hall was designed to be a suitable vehicle for a sumptuous textile display. Unlike Eltham, the smaller scale of Crosby Hall made it possible to dispense with buttresses to take the thrust of the spectacular roof. The striking semi-octagonal bay window with stone-vaulted ribbed ceiling incorporates Crosby's crest. The large fireplace opposite it seems to be original, with the central hearth and louvre essentially for decorative and status purposes.[17] The original floor was unpolished Purbeck marble. It is not clear whether there was a dais. None was detected in the dismantling. The position of the window in the second bay from the end is unusual but this occurs at Fawsley Hall, Northamptonshire (c.1510). Possibly the dais extended across both bays with the end-bay doorway leading directly into the parlour. The highly ornate roof is a false ceiling below the outer roof. It is divided into eight bays of four-centred arched principals supported on stone corbels. Each bay is divided into four rows of boarded panels separated by pendants. The result is a ceiling of thirty-two compartments and twenty-seven ornamental pendants. Between the pierced spandrels at the window heads and the ceiling is a cornice of quatrefoils and an embattled head. The roof was possibly designed by Edmund Graveley, appointed to the office of the king's chief carpenter in 1461 and a warden of the Carpenters' Company in 1462–3. His work is an early secular example of a curved, panelled ceiling, for panelling had hitherto been confined to wall decoration.

The standing and documentary evidence of the lost structures show that the gap between this property of a merchant-prince moving in royal circles and a royal residence was relatively narrow. Crosby's splendid survival should be compared with Edward IV's hall at Eltham Palace erected less than ten years later. Though the latter was nearly twice as large, it is probable that the royal master-mason Thomas Jurdan was responsible for both structures, with their similar fenestration pattern, mouldings, and bay window vaults.

NOTES

1 P. Norman, *Archaeologia* 57 (1901) 257–84. He suggests that the undercroft, 40 feet by 20 feet, may have lain below the crenellated hall, with the vaulted passage below the screens, and the offices under the two end

chambers. Also C. L. Kingsford, *London Topographical Record*, II (1917) 74–8; Schofield (1995) 76, 193–4. Part of the Inn was rediscovered during excavations in 1994–7, T. Bingham and A. Woodger, *Roman and Medieval Townhouses on the London Waterfront* (2001) 61–7.

2 Schofield (1995) 216–17.

3 V. Harding, *London Topographical Record*, 24 (1980) 11–30; Schofield (1995) 217–18.

4 J. Imray, *The Charity of Richard Whittington* (1968).

5 Schofield (1995) 44, 223–5.

6 L. F. Salzman, *Building in England* (1952) 38.

7 John Stow, *Survey of London* (1603), ed. C. L. Kingsford (1908).

8 Illustrated in Schofield (1995) 67.

9 There is no evidence that there was a chapel in this range.

10 J. Schofield, *The Building of London* (1984) 123, and *London Medieval Houses* (1995) 160–3.

11 The actual offer was made to Richard at his mother's town house at Baynard Castle.

12 Goss (1908) for details of earlier owners and tenants.

13 Lot 291, Sale catalogue of Cottingham's Museum, Waterloo Road, London (1850).

14 Part of the great chamber ceiling was utilised for the family pew, while the screens to the tower, south-west chapel, and vestry are also claimed to originate from Crosby Place.

15 Among the more bizarre proposals was one to rebuild it on the roof of Selfridges's store in Oxford Street, London.

16 S. Thurley, *Country Life* (October 2003).

17 W. Godfrey in *Survey of London*, IX (1908) 47.

C. W. F. Goss, *Crosby Hall* (1908)

P. Norman, *Survey of London*, IX, *Crosby Place* (1908)

A. Clapham and W. Godfrey (eds.), *Famous Buildings and Their Story* (1913) 121–38

J. Schofield, *London Medieval Houses* (1995) 160–3

ELTHAM PALACE, Kent

In 1295, the manor of Eltham was acquired by Anthony Bek, bishop of Durham, who initiated the development of the present site. He erected a defendable stone wall round a wide moat approached from the north as today. Little is known about the form of his courtyard house but Bek gave the manor and park to Edward, prince of Wales in 1305, though he continued to occupy the property until his death in 1311.[1]

Now that the house was a royal residence, Edward II strengthened the west moat wall with buttresses and gave it to his wife, whose second son, John, was born at Eltham in 1316. Edward III expanded the house, particularly between 1350 and 1359, including new lodgings for himself and his wife on the east side of the inner court. It was probably during the later fourteenth century that the outer court began to be developed to provide additional household and staff accommodation. The palace continued to be popular with Richard II and Henry IV who erected a range of timber-framed apartments linked to the earlier work, with a corresponding set for the queen (1400–7). Henry VI extended the latter for his bride, Margaret of Anjou (1445). Between 1475 and 1483, Edward IV was responsible for the majestic great hall that is the principal medieval feature of the site today. He added a new range of lodgings[2] and was probably responsible for the existing north bridge across the moat.

The palace continued to be much favoured throughout the fif-

teenth and sixteenth centuries, with Henry VIII as well as Edward III and Henry VI spending much of their youth here. Henry VII had remodelled the royal apartments and rebuilt much of the outer court, but Henry VIII modified the king's lodgings, altered those of the queen, and built a new chapel in Reigate stone as large as the great hall (1519–22). By that time, the palace was one of the few that could accommodate the entire court of up to 800 people in the multi-courtyard residence depicted in John Thorpe's well-known ground plans of about 1603.[3] By then, the palace was beginning to decline in favour of Greenwich Palace. Queen Elizabeth only visited it occasionally, though the royal apartments were given a new front in 1585–8 and those of the queen were altered by James I for his wife in 1603–4. The subsequent reports increasingly mention decay and near collapsing structures, hastened by Civil War ransacking and partial demolition thereafter. In 1656, John Evelyn noted that the palace and chapel were 'in miserable ruins'.

During the eighteenth century, the property was converted to agricultural use, with some of the rooms used as a farm and the hall as a barn, but its proximity to London attracted antiquarian interest. Wyatville's proposal to dismantle the roof of the hall and reuse it to crown St George's Hall at Windsor Castle was vigorously opposed, and abandoned in favour of summary repairs by Sir Robert Smirke. The outcry resulted in an early study, *Plans and Elevations . . . of the Great Hall . . . of Eltham* by H. Dunnage and C. Laver (1828). Early twentieth-century repairs were followed by a more radical dismantling, strengthening, and reassembling of the hall roof and renewal of the bay window tracery (1911–14), but it was the development of the site by Seely and Paget for Samuel Courtauld and his wife (1933–6) that was responsible for the present layout, mansion house, and hall refurbishment.

OUTER COURT

Although Eltham has become a suburb of London, the palace benefits from a tree-lined approach and retains open countryside to the south. The site of the outer court is taken up by early twentieth-century houses standing in their own grounds, with the two sixteenth-century timber-framed houses at the north end as the only standing evidence of the outer court buildings.[4] Thorpe's plan of c.1603 shows that the court, formerly lined on three sides with the fourth open to the moat, included kitchen and service facilities, lodgings, and accommodation for the royal household. This was its final form, developed over two centuries, with Thorpe showing its final late Tudor layout.[5] Taken together, the outer and inner courts and moats at Eltham covered an area of just over 8 acres. At the close of Henry VIII's reign, Hampton Court covered little more than 6 acres.

INNER COURT

The site is surrounded by an extremely broad moat between 100 and 130 feet wide. A canalised version was introduced on two and a half sides by the Courtaulds in the early 1930s as part of their landscaping of the grounds. The approach is spanned by two bridges. The principal stone bridge of four ribbed arches is probably of Edward IV's time. The added brick parapet is topped by coping that Courtauld is said to have reused from the hall's embattled parapet.[6] Two brick outer walls stand of the porter's lodge at the inner end of the bridge. The south bridge to the privy garden is a 1930s wooden

PLATE 88 Eltham Palace: bishop Bek's inner court from the south with Edward IV's hall in distance

walk on a much earlier stone base with brick piers, probably of Henry VII's time.

In the years close to 1300, bishop Bek constructed a rubble-stone, flint, and brick retaining wall round the 3 acre inner court of quadrilateral shape with angle bastions. His much patched wall stands in part on all sides from moat to courtyard height, now with a brick topping, with the corner bastions similarly crowned.

In the inner court, a grass sward and tarmac turning-circle overlie the north-west quarter closed by Courtauld's house and Edward IV's hall. Excavations in 1976–7 revealed part of bishop Bek's manor house of c.1300, including his north–south hall at right angles to the present one and in front of it, and a vaulted undercroft. The remains of Henry VIII's chapel of the 1520s were also revealed next to the undercroft, but have been reburied.[7] The west side of the court was lined with the late medieval royal apartments. Bek's original west wall had to be strengthened in 1315 by a new one in front of it with arched buttresses supporting the older retaining wall and the area in between rubble-infilled.[8] From the landscaped moat, the early fourteenth-century Reigate stone and buttressed walling is interrupted by five projecting Elizabethan bays in diapered brick at the south end (1585–8) and seven stone bays at the north end (four of 1603–4). They mark the king's lodgings (south) and queen's lodgings (north) respectively, with the latter terminating at the north-west angle in a bastion of lightly coloured brick, possibly incorporating part of Bek's work. At courtyard level, the brick foundations of the king's apartments were uncovered during the 1950s, and the stone footings of the queen's at a lower level dating from the later fifteenth and early sixteenth centuries. The former include an early Tudor polygonal bay window (second from the south end) recalling those at Thornbury Castle, and the latter were linked by an open corridor towards the courtyard. Between them was a line of shared apartments, accessed from the dais end of Edward IV's hall, now marked by the seven exposed stumps of the stone arched buttresses built in 1315 to support Bek's unstable wall. Peter Stent's drawing of c.1653 shows this bayed frontage complete, with the hall and chapel roofs rising behind it.[9]

Although a farmstead occupied the north-east quadrant of the court during the eighteenth and nineteenth centuries, only a three-gabled timber-framed frontage was visible evidence of the earlier royal structures. It was part of the service block beyond the buttery and pantry. The intention to preserve it in situ in 1933 did not prove possible, so that the upper part had to be dismantled and incorporated as a lifeless remnant in the Courtauld house.

John Thorpe's detailed plan of the palace complex shows that the present south lawn was occupied by the kitchens, offices, and five small courtyards, an area awaiting detailed examination.[10] Across the moat lay a privy garden during the fifteenth century, enlarged by Henry VIII, with parks beyond for hunting.

PLATE 89 Eltham Palace: drawing of royal lodgings by Peter Stent
(c.1653)

GREAT HALL

In 1475, Edward IV demolished Bek's hall and built a larger one at right angles to it. His replacement, 101 feet by 36 feet and 55 feet to the roof apex, is among the largest in medieval England. It was brick-built, faced with Reigate stone on the north side and squared Kentish ragstone below the window sills on the south. The lower half of the buttressed walls is blank stonework with the upper half filled with buttress-separated windows of twin cinquefoil lights under a four-centred head. The square-headed entrance, without drawbar, is enlivened by Edward IV's *rose en soleil*. It led directly into the cross passage and service end with simple arches (blocked) in the lower end wall to the buttery and pantry, with the kitchen in a court-yard beyond the south door. Earlier structures no doubt prevented the kitchen from being in its more usual position beyond the services.

The upper end of the hall was marked by a dais, lit from each side by fine bay windows. The hearth was positioned in the fourth bay close to the dais, but the louvre, shown in Peter Stent's seventeenth-century sketch, has disappeared apart from the internal framing reinstated in 1911–14.[11] The magnificent roof is of false hammer-beam construction, finely traceried.

The hall at Eltham was the first important royal residential work since the completion of Henry V's palace at Sheen in the 1430s. It was fostered by the more stable political conditions following the death of Warwick the Kingmaker in 1471, an improvement in the royal finances, and the acceptance of Louis XI's proposal in July 1475 to pay Edward 75,000 gold crowns for withdrawing his army from northern France and an annual payment of 50,000 gold crowns thereafter. Work on the new hall started shortly afterwards, with an account for the roof surviving from September 1479 suggesting completion by about 1480. The hall was designed by Thomas Jurdan, the king's master-mason, with the roof designed by Edmund Graveley, the king's master-carpenter.[12] It is possible that Edward IV also rebuilt the hall offices and great kitchen.

Several elements warrant further comment.

- The entrance front has a continuous window and buttress rhythm of blank walling in the lower register and a linked line of windows above, terminating in a bold bay window drawing attention to the dais end.[13] However, the latter is not offset by a matching porch at the lower end, while the entry is surprisingly modest.

- The hall depends for its external impact on massing, not decoration, which is limited to buttress stepping and modest gargoyles to the parapet string course. The parapet is a 1930s replacement of the original embattled one shown in Buck's engraving of 1735, and the roof was initially lead covered. The window tracery is plain, tall cinquefoil lights with a small quatrefoil head.

- The two square dais bays were an afterthought, set back from the line of the hall outer wall which partly covers one light in both cases.

- The south wall is of poorer-quality stone as it faced the narrow kitchen court, not the open sward of today. The south cross-passage doorway is similarly modest, with continuous simple moulding to a two-centred head. The remains of a corbel and the position of one to the right would have supported a small canopy. The two service entries, centrally positioned with continuous mouldings to four-centred heads, are also plain.

- The absence of a porch, the lack of ornamentation, and the modest roof corbels – embattled rather than figured – suggest that money was tight. The restrained style of Edward's hall is particularly marked compared with Sir John Crosby's ornate hall at Bishopsgate (1466).

- The generous dais bays introduce a more exotic note internally, with a tall, broad opening reaching almost to wall-plate level. The three two-light windows extend almost to ground level, and both bays are crowned by a two-bay stellar-type vault with bosses at all rib joints.

- The hall bays have doors to the king's apartments (south) and the queen's apartments (north). Above the doorways is blind panelling mirroring the windows. However, both bays have high rear arches with the north side retaining a two-light first-floor window. It is probable that the upper blind arcading was originally open, serving as a view-point looking down on to the hall scene.

- The six-bay roof is literally and metaphorically the hall's crowning glory. Because the hammer posts are morticed into the ends of the hammer beams rather than resting on the beams, architectural historians have dubbed the construction a 'false' one. This is regrettable and gives the unjustifiable connotation of fakery. It is a gloriously robust structure. The wall plates and trusses are richly moulded and generously proportioned. The lack of stone decoration in the hall is amply rectified by a roof with gorgeous deep pendants,[14] two lines of open tracery above the collar beams, and three lines of cusped wind braces, the lowest in counter-curves, the next in opposing curves, and the uppermost in regular form. Unlike the much admired roof at Penshurst Place hall, the purlins at Eltham are chamfered, while the roof corbels commence at a much higher level than at Westminster Hall for the weight borne by the hammer beams is not very great owing to the low pitch of the principal arches. This gives a less lowering effect at Eltham than at Westminster. Some of the woodwork was at one time gilded, for Courtauld found traces on the under surfaces of the yellow pigment which formed the base for gilding.

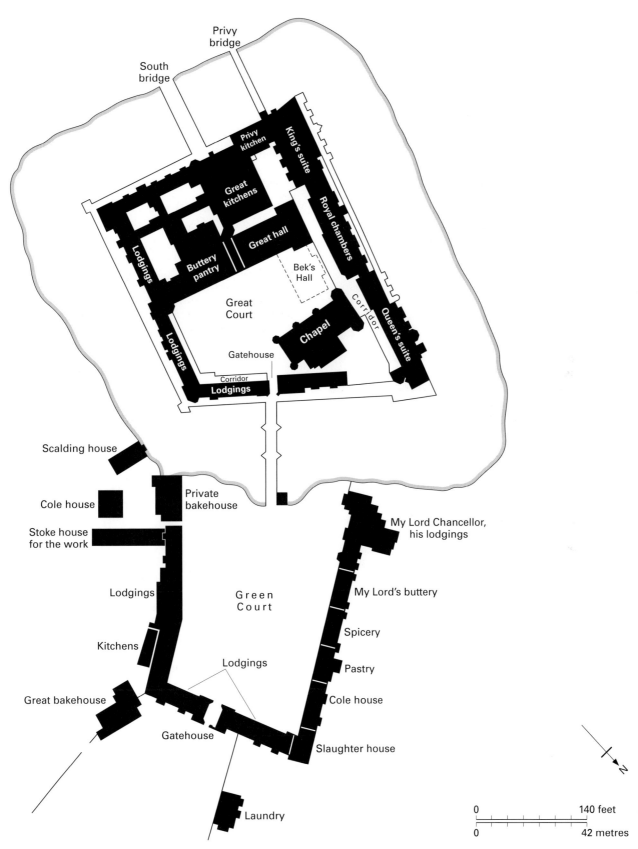

Privy
bridge

South
bridge

Privy
kitchen

King's suite

Great
kitchens

Royal chambers

Great hall

Lodgings

Buttery
pantry

Bek's
Hall

Great
Court

Corridor

Chapel

Queen's suite

Lodgings

Gatehouse

Corridor

Lodgings

Scalding house

Private
bakehouse

Cole house

My Lord Chancellor,
his lodgings

Stoke house
for the work

Lodgings

Green
Court

My Lord's buttery

Spicery

Kitchens

Lodgings

Pastry

Great bakehouse

Cole house

Gatehouse

Slaughter house

Laundry

N

0   140 feet

0   42 metres

FIGURE 53 Eltham Palace: John Thorpe's plan *c.*1603, with the added site of bishop Bek's hall

PLATE 90 Eltham Palace: north bay of hall

NOTES

1 For this and all following documentation, Colvin, *HKW*, II (1963) and IV (1982).
2 It was an extended range on the site of the later royal apartments, divided into the king's suite and the queen's suite, with the latter bayed like the range he built at Nottingham Castle (1476–80). From the queen's suite extended a long gallery, solely intended as a recreational facility. S. Thurley, *The Royal Palaces of Tudor England* (1993) 20–1.
3 Hatfield House, CPM 1.5 for the buildings and the moat, and PRO MFF 228 for those of the outer court.
4 Formerly a single residence of hall with great chamber at one end and parlour at the other, it was a remodelling from an earlier, narrow two-storey building, probably mid-fifteenth-century, which survives at the rear.
5 H. W. Clapham and W. H. Godfrey, *Some Famous Buildings and Their Story* (1913) 49–66. The overall accuracy of the drawings has been supported by the excavations, though it can be corrected in detail, e.g. Henry VIII's chapel was several feet nearer the hall than shown by Thorpe. See *HKW*, IV pt II (1982) opp. 86.
6 The fifteenth-century stone window in the moat wall is a 'find' inserted here by Courtauld to light the heating plant of the house.
7 H. Woods, *Trans. London and Middx Arch. Soc.* 33 (1982) 215–65; Strong (1983) 4–5.
8 *HKW,* I (1963) 930–1.
9 Only a copy of this drawing is known, left at Eltham by Stephen Courtauld.
10 Dr Strong states that the foundations here 'belong, in the main, to Bek's fortified manor and to work carried out in the later fourteenth century': (1983) 18.
11 The louvre was an afterthought for the timbers were cut to receive it.
12 J. Harvey, *Eng. Med. Arch.* (1984) 165, 123.
13 The bays were separately gabled but whether this was an original feature or a consequence of replacing the original lead roof with tiles during the later seventeenth century has not yet been determined.
14 Restored by Courtauld in 1934–5 on the evidence of the single survival drawn by Buckler just before it fell down in 1817.
15 See interior by S. H. Grimm in *Archaeologia* 6 (1782) 368.
16 The remains of a tiled floor were found in 1935, 18 inches below the present level.
17 *The Complete Poems of John Skelton*, ed. P. Henderson (1948) 2.
18 Brook (1960) 30–2.

J. C. Buckler, *An Historical and Descriptive Account of the Royal Palace of Eltham* (1828)

H. Dunnage and C. Laver, *Plans, Elevations, Sections . . . of the Great Hall of the Royal Palace of Eltham* (1828)

C. Hussey, *Country Life* (May 1937)

R. Brook, *The Story of Eltham Palace* (1960)

H. M. Colvin *et al.* (eds.), *History of the King's Works*, II (1963) 930–7; IV (1982) 78–86

D. E. Strong, *Eltham Palace Handbook* (1983 edn)

M. Turner, *Eltham Palace Handbook* (1999)

E. J. Priestly, *Eltham Palace* (forthcoming)

• The apartment is a classic example of high-status, late medieval hall design – blank lower walling for tapestries, a well-lit upper register (markedly so in this case), and a spectacular roof. This is an extremely spacious and generously proportioned hall, well fitted for receptions and entertainment. The reinstated Courtauld hangings give a reasonable impression of royal use, as does the cross-passage screen. The original one which survived the eighteenth but not the nineteenth century[15] was divided into five divisions, two of which were archways, as in the present one which incorporates the slight fragments of the original screen. The dais panelling, stone floor, and minstrel's gallery are early twentieth-century antiquarian inventions.[16]

Edward IV favoured Eltham above all other royal residences (after Westminster) listed in John Skelton's eulogy on his death.[17] The palace was large-scale, conveniently close to London, suitable for entertaining important visitors, and extensive enough to hold the whole court.[18] Edward's work created a new and spacious courtyard approach, different from that which he had inherited where Bek's hall was differently aligned. His front included the three-gabled service block so that it was a combination of stone and timber-framing, formal and informal. Edward's hall set a new standard in architectural magnificence – astringent externally, imposing internally. His line of royal apartments with gallery extension complemented it, but the apartments were replaced by his immediate successors, while Henry VIII's chapel dramatically reduced the scale of Edward's front court.

ELY PLACE and London episcopal residences

Apart from the house of the bishop of London, the earliest ecclesiastical residences were developed in the suburbs rather than within the city – the bishop of Lincoln in Holborn, Canterbury at Lambeth, and Winchester and Rochester in Southwark.[1] All five properties were established before 1200, but the practice of choosing sites outside the city was maintained for the twelve episcopal houses built during the next hundred years, and for the final three (Coventry and Lichfield, Exeter, and St David's) in the early fourteenth century. These later houses were sited on the north side of the river.

Every see in England and Wales had a London house except St Asaph, but only two were established within the city (London, Hereford). The three early foundations stayed south of the river, while four sees chose Holborn (Bangor, Chester, Ely, and Lincoln). However, the majority preferred to develop their houses on the more open land close to the river in an arc like a necklace of eleven pearls between the city and Westminster[2] (see fig. 51).

There is more standing evidence of episcopal than of lay residences, helped by the accident of survival as much as by longer institutional ownership. This particularly applies to Lambeth Palace, by far the finest palace survival and still the home of the Primate of All England (q.v.). Part of the bishop of Winchester's hall of *c*.1225 stands as a ruin, while the chapel of *c*.1290 of the bishop of Ely was reopened for worship in 1876. To these can be added the later fifteenth-century foundations of the archbishop of York's palace in Whitehall, excavated in the late 1930s, the partial excavation of the Inn of the bishop of Bath and Wells in the Strand forty years later, and the dean of Lincoln's early fifteenth-century hall in Holborn (page 223).

The majority of episcopal residences were not unlike those of the see of Durham or Bath and Wells in scale and ownership changes. *Durham Place*, first established by bishop Poore of Durham (1228–37), was extended by bishop Bek (1285–1311) and again by bishop Hatfield (1345–81). A plan of 1626 shows that it was a double courtyard residence with the hall and principal residential block at the rear of the inner court, overlooking the river. Hollar's drawing of 1630 shows the impressive river frontage of the aisled hall (by Bek?) with the screens passage terminating in a water gate and the embattled head of the hall carried on a line of corbelled arches separated by mini buttresses. The four-storey tower at the upper end was a residential block, a later rebuild (by Hatfield?) adding to the imposing character of this house of a palatinate prince whose principal residence was the overpowering castle next to his northern cathedral. Durham Place was occupied by Wolsey between 1516 and 1518 while York Place was being rebuilt for him, and thereafter as diplomatic lodging. Most of it was demolished in 1660, but the remnants of the palace were not cleared away until the area was acquired for the Adam brothers' Adelphi of 1769–70.[3]

Hollar's engraving of 1646 shows that the courtyard *Inn of the Bishop of Bath and Wells* between St Clement Danes church and the river reflected the piecemeal development of many of the larger houses, the courtyard form, the use of different building materials, and the retention of the medieval hall as the nucleus of the house as late as the mid-seventeenth century. First mentioned in a deed of the 1230s, the five-bay stone-built hall with its two-storeyed porch, high-pitched roof, and central louvre seems to be a development close to *c*.1300. The buttress-separated windows that might have dated it more precisely were remodelled much later as double-transomed windows reaching almost to the ground. Above the stone-built offices rose a timber-framed retiring chamber with an inserted oriel, while the detached kitchen and offices round their own courtyard lay further east (screened in Hollar's engraving by an open stable). This extended line of buildings, allowing the courtyard to be generously scaled, was enclosed by a hotch-potch of buildings by the late sixteenth century that included a lodging range, barn, stables, and storehouse.[4]

PLATE 91 London, Winchester House: hall gable window

It was the episcopal courtyard residences lining the Strand and Holborn that made them superior suburbs, but the Reformation brought fundamental changes. Most of the monastic inns were taken over for lay use with little need for any modifications. The same applies to the majority of episcopal houses, so that the riverside between the Temple and Westminster was rapidly occupied by the nobility well before the close of the century, though their alterations tended to be more extensive. The Inn of the Bishop of Bath and Wells passed to Sir Thomas Seymour in 1545 and was purchased by the earl of Arundel four years later. They were responsible for a sequence of developments which replaced and extended the bishop's private apartments and included the gallery that housed the 14th earl of Arundel's collection of antique statues depicted in Daniel Mytens' magisterial portrait of the earl in 1618. Excavations in 1972 not only revealed a fourteenth-century vaulted cesspit of the bishop's house and some contemporary wall evidence, but were notable for the recovery of six of the earl's collection of Greek and Roman sculptures.[5] Unfortunately, the whole of the Strand area has suffered from extensive terracing as well as multiple rebuilding, destroying several layers of London history.

The site of *Winchester House* in Southwark is far from the haven of peace that is Lambeth Palace, but it retains part of the one primary medieval element missing from that residence, its hall. Southwark developed as the suburb approach to London Bridge, the lowest crossing of the River Thames. As the gateway to and from south-east England, Southwark was inevitably in the shadow of London, though it was not so susceptible to the city's commercial and political pressures. Because the suburb lay in the extreme north-east of the diocese of Winchester, bishop Blois acquired a 7 acre site upstream from London Bridge during the 1140s for a permanent London residence, completed by 1170. Documentary research has shown that the bishops of Winchester initially used their Southwark residence as a depot for produce and livestock from their other manors. Some was needed for the palace but most of the produce was sold or given away to the poor. Wool was also brought here prior

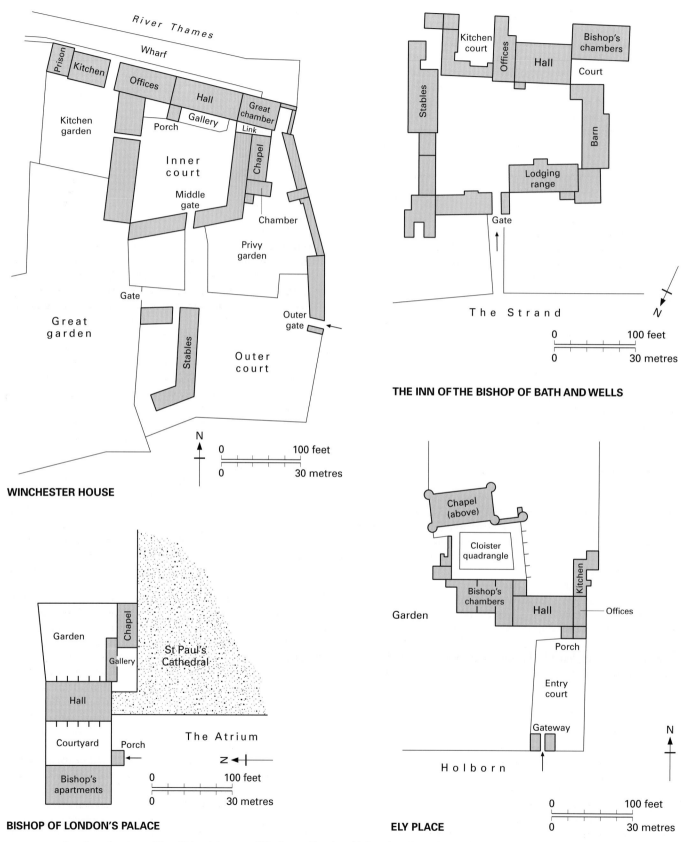

FIGURE 54 London: site plans of four bishop's houses – Winchester (Southwark), London (St Paul's), Bath and Wells (The Strand), and Ely (Holborn)

WINCHESTER HOUSE

THE INN OF THE BISHOP OF BATH AND WELLS

BISHOP OF LONDON'S PALACE

ELY PLACE

to its sale on the London market, but by the second half of the thirteenth century the property no longer served as a distribution centre at all. Substantial building additions were part of its development as a stately residence and episcopal administrative centre.[6] The bishops ceased to use the palace after 1626 and it was broken up three decades later into tenements and warehouses.[7] Fire gutted the building in 1814 and most of it was demolished shortly afterwards.

The only standing remains are the west wall of the hall with its dramatic rose window and part of the south wall, viewable as an open site from Clink Street. Excavations in the 1960s and in 1983–4 revealed some of the later twelfth-century footings and confirmed the early thirteenth-century rebuilding of the hall parallel with the Thames, and the addition of a long range of buildings on one side of an inner court. The hall block, 146 feet long and 40 feet wide externally, was carried on three massive parallel stone bases above timber piles – the two outer walls and a central one supporting an arcade dividing the ground-floor vaulted undercroft. An external stair and porch led to the first-floor hall and great chamber, the latter half the size of the former. The service rooms were in a separate structure beyond the buttressed west wall with a passage to the detached kitchen. Dendrochronology of the piles confirmed the documentary evidence for construction from 1221 to 1225.[8] The west gable and rose window were alterations of the second quarter of the fourteenth century, possibly in association with a new roof structure. The window is contemporary with the similar one at the lower end of bishop Gower's ceremonial hall at St David's (c.1330–40).[9] The three service doors below were inserted later, when the separate service rooms were integrated into the west end of the hall.

The inner courtyard lay south of the hall and offices, approximately on the site of the present Winchester Square. Developed in the middle of the thirteenth century, both east and west ranges housed the bishop's knights and clerks, squires and grooms, and were almost certainly two-storeyed, with social distinction between ground- and upper-floor occupation. South of the courtyard lay the outer court, surrounded by stables and prison buildings, while east of it was that adjunct of any substantial London house, a privy garden. Part of it was used in 1357 for a new two-storey chamber block for the bishop, together with a private postern to his barge moored at the riverside.[10]

Increasing business demands in London as treasurer and chancellor to Edward I persuaded bishop Kirkeby of Ely (1286–90) to acquire properties over a large area of Holborn when it was still an almost entirely rural area outside the city walls. He initiated one of the largest and most elegant episcopal residences in London, *Ely Place*, probably completed by his successor, bishop Luda (d.1298). The gatehouse fronting the street, rebuilt by bishop Arundel (1374–88), opened into a large outer court with dormitories and stables for the bishop's entourage. The majority of buildings that survived until the 1770s were those of the late thirteenth century, including the hall opposite the entry gate. A two-storeyed porch (partly rebuilt in brick in c.1500) opened into this spectacular apartment, 72 feet by 32 feet and 30 feet high. Its five bays were lit by four windows in both side walls of twin trefoiled lights under a quatrefoil head. The kitchen lay north of the offices, while the storeyed chamber block beyond the hall dais consisted of three principal rooms in 1357. A large rectangular cloister with chambers above at least two alleys separated the bishop's private apartments from the still-standing chapel of St Etheldreda.[11] With its gardens and vine-

yards, this was a country mansion in all but name, and continued to be so despite extensive lay intrusions in its grounds by the Hatton family after the property had been leased to Sir Christopher Hatton in Elizabeth's reign. Its components continued in a fair if abused state for a further 200 years until the hall, episcopal apartments, and cloister were pulled down in the mid-1770s to make way for Ely Place, the short street of houses flanking the chapel that was suffered to survive for the new householders. Fortunately, a ground plan and engravings of the buildings were made immediately before their destruction.

Like the early thirteenth-century chapel at Lambeth Palace and that formerly at Winchester House, St Etheldreda's was raised above an undercroft with a plain entry and cusped lights.[12] Its braced ceiling joists, stone-pillar-supported since 1872–3, are original. The broad and spacious episcopal chapel is not buttressed but supported on 8 feet thick walls. This little-known jewel of Edward I's reign is approached from a triple-pillared and multi-arched entrance at the head of a flight of steps at the end of the reconstructed cloistered corridor. Divided into six bays, the body of the chapel is marked by two-light traceried windows, with a further bay at each end filled with blind tracery because of lost abutting buildings. Vast five-light windows with Flamboyant traceried heads fill the end walls, flanked, as are all the windows, by tall niches under gabled heads, repeated externally. The plain Victorian roof is dark but inoffensive, while the stained glass of 1952–64 imparts a richness befitting its architectural setting. It was completed during the closing years of the thirteenth century, and the contrast between the austerity of Lambeth Palace chapel and the richness of that at Ely Place is symptomatic of a fundamental development in an architectural style that was to reach its apogee in the mother church of Ely a generation later.

York Place, conveniently close to Westminster Palace, originated as the residence of the treasurers of Henry II and Hubert de Burgh, chief justiciar at the beginning of Henry III's reign until his fall in 1232. Burgh's trustees transferred the property to the see of York so that it became the London home of successive archbishops. It was largely rebuilt in brick with stone dressings by archbishop Neville (1465–76), including a new great hall and cloister as well as a subsidiary hall with three chambers.[13] Such grand-scale activity befitted this northern aristocrat, as did the additions by Wolsey after 1514, until this episcopal residence fell, like all his properties, into the royal lap. As a consequence of the fire at Westminster Palace in 1512, Henry VIII converted the cardinal's property into a new palace and centre of royal power, renamed it Whitehall, and left the financial and legal machinery of government in the former royal palace where they were joined shortly afterwards by the houses of Parliament.

The bishop of London's palace was initially on the south side of St Paul's Cathedral, but a novel plan was adopted when it was moved to the north side during the thirteenth century. A gatehouse immediately north of the cathedral's west front opened into a rectangular court with the large buttressed great hall filling its east side, but the bishop's private apartments were apparently on the opposite side. A gallery from the hall alongside the bishop's garden led to the detached two-storeyed chapel adjoining the north aisle of the cathedral nave. The bishop ceased to use the residence in Mary's reign and the property was pulled down in 1647.[14]

The bishop's principal residence now lay further west in Fulham. Though this had been an important country estate since the twelfth

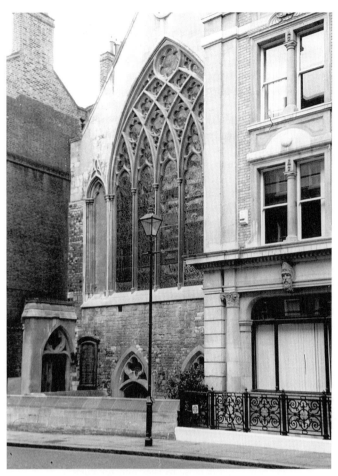

PLATE 92 London, Ely Place: chapel from the east

2 About twenty-five of the more wealthy monasteries also had houses in or close to the city. A few were established in the twelfth century, but the majority were spread equally between the thirteenth and fourteenth centuries, with Glastonbury and St Mary's, York as fifteenth-century latercomers. For details, M. Lobel (ed.), *British Atlas of Historical Towns*, III, *City of London* (1989).

3 *Survey of London*, 18, Strand pt 2 (1937) 84–94; Schofield (1995) 212.

4 M. J. Hammerson, *Trans. London and Middx Arch. Soc.* 26 (1975) 209–51; Schofield (1995) 210–12; J. Proctor, *Trans. London and Middx Arch. Soc.* 51 (2000) 45–79.

5 Hammerson, *Trans. London and Middx Arch. Soc.* 26 (1975).

6 M. Carlin in Seely (forthcoming).

7 Hollar's panorama of 1647 shows the palace's state at that time with its extended riverside frontage.

8 Carlin (1985) 37; Yule (1989) 31–9.

9 The rose window at the east end of St Paul's Cathedral had been inserted about thirty years earlier.

10 C. Phillpotts, *London Arch.* 9 (1999) 48–9 with plan.

11 Building work in 1985 exposed part of the west alley, floored with late medieval tiles in chequerboard pattern.

12 It lacked both altar footing and piscina until converted for chapel use in 1873–6 when the floor level was lowered by 2½ feet and the street entrance was inserted. The late twelfth-century chapel of the bishop of Winchester may have been at first-floor level: its early thirteenth-century successor was clearly so, running north/south, with the room below used for storage. The only known double chapel in London was that initiated by Edward I and completed by his two successors at the palace of Westminster.

13 Thurley (1999) 1–12; H. J. M. Green and S. J. Thurley, *Trans. London and Middx Arch. Soc.* 38 (1987) 59–130.

14 W. S. Simpson, *Trans. London and Middx Arch. Soc.* 1 (1905) 13–73; G. H. Cook, *Old St Paul's* (1955) 65–6.

General

R. S. Rait, *English Episcopal Palaces: Province of Canterbury* (1910)

T. B. James, *The Palaces of Medieval England c.1050–1550* (1990)

J. Schofield, *Medieval London Houses* (1995)

M. Thompson, *Medieval Bishops' Houses in England and Wales* (1998)

Winchester House

S. Toy, *Surrey Arch. Coll.* 49 (1944–5) 75–81

H. Roberts and W. H. Godfrey (eds.), *Survey of London*, XXII (1950) 49–50

M. Carlin, *London Topographical Record*, 25 (1985) 33–58

B. Yule, *London Arch.* 6 (1989) 31–9

M. Carlin, *Medieval Southwark* (1996)

C. Phillpotts, *London Arch.* 9, no. 2 (1999) 47–53

D. Seely, *A Palace in Southwark of the Medieval Bishops of Winchester* (forthcoming)

Ely Place

C. R. Keene, *Trans. London and Middx Arch. Soc.* 5 (1881) 494–503

C. L. Kingsford, *London Topographical Record*, 10 (1916) 44–144

B. Barber and K. Pitt, 'Archaeological excavations at 33 Ely Place', unpublished DGLA Report, 1990

York Place

S. Thurley, *Whitehall Palace* (1999)

Fulham Palace

RCHM, *London*, II (1925) 34–6

century, its redevelopment by bishop FitzJames in 1510–20 within one of the broadest moats in England (until 1921) made it far more attractive than the crowded streets of London. Built entirely in brick, it is a relatively late example of this episcopal practice, adopted for many rural palaces during the last quarter of the fifteenth century. English bishops were among the pace-setters of this new material (Buckden, Esher, Farnham, Hatfield, Otford), with Fulham still displaying the courtyard plan that has otherwise disappeared in comparable London mansions through rebuilding and commercial development. The palace, set in seventeenth-century landscaped gardens, was subject to major alterations during the eighteenth century by Stiff Leadbetter and S. P. Cockerell.

Little survives of the other residences in this relatively small diocese. Apart from the early castle at Bishop's Stortford, the only surviving structure is the brick-encased timber-framed house of the early sixteenth century at Much Hadham. Nothing remains of the bishops' houses at Haringay or Stepney (Greater London), Broxbourne (Hertfordshire), or Berden (Essex), and only earthworks at Orsett and the moat at Wickham Bishops (Essex).

NOTES

1 The two bishops' houses in Southwark were soon joined by early town houses for the heads of Lewes Priory and Battle Abbey, and for St Augustine's, Canterbury a little later.

LAMBETH PALACE, London

Apart from the palace of Westminster, that at Lambeth is almost the sole representative of such a residence in London. It is certainly the most complete, maintaining its original function as the seat of the Primate of All England for over 800 years. And though the River Thames has been embanked, and the medieval towers that initially dominated the district have been dwarfed by those of modern commerce, this still-occupied archiepiscopal residence has retained the garden and wooded grounds that were once the perquisite of most early mansions in London. It is a rare survival of *rus in urbe*.

Initially known as the archbishop's manor house of Lambeth,[1] it encompasses a span of buildings from the early thirteenth to the early nineteenth centuries, divided into those pre-dating and post-dating the Commonwealth. Its early development is clarified by the river view by Wenceslaus Hollar of 1647 and the parliamentary plan of the buildings prepared in 1648 to establish their worth a year before the great hall was pulled down for the value of its building materials.[2]

These two sources show that random development had resulted in a disjointed plan round four variably sized courts or yards. The gate-tower opened into a narrow court, with the hall lying parallel to the river and east-facing extensions at both ends. That at the lower end was the kitchen and offices range; that at the upper end was a sequence of private apartments. Immediately to the rear of the hall was the cloistered Pump Court with the thirteenth-century chapel on its north side flanked by three towers, two to the west and a third at the north-east angle. Post-Reformation developments have included rebuilding the hall on the same site as the earlier one in 1660–3, pulling down the kitchen wing in 1829, and replacing the entire residential wing by the existing one in 1829–33.

Superficially of medieval character throughout, only part of the palace is genuinely so – the early thirteenth-century chapel, the early fourteenth-century withdrawing chamber, the fifteenth-century Water Tower and gatehouse, and the early sixteenth-century Cranmer Tower.

Except for the great hall, the palace has always been designed for first-floor living, with the earlier buildings in stone and those of the late fifteenth to the late seventeenth centuries in brick. Some are individually interesting though not remarkable, but they do not coalesce into a satisfactory whole. It was never a homogeneous residence so that the benefit of dividing it into two separate functions was recognised two centuries ago when Edward Blore erected his new archiepiscopal residence to the north-east of the older buildings, which were converted into a library, diocesan record office, and episcopal secretariat. That division has held to the present day, so that the buildings are best noted in the order of construction. That they are summarily described lies in their remodelled interiors through continuous habitation, ecumenical administration, and Second World War repairs to the gutted chapel, hall, and Water Tower. It is its present purpose as a home, research library, and power-house of the world-wide Anglican Communion that enables this palace to maintain its original functions beyond those of residence and administration, hospitality and fellowship.

Archbishop Anselm (1093–1109) had a house at Lambeth[3] but it was archbishop Hubert Walter (1193–1205) who acquired the church and manor of Lambeth from the bishop of Rochester in exchange for land. As it was intended to be a permanent residence for a leading dignitary of the state as much as for the Primate of England, the choice of this site opposite the royal palace of Westminster was deliberate. No buildings can be ascribed to the twelfth century, though the fractured layout suggests the existence

PLATE 93 London, Lambeth Palace: engraving from river Thames by Wenceslaus Hollar (1647)

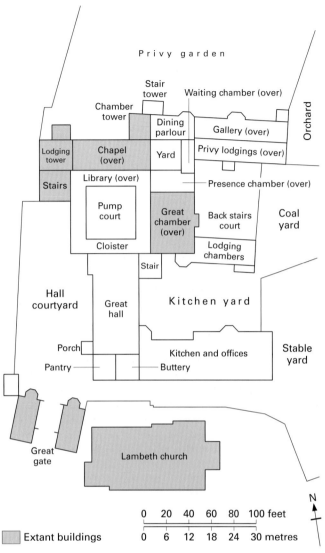

FIGURE 55 Lambeth Palace site plan *c.*1648

Extant buildings

A hall existed by 1234, when it is mentioned in the earliest sur-viving accounts, but whether it was that or a late medieval replace-ment which is shown in Hollar's engraving of 1647 is open to question. A hall by Langton would have been aisled (like that by him at Canterbury Palace), which is unlikely to have been accept-able by the fifteenth century. Hollar's engraving shows that the river façade was divided into three by 1647 – a two-storeyed porch, a line of four windows lighting the body of the hall, and a rectangular dais bay window – surmounted by an embattled parapet and a steeply pitched lead-covered roof. The 1648 plan shows that the porch opened into a screens passage in the second bay, allowing the end bay to be divided into a buttery and pantry. The opposing cross-passage door accessed the kitchen and offices, a range at right angles (a plan repeated at Ely Place) and almost as large as the hall. This last was a five-bay apartment with its body lit by a pair of extended windows of early Perpendicular character in each bay, and the dais bay similarly with a pair of windows. Opposite was the door access-ing the staircase leading to the archbishop's apartments. This hall might possibly have been the work of archbishop Courtenay (1381–96), built after the palace had been sacked by the mob during the Peasants' Revolt in 1381. Yet the fenestration is too indistinct in the engraving to be a guide, so that its ascription to archbishop Chichele (1414–43) is equally valid. If so, it is possible that the deliberately conservative arch and hammer-beam truss roof of Juxon's hall of 1660–3 echoed its predecessor, demolished only eleven years earlier.[6] Like that at Arundel Castle, the Lambeth apartment is one of the major lost halls of late medieval England.

The cloister, possibly of late twelfth-century origins, linked the chapel with the great hall as did that at Ely Place. It seems to have been of timber construction, with first-floor galleries added by Chichele during the early fifteenth century. These held the arch-bishop's library as early as Elizabeth's reign until the whole struc-ture was replaced by a new cloister in 1830, initially for kitchens and domestic offices, but now used as a reading room and for book stacks.

Although the palace developed into a substantial complex between the mid-thirteenth and late fourteenth centuries, we have few details and only scrappy documentation. We know that the archbishop had a small complex of chambers by Courtenay's time, including a waiting chamber and inner presence chamber, pre-ceded by the great chamber. This had probably been built much earlier in the fourteenth century at the head of the stair from the hall dais. Called the High Commission Court in 1648 and the Guard Chamber until the mid-eighteenth century (by which it is still known), the character of this major apartment has been jeop-ardised since Blore had the roof propped up while he replaced the original walls with those of his design. The floor height and pro-portions remain unaltered, 56 feet by 27½ feet, divided into four bays by collar trusses supported by two-centred arches. The span-drels are pierced with quatrefoils and cusped daggers, and the roof is given heightened effect by similarly decorated and elongated wind and side-wall braces.[7] The apartment formerly opened into the more private rooms east of the chapel built before the close of the century, with an oratory added by archbishop Arundel (1397–1414).

Archbishop Chichele was responsible for initiating the five-storey Water Tower abutting the west end of the chapel. It provided

of at least a hall and a residential unit from that time. Walter's initial proposal to build a new grand house in 1197–8 was overtaken by the decision to establish a Premonstratensian abbey on the site in 1199. This may have dictated the layout of the present palace round a clois-ter, for the proposed church was probably on the south side of the cloister (where the great hall was later situated), while the walls of the chapel undercroft were probably those of the canons' refectory.[4]

Now almost engulfed by later buildings, the chapel is raised above a four-bay vaulted undercroft with a central line of circular Purbeck marble columns, an area initially divided into rooms. Externally gaunt, the chapel is wide, internally austere in character, with each of its four bays lit by three graduated lancets outlined by tall shafts of Purbeck marble, with five-lancet windows filling both end walls.[5] Built for archbishop Langton (1206–28) after he returned to England following the interdict of 1208–13, the chapel was burnt in 1941 so that the vaulting, glass, and most of its furnish-ings are reinstatements of 1954–5.

PLATE 94 London, Lambeth Palace: Great Gate from the west

work for quoins, windows, and doorways. The two-storeyed central block, of separate vaulted carriage and pedestrian entrances with a single large chamber above, is flanked by square five-storey towers, the roof line enhanced by battlements, turrets, and tall chimneys. This substantial structure served as the gatehouse to the palace with porter's lodge and prison with iron rings, as the registry for the archbishop's prerogative court, and as eight lodgings for senior members of the archbishop's household. They comprised a large heated outer chamber and an inner chamber with garderobe (west), and a slightly smaller group with the garderobe near the stair (east). Compared with contemporary brick gatehouses such as Hadleigh Deanery or Oxburgh Hall, Morton's entrance is four-square and plain, though it can best be compared with St John's Gatehouse at Clerkenwell in date and form. Since the 1860s, the Albert Embankment has cut off the gatehouse from the river, and it is now used as an archive repository.[9]

Archbishop Cranmer (1532–56) built a tower north-east of the chapel with his study opening directly into it, and probably the gallery, 90 feet long, east of the chapel usually attributed to cardinal Pole.[10] This work, extending the complex of private apartments, was sympathetic to the earlier buildings, as was Juxon's hall of 1660–3, deliberately coloured by the medieval past for symbolic reasons. The same could be said of Blore's residential range which replaced Cranmer's red-brick apartments. Cranmer's double-pile range included a great parlour and long gallery facing the garden, backed by the archbishop's privy lodgings above an arcaded stone gallery. Described by Blore as 'miserably deficient' and therefore to be pulled down, the same could be applied to his aesthetically arid replacement, particularly the unbroken garden frontage (1829–33), though his internal plan of ground-floor staff quarters (now offices) below the archbishop's apartments has proved adequate enough.[11]

The 1648 plan shows that the formal gardens and orchard north of the palace and part of the east court were still moat-enclosed and continued to be so until the mid-eighteenth century. Today, the 12 acre garden and park are a haven of calm, with the latter used since the mid-twentieth century as a public recreation ground.

high-quality accommodation overlooking the river, which was closer to its walls than today. The cellar and two floors were constructed with Kentish ragstone in 1434–5 by Thomas Attenhille at a cost of £291 19s. 4½d. in place of an earlier stair tower serving the chapel.[8] The tiny newel was replaced with a larger stair and garderobe turret on the north side and two further floors were added to Chichele's structure. These were built in brick, faced with good-quality Kentish ragstone to the front and therefore unlikely to be before the late fifteenth century, probably by archbishop Morton. Finally, a three-floor tower was built against the south side, the so-called Laud's Tower, by the early sixteenth century. Today, the river face displays a regular pattern of windows for each floor, with an embellished niche (with a statue of St Thomas Becket by John Thirsk) separating those marking the middle stage. The ground floor retains a good timber ceiling with elaborate mouldings, the cross beams formerly supported on a central post which gave the room its name, the post room. The room above was an antechamber (now vestry) to the chapel, while the three uppermost floors were comfortable lodgings of outer and inner heated chambers, served by the added stair and garderobes. At the top of the stair is a purpose-built prison with barred windows, iron wall-rings, fireplace, and incised inscriptions.

In about 1490, archbishop Morton (1486–1500) replaced the earlier entrance with the great towered gateway to give greater dignity to the palace approach from the river. Incorporating the gate mentioned in 1322 when archbishop Reynold carried out improvements to the palace, Morton's structure was entirely brick-built with occasional diapering contrasting with the dressed stone-

NOTES

1 It was called Lambeth House in Stuart and Georgian times until given palace appellation in the early nineteenth century.
2 Tatton-Brown (2000) 106–7.
3 *Ibid.* 15.
4 *Ibid.* 24–6. The lowest levels of the undercroft walls are of different building materials from the upper structure and it lacked buttresses.
5 P. M. Johnson, *Surrey Arch. Coll.* 32 (1919) 131–52; V. Jansen in *England in the Thirteenth Century* ed. W. M. Ormrod (1985). Part of the thirteenth-century glazed tile flooring survives under the present wood flooring and stalls. S. Degnan and D. Seely, *London Arch.* 6, no. 1 (1988) 11–18.
6 Since 1829, it has been used as a library and exhibition room.
7 Until determined by dendrochronology, estimates of its date vary from the late fourteenth to the later fifteenth century. The chamber was converted from an armoury to a dining room in the mid-eighteenth century, and now serves as a meeting room and portrait gallery.
8 Dodwell (1958) 28; Tatton-Brown (2000) 48–50.
9 Tatton-Brown (2000) 53–4.
10 *Ibid.* 62.
11 Blore prepared a number of valuable plans and watercolours of the archbishop's private apartments before their destruction.

A. C. Ducarel, *The History and Antiquities of the Archiepiscopal Palace of Canterbury* (1785) in *Bibliotheca Topographica Britannica* II, no. 4

W. Herbert and E. W. Brayley, *A Concise Account, Historical and Descriptive, of Lambeth Palace* (1806)

RCHM, *London*, II (1925) 79–86

D. Gardiner, *The Story of Lambeth Palace* (1930)

H. Roberts and W. H. Godfrey, *Survey of London*, XXIII (1951) 81–103

C. R. Dodwell, *Lambeth Palace* (1958)

R. Haslam, *Country Life* (October 1990)

T. Tatton-Brown, *Lambeth Palace* (2000)

LOW HALL MANOR and lesser houses of London's hinterland

The tentacle spread of London during the last 200 years has swept away most of the historic evidence within a 15 miles radius of the city, the area officially referred to as Greater London since 1965.[1] It contained several market towns, over 300 villages and settlements, and an unknown number of manor houses, but all have been thoroughly blighted or destroyed by rampant 'development' and building schemes – railways, offices, factories, estate housing, supermarkets, commercial centres, and motorways. Only an occasional heavily restored parish church and possibly a drastically altered building survives as evidence of any medieval settlement.

Archaeological excavation is severely limited and usually incomplete in densely built-up suburbs, so that our appreciation of London's hinterland is sketchy. Since the 1950s, our knowledge on the royal palaces has been extended considerably through excavations at Eltham, Greenwich, Kennington, and Rotherhithe. Further upstream, bishop Booth of Durham (1457–76) had built a fortified house at Bridgecourt, Battersea, begun under licence in 1474.[2] Subsequently bequeathed by archbishop Booth to the see of York and renamed York House, the moated site was excavated in 1996–8, to reveal that all medieval structures had been comprehensively demolished for post-medieval buildings. Even so, an octagonal corner tower, a line of five rooms, and two courtyards were identified.[3]

Further distant from the Thames, a handful of standing structures have been examined such as Franks Farm, Upminster, and Walnut Tree Lodge, Leyton,[4] or Ickenham Manor Farm,[5] but little prime-quality evidence has survived later alterations. Excavations have often proved of restricted value. Northolt, excavated in 1950–74, was primarily a mid-fourteenth-century house that proved to be a six-period site.[6] West Drayton House was built by Sir William Paget in 1546–9 and demolished in 1750–60 except for the mutilated red-brick gatehouse. Work in 1979–80 uncovered features relating to the earlier manor house here held by the canons of St Paul's Cathedral. Two main periods of building were identified, in the twelfth and fifteenth centuries. The excavations of the double moated site at South Norwood in 1972 were disappointing. Fragments were recovered of the medieval timber bridges across both moats, but the platform interior had been levelled in the nineteenth century, destroying the building evidence.

The paucity of work on manorial, professional, and merchant houses through documentary study, architectural analysis, or excavation means that our knowledge of them in the Greater London

PLATE 95 London, Low Hall Manor: site excavation (1997) with the services wing to the left of the central hall and the extended private quarters to the right

area is very patchy. We are not yet clear whether the examined house sites are typical or not. It has not been possible to determine whether they were isolated or close to communities. And more work needs to be undertaken before it can be determined to what extent they were influenced by or reflected the growth and wealth of London.

The excavation of *Low Hall Manor*, Walthamstow, and consideration of two other properties highlight some of the problems of sites in this region. A seventeenth-century farmhouse at Low Hall was destroyed by a bomb in 1944. The property remained neglected for fifty years until local housing expansion made its development financially attractive. In 1997, excavation revealed the total and pristine plan of a mid-fourteenth-century manor house, virtually free from post-medieval development. And because the housing programme was intended to cover the whole site, it was completely stripped rather than the more usual limited trenching or keyhole excavation that existing buildings, developer financing, and time limitations often impose. By 1999, a suburban estate had obliterated all previous historic evidence.

The excavation results were impressive. In 1352, Low Hall Manor was in the hands of the city merchant Simon Fraunceys, twice lord mayor. On his death, the property passed via his wife to

Thomas, earl of Warwick (d.1401) and was held by his successors until the death of the Kingmaker at Barnet in 1471. The manor was held by the crown until 1550 when it passed into private hands. Occupation continued until the seventeenth century, when the medieval house was completely levelled and replaced by a smaller one over part of its site which stood in declining condition for three centuries.

Total excavation of the moated platform revealed the stone foundations of a classic-plan mid-fourteenth-century single-storey hall and two-storeyed end wings, all of single build. Parallel with the entry arm of the moat and comfortably positioned half-way from it on the platform, the hall lay opposite the entrance approach with its porch almost in line with the bridge. Approximately 41 feet by 27 feet, the apartment had a central hearth. The offices wing extended beyond the rear line of the hall, with a detached kitchen nearby. The rectangular residential block, in line with the hall, was generously proportioned. There was an absence of datable finds except for a substantial quantity of fourteenth-century geometrically decorated floor tiles from Penn in Buckinghamshire. That they were found in the moat rather than within the ground-floor rooms suggests they came from the high-quality upper rooms and were used as moat infill at the time of the house's destruction. A baseplate frame of the contemporary bridge over the moat was revealed, dendrochronology dated to the summer of 1344, with evidence of a drawbridge associated with the ragstone abutment cut into the platform edge.

Low Hall Manor vividly revealed the two stages over the next 150 years necessary to meet the demand for additional rooms and greater privacy. The extensions almost doubled the size of the house but they continued to retain and respect its early core. The residential block was initially enlarged with an L-shaped addition wrapped round two sides, containing two small and a large rear room at both levels. At the same time, a stone gatehouse was added at the side of the earlier bridge abutment. In the second phase, a new wing was built at right angles to the enlarged residential block parallel with the north arm of the moat. Built on chalk footings and possibly timber-framed (in part?), it consisted of a large outer and smaller end chamber, the former with a central fireplace and the latter with a privy discharging into the moat. The wing was almost certainly two-storeyed, with the upper floor repeating the ground-floor facilities.[7]

The moat enclosing *Headstone Manor*, Harrow, one of only seven known in north-west London, is the finest of them and still water-filled. The south-west arm has portions of brick revetment, and a central red-brick bridge gives access to the platform. The manor house standing in the south-west quarter of the rectangular island reveals occupation evidence spanning the ninth to the nineteenth centuries. This timber-framed house not only is the earliest in the region, but retains high-quality work of the fourteenth, seventeenth, and eighteenth centuries. Within the outer court is a superb ten-bay timber-framed barn of *c*.1505, and the frame of a smaller barn of similar date.[8]

This manor was owned by the archbishop of Canterbury between *c*.825 and 1535, after which it passed through the hands of several different families. Resistivity and dendro surveys have revealed that the aisled hall of *c*.1315 by an ecclesiastical tenant originally extended further southwards, the cross wing is contemporary, and further earlier buildings exist within the outer courtyard area. The house was purchased by archbishop Statford in 1344 to become the

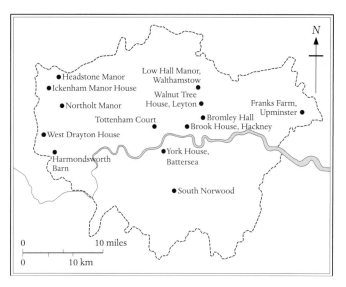

FIGURE 56 Greater London houses mentioned in text

prime if rarely visited archiepiscopal residence in Middlesex. Major developments were undertaken during the later sixteenth century affecting the high end of the hall, for this is a substantial domestic complex of major significance which has yet to reveal its full potential.[9] As the property has been owned by the local authority since 1934, it is now a question of whether that authority responds more sympathetically and willingly to its responsibilities in the twenty-first century than in the past.

Brooke House, Hackney, visibly a house of 1535 until its destruction, was developed round a late fifteenth-century property. Much of it was built in 1476 and grew round two courtyards. Wartime bomb damage was considered sufficient in 1954–5 to justify total destruction and the erection of the pathetic Hackney College on its site. Fragments of the late fifteenth-century wall painting recovered from the chapel and now in the Museum of London show high-quality workmanship. It dates from the time when the property was owned by William Worsley, dean of St Paul's. This rare metropolitan survival depicts a mitred saint with staff and a kneeling figure against a multi-patterned background design carrying the dean's initials.[10] The late seventeenth-century *Bromley Hall*, Tower Hamlets, developed round a square brick tower-house, at least three storeys high, dendro dated to 1482–95. It had narrow octagonal corner turrets and a projecting newel on the north side. The second floor (and above) may have been timber-framed and jettied from the brick walls. Internally, the tower was divided by timber-framed walls with heated rooms on each floor. On land held by the titled Devereux, Sadler, and Cecil families, the earliest known occupant seems to have been the wealthy courtier Sir John Blount in 1509. This elaborate structure may have been emulating Henry VII's tower-house nearby at Greenwich Palace.[11]

NOTES

1 The area had previously included Middlesex and parts of Essex, Hertfordshire, Surrey, and Kent.

2 *Cal. Charter Rolls: 1427–1516*, 242.

3 D. Hawkins *et al.*, *London Arch.* 9, no. 5 (2000); *Med. Arch.* 47 (2003) 246–9.

4 Recorded by Museum of London, 1975–85.

5 P. A. Clarke, *Trans. London and Middx Arch. Soc.* 42 (1991) 101–13. The house retains part of a mid to late fourteenth-century timber-framed hall.

6 *Med. Arch.* 5 (1961) 211–99; 8 (1964) 272; 9 (1965) 202.

7 I. Blair, *Essex Archaeology and History* 33 (2002) 191–220.

8 The famous timber barn, 192 feet long, at Harmondsworth in the shadow of Heathrow Airport stands virtually unaltered since its construction by Winchester College in *c*.1426–8. Virtually all the timbers in its twelve aisled bays are original. Purchased by William Wykeham in 1381, the manor was among the college's prime sources of revenue. The present farm buildings are post-medieval. D. Pearce, *Country Life* (December 1990); *Vern. Arch.* 24 (1993) 52.

9 VCH, *Middlesex*, IV (1971) 204, 221, 229; *Vern. Arch.* 33 (2002) 110–11; P. A. Clarke, *Trans. London and Middx Arch. Soc.* 51 (2000) 157–82; A. Bond, *English Heritage, Reports and Papers*, 52 (2001).

10 F. H. Sheppard (ed.), *Survey of London* XXVIII, *Hackney* (pt 1) (1960).

11 *Med. Arch.* 47 (2003) 245; 48 (2004) 268; *Vern. Arch.* 34 (2003) 93.

THE SAVOY and London magnate residences

London can show no medieval magnate's residence in whole or part, and though *the Savoy* is synonymous with John of Gaunt (though built by his father-in-law), we know more about it than most other baronial mansions. At the request of his wife, Eleanor of Provence, Henry III granted an area of land between the Thames 'and the Strande' in 1246 to her uncle, Peter of Savoy, the seventh son of the count of Savoy. He retired to Chillon Castle in 1268 and Eleanor bought back the manor two years later.[1] In 1284, she gave it to her second son, Edmund, 1st earl of Lancaster, who obtained a licence to crenellate his house called the Sauvoye three years before his death in 1296.[2] The property descended in turn to his two sons, but it was his grandson Henry, earl of Lancaster and Derby, who erected one of the most imposing mansions in medieval London.

In autumn 1345, Henry had captured the castle and town of Bergerac in the Dordogne and been granted them by Edward III nearly two years later for his services in Aquitaine.[3] The immediate booty and ongoing dues funded Henry's aspirations for his magnificent new London residence. Between 1347 and 1350, he purchased a clutch of nearby properties to clear access and enhance the mansion he had in mind, including the land and houses of Sir Henry Scrope.[4] By then, the manor of the Savoy was an area of considerable extent, stretching from the Temple to the present site of Cleopatra's Needle. It was divided into four wards, three of them edging the riverbank – the royal ward next to the Temple, the middle ward astride Howard Street, and the Savoy ward subsequently covered by Somerset House and the Hospital. The elongated fourth ward to the north, church ward, extended from St Clement Danes to St Mary le Strand.

The palace was built in the third ward on land next to Waterloo Bridge, now covered by Waterloo Street, Lancaster Place (*c*.1903–2, the Duchy's present headquarters), the Institute of Electrical Engineers (*c*.1892), and the Savoy chapel and churchyard. We have no contemporary description, and the building documentation is patchy, but the mansion was clearly of a scale that befitted the newly created duke of Lancaster (March 1351). We learn from his successor's registers that the property was stone-built throughout but with

some roofs thatched, a material banned within the city since 1212. The complex was developed round two courts rather than a single one, and included hall, chapel,[5] and group of private apartments, facing inwards rather than towards the river. The property included a cloister[6] as well as bakehouse, brewery, laundry, smithy, stables, fishpond, and a hedge-protected fruit and vegetable garden.[7] This last was tended by Nichol Gardiner, who was paid 2d. a day and allowed to take all the produce not needed by the duke's household.[8] The whole was enclosed by a stone wall (partly mud-built on the west side) with a large street gate towards the Strand and a smaller water gate to the Thames.[9] The palace chapel was an important structure, and Loftie's suggestion that it may have been chosen as the site for the later (and still existing) chapel at the north-west corner of Henry VII's hospital is possible.[10] What is clear is that the palace replaced any earlier building in a swiftly completed development programme between about 1350 and 1357 that cost the enormous sum of 52,000 marks (£35,000) according to Knighton.[11] King John of France was confined here in 1357, and though he subsequently stayed at Windsor Castle, his entourage were accommodated at the Savoy until the king returned to France in 1360. It was his home again in 1364 after his son had broken parole, though only for the short time before his death in April of that year.

With the demise of the 1st duke at Leicester in 1361, a victim of the plague, John of Gaunt inherited the property through his wife, Blanche, the duke's sole heiress. He frequently resided at the Savoy during the next twenty years and commissioned some modest alterations from Henry Yevele and William Wintringham in 1375–7.[12] In May 1381, Gaunt left the palace to lead an expedition to the Scottish marches and he was in Yorkshire when the Peasants' Revolt broke out in south-east England. Gaunt's insensitivity and overweening influence over the young Richard II fostered the London mob's ferocious hostility towards him. Hertford Castle and his manor at Little Chesterford in Essex were ransacked, but the undefended character of the Savoy, 'a lodging unrivalled in splendour and nobility within the kingdom',[13] meant that it fell victim more easily to the mob's fury on 13 June. It was the immediate and visual symbol of Gaunt's wealth, eminence, and status. Five wagonloads of furnishings, plate, and jewels were consumed by the flames, swiftly joined by the hated court rolls and duchy records that symbolised Gaunt's power. Gold and silver vessels were hacked to pieces and thrown away, while the fact that his jewels and plate were destroyed rather than looted bespeak the mob's virulent hatred of the absent duke.[14]

The searing memory of mob rule which had initially surfaced five years earlier[15] quashed any thoughts of rebuilding in Gaunt's lifetime, and the property is not even mentioned in his will. Shortly after the conflagration, lead from some roofs was taken for reuse at Hertford Castle, damaged timber was sold, and new timber purchased for replacement gates for the street entrance.[16] Gaunt left the ruins to stand as a memorial to the bitterness of Londoners towards him, and the fragility of worldly splendour.[17] His successors had no need of this property when they enjoyed the benefit of all crown residences, so that the palace remained a ruin for over 130 years.

Summary repairs were made in 1393–4 by Stephen Lote to a tower called Symeon Toure and to the water gate. They and the street gate seem to have been the only retained roofed buildings, with one of them used as a prison by 1394[18] and throughout the fifteenth century. Some leases were granted for new houses and shops on land nearby[19] but the manor otherwise remained neglected

Early in the sixteenth century, Henry VII sought to establish a hospital for poor people here, and although work had begun in 1508, it had not proceeded far before his death. Shortly after the site had been conveyed to the executors of Henry VII's will in 1511, a large number of workmen were employed on the hospital's construction throughout the remainder of the decade. Use was made of some of the earlier walls, particularly along the river front, but the site was dominated for three centuries by the enormous cruciform hospital building that is the focal point of Vertue's early eighteenth-century engraving. The foundation gradually degenerated into squalor, was dissolved in 1702, and divided into barracks, a prison, tenements, and Lutheran and Calvinist churches. The buildings were pulled down between the early and mid-nineteenth century, leaving only the chapel and graveyard of St Mary (the Savoy Chapel) as testimony to the site's rich history.[20]

The only detailed view of the Savoy is that of 1736 by George Vertue depicting Henry VII's hospital from the river.[21] An extended two-storeyed range above a raised basement rises from the water's edge, with short end ranges at right angles (that to the west forward into the river), and a high river-projecting tower off-centre. The cross-like hospital rises behind, flanked by ancillary buildings.

Vertue delineates the different building materials and textures with great care. The walling of the river range to a height of about 12 feet above the water level is of rubblework as against the dressed

stonework of the floors above, suggestive of two building phases. They are usually attributed to the mid-fourteenth and early sixteenth centuries respectively, even though the lower parts of the two river projections were also built of better-quality dressed stone, necessitated by the garderobe discharge outlets washed by the tide. Closer examination also shows that this range and the central tower have plain embattled parapets, whereas the upper parts of the end ranges were built of chequered stone of early Tudor character (repeated in the belfry tower of St Mary's chapel and the south transept gable of the hospital). In contrast, all the parapets to the buildings behind this range are elaborated with diamond patterns of early Tudor form. It is therefore probable that virtually the whole of the river range was mid-fourteenth-century work, with the first- and second-floor line of single and twin uncusped lights under square hoods inserted for hospital use in a relatively plain wall, or possibly in the position of (occasional) earlier windows. The narrow character of the water gate also suggests it lies in the earlier position, while the short enclosing wall further left certainly looks medieval. Hollar's drawing of the hospital of 1650 is less detailed, but it shows the river range with the tall chimneys that might have been expected and which had been taken down nearly ninety years later.[22]

The evidence for *magnate houses*, leased or owned in the city, is essentially documentary.[23] At least forty-five houses have been identified as high-status dwellings, thirty-five within the city walls and ten without. By the late fifteenth century, two-thirds of them were courtyard properties.[24] The foundations have been traced of part of

PLATE 96 London, The Savoy: engraving from the south by George Vertue (1736)

the thirteenth/fourteenth-century riverside house of the Bigod family, later earls of Norfolk, at Broken Wharf.[25] Cannon Street Station covers The Erber, the extensive mansion of the Scrope family (1340–99) who then moved to Scrope's Inn and sold the earlier property to a sequence of high-status occupants including the earl of Wiltshire (1399), Warwick the Kingmaker (1460–71), and George, duke of Clarence (1472–8).[26] Ralph, Lord Neville (d.1357) had purchased an inn in Silver Street which was enlarged by his son (d.1388) when it was described as a great tenement and occupied by his successors until the sixteenth century.[27] The earls of Northumberland had acquired the site for Northumberland Inn, St Martins Lane by 1343, but it was forfeited to the crown after Scrope's rebellion in 1403, though recovered by the 4th earl in the late fifteenth century. During its sequestration, the earls leased premises in Aldgate, known as Northumberland's Inn, which excavations in 1982 showed had a timber-framed hall.[28] The earls of Warwick were fortunate in retaining their large town house from at least 1351 to the early sixteenth century, the scene of a particularly spectacular household under the Kingmaker.[29] The earls of Oxford maintained their stone and timber inn from c.1348 until 1590, a similar period to the great stone and timber house of the earls of Pembroke and their successor, Barons Bergavenny.[30]

The earl of Lincoln took over Holborn Old Hall with its hall and chapel from the Dominican friars in 1286, and held the property until 1602.[31] During the fifteenth century, Mountjoy's Inn was occupied by Thomas, Lord Stanley (d.1459), the Speaker, Sir John Saye (d.1478), Margaret, countess of Richmond (d.1509), and Charles, Lord Mountjoy (d.1545). The origins of the present College of Arms lie in the courtyard house built by Thomas Stanley, 1st earl of Derby (d.1497),[32] while those of La Riole lay in a thirteenth-century house. This property was virtually rebuilt at the same time that a tower was added for Queen Philippa in 1348–55 when it became her wardrobe (storehouse) and was referred to as Tower Royal. It was subsequently occupied by the earl of Nottingham (1397), the duchess of Clarence (d.1440), the dukes of Somerset and Norfolk, and the countess of Richmond who had married the earl of Derby.

Minor magnates followed their richer and more powerful brethren. The Lovell family owned Lovell's Inn for much of the fifteenth century, acquired through marriage from Lord Holand.[33] Zouche's House, held by several generations of the Zouche family of Harringworth from 1382 to 1431 and possibly longer, had become a very substantial property of sixty-two rooms by 1607 when a detailed schedule was drawn up.[34] The Leaden Porch near London Bridge, first mentioned in 1398, was in the ownership of Lord Bardolf in the mid-fifteenth century but rose in status through occupation by John Howard, duke of Norfolk, later that century.[35]

These and most other magnate houses were within the city walls, but there was a scattering of lay mansions within the arc of ecclesiastical residences stretching from the Temple to Westminster. The site of the large-scale mansion of Lord Hungerford, erected in 1419 and burnt down in 1669, is now covered by Charing Cross Station. And while the Savoy was long held in awe as the greatest mansion of the riverside, it was supplanted in the early sixteenth century by one built just within the city wall. Standing east of the Temple, the earl of Salisbury's residence was rebuilt by Humphrey, duke of Gloucester, as a courtyard house after a fire in 1428. Misleadingly called Baynard's 'Castle' in 1453 through the resem-

blance of its end turrets to its predecessor of that name in the locality,[36] it continued to be owned by the York family, so that Edward IV was proclaimed king here in 1461 as was Richard III in 1483. The property was substantially rebuilt by Henry VII in c.1501 as his principal London residence, with the frontage hurriedly excavated in 1972 in advance of site development.[37]

Lower down the social scale, several élite *gentry* had *town houses*, such as the wealthy Thomas Bukeral in the mid-thirteenth century (The Barge, Buckersbury). Though partly demolished by Stow's time, it was still capable of being described as 'a great stone house'. In 1360, Sir Ralph Basset of Drayton House, Northamptonshire, owned Basset's Inn, while Sir Thomas Berkeley's mid-fourteenth-century stone house passed through marriage in the early fifteenth century to the earl of Warwick.[38] Late in the fourteenth century, Richard II granted the sequestered house of the abbot of Fécamp near the Blackfriars to one of his favourites, Sir Simon Burley. Sir John Fastolf built Fastolf Place in Southwark during the 1440s, and the western edge of this large moated site and adjacent tidal mill were excavated in 1992.[39] As at Caister Castle, Fastolf's death in 1459 brought a host of acquisitive claimants for such a desirable property, including the duke of Exeter, the earl of Wiltshire, the duchess of York, and the bishop of Winchester.[40]

NOTES

1 Somerville (1960) 4–5.
2 *Cal. Pat. Rolls: 1292–1301*. This licence was possibly protection against the suspension of the city's liberties between 1285 and 1299 by his brother, Edward I. It was the first licence issued for a town house in England. Nearly all the other applications for licences in London were made during the first half of the fourteenth century, with only one further application in 1385. Two were from bishops, but the others were from private citizens (see appendix 4). Building did not necessarily follow, though the embattled parapet crowning Sir John Pulteney's residence (1341) is clearly visible in Wyngaerde's panorama of 1540.
3 They were still in Lancastrian hands as late as 1395. R. Somerville, *History of the Duchy of Lancaster*, I (1953) 55.
4 Loftie (1878) 41.
5 The first chancellor of the duchy, the priest Thomas Thelwall, was sworn into office in the chapel in 1377, Loftie (1878) 56.
6 The basis for the double-courtyard ascription. Lambeth Palace and Ely Place had cloistered courts before the close of the thirteenth century, separating the hall and chapel. A slightly later cloister of the 1370s still survives at the Charterhouse through its conversion into a mansion after the Dissolution, and into a school in 1611. Winchester House was also double-courtyard before the close of the thirteenth century.
7 The details come from *John of Gaunt's Register: 1372–6*, ed. S. Armitage-Smith (1911) nos. 1222, 1223, 1228.
8 Loftie (1878) 56.
9 There is no evidence of any moat.
10 Loftie (1878) 64; Cowell (c.1921) 32. John Sampull was buried here in 1510 before the hospital construction was thoroughly underway, and in a chapel that unusually stands north–south, suggesting an earlier site association. However, the shell of the present chapel is entirely contemporary with the remainder of the hospital, brick-built with stone facing. Somerville (1960) 19–20.
11 *Chronicon*, ed. J. R. Lumby, II (1895) 118.
12 J. Harvey, *Eng. Med. Arch.* (1984) 337, 360; A. Goodman, *John of Gaunt* (1992) 322. £30 was spent in 1375, £20 in 1376, and £40 in 1377.
13 Walsingham, *Historia Anglicana*, ed. H. T. Riley, I (1863–4) 456–7.
14 *Anonimalle Chronicle*, ed. V. H. Galbraith (1927) 142. This author seems to have been an eye-witness to the palace's destruction. He notes that the

mob found three barrels of gunpowder but, mistaking them for containers of gold and silver, threw them on to the fire, creating greater havoc and loss. Also Walsingham, *Historia Anglicana*, I (1863–4) 456–8; *Chronicon Henrici Knighton*, II (1889–95) 132–4; *Froissart*, ed. G. C. Macaulay (1895) 255–6; and Ranulph Higden, *Polychronicon*, ed. C. Babington and J. R. Lumby 9 (1865–86) 1–2.

15 Rioters assembled outside the palace gateway in 1376 clamouring for the duke. He was dining elsewhere, but the princess Joan was able to assuage the mob's anger.

16 *John of Gaunt's Register: 1379–83*, ed. E. C. Lodge and R. Somerville (1937) no. 738; *Archaeologia* 24 (1836) 306.

17 A. Goodman, *John of Gaunt* (1992) 79–80.

18 *Archaeologia* 24 (1836) 299.

19 Loftie (1878) 82.

20 For its history from Henry VII's foundations onwards, Somerville (1960).

21 PRO, MPC 103. Published in 1750 in association with a plan of the building by the Society of Antiquaries of London.

22 None of the late eighteenth-century drawings and engravings of the hospital buildings such as those by J. Hooper (1787) or S. Rawle (1798) or the watercolour by S. Ireland (1794), or the photographs of the last hospital ruins (Duchy of Lancaster office), suggests work earlier than the time of Henry VIII.

23 Apart from the Guildhall and the relocated Crosby Hall, the only medieval secular structures to survive within the City of London are five medieval undercrofts and the remains of five inns of lawyers.

24 They are marked on the maps of the city in *c.*1520. Lobel (1989).

25 Schofield (1995) 215.

26 *Ibid.* 179.

27 *Ibid.* 209–10.

28 *Ibid.* 202, 181.

29 *Ibid.* 226–7. The cellars that have been excavated on part of this site suggest a particularly large complex. Also *Med. Arch.* 11 (1967) 294–5.

30 Schofield (1995) 158.

31 *Ibid.* 209.

32 *Survey of London*, XVI *The College of Arms* (1992); Lobel (1989) 79, 81, 84.

33 Schofield (1995) 193.

34 *Ibid.* 194–5.

35 *Ibid.* 178–9; Lobel (1989) 78–9.

36 *Med. Arch.* 17 (1973) 162–4; 26 (1982) 192. The Norman castle, probably founded by the Conqueror to defend the south-west corner of the city, was rendered unusable by King John in 1212. The site was given to the Blackfriars for their friary in 1275. J. Schofield, *The Building of London* (1984) 38–40, 70.

37 T. Dyson, *The Medieval London Waterfront* (1989) 9–12.

38 Lobel (1989) 65, 67.

39 D. Bluer, *London Arch.* 7, no. 3 (1993) 59–66.

40 M. Carlin in *Richard III, Crown and People*, ed. J. Petre (1985) 44–7.

The Savoy

S. Appleby, *History of the Savoy* (1834): Manuscript L2 (1), Duchy of Lancaster Office

W. J. Loftie, *Memorials of the Savoy* (1878)

L. A. Cowell, *The Story of the Precinct of the Savoy* (n.d., *c.*1921)

R. Somerville, *The Savoy* (1960)

London houses

C. L. Kingsford, *London Topographical Records*, 10 (1916) 44–144; 11 (1917) 28–81; 12 (1920) 1–66

D. Pearce, *London's Mansions: The Palatial Homes of the Nobility* (1986)

M. Lobel (ed.), *The British Atlas of Historic Towns*, III, *The City of London* (1989)

J. Schofield, 'Medieval and Tudor domestic buildings in the City of London', in *Medieval Art, Architecture and Archaeology in London*, ed. L. Grant (1990) 16–28

J. Schofield, *Medieval London Houses* (1995)

C. Barron, *London Journal* 20 (1995) 1–16

SHEEN and the residences of the English monarchy near London

As the Norman and Angevin kings of England and parts of France were incessantly on the move, they necessarily established a broad spread of accommodation across the greater part of England. Some residences such as those at Cheddar, Westminster, and Winchester were taken over from late Saxon rulers, but they were swiftly joined by a much broader range of accommodation. The majority of additions were dictated by afforestation – hunting lodges close to the swiftly established network of royal forests. They included those at Brigstock (Rockingham Forest), Brill (Bernwood Forest), and Clipstone (Sherwood Forest), but others were early castles associated with nearby forests such as Pickering, Rockingham, Northampton, and Windsor. There were also three palaces – Westminster, the Tower of London, and Guildford.[1] King John collected houses as some people collect stamps, nurtured by his predilection for confiscating other people's property (Cranborne, Gillingham, Bere). Henry III indulged a massive building programme at selected properties, particularly at Clarendon (£3,600), Havering (£2,100), Westminster (£10,000), and Woodstock (£3,300).[2]

Further additions came from gift, purchase, forfeiture, marriage, and escheat. Some properties were retained for only a few years such as Faxfleet (1322–6) and Fulmer (1323–7): others were taken into permanent usage for nearly a century or more, including East Tytherley (1335–1402) and Isleworth (1312–1421). There was considerable movement during Henry III's reign, but a gradual settlement and reduction followed during the next two centuries. Edward I inherited twenty houses from his father, but though this rose to twenty-five early in Edward III's reign, it had fallen to seventeen houses by the close of the century, twelve under Henry VI, and ten with the advent of Henry VII. This reduction arose from a number of factors – the alienation of the royal demesne, more imperative calls on the crown's financial resources, higher living standards which made early houses financially prohibitive to update, less extensive court travelling, and the centralisation of government at Westminster. This last was particularly important in determining the more limited number of houses and their geographical distribution.

During the fourteenth century, the consolidation of power and central administration at Westminster became increasingly dominant. Whereas the royal houses had been scattered across the Midlands and south in Henry III's reign, nearly all those retained in royal hands a century later were within a day's journey from Westminster. Burstwick and Cowick in Yorkshire, acquired for their convenient access to Scotland, were granted away in 1355 and 1370, leaving Clipstone (Nottinghamshire) and Cheylesmore (Warwickshire) as outliers, the only ones north of the Chilterns. This concentration on accommodation in the south-east was initiated by Edward II. He had already acquired King's Langley and

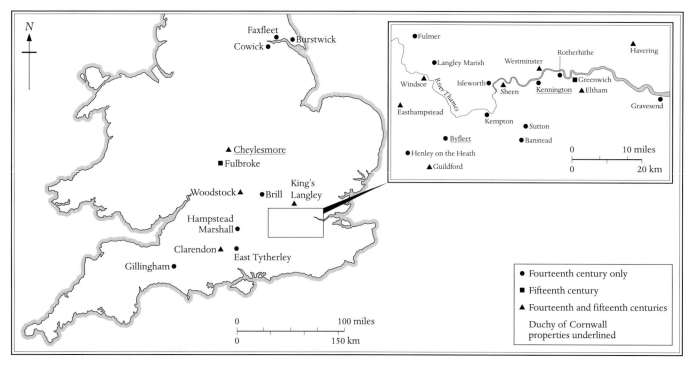

FIGURE 57 Royal houses: 1300–1500

Byfleet when he was prince of Wales but they were joined in 1311 by the gift of Eltham from bishop Bek of Durham and Sheen in 1313 from Otto of Grandston. Easthampstead and Henley on the Heath were purchased by Edward II as was the Rosary (c.1325), a riverside retreat opposite the Tower of London, excavated in 1988.[3] Isleworth came to him by escheat. Edward III built a house for himself at Rotherhithe and acquired Kennington for his son, but his purchases extended as much to the chase as to proximity to government. He added hunting lodges at Foliejohn, Hampstead Marshall, and Wychemere to be close to Windsor Forest, and a large if enigmatic fortified house at Moor End in Northamptonshire. Edward also spent far more than his immediate predecessors or successors on improving his residences, domesticating Hadleigh, Leeds, and Windsor castles as well as his houses at Havering and Sheen. Not surprisingly, some houses became particular favourites, such as King's Langley under Edward II and III, Kennington and Sheen under Richard II, and Eltham under Edward IV. Some fell out of favour such as Guildford 'palace', Banstead, and Gravesend, while those of the duchy of Cornwall which had been established in 1337 to provide for the heir to the throne (Cheylesmore, Kennington, Byfleet, and Beckley hunting lodge) could be occupied by the king in the absence of a son.[4]

The principal differences in the planning of royal houses from major baronial houses lay in three areas. The first was the creation of a separate group of lodgings for the queen, distinct from those for the king. This had occurred as early as Henry II's time at Windsor, and was firmly established by Henry III's time at Westminster and Clarendon, and subsequently at Windsor and Greenwich. The second was the diminution of the hall for communal life in favour of its ceremonial function, with a smaller hall for the king's and queen's use, in association with a withdrawing chamber as at Westminster.

The third was the establishment of separate lodgings for the principal household members, as at Windsor and Eltham during the second half of the fourteenth century. To these should be added the growing popularity of a regular quadrangular layout, usually a double courtyard as at Rotherhithe under Edward III and Sheen under Henry V where brick was first employed in royal works on a major scale. Sheen also reminds us that timber-framing was far more common than has usually survived, though a late example from the outer court remains at Eltham.

'The King's Pallaces are of such magnificent building, so curious art and such pleasure and beauty for gardens and fountains, and are so many in number as England need not envie any other Kingdome therein.' Though Fynes Moryson's approbation of 1617 applied to many of those acquired and developed by Henry VIII, it was equally true of the smaller number in crown hands at the time of his father's accession. Three such residences in the London area survive to a greater or lesser extent – Westminster, the Tower of London, and Eltham. Foundation evidence has been recovered at Kennington (c.1340–63), Rotherhithe (1353–6), and Greenwich (1426–1506), and there is considerable documentary evidence for that at Sheen (1414–c.1450). Nothing survives at Banstead, Gravesend, Henley on the Heath, Isleworth, Kempton, or Sutton in Chiswick.[5] The five Thames-side residences – The Tower, Kennington, Rotherhithe, Sheen, and Greenwich – are considered in that order of acquisition; Westminster and Eltham are discussed separately.

THE TOWER OF LONDON

The only royal residence within the boundaries of the capital was the Tower of London, founded by William the Conqueror. The White Tower (c.1078–c.1097) was always intended to dominate the city, and did so (with St Paul's) until the beginning of the nineteenth

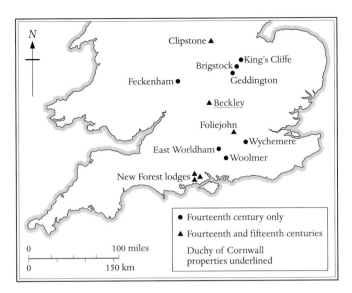

FIGURE 58 Royal hunting lodges: 1300–1500

PLATE 97 Tower of London: royal lodgings and river frontage (c.1500)

century. But the White Tower was not just a military keep, but a magnificent hall with state chambers and an apsidal chapel. From its inception, the Tower was as much a royal residence as an intimidating symbol of regal power and strongly defendable crown refuge. This *arx palatina*[6] was enclosed by a stone curtain with towers during the 1190s, but it was primarily two monarchs who were responsible for the castle's present form during the mid and late thirteenth century respectively. Henry III's work was twofold. He enlarged the castle's defensive circuit, initially towards the river (1220–38) and subsequently landwards (1238–72). During the 1230s, he also initiated the redevelopment of the royal lodgings with a stone hall (with kitchen nearby) and a two-storeyed rectangular chamber block at each end. With the principal room at first-floor level, that used by the king was linked with his presence chamber (with oratory) in the recently completed Wakefield Tower[7] and that for the queen with her lodgings in the Lanthorn Tower. A pentice with a river-facing gallery connected these two royal suites (by c.1260).

At a cost only exceeded by that at Caernarfon Castle, Edward I converted the fortress into a concentric one on all four sides with a new moat, low revetment wall, barbican, two entry gatehouses, and a new river frontage centred on St Thomas' Tower, a water gate with a privy suite of royal apartments above (1275–85). His first floor *magna camera* with oratory, and inner chamber with closet and garderobe, were linked with but replaced his father's lodgings in the Wakefield Tower.[8] Henry III's hall and chamber blocks have long since been pulled down (hall footings revealed) and the Lanthorn Tower was rebuilt in the late nineteenth century, but this extended residential *ensemble* is splendidly depicted in the manuscript illustration of the Tower in the poems of the duc d'Orléans (c.1500).[9]

By the close of the thirteenth century, the Tower of London had assumed its present circuit. All subsequent work is minor, but lavish expenditure did not walk hand-in-hand with frequent occupation. In the forty-five years between 1227 and 1272, Henry III only stayed in the palace-fortress on eleven occasions, totalling no more than thirty-two weeks, and seven of those visits were in 1261 when it was his place of refuge at a time of political crisis.[10] Edward I's

visits were equally rare. He occupied the royal lodgings in 1285 when he sought to dominate the city, but came only six times thereafter.[11] The turbulent reign of Edward II meant that the Tower primarily served as a refuge (1308, 1321, 1326) but that did not prove necessary under his son.

Edward III reroofed the inner courtyard hall and partly rebuilt the original water gate (Bloody Tower) in 1360–2 with its comfortable first-floor chamber with contemporary tiled floor.[12] There is another one on the first floor of the Byward Tower, though this chamber is more important for its painted ceiling beams and high-quality (though mutilated) wall painting of the Crucifixion.[13] This work of the 1390s reminds us that Richard II's brilliant court was often at the Tower, usually seeking refuge, for it had developed not only as the centre of the royal treasury but also as the chief arsenal of the kingdom. The structure did not change during the next hundred years when the opportunity was taken to reroof the White Tower. Otherwise, the complex slid out of use as a royal residence under Henry VIII to become an armoury and prison, and a repository for records, jewels, and animals.

KENNINGTON PALACE

The Black Prince acquired the manor of Kennington in 1337. The earlier manorial complex was swept away about three years later to be replaced by a new residence appropriate to the prince, built in two phases, c.1340–52 and c.1353–63. It survived relatively unaltered until it was totally demolished by Henry VIII in 1531 to provide building materials for his palace at Whitehall.

The site lies west of the junction of Kennington Lane with Kennington Road, with much of it excavated in 1965–8 prior to the erection of a characterless office block for the duchy of Cornwall. Though the core apartments were identified, no more than two courses survived of the hall, great chamber block, kitchen, and stables. The first three were in series with the stone-built hall raised over a low-vaulted undercroft, possibly freestanding at both ends until it was modified or rebuilt in about 1356–7 because of structural weakness.[14] Raised about 6 feet above ground level, it was porch-approached, had three fireplaces in the dais wall (as in the hall of the ducal palace at Poitiers, 1384–6), and had two opposing stairs to the stone-built chamber block. Positioned at right angles to the hall and initially separate from it, both floors of this block were residential with the principal apartments at the upper level with an inner chamber, garderobe turret, and oratory projecting beyond the south line of the hall. Documentation shows there was a separate chamber block for the prince's wife (and later for the queen under Richard II), tentatively identified beyond the great chamber in the excavations.[15] The kitchen was a detached timber-framed structure, though more substantial evidence was found of the stables, half-timbered on stone foundations close to the main gate and the enclosing wall along Kennington Lane built by Henry Yevele in 1358. Several independent chamber units were recovered, with suggested occupation by the treasurer, controller, and steward of the household.

The palace was chalk-built, with Reigate stone for dressed work. Evidence was recovered of painted wall plaster, floor tiles, architectural mouldings, and a little glass, but the site destruction had been wholesale. Even so, the paucity of recovered building and occupational material is at odds with the documentary evidence for its considerable use as a residence and administrative centre during the first hundred years and the archaeological evidence for its continued habitation until its destruction.[16] Wholesale destruction and a high standard of cleanliness are probably responsible for this paradox. For its date, the palace is curiously archaic in its planning. It sits astride the development from independent to united building units, still has separate residential units, presumably linked by covered ways, and lacks any obvious attached buttery and pantry at the lower end of the hall. This looks backwards to Clarendon Palace rather than forward to the ceremonial sequence of rooms at Windsor Castle and Kenilworth Castle, and the layout was not rectified at a later date.

ROTHERHITHE MANOR HOUSE

This was a short-lived royal house, built by Edward III between February 1353 and 1356 on the south bank of the River Thames within sight of the Tower of London. Incorporating part of an earlier house on the same site, it cost about £1,100 to rebuild[17] and was a favoured residence during Edward's later years. He bequeathed the property to his foundation of St Mary Graces by the Tower in 1377 when it passed out of royal hands.

Edward's residence followed the double-courtyard plan – an embanked outer court with timber buildings facing inland, and a stone-built and moated inner court close to the riverside. Between this court and the river was a wharf, reached by a river gate and bridge and now covered by the modern river embankment and road. The inner court and moat stands as an open grassed area with some of the outer walls left exposed to a height of about 6 feet after excavation between 1986 and 1991, but the outer court has since been covered by a line of houses.

Rotherhithe was a small country house with a compact inner court, 100 feet by 66 feet, enclosing two-storeyed ranges with outer walls 3 feet thick. The hall and privy entry gate at its side faced the river. This gate-tower with internal newel opened into a narrow passage with direct access to the hall, lit by windows in both side walls, and with an end wall fireplace. The buttery, pantry, and stone-built kitchen filled the east range. The southern part of the site was left unexcavated for future generations.[18]

The north wall of the hall range, destroyed in the 1930s, had been recorded in 1907 when it was standing 16 feet high.[19] This shows a range with two lines of fifteenth-century windows, five at ground level and four above, of two cinquefoil and transomed lights under depressed heads. Within a century or more after construction, the hall had been floored and a chamber created above.

SHEEN PALACE

Kennington and Rotherhithe have been identified by limited excavation, whereas Sheen (now Richmond) can only be recovered from documentary and pictorial evidence. Edward III first developed the earlier manor house at Sheen into a royal palace (1358–70) and it became a much favoured residence of Richard II and his wife. He was responsible for building a timber-framed summer retreat on an island in the River Thames which included several chambers with fireplaces and a kitchen, but was destroyed at the same time as the palace to assuage the king's grief after the death of Queen Anne from the plague (1394).[20]

Nearly twenty years later, Henry V redeveloped the site by building a 'grete work' and founding a charterhouse nearby.[21] His palace was built over the gardens of the earlier one, under the direction of the master-mason Stephen Lote. Work was initiated by transferring part of the timber-framed royal manor house from Byfleet as temporary accommodation, supplemented by materials from a royal house at Sutton in Chiswick. At the same time, new materials were brought from a geographically wide area – freestone from Caen, Devon, Oxfordshire, and Yorkshire, bricks from Newenden Bridge near Calais, lead and plaster from Lancashire, timber from Surrey, glass from London, and garden trees from Rouen.[22]

Work proceeded along two parallel tracks, with an expenditure of nearly £8,200 in the first five years (1414–19). The re-erected Byfleet building was a substantial one with a king's ward, queen's ward, chapel, and kitchen, and though much of it was timber-framed, stone was used for the chapel and the two towers erected on the east side between 1419 and 1422 with virtual completion by the king's death that year. This structure was entirely domestic in character, unimpaired by the moat, outer wall, and two towers (for garderobes?). It was a temporary house until the main stone building had been completed, as had similarly occurred at Windsor Castle in the 1350s.

The main palace building was far less developed when work ceased in 1422, until young Henry VI was crowned in 1429 and ordered that the palace should be completed. This took nearly twenty years, with incomplete documentation giving only partial information on expenditure and scale, though both were clearly substantial. Doors were being hung in the hall and glass inserted in the chapel windows between 1436 and 1439, at the same time that the site of the old palace and the new one were separated by a broad moat, 25 feet wide and 8 feet deep.[23] In 1444–7 a cloister with a central lead cistern was erected and William Clere, clerk of works,

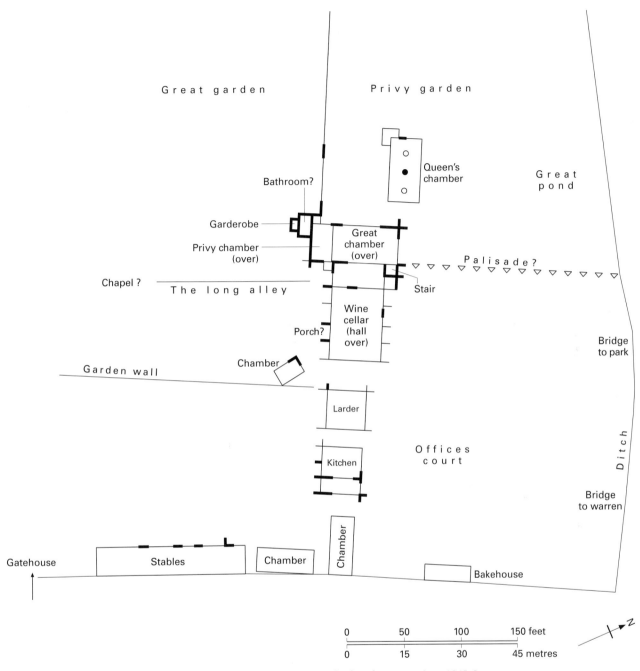

Great garden

Privy garden

Great
pond

Queen's
chamber

Bathroom?

Garderobe

Privy chamber
(over)

Great
chamber
(over)

Palisade?

Chapel ?

The long alley

Stair

Wine
cellar
(hall
over)

Porch?

Bridge
to park

Chamber

Garden wall

Larder

Offices
court

Ditch

Kitchen

Bridge
to warren

Chamber

Chamber

Gatehouse

Stables

Chamber

Bakehouse

| 0 | 50 | 100 | 150 feet |
| 0 | 15 | 30 | 45 metres |

N

FIGURE 59 Kennington Palace: site plan based on excavations, 1965–8

was ordered to build 'the grete quadrangle with a gatehouse all of new to be made for the necessary logging of the worshipful household, with a closer of brike toured about (for the king's) garden there'.[24] Cloake suggests that this great quadrangle with its household lodgings equates to the outer court of the Tudor palace facing Richmond Green, and that the garden was also extended at the side to the same frontage, facing the Green and enclosed with a towered brick wall.[25]

Looking northwards from the Thames, this palace developed as a sequence of separate units over a hundred year period.

1. The site of Edward III/Richard II palace, destroyed in 1395, was planted as an orchard during the second quarter of the fifteenth century. It lay next to

2. The river-facing palace, initiated by Henry V in 1414. It developed as a rectangular block with its outer faces broken by corner towers and bay windows, not unlike the form of Herstmonceux Castle (c.1438–49). The enclosing moat and garden separated the palace or 'privy lodging' block from

3. The stone and timber-framed Byfleet building to its right.

4. North of Henry V's palace lay the middle court flanked by the hall and chapel on opposing sides.

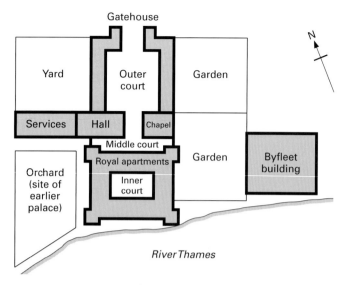

Gatehouse

Yard

Outer court

Garden

Services | Hall | Chapel

Middle court

Orchard (site of earlier palace)

Royal apartments

Garden

Byfleet building

Inner court

N

River Thames

FIGURE 60 Sheen Palace: diagrammatic plan

5. In 1444–7, the complex was developed further towards Richmond Green with a gated outer court, lined with lodging ranges. At the same time, the palace garden was extended northwards to be in line with this added 'great' court.

The palace was seen by William Worcester in 1480, who noted that a recent banquet here, consisting of three courses of fifty-seven dishes each, cost £100.[26] The complex had remained unchanged for nearly fifty years until a fire in December 1497 destroyed the chapel and probably much of Henry V's palace block. Its foundations seem to have been used as the basis for the rapidly completed rebuilding between 1498 and 1501. It included a four-storeyed 'canted tower' with a handsome room on each floor. Cloake considers that this was not the entrance tower in the middle of the north face[27] but the residential north-east tower opposite the chapel.[28]

GREENWICH PALACE

Humphrey, duke of Gloucester acquired the manor of Greenwich in 1426 and obtained a licence seven years later to wall, crenellate, and build a tower of stone in the park.[29] On Humphrey's death in 1447, his country house reverted to the crown and was taken over by Queen Margaret of Anjou, who spent nearly £300 on alterations. This two-courtyard residence included a great chamber, parlour, chapel, and a gallery overlooking the garden with heraldic glass in its windows.[30] In 1499–1506, Henry VII redeveloped the property at a cost of over £3,000, using more than 600,000 bricks made in 1499.[31] A similar scale of expenditure was incurred by Henry VIII, but all late medieval and Tudor structures of this favoured residence were pulled down in 1661–5 in preparation for Charles II's new palace.

It was long used as a naval college and hospital, but its great quadrangle was excavated in 1970–1 to reveal evidence of a small timber-framed house of fourteenth-century date, the footings of a two-storeyed apartment range of duke Humphrey, taken down when Henry VII initiated his brick palace following the earlier alignments.[32] The principal feature of the excavation was the recovery of the base of the great tower which formed part of the river frontage, shown in some detail by Antonius van den Wyngaerde in

his view of 1558.[33] This depicts the chapel at the end of a two-storeyed range that commenced with a river gateway, followed by a line of state apartments on the upper floor with semi-octagonal bays in both faces. The frontage is interrupted by the five-storeyed great tower with a short added wing to the river edge, and the body of the range continuing for a short length before terminating in the kitchen turret. Behind lay a courtyard, enclosed on at least three sides. The chapel and apartments still lie under the Queen Anne block, but the kitchen west of the tower was also exposed.

The tower, 39½ feet by 33 feet internally, had two bays (one for a stair) to the river, and a four-tier garderobe projection in the middle of the courtyard wall. It was almost the last of the great tower-houses that had been such a feature of major residences since the second quarter of the fifteenth century[34] and was not repeated in any subsequent royal works.

NOTES

1 Only Westminster has been consistently referred to as a palace since the mid-thirteenth century. The term for the Tower was more specialised, while the reference to Guildford Castle was restricted to the reign of Edward I. S. Thurley in *The Age of Transition*, ed. D. Gaimster and P. Stamper (1997) 93–4.

2 *HKW*, I (1963) 120.

3 It stood on the site of Hay's Wharf. It was a moated building shown in Ralph Agas' sixteenth-century map of London, of which a courtyard wall 125 feet long was excavated. *London Arch.* 7, no.3 (1993) 61–2.

4 Byfleet was pulled down by Henry V so that the materials could be used for his new palace at Sheen. Kennington was similarly demolished for the benefit of Whitehall Palace in 1531. Beckley was replaced by a new house in the sixteenth century, but the gatehouse still stands at Cheylesmore. A. Emery, *Greater Med. Houses*, II (2000) 366–8.

5 *HKW*, II (1963) 896–8; 946–8; 960–2; 963–5; 965–7; 1003–4.

6 William FitzStephen, *Life of Archbishop Becket*, ed. J. C. Robertson and J. B. Sheppard (1875) 3.

7 P. E. Curnow in *Ancient Monuments and Their Interpretation*, ed. M. R. Apted *et al.* (1977) 155–89.

8 S. Thurley, *Architectural History* 38 (1995) 36–57.

9 Brit. Lib., Royal MS 16 F 11, f.73. This also shows the wharf built along the river front during the fourteenth century, isolating the fortress and its moat from the Thames.

10 D. Carpenter, *London Journal*, 19 (1994) 95–107.

11 Thurley, *Architectural History* 38 (1995) 36–57.

12 P. E. Curnow in *The Tower of London*, ed. J. Charlton (1978) 55–61.

13 E. W. Tristram, *English Wall Painting of the Fourteenth Century* (1955) 36–8, 193–4; *The Age of Chivalry*, ed. J. Alexander and P. Binski (1987) 509–10.

14 *HKW*, II (1963) 967; Dawson (1976) 47.

15 Dawson (1976) 52.

16 Initially described as a manor, it was called a palace by 1438 and thereafter until the term 'place' was used by the sixteenth century. *Ibid.* 188.

17 *HKW*, II (1963) 990–4. A further £126 was incurred in the next five years.

18 Norton (1988) 395–401; S. Blatherwick, *A Royal Residence at Rotherhithe* (in preparation).

19 P. Norman, *Surrey Arch. Coll.* 20 (1907) 132–42.

20 *HKW*, II (1963) 994–8.

21 *A Chronicle of London 1089–1483*, ed. H. H. Nicholas (1827) 99. The charterhouse lay just south of the King's Observatory in Richmond Old Deer Park.

22 Cloake (1995) 30–1.

23 *HKW*, II (1963) 1000; Cloake (1995) 32.

24 *Ibid.* 32–3.

25 *Ibid.* 33. For a site plan of 1611, see *Post-Medieval Archaeology* (2001).

26 *Itineraries*, ed. J. H. Harvey (1969) 271. Worcester noted that the hall, about 77 feet by 40 feet, had once stood at Byfleet, and that the (outer?) court, built round with chambers, was about 208 feet by 175 feet.

27 *HKW*, IV pt 2 (1982) 224–7.

28 Cloake (1995) 60, 69–70.

29 *Cal. Pat. Rolls: 1429–36*, 20. It was reissued four years later with the park area adjusted. *Ibid. 1436–41*, 74.

30 *HKW*, II (1963) 949.

31 *HKW*, IV pt 2 (1982) 97–9.

32 P. Dixon, *Excavations at Greenwich Palace* (1972).

33 Ashmolean Museum, Oxford. Wyngaerde made two sketches, one from the river and one from the park. An early seventeenth-century painting at Kingston Lacy shows the dominating character of the tower particularly clearly.

34 A. Emery, *Greater Med. Houses*, II (2000) 349–55.

General

H. M. Colvin *et al.* (eds.), *The History of the King's Works*, 6 vols. (1963–78)

T. B. James, *The Palaces of Medieval England c.1050–1550* (1990)

S. J. Thurley, *The Royal Palaces of Tudor England: Architecture and Court Life, 1460–1547* (1993)

J. Steane, *The Archaeology of the Medieval English Monarchy* (1993 edn)

Tower of London

J. Charlton (ed.), *The Tower of London: Its Buildings and Institutions* (1978) with bibliography of earlier works

R. A. Brown and P. E. Curnow, *The Tower of London: Handbook* (1984)

Kennington

H. Roberts and W. H. Godfrey (eds.), *Survey of London*, XXIII (1951) 5–11

H. M. Colvin *et al.* (eds.), *HKW*, II (1963) 967–9

G. I. Dawson, *The Black Prince's Palace at Kennington, Surrey* (1976)

Rotherhithe

H.M. Colvin *et al.* (eds.), *HKW*, II (1963) 989–94

E. Norton, *London Arch.* 5, no.15 (1988) 395–401

S. Blatherwick, *A Royal Residence at Rotherhithe: Excavations at Edward III's Manor House at Platform Wharf, Rotherhithe, 1985–94* (in preparation)

Sheen

H. M. Colvin *et al.* (eds.), *HKW*, II (1963) 994–1002

J. Cloake, *Palaces and Parks of Richmond and Kew*, I, *The Palaces of Sheen and Richmond* (1995)

Greenwich

H. M. Colvin *et al.* (eds.), *HKW*, II (1963) 949–50; IV pt 2 (1982) 96–123

P. Dixon, *Excavations at Greenwich Palace* (1972)

WESTMINSTER ABBEY ABBOT'S HOUSE and
London monasteries

Westminster Abbey, the West Minster or Benedictine foundation of St Peter to distinguish it from the East Minster or civic church of St Paul in the city of London, has not always enjoyed the over-

whelming patronage that it did under Edward the Confessor and Henry III. No other European ruler bore the entire cost of a Gothic church on a cathedral scale as Henry III did through rebuilding the Confessor's church.[1] On the other hand, Edward I was markedly unenthusiastic about continuing his father's work, while Edward II showed almost no interest in it at all. Edward III's attention lay in his secular projects and collegiate foundations at the palaces of Windsor and Westminster, while Richard II sought the credit for completing the nave on an annual subsidy of £100 after declaring himself of age in 1387.

Naturally, monastic funding at Westminster had been very modest during the thirteenth century in the face of such royal munificence and initiative so that it was not until some of the precinct roofs had been damaged by fire in 1298 that the foundation had to look to its own resources.[2] The chapter-house and cloister walk, damaged in the fire, were only repaired slowly, while it took two generations to build the remainder of the cloister. The forceful abbot Litlyngton (1362–86) initiated two projects. The first was the completion of the scarcely begun nave from 1375 onwards through the financial generosity of his predecessor, Simon Langham, though the work dragged on until the early years of the sixteenth century before it was roofed and vaulted. The second was the construction of a new house for himself at the north-west end of the claustral complex.

The *Abbot's House* is the only complete medieval London house on the north side of the Thames. It was a very grand residence and is still used in a manner close to its original function. It consists of ranges round four sides of a small court, built in two phases with the three-storeyed block of abbot Islip (1500–32) extending the original accommodation erected by abbot Litlyngton between 1370 and 1379.[3] Litlyngton built and paid for a sequence of rooms round two sides of an oblong paved and cobbled court abutting the south-west corner of the abbey church which towers over it. This court was initially enclosed on the east side with a covered gallery giving Litlyngton private access to his camera, subsequently raised after it was incorporated into the seventeenth-century dean's house, and rebuilt after bomb damage in 1952. The principal range on the left-hand side is made up of the abbot's camera, completed by 1372, the dining hall built between *c.*1372 and 1375–6 when the glass was inserted in the windows, and the kitchen with a chamber above. All three units are in line, with the camera, hall, and offices raised above a low ground floor overlooking a garden to the west extending as far as the (lost) abbey gatehouse. This area from the Crimean Memorial to Sir George Gilbert Scott's gateway and houses (1860s) is now part of the streetscape, with the low ground floor concealed by the abbey shop (1950s). The remainder of the lodging, at right angles to the hall range, consists of the entry passage and store with chamber above.

A short passage extending from the south-west corner of the abbey cloisters[4] accesses the two-bay, tierceron-vaulted entry to the abbot's house, the outer arch retaining the head stops of abbot Litlyngton and Richard II. As the hall stands above low storage rooms with plain joisted ceilings, it is still approached by that rare, though renewed survival, a covered wooden stair to the late fourteenth-century doorway. The four windows in both side walls are of two-transomed cinquefoil lights with a tracery head similar to that built by Litlyngton a little earlier in his cloister walks (1352–66). Some of the glass inserted with his initials NL in 1375–6

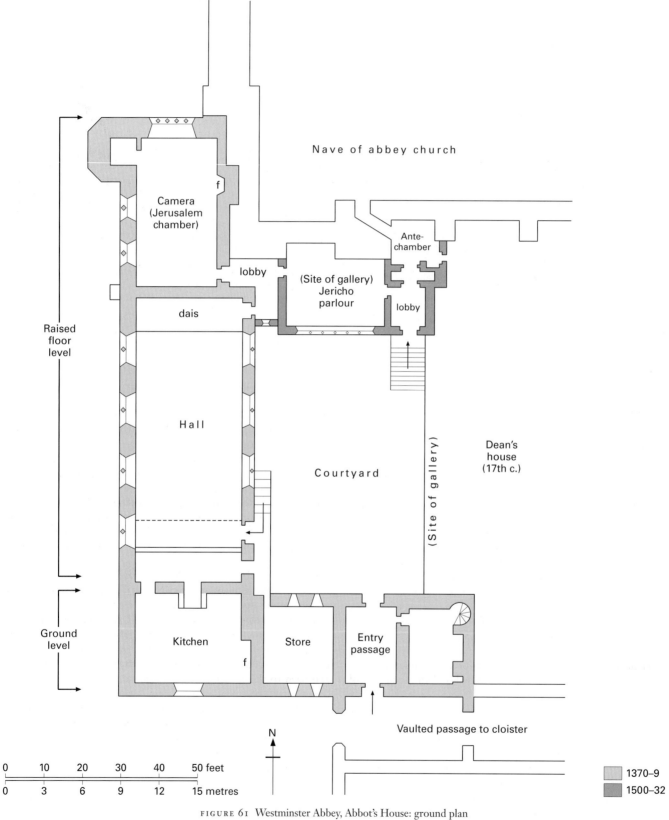

Nave of abbey church

Camera (Jerusalem chamber)

f

lobby

Ante-chamber

(Site of gallery) Jericho parlour

lobby

dais

Raised floor level

Hall

Courtyard

Dean's house (17th c.)

(Site of gallery)

Ground level

Kitchen

f

Store

Entry passage

Vaulted passage to cloister

N

| 0 | 10 | 20 | 30 | 40 | 50 feet |
| 0 | 3 | 6 | 9 | 12 | 15 metres |

1370–9
1500–32

FIGURE 61 Westminster Abbey, Abbot's House: ground plan

PLATE 98 London, Westminster Abbey Abbot's House: hall (left) and Jericho Parlour from the paved court

is still in place. The low-pitched roof is spanned by five heavy tie beams (end ones original) on arched braces with open traceried spandrels and small king posts. The braces rise from substantial stone corbels of angels holding shields with the arms of the abbot and abbey. The original third bay louvre is now closed but the hearth was in use until 1847. No other original fittings remain[5] but this hall has that second rare virtue of no added hearth and chimney stack.

Like the hall, the abbot's camera is built over a low ground floor divided by a row of braced oak posts. It has been known since Henry IV's demise here (1413) as the Jerusalem Chamber, probably from the subject matter of wall paintings or early tapestries rather than their successors. The two west windows are similar to those in the hall but the large multi-light north window was inserted by abbot Islip. The low-pitched three-bay roof of braced tie beams has Litlyngton's initials and mitre, and a crowned R for the abbey's royal patron. The fireplace is fifteenth century (1928 lintel), with an over-mantel added in 1624. The room was restored by Gilbert Scott in c.1870 when the cedar panelling was added and the sequence of mid-thirteenth-century glass medallions inserted from the abbey church. The present lobby approach from the hall, part of Islip's extension, probably follows an earlier form.

The offices, within the body of the hall but timber-framed partitioned from it, have a central late fourteenth-century entry flanked by buttery and pantry serving hatches. The east wall kitchen fireplace is post-medieval but probably on the site of the original hearth. The room at the side with small unglazed lights to the courtyard has always been used as a store. The rooms above the entry, store, and kitchen – now the ante-room and drawing room of

the dean's house – have remade or reopened fourteenth-century windows overlooking the court. The original approach to them and their function is no longer clear, but they may have been associated with the two rooms at a higher level over the cloister extension, remodelled by Litlyngton, to serve as his personal suite.

This part of the house was supplemented or replaced by Islip's three-storeyed block on the north side of the court. Built of a lighter coloured grey stone than that used by Litlyngton, this compact unit rises no higher than his hall roof and has a common parapet level.[6] The window form of uncusped segmental lights set in square frames is common throughout. The ground floor, now used for utilities, incorporates a late fourteenth-century east–west wall, part of Litlyngton's covered gallery. A replacement straight flight of external steps from the court is the approach to the principal first-floor room, the Jericho Parlour, with its eight-light window to the court, original fireplace, and early sixteenth-century linenfold panelling. It is flanked by lobbies. That to the east has a contemporary inner closet; that to the west has an original lamp niche and is the approach to the earlier Jerusalem Chamber. The second floor is divided into three rooms with original windows to the courtyard, two with contemporary moulded ceilings and one panelled in 1605, and Islip's galleried chapel looking into the abbey church.

Though the abbot's house is now divided between three occupants, it still functions to its original purpose with the hall, offices, and kitchen used for dining by Westminster School, the Islip block and Litlyngton's camera occupied by the dean and chapter, and the chambers over the kitchen, offices, and entry part of the dean's private house. Equally important is the high calibre of its original layout and character, the little-touched state of its hall and panelled or tapestry-hung rooms, and retained features that have so often been emasculated or replaced elsewhere. That they should survive in the heart of London where modernisation and rebuilding is a way of life is a tribute, in this instance, to a particularly conservative (and independent) institution.[7]

Not surprisingly, the city was not conducive to *monastic foundations* inside its walls – the Augustinian priory of the Holy Trinity, Aldgate, and the Benedictine nunnery of St Helen, Bishopsgate, were the only representatives.[8] Three major houses close to the city stand to a greater or lesser extent – part of the Augustinian priory church of St Bartholomew,[9] the Charterhouse in its remodelled mode as an Elizabethan house and Jacobean school,[10] and the heavily rebuilt Augustinian church of St Mary Overie (now Southwark cathedral). Apart from the Benedictine abbey next to the royal palace at Westminster, the majority of foundations of London's hinterland lay in comparative isolation in the countryside. Virtually all of them now lie under densely built suburbs, occasionally revealed when their sites are subject to redevelopment. Some of the most substantial excavations from 1980 to 2000 have been on such sites, but the work is frequently partial, as the original precincts often covered larger areas than are needed for commercial exploitation. The church has been revealed of the extremely wealthy Cistercian abbey at Stratford Longthorne. Church and claustral ranges have been recovered at Bermondsey Abbey (Cluniac),[11] Merton Priory (Augustinian), and Edward III's far from remote Cistercian foundation of St Mary Graces at Tower Hill. A guests' range has been excavated at Barking Abbey (Benedictine), and the whole site of Lesnes Abbey (Augustinian) has been stripped and exposed since 1913.

One of the most surprising recoveries has been at St John of Jerusalem, Clerkenwell, the headquarters of the Knights Hospitallers in England, which developed more like an ecclesiastical palace than a monastery. Prior Docwra's brick-built but ragstone-faced gatehouse of 1504 stands astride St John's Street and the foundations of the earlier church are under its eighteenth-century successor, but keyhole excavations have shown that the Priory had courtyards rather than cloisters, a great hall, and a great chamber. In layout, the foundation was far closer to Lambeth Palace than a monastic precinct, just as its gatehouse emulates the episcopal entry. The prior was a leading magnate of the realm, with enormous political influence and financial power who preferred secular standards and lifestyle to those of a conventual house.[12]

The excavations at Merton Priory showed that the early infirmary hall and cloister walk had been subdivided with wooden partitions during the fifteenth (?) century to give each monk his own private room. But no stand-alone lodging for the head of any of these properties has been recovered so far, leaving that at Westminster Abbey in splendid isolation. Yet these foundations, relatively close to the royal house and the mercantile centre of the country attracted support not only from the crown but equally from magnates and merchants as well as from more humble citizens. They were among the wealthiest foundations in the country. Stratford Langthorne was second only to Fountains Abbey in the order's financial standing in 1460. Merton was second only to Cirencester Abbey. It might be expected that the priority and funding expended on such lodgings elsewhere in the country would certainly be reflected in those foundations close to London. It might also be anticipated that such lodgings would be as much in

the vanguard of architectural development as their churches had been in an earlier age, and that they similarly adopted up-to-date structural and decorative features. Yet such evidence has not been recovered so far, though the reconstruction of the extremely wealthy priory of Holy Trinity, Aldgate suggests that the multi-roomed prior's house above the west cloister range was equally lavish in scale as that at Westminster.[13] Nor was it likely to have been an isolated example.

NOTES

1 C. Wilson, *Westminster Abbey* (1986) 23.
2 P. Binski, *Westminster Abbey and the Plantagenets* (1995) 175, 205.
3 Robinson (1911) 16–22.
4 Initially the abbey outer parlour, opened up and vaulted in the later fourteenth century. Part of the Norman abbot's lodging lay above it, remodelled by Litlyngton in the 1360s.
5 Screen, balcony, and tables early seventeenth century; panelling 1733; paved floor mid-nineteenth century.
6 Plain to the courtyard, embattled to the street, both renewed.
7 This house 'has special beauties which must always have been exceptional'. W. R. Lethaby, *Westminster Abbey Re-examined* (1925) 147.
8 The nuns' church survives as the parish church, but nothing of the priory buildings.
9 The oriel window in the choir south aisle, inserted as an oratory by prior Bolton in the early sixteenth century, was reached from his adjacent lodging south of the ambulatory and east of the chapter-house.
10 Some late fourteenth-century doorways, a fifteenth-century gatehouse with early oak doors, the chequer-worked boundary wall, and the overall plan betray its monastic origins. M. D. Knowles and W. F. Grimes, *Charterhouse* (1954); W. F. Grimes, *The Excavation of Roman and Medieval London* (1968) 175–80. Dendrochronology in 1995 revealed that parts of the existing roofs are also of the late medieval period.
11 A. R. Martin, *Jour. Brit. Arch. Assoc.* 32 (1926) 192–228; W. F. Grimes, *The Excavation of Roman and Medieval London* (1968) 210–17.
12 H. W. Fincham, *The Order of the Hospital of St John of Jerusalem and its Grand Priory in England* (1915).
13 J. Schofield, *The Building of London* (1984) 48, depicts the complete monastic extent, mainly based on a ground plan of 1592 by John Symonds. The claustral west range was excavated in about 1980.

J. Armitage Robinson, *The Abbot's House at Westminster* (1911)
RCHM, *London*, I (1924) 86–8
L. Tanner and Lord Mottistone, *Trans. Anc. Mon. Soc.* 2 (1954) 71–86

WESTMINSTER PALACE, London

Though the Saxon kings may have had a palace somewhere in London, the identification of a late tenth- or early eleventh-century bridge and approach road in 1996 suggests there may have been a palace at Westminster from that time. Yet it was from the reign of Edward the Confessor that the building next to the abbey he founded became the prime residence of the kings of England, and it continued to be so for nearly five centuries until a fire in 1512. During this period, it developed in scale and function round three courts to serve as a residence and a number of different government purposes. The southern part consisted of the private apartments of the monarch until the first years of Henry VIII's reign. The northern buildings, initially a ceremonial centre based on William II's great hall, became the heart of royal finance and justice, the seat of the exchequer and the law courts by the mid-fourteenth century.

The outer court from the entry gate to the front of Westminster Hall was the approach for the general populace.

In the mid-sixteenth century, the empty royal apartments were put to institutional use. In 1547, St Stephen's chapel was assigned as a permanent home for the House of Commons, with the White Chamber occupied by the House of Lords. For nearly 300 years, this warren of medieval buildings continued to serve as the seat of parliament and the centre of all government departments until the conflagration of 1834 destroyed most of the palace.

Only three structures were left after the ruins had been pulled down. The great hall, the lower chapel, and the remains of the adjoining cloister, all integrated in Sir Charles Barry's new Houses of Parliament (1840–52), arguably the most important building of Victorian Britain. The independent Jewel Tower, outside the range of the fire, continued to serve as a government office until 1938. The following text concentrates on these four survivals of the primary royal palace of medieval England, the sources relevant to their much altered condition, and the lost royal apartments.

Medieval palaces grew piecemeal and Westminster was no exception. The present structure was initiated by William II's ground-floor hall of gigantic size, north of the nucleus established by the Confessor. The remainder of the palace, developed over the next two centuries, was essentially two-storeyed, with the ground level used for services and stores, and the upper floor reserved for royal occupation and high-status officials. Henry III reconstructed the royal bedchamber and the apartments of the queen, the three Edwards rebuilt St Stephen's chapel over a seventy-year period, while Richard II remodelled the ceremonial hall and erected the cloisters serving St Stephen's college. The palace was never a permanent place of occupation, but it became the principal residence for a peripatetic court throughout the middle ages. Its position on the banks of the River Thames next to Westminster Abbey complemented the royal stronghold of the Tower dominating the city of London 2 miles downstream, with a residential and administrative interchange between the two that is often overlooked in their separate consideration.

SOURCES

Though the record is not as detailed as we would wish, we know a great deal about the construction, layout, and decoration of the palace from an abundance of medieval documentation and an extensive portfolio of pictorial evidence. The architectural history has been covered in the volumes of *The History of the King's Works* (1963–84), with the medieval evidence detailed in volume I. Nearly all the pictorial material has been brought together in volume 9 of *Architectural History* (1966). It is spread among a number of centres in London including the British Museum, the British Library, the Society of Antiquaries, the Palace of Westminster, and Westminster City Archives Centre. Even so, new records can be discovered such as the drawing showing the north end of the palace, recently identified in the Bibliothèque Nationale, Paris.

The earliest reliable view of the palace was drawn by Antonius van den Wyngaerde in about 1558 showing the overall shape of the palace buildings and the dominating presence of Westminster Hall and St Stephen's chapel before the loss of its clerestory (Ashmolean Museum, Oxford). Nearly a century later, two of Wenceslaus Hollar's eight views of London show the palace from the Thames, and New Palace Yard from the east (1647). Wyngaerde's and

Hollar's views necessarily lack detail. In 1739, Samuel Scott prepared a watercolour panorama of Westminster from the south-east showing the embankment in the foreground and the hall mainly hidden in trees (Brit. Mus., P. & D. 1865–8–10–1323).

Artistic output grew apace from 1780 onwards. John Carter's extensive body of drawings included the interior of the Painted Chamber in 1788 and St Stephen's chapel in 1791 before Wyatt's destructive changes. They were prepared under the greatest difficulty, though the accuracy of his zealous work needs to be checked against other sources. They were the basis for J. Topham and others, *Some Account of the Collegiate Chapel of St Stephen, Westminster* (1795). H. C. Englefield's edition of 1811 included additional illustrations by Richard Smirke and John Dixon of the wall paintings discovered in 1800. J. T. Smith, allowed to see parts of the chapel denied to Carter, published his fruitful labours as *Antiquities of Westminster* (1807, additional plates 1809). William Capon's thirty years of careful drawings, nearly all coloured, included fundamental work on the sculpture and wall paintings of the Painted Chamber (Westminster City Archives Centre, Box 57, nos. 53–55), an oversize view of the Prince's Chamber (Westminster City Archives Centre, E133, no. 109), and a vital plan of the palace published in *Vetusta Monumenta*, V (1835).

A body of illustrations was made while the fire was still raging and in its aftermath, including work by Constable and George Scharf who painted the roofless cage of St Stephen's chapel and the cloisters of St Stephen (Palace of Westminster 3793). Within two years of the tragedy, E. W. Brayley and J. Britton had published *The History of the Ancient Palace and Late Houses of Parliament at Westminster* (1836). It is a mine of information if treated with care. The drawings by F. Mackenzie in his *The Architectural Antiquities of the Collegiate Chapel of St Stephen* (1844) are brilliantly executed but extremely unreliable. He is only of value where he drew what he actually saw.

The archaeological record for this site is distressingly poor. No excavation or professional analysis of the ruins was made prior to the construction of Barry's Houses of Parliament.[1] The record is scarcely better with the reconstruction of war damage in 1948, the creation of the car park under New Palace Yard in 1972–4, or the examination of the site boundaries in 1996–7 occasioned by the nearby underground station. Like the imperial palaces at Istanbul, Aachen, and Trier, or the royal palace of the Louvre, part of the Westminster site is bisected by modern roads which have also destroyed the palace's vital relationship with the adjacent abbey. A detailed study of the medieval structure and surrounding area, bringing together the documentary, architectural, pictorial, and archaeological evidence, is urgently required for this key site in English medieval history. A plan of all that is known of the buildings so far was published to accompany the first two volumes of the *History of the King's Works*, but a comprehensive re-evaluation of all the sources awaits its master.

GREAT HALL

William II built his great hall between 1097 and 1099, and its side walls survive, refaced internally in 1835–7. At 239½ feet by 67½ feet the largest hall at that time in Europe, it is probable that its enormous roof was supported on two rows of pillars, though a single clear span has been suggested.[2] The high-set windows, not always strictly opposite each other,[3] were prefaced on all four sides by an

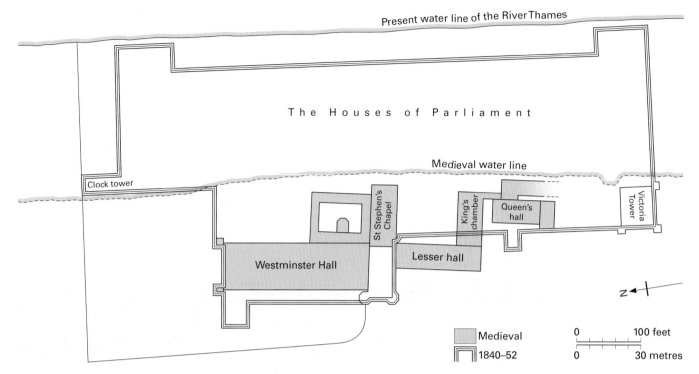

FIGURE 62 Westminster Palace: site layout

elaborate arcaded wall passage which can still be traced (longitudinal section by S. Smirke (1835), Society of Antiquaries, H. of P. Red Portfolio, 354–5). The main entrance is presumed to have lain at the north end, with the high table against the south wall of the hall.[4] Westminster Hall was never intended to be a grandiloquent domestic apartment but an appropriate setting for the great coronation feasts and crown-wearing ceremonies of the *arriviste* Norman rulers.

By the late fourteenth century, the structure looked old-fashioned and gloomy.[5] Richard II initiated improvements in 1385, structurally by adding flying buttresses on the east side, and authoritatively by commissioning thirteen statues of kings of England from Thomas Canon. Six were positioned internally on the south wall with the remainder held in store. In 1393, the decision was made to remodel and reroof the hall. Henry Yevele heightened the walls by 2 feet and added a richly decorated string course with heraldic shields and royal emblems. Though blind panelling was a key motif of the Perpendicular style (as in the newly erected halls at Windsor and Kenilworth castles), its marked absence at Westminster was probably to allow tapestries to be hung on feast days and for the temporary erection of law courts and shops against the walls.

The Norman arcaded clerestory was replaced by two-light traceried windows in the side walls, and large Perpendicular windows in the rebuilt end walls. The south window, decorated with large corbels of Richard II's white hart, rose behind a marble throne. This was flanked by three niches on each side by Yevele's deputy, Walter Walton, filled with Canon's earlier highly coloured and gilded statues. This original aspect of the south wall is shown in a pen and ink drawing of the hall's interior of about 1620 (Brit. Mus., P. & D.1848-9-11-748). Aesthetically important but artistically modest, these statues have survived to the present day, though the pinnacled

niches are a close reconstruction by Barry in the 1850s and the swords, sceptres, and orbs carried by the figures are copies of that time.[6] Their form and position were possibly a deliberate contribution to Richard II's attempt to emphasise his God-given monarchical status.

Hugh Herland's magnificent roof of 1396–7, supported by massive buttresses, dispensed with all internal support. It combined the two great principles of roof construction – arched braces from collars, and hammer beams. The thirteen massive transverse arches were a development of those employed a generation earlier at Edward III's ceremonial hall at Windsor Castle, while the hammerbeam form had been growing in technical assurance since the beginning of the century. The two roof lanterns were raised in 1397–8, with the decorative tracery almost completed by 1401 (John Buckler, Brit. Lib., Add. Ms. 36436 ff.430–5). The result was, and is, the most technically and aesthetically impressive hall in medieval Europe, even though there is still no consensus how Herland achieved structural stability.[7]

The last phase of this project was carried out between 1398 and 1401 when the north front was rebuilt as an impressive entrance façade, with two added towers flanking the new north window and a new central door framed by a porch. The lower walling was filled with a row of niches on each side of the porch and by two on each tower at first-floor level. They were filled, in part, with Canon's figures that had been held in store, supplemented by others added by later generations. The result was unique in English hall design in being an impressive and church-like statement of internal ceremonial function. The niches are now empty but five of Canon's statues have been found, though badly eroded, and stand on window sills inside the hall.

PLATE 99 London, Westminster Palace: hall interior

The north forecourt was the more public face of the palace, known as the Outer Court until 1517 when it was called New Palace Yard. Wall-enclosed, it was entered from either the great gate[8] or the water gate. A clock tower was erected by Henry Yevele opposite the north door of the hall in 1365–7 (pulled down in 1698), while excavations in 1972–4 revealed the remains of the mid-fifteenth-century great conduit that flowed with wine at coronations.[9] The lower part of the hall's show frontage had been almost covered with satellite buildings by the end of the seventeenth century (Brit. Lib., Add. Ms. 32450A). They had been extended fifty years later to include ale and coffee houses (Westminster City Archives Centre, Box 58 and E133). The state of the frontage in 1814 is shown in detail by J. Buckler (Brit. Lib., Add. Ms. 36370 ff.211, 213) before it was reconstructed by Soane to the original design in 1819–22.

Westminster Hall has been the scene of many historic events – royal and parliamentary ceremonies, banquets and coronation feasts, tournaments, state trials – and was the heart of the law courts until they were moved to the Strand in 1883. Thirty years earlier, Sir Charles Barry had remodelled its south wall after completing his Houses of Parliament. He took down Richard II's window, reset the end of the hall several yards back, and built the present theatrical steps and south window to create a ceremonial passage from this magnificent medieval hall to his newly built St Stephen's Hall.

ST STEPHEN'S CHAPEL

This was the main centre of worship in the palace, built on two levels. The lower chapel, dedicated to the Virgin, was used by the court: the upper chapel, dedicated to St Stephen, was reserved for the royal family and their immediate entourage. Constructed in place of an earlier chapel, and in emulation of and influenced by the Rayonnant style of the French king's Ste Chapelle in the main royal palace in Paris (begun 1241–3), the English structure was a stop–start enterprise over a seventy-year period, reflecting the political fortunes of three monarchs. It was initiated by Edward I in April 1292 under the master-mason Michael Canterbury. The lower chapel dates from this period (though probably not the vault) and the sills of the upper windows, until work was halted by a financial crisis in the summer of 1297 occasioned by Edward's war against Scotland. There was a gap of nearly twenty-five years until Edward II found sufficient money between about 1320 and 1326 to

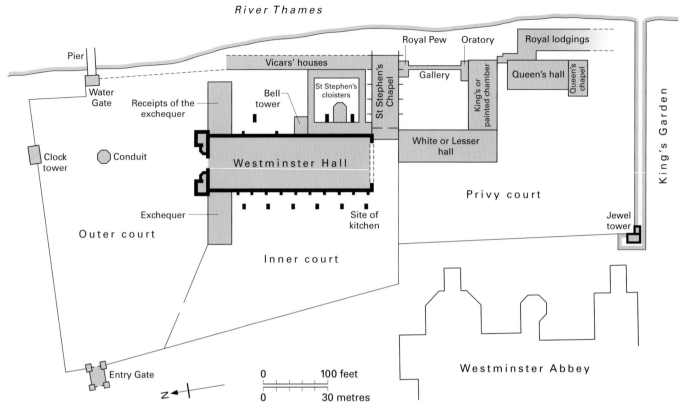

FIGURE 63 Westminster Palace: principal buildings *c*.1510

begin the walls of the upper chapel and plan for the addition of the clerestory. The crisis of Edward's deposition brought cessation until Edward III gave instructions in 1331 for building to recommence, allowing prepared stone and stored timberwork to be used. Despite a temporary halt in 1334–7 through the pressure of Scottish affairs, William Ramsey completed the structure by 1348. In that year, Edward turned the chapel into a college of canons as he was doing at Windsor, before glazing, internal furnishings, and decoration were initiated, with conclusion in 1363.

St Stephen's chapel is symptomatic of the main thrust of royal patronage from religious activity under Henry III to a secular environment under the first three Edwards. It was this chapel rather than any royal monastery such as Westminster or Vale Royal that served as the major engine of architectural and aesthetic innovation after the late thirteenth century. Furthermore, it was master-masons such as Michael Canterbury, William Ramsey, Henry Yevele, John Lewyn, and William Wynford with their influential practices rather than artistic patrons such as Henry III who determined the fundamental changes and developments in fourteenth-century English architecture.

With the palace's abandonment as a royal residence, the upper chapel was used to accommodate the House of Commons until the fire of 1834.[10] The principal structural change wrought on the fabric was the removal of the vault and clerestory and the lowering of the roof by Sir Christopher Wren in 1692, followed by James Wyatt's wall replacement in 1800 to accommodate additional members of parliament. The lower chapel was used after the Reformation as the Speaker's dining room, kitchen, and store until

it was reinstated for chapel use, 'terribly scraped and garnished'[11] by Edward Barry in the 1860s.

Apart from Wyngaerde's view, an anonymous drawing of *c*.1600 (V & A Museum, E.128–1924) is the only other one that shows the chapel before the removal of the clerestory, but antiquarian interest was only stimulated by the discoveries made during Wyatt's building activity, and the decorative stonework revealed by the 1834 conflagration. John Carter's careful drawings, used to illustrate Topham's work of 1795, are an invaluable record, though his detailing has to be treated with care for the chapel was totally masked at that time by the panelling and galleries of the House of Commons. The interior is best illustrated by the large varnished watercolour made by Adam Lee between 1820 and 1830 (Museum of London A 15454). Lee's architectural study shows elements of imagination rather than fact in its detailing, roof form, and heightened perspective, but his watercolour evokes the richness of the chapel better than any other source.[12] After the fire, George Moore also made some watercolours showing the decoration that covered every part of the revealed stonework (Palace of Westminster 260 and 1254). It is only with Maurice Hastings' analysis of the evidence in *St Stephen's Chapel* (1955) that the architectural importance of this remarkable building has been added to its already recognised aesthetic significance.

The chapel was intended to be tall, slender proportioned, richly decorated, and small – a jewel casket of unsurpassed taste. At 90 feet long and just under 30 feet wide, the chapel exceeded its French prototype by rising nearly 100 feet high, through the addition of the clerestory, not for light but for visual effect. The structure consisted of five bays, massively buttressed, with octagonal turrets at both ends and an entry porch. The low ground-floor vaulted undercroft, entered by a central west door, has ogee-arched window tracery (the earliest known) and lierne vaulting. The upper chapel was approached from a newel in the north-east turret or by a door in the first-floor White Hall opening into the vestibule.

Externally, the windows in each bay were distinguished by mullions from the principal windows extending in front of the lower windows to the ground. Internally, the sides of the upper chapel were divided by a crested parapet separating the main windows from the clerestory above. The lower part of each bay was filled with a wall arcade surmounted by a decorative frieze. Above rose the four lights of the principal window, the base solid for paintings on plaster, and the upper part with a curvilinear traceried head. The clerestory windows were shorter but probably with similar heads below the wooden vault springing from three-sided piers between each bay. Large six-light windows filled the east and west ends to create a multi-windowed envelope not unlike the more modest version at Ely Place (c.1300). The royal chapel was divided by a screen into a two-bay ante-chapel and the three-bay chapel proper (with choir stalls).[13]

St Stephen's chapel is as fundamental to the development of the Perpendicular as to the Decorated style: the one with its emphasis on vertical mullions extending from the upper windows and past the lower ones to the ground;[14] the other through the micro-decoration that has taken over the constituent elements of elevation, externally and internally. The evidence and assessment of this transitional building is not free of controversy, particularly as the tracery of the upper windows is still in doubt, but this royal chapel joins that small group of buildings in the pantheon of proto-Perpendicular structures.[15]

It took fifteen years to carry out this chapel's stunning internal decoration, entirely the work of Edward III rather than of his father or grandfather. The wall arcade, divided by Purbeck columns covered with gold spots, was filled with life-size angels holding decorated drapery under each arch. The frieze above was elaborately carved with heraldic shields and supporting beasts beneath a crenellated parapet, painted, gilded, and inset with pieces of coloured glass. (Illustrated in a pen and ink drawing by R. Smirke c.1800, Society of Antiquaries, St Stephen Ch., Red Portfolio 29–49.) The bases of the windows were painted with biblical scenes above descriptive verses. The body of the windows was filled with stained glass illustrating stories of the Old and New Testaments. The projecting parapet was elaborately carved, painted, and gilded and it is possible that the clerestory had a frontal arcade. The roof, marked to imitate stone, was painted sky blue with gold stars. The fronts of the piers between each bay were filled with coloured statues of angels under carved canopies with painted figures of military saints on the narrower sides. At the east end, the wall arcade beneath the window was painted and embellished with figures of Edward III and his sons on one side of the altar and Queen Philippa and the daughters on the other, both with their patron saints, beneath scenes of the infancy of Christ (R. Smirke, c.1800, Society of Antiquaries and St Stephen Ch., Red Portfolio 16/4 and 17/2).[16]

Like the Ste Chapelle, the chapel had been conceived as a vessel for figurative stained glass. Commissioned in 1349, none of the glass survives, but the illustrations of fragments made in 1800 by J. T. Smith suggest a close connection with the glaziers of Ely lady chapel. A small number of stone and painted wall fragments spanning the years from 1350 to 1363 were saved in 1800 from Wyatt's butchery and are displayed in the British Museum. Though badly damaged, they still hint at the blinding colour of the chapel's interior through (i) a pierced and crenellated parapet surmounting the wall arcading (Brit. Mus., MLA 1814, 3–12, 2); (ii) moulded stone fragments, richly painted with stamped and gilded flowers in red lead and chalk applied to the mouldings (Brit. Mus., MLA 1883, 3–10, 1–2); (iii) fragments of the wall painting below the main windows of both side walls. These remains are from the scenes from the Book of Job, painted on the plasterwork with raised gilded and gesso work (Brit. Mus., MLA 1814, 3–12, 2). These painted scenes, about 2 feet high, had painted texts underneath explaining the action shown. Totalling about 160 scenes, they were not parochial but display a combination of English with continental, particularly Italian-influenced, techniques.[17]

Though the chapel's decorative scheme may have been laid down in 1292, it had been modified by 1350 to include military undertones, with armed figures of martyrs and saints, battle scenes, and St George rather than St Edward at the head of the royal family on the east wall.[18] It was because of this aesthetic modification under Edward III that the bases of the windows were masonry-filled to take the painted decoration that had now become such an essential element of the chapel's decoration.

The whole structure was ablaze with colour in what must have been an overwhelmingly impressive and fantastically lavish interior. Despite the lack of a clerestory and any hint of colour, the closest architectural parallel in shape, multi-fenestration, vaulting, and overwhelming richness of ornamentation is the lady chapel of Ely Cathedral Priory (1322–49). The closest pictorial parallels are the contemporary decorated rooms in the Papal Palace, Avignon, and Karlstein, Prague. St Stephen's chapel was the most important building of its date in England. At a cost of about £9,000,[19] it was the most splendid private chapel in the country, so that its destruction is one of the great losses of medieval England.

ST STEPHEN'S CLOISTERS

The vicars' houses, cloister, and bell tower were built at royal expense, but though the tower was initiated in 1353–4, the houses and cloister were not constructed until 1384–96. The existing two-storeyed cloister was a replacement by Dr John Chambers of 1526–9 which incorporated some of the earlier structure. The walks were fan-vaulted and there was a projecting oratory on the west side (plans of c.1593, Hatfield House, Cecil Papers 24/61–2). The painting by George Scharf (Palace of Westminster 3793) and the drawing by John Taylor clearly illustrate its damaged state after the fire. The ruins were largely pulled down by Sir Charles Barry, though the form and overall design of the cloister was retained in his replacement Cloister Court, and in the two walks rebuilt after war damage in 1948–50.

THE ROYAL APARTMENTS

If Henry III's magisterial patronage was primarily devoted to rebuilding Westminster Abbey church, he also favoured updating his residence and seat of government nearby. By his time, two groups of royal apartments had developed: a dining hall (White or Lesser Hall) and bedchamber (King's or Painted Chamber) for himself, and a hall and private chapel for the queen.

The empty room and its tapestry-covered walls were depicted by John Carter (1788–90, Westminster City Archives Centre, Box 57 no. 27, 33A) and William Capon (1799, Society of Antiquaries, H. of P. Carter & Capon Portfolio). In 1819, the series of wall paintings that had given this room its name were uncovered and copied independently by Edward Crocker (Ashmolean Museum, Oxford, WA 1863, 1450–72) and Charles Stothard (Society of Antiquaries, Stothard Box, 236c) published in *Vetusta Monumenta*, VI (1842). Their watercolours depict the schemes of Henry III as well as those of his successor, both undertaken by Walter Durham who had assisted William Westminster in the earlier programme.[21]

Behind the king's bed was an oratory with three oval-shaped windows. It had been destroyed by 1790 when John Carter drew his exterior view of the Painted Chamber (Westminster City Archives Centre, Box 57, nos. 27–29) but he shows that the vault springers above the windows carried corbels with the arms of the Empire impaling Bohemia. There is little doubt that this oratory was vaulted when Anne of Bohemia was queen (1382–94). It was linked by a first-floor gallery with St Stephen's chapel.

Henry III built or remodelled an earlier large apartment further south for his wife, and added a lancet-lit chapel in 1237–8. The former (White Chamber) came to be used as the House of Lords in the sixteenth century, and the latter (Prince's Chamber) as a robing room. A plan of these two chambers was made by Soane before he demolished them in 1823 (photo. neg. held by the National Archives, Kew, WORK. 29/18) and a view of the remains of the Prince's Chamber by Capon (Westminster City Archives Centre, E133, 109 and Box 57 nos. 53–55A). A further range of apartments, built by Henry III for his son, the Lord Edward, created a distinct area – the prince's palace – for the heir apparent. Little is known of it or its position towards the abbey precinct, though it was fully repaired by Edward II and used by his grandson. It was mostly destroyed in the fire of 1512 which signalled the abandonment of this palace as a royal residence in favour of Whitehall Palace.

THE JEWEL TOWER

This L-shaped tower, three storeys high, was built by Henry Yevele in 1365–6 on land belonging to the Abbey of Westminster beyond the south-west corner of the private palace but now taken into the royal precinct. Constructed of Kentish ragstone and moat-surrounded, it was designed to house the personal treasure of the king. The angle stair turret gave access to a large outer and small inner chamber on each floor. The larger rooms were heated and the smaller rooms retain close-stool recesses. Both ground-floor rooms are vaulted, and the uppermost floor held the sovereign's gold and silver plate and jewels until the death of Henry VIII. The Jewel Tower was an offshoot of the great wardrobe in the Tower of London, but as accessions and disbursements were made to and from members of the royal family and magnates, and through purchase and attainments, the tower also held an office for the keeper and clerk.

From the early seventeenth century, the tower was used to store parliamentary records, and in 1718–19, the windows were replaced with round-headed openings of Portland stone, while other medieval features such as the gargoyles and crenellated parapet were stripped away. It was used as the Weights and Measures Office from 1869 until 1938, but was restored to its early condition as far as possible in 1948–56 and opened to the public.

PLATE 100 London, Westminster Palace: Jewel Tower

The White Hall and King's Chamber were upper-floor twelfth-century apartments. The former, 120 feet by 38 feet with Norman moulding revealed in 1834, was thoroughly repaired after the fire of 1298. The Painted Chamber, at right angles to it, was extensively remodelled by Henry III. He used it as his state bedchamber and audience chamber, though the apartment occasionally served as a meeting place for parliament from the fourteenth century onwards. It was 80½ feet long, 26 feet wide, and 32 feet high, and Henry inserted elegant two-light windows overlooking the Thames, and redecorated the chamber after a fire in 1263. The walls were covered with paintings of virtues and vices between the windows, and the coronation of Edward the Confessor above the king's bed (1266–7). The ceiling was initially decorated with figurative paintings (two panels, rediscovered in 1993, Brit. Mus., MLA 1995–4–1, 2), but the scheme was soon abandoned in favour of a flat oak-panelled ceiling with decorative *paterae*, probably originally coloured (example in Sir John Soane Museum, M 118/363).[20]

Between 1292 and 1297, the walls were repainted for Edward I with a cycle of Old Testament scenes including several battles. Towards the close of the fifteenth century, the chamber was hung with tapestries of the Trojan wars. They were probably made late in Edward IV's reign and were bought by Henry VII in 1488 but are now lost.

NOTES

1 Sir John Soane rescued a fourteenth-century gable from St Stephen's chapel and two fifteenth-century arches and some miscellaneous masonry fragments from the palace, and made two casts of corbels of Richard II's time from Westminster Hall that have since been destroyed. They are part of Soane's museum collection in Lincoln's Inn Fields.

2 Wilson (1997) 43–4.

3 This misalignment, as well as the slight outward bowing of the side walls, *may* reflect the timber framework of an earlier structure.

4 A thirteenth-century marble trestle that supported the dais table is preserved in the Jewel Tower. Nine sculptured Norman capitals, found built into the later medieval fabric in 1835 and possibly from the hall, are also displayed in the Jewel Tower.

5 By this time, it also housed several law courts and was lined with shops, cleared away when the hall was needed for ceremonial purposes.

6 M. Hay, *Westminster Hall and the Medieval Kings* (1995); P. Lindlay, in *The Regal Image of Richard II and the Wilton Diptych*, ed. D. Gordon (1997) 74–83.

7 F. Baines, *Report on the Condition of the Roof Timber of Westminster Hall* (1914). His papers, held in the House of Commons library, include several extremely detailed and beautifully coloured drawings. H. Cescinsky and E. R. Gribble, *Burlington Magazine* 40 (1922) 76–84; J. Heyman, *Proc. Institute of Civil Engineers* 37 (1967) 137–62; L. T. Courtenay, *Jour. Soc. Arch. Hist.* 43 (1984) 295–309; L. T. Courtenay and R. Mark, *ibid.* 46 (1987) 374–93; L. T. Courtenay, *Jour. Brit. Arch. Assoc.* 143 (1990) 95–111; *The Development of Timber as a Structural Material*, ed. D. T. Yeomans (1999).

8 Replaced by Richard III in 1484, it was left unfinished and was pulled down in 1706 because it obstructed traffic.

9 V. Horsman and B. Davison, *Antiq. Jour.* 69 (1989) 279–97.

10 The story is told by Hastings (1950) 77–118.

11 W. R. Lethaby, *Westminster Abbey and the King's Craftsmen* (1906) 181.

12 The Museum of London holds seven watercolours by Lee, a sixth of those exhibited in 1831, evoking the fourteenth-century splendour of St Stephen's chapel. *Trans. London and Middx Arch. Soc.* 34 (1983) 231–44.

13 For a tentative impression of the interior, Hastings (1950) 75 and (1955) frontispiece.

14 Mackenzie (1844) 6.

15 J. H. Harvey, *Burlington Magazine* (August 1946) and *Studies in Building History*, ed. E. M. Jope (1961) 134–65. Also Hastings (1955); *HKW*, I (1963) 524–5, and Wilson (1980).

16 E. Howe describes and illustrates these altar wall murals and suggests they not only were a dynastic display but reflect the Plantagenet view of divine kingship, *Antiq. Jour.* 81 (2001) 259–303. Also E. W. Tristram, *English Wall Painting in the Fourteenth Century* (1955) 48–58, 206–19. He suggests the altar wall was probably painted after 1355, *ibid.* 53.

17 *The Age of Chivalry*, ed. J. Alexander and P. Binski (1987) 498–500; P. Binski, *Westminster Abbey and the Plantagenets* (1995) 184–5.

18 Binski, *Westminster Abbey* 183.

19 *HKW*, I (1963) 522.

20 P. Tudor-Craig, *Arch. Jour.* 114 (1957) 92–105.

21 *The Age of Chivalry*, ed. J. Alexander and P. Binski (1987) 341–4.

General

RCHM, *London*, II (1925) 123–5

H. M. Colvin *et al.* (eds.), *The History of the King's Works*, I (1963) 491–552

H. M. Colvin (ed.), *Architectural History* 9 (1966) 23–184

R. Cooke, *The Palace of Westminster* (1987)

J. A. A. Goodall, in *The Houses of Parliament: History, Art, and Architecture*, ed. C. and J. Ridding (2000) 49–68

Hall

I. M. Cooper, *Jour. Brit. Arch. Assoc.* (1937) 3–63

H. St G. Saunders, *Westminster Hall* (1951)

C. Wilson, 'Rulers, artificers and shoppers: Richard II's remodelling of Westminster Hall, 1393–99', in *The Regal Image of Richard II and the Wilton Diptych*, ed. D. Gordon *et al.* (1997) 33–59

Chapel

F. Mackenzie, *The Architectural Antiquities of the Collegiate Chapel of St Stephen* (1844)

M. Hastings, *Parliament House* (1950)

M. Hastings, *St Stephen's Chapel* (1955)

C. Wilson, 'The origins of the Perpendicular style and its development to *c.*1360', PhD thesis, University of London (1980)

Royal apartments

P. Binski, *The Painted Chamber at Westminster* (1986)

Jewel Tower

A. J. Taylor, *The Jewel Tower: Handbook* (1956)

9

SOUTH-EAST ENGLAND:
HISTORICAL BACKGROUND

CHURCH AND COAST

IT might be anticipated that the position of Kent between London and Europe would encourage the building of royal and baronial residences but this was not so. Much of the reason for this lies in the fact that well over half of the cultivated land of the county was owned throughout the middle ages by the two wealthy monastic houses at Canterbury – Christ Church Cathedral Priory and St Augustine's Abbey, with many of their estates in east Kent (and increased by the quite separate and widespread holdings of the archbishop) – and to a much lesser extent by St Andrew's Cathedral Priory at Rochester with its estates in north-west Kent. There were also a number of smaller church holdings, including the rights of Battle Abbey over much of the Weald, so that the county was primarily in ecclesiastical rather than secular hands.

The development of large baronial estates was also hindered by the inheritance law of gavelkind, a form of tenure well established before the Norman Conquest and essentially limited to Kent, whereby an estate was not inherited by the eldest but was divided equally between all male heirs. Such lands were freely negotiable on the open market and could be sold at will without reference to any lord. Some people preferred to retain their small holdings and security of tenure while others opted for a sum of money in their pockets rather than a tiny area of land. The former encouraged the development of the many late medieval farmhouses in Kent, while the latter contributed to the slow development of some of the larger estates. Knole Park developed from such a practice over a period of two centuries where three local families built up substantial holdings in and around Sevenoaks which were all bought up by archbishop Bourchier in the 1450s and formed into the single estate of Knole.[1] This patterning of small holdings across the county continued after the Dissolution, for Henry VIII retained few ecclesiastical estates in his hands but gave or sold most of them to a broad range of private individuals.

South-east England was not particularly wealthy. The coastal lands of both Kent and Sussex were the richest areas, particularly the lower Medway valley and the chalklands of the Isle of Thanet, and the Sussex coastal plain.[2] This was partly due to soil fertility and easy coastal transport, but in the case of north Kent, it was helped by the effective agricultural practices of the Benedictines at Canterbury and Rochester. The downland ridges and forest areas of the Weald separating them were among the poorer lands of England until the development of the cloth-making and iron-smelting industries during the later fifteenth and sixteenth centuries. This sudden population rise in a woodland region and its piecemeal colonisation encouraged the development of the many timber-framed houses which characterise the region. One type

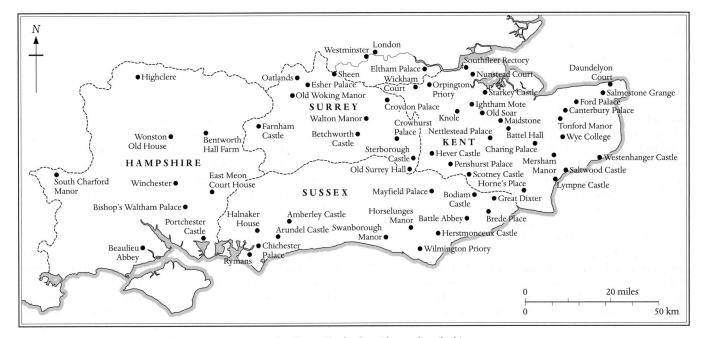

FIGURE 64 South-east England: residences described in text

dominated, paradoxically known as Wealden but which occurs in many other areas of south-east England. They survive in their hundreds, standardised as so much timber work is in Kent, with few datable to before the later fifteenth century and falling out of favour by the later sixteenth century.[3]

Kent was a county without major residential members of the baronage, as much in the later middle ages as in the seventeenth century.[4] There were none of the large feudal estates common in so many other parts of England, for the bulk of the land not in ecclesiastical hands was held by lesser gentry. The principal exception was the earl of Stafford who held the honour of Tonbridge, but after the death of Ralph, 2nd Lord Stafford at Tonbridge Castle in 1372, the line passed through a succession of minorities and short-lived members for over fifty years when the focal point of their activities and estates lay elsewhere. The majority of the county was run by a small number of minor holders – knights and esquires who served as justices of the peace and sheriffs and represented the county in parliament – men like the Cobhams of Hever, Allington, and Sterborough castles or Roger Ashburnham of Scotney Castle.

The peninsular position of Kent has always tended to isolate the county, so that even today this characteristic can still be experienced by traversing the narrow high-hedged lanes in the central and western parts of the county and which run to the very edge of London's sprawling conurbation. For despite its proximity to the metropolis, the impact on the county was far less forceful before the early twentieth century than in Surrey. There was some movement from London into the western part of the county from the middle of the fourteenth century, helped by the war with France. Sir John Pulteney, a draper and four times lord mayor, bought himself an estate at Penshurst, while Sir John Devereux who subsequently owned it had been Richard II's constable at Dover Castle and Warden of the Cinque Ports. The grocer and lord mayor Sir John Philipot built the now ruined chapel at Grench Manor, Gillingham,

before 1389. The subsidy roll for London in 1436 shows that of the 358 men listed with assessments of over £5, slightly more held land in Kent than in Essex or Middlesex.[5] At the same time, the duke of Gloucester was developing his mansion at Greenwich, while Lord Saye was building up his Knole estate. But it was not until the later sixteenth century that Lambarde noted any substantial influx of courtiers, lawyers, and merchants into the gentry of the county[6] and even then, this was essentially in the north-west so that its parochial character was unaffected by London's social and political attitudes until the later nineteenth century.

F. R. H. Du Boulay pointed out that the attractiveness of north-west Kent over and above other parts of the county appears in will after will. If the principal residences in the fifteenth century were mapped, then a heavy concentration would be seen along the south bank of the Thames estuary and immediately inland.[7] But little work has been carried out surveying and analysing the existing remains of such residences or the contents afforded by the better off. In 1400, James Pekham, of minor gentry at Wrotham, left good-quality furnishings for his kinsmen including green tapestries powdered with popinjays, and a number of books in French.[8] We could do with learning more about such people as well as their homes.[9]

Proximity to Europe and the danger of invasion also meant that there were more castles in Kent and Sussex than in other southern counties. The king held the powerful castles at Dover and Rochester as well as Canterbury,[10] and also Leeds from 1278 which he frequently vested in the hands of his queen. Not surprisingly, local landowners also tended to build strongholds which continued to be occupied during the later middle ages: the Badlesmere at Chilham, the Cobhams at Allington, and various tenants at Leybourne.[11] The houses of Kent, therefore, are numerous but not particularly large. Even Penshurst Place was no exception to this until Sir Henry Sidney made his extensive additions in the later sixteenth century.

PLATE 101 Ightham Mote: north range

Small manors abounded, often little more than large farmhouses, and there was a growing number of modest gentry estates like Ightham Mote or Wickham Court, most of them painstakingly built up from small properties as families died or sold out. But to the many travellers between the continent and London – pilgrims to Canterbury, traders to and from Europe, and distinguished foreign visitors – it was the archiepiscopal palaces such as Canterbury, Charing, Knole, Maidstone, and Saltwood which identified where so much of the wealth of medieval Kent lay.

Kent stepped into the political limelight in the mid-fifteenth century when the locally based rebellion led by Jack Cade in June 1450 gained support from south Essex, Surrey, Sussex and, for a time, a considerable element of the London populace. It was played out at Blackheath, Southwark, and the city of London with sporadic support elsewhere because the revolt was aimed at the dismissal of the king's ministers and advisors rather than the king himself.[12] A considerable number of London properties suffered spoliation or destruction, including the houses of the hated favourites (Lord Rivers, Lord Saye, Sir Thomas Stanley) or those who opposed the rebels (the merchant alderman Malpas), but there was little damage to residences in Kent even though the wide-ranging tranche of grievances had included resentment against London entrepreneurs buying or seizing local estates.[13] Whereas the revolt of 1381 was a

broad-based rural movement determined by economic and social problems, the 1450 rebellion was a more narrowly based rising from a catalogue of local grievances. The rebellion was short-lived but brutish. It was corrupt officials and their London houses that suffered initially but only the rebels rather than their properties paid the consequence in the aftermath of the revolt[14] which fostered the increasing country-wide loss of confidence in Henry VI's disastrous rule.

Many of the developments noted in Kent were repeated in Surrey. The medieval houses of the crown close to London – Kennington, Sheen, and Weybridge – have disappeared, leaving the episcopal residences at Farnham, Croydon, and Esher as the primary survivals. Nor was Surrey extensively populated in the middle ages, as a consequence of its poor soils – a sequence of sandy heath, clay and chalk with the Weald stretching southwards as an unpromising barrier. So many parts of Surrey were forest or woodland, as they still are in the south, that Henry II asserted that the whole of Surrey was within forest law. Although this claim was periodically surrendered and reasserted until the mid-fourteenth century, it did not encourage magnates to choose Surrey for their principal seats. The earls of Clare and Warenne dominated the county between the twelfth and fourteenth centuries, but the division of the Clare estates between three co-heiresses in 1314 and the end of the house of Warenne in

1347 meant that a handful of minor landowners such as the Cobhams of Sterborough or the Gaynesfords of Crowhurst played a primary role in the county until the early sixteenth century. It was only with the development of the royal palaces by Henry VII and his son on the southern edge of London – Richmond, Woking, Oatlands, Hampton Court, and Nonsuch – that major landowners developed estates nearby centred on houses such as Sutton Place, Loseley, Baynards, and Great Fosters.

Until that time, the county was essentially one of small holdings, scattered farms, and sparsely populated parishes. There are very few late medieval churches, little industry, and only a handful of small towns. The fact that about 150 moated sites have been identified might suggest that the present survivals underrepresent the situation. Moated sites are widely scattered across the county except for the North Downs, with the largest concentration on the Wealden claylands in the south-east, but their status and function are so broad that it is not yet possible to determine how many protected major residential sites and how many served farmsteads or lesser sites.[15]

As in Kent, the absence of powerful secular landlords meant the presence of many yeoman farmers, and although the county lacked good building stone, it had an abundance of woodland. A considerable number of small-scale timber-framed houses of later fifteenth- and sixteenth-century date survive, particularly on the eastern half of the Wealden arc. They are generally hall houses rather than the Wealden form, and do not attain the exuberance of those in Kent and Sussex.[16] One or two houses are of considerable scale, such as Crowhurst Place and Old Surrey Hall, and these are close to the Kent border. Nor is it surprising that their most impressive feature is the hall roof presaging those of the Henrician palaces.

Sussex, like Kent, is a county of castles and fortified houses, nearly all of them within reach of the coast and the river valleys cutting through the chalk downs. With the exception of Mayfield Palace, the rich farm lands and easy lines of communication meant that the few manor houses were also on the coastal plain. Yet the coastline has changed more radically here than in most parts of the country. Arundel and Bodiam castles are no longer on estuaries, three or four of the episcopal houses on Selsey peninsula have been washed away or left inland, Herstmonceux no longer overlooks inlets and marshes, while several towns of east Sussex have been stranded by the receding sea.

Initially, Sussex prospered under the Normans, with at least eighty churches built from that period, the cathedral at Chichester, and the monasteries at Battle and Lewes, followed by those at Bayham, Michelham, Robertsbridge, and Wilmington during the thirteenth century at the same time that a broad span of churches characterised the county. Battle Abbey's manor at Alciston – farmhouse, tithe barn, and dovecote – mirrored the sheep farming and wheat crop patterns of local secular estates[17] while Lewes Priory's grange at Swanborough was indistinguishable from contemporary manor houses. Edward I founded the town of New Winchelsea to replace the old settlement that had been destroyed by the sea in 1288 but his scheme was too ambitious and the port silted up. The fourteenth century witnessed the abandonment of other eastern harbours as the county passed the height of its early prosperity. At the same time, the house of FitzAlan had become the dominating family in the region, particularly after its acquisition of the southern estates of the house of Warenne in 1347.

PLATE 102 Portchester Castle: hall range

The proximity of Kent and Sussex to the French coast meant that both counties were constantly in a state of military activity. Throughout the greater part of the Hundred Years' War (as in centuries earlier), much military coming and going across the region disrupted business, and brought ill-disciplined forces and considerable anti-social behaviour. But the area also enjoyed the benefits of foreign goods in times of peace as well as providing victuals, ships, and supplies in times of war. Sussex, in particular, suffered from the French attacks and invasions that began after 1360, peaked in 1377, and continued to a lesser extent until the closing years of the century. The coastal trade never recovered its former prosperity and a long period of economic decline was exacerbated by further piratical raids during the mid-fifteenth century.

As the fifteenth century progressed, glass-making and the iron industry of the Weald replaced the older shipbuilding activity along the coast. This encouraged the development of properties by the lesser gentry and yeomanry who were numerically large and financially independent.[18] It is from this period that a number of timber-framed houses survive such as Great Dixter with its fine hall and the slightly later Horselunges Manor. Sussex, like Surrey, began to attract leading Tudor courtiers such as Lord de la Warr at Halnaker and the king's cousin Sir David Owen at Cowdray, with further mansions following at Laughton, Legh, Bolebroke, Cuckfield, and Slaugham. By that time, the iron industry had developed sufficiently to bring some much needed prosperity to the region.

HAMPSHIRE

Hampshire is a county of relatively infertile clays, gravel, and sands in the far north and far south, with a great swathe of chalkland in between. It was and still is a good-quality agricultural area with much of the downland now beech covered, broken by a sequence of smaller river valleys – Meon, Itchen, Test, and Avon in the west. They facilitated communication but were not important for navigation, though the bishop of Winchester made the Itchen navigable in the early thirteenth century between Alresford and Southampton, while the broken coastline fostered speedy means of transport. An analysis of lay wealth in 1327 shows that the area close to Portsmouth and Hayling Island (spreading eastwards to the River

PLATE 103 Winchester College: inner gate to Chamber Court

Adur) was the most wealthy, followed by the chalkland in the north, with the New Forest as the poorest.[19]

The church was the leading landowner, holding a quarter of the county.[20] Five of the fifteen monasteries had benefited from the lavish grants of the late Anglo-Saxon kings (St Swithun's Priory, St Mary's Abbey, Hyde Abbey, all in Winchester, Romsey Abbey and Wherwell Priory) while King John's foundation at Beaulieu (1204) and Peter des Roches' at Netley (1239) had been generously funded even though they necessarily held some of the less fertile blocks of chalkland. By the fourteenth century, the estates of the bishop of Winchester were pre-eminent, followed by those of the prior of St Swithun's and the abbeys of Hyde, Romsey, Beaulieu, and Titchfield, and the priories at Wherwell, Christchurch, and South-wick. There was no comparable secular overlord. Initially, there had been some minor lords such as the Port family who originally held Basing Castle and built a timber-framed house at Wickham and a stone one at Warnford in the early thirteenth century not long before their decline, but otherwise it was an area of modest territorial holdings. Leading Hampshire gentry, like the de Scures at Wickham between 1268 and 1381 followed by the Uvedales until 1696, frequently holding the office of sheriff, might enhance their residences with a moat but little else.[21] Compared with Sussex, Wiltshire, or Dorset, Hampshire has few late medieval secular houses of any scale outside the episcopal residences, and though Wiltshire was more wealthy, Sussex and Dorset were not.

Like Sussex, Hampshire prospered throughout the twelfth and thirteenth centuries but the agrarian crisis during the early fourteenth century was compounded by the drastic demographic and economic changes consequent upon the Black Death and its return in 1361 and the 1370s. The extended sequence of episcopal records has long made Hampshire central to studies of the plague. It was one of the earliest areas to be affected, with probably about half the population dying in 1348–50, though it was higher in some areas such as the manor of Bishop's Waltham (65 per cent) and coastal manors such as Titchfield (80 per cent) and Crofton (92 per cent). In addition to the short- and long-term social and economic consequences of the disaster, evidence is now being identified of its effect on art and architecture.[22] But changes in architectural style and decoration, parish church closures such as the nineteen in Winchester,[23] park expansion (as at Highclere, Standlynch), and the abandonment of small monastic houses such as St Cross Priory, Newport[24] are easier to identify than the effect on manor houses. The excavation of the manorial complex at Faccombe, Netherton, revealed a dramatic decline between its prosperous state in the 1320s and thirty years later when rat bones increased, the coin sequence halted, and the pottery sequence ceased. A survey of 1356 showed that attempts to revive cultivation of the demesne were unsuccessful, the manor house was abandoned, and the dovecote had disappeared. Tiles and timber were stolen from the house in the 1360s and animals were occupying the ruins of the hall by 1379.[25] A similar story is emerging through excavation at Mersley Farm, Knighton, Isle of Wight.[26] It was partly because so many clergy had fallen victim to the plague that William Wykeham established his collegiate foundations at Oxford and Winchester (the pestilence is identified in its statutes) to make up for this loss. Whether the absence of timber-framed farmhouses before the late fourteenth century is a consequence of the plague or not is arguable, but there is little doubt that a more austere decorative style was preferred in high-status buildings such as

Richard II's apartments at Portchester Castle and East Meon Court House, and that the complex roof structures and experiments of the early fourteenth century were eschewed in favour of comparatively plain ones as at Winchester College hall.

In the short term, many holdings lay vacant. In the long term, the change from arable to pasture and the dramatic increase in sheep farming, particularly on the poorer lands, was embraced by the church as much as by lay owners. At the same time, demesne or direct farming on the more wealthy estates gradually gave way to tenant farming, markedly so by the second half of the fifteenth century, though the bishop seems to have kept his Hampshire properties in demesne considerably longer than his neighbours.[27] Cloth making had spurred the development of small towns in north Hampshire such as Basingstoke, Andover, and Alton, but the county never enjoyed the financial and economic benefits that drove the late medieval economy of Wiltshire.

Winchester was the exception. The city had declined as a royal centre during the later twelfth century and had been overtaken by Westminster before 1200 as the heart of royal finance and administration. The royal castle was never important again after the fire of 1302 had burnt down the royal apartments, while the importance of St Giles' Fair also declined before the end of the fourteenth century. Yet the latter coincided with a renaissance, architecturally as well as economically, through the developing wool trade and the setback in Southampton's trading prosperity from the extended war with France.[28] The cathedral took its present form, several notable residences were added to the close, Winchester College was built, and the accommodation of the Hospital of St Cross was redeveloped on a lavish scale between 1380 and 1450.

Society had not remained static since the fourteenth century but there were still no outstanding laymen by the early sixteenth century. The Lisles and Poles held eight or nine manors and Lord de la Warr held three, but the Sandys and Pophams held only three manors between them. This absence of major lay houses is offset by the considerable number of late medieval yeomen properties,[29] though this ownership pattern changed dramatically with the Dissolution of the Monasteries and the vast sale of monastic land that followed in the 1540s.[30]

NOTES

1 F. R. H. Du Boulay, *Arch. Cant.* 89 (1974) 1–10. This author has sounded a note of caution in attributing gavelkind to some of the richer members of society who were clearly anxious during the later middle ages to preserve the bulk of their estates in the hands of their eldest son: *The Lordship of Canterbury* (1966) 159–61.

2 R. E. Glasscock, *Arch. Cant.* 80 (1965) 61–8.

3 Stuart Rigold's comment that 'halls of the fifteenth and early sixteenth centuries survive in Kent in their thousands, while known timber halls earlier than say 1370 can be counted on the fingers' needs to be modified in the light of the RCHM study, *The Medieval Houses of Kent* (1994).

4 B. Webster, *Arch. Cant.* 100 (1984) 219–20.

5 A. Brown, *Arch. Cant.* 92 (1976) 145–55.

6 W. Lambarde, *A Perambulation of Kent* (1826) 6.

7 *The Lordship of Canterbury* 149 note.

8 The Register of Archbishop Arundel, Lambeth Palace Library, f.176v.

9 It is significant that Stuart Rigold's survey of medieval archaeology in Kent covered most standing structures with the exception of houses after 1300. *Archaeology in Kent to A.D. 1500*, ed. P. E. Leach (1982) 84–6.

10 Canterbury Castle was never of major importance and was derelict by the mid-fourteenth century.

11 This pattern came full circle with the rehabilitation of these castles during the early twentieth century. This extensive Kentish practice had begun as early as 1822–5 at Leeds Castle (never in ruins or a farmhouse), followed by the gatehouse at Saltwood 1882–4, the castles at Hever 1903–7, Allington 1905–29, and Lympne 1906–12, the keep at Chilham in the 1920s, and Courtenay's hall and tower at Saltwood in 1936–40.

12 R. Griffiths, *The Reign of King Henry VI* (1981) 610–85.

13 Including Alderman Malpas in Essex. The opportunity was taken at this time by some of the rebels to raid the duke of Buckingham's park at Penshurst for game. C. Rawcliffe, *The Staffords, Earls of Stafford and Dukes of Buckingham* (1978) 178.

14 The exception occurred mainly in Wiltshire where William Ayscough, the hated bishop of Salisbury who was an influential advisor of Henry VI, was murdered outside Edington priory church, followed by the sacking of the monastery. The bishop's palace at Salisbury was wasted and the episcopal records burnt, his manor houses at Potterne, Ramsbury, and Woodford were sacked, and his valuable sheep flocks were decimated. But this supplementary rising was not only in support of the Kentish rebels but a reaction to the recession that had attacked the buoyant cloth industry in the Salisbury and west Wiltshire region. J. N. Hare, *Southern History* 4 (1982) 13–32. The palaces of other royal bishops, Waynflete at Winchester and the queen's chancellor Booth at Lichfield similarly suffered.

15 D. J. Turner, 'Archaeology of Surrey: 1066–1540', in *The Archaeology of Surrey*, ed. J. and D. G. Bird (1987) 231.

16 In Charlwood parish, for instance, where fifteenth- and sixteenth-century timber-framed houses of vernacular character are numerous, there are no houses of Wealden form. J. Harding, *Four Centuries of Charlwood Houses* (1976).

17 J. Brent, *Sussex Arch. Coll.* 106 (1968) 89.

18 J. Cornwall, *Sussex Arch. Coll.* 114 (1976) 1–26.

19 *Archaeology in Hampshire*, ed. D. A. Hinton and M. Hughes (1996) 42–3.

20 J. Kennedy, *Proc. Hampshire F. C. & A. Soc.* 27 (1970) 67. This figure excluded estates held by the Hampshire monasteries outside the county or land held within the county by more distant foundations.

21 R. Whinney, '*All that capital messuage called Wickham Place*' (1980) 19.

22 P. Lindley in *The Black Death in England*, ed. M. Ormrod and P. Lindley (1996) 124–46; *The Black Death in Wessex*, ed. T. B. James (1999); T. B. James, *The Black Death in Hampshire* (1999).

23 D. J. Keene, *Survey of Medieval Winchester* (1985) 93.

24 Between 1350 and 1381, the church, prior's hall, and chamber had fallen into ruin, and though French attacks may have contributed, pestilence was the fundamental cause of this priory's abandonment. S. F. Hockey, *The Isle of Wight in the Middle Ages* (1982) 50–5. Even so, the island's prominent position made it a frequent target for invasion scares, culminating in the successful attack of 1377 when Yarmouth, Newport, and Newtown were razed to the ground and only Carisbrooke Castle withstood the onslaught. It was not until the late fifteenth century that there was a significant improvement in the island's well-being.

25 J. R. Fairbrother, *Faccombe, Netherton: Excavation of a Saxon and Medieval Manorial Complex* (1990) 53–4, 73–9.

26 James, *The Black Death in Hampshire* 7.

27 E. Miller (ed.), *The Agrarian History of England and Wales: 1348–1500* (1991) 144.

28 Winchester was more than twice as populous as Southampton with 8,000–10,000 in 1300 and 3,000–5,000 in 1377, compared with Southampton's 2,500 pre-plague population which had fallen to about 1,600 in 1377. James, *The Black Death in Hampshire* 9.

29 E. Lewis, E. Roberts and K. Roberts, *Medieval Hall Houses of the Winchester Area* (1988).

30 J. Kennedy, *Proc. Hampshire F. C. and A. Soc.* 27 (1970) 65–85; J. Hare, *The Dissolution of the Monasteries in Hampshire* (1999).

10

SOUTH-EAST ENGLAND: ARCHITECTURAL INTRODUCTION

THREE factors distinguish the greater houses of the south-east from those of central and south-west England. The first is the large number of episcopal residences in the region. Even leaving those of London to one side, they contribute nearly a third of the properties covered in the detailed survey. The second is the paucity of major secular houses in Surrey and Hampshire and the limited number in Kent and Sussex. The third is the response across the region to the fear of French attack and possible invasion during the last quarter of the fourteenth century, and this is considered in detail in the essay that follows.

EPISCOPAL RESIDENCES

The spread and survival of episcopal palaces in England and Wales is patchy but the south-east retains a greater range in extent and quality than in any other part of the country. The political standing of the archbishop of Canterbury was of major significance throughout the middle ages. The relative wealth of his diocese and its position astride one of the key routes between London and Europe are at variance with its comparatively modest size. More than ten roofed properties survive, ranging from palace and castle to country houses, plus some ruined buildings and lost but documented residences. The diocese of Winchester is close on Canterbury's heels numerically and qualitively, with the benefit of even greater financial resources throughout the middle ages. Nine properties can still be examined, five roofed and four in ruin, plus the well-documented loss at Highclere. The see of Chichester is represented by residences at Chichester and Amberley, while the bishop of London's country house at Nurstead retains half of its timber-framed hall of *c.*1314. Rochester was always the poor relation.

Stephen Langton (1207–28) put his *imprimatur* on the archbishopric by completing the great hall at Canterbury initiated by his predecessor that was only second in scale to Westminster Hall. By the close of the thirteenth century, the archbishop's residences at Lambeth and Canterbury were both palace-like, necessary for prelates often deeply involved in royal and papal affairs. Architectural interest during the next two centuries therefore moves to the expansion of the several country houses held by the see and which proved such useful stopping places for much travelled men of state. These houses needed to be commensurate with the archbishop's status so that, although they are now reduced or ruined, they were built by leading craftsmen demonstrating up-to-date styles and materials.

The fine halls at Charing and Mayfield (both with post-medieval roofs) are early fourteenth-century structures by archbishop Winchelsey (1294–1313) and by Meopham (1328–33) or Stratford (1333–48) respectively, with Mayfield sharing affinities with the halls at Ightham Mote and Penshurst Place. Saltwood Castle was

PLATE 104 East Meon Court House: hall interior towards dais

survive close to London, despite losing its brick-built gatehouse and lodging court in 1808. These had been added by Morton, who favoured brick as more fashionable and quicker to use than stone. It was the chosen material for his rebuilding of Ford, of which little remains today though it was initially as large as Knole, developed round four courts and included a lodging tower 52 feet high. Not surprisingly, the scale of such palaces built by the early Tudor archbishops attracted the envy of Henry VIII.

Second only to Canterbury was the see of Winchester, with Winchester House in Southwark vying in scale with the palace at Lambeth. Developed by Peter des Roches (1205–38), with only a fragment of the great hall standing today, its size and layout can be reconstructed from documentary sources. The early palace at Wolvesey, always the centre of the bishop's domain, has similarly suffered, though the medieval walls have been consolidated and the ground plan laid out, with the mid-fifteenth-century chapel incorporated in the adjacent Caroline residence. Bishop Wykeham's career spanned the second half of the fourteenth century, extending from involvement in the royal work at Windsor Castle under Edward III to his major collegiate foundations at Winchester and Oxford. Less well known are his alterations and additions at Highclere, Bishop's Waltham Palace, and East Meon Court House – the first lost, the second ruined, and the third still roofed and occupied. At his palace at Wolvesey, he remodelled his own chambers (1372–6) and improved the palace defences in view of the likelihood of foreign invasion.

Like Lambeth Palace, Farnham Castle is still occupied but has not been subject to the same architectural analysis as its Thames-side sister. Dominated by the ruined shell keep, the bishop's apartments in the bailey centre round his late twelfth-century hall and slightly later camera. Bishop Waynflete's brick gateway of 1470–5 was ostensibly the approach to the earlier aisled hall but it served primarily as a lodging tower for honoured guests, a variant on the great brick towers at Tattershall Castle and Buckden Palace. Waynflete's brick gatehouse at Esher Palace was more conventional, now standing alone and prettified by William Kent in the 1730s.

The palace at Chichester has retained its experimental kitchen of c.1300 with hammer-beam trusses, though the associated hall no longer remains. Like Farnham and Bishop Auckland, the castle at Amberley is among the more complete episcopal fortresses, in this case converted from a manor house to a residence of limited defensive capacity during the early years of Richard II's reign.

ROYAL RESIDENCES

Episcopal building in south-east England was regular and extensive throughout the late middle ages; royal activity was modest. Edward III built lavishly but reduced the number of royal houses scattered across central and southern England by concentrating on those in the Thames valley. At the same time, the expansion of the royal household and the scale of the residences to hold such large numbers limited mobility. Outside London and Windsor, there is little evidence of royal work in south-east England apart from the shadow of Edward I's additions at Leeds Castle, and more particularly the gloriette favoured by several queens. The exception is Richard II's hall and apartment ranges within Portchester Castle, preceded by the rebuilding of Southampton Castle (1378–85) with a replacement cylindrical keep, and the refenestration of the earlier hall at Winchester in the 1390s.[1] The mini-palace constructed

given a sequence of generous apartments against the curtain wall extending from the mid to the late fourteenth century, complete with a great chamber by archbishop Courtenay (1381–96), reroofed in the 1930s. By this time, Lambeth Palace also possessed a fine great chamber with a high-quality roof frequently attributed to Courtenay. He was a prolific builder, adding the most atmospheric chamber today at Maidstone Palace which had been initiated by Walter Reynolds (1313–27) and extended by Simon Islip during the 1350s.

The archbishops tended to be less frenetic in their visits during the fifteenth century and stayed longer in their houses. Archbishop Chichele (1414–43) erected the lower part of the Water Tower at Lambeth in the mid-1430s with the upper floors and further tower added at the close of the century in brick, as was the five-storey gateway by archbishop Morton (1487–1500). But Morton's predecessor, archbishop Bourchier (1454–86), had bought the manor of Knole in 1456 and started a double courtyard house which forms the core of the present Jacobean mansion. The gatehouse, lodging ranges and private chapel still testify to the scale of his planning as does archbishop Stafford's roofed hall at Croydon (c.1445–50) with its extensive sequence of chambers completed by his two successors. Croydon is the finest large-scale fifteenth-century residence to

PLATE 105 Carisbrooke Castle: fourteenth-century residential block

within the earlier walls at Portchester should be compared with the preceding development within earlier walls at Bishop's Waltham Palace. Both consisted of two-storey ranges – first-floor hall, kitchen, and offices in one arm, private apartments in the other. More than a century later, the Tudor monarchs still barely strayed further afield from the Thames, despite Henry VIII's new residences at New Hall and Beaulieu in Essex, and Nonsuch, Woking and Oatlands in Surrey.

DEFENDABLE RESIDENCES

Defendable residences as a status and social statement are not confined to the south-east but the region displays some high-quality examples. The licensed houses at Westenhanger and Sterborough and much of Lympne date from the mid-fourteenth century, when the possibility of foreign invasion was not entertained. The redevelopment of the older castle at Arundel into a palace-fortress by the 3rd earl of Arundel (d.1376) in imitation of the royal work at Windsor Castle took this élite aspect of the movement to new heights in southern England as the Percys and Nevilles were similarly doing in the north. Though the earl's hall and residential apartments failed to survive the Civil War and nineteenth-century romanticism, the far more modest apartments remain at Carisbrooke Castle, developed by William Montagu, earl of Salisbury beyond the upper end of the earlier hall (1385–97).[2] The splendid mid-fifteenth-century castle at Herstmonceux continues to impress all visitors until they penetrate to the interior, where twentieth-century practicality has replaced historical accuracy. But the significance of Herstmonceux lies in its bristling exterior, its well-documented and ingenious internal plan, the almost total use of brick, and its construction by a knight on a scale which vied with that at Arundel eighty years earlier by the richest magnate in England.

Fear of foreign attacks against south-east England that had dogged the closing years of Edward III's reign became a reality under his son. The years between about 1360 and 1400 witnessed an extended attempt to put many leading properties in a state of

defence and to expand the military defences of the region. Castles were built at Queenborough, Cooling, and Bodiam while houses such as those at Amberley, Halnaker, Penshurst, and Scotney were given protective towers, walls, and gatehouses. Even the grange-like priory at Wilmington was hastily guarded by a three-storeyed tower and portcullis-defended entry. This response will be considered in more detail below, together with Bodiam as the central pivot in the current debate as to whether that castle was primarily a fortress with residential provision to defend the locality from French attacks, or whether it was essentially a residence in a military style.

GENTRY HOUSES

The south-east holds a modest span of stone-built houses of the gentry and those who aspired to that position in society. At first, they were relatively plentiful in Kent, and though the builder of Old Soar of c.1290 is not known, he was possibly a member of the Hore family who contributed to the Kent lay subsidy of 1334–5. Only the solar block survives, with its diagonal garderobe and chapel projections and hints of a defendable capability. It forms a vivid contrast to the old-fashioned episcopal hall of c.1314 at Nurstead Court where chamber, aisled hall, and services were under a common roof though only the upper end of the structure survives. Battel Hall of c.1330 may well have been erected by a member of the household of Queen Isabella who lived nearby at Leeds Castle. The hall and upper chamber block show not only good-quality workmanship but also a defensive element separating the two units. Isolde Inge and her husband seem to have been responsible for the initial development of the courtyard house at Ightham Mote between c.1330 and 1342 with its unusual feature of two solars abutting the chapel block, with the former always timber-framed. Southfleet Rectory, attributed to the wealthy incumbent during the 1340s, illustrates a similar but less ambitious development of a solar block in line, while Walton Manor with its chapel unit opening off the hall also bears similarities with Ightham. Far more complex was the development of the courtyard house at Penshurst Place, initiated between 1338 and 1349 by the first London merchant to be knighted. A classic example of the fully fledged medieval house, John Pulteney's hall enjoys the accolade as the finest of its period in southern England and helps to point the contrast between the provincial character of Ightham and a metropolitan realisation at Penshurst, which was defensively enclosed during the early 1390s. Penshurst's qualities attracted the attention of Henry V's brother whose residential range added a French element to a still rural mansion.

The fifteenth century opens with Rymans near Chichester harbour, an idiosyncratic house like Mortham Tower in Yorkshire where a residential unit was added to the hall in vertical rather than horizontal mode. It was made up of a relatively dark chamber, possibly for storage, with William Ryman's withdrawing chamber and bedchamber above. At the side was an independent office for his legal activities with an inner chamber above. This was a comfortable gentleman's residence close to the coast, as were all the late medieval houses in the county. Sir Reginald Pympe, sheriff of Kent in 1409, was responsible for expanding the thirteenth-century residential range at Nettlestead Place, the enigmatic and only survival of a larger house. Richard Haut never received the knighthood to which he aspired but his stone and timber additions to his house at Ightham between 1474 and 1487 were extensive and ingenious within a moat-restricted site.

PLATE 106 Herstmonceux Castle: gatehouse

Brick had already been used on a small scale in Kent in the window reveals at Allington Castle (c.1290), in the undercroft vault at Horne's Place chapel (1366), and more extensively at Daundelyon Court (before 1445), as well as at Tonford Manor where the diapered brick is mixed with flint. Tonford was one of five properties that Sir Thomas Browne, a deputy treasurer to Henry VI, sought to crenellate in 1448 but only the towered walls near Canterbury and the cheerless remains at Betchworth Castle in Surrey testify to his industry. Brick had been embraced wholeheartedly at Herstmonceux Castle and subsequently at Farnham Castle, but it was far more tentative in Hampshire where it was limited to South Charford Manor and Bishop's Waltham Palace. Brick usage moved closer to London when Sir Henry Heydon forsook Baconsthorpe Castle in Norfolk for West Wickham in Kent after marrying into the Boleyn family in 1469. Wickham Court is an unusual brick rectangle with octagonal corner turrets and rooms grouped round a small light-well. Externally it looks complete (if Victorianised) but the internal changes have been so comprehensive that the layout and division between family and staff rooms has to be sought in one of John Thorpe's plans of c.1600.

Recent work in Kent has confirmed that following the Black Death and its extended aftermath, timber-framed houses associated with the county gentry were rare before the last quarter of the fifteenth century. Stone prevailed until then, with brick becoming more fashionable from the mid-century onwards. Earlier framed

houses such as the Manor House, Benenden (possibly late fourteenth century by a knight) and at Horne's Place are rare. Brede may have been built during the early fifteenth century but all was destroyed in 1979 except the outer walls and chapel. Stoneacre erected by the Ellis family in c.1500 is more typical of the new mood for hall houses with cross wings by those of modest status in a region that was becoming less circumscribed by a small-holder economy.[3] In Sussex, Great Dixter and Horselunges Manor are within the same time-frame. The former was built during Edward IV's reign by Sir John Elrington when he was treasurer of the king's household, while Horselunges with its ground-floor hall, great chamber over, and continuous jettied front elevation marks an important building development by Sir John Devenish at the close of the century. Crowhurst Place and Old Surrey Hall were near contemporaries built by members of the Gaynesford family, minor Surrey gentry who enjoyed the profits of law. With their massive close framing, silver-grey woodwork, and heavy roofs of Horsham stone, these houses achieved a warm dignity which eschewed the florid mannerisms that were already affecting contemporary structures in Lancashire and the Welsh marches. That aspect came several centuries later when these two surviving halls with their experimental roofs combining tie-beam and hammer-beam structures[4] were cocooned in an excess of twentieth-century enthusiasm for timber-framed additions.

Hall Farm, Bentworth, the home of the Bentworth family, reminds us that the church was not the only landowner of importance in Hampshire, though there were few great lay houses. Those that exist seem to have been centres of small estates or subdivided manors as at Hall Farm. Of mid-fourteenth-century date, the house has been so heavily altered internally that its form has to be established from its walls, though it retains a detached chapel. Wonston Old House is early fifteenth-century flint-built, with a greater retention of its original form including an extension to the upper chamber block and timber-framed kitchen.[5] Timber continued to be the primary building material in the area for all but the most wealthy houses by the clerical élite. Wonston may have been a rectorial holding from the beginning but other examples include the aisled hall of c.1328–9 incorporated in Burghclere Manor House, and the extended stone chamber block of the Priory, Odiham (1448–9). Hampshire has a substantial number of smaller framed houses on the open plan, but of more modest scale than in Kent or Sussex as befitted yeomen farmers and prosperous traders.[6] But there was always a substantial gap between these and the houses of superior (mainly ecclesiastical) landowners.

This extensive use of timber led to innovations in roof construction across the region, including the Old Deanery, Salisbury (c.1258–74), the kitchen at the Bishop's Palace, Chichester (c.1300), the Pilgrims' Hall range, Winchester (c.1310–11), and Marwell Hall (c.1315–25), possibly by the same carpenter as the Pilgrims' Hall.[7] Though a 130 years later, the hall roof of the prior of St Swithun's, Winchester, is a particularly magnificent arch-braced collar structure. A number of crown-posts roofs exist as at East Meon Court House, but the majority are side-purlin-trussed structures with large curved wind braces. One unusual though badly mauled structure is the timber frame that crowned the three-storey brick tower at South Charford Manor, built by Sir John Popham, a veteran soldier and diplomat in the mid-fifteenth century. The platform timbers survived the destruction of the framed walls and roof

PLATE 107 Battel Hall: hall cistern

they supported, now hidden under the present seventeenth-century pyramid roof.

MONASTIC BUILDINGS

More residential structures survive from Hampshire's monasteries than might be expected through their heavy destruction. Two early houses stand – the Prior's Lodging (now the Deanery) of Winchester Cathedral Priory with its splendid fifteenth-century roof, and the smaller thirteenth-century ruined 'abbot's' house at Netley. This is a detached stone building with an outer and inner chamber and chapel on both floors with the lower rooms vaulted, but it is unclear whether it was used by the abbot or by special guests. The Pilgrims' Hall, Winchester, is a stunning monastic survival, as is the early thirteenth-century coupled-rafter roof of the refectory at Romsey Abbey through its conversion into houses known as 11–15 The Abbey. The refectory at Beaulieu survives through its adaptation to parish church use, while that abbey's early fourteenth-century gatehouse, domesticated and enlarged in the late nineteenth century, is of unusual design with its two ground-floor vaulted halls and twin chapels above.

Moving into Sussex and Kent, the fine gatehouse of c.1338 at Battle Abbey was a more obvious symbol of abbatial wealth and influence, though mindful of military pretension. Michelham Priory was by no means as wealthy, but the precautionary gatehouse of c.1400 is equally telling, if more modestly so.[8] The prime abba-

tial lodging is the thirteenth-century example at Battle with its fifteenth-century hall, but the former has suffered from house and school conversion while the restoration of the hall after fire damage in 1931 was competent but dull. The prior's house at Orpington, though relatively complete, has similarly been stripped of detail through continuous occupation. Though Wilmington was a priory in name, the buildings were those of a grange-type residence where the thirteenth-century domestic unit was expanded twice during the following century when the hall was rebuilt. Swanborough Manor was a true grange of Lewes Priory, altered in the early fifteenth century when the Norman hall was floored and enlarged for the prior's own use. Yet the most complete grange is at Salmestone, near Margate, centred on a mid to late thirteenth-century domestic unit with a scrumptious chapel of 1326 and a still-occupied hall frame of 1370–80, now converted into a house.

COMMUNAL RESIDENCES

More important and significant for the development of domestic architecture were the three episcopal communal foundations: Winchester College and New College, Oxford for academic study erected between 1380 and 1400, and the rebuilt Hospital of St Cross, a home for pensioners, between c.1380 and 1450. While bishop Blois had been a driving political and architectural force in England throughout the mid-twelfth century, bishop Wykeham was equally so throughout the later fourteenth century. But his financial activity and vision were matched by the drive and achievements of his architect. This combination of patron and architect created a dynamic centre at Winchester comparable to that led by John Lewyn and the group of northern magnates centred on Durham, and Henry Yevele working for Richard II and his courtiers based on London. These three movements were a critical factor in the large-scale thinking that marked the second half of the fourteenth century from the crown at Windsor and Westminster to the baronage at Kenilworth and northern England, and Wykeham at Winchester. The work by this bishop and William Wynford is of European significance with consequences extending far beyond the patronage of Wykeham's immediate successors. The scale and little-altered condition of the bishop's twin foundations, as well as their residential and educational purpose and display of the newly developed Perpendicular style over a short time span are of paramount importance for domestic studies. Equally so are those of the Hospital of St Cross where the scale and magnificence of Blois' church was matched by the late medieval hall, kitchen, and gateway, concluding in about 1450 with the spectacular and highly comfortable lodging ranges which set a standard not achieved again until the palaces of the early Tudor monarchs.

NOTES

1 The castle had now become an administrative and legal centre. *HKW*, II (1963) 862–3; M. Biddle and B. Clayre, *Winchester Castle and the Great Hall* (1983); M. Biddle, *Winchester Castle* (promised). For a valuable paper adopting a wider approach than usual to castles in Hampshire, M. Hughes, *Landscape History*, 2 (1989) 27–60.

2 The building was wholly altered in 1856 and again in 1900 when the rectangular windows were inserted. Two fireplaces date from Montagu's time including that in the earlier hall carrying the arms of Montagu's second wife. *HKW*, II (1963) 591–5; P. G. Stone, *Architectural Antiquities of the Isle of Wight* (1891) 74–103; VCH, *Hampshire and the Isle of Wight*, V (1912) 222–7.

PLATE 108 Leeds Castle: from the west

3 RCHM, *The Medieval Houses of Kent* (1994) 128–35.

4 The tone had been set by the hall roof of archbishop Stafford at Croydon Palace in *c.*1445–50 and was followed by the Carew family at Beddington attributed to *c.*1500 under the influence of that at Eltham Palace. B. Weston, D. Cluett, and J. Phillips, *Carew Manor, Beddington* (1982) and *London Arch.* 4, no.9 (1982).

5 Two further Hampshire stone houses retain interesting structural elements. Chale 'Abbey' near the southern tip of the Isle of Wight, erected by John Langford (d.1342) constable of Carisbrooke Castle, retains his two-storeyed hall block. VCH, *Hampshire*, V (1912) 236. The Priory, Odiham, a mid to late fifteenth-century stone house, remodelled in *c.*1700, may have been a house for chantry priests though it has markedly superior accommodation above low-ceiled service rooms. G. I. Meirion-Jones, *Arch. Jour.* 128 (1971) 166–73.

6 They were mainly of cruck construction in the western and central part of the county, with a few of Wealden type to the east. Seventy-five of these smaller houses in central Hampshire are described by E. Lewis, E. Roberts and K. Roberts, *Medieval Hall Houses of the Winchester Area* (1988). See also E. Roberts, *Hampshire Houses: 1250–1700* (2003).

7 This late eighteenth-century named hall in Winchester Close consists of two abutting halls that may have been erected to provide guest accommodation for St Swithun's Priory. The stone-built hammer-beam hall was possibly reserved for high-ranking guests with the adjacent framed base-cruck hall for less prestigious people. J. Crook, *Archaeologia* 109 (1991) 130–59 superseding his paper in *Proc. Hamp. N. H. and A. Soc.* 38 (1982) 85–101; E. Roberts, *Hampshire Houses 1250–70* (2003) 7–10, 251.

8 The secular gatehouses of prestigious entry at Chichester Palace (1327) and Mayfield Palace (fifteenth century) were followed during the sixteenth century at Ratton House (timber-framed), Old Buckhurst (stone), Bolebrooke (brick), Cuckfield Park (brick), and Loxwood (stone). This last was moved to Bailiffscourt by Lord Moyne in the early 1930s when he created a romantic evocation of a late medieval courtyard house near Climping. When the Georgian farmhouse on the site was demolished, it was found to be embedded with arches, doorways, and stones from an earlier courthouse. The stunning fake that Amyas Phillips developed also included other fifteenth-century features including windows, contemporary ceilings from Surrey and Somerset, and a two-light timber window from a house near Muchelney Abbey.

11

THE IMPACT OF THE HUNDRED YEARS' WAR ON ENGLISH DOMESTIC ARCHITECTURE

INTRODUCTION

THE phrase 'The Hundred Years' War', first used by Desmichels in 1823, may be a highly convenient term to describe the attenuated late medieval conflict between England and France, but it is conceptually misleading. It is not so much that this struggle for supremacy extended well beyond the traditional limits of 1337 to 1453, but the fact that it was not a continuous war but a series of vicious conflicts, separated by extended periods of uneasy peace or truce marred by sporadic hostilities. Nor was it simply between the Plantagenet and Valois dynasties, but also between them and fiefs such as Brittany, Flanders, and Burgundy who chose to support one side and then the other as the political or economic situation demanded. To a lesser extent, it also involved Scotland, the Holy Roman Empire, Castile, Navarre, and Portugal, creating a complex pattern of political, financial, economic, military, and social consequences. Though this essay is precise in its scope, one consequence common to this as to most other aspects of the War is that a conflict which began between protagonists who only knew the feudal order was concluded about 150 years later by an increasingly meritorious society at the dawn of the Renaissance.

The origins of the conflict were deep rooted and lay at least as far back as the Angevin inheritance of Aquitaine in the mid-twelfth century. The more immediate cause was the dynastic crisis in France in the years following the death of Philip IV in 1314 and his short-lived successors, and the feudal responsibilities and family conflict inherent in the close relationship between the royal houses of France and England. It was also about the gradual development of national characteristics and consciousness, particularly in France with the associated concept of a single state centred on Paris, and its opposition by a number of great princes and vassals of the French crown anxious to develop their own political independence, particularly the count of Flanders and the king of England as duke of Aquitaine.

Nor were the key protagonists equal. France was the wealthiest kingdom in western Europe with a population estimated at between 15 and 21 million inhabitants. Agriculturally rich, it covered an area not dissimilar to that today, though the royal domain embraced only about half the kingdom with the remainder held by four almost independent fiefs of the French king – Aquitaine, Brittany, Burgundy, and Flanders. The machinery of government, centred on Paris, was expanding though with difficulty in the mountainous south, but Philip IV (1285–1314) had won his conflict with the papacy, with the added benefit of the pope's proximity after his relocation from Rome to Avignon in 1309. England and Wales was a poorer country with a population of about four and a half million, principally spread across central and southern England, and lacking

PLATE 109 Hever Castle: engraving from the south-east by S. and N. Buck (1735)

the benefit of a substantial manufacturing industry. On the other hand, it was far more cohesive than France, with a well-oiled central administration, a more efficient means of levying taxes and raising an army, and far greater loyalty from the leading magnates. There was, though, a potential danger along the northern frontier if Scotland formed an alliance with France. Neither country believed that the conflict was more than a quarrel about feudal sovereignty nor that it would extend beyond a few seasons of warfare. This might have been so had not Edward III formally assumed the title and arms of the king of France in 1340, inaugurating a new posture in Anglo-French relations, and making it impossible for either side to compromise.

The extended period of tension and conflict that makes up the Hundred Years' War can be divided into four key phases. After an initial period of uncertainty for Edward III, a string of successes including Crécy (1346), the taking of Calais (1347), and victory at Poitiers (1356) culminated in the treaty of Brétigny (1360). Within less than twenty-five years, France had been brought to its knees, its king captured, and the chivalry of France left in disarray. In the second phase, a measure of peace lasted until 1369 when the French took the offensive under the reforming and capable Charles V (1364–80) and recovered most of the lands they had lost within seven years. The death of the key protagonists, the Black Prince (1376) and Edward III (1377) in England and du Guesclin (1380) in the same year as Charles V in France, combined with the accession of royal minors, a sequence of political crises, and financial exhaustion in both countries by the mid-1380s led to the truce of 1396 that lasted for twenty-eight years.

France remained impotent for three decades, even after the ambitious Henry V took the initiative to reopen the War (1415), won a resounding victory at Agincourt, and systematically conquered Normandy before capturing Paris. He replaced the scorched-earth practice of the previous century with a policy of land settlement, and by the treaty of Troyes (1420) he was recognised as heir to the throne of France. The fourth phase of the War initially favoured the English, but with their failure to capture Orléans (1428–9), the die was cast for their gradual expulsion by an enemy fortified by the moral high ground of a legally crowned French sovereign. Paris was regained (1436), followed by English withdrawal towards the Channel and expulsion from Aquitaine until Calais remained England's sole possession (1453). The War petered out, unmarked by any truce or formal declaration, though the conflict did not cease for the French until the duchy of Burgundy had been absorbed into the royal domain in 1477.

War brought fame to men on both sides, and this was of vital importance to the greater and lesser aristocracy, particularly as both sides considered they were fighting a 'just' war. Fame meant honour and the esteem of a person's peer group, and it increased his standing in society. And the most obvious way of demonstrating this – be he duke, magnate, or knight – was to prove his prowess on the battlefield, display his coat of arms on every public occasion, and build a palace-fortress, castle, or fortified house commensurate with his position. So what was the effect of the War on domestic architecture in England? Were many houses built on the spoils of war? Did the constant stream of English magnates, knights, and gentry to France affect building practices in England, and if so, were the consequences fundamental or limited to decorative techniques?

It is impossible to assess the particular impact of such an extended and bitter conflict simply by considering the relevant buildings in isolation. It is essential to place them in the context and changing circumstances of the time, to consider the range of options and benefits available to the participants, and to recognise how financial motivation and realisation changed over a century or more. War brought devastation as well as benefits to many combatants. Some participants squandered their rewards as much as others judiciously husbanded their prizes. And these were spread across a broad spectrum of society of which building – domestic, collegiate, or ecclesiastical – was only one option, albeit the most conspicuous and long-lasting.

275

One factor is fundamental to this situation throughout the long struggle. The War was fought almost entirely on French soil. That was not how the French intended the War to begin or to develop. In March 1336 Philip VI transferred the fleet that had been assembling for a crusade from the Mediterranean to the mouth of the Seine preparatory to an invasion of England in support of his Scottish ally. Plans to dispatch armed galleys from Rouen and Bruges to England in 1339 (confirmed by the discovery of the supposed French invasion plan at the sack of Caen seven years later) were serious enough for Edward III to counter with the destruction of the French fleet at Sluys in 1340 and prevent any such invasion for the next twenty years. Preparations made in the 1370s and 1380s were a valid attempt to convert the invasion of south-east England into a reality, but despite some pocket raids at that time, no French army invaded English soil. Lowland England never suffered from the depredations and destruction of French troops. Across the Channel, France suffered from a 120 year span of devastating attacks by the English and other military forces in a harrying that permanently scarred the country. The havoc was particularly severe during the earlier phases of the war, but the English conquests were more easily won (and recovered by the French) with fewer ravages during the latter phases.

THE RESPONSE TO WAR

The response to joining Edward III overseas was in marked contrast with the brief conflicts in France under his two predecessors (1294–7 and 1324). Although Edward's first campaigns achieved little success and necessitated large numbers of mercenaries, nothing begat enthusiasm for a cause better than overt success. The initial reluctance of the higher and lower aristocracy to participate was overcome by a combination of political circumstances, financial persuasion, and material gains. The eagerness to be reconciled with the king after the political rift of 1339–41, the persuasion of royal propaganda including the establishment of the Order of the Garter by 1348, the developing momentum of a chivalric *esprit de corps*, and the military triumphs at Crécy and Calais made war overseas a desirable and honourable activity.

There were also financial inducements for people at all levels of society to serve overseas. The king offered to pay all ranks on a sliding scale, often quarterly in advance. He put his captains on short-term written indentures, paid bonuses for them to take up posts of command, compensated them for horses killed on the battlefield or in service (until the 1370s), and gave letters of protection for any legal actions against their estates in England while they were serving abroad.[1] The appetite for continental campaigning was now as attractive to the lower gentry as to the magnates. They also had estates to maintain in England as well as judicial and local administrative responsibilities, but short-term indentures meant limited absence with possible financial benefits combined with the optimum use of their military potential. Soldiers were pardoned for any previous criminal offences, were paid a wage and, like their captains, shared in the spoils of war. A volunteer rather than a conscripted army helps to explain the rolling and ever wider enthusiasm for the war.

Paid military service – with obligations as much as benefits – had been practised during Edward II's reign to defend the Scottish border in the absence of the king. It became increasingly widespread, particularly towards the closing years of Edward III's reign when the king was no longer leading the army in person and the royal household was not present to deal with the distribution of wages and related matters. The introduction and development of this 'military revolution' has led to considerable historical discussion,[2] but it was the usual method of raising armies by the second phase of the War from 1369 onwards. By the time of Henry V, all armies were raised by indentures of war, greatly enhancing their effectiveness and enthusiasm for overseas campaigns. But agreement to pay and payment achieved were not necessarily the same. Even before the close of Edward III's reign, John of Gaunt and Thomas of Woodstock, later duke of Gloucester, sometimes had to wait years before they received payment in full from the Exchequer for their services and those of their retinues,[3] and by the last phase of the War, the dilatoriness of the overstretched Exchequer had become notorious.[4]

MILITARY CAREERS AND PROFESSIONALISM

Unlike the wars of the first two Edwards, the Hundred Years' War gradually brought the prospect of political influence, personal honour, and social advancement to all ranks of society. The king led all military operations initially, but with the decision to attack several regions of France simultaneously in the mid-1340s – Brittany, northern France, Aquitaine – the delegation of command went hand-in-hand with the growth in the power and privileges of a new generation of talented magnates and leading military knights. The strategy had been prompted by the high success achieved by a campaign in 1342 supporting a succession dispute in Brittany led by the young earls of Northampton and Oxford and knights such as Sir Walter Manny, Sir Richard Stafford, and Sir Walter Bentley. The king was able to join them five months later. In 1345, Northampton and his lieutenant, Sir Thomas Dagworth, followed up their initial success with a second campaign to Brittany, and the recently ennobled earl of Lancaster headed a campaign force to Aquitaine,[5] while in 1346 the king led a mammoth plundering expedition to Normandy supported by the sixteen-year-old prince of Wales and the earls of Northampton, Warwick, and Arundel. The approaching French army forced Edward to turn towards his troops in Flanders that he had put under the command of Sir Hugh Hastings. All three theatres of war were politically successful, extremely profitable, and marked by several career successes and many deeds of prowess culminating in the royal victory at Crécy.

Almost all magnate families served overseas during the 1340s and 1350s under Edward III or the Black Prince, bringing glory and renown to their names. Support for the War was one of relaxed co-operation between the crown and the nobility who recruited and led the contract armies that became an increasingly significant factor in England's success.[6] But comparable expectations and triumphs were not fulfilled after the War was renewed in 1369, so that the new generation of nobles became more critical of the government from the mid-1370s onwards and experienced increasingly less profitable returns. During this period, John Lord Neville of Raby and John of Gaunt played the dominant role in England's beleaguered strategy, followed after the succession of the ten-year-old Richard II by the new earl of Arundel and Thomas of Woodstock, who were equally unsuccessful in northern France. This period was also marked by a diminution of the number of knights going overseas. This was partly the consequence of an overall reduction in their number as a class of society, but also because of a reduction in the number of fighting knights needed in the theatres of war. By this time, fewer than 10 per cent of an army's men-at-arms were knights compared with 20 per cent or more earlier in the War. And this reduction continued during Henry V's reign.[7]

This diminution had been offset by the growing number of professional soldiers of esquire or non-aristocratic birth – younger sons, young bloods, adventurers, and seekers of fortune. Some found permanent service with the Black Prince or Gaunt in their extensive campaigns, or stayed permanently in Aquitaine as many men did from Cheshire and Lancashire. But this knightly decline was also offset by the rising number of mounted archers drawn from the ranks of yeoman farmers, particularly during the fifteenth century.[8] They were less expensive than knights but tactically as effective. The combination of men-at-arms and mounted archers modified the social composition of the army and meant that the spoils of war spread further down the social scale. Late in life, Sir Thomas Gray, disapprovingly old-fashioned, wrote that 'young fellows [in the late 1350s] who hitherto had been of small account . . . became exceedingly rich . . . many of them beginning as archers and then became knights, some captains'.[9] Though Sir Robert Knollys was the exemplar[10] others were equally successful despite not being born into the chivalric class.

Birth was becoming less important than reputation, and reputation was all-important to a rising family. While Sir Hugh Hastings' success was commemorated on his stunning brass in Elsing church (1347) and Sir Thomas Bradeston placed the arms of his associates and commanders in the great east window of Gloucester Cathedral (1348–50), more worldly returning captains such as Sir Warin Lisle and Sir Edward Dalyngrigge flaunted their achievements by building new homes to proclaim their financial and battlefield successes. The reverse side of the coin was that campaigning in France could also devastate families, preventing young men from entering their inheritance such as the five Gloucestershire knights and squires who died in France between 1338 and 1363 before succeeding to their estates.[11] Nor did overseas service necessarily bring the anticipated fruits. Sir John Hardeshull (d.1369) saw no tangible benefits for his years in Brittany during the 1340s. He took no notable prisoners, was himself captured, did not buy any new properties or invest in land, and lived his final years at Saleby in Lincolnshire as a modest country gentleman.[12]

As in Edward III's reign, leadership during the third phase of the War was held by the king, his immediate family (three brothers), and many nobles led by the earls of Warwick and Dorset. As Henry V's policy of conquest and occupation extended from Normandy to Paris and under Bedford from Maine towards the Loire, it was necessary to turn to the lower echelons of society to find persons capable of the more passive duty of garrisoning towns and fortresses on a permanent basis rather than displaying their skills on the battlefield. Soldiers of talent and experience, controlling small bands of forces, were given positions of responsibility. Birth was no longer the primary criterion: career professionalism was. Furthermore, the new strategy of virtually permanent armies and garrisons in the field meant that men frequently served several extended tours of duty in France. Under Bedford as much as Henry V, the risk of capture or death was less likely than in the previous century but so were the prospects of booty or ransom once the initial conquest had been completed.

PLATE 110 Michelham Priory: gatehouse

Henry VI failed to lead his armies into battle. He was a minor until 1437 with the loss of Paris and Upper Normandy still ringing in his ears. At the point when he might have taken up arms, he became increasingly committed to peace, not war. The higher nobility therefore, again filled the gap during the last phase of the War. Some such as the dukes of York (between 1436–7, 1440–6) and the inept Somerset (1438–40, 1443–4) and earls such as Salisbury (Richard Neville 1436–7), Arundel (1431–5), and Warwick (1437–9) served for relatively short periods, with early deaths curtailing the last two. Others such as Lord Talbot and Lord Scales became permanent war leaders. Knights such as Sir John Fastolf, Sir John Handford, and Sir John Cressy spent much of their mature years in service in France, with the last named (d.1445) undertaking expeditionary and garrison services from the late 1420s to the mid-1440s.[13] But aristocratic and knightly involvement became increasingly affected by the deteriorating political situation in England and disenchantment with a failing cause abroad, particularly at gentry level whose representatives sat in the Commons and held (or rather withheld) the purse strings.[14] Yet by the time the War ended, four generations of the aristocracy and tens of thousands of Englishmen had fought, served, or lived in France – probably about 4 or 5 per cent of the adult male population of England at any one time during the conflict.[15]

THE GAINS OF WAR

The heady anticipation of financial and social advancement was highly successful in mobilising support for the ongoing claims by Edward III, Henry V, and Bedford (on behalf of Henry VI) to the throne of France. But though men might state that they were fighting for their king and honour, the prospect of the spoils of war was considerably more potent.

By the laws of war, captured prisoners were the private property of the captor. They might ransom or sell them, as Sir Thomas Holand sold the count of Eu to Edward III for 80,000 florins. The sum to be paid depended on the social standing of the person captured and was determined by negotiation on what he could afford. King John was ransomed for 3 million gold crowns after his capture at Poitiers. It was the most spectacular ransom of the War and though it made great demands upon France in the 1360s (though less than half was eventually paid), it was nevertheless a staggering sum for the English coffers. Sir Walter Manny took over £11,000 worth of prisoners between 1337 and 1340 and fared just as well over the next three years. The Suffolk knight Sir Thomas Dagworth captured Charles of Blois, the French candidate to the duchy of Brittany, at La Roche-Derrien in July 1347 and sold him to Edward III for 25,000 gold écus. According to Knighton, Henry, earl of Lancaster made £50,000 from the ransoms of Auberoche in October 1345, and if this seems excessive, he had taken a third of that only two months earlier from the prizes at Bergerac, plus a barrel of gold. Fourteen of the thirty-five nobles taken at Poitiers were bought from their captors by the Black Prince for £66,000 and shipped from Bordeaux to Plymouth along with their king to secure the maximum terms from the French. And the same practice was adopted with similar success immediately after Agincourt.

Spectacular ransoms grabbed the headlines but they were not particularly numerous, and in the later phase of the War, the smaller number of battles meant fewer aristocratic prisoners. Far more common was capturing combatants of lesser rank such as those seized at Caen in 1346 who, apart from the constable, included about 100 knights, over 120 squires, and a large number of wealthy citizens. When the earl of Lancaster set out on a *chevauchée* from Gascony later that year, the Gascon soldiers agreed to serve without pay for a month in anticipation of the ransoms and booty they hoped to take. Ransoms applied to both sides. The earls of Salisbury and Suffolk were both captured in the Low Countries in April 1340 and paid the consequences, as did the young earl of Pembroke in 1372-5, with imprisonment hastening his death. Ransoms could be easily squandered and no doubt many of the families of soldiers in France never saw any such money, but it has to be conceded that some of the houses built in England during the mid-fourteenth century – a period when many magnates were hard pressed to fund their adventures overseas – were the consequence of French *livres* handed to the victor.

Most of the spectacular ransoms occurred during the first phase of the War. Booty and plunder could be just as impressive but they were spread between a wider range of people and across a broader span of years. They were particularly the reward of *chevauchées*, swift and brutal raids by troops sweeping across the countryside in a campaign of pillaging, booty, property destruction, and land wastage. By deliberately avoiding battle confrontation, they challenged the political and moral authority of the French crown to defend its territories, destabilised tax collection and payment, and brought the promised return of the spoils of war. Rules were laid down to ensure that the spoils were shared in a reasonable and equitable way. Men were specially appointed to collect and assess the value of booty and to arbitrate on disagreements about its distribution. Initially the division was by halves, but by the early 1370s, it was customary for a soldier to give a third of his gain to his captain, who gave a third of his gain, and a third of that passed on to him by his soldiers, to the king. This helped to ensure that the profits of war were not limited to the leaders but extended across a fairly wide number of participants at all levels.[16]

The earliest of the great *chevauchées* were led by the royal house (before Crécy 1346, Poitiers 1355-6, and Reims 1359-60). Those after the renewal of war in 1369 were led by Sir Robert Knollys (1370), the duke of Lancaster (1373), the earl of Buckingham (1380), and others. After Henry V's first campaign, the practice ceased, for the king forbade looting or ravaging if his policy of permanent territorial occupation was to succeed. It has been argued that the lack of detailed evidence for all but the royal family and a relatively small number of commanders and captains invites caution in accepting reports of massive profits won during the War.[17] It is usual to cite the careers of leading magnates and captains such as Sir Hugh Calveley, Sir John Chandos, or Sir Robert Knollys, who was said by Froissart to be in London at the time of the Peasants' Revolt in 1381 guarding his treasure which Walsingham recorded was almost of royal proportions. Such people were undoubtedly enriched by the War, but there is limited evidence to assess how the majority of knights fared and considerably less for the squires. By 1380, the age of quickly garnered spoils had essentially passed, and in the period of low prices during the last two decades of the century the gentry could not look to the profits of war to supplement their reduced income from land. In any case, such profits were unpredictable and uneven in scale and distribution, and though some individuals fared exceedingly well, returns were not always as substantial as expectations.

The aspirations of the nobility and gentry when Henry V led his army to France were the same as those under Edward III – honour and profit. This was particularly so as the English expedition of 1412 – two dukes, four earls, eight barons, twenty-eight knights, and 6,500 men-at-arms and archers – supporting the Orleanist faction seeking power over the mad French king had been most handsomely bought off. Within two years, Henry V had developed his policy of conquering France by force and maintaining that conquest through settlement based on the redistribution of confiscated estates to his supporters. Every Frenchman in Normandy (and later in Maine) who failed to take the oath of allegiance to the English crown forfeited his lands to an Englishman. To the potential 'advantages' of war – glamour, status, ransom – plunder was replaced by the more financially secure one based on land grants and offices. The immediate recipients were the nobles and captains who had supported Henry and took responsibility for the maintenance and control of their newly acquired French estates. However, most of the grants were to the lower ranks, mainly lesser gentry and minor landowners, who were expected to live there and contribute to the defence of their property. Many did so and fostered a vested interest in the maintenance of the Lancastrian conquests. Some took the opportunity afforded by this new revenue source to enhance their capital with savings made through not living at home, while the more sagacious invested their returns in land in England. In addition to his extensive portfolio of acquired land grants during the

PLATE III Amberley Castle: gatehouse range

1420s and 1430s, Sir John Fastolf particularly benefited from numerous military and administrative posts and captured members of the French aristocracy.[18] The Dane, Sir Andrew Ogard, formerly Anders Pederson who obtained letters of denization in 1433, joined the English forces to acquire the monies that would allow him to purchase estates in England and build the brick house at Rye in Hertfordshire (c.1443). Sir Leonard Hastings (d.1455) similarly fared well enough in France to move his *caput* from Yorkshire to Kirby Muxloe near Leicester.

Fastolf vigorously exploited his overseas estates, but to do so he and other landholders needed officers and administrators to organise their properties as well as their households. Such was the young Ralph Cromwell under Henry V and Clarence, Sir William Bowes under Bedford, and Sir William Oldhall under the duke of York. They equally enjoyed the opportunity to acquire conquered territories as well as to serve their king (and themselves) without the need to face the battlefield any more than did the accountants and lawyers necessary to serve the permanent English presence in France. Yet Fastolf's spectacular success was not typical. The majority seem to have made an efficient living rather than substantial profits, with the spoils of an earlier generation replaced by the more mundane though steadier returns to be made from sequestered land and the rights of lordship due to the new holder.[19]

As in war of any age, entrepreneurs took advantage of this particular conflict mainly by staying at home, to make considerable profit for themselves through servicing its needs. The Hundred Years' War not only demanded large sums to pay for it, but they needed to be raised quickly, particularly to pay all indentured soldiers an advance on their wages. It was Edward III's failure to achieve this that partly explains his difficulties in 1339 and his crisis in 1341, as well as the rise of commoners such as John Pulteney and William de la Pole who were capable of advancing the substantial sums that the king desperately needed. The rewards were a knighthood and grants of land, which helped Pulteney to build Penshurst Place (c.1341–9) and to die a rich man. Within four generations, the family of de la Pole had risen from commoner to duke, and from a brick house in Hull to Wingfield Castle in Suffolk. Sir Peter le Veel, who served in the retinue of the Black Prince from 1362 to 1367 and frequently returned to France during the 1370s, lent money on a substantial scale, as did the earl of Arundel (d.1376) who used his £50,000 fortune as much to increase his influence with the king and fellow magnates as to enhance his personal fortune. Even more anxious to buy influence was cardinal Beaufort, a particularly wily operator, who used his episcopal and personal wealth to underpin the War throughout its last phase. His sequence of massive loans totalling £220,000 over the thirty-three year period 1413–46 were not necessarily usurious, but they certainly brought him control over the royal finances and helped to sustain the Lancastrian regime until his death in 1447.[20]

THE HOUSES OF WAR

'The relationship between crown and nobility, and the part played by war in shaping English government and politics and the English sense of themselves, remain at the heart of any interpretation of late medieval English politics.'[21] Furthermore, the War strengthened and enhanced the role and finances of the nobility and gentry, but this was secondary (though highly supportive) to their primary concern – the consolidation and extension of their inheritance, lands, and offices. These were the basis of their wealth and power, which they intended to hand on to their heirs, while the size of the household, the scale of their residences, their patronage and generosity were the outward manifestation of their rank and territorial standing. The 'benefits' of war were uneven in scale and not necessarily fairly distributed, but they helped to resource a number of major building projects by commanders and captains, which symbolised their relationships and standing, not only with their peer group, but with others of higher or lower status.

In their different ways, it has recently been appreciated that Edward III and Richard II used language and imagery to emphasise their majesty,[22] as Henry V similarly did, and to encourage pride in nationhood.[23] While building was only one of the options open to the monarchy, it was a primary tool for magnates and gentry alike as a statement of authority and military success. English houses had no more outward or specific identification of the martial achievements of the owner or the war funding of his property than the funerary monuments of the commanders and captains of the War.[24] The apparently original enamelled copper plate on the machicolated outer gate of Cooling Castle is unique in its declaration that the castle was 'mad[e] in help of the cuntre'. The heraldic displays such as those at Hylton, Lumley, or Bodiam castles were a declaration not of battlefield success but of the builder's status, descent, and affinity. But by their construction, they made an immediately recognisable proclamation of success as much as did Hardwick Hall, Burleigh House, Audley End, Houghton Hall, Wentworth Woodhouse, or Waddesdon to later generations.

Almost before the War had finished Edward III was seen as embodying the ideals of kingship and valour, and this was stressed when Edward IV went to war with France in 1475.[25] The many deeds of valour by captains of war, particularly those achieved during the first phase, were popularised so that by the mid sixteenth century the War was being perceived as a chivalric-inspired romance, with the victories highlighted and the ultimate disastrous defeat brushed aside.[26] John Leland was not part of that movement, but he did repeat the testimonies from eight owners or custodians that their houses had been built *ex spoliis nobilium bello Gallico captorum*. Such statements were based on tradition rather than original documentation and Leland was sometimes sceptical of their accuracy.[27] Fortunately, his comments are supplemented by a number of other sources to give a more balanced picture.

Building brooked no delay and certainly did not wait upon truces or peace before returning magnates began investing their gains during the 1340s. According to Knighton, Henry duke of Lancaster (d.1361) made so much money from the prizes at Bergerac in Aquitaine in 1345 that he was able to rebuild the Savoy Palace in

the Strand at the cost of 52,000 marks.[28] Thomas, 3rd earl of Warwick, one of the pre-eminent commanders of the first phase, developed the imposing entrance frontage of Warwick Castle between *c*.1340 and 1369, while a recent authority on that structure agrees that the seventeenth-century tradition may well be true that Caesar's Tower was built out of the £8,000 ransom of the archbishop of Sens captured at Poitiers.[29] After his Scottish war service and as admiral, William Clinton, earl of Huntingdon, built a totally new castle at Maxstoke in his late thirties (*c*.1342–6), while the earl of Stafford who was sent to Gascony as seneschal in 1345–6 and defended Aiguillon, rebuilt the keep at Stafford Castle (1347–*c*.1368). Leland noted that Thomas, 3rd Lord Berkeley, 'taken prisoner in France', later recovered his losses by taking French prisoners, including some from the battle of Poitiers. Consequently he was able to build Beverston Castle, though in fact his work was limited to the residential tower and the west wing (*c*.1330–*c*.1350).[30] More fundamental was the new castle with unusual design features built at Mettingham (1343–*c*.1350) by Sir John Norwich who had fought extensively in Gascony.

Not surprisingly, some of the largest building projects at this time were undertaken by the crown and the royal princes. Edward III and the Black Prince, in particular, enjoyed the benefits of ransoming notable prisoners. The Black Prince rebuilt Kennington Palace in a two-phase development of *c*.1340–52 and 1353–63, overlapping Lancaster's activity at the Savoy between 1350 and 1357, while the rebuilding of the residential apartments and upper court at Windsor Castle (1352–*c*.1377) was the most expensive royal building project of the later middle ages.

Most of this first-phase activity was magnate led (Sir John Norwich was ennobled in 1360). The structures varied considerably in scale and form, reflecting the attitudes and financial resources of their builders. They ranged from the modest tower-house at Beverston Castle to the crowning one at Stafford. The spectacular frontage of Warwick Castle, possibly influenced by the field experience of Thomas, 3rd earl of Warwick, is one of the most formidable defences in England, while only a few miles away the contemporary work at Maxstoke is more of a reflection of the image of war. The commanding gatehouse is at odds with the low walls, berm, and corner towers, and it is they which betray that the interior was filled with a hierarchy of family apartments, household lodgings, and guest chambers round four sides of the courtyard. By their nature, the less expensive unprotected houses did not have the same immediate *cachet* unless they were on the largest scale such as Kennington Palace or the Savoy in London.

Yet the profits of war were not the only factors pertinent to these developments. The heiress daughter of Sir Thomas Leybourne brought an estate of forty manors to bolster the modest patrimony of William Clinton when she married him in 1328. The failing Stafford fortunes were reversed by the conjunction of war service with marriage to the Audley heiress. The remodelling of Beverston Castle was at least the result of Lord Berkeley's extensive sheep rearing activities and astute estate management as much as any funding from France. Most of these projects had been initiated – and in some cases completed – before the Black Death with the attendant collapse of land values and baronial incomes. The Warwick and Stafford castle programmes were delayed, but the impact of the plague on such projects can be overstated.[31] In particular, it failed to affect the redevelopment of the keep at Windsor

Castle preparatory to the conversion of the upper ward into a vast palace-complex as befitted a monarch finally recognised as one of European standing.

The reversal in English fortunes and the loss of hard-won lands did not diminish building fervour in England between the 1360s and 1390s. The wealth of the 3rd earl of Arundel had been almost doubled by the acquisition of the Warenne inheritance in 1347, but it was enhanced still further by the earl's long participation on the battlefield, from Crécy until his death in 1372, and by his diplomatic missions. This treasure chest was the basis for his rebuilding of Arundel Castle in emulation of Edward III's work at Windsor Castle. Twenty-five years' war service, particularly under the Black Prince and Gaunt, funded Lord Scrope's land acquisitions early in his career and the subsequent construction of Bolton Castle (c.1377–c.1396). Ralph, Lord Neville (d.1367) was probably responsible for initiating Brancepeth Castle (c.1360–80), completed by his son. The ransoms obtained in Gascony by John, 3rd Lord Neville contributed to his development of Raby Castle (c.1367–c.1388), claimed by Leland as the largest inhabited castle in northern England.[32] He also initiated Sheriff Hutton Castle (1382–c.1410) with its impressive hall and massive corner towers. These northern palace-fortresses were more formidable than most magnate projects of a generation earlier and were as much a political statement of semi-independence from a weakened crown as an updating of residential apartments.[33] The second phase of the War also witnessed the construction of several smaller castles by returning soldiers such as Sir Warin Lisle at Shirburn (1377–c.1382) who fought under two dukes of Lancaster, Sir Richard Abberbury at Donnington (c.1386) who served under the Black Prince, and Sir Edward Dalyngrigge who served under Sir Robert Knollys and included the latter's shield on the postern gate of Bodiam Castle (1385–c.1391). Despite the claim in Dalyngrigge's licence to crenellate that Bodiam was built for the defence of the neighbourhood, its construction – as with its fellow castles – benefited from the spoils of war. Their superficial military character essentially emphasised their builders' social position consequent upon battlefield success overseas.[34]

The returns from Henry V's initial subjugation of Normandy helped him to continue with, though not to finish, the new palace at Sheen that he had initiated in 1414. Sir John Cornwall, who had married Henry IV's sister in 1400 and received 21,375 crowns through being bought off by the French in 1412, developed Ampthill Castle, possibly in the 1420s.[35] Sir Walter Hungerford probably expanded his father's castle at Farleigh Hungerford at this time after a period of distinguished war service under the king, though his treasurership of England (1426–32) and his father's services as Gaunt's steward rather than the ransom from the ascribed capture of the duc d'Orléans at Agincourt mentioned by Leland were more probably responsible for funding the development of this fortified house.[36] William Worcester claimed that the capture and ransom of the duc d'Alençon by Sir John Fastolf at the battle of Verneuil (1424) paid for Caister Castle, but as part of the debt of £18,000 was still owed to Fastolf by the crown thirty-one years later, its contribution to the castle's construction is doubtful.[37] In any case, Caister was built between 1432 and 1455, during the later stages of Fastolf's long military career, principally resourced from his substantial landed income, from the sale of lands in France before his last visit there in 1446, and by the acquisition of a considerable amount of building material without charge.[38]

The deteriorating situation abroad from the 1430s onwards was not reflected in building at home. A wealthy marriage and the return from local offices rather than war service in Normandy enabled Sir William ap Thomas to initiate the rebuilding of Raglan Castle (1432–45), though it was his son who was responsible for converting it into the formidable palace-fortress that stands today. Leland makes no reference to Raglan but he accords several contemporary projects to the funding of war spoils. Sir William Bowes, chamberlain to the duke of Bedford for seventeen years, 'grew so rich that when he returned home, he increased his estate and his standing by rebuilding the manor house at Streatlam from its foundations' during the 1430s.[39] Sir Richard Lenthall 'took many prisoners at Agincourt and with their ransoms, began to build Hampton Court [in Herefordshire] . . . until he left off on the death of his son' with construction in hand between 1434 and his son's early death in 1447.[40] Sir Ralph Boteler served under Bedford throughout his rule, but despite Leland's attribution that Sudeley Castle (1441–58) was built on spoils won in France, his marriage to a wealthy widow and the returns from a sequence of crown offices were at least as important.[41] Though nothing survives and there is little indication of its construction date, Leland identifies that 'the excellent gatehouse and façade of Lord Stourton's house at Stourton . . . with the magnificent façade of the inner courtyard with high battlements like a castle' was built 'from spoils taken during the war with France'.[42] Lord Stourton (d.1462) was deeply involved with the defence of Calais during the closing stages of the War, and his house was the temporary home of the duc d'Orléans in 1438–9.

All the houses in the last two phases of the War were built by professional soldiers, captains of war rather than by magnates. They reflected their achievements overseas and status at home as much as their predecessors', and similarly differed in form. Ampthill, Hampton Court, and Sudeley Castle were highly comfortable quadrangular houses, while Caister, Farleigh Hungerford, and Stourton were courtyard residences dressed in an outer coat of military pretension.

Most of the properties named so far are given the nomenclature 'castle' though military terminology has been misappropriated to a range of residences of the later middle ages of totally different character and design.[43] Few 'castles' built during this era were fortresses. The frontage of Warwick Castle and the redevelopment of Raglan Castle are the last formidable displays of medieval defensive architecture and they were separated by a hundred years and the respective rank of their builders.[44] Otherwise, the word 'castle' embraces a range of residences from palace-fortresses to trophy houses, fortified houses and tower-houses, in fact any residence with a martial air. Yet, the military panache of Bodiam is as restrained as the fantasy element is controlled at Herstmonceux. The use of such a fashionable material as brick at Caister (as in the contemporary 'castles' at Tattershall and Herstmonceux) hardly makes a convincing statement of defensive durability when brick was being used at the same time for country houses, churches, almshouses, academic colleges, and episcopal palaces. From the distance, the impressively sited castle at Donnington is demonstrably castellar, but a closer examination shows that the fortification is relaxed, a knowing hint that this was essentially a retirement home. The dominating gatehouse with decorative vaulting, enriched string course, windows of some size, and built-in facilities barely conceals its function as one of high-status apartments. The courtyard walls and turrets were of low scale, relatively thin, and wholly secondary to the castle's domestic *raison d'être*. Maxstoke Castle had demonstrated the same characteristics of a castellated country house, though with considerably more panache.[45] The all-embracing use of this single word has long hindered our appreciation of the radically different character, purpose, and architectural form of the houses of late medieval England. The existence of a moat, towers, and battlements nearly always represented social pretension, not protection from fears.

A number of houses lacking any martial face can also be identified as war-funded. The Savoy, the duke of Lancaster's London residence, Penshurst Place, Sir John Pulteney's country estate, and de la Pole's houses in Hull and Wingfield have already been mentioned, but there are others such as the first phase of Faulkbourne Hall (*c.*1439) by Sir John Montgomery who served under the duke of York in the 1430s. An equally refined residence was that built by Sir Andrew Ogard at Rye, Hertfordshire, in 1443 and similarly of brick of the highest decorative quality. John Leycester (d.1398), a bully from Cheshire, built the timber-framed Tabley Old Hall, jutting out into a mere that eventually contributed to its collapse in the 1950s. Leland records that a house in Eaton near Leominster was built by William Hakluyt who had fought at Agincourt and taken a French nobleman called St George.[46] Lower down the social scale, William Jauderel, an élite archer who served under the Black Prince during the early 1350s, was rewarded after his return to England in 1356 with two oak trees from the royal forest of Macclesfield to repair his house at Whaley Bridge in Derbyshire.[47] There is little doubt that further research will reveal more houses that similarly benefited in kind as well as from war gains through service abroad.

Many of these properties were furnished with the material benefits of fighting overseas. There was pardonable exaggeration in Walsingham's claim during Edward III's campaign of 1346–7 that 'coats, furs, quilts and household goods of every kind, table cloths, necklaces, wooden bowls and silver goblets, linen and cloth could be seen in every home . . . There was not a woman in England of any account who did not enjoy the pickings of Caen, Calais, and other towns.'[48] Yet numerous French items recorded in English inventories and wills over the next hundred years bear out the measure of the chronicler's comments. France may have been the enemy, but their finery, plate, jewellery, manuscripts, furnishings, and tapestries were of the finest quality. Their display enhanced the wealth and standing of the acquisitor, identified success overseas, and was a long-term investment. The Black Prince's residences displayed the magnificent salt cellar in the shape of a silver ship belonging to the French king which John Jauderel (William's brother), with other archers, had looted after the battle of Poitiers.[49] In the 1340s, Sir Thomas Ughtred of Kexby in Yorkshire bequeathed to his son the bed hung with tapestries 'covered with images of the magnates of the kingdom of France, armed with their arms, with images of the common people of the same kingdom around the fringes'.[50] The inventory of 1448 for the furnishings of Sir John Fastolf in his castle at Caister included ten white beds from France, some Norman arms, and nineteen books written in French.[51]

Others preferred to invest their returns in more spiritual projects. Sir Walter Manny, a Hainaulter by birth but an adoptive Englishman and leading captain of the 1340s, was a highly successful practitioner of ransoms, particularly in Brittany in 1342. In 1371, he founded the London Charterhouse and employed Henry Yevele to build the great cloister and church. Other leaders founded colleges of secular canons, including Henry, duke of Lancaster at Leicester (1356), John Lord Cobham at Cobham (1370), Sir Robert Knollys at Pontefract (1385), and Sir Hugh Calveley at Bunbury (1386). Calveley may have been responsible for widening the nave at Steventon church and reroofing the nave and chancel,[52] while Sir William Echyngham virtually rebuilt Etchingham church (1370–80), with the heraldic shields of Edward III, the duke of Brittany, the Black Prince, and Gaunt in its east window. Though building was the most prominent, charitable donation, lavish entertainment, and enlarged households were further ways of flaunting battlefield success.

The architectural achievements of the War took many forms but there were sometimes more subtle associated concepts. This was particularly so with the monarchy. Edward III's remodelling of Windsor Castle was only one element of his development of an aristocratic *esprit de corps*. His projection as the new King Arthur, his foundation of the Garter, his encouragement of tournaments as a theatrical display, and the cult of chivalry were integral to his conversion of Windsor into a palace-fortress. This courtly enhancement was mirrored in the households of his sons and emphasised under Richard II with Westminster Hall decorated with his personal insignia as well as the royal arms. It is also from this reign that the earliest realistic panel paintings of a king have survived, the Westminster portrait and the Wilton Diptych. Henry V emphasised his personal piety with his Carthusian foundation next to his grand new palace at Sheen, and with the most elaborate chantry chapel in England, that in Westminster Abbey, completely covered with heraldic carvings, the depiction of kings, saints, and royal emblems.[53]

For the great majority of English people, the War was a distant trumpet. They never experienced the hardship and tragedy of the battlefield, the devastation of army occupation, or the vicious wasting and pillaging of the countryside. The War brought heavy taxes, the times were filled with rumours, and most people knew of friends or a member of the family who never returned from the battlefield. For them, the most striking and long-lasting images were the castles and imposing houses that were raised across the countryside. They were just as much a symbolic as a visual statement of achievement in the War. They were a mirror of English confidence and an assertive declaration of success. They were also a power-statement of lordship and locality, an attempt to remind the neighbourhood that the War had changed nothing, whereas the reality – in due course – was wholly different.

THE ARCHITECTURAL INFLUENCE OF THE WAR

The influence of building design and the transmission of architectural ideas between one country and another is not about detailing but about the cross-fertilisation of planning concepts, style, and design features, and to some extent scale. Copying an admired model was considered worthy. In 1398, John Middleton was contracted to model the walls of the new dormitory of Durham Cathedral Priory on those of the Constable's Tower at Brancepeth Castle, while the masons and overseers of Totnes church were sent in 1449 to study the towers of Ashburton, Buckland, and Tavistock before building that at Totnes.[54] Indigenous architecture had been erased in favour of that from northern France since the Norman Conquest, fostered by the subsequent mobility of masons and by common building standards by the European monastic orders. After its destruction by English forces in 1385, Melrose Abbey was rebuilt under the supervision of John Morow who came from Paris, while Batalha Abbey in Portugal was constructed towards the close of the fourteenth century under English direction.[55]

For over a hundred years, English commanders and administrators besieged, sacked, and lived in French fortresses and houses. It is therefore frequently claimed that defensive buildings in late medieval England such as Nunney Castle were influenced by or copied French models. Though this leads to historical contortions,[56] there is a world of difference between seeing the buildings of a foreign state and adopting some of their characteristics, particularly when they are those of the enemy. And francophobia had been sedulously encouraged for some generations.

It is possible that some of the English castles built during the first phase of the War may have been influenced by the sudden wave of military construction in France. Many French towns, hitherto lacking stone walls, set about rectifying their vulnerability with formidable enceintes, from Guérande (1343) in Brittany to Vézelay (c.1360) and Semur en Auxois (c.1372) in Burgundy, to Avignon (1355–77) and Villeneuve-lès-Avignon (c.1362–8) in Provence. It is difficult not to feel that the earl of Warwick who spent so many of his years between 1339 and 1369 as commander in Flanders, Brittany, northern France, and Aquitaine was influenced by what he saw and experienced when redeveloping the entrance frontage at Warwick Castle. The highly unusual plan of Mettingham Castle may have been similarly affected by what Sir John Norwich witnessed abroad, while the windows of Harewood Castle are like those in the contemporary hall at Angers Castle. The completion of St Stephen's chapel in the palace of Westminster was in emulation of the house of Valois, while reports on the donjon at Vincennes may have influenced the design of Henry V's palace at Sheen.[57] However, it is not possible to lay down any hard and fast judgment. No one left records of their aesthetic influences and assessments, though scholars have waxed and waned on a non-provable subject.

The hexagonal form of Old Wardour Castle can be paralleled with that adopted by the duc de Berri at Concressault[58] but there is no evidence that Lord Lovel or his probable designer, William Wynford, visited what was a relatively modest castle in the duke's portfolio. It is all too easy to identify similar features and planning characteristics between contemporary castles and adumbrate a more personal link. Four castles in central Burgundy, for instance, built between the late fourteenth and mid-fifteenth centuries can be readily paralleled with contemporary structures in England. La Motte-Josserand has a similar quadrangular plan to the contemporary castle at Bodiam (c.1385) with its bold circular corner towers, rectangular projections in the middle of two sides, and opposing entries in the other two. The drawbridge-protected entry across the now filled moat was not so formidable as that of the English fortress and the towers have also been curtailed by later roofs, but the internal ranges against the outer walls are still complete and inhabited.[59] Chevenon is a five-storey residential tower-house in the form of a gateway, built by Jean III de Chevenon between c.1395 and 1406. It is similar in scale, design, and internal layout to Hylton Castle

(c.1395–1405) with its two central tourelles, end towers, and machicolated parapet. It has similarly lost its enclosure to the rear.[60] Rosières is a rectangular tower-house, three-storeyed with a roof-covered machicolated parapet and corner bartisans, close in form to such northern tower-houses as Chipchase and Belsay (c.1370–80). Corabœuf is a more slender but taller tower-house with ground-floor entrance and bartisans. Built a little before 1450, it is more overtly residential and not unlike Rochford Tower, Boston (c.1445–60).

The uneasy peace between the two countries in the late fourteenth and early fifteenth centuries and Burgundy's stance as an ally after the renewal of war – even if an unreliable one – may have encouraged some travel abroad. But did Sir Edward Dalyngrigge take the opportunity to see Jean de Bazoches' castle at La Motte-Josserand before initiating work at Bodiam? Rosières used to be attributed to the late fourteenth century and therefore the comparison with the Northumbrian tower-houses seemed valid, but it has recently been reattributed to 1470–80 so that the similarity collapses.[61] Corabœuf is typical of many residential tower-houses in both France and England, but again it is not a case of copying. Rather it is the practice of using a common lexicon of architectural concepts, and similar defensive and residential forms. Moreover, the almost perpetual state of hostilities across the body of France, caused as much by internal feuding as by international war, meant that their castles and fortified houses were prefaced and surmounted by a formidable and often awesome defensive display until the close of the fifteenth century.[62] England lacked such features or the need for them (except at Raglan and possibly Hunsdon). Where they otherwise exist as at Caister, Tattershall, and perhaps Pontefract (to judge from the early seventeenth-century painting), they were drawn from the architectural vocabulary of western Europe rather than specifically from France.

THE DEFENCE OF SOUTHERN ENGLAND

There were few periods during the fourteenth century when part of England was not under the threat and sometimes the reality of invasion. The marcher borders suffered uncertainty though not reprisals from Edward I's conquest of Wales and Scotland, whereas northern England experienced the bitter wrath of Scottish raiders throughout much of Edward II's reign, with widespread damage as far south as central Yorkshire and Lancashire. During the early years of Edward III's rule, the south coast began to experience short-lived raids by French privateers, culminating in attacks on Portsmouth and Southampton (1338),[63] Dover, Hastings, Portsmouth, and Plymouth (1339), and Portsmouth again in 1342. They showed up the defensive weakness of the Channel coastline though no practical steps were taken to rectify the situation.

Widespread fear of French invasion in 1359–60 drew attention to the vulnerability of London and the Thames estuary to foreign naval attacks. The crown was persuaded to update and partly rebuild the defences at Hadleigh Castle on the north side of the Thames (c.1360–70)[64] and to construct an entirely new fortress on the south side. Queenborough Castle on the Isle of Sheppey (1361–c.1375) safeguarded the main shipping channel of the Swale and its confluence with the Medway, but more importantly, it commanded the broad approach to the Thames estuary.[65] The inhabitants of some of the towns on the south-east coast also became jittery. A severe French attack on Rye and Winchelsea in March

1360 worried the men of Rye,[66] persuaded Lewes Priory to protect its precinct with crenellated walls (July 1360),[67] and frightened the burghers of Southampton into initiating the sea-facing defences, still unfinished by 1386 when the king's help was sought to complete the project.[68] Whereas Southampton was mainly a trading port, Portsmouth was essentially a naval port used for mustering ships throughout the War. In 1369, the crown reviewed the defences of the harbour's guardian fortress, Portchester Castle, and heightened its walls and towers, with the added floors of Assheton's Tower dominated by early examples of gunports.[69] No private individuals took similar protective measures during this period of impending war clouds.

The thirty ships that landed forces at Portsmouth and burnt the town in 1370 pointed up the inadequacy of English control of the Channel, which was confirmed by the defeat of an English expeditionary force by a Castilian fleet in a fierce battle off La Rochelle two years later. Edward III's claim to be lord of the sea was shown to be illusory, encouraging the French to expand their own fleet rather than rely on a Castilian ally whose support might not always be so readily available.[70] French attacks against vulnerable south-east England became increasingly severe, peaking in 1377 with two waves of enemy forces. The first in June burnt Rye, Hastings, Dartmouth, and Plymouth, trashed the countryside round Lewes, and retreated unhindered across the Channel.[71] The second offensive in August virtually captured the Isle of Wight, besieged Carisbrooke Castle, and extracted a ransom of 1,000 marks from the populace before crossing the Channel to attack Calais. These were little more than pinpricks of war but they panicked the southern counties and initiated a wave of defensive building that embraced royal, civic, and private enterprise working to a common end (1378–c.1392). Rumours throughout 1379 that a French invasion was imminent seemed to be confirmed in the following year when a combined French and Castilian force harried the north Kent coast between Hoo and Gravesend. Fear that the very gates of London would be under siege intensified the urgency of the national building programme.

The king protected the waters of the Solent and the Isle of Wight by rebuilding the keep at Southampton Castle (1378–82), which was understandably ordered to be completed quickly under the king's master-mason, Henry Yevele.[72] The latter was also responsible for heightening the mid-fourteenth-century gatehouse of Carisbrooke Castle with its high-level gunports and machicolated gallery (1380–3).[73] Rochester Castle was strengthened still further by a bastion gateway dominating the strategic bridge across the lower Medway and the main road from Dover to London (1378–83).[74] At the same time, all castellans from Kent to Caernarvonshire were put on alert, and even the defences at Conwy, Beaumaris, and Caernarfon castles were reviewed and some new lookout positions created.[75] Later crown involvement extended to supporting the town defences at Southampton and Canterbury, which had stretched the resources of the local citizens.

With royal encouragement, two or three leading magnates contributed important works in the south-east. Lord Cobham began building a new castle at Cooling on the recently attacked marshland overlooking the narrowing estuary of the Thames (pl. 113), although there is evidence here, as elsewhere, that work was begun at least eighteen months before the licence to crenellate was issued in February 1381.[76] Archbishop Courtenay extended the defences

PLATE 112 Carisbrooke Castle: gatehouse

at his residence at Saltwood with an impressive gatehouse and newly towered outer bailey (c.1382–c.1385). Bishop Wykeham similarly repaired the precinct wall of his episcopal palace of Wolvesey and helped with that enclosing the city.[77]

Private landowners further from the coast similarly sought to protect their properties. As far as we know, their work was not part of any concerted scheme but an individual reaction to anticipated foreign attack. The fortified houses at Scotney (c.1378) and Hever (1383)[78] were essentially new works, whereas the fortifications at Amberley (1377) and Halnaker[79] were additions to earlier domestic residences. The three-storey tower and defended entry added at Wilmington Priory were probably part of this response, as was the gatehouse at Michelham Priory (pl. 110). Some additions were more modest, such as the machicoulis added to the gatehouses at Allington and Leeds castles.[80] The owner of Westenhanger must also have been pleased that the walls and towers begun under licence in 1343 had probably been completed by 1381 when a private vendetta assault on the castle gave a foretaste of more serious problems ahead.[81]

Most of the civic defences in the vulnerable south-east were erected in response to this threat of French invasion. The refortification of Canterbury, initiated by the burgesses in 1378, was supported by archbishop Sudbury who starter-funded the imposing west gate in 1380. Richard II gave further encouragement five years

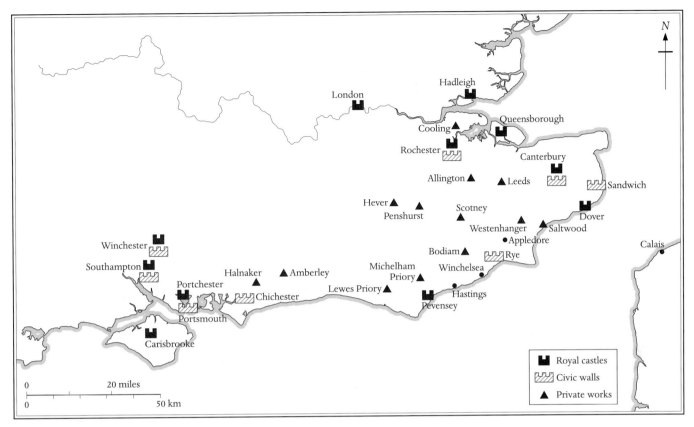

FIGURE 65 Defence in southern England, 1360–1400

later with a grant of £100,[82] with work continuing throughout the 1380s and 1390s when the towers and walls along the banks of the River Stour were erected.[83] New walls were built or existing ones repaired by burgesses at Rochester, Dover, Rye, and Chichester though newly made ditches, earthen banks, and timber palisades were deemed adequate at Portsmouth and Sandwich.[84] As it was held that the south-east was at the greatest risk, comparable work in East Anglia at Harwich, Yarmouth, Norwich, and Kings Lynn was relatively minor.[85] London was reasonably well protected but plans were drawn up by the city in 1390 for building a tower on each side of the Thames below the port of London to protect its shipping.[86]

It is difficult at this distance of time to appreciate the fear that invasion can engender. News, alarm, and hope spread as rapidly as intelligence confirmed or contradicted earlier rumours. Some idea of the same local response to a comparable situation can be seen at Cobb's Hall, Aldington, overlooking Romney Marsh, an early sixteenth-century timber-framed house where the rear face has been completely covered with a massive stone wall with tiny openings for muskets. If this was the local reaction to the Napoleonic scare, how much more frightening must it have been in the late fourteenth century when rumour and counter-rumour were even more rife.

The government's strategic response was to launch a *chevauchée* across northern France led by the earl of Buckingham (1380), take key French coastal fortresses to combat the naval activity, and regain control of the Channel. Leases were negotiated on Brest and Cherbourg but attacks on St Malo, Harfleur, and Nantes were repulsed, while the 'crusade' in Flanders led by the belligerent bishop of Norwich (1383) was a fiasco. A truce followed in 1384, but earlier in that year the French king's uncle, Philip duke of Burgundy, had inherited the county of Flanders he had long coveted, and with the loss of English influence there the French now pressed home their plans to take the war across the Channel. The possibility of an invasion of England by a Franco-Burgundian force which Philip was now urging upon the young Charles VI became frighteningly possible. Rumours of an impending invasion were rife throughout England in 1385, with the south coast particularly vulnerable as Richard II ineffectively led an army to Scotland to root out the French forces there. It was against this background that Sir Edward Dalyngrigge was granted a licence in October 'to construct and make into a castle his manor house at Bodiam near the sea in the county of Sussex for the defence of the adjacent country and resistance to our enemies'.[87] Some expenditure was also incurred in putting Dartmouth, Plymouth, and the royal castles at Trematon and Tintagel in good order as it was feared the French might attempt a secondary landing in the south-west.[88]

Despite marginalisation by some historians,[89] the danger was real enough. Ships, men, materials, and supplies poured into the Zwin estuary in Flanders throughout 1386, giving credence to the likelihood of imminent invasion.[90] Troops were deployed along the south coast, while the possibility of Scottish attacks across the northern border in support of the French warranted enhancing the defences at Tynemouth and Carlisle castles.[91] By August, London and the south-eastern counties were in panic, for it was

PLATE 113 Cooling Castle: inner gatehouse from the south

accurately reported that the armada at Sluys was ready to sail. Yet the French aborted the enterprise in November on financial grounds, and any thoughts of postponing the project for a few months was thoroughly dampened by the incisive naval successes scored in the following year. In March the earl of Arundel captured fifty ships of the combined French and Flemish fleet, and in September the earl of Northumberland's son defeated a French naval attack on Brest.

The widely held desire for peace by both countries led to a three-year truce (1389), subsequently renewed each year as a prelude to a more lasting reconciliation. Though there was an increasing number of voices in favour of peace with France,[92] the invasion scare had fuelled resentment and bitterness against the French so that rebuilding the walls and towers at Canterbury continued, financially supported by archbishop Courtenay and prior Chillenden. The crown now proposed to repair the decayed keep at Canterbury Castle (1390),[93] while Winchester refronted the west gate to include gun ports (c.1392–4)[94] and put the castle in good order (from 1390 to 1403).[95] It is possible that the licence granted to Sir John Devereux in 1392 to enclose his entirely domestic residence at Penshurst was a similar response, but it is more likely to lie in local politics in Kent at this time.[96] The French king's bouts of insanity from 1392 onwards spurred attempts between the two demoralised countries to reach a grudging but mutual reconciliation. The threat of invasion receded as negotiations led to the relatively permanent truce in 1396, confirmed by the marriage of the recently widowed Richard II to the six-year-old daughter of the French king.

These thirty years of crisis witnessed the most important spate of fortress-building activity between Edward I's subjugation of north and central Wales and Henry VIII's defence of the south coast in the late 1530s. The strategy adopted in the later fourteenth century was similar to that of a hundred years earlier in its combination of royal and magnate activity, but the Ricardian work was marked by rigorous financial constraint and severe limitations of manpower resources.

The threat of enemy invasion was met by three differing responses in terms of defensive architecture. Queenborough Castle was the only royal castle built on a fresh site throughout the later middle ages. It was a concentric design of circular rather than the rectangular form adopted by Edward I, with a central towered 'rotunda' protected by a low enclosing wall and moat. It was pulled down shortly after 1650 and is poorly documented, regrettably so in view of its design importance when few military structures were being built in England.[97] Cooling Castle was a hastily built defensive station. It was made up of two rectangular wards within encircling moats, the inner ward a quarter of the size of the outer one. Both were summarily protected by enclosing walls and modest angle towers reminiscent of mid-thirteenth-century work, but the outer ward (as at Saltwood Castle) was capable of accommodating a large number of troops. To ensure that work was completed quickly, at least three contractors were involved, the design was of the simplest, and the outer and inner wards were built virtually independent of each other.[98] In contrast, Bodiam Castle promised serious military defence but was essentially a show castle in a contrived landscape and garden setting. All three castles were entirely new strongholds, unaffected by earlier structures, which certainly existed at Cooling and Bodiam. This period also saw the use of cannons in the field and the earliest exemplars in England of circular and keyhole-shaped gunports.[99] Queenborough was the earliest castle to deploy artillery in this country as well as the more traditional and still effective weapons such as mangonels. The earliest extant gunports are a few years later, spread across royal, civic, and private structures in Hampshire, Sussex, and Kent.[100] Finally, the expansion of the water defences which had been such a prominent feature at Leeds Castle since the thirteenth century were mirrored at Saltwood and to a lesser extent at Scotney and by the wide moats at Cooling, Bodiam, and Westenhanger castles.

Nor were these years without their effect on the form of domestic houses in the south-east, although again there was no common solution. Hever anticipated Bodiam and Westenhanger in adopting the moated rectangular plan, though with miniature corner towers and gateway, while the residential core at Halnaker was protected by a more formidable frontage. The two courts at Scotney were an adoption of the Cooling design to another lowland site but with the now destroyed residential cross range rising above the low angle towers and enclosing walls. The earlier houses at Amberley and Penshurst were now protected by high perimeter walls and towers – circular at Amberley, rectangular at Penshurst.

These castles and defended houses reflect the haphazard and limited financial arrangements imposed by the scarcity of royal funds and the need to rely on private resources. The new castles supplemented the long-established but maintained fortresses at Rochester, Dover, Pevensey, Lewes, Portchester, and Carisbrooke, whereas the fortified houses were an individual reaction to the anticipated invasion. The decision to build a new one, or to extend an earlier house defensively, was particularly likely with war veterans such as Cobham, Dalyngrigge, and Lord St John of Basing (Halnaker) who had experienced the tension, fear, and material destruction of invading forces abroad. Their houses may have been out of the immediate reach of short-lived coastal attacks but they were just as powerful a reaction to the prospect of invasion as the sea-facing fortresses.

The coastal raids on southern England during the early and mid-fifteenth century were a coda to the justified fears of Richard II's time. They were essentially the consequence of piracy rather than

PLATE 114 Halnaker House: gatehouse range

invasion and were aimed towards the developing ports of Portsmouth, Poole, Dartmouth, Plymouth, and Fowey rather than the decaying Cinque ports of Kent and Sussex. Recent research has suggested that Henry IV used privateering as a controlled form of safeguarding the Channel, and not surprisingly there was retaliation.[101] The defences were strengthened at Portsmouth and Poole[102] and further west at Dartmouth, Plymouth, and rather later Fowey, where individuals as much as the towns took the initiative to protect themselves.[103] Private measures even extended to defendable frontages at Compton and Berry Pomeroy castles (c.1450–95) and more modestly at Pengersick (c.1520).

The French successes of the late 1430s initiated the inexorable reversal of English fortune in northern France and the likelihood of French retaliatory expeditions across the Channel. A tower seems to have been added at about this time at Lympne Castle overlooking Romney Marsh,[104] while a two-storey brick gun tower, The Bulwarks, was built in 1451 to defend Sandwich. It was the only town to be raided six years later. Severe fighting led to badly damaged suburbs, but the densely built-up heart of the town was saved. It was only now that the ditches and earthen banks were replaced with walls – the last town defences erected in medieval England.[105]

One consequence of the earlier invasion threat and the reality of coastal raids was that gunports came to be added to the portfolio of military features in a domestic context. The defensive arcade at Southampton and the West Gate at Canterbury show a surprising sophistication in their distribution of gunports to achieve interlocking fields of fire. This was repeated at Raglan Castle in the mid-fifteenth century where their siting at waist level as well as their careful flanking capabilities show they meant business. On the other hand, those at Minster Lovell Hall, Sudeley Castle, and Kirby Muxloe Castle are at odd levels or in newel stairs, either incapable of being operated or, at best, used for firing salutes to impress visitors. At least, their inclusion shows that the owner was up-to-date in his symbolism.

IMPOVERISHMENT AND BANKRUPTCY

It is highly arguable whether the cost of the War to England was offset by the profits that were derived from it, or whether the conflict was a major drain on the country's resources leading to economic stagnation for most of the fifteenth century.[106] The debate continues to be vigorous, but in one respect the weight points in the latter direction.

The War imposed huge financial demands on the English crown, forcing it to raise vast sums to pay for wages, weapons, supplies and provisions, ships to transport troops across the Channel, and allies abroad. Within the first three years of hostilities, Edward III had spent a sum approaching £500,000, had exhausted his credit, and had drained the financial capacity of his subjects. The reorganisation of the country's financial system during the 1340s with its much greater emphasis on indirect taxation, particularly on wool exports, created a more viable and stable financial resource to support the country's long-term military policies. This, together with the spoils of war and English military successes during the later 1350s, encouraged Edward to embark on the most substantial royal work of the later middle ages, the reconstruction of the royal apartments and upper court at Windsor Castle. Edward also undertook several lesser building projects at Westminster Palace, Eltham, Rotherhithe, and Hadleigh, while the Black Prince redeveloped Kennington Palace. But the renewal of war late in Edward's reign and near bankruptcy during the 1380s meant that Richard II had to limit himself to no more than the rebuilding of Westminster Hall and adding new apartments at Portchester Castle at the close of the century (pl. 102).

Henry V initiated the building of a new palace at Sheen in 1414 but it was not completed for twenty-five years. The renewal of war again put an intolerable strain on the crown's financial and military capacity. Financial exigency even forced Henry V to imprison the queen mother for three years (1419–22) so that her vast dower (nearly 10 per cent of the total royal revenues over a thirty-year period) could be put at the disposal of the royal treasury. Henry VI concentrated on his religious and educational foundations at Eton and Cambridge, hindered by the financial crisis and near bankruptcy of the 1440s, while Edward IV wisely husbanded his resources until Louis XI's pension funded the replacement hall at Eltham Palace (1475–c.1480). Royal domestic building after the first phase of the War was modest, and though the works of John of Gaunt were impressive, his precept was not followed to any major extent by later members of the royal family, by the dukes of Gloucester, Clarence, or Bedford, or by the semi-royal houses of Beaufort, March, or York.

The financial difficulties of the French monarchy were as formidable as those of the English crown. France suffered from two periods of overwhelming distress and near bankruptcy. The first was between Crécy and the treaty of Brétigny when the appalling consequences of the Black Death were followed by the capture of the French king and government of an impoverished land by the young dauphin. His difficulties were compounded by the activities of the *grandes compagnies* (mercenary armies), an uprising in Paris, and a series of *jacqueries* (peasant revolts) in the provinces against the nobility (1358). The second and more extended period of financial and political collapse was between 1380 and 1430, when the three fiefs of Anjou, Berri, and Burgundy created by John the Good for his three younger sons virtually became autonomous states functioning almost independently of the monarchy. After Charles VI's madness from 1392 onwards, much of the royal treasury was siphoned into the coffers of the king's three uncles. By 1400, for instance, nearly half of the revenues of Philip, duke of Burgundy, were drawn from the French crown in the form of gifts, pensions, and taxes. Even so, the finances essentially remained within the borders of France if not within crown-held lands.

It is instructive to compare the relative modest scale of the building projects of the English royal house between about 1360 and 1430 with the still extant secular buildings of the French royal family. Charles V (1364–80) was tenacious in reviving the authority of the crown, but while the country was wracked by taxation he enjoyed luxury and majesty just as much as his Valois predecessors. The excavation and display of the medieval Louvre since the mid-1980s has drawn attention to the remodelling of this château into a palace-fortress for Charles between c.1364–71 when his architect, Raymond du Temple, added a further storey to the royal accommodation, machicolated the towers, and erected a magnificent newel stair linking the queen's lodgings with those of the king. The château of Vincennes with its spectacular residential tower-house and courtyard complex, both moat-enclosed, was initiated by John II between 1361 and 1364 but was essentially erected by his son. The tower-house complex completed by 1370 was encircled within a massive towered *enceinte* covering 15 acres to encompass the royal residence, the earlier *manoir*, and several *hôtels* accommodating senior household staff, knights, and favourites, as well as the large chapel initiated in 1379 (though not completed until 1522–9). Charles' combination of the practical and the aesthetic encompassed strengthening the city walls round Paris, constructing the eight-towered Bastille fortress (1370–83), and building the Hôtel St Pol, a town house for himself nearby. At the same time, Charles also gathered artists and scholars round him such as the ballad writer Guillaume de Machault, the laudatory poetess Christine de Pisan, and the painter Girart d'Orléans, and he built up a justly famous library in the Louvre. Paris was transformed, physically and culturally. It again became a leading centre of artistic activity and remained so until Henry V's occupation of Paris and Bedford's regency.

Charles V's relatively brief but highly active reign was followed by the extended anarchy of Charles VI (1380–1422) when his three uncles gave full reign to their ambitions and vanity. The eldest, Louis I, duke of Anjou (d.1384) had already shown the way when he initiated the château at Saumur in 1367 and had completed most of it before his death. Towering over the middle reaches of the River Loire, it was a far larger and more spectacular palace-fortress than Bolton, Sheriff Hutton, Raby, or any other contemporary castle in England. Sixty-nine of the Apocalypse tapestries woven for Louis between 1373 and 1380 to decorate the chapel of his castle at Angers are still displayed in galleries there. They stand as a small survival, comparable to the 180 tapestries acquired by Charles V and the even finer collection of Philip, duke of Burgundy, with their range of subjects that included pastoral scenes, chivalric encounters, hunting occasions, tournaments, and armorial devices.

Charles V's second brother, Jean duc de Berri (d.1416), was a builder *extraordinaire* with his portfolio of two Paris mansions and seventeen castles in the lands of Berri, Poitou, and Auvergne. The most valued were brilliantly and accurately depicted in beguiling landscapes by the Limbourg brothers in *Les Très Riches Heures* (c.1400–15). His great wealth, achieved by crippling his subjects with the highest taxes in France, fed his vicious vanity. Guy de Dammartin remodelled the still-roofed hall of his palace at Poitiers (1384–6), nearly twice as long as Gaunt's hall at Kenilworth Castle,[107] with a magnificent end-wall triple fireplace with balustraded gallery, end spiral stairs, elegant traceried windows, and statues of the king and duke with their wives. He subsequently raised the Maubergeon tower next to the palace, modelled on that at Vincennes (1386–95) though entirely residential, with elegant vaulted apartments and a crown of twenty statues. The duke's smaller country residence at Mehun-sur-Yevre near Bourges (1367–90), well over twice as large as the contemporary castle at

Wardour, is shattered but the two standing towers illustrate the richness and comfort that the duke enjoyed at what Froissart described as 'the most beautiful house in the world'. The remains (like those at Saumur) confirm the aesthetic development initiated by Raymond du Temple that the lower part of a residence should still be forbidding but the roofline could be transformed by machicolations, decorative turrets, gablets, pinnacles, and arcading to create a lacy profile against the sky. As with all his properties, the duke vied with his brothers to employ the finest sculptors, artists, illuminators, and goldsmiths for ostentatious furnishings and decorative objects, though he was always impatient to possess the finished works.[108]

The marriage of the king's third brother, Philip the Bold, duke of Burgundy (d.1404) to the heiress daughter of the count of Flanders created the Flanders–Burgundy axis that dominated French politics and culture for much of the fifteenth century. Little enough building survives of his politico-centric court at Dijon where only a tower, kitchen, and hall block of his palace remain, enveloped in the city's Musée des Beaux-Arts and Estates General building together with a handful of associated treasures (paintings and tombs). In 1383, he founded the Charterhouse of Champmol nearby, summoned the Flemish sculptor Claus Sluter to create the dynastic mausoleum there, and welcomed a stream of other Flemish sculptors, painters, and goldsmiths to his court, a foretaste of similar splendours under his son John the Fearless (d.1419). Immediately after his father's murder, Philip the Good relocated the Burgundian court to Ghent and Brussels, hastening the decline of Paris as the centre of cultural activity for the remainder of the century in favour of the Low Countries.

As soon as Charles VI's younger brother Louis (d.1407) exchanged his *apanage* of Touraine for the duchy of Orléans in 1392, he added to the three existing fortresses that already protected his newly acquired territory[109] by initiating Pierrefonds and La Ferté-Milon (1398–1407), where the highly decorated entrance frontage still stands like magnificent stage scenery. Despite Viollet le Duc's reconstruction of the shattered ruins, Pierrefonds is fundamental to appreciating the development of royal architecture at the opening of the fifteenth century. Developing it round a tower-house of *c.*1393–4, contemporary with that at Warkworth, Louis expanded this *manoir-donjon* into a palace-fortress with eight towers, sumptuous courtyard ranges, a free-standing chapel and massive machicolated enclosing walls (*c.*1397–1407).[110]

A visit to these sites underlines the financial and human resources available to the French royal family. Even at a time of financial distress for the crown, their scale reflects the resilience, comparative prosperity, and retained wealth of northern and central France as well as the priority given to artistic patronage. Bankruptcy is relative, but the number and scale of the building activities of the French royal court during this period simply underlines England's far more modest resources and long-term financial limitations compared with its enemy across the Channel.[111] Far less survives of the associated frenzy of artistic patronage in France, though inventories record the extent of this era of extravagant luxury and priceless treasure, which was barely matched in England. The difference was continued by the house of Anjou under the adventurous Louis II (d.1417) and King René (d.1480) who developed the Bastille-influenced castle at Tarascon in Provence (1400–50),[112] by the artistic plenitude of the house of Burgundy under Philip the Good

(d.1467), and by the revival of the royal court under Louis XI (d.1483) in contrast with the cultural paucity of Henry VI of England and his two Yorkist successors.

As England never experienced the onslaught of foreign armies at any time throughout the War, castles became residential and undefended houses proliferated. In contrast, hardly any unprotected houses have survived the decades of trenchant attacks that afflicted most parts of France. A sure target for plunder and destruction, only properties within walled towns escaped and those built in the almost independent Brittany where the dukes astutely kept all factional forces at bay after 1380. Otherwise, most earlier fortresses were repaired and extended to provide truly formidable protection and defence throughout the extended conflict. Fortified houses and 'strong' houses necessarily became more formidable as the War progressed so that the many hundreds that still stand are the overwhelming visual reminder of the conflict in France. The contrast with the several hundred unprotected houses in England is striking, but Berry Pomeroy Castle withers in comparison with Bonaguil (*c.*1493–1500), Herstmonceux is no match for the brick defences at Rambures (*c.*1420–65), while the mansion by Henry VI's treasurer of the mid-1440s at Sudeley is old-fashioned alongside that of Louis XI's treasurer at Le Plessis-Bourré (1468–73). Lord Cromwell's expansive residence at Wingfield, his tower-house at Tattershall, and Sir William Herbert's redevelopment of Raglan Castle are the equal of their *confrères* overseas. But as an expression of greater and lesser aristocratic pretension and standing during the later stages of the War, English houses rarely compare with the scale and magnitude of contemporary châteaux or other residential forms of lordship, or with their range from decorative seigniorial display to bellicosity.

Despite the havoc wrought across the country and the incredible hardship and losses suffered by the people, France was in a far stronger political condition and poised to become more united as a nation-state by the 1470s than would have been deemed feasible two generations earlier. When the aftermath in both countries is taken into account – the failure of Yorkist rule in England, the royal centralisation in France – then the latter emerged once more as the leading country of western Europe. Exhaustion and destitution throughout the second quarter of the century had virtually stifled all building activity by crown and noble, but peace brought recovery and prestige to both. Beginning in the Loire valley,[113] Louis XI could now adopt a more open style of residence at Langeais (1461–7), followed by his treasurer (Le Plessis-Bourré 1468–73), his chamberlain (Le Plessis-Macé 1470s), his chancellor (Fougères 1475–97), and other court members (Chaumont 1462–81, Meillant 1473–81). This combination of atrophied fortifications protecting comfortable residences rapidly spread across the country, and though there was an occasional austere manor house like Louis XI's favourite, the brick-built Plessis-les-Tours (after 1463), the French *manoir* had also become a viable proposition by the closing years of the century.

NOTES

1 Although authority on the battlefield was vested in the commander's standard, the thinking behind a leader's tactics frequently rested on the experience and advice of his valued captains. As the war progressed the value of military-minded and battle-hardened veterans became increasingly critical, particularly when the ennobled commander was militar-

ily inexperienced or followed ingrained out-of-date practices of warfare.

2 A. Ayton, 'English armies in the fourteenth century', in *Arms, Armies and Fortifications in the Hundred Years War*, ed. A. Curry and M. Hughes (1994) 21–38.

3 S. Walker, *The Lancastrian Affinity: 1361–1399* (1990) 58–80.

4 In 1421 and 1424, cardinal Beaufort insisted that his war loan should be recorded on the roll of Parliament to ensure its repayment by an almost bankrupt Exchequer. The crown jewels he held as collateral in 1424 were only partially returned in phases between 1427 and 1432, with the remainder restored by his executors in 1449. G. L. Harriss, *Cardinal Beaufort* (1988) 126–7, 147–9, 380–1.

5 The duchy of Aquitaine was the vast area between Anjou and the Pyrenees from the Bay of Biscay to the Massif Central that came to Henry II as his wife's dowry in 1152. By the early fourteenth century, the English-held lands had been reduced to the duchy of Gascony, the area between the Garonne river and its tributaries, and Bayonne close to the Pyrenees. This valuable wine-producing region had a political and economic symbiosis with England, which made the French challenge of suzerain in the mid-1330s the immediate cause of the war. The sharp rivalries of powerful pro-English and pro-French families made it a constant battlefield throughout the war, with fluctuating borders, while expulsion of the English from Gascony in 1453 marked the end of the conflict.

6 One supplementary benefit extended to initially reluctant commanders was that they were now in receipt of the king's goodwill at home. The honour and castle at Pontefract was restored to the earl of Lancaster 'having regard to the good service . . . which our cousin has done in Gascony'. The earl of Warwick was appointed sheriff of that county and Leicestershire for life, and the earl of Arundel was similarly granted that of Shropshire. A. Tuck, *Crown and Nobility* (1999) 111. Lower down the social scale, many yeomen who fought under the Black Prince in Aquitaine during 1355–7 received grants or land or offices at home. H. J. Hewitt, *The Organisation of War under Edward III, 1338–62* (1966) chapter 2.

7 Ayton in *Arms, Armies and Fortifications in the Hundred Years War*, ed. Curry and Hughes 28–30. An analysis of the knights of Gloucestershire has shown that less than half undertook military service overseas, but nine went to Flanders in 1337, eleven knights and squires in 1340 and 1342, and seventeen knights at the great siege of Calais. Eight accompanied Edward III in 1359–60 and six were part of Buckingham's *chevauchée* of 1380–1. Some experienced a single campaign, a greater number gave intermittent service, while a few made repeat visits, with seven present at more than four campaigns, one enjoying eight, and one fourteen. N. Saul, *Knights and Esquires: The Gloucestershire Gentry in the Fourteenth Century* (1981) 30–5, 50–3.

8 A. Curry in *Arms, Armies and Fortifications in the Hundred Years War*, ed. Curry and Hughes 45–7.

9 *Scalacronica*, ed. H. Maxwell (1907) 131, 134.

10 Though the succession dispute and therefore the war in Brittany was settled by agreement with France in 1365, many Englishmen, including Knollys, stayed on in the duchy. War in Brittany flared up again in 1372–5 and again later.

11 Saul, *Knights and Esquires* 57–8.

12 M. Jones in *England in the Fourteenth Century*, ed. W. M. Ormrod (1986) 109–17. Also R. C. Dudding, *History of the Manor and Parish of Saleby* (1922) 147–58.

13 Curry in *Arms, Armies and Fortifications in the Hundred Years War*, ed. Curry and Hughes 65–7, 196.

14 M. Keen in *England and Her Neighbours, 1066–1453*, ed. M. Jones and M. Vale (1989) 299–303.

15 M. M. Postan, *Essays on Medieval Agriculture and General Problems of the Medieval Economy* (1973) 63–5, gives an estimation of 10–15 per cent but Anne Curry tells me that her calculations indicate a considerably lower figure.

16 D. Hay, 'The divisions of the spoils of war in fourteenth century England', *Trans. Roy. Hist. Soc.* 4 (1954) 91–109.

17 K. B. McFarlane, *Past and Present* 22 (1962) 3–13; M. M. Postan, *Past and Present* 27 (1964) 34–53 and his *Essays on Medieval Agriculture* 63–80; J. Bridbury in *Trade, Government and Economy in Pre-industrial England*, ed. D. C. Coleman and A. H. John (1976) 80–95; A. Tuck, *Crown and Nobility 1272–1461* (1998) 106–29. The jury is still out on the assessment of the evidence.

18 K. B. McFarlane, *England in the Fifteenth Century* (1981) 178. In this and the previous chapter in the volume, McFarlane showed how war was seen as a business with profit as a prime motivation for service abroad by esquires as well as by leading knights, *ibid.* 151–97.

19 C. T. Allmand, *Lancastrian Normandy 1415–1450* (1983) 50–80.

20 G. L. Harriss, *Cardinal Beaufort* (1988) 392–5, 402–6. Keen in *England and Her Neighbours 1066–1453*, ed. Jones and Vale 303–6. A. J. Pollard points out that even Talbot, with all his captaincies and offices, did little more than break even, after meeting his household, estate, and garrison expenses. *John Talbot and the War in France* (1983) 120.

21 Tuck, *Crown and Nobility* 299.

22 W. M. Ormrod, *The Reign of Edward III* (1990); N. Saul, *Richard II* (1997) and several authors in *The Regal Image of Richard II and the Wilton Diptych*, ed. D. Gordon, L. Monnas, and C. Elam (1998).

23 C. T. Allmand, *Henry V* (1992) 419–25.

24 B. Kemp in *Arms, Armies and Fortifications in the Hundred Years War*, ed. Curry and Hughes (1994) 195–6, 210–11, notes that only four or five knights had any military achievements inscribed on their tombs throughout the length of the war.

25 D. A. L. Morgan, 'The political after-life of Edward III: the apotheosis of a warmonger', *Eng. Hist. Rev.* 112 (1997) 856–81.

26 Historical writings were markedly stimulated during the course of the Anglo-French struggle, as the chronicles of Froissart and Jean de Venette and the memoirs of Philippe de Commynes testify. But enthusiasm for the war became far more didactic under the self-confident Tudors, honouring the great heroes of English chivalry culminating in the anonymous drama *Edward III* and the historical plays of Shakespeare. In houses, it is reflected in the Jacobean statues at Doddington Old Hall of knights who had fought at Poitiers. A. Emery, *Greater Med. Houses*, II (2000) 531. See also P. Morgan, *War and Society in Medieval Cheshire* (1987) 3–8.

27 Ampthill, Farleigh Hungerford, Sudeley.

28 *Chronicon Henrici Knighton*, ed. J. R. Lumby, II (1895) 118.

29 R. Morris in *England in the Fourteenth Century*, ed. Ormrod 172. C. Given-Wilson and F. Bériac, 'Edward III's prisoners of war: the battle of Poitiers and its context', *Eng. Hist. Rev.* 116 (2001) 802–33.

30 *Itinerary*, IV, 133.

31 P. Lindley in *The Black Death in England*, ed. M. Ormrod and P. Lindley (1996) 136–44.

32 *Itinerary*, I, 75.

33 In Leland's view, no house in the north was so much like the palace of a prince as Sheriff Hutton Castle, *ibid.* I, 65. Recent research is suggesting that much of this castle may have been built by Lord Neville's son, the earl of Westmorland (d.1425), who spent most of his career between 1389 and 1424 on the Scottish border.

34 But the evidence for Nunney Castle (*c.*1373) is cautionary, see note 56.

35 *Itinerary*, I, 102–7. Leland was sceptical of the claim of French spoils, preferring his marriage to the wealthy widow.

36 *Itinerary*, II, 137–9. M. A. Hicks, 'Counting the cost of war', *Southern History* (1986) 13–14, concurs. There is no proof that Hungerford captured the duke at Agincourt.

37 McFarlane, *England in the Fifteenth Century* 175–97.

38 109 tons of freestone, 900 pounds of lead, and a considerable amount

of plaster of Paris. Fastolf's career and success is claimed to have been exceptional, but it was not *that* exceptional during the period. It is simply the best documented.

39 *Itinerary*, II, 11–19.

40 *Ibid*. II, 72.

41 *Ibid*. II, 56.

42 *Ibid*. V, 223. Leland's source was Lord Stourton, with whom he may have stayed.

43 The earliest study on the subject, *Medieval Military Architecture of England* (1884) by the engineer G. T. Clark, got it right. His text and descriptions cease with the reign of Edward I, with his account of Bodiam Castle as a footnote. The problem developed under his successors who extended the subject to include all late medieval properties ascribed 'castle' and then to denigrate their lack of military competence. So Ashby de la Zouch Castle and Broughton Castle were included, whereas Haddon Hall and Ightham Mote were not. The fact that Broughton was only elevated to castledom by a pretentious owner in the late Victorian period was overlooked. The problem was still a fundamental one with D. J. Cathcart King, *Castellarium Anglicanum*, 2 vols. (1983). The tide began to turn with Michael Thompson's prescient text, unhappily titled *The Decline of the Castle* (1987), and has been rigorously accelerated by Charles Coulson, 'Cultural realities and reappraisals in English castle study', *Jour. Med. Hist.* 22 (1996) 171–207; in *Fourteenth Century England*, ed. N. Saul (2000) 133–51 and *Castles in Medieval Society* (forthcoming).

44 Their military character, by a magnate and knight respectively, was circumscribed by very specific circumstances, as were minor contenders such as Bodiam, Hunsdon, and Berry Pomeroy Castle. For details, see individual text entries.

45 C. Coulson in *Fourteenth Century England*, ed. Saul 142–7.

46 *Itinerary*, II, 75. His source was the current head of the Hakluyt family. Also A. Emery, *Greater Med. Houses*, II (2000) 532–3.

47 R. Hardy in *Arms, Armies and Fortifications in the Hundred Years War*, ed. Curry and Hughes (1994) 162–4, quoting *Register of the Black Prince*, III (1933) 264–5.

48 *Historia Anglicana*, ed. H. T. Riley, I (1863) 272.

49 See note 47.

50 *Testamenta Eboracensia*, ed. J. Raine (1836) 243.

51 Magdalen College, Oxford: Fastolf Papers 43.

52 J. Fletcher, *Trans. Newbury Dist. Field Club* 12, no.1 (1970) 75–85.

53 Even major churches such as Salisbury and Canterbury cathedrals now decorated their choir screens with statues of English kings as well as Old Testament rulers, with the choir screen of York Minster possibly commemorating Henry V's conquest of Normandy. J. H. Harvey in *A History of York Minster*, ed. G. E. Aylmer and R. Cant (1977) 181–6. Also W. M. Ormrod in *Arms, Armies and Fortifications in the Hundred Years War*, ed. Curry and Hughes 96–101.

54 J. Harvey, *Eng. Med. Arch.* (1984) 204, 126.

55 One of the unexpected architectural consequences of the war was the erection of a fully developed Perpendicular abbey church in the middle of Portugal. The victory of Aljubarrota in 1385, when Portuguese forces (with some English support) defeated the Castilian army, led to the marriage of John of Gaunt's daughter to the heir of the Portuguese throne. The abbey founded at Batalha, close to the field of victory, clearly involved English as well as Portuguese architects. With its Founder's Chapel completed in 1435, this abbey church gives a vivid impression of what a totally Perpendicular cathedral in England might have been like had one been erected. The English influence is emphasised by comparing Batalha with the contemporary archaic simplicity of the choir and apse of the convent of Carmo in Lisbon (1389–1423) founded by the Constable of Portugal.

56 S. E. Rigold considered that 'the completely French fashion of Nunney castle is alone sufficient witness that Sir John de la Mare had served in

France' (*Nunney Castle: Handbook* (1957) 4), though there is no record of him having been abroad. For Colin Platt, Sir John 'would have seen castles like Anjony . . . on which to model his own fortalice at Nunney' (*The Castle in Medieval England and Wales* (1982) 121), though Anjony was not built until sixty years later, between 1435 and 1439. Similar overstretched claims are made for the 'pronounced French influence upon the design of Raglan Castle' (J. R. Kenyon, *Raglan Castle: Handbook* (1988) 17) though the unique double drawbridge to the tower-house occurs in contemporary Italian fortresses just as much as those in France.

57 Henry did not see Vincennes before December 1420 at the earliest.

58 Firmly so by A. D. Saunders, *Old Wardour Castle: Handbook* (1968) 12, and more tentatively in the replacement handbook by B. K. Davidson (1999) 24. Also Colin Platt, *The Castle in Medieval England and Wales* (1982) 124–5. Platt is a proponent of the 'Frenchifying' of English castles by returning soldiers but his comparisons between Wardour and the complex tower-houses added to earlier fortresses at Largoet (1374–1414) and at Septmonts (1373–1404) are hardly valid parallels.

59 Posanges follows the same basic plan as La Motte-Josserand but with a reinstated moat, with the corner towers virtually water encircled, and a bolder entry, machicolated to the inner court as well as to the approach. Though Posanges was built nearly fifty years later (1437–53) by Guillaume Du Bois, it helps to make up for some of the losses incurred at La Motte-Josserand since its rehabilitation in 1964–74. J. H. de Vaivre, *Congrès Archéologique de France* (1986) 211–34.

60 J. P. Bardin, *Chevenon* (1987).

61 J. Mesqui, *Châteaux forts et fortifications en France* (1997) 430.

62 Overhanging machicolated parapets are relatively rare in England and are usually limited to gatehouses. Roofed machicolated galleries are virtually unknown this side of the Channel, and there is no record of those high-pitched circular tower roofs sweeping over the galleries that help to make Pierrefonds, Châteaudun, and Culland so belligerant.

63 Major excavations in Southampton between the late 1950s and the 1980s have confirmed the documentary evidence for the destructive character of these raids. Between 40 and 50 per cent of all buildings were destroyed in 1338, followed by the abandonment of many sites for several decades. Overseas merchants took their business elsewhere, creating a prolonged recessionary period which lasted until the close of the century. M. Hughes in *Arms, Armies and Fortifications in the Hundred Years War*, ed. Curry and Hughes 126–31. Also C. Platt, *Medieval Southampton: The Port and Trading Community, AD 1000–1600* (1973) and *The Southampton Terrier of 1454*, ed. L. A. Burgess (1976).

64 *HKW*, II (1963) 662–6 and I (1963) 236–7. Two of the towers and some foundations survive. The opportunity was also taken to make the castle serve as a royal residence but the apartments built for the ageing king have since slipped into the marshes below. P. J. Drewett, *Jour. Brit. Arch. Assoc.* 37 (1975) 90–154.

65 *HKW*, II (1963) 793–804. Work on the 'rotunda' was carried out with speed between 1361 and 1366, with the outer defences essentially completed in the next three years. At the same time, the badly neglected defences at Rochester Castle were put in hand. *Ibid.* 811–12; R. A. Brown, *Rochester Castle: Handbook* (1985) 19, 30–2, 35.

66 It was nine years after the war had re-opened before they obtained a licence to wall the town. *Cal. Pat. Rolls: 1367–70*, 224.

67 *Cal. Pat. Rolls: 1358–61*, 444. The walls have not survived.

68 The novelty of these defences is that they incorporated the outer walls of the merchants' houses next to the quays, subject to the blocking of all pertinent windows and doors. Platt, *Medieval Southampton* 119–32; A. D. Saunders in *The Southampton Terrier of 1454*, ed. Burgess, 22–34.

69 Assheton's Tower was completed by 1385. B. Cunliffe and J. Mumby, *Excavations at Portchester Castle*, IV (1985) 95. The castle had been kept in a state of readiness since the 1320s. *Ibid.* 124–8.

70 The long-term importance of sea engagements such as Sluys (1340) and

Les Espagnols sur Mer (1350) was exaggerated by chroniclers at the time and by historians since. C. F. Richmond in *The Hundred Years War*, ed. K. Flower (1971) 96–121. Even so, the English fleet had dwindled from twenty-seven ships in 1369 to only five in 1378, while the French fleet at Rouen was at the peak of its medieval strength of over forty vessels, with up to eight more from Castile. N. Saul, *Richard II* (1997) 31–2.

71 These attacks were not by large forces but by a number of small galleys, flat-bottomed vessels that swiftly crossed the Channel and landed teams of men capable of inflicting substantial damage and alarm over a period of only a few days. The earls of Arundel and the duke of Lancaster had failed to garrison their castles at Lewes and Pevensey. *VCH, Sussex*, VII (1940) 16; I (1905) 509–11; II (1907) 139–40.

72 *HKW*, II (1963) 842–4; C. Platt and R. Coleman Smith, *Excavations in Medieval Southampton 1953–69* (1975) 178–81; *Excavations at Southampton Castle*, ed. J. Oakley (1986) 114–17. The cylindrical keep on its motte was further protected between 1383 and 1388 by a barbican and enclosing mantlet. The keep was described by Leland as 'both larg, fair, and very stronge, both by worke and the site of it', *Itinerary*, I, 277. It had fallen into disuse by the seventeenth century and was replaced, in turn, by a windmill, a castellated mansion, and in 1967 an ill-designed and over-prominent block of 1960s flats.

73 *Cal. Pat. Rolls: 1377–81*, 486; *HKW*, II (1963) 594–5. It is claimed that the earliest gunports in Britain are the two loops in the north precinct wall of Quarr Abbey, 6 miles from Carisbrooke. D. F. Renn, *Arch. Jour.* 125 (1968) 301–3. They may be associated with the crenellation licence of October 1365 but they offered gesture rather than meaningful protection. They do, however, show an awareness of a very new weapon.

74 *HKW*, II (1963) 813. The lower part remains, pierced by a horrendous arch of 1872.

75 *Ibid.* I (1963) 237; *Cal. Pat. Rolls: 1377–81*, 467.

76 *Cal. Pat. Rolls: 1377–81*, 596. Payment was made in 1379 for building work already completed. For this and other work at Cooling, *Arch. Cant.* 2 (1859) 95–102; 9 (1877) 128–44; 46 (1934) 52–6; and for a building contract of October 1381, D. Knoop, G. P. Jones, and N. B. Lewis, *Transactions of the Quatuor Coronati Lodge* 45.1 (1932) 52.

77 M. Biddle, *Wolvesey: Handbook* (1986) 18–19.

78 Scotney is dated on architectural grounds, Hever by licence, *Cal. Pat. Rolls: 1381–85*, 326.

79 Amberley is dated by licence, *Cal. Pat. Rolls: 1377–81*, 76; Halnaker's attribution is on architectural grounds.

80 The expenditure at Leeds Castle between 1367 and 1373 was primarily residential but the machicolated outer gateway has been attributed to the accounts for the period December 1369 to April 1373. *HKW*, II (1963) 701.

81 *Cal. Pat. Rolls: 1343–45*, 106; D. and B. Martin, *Arch. Cant.* 121 (2001) 203–34.

82 *Cal. Pat. Rolls: 1377–81*, 450 and *1385–89*, 103. As at Southampton, a commission of inquiry had been ordered in 1363 but there is less evidence of immediate action. *Ibid. 1361–64*, 373. For other crown measures taken to help defend the coast, J. R. Alban in *Patronage, the Crown and the Provinces*, ed. R. A. Griffiths (1981) 57–78.

83 *Arch. Jour.* 86 (1929) 275–8. S. S. Frere *et al.*, *Excavations on the Roman and Medieval Defences of Canterbury* (1982) 21–2, 107–11; H. Turner, *Town Defences in England and Wales* (1971) 149–54.

84 Turner, *Town Defences* 154, 155, 158, 164; Hughes in *Arms, Armies and Fortifications in the Hundred Years War*, ed. Curry and Hughes 149–54.

85 Turner, *Town Defences* 126, 129, 141, 195, 198. The most substantial survival is Cow Tower at Norwich, an isolated blockhouse on the bend of the River Wensum outside the city walls. This three-storeyed brick-built tower was constructed in 1385–6 with cross slits intended for gun-loops. A. D. Saunders, *Med. Arch.* 29 (1985) 109–19; B. S. Ayers, R. Smith, and M. Tillyard, *ibid.* 32 (1988) 184–207.

86 J. Harvey, *Eng. Med. Arch.* (1984) 361.

87 *Cal. Pat. Rolls: 1385–89*, 42. Two hundred years later, Sir Moyle Finch still sought a licence to crenellate Eastwell Manor in Kent for fear of Spanish invasion.

88 The stone curtain and an angle tower at Dartmouth Castle date from 1388 when 'a fortalice by the sea' was under construction. A. D. Saunders, *Dartmouth Castle: Handbook* (1986) 14. Also *HKW*, II (1963) 847, 846 and I (1963) 472; R. Higham in *Security and Defence in South-West England before 1800*, ed. R. Higham (1987) 40–9. The modest works at Trematon and Tintagel castles are only recorded because these duchy of Cornwall fortresses had reverted to the crown as there was no prince of Wales.

89 This particularly applies to some of the assessments of Bodiam Castle determined with hindsight.

90 French chroniclers exaggerated when they estimated that 900 ships and 60,000 men were assembled, but the scale of the operation was clearly impressive. N. Saul, *Richard II* (1997) 152–6, 167–9, assesses that 'England stood in graver danger of being overwhelmed than at any time since the beginning of the long struggle with France in the 1330s', *ibid.* 153. Also J. J. N. Palmer, *England, France and Christendom 1377–99* (1972).

91 *HKW*, I (1963) 237. For the residential gatehouses at Tynemouth and Carlisle, A. Emery, *Greater Med. Houses*, I (1996) 141–3, 199–200. Similar work was undertaken at Roxburgh Castle and unspecified work at Berwick.

92 Saul, *Richard II* 205–34.

93 *HKW*, II (1963) 590. This royal castle had been derelict for the previous fifty years but the work proposed was not carried out, probably as a consequence of the improving political situation.

94 B. H. St J. O'Neil, *Proc. Hampshire N. H. and F. Club*, 16 (1944) 56–8; Turner, *Town Defences* 179–80.

95 *Cal. Pat. Rolls: 1377–81*, 111; *HKW*, II (1963) 863–4; Harvey, *Eng. Med. Arch.* (1984) 363–4.

96 *Cal. Pat. Rolls: 1391–96*, 164. B. Webster, 'The community of Kent in the reign of Richard II', *Arch. Cant.* 99 (1984) 217–29.

97 A. Clapham and W. Godfrey, *Some Famous Buildings and Their Story* (1913) 269–75; *HKW*, II (1963) 793–802. A few mounds and the central well survive close to the railway station. Although built in the early fourteenth century with a taller rotunda, Bellver Castle, Majorca, is similar in plan and in its combination of residential and military features.

98 *Arch. Cant.* 9 (1877) 128–44. The similarities between Cooling's inner gateway and Canterbury's west gate lie in John, Lord Cobham's supervisory responsibility for the construction of Canterbury's defences.

99 T. F. Tout, 'Firearms in England in the fourteenth century', *Eng. Hist. Rev.* 26 (1911) 666–702; B. H. St J. O'Neil, *Castles and Cannons* (1960) 1–21; J. Kenyon, *Arch. Jour.* 138 (1981) 205–40; A. D. Saunders, *Fortress Britain* (1989) 1–14. There is no recent study in English on the first century of artillery and gunpowder in Europe from *c.*1325 to 1425 outside P. Contamine, *War in the Middle Ages*, trans. M. C. E. Jones (1984); M. G. A. Vale in *War, Literature and Politics in the Late Middle Ages*, ed. C. T. Allmand (1976) 57–72; and K. de Vries, *Guns and Men in Medieval Europe 1200–1500: Studies in Military History and Technology* (2002). European studies include Luis de Mora-Figueroa, *Glosario de Arquitectura Defensiva Medieval* (1994), and M. Mauro, *Rocche e Bombarde: fra Marche e Romagna nel xv secolo* (1995). The earliest documentary reference to a cannon occurs in a decree of 1326 issued by the Council of Florence at about the same time as the only known fourteenth-century pictorial evidence. This occurs in two manuscripts of 1326–7 prepared for Edward III. The much-reproduced illustration in the volume by Walter de Milemete on the duties of a king (Christ Church, Oxford) is possibly pre-dated by the similar illustration on the duties of a prince (Brit. Lib., London). The earliest

known artillery are two handguns in the National Museum, Stockholm, possibly of fourteenth-century date. R. D. Smith in *Arms, Armies and Fortifications in the Hundred Years War*, ed. Curry and Hughes 153–4.

100 Building evidence supports the documentary evidence that artillery only became important during the last three decades of the fourteenth century, when much larger guns were developed, mounted on wooden beds. However, the gunloops in English castles and town walls during this period were only for hand-held guns. Smith in *Arms, Armies and Fortifications*, ed. Curry and Hughes 155–60. The earliest are simply circular holes, as at Quarr Abbey and Carisbrooke Castle gatehouse, while Cooling uses the keyhole form as well as circular gunports. The development of the keyhole form seems to be a south coast phenomenon from Southampton (1370s) through to Canterbury, Cooling, and Bodiam (1380s). The gunports at Cow Tower, Norwich and in the city walls there of ten years later are quite different. An unexplained factor is how England came to use keyhole gunports a generation earlier than Europe. See also J. Kenyon in *Fort* 1 (1976) 22–5 and 4 (1977) 75–85.

101 C. F. Richmond in *The Hundred Years War*, ed. K. Fowler (1971) 96–121; C. J. Ford, *Trans. Roy. Hist. Soc.* 29 (1978) 63–77.

102 Two towers were built either side of Portsmouth harbour in 1417 and 1420–2. *HKW*, II (1963) 792; *Cal. Pat. Rolls: 1429–36*, 298; Turner, *Town Defences* 198.

103 Individuals helped at Fowey and Dartmouth where a crenellated tower 'for defence against the king's enemies' was built in 1402. A. D. Saunders, *Dartmouth Castle: Handbook* (1986) 14–16 (the present castle dates from 1481–94); *Cal. Pat. Rolls: 1401–05*, 346; Leland, *Itinerary*, I, 203–4. Leland also records that Penrhyn College at the head of the Fal estuary was defensively enclosed and towered, though with no indication of responsibility, *ibid.* I, 197. Of course, some of the raids were from neighbouring rivals.

104 The reaction of Herstmonceux Castle (*c.*1438–49) facing Pevensey Levels was nothing to do with any potential invasion. Nor was this worry relevant to the licence granted to bishop Moleyns of Chichester in 1447 to crenellate all twelve episcopal country houses within his Sussex diocese. Moleyns was keeper of the Privy Seal and a supporter

of the duke of Suffolk. Both were held responsible for the recent failures in France and the collapse of Normandy in 1449–50; both were murdered at the hands of a mob.

105 *Arch. Jour.* 126 (1969) 221; *Arch. Cant.* 100 (1984) 211–13. The lower part of Fishergate overlooking the River Stour and the only surviving gate may have been initiated in 1384.

106 The respective views of McFarlane, *England in the Fifteenth Century* 139–49, and Postan, *Essays in Medieval Agriculture* 49–80, have not yet been resolved by their supporters.

107 Poitiers, 165 feet by 55 feet; Kenilworth, 90 feet by 45 feet.

108 The pay-off to the duke of Clarence's expedition to leave France in 1412 included treasure from the duke's chapel at Bourges, valued at 66,375 écus, as a pledge for the negotiated payment of 150,000 écus within two months (it took thirty years to achieve). The treasure included a great golden cross, a golden crucifix with diamonds and a ruby, and a reliquary of the Cross. J. D. Milner, 'The English enterprise in France 1412–13', in *Trade, Devotion and Governance: Papers in Later Medieval History*, ed. D. J. Clayton, R. G. Davies, and P. McNiven (1998) 80–101.

109 Montépilloy, Crepy, and Vez.

110 J. Harmand, *Pierrefonds, la Forteresse d'Orléans: les réalités* (1983). His bastard son initiated the redevelopment of Châteaudun with its chapel and residential Dunois wing (1451–68).

111 Similarly, the fortifications of English towns were never as massive or as sophisticated as those of northern France. The poor-quality construction of the walls at Southampton has been confirmed by excavation, while the comparatively modest character of the defences at Norwich, Great Yarmouth, Canterbury, and Winchester contrasts with the formidable late medieval circuits at Falaise, Fougères, Caen, and Saint-Malo.

112 In his attempt to create an axis between Anjou, Provence, and Naples where he attempted to become king, Louis sold most of his father's 3,000 luxury objects.

113 By Charles VII's supporters during the closing years of his reign, King René of Anjou at Angers (Châtelet 1453) and John, bastard of Orléans at Châteaudun (1451–68).

12

SOUTH-EAST ENGLAND:

BIBLIOGRAPHY

KENT

W I L L I A M Lambarde, *A Perambulation of Kent* (1576, new edn R. Church, 1970), is the earliest published history of any English county and is still of some value. Two centuries later, Edward Hasted, *A History and Topographical Survey of the County of Kent*, was a four-volume work, issued in 1778–99, and much revised for the second edition in twelve volumes, 1797–1801 (reprinted 1972). It is a mine of information and the bedrock of subsequent Kentish studies. It also stifled subsequent historical research.

The Victoria County History for *Kent* has never progressed beyond three early volumes (1908–32) and no further volumes are planned. A multi-volume history of Kent has been promised by the Kent History Project, established in 1989, but only one title, on the seventeenth century, has yet seen the light of day. In the meantime, F. Jessup, *A History of Kent* (1974) and C. Wright, *Kent Through the Years* (1975), provide brief surveys, while P. Brandon and B. Short, *The South-East from A.D. 1000* (1990), cover London south of the Thames as well as Kent, Surrey, and Sussex. Kent has no record society, adding to the problems awaiting the recorder(s) of its historical development, but the archive repository at Maidstone is a particularly rich one which has published the series *Kentish Sources*. They are subsequent to *Kent Bibliography* by G. Bennett (1977) and its *Supplement* of 1981.

Medieval Kent has been badly served by historians but three Canterbury studies cover a wider scope than their titles suggest: R. A. L. Smith, *Canterbury Cathedral Priory: A Study in Monastic Administration* (1943), F. R. H. Du Boulay, *The Lordship of Canterbury: An Essay on Medieval Society* (1966), and W. Urry, *Canterbury under the Angevin Kings* (1967).

For the buildings of Kent, the outstanding work was prefaced by a minor one. The latter was J. Archibald, *Kentish Architecture as Influenced by Geology* (1934). The primary work is John Newman, *The Buildings of England: North East and East Kent* (1969) and *West Kent and The Weald* (1969). Newman's two volumes in this series are the most satisfactory of all the first editions of Pevsner's county volumes. Newman did his own preparatory research and his descriptions are therefore particularly soundly based. His intimate knowledge of the county meant that he also included more of the lesser buildings than was possible in some of the other volumes. He brought an unprejudiced eye to the material, often suggesting new attributions (Penshurst, Knole) and, more importantly, included many felicitous phrases which are apposite summations.

Kent has been far more fortunate in its coverage of country houses than of its history. Arthur Oswald, *Country Houses of Kent* (1933), offers a broad survey of all major residences. Anthony

Quinney, *Kentish Houses* (1993), provided a far more detailed and thorough analysis covering the whole range of domestic architecture from the twelfth to the close of the twentieth century. Within a year, the RCHM, led by Sarah Pearson and her colleagues, published three linked books on rural medieval houses in almost overwhelming detail, *The Medieval Houses of Kent: An Historical Analysis*, *The House Within: Interpreting Medieval Houses in Kent*, and a *Gazetteer of Medieval Houses in Kent* (1994). R. J. Brown, *Old Houses and Cottages of Kent* (1994), covers the smaller houses of yeomen farmers and traders under the building materials used. K. Gravett, *Timber and Brick Building in Kent* (1971), reproduces the pen and ink drawings of J. Fremlyn Streatfield made during the 1830s and 1840s. R. T. Mason, *Framed Buildings of the Weald* (2nd edn 1969), has been superseded. Castles have not been subject to the same detailed analysis as houses. J. Guy, *Kent Castles* (1980), is an overview but A. Saunders and V. Smith, *Kent Defence Heritage* (2001), cover all military and defensive sites from Roman forts to the late twentieth century. The three volumes include thematic summaries and two gazetteer volumes.

The Kent Archaeological Society was founded in 1857 and published its first volume of transactions *Archaeologia Cantiana* in 1858. Two volumes of useful studies published in recognition of a former editor of the Society (1970–99) are *Collectanea Historica*, ed. A. Detsicas (1981), and the *Memorial Volume* 121 (2001). The *Kent Archaeological Review* is a quarterly journal, published since 1965, to cover current activity in the county. The *Report* of the Royal Archaeological Institute Summer Meeting at Canterbury published in 86 (1929) covers mainly ecclesiastical sites, but more secular and domestic properties were included in the volumes 126 (1969) and 150 *Supplement* (1994).

SURREY

The standard county history is Owen Manning and William Bray, *History of Surrey*, 3 vols. (1804–14) with an illustrated edition in thirty volumes (1847) and a facsimile edition introduced by J. Simmons (1974). It was followed in 1850 by E. W. Brayley, *Topographical History of Surrey* and the four volumes of the Victoria County History, *Surrey*, rapidly completed between 1902 and 1912.

There has been no successor to J. Blair, *Early Medieval Surrey* (1991), covering the history, institutions, and economy of the county up to 1300. Its history uncovered through archaeology is summarised in R. Hunt, *Hidden Depths: An Archaeological Exploration of Surrey's Past* (2002). The *Archaeology of Surrey to 1540*, ed. J. Bird and D. G. Bird (1987), includes a far more valuable and effective chapter on archaeology from 1066 to 1540 by D. J. Turner, covering castles, moated sites, religious sites, housing, towns, and rural settlements. The county council has published several editions of an annotated *Antiquities of Surrey* since 1954. The well-illustrated sixth edition, *List of Antiquities and Conservation Areas . . . in Surrey* was published in 1976.

Ian Nairn was mainly responsible for *The Buildings of England: Surrey* (1962) by Nairn and Pevsner. The Surrey Archaeological Society has published its annual *Collections* since 1858, but Surrey enjoys a number of smaller historical societies that publish bulletins including the Bourne Society of Caterham, Warlingham, Coulsdon, Purley, and Godstone; the Croydon Natural History and Scientific Society; the Egham-by-Runnymede Historical Society; and the Farnham and District Museum Society.

SUSSEX

Unlike Kent, Sussex was late in attracting serious interest in its history. Apart from several town studies (Arundel, Lewes, Hastings), the first large-scale county history was Edmund Cartwright and James Dallaway, *History of the Western Division of Sussex*, 3 vols. (1815–32), a seriously flawed work, followed by the more useful T. W. Horsefield, *History of Sussex* (1835). Where Sussex surpasses Kent is in its illustrative material. Samuel Grimm and the two James Lamberts (uncle and nephew) were employed by Sir William Burrell between 1770 and 1796 to prepare watercolours and drawings of churches, castles, houses, and ruins for Burrell's projected history of Sussex. Nearly 1,200 drawings survive in eight folios in the British Library (catalogued in *Sussex Arch. Coll.* 28 (1878)). Other valuable source material is kept in the two county record offices at Chichester and Lewes, and the reference collection of the Sussex Archaeological Society at Lewes. A selection of these was assembled by W. H. Godfrey and L. F. Salzman, *Sussex Views* (1951), and a more lavish volume was published fifty years later with the inclusion of views from other sources in J. H. Farrant, *Sussex Depicted: Views and Descriptions 1600–1800* (2001). Equally valuable are Sir William Burrell's notes, forty-two volumes deposited in the British Library and a well-used quarry for later historians.

The Victoria County History, *Sussex* is steadily spanning the county. Ten volumes have been published to date, with three more planned on Arundel Rape, leaving only Pevensey Rape to be covered. P. Brandon, *The Sussex Landscape* (1974) in the *Making of the English Landscape* series was the first study of the subject. For general histories, see J. R. Armstrong, *A History of Sussex* (1974) and J. Lowerson, *A Short History of Sussex* (1980). For more academic work, see N. Saul, *Scenes from Provincial Life: Knightly Families in Sussex 1280–1400* (1986), E. Searle, *Lordship and Community: Battle Abbey and Its Banlieu, 1066–1538* (1974), and some of the titles in S. Farrant, *Medieval Sussex: A Bibliography* (1980). A research report, *Archaeology in Sussex to 1500*, edited by P. Drewett (1977), is now out of date, while *An Historical Atlas of Sussex*, edited by K. Leslie and B. Short (1999), is necessarily map-driven. The Sussex Record Society, founded in 1900, has published nearly a hundred volumes to date.

The buildings are covered by I. Nairn and N. Pevsner in *The Buildings of England: Sussex* (1965) with some sharp comments by Nairn. J. Guy, *Castles in Sussex* (1984), gives a broad-based survey. Individual descriptions of the summer meeting centred on Chichester (1935), Brighton (1959), and Chichester again (1985), published in *The Archaeological Journal*, can be more detailed. The Sussex Archaeological Society, founded in 1846, has published its annual *Collections* covering the history and archaeology of East and West Sussex since 1853. It is the only such society to own several historical sites open to the public. *Recologea Papers* has been the journal of the Robertsbridge and District Archaeological Society since 1964, while West Sussex in particular, and southern archaeology in general, are covered by the annual reports *The Archaeology of Chichester and District*. East Sussex has a very active field archaeology unit which has been responsible for recording and analysing over 1,200 historic buildings in the eastern part of the county. Their publications, Historic Buildings in Eastern Sussex, include D. Martin and B. Martin, *Dated Houses in Eastern Sussex: 1400–1750* (1987) and *Domestic Building in the Eastern High Weald: 1300–1750* (1989). Several books have been published on timber-framed buildings, including R. T. Mason, *Framed Buildings of the Weald* (1964), H. M. Lacey and U. E. Lacey, *The Timber-Framed Buildings of Steyning* (1974), and D. Chatwin, *The Development of Timber-Framed Buildings in the Sussex Weald* (i.e. the parish of Rudgwick) (1996). M. Beswick, *Brickmaking in Sussex: A History and Gazetteer* (1993), is more useful than B. Dawson, *Flint Building in West Sussex* (1998).

HAMPSHIRE

Despite several attempts, Hampshire lacked a soundly based county history until the publication of the Victoria County History for *Hampshire and the Isle of Wight* in five volumes from 1903 to 1914. It was among the first of that series to be completed. The Hampshire landscape is briefly covered in an assessment of that title published by the county council in 1993. For the New Forest, see C. R. Tubbs, *The New Forest: History, Ecology and Conservation* (2nd edn 2001). B. Carpenter-Turner's brief study, *History of Hampshire* (1963), *A Survey of Southampton and Its Region*, ed. F. J. Monkhouse (1964) and *The Portsmouth Region* (1989) are still of value. To these should be added P. A. Stamper, 'Medieval Hampshire: studies in landscape history', PhD thesis, University of Southampton (1983), and the more broad-based J. H. Betty, *Wessex from A.D. 1000* (1986) and M. Aston and C. Lewis (eds.), *The Medieval Landscape of Wessex* (1994).

The Hampshire Field Club and Archaeological Society was founded in 1885 and regularly issued an annual *Proceedings* of three parts to a volume until 1996. In that year, the title was changed to *Hampshire Studies* and it has since been published in a single volume per year. In addition to the usual Department of Environment lists, the county council has been producing a parish record since 1972 listing all features of aesthetic, archaeological, historic, scenic, scientific, and traditional interest that contribute to the heritage of the county. The material is synthesised in the volumes *Hampshire Treasurers*, of which twenty-six have been published to date. The county record office has been issuing a series of *Hampshire Papers* since 1990 covering historical and architectural subjects in addition to its long-standing *Record Series*. The *Proceedings* of the Isle of Wight Natural History and Archaeological Society, initiated in 1921, are essentially concerned with the flora, fauna, and geology of the island.

The present state of archaeology is covered by *The Archaeology of Hampshire*, ed. S. J. Shennan and R. T. Schadla-Hall (1981), and *Archaeology in Hampshire: A Framework for the Future*, ed. D. A. Hinton and M. Hughes (1996), particularly pp. 40–54. The county's buildings are well described in *The Buildings of England: Hampshire* by N. Pevsner and D. Lloyd (1967), with a second edition in preparation. They are summarily covered in part I of *Hampshire's Heritage* (1979) and in more detail in the Summer meetings held at Winchester and Southampton, published in the *Archaeological Journal*, 81 (1924) and 123 (1966). Recent titles on the county town, are B. Carpenter-Turner, *History of Winchester* (1992), T. B. James, *Winchester* (1977), A. W. Ball, *Winchester Illustrated* (1999), and the volumes of that long-term project since 1976 *Winchester Studies*, ed. M. Biddle. E. Roberts, *Hampshire Houses 1250–1700: Their Dating and Development* (2003), exhaustively covers the span of timber-framed structures, with occasional reference to high-status stone- and brick-built houses. For the Isle of Wight, H. V. Basford, *The Vectis Report* (1980), provides a well-illustrated survey of the archaeology of the island and its complexity, while C. W. R. Winter, *The Manor Houses of the Isle of Wight* (1984), includes several with early workmanship among the hundred or so of the sixteenth to eighteenth centuries.

13

SOUTH-EAST ENGLAND: SURVEY

AMBERLEY CASTLE, Sussex

The boundaries of the diocese of Chichester have remained virtually unchanged and coterminous with the county of Sussex since the late seventh century, with the majority of the bishop's medieval manors in West Sussex. Amberley was the most favoured residence, with Aldingbourne, Cakeham, and Drungewick next in popularity. Some thirteenth- and early sixteenth-century structures survive at Cakeham and the moated site at Drungewick, but the extensive remains at Amberley encompass at least seven building phases.

1. The castle was held by the bishops of Chichester throughout the middle ages. Part of a late Norman arch with chevron ornament survives at the entrance to the chamber beneath the first hall (present dining room). This mid-twelfth-century feature may or may not be an insertion. No other element within the castle has such clear late Norman character.

2. The south-east corner of the castle is essentially an early-thirteenth-century house. T-shaped, it is made up of a hall with several ancillary rooms at right angles to it along the line of the outer wall. All the principal rooms were at first-floor level. The external evidence for them is a two-light window in the upper end wall, and the two single lights of the large chamber against the outer wall, heavily restored and altered by the duke of Norfolk in 1908. This early thirteenth-century house was built of rubble, whereas ashlar was used for all later work.

3. During the early to mid-fourteenth century, the great hall with end chamber blocks was developed astride the court, touching a corner of the earlier hall. It may have been built by John Langton (1305–37) rather than Robert Stratford (1337–62) in emulation of the new archiepiscopal halls at Charing, Mayfield, and Maidstone.

4. The house was converted into a castle by bishop Rede (1370–85), who erected the gatehouse and curtain walls under a licence to crenellate granted in December 1377.[1] At the same time, he added the lodging ranges and converted the earlier two-storey hall into a single-storey chapel.

5. Bishop Sherburne (1508–36) inserted new windows and fireplaces in the upper residential block, and again divided the early hall at right angles to it into two floors, and added the bay window.

6. The castle had passed from ecclesiastical to secular ownership by the seventeenth century. After it sustained damage in the Civil War, some of the rooms were restored in Charles II's reign, including the main staircase. During the eighteenth and nineteenth centuries, the castle was occupied by several farming households.

PLATE 115 Amberley Castle: aerial view

PLATE 116 Amberley Castle: hall porch and window from the outer court

7. The curtain walls and battlements were restored by the 15th duke of Norfolk in 1908–13, with the present house restored and enlarged by Thomas Emmet in 1927–8. The cottage and adjacent outhouses against the south wall were repaired in 1962. The castle was adapted as a hotel in 1988.

Bishop William Rede, a friend of William Wykeham, a distinguished scholar and book collector, fortified a previously domestic residence. Until then, Amberley was a country house sitting on the end of a low ridge of Upper Greensand next to the parish church and above the flood plain and marshes of the River Arun. It may have been palisaded or hedge enclosed but no earlier defensive structures have been identified. It is possible that Rede initiated the redevelopment of his house a little before receiving crenellation authority[2] but building was still in hand in August 1382.[3] Rede's residence became an elongated rectangle in plan. The curtain walls and gateway are almost complete, but the residential apartments and chambers are either ruined or destroyed. In this respect, the castle is like that at Bodiam. Rede enclosed the site with an almost unbroken perimeter wall lacking the projecting angle towers common at this period. Apart from the slightly projecting gatehouse towers the enceinte is broken only by the garderobe and massive kitchen tower, the latter built on an artificial platform protected by the marshes. The corner towers were within the angles. Internally, the hall with its end chamber blocks effectively divided the castle interior into an outer and inner courtyard – an early version of the increasingly popular double courtyard plan.

GATEHOUSE

The twin-towered entrance is modest. The drum towers project beyond the line of the enceinte, but the gatehouse was integrated with the two-storeyed ranges encircling the greater part of the outer court. A moat, now partly filled, protected the entrance. There is no evidence of a drawbridge, neither rebate nor holes for chains, and there were no machicolations. The passageway is wide and was defended by a portcullis and stout doors. There was a large single chamber above. The porter's lodge was on the left-hand side, with a fireplace and an oubliette discovered in 1985. The lower part of the drum towers enclosed staircases giving access to the first-floor rooms in the flanking wings. Outside the gateway, the entrance frontage was an unbroken face of walling, punctured by an

occasional slit, but the present windows and doorways are post-medieval[4] (pl. 111).

OUTER COURT

The three sides of the outer court were enclosed by two-storeyed ranges against the outer wall, with three-storeyed towers in the angles. The principal rooms were at first-floor level with the windows and fireplaces not repeated in the more modest rooms below. All internal walls have gone, apart from a section adjacent to the porter's lodge lit by single windows with cusped heads, and the north-west angle tower.

The two north-facing towers consisted of a large room on three floors lacking fireplaces and garderobes. The upper rooms were lit by narrow slits in the two outer walls. The internal walls of the south-west tower no longer survive but the abutting ranges prevented any light from penetrating the lower rooms of both west-facing towers.

The west range was divided into at least three rooms (see fireplaces) at first-floor level, with narrow slits in the outer walls. One chamber had a garderobe. The ground-floor rooms were spartan.[5] The two-storeyed pattern continued on the north side. There was a communal garderobe at ground level adjacent to the north-west tower, a bakehouse with an oven, and an upper storey between serving an unknown purpose. It seems that this was an area of offices. The plan of accommodation was then broken by a group of four lodgings, two on each floor, placed in the middle of the range. All inner walling has disappeared so that the means of access to the upper chambers is conjectural, although an outer staircase is most likely. Both ground-floor chambers were furnished with a loophole, fireplace, and garderobe in their outer wall, while the upper rooms had similar features except that the loopholes were replaced by attractive two-light windows with ogee heads, originally glazed, and larger fireplaces. The garderobes, with their paired doors, eyelet loopholes, and seats survive in excellent condition, and there was a small chamber above them, reached from the wall walk with its own fireplace and garderobe. It had squinched sides, most clearly seen from the path below the castle wall.

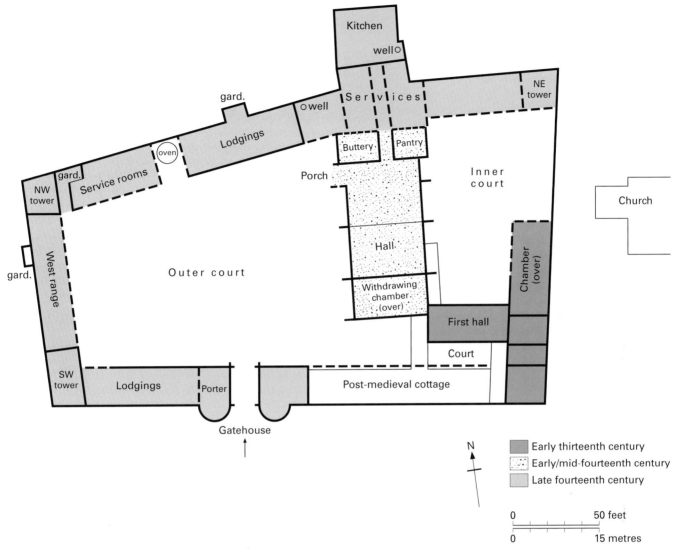

FIGURE 66 Amberley Castle: ground plan

Three standards of accommodation were provided. The simplest were the chambers lacking fireplaces or garderobes, and lit by narrow openings (west range angle towers). The upper rooms of the west range were heated, while the most comfortable rooms were the four lodgings in the middle of the north range. Even here, the differentiation between ground- and first-floor rooms was repeated. It is also possible there was a staff hall or offices near the north-west tower (oven, communal garderobe). The value of Amberley's outer court lies in the social distinction of its accommodation standards, sixty years earlier than the well-known exemplar at Wingfield Manor.

GREAT HALL AND SERVICES

Most of the great hall has disappeared. The attractively moulded entrance arch with its weathered head stops of a king and bishop still stands, formerly porch-protected. The spring of the arch of the opposing cross-passage doorway also survives, as do the three arches to the services, with hacked hood mouldings.

Little remains of the hall, 57 feet by 37½ feet, although its foun-dations remain under the lawn. It was lit by two large windows in each side wall. Their form is unknown (although probably of two lights), but their recesses came down almost to floor level. Half the hall area was roofed in 1927–8 when the present window in the library and the room above was created. It incorporates the head of a medieval arch. The hall was apparently roofed in two and a half bays, the latter lit by a three-light window in the lower gable wall. It seems to have been a simple arch-braced collar-beam structure. An arch in the upper end wall of the hall dais led to the ground floor of the upper residential block.

The buttery, pantry, and kitchen passage with chamber above were an addition. The two shallow buttresses supporting the end wall of the hall, and the offset at its foot, survive inside the offices, suggesting that the earlier structures may have been timber-framed.

The kitchen tower is a substantial projection breaking the line of the north wall. It stands only to ground-floor level. Its unusual position can only be explained by the need to have it totally detached from the remainder of the castle for fear of fire. There is evidence that the kitchen was enlarged, possibly under Rede, while the area between the tower and the offices was divided by framed partition walls into further service areas.

UPPER RESIDENTIAL BLOCK AND INNER COURT

The two-storeyed upper chamber block, 38 feet by 17 feet, has been heavily altered. It originally consisted of a single chamber at ground- and first-floor level but the rooms have been divided (entrance hall and withdrawing room; upper staircase and bedroom). Only the outer walls are original, and a window not dissimilar to those in the north range lodgings. There is also an archway in the bedroom which may have led to a garderobe. The stair is later seventeenth century, possibly replacing an internal one from the parlour for the early approach to the upper floor is no longer clear. An arch (now blocked) at right angles to that from the great hall (visible on the staircase landing) seems to have given access from a straight covered staircase against the outer wall leading to a gallery in the thirteenth-century hall.

The early hall block was converted by bishop Rede into a single-storey chapel. The floor was removed and a large window, not dissimilar in size to those in the great hall, was inserted into the south wall (now blocked). The piscina for this chapel also survives. Bishop Sherburne, the last bishop to reside at Amberley, divided the hall again in the early sixteenth century and decorated the upper room with panels, now in Chichester Museum.[6]

The north side of the inner court continued the standards of the outer court. The north-east angle tower, lacking its inner walls like that in the diagonally opposite corner of the castle, was again three-storeyed, similarly lacking fireplaces and garderobes, with only one window in the outer wall. The east curtain, without windows and free of buildings at this point, allowed the rooms to be windowed in the destroyed courtyard-facing wall.

There seems to have been a single-storey range between this tower and the kitchen services. Unlike most inner courts, it seems to have been a continuation of the bishop's staff accommodation.

REVIEW

The first impression of Amberley Castle is that it is a major defence rather than an ecclesiastical residence. The fact that it was built on the cliff-like edge of a ridge end adds considerably to the height of the walls on the north and west sides overlooking the protective marshland. These two sides of the castle were remarkably secure. On the south side, the gatehouse guards a gap in the South Downs, while the whole was secured by a moat. The lack of windows in the outer walls adds to its defensive capacity.

But the defences were limited. The marked absence of projecting towers at the corners or midway along the curtain (except for the kitchen tower) was a major weakness. The enfilade was hardly protected, flanking fire was barely possible, while the different levels show that the moat next to the entrance frontage was a dry one. The lack of serious defences in the gateway such as machicolations or drawbridge, the obvious weakness of the east side next to the churchyard, and the ease with which the castle was commanded from the church tower show that Amberley was not built as a major fortification. It was doubtless developed in response to possible French attacks during the early years of Richard II's reign, particularly as it overlooked the upper navigable section of the River Arun. But it is 8 miles from the coast and the area was protected to some extent by Arundel Castle nearby. The defences at Amberley are not as strong as they seem at first sight, but once within his castle, the bishop was well

protected from the outer world. It was certainly capable of keeping marauders at bay, but the opportunity to expand his residence may not have been unwelcome. Rede was a learned bishop whose work encompassed residential comfort as much as superficial defence.

NOTES

1 *Cal. Pat. Rolls: 1377–81*, 76. A second licence was granted to bishop Moleyns in October 1447 as part of a multiple application covering all his episcopal manors, but there is no structural evidence from that time of any building activity at Amberley.
2 Peckham did not support this view when it was put forward, based on internal evidence by P. M. Johnston, *Sussex Arch. Coll.* (1921) 29, although the lower end of the hall and the adjacent buttery and pantry is work of two periods (see text). The outer and inner entrance arches of the gateways are four-centred – more likely to be of the fourth rather than the third quarter of the century. The windows of the upper lodgings are also early Perpendicular style.
3 Date of bishop Rede's will, Lambeth MSS Reg. Courtenay f.212. No episcopal registers survive prior to 1397.
4 Much of the curtain wall from the gatehouse towards the church had been badly damaged and was rebuilt in the early twentieth century.
5 During the early sixteenth century, bishop Sherborne remodelled the garderobe (see outer face), the large first-floor opening leading to it, and the similar ground-floor doorway breaking the defensive enceinte.
6 Arscott (2003) 51–5.

W. D. Peckham, *Sussex Arch. Coll.* 62 (1921) 21–63
D. Arscott, *Amberley Castle* (2003)

ARUNDEL CASTLE, Sussex and the FitzAlan family

Arundel Castle, the home of the FitzAlan family from 1232 to 1580 when it passed by marriage to the present Howard family, was one of the primary residences of late medieval England. The domestic ranges were more extensive than those at Warwick Castle, whereas its powerful defences do not seem to have been extended after the late thirteenth century. Yet little of this is apparent today through the ruination of both wards during the Civil War siege of December 1643 to January 1644 and its slighting in 1654. The residential ranges lining the three sides of the south ward remained roofless for over seventy years until the south-facing family apartments were rehabilitated by the 8th duke of Norfolk (d.1732).[1] The Tudor-modified east range of household lodgings was remodelled as the entry hall, but the medieval great hall and offices on the west side of the ward were left as a shell. In 1749, Horace Walpole described the fortress as 'only a heap of ruins, with a new indifferent apartment clapt up for the Norfolks when they reside there for a week or a fortnight'. Shortly after his succession in 1777, the 10th duke decided to restore Arundel as the principal family seat, although his early death in 1786 meant that it was left to his son to carry out his intentions. With a few exceptions at the lower levels, the 11th duke swept away the medieval and Tudor residential structures and replaced them between 1787 and 1812 with ranges to his own design on three sides of the lower court following the line of the earlier work.[2] Within fifty years, the 14th duke had initiated a rebuilding programme to designs by M. E. Hadfield, but his early death in 1860 precluded much activity. It is one of the mysteries of ducal intelligence why virtually all previous work was totally remodelled or replaced by Charles Buckler for the 15th duke of Norfolk between 1875 and 1903 with the present sterile buildings

PLATE 117 Arundel Castle: from the south

of misdirected energy and overwrought expenditure.[3] The crafts-manship is superb but the overwhelming effect is one of stony omnipresence.

Similar in age and shape to Windsor Castle, with the central motte flanked by walled baileys, the constricted quarters within the shell keep were superseded by a range of apartments lining the south side of the castle on the edge of a spur overhanging the for-merly tidal River Arun. They were built by Henry II during his short tenure of the castle between 1178 and 1189 and have contin-ued to be the residential nucleus of the castle to the present day. Elements of these late twelfth-century buildings have been pre-served under the three post-medieval rebuildings. The vaulted undercroft, 45 feet by 25 feet, is spanned by four irregularly posi-tioned semi-circular ribs dying into the side walls. The room is at a lower level than the plain broad Norman doorway with two splayed contemporary windows nearby. This wall was formerly external to the courtyard but has been corridor-protected since the eighteenth century. The great hall lay above (now nineteenth-century drawing room) with truncated pilaster buttresses and two fine twin-light windows under semi-circular heads, visible in the outer wall. There is no structural evidence to support the view that Henry II's chapel (more probably his withdrawing chamber) has been incorporated in the early eighteenth-century chapel (now dining room) next to it.

During the third quarter of the fourteenth century, the prodig-iously wealthy Richard, 3rd earl of Arundel (d.1376) undertook a major rebuilding campaign round three sides of the south ward that converted the castle into a palace-fortress. The late Norman hall was replaced by an entirely new one on the west side of the ward, badly damaged during the siege of 1644–5 from guns on the parish church tower. Evidence for its form comes from three sources – pic-torial, documentary, and comparative. Wenceslaus Hollar's engrav-ing prepared in 1643 shows the high-roofed hall immediately prior to its destruction while its two-storey entry porch survived until 1806 when the 11th duke built his barons' hall. The entry and much

of the hall courtyard wall is depicted a little before this event in the important elongated grey and brown wash drawing detailing the buildings round three sides of the south ward towards the close of the eighteenth century.[4] Dallaway's plan of 1789 suggests that the porch had been retained to give access to the coach house, stables, and yard developed on the site within the remains of the hall.[5] Tierney's engraving of its entrance with several lines of deep mould-ing indicates a mid to later fourteenth-century date,[6] making it the work of Richard FitzAlan, 3rd earl (d.1376). Horsfield, quoting Cartwright,[7] states that the roof resembled those of Westminster Hall and Eltham Palace, which suggests it may have been of hammer-beam form. Hollar also shows that the hall roof was steeply pitched, with a large window in the south gable and a crowning central louvre. The apartment rose high above the castle walls with all adjacent structures at a lower level.[8] The kitchen and offices lay north of the hall towards the earlier gatehouse.[9] During the first years of the nineteenth century, a Norman-Gothic barons' hall of octagonal shape was erected, followed by a chapel, both replaced by the present grandiloquent structures between 1860 and 1894.

In making Arundel the centre of his estates, the 3rd earl remodelled Henry II's south-facing apartments. The end of the Norman undercroft is now closed by an eighteenth-century brick partition wall, partially covering one of the Norman windows inter-nally and supporting the division between the two rooms above. It separates the Norman structure from a later extension. Approxi-mately 24 feet square, it is barrel vaulted in stone without ribs, lit by a single square-headed loop high in the east wall. The vault dif-ference and single loop point to the fourteenth or fifteenth centu-ries, with a preference towards the earlier period. It is the primary surviving evidence of Richard FitzAlan's domestic augmentations, for apart from adding this new east chamber (now duke's study), he divided the adjacent Norman hall into apartments. A stair was inserted in the south-east corner between the added room and undercroft filling a corner of the latter, possibly in Tudor times, but now blocked and featureless.

301

Hollar's engraving of 1643 of the castle and town from the south-west shows that the embattled frontage was recessed between slight projections at each end, the south-west with a higher turret and the south-east with a steeply gabled roof. Buck's engraving of 1737 shows that large rectangular windows were inserted in late Tudor times (probably 1570s) but Civil War damage and abandonment meant that rehabilitation was drastic (1708–18). The range was widened with an added red-brick frontage towards the courtyard but the earlier walls and room shapes were deliberately retained internally and still remain today after three Gothic remodellings.[10]

The third phase of Arundel's work was the erection of a new range of household lodgings for his staff along the east side of the ward.[11] Details are scanty for it was remodelled in the earlier six-teenth century when a gallery 120 feet long was created, lit by eight windows overlooking the courtyard. The line of ground-floor lodgings was not altered. Eighteenth-century paintings of the castle show that the range had been developed in stages of varying height, but all earlier work was swept away in the years following 1800 when the present library and ante-library were developed. They were subsequently incorporated in a new east wing of the 1870s, built as a self-contained house by Buckler in his all-embracing thirteenth-century style.

THE FITZALAN FAMILY

The fortunes of the FitzAlan family were founded on the Welsh Marches. It was upon the death without heirs of Hugh d'Albini in 1243 that the castle and honour of Arundel devolved on his nephew, John FitzAlan, whose father had married Hugh's sister. This accident more than doubled the value and extent of the FitzAlan estates and helped to change their owner from a secondary marcher lord to a leading member of the baronage.

It was not until the mid-fourteenth century that the centre of their interests and investments turned from Shropshire to Sussex, possibly as part of the 3rd earl's policy to restore the family fortunes following the attainder of his father (1326). In this, Richard FitzAlan (d.1376) was substantially helped by dynastic mishap, the profits of war, the financial and political benefits of high office, and astute estate management.[12] Richard's territorial wealth benefited in 1347 from the failure of the house of Warenne which brought him the earldom of Surrey and most of his uncle's southern estates which nearly doubled the Arundel patrimony. His career almost coincides with that of Edward III whom he served loyally, either as soldier or as diplomat, at every stage of the war with France including command in Scotland, at the battles of Sluys and Crécy, the capture of Calais and a final appearance on the field in 1372. Not surprisingly, an active career in the king's service abroad as well as his influence at court brought financial rewards. His second marriage was to Eleanor, daughter of the earl of Lancaster, and he proved an extremely capable manager, systematically purchasing economically valuable manors and running them efficiently. Consequently, Arundel became a money-lender on a large scale, assisting the king, the Black Prince, and John of Gaunt, as well as several leading ecclesiastics, members of the baronage, and London merchants. The scale of his lending enabled him to demand and obtain speedy repayment through first claim on the London customs.[13] We have no documentation that clarifies who initiated the redevelopment of the castle, but it was almost certainly begun by the third earl and any work left unfinished at his death was completed by his son. His work converted the castle into

a palace-fortress as much as those held by the Percy and Neville families in the north of England. It also bears close similarities to the almost contemporary work at Windsor, reflecting, as did the original site, its development under Edward III of hall, family apartments, and lodging ranges round three sides of the main ward.

The 3rd earl died in January 1376 possessed of the enormous sum of 90,359 marks (£60,249), nearly half held in gold and silver in a chest 'in the high tower of Arundel' as well as 17,143 marks at St Paul's Cathedral, 19,431 marks in his Welsh marcher castles, and 8,484 marks in his son's hands. A further 8,478 marks in outstanding loans and a valuation of 9,546 marks on the earl's moveable goods brought the total to 153,442 marks (£102,295).[14]

The 4th earl consolidated and extended the family estates. Not only was he the most powerful landowner in Sussex, investing in arable and pasture of high quality, but he was also the leading land-owner in north Shropshire and the nearby marches, and to a lesser extent in Surrey and five other counties. Like his father, he was probably the richest magnate of his day but his dislike of the young Richard II and his policies meant that he extended no loans to the beleaguered monarch.[15] His second marriage in 1390 to an heiress added to his landholding and included a third part of the lordship of Abergavenny. He was one of the principal wool exporters in the south-east, with over 15,000 sheep in Sussex alone – an economic prosperity jeopardised by Richard II's policy towards France and Flanders in the 1380s leading to coastal attacks and the closure of the Flemish wool market.[16] He was a particularly capable financial administrator, was literate, and held several national offices bringing him the profits of court positions, but his tactlessness, aggressive temper, and militant tastes grated on Richard II. Initially loyal to the crown, he became a political opponent and virulent critic of the king, culminating in his treacherous arrest and execution on Tower Hill in 1397 at the age of fifty-one.

Any building work left unfinished at Arundel was completed by the 4th earl, for several of his friends, particularly lords Cobham and Scrope and his supporter in east Sussex, Sir Edward Dalyngrigge, were rebuilding their family homes, as were members of Richard's close-knit family such as his niece, the duchess of Gloucester at Caldicott Castle and his brother, archbishop Arundel at Oriel College, Oxford and Ely Place, Holborn. The genuine piety of the 4th earl was reflected in his rebuilding Arundel church as a major collegiate foundation (1380–97),[17] with the residential buildings ready for occupation in 1381 though the church took rather longer. He also established a hospital for twenty poor men (1395)[18] and made a substantial contribution to his brother's reredos in the lady chapel of Ely Cathedral.[19] Little of this would have been possible without the benefit of his inherited wealth though it had been astutely increased so that he had an annual income of £3,700 by 1397 excluding the substantial sums arising from his wool sales.[20] The 4th earl, like his father, was the medieval equivalent of a multi-millionaire.

The execution of the 4th earl in 1397 resulted in a series of inventories of his goods and estates which, taken with his will of four years earlier, reveal the scope of his possessions and lifestyle.[21] The castle was used by the earl as his treasury but it was also his repository of battle and tournament armour with many pieces from foreign workshops such as *bacinets* or head pieces from Milan with the vizor and collar garnished with silver, smaller head pieces and breast plates from Flanders, and an *aventail* (probably a detachable

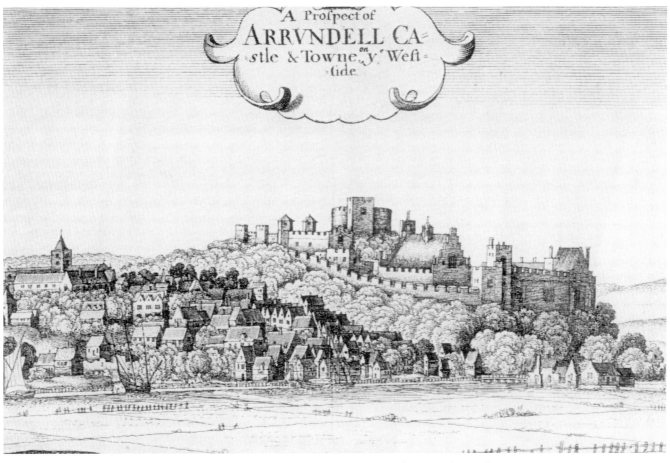

PLATE 118 Arundel Castle: engraving from the south-west by Wenceslaus Hollar (1644)

vizor), from Lombardy and Westphalia.[22] Some of the forfeited furniture taken to Windsor Castle must have come from Arundel, but none of it was so identified although it included nine beds, eight of them with triple sets of curtains, as well as forty-five cushions or pillows, fifty-nine rugs, and three coverlets.[23] The curtains were embroidered with the arms of Arundel, and Warenne with Arundel, as well as with crowned unicorns, wild men, and roses. Other inventories and his will of 1393 are evidence of the luxurious furniture, furnishings, plate, and jewels that were part of Arundel's lifestyle.[24]

Like his grandfather, FitzAlan's son Thomas was anxious to recover his forfeited inheritance. He married the illegitimate daughter of King John of Portugal and played an active part under Henry V in campaigns against the Welsh and French. But he died without heirs in 1415, shortly after the siege of Harfleur. His very considerable inheritance was divided between the family, with the Warenne and Shropshire estates going to Thomas' sisters, while his cousin, Lord Maltravers (d.1421), became the leading Sussex landowner with his estates centred on Arundel Castle. The last FitzAlans were all prominent soldiers and courtiers, but they left little mark on the castle except for modifications under the 12th earl (d.1580) including the erection of an enclosing fourth range of brick against the motte (1540s). However, the principal survival of the later earls is their magnificent tombs from the 5th to the 12th earl (1415 to 1580) filling their collegiate chapel to form one of the glories of late medieval England.

NOTES

1 Tierney (1834) 79.
2 Steer (1976). This record prepared between 1786 and 1801 was discovered in 1975. Also J. M. Robinson, 'Gothic revival at Arundel: 1780–1870', *The Connoisseur* (March 1978) 163–71.
3 For an enthusiastic appraisal, C. Wainwright, 'Arundel Castle from 1850', *The Connoisseur* (March 1978) 172–85. The twelfth-century gateway and keep as well as the late thirteenth-century Bevis Tower, Well Tower, and Barbican were also rehabilitated by the 15th duke. G. T. Clark records that his request in 1870 to examine the earthworks of the upper ward 'was evidently regarded as a sort of treason'. Clark (1884) 200.
4 The drawing is undated but attributable to between 1786 and 1801. It is the frontispiece to Steer (1976).
5 Plan in Dallaway (1832).
6 Tierney (1834) 51–2.
7 Horsfield (1835) 126.
8 The hall was modified in Tudor times when there was refenestration, and a courtyard stack and chimney were inserted, and a cellar under the hall's lower end. A Tudor doorway opens into this chamber 16 feet square, spanned by six depressed semi-circular stone ribs with brick infill.
9 John Goodall has suggested to me that the barbican usually ascribed to *c*.1285 is probably later, possibly by the 3rd earl.
10 J. M. Robinson, *The Connoisseur* (March 1978) 165 and *Arundel Castle* (1994) 8; *Castle Studies Group Bulletin* 19 (2005–6) 10–23..
11 As expected with a lodging range, it has no undercrofts or cellars.
12 For the development of FitzAlan's wealth between 1306 and 1397, C. Given-Wilson, *Eng. Hist. Rev.* 106 (1991) 1–26.

13 *Ibid.* 10–11.

14 M. Clough, *Two Estate Surveys of the FitzAlan Earls of Arundel*, Sussex Rec. Soc. 91 (1969) xxvi; L. F. Salzman, 'The property of the Earl of Arundel, 1397', *Sussex Arch. Coll.* 91 (1953) 33–4.

15 Given-Wilson, *Eng. Hist. Rev.* 106 (1991) 15.

16 A. Goodman, *The Loyal Conspiracy* (1971) 105–14.

17 W. H. St J. Hope, *Archaeologia*, 61 (1908) 61–96. The 3rd earl's unful-filled collegiate endowment of 1375 for six chaplains and three choristers based on the chapel in a castle tower was expanded by the 4th earl into a collegiate foundation outside the castle walls, perhaps prompted by the recent coastal raids which might lead to the foundation's destruction if the castle was besieged, as suggested by Goodman, *The Loyal Conspiracy* 107–8, but more probably as the consequence of the decayed condition of the parochial church which the earl totally rebuilt. John Harvey drew attention to the pattern similarity between the windows of Arundel church and those by William Wynford in the cloisters of New College, Oxford and Winchester College. *Eng. Med. Arch.* (1984) 355.

18 K. J. Evans, *Sussex Arch. Coll.* 107 (1969) 65–78. The building was finished by the close of 1396. Approached by a gateway, it consisted of four ranges round a small quadrangle: the chapel on the north, the refectory and kitchen on the east, and accommodation for the inmates on the south and west sides.

19 M. Aston, *Thomas Arundel* (1967) 277.

20 Goodman, *The Loyal Conspiracy* 114; Given-Wilson, *Eng. Hist. Rev.* 106 (1991) 17.

21 Salzman, *Sussex. Arch. Coll.* 91 (1953) 32–52.

22 *Ibid.* 46–9.

23 *Ibid.* 49–50. In 1397, Stanstead, a medieval hunting lodge of the family close to the Hampshire border contained ten table boards, nine forms, eight pairs of trestles, four cupboards, a chair from Flanders, and four stools, *ibid.* 41. The house was destroyed during the Civil War but it retains two cellars in adjoining ranges of thirteenth-century date, with three bays of quadripartite vaulting carried on two central pillars. The present house on the same site was rebuilt in 1686 and again in 1903. The chapel, a quarter of a mile away, is said to incorporate the ruins of a brick castellated house built by Lord Maltravers, son of William, earl of Arundel in about 1480. It is illustrated in Kip's *Britannia Illustrata* (1708) and by Grimm, Brit. Lib., Add. MS 5675, f.39. In 1818, the two-storeyed porch and turreted front were incorporated in a box-like chapel of Regency character. *VCH, Sussex*, IV (1953) 121.

24 His will of 1393 was drawn up at Castle Phillipp which Anthony Goodman suggests was Shrawardine Castle in Shropshire. Palgrave, *Ancient Kalenders* 3, 303–7, summarised by Salzman, *Sussex Arch. Coll.* 91 (1953) 50–1, shows that Shrawardine was equally richly furnished in 1396.

C. Caraccioli, *The Antiquities of Arundel* (1766)

F. Grose, *The Antiquities of England and Wales*, V (1787), 119–22

C. Wright, *The Antiquities of Arundel* (1818)

J. Dallaway, *History of the Western Division of the County of Sussex*, II pt 1 (1819) 96–115, 187–91

M. A. Tierney, *The History and Antiquities of the Castle and Town of Arundel*, I (1834) 30–100

T. W. Horsfield, *History, Antiquities and Topography of the County of Sussex* (1835) 126

W. S. Elwes, *A History of Castles, Mansions, and Manors of Western Sussex* (1876)

G. T. Clark, *Medieval Military Architecture*, I (1884) 195–203

P. M. Johnson, *Country Life* (December 1914); reprinted in A. Tipping, *English Homes* Pd I, vol. 1 (1921) 21–40

A. Steer, (ed.) *Plans, Elevations . . . of Arundel Castle*: 1786–1801 (1976)

W. Allan, (ed.) Arundel Castle, articles on its owners, contents, Regency and Victorian architecture. *The Connoisseur* (March 1978)

J. Martin Robinson, *Country Life* (January/February 1983)

J. Martin Robinson, *The Dukes of Norfolk* (1983)

J. Martin Robinson, *Arundel Castle* (1994)

BATTEL HALL, Kent

Leeds Castle near Maidstone came into royal possession in 1278 to become a favoured residence of Edward I who developed and strengthened it. The surrounding lake was probably established by him at the same time that the three water-enclosed islands were redeveloped as the barbican, the gated and wall-protected courtyard, and the 'gloriette' with its king's and queen's apartments on two floors round a tiny court. All three parts of the residence retain structural elements from this time which, more interestingly, became a pleasaunce rather than a castle.[1] It was developed as a major country house in 1618–30[2] (pl. 108). Battel Hall, on rising ground half a mile from the castle, was built during the second quarter of the fourteenth century with a richness of decoration that may have been the consequence of its proximity to the royal residence.

Battel is not a large house but it is a particularly rewarding one. It consists of a single-storey hall flanked by two-storeyed chamber blocks under a common roof ridge, with a narrow extension at right angles to the upper block. The hall was divided in the late fifteenth century and the lower block was replaced in the seventeenth century, but because the property was used as a farm until the 1930s, it survived in a relatively unaltered state with detailed restoration in the 1950s.

The two-bay hall retains its essential features of opposing entries at the lower end and two-light transomed windows under square heads in both side walls (replaced on the east or garden side in the late fifteenth century). The tall windows were reconstructed from elements found on the site in the 1950s, and although they included the cinquefoiled cusping under the transoms, no remains were found of the original traceried heads. Nevertheless, it is the quality of the decorative details, and one particular element of its planning, that makes Battel Hall important. This is not apparent externally; indeed both entrance doorways have unbroken mouldings of modest form. Internally, their inner hood mouldings terminate in fine heads and these are repeated on the rear arches of the hall windows and on the spectacular laver close to the west doorway. This domestic piscina consists of an ogee arch on shafts with split cusps and crocketed head rising from a projecting sink and enclosing a cistern in the form of two embattled towers with lion head spouts[3] (pl. 107). This laver may not be in its original position for it is likely to have been in the lower end wall like those at Harewood Castle and Wingfield Manor and relocated when that wall was rebuilt. Nevertheless, it is the most elaborate laver to survive in England. The renewed archbrace and crown-post roof of the hall was spanned by a stone arch which was taken down in the sixteenth century when the apartment was divided longitudinally and partitioned vertically so that only the base of the arch and its supporting crouching corbel figures survive.

The undercroft north of the hall was lit by narrow loops and was formerly barrel vaulted. It was approached from the now destroyed stair projection whose form – newel, straight flights, or in a wing – awaits excavation. However, it is clear there was no direct access from the high end of the hall to the undercroft. The comfortable withdrawing chamber above, 22 feet by 17 feet, retains its impres-

PLATE 119 Battel Hall: from the east

sive hooded fireplace complete with embattled cresting, and evidence of three ornate two-light windows with seats. Yet the hall doorway at the foot of the stair turret has the surprising feature of portcullis defence creating a private and independent two-chamber unit, with the undercroft serving as a subsidiary element to the withdrawing chamber above.

The narrow two-storeyed wing at right angles may have been a garderobe projection, although its size (18 feet by 11 feet) makes its upper-floor use as an inner chamber feasible. The first-floor doorway in the re-entrant angle is probably an insertion, as access at this point would cut across the adjacent window of the great chamber and invalidate its protected character.

The block below the hall, presumably offices with chamber above, has been rebuilt. It may initially have been a timber-framed structure but the stone rebuild now has Gothick windows. The projecting wing, balancing the earlier one opposite, was added in the late fifteenth century.[4] The location of the kitchen is not known although there used to be a water facility on the site of the present forecourt. This factor, a possible garderobe projection nearby, and the addition of a hood moulding above the hall doorway to the garden suggest that Battel Hall was initially approached from the east, the opposite of current practice.

There is no documentary evidence for the construction of this compact stone house, but the detailing suggests a date during the second quarter of the fourteenth century. The decorative work of the laver, for instance, is c.1330 and this accords with the other work at Battel, while the use of stone arches occurs in other substantial

halls nearby, e.g. Mayfield Palace and Ightham Mote, within ten years of this date. The house was not a defensive one but the comparison with the undercrofts and more defensive upper block at Old Soar, Plaxtol, is intriguing. Battel Hall was well windowed and comfortable, and displays considerable decorative work of high quality. Stuart Rigold's consideration that it may have been built by some favoured member of Queen Isabella's household is persuasive.[5] Queen Isabella lived at Leeds Castle after the execution of Edward II in 1327 until her death thirty years later.[6] An association between the two households accords not only with the quality of detailing but with the defensive precaution extended to the residential chambers beyond the hall.

NOTES

1 The late thirteenth-century barbican is protected by a gate-tower with a three-storeyed fortified mill alongside. The gateway of c.1200–50 is prefaced by a gatehouse of 1296–9, machicolated in Richard II's time. The principal courtyard with its lowered wall was defended by D-shaped bastions, with the medieval hall above the thirteenth-century undercroft at the north-west angle. The lower walling of the gloriette of c.1278–90 includes a fine pair of conjoined windows lighting the so-called 'chapel'. The timber-framed inner courtyard wall was rebuilt in stone after an early nineteenth-century fire. Like the early twentieth-century restoration of Berkeley and St Donat's castles, that at Leeds included several internal fittings from French properties.

2 C. Wykeham-Martin, *History and Descent of Leeds Castle* (1869); *HKW*, II (1963) 695–702; *Country Life* (December 1913; November/December 1936; April 1983; May 2003); D. A. H. Cleggett, *History of Leeds Castle*

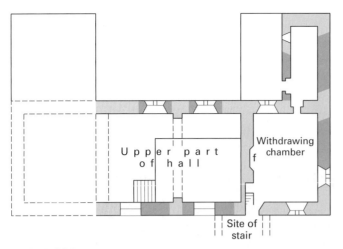

FIRST FLOOR

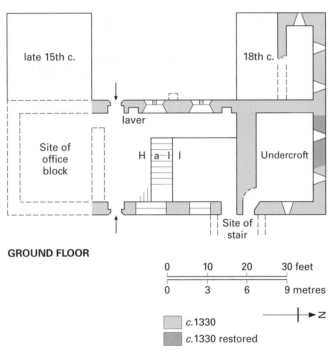

GROUND FLOOR

FIGURE 67 Battel Hall: floor plans

and Its Families (1992), revised 2nd edn Leeds Castle through Nine Centuries (2001).

3 Engraved in J. H. Parker, *Some Account of Domestic Architecture*, II (1953) 46. Also 285–6.
4 Since the 1950s, this block has been used as two sitting rooms with bedrooms above. The hall staircase was inserted at the same time.
5 Rigold (1969) 255.
6 *HKW*, II (1963) 698–9.

S. E. Rigold, *Arch. Jour.* 126 (1969) 255–6
S. Pearson, P. S. Barnwell, and A. T. Adams, *A Gazetteer of Medieval Houses in Kent* (1994) 78–9

BATTLE ABBEY, Sussex

Even before William the Conqueror's death, his endowments to his Benedictine foundation of *c*.1070 at Battle made it the fifteenth most wealthy abbey in England. Sound estate management during the twelfth and thirteenth centuries funded an extensive rebuilding programme during the reigns of Henry III and Edward I affecting church and cloister. Though much of this work has been destroyed, the abbey retains two outstanding structures of secular character – the abbot's house and the gatehouse.

The abbot was one of the great barons of England and the scale of his residence made this abundantly clear. Such a residence was equally necessary for the number of important visitors and benefactors the abbot received, some of them with extensive retinues. Not surprisingly, his accommodation needed little modification to become the centre of Sir Anthony Browne's new mansion in 1538. In richness and complexity, it can be compared with the houses at Castle Acre, Forde, and Cleeve, in this instance with a virtually unaltered sequence of ground-floor vaulted rooms. At the same time, the range shows how the earlier accommodation was adapted to meet the different country-house lifestyles and taste of its occupants and those of a school since the 1920s.

The house consists of a broad ⌐-shaped block of mid-thirteenth century date with the fifteenth-century great hall projecting southwards, and with further post-medieval extensions (mainly 1850s) of country-house function. The west front and hall porch are basically thirteenth century, refaced in the later sixteenth century when the end stair turret was added. The windows and hall entry were remade in 1810.

The broad porch, divided into two bays in 1810, opens to the later fifteenth-century entry and cross passage of a hall, 57 feet by 31 feet. A fire in 1931 gutted this apartment and most of the upper floors of the earlier house. They were reconstructed by Sir Harold Brakspear. The fire revealed that the three-light windows on the west side of the hall had originally been lower but were infilled in the later sixteenth century. As the abbot continued to use his earlier private rooms at the lower end of the hall, the dais wall was enhanced with a five-light window. The form of the roof is not known, for that destroyed in the fire was a hammer-beam structure erected in 1810 by Sir Godfrey Webster. Brakspear restored the window tracery, Tudor fireplace, roof, balcony, and plaster wall lining to their state before the fire. Only the shell of the apartment is original.

Site layout dictated that the door from the hall dais opened not into the abbot's withdrawing chamber as usual but to the kitchen and offices that served his hall. Of late thirteenth-century origin, they lay next to the great kitchen serving the abbey refectory. These last two buildings were destroyed in the seventeenth century, with the abbot's own kitchen converted into rooms with Gothick windows in 1810 and a made-up triangular projection at the angle.

North of the fifteenth-century hall is the thirteenth-century abbot's house with his apartments above the sequence of vaulted apartments, superficially partitioned in the 1810s. The house was approached by a broad porch (originally single storey and now prefaced by school buildings) opening into a dark vaulted room below the abbot's hall (now partitioned). The vault below the great chamber is higher than the others but was decoratively 'enhanced' in the early nineteenth century. These rooms with a high standard of

PLATE 120 Battle Abbey: abbot's hall interior (c.1900)

workmanship were used for guests, staff, and storage. The abbot's own apartments were on the first floor, though they have been much damaged by post-medieval alterations as well as the fire of 1931. The original sequence was the abbot's hall (little remains) and his better-preserved withdrawing chamber and bedchamber (essentially Regency Gothick) backing on to the hall, with a chapel over the porch. This last was only discovered after the fire, when the original windows, altar recess, cupboard, and wall decoration were revealed. In the mid-fourteenth century, abbot Alan of Katling added rooms over the two chambers and another chapel over the porch, but the integrity of this accommodation is badly damaged by school use.

The gatehouse dominates the market place and town of Battle, a symbol of abbatial wealth and influence. Built of Wealden sandstone under a licence to crenellate granted to abbot Alan of Katling in 1338,[1] it adapts the defensive form to a monastic environment. The octagonal angle towers were miniaturised, the moat, portcullis, and drawbridge were dispensed with, and the whole was embellished with filigree decoration. The practical purpose of the turret cross loops is arguable. Three storeys high, the contemporary lower range on the right-hand side incorporated the Norman predecessor, but the more extended two-storeyed range on the left is a mid-sixteenth-century court house above a covered market.

The frontage is composed in four planes separated by string courses, with the lower ones continuing across the contemporary west wing. Above the off-centre entrance of deeply moulded carriage arch and lower pedestrian arch is a band of blind cinquefoil lights with ogee heads carried round the turrets. The third level has two niches with ogee heads for statues and a higher central window with an elaborate blind head. The highest level is topped by a corbel-supported embattled parapet with cusped merlons. The turrets rise to a higher level, with those to the rear holding stairs. The courtyard façade is a mirror image with less-worn detailing. Both entry passages are vaulted in two bays with stone bosses carved with animal and human heads and mythical beasts. The porter's lodge was provided with a fireplace, an entry squint, a garderobe, and a vaulted closet with a wall drain in the front turret.

The stair to the first-floor chamber was portcullis-protected, and

PLATE 121 Battle Abbey: gatehouse from the monastic precinct

with two murder holes in front for missiles in case of attack. The defensive-looking frontage was not entirely for show. The principal chamber was reinstated from school use in 1992 when the fireplace was reconstructed from fragments found in the hearth blocking. The room is generously lit by two-light windows in both outer faces with window seats and well-moulded rear arches. The walls retain original plaster evidence. The second-floor interior is totally modern. The upper room of the west wing, initially a separate lodging with independent stair access, repeats the window and fireplace form less elaborately. The area was possibly partitioned into two rooms with the doorway in the outer one leading to a double garderobe.

Apart from trumpeting the abbey's wealth and standing, the gatehouse was probably used as an estate office with comfortable accommodation for the stewards and senior officials responsible for administering the abbey's extensive holdings which were exempted from episcopal and royal jurisdiction. The porch to the south-east turret was added not long after construction to emphasise the importance of the first-floor chamber.[2]

NOTES
1 *Cal. Pat. Rolls: 1338–40*, 92.
2 For a contemporary secular structure a few miles south, the moated manor at Ewhurst retains its modest early fourteenth-century stone gateway with vaulted passage and room above. The house is a sixteenth-century replacement.

H. Brakspear, *Archaeologia* 83 (1933) 139–66

E. Searle, *Lordship and Community: Battle Abbey and Its Banlieu, 1066–1538* (1974)

J. Coad and A. Boxer, *The Battle of Hastings and the Story of Battle Abbey* (1999)

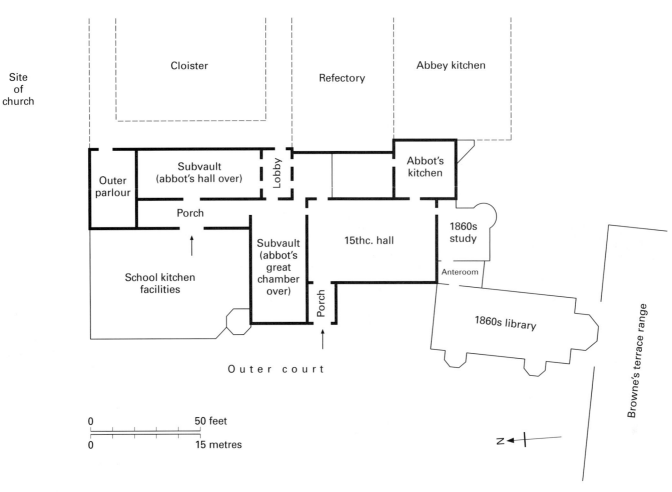

FIGURE 68 Battle Abbey, Abbot's House: site plan

BEAULIEU ABBEY and monastic gatehouses in south-east England

The monastic houses in south-east England show a range of gatehouses from the spectacular to the modest but only four stand out – those at Beaulieu, Battle, Michelham, and St Augustine's, Canterbury, representing the spiritual and the more secular approach to such establishments. The high-quality gatehouse to the Cistercian abbey at Beaulieu befitted King John's foundation of 1204. However, it lost its four-square, free-standing character when it was domesticated by the Wriothesleys in the later sixteenth century and extended early in the eighteenth century into a castle-like house.[1] Its striking character was thoroughly subsumed in its embracement by the large-scale residential development of 1871–4 for the Montagu family. Except for the added attics, all post-medieval work was removed in favour of Sir Reginald Blomfield's heavy-handed conversion to late Victorian domesticity.

Standing closer to the River Beaulieu than the abbey church, the modest thirteenth-century outer gateway gives way to the far more impressive inner or great gatehouse – an example of the early fourteenth-century monastic enthusiasm for a striking approach as at Kirkham, Bury St Edmunds, and Butley Priory. Beaulieu has the unusual plan of a central division at both levels, creating an outer and inner hall at ground level supporting two parallel chapels above.

The outer hall was an open porch with a large central arch with double ogee mouldings and a small doorway for foot passengers to the left. The inner hall is the gateway proper, window-converted by Blomfield who inserted a balancing foot entry to the right. The inner hall had a broad central exit, a smaller side doorway, and evidence of a screened section to the right for a heated porter's lodge.[2] Both halls have unusually rich tierceron star vaults in three bays. Though the columns and capitals are original, Brakspear was not certain that the vaulting was quite of the same period.[3] A slightly later date for this work might account for the massive frontal buttresses.

The upper floor was reached by a turreted newel on the west side, infilled at ground level but still extant above. This floor has the highly unusual arrangement of two parallel chapels with piscinas and aumbreys, separated by open double-ogee arches, though both chapels have been converted into rooms. The south chapel has a Flamboyant east window of three cinquefoil lights and replacement decorated head, and two windows overlooking the abbey approach of two lights with quatrefoil heads (replacing sash windows). The ogee-decorated piscina is original but the thirteenth-century-style west window of three lancets is a Blomfield replacement, apparently

308

PLATE 122 Beaulieu Abbey: gatehouse

based on clear evidence. One of the arches separating the south from the slightly larger north chapel was infilled when the latter was converted into two Victorian rooms and given new ceilings. The three-light east window has a replacement reticulated head in a square frame and a north window by Blomfield.

First-floor gatehouse chapels are unusual (Whalley is a rare exception) and two even more so. The contrast between Beaulieu and the near-contemporary entry to Battle Abbey (q.v.) could not be more marked. Purposefully dominating the town of Battle, its secular character is immediately apparent, a defendable approach, a busy estate office with high-quality accommodation proclaiming a royal foundation of wealth and considerable influence.

Even more secular in character is the defendable gateway to the moat-protected Augustinian priory at Michelham near Hailsham. No records exist for the construction of entry or moat but the two cannot be divorced. The moat was created after the erection of the medieval hall excavated in the southern angle of the enclosure in 1971–5.[4] The hall was probably built in the late thirteenth century, certainly between 1280 and 1350, but the water level of the moat and the floor level of the hall are incompatible. The hall was abandoned for regular residential use, possibly by the late fourteenth century, and put to industrial purposes. The gateway can be attributed on architectural grounds to the late fourteenth or possibly the early fifteenth century. Prior Leem (1373–1417) took out a sizeable mortgage in 1388 which may have been used to fund the construc-

tion of this entry, a smaller version of that at Battle and as much a symbol of prestige as a deterrent to anticipated foreign raiders during these unsettled years (pl. 110). The fourteenth-century moat was either contemporary with the gateway or preceded it by a few years.

The entrance was protected by a drawbridge which filled the rebate above the arch when raised. There was a single entrance opening into the broad hall passage. Any division was simplistic, i.e. wooden partitions, and there was probably none. The two upper floors were put to residential or administrative use. There was a single chamber on each floor with large twin-light windows with embattled transoms and square hoods, a fireplace, and a garderobe leading off the rear spiral stair that served all levels. The gateway's defensive capacity was limited, for though the front and side faces are well windowed the rear is entirely blank!

The only other regionally significant monastic gateway is that to St Augustine's Abbey, Canterbury, where abbot Fyndon (1283–1309) built himself a new house in the west cloister range, added a new outer court to the abbey, and prefaced it with a striking entrance in 1308 under a licence to crenellate. In 1539, the abbot's house was converted into the 'King's New Lodgings' as a stopping point for Henry VIII on his many journeys and it survived until the seventeenth century. The gateway was retained, handsome enough for the king as it had been for abbot Fyndon. It is a display of high-quality decoration between ill-proportioned turrets. The wide double-arched entry extends from turret to turret with the upper part of the frontage elaborately filled with a pattern of gablets between running friezes, a line of cusped triangles, and panelled battlements. The two windows are almost lost in this exuberant display. The passage is two and a half bays deep, vaulted, and with fine unrestored decoration. The Cemetery Gate to the abbey, built in 1391 by the sacrist Thomas Ickham at a cost of £466 13s. 4d., repeats the form of octagonal turrets flanking the entry arch but it is a stripped down version, notable for the defensive looking row of corbelled machicoulis.[5]

NOTES

1 J. Cornforth, *Country Life* (October 1992).
2 Hope and Brakspear (1906) 145.
3 *Ibid.*
4 L. and P. Stevens, *Sussex Arch. Coll.* 129 (1991) 45–79. Also K. J. Barton and E. W. Holden, *Sussex Arch. Coll.* 105 (1967) 1–12.
5 The gatehouses still standing at Hyde (Hampshire), Lewes and Bayham (Sussex), and Dover, West Malling, Minster, and Aylesford (Kent) do not call for special comment.

Beaulieu
W. H. St J. Hope and H. Brakspear, *Arch. Jour.* 63 (1906) 145–7
VCH, *Hampshire*, IV (1911) 652
J. K. Fowler, *A History of Beaulieu Abbey* (1911)
S. F. Hockey, *Beaulieu, King John's Abbey* (1976)

Michelham Priory
G. M. Cooper, *Sussex Arch. Coll.* 6 (1853) 129–63
W. H. Godfrey, *Sussex Arch. Coll.* 67 (1926) 1–24
J. Bellam, *Michelham Priory: Guide Book* (1992 edn)

St Augustine's, Canterbury
R. Gem (ed.), *St Augustine's Abbey, Canterbury* (1997)

BENTWORTH, HALL FARM, Hampshire

Hall Farm, 3 miles north-west of Alton, is typical of many late medieval hall and cross-wing houses in the county, but it is one of the very few that was stone-built and by a lay owner. The framework survives relatively complete to enable its plan and some of its character to be established, but continuous occupation has resulted in drastic changes. Yet at least two features – the porch and the chapel – testify to the standing of such houses. It is a smaller version of Hendred House in Berkshire.

The house was constructed in the early to mid-fourteenth century with a detached chapel close to the upper cross wing. This wing was reconstructed in the late fifteenth century, and the three-bay hall was thoroughly remodelled over a century later with an inserted floor and replacement roof. It is a consequence of the change from farm usage to residential occupation in the late twentieth century that the property has revealed some of its earlier features.

Built of flint with dressed stone, refenestration and rendering disguise the early style and date of the house apart from the porch. This retains its outer and inner arches and a single trefoiled light, characteristic of the first half of the fourteenth century. The much restored outer arch has a two-centred double-chamfered head with stops, while the broader inner arch is more elaborate, with moulded and chamfered orders. It opens into a broad passage with access to the hall on the right blocked by an exposed stone wall – the rear face of a post-medieval inserted stack.

The hall, originally 33 feet by 20 feet and open to the roof, is now two-storeyed with frontal gable, casement windows, and an added outshut at the rear with a cat-slide roof. Internally, hearth and stack, room division, and roof are probably early seventeenth century, though the roof made use of some earlier timbers and retained a tie beam at the west end. The lower half of the stone frame of a tall two-light window with effete mouldings in the north-facing wall hints at this hall's early character.

The two ground-floor rooms of the lower cross wing retain square-headed rectangular lights, one blocked, one partial, while the upper chamber has a two-light window in the south wall, now lacking its head. This wing has been subject to extensive rebuilding.

The upper cross wing, curtailed at the rear, also has several rectangular lights to both floors but interest centres on the upper floor, presumably a single chamber divided into two in the late fifteenth century. The north-facing room retains its fireplace with roll moulding and steeply pitched head, the frames of blocked windows

PLATE 123 Bentworth Hall Farm: from the north

on either side, and the tie-beam, queen-post, and collar roof with wind braces. This room has considerable remains of Elizabethan wall paintings. The second room, lobby-approached, has a door frame with four-centred head, and wind braces to the twentieth-century rebuilt south wall.

The flint-built chapel stands forward of the house and was possibly pentice-linked to it. The chamfered entry arch with depressed head is a late fifteenth-century replacement. The east window is a single trefoiled light with (infilled) quatrefoil and steep two-centred head. A modest window for its position, it has the same character as the porch light. The rebuilt angled west wall and blackened roof timbers are the consequence of extended agricultural use, but the multi-raftered roof supported by two pairs of purlins is original.

The medieval stone houses in Hampshire (compared with framed structures) were usually associated with seigniorial or ecclesiastical occupation. In this case, the Bentworth family seem to have been responsible for its construction. The manor of Bentworth was held by the archbishop of Rouen between the early twelfth and fourteenth centuries, then passed via William Melton, archbishop of York (d.1340) to the Melton family for the next two centuries. Hall Farm, called Hall Place and then Manor Farm in the nineteenth century and Bentworth Hall in the eighteenth century, was a sub-manor held by the Bentworth family by the beginning of the fourteenth century.[1] William Bentworth (d.1317), sometime constable of Farnham Castle, held considerable land in the area, while his wife Maud was permitted to hold services in the oratory of her manor between 1333 and 1345. The property had passed to the Windsor family by the 1370s who held it for the next two centuries and were ennobled in 1529. It is their arms of later sixteenth-century date that survive over the dais. Robert Hunt, whose arms are over the porch entry, was the first of that family to hold the manor of Bentworth Hall, from 1590 until the beginning of the eighteenth century when it began an era of tenant farmer occupation.[2]

NOTES
1 VCH, IV (1911) 69.
2 Bramshott Manor can be added to the very small number of lay stone houses in Hampshire. Its three chamber blocks, partly stone-built, were erected between the fourteenth and early sixteenth centuries.

VCH, *Hampshire*, IV (1911) 68

BETCHWORTH CASTLE, Surrey

The manor of West Betchworth was granted to Richard, 3rd earl of Arundel in 1373 and was held by that family until 1437 when it passed by marriage to Thomas Browne. It was in the possession of the Browne family until 1690.

A licence to crenellate was granted to Sir John Arundel, the earl's younger son, in July 1379,[1] and another licence was granted to Sir Thomas Browne in 1448 in response to his request to enclose with walls of stone and mortar, crenellate and provide with battlements five manors in Kent and Surrey and make them towers and fortresses.[2] Arundel was Marshall of England in 1377 and from April 1378, but he was drowned at sea in December 1379 before he was able to establish Betchworth as his family home. The core of the present unkempt remains, nearer Dorking than Betchworth village and on the edge of a golf course, dates from the fifteenth century. The site, on a knoll sharply dropping to the River Mole, is a modestly defensive one and there was almost certainly earlier occupation, but the standing remains are entirely domestic. They have never been excavated and the stumps of walling are not easy to interpret beneath their cover of trees, suckers, and ivy.

Betchworth was a two-storeyed house above a low basement with contrasting quoins at the angles. Its core are two tall back-to-back chambers at ground level with that overlooking the river dominated by three large windows, now bereft of tracery but with the head

PLATE 124 Betchworth Castle: engraving by S. and N. Buck (1737) before ruination

of one still giving evidence that it was of two cusped lights.[3] Foundations extend either side but Watson's engraving of 1782 from the east indicates that only the buttressed two-bay block to the south was contemporary.[4] The house was extended in the later sixteenth century to create an E-shape with further alterations in 1705 and 1799. The castle is depicted in a distant view of Betchworth House of 1739 by Robert Griffier[5] but the most detailed illustration is that two years earlier by Samuel Buck showing an embattled structure of several blocks with Tudor windows and an early Tudor bay like those at Thornbury Castle. The house was abandoned by the 1830s.

The doorways and first-floor fireplaces with low four-centred heads are indicative of fifteenth-century work and the cusped lights suggest that they may be attributable to Browne. The remains differ from his work at Tonford, Kent (q.v.) and do not coalesce into any immediately identifiable plan, but they could be part of a residential block on one side of a lightly defended enclosure.[6]

NOTES

1 *Cal. Pat. Rolls: 1377–1381*, 380. He is held to have been summoned to parliament in 1377 as Lord Arundel.
2 *Cal. Charter Rolls: 1427–1516*, 102.
3 The standing remains suggest that the origins of the castle may have been a two-storeyed square building of Norman date with accommodation in two ranges, as identified at Bletchingley 8 miles away, Castle Acre, Norfolk, and Walmer, Kent. *Arch. Jour.* 139 (1982) 138–302 and *Med. Arch.* 39 (1995) 174–5.
4 J. Watson, *Memoirs of the Earls of Warren and Surrey*, II (1782) 11.
5 J. Harris, *The Artist and the Country House* (1995) 66.
6 Excavation would clarify, as it has at Guildford Castle, establishing the character of this royal palace between the twelfth and early fourteenth centuries (R. Poulton, *The Royal Castle and Palace, Guildford* (c.1996)), and at the equally significant excavation of the manor of Hextalls at Little Pickle, Bletchingley. This developed from a thirteenth-century timber-framed hall and chamber block for the keeper of the deer park, with a stone replacement chamber of c.1325, to an enlarged hall and cross-wing house with a detached kitchen in c.1425. It was converted to a modest early Tudor house for a leading courtier, Henry Hextall, in c.1490, and demolished in the 1550s. R. Poulton, *The Lost Manor of Hextalls, Little Pickle, Bletchingley* (1998).

O. Manning and W. Bray, *The History and Antiquities of Surrey*, I (1804) 555–60
J. D. Mackenzie, *The Castles of England*, I (1897) 92–3
VCH, *Surrey*, III (1911) 147

BISHOP'S WALTHAM PALACE, Hampshire

The palace of the bishops of Winchester, 9 miles south-east from their *cathedra*, was one of the largest episcopal country houses in England, comparable with that of the bishops of Durham at Bishop Auckland. It was developed by four of its most prominent holders across a time-span of more than three centuries. From its inception, the palace was among the grandest of the richest see in England, and it subsequently encompassed an outer court, an inner court, an extensive garden, a great park to the south, and fishponds to the west. The outer court is now covered by part of the relief road round the town and the associated services.[1] The bishop's garden is still open land, while the ponds survive in shrunken form. The

present approach is from close to the lost outer gate, but instead of crossing the span of the outer court to the gatehouse, visitors use a replacement services bridge over the still partly water-filled moat to enter the inner court at an oblique angle.

As we possess an almost complete sequence of annual accounts for the estates of the bishopric of Winchester from 1208–9 onwards, we have considerable detail on the building work carried out at Bishop's Waltham. The estate of Waltham was acquired by the bishops in 904 and the timber buildings excavated in the outer court may have been part of a late Anglo-Saxon episcopal residence.[2] The present palace was developed in four major phases – in the mid to late twelfth century by Henry of Blois, in the later fourteenth century by William Wykeham, in the early to mid-fifteenth century by Henry Beaufort, and to a lesser extent at the close of the fifteenth century by Thomas Langton. Much of the inner court is grassed over, but nearly all the substantial craggy flint walls facing the visitor round two and a half sides of the court are the consequence of the rebuilding programme of William Wykeham.[3]

Henry of Blois (1129–71), King Stephen's brother, established the shape of the palace, probably after his return from exile in 1158. The hall and service rooms were sited on the west side of the court, corridor-linked to his private apartments at right angles. A detached chapel lay further east. A three-storeyed tower was added at the junction of the hall and apartment range in a second-phase development late in the century, possibly by Richard Ilchester (1174–88), and there was formerly a second tower at the south-east angle of perhaps the same period. At this stage Waltham, like the bishop's palace at Wolvesey, might be considered a fortified house with timber and earth ramparts, a wet moat, and twin corner towers.

Most of this Norman work was incorporated or swept away by Wykeham during his transformation of the palace over a twenty-five-year period, but enough survives to confirm its scale. The lower walling of the hall, services, and kitchen is Norman, though not obviously so, but the mid-level arcading of the hall dais wall is clearly of that time. The link range to the west tower retains a fairly complete first-floor Norman window, and a blocked one in the outer walling of the great chamber in the residential range. The most obvious survival from this period is the excavated walling of the apsidal chapel crypt.

William Wykeham (1367–1404) retained the earlier plan but transformed the palace by rebuilding the two principal ranges on a majestic scale in an up-to-date style. All the important apartments were sited at first-floor level, including the public and service rooms as well as his private suite. They were laid out in a more orderly sequence, but his development was not radical enough to encompass an integrated courtyard plan as at Windsor Castle or some of the northern palace-fortresses. Building was carried out in four phases. It was initiated in 1378–8 with the construction of a new bakehouse and brewhouse on the east side of the inner court to enable the hall and services to be totally redeveloped in 1379–81. The timber services were rebuilt on a larger scale in flint and stone with a chamber above between 1387 and 1393 when the adjacent kitchen was reconstructed and heightened. The third phase followed in 1394–6 when the tower and residential range were remodelled to improve Wykeham's personal accommodation. The bulk of the palace had now been transformed but Wykeham undertook some subsidiary work in 1401–2 including the reconstruction of the gateway to the outer court.

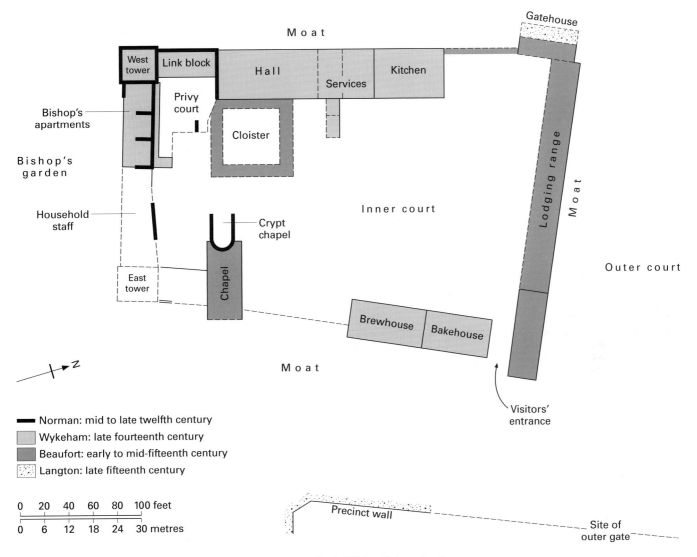

FIGURE 69 Bishop's Waltham Palace: site plan

Wykeham incurred a little over £1,500, not a vast sum considering the scale of his work. It was carried out under the direction of William Wynford, his master-mason, though Henry Yevele, the royal master-mason, was also involved in the rebuilding of the hall (1380–1). Hugh Herland, the master-carpenter, was responsible for some of the roofs as were Robert Brewes and William Ickenham, while Thomas Glasyer undertook the window glass. The triumvirate of Wynford, Herland, and Glasyer were also responsible for Wykeham's collegiate foundations at Winchester and Oxford and the redevelopment of the bishop's house at Highclere (not Herland). Flint was collected from the surrounding area, stone was brought from Beer in Devon and the Isle of Wight, timber was felled in the nearby woods, while the clay roofing tiles were made locally.[4] Some of the flint walls of the prestigious buildings were plaster-covered as was the case with the west tower.

The range of five windows rising to roof level in the outer wall of the hall is one of the most distinctive features of a site that is otherwise a sequence of battered flint walling. Wykeham retained the Norman dais wall but pulled down the remainder of the hall to its lower walling, infilled to a height of 4 to 5 feet, and rebuilt his new hall at the higher level. The flight of steps (probably porch-protected) and courtyard wall of Wykeham's new first-floor apartment were thoroughly robbed by the eighteenth century, as was the lower end wall so that only two sides of the hall survive. The upper two thirds of the outer wall are filled with the deep splays of a line of Perpendicular windows, framed internally by slender columns to depressed four-centre rear arches. The transomed windows were of two cinquefoiled lights, now mainly destroyed except for the tracery ends. There was presumably a similar line of windows in the lost wall opposite. The form of the low-pitched roof is not known for only the slots for its trusses and two carved corbels of 1381 remain. This first-floor hall is one of a number associated with the court during the second half of the fourteenth century, beginning with Edward III at Windsor followed by Gaunt at Kenilworth Castle, Wykeham at Bishop's Waltham, New College, Oxford, and Winchester College, and concluding with Richard II's hall at Portchester Castle.

PLATE 125 Bishop's Waltham Palace: hall interior towards windowed outer wall

While the service rooms stand at their Norman level today, Wykeham retained only the lower courses of the earlier walls to support the infilling that brought their floor level to the common height of the hall and kitchen, the latter fixed by the surviving doorway jamb. There were two service rooms opening from the servery passage between the kitchen and hall.[5] The three areas were separated by timber-framed partition walls, lit by well-moulded trefoiled lights, and with hatches opening from the buttery and pantry into the servery passage. The substantial room above, with the frames of two large windows and the base of a fireplace opposite, must have been an important chamber, but its proximity to the services made it fairly noisy and unsuitable for honoured guests.

The size of the kitchen, 50 feet by 29 feet and rising through two storeys to an open roof, is powerful evidence for the scale of the bishop's household and his entertaining needs. The smaller Norman kitchen had been enlarged in 1252 and it was this modified structure which was the basis for Wykeham's apartment, again rising from an infilled base. On the thicker earlier walls, he raised thinner higher walls with an entirely new one towards the services. The original fenestration was inadequate, for Wykeham replaced it in 1400 with the present windows on three sides of his new upper walling with similar shaped heads to those in the hall. The whole structure was crowned by an elaborate louvred roof by Hugh

Herland, probably of pyramidal form as there is no evidence of gable ends. The essential hearths and ovens are represented by some modest survivals in the west wall, while the head of the internal well is at the Norman floor level, not Wykeham's higher one.

Wykeham added a further floor to the earlier two-storeyed link block between the hall dais and the west tower, and replaced the whole of the inner wall. The ground floor was remodelled as courtyard-approached accommodation with a fireplace in its outer wall and two single lights opposite. The corridor above had always been a feature of the palace but Wykeham widened it into a gallery 13 feet wide. Only two featureless crags remain of Wykeham's heated room above, but it served as an inner chamber to the second floor of the west tower.

The late Norman west tower was raised from three to four floors by Beaufort rather than Wykeham. The ground floor with its central sleeper wall was always windowless and reached only from the floor above. The first-floor chamber with the robbed openings for two early but large round-headed windows marks the separation between the semi-private and private apartments of the bishop. It could have been as much an ante-chamber or lobby to the bishop's apartments as a withdrawing chamber to the hall. The second floor was always a high-quality chamber with a mural garderobe in the south-east angle. Wykeham inserted large windows in the west and

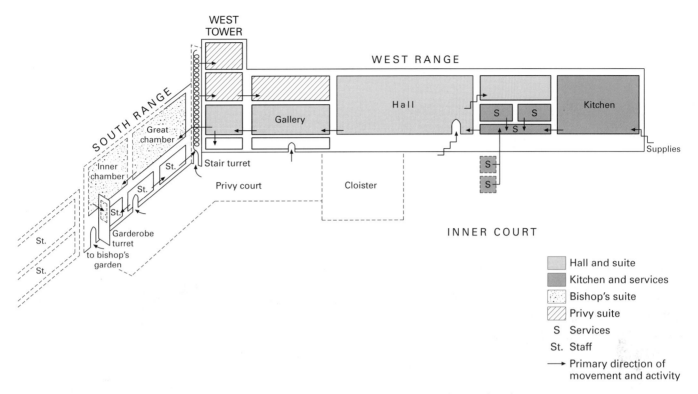

FIGURE 70 Bishop's Waltham Palace: planning and movement diagram of west and south ranges c.1450

south faces (1395), but cardinal Beaufort filled the latter with a fire-place and inserted new windows on each side. This chamber could have been for the bishop's personal use, under Blois as much as Wykeham,[6] though it is just as likely that it served as guest accommodation for many royal and high-status visitors who stayed at the palace, particularly after Wykeham had associated it with his new chamber in the link block to create a two-roomed lodging.[7] This is even more likely after Beaufort added the third storey in 1406.[8] It created a three-roomed unit of considerable privacy, the uppermost chamber flooded with light from five windows and warmed by a broad fireplace – now among the best-preserved features of the palace.

It is unfortunate that the range of private apartments has been so badly mauled. Only one end survives to any extent, for the remainder is the lower walling of three Norman undercrofts. Wykeham remodelled and heightened the outer wall but built an entirely new inner wall 5 feet from the earlier one to create a wider and more imposing sequence of apartments. The parallel footings survive, with Wykeham's terminating in a garderobe pit serving his first-floor chamber. The principal rooms had always been on this upper floor, but after Wykeham's work, it extended for about 70 feet, roofed at a lower pitch than originally (see tower face). His range was approached from a lost doorway in the east wall of the tower, with the spiral stair (base only) serving tower and range for staff use. The range was probably divided into a larger heated outer and smaller inner chamber, lit on both sides by vast windows of which only one jamb survives.

The angle between the link range and the bishop's apartments was always separated from the inner court to improve its privacy, but the scrappy walling is of different periods and this privy court

retains little detailing. Nor has the south-east segment of the site been excavated. The three lines of walling suggest an extension of the bishop's apartment range, terminating in the east tower recorded in documents. The date of these structures, probably for household knights, clerks, and esquires, is not known.

Much of the east side of the court (the cross wall is seventeenth century) is taken up with Wykeham's earliest building, the bake-house and brewhouse. It was apparently a single-storey structure with elongated lights and two-centred doorways until cardinal Beaufort added the upper floor.[9] Though the upper walling is thinner than that below (a Wykeham practice), the 4 feet thick ground-floor walling is more substantial than would be expected for single-storey service rooms, even without the batter usually adopted for storeyed structures. The full-height gable ends betray no obvious building line[10] while the upper windows are similar but smaller than those below. It is possible that Wykeham was responsible for the entire range, for the documents only record Beaufort's responsibility for improving the approach to the upper-floor accommodation by adding the timber gallery, supported on columns and joists set into the outer wall, with the higher row of bricklined holes carrying the roof in extension of that rebuilt in 1439. This upper floor with its single fireplace was dormitory staff accommodation.

The additions made by cardinal Beaufort (1404–47), Henry IV's half-brother, were similarly spread over an extended period. His first project was the addition of the top floor to the west tower in 1406 to improve the quality of the high-status lodging. It was followed by the construction of a new chapel in 1416–17, though this project was held up for ten years until Beaufort was back in favour with the king. The third phase from 1438 to 1442 was the most

315

PLATE 126 Bishop's Waltham Palace: truncated lodging range with bakehouse/brewhouse block to the right

substantive for it encompassed upgrading some of the apartments by panelling the tower rooms and glazing the hall windows, creating a cloister area, building a new gatehouse to the inner court, and constructing the great lodging range that lined its north side. Initially, Beaufort continued to use the same building materials as his predecessors, but his later work made considerable use of timber framing and brick. This last had become a fashionable material in the 1430s and the line of chimney stacks at the rear of the lodging range, decorated in diaper pattern, was undoubtedly intended to be conspicuous. Though some of the relevant accounts are incomplete, Beaufort's early expenditure was at least £300, while his later activity cost over £1,200.[11]

Beaufort's expenditure was similar in cash terms to that of Wykeham, but apart from the added storey to the tower and one end of the lodging range, his activity has been reduced to foundation level. This includes his rectangular chapel next to the Norman chapel crypt, and the cloister in front of the hall, first mentioned in 1441. Nor is the gatehouse evidence much more articulate. It consisted of a central passage with side chambers, but only the end walls stand, with fireplaces and a garderobe pit. The upper floor has been destroyed.

This leaves the lodging range. Only a quarter of it stands at the east end but it does so as a roofed building because it was adapted as a farmhouse in the late seventeenth century. It was initially part of a 243 feet long, two-storeyed timber-framed range on stone foundations, with galleried frontage, and a line of brick chimney stacks at the rear. Conversion of this survival to farmhouse usage resulted in the balcony being replaced by a roofed corridor, and the frontage faced with a mixture of brick and flint.[12]

Both floors consist of three rooms, approached from the courtyard at ground level and by a gallery at the upper. Each room, 22 feet by 17 feet, was lit by a window in each outer wall, and warmed by a fireplace in a projecting stack. The lower rooms were 8½ feet high as against the 12 feet of the upper rooms, but neither enjoyed the garderobe provision found in most lodging ranges.[13] As the ground floor was substantially altered for farmhouse use, the three rooms essentially reflect the features of that time. Only the frame of the courtyard door to the second room remains, minus its head.

Some of the alterations to the upper floor have been removed to show the early character of the three rooms more clearly. The end chamber lacks the majority of its partition wall to the next room in favour of a farmhouse one 4 feet further west. However, the slots in the frame show its position, as does the wattle and daub survival immediately above. The gallery doorway and fireplace are original but the closet to the rear of the stack is a later sixteenth-century addition. The windows are replacements in their original positions. The two-bay roof of braced tie-beam trusses supporting crown posts and collar purlins is little altered. The second room has a fifteenth-century fireplace brought from elsewhere and a late fifteenth-century two-light replacement window. The third room retains its gallery door frame, though the 5 foot wide gallery was replaced in the late seventeenth century by the present attic corridor.

The remainder of this timber-framed range is marked by the flint foundation of its outer wall with its line of chimney stacks overlooking the wet moat. This establishes that the range included eleven self-contained rooms at ground level and eleven at first-floor level, with the higher first-floor rooms used by people of superior social status – household officials or guests, though not of the highest rank in view of the lack of garderobes. The first-floor gallery was linked by a short wooden bridge to that added by Beaufort to the dormitory above the bakehouse and brewhouse. These galleries, like the pentices and alleys across the inner and privy court, have disappeared.

The visible contribution of bishop Langton (1493–1501) is minor, but Leland wrote that 'most part of the 3 partes of the base court was buildid of brike and timbre of late dayes by Bisshop Langton'.[14] Much of this occurred from 1495 onwards, and though the outer court no longer exists, Langton's activity also included facing Beaufort's lodging range with red brick with black diapering, and adding a block in front of Beaufort's gatehouse in 1499. This has been pulled down, though the dated arms that decorated it were discovered during rubble clearance in the 1950s. Langton was also probably responsible for the brick precinct wall and two (originally three) corner turrets enclosing the bishop's garden. The property continued to be an active episcopal residence until the Civil War without further structural developments, but it was used as a building source by bishop Morley to repair Wolvesey Palace in the 1660s and quickly fell into ruin.

NOTES

1 It included a gatehouse, chambers, stables, and several barns, with the last survival, the thirteenth-century great barn, demolished as late as 1967.
2 Lewis (1985).
3 Hare (1988) 222–3, correcting the dating given by S. E. Rigold, *Arch. Jour.* 123 (1967) 217.
4 Hare (1988) 222–46 for the supporting documentation in these two paragraphs.
5 Nothing survives of the pantry and larder on the courtyard side of the passage.
6 Hare (1987) 25; (1988) 233.
7 Royal visitors included Henry II (1182), Richard I (1194), John (1208, 1210), Henry III on several occasions, Henry V (1415), Henry VI (1450), Edward IV (1476), Edward VI (1552) and Mary (1554).
8 In his will of 1447, Beaufort bequeathed Henry VI's wife his 'blue bed of gold and damask at his palace at Waltham in the room where the Queen used to lie when she was at the Palace, and 3 suits of the arras hangings in the same room'.
9 Hare (1987) 29; (1988) 236–7; G. L. Harriss, *Cardinal Beaufort* (1988) 369.
10 That at the north end carries the chimney that served the formerly projecting double ovens of the bakehouse.
11 Hare (1988) 232–3.
12 A detailed illustrated account by R. Warmington is given as an appendix to Hare (1988) 246–51.
13 Slight evidence of chutes to one side of some of the stack plinths might suggest small private latrines (Hare (1988) 247), but surely there would have been some door evidence to such closets in the relatively well-preserved portion that survives. The only clear garderobe evidence is at the end of the range next to the gatehouse.
14 *Itinerary*, I, 285.

E. Lewis, *Proc. Hampshire F. C. and A. Soc.* 41 (1985) 81–126
J. N. Hare, *Bishop's Waltham Palace: Handbook* (1987)
J. N. Hare, *Arch. Jour.* 145 (1988) 222–54

BODIAM CASTLE, Sussex

More books and articles have been written on this castle than on any other in England or Wales. It is much photographed, is extremely popular with visitors, and has recently become the subject of a vigorous debate as to its purpose and function.

Bodiam Castle was built by Sir Edward Dalyngrigge under a licence to crenellate issued on 20 October 1385. It granted him permission thus: 'strengthen with a wall of stone and lime, crenellate, and may construct and make into a castle his manor house of Bodiam, near to the sea, for the defence of the adjacent country and resistance to the king's enemies, and may hold his aforesaid house so strengthened and crenellated and made into a castle for himself and his heirs forever'. The result is a rectangular structure enclosed with high walls, bold round towers at the corners and square mid towers on each side, with one serving as the postern and that opposite doubled to become the imposing gatehouse. Each side of the interior is lined with high-status domestic ranges following the classic medieval plan of hall, offices, and kitchen opposite the entry, with the family apartments on one side, and some large unheated rooms opposite, probably for the household, with storage and lodgings above flanking the entrance. The whole site is moat-surrounded, with an independent barbican protecting the gatehouse.

One of the fascinating aspects of this castle is the way that our interpretation of it has changed over the past 200 years, for this has relevance to the study of many contemporary houses.

- During the eighteenth and nineteenth centuries, the castle was ivy-covered and viewed as a romantic ruin, stimulating thoughts of Arthurian knights, daring deeds, and ladies on caparisoned palfreys.
- The first professional assessment was made in 1884 by an engineer, George T. Clark.[1] His study of castles ceased with those of Edward I but he made one exception for a 'great fortress (that) is wholly original'.[2] A more extreme view of Bodiam's military capability was made by another engineer, Harold Sands in 1903,[3] with A. Hamilton Thompson confirming the castle's military purpose and design a few years later. For him, it 'represented the highest efforts of perfected castle building in England'.[4]
- Lord Curzon bought the castle in 1917, initially planning to make it habitable, but his romantic enthusiasm was curbed and put to better use in consolidating the standing structure and excavating the moat. His work culminated in his lavishly produced book *Bodiam Castle*, published posthumously in 1926, which maintained the view that it was a military stronghold.
- Between 1939 and 1946 W. D. Simpson suggested a variation on

that interpretation based on his view that many late castles demonstrated an owner's reaction to the anarchy of late medieval society as expounded by the Rev. Denton in the late nineteenth century. In his interpretation of 'bastard feudalism', those of high social status had to protect themselves from being attacked by mutinous retainers, and Simpson applied this to the layout of Bodiam with its independently secure gatehouse, isolated quarters for 'hard-boiled mercenaries', and independently controlled lord's accommodation.[5]

• In 1963, Patrick Faulkner published an important paper on household planning in fourteenth-century castles which drew attention to this hitherto neglected aspect of fortress studies.[6] As castles became more ordered and regular in their planning during that century, they had to take into account the growing demand for high-quality residential accommodation. The reconciliation of these conflicting demands of contraction and expansion led to their integration in a single concept as exemplified at Bodiam with its more open and domestic character.

• Thirty years later, Dr Charles Coulson blew the debate wide open in his seminal paper analysing many aspects of the castle.[7] He showed through close argument that there had been a too literal acceptance of the local defence phrase of the licence, that many of the defences were not serviceable militarily, and that the castle was a grand house with the trappings of defence to impress visitors with Dalyngrigge's past career and standing in the region. Almost at the same time, Paul Everson demonstrated that the landscape surrounding the castle was an elaborate and contrived water and garden setting for the building.[8] Coulson was able to incorporate these findings in his own paper and thereby strengthen his arguments.

• The castle became pivotal in a scholarly debate about whether the castle was essentially a fortress with residential provision, built to defend the country from French attack, or whether it was primarily a residence in a fortified style.[9] The wider ramifications of this extend to the interpretation of the many castles built in England and Wales after the group of fortresses erected by Edward I to consolidate his conquest of north and central Wales.[10]

• Attention has recently been drawn to learning more about Dalyngrigge's upwardly mobile career.[11] A participant in the war in France between 1359 and 1387 and prosperously married, he became active in local politics from the mid-1370s but was bested in his quarrel with John of Gaunt's agents in Sussex during the early 1380s. The castle may have been Dalyngrigge's belligerent response to his wounded ego.[12]

• The benefit of these and other allied studies is that the shackle of military historians on the interpretation of castles in this country since the late nineteenth century has been broken. This particularly applies to castles of the later middle ages, hitherto dismissed as illustrating an era of 'decline', vainly trying to maintain the old traditions of the feudal stronghold.[13]

• However, a sense of proportion needs to be maintained. This is particularly necessary in the case of Bodiam between the extremes of fortress *aficionados* and those who consider it 'an old soldier's dream house'.[14] This castle looks formidable but has serious military vulnerability. It was a house of swagger, with the architectural trappings of defence set in a deliberately conceived

PLATE 127 Bodiam Castle: from the north-east

landscape. Yet it is also markedly impressive, irrespective of its owner's intent or mindset. It was expensive to build and speedily completed. It is a sophisticated and complex residence which was the culmination of several strands in Dalyngrigge's career, though it probably failed to be crowned by ennoblement through his relatively early death in 1393.

• The strength and range of the debate warrants caution. It is all too easy to jettison all earlier assessments in favour of the new orthodoxy. There is evidence that this is occurring in the aftermath of the Bodiam discussion,[15] of an uncommon intensity which 'promises to revolutionise our understanding of castles'.[16] Late medieval residences that claim that appellation were markedly individual, reflecting their owner's personal requirements, so that each structure needs to be considered independently and in the light of its owner's identity rather than shoe-horned into the prevailing view of martial development or seigneurial symbolism.

NOTES

1 *Medieval Military Architecture*, I (1884) 239–47.
2 Even so, he pointed out the ease with which the moat could be drained by any attacking force and had a sceptical view of some of the building's defensive capabilities.
3 *Sussex Arch. Coll.* 46 (1903) 114–33.
4 *Military Architecture in England during the Middle Ages* (1912) 322–7, 360.
5 His views were not mentioned in his useful paper on the castle, *Sussex Arch. Coll.* 72 (1931) 66–99, but were developed in *Jour. Brit. Arch. Assoc.* 5 (1939) 39–54 and *Antiq. Jour.* 26 (1946) 145–71. Bastard feudalism was a term of abuse coined by Rev. Plummer in 1885 and developed by Rev. Denton, *England in the Fifteenth Century* (1888). The subject was totally reassessed by K. B. McFarlane during the 1940s and published in his collected papers *Nobility of Later Medieval England* (1973) and *England in the Fifteenth Century* (1981). Simpson's application of Victorian sentiment to castle studies promptly collapsed.
6 *Arch. Jour.* 120 (1963) 215–35.
7 In *The Ideals and Practice of Medieval Knighthood*, ed. C. Harper-Bill and R. Harvey (1992) 57–107.

8 *Château Gaillard* 17 (1996) 79–83. Also C. Whittack, *Sussex Arch. Coll.* 131 (1993) 119–23.

9 A foretaste of Coulson's views in *Jour. Brit. Arch. Assoc.* 132 (1979) 73–90 had prompted a riposte from D. J. Turner as to whether Bodiam was an old soldier's dream house or a true castle as he believed. *England in the Fourteenth Century*, ed. W. M. Ormrod (1986) 267–77.

10 M. Johnson, *Behind the Castle Gate* (2002) with Bodiam discussed at 19–33; M. Morris, *Castle* (2003) 142–82. J. Goodall's views on Bodiam are summarised in *Country Life*, 16 April 1998 and the guidebook *Bodiam Castle* (2001) pending his forthcoming book on castles.

11 N. Saul, 'The rise of the Dallingridge family', *Sussex Arch. Coll.* 136 (1998) 123–32; *The History of Parliament: 1386–1421*, ed. J. Roskell *et al.* (1992).

12 S. Walker, 'Lancaster v. Dallingridge: a franchisal dispute in fourteenth century Sussex', *Sussex Arch. Coll.* 121 (1983) 87–94; Morris, *Castle* 150–66.

13 The title of M. W. Thompson's book, *The Decline of the Castle* (1987); H. Braun, *The English Castle* (1936) 108.

14 Christopher Holler's telling phrase in *The Flowering of the Middle Ages*, ed. J. Evans (1966) 114.

15 M. Johnson, *Behind the Castle Gate: From Medieval to Renaissance* (2002), rejects military decline and social display in favour of essentialism, new historicism, cultural materialism, and gender studies.

16 J. Goodall, *Country Life* (16 April 1998).

BREDE PLACE, Sussex and HORNE'S PLACE, Kent

Brede Place suffered from such a devastating fire in 1979 that only the outer walls and the chapel and chamber extension survived. The latter would not have done so had they not been separated by the only stone party wall in the house. A bold but imaginative restoration took place between 1979 and 1983, with the principal block, altered in two phases during the sixteenth century, totally cleared to create a single chamber combining hall and parlour open to the roof, with three tiered rooms at the north end separated from this extremely spacious new chamber by glass partitions.

Brede Place is a compact block built of buff-coloured sandstone on a steep slope above the River Brede. The Victoria County History suggested that the house was originally a timber-framed structure of fourteenth-century date with a slightly narrower hall, and wings that were jettied and gabled. It was remodelled in stone by Robert Oxenbridge during the early fifteenth century, when the chapel and a further chamber block were added at the south end. The fierceness of the fire proved that the stonework was simply a casing over the timber framing. All that evidence was destroyed in 1979, although the single party wall still stands to confirm the chamber extension development.

PLATE 128 Brede Place: from the west (1968)

The main rectangular block, 80 feet by 34 feet externally, was divided by partitions into a two-bay hall, 38 feet by 29 feet and originally open to the roof, flanked by offices with chamber above at the lower end and a parlour with withdrawing chamber above at the upper. The galleried chapel and two-storeyed chamber extension behind it abutted the parlour cross wing. In the mid-sixteenth century, two brick additions were made to the frontage – a prominent two-storeyed gabled porch with porter's lodge and a polygonal bay, possibly for a newel, between hall and parlour. Many of the principal windows and some of the fireplaces were replaced at the same time, but the massive chimney stack inserted in the middle of the hall was a late Tudor addition.

The few original elements that survived the fire include the early fifteenth-century entrance doorway with continuous moulding, a garderobe doorway opening off the chamber above the offices, and the chimney stack in the parlour wall. A doorway from the parlour that seems to be original gave access to the added chamber unit, a single room on each floor with garderobe, fireplace with simple chamfered head, and single and double cinquefoil lights. The primitive ladder to the upper chamber and king-post roof were destroyed in the fire.[1] The parlour doorway to the chapel is a post-medieval insertion for it was originally an independent unit built at a slightly lower level than the body of the house. It is approached by a badly worn two-centred doorway in the north wall and lit by square-headed windows of two cinquefoil lights at ground and upper level, and a more elaborate traceried window in the south wall lighting the altar. This has three long cinquefoil lights with split panels in the head. The gallery was warmed by a fireplace (Tudor head), but the three original wooden stalls with misericords in the chapel were stolen immediately after the fire.

Robert Oxenbridge purchased Brede Place in the early fifteenth century and his family held it until the mid-seventeenth century. In his remodelling shortly after acquisition, Oxenbridge used local ashlar sandstone for the frontage but rubble with ashlar dressings for the remainder. The house has been in continuous occupation but has never been extended beyond the fifteenth-century chapel which is its principal survival today.

Ten miles north-east stands a far finer chapel built two generations earlier. Horne's Place near Appledore was the residence of justices of the peace in the late fourteenth century and sheriffs and knights of the shire in the fifteenth century. The house was timber-framed, since replaced, but the stone-built chapel of high decorative quality remains. It dates from the mid-1360s when William Horne received a licence to hold divine services in his chapel and is of two storeys.[2] The lower walls of the undercroft are of stone but its upper inner walls and vault are of brick inserted after a fire in 1381.[3] It retains no original features other than the entrance doorway, for the one opposite the house is a later insertion. No more than 8 feet high at the apex, the area was probably used for storage.

The chapel above, 22 feet by 12½ feet internally, is built of large square ragstone blocks. It rises 23 feet high so that it is almost half a cube and therefore tall but short. A three light window with Perpendicular tracery fills most of the east wall, and there are smaller but slightly different versions in the adjacent side walls. These have cusped lights with ogee heads beneath exquisitely detailed rear arches of a more Decorated character and this is even more obvious externally. In fact, it is the quality of the internal

details such as the minutely carved capitals, the hood moulding, the strapwork and stone corbels with Catherine wheels that are the outstanding features of this chapel. The details are of the utmost refinement, far above the level of parish churches in this area.[4] There is a barrel-vaulted arch-braced roof of three bays.

There was a communicating door to the house and a balcony formerly reached by an external stair at the angle and probably added in the late fourteenth or earlier fifteenth century when the outer door and window were inserted. The position of the squint, 8 feet above the ground, suggests that there was a further building south-east of the chapel where the external off-set stops and the walling have been rebuilt in rougher stone and yellow brick as also occurs at the south-west angle.

This building is a particularly splendid example of a domestic chapel illustrating the stylistic crossover that marks the third quarter of the fourteenth century and the refined standards obtainable by a family prominent in the county establishment during that period. William Horne was appointed a justice of the peace in 1378, and suffered in Wat Tyler's rebellion three years later when two men from Cranbrook raised a number of men in Tenterden who broke into his house and took away goods and chattels worth £10.[5]

NOTES

1 It has been suggested that this may be a separate priest's lodging (VCH, IX (1937) 167; N. Pevsner, *Buildings of England: Sussex* (1965) 424) but no internal chapel or external door has been traced.
2 1366, *Archbishop Langham's Register*, f.48.
3 Information from Ken Gravett.
4 John Newman, *West Kent and the Weald* (1969) 127.
5 J. Whinfrith, *A History of Appledore* (1983) 15–17. Two or three other stand-alone chapels survive in Kent. The fourteenth-century flint and stone two-storeyed chapel of Thorne Manor near Minster in Thanet survived the otherwise total destruction of the manor in the nineteenth century. Even so, the undercroft and chapel were converted into a house, so that no internal features survive. The walls also survive of the chapel at Horton Manor near Canterbury but in a much abused state. It was built by the Badlesmeres in the late thirteenth century and altered by Christopher Shuckborough in *c*.1380 who inserted a crown-post roof in the nave. T. Tatton-Brown, *Arch. Cant.* 98 (1982) 77–105.

Brede
H. A. Tipping, *Country Life* (November 1906)
T. Garner and A. Stratton, *The Domestic Architecture of England during the Tudor Period*, I (1911) 47–9
VCH, *Sussex*, IX (1937) 165–7, 169

Horne's Place
S. Robertson, *Arch. Cant.* 14 (1882) 363–7

CANTERBURY PALACE and the residences of the archbishops of Canterbury

The archbishop's palace in Canterbury, initially developed by Lanfranc in the years close to 1080, was demolished in about 1650. It was replaced by a smaller residence in 1899–1901 by W. D. Caroe, used essentially at weekends, with Lambeth Palace as the primate's principal seat.

The first palace was one of the most important houses of medieval England. It lay north-west of the cathedral, with Lanfranc's original T-shaped development surviving until supplanted during the thirteenth century. Archbishop Walter initiated a vast new hall in 1199, completed by Stephen Langton by 1220, which was second in scale only to Westminster Hall. At 165 feet by 21 feet internally, this aisled hall was divided into eight bays, each filled with two double-transomed windows of plate tracery form with a quatrefoil above in a buttressed transverse gable. Part of one of these windows and most of the porch were incorporated in Walpole House nearby in the eighteenth century. The aisles were divided by pillars of clustered shafts of Purbeck marble. This hall was on regal scale, larger than Henry III's hall at Winchester (1222–35) to demonstrate the archbishop's standing to King John and his successors. Immediately east of this hall is a pillared undercroft which must have supported the archbishop's great chamber. North-west of the hall lay a detached kitchen of which part has been incorporated in a detached house of King's School. During the late fifteenth century, Lanfranc's north–south chamber block that linked his Norman hall with that built by Walter was reconstructed, and part of this was incorporated in Caroe's development, the first occupiable residence for the primate in his archiepiscopal seat since 1650.[1]

The lordship of Canterbury was as much a secular as an ecclesiastical estate. The many manors that made up this lordship were quite separate from the estates of Christ Church Priory, the mother church of the diocese, and were held 'of the archbishop in right of his church of Canterbury'. The archbishop was the largest land-owner in Kent between the Conquest and the Reformation, and from the close of the thirteenth century his estates – varying in size from villages to scattered settlements and patches of woodland and marsh – were grouped into seven administrative units or bailiwicks. The largest was in north-east Kent centred on Wingham and the richest was in south-east Kent centred on Aldington. A more scattered group in mid-Kent was based on Maidstone and in north Kent on Otford. A number of manors north and south of London looked to Croydon and there were two groupings in Sussex – in the east centred on South Malling and in the south-west on Pagham.

There were archiepiscopal residences in each of these bailiwicks, varying from the extremely large such as that at Lambeth to a relatively small house like that at Teynham. Nor was this situation a static one. Most of his dwellings were in existence by the close of the thirteenth century and came to number twenty-four, seventeen in Kent, three in Surrey, three in Sussex and one in Middlesex. Some such as Wrotham and Lyminge were allowed to lapse during the fourteenth century, and some were newly built such as Knole and Ford in the later fifteenth century. Nothing survives of his residences at Bekesbourne, Bishopsbourne, Boughton under Blean, Gillingham, Lyminge, Northfleet, Wingham, and Wrotham in Kent or Wimbledon in Surrey.

Yet there is a surprising number of extant remains at the remaining fourteen sites, varying from the stump of a tower at Slindon, to the moated platform and aisled hall of c.1315 at Headstone Manor, and the still maintained palace at Lambeth. Until the later fifteenth century, only two can be described as palaces – Lambeth and Canterbury – where the question of scale and splendour at a centre of power are the determining factors. The others were essentially manor houses, albeit substantial ones. Yet even the archbishop's lesser houses were on a large scale compared with those of the nearby bishop of Rochester who, apart from his residence next to the cathedral and a house at Lambeth (later at Southwark), had only

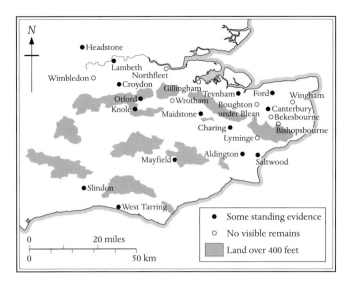

FIGURE 71 Residences of the archbishops of Canterbury

four small dwellings at Stone, Trottiscliffe, Halling, and Bromley.[2] On the other hand, Mayfield, Croydon, and Charing were comparable in size with those of many contemporary magnates, for the archbishop took the majority of his household on his travels. As the mansions towards the close of the middle ages had to be on a scale capable of accommodating his household, Knole, Ford, and Otford were as large as any in the land and may be truly described as palatial.

The archiepiscopal residences were mainly positioned on two routes across Kent, the present A2 and A20, which formed the twin axes of the diocese. The first extended from Canterbury to Lambeth via Teynham, Gillingham, and Northfleet. These residences have all been destroyed, for the second route was the preferred one throughout the later middle ages. This ran from Canterbury to Lambeth via Charing, Maidstone, Otford (and Knole after the 1450s), and Croydon. Ford and Saltwood were outliers to the north and south of Canterbury respectively, though the latter was a valuable stopping place on the way to Mayfield and the archbishop's Sussex estates via Aldington. All these residences were within a relatively easy day's journey of about 15 miles, necessary when the cortège usually included a large retinue. In 1326, archbishop Reynolds and his party, admittedly frightened by the murder of bishop Stapledon of Exeter, rode the 20 miles from Lambeth to Croydon and then on to Otford in the evening, and the next day continued to Maidstone where they stayed.[3]

Archbishops were in constant movement throughout the middle ages. Like any lord, secular or spiritual, it was wise to traverse their estates and an archbishop's spiritual duties enhanced that need. His duties, in particular, necessitated frequent attendance in London, and for that reason the residences nearest to the Thames became particularly important later in the period. From the early fourteenth century, his household not only grew larger but became more elaborate and formal. In 1349, that of archbishop Stratford was divided into eight departments – hall, chapel, wardrobe and armoury, treasury, kitchen, pantry and buttery, larder, and stables. The books, vessels, jewels and vestments of the chapel were, of course, of especial high value as befitted the primate of England, but the jewels and personal contents of his wardrobe were also of considerable worth. Two household rolls for the same archbishop show that the majority of his disposable income was taken up by his household. Not surprisingly, the kitchen was the prime area of expenditure, particularly when the drink, bread, and fowls of the buttery, pantry, and poultery were added. Next came the stables, with the feed for the horses of the household and its guests and the shoeing of the household's mounts. The hall covered the provision of heat and light, while the wardrobe included a wide range of domestic expenses extending from domestic plate and dishes to sheets and furnishings for guests' chambers. As Du Boulay notes, 'The overall impression of Stratford's household rolls is of a curious combination of luxury and discomfort: the routine fatigues of perpetual motion and the privileged plenty of delicacies brought in great variety from all quarters to the tables in the hall.'[4]

Hospitality was generous, with guests frequent and numerous. Stratford entertained important visitors on twenty-six out of forty days in part of December 1341 and March 1343. Just over a century later, the scale and variety of provisions under Bourchier had not appreciably altered but the accounts for October 1459 record that there were two meals a day in the hall – dinner and supper – although there was no supper on Fridays and vigil. At each of these meals, attending people were divided into guests and household, and the latter were grouped into gentry and 'others'. On average, there were four important and eighteen less important guests in hall each day, while the household averaged twenty-two gentry and fifty-two 'others' to dinner, and sixteen gentry and forty-six 'others' to supper.[5] Not surprisingly, hospitality was highly expensive, but the standing it conferred was even more important, and its organisation equally so until the Dissolution brought it all to an abrupt end.

More complete palaces and country houses survive from the diocese of Canterbury than for any other see in the country. The earliest residences date from the late eleventh century, immediately after the arrival of Lanfranc from Normandy. Excavations at Canterbury have revealed evidence of his hall, and the chamber above an undercroft immediately west of the church at Maidstone can also be attributed to this period. The palaces at Canterbury and Lambeth were reconstructed during the first quarter of the thirteenth century after the election of Hubert Walter in 1193, the first of a line of secular and state-involved archbishops. The proposal that Lambeth should be a college was abandoned and the property was developed instead as a palace, complete with a cloister that was a survival of the earlier plan. The chapel and probably the lost hall were initiated by Walter and completed by Langton. Both residences had become extensive by the late thirteenth century, though little work survives from the following one.[6]

The majority of the archbishop's residences took shape between the early fourteenth and early sixteenth centuries so that their development spans almost the whole of the medieval period. Lambeth is the only one to continue to serve its original function since that at Canterbury is now a Victorian Tudor-style house. The other residences are in public or private hands but in two cases where virtually nothing exists above ground (Teynham and Ford), archaeological and documentary evidence has enabled their original form to be identified. Unfortunately, documentary material for episcopal building work during the fourteenth and fifteenth centuries is very patchy as a consequence of the wholesale destruction of

the archbishops' records in the revolt of 1381, the losses occasioned by a household constantly on the move, and the fact that temporal records became increasingly fragmented after 1400 rather than centralised as had been the practice with the archbishops' registers.[7]

Teynham, near Faversham, was a minor residence used for short-term visits only. Rescue excavations in the early 1980s found some scanty remains of masonry buildings from the twelfth to the fifteenth centuries, including one range incorporated in the present churchyard wall indicating that the parish church was a key element in the layout of this site.[8] The hall of the 1330s at Mayfield by Simon Meopham (d.1333) or his successor served a comfortable Sussex manor house. It lay in ruin until the shell was roofed and converted into a convent chapel in 1863–6, now the school assembly hall. Rather more survives at Charing, long used as a farm with the early fourteenth-century hall serving as a barn and two mid-fourteenth-century lodging ranges of extremely early form next to the ruined gatehouse.

Archbishop Islip (1349–66) enhanced two residences. The more substantial was at Saltwood Castle where he added an impressive first-floor reception chamber at the lower end of the slightly earlier hall within this twelfth-century castle. At Maidstone, he rebuilt the audience hall and made use of materials from Wrotham Palace which Islip recorded in 1352 was in ruin through pestilence and lack of funds. His successors extended the private apartments in a still-roofed complex of comfort but little individuality through post-medieval occupation. It is used today for municipal weddings rather than episcopal receptions.

Insurgents attacked the episcopal residences at Lambeth, Croydon, and Otford during the rebellion of 1381, not because they were symbols of the archbishop's personal unpopularity but because they held manorial documents of labour services which were restrictive and rents which were high. Courtenay (1381–96) made good the damage, repairing roofs, fences, tables and chairs, for instance, at Otford in 1382–3, but he also embarked on a major rebuilding programme centred on the three halls.[9] Nothing remains of that at Otford replacing a mid-thirteenth-century structure, but it is known that it was buttressed and battlemented and sufficiently grand to be incorporated in the palace built by Warham in the early sixteenth century.[10] The two-storeyed porch and some adjacent walling remain of the hall at Croydon which was reconstructed two generations later. The contemporary fragment of c.1380 with its blocked windows at Aldington has been incorporated into a nineteenth-century house next to the church. This property gives little evidence today that the site enclosed a large hall, a chapel, five kitchens, six stables, and eight dovecotes within a park of over a thousand acres.[11]

But Courtenay's most impressive survival is at Saltwood Castle where, apart from the spectacular gatehouse and other substantial defensive works added by him, an equally impressive first-floor hall was raised, approached by a grand staircase, with an associated chamber tower and large two-storeyed chapel block. Only the foundations survive of the last named, but the remaining work compares with that at Dartington Hall, similarly restored in the early twentieth century, to recreate some of the most important residential evidence of the late fourteenth century. Courtenay's apartment repeats the Canterbury pattern of providing a second magnificent reception hall, comparable in scale to the contemporary royal halls at Kenilworth and Portchester. Part-ruined, part-occupied and

PLATE 129 Charing Palace: great hall

romantically secluded, Saltwood is one of the most complex yet least studied castles in southern England.

Archbishop Arundel (1397–1414) continued the work begun by Courtenay at his college of priests at Maidstone, and rebuilt the great chambers (the guard halls) at Lambeth and Croydon. This last residence was developed over an extended period between c.1380 and 1490 and has been in continuous occupation ever since, currently serving scholastic and educational needs.[12]

Between 1445 and 1450, archbishop Stafford (1443–52) rebuilt the late fourteenth-century hall at Croydon. Thomas Bourchier (1455–86) added a long gallery there which survives, whereas his gallery at Knole does not. Bourchier had bought the manor of Knole from Lord Saye and Sele in 1456 to begin an entirely new residence for himself which he presented to the see of Canterbury in 1480.[13] Even today, when much of Bourchier's work round the Stone and Water courts was remodelled in 1603–8, the gate-tower, the two-storeyed chapel, and the range of lodgings show that he built on the grandest scale.

John Morton's activity (1486–1501) was spread across several residences.[14] Important work occurred at Croydon, including the gatehouse and lodging ranges destroyed in 1808, the great brick gatehouse at Lambeth, some apartments at Charing (though Leland intimates there was far more), stables at Maidstone, and extensions at Knole. Morton's development at Ford was more extensive. This was nothing less than a new house on a scale commensurate with that at Knole. Built of brick, it was demolished in 1658 and the only fragment to survive is part of the stable range incorporated in a farmhouse on part of the site. Yet the remains of a map of 1624 and the parliamentary survey of 1647 show that it included an outer court, a gatehouse leading to a second court with

a cross range of hall and services, and two further small courts – a base court with domestic offices and an inner court surrounded by lodgings. Where it differs in particular from Bourchier's slightly earlier residence is in the inclusion of a five-storeyed residential tower on one side of the hall court.

Archbishops tended to have their favourite residences: Stafford liked Charing, Courtenay preferred Saltwood, Bourchier loved Knole, Morton enjoyed Aldington, and Warham Otford. From the beginning of the thirteenth century, Lambeth rather than Canterbury had been their principal residence but no one could fail to see that the sumptuous palaces of Knole, Ford, and then Otford had added very considerably to the assets of the lordship.

Archbishop Warham (1504–32) planned his palace at Otford on an enormous scale (1514–18). The earlier manor house was demolished except for the walls of the hall and chapel and the now widened moat. This enclosed a 3 acre site with an open cloister, galleries and lodgings round it, that clearly anticipated Wolsey's palace at Hampton Court of similar scale.[15] It is not surprising therefore that in the atmosphere generated by the Dissolution of the Monasteries, the extent and richness of the lordship of Canterbury should excite the avaricious temperament of Henry VIII. Between 1536 and 1546 the majority of lands which had supported the archbishops for centuries were compulsorily exchanged by Cranmer for others of inferior value. It was the recently built palaces relatively close to London that the king coveted. Despite Cranmer's plea that Knole was too small for the king, Henry pointedly remarked that '"if I should make myne abode here, as I do suerlie mynde to do nowe and than, I myself will lye at Knolle and moste of my house[hold] shall ly at Otteforde". And so by this meanes bothe those houses were delivered upp into the kingis handes'.[16] Royal expenditure and occupation at both residences followed shortly afterwards. Other residences such as Maidstone, Charing, and Mayfield were sold or leased to courtiers and crown servants. The archbishop retained Croydon and Lambeth, but the former amplitude of accommodation rapidly gave way to relatively spartan circumstances.

In 1544, Henry VIII returned Bekesbourne, 3 miles south-east of Canterbury, to Cranmer who promptly started a new brick palace there. Apart from the gatehouse with its initialled datestone TC 1552, the residence was destroyed in the mid-seventeenth century. Extended by Parker and Whitgift during its single century of occupation, it was the only post-Reformation palace built by the archbishops prior to Caroe's house at Canterbury.[17]

NOTES

1 J. Rady, T. Tatton-Brown, and J. A. Bowen, *Jour. Brit. Arch. Assoc.* 144 (1991) 1–60; J. M. Freeman, *Country Life* (April 1991).

2 Rochester was always a small see with fewer medieval houses than any other in England. Nothing remains of any of them apart from a mid-thirteenth-century wall at Halling, and a faceless mid-fifteenth-century block at Rochester incorporated in eighteenth- and nineteenth-century ecclesiastical houses. It is the least impressive episcopal residence in England. A. J. Pearman, G. A. Tait, and H. P. Thompson, *Arch. Cant.* 33 (1918) 131–51.

3 Du Boulay (1966) 115.

4 *Ibid.* 259.

5 For the last two paragraphs, *ibid.* 254–64.

6 The two-storeyed thirteenth-century flint-built solar unit to a fourteenth-century hall remains at West Tarring. They were both remodelled in

*c.*1400. The building is now used as the village hall. *Sussex Arch. Coll.* 64 (1923) 140–79.

7 Du Boulay (1966) 7–15.

8 B. Philp, 'The discovery of the archbishop's palace at Teynham', *Kent Arch. Rev.* 72 (Summer 1983), 42–3. Archbishop Hubert Walter died here in 1205.

9 For Courtenay's career, J. Dahmus, *William Courtenay, Archbishop of Canterbury 1381–96* (1966).

10 B. Philp, *Excavations in the Darenth Valley, Kent* (1984) 137, 159. Courtenay also enlarged the site and in 1391–2 glazed the windows in the chapel which was also retained by Warham. D. Clarke and A. Stoyel, *Otford in Kent* (1975) 71–3, 79–85.

11 E. W. Parkin, *Arch. Cant.* 86 (1971) 15–24.

12 For Arundel's career, M. Aston, *Thomas Arundel* (1967).

13 For Bourchier, R. Du Boulay, *Registrum Thome Bourgchier* (1957).

14 For Morton's career, C. S. L. Davies, *Eng. Hist. Rev.* 52 (1987) 2–30.

15 Philp, *Excavations in the Darenth Valley* 137–65; B. Philp, *Archaeology in the Front Line* (2002) 112–16.

16 Du Boulay (1966) 324.

17 *Arch. Cant.* 96 (1980) 27–57; Tatton-Brown (2000) 73–4.

F. R. H. Du Boulay, *The Lordship of Canterbury* (1966)

E. Carpenter, *Cantuar, the Archbishops in their Offices* (3rd edn 1997)

T. Tatton-Brown, *Lambeth Palace: A History of the Archbishops of Canterbury and Their Houses* (2000)

CHARING PALACE, Kent

The palace at Charing was one of the archbishop of Canterbury's lesser country houses and was developed piecemeal. Although constructed round two courts separated by the hall, all the principal structures were positioned irregularly round the front or outer court. Nothing remains of the kitchen and the associated facilities round the services court to the east.

The manor of Charing had been held by the see of Canterbury since the eighth century and became the archbishop's property in the late eleventh century. Like many of the archbishop's houses, Charing was built next to the parish church and makes a striking adjunct to it, using knapped flint with stone dressings until the introduction of brick in the late fifteenth century. The standing structures were developed in five phases – the first chamber block and chapel in the late thirteenth century, the hall during the early fourteenth century, the gatehouse and lodging ranges by the mid-fourteenth century with the second chamber block a rebuilding of the later fourteenth century, heightened in brick a century later. Some of the buildings are ruined but the initial impression of substantial architectural interest stimulated by the roofed structures becomes one of some disappointment as it becomes clear that the hall has suffered drastically through barn conversion in the eighteenth century, while extended farm occupation of the second chamber block and the conversion of part of the lodging ranges into two cottages has denuded them of primary architectural value.

The first chamber block was two-storeyed but only two walls stand, the south with central ground-floor entry and the east wall abutting the still-roofed second chamber block. Attributable to the late thirteenth century, the principal chamber was at first-floor level with a mural fireplace and large south-end window. The first-floor chapel lay to the north-east, linked to the great chamber by a lost

extension. Only part of its beamed undercroft survives as an outhouse, though much of the chapel was still standing in the late eighteenth century when Hasted noted three windows on the south side and a larger one at the east end.[1]

Much of the hall walling stands (with extensive rebuilding) but the double-pitched roof is eighteenth century, supported on central posts inserted at the same time as the barn entries were forced through the side walls and an oast erected in the south-east corner. The two-storey porch retains its outer and inner entry, a narrow side doorway to a vaulted mural stair, and blocked trefoil lights at both levels.[2] The hall, 71½ feet by 35 feet, is one of the largest unaisled halls in the country. It was of five bays, lit by transomed windows on the west side (probably opposite too), of which one partly survives of two trefoiled lights under an octafoil head. More difficult to appreciate but more impressive was the lost roof of Charing's hall, at least twice as high from the top of the walls as the present one. Rising 50 feet from floor to roof ridge, its trusses were supported on wall posts rising from low-set corbels between the windows, of which two remain.[3] The form of the roof structure is not known (pl. 119).

The frame of the east cross-passage doorway has been removed but the low end of the hall retains three doorways (and an inserted fourth). The two brick-rebuilt central doorways opened into service rooms with the doorway at the far end probably accessing a stair to a room over the services. At present, this area is single-storey with a rebuilt south wall and lean-to roof, but comparison with other episcopal halls such as that at Wells (*c.*1290),[4] the need for a high-quality reception chamber, the presence of an unusual mural passage,[5] and the stair entry point to a spacious apartment over the services. There is no firm date for this hall but the window evidence points to the early fourteenth century, and its scale suggests comparison with the nearby halls at Mayfield (1330s) and Penshurst (early 1340s), with the stone arches at the archbishop's house at Mayfield repeated in the smaller halls at Battel Hall (1330s) and Ightham Mote (1337). Dendro analysis of the present hall roof revealed a reused rafter and brace with a date range of 1326–51[6] so that the hall's construction at the end of the first quarter of the century is not unlikely.

The gatehouse and lodging range lining the street frontage with the associated north wing is made up of several contiguous units – the ruined gatehouse, a lodging occupied as a cottage, the buttressed end of a ruined lodging block at right angles to the street, and a large garderobe projection incorporated into a second cottage with a similar but less altered projection to the north. The gatehouse with separate vehicular and pedestrian entries was formerly vaulted. A porter's lodge lay to one side, with a stair (blocked doorway) to the well-appointed chamber over the entry with hooded fireplace and garderobe. Occupation has destroyed the form and detailing of the first lodging but it seems to have been unitary. The much larger second lodging block was at a sharp angle to the first, closing the west side of the court. Its outer walls stand to roof level but the inner wall has been reduced to ground height. The block consisted of two rooms at both levels, a south room 55 feet long and a north room 40 feet long with the two visible doorways supplemented by the pictorial evidence of a third to the upper floor.[7] The two large projections – one incorporated in the cottage and the other used for storing farm equipment – were garderobes

PLATE 130 Charing Palace: garderobe projections, lodging ranges, and gatehouse from the Market Place

with arched ground-floor openings. They were large enough for communal use and therefore served two dormitories rather than partitioned rooms. This would also apply to the two lower rooms if the scale of the projections is taken into account.[8] The trefoil-headed single and double lights suggest a date not much later than the hall during the second quarter of the fourteenth century, possibly by archbishop Stratford (1333–48).[9] These three lodgings are among the earliest examples in the country. The unitary lodging would probably have been for officials or guests. The two ground-floor rooms could have housed up to about fifteen and ten staff respectively, with fewer in the two rooms above if they were occupied by more senior staff.

The T-shaped second chamber block abutting the earlier one is almost certainly a replacement attributable to the late fourteenth century. Initially two-storeyed, a third one was added in brick by archbishop Morton (1486–1500), whom Leland claimed made 'great building at Charing'.[10] The rear extension is a further brick replacement of the seventeenth century. These rooms were the archbishop's private quarters, but continuous occupation and division has left little original evidence, though a first-floor great chamber, parallel with the earlier one, is probable. At Charing, the archbishop's accommodation was always totally separate from the hall. The 60 feet gap between the two structures would have been pentice-linked originally, but this was replaced by the more comfortable passageway in the late fourteenth century. There is a fascinating contrast between hospitality and privacy at this house, between the size of the hall and the modest scale of the archbishop's apartments, between their usual position backing on to the high end of the hall and their clear separation here. The archbishop wished to demarcate the two functions, and in so doing retained his personal seclusion.

Charing was one of the archbishop's lesser country houses compared with Lambeth, Croydon, and Mayfield, but it was a valuable stopping point between London and Canterbury 14 miles away. It was primarily a short-term stay for archbishops and kings[11] until it was handed over to the crown by Cranmer in 1545. The buildings

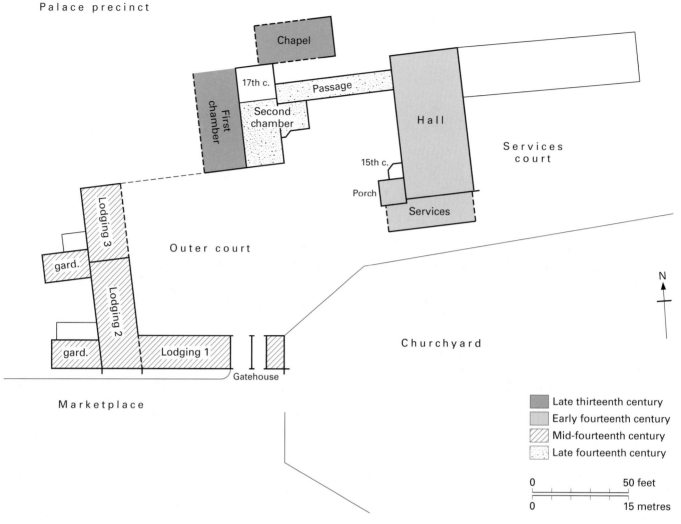

FIGURE 72 Charing Palace: site plan

still show the irregular and independent disposition round a court common until the later thirteenth century, with the gatehouse and lodging range introducing a more formal approach. Despite the damage they have all suffered, each building represents a key component in the structure of a major household. The absence of an aggressive post-medieval insertion also means that the site retains rare ensemble value. However, some essential structures are missing such as the kitchen, bakehouse, brewhouse, and stables, while the standing buildings have lost most of their architectural detailing. The absence of any building documentation compounds this lack of dating precision. The archbishop's quarters were almost certainly more extensive than today while Leland's claim of 'great building' by Morton is not apparent, though it might be revealed by geophysical survey or archaeological excavation. Until the close of the twentieth century, the property was a working farm, but this has ceased and its future is uncertain. There is no doubt that considerably more remains to be discovered about the palace's character and architectural development as well as that of the associated earthworks in the still-open precinct to the north and the grassed area to the south.

NOTES

1 *The History and Topographical Survey . . . of Kent* (1798) 430.
2 The north stair turret is a late fifteenth-century addition.
3 Pearson (2001) fig. 5, 327.
4 As at Charing, the bishop's private accommodation at Wells was some distance from the ceremonial hall.
5 It may have been linked to a two-storeyed range on the south side of the services court. Pearson (2001) 331.
6 *Ibid.* 328. The relevant archbishops were Walter Reynolds (1313–27) and Simon Meopham (1327–33). Also *Vern. Arch.* 30 (1999) 94.
7 Pearson (2001) 333–4.
8 None of the rooms seems to have been heated.
9 Sarah Pearson shows that the extension of the palace grounds to take these buildings was planned as early as 1298: (2001) 322–4.
10 *Itinerary*, IV, 62. The roof timbers have been dendro dated to between 1496 and 1521. Pearson (2001) 320.
11 Edward I in 1297–1299, Henry VII several times between 1498 and 1508, Henry VIII in 1511–13, 1520, and the early 1540s.

P. K. Kipps, *Arch. Jour.* 90 (1933) 78–97
S. E. Rigold, *Arch. Jour.* 126 (1969) 267
S. Pearson, *Arch. Cant.* 121 (2001) 315–49

CHICHESTER, BISHOP'S PALACE, Sussex

The earliest evidence of the bishop's residence at Chichester includes two Norman windows by the south wall of the great kitchen, an inserted Norman doorway, and the scars of two vaulted ground-floor bays of a two-storeyed building. This was part of the palace burnt in 1187 and was replaced under bishop Seffrid (1180–1204). Of this later building the chapel range survives.[1]

This range was two separate buildings initially, the 'hall' and chapel, with a passage between them. The 'hall', 49 feet by 19 feet internally, has left little evidence other than its shell, floored and re-roofed by the close of the middle ages and remodelled in 1725–7 to form the heart of the present bishop's residence. Though usually described as the 'hall', it is too narrow to have served that purpose and there is no evidence in the patched flint walling that it was an aisled structure of which only the central portion survives. It is most likely that it was a residential unit, probably with an inserted floor by the thirteenth century if not earlier, which has retained its original east gable and stone cross when the upper chamber was heightened and covered with a new roof during the fifteenth century. The opportunity was taken to extend this roof across the passage although the present timber work is of no great age.

The original hall and its porch lay between the two wings but was pulled down in the mid-seventeenth century, converting the palace from a large block-like structure to its present H-shape. The screens and offices lay on the site of the south-east wing with the surviving kitchen beyond. The hall was about 67 feet by 34 feet and probably built in the late thirteenth century,[2] with the offices flanking a central passage to the kitchen marked by a thirteenth-century doorway in the west wall of the south-east wing.[3] The central apartment can be attributed to Gilbert of St Leofard (1288–1305).

The former free-standing kitchen seems to have been built at the same time as the hall, close to the twelfth-century block noted earlier. It is built of flint rubble with shallow buttresses carrying the wooden roof of paired hammer beams supporting a hammer post in each corner. The structure has been dendro dated to about 1300.[4] At 34 feet square internally, it is a particularly large structure, but as the hammer beams preclude the normal angle hearths it is conjectured that they were in the middle of the apartment. This is not particularly practical without a massive stone support (as at Alcobaça in Portugal) while the central louvre, ceiled in the early twentieth century, precluded any such superstructure.[5] However, this roof was markedly experimental, with recent work showing that the pyramid crown is not original. It rose from a clerestory, now removed.[6] The small windows are entirely of nineteenth-century form, but the west wall retains the usual three service doorways, the principal one with a cinquefoil segmental head not dissimilar to the window heads of the gatehouse of c.1327.

The enriched chapel of c.1200 survives little altered. It is divided into two bays by sexpartite vaulting, but the windows in the north and east walls indicate remodelling in the 1320s when the lancets in the south wall were blocked.[7] At the same time, bishop Langton inserted the screen, now surmounted by a Victorian beam. On the south wall is the famous mid-thirteenth-century roundel of the Virgin and Child, rediscovered in 1829.

The medieval boundary wall with its early Tudor brick crenellation still encloses two sides of the outer court, with a late med-

PLATE 131 Chichester, Bishop's Palace: from the south

ieval range on the east side with crown-post roof, used for stabling with lodgings over. The compact gatehouse, built in 1327 by bishop Langton (1305–37),[8] had ribbed vaults over both entry passages and a small porter's lodge. The stair nearby leads to a fine first-floor chamber with twin-light windows with cusped ogee heads on three sides, an original fireplace in the west wall, and garderobe evidence near the roof stair.

The south-west wing was erected by bishop Sherborne (1508–36) with late Perpendicular windows, a fine painted ceiling in the parlour, and great chamber above. The north-west wing in brick with projecting garderobe tower was also by Sherborne but the massive external footings on the north side suggest that it replaced an earlier structure.

NOTES
1 *Chron. Rogeri de Hovedon*, ed. W. Stubbs, II (1871) 333.
2 Tatton-Brown (1994) 229–30.
3 Excavations in 1989 and a resistivity survey revealed no foundation evidence but the documentary evidence supports this location.
4 *Vern. Arch.* 24 (1993) 52–3; Munby (1985) 15–16, 32.
5 Surviving kitchens at the Bishop's Palace, Lincoln (early thirteenth century), Magdalen College, Oxford (late thirteenth century of St John's Hospital), Berkeley Castle (1330s), Glastonbury Abbey (1330s), Durham Priory, and Raby Castle (1370s) all have either angle or lateral hearths, as do those excavated at Furness Abbey and St Augustine's, Canterbury (late thirteenth century). The kitchen excavated at Northolt Manor (first half of fourteenth century) did have a central hearth but the building was a flimsy structure and little cooking seems to have taken place in it. J. G. Hurst, *Med. Arch.* 5 (1961) 215.
6 *Vern. Arch.* 24 (1993) 53.
7 This would have been necessary if there was an extension south of the chapel towards the kitchen although the present area is essentially late fifteenth century and featureless internally.
8 It was described as 'newly built', Bishop Langton Episcopal Rec., Liber B, f.76.

I. C. Hannah, *Sussex Arch. Coll.* 52 (1909) 1–23
VCH, *Sussex*, III (1935) 148–60
J. Munby, *Arch. Jour.* 142 (1985) 15–16, 32
R. Haslam, *Country Life* (August 1985)
T. Tatton-Brown, *Chichester Cathedral*, ed. M. Hobbs (1994) 228–32

CROWHURST PLACE and OLD SURREY HALL,
Surrey

These two timber-framed houses, built within 5 miles of each other by members of the Gaynesford family towards the close of the middle ages, were again in the hands of a common owner 400 years later who extended and pomaded the structures out of all recognition of their original selves. Both retained little outside their halls when purchased by George Crawley in 1912 and 1922 respectively, but that was the core that spurred their rhapsodic transformation on a medieval theme.

Crowhurst Place was the prime residence of the Gaynesford family, who had settled in the parish of Crowhurst in 1338 and grew rich on the proceeds of law. The mid-fifteenth-century Gaynesford Cartulary records over 200 title deeds and the rent rolls of their manors across four counties.[1] In 1418, John Gaynesford III (d.1420) purchased a moated residence at Crowhurst which included hall, chapel, chambers, pantry, kitchen, bakehouse, and brewhouse at the time of his son's death in 1450. The family replaced it with a new house towards the close of the fifteenth century, centred on the present close-framed two-bay hall.

Its roof, spanned by arch-braced tie beams, was an experimental structure with the ridge and three side purlins separated by ashlaring (with wind braces) and three lines of coving which give it an assured lightness. Decoration was essentially limited to the mould-

ings of the tie beams, wall plates, purlins and upper collar. Crawley found traces of a louvre, for the fireplace is a post-medieval insertion, while the entrance porch, semi-circular bay window, and stairs were added by him in 1912.

Four doorways in the screens passage gave access to the offices, kitchen, and stair to an upper chamber, but the wing has been too drastically altered to be of value. The upper cross wing may be a secondary feature, for the foundations traced in 1912 immediately east and south of the present structure were considered evidence of the earlier house. Crowhurst Place and grounds were enriched by Crawley to such an extent that it became a theatrical ensemble quite unlike that known to its builder. Yet Crowhurst is among that group of late fifteenth-century timber-framed houses in south-east England which vied in scale with contemporary stone structures.[2] It awaits dendro analysis to determine whether the house was built by John Gaynesford VI (1460–91) or his son Sir John Gaynesford VII (1491–1540).

Old Surrey Hall lies on the northern slope of a secluded valley of the upper Medway stream, close to the junction of the Surrey, Kent, and Sussex borders near Lingfield. It stands within a large moated site, approximately 56 yards by 72 yards internally, served by a spring above the north arm. There is no immediate evidence of occupation prior to the single medieval survival spanning the middle of the site. The hall, floored and partitioned, was occupied as a farmhouse until 1922 when Crawley restored it as the heart of the present fairy-tale residence. The two wings he added were joined by a further extension in 1937 by Walter Godfrey in a more debased Tudor style, closing the courtyard to make the house quadrangular. Ian Nairn considered the work to be 'imitation carried to the point of genius'.[3]

The timber-framed hall, 46 feet by 24½ feet and about 42 feet high, rises from a stone plinth with herringbone brick noggin filling

PLATE 132 Crowhurst Place: from the north-west

the close framing.[4] The roof of Horsham tiles is supported on deeply projecting eaves carried on original curved brackets. Internally, the hall is divided into three bays by four heavily moulded tie beams at eaves level, two against the end walls, supported by moulded braces from replacement corbels. There are no signs that the beams carried crown posts. But an attempt was made to offset their heaviness by creating a barrel vault effect through a close network of scissor rafters with four-centred heads. To some extent, it is a more elegant structure than its sister hall at Crowhurst.

There are original cross-passage entries at the lower end and bay windows at the upper. The west bay window is original, with the east one reconstructed in 1923–4 on original internal evidence, although both gables are twentieth-century additions. Apart from the reconstruction of the bay window, new windows were inserted in the body of the hall, and the narrow wooden buttresses and louvre framing were added, a cellar created, the post-medieval chimney rebuilt and refurnished[5] and a screen built on the line of the first bay to create a separate dining room. Two of the original timber-framed office doorways survive, with the wider four-centred archway to the kitchen passage probably flanked by a further doorway on the site of the (blocked) fireplace.

The date of the hall is not known. As there is neither decorative, heraldic, nor documentary evidence for its construction, this can only be determined by dendrochronology. The hall is usually ascribed to *c.*1450, but in planning terms the occurrence of the double bay windows at the upper end suggests a post-Eltham hall date, while the mouldings of the tie-beam braces are of a form common until the mid-sixteenth century. It is therefore unlikely that the hall was built before the close of the fifteenth century.

The estate, originally known as Blockfield, only emerges as a distinct entity in the mid-fifteenth century when it was purchased by the Gaynesford family. Old Surrey Hall, more isolated than Crowhurst Place 5 miles north, was built by a junior branch of the family but on a more impressive scale. It is the largest of the medieval open-hall houses of the Weald, and slightly larger than those at Ockwells, Little Sodbury, and Athelhampton. Its position and the discovery of foundations eastwards[6] suggest that it may have been part of a double courtyard house – a comment on the rapid rise of this younger branch of the family.

The earliest recorded holder of the manor was Richard Gaynesford in 1477 (d.1483) followed by his younger brother, John, who was High Sheriff of Surrey in 1501–2 and served on the grand jury at the trial of Buckingham in 1521. The Gaynesford family sold the property in 1679 and it declined in status and condition until the hall stood alone as a farm labourer's cottage awaiting its metamorphosis in 1922 by George Crawley.

NOTES
1 Brit. Lib., Harleian MS 392.
2 The Gaynesford coat of arms occurs on the hammer beams of the hall roof at Great Dixter.
3 I. Nairn and N. Pevsner, *The Buildings of England: Surrey* (1962) 334.
4 As at Ockwells, Old Surrey Hall raises the question whether the brick noggin is original or a post-sixteenth-century replacement of plaster infill.
5 The restorer found traces of a hearth in the middle of the hall. Clifford (1959).
6 Arthur Oswald (1929) referred to the discovery of foundations which

suggested that an early court lay to the east of the hall. H. Dalton Clifford (1959) noted thirty years later that the foundations suggested that the original plan was H-shaped with the hall in the middle, and that the eastern wings may have been enclosed to form a courtyard.

Crowhurst Place
C. Bailey, *Surrey Arch. Coll.* 4 (1869) 271–8
W. D. Gainsford, *Annals of the House of Gainsford between AD1331 and AD1909* (1909)
VCH, *Surrey*, IV (1912) 275–8
M. Conway, *Country Life* (July 1919); edited in H. A. Tipping, *English Homes*, Pds I and II, vol.2 (1937) 155–62
R. H. C. Headlam, *George Crawley: A Memoir* (1929)
R. W. McDowall, *Surrey Arch. Coll.* 64 (1967) 148–53

Old Surrey Hall
A. Oswald, *Country Life* (September 1929)
H. D. Clifford, *Country Life* (October 1959)

CROYDON PALACE, Surrey

Unlike Eltham Palace, the initial country atmosphere of Croydon Palace has been overwhelmed by the development of Croydon as a suburb of London. Since the nineteenth century, most of the palace site has been cut up by roads, houses, light industrial premises, and car parks so that only the core structures survive but none of the subsidiary buildings or setting. The palace formerly covered 8½ acres and some of its water-enclosed gardens, fishponds and meadows existed until the late Victorian years, but the medieval remains are now squashed between the rebuilt parish church and some mean streets so that it looks increasingly like the school complex that it is.

The site has a building history dating back to the late eleventh century, with some stone elements traceable to at least the twelfth century.[1] The present palace[2] is essentially a late medieval residence developed in two phases: the first commenced towards the close of the fourteenth century, with the other extending throughout the second half of the fifteenth century. Documentary evidence for building activity at Croydon is extremely scanty but some of the major work can be identified from the heraldic corbels.

The last episcopal occupant was archbishop Herring (1747–57), who undertook considerable repairs, but after his death a period of unoccupation gave way to neglect and its sale in 1781. For a hundred years, the buildings and grounds were used for calico printing and bleaching and multi-residential use. The gatehouse and part of the stable block were pulled down in 1806 (except for the inner arch), followed two years later by the demolition of the west range of lodgings so that the churchyard could be enlarged. The kitchen, buttery, and pantry were torn down in 1810 and the lower end of the great hall collapsed in 1830. The east range of lodgings was destroyed by 1880 and with it the last vestiges of the outer court.[3] The remaining buildings were rescued from a very parlous state by their conversion to a school in 1889 and it still fulfils the same function today.

With the destruction of the outer court, offices, gardens and grounds, only the archbishops' residential suite survives, together with the great hall which gives access to it. The apartments are irregularly grouped round two small courts and are more cramped than the similar accommodation at Saltwood Castle or Knole, for the adjacent churchyard curtailed any generous development plans. Yet despite their very chequered history and abuse, the hall and apartments at Croydon are one of the most complete and important survivals of late medieval accommodation in south-east England and the present multi-purpose use of every room in the palace maintains its integrity.

Part of the large *outer court* is a cemetery extension but the majority is used today for classrooms and car parking. The description and engravings of the court published by Ducarel in 1790[4] show that it was formerly enclosed on two sides by ranges of lodgings, with the gatehouse in the north-east corner (not opposite the hall porch) and a barn and stabling closing the street approach. Built of brick with a regular pattern of doors and windows and an internal corridor giving access to all chambers and stairs, the longer line of lodgings on the east side was of a higher standard than that opposite. This range consisted of six lodgings on each floor with projecting chimney stacks, two with adjacent garderobes, flanked by a smaller unheated chamber at either end. The ground-floor corridor was joined to the hall porch by a buttressed link-building screening the kitchen and offices. The lodgings on the opposite side of the court consisted of eight smaller chambers on each floor with wall fireplaces, no garderobes, and a single staircase to the upper floor. The parallel with the overall layout, lodgings, and buttressed link of the outer court at Dartington Hall is particularly close, including the facility differences between the two ranges indicative of separate building phases. The episcopal work dates from the mid-fifteenth century when brick and diaper work became common at Croydon, while the thirty-two lodgings benefited from corridor access rather than the individual approach adopted half a century earlier at Dartington Hall. The lower half of the gatehouse was of stone with entrance archways of late fourteenth-century date, but the two upper storeys in diapered brick were probably added by Morton (1486–1500) a century later.[5] Excavation in 1970 revealed that the barn and stable block had been rebuilt on at least two occasions – initially under archbishop Arundel (1399–1400),[6] and again by Sir William Brereton in the 1640s/50s.[7]

The origins of the *great hall* are thirteenth century[8] but the earliest survival is the two-storeyed porch. Built of flint rubble with stone dressings, the buttressed outer walls (and those of the hall) have been heavily renewed and refaced, the stair turret on the east side has been removed, and the upper chamber rebuilt. Internally, the porch has an octopartite vault with foliated bosses, and a two-centred inner archway, considerably simpler than the contemporary outer archway. The porch is reasonably attributed to archbishop Courtenay (1381–96), but it may be by archbishop Arundel during the first years of his episcopate. He built a timber-framed hall in 1399–1400, though probably not the origin of the present one.[9]

The hall was remodelled by archbishop Stafford (1443–52) between c.1445 and 1450. At 56 feet long, 38 feet wide and 55 feet high, this spacious apartment is just 6 feet shorter than the hall at Penshurst Place. Stafford inserted the line of windows high up in the earlier side walls – three uncusped lights under four-centred heads – and crowned the apartments with a complicated form of arch-braced roof of four bays with two levels of collar beams and two lines of purlins. The trusses are supported externally on substantial buttresses and internally on timber columns with moulded

PLATE 133 Croydon Palace: hall from the north-west

capitals and bases rising from corbels of angels carrying the contemporary shields of Stafford (twice), his kinsman Humphrey, earl of Stafford created duke of Buckingham in 1444, and Richard duke of York.[10] Stafford's cross-passage doorway survives and the inner arch of the single-storey bay window at the upper end, but not the central hearth or louvre.[11] The elaborate canopied arms of Henry VI in the middle of the upper end wall were rescued from the destroyed east wall in 1830, having been moved less than a century earlier from a passage at the rear of the hall.[12]

The lower end wall is a nineteenth-century rebuild occasioned by its collapse after the destruction of the adjacent offices and kitchen where Old Palace Road and a row of suburban houses now stand. Pugin's engraving of 1829[13] suggests that the three service doorways, the central one higher than its companions, were fourteenth-century work contemporary with the hall porch, while Ducarel suggests that the kitchen and buttery may have been no later than this period.[14] There was also a large window and three gable slits in the end wall,[15] and although this was entirely destroyed, medieval elements in the present end wall indicate that its collapse in 1830, graphically shown in Joseph Nash's contemporary lithograph, was not so wholesale as he suggests.

The reason why Stafford rebuilt the upper part of the hall is unclear. It may have been unsafe, for the close and complex network of purlins and rafters suggests that stability considerably exercised the minds of the master-carpenter and his patron (and Herring in the mid-eighteenth century), or it may have been to get rid of the inconvenience of an earlier aisled hall which survived the fourteenth-century modifications.[16] London and its suburbs have an outstanding group of late medieval halls beginning with that of the abbot of Westminster and the extraordinary royal hall nearby. The group concludes with the early Tudor structures at Beddington and Hampton Court, and between them are three fifteenth-century structures at Croydon, Crosby, and Eltham respectively, all on a sumptuous scale with that at Croydon as the least known.

The *private apartments* of the archbishop lie on the upper floor of a series of two-storeyed ranges with the ground-floor rooms of low proportions for domestic and office use. The two chambers beneath the private hall, separated by a wall with a fourteenth-century doorway and marked externally by an angle pilaster buttress, show evidence of loops with semi-circular heads of possibly late twelfth-century date.[17] This suggests there was either a two-storeyed residential block immediately to the rear of the hall or a corridor link as at Charing and Mayfield palaces. Whichever applied, it has left no pre-fifteenth-century trace linking the great hall with this early building 20 feet from it. Rebuilding the private apartments was undertaken by Arundel (and possibly Courtenay) at the very beginning of the fifteenth century, and continued from the middle of the century by Stafford, Bourchier, and Morton in virtually a single programme until the close of the century. Only Chichele (1414–43) failed to make a contribution in the fifteenth century, but he concentrated on completing the parish church begun by Courtenay.

Stafford's doorway in the end wall of the great hall opens into a lobby initiated by him and still marked by a continuation of the hall's ashlar offset. The early seventeenth-century staircase replaces the original approach to the private hall (the 'Guard Room'). This imposing chamber, 51 feet long and 22 feet wide, was rebuilt by archbishop Arundel (1397–1414), possibly completing work planned or begun by Courtenay. It was the archbishop's inner hall and is now used as the school library. The four-centred barrel roof has been ceiled but the moulded principals dividing it into three bays are exposed. They are supported on finely carved corbels, of angels holding musical instruments in the corners of the room, of the arms of Arundel (twice) and Canterbury, and of the instruments of the passion in the central bay. The oriel is early Tudor (rebuilt 1910), the windows and fireplace are early eighteenth-century insertions, and the doorways are brutally modern.

The extent of the Courtenay/Arundel remodelling at Croydon Palace is conjectural. Apart from the alterations to the great hall and the newly built private hall, their rebuilding programme seems to have included two further elements. The privy chamber block with its newel staircase opening off the upper end of the private hall was similarly built of stone and flint rubble and may have contained the private chapel which Courtenay is known to have erected at Croydon.[18] The other structure incorporating flint-rubble walling is the lower part of the chapel block, but its form and linkage with the private hall are not known.

The next phase commenced in the middle of the century with Stafford's aforementioned reconstruction of the great hall and lobby. Later alterations have made it difficult to establish whether he or Bourchier was responsible for remodelling the chamber block immediately behind the great hall, but the original location of the canopied royal arms in a passage at the rear of the hall suggests the work of Stafford.

A more extended programme was undertaken by his successor, archbishop Bourchier (1454–86), who redeveloped the *chapel*. It is like a patchwork quilt. The ground floor has flint walls suggesting work fairly close to 1400, and the three central bays of the upper chapel may be of similar date, possibly under construction when Arundel ordained in an oratory in the palace in 1401.[19] This stand-alone structure was extended and refaced in brick by Bourchier and provided with independent covered access from the outer court. As in the great hall, the side windows are in the upper walling, with an extended seven-light window at the east end. The work can be compared with Bourchier's chapel at Knole, but most

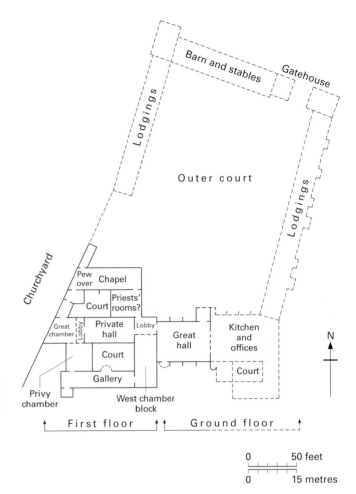

FIGURE 73 Croydon Palace site plan

of the fittings are seventeenth century apart from some of the stalls and Morton's screen. The three-storeyed link between the altar end and the principal apartments, possibly priests' rooms or vestries and with the only original surviving staircase in the palace, may be attributed to Bourchier rather than his successor, John Morton (1486–1500).

It was probably Bourchier rather than Morton who created the second court with a *gallery* linking the west chamber block with the privy chamber.[20] This gallery was a two-storeyed timber-framed structure with the principal gallery on the upper floor. The walls were encased with brick on the south side by archbishop Wake (1716–37) and plastered on the courtyard side, but the restoration of the short south wing in 1963[21] revealed the original structural form. The upper gallery, panelled and ceiled in the seventeenth century, rewindowed in the early eighteenth and now divided into classrooms, gives little hint that this is one of the earliest long galleries to survive in England. Corridor galleries, often two storeys high, were built in some of the largest houses in the fifteenth century, including Herstmonceux Castle (c.1438–49), and by Bourchier at Knole, as well as at Croydon, to give access to lodgings or rooms opening directly off them. Garden galleries, again of two storeys, occurred in some of Henry VII's residences and were essentially intended for recreation or viewing the privy garden as at

Richmond Palace. But the gallery at Croydon, 75 feet long and 15 feet wide and with windows on both sides, was not primarily a means to reach further rooms but an end in itself. Furthermore, the inner framing survives for a timber oriel and possibly a narrower screen on either side overlooking the small inner court.

Morton's work extending the private apartments towards the church was the last major building development at Croydon Palace. Built of brick, the acutely angled wall of the churchyard determined their layout, with diaper patterning particularly prominent on the west face where their form (and the crossed keys of St Peter in the chapel gable) can be most readily appreciated. A lobby beyond the private hall, 7 feet wide, gave access to a new great chamber (the 'dining room') which retains Morton's ceiling and fireplace but has been divided into two school rooms and a corridor. The lobby also provided access to the earlier privy chamber on the south side of the apartments, now distinguished by one original paired window and school furniture concealing an internal spiral staircase.

A three-storeyed corridor on the line of the churchyard wall with several original windows leads from the great chamber to an ante-room with fireplace, and the chapel. The corridor above, again approached by a replacement seventeenth-century staircase, repeats the pattern but gives access to a bedchamber open to the roof and the archbishop's private pew.

Morton's final work may have been remodelling the lobby at the north end of Stafford's residential range immediately west of the hall, for the ceiling timbers on both floors are like those in Morton's west rooms.[22]

The manor at Croydon illustrates the growth of a relatively small twelfth-century house to a late medieval palace complex. It began with a small block of private chambers and was extended by the construction of a large stone and flint-rubble hall. During the late fourteenth and early fifteenth centuries, the archbishop's suite was replaced by a more private hall, chapel, and several personal chambers, followed by the refurbishment of the great hall and the semi-public chambers behind it. A larger chapel was created, a timber-framed gallery was erected, and the outer court was filled with lodgings with corridor access. The first of the Tudor archbishops extended his private apartments in diapered brick, with site limitations making it one of the last irregularly planned palaces before the more formal double-courtyard plan became the accepted pattern for all major site developments, as Bourchier had demonstrated in tandem at Knole.

This late medieval manor developed from the plan adopted by John Holand at Dartington Hall at the close of the fourteenth century. The outer court with its twin range of lodgings, entrance approach, and adjacent barn was very similar in planning terms to that built in Devon. Although Holand's residential apartments beyond the upper chamber block were similarly subject to extensive changes in the mid-fifteenth century, they were also haphazardly grouped round a second court that subsequently included a gallery. The private apartments at Croydon were also irregularly patterned round a further court, but one between the upper chamber block and the churchyard wall which cramped their piecemeal development into a squashed double courtyard form.

In its final development stage, Croydon reflects several key planning elements during the later fifteenth century – a pattern which can be paralleled at Lord Cromwell's manor at Wingfield. The great hall continued to fulfil its long-established function as a

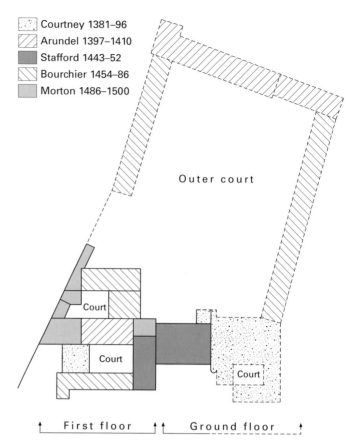

Key:
- Courtney 1381–96
- Arundel 1397–1410
- Stafford 1443–52
- Bourchier 1454–86
- Morton 1486–1500

Outer court

Court

Court

Court

First floor ↕ Ground floor

FIGURE 74 Croydon Palace development phases

formal reception and dining apartment, particularly useful in view of the many royal visitors to Croydon. A door at the upper end gave access to a lobby and stairs in part of the upper chamber block leading either to a semi-public room in the remainder of the block, or ahead to the archbishop's imposing private hall and chambers. From the latter, a corridor on the line of the church-yard wall led to the chapel and the archbishop's pew, what may have been a lower chapel for lesser staff, and priests' room and vestries closing the east side of the court between the chapel and the upper chamber block. At about the same time, this semi-public chamber behind the great hall was extended by the long gallery which gave facilities for more private conversations and business with access at the upper end for the archbishop to retire to his private apartments.

The mutilation of the palace between 1781 and 1887 and its adoption as a school has stripped the buildings of much of their character. The bones still exist but little of the flesh. The plain windows, minimal decoration, and utilitarian occupation inevitably make a visit to the palace rather a joyless experience, though it is possibly the most complete late medieval manor to survive close to London.

NOTES
1 Lower walling of undercroft, round-headed light near great parlour. Walder (1990) 18–21.
2 It was not until the episcopacy of Whitgift (1583–1604) that the manor or archbishop's residence at Croydon was referred to as a palace.

3 L. Thornhill, *Proceedings of the Croydon Natural History and Scientific Society* 17 (1987) 209–48.

4 Ducarel (1790) 45, pl. 3; also Oswald (1965). A suggested ground plan of the court is given in Faulkner (1970) 137.

5 Both gatehouse frontages are illustrated by Ducarel (1790) pl. 4.

6 Anderson (1879) 295–6 repeating E. R. Mores in *Bibliotheca Topographica Britannica* (1790) 54–6.

7 Chadwick and Phillpotts, *Surrey Arch. Coll.* 89 (2002) 40 replacing P. Drewett, *Arch. Jour.* 128 (1971) 162–5.

8 Faulkner (1970) 134 suggests that two lines of quoins in the rebuilt east end are evidence of buttresses supporting a thirteenth-century aisled structure. A window jamb and a blocked opening of the earlier hall are also visible in the lower part of the north wall.

9 Suggested by Chadwick and Phillpotts, *Surrey Arch. Coll.* 89 (2002) 45.

10 The other shields are later – Laud and Juxon, and Herring who inserted the additional roof ties in 1748.

11 The bay window was destroyed in the mid-nineteenth century when the hall was used as a bleaching house. Ducarel refers to the former central hearth and louvre. The brick parapet is sixteenth century.

12 J. Milles writing in 1754 in *Bibliotheca Topographica Britannica* (1790) 60–7.

13 *Examples of Gothic Architecture* (1838) pl. 38.

14 Ducarel (1790) 46.

15 E. Blore, Brit. Lib., Add. MS 42, 022, ff.56 and 57.

16 Faulkner (1970) 135.

17 *Ibid.* 133–4. The blocked loop is now covered but the pilaster buttress has been more clearly revealed since 1970. Archbishop Langton stayed at the residence on this site in 1213–15.

18 Hobson (1909) 229–31; Walder (1990) 30–5.

19 Anderson (1879) 295, 296.

20 R. Coope, *Arch. Hist.* 29 (1986) 68 n.27.

21 The purpose of this projection providing only two small rooms is unclear. There is a dearth of garderobes at Croydon and the projection may have served to relieve the pressure. It has been moved eastwards from its original site, stands on 2 feet of brickwork, and incorporates a badly weathered fifteenth-century doorway at ground level. Walder (1990) 33.

22 *Ibid.* 64.

A. C. Ducarel, 'History and antiquities of Croydon', in *Bibliotheca Topographica Britannica*, II (1790)

J. C. Anderson, *The Archiepiscopal Palace at Croydon* (1879)

J. M. Hobson, *The Reliquary* 15 (1909) 225–39

B. Fletcher and J. M. Hobson, *Surrey Arch. Coll.* 24 (1911) 81–91

VCH, *Surrey*, IV (1912) 206–13

A. Oswald, *Country Life* (April 1965)

P. A. Faulkner, *Arch. Jour.* 127 (1970) 133–8

E. A. Walder, 'Croydon Palace in its context to 1500', MA thesis, St David's University College, University of Wales (1990)

A. M. Chadwick and C. Phillpotts, *Surrey Arch. Coll.* 89 (2002) 27–52

EAST MEON COURT HOUSE, Hampshire

This is a most splendid survival, harmoniously sited close to the Norman-towered church and next to the smooth grass slope of a Hampshire Downs hill. It was subject to a sympathetic restoration by Morley Horder (d.1944) in the early 1930s after he had rescued the property from farm occupation, and he added an exemplary extension to the seventeenth-century timber-framed farmhouse for

PLATE 134 East Meon Court House: from the west

his own use so that the hall need not be domesticated. East Meon joins a handful of houses that includes Haddon, Penshurst, Dartington, Martock, and Stoke Sub Hamdon where the properties are of sufficient occupational scale to allow the roofed halls to remain in their barely furnished medieval state.

East Meon was a hall and cross-wing house, built of flint and occasional stone, with a clay-tiled roof. The 4 foot thick walls are well worn, as is the dressed sandstone of the windows and doorways, but neither has needed substantive remedial treatment. The hall, chamber, and kitchen of the bishop's house at East Meon are recorded in the first extant pipe roll of the bishopric for 1208–9.[1] There is no record of substantial building activity until the close of the fourteenth century, when the hall, stair lobby, and lower cross wing with garderobe block were rebuilt by William Wykeham. The upper cross wing was remodelled forty years later, but it no longer exists, leaving the hall and lower cross wing as the well-preserved record of Wykeham's work of 1395–7. This was carried out under the supervision of his master-mason William Wynford, at a cost of just over £110.[2]

The accounts confirm there was an outer court with a timber-framed gatehouse rebuilt by bishop Beaufort in 1438–9, while nineteenth-century maps, identifying post-medieval farm buildings, point to the earlier larger scale of this property. The area is now marked by an eighteenth-century thatched barn and a formal yew-enclosed garden by Horder. The imposing cross-passage doorways to the hall, neither porch-protected, have plain continuous chamfers and two-centred heads with higher four-centred rear arches. They access the hall, 48 feet by 26 feet internally and 46 feet high to the open roof. The walls are unplastered, but Horder floored the area with York paving slabs laid a foot lower than originally, leaving oddly positioned stops to the doors.

The three-bay hall is lit by a tall single window in the first and third bays, and opposing windows in the second one, all of two cinquefoiled and transomed lights set in broad splays with a plain depressed head. The windows were initially shuttered, not glazed until 1441, and there were no window seats. Nor was there a mural fireplace, but an open hearth which heavily sooted the roof timbers, though there is no extant evidence of a louvre. The relatively small doorway in the end bay opened into what the building accounts called an 'oriel' – a lobby to the upper cross wing – now pulled down, with the entry blocked externally. The oddly angled line of the end wall can only have arisen because of the position of a pre-existing structure, and this is confirmed by masonry joints and its different wall texture. Horder removed a two-storeyed farm tenancy against its inner face which has scarred it, and inserted the rectangular-framed fireplace which he found in the grounds of the house. The lintel of six blind quatrefoils with blank shields is early to mid-fifteenth century (pl. 104). The arch-braced tie-beam and crown-post to collar-purlin roof is supported on eight stone corbels of alternate carved heads of a bishop and a bearded king. The roof is competently made but markedly plain for an episcopal house.

Nothing survives of the upper cross wing which preceded Wykeham's building programme and had become so dilapidated that bishop Beaufort remodelled it in 1439–42.[3] The accounts show that it included a chapel next to the lord's (i.e. bishop's) chamber, and that this had glazed windows, a stone chimney, and a screen beside the bishop's bed.[4] It is possible that the fine fireplace, now in the hall, and the stone chimney cap currently used as a garden orna-

PLATE 135 East Meon Court House: hall interior towards the services

ment, may have come from this suite. The wing could not have been more than 15–16 feet wide because of falling ground, while foundations traceable in dry weather suggest it may have projected further west than its fellow wing.[5] This structure was modified in the late sixteenth/seventeenth century when a brick chimney flue was inserted in the hall wall, while subsidence may have hastened the destruction of this wing.

The lower chamber block is a tall gabled cross wing with a smaller gabled extension. The ground floor was divided into two offices entered from the hall by single chamfered doorways which repeat the higher rear arches of the cross-passage doorways. The framework of the hall screen with a central and two side entries existed in 1908, but Horder removed this and the wooden partition separating the two service rooms as he considered them inferior, secondary work.[6] The services partition, now marked by lines on the end wall and central wooden post, divided the area into a slightly smaller and larger room, both with two single-light windows. The west room accommodated the stair underside and the door to an inner chamber. With its high single light and retained old shutter, this relatively tall room was probably used for storage.

The upper floor was approached not from the cross passage but

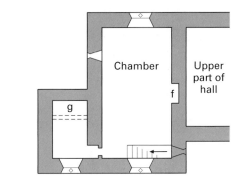

UPPER FLOOR

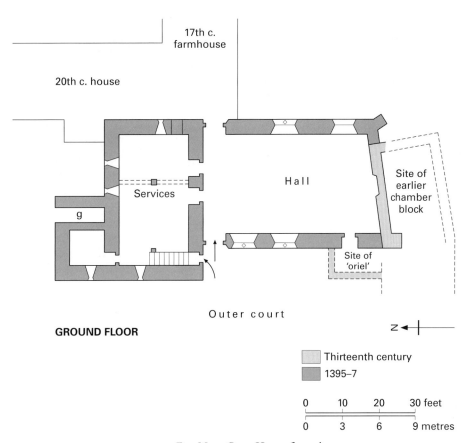

GROUND FLOOR

FIGURE 75 East Meon Court House: floor plans

from an external doorway opening on to a stair fortuitously retaining its original solid timber steps. This substantive chamber, 36 feet by 18 feet, has two trefoiled lights at each end (one converted by Horder to a door) and a single north light.[7] The contemporary fireplace in a revealed stone stack in the hall end wall has a slightly curved head but it is otherwise plain. The three-bay roof repeats the hall form but the tie beams rest on wall plates rather than corbels, and the crown posts are not chamfered.

The doorway at the head of the stair – the only one now at the correct floor level – opens into a closet with garderobe facility. It has a two-light window but no fireplace, and as it has lost the garde-

robe partition, it is a single room 16 feet by 11 feet to the uninterrupted collared roof. However, the garderobe chute survives below, with its pit floored in 2000.

East Meon was not a first-rank residence like that at Bishop's Waltham, nor was it just a manorial farm like Lodge Farm, Odiham. The quite separate approach to the upper floor of the lower cross wing supports its possible use as a court room twice a year with an inner closet for the clerk, though the name 'Court House' was not used before 1647.[8] But it was far more a record and accounting centre for the large estate of about 19,000 acres[9] and is likely to have been the steward's lodging and business area. Initially it was called the 'new chamber' to distinguish it from the lord's chamber, and that occupational distinction continued after Beaufort remodelled the bishop's suite.[10] The body of the house would have been a periodic residence for household officials and servants, and was occasionally used by the bishop, though not apparently by Wykeham. It was (and is) a particularly pleasant rural retreat, one where the bishop could hunt or relax for one or two days with a small group of companions. It was also used by the bishop's friends, but in the hierarchy of episcopal properties East Meon was a minor, though valuable, multi-purpose residence.

What characterises the house is its economy of style. All door and window arches are two-centred rather than the more fashionable four-centred. Doorways are single chamfered, and the windows lack elaborate traceried heads, seats, and glazing initially, while the roofs are markedly plain. This contrasts with the greater elaboration of the other Wykeham (and Wynford) buildings, particularly Winchester College, but also Bishop's Waltham Palace, and points up the lower status of this house, though the simplicity of timberwork has been claimed as a regional characteristic.[11] Yet the principal doorways and windows are tall, the rooms are particularly well proportioned, and the restrained decoration may not necessarily have extended to the bishop's suite had that been part of Wykeham's programme.

NOTES

1 *The Pipe Roll of the Bishopric of Winchester 1208–9*, ed. H. Hall (1903) 47. Part of the church was built by bishop Henry of Blois (d.1171) who may have initiated a residence on the site of the present Court, used by King John in 1211.
2 Roberts (1993) 458–66.
3 This wing may have stood since at least the opening of the thirteenth century, see note 1.
4 Roberts (1993) 462.
5 Without excavation, it is difficult to distinguish any stone/flint foundations from the brick walls of known farm buildings to the south-west.
6 Oswald (1937) 510.
7 The two gable lancets and that over the stair entry are Horder insertions in concrete to identify his work, as elsewhere in the house.

8 Roberts (1993) 479.
9 It retained this extent until the mid-nineteenth century. VCH, III (1908) 64, 76–8. The farm buildings that made the property so useful between the seventeenth and nineteenth centuries may have originated in those mentioned in the medieval accounts. They included hay and barley barns, a granary, and a cowshed. Roberts (1993) 461–2.
10 Roberts (1993) 472 suggests otherwise.
11 R. Warmington in J. N. Hare, *Arch. Jour.* 145 (1988) 246, though he is referring to a lodging range of 1438–42 at Bishop's Waltham Palace.

VCH, *Hampshire*, III (1908) 65–6
A. Oswald, *Country Life* (May 1937)
E. Roberts, *Arch. Jour.* 150 (1993) 456–81

ESHER PALACE, Surrey

The bishop of Winchester's house at Esher, like Farnham Castle, was a convenient stopping point between Southwark and Winchester. The see had purchased the manor in 1245 and constructed a small lodging there shortly afterwards which had proved particularly popular with William Wykeham and Henry Beaufort, but it was William Waynflete who initiated the redevelopment of the site during the mid-1460s.[1] We have no building accounts for this work but the gatehouse had been completed before April 1484 when 'the flore of the chambyr in the towre over the gate of the manor of Essher' was taken as the model for that of the bishop's grammar school under construction at Wainfleet in Lincolnshire.[2] The palace was an irregular group of buildings on the banks of the River Mole, with the gateway originally facing towards Esher Green rather than the river as today. A drawing of 1606 shows that Waynflete's gatehouse was approached through a stable yard and gave access to a quadrangle with a range of buildings on either side. Opposite was the porch of the hall, leading to a group of three-storeyed residential apartments built on a promontory in the river at the right-hand angle of the courtyard.[3] The extent of Waynflete's responsibility for this work is uncertain, but excavation in 1912 suggested that it

PLATE 136 Esher Palace: engraving from the north by S. and N. Buck (1737) showing William Kent's alterations

included much of the quadrangle and the hall, but excluded the residential apartments.[4]

In 1718, Aubrey recorded that the timberwork in the hall was 'not unlike that in Westminster Hall',[5] but much of the bishop's work had already been pulled down in 1678. The site was refashioned by William Kent in the early 1730s, but it passed through several hands during the nineteenth century until the estate was broken up in the early 1930s. The sole surviving element of the palace is therefore approached today through roads of individual suburban houses in a sequence of eclectic styles.

The gatehouse stands as an isolated tree-embowered remnant. It was so substantially altered by Kent that it looks more like an over-sized Gothick folly than a late medieval gatehouse. It is a four-storeyed structure with polygonal angle turrets rising above the roof line and was originally flanked by curtain walls.[6] The extensive use of diapered brickwork on the two principal façades remains its most striking feature – apart from the replacement windows inserted by Kent. Each floor is marked by a bold string course (upper two heavily restored) which break up the brickwork patterns. The battlements were carried on miniature blind corbels and the original brick drip mouldings survive, but none of the window fitments. The rib-vaulted passageway, protected by a portcullis at either end,[7] was flanked by a chamber on either side. A brick staircase in the north-west angle, similar to contemporary work at Kirby Muxloe Castle, rises through all floors, which may have consisted of a large outer and small inner chamber at each level, with a garderobe behind the staircase.

After the politician Henry Pelham bought the estate in 1729, William Kent was asked to update the house and its later wings. He added a single-storey fretted porch between the turrets, altered all the windows, and inserted several striking quatrefoil openings to create one of the earliest examples of Rococo Gothick. Waynflete's rib-vaulted entrance hall was stuccoed and pretty niches were added along its walls.

Compared with his residential tower at Farnham Castle, Waynflete's building at Esher was a conventional gatehouse, albeit one providing three suites of lodgings. Both structures are decorated with close-set diapering, but dressed stonework is used at Esher which breaks up the patterning. The Esher gatehouse is less severe and lacks the more sophisticated elements introduced at Farnham such as the cusped corbelling, the prominent line of machicolations, and the unbroken diaper display. Whilst the Farnham tower of 1470–5 may reflect the uncertain political climate immediately following Edward IV's deposition and restoration, the prettier Esher gatehouse is more closely in tune with the relaxed mood of the king's later years.

NOTES
1 Floyer (1919–20). For Waynflete's building activities, V. Davis, *William Waynflete* (1993) 99–116.
2 Thompson (1960) 90.
3 Illustrated in Floyer (1919–20) 71.
4 *Ibid.* 70.
5 John Aubrey, *The Natural History and Antiquities of Surrey*, III (1718) 120–1. Aubrey also noted the existence of Waynflete's arms on the gatehouse, and on the still-existing keystone of the passage vaulting.
6 That on the west side was excavated in 1912. *Society of Antiquaries Prints and Drawings BP55*. The walls on either side were replaced by residential wings which were remodelled by Kent and destroyed early in the nineteenth century.

7 Covered by Kent's work, but the grooves still remain under the floor above the passageway.

R. Nevill, *Surrey Arch. Coll.* 7 (1880) 214–21
G. Lambert, *Esher Place* (1884)
J. K. Floyer, *Proceedings of the Society of Antiquaries* 32 (1919–20) 69–79
M. W. Thompson, *Surrey Arch. Coll.* 57 (1960) 85–92
Surrey County Council, *List of Antiquities in . . . Surrey* (5th edn 1965): floor plans and east elevation of gatehouse opp. 56 and 58, and plan of 1606 opp. 54

FARNHAM CASTLE, Surrey

A major residence of the bishops of Winchester from the twelfth century to 1927, Farnham Castle – like the similarly disordered archiepiscopal complex at Croydon – is still in occupational use. Farnham was a convenient stopping point just over half-way between the bishop's palaces at Southwark and Winchester and was in constant use throughout the middle ages. Always outside but dominating the town, the castle was a motte and bailey structure with a heterogeneous but highly important assemblage of domestic buildings in the bailey spanning eight centuries.

To place this late medieval work in context, the following summarises the primary development phases of this little studied complex. The castle was possibly an early country house, fortified with a square tower surmounting a conical mound during the

PLATE 137 Farnham Castle: Waynflete's Tower from the south

1130s. Later that century, the tower was pulled down and the mound encased by the masonry of the present shell keep which formerly rose higher. There also seem to have been two stages in the early development of the hall, initiating the three-sided enclosure of the bailey with the keep filling the fourth. The first hall was possibly a two-storeyed structure to judge by the chiselled-off arcading on the south wall face,[1] followed by the present aisled hall with its wooden arcade and contemporary chapel of the late twelfth century.[2] The kitchen at the lower end of the hall and the newel-approached bishop's *camera* with its concealed scissor-beam roof at the upper end were developed early in the thirteenth century, probably by Peter de la Roche (1205–38).[3]

Under bishop Edington (1346–66), the network of rooms within the keep was improved by the construction of a small hall and chapel,[4] while a large chapel was initiated in the bailey in 1347–8 and completed in 1353 in extension of the great hall and spreading beyond the original bailey ditch.[5] In 1378, the outer wall of the hall was raised by bishop William Wykeham (1367–1404) and lit by twin-light clerestory windows,[6] possibly at the same time as the two-light transomed window with cusped heads (now blocked) was inserted in the *camera*.

The most extensive late medieval programme was undertaken by bishop Waynflete (1447–86) culminating in the impressive entry tower erected between 1470 and 1475.[7] The west side of the bailey was closed during the sixteenth century by a three-storeyed timber-framed lodging range for guests with first- and second-floor balconies. The last major addition was the chapel opposite, added in the 1660s by bishop Morley after the Restoration, though he also gave the hall its present character and built the great stair. Keep and bailey remained in residential use throughout late medieval and Tudor times, but with the slighting of the keep in 1648 its occupation was abandoned and it fell into ruin. The bailey buildings remained the centre of the episcopal household until 1956[8] when it became the Centre for International Briefing preparing people for living and working abroad.

Waynflete's entry replaced a bridge and earlier stone porch tower which stood on foundations still below its brick replacement. The replacement entry continued to be in line with Castle Street rising from the town centre, but although it gives formal access to the hall and domestic buildings, it was essentially a residential tower built on a bulky scale. In plan, it is a square, four-storeyed structure with shallow semi-octagonal towers to the front and a substantial projection on the east side. Entirely built of red brick heightened with mortar mixed with red ochre,[9] the unbroken façades of the tower are densely patterned with dark headers in diamond shapes up to battlement level. A plain, four-centred brick archway, formerly portcullis-protected, gives access to a broad flight of steps and passage leading to a contemporary stone doorway opening into the hall. The passage was flanked by a porter's lodge and a narrow room approached internally, all above a vaulted basement. All early windows were replaced in the eighteenth century with larger sash openings 'of more than ordinary dullness'.[10] The tower is crowned with a battlemented parapet carried on miniature cusped corbelling broken by false machicolations on two sides, with similar corbelling carrying the turret battlements. As the tower was not free-standing but built against earlier stone walling, the battlements and angle towers are limited to three and two sides respectively.

The entrance to the hall was incidental and is played down.

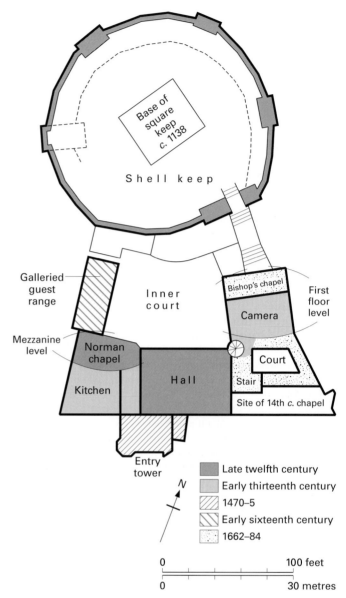

FIGURE 76 Farnham Castle: site plan

However, it determined the position of the tower, even though it necessitated positioning the approach on one side to be in line with the screens passage and consequently broke the line of the right-hand angle tower. As Waynflete's building was constructed in the former bailey ditch, it rises from a lower level than the earlier hall and kitchen flanking it.[11] There is a slight plinth, but no offset or string course to lighten the elevation until the level of the machicolations and corbelling carrying a very solid battlemented parapet. There is an absence of contrasting stonework for windows or doorways, while the angle towers are unrelieved by any openings. These factors created a severe frontage necessary to achieve unrelieved surfaces to display the newly developed fashion for all-over diaper, of which this is an early example. Unfortunately, the superstructure is top heavy, with an overemphatic parapet, machicolations which are too narrow to provide adequate contrasting light and shade, and a cardboard appearance to the side elevations through failing to give

338

the rear elevation corbelled turrets similar to that topping the stair projection. Ian Nairn, however, sees the tower as extraordinarily sophisticated architecture, with the entrance arch showing alarming suavity and the gatehouse as a whole displaying subtle detailing without contemporary peer.[12]

Internally, the upper floors of the tower were divided into corridors and rooms in the eighteenth century (when the attic rooms may have been created) and all fittings date from this period. No original fireplaces, garderobes, windows or stairs survive and therefore its internal planning is conjectural. The brickwork between the front windows is disturbed and not diapered (clearer in some photographs than on site) which suggests that some of the eighteenth-century openings are not replacing earlier windows, although this is more true of the enlarged side windows. The absence of projecting chimney breasts also seems to be part of the scheme for creating unbroken façades. It is likely that the present staircase replaces an earlier one in part of the projection, with the remainder occupied by small chambers or garderobes lit by windows, now blocked. How the accommodation was patterned is guesswork. The first floor could have been an audience hall with a withdrawing chamber above for the bishop, although this would have been more convincingly built at the upper end of the hall range, and he still made considerable use of the accommodation within the shell keep. It is more likely, therefore, that this impressive tower provided suites of lodgings for honoured guests, including sovereigns, who were particularly frequent visitors during the fifteenth century.[13]

Waynflete, as executor to Sir John Fastolf and Lord Cromwell, is likely to have been inspired by their brick residences, and particularly by the great tower at Tattershall. But why did Waynflete adopt the form of a keep-like tower here while his gatehouse at Esher was so traditional in form? The difference lies in their purpose – the one was principally an entry with some accommodation over, while those roles were reversed in the massive brick tower. Furthermore, the military head of the tower not only emphasised that Farnham was a palace-fortress but gave the castle (and incidentally the town) a new focus of attention. It may have been a reflection of the uncertain times immediately after Edward IV's readeption, but it was the combination of the new building material and the accommodation potential that appealed to the bishop of Lincoln in determining to follow suit at Buckden Palace.

NOTES

1 M. W. Thompson, *Medieval Bishops' Houses in England and Wales* (1998) 92. Also N. Riall, *Med. Arch.* 47 (2003) 115–29.

2 The single wooden arcade post has been dendro dated to *c*.1180. *Vern. Arch.* 27 (1996) 91.

3 At the same time, the whole site was enclosed with a curtain wall interrupted by square towers, extensively rebuilt or refaced in brick, followed by the outer gatehouse (with nineteenth-century additions above).

4 Thompson (1961; 1989 edn) 20.

5 Brooke (1985) 15–17; Robo (1935) 139–40.

6 Brooke (1985) 7.

7 Thompson (1960) 85–9. For Waynflete's extensive building activities, V. Davis, *William Waynflete* (1993) 99–116.

8 Farnham Palace was transferred to the new see of Guildford in 1927.

9 Thompson (1960) 88.

10 C. Peers in VCH, II (1905) 602.

11 Brooke (1985) 6. The banks protecting their bases have also been removed, adding to the patchiness of the south frontage.

12 I. Nairn and N. Pevsner, *The Buildings of England: Surrey* (1962) 200–1.

13 The extensive Winchester pipe rolls show that they included Edward IV in 1477, Richard III in 1483, and Henry VII and his queen in 1487.

VCH, *Surrey*, II (1905) 599–605
E. Robo, *Medieval Farnham* (1935) 121–53
A. Oswald, *Country Life* (1939) 652–6, 682–6
M.W. Thompson, *Surrey Arch. Coll.* 67 (1960) 85–92
M. W. Thompson, *Farnham Castle Keep: Official Handbook* (1961 and later editions)
P. D. Brooke, *Farnham Castle: The Forgotten Years* (1985)
Centre for International Briefing, *Farnham Castle: History and Guide* (1965 and later editions)

FORD PALACE and DAUNDELYON COURT, Kent

Very little stands of these two fifteenth-century brick residences in north-east Kent. Ford Palace near Reculver was developed by archbishop Morton between 1486 and 1500. Some brick walling survives at an angle of the outer court, and the walls and crown-post roof of part of the stable range incorporated in a farmhouse on that site. Yet this was a residence on a scale comparable with that built a generation earlier by archbishop Bourchier at Knole. It can be identified from a fragment of a map dated 1624, supplemented by a parliamentary survey of 1647.[1]

Leland noted that Morton 'made almost the hole house', but from the shaping of the plan it seems to have incorporated remains of an earlier residence of *c*.1300.[2] Built round four courts, the elongated outer court was like that at Eltham Palace, gatehouse-approached, and irregularly shaped. The area included the stables on the north side with an entry to the inner court which faced the buttressed great hall opposite. At 52 feet long and 27 feet wide, the hall rose through two storeys with the massive kitchen beyond the services at its lower end. Beyond the hall were two smaller courts separated by a longitudinal passage in line with the screens

PLATE 138 Daundelyon Court: gateway (1796)

339

passage. The hall formed one side of the privy court, with chambers and lodgings on two sides and a long gallery above on the east side facing the deer park. The fourth or base court beyond the services and kitchen was essentially for domestic offices.

This palace was the first major building in Kent to be constructed almost entirely of brick and was on a scale that vied with the residences of Henry VIII and those of his leading courtiers. It was distinguished, however, by a five-storey residential tower, 52 feet high, on the north side of the inner court. As it lay close to the hall and adjacent to the stone chapel, it may have been intended for Morton's private apartments, but it is more likely to have served as a guest tower like that at Wingfield Manor. The palace was demolished in 1658.

A house of some magnificence, 9 miles north-east, was similarly stripped of materials after it had burnt down in the eighteenth century. No more than a high-quality brick gatehouse survives of the residence of the Daundelyon family on the flatlands behind Margate. A little earlier than that erected by Morton at Ford, the so-called Dent De Lion gatehouse consists of a broad passage, 3 feet lower than originally, flanked at both ends by lofty turrets. The entry passage is spanned by two arches: a particularly tall four-centred one for carriages and a two-centred pedestrian archway. A single tall arch with capitals spans the rear. There was no chamber above the passage, which supported a wooden roof, but there are lodgings in each of the front turrets at ground and passage roof level, and a stair in the north-east rear turret.

The notable feature of this gatehouse is that it was designed with style. The frontage is built of narrow alternating bands of knapped flint and brick with stone dressings, so that it presented a show façade of contrasting colours – red brick, grey flint, and cream stonework – to striking effect.[3] The string course above the entrance was decorated with the coat of arms of the Daundelyon family in the middle, with corbelled lion heads with tongues at either end. Battlements and two gun ports gave the approach superficial pretensions of defence.

The shield dates this fine gateway to before 1445 when John Daundelyon, the last of this short-lived family, died.[4] The gatehouse now adjoins farm outbuildings of the 1830s, converted to residential purpose in the 1980s. Nothing stands of the family house a little to the north, though the gatehouse suggests that it was of some considerable style.

NOTES
1 Lambeth Palace Library: Comm. XIIa/23; A. Hussey, *Arch. Cant.* 26 (1904) 119–32; Gough (2001) 257–60.
2 Gough (2001) 253.
3 The same materials were used less formally in the body of the gatehouse, i.e. flint pebbles supported on a few courses of dressed stone with brick quoins. The tops of the turrets were rebuilt in yellow stock brick in the nineteenth century.
4 His armoured brass is in Margate Church. Professor Du Boulay suggested that his father may have been a farmer of Bishopsbourne during the 1390s: *The Lordship of Canterbury* (1966) 221.

Ford Palace
B. J. Bennet, *Arch. Cant.* 45 (1933) 168–73
K. McIntosh and H. E. Gough (eds.), *Hoath and Herne* (1984) 36–40
H. Gough, *Arch. Cant.* 121 (2001) 251–68

Dent De Lion gate
C. E. Woodruff, *Arch. Cant.* 25 (1902) 57–63

GREAT DIXTER, Sussex

Like Horselunges Manor, Great Dixter is a fifteenth-century vernacular residence that aspired to higher standing by its scale and high-quality detailing. In contrast with the many smaller stone manor houses, Great Dixter near Northiam may stand as the representative for that wealth of late medieval framed houses that span Sussex and the adjoining counties.

The house followed the standard plan of a hall open to the roof with a services cross wing at the lower end and a residential cross wing at the upper. Hall and upper cross wing still stand, with the hall, once more open to the roof, prefaced by a boldly projecting porch which gives the house a homely character. The two-storeyed office wing, long taken down, was replaced by a new one by Lutyens in 1910 when he added an earlier timber-framed hall house with chamber blocks under a single roof ridge brought from Benenden in Kent.[1]

Interest centres on the hall, 40 feet by 25 feet and 31 feet high, divided into four unequal bays but essentially separated into two by a massive braced tie beam spanning the middle of the chamber. There is a lesser tie beam at the lower end but the subsidiary bays support pseudo-hammer-beam trusses with the bracing of the hammer posts dying into the principal rafters. That at the upper end is not even tied into the adjacent wall but stands a foot away from it. The upper walling is close studded, rising from a moulded wall beam at mid level. Restored bay windows rising the height of the hall fill the third bay but the other windows and the fireplace at the lower end are Lutyens insertions made when the post-medieval floors, partitions, and windows throughout the house were removed in 1911. Evidence that some of the windows had originally been served by shutters sliding in grooves was happily mirrored by the survival of windows with wooden mullions and an original shutter in the Beneden house.

The two-storeyed cross wing with barge board gables and massive chimney breast is a three-bay structure divided by braced tie-beam trusses with king posts supported on moulded posts rising

PLATE 139 Great Dixter: first-floor chamber of upper cross wing

from the floor as in the great hall. The staircase at the rear of the hall and parlour, and the oriel windows, are Lutyens replacements. The dragon-jettied two-storeyed porch is a slightly later addition fitted against a jettied projection which had to be removed to accommodate it.[2] It is possible that the gabled end walls of the cross wing are also a secondary feature replacing the jettied frontage of a traditional Wealden type house under a continuous roof.

Great Dixter has a crude hall roof of mixed structural techniques and uneven bay design. The heraldic devices on the six hammer beams suggest a structure not later than the third quarter of the fifteenth century. The property was owned by the Etchingham family from the late fourteenth century. Its ownership passed by marriage from the Etchingham to the Wakehurst, Elrington, and Windsor families, complicated by rival claims on the property during the third quarter of the century.[3] The house was built by Sir Thomas Etchingham between 1464 when he inherited it from Elizabeth Wakehurst by default of her male line, and 1479 when he settled the property on his daughter Margaret, and her second husband Sir John Elrington. He was one of Edward IV's loyal household servants, promoted from gentry rank, knighted, and appointed cofferer from 1371 to 1374, and then promoted to treasurer of the king's household from 1474 until his death in 1483. The house was probably built between 1464 and 1470 when the line of Dalyngrigge of Bodiam died out, whose arms (with those of Gaynesford of Crowhurst) are on a hammer beam. As Sir Thomas Etchingham already held major properties at Etchingham and Udimore, Great Dixter was never more than a lesser house for him, but it was one of suitable size and rank for Sir John Elrington, though he did not implement the licence to crenellate he obtained in 1479.[4] Elrington's daughter married Andrew, 1st Lord Windsor and their badges occur in the solar fireplace spandrels, possibly at the time that modifications were made to this wing.

NOTES
1 C. Hind, *Country Life* (November 1993).
2 Ray (1909) 147.
3 Weaver (1913) 18–22; Martin and Martin (1987) 18.
4 *Cal. Pat. Rolls: 1476–85*, 162. An earlier moated residence had lain immediately south-west of the present house.

J. E. Ray, *Sussex Arch. Coll.* 52 (1909) 132–55
L. Weaver, *Country Life* (January 1913)
VCH, *Sussex*, IX (1937) 270–1
D. Martin and B. Martin, *Dated Houses in Eastern Sussex 1400–1750* (1987) 18–22

HALNAKER HOUSE, Sussex

Halnaker House is a little-known but extensive ruin 3 miles northeast of Chichester. Built of flint rubble, the principal elements were irregularly grouped round a courtyard on rising ground. The thirteenth-century chapel and fourteenth-century hall on two sides of the courtyard were formerly linked by a large residential range of medieval origin which has completely disappeared. The remainder of the site was enclosed by retaining walls and a defensive residential frontage added in the later fourteenth century. Drawings made in 1781 by S. H. Grimm are particularly valuable in illustrat-

ing its final if much altered form prior to the abandonment of the house in *c*.1800.[1]

The early thirteenth-century chapel is an oblong shell with lancet windows, in design not unlike the chancel at Appledram or the bishop's chapel at Chichester. The hall and offices range was rebuilt during the mid-fourteenth century but is now much ruined. The relatively small hall, 42 feet by 29 feet, was lit by a pair of windows towards the courtyard of two cusped and transomed lights under a quatrefoil and square hood mould.[2] The opposite wall has been completely destroyed but excavations in the 1950s showed that it was a hall of three and a half bays with a later fireplace in the north wall and a projecting stair turret giving access to the now destroyed solar. The destroyed upper residential block seems to have been three-storeyed with a blocked door from the dais opening into the ground-floor room and the existing door and steps in the south-east corner giving access to an undercroft with its ceiling marked by the line of corbels just above the present ground level. The two-storeyed porch to the hall is a late fourteenth-century addition, built against part of the earlier cross-passage arch, and it is matched by an early Tudor bay window abutting the dais-end bay of the hall but opening from the adjacent residential block.

The double block at the lower end of the hall was similarly three-storeyed, extended in line with the hall porch, gabled and bay windowed in the early sixteenth century. Part of the earlier offices block survives, with evidence of a central doorway and a low arch to its left, possibly a hatchway. The kitchen was in line with the offices,

PLATE 140 Halnaker House: gatehouse from the south

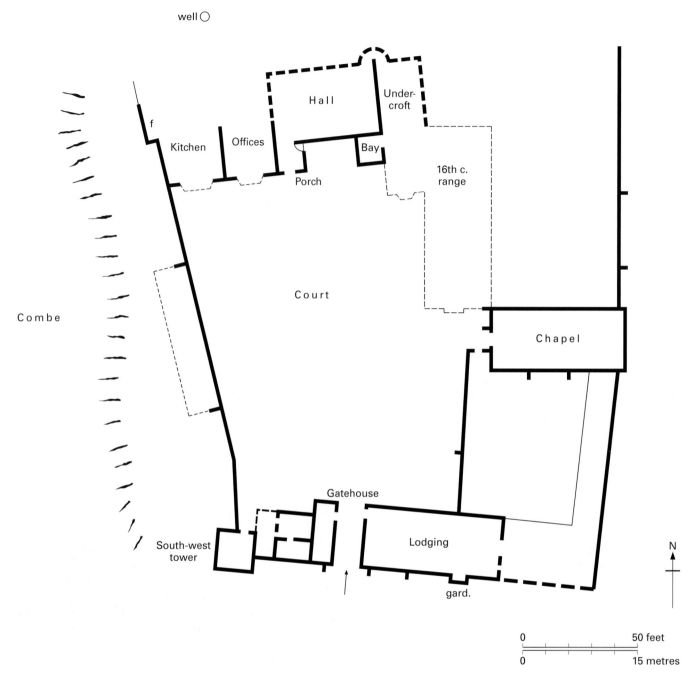

well ○

Hall

Under-croft

f

Kitchen

Offices

Bay

Porch

16th c. range

Court

Combe

Chapel

Gatehouse

South-west tower

Lodging

gard.

N

0   50 feet

0   15 metres

FIGURE 77 Halnaker House: site plan

with evidence of a lateral fireplace in the west wall.[3] A well exists north of the kitchen (adjacent to the swimming pool steps) but no evidence of a second court was discovered in this area when the nearby house, Little Halnaker, was erected in 1961.

Halnaker sits on elevated ground at the point where the South Downs rise from the coastal plain. It looks across the lowlands towards the spire of Chichester Cathedral and it was because of the possibility of attack from the sea in the late 1370s that the south-facing defensive frontage was added at the same time that similar steps were being taken nearby at Amberley Castle. The two-

storeyed frontage was composed of a gatehouse flanked by a three-storeyed tower at the south-west angle, and a lodging range with a garderobe turret to the east. With tiny slits to the ground-floor rooms and paired windows above, this frontage was not the balanced composition it seems today owing to the destruction of the outer wall beyond the garderobe turret. Similarly built of flint rubble as the rest of the house, the gatehouse façade was enhanced with dressed sandstone and knapped flint (pl. 114). The large entrance archway was flanked by two buttresses supporting half-octagonal turrets at roof level carried on squinches.[4]

The entrance, protected by a portcullis and double doors, opened into a vaulted passage. As with the hall porch, the four-centred mouldings of the rear arch die into the side walls. The gatehouse is flanked on the west by a two-storeyed block, badly damaged but consisting of a porter's lodge with passage against the outer wall opening into a chamber towards the courtyard. The projecting stair turret gives access to a similar pattern of rooms at first-floor level and the portcullis chamber. Right of the entrance passage is a two-storeyed lodging range with a high-pitched roof. The ground floor was fairly low and dark, with two windows towards the courtyard and a secondary door creating at least two chambers. The upper floor, divided into three chambers, benefited from windows towards the field and courtyard, a square-headed fireplace, and garderobe facilities. The roof gave access to the turrets above the gatehouse and garderobe. The remainder of the enclosure at the south-east corner is soil-filled and overgrown. The square angle tower projecting well forward towards the field was entirely residential. The generous first-floor chamber with fireplace was rewindowed in the early sixteenth century.

There is no documentary evidence for the construction of this frontage, but the use of two- and four-centred arches[5] and other features[6] are consistent with a late fourteenth-century date. It was a formal and carefully designed façade with sophisticated knapped and dressed stonework. Nor was it simply a routine gateway and protective wall, but designed to provide considerable residential accommodation of a high standard for different social levels. The site was not a particularly defensive one although it was protected by a combe on the west. The frontage certainly changed Halnaker into a fortified house, with the buttressed enclosing wall giving the property an additional measure of protection, but it also converted Halnaker into a larger and more stylish residence.[7]

The form of the hall windows and the cross-passage arch suggests the work of Sir Luke Poynings in the mid-fourteenth century (d.1376) but the entrance frontage would have been an early work of his son, Thomas Poynings, 5th Lord St John of Basing. He was a commissioner of array in Sussex and Hampshire who died fifty-three years after inheriting the property. As he died without heirs (1429), Halnaker became part of the inheritance of the Poynings family that descended to Elizabeth Bonville who married Thomas, 9th Lord de la Warr before August 1494. Extensive alteration by Thomas in Henry VIII's reign, much of it in brick, included remodelling and gabling the north and east wings and refurbishing the interiors. Yet hardly any of this is apparent today, for though the house continued to be occupied for two centuries after Lord de la Warr's death in 1544, it was sold in 1765 to the 3rd duke of Richmond of nearby Goodwood, stripped, and left to decay. Several bay windows, fireplaces, and other stonework details were removed to Chichester in c.1840[8] so that the ruins have reverted closer to their late fourteenth-century form, now rose-bowered and set amidst mown lawns and landscaped grounds.

NOTES
1 Brit. Lib., Add. MS 5675. Three of them are reproduced in Garner and Stratton (1911).
2 *Ibid.*
3 More of it remained in 1859, H. T. Turner and J. Parker, *Some Account of Domestic Architecture in England*, III pt 2 (1859) 318.
4 The description by Dr Gromet, *Archaeologia* 29 (1842) 380–1, cannot be reconciled with the existing remains.

5 As at Amberley and Scotney castles.
6 Comparable square-headed fireplace lintels occur at Nunney and Wardour castles and Dartington Hall, where there are also windows with shouldered heads as shown by Grimm in the upper outer face.
7 Grose's engraving of 1783 shows its still-occupied form. Supplement to *Antiquities of England and Wales*, II (1787).
8 Most of this early sixteenth-century work was incorporated in The Grange, Tower Street (destroyed in 1962) and The Chantry, but the latter includes a fourteenth-century window. Steer (1958) and F. W. Steer, *The Grange, Tower Street, Chichester* (1963).

J. L. André, *Sussex Arch. Coll.* 43 (1900) 201–13
T. Garner and A. Stratton, *The Domestic Architecture of England During the Tudor Period* I (1911) 86–7
W. H. Godfrey, *Sussex Arch. Coll.* 82 (1942) 59–64
VCH, *Sussex*, IV (1953) 142–4
F. W. Steer, *A Short History and Description of Halnaker House* (privately printed) 1958

HERSTMONCEUX CASTLE, Sussex

The appreciation of this magnificent castle necessitates visits to Herstmonceux, Lewes, and London. The first is to assess the castle's position and study the site and existing structure. The second is to the headquarters of the Sussex Archaeological Society at Lewes to examine the important record of the castle's interior made immediately prior to and during its demolition in 1776. The third is to the Print Department of the Victoria and Albert Museum in London to examine the further drawings prepared during the 1770s. Together, they constitute an outstanding body of evidence about one of the pre-eminent buildings of fifteenth-century England.

THE FIENNES FAMILY

The Herstmonceux estate (Herste, a clearing in the wood; de Monceux, a barony near Bayeux) was held by the de Monceux family from the beginning of the thirteenth century until it passed by marriage into the Fiennes family upon the death of the last de Monceux without heirs in 1330. The Fiennes were local landowners of modest means who developed their patrimony during the fourteenth century. Sir William Fiennes was mayor of London, and sheriff of Sussex and Surrey in 1396 and again in 1398. He died in 1403 and was buried in Herstmonceux church under a fine memorial brass.

He had two sons, Roger and James, who became prominent figures during the personal rule of Henry VI. The younger son, James, was sheriff of Sussex and Surrey in 1438, was member of parliament for Kent during the 1440s, and helped to negotiate the marriage of Henry VI to Margaret of Anjou. He was created Baron Saye and Sele in 1447, and appointed Treasurer of England in 1449. But his career was cut short by Jack Cade's rebellion in 1450 when he was caught and executed by the rebels.

Roger Fiennes was born in 1384 and baptised in Herstmonceux church. He had taken eight men-at-arms and twenty-four archers from Herstmonceux to support him during the Agincourt campaign, and served in subsequent campaigns in France with four times as many supporters. He was knighted in 1422, appointed sheriff of Sussex and Surrey in 1422 and 1434, was member of parliament for Sussex in five parliaments, and was keeper of Portchester Castle from 1421 until his death. Sir Roger's career was crowned by his appointment in 1439 as treasurer of the household of the young Henry VI which he held for seven years, and that of chief steward of the Duchy of Lancaster in the South from 1441 to 1447. In addition to the rich financial benefits of these two offices, he was also responsible for organising the coronation of Margaret of Anjou in 1455. Ralph Griffiths suggests that after giving up the treasureship of the royal household in 1446, 'Fiennes retired from crown service, possibly willingly through ill-health or the like'.[1] He died in November 1449 aged 65.

Sir Roger lived most of the time at Hever Castle in Kent, but as he became a more important and wealthy Sussex landowner, he decided to build a larger and more up-to-date residence on the principal family estate. The licence to crenellate was granted to him when he was 56 and the building of his brick castle occupied his concluding years. The financial resources necessary to build such a major residence were not the consequence of the spoils of war[2] as for Fiennes' appointments and offices later in life. This was particularly so after 1436 when he benefited more than most through being a leading member of the royal household. At first, Roger and his younger brother were essentially prominent Sussex gentlemen, but when they became royal and county officials, their fortunes prospered in proportion. Furthermore, the Fiennes brothers became supporters of Suffolk and his faction during the mid-1430s and it was this combination of ability in the royal household and support for Suffolk which enabled them to dominate south-east England for the next fifteen years. As E. F. Jacob noted, 'Roger and his friends ruled Kent, Surrey and Sussex in the 1440s . . . while the execution of his brother bears witness to the indignation against his harshness and monopoly exercised over county politics.'[3]

Sir Roger and his brother were among the 'new men' of Henry VI's personal rule. They owed their power base to him and it was manifested in several major building programmes. Herstmonceux Castle was the public demonstration of Sir Roger's social and political position, as was the purchase of the Knole estate in Kent by his brother, the development of Wingfield Manor and Tattershall Castle by Ralph, Lord Cromwell when treasurer of England (1433–43), Sudeley Castle by his successor (1443–46) and Stourton House by Roger's successor as household treasurer (1446–53).

Sir Roger Fiennes was succeeded by his son Richard, who married Joan, the heir of the Dacre family. He was granted the title of Lord Dacre of the South to differentiate his line from the northern branch of the family. He and his brother were able to perpetuate their father's and uncle's influence in the south-east[4] while Richard was appointed chamberlain to Edward IV's queen. He died in 1483.

The Dacre family held the castle until they sold it to the Naylor family in 1708. That family occupied it until 1727, as did their relations until they vacated the property in 1740.

ARCHITECTURAL HISTORY

The castle was erected by Sir Roger Fiennes under the licence granted on 5 February 1441 to 'enclose, crenellate, entower and embattle his manor of Herstmonceux with walls and lime'.[5] It is quite possible that work had begun before this date, for the three men from the Flemish town of Malines living at Herstmonceux in 1436 are known to have been brickmakers.[6] We have no building documentation or other evidence determining how long the castle took to construct, but its homogeneous design and limited internal decoration suggest that work progressed quickly and had been all but finished before Fiennes' death late in 1449. Assuming it would take a little time to prepare sufficient bricks from about 1436 and carry out site preparation, construction could have been initiated by about 1438 with completion by 1449. That work probably began before the crenellation licence was granted was not uncommon, as those for Stokesay and Bolton castles show, as well as the several pardons for work completed without any such permission. An unconfirmed tradition stated that the castle was built at a cost of £3,800, which can be compared with the sum of £994 18s. 2¼d. incurred forty years later on building Kirby Muxloe Castle (1480–4), until it was abandoned before completion.

Subsequent alterations were relatively minor. In the last decade of the sixteenth century, the staircase to the private apartments and the 'dairy' block were rebuilt, and some new windows and armorial chimney pieces inserted by Baroness Dacre (1594–1612). In the late seventeenth century, the principal apartments either side of the north-east corner were refurbished with sash windows and wainscot by Lord Dacre, Earl of Sussex (1654–1715). The castle fell into neglect after 1740 through unoccupation, and it was gutted in late 1776 and early 1777 on the advice of Samuel Wyatt for reuse in the construction of Herstmonceux Place nearby. Most of the castle interior had remained untouched for over three centuries. Although it had no doubt suffered from neglect, particularly during the preceding thirty years after the Naylor family had vacated the property, Walpole noted in 1752 that there were still a few necessary beds and chairs at that time. The need for comprehensive destruction is not supported by the evidence of the drawings made in 1776, nor by the state of the external brickwork during the next one and a half centuries. Wyatt's survey and advice that the castle was dilapidated beyond economic repair – like that given by his brother James Wyatt at Hereford Cathedral – was expedient and carried out with ruthless efficiency.

The castle remained a ruin until 1911, when partial restoration of the shell was begun by Colonel Claude Lowther, with the work completed by Sir Paul Latham between 1932 and 1935. The property was bought by the Admiralty in 1946 for use as the Royal Observatory but vacated in 1988, when it became a study centre of Queen's University of Ontario.

When Colonel Lowther began his work of restoration in 1911, the castle was an ivy-covered shell. Yet as the exterior walls were secure even after years of decay, no substantial reconstruction was needed to restore them to their original condition. Lowther, followed by Latham, strengthened the brickwork, replaced all lost and broken battlements, and refilled the moat. Consequently, the exterior of the castle looks today much as it did in the mid-fifteenth century, apart from the seventeenth-century windows inserted in the northern and eastern ranges. The only important modification was Lowther's doubling the width of the moat on the entrance side, extending the original bridge, and lowering the outer banks to improve the view.

All the internal buildings were stripped in the late 1770s so that, except for occasional footings, hardly any evidence remained at the beginning of the twentieth century of the four courts into which the inner area had been divided.[7] Because of this, the buildings added by Lowther and Latham in a pseudo late Gothic style made no

PLATE 141 Herstmonceux Castle: from the south-east

attempt to follow the original plan but were erected against the outer walls to create a large central courtyard. The south range and part of the east and west ranges, up to and including the great hall and chapel, were built up by Lowther (his own architect with the help of Cecil Perkins), but the great hall was still without its roof at the time of his death in 1929. Latham completed the remaining ranges of the castle, and added the service supply platform with a new entrance at the north-west angle. There was one significant difference, though, between the two phases of this work. Whereas Lowther had aimed at 'castle-type' buildings with flat roofs, Latham, under the advice of his architect, Walter Godfrey, adopted the original form of pitched roofs and tall brick chimneys rising above the battlements to give the castle an external appearance close to that shown by S. and N. Buck in 1737.

The restoration caused much controversy at the time, ranging from 'a perversion of history' to 'abandoning archaeological precision in favour of artistic licence'.[8] But it was a totally practical solution to a large site, built in compatible materials and character.[9] The contrast with the reconstruction of Arundel Castle in the same county only a generation earlier is particularly instructive. Not only is the former heavy-handed architecturally, but the principal apartments had to be all but abandoned as a permanent residence within two generations of its reconstruction.

DESCRIPTION

The site

The castle sits close to the rivulet of a minor valley sheltered by rising ground on three sides but open to Pevensey Levels and the sea 4 miles away. In early medieval times, the site was near an inlet of the sea which had been subject to silting from at least the thirteenth century onwards. Any defensive purpose at the time of its construction in the fifteenth century is not immediately apparent, while the suggestion that it was built in reaction to fear of French invasion[10] is unconvincing. On the other hand, Fiennes was replac-

ing an earlier house on an unknown site but one which was probably not far from the present structure. The castle was built totally anew with no evidence of any previous structure.[11] Nevertheless, the site chosen was a weak one, built in a hollow with rising ground on three sides, though encircled by a serious moat.

Building materials

Excluding some minor brickwork in Kent, at Allington Castle (late thirteenth century), Horne's Place Chapel (1366), Grench Manor (1378), and Daundelyon Gatehouse (by mid-fifteenth century), Herstmonceux was the first major building in south-east England to be constructed of brick. It was in the forefront of use as a fashionable material and was contemporary with work at Caister (1432–c.1445) and Tattershall (c.1440–6) – a group of castles which adopted this building material on a major scale for the first time. A generation separated Herstmonceux from the next important building in the south-east, Waynflete's gatehouse at Farnham Castle (1472–5).

The bricks used vary between 9¾ × 4½ × 2¼ inches and 9½ × 4¾ × 2⅛ inches. A brick in the fifteenth century was often 2 inches thick but those at Herstmonceux range between 1¾ inches and 2⅛ inches. They are laid in English bond. Nathaniel Lloyd pointed out that some of the bricks used in the batter on the south front were Flemish imports.[12] The gatehouse towers were diapered with dark heads arranged in geometrical designs of two lozenges linked vertically, four such lozenges, and a large saltire.[13] This work is limited and tentative, for the castle is one of the earliest buildings in England to show a feature which was to become so popular during the following years. The bricks were probably burnt on site, possibly using material dug from the moat.[14] Although Flemish brickmakers were employed, there is no reason to believe that the majority of the castle was not built by English workmen. Local greensand stone was used for all windows, door surrounds, parapets, machicolation corbels, and internal buttresses.

The exterior

The castle was built on an almost square plan with symmetrical fronts terminating in an octagonal tower at each corner (193 feet by 183½ feet excluding the towers). There are three intermediate towers in each front displaying five sides of an octagon, with the central tower rising a stage higher (15 feet) above battlement level. That on the north was the postern tower, the eastern tower was the apse of the chapel, that on the west was the bakehouse (now the bay window of the twentieth-century great hall), while the entrance gatehouse with its double towers dominated the south front. The batter which rises for 13 feet from the base of all walls and towers is continued prominently up the towers to the battlements. This batter may have helped to protect the castle as much from damp as from siege engines[15] while the steeper continuation up the towers was essentially for strength. The brickwork was relieved by dressed stonework for all openings, as well as by the moulded plinth at ground level and the string course immediately below the battlements. The main gateway was approached by a bridge of which the outer section was an extension by Lowther. The three arches near the gateway are original, with a small open area initially in front of the entrance to take the drawbridge (pl. 106).

The south front, and in fact the whole castle, is dominated by the central gatehouse, 84 feet high, not unlike a gigantic pair of binoculars. The two octagonal towers flanking the portal, change above the upper string course to a circular plan. They are devoid of windows but have crossed arrow loops at each floor with circular gunports at ground level commanding the approach. Boldly projecting machicolations support the arrow-looped battlemented *chemin de ronde*, spanning both towers and the frontage between them. The towers are topped with circular watch towers rising from the machicolated gallery. The entrance and the room immediately above it are recessed within a striking and extremely lofty four-centred arch of moulded stone concealing 'murder holes'. The entrance is a single opening, while the two-light transomed window above is boldly rebated to form a prominent feature. The long vertical slots which received the beams supporting the drawbridge are another distinctive element of this recessed front. There is a further large chamber immediately below the machicolations lit by two twin-light windows separated by a stone panel carved with a banner displaying the arms of Sir Roger Fiennes held by a wolfhound.

The three-storeyed postern tower on the north front is similar to the angle towers and has a narrow entrance within a recess spanned by three machicolations. Drawbridge slots and a murder hole occur again, while the bridge also stopped short of the entrance door. The toothed brickwork terminates abruptly here, probably intended for a barbican which was never completed. The drawbridge slots suggest there was a second fixed bridge and gap here.

The symmetry of the castle exterior, as at Bodiam, is a striking feature of the site with the rhythm of multi-angled towers and lesser turrets that the more extended frontages permitted giving Herstmonceux a sophisticated presence not seen before. This symmetry is broken only by the slightly irregular patterning of the transomed windows reflecting the disposition of the interior apartments. The windows are square-headed and plain rectangular lights. Their form suggests that they were replacements of the original openings made in the late sixteenth century, but they are original. The castle was subject to little alteration internally (see later) and the total modification of every window in each one of the fronts

ages and in every tower would be extremely unusual. They all retain their original brick relieving arches internally, and whereas some of the windows in the east range were blocked in the late seventeenth century, their original square-headed form can still be made out either as single lights or as transomed double lights with uncusped heads. They are an early example of a form that proved enduring for the next two centuries, though it had occurred a little earlier in the brick-built castle at Caister (1432–45).

The window with cinquefoil tracery in the gatehouse is original, as are all the transomed chapel windows with restored heads.[16] The semi-circular bay window nearby (similar to those at Kirby Hall) was added in about 1600. The sash windows north of the chapel and round the corner in the north range were inserted by the 1st earl of Sussex in about 1670. Some of these on the east side are in different positions from the original openings which can be traced as blockings in the brick façade. The few transomed double lights that are known to have existed lit the principal apartments but these larger openings were protected by the considerable width of the moat.[17]

Present internal features

The buildings within the perimeter wall were originally built round four courts. Because of their wholesale destruction in 1777, the only original work to survive to the twentieth century was the bulk of the gatehouse block with some of the brick vaulting of the entrance hall, part of the inner walls of the north and south ranges, and the south-facing wall of the chapel.[18]

There was a single entrance into the brick-vaulted entrance hall rather than the usual main and subsidiary foot entrance, and it is fitted with the original oak doors (restored). The ribs of the modest brick vault die into the walls without corbels (repaired by Lowther), a feature which may have its origin in the Low Countries.[19] The fireplace in the entrance was inserted in the seventeenth century. Openings in the side walls gave access to the watch turrets and to the guardroom on the west side. The brick newel adjacent to the entrance hall is original, although the steps above the second floor have been replaced by wooden ones and a wooden central post, probably in the late sixteenth century. On the opposite side is a straight stair.

Three historic items were inserted in the ranges built by Lowther and Latham. The Jacobean staircase in the staircase hall was formerly at Cecils' Theabalds (Lowther), the Charles II staircase and doors in the west entrance hall of *c*.1680 came from Wheatley Hall, Doncaster (Latham), and the early seventeenth-century oak gallery chimneypiece and overmantel from Madingley Hall near Cambridge (Latham).

ORIGINAL INTERIOR DESIGN

It is extremely fortunate for the study of Herstmonceux Castle that a substantial body of eighteenth-century material exists illustrating the castle interior shortly before its destruction. This includes two tinted floor plans prepared between 1708 and 1710 during the early occupation of the Naylor family,[20] the external appearance of the south and west fronts by the brothers Buck (1737), and two portfolios of detailed pencil drawings of the interior by James Lambert junior of Lewes, made immediately prior to and during its destruction in 1776–7. The two finished plans and nineteen of Lambert's drawings are held in the library of the Sussex Archaeological

Society at Lewes, while the preliminary plans and nine further drawings are held in the Prints Department of the Victoria and Albert Museum, London.[21] Four finished tinted drawings (three in the Museum and one at Lewes) were subsequently made from this record by Lambert's uncle, also James.

These portfolios of plans and drawings showing the original disposition and character of the castle interior are of the utmost importance. They reveal that the interior had never been subject to major alterations, only minor modifications, and are of outstanding value for the study of fifteenth-century domestic architecture when so much contemporary work has been lost or altered beyond recognition.

The confines of a compact site and the adoption of the two-storeyed form virtually throughout the building meant that the spreading form of Caister Castle or Wingfield Manor was impractical. Division into distinct areas centred round four courts of unequal size helped to overcome the problem, though it must have made the castle a veritable rabbit warren.[22] Three of these courts were cloistered in part or whole. The vaulted entry hall opened into the cloister walks of the principal court, the Green Court leading to the great hall and chapel on the far side. The screens passage gave access to the Butler's Pantry Court, but this second cloister court was modified in Elizabethan times by the construction of a new 'great' staircase leading to the principal apartments. The latter had been located in the usual position at the upper end of the great hall, in part of the east range on the ground floor and the whole of the east and north ranges of the upper floor. It also extended at this level as far as the gatehouse. Fiennes was extremely comfortably housed in rooms of increasing privacy on those sides away from the hurly-burly of castle life and its sun-filled rooms.

The remainder of the rooms in the castle were devoted to Fiennes' household. The stewards' rooms were near the entrance on the south and west sides of the principal court, while the kitchen and associated offices were clustered round the Pantry, Poultry, and Pump Courts. The last two were separated by a passage linking the kitchen with the great hall. The kitchen, built against the west wall, was 21 feet by 31 feet and open to the roof. It contained three vast fireplaces, two filling the west wall and a further one in the south wall with massive chimney breasts built against the internal walls sweeping upwards in a diminishing curve towards the plain beamed ceiling. Light came from windows close to the flat ceiling.

The office facilities were particularly extensive. Those round the Poultry Court were service adjuncts of the kitchen, while the Pump Court was surrounded by the bakehouse (with a vast oven), brew-house, laundry and storage areas. The upper rooms in the south-west angle were probably staff dormitories. The east wall of the Pump Court was supported by two massive buttresses against a three-storeyed block (the only known one in the castle) with a line of lodgings at first floor level, possibly for guests or household officials. The uppermost storey of the two south facing corner towers were dovecotes: that in the southeast corner survives unaltered. Walter Godfrey records that a vaulted passage-way traversed the principal buildings below the level of the inner courts, used in the twentieth-century reconstruction for water and electricity supply.[23] It may well have been a post-medieval insertion like that at Ashby de la Zouch Castle.

All the buildings were surmounted by tiled roofs of steep pitch and crowned by tall slender brick chimney stacks. The utilitarian

Pump Court lacked the embattled parapet used elsewhere though it had dormer windows with stepped gables, another Low Countries influence. Lambert's drawings show that there was a square tower with single-light windows at the upper end of the hall rising two storeys above the junction of the roofs of the hall and the chapel. Possibly a belfry turret, it was not unlike those raised higher in the eighteenth century at the angles of the Cloister Court at Eton College. The survey of the castle made in 1570 notes that the hall had 'a square tower at every end embattled'.[24]

At first sight, the plan of Herstmonceux looks complex and quite different from the normal late medieval plan for a major residence. But upon analysis, the plan of the castle divided into three parts – the family and guest apartments on part of the east and north side, the offices and service quarters on the west side, and the administrative rooms on the south and part of the east sides of the castle. The pattern is also essentially of two courtyards separated centrally by the great hall and offices, although at this particular site, they were divided further by subsidiary central ranges at right angles to make four courtyards of unequal size. Furthermore, the normal hall, screen, offices, buttery, kitchen passage, and kitchen in line was followed. Within this framework, the planning of a large household was achieved with extraordinary skill.

According to Avray Tipping, four-fifths of the ground floor and half of the upper floor were needed for the work and lodging of servants and retainers.[25] The proportions of nearly three-quarters of the ground floor and a quarter of the upper floor are more accurate. Four features warrant further attention.

The cloistered courts

The ground floor of Green Court, the entrance court, was cloistered on all sides. Each of the four alleys was made up of eight bays of open brick arches separated by slender stone buttresses which continued up the face of the wall to roof level. As the arches died into the sides of the buttresses, the effect was of an almost continuous arcade round each side of the cloister. A low wall at the base of the openings inhibited access to the central garth. Lambert's drawing of 5 November 1776 made during demolition shows that the hall walk was diapered but there is no evidence that this or the other walks were brick vaulted.[26] Nor is this drawing entirely clear whether there was an upper corridor on the hall side. Lambert shows the buttresses terminating at a bold string course at ground-floor roof level whereas the plan identifies a first-floor gallery blocking the large hall windows.

The glazed upper galleries above the three remaining walks were lit by twin lights with transoms in alternate bays. The upper windows had cinquefoil heads. Lambert's drawings at Lewes show those on the south side with uncusped heads whereas the finished drawing at the Victoria & Albert Museum depicts cusped windows. The buttresses were marked by an unusual billowing offset at the string course separating the ground and first floors. They terminated abruptly at roof level which was not battlemented by the eighteenth century. However, as Lambert's drawings show that the other cloistered courts had embattled parapets, and there is a record of their existence here in 1570, it may be accepted that this feature was original to the Green Court.

The Butler's Pantry Court was cloistered on two sides with buttresses marked by curved rebates to the offsets. The east side of the court was replaced in the late sixteenth century with a three-

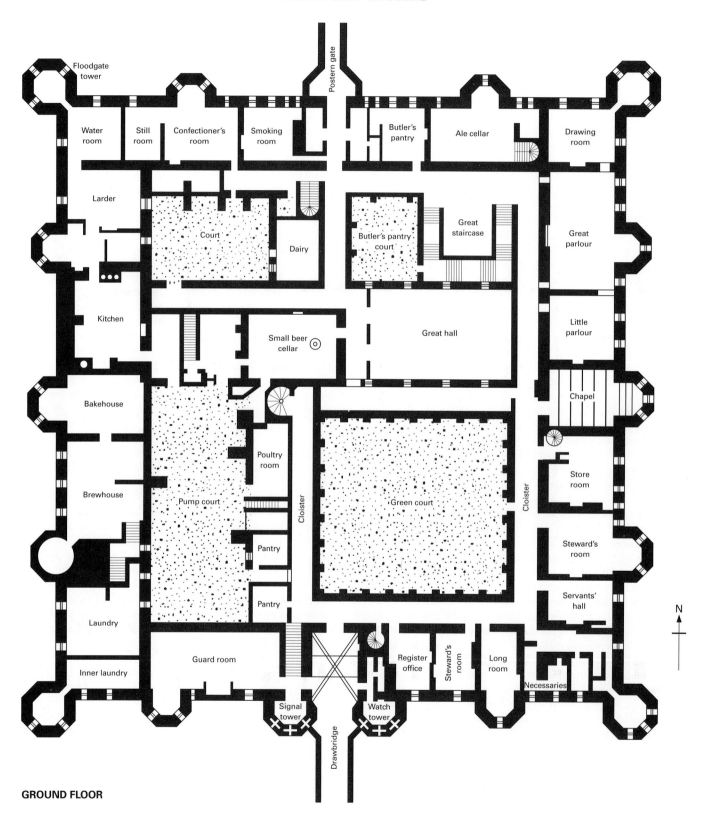

GROUND FLOOR

FIGURE 78 Herstmonceux Castle: floor plans prior to 1776

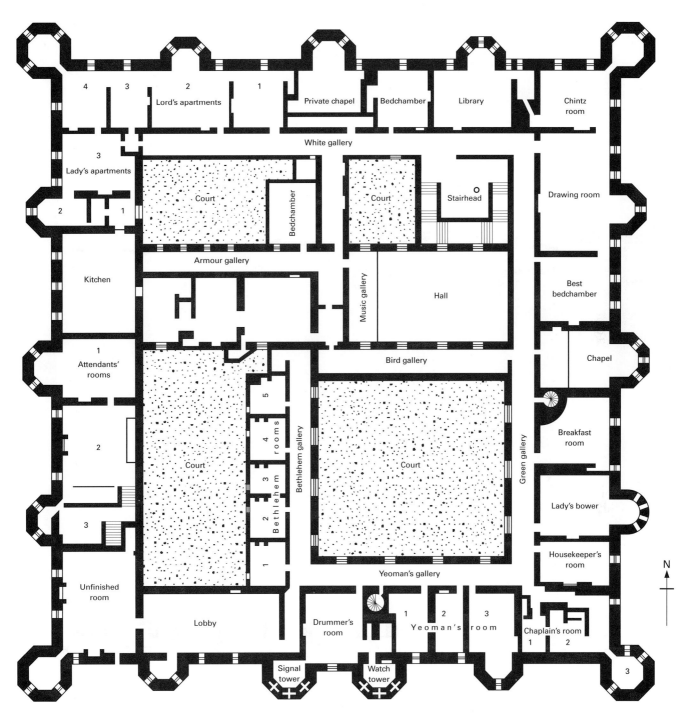

FIRST FLOOR

PLATE 142 Herstmonceux Castle: Green Court by James Lambert (1776)

storeyed staircase block with large square-headed windows with leaded lights and a crow-stepped gable. The presence of two-centred doorways at the end of the cloister corridor and opening into the Elizabethan stair-well from the court, and a string course similar to that beneath the windows in the great hall suggest that the outer wall of this insertion was built on the line of Fiennes' staircase.

The north side of the Poultry Court (Chicken Court on Hare's plan of 1851) was also cloistered and there was a stair turret in the corner, partly concealed in the late sixteenth century by the insertion of the dairy and privy chamber block with a sharply pitched roof.

The marked similarity and relationship between the cloistered courts with glazed galleries above and the Green Court in particular with the contemporary Cloister Court at Eton College (1441–c.1448) will be discussed later. In any case, the use of cloistered walks in residences was a talking point at the time as evidenced at Ewelme and Ockwells, but Herstmonceux was the earliest known house to adopt this form with such vigour and enthusiasm.

Great hall

It was usual in military architecture for the hall to be built against one of the outer walls. As at Kenilworth and Raglan castles, Herstmonceux adopted the normal late medieval plan with the hall separating two courts. The apartment was 54 feet by 28 feet and 26½ feet high. Approached from the Green Court, the entrance door had shields in the spandrels. There were two doors in the screens passage leading to the beer cellar and kitchen passage respectively, while Lambert's tinted drawing shows the original screen of simple form with a gallery frontage of blank cusped panels with the lower panels and two gates of seventeenth-century date.[27]

The hall was of five bays, lit by four two-light windows with cusped heads in the upper half of the side walls. A boldly moulded string course immediately below the roof corbels rose to window level at the dais end. The lower half of the walls were blank – a feature common enough in near contemporary grand halls as at Minster Lovell, Wingfield, and Eltham to allow for tapestry display below.[28] The roof was spanned by tie beams supported on sweeping

PLATE 143 Herstmonceux Castle: hall interior by James Lambert (1776)

curved braces resting on corbels carved with the Fiennes wolf-hound. The spandrels of the braces were filled with open cusped lights, while Lambert shows a high-pitched unsupported raftered roof. This must be conjecture arising from the destruction already in hand in 1776.[29] As the overall design was modest, a low pitched roof is most likely. There were no wall fireplaces and Lambert's drawings neither of the interior (V & A) nor the exterior (Lewes) give any indication of a louvre. One was possible, but heating may have been provided by portable braziers. By the eighteenth century, the lower walling was plain panelled and the floor was of square, pink-coloured pavement slabs.

Family apartments

A door in the dais wall accessed the private apartments. These were in their normal position at ground- and first-floor levels with three major apartments on the north-east side terminating in the centrally positioned chapel. These apartments were originally lit by twin-light transomed windows (see exterior face). The chapel rose through two storeys and made use of the central tower to create a semi-octagonal apse with three tall windows, 16 feet high, divided by transoms. The body of the chapel was presumably used by the household with the first-floor gallery reserved for Sir Roger and his family. Lambert's drawing of the chapel shows that it had a totally plain flat ceiling and equally plain furnishings by that time – a seventeenth-century pulpit with tester, and pews, altar, and altar panelling of possibly the same date. Some stained glass remained in the windows, described by Walpole in 1752 as 'seven long lean saints, ill done'.

The original approach to the upper floor of the apartments is not clear, but for reasons given earlier, it is probable that the Elizabethan staircase replaced an earlier one in the same position. This would have been approached from the ground-floor corridor at the rear of the dais rather than direct from it. The upper apartments extended the length of the east and north ranges, and included part of the south range as far as the gatehouse. Their extent is indicated by the galleries from which the rooms opened. They also include a line of lodgings, possibly for guests, overlooking the

351

Pump Court. The extent of these apartments for Fiennes and his family and guests is striking, as is their privacy. Equally significant is the absence of a hierarchical parade of large apartments. Fiennes preferred a greater number of smaller-scale rooms.

First-floor galleries

Except for the rooms on the southwest side which were probably used by household staff, galleries were built to link all first-floor rooms. The usual medieval practice of entering each room from the one adjacent to it in sequence was thereby avoided. This unusual feature may have developed from planning within a constricted site but that cannot be the sole explanation for these internal galleries. Privacy was an increasing prerequisite of any major household, and Herstmonceux is its mid-century exemplar with more modest contemporary examples at Wingfield Manor and Ockwells. Some of these upper lodgings were probably for senior household staff, but the apportionment of rooms can only be guesswork.

Grose noted that the windows lighting these galleries were decorated with the wolfhound of the Fiennes family.[30] Lambert's drawings show that the family badge was inserted in a circle with a ground colour of blue or red, and the whole closely surrounded by flowers in yellow ground diamond-shaped quarries. Other windows were decorated with the Fiennes motto and the entwinned initials of Roger and his wife Elizabeth. The approach to these galleries was by 'many winding staircases, curiously constructed in brickwork without any timber'.[31] Such a staircase still survives in the gatehouse.

DESIGN CHARACTERISTICS

The pre-eminent design characteristics of the castle were compactness and taut planning with limited decoration. The realisation and unification of the concept suggests that it was completed before Fiennes' death in 1449. Only one element was left unfinished and that was the walling of the postern tower, which may have been intended for a barbican. The residence was a large one, but controlled by a very measured design. As at Bodiam, a compact quadrangular form was adopted rather than the more extended double courtyard design followed at Caister Castle. Brick was chosen even though it was a relatively new building material for a large-scale residence, but its success furthered its growing popularity within court circles.

Externally, the castle's defences had some purpose (see below), otherwise the moat, the formidable gatehouse, the small outer windows, and the defensive superstructure have no meaning. Internally, it would have been easy to have designed the accommodation against the perimeter wall to enclose a large central courtyard (as at Bodiam Castle). For more high-status families, a centrally positioned hall creating two courtyards was not unusual. For Fiennes, a more complex design was adopted to accommodate his large supporting household. Yet this was intended not to create a large number of lodging ranges as at Wingfield Manor, Knole, or Croydon Palace but to create substantial offices and service accommodation for entertaining on a lavish scale. The introduction of cloisters and internal galleries provided an exceptional amenity offering speedy movement between the different functions within the castle, with no interference from other activities. The first-floor galleries giving privacy to the principal residential apartments were even more so.

Decoration was minimal. Continuous moulded arches for doors and windows as at Wingfield, Tutbury Castle, and Eton College were characteristic of the 1440s. Only three forms were used for windows – square-headed (frequently), uncusped heads for the more important rooms (family apartments and chapel), and occasionally cinquefoil heads (galleries). The brick vaulting in the entrance hall and the cloister arches dies into the adjacent walling, while the hall roof, like the entrance vaulting, was of modest design. Even the chapel had uncusped lights and a plain ceiling. As at Wingfield Manor, the chimneys were particularly tall, a more striking statement of internal comfort than the twentieth-century replacements.

The only decorative work evident was the unusual design of the cloister buttresses with their bulging offset, and the use of the Fiennes wolfhound for the hall corbels and gallery windows in association with the family motto. The chapel windows were decorated with saints and the arms of Sir John's wife.[32] In 1752, Walpole observed that all the internal walls except in the principal chambers were in their native 'brickhead'.

The diapering, brick vaulting ribs, and stepped gables over the dormers suggest Flemish or Low Countries influence but otherwise Herstmonceux is totally English in design and layout. It is not beholding to fanciful memories of Fiennes' French campaigns.[33]

ITS DEFENSIVE CHARACTER

Herstmonceux is a vision. The soft red brickwork reflected in the wide moat against a verdant background creates a picture-book scene. The design is helped by the pronounced batter of the towers which gives them a more graceful appeal. Equally important is the castle's external symmetry. Herstmonceux is proof that the balanced design had reached England two or three generations before the Renaissance reached these shores. However, the castle reflects some of the conflicting discussion that Bodiam has fostered, though to a lesser extent. It has been described as 'one of the most magnificent pieces of quasi-military architecture in Britain'.[34] It is an excellent example of that combination of a major residence hiding behind an apparently military cloak. Like Dalyngrigge's residence 15 miles to the east, Herstmonceux hides a domestic interior behind a defensive exterior, and the two are married together so that the one gives no hint of the other.

The attractive setting and the warm-coloured brick do not lessen the fact that Herstmonceux was capable of withstanding a superficial attack. The spring-fed moat was a wide one and extended round the north side until the Elizabethan garden was raised above the water level. It becomes a small lake on the east side to reach the bed of a small stream and was held back by the causeway that still exists south of the castle.[35] The outer bank was surmounted by a low crenellated brick wall extending on all sides from the bridge and shown complete in Buck's engraving of 1737. Like Bodiam, the site was not inherently strong, and shares the disadvantage of being overlooked by rising ground.

The entrance is a militarily capable if showy gatehouse, of considerable bulk. The machicolated *chemin de ronde* and murder holes are genuine enough, with the drawbridge covering the two-light window above the entrance in an emergency. Those lighting the room above would have been considered out of range of attack. Similar protective features occur on the postern tower too, but as at Bodiam, the archery loops and artillery gunports look fierce externally but had

PLATE 144 Herstmonceux Castle: gatehouse

Construction determined by such factors is engaging but made with the benefit of hindsight – so often the grounds for a reasonable explanation, but less so in the case of Herstmonceux if planning and construction had been initiated in the late 1430s. The uneasy atmosphere of the time cannot be totally dismissed and the military flavour is genuine, but the castle is primarily 'a magnificent parade of feudal pride'.[36] It is a statement of achievement, of regional and national power, and personal success. It is far less formidable-looking externally than Bodiam, but as there, the trappings of defence cannot be totally dismissed. They are more than chivalric display and social advertisement. Herstmonceux is a complex building – expensive, sophisticated, and one built by a knight on a scale that vied with magnate and even royal magnificence. It sends out mixed rather than ambiguous signals and therein lies its power, its interest, and its complexity.

INFLUENCES

The late fourteenth-century castle at Hever had been Fiennes' early home. Its tight rectangular form, strong gatehouse, and two-storeyed ranges internally, may have influenced Fiennes' plan. Another late fourteenth-century structure, Farleigh Hungerford Castle in Somerset, enlarged by Fiennes' contemporary, was essentially a major rectangular residence confined within a defensive perimeter. There were the central gatehouse and corner towers. Internally, there were a number of courtyards with the hall off-centre from the gatehouse across the principal one. Herstmonceux is simply a modification and extension of this plan on a larger scale two generations later.

Of the contemporary buildings of Lord Cromwell, his tower-house at Tattershall was similarly built of brick, while Wingfield followed a generous courtyard plan affording accommodation for a very large household. On the other hand, Wingfield lacks the compactness and overt defensive features of the Sussex stronghold and makes comfort its predominant imprint. Herstmonceux combines some of the characteristics of both these contemporary residences in a single residence that had the best of both worlds – protective and domestic.

This is not the place to follow the development of brick architecture in England but there is little doubt that Herstmonceux was influenced by Henry V's palace at Sheen (1414–22) with subsequent completion between 1429 and 1439. Using brick on a dramatic scale, it adopted a quadrangular form with multi-angled corner and side towers as did Herstmonceux which similarly made a statement about Fiennes' standing and his wish to be seen as trend-setting. It is equally significant in the construction of Henry VI's religious establishment at Eton, founded in October 1440 with construction initiated in 1441 and continuing uninterrupted for the next seven years. That there was close involvement and familiarity between the two structures is obvious in their choice of materials, planning, and decorative features. Eton's Cloister Court was altered during the eighteenth century by the addition of a third storey on two sides and a complete replacement on the hall side by a new library. Nevertheless, the original form is clear, particularly from an examination of the west side and Loggan's engraving of *c*.1688 showing the untouched east side of Cloister Court. Both courts were built of brick with stone dressings and diaper patterns.[37] Both are distinguished by a lower open arcade with low walls supporting an enclosed and glazed upper gallery, with each bay separated by

limited value in practice, particularly as the gunports do not allow hand guns to traverse. The curtain walls are only 3 feet thick, not of fortress quality, though the impression of defence as seen from across the moat would have been heightened by the many single-light windows. Except for those above the main entrance, only the chapel (as at Bodiam) and the rooms in the north-east angle were allowed to have windows larger than elsewhere, but those in the strongly projecting corner towers commanded a wide field.

The gatehouse was formerly a self-contained unit. There was no communication between the entrance hall and the large guardroom to the west or the apartments to the east. Nor was there any internal communication between the ground and upper floors of the gatehouse. The newel staircase opening off the courtyard gave direct access to the second floor and the roof. The apartment immediately above the entrance hall contained the drawbridge machinery and could only be entered from one of the galleries round the Green Court.

To twentieth-century eyes, Herstmonceux looks less capable of withstanding an attack than it did to any fifteenth-century warmonger, partly because of its romantic setting, partly because of the larger windows inserted at a later date, and particularly because the building materials used throughout the whole structure impart a warm and homely feeling alien to its external character. Fiennes was a member of the unpopular Suffolk party during the 1440s and his brother was murdered, so that some sort of protective face might be thought reasonable. The bishop of Chichester was keen to renew his licence to crenellate his houses in 1447, while Rye and Winchelsea were burnt by French marauders in 1448.

buttresses rising to parapet level. Embattled parapets are common to both buildings, as are paired doors opening off the corridors, windows with cuspless four-centred heads, and tall chimney stacks. There are some minor differences. The bays at Eton have continuous moulded stone arches whereas the arcades at Herstmonceux sprang direct from the buttresses. The latter were distinguished by a decorative offset. There were no angle stair turrets at Herstmonceux and there was a more sparse pattern of windows lighting the galleries, while the projecting turrets at the rear of the royal ranges are crude compared with the turrets marking Fiennes' frontage.

Sir Roger Fiennes was a paymaster of the royal project from its inception, while his brother James was closely involved in the establishment, with the first building account ascribed to 'good master James Fenys squier for the kyngs body'.[38] Brickmen for one of the Fiennes brothers was noted in the Eton account book for 1442–3 but which of the two buildings was the leader is an open question. It is usually assumed that courtiers followed and copied crown initiative but the possibility that Fiennes began his castle shortly before the licence to crenellate was granted in 1441 suggests that, in this instance, the rôles may have been reversed. Nor does the castle seem to have been affected by the many constitutional and structural changes that affected and prolonged the development of Eton College.

Herstmonceux learnt from and stimulated college planning, particularly in the disposition of the entrance court and hall, the introduction of cloisters, the construction of a dominating entrance, and planning compactness. The cloistered quadrangle plan first adopted in the late fourteenth century by William Wykeham at Oxford and Winchester became common in the following century at St John's (1436) and All Souls (1437) at Oxford followed by King's College (1441) and Queens' College (1448) at Cambridge.[39]

Herstmonceux's influence was little felt locally. Brick was looked upon as an exotic material in the immediate area except by Sir John Scott when he built Mote Manor, Iden, in the 1460s, but this was demolished in the late seventeenth century and is only known from the surviving accounts.[40] The only other buildings were the Dacre chapel added to Herstmonceux church and the church at East Guldeford near Rye, built by Sir Richard Guldeford in 1499.

Herstmonceux's influence lay with high-status buildings. A plan using four courts was followed by archbishop Bourchier at Knole, which he purchased from Sir James Fiennes' son in 1456 and built from anew. The imposing entrance was repeated, the hall was on the far side of the first court, corridors were used to facilitate circulation at both ground- and first-floor level round this first court, and there were two subsidiary courts. The planning of Knole is basically a less constricted Herstmonceux without its outer defensive character. An East Anglian version of Fiennes' residence was built to a comparable scale by Sir Ralph Shelton at Shelton Hall between 1465 and 1480. Similarly moated, brick-built, with central gatehouse, corner towers, and several courtyards, it initiated the major sequence of brick-built mansions in early Tudor Norfolk.[41] At the same time, a more complex courtyard residence was being developed by Edward IV and his successors at Eltham Palace. The Inner Court of the royal palace is more than twice the size of the Sussex building and it lacks the symmetrical fronts of Herstmonceux, owing to the fact that Edward IV had to build within the limits of an irregular shaped site developed over the previous two centuries. Nevertheless, in both

cases, the apartments and offices are grouped round a number of courts within the confines of a moated area. At Eltham, the entrance court was surrounded by a corridor on nearly three sides and the hall was in the same relation to the principal court and its entrance as at Herstmonceux. Roughly speaking, Fiennes' apartments were facing east (and also north on the first floor), the offices faced west, and the administrative rooms faced south. We have limited knowledge about the internal room disposition at Eltham but the royal apartments lay in the same relation to the great hall as at Herstmonceux, although the kitchen was immediately north of the great hall, and the 1520s replacement chapel filled one corner of the entrance court.

OVERVIEW

Herstmonceux Castle told a different story to a fifteenth-century visitor than to one today. No one could doubt its commanding presence, its bristling face, the daring use of brick on such a scale, and its hint of internal comfort. Yet it was built by a knight – not a baron, a leading prelate, or a member of the royal family – with a scale and panache that was breath-taking. Any visitor would have been overawed, even more so when the castle was alive with banners, trumpets, household staff, and attendants. Once inside, the complexity of the site would be revealed, with its unusual planning features and visible symbols of seigniory. Though Herstmonceux has the superficial character of a palace-fortress, albeit a softened southern version of one, it is a leading trophy house of the period. It was developed on a new site and completed within its owner's lifetime, was essentially a residence with (in this case) the superficial trappings of defence, was multi-courtyard to allow for extensive entertaining as well as personal accommodation, and was a prestigious reflection of the owner's standing and position in society. Even in its present modified state, Herstmonceux Castle can be seen to have been innovative. It stands as part of the great flowering of fifteenth-century English architecture, and would have done so even more if Wyatt had not destroyed its internal structure. Nevertheless, it is an immensely important survival, a testimony to the richness, vigour, and invention of the Lancastrian court circle with a sophisticated design, externally and internally, that was ground-breaking.

NOTES

1 *The Reign of King Henry VI* (1981) 293. For Fiennes' career, J. C. Wedgwood, *History of Parliament: 1439–1509* (1936), and J. S. Roskell *et al.*, *History of Parliament: 1381–1421* (1993) 70–3.
2 Such as J. Wight, *Brick Building in England* (1972) 124.
3 *The Fifteenth Century* (1961) 333.
4 R. Griffiths, *The Reign of King Henry VI* (1981) 340.
5 *Cal. Charter Rolls: 1327–1516*, 13–14.
6 *Cal. Pat. Rolls: 1429–36*, 539. One of them, John Roweland, is named as a brickmaker in the Eton Account Book of 1442–43 plus 'two of his men with Fiennes'. Eton College Mss. Coll. BA/3.
7 No detailed archaeological survey was attempted by Lowther or Latham but standing evidence was shown on the ground plan by Walter Godfrey in VCH, IX (1937) opp. 132.
8 Tipping (1937) 282, 302.
9 For the present ground plan, VCH, IX (1937) opp. 132; for the first-floor plan with room description, Tipping (1937) 298, 303–6.
10 B. O. St Neil, *Castles and Cannons* (1960) 29.
11 Venables drew attention to 'a little rude grouted work in some interior walls' which he thought might have been reused material from the former manor house. *Sussex Arch. Coll.* 4 (1851) 169.

12 *A History of English Brickwork* (1934) 12.

13 T. P. Smith, *The Medieval Brickmaking Industry in England 1400–1450* (1985) 13, 14.

14 Simpson (1942) 110–22. T.P. Smith concurs with construction in home-made bricks: *The Medieval Brickmaking Industry* 36.

15 Wight, *Brick Building in England* 124.

16 VCH, IX (1937) 132.

17 The garden north of the castle is enclosed by a brick wall approximately 300 feet by 200 feet, built after the moat had been drained shortly before 1570. The survey of that date mentions a walled arbour, an orchard, and a brick-built banqueting house four storeys high. The present garden is divided at three-quarters of its length by a low wall to create a small terrace.

18 Some later rooms inserted below courtyard level were blocked by the Admiralty in the late 1940s.

19 Goodall (2004) 521. He also draws attention to the likelihood that the diaper patterning on the walls shown by Lambert was painted, *ibid.*

20 Many of the room names given by Lambert differ from those marked on the mid-eighteenth-century plans reproduced by Venables in 1851. As there are no other differences, the later plans are reproduced here for clarity.

21 Sussex Arch. Soc. Picture Collection, LEWSA, VR 3531–51 and V & A Museum Print Dept E402–15 Q3A. Eighteen finished drawings and watercolours by Lambert from the Ashburnham Collection are at Yale University.

22 The internal courts would have been smaller than Lambert's drawings suggest. J. H. Parker, *Some Account of Domestic Architecture in England*, III (1859) 319 and S. Toy, *The Castles of Great Britain* (1953) 215–16 consider that the original plan consisted of ranges of buildings built against the outer walls with a hall dividing the spacious courtyard into two. They see the pattern of four courts as probably a development of the sixteenth century and later. The early eighteenth-century plans and Lambert's drawings are sound evidence to the contrary.

23 VCH, IX (1937) 134.

24 Simpson (1942) 118.

25 Tipping (1937) 294–5.

26 Lewes, LEWSA, VR 3536.

27 V & A Museum, Print Dept E412.

28 The plans of 1708–10 and the mid-eighteenth-century ones mark the windows at ground- and first-floor level. However, the earlier plans do not show the south windows at the upper level.

29 Goodall (2004) 522–3.

30 *Ibid.* 187, and F. Grose, *Antiquities of England and Wales*, V (1797) 157–8. A few fragments of glass from the castle are held in the Bob Jones Art Museum, Greenville, South Carolina.

31 Venables (1851) 179.

32 *Ibid.* 132.

33 The view of C. Platt, *The Castle in Medieval England and Wales* (1982) 167. D. J. Cathcart King, *The Castle in England and Wales* (1988) 161 noted during a Château Gaillard conference in 1966 that the large French contingent standing in front of Herstmonceux asserted they had nothing like it in France. Smith, *The Medieval Brickmaking Industry* 18–19 suggests that the *machicoulis* archlets may show Baltic influence as at Caister Castle. W. D. Simpson claimed the same feature as a French mannerism: *The Building Accounts of Tattershall Castle* (1960) xxiv.

34 W. D. Simpson (1942) 113. A. H. Thompson considered that it had no military advantages and compared it with Compton Wynyates: *Medieval Military Architecture* (1912) 132.

35 The moat was drained shortly before 1570. VCH, IX (1937) 132. The possibility (also mentioned by Goodall (2004) 518) that Herstmonceux also enjoyed a designed landscape like that enclosing the castles at Bodiam and Saltwood warrants further examination.

36 Simpson (1942) 110.

37 Goodall suggest that foreign craftsmen (present in both buildings) were responsible for the diapering pattern at Eton, *Windsor: Medieval*

38 *Ibid.* 256 and n. 55.

39 The cloistered court at Queens' College to which the Green Court is sometimes compared was not added until *c.*1494–5.

40 M. Beswick, *Brickmaking in Sussex: A History and Gazetteer* (1993) 18.

41 A. Emery, *Greater Med. Houses*, II (2000) 149–51.

E. Venables, *Sussex Arch. Coll.* 4 (1851) 124–202

H. A. Tipping, *English Homes*, Pds 1 and 2, II (1937) 281–306: the Herstmonceux entry by Christopher Hussey

VCH, *Sussex*, IX (1937) 131–4: article by Walter Godfrey

W. D. Simpson, *Arch. Jour.* 99 (1942) 110–22

D. Calvert and R. Martin, *A History of Herstmonceux Castle* (1994)

J. A. A. Goodall, *Burlington Magazine* 146 (August 2004) 516–25

Archaeology, Art and Architecture in the Thames Valley, ed. L. Keen and E. Scarff (2002) 255.

HEVER CASTLE, Kent

Hever Castle lies next to the little River Eden which William Waldorf Astor diverted in 1903–7 when he transformed the moated farmhouse and meadows into the present entrepreneurial showpiece. More than 500 years earlier, Sir John Cobham 'of Devonshire'[1] had received a licence in 1383 to crenellate Hever. The strong gateway and modest outer walls are of this time.[2]

Like Ightham Mote (*c.*1330), Hever is approximately square, moated, and planned round a small courtyard with the hall opposite the entrance approach.[3] Hever was slightly smaller and the overall plan is more simple, but it has a strongly defended entrance approach as befits the troubled early years of Richard II's reign. The other façades of the castle show no defensive features. They were relatively flimsy enclosing walls of modest height, with an offset 4 feet from the ground and a strong string course supporting broad battlements.[4]

The three-storeyed oblong entrance block with its off-centre passageway is the principal defensive element of Cobham's residence. The majority of the castle is built of irregularly coursed Wealden sandstone, darkly streaked, creating a warm golden brown texture, but the narrow entrance frontage, slightly projecting from the body of the gatehouse, is built of smooth square blocks as if to emphasise its more formal character. It is designed in four planes. Above the entrance archway, flanked by buttresses, is a decorative section of seven quatrefoils with seven blind trefoil panels, with the central one open but barred (see engraving of 1735, pl. 109). The upper part of the buttresses are similarly treated and separate a blank section broken by a central loop and gunport. A row of machicolations and battlements complete the façade. The passageway, only 8½ feet wide, provides compact protection. It is divided into two rib-vaulted bays with 'murder holes', separated by three portcullises and two pairs of doors. The outer and inner porters' lodges were separated by a portcullis. The two upper floors, now a single area with a corner garderobe, may have been divided into an outer and inner chamber. This gateway was a serious defence, supported by a drawbridge and further gunports in the upper faces of the side walls, but its integrity was subsequently diminished by the two- and three-light windows inserted by Sir William Boleyn (1464–1506) after his father had purchased the castle in 1462.[5]

The frontage is completed by small angle turrets which give

PLATE 145 Hever Castle: from the south

Hever the appearance of a toy fort. In fact they are so minute and lacking in windows that they look like eighteenth-century pastiches. They abruptly cut the line of the string course and battlements (as does the gateway) and are not matched by comparable turrets on the north façade. Their small scale complements that of the entrance approach but they do not look comfortable in a late fourteenth-century context. However, they are shown in Buck's engraving together with the narrow loops, and have four-centred arches internally, matching those elsewhere in the castle. They provide small closets opening from the corner rooms, with the first floor serving two chambers, the upper one originally reached by a ladder as at Thornton Abbey gatehouse (c.1382). A change of texture on the west and east faces indicates that the upper sections are rebuilds when they may have been unnaturally heightened.[6]

Hever Castle is essentially a late fourteenth-century framework with very little original internal domestic content. The hall was in the same position as the present one which is of early sixteenth- and early twentieth-century character, but although the screens entrance looks late fourteenth century, its narrowness and style suggest that it was an Astor importation.[7] The kitchen with its well (filled in) and fireplace lay to the east and retains single cusped lights at ground- (renewed) and first-floor levels. The string course gargoyle on the outer face is appropriately open-mouthed! There were two-storeyed ranges on the west side (with a triangular chimney breast projection like that in the gateway), but the present timber-framed courtyard walls, ghosts of Cobham's original work, were replaced, gabled, and dormered in 1903–7 when the north front was also brought forward. No original roofs survive.

Hever was a fortified house protected by a strong gatehouse and modest enclosing walls. It was moat-surrounded (the beflowered berm is early twentieth century) with the castle rear protected by the River Eden, moved 100 yards northwards in 1903. The remains of a second moat round the castle were heavily modified as part of Astor's landscaping of the grounds. In planning terms, Hever's defence lay only in its façade, supported by double wet moats.

Stylistically, Cobham used a mixture of forms – two- and four-centred arches as in the gateway passage, and single lights with old-fashioned trefoil and shouldered heads. There would have originally been various outbuildings but any putative remains of the medieval or later centuries were swept away in the tidiness of 1903–7.[8]

No alterations were made by any of the well-known families who held Hever during the first half of the fifteenth century – Scrope, Fastolf, and Fiennes – until it was purchased in 1462 by Sir Geoffrey Boleyn (d.1464), the former lord mayor of London (1459). Like his equally ambitious Norfolk neighbours, the Heydons of Baconsthorpe who purchased Wickham Court to be close to London, Boleyn of Salle initially added Blickling in Norfolk and then Hever as steps in his path of social aggrandisement. It was probably his son, Sir William Boleyn (d.1506), who began to open up Hever (cinquefoil cusped lights under square hood moulds), followed by Sir Thomas Boleyn (d.1538, windows with plain heads) and Sir Charles Waldegrave in 1584 (mullions and transomed windows, gables and chimneys). After extended farmhouse use, the whole was spectacularly transformed by Viscount Astor in 1903–7 when more windows were inserted, the internal ranges revitalised, and the principal reception rooms subject to the same oppressive atmosphere that Astor had created at Cliveden through introducing too much elaborate reproduction panelling.

NOTES

1 John Cobham of Rundale (d.1362) had held the manor of Hever and Allington. His son, Sir Thomas held Allington and John Cobham was therefore related to him rather than to the elder Cobham branches of Cobham or Sterborough. According to the licence to crenellate, John Cobham came from Devonshire and the only John Cobham who could have built Hever was John Cobham of Blackborough who married Katherine and died without heirs in 1389. T. May, 'The Cobham family in the administration of England 1200–1400', *Arch. Cant.* 82 (1967) 1–31.

2 *Cal. Pat. Rolls: 1381–86*, 326. In his guidebook of 1966, Gavin Astor attributed the castle to Edward I's reign. Hasted had claimed construction by Edward III with a mythical licence to crenellate. R. Allen Brown dated it to c.1482, *English Castles* (1976) 146, and Clive Aslet (1981) limited the central gatehouse bay to this period.

3 Hever, 90 feet by 100 feet; Ightham, 114 feet by 125 feet.

4 The two single lights with shouldered heads in the north-west outer wall are sometimes cited as evidence of late thirteenth-century work, but the form was common enough a century later, and the outer wall shows no sign of having been built at two different periods.

5 A similar and contemporary three-light window was inserted in the gate tower at Ightham Mote.

6 Some restoration of the castle occurred in 'about 1830 when the room over the gateway was fitted up in imitation of the old style'. Turner and Parker (1859) 305.

7 Viscount Astor kept no record of his work at Hever, but it is known that he made considerable use of the timberwork from the demolished stables and lodgings in front of the castle for different parts of his 'Tudor village'.

8 The foundations of an early building were revealed in front of the castle in 1903–4, but no records were kept indicating its form. Astor (1966) 26. Timber-framed stabling and first-floor lodgings reached from an open gallery also existed close to the castle's frontage until 1898. They were possibly of early sixteenth-century date. Illustrated in K. Gravett, *Timber and Brick Building in Kent* (1971) 95, 22. It is possible that Hever was the exemplar of a more modest version at Horton Kirby, 15 miles to the

north. The Court Lodge now looks like an entirely nineteenth-century range but it was the entrance frontage of a simple fortified house. Almost identical in size to Hever (98 feet by 105 feet), it was similarly protected by a moat (with a berm), and had a simple projecting gateway, and ranges on at least two but not necessarily on all four sides of the courtyard with inner timber faces. Unfortunately, there is insufficient evidence to establish its date, although the few openings suggest that it was before the second quarter of the fifteenth century. P. J. Tester, 'The Court Lodge, Horton Kirby', in *Collectanea Historica*, ed. A. Detsicas (1981) 163–72.

T. H. Turner and J. H. Parker, *Some Account of Domestic Architecture in England*, III (1859) 304–5
A. Oswald, *Country Houses of Kent* (1933) 9–10
G. Astor, *Hever Castle and Gardens* (1966)
C. Aslet, *Country Life* (January 1981)

HORSELUNGES MANOR, Sussex

Horselunges Manor moves on a stage from the hall house exemplified by Great Dixter (q.v.). It is a prime and large example of a continuous jettied, timber-framed house of about 1500, with a ground-floor hall rather than one open to the roof. Like Crowhurst and Old Surrey Hall (q.v.), Horselunges Manor was spectacularly restored and extended in the early twentieth century although in a more controlled manner with a parallel range to the rear.

Two miles north of Hailsham, the principal range of seven bays, close studded with plaster infill, has a wide axial entrance with the hall of three bays to the left and the offices area of three bays to the right. The end bay incorporates a large blocked archway, believed to be an insertion when a carriageway was created giving access to the rear of the house.[1] The upper floor is carried on a continuous jetty supported on bracketed shafts, but all the windows of the entrance frontage were replaced in the mid-sixteenth century. The present sequence of slightly forward ground-floor bays and upper-floor oriels are part of the restoration by Walter Godfrey in 1925 on the evidence of a single survival, with the replacement gables based on the likely treatment of the roof line.

Internally, the single-storey hall has two heavily moulded cross beams on brackets and a longitudinal beam dividing it into six compartments. The staircase, inserted in the mid-sixteenth century,

PLATE 146 Horselunges Manor: principal range before restoration (1924)

gives access to the great chamber, which is slightly wider than the hall underneath because of the jettying. Partially open to the roof, it is spanned by great tie beams braced to the wall posts but without supporting crown posts. What survives today at Horselunges is not the whole story. Doorways in the end wall of the hall and parlour show that there was an extra bay and a south wing and there is evidence that the opposite end has been truncated. Godfrey considered that the house may have been of quadrangular courtyard form with the hall initially in a destroyed range but this is no longer considered so.[2]

From the early fifteenth century, the moated site of 1½ acres was occupied by the Devenish family of Hellingly. The present timber-framed structure within the moat may be attributed to Sir John Devenish at the close of the century. He entered into his patrimony in 1477, was knighted in c.1490, and married Elizabeth, a co-heiress of Lord Hoo. He had died by 1518. Horselunges is a splendid example of regional timber framing on the grand scale and illustrates the transition of such a house during the sub-medieval period followed by many smaller houses in Sussex. The workmanship is of a high standard throughout, with playful animals in the doorway spandrels, heads stopping the chamber cross beams, and elaborate mouldings extending from the jettied frontage to the purlin and wind-brace roof of the great chamber.

NOTES
1 Godfrey and Budgen (1925) 11.
2 R. T. Mason, *Framed Buildings of the Weald* (1969) 88.

W. Godfrey and W. Budgen, *Sussex Arch. Coll.* 66 (1925) 1–17, 18–33
W. H. Godfrey, *Country Life* (January 1935)

IGHTHAM MOTE, Kent

Ightham Mote, nestling in a still-secluded wooded valley 5 miles east of Sevenoaks, is one of the most romantic-looking houses in southern England. It is also an architectural hotchpotch, for although it appears to be a textbook example of a moated medieval house, much of its interior dates from the Tudor and Stuart periods when the families were anxious to make the house more habitable and convenient to use. This diffuseness of a complex site is compounded by the lack of early documentation and a considerable amount of late nineteenth-century restoration simulating early work.

The property stands on a tongue of clay in a tributary valley emerging from a larger one out of the Greensand ridge to the north. The area has always been richly wooded, broken by trackways with no evidence of local habitation prior to the present site development.[1] The house was established here either because the land was of little value to the lord of the manor of Ightham, or because it evolved from a mill and embanked mill pond which was modified to become the constantly spring-fed moat. This probability arises because the moat was not dug into the clay but was built up with brought-in-material, though no structural or excavated evidence of an earlier building has been identified.[2] The house reflects the local landscape by using stone from the nearby Greensand quarries, lime from the adjacent chalkland, and timber from the local woods.[3] The property has never been subject to a landscaped park or tree-lined vistas but still reflects its long-established past – isolated and tranquil.

From the first, the house was a combination of stone and timber-framing. The hall and chapel erected during the second quarter of the fourteenth century were stone built, but the two contemporary solars were timber-framed. This combination was repeated throughout the house's development, but the post-medieval replacement of timber with stonework and vice versa occurred on such a scale that its early charm of combined materials has been replaced by one of different aesthetic appeal, though using the same materials. Fortunately, phased restoration by the National Trust between 1989 and 2004 has dramatically enhanced our understanding of the house's development and modified earlier assessments.

The builder of Ightham Mote has not yet been identified. No documentary evidence directly relating to the property has been traced earlier than 1372 when it was held by Sir Thomas Cawne, but as there is no evidence for Sir Thomas at Ightham before then or in Kent before 1363, and as his children were very young at that time, construction by the previous holder of the manor is more likely.[4] This was Isolde Inge who held the estate as a widow in 1340 and who had remarried a St Pere by 1347. Dendrochronology has given us a precise sequence for all phases of the house's development including its initial construction during the 1330s which may have been the work of Isolde or her husband, but there is no certainty.[5]

PHASE I: 1330–50

The hall, two solars, chapel, and entry gate were erected between 1330 and 1342 – not in that order but starting with the east–west solar (1330) followed by the north–south solar (1331), the entry gate (1332), the hall (1337), and the chapel block (1342).

Hall

The hall entrance is no longer porch-protected but evidence was found in 1991 that a contemporary one existed, wider than the doorway and capable of taking a stair to the chamber above the services. It was a timber-framed structure.

The hall, 30 feet by 20 feet, has been little altered since its construction, though its present state is not without problems. It retains two of its three service doorways, an original window of two cinquefoil lights with an octofoil above south of the fireplace, and a five-light window of the 1480s in the west wall with glass of *c*.1521 by Richard Clement in tribute to Henry VIII. The roof is a crown-post structure supported on trusses against the end walls, and a stone arch offset from the centre dividing the hall into a lower one-third bay and an upper two-thirds bay. The stone arch is one repeated in a small group of élite contemporary houses in the area with the double crown post here simply sitting on it. In a hall of limited space, the high-pitched roof, 37½ feet to the ridge, creates an apartment of uncomfortable proportions. The six humorous corbels supporting the three arches are a valuable addition to the hall's limited character in view of the dour panelling and frieze introduced by Norman Shaw in 1872.

It is arguable whether there was a cross-passage doorway or not opposite the hall entry. There is no obvious structural evidence, but the walling here is very badly damaged, and in part rebuilt. Opposing doorways were common by this time and might be expected in a high-quality house like this as well as being particularly desirable to reach the kitchen court to the east. Such a doorway

PLATE 147 Ightham Mote: east–west solar block, north–south extension, and guest lodging

would be squashed at the side of the original window[6] though not impossible if it was no larger than the office doorway at the side. As access to the kitchen court could otherwise be from the kitchen, as at Dartington Hall, the matter lies unresolved.

There were originally three doorways in the lower end wall to the service (see below), but any screen from the hall entrance would have cut into the middle of the window opposite! The fireplace is a Tudor insertion for evidence was found in 1998 of a second window in this position under the plasterwork, including its upper splayed quoins and part of a voussoir. The roof timbers are very sooted, and though no louvre exists Major Luard-Selby reported he had found indications of one in 1863,[7] while the peg holes for fixing it have been traced in the central rafters. The roof timbers have been painted Tuscany red, probably medieval rather than the brighter Tudor colours. The corbels against the end walls are 'flying' corbels supporting nothing. No comparable examples have been traced, though the practice may have been repeated in the 'old' chapel where there is adequate space for a similar decorative rather than structural feature where the timbers stop short of the end walls. There was no dais in this hall but the upper-end doorway opening on to the stair is similar in date and style to the hall entrance, although its rear arch has been crudely rebuilt.

The solar blocks

The staircase opening from the hall is a Jacobean-style make-up on the site of an earlier structure similarly giving access to the solar blocks.[8] These do not conform to the standard plan and contribute to the puzzles of Ightham. Basically, there are two solar units to the rear of the hall – one lying from east to west followed by one north to south. Both are timber-framed, but abutting them is a further two-storey stone block running to the edge of the moat and so creating an irregular T-shaped group of apartments. The upper chamber of the stone block has long been known as the 'old' chapel because of its vaulted undercroft, its position facing eastwards, and the first-floor squint from the adjacent residential room. The two solar blocks were the first structures to be created and at the same time, for apart from identical dendrochronology, the wall plate of the east–west range carries the gable truss of the north–south range. The failure to create a common courtyard façade is odd, while they hold none of the decorative features found in the stone structure added ten years later and heightening the uncomfortable relationship between them. These factors are probably a reflection of changes in the initial development of the house.

The solar blocks were of two bays each but they have been so badly mauled that the ground-floor rooms in particular, are of minimal interest. From the stair hall, a plain two-centred archway opens into a large ground-floor chamber to the rear of the hall. The insertion of a sixteenth-century fireplace, a late eighteenth-century window in a galletted seventeenth-century courtyard wall, and later partitioning changes to create a larger room and passageway mean that its medieval character is non-existent. The same is true of the remaining rooms divided by brick walls in the nineteenth century to form a strong room and staff quarters. The plain stair lobby doorway to these rooms suggests that the ground floor was always used for storage or staff attendant on the family.

We have no idea what the original stair to the upper floor was like but it was probably of stone rather than timber in this high-status link. It had to be fairly wide to allow access to the undercroft and ground-floor rooms as well as separate entries to the chapel and first solar.

The two upper rooms are not much more rewarding to the medievalist. Externally, the timber façade of both blocks looks picturesque early Tudor work with barge boards inserted by Sir Richard Clement with the emblems of Henry VIII and Catherine of Aragon and a contemporary oriel window in the earlier close-studded wall. However, the wall and gable of the north solar had been brought forward from the original line in the later fifteenth century. Most of the internal features are of the Tudor or Stuart period, except for the roof structure which reveals the original form of both apartments. The east–west range, marked by the proportions of the present oriel room, retains its original strongly braced central tie-beam and crown-post roof (but with the crown post moved by one truss in 1890–91). The floor has also been raised by a foot, making the chapel squint lower than originally. The present fireplace in the hall wall is probably on the site of the original one as this was an important retiring room.

The further two-bay solar to the north at right angles similarly retains its crown-post roof but has been more drastically altered through division into two rooms in 1890–1 and the post-medieval insertion of the doorway from the chapel.

The chapel block

The undercroft below the first chapel floor with the thickest walls in Ightham (3½ feet) is the least altered part of this fourteenth-century house. It is divided into two bays (19½ feet by 11½ feet internally) with a quadripartite vault with the ribs dying into the walls. A two-light window close to the water level is of mid-fourteenth-century form with ogee heads, but the original entrance (rather than the present late medieval insertion similar to the rear archway of the gate-tower) opened directly from the stair lobby in the south-east corner of the room (now blocked).

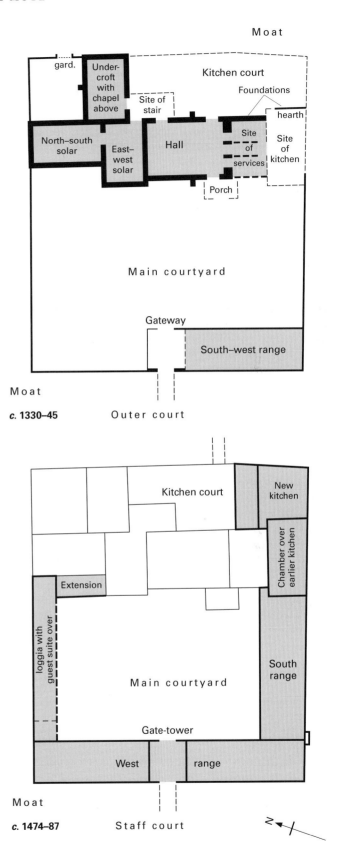

FIGURE 79 Ightham Mote: site plans, c.1330–45 and c.1474–87

The chapel at the head of the stair (22 feet by 14 feet internally) retains less original character through horizontal division between the mid-sixteenth and mid-twentieth centuries. A fourteenth-century doorway survives and the simple collar-raftered roof with its moulded cornice and foliated stops as in the hall, but the majority of the string course round the room, 3 feet from the ground, has been hacked away except in the east corner. The lower part of the tall east window survives, but the upper part, the fireplace, and the doorway from the staircase are a consequence of the room's division. Timber studding inserted at the same time in a large gap in the north wall may fill the site of a former window.

It is usually considered that the original entry was blocked by the Tudor fireplace within the chapel and the landing cupboard outside it, but the only evidence for this is a modest line of dressed stonework internally. Such a position would be unusual, while an entry near the lower end would be more appropriate and would fit the stair access better. The present entry to the chapel from the second solar is an insertion, with the reused fourteenth-century doorway positioned the wrong way round, i.e. inside rather than outside the chapel. The use of this chamber as a chapel is impaired by the absence of a piscina but the string course rises over the ogee-headed squint to suggest that it is an original feature with no evidence of insertion, even though there was a ten-year difference between the erection of the two units.

Additional residential unit

The small court created at the north-east angle between the chapel, the solar blocks, and the outer wall against the moat was partially infilled in about 1532 when the lower windows of the new two-storeyed range were inserted in the fourteenth-century outer wall, and the whole area was heavily restored in 1890–1 when the timbered façades were re-created. Yet there may have been a fourth early unit in this corner of the house. Though the middle of the chapel north wall was buttressed and therefore external, the east wall against the moat retains the remains of a double garderobe chute, the only surviving medieval facility of this nature serving this part of the house. The remains include the stub and chase evidence of its outer walls and much of the central stone division. The shafts are primary work for the undercroft window was offset to the vaulting to accommodate them. They were either corridor approached against the side of the chapel or indicative of a subsequently destroyed additional solar unit.

Offices and chamber block

Repair work in 2001 confirmed there were the usual three doorways to the buttery, pantry, and kitchen at the services end of the hall. The central one to the kitchen passage was higher and remains, as does the lower one to the east. The jamb of the third arch was traced within the Victorian porch created by Norman Shaw for Mrs Luard-Selby in 1872.

Stone foundations of an offices wall towards the moat were found under the buildings in 1991, but the bulk of the structure was always timber-framed. The straight joint between the hall and offices, and the slightly lower roof line, show that the latter was constructed separately from the hall. There was a substantial chamber above the offices, approached from the hall porch, but all the present rooms in this area are post-medieval.

The kitchen extended to the south wall of the site. Its hearth was

PLATE 148 Ightham Mote: from north-east showing stone chapel block, garderobe chute of additional residential block, and post-medieval framed additions

found during consolidation work in this area though nothing else remains of the original structure. A new one was built next door to it in the 1470s which has since served as the kitchen to the house. The entry from the kitchen court giving access across the moat is probably a Tudor facility rather than an original one breaking the security of the site.

Entrance range

The original fourteenth-century entry to the main courtyard is that incorporated in the later gatehouse. It was simply a drawbridge-protected doorway in the curtain wall. No evidence has been found of any contemporary superstructure.

Much of the ground-floor stonework extending south from the gateway has mortar similar to that used in the 1330s construction phase. Towards the north end, the room (but not the structure) seems to have extended into the gate-tower with no evidence of a partition. The ground floor ceiling timbers have been dendro dated to between 1320 and 1345, while the fifteenth-century roof has a daub partition on studs of 1330–45. This suggests that the upper floor was of the same plan as at present – an outer room 33 feet long and an inner room 11 feet long at the south end.

No other fourteenth-century structures have been identified round the sides of the walled court, but there would probably have been accommodation for senior staff, possibly in timber-framed lodgings.

PHASE 2: 1474–87

Ightham Mote came into the hands of Sir Thomas Cawne at a time not yet known, though he bequeathed the house to his son, Robert, in 1374.[9] It descended through his daughter to Sir Nicholas Haut in 1399, whose family held the property until 1519. They were minor gentry but Richard Haut rose to a position of some importance during the third quarter of the fifteenth century.[10] He was a cousin of Edward IV's queen, Elizabeth Woodville, and was appointed treasurer of the household of Prince Edward. No work had been undertaken at Ightham Mote for over a century and the house was looking old-fashioned. Marriage to a rich widow enabled Richard Haut (1462–87) to undertake a sequence of developments that shaped the courtyard as it stands today. Work seems to have been initiated with a new kitchen (1474) and the creation of a superior chamber above the earlier kitchen (c.1474). The west or entrance range was developed between 1474 (south end) and 1479 (north end) at the same time as the north range, possibly followed by the south range during the 1480s.

Entrance range

The three-storeyed gate-tower in the middle of the west range is flanked by lower wings with two-light windows of early Tudor form. With its slightly rougher stonework and drawbridge-protected entrance arch of fourteenth-century character, it is reasonable to assume that the entrance incorporates some of the earliest work at Ightham and that the remainder of the range dates from c.1520. Its development was more complex.

The lower walling overlooking the moat is of uniform construction throughout its length including the entrance up to the spring of the fourteenth-century arch.[11] The present bridge is of late date and was originally wider if the early squint on the north side is to have had any value. A simple passageway gives direct access to the courtyard with no porter's lodge in the side wall or any secondary defensive features.[12]

During the 1470s, a framed superstructure was erected above the earlier entry, for a tie beam of that date has been found behind the brickwork of the south elevation. It is open to question whether the gatehouse ground floor was entirely stone-built or timber-framed. The stone north wall seems to be original but the south wall was definitely framed. This was replaced by the present stone structure to create a commanding entry. It was in existence by the early sixteenth century and may have been erected in the late fifteenth century.

The gate-tower is flat fronted and of no military character, with large cinquefoil windows showing that the question of defence had long since been superseded by those of display. The joggled and patched stonework either side of the entrance arch resulted from the additional weight it now carried, though the brick parapet, south wall, armorial glass, and informal staircase are late Tudor additions. The stairs were reconstructed in 1890–1 by Sir Thomas Colyer-Fergusson (1889–1951) above the so-called 'oubliette'

created earlier in the century, when Major Luard-Selby inserted the chimney stack in 1856.[13] Colyer-Fergusson also took the opportunity to rebuild the brick wall on the north side of the passageway in stone and over-point the opposite wall.

The wings either side of the gate-tower are entirely of stone but this was not always so. The changes are most obvious south of the entrance, where the lower walling of 1330–45 is interrupted by a row of mid-Tudor ground-floor windows. Immediately above them is a line of square holes filled with stones. The stonework above is of a slightly different texture and retains the ghosts of the initial timber framing of c.1480. This is particularly noticeable where the wing meets the gate-tower at first-floor level and the straight joint outlines the timber post which supported the end roof truss spanning this wing. The south gable was similarly timber-framed initially. The timber replacement with stone infilling occurred during the early seventeenth century after Sir William Selby I (1591–1612) had purchased the property for £4,000. By the time John Buckler drew this frontage in 1830,[14] the present upper line of windows had been inserted and the end gable rebuilt in stone.

Internally, the roof was replaced in about 1480 by the present fine structure of moulded posts, roof plate, cranked tie-beams, and good crown posts. However, the smaller end room roof is of such poor quality that it was probably always ceiled to give it standing. They were possibly rooms for senior household staff. They were not corridor linked to the gatetower rooms until Victorian times when a forced entry and floor level change was made. Nor is it clear how this upper floor was approached, though an outer stair is postulated.

The slightly later north wing was originally of comparable design with common evidence of the straight joint and the timber framing abutting the gate-tower. It may originally have been a dormitory for staff serving the adjoining guest suite in the north range. However, the upper floor was removed by Sir William Selby I in 1611 and rebuilt in stone, with the roof crudely reconstructed at a higher level, lit by mullioned and transomed windows in the outer wall, and warmed by a fireplace against the gate-tower with the arms of William Selby II (1612–38). The Venetian-style window was inserted in the earlier eighteenth century and the remaining windows blocked and wallpaper-covered in the early years of the following century (although two are still visible in the west wall) when a single 'Tudor' type window was inserted by Thomas Selby (1797–1820).

North range

Dated roof timbers of the 1470s identify the construction of the north range by Richard Haut. Built above an open arcade or loggia, it seems to have consisted of three rooms, a lobby, a large outer chamber ('new chapel') and small inner chamber (corridor room), approached from a smaller stair than the present early seventeenth-century one at the west end. The larger room was always spanned by the barrel-vaulted ceiling, originally painted deep red. Though there is no evidence of a wall fireplace in either room, it may have been a high-quality guest suite – a lobby-approached and imposing reception chamber with an inner bedroom. Entered from the original oak door, the suite was not linked to the solar blocks to preserve its privacy. The outer jetty facilitated wider accommodation internally as well as emphasising the suite's status externally (pl. 101).

Both floors have been drastically altered. The loggia and walling above were brought forward during the nineteenth century and the ground floor converted into a conservatory in 1890–1. The upper

PLATE 149 Ightham Mote: eighteenth-century chapel conversion from guest lodging

floor was modified by Sir Richard Clement between 1521 and 1529 whose marriage to a rich widow enabled him to buy Ightham Mote. He improved the lodging with stained glass windows and decorated the ceiling with the emblems of Henry VIII and Catherine of Aragon.[15] The entry stair was modified in *c*.1611 at the same time that the doorway was forced through to the family apartments. The room was not converted into a chapel until the early eighteenth century when the medieval and later furnishings were introduced.[16] The panelling, though antique, was fitted in 1906, as were further ecclesiastical additions.

South range

The lower stone walling is first-phase work but the range is essentially of 1480–1 when the floor joists were jettied over the moat, though (unusually for Ightham Mote) the courtyard wall was framed up to the eaves. Twin garderobes were added at the junction with the west wing, capable of serving both ranges. The crown-post roof is of poor quality, ceiled in 1560–5. Initially both floors of this four-bay range were divided into two chambers but they have witnessed many alterations. The courtyard façade was rebuilt in stone

during the late eighteenth century, internal corridors were added and removed in the mid-nineteenth century, while the external framing was rebuilt in mock half-timber in 1906 in place of the plaster covering the initial timber framework. This range always seems to have been of secondary standard and use throughout most of its life and was found to be the most neglected of the whole house during the 1989–2004 restoration.

East range extension

In *c*.1485, two rooms were added against the north–south solar which may have served as a first-floor gallery to improve circulation, though the area was wide enough to be used as a room.

Kitchen

A new kitchen was built in the south-east corner of the site next to the original one. A high-status room was added over the original structure during the 1470s, a practice repeated at Ashby de la Zouch Castle and a little later at Cotehele. The lower end of the hall was no longer seen as an inferior area of the house, probably because of the pressure for good-quality accommodation when that at the upper end was already taken up. The newly created chamber was partitioned in the early eighteenth century but still retains its original proportions. The room has been ceiled but evidence was found in 2000 of a corbel support for the braced truss that initially spanned this room. A short gallery was added next to it in the later sixteenth century marked by the massive four-light transomed window in the east front.

Staff court

Ightham Mote has been moat-bound throughout its development and has never expanded beyond it so far as any primary accommodation is concerned. The staff court outside was developed in about 1475 to give greater privacy to those within the house as well as provide better accommodation for the staff than they had hitherto enjoyed. The range was initially timber-framed throughout, with the house-facing elevations jettied, but those facing away were built in one plane. As elsewhere at Ightham, part of it was replaced with stone – the ground in this instance – with fire destroying that half of the quadrangle facing the house in Victorian times.

PHASES 3–6: POST-MEDIEVAL

Some of the changes introduced by Sir Richard Clement (1521–38) have been noted for he essentially brought Ightham Mote to the form that exists today. The penultimate phase occurred during the early seventeenth century when Sir William Selby in particular (1611–38) made a number of internal modifications to make the house more comfortable, including the development of the north end of the gatehouse range. The last phase was a sequence of Victorian modifications including repairs in 1846 for Prideaux Selby (1846–67), work by Norman Shaw in the 1870s for Mrs Luard-Selby (1867–89), and the many changes carried out by Sir Thomas Colyer-Fergusson (1889–1951) after the sale of the house to him in 1889. His restoration of the property between 1890 and 1906 left few areas untouched. But though four centuries of modifications and adaptations to meet the needs and fashion demands of post-medieval occupants are of considerable interest, they are less significant than the early development of this moat-circumscribed house.

REVIEW

Although the name Ightham Mote derives from the Anglo-Norman meaning Ehta's moated homestead, no structural or archaeological evidence of occupation has been found prior to the early fourteenth century. The house was built, developed, and occupied throughout its 650 years' history by gentry – knights, squires, local administrators, members of parliament, and occasionally courtiers. It never aspired to grandness though it was initially a house of aspiring status. Its post-medieval development was modest and primarily concerned with family convenience – corridors, bedrooms, service facilities, heating, and drainage rather than imposing reception rooms or suites of apartments.

The house was situated in a valley bottom to take advantage of the spring which fed the moat as well as the upper lake and a lower pond (a stew or fish pond) immediately north of the house (now lawn). The moat seems to be contemporary with the house rather than of thirteenth-century origin. Ightham is a classic example of a moat-restricted site. Penshurst Place, not far distant, never had one, so that the family apartments could be positioned increasingly further from the services to give greater privacy. As the north–south axis at Ightham was filled from the first, expansion was necessarily limited and tight. Though the present outer court buildings are of later fifteenth-century origin, the site almost certainly existed a century earlier to accommodate stables, workshops, outhouses, etc.

It seems that the house was initially planned as a timber-framed structure. The two solar blocks were so built, but possibly as a consequence of increased funding, stone was preferred for the hall and chapel block, six and eleven years later.

The hall and services followed the increasingly standardised layout of extending in line with the solar blocks also facing the entrance on the opposite side of the courtyard. Although the hall was erected in about 1337, doubts about the provision of a fully developed screens passage and its uncomfortable proportions suggest the work of a parochial master-mason compared with the mature standards demonstrated nearby at Penshurst Place during the 1340s. Yet this was a high-quality house, with the hall boasting a stone arch comparable to those in such episcopal and élite houses nearby as Charing (c.1320–30), Mayfield (1330s), and Battel Hall (c.1330).[17]

It had a complex group of family apartments displaying greater domestic plenitude than the rather small hall implies. A stone chapel in association with a timber-framed solar block is not particularly unusual, but a double solar block is rare. The possibility of a contemporary third block against the chapel terminating in a double garderobe heightens the complexity of the family accommodation. The early fourteenth-century manor of Walton on the Hill in Surrey (q.v.) has a stone hall and chapel block of comparable scale, attributed to the bishop of Bath and Wells. A more pertinent parallel is Broughton 'Castle' in Oxfordshire (q.v.), a development of similar scale and greater complexity initiated during the later thirteenth century but developed during the early fourteenth by a modest landowning family of which only one member was knighted. The lower end of Ightham followed the standard pattern of offices and kitchen in line, while at least one contemporary range stands on one side of the gated court, probably for high-status staff.

The second and third phases by Richard Haut and Sir Richard Clement, both reflected the work of 'new' men at the courts of Edward IV and Henry VIII. That of Richard in particular, exemplifies his need for higher-quality accommodation for himself and his household. Site restrictions necessitated the development of good-quality accommodation at the lower end of the hall, as well as high-status guest rooms and improved ranges for household officials and staff. The better staff facilities outside the moated platform not only reflected the increased scale of the household but the pressure for greater family privacy.

Ightham Mote was never an élite residence like Penshurst, Knole, or Mayfield Palace but the home of minor landowning families from the fourteenth to the mid-twentieth centuries. It is not a repository of quality furnishings or spectacular internal decoration but a reflection of gentry lifestyle over six centuries. For instance, the centre of the household extended from the initial solar complex to the lower end of the hall a century later and then moved to the north-west range (the drawing room) during the early seventeenth century. Changing circulation patterns can be identified in the upper floor of the west ranges, with corridor insertions linked by forced entries. The different building materials used – stone, timber, and brick as well as replacing timber-framing with stone facing (entry range) – were the contrasting solutions to the financial circumstances, attitudes, and lifestyles of different generations who loved this still-enchanting house.

NOTES

1 Flint evidence of prehistoric settlement was found in the neighbourhood during the nineteenth century: N. Bannister, *Ightham Mote Estate: An Archaeological and Historical Landscape Study* (1999) ch. 2, I. The strip lynchets within the valley have not been dated but a a thirteenth-century jug strap handle was found a few years ago by the farmer in a field 200 yards from the house.

2 Timbers high in the kitchen roof have been dendro dated to the 1280s, but in an otherwise late fifteenth-century context. They had not been obviously reused but were too high to be an integral part of an earlier house.

3 The earliest tree rings from timbers felled for the house in the fourteenth century were from oaks planted 160/180 years earlier.

4 S. Pearson (RCHM) Report on Ightham Mote (1987) 1. Also E. Harrison, *Arch. Cant.* 48 (1936) 169–218.

5 For the dates, *Vern. Arch.* 25 (1994); 26 (1995); 27 (1996); 28 (1997). They and subsequently corrected dates will be published in the detailed report being prepared under the editorship of Peter E. Leach. This will supersede all previous (and brief) descriptions such as those by J. O. Scott, *Arch. Cant.* 24 (1900) 189–92, A. Vallance, 45 (1933) 116–23; and H. A. Tipping, *English Homes*, Pds I and II (1937) 1–16.

6 This may have been moved, for it is not central to the bay, interrupts the stone rebate, and shows considerable evidence externally of damaged and rebuilt walling.

7 *Arch. Jour.* 20 (1863) 387. The roof timbers were heavily renewed in the late nineteenth century.

8 The present stair, probably nineteenth century, incorporates timbers from at least four structures, including arcading from the stables.

9 *Arch. Cant.* 4 (1861–2) for the will of Sir Thomas. It is undated but Sir Thomas' widow recovered his lands from the feoffees in 47 Edward III, i.e. 1373–4. For a brief note on the former owners, C. E. Woodruff, *Arch. Cant.* 24 (1900) 195–200, but much more research needs to be carried out in this field.

10 P. W. Fleming in *England in the Fifteenth Century*, ed. D. Williams (1987).

11 It has a slight batter immediately above the level of the moat, continued along the north side but absent from the south range.

12 The nail-studded rear door is probably early sixteenth century.

13 *The Builder*, July 1873.

14 Brit. Lib., Add. MS 36368 f.45.

15 The date of the windows is uncertain. Their framing is integral with dendro dated walling of 1474 but their form, square headed and without cusps, does not seem earlier than the 1520s. Dr Starkey suggested that the ceiling boards could have been reused from a temporary wooden pavilion built for a royal festivity (*Archaeologia* 107 (1982) 153–63), but further examination in 1997 has shown that the ceiling was inserted in the 1470s and was painted *in situ* about fifty years later.

16 They are shown minus the linenfold panelling, in drawings of the chapel's interior by William Twopenny in 1827 and 1828.

17 J. O. Scott suggested that the similarities in the mouldings of the arches at Mayfield and Ightham pointed to a common master-mason (*Arch. Cant.* 24 (1900)), but work at Mayfield was far closer to Penshurst Place than to Ightham.

T. H. Turner and J. H. Parker, *Some Account of Domestic Architecture in England*, II (1853) 282–4

H. Taylor, *Arch. Cant.* 27 (1905) 1–29

M. Hall, *Country Life* (June 1990)

The National Trust, *Ightham Mote: Guidebook* (2005 edn)

P. E. Leach (ed.), *Report on the Restoration of Ightham Mote* (forthcoming)

KNOLE, Kent

The study of the late medieval plan and early development of Knole is hampered by a number of historical factors. The most obvious is that the original fifteenth-century buildings have been altered, enlarged, and enveloped to such an extent that what began as an extensive courtyard house has become a vast complex, frequently compared to a medieval village in shaping and size. Matters are made more difficult by the use of the same local ragstone for nearly all work throughout all building periods. This soft-textured material has meant that from an early stage the builders of Knole adopted the two- and occasionally three-light uncusped window with a four-centred head as an easy-to-work form. It became the *leitmotif* of Knole. Used from the late fifteenth to the eighteenth century, it makes the identification of different building periods extremely difficult. Although roof trusses often provide vital clues to historical development when alterations have completely changed the apartments they cover, this is not true of Knole. At the beginning of the seventeenth century, the earl of Dorset destroyed nearly all the earlier roofs, added a second storey above most of the ranges, and crowned them all with new structures. To add to the difficulties of analysing this house, it is a property which is in multi-occupation. The extensive state apartments are furnished and have been open to the public for more than 150 years. A greater proportion of the residence is in private occupation by families of the Sackville line. Some of the ranges are used by the estate staff, but others are empty and uninhabited. Knole shares with Wentworth Woodhouse the dubious distinction of being the largest private house built in England so that examining every apartment and room is physically enervating.

Fortunately, there are some compensating advantages. As at Haddon Hall, nothing at Knole has changed structurally since the first half of the seventeenth century. From the point of view of internal decoration and furnishing, there has again been little modification since the close of that century. The sheer scale of Knole is

PLATE 150 Knole: Bourchier's Gatehouse from Green Court

challenging, and the skill and warmth with which the Sackvilles have cared for this complex over many generations is exemplary.

Archbishop Bourchier of Canterbury (1455–86) bought the manor of Knole from William Fiennes, 2nd Lord Saye and Sele in 1456. It is known that a house existed at Knole before the mid-fifteenth century but its position has not been located. No evidence has been found of occupation on the present site prior to Bourchier's work of the late 1450s which had progressed sufficiently for him to stay there in 1464. In 1467, the account rolls at Lambeth Palace record repairs to the roof and building a new tower which suggests that the house was completed in part and possibly in whole. This is likely to have been by 1480 when Bourchier presented the palace he had built for his own use to the see of Canterbury.[1]

Bourchier's two successors, archbishops Morton (1486–1501) and Warham (1504–32), both spent substantial sums on Knole. In 1537, Cranmer reluctantly offered the house to a determined Henry VIII, who showed particular affection for the property and made further additions to it during the 1540s.

In 1566, Elizabeth I granted the estate to her cousin, Sir Thomas Sackville, later earl of Dorset. He leased out the property until 1603, but took it back into his own hands and remodelled it thoroughly between 1603 and 1608. He inserted an attic level in several ranges, renewed most of the roofs, inserted many plaster ceilings and much panelling, created a series of magnificent state rooms, and left Knole internally in the form it is today – a showhouse of Jacobean splendour, enhanced by its outstanding collection of late Stuart furniture.

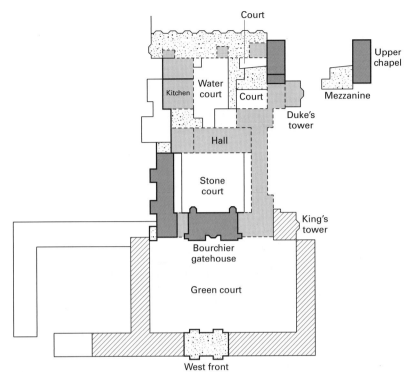

FIRST FLOOR

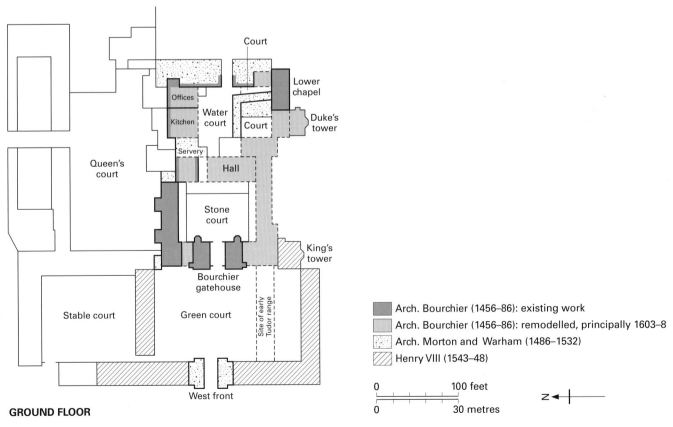

GROUND FLOOR

Arch. Bourchier (1456–86): existing work

Arch. Bourchier (1456–86): remodelled, principally 1603–8

Arch. Morton and Warham (1486–1532)

Henry VIII (1543–48)

0   100 feet

0   30 metres

N

FIGURE 80 Knole: floor plans

BOURCHIER'S GATEHOUSE

Bourchier's gatehouse fills the bulk of the east frontage of Green Court. The central section is two-storeyed, but it is enveloped by three-storeyed towers on either side with garderobe turrets rebated from the frontage. Note that the stonework of the towers is coarser and more random than the central section, while the string courses do not match. The clock tower (removed from the great hall) and the stone tower supporting it were added in 1745 when the curious fretted 'window' was added. The entrance arch with its simple mouldings is surmounted by a broader four-centred arch with angels carrying shields in the spandrels. There are blind machicolations, simply decorative and now broken by the insertion of the mis-aligned oriel window at first-floor level.

The two-bay entrance passageway has simple ribbed vaulting on plain corbels. The rear façade is more orderly, but this may be due to a reordering in 1604 when the lead pipes and hoppers were inserted. Apart from the entry passage, the ground floor is made up of two large rooms at ground level, and three large chambers at first-floor level linked by a rear passage with open windows. All outer rooms were garderobe-provided, and accessed from the newels in the two widely spaced turrets boldly projecting towards the courtyard. The front-facing oriel is the grandest surviving fifteenth-century feature in the house. It is an impressive window internally, with side columns and a ribbed panelled ceiling like that in the lower chapel. A corbel in this oriel chamber is decorated with Bourchier's emblem, a Stafford double knot.

Initially, the gatehouse seems to have consisted of a two-storeyed structure with a room above the entry passage, extended shortly afterwards into a much larger three-storeyed structure, when the oriel may have been inserted. Both phases are architecturally attributable to Bourchier, with the narrow garderobe arches stylistically comparable to those by him in the north range. In its final form, the gatehouse is clearly of residential importance and should be compared with the slightly earlier suite of similar apartments over the entrance to Herstmonceux Castle (c.1438–49) and the slightly later suite at Oxburgh Hall (1480s).

The remainder of the east frontage facing Green Court retains no further evidence of original work though the line of walling is probably so. The end towers are additions but the small one on the left with its thinner walling seems to have been added not long after the initial work had been completed, because of its relationship to the adjacent rooms.

STONE COURT

The wide corridor on the north and south sides of Stone Court was added in the early seventeenth century, protecting the post and panel walls with windows that were originally the outer faces of the side ranges towards the court.

Falling ground north of the north range creates a cliff-like frontage externally which reveals the form of Bourchier's work. The pattern of fireplaces and garderobe projections at ground- and first-floor levels indicates the range was a sequence of lodgings above cheerless lower-ground-floor chambers. Although the windows and fireplaces have been altered internally, the same plan was adopted at both levels and consisted of three suites: a single lodging at the north-west angle (with garderobe, subsequently replaced by a larger turret) followed by two paired lodgings – an outer room with fireplace and an inner one with garderobe.[2] The narrow two-centred garderobe doorways on the first floor are original as is the end ground-floor doorway. The trusses above the Georgian ceilings are reported to be contemporary.[3] That Bourchier was responsible for this range is made clear by his arms and the figures painted on the plastered inner wall of the lower ground floor.

The south range retains few original features as a consequence of later fittings and decorative schemes. There are two fifteenth-century doorways at either end of the ground-floor Colonnade Room and one in the Cartoon Gallery above (though not in line) which may be original openings rather than insertions in the timber-framed partitions. All fittings at both ground- and first-floor level are early seventeenth century, as is the second-floor gallery and roof structure above. It is likely, however, that the south range was initially made up of suites of lodgings like those on the north side of the court.[4]

Bourchier's great hall stood on the site of the present hall, for the buttery and pantry doorways are original, but nothing else survives earlier than the beginning of the sixteenth century.[5] An examination of the stonework during its restoration in 1981 confirmed the absence of any fifteenth-century features, while the roof was removed in the early seventeenth century when the earl of Dorset raised the height of the whole range and inserted an upper gallery throughout its length.

WATER COURT

Before a range divided Water Court in the late fifteenth century, the south side of the court was composed of an irregular group of private apartments terminating in a two-storeyed chapel. There are two large rooms at ground- and first-floor level. They are currently the dining room and inner sitting room of Lord Sackville at ground-floor level, and the ballroom and guest bedroom of Lord Sackville at first-floor level. Their position, with the bedroom giving access to the private pew in the chapel, suggests that they are the position of the original withdrawing and inner chamber at each level. There is no visible, architectural evidence to confirm this supposition although Faulkner reported a blocked window with Bourchier detail.[6] Nor is it clear how the first-floor rooms were initially approached. It may have been by stairs on the site of the present Stone Stair south of the hall, or on the site of the seventeenth-century Great Staircase.

This accommodation quickly became inadequate and further chambers were built in a tower, the Duke's Tower. That this is an addition can be seen from the walling at basement level and the way the east wall has been scooped away to give light to the chapel window. It provided additional rooms at three levels, now a sitting room (ground) and bedrooms (first and second). As the basement of the tower is divided into two, the floors above may have been so constructed originally to create paired lodgings.

Although the stained glass window at first-floor level with the Bourchier double knot could be an insertion, that affectionate recorder of Knole, Vita Sackville-West, noted its occurrence in the fireplace spandrel.[7] As Faulkner suggests, this tower may have been added in 1480 when Knole became an official residence so as to free the principal first floor for use as an audience chamber.

The two-storeyed chapel is basically a mid-fifteenth-century structure built in stages. The lower and upper chapels were originally approached from the private apartments by a newel stair in a turret, but this was replaced in the early Tudor period by the present

PLATE 151 Knole: chapel and east range

chapel stair (with its seventeenth-century staircase). There was a separate entrance from Water Court to the lower chapel, which is now featureless except for its east window and a curious bonded projection high up the wall which looks like a chute.

The upper chapel, built at mezzanine level, is divided into three bays, with a three-light window in each one on the south side and a large east window of five lights. These windows exhibit the only cusped tracery at Knole apart from the oriel in the Bourchier gatehouse. There was formerly a window on the north side close to the entrance, but a building has always abutted against the remainder of this wall towards the east. The ceiling is eighteenth century, but the apartment is still a fine example of a private chapel of its period.

It is possible to determine the position and form of the original east front by following the rebate through existing unoccupied rooms. It consisted of three small turrets, one against the chapel wall, a central one with a passageway, and a further turret towards the kitchen and offices area. The inner entrance arch of the passageway towards Water Court is unaltered and the rebates for the outer arch have been revealed by stripping the plasterwork on either side of the passageway. The large arch adjacent to the north turret served a fireplace in the service area and has been subsequently cut through (fig. 81).

The turrets and the frontage between them were subsequently enveloped by the parallel east range that forms the present domes-ticated garden-facing frontage. The stone base of this addition has a series of two-light windows with uncusped tracery, possibly early sixteenth century. It is surmounted by a half-timbered façade (subsequently plastered), marked by eight oriel windows and matching gables in a seventeenth-century roof structure (possibly after a fire of 1623). There is a late medieval stone chimneypiece in the first-floor Leicester Gallery which may be a later insertion. The stair turret and late fifteenth-century door at the north-east angle of Water Court, seemingly medieval, are eighteenth-century additions.[8]

The kitchen was a detached building. The majority of the walling, including the hearths, is original but the uppermost section was a subsequent rebuilding in brick when the present ribbed roof was inserted with its non-supportive corbels. There is no evidence of the louvre which the kitchen must have originally had. The bread ovens associated with the hearths have been filled up.

Water for the kitchen and the offices beyond (see the broken arch mentioned above) must have been drawn from a well in Water Court. This was so named prior to the reservoir tanks being inserted under Stone Court by Dorset in the early seventeenth century.

The servery, before the kitchen, could originally have been an open court, subsequently roofed shortly after completion, when the present attractive ribbed ceiling was inserted.

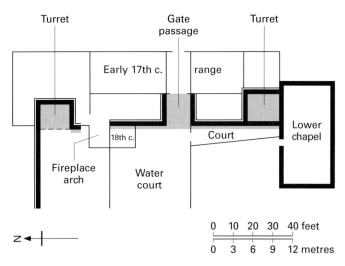

FIGURE 81 Knole: east frontage with seventeeth-century added range

GREEN COURT

Either Morton or Warham may have been responsible for the construction of Green Court, an outer court preceding Bourchier's gatehouse. The entrance is slightly earlier in style than that adopted for the royal palaces under Henry VIII,[9] while a line of lighter grass, possibly marking a wall or range, has been noted on several occasions on the south side, parallel with the orangery and approximately in line with the outer wall on this side of Stone Court.[10]

SUMMARY

Knole is one of the most complex houses in England and has not yet benefited from the detailed architectural appraisal it so richly deserves. A review of its late medieval form will therefore help to distinguish core work from the many extensive additions. From the first, Knole was a double-courtyard house of two-storeyed ranges surmounted by an embattled parapet. As with the contemporary residences at Wingfield, Sudeley, and Herstmonceux, it was built on totally clear ground, making no use of earlier buildings.

- Knole was developed by archbishop Bourchier over an extended period from about 1456 to 1486.
- The house was initially approached through the Bourchier gatehouse. Shortly after its erection, the original two-storeyed entrance was converted into a large residential block by the addition of flanking three-storeyed towers with garderobe facilities.
- Bourchier erected a two-storeyed range of lodgings on the north side of the first court (Stone Court), but the form and use of the range on the south side is not clear, although further suites of lodgings here would not be unreasonable.
- Bourchier's great hall was in the same position as the present one, but the existing structure is early sixteenth century.
- The private apartments consisted of a large withdrawing chamber and inner chamber at ground- and first-floor levels, terminating in a two-storeyed chapel with a private pew at the upper level. A tower providing further private accommodation was added shortly afterwards.
- The kitchen was an almost independent building on the north

side of the second court (Water Court) with offices beyond. At first, it faced the private apartments.
- This second court was closed by a wall broken by three small projecting turrets with a passageway in the central one.
- By the later fifteenth century, Water Court had been divided to screen the private apartments from the kitchen and offices.
- Green Court was laid out not long afterwards, creating a four-court residence. One of similar number and scale had been developed by archbishop Morton at Ford by the close of the fifteenth century.
- Although it is possible to determine the early form of the house, very few internal features survive attributable to the mid or late fifteenth century. None of the rooms – except the chapel – gives much indication of its medieval character.

Archbishop Bourchier's house was built on the grandest scale with large courtyards, open corridors, ranges of lodgings, and extensive private apartments, even though the last were still irregularly planned. There are immediate parallels between Herstmonceux Castle (c.1438–49) and Knole, the former built by Sir Roger Fiennes, the brother of Knole's previous owner, even though their common four-courtyard plan was not an initial element at Knole.

Knole clearly inspires affection, as a family chronicler recorded four and a half centuries later. But for all its seventeenth-century splendours, it commands respect rather than warmth, and its formal interiors give little hint of its episcopal origins. Bourchier's work makes so little display that it survives as a palimpsest rather than as a palace. In design terms, his work is sober, almost severe. It lacks decorative character, for example in the entry passage where the vaulting and corbels are plain, as are the window and doorway arches. Yet the wall painting in the north range hints at an internal richness that would have extended throughout the mansion he loved and frequented so often.

NOTES
1 Du Boulay (1974).
2 At Haddon Hall, the outer room benefited from a garderobe and a fireplace, and the inner room possessed neither. One or two of the fireplaces at Knole are later insertions.
3 Faulkner (1970) 142.
4 The three-storeyed King's Tower is an addition of mid-sixteenth- rather than late fifteenth-century date.
5 In 1465, a room at the end of the hall was specially set aside for Bourchier's auditor and comfortably furnished with beds and hangings. F. R. H. Du Boulay, *The Lordship of Canterbury* (1966) 274. Cecil Hewitt was unable to identify any woodwork in the present hall earlier than c.1510.
6 Faulkner (1970) 142.
7 Sackville-West (1922, 1947 edn) 7.
8 Information from Cyril Hasyon, house stonemason.
9 *HKW*, IV pt 2 (1982) 218.
10 For the development of the park and gardens, K. Taylor, *Arch. Cant.* 123 (2003) 153–84.

V. Sackville-West, *Knole and the Sackvilles* (1922, revised edition 1947)
C. J. Phillips, *The History of the Sackville Family* (1929)
H. A. Tipping, *English Homes*, Pd. 3, I (1929) 222–68
F. R. H. Du Boulay, *Arch. Cant.* 89 (1974) 169–82
P. A. Faulkner, *Arch. Jour.* 127 (1970) 140–6

LYMPNE CASTLE, Kent

Archbishop Lanfranc detached Lympne from his estates and gave it as an endowment to the archdeacons of Canterbury, who held it until 1860. Under the eye of the archbishop's castle at Saltwood less than 3 miles away, Lympne was essentially a country residence for the archdeacons of the diocese, as one of its former names, Court Lodge, more accurately suggests.

The forecourt must have been approached by a gateway, but apart from the outer wall of a stone barn, only the principal range survives, commanding impressive views from its escarpment position across Romney Marsh and the Channel. Built of ragstone, the hall block of *c*.1350–75 is flanked by an earlier square tower at the lower end and a D-shaped tower at the upper. This was added in the fifteenth century, possibly by archdeacon Chichele (1435–61), brother of the archbishop, in response to recurrent French raids.[1] Sir Robert Lorimer rescued the castle from an extremely neglected condition between 1906 and 1910 when he built the adjacent house, but as John Newman appositely points out, Lorimer anaesthetised the interior and stripped the castle of its history.[2]

Two storeys high with walls 5 feet thick, the low but substantial square tower possibly began life as a strong chamber-block tower of Longthorpe type. It has no early datable features but is probably thirteenth or early fourteenth century, converted after the construction of the hall into a kitchen with a residential chamber above. To create a service unit, two rooms were added on the south side, one of which survives and since the early twentieth century has been fully opened into the kitchen. The second service room has disappeared but some of its foundations have been incorporated in the rampart wall. The usual means of access to these rooms from the screens passage was blocked by the circular stair so that it was necessary to adopt the more inconvenient arrangement of access via the cross-passage door and a chemise. There was at least one chamber above these service rooms, serving as an inner chamber with garderobe (fig. 82).

The hall and parlour block is a single build, attributable on architectural grounds to the third quarter of the fourteenth century. The two-storeyed porch retains its original form, including its three upper windows, but the vaulted ceiling in the upper room is a Lorimer insertion. Entry to that room was probably always from the adjacent square tower so that the principal chamber (above the kitchen) was supported by two subsidiary chambers to the west and south.

The four-bay hall is lit by two transomed twin-light windows in both side walls. The lights are cusped – trefoil below, cinquefoil above – with a quatrefoil in the head, restored by Lorimer from the almost complete tracery found in one of the window blockings. At the same time that the hall was built, an entrance was broken through the lower end to give access to the newly created kitchen in the square tower, and a circular stair was added giving access to the principal chamber above. The screen was still in existence until the late nineteenth century, but the fine tie-beam and crown-post roof is original. The central hearth was replaced during Tudor times with the end-wall fireplace.

Twin doors at the hall high end access a now characterless parlour. Usually considered to have been a single room with little light, it seems to have been initially partitioned – either centrally or

PLATE 152 Lympne Castle: from the south-west

towards the north side. The withdrawing chamber above, with crown-post roof, was formerly reached by a door in the south-west corner of the hall (now blocked) opening on to a stair against the outer wall. A line of corbels below the string course marks the position of the roof protecting both stair and upper doorway (now a window).

The parlour is followed by two small rooms, with the south one, foreshortened by Lorimer, originally extending to the edge of the rampart where there were garderobe chutes. These rooms are attributed to the fourteenth-century build, but in the absence of any clear function or association at upper level with the withdrawing chamber, they are more likely to be contemporary with the abutting D-shaped tower. This curious addition is three-storeyed, providing a room at each floor and a small fourth-floor room below battlement level. The rooms are lit by single and double cusped lights, with the uppermost floor possibly divided to create a two-room lodging.

Lympne represents the typical late medieval house plan, with old-fashioned access arrangements to the withdrawing chamber, and room(s) underneath of mundane purpose. On the other hand, prime residential use was made of the upper rooms at the lower end, as was the case at Penshurst. Although perched on the cliff edge and protected by a narrow rampart on its line, it was only in the fifteenth century that Lympne essentially became 'lyke a castelet embatelyd'.[3] The opportunity was also taken to enlarge the parlour block accommodation.

NOTES

1 Leland notes that Lympne 'was sumtyme a famose haven, and good for shyppes that myght cum to the foote of the hille'. *Itinerary*, IV, 65.
2 *West Kent and The Weald* (1969) 379. No record was kept of Lorimer's work, although evidence was found of other building including marble shafts from a thirteenth-century (?) hall. Fortunately, Lorimer built a new country house for his plutocrat client, Henry Tennant, just touching the north-west corner of the castle rather than incorporating it in his development. To shield the castle from the village, he prefaced his work with a medieval-style gateway and extensive stable block.
3 Leland, *Itinerary*, IV, 66.

Harry Margary, *Guide to Lympne Castle, Kent* (n.d., *c*.1960)
S. E. Rigold, *Arch. Jour.* 126 (1969) 260–2

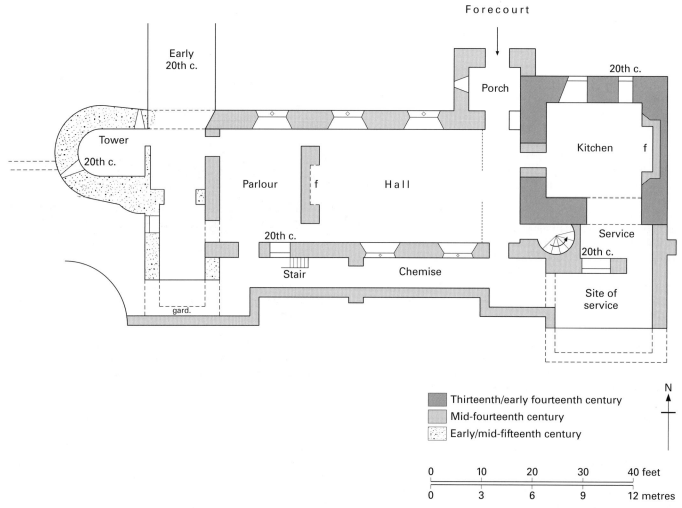

FIGURE 82 Lympne Castle: ground plan

MAIDSTONE PALACE and the archiepiscopal precinct, Kent

Maidstone possesses a rare group of fourteenth-century buildings – an episcopal palace, a major parish church, and a college of priests – but time has not dealt kindly with this complex. The college was partially destroyed after the Reformation and subdivided by an almshouse development in 1887. The palace has been continuously inhabited and modified since the late sixteenth century, the church lost its spire in 1731, and the whole group was violated during the twentieth century by an arterial road system.

The palace was developed by a sequence of archbishops between the mid-fourteenth and mid-sixteenth centuries on the site of an earlier residence at the confluence of the rivers Len and Medway. It was erected close to the parish church (as at Charing and Howden) with the principal apartments overlooking the Medway. Late in the fourteenth century, archbishop Courtenay created a major precinct by rebuilding the church as a collegiate foundation and erecting the college nearby, although the majority of this work was carried out after his death. Local grey, crumbling Kentish ragstone was used

throughout. The town subsequently developed north and west of this grouping and independent of it.

ARCHBISHOP'S PALACE

The archbishops of Canterbury had long held an estate at Maidstone, with evidence of an early Norman house incorporated in the walls of an outbuilding next to the church. Extensive repairs with dendrochronology analysis by Maidstone borough council in 1991–3 revealed that the present country house of the archbishops had been initiated in the early fourteenth century and had developed over the next two centuries in a sequence of phases as a two-storeyed residence with all the principal apartments on the upper floor. At the Reformation, the palace was purchased by the crown, who sold it to Sir John Astley in 1580. He was responsible for refronting the residence, while subsequent domestic occupation led to internal subdivision, and the demolition of the palace chapel in 1780 followed by the lodging and service ranges which had made the palace quadrangular. The borough council purchased the property in 1887 and it is now used by Kent County Council as their Register Office.

The surviving range is that of the episcopal apartments, developed between 1325 and 1535 by at least six archbishops in a sequence of two-storey blocks encompassing a low ground floor and taller apartments above, with the earlier work open to the roof. Ongoing occupation has made the ground floor a warren of rooms, stairs, and partitions but the upper floor retains the volumes and to some extent the character of the principal rooms.

The thirteenth-century ground-floor hall no longer survives. Excavations in the courtyard in the 1990s revealed considerable foundations which may have encompassed this apartment.[1] If so, it probably abutted against the standing range which was initiated by archbishop Reynolds (1313–27) when he built the great chamber with its undercroft as the earliest of the surviving structures in c.1325. During the 1350s, archbishop Islip (1349–66) replaced the earlier audience hall or withdrawing chamber with the present first-floor structure at right angles to the great chamber. It is approached today by an external stair from the courtyard, whereas originally it would have been via an internal stair from the ground-floor hall. In 1395–6, archbishop Courtenay (1381–95) added an inner chamber block leading off the upper end of the great chamber, overlooking the river in a short unit parallel with the hall. There was a gap of a hundred years when more modest additions were made at each end of this central core. In 1491, archbishop Morton (1486–1501) rebuilt the services unit at the south end with a high-quality upper room, while archbishop Warham (1504–32) replaced units at the north end of the range in 1525 with a small lodging block for himself. Cranmer (1533–56) added a further unit here ten years later as the last of the episcopal work, only two years before the property was sold to the crown. Sir John Astley refronted the property during the 1580s to give it the character of an Elizabethan residence marked by the three projections that face the visitor today. This is in contrast to the apparently medieval character of the river frontage, with windows that are nearly all 1909–10 'reconstructions' on inadequate evidence giving an impression rather than an accurate realisation of its early character. The two end wings to the front with timber-framed structures above stone ground floors are similarly pastiche – eighteenth century to the south and a 1910 rebuild to the north.

All ground-floor rooms retain their timbered ceilings but little of their initial character. The area below the audience hall was mainly used for storage, with racking evidence and door access to the river by the late fifteenth century. The area was converted into a kitchen in Elizabethan times, with a staircase added in the following century and further division thereafter. The great chamber undercroft retains a window in its south wall blocked by Islip's addition. The ground floors of the Courtenay, Morton, and Warham additions have been modernised but Warham's incorporated a fourteenth-century east wall, possibly by Courtenay, with garderobe evidence.

The left-hand projection of Astley's Elizabethan frontage replaced the original approach to Islip's mid-fourteenth-century audience hall. It retains the fifteenth-century entrance with continuous moulding to an apartment that was foreshortened by 8 feet during the eighteenth century when the stair hall and panelled withdrawing room were created. Islip's hall is essentially a late sixteenth-century chamber with contemporary windows, fireplace, porch chamber, and panelling.

The slightly earlier great chamber in a cross wing to the audience hall is less altered. The first third was partitioned in the fifteenth

PLATE 153 Maidstone Palace: from the south-west

century (now glazed) to form an ante-chamber (now stair and lobby), ceiled in the late sixteenth century when Astley created a long gallery in the roof space. The remainder of the great chamber is open to the roof, dendro dated to 1325 though some of the timbers have been reused, possibly those removed from Wrotham Palace which Islip stated in 1352 was in ruin because of pestilence and decay through lack of funds.[2] The fireplace lintel bears the arms of Warham while the large bay window is a conceit of 1912.

The first of Courtenay's two chambers of 1395–6 is the least altered in the palace with retained individual touches. It was panelled in flushed oak in the later fifteenth century, possibly by archbishop Bourchier (1455–86), a rare survival with decorative mouldings superimposed in the eighteenth century when the panelled doors were introduced. The ogee-headed doorway separating it from the second room, the traceried squint, and the low-pitched timbered ceiling are original, though half the ceiling had to be replaced after a fire in 1900. The 1910 windows replaced Georgian sashed insertions.

The Morton room with its timber frontage facing the river also enjoys an attractive low-pitched panelled ceiling with well-moulded timbers below a crown-post roof. The fireplace in the Warham suite carries his arms with the six Tudor-style doorways of one room reflecting its multi-purpose use over the centuries. The Cranmer room added ten years later retains original doorheads and fireplaces, Jacobean panelling, and the only sash window of the many inserted during the eighteenth century.

The courtyard was gatehouse-approached but only three structures survive round an area slashed in half by the traffic-laden road. The building at the side of the River Len is a small two-storeyed house with the principal room at first-floor level, and a single-storey extension. It has been heavily restored but retains a thirteenth-century (?) doorway and single-light windows of fourteenth-century date. It may have originally been part of a lodging range next to the gatehouse. It is currently used as offices. The outbuilding between the house and the church – a chamber above an undercroft – is a survivor of the much earlier layout for it incorporates fragments of two late eleventh-century walls of the archbishop's early house, altered in the fourteenth century. The stables on the opposite side of the courtyard to the palace are the least altered survival. This two-

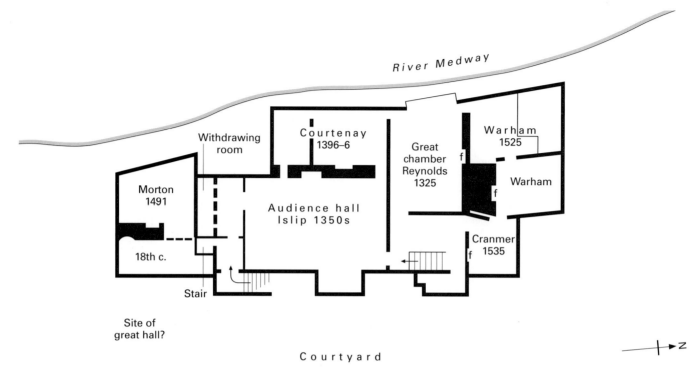

River Medway

Withdrawing room

Morton
1491

18th c.

Stair

Site of
great hall?

Courtenay
1396–6

Audience hall
Islip 1350s

Great
chamber
Reynolds
1325

Warham
1525

Warham

Cranmer
1535

Courtyard

FIGURE 83 Maidstone Palace: first-floor plan

storeyed buttressed structure of eleven bays with staff lodgings above the stables is fifteenth century. The outer stairs and porch chamber are original (although the brick noggin is a twentieth-century replacement for plasterwork). A number of doors (four large, two small) gave access to the stables, which were divided by a central line of posts. The first-floor lodgings for servants and grooms consisted of an open space with the roof supported by crown posts and raking struts carried on tie beams. There were single-light openings and an end-wall fireplace.

COLLEGE OF PRIESTS

Towards the end of his life, Archbishop Courtenay founded his college of secular canons at Maidstone in June 1395, and strengthened it by incorporating the mid-thirteenth-century hospital of Newark across the river in his foundation.[3] The college consisted of a master and twenty-four chaplains. It was built on a generous scale that complemented the adjacent palace. Building work began immediately, and although Courtenay died in 1396, the construction of the college continued without a break for the next few years with money bequeathed in his will.

Courtenay was the brother-in-law of Sir John Cobham who had started building his college of priests at Cobham twenty-five years earlier, but Courtenay's foundation was richer and developed on a much larger scale, complete with several gatehouses.[4] Its design in an austere style has been attributed to Henry Yevele, though he was an old man by this time.[5] The college was suppressed in 1547, and after passing through a series of titled owners and a disparate range of uses including partial demolition, it was bought by Maidstone Borough Council in 1949 who restored it for occupation seven years later. At the time of writing, its future is still under discussion.

Courtenay's foundation incorporated a house of c.1360 which

served as the master's residence with the college built round it. The present remains include three gatehouses – one from the town (complete), one from the country (ruined), and a subsidiary gateway (complete) which may have been the river approach. The three-storeyed north gatehouse facing the town was designed to impress. It is flat-faced, does not project from the remainder of the frontage, and is unsupported by buttresses, giving it a cliff-like character. It adopted the common practice of a tall carriageway and lower pedestrian passage, opening into a single vaulted bay rising through two floors. There was a single inner arch. With ground- and mezzanine-floor rooms either side the entries, the uppermost floor was a single chamber with end-wall fireplace. Excavations on the east side of this gatehouse in 1956 indicated there may have been a kitchen here, possibly for alms given at the gate.

The ruined south gatehouse repeats the separate carriage and pedestrian entries at both ends of the passage. There is no evidence of vaulting but the scale of the gatehouse shows that it was intended to impress. There are traces of a barn on each side but this approach has been separated from the remainder of the precinct by the alms-houses of 1887. The inner gatehouse faces the river and was accessed from it, although set well back from the river bank and the line of the other buildings. It marked the division of the college into two courts. A projecting stair turret served the upper room with fireplace.

Nothing remains of the chambers round the inner court for the twenty-four priests. It is assumed they were housed individually as at Cobham, though this awaits confirmation. The refectory range was built on falling ground next to the north gatehouse. Apart from a single light above the courtyard entrance (corridor covered), the body of the hall is lit towards the courtyard by mullioned and transomed lights with cusped heads (lower lights trefoil, upper cinque-

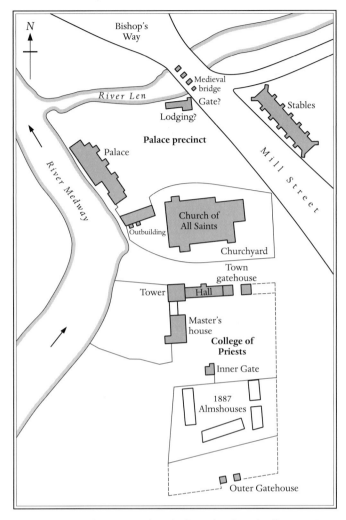

FIGURE 84 Maidstone: site plan of palace, church, and college precincts

popular episcopal country house. Apart from Courtenay's room, post-medieval occupation has stripped the residential range of substantive personality but the building capably reflects the archbishops' desire for more personal accommodation. Courtenay's college was not unlike an academic foundation, with the hall and treasury tower reflecting that of Wykeham's Oxford establishment, but with imposing gatehouses comparable in scale to the contemporary one at Ely cathedral priory. The contrast between the imposing town gatehouse and the more commanding but astringent one at Saltwood Castle reflects two quite different approaches to the same type of secular structure.

NOTES
1 S. Pearson, *Arch. Cant.* 121 (2001) 338; B. Philp, *Archaeology in the Front Line* (2002) 170–3.
2 *Literae Cantuarienses*, ed. J. B. Sheppard (1888) 79.
3 A document of 1425–6 in Maidstone Record Office shows that the hospital was not suppressed.
4 The scale of Courtenay's foundation can be gauged by comparing it with the chantry college established in 1392 by Robert Bradegare (d.1409), a clerk of the Canterbury diocese, at his birthplace. His foundation was for a chaplain and two clerks, enlarged in 1398 to take two poor scholars and a master. Looking like an eighteenth-century house opposite Bredgare church, the college had a central hall open to a crown-post roof. The services, with the clerk's room over, were below the cross passage, as was the kitchen open to the crown-post roof. The chaplain's room, at the upper end of the hall above two vaulted chambers, was extended into the hall in 1398. E. W. Parkin, *Arch. Cant.* 91 (1975) 87–97.
5 J. Harvey, *Eng. Med. Arch.* (1984) 365 with suggested completion by Stephen Lote.
6 Rigold (1969) 253.
7 *West Kent and the Weald* (1969) 389.
8 Rigold (1969) 253.
9 J. Cave-Brown, *The History of the Parish Church of All Saints, Maidstone* (1889).

Beale Post, *History of the College of All Saints, Maidstone* (1856)
S. Rigold, *Arch. Jour.* 126 (1969) 252–4

MAYFIELD PALACE, Sussex

The archbishop of Canterbury's palace at Mayfield centres on the little-known but splendid hall restored by E. W. Pugin in 1864–6 when the palace ruins were converted into a convent and school. Although this outlier of the archbishop's estates lay within the diocese of Chichester, it dominated medieval ecclesiastical life in the area and is architecturally related to a number of buildings on the north-east edge of the Weald.

The residence was developed round a courtyard of late thirteenth-century date with the principal apartments on the first floor, but any early hall was replaced in the following century by the present impressive structure and associated lower chamber block. This four-bay hall, 69 feet by 39 feet and over 50 feet high, is dominated by three spectacular stone arches spanning its width. Nearly 4 feet wide, they rise from finely carved foliated brackets resting on figures or half-figures and carry a stone partition wall, originally panelled,[1] supporting the Victorian replacement roof. Their size and that of the supporting buttresses suggest that the original roof at Mayfield was an experimental structure. Late eighteenth-century

foil). Rigold considered the two separate rows of paired cinquefoil lights towards the town meant that there was a gallery on the north side,[6] although Newman suggested that the refectory and kitchen were on the ground floor and the chaplains' rooms above.[7] Services were at the lower end with an external door. The three-storeyed treasury tower at the end of the hall range on falling ground towards the river typifies the college's austere style, particularly the face towards the town. As traces have been found of a large drain leading towards the river, was the ground floor used as a kitchen as at Lympne Castle?

The Master's House retains several lights with ogee-shaped heads of *c.*1360. It was a two-storeyed structure with trussed rafter roofs but has been so drastically altered that its original plan is conjectural. Rigold stated that it was a first-floor hall with a chapel in the cross wing above an undercroft with ogee lights.[8] A replaced pentice linked this house with the dining hall.

The parish church was made collegiate in 1395 and rebuilt on a scale appropriate to the college. It is the largest Perpendicular church in Kent, low but broad and cuboid in its elements. It is not an inspiring one by East Anglian standards.[9]

Maidstone Palace reflects the late medieval development of a

PLATE 154 Mayfield Palace: hall from the outer court

drawings and pre-restoration photographs show a line of joist holes immediately above the dais gable window, with a chase and corbel on either side for supporting braces. Similar chases existed in the partition walling above the arches, indicating longitudinal support throughout the hall.[2]

Equally impressive are the tall windows 30 feet high, of two lights with transoms and rear arches, virtually filling each bay. The upper lights are trefoiled and the lower ones cinquefoiled. The head of each window is filled with a spherical triangle with cusped tracery of ogee form and stops on the inner points. They are set in deep splays with slender shafts and foliated capitals, and are recessed externally beneath arches between the buttresses to support the parapet as at Penshurst Place. The small diamond-shaped panes of fleur-de-lis on a lead-patterned background found on site and copied by Pugin may have been contemporary work.[3] The window at the north end of the dais was lowered at a late date and converted into a bay window.

The generous entrance of the two-storeyed porch opens into a single bay, 20 feet deep, spanned by a quadripartite vault with figured corbels and foliated central boss (pl. 184). There were no side benches and the ruins of the upper chamber were rebuilt by Pugin. The outer and inner archways are shafted with leaf capitals but the opposing doorway in the north wall and the window above were replaced by Pugin with a full-length window to match its fellows.[4]

The lower and upper chamber blocks lay at right angles to the hall and were three-storeyed by the early sixteenth century and may have been so earlier. The three service doorways with continuous chamfers betokening their utilitarian purpose were joined by a fourth archway close to the porch formerly giving newel access to the upper chambers. The room in line with the porch is an unusual feature but most of the service area has been opened up to create an ante-chapel for the school. The majority of the hall end wall existed in 1864 (see photos) but two-thirds of it was rebuilt at the same time as the upper chambers were created, and the staircase was reinstated in the tall early sixteenth-century turret.

The larger doorway at the upper end of the hall (with an inserted window of *c*.1500 above) opened on to a lobby with a grand flight of stairs rising to the archbishop's private apartments. The lesser doorway opened into a garderobe tucked inside the buttress. The string course round the hall is at a higher level above the dais, and in the middle of this wall were the remains of the archbishop's seat with stone diapering of flower petals set in squares and now moved northwards. According to Parker, it seems to have been surmounted by a stone canopy, already destroyed in his day.[5] Above it was a triangular trefoil window in the gablehead, blocked by Grose's day but reopened by Pugin.

Rather than restore the extensive remains of the residential apartments beyond the hall, Pugin completely cleared the site. Evidence of their thirteenth-century origins existed in at least two ranges round the courtyard[6] and there seems to have been some fourteenth-century work.[7] The grand stair rose to the archbishop's great chamber, which was separated by a small court from the hall. A similar separation occurred at Charing and Buckden palaces, with the passage link still surviving at Charing. The great first-floor chamber at Mayfield was either late thirteenth or early fourteenth century but the grand stair was a later replacement of the original linking passage. This may have been by archbishop Warham (1503–32) who reconstructed these apartments, though only their overall shape and style were adopted by Pugin when he destroyed the stair as part of his replacement convent accommoda-

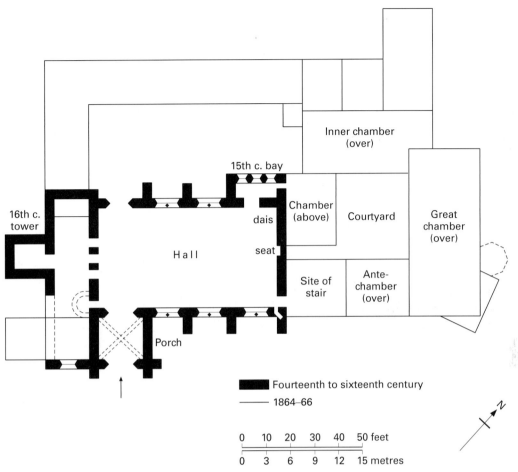

FIGURE 85 Mayfield Palace: ground plan

tion. A late thirteenth-century fireplace (transferred) and some early sixteenth-century doorways and windows round the original courtyard area (roofed in the 1970s) were permitted to remain.

The fifteenth-century gatehouse from the street to the outer court was altered for farmhouse use in *c*.1750 and for the school in the 1870s.

Held by the see of Canterbury since the ninth century, Mayfield was a favoured residence, particularly during the fourteenth century. Simon Meopham (1328–33) held a provincial synod here in 1332 (Concilium Maghfeldense), and John Stratford (1333–48) frequently 'sought quiet retirement' at the palace, whilst Simon Islip (1349–66) was in almost continuous occupation. All three archbishops died at Mayfield. A further provincial synod was held in 1362 but the manor proved less popular in the fifteenth century until Warham made his substantial alterations. The palace was handed over by Cranmer to Henry VIII in 1545 and was used by the Gresham and Baker families until the latter abandoned it in 1740. The buildings became a local quarry for over a hundred years, until the property was bought by the duchess of Leeds in 1863 and given to the nuns of the Holy Child School, St Leonards, on condition that they restored the ruins.

Arches spanning particularly wide halls were adopted at Conwy Castle in 1346–7 and more locally at Battel Hall (1330s) and Ightham Mote (*c*.1337). The Mayfield hall has an even closer affin-

ity with that at Penshurst Place (early 1340s), which is comparable in its proportions, layout, experimental roof, and the use of large two-light transomed windows under wide external arches supporting the parapet. The hall can therefore be dated on architectural grounds to the second quarter of the fourteenth century and more precisely to the 1330s, an early activity of archbishop Stratford or his predecessor's synod of 1332 possibly occasioning its earliest large-scale use. Built of local sandstone, the hall is one of the finest to survive from the fourteenth century, for everything about it speaks of the position and standing of its archiepiscopal builder. The spacious porch and boldly projecting buttresses taking the thrust of the spectacular roof arches betoken strength. The beautifully proportioned windows with their seats and inner columns filling most of the side walls and flooding the hall with light suggest grace. Mouldings are deep-cut while foliated and figure capitals and corbels create movement. The replacement glass and the rare seat of state hint at the colour and richness that this apartment formerly possessed and which its present use as the school chapel, with a mid-fourteenth-century Italian crucifix, quietly supports.

NOTES

1 See early nineteenth-century watercolour in the school library.
2 Turner and Parker (1853) opp. 290.
3 Turner and Parker note that there were no grooves for glass in the

mullions but the profusion of hooks on the inside jambs suggested that the glass was in casements. The original panes discovered in 1864 have been framed and are kept in the school courtyard.

4 Turner and Parker (1853) opp. 292, and photos of 1864 held by the school.
5 Turner and Parker (1853) 292; Grose (1787) 55.
6 According to Bell-Irving (1903).
7 Parker (1853) 292.

F. Grose, Supplement to *Antiquities of England and Wales*, II (1787) 53–7
T. H. Turner and J. H. Parker, *Some Account of Domestic Architecture in England*, II (1853) 290–3
E. Roberts, *Jour. Brit. Arch. Assoc.* 23 (1867) 333–67
E. M. Bell-Irving, *Mayfield: The Story of an Old Wealden Village* (1903)

MERSHAM MANOR, Kent

The distinction between small manor houses and large farm houses in Kent during the late medieval period is a grey area. Kent was a county of minor manors – often no more than a demesne farm and the scattered lands of a small number of freehold tenants. On ecclesiastical estates such manors – often called court lodges – were little more than wealthy farm houses and they are particularly prevalent in east Kent. Such lodges, usually of stone but not necessarily so, housed a bailiff or tenant farmer responsible for some of the extensive monastic estates which, in the case of Mersham, belonged to Christ Church Priory, Canterbury.

Today, the whitewashed frontage of Mersham Manor near Ashford looks like one of the many farmhouses in the area, but the steeply pitched hipped roof suggests an early date and the evidence at the rear reveals its form.

The house consisted of a hall with integrated services and chamber accommodation at the lower end. The cross-passage

PLATE 155 Mersham Manor, from the east

doorways are now blocked but the much altered hall retains a transomed two-light window with hexagonal oculus rising almost to roof level. The first-floor window with ogee trefoil lights shows that there was a high-quality chamber above the kitchen with garderobe access, but it was not the solar as in the priory's house at Great Chart.[1] The *Memorandum Book* of Prior Eastry records the erection of a camera in 1322–3.[2] This no longer survives but it meant that the present hall building was erected against an earlier upper end and that it was always a separately roofed structure like the present one of *c.*1800. The house, with its original scissor-braced roof, can therefore be attributed to between 1325 and *c.*1340.

As it stands, the building is similar to Court Lodge, Great Chart, built by the priory in 1313 and which preceded the more developed Mersham plan by a decade or two. It has been suggested that court lodges were built to a specialised plan required by the clergy,[3] but even if this is so, they stand between the grander stone houses of the gentry and the incunabula of the Wealden framed house.

NOTES
1 See page 383, note 7.
2 RCHM (1994) 91.
3 A. Baker and S. E. Rigold, *Arch. Cant.* 85 (1970) 61.

RCHM, *A Gazetteer of Medieval Houses in Kent* (1994) 90–1

NETTLESTEAD PLACE, Kent

Nettlestead Place, on the banks of the River Medway south-west of Maidstone, consists of an extended two-storeyed residential building of thirteenth- and fifteenth-century date, incorporated in a house of 1921–2 by Morley Horder. Built of Kentish ragstone, the medieval structure is part of a larger house of unknown scale. It consists of two ranges in roughly coursed rubble. The ground floor of the larger west range is a mid-thirteenth-century vaulted undercroft. The narrower room to the east has only fifteenth-century characteristics, as does the combined upper floor, now covered with twentieth-century roofs.

The south or garden frontage with its upper line of spacious fifteenth-century windows is interrupted by three projections abruptly curtailed at roof level. They do not serve the ground-floor rooms and are not obviously bonded into the wall, although they maintain the hollow-chamfered plinth 2 feet from the ground. Either the undercroft and the chamber above are mid-thirteenth-century work and the projections date from that period as the common string course suggests, or they are fifteenth-century additions contemporary with the refenestration which their restricted upper-floor usage supports. However, as these projections have determined the position of the upper windows, it is probable that they date from the earlier period, with the easternmost projection of slightly different form (see higher offset) dating from the later period. Thus it seems likely that the undercroft and upper chamber are thirteenth century, with the latter refenestrated in the early fifteenth century when the extension was added.

The smaller ground-floor chamber of the east range is approached by a two-centred doorway with continuous deep hollow chamfers separated by a roll. It is lit by a window of two

PLATE 156 Nettlestead Place: from the south

lights with cusped heads under a bold hood mould externally and a broad four-centred rear arch. (The single light and adjacent door are a very late fifteenth-century insertion contemporary with the church porch constructed after 1496 with money bequeathed by John Pympe.) The upper floor is approached by a doorway identical with that below, probably approached by an external staircase which still existed in 1908.[1] Similar generous windows to that below were introduced here and throughout the upper floor of the west range. One window is paired but the others are irregularly spaced. They are all deeply recessed, have flat sills rather than window seats, and jambs heavily incised with masons' marks. The three projections, apparently solid at the lower level (though never thoroughly investigated), hold a small room at the upper level, one with a small rectangular light and the easternmost with a late sixteenth-century round window.

The upper area of the west range, in both its thirteenth- and fifteenth-century forms above an undercroft of some importance, suggests a great chamber. But although one garderobe projection towards the corner might be anticipated, a second centrally positioned one is highly unusual. It is possible that this upper chamber was divided into a larger and small inner room, both garderobe-

provided, though this would be idiosyncratic. There are no other medieval features internally, not even the fireplace that might be expected, while the mid projection, appropriately positioned for such a feature, is far larger than usual for a stack.[2] The different fenestration of the east range also points to two-room division, but it should be noted that the projection here seems to overlie the hood mould of a late fifteenth-century ground-floor window so that its date is questionable. The layout and function of this upper floor is unclear and warrants further investigation. The two areas were united by Horder, the separating east wall was removed, and a continuous roof was inserted in the 1920s in the belief that both rooms were contemporary. He also rebuilt the west wall on original lines.

The range, in its thirteenth- and fifteenth-century forms, suggests good-quality accommodation at the upper level, with the body of the house lying to the north or north-east. Parker noted in 1859 that the house 'was much more extensive, a large portion including apparently the hall, having been destroyed'.[3] That this was so is suggested not only by the size of the existing range, but by the location of the gateway, 100 yards from the medieval range. It is a non-defensive stone structure with an extremely tall entrance passage

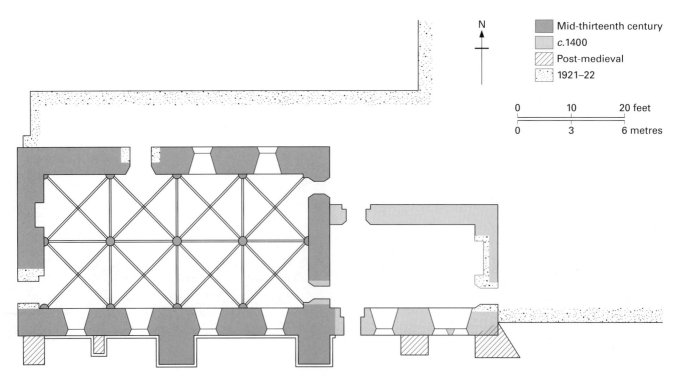

Mid-thirteenth century
*c.*1400
Post-medieval
1921–22

0   10   20 feet
0   3   6 metres

N

FIGURE 86 Nettlestead Place: ground plan

and porter's lodge surmounted by a timber-framed chamber jettied over the front arch. Two tie beams support the crown posts ubiquitous in Kent from the fourteenth to the mid-sixteenth century. The pretty wooden cusped window tracery seems original. The narrow-shouldered arch of the large doorway suggests a fourteenth-century date for this structure.

During the thirteenth century, Nettlestead Place was held by the Wahull family, with Walter Wahull (1242 to after 1262) as the most likely builder of the earlier remains of the house. The early fifteenth-century work may have been carried out *c.*1420 by Reginald Pympe, who entered into the estate as a minor in 1375 and died over sixty years later in 1438. His family had acquired Nettlestead before the close of the thirteenth century and had risen to local prominence in the mid-fourteenth century. Sir Reginald, appointed sheriff in 1409, may well have enlarged other parts of the house that no longer survive. He employed masons from the Maidstone district, for the two early fifteenth-century doorways are identical with those of the Corpus Christi Hall at Maidstone built by 1422, and favoured broad four-centred rear arches and deep hood moulds. Pympe was also responsible for rebuilding the nave of the adjacent church, with its particularly tall windows still in part displaying his gift of contemporary glass inserted between 1425 and 1438.[4] This, as was often the case in the later middle ages, displayed his family connections and standing with the earls of Stafford (who held Tonbridge Castle) and the gentry within a 25 mile radius of Nettlestead. Yet the form of the window tracery and crown-post roof suggest that Corpus Christi Hall was built well before 1422, while the Nettlestead doorways can be paralleled with late fourteenth-century examples such as the Rectory, Cliffe-at-Hoo, and those in Maidstone parish church post 1395.[5] A date close to 1400

is most likely for this stage in Sir Reginald's development of the house which his family continued to occupy throughout the remainder of the fifteenth century.

NOTES
1 *Arch. Cant.* 28 (1908) 168.
2 Sarah Pearson has suggested to me that a stack of such purpose may have been converted into a small oriel in the sixteenth century.
3 T. H. Turner and J. H. Parker, *Some Account of Domestic Architecture in England*, III (1859) 307. Oswald (1958) records that a late eighteenth-century manuscript said that it was the largest in this part of the country.
4 *Arch. Cant.* 28 (1908) 157–282 and 76 (1960) 40–3.
5 Sarah Pearson drew my attention to these contemporary examples.

A. Oswald, *Country Life* (October 1958)
RCHM, *A Gazetteer of Medieval Houses in Kent* (1994) 93

NURSTEAD COURT, Kent

This early fourteenth-century house, 3½ miles south of Gravesend, has been so severely truncated and divided internally that its original form and significance are not immediately apparent. It was, however, an aisled timber structure of four bays under a steeply pitched hipped roof. Beneath this common covering was a hall, flanked by a partitioned bay at either end.

In 1825, exactly half this structure was pulled down and replaced by a Regency villa by Edward Blore, extended and heightened nearly thirty years later, so that the Court is incongruously made up today of a many-gabled Victorian house with what looks like a cottage extension at the rear under a tremendous roof sweeping close to the ground. The architectural importance of Nurstead lies hidden within this cottage-like projection.

The original structure was built of thick rubble flint walls, unbuttressed, and only 11 feet high. It was 28¾ feet wide and approximately 76 feet long internally, and open to the roof throughout. Approached by cross-passage doorways, the central hall was lit by two large gabled and transomed windows in both side walls, but the evidence for the partitioned end bays indicates they were served by modest single lights. The arch-braced timber roof, rising to a height of 36 feet at the ridge, was supported on three pairs of oak columns, 16¼ feet apart, and the associated wall columns created narrow aisles less than 4 feet wide. The end bays were used as a private chamber and for services respectively and the sharply pitched roof was probably thatched.

Only the upper half of the hall and the end bay survive to the rear of the Regency and Victorian structure, now divided into two floors and an attic. However, the massive oak piers and aisle columns are immediately apparent among the later corridors and reception rooms, while the roof structure dominates the bedrooms and attic. The present owner has considered removing all these later, mainly nineteenth-century additions to reveal the Court's original form, but the result would be an academic re-creation at the expense of several practical and much used family rooms.

The four surviving wooden piers and two columns of the north aisle identify the upper bay of the hall and the chamber beyond. Two of the piers and the columns are surmounted by leaf carving of a high standard, and this feature is repeated on the stops of the wall plates. The central piers are totally round but those at the upper end prove to be half columns with their rear faces cut back to take a partition wall or screen.[1] The rebates for this still survive cut into the columns, while the partition directly above in the attic shows obvious evidence of soot on one side and not on the other, indicating that the partition rose the height of the building. The capitals of the piers against the partition differ still further from the other columns by the absence of any leaf decoration, for reasons no longer clear. The back of the dais may have been enhanced by a hanging, panelling, or some other fixture which conflicted with any decorative work, although the beams above were painted with rosettes which are still dimly visible.

The hall was well lit by four tall double-light windows with mullions and trefoil heads rising to a quatrefoil under individual gables. Much of the upper window survives on the north side and pictorial evidence exists for the second window in the same wall.[2] There were similar windows on the south side, for evidence of one was traced when the roof was relaid in 1988. The circular piers supported substantial two-centred moulded arches which cut into the underside of each tie beam at the central point where it supported a crownpost structure (particularly well displayed in the attic). The hall would have been warmed by an open hearth.

Access to the upper end bay was by one of the two aisle arches (one now missing). The north aisle arch has been partially reconstructed and opens into an area, possibly always at a higher level than the hall, lit on the north side by a single-light window with a door in the corner giving external access. The moulded cornice at the top of the aisle wall above this contemporary stone doorway is the same height as the cornice in the hall and identical in character. This area was therefore initially planned as a single room open to

PLATE 157 Nurstead Court: hall aisle column and capital

the roof.[3] However, an upper floor was inserted shortly after the hall had been built (see moulded profiles) though it is not known whether the ground-floor room was subsequently divided or not.

The lower half of the hall and the service bay can be reconstructed from drawings by William Twopenny (1822) and Edward Blore (1824).[4] The destroyed portion was of the same area as the surviving bays, so that the end wall was on the site of the present Victorian entrance façade. The early nineteenth-century drawings indicate there was an external doorway in the middle of the end wall with a high-positioned lancet on either side. On comparative evidence, this doorway would have served a detached kitchen reached by a central passage in the end bay, flanked by offices used as a buttery and pantry respectively. The drawings also show a cross-passage door opening direct into the hall, presumably matched by one on the south side, flanked by a further high lancet above a low-set door (possibly inserted) with a depressed head. Though the end-wall dormers are post-medieval, the placement of the lancets suggests they may have lit a contemporary chamber above a low-ceiled buttery and pantry, though the fact that the upper-end bay was open to the roof makes that view debatable.[5]

This hall and chamber block could not have existed without some associated structures but the only one to survive is the oblong rubble flint building of unknown purpose touching the north angle of the upper-end bay. A two-storeyed building above a basement, 15½ feet by 22½ feet internally, its ruined walls 5 feet thick survive to a height of about 10 feet but they are not bonded into the hall structure. The basement, 8 feet below ground level, could only be accessed internally. The first floor was externally stair-approached with a window or another door adjacent to the house, while a spiral stair led to the upper level.[6] The date and purpose of this structure are unclear. P. J. Tester favoured the late fourteenth century;[7] Martin Cherry states, on unclear evidence, that it was earlier than the hall.[8]

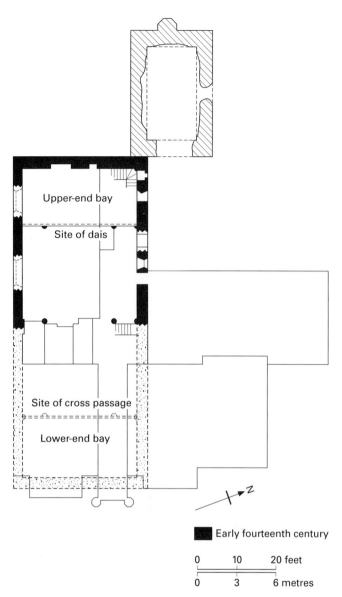

Upper-end bay

Site of dais

Site of cross passage

Lower-end bay

■ Early fourteenth century

```
0        10        20 feet
0        3         6 metres
```

FIGURE 87 Nurstead Court: ground plan

Stephen in 1299, and his nephew Stephen Gravesend (bishop 1318–38). The property is not mentioned in bishop Richard's will or in the extensive accounts of his executors, while dendrochronology analysis in 1987 established a felling date for the wood ranging from 1299 to 1334 with *c*.1314 as the most probable date.[9] The Court was therefore built by Stephen Gravesend, who acquired the estate in 1303. In 1313 he was appointed canon of St Paul's cathedral in London and he may have built Nurstead just before or during his early years of episcopal office.

Nurstead Court was built by a bishop as a country house, less than 25 miles from London by boat or horse. For its date, it was a conservative building in construction and decorative detail, although enriched to a high standard. Its architectural importance lies in the quality of its workmanship and the recovery of its original form despite its regrettable truncation. Nurstead is a remarkable example of a timber-aisled hall of high social standing in southern England, but though it displays an early form of the fully fledged medieval house plan – hall flanked by upper and lower end chambers under a common roof – this basic layout was old fashioned and only one of several primary buildings making up the manorial complex. Major developments in roof construction were already making pillared aisles obsolete. The lack of upper-storey accommodation at the high end of the hall and *possibly* at the lower is surprising when the two-storeyed form of end bays was already popular (and soon rectified at this property too). End bays usually projected beyond the line of the hall in cross wings to allow greater room and avoid vast unbroken and difficult-to-reach roof areas. Wealthy though the bishop was, these major strides in house development bringing all the principal accommodation in a single structure could not be better demonstrated than by contrasting Nurstead with the gentry houses developed by the next generation at Battel Hall, Ightham Mote, and Penshurst Place.

NOTES

1 First noted by Smith (1955) 85.
2 See Ambrose Poynter's drawing of *c*.1831, Notebook in RIBA Library, He/53. The drawing is reproduced in Smith (1955) pl. XII.
3 Smith (1955) 85 suggested that the upper floor was probably an original feature, but the clearance of post-medieval cladding has revealed the early form. Cherry (1989) 455–6.
4 William Twopenny, *Engravings for Ancient Capitals* (1837); E. Blore, *Gentleman's Magazine* (1837) 364–7. Also Blore's drawing in Brit. Lib., Add. MS 42,018 nos. 8, 9, 10. Blore's drawing of the hall interior showing it in pristine condition includes evidence that was conjectural as well as extant in his day.
5 Cherry prefers a single-storey bay at the lower end: (1989) 456.
6 Pryor (1988) Postscript 31.
7 Hasted noted it in the late eighteenth century as a chapel, *History of Kent*, III (1797) 354, while Turner and Parker (1853) 281, suggested that it was 'a strong tower'. P. J. Tester, reviewing the evidence of 1982, noted the use of flint and chalk chequerwork internally and banded flint and ragstone for the lower courses externally – a local fourteenth-century feature. He considered that the structure was probably defensive, associated with the later fourteenth-century raids, or less likely, that it was a solar tower as at Lympne Castle. *Arch. Cant.* 98 (1982) 243–5.
8 Cherry (1989) 458–60.
9 *Vern. Arch.* 19 (1988) 48.

T. H. Turner and J. H. Parker, *Some Account of Domestic Architecture in England*, II (1853) 281–2

There must have been a detached kitchen east of the hall block, while a further drawing by Blore in the British Library also suggests that there were some ancillary buildings north-east of the hall with a hipped roof at right angles to the hall range but detached from it. This may be later or post-medieval work, but possibly on the site of earlier structures.

Nurstead Court has been attributed on architectural grounds to the late thirteenth or early fourteenth century. The decorative work is of a very high quality, commensurate with ecclesiastical connections, while the style of the window tracery and the carving of the capitals suggests a date close to the turn of the thirteenth century rather than one towards the second quarter of the following century. The house was owned at that time by the Gravesend family and two members were appointed bishops of London during the potential periods of construction – Richard Gravesend (bishop 1280–1303), who entered the manor on the death of his father Sir

A. Oswald, *Country Houses of Kent* (1933) 14–15

J. T. Smith, *Arch. Jour.* 112 (1955) 84–6

E. A. Pryor, *Nurstead Court* (1988, privately printed)

M. Cherry, *Arch. Jour.* 146 (1989) 451–64

OLD SOAR MANOR, Kent[1]

Old Soar Manor lies on the eastern slope of the Bourne valley in west Kent, close to the villages of Plaxtol and Crouch. The house stands alone, surrounded by its farm buildings, in a situation that is made remote, even today, by reason of the deep, narrow lanes that lead to it. Six hundred yards to the east begins the great woodland called the Hurst, which in medieval times ran towards Maidstone for a distance of about 7 miles. The manor of 'Sore alias Hores' was a sub-manor of the archbishop of Canterbury's manor of Wrotham. It may have been created not later than *c*.1290 when sub-infeudation was prevented by the statute of *quia emptores*. There has been general agreement that the house dates from between 1280 and 1300 on stylistic grounds.[2]

The manor house consisted of an aisled, timber-framed hall which has gone, and a fortified solar end built of local, rough-coursed, galleted ragstone which survives. There is negligible evidence for a service end and no clue as to the existence of a gatehouse or encircling wall. The sloping site with its underlying stone would make a moat unlikely.

The remoteness of the situation perhaps contributed to the partial survival of the house. The aisled hall, or a later successor, was replaced in 1780 by the present brick farmhouse attached to the south-western side of the stone solar block.[3] The only remains of the hall are at the upper end backing on to the solar. The corbel to the south-west of the doorway on the hall side is elaborate with three colonettes carved with foliage on the cap and at the base. This was a respond to the north-western arcade of the aisled hall. A large block of Bethersden marble sits on top of the corbel supporting a beam that probably relates to the post-medieval flooring of the hall. Rough stonework close by, at the base of the solar wall, is the remains of a dais. The segmental-arched doorway to the solar staircase also remains.

The Y-shaped end block is made up of three units of common plan at both levels. The principal or upper floor consists of the solar of the same 39½ feet width as the former hall, with a large projecting garderobe attached by the width of a doorway at the north corner and a chapel attached by a similar feature at the east corner.

The three ground-floor rooms are undercrofts or cellars. Each undercroft has its own external entrance and they do not interconnect internally. That beneath the solar has a stone barrel vault. The other two have replacement wooden floors. The room under the

PLATE 158 Old Soar Manor: solar interior

381

solar has an entrance into the former hall at the foot of the spiral staircase. These undercrofts were used as storage space by the lord of the manor and were vulnerable points that had to be integrated into the protective system of the house.[4] The weakest point for an intruder is the outer entrance to the solar undercroft in the south-east wall. Renn debates whether the opening was a window or a doorway as previous authors show both.[5] No opening at all would have been the best defensive policy but this would have left the interior poorly lit by a single arrowloop. Clarification is provided by a photograph taken by the Ministry of Works in 1949 when restoration was in progress, showing the doorway in the process of being cleared of five courses of brick above the threshold along with lath and plaster infill above. The lath and plaster had been used to block up the window seen by Wadmore in 1897 but the segmental-headed arch and jambs are those of a complete and original doorway.

The floor of the solar undercroft is reached by three downward steps. The undercroft has a ragstone barrel vault on which can be seen the mortar lines marking the edges of the boards used for shuttering during construction. An arrowloop in the north-west wall covers the area between the staircase tower and the doorway to the garderobe undercroft. In the west corner two steps rise to reach the base of the spiral staircase and the hall entrance.

The doorways are narrow and the clockwise staircase is steep and constricted, to the disadvantage of an intruder. The stair has a stone vault and is dimly lit by two arrowloops. The door at the top opens outwards across the head of the stair in the face of an enemy. A recess in the outer wall of the turret allows the door to remain open without obstructing traffic on the stair. The door may be fifteenth century. The stair extends beyond the segmental arched doorway, continuing the spiral of the staircase into the floor of the solar, bringing a visitor face to face with the room's south-west wall. This may be a disorientation ploy against an enemy. It also suggests that the staircase once continued further, perhaps into a lookout tower over the valley, or to a viewpoint over the hall, or that such a plan was abandoned after an initial essay. The stone newel continues above the last step for another four and a half courses strongly suggesting missing steps. At some time the west corner of the solar was walled across the stone newel to the south-west wall to a height of 6½ feet. This walling hides any evidence there may be of the original plan.

The solar is an elegant and lofty room lit by two large Y-tracery windows on the north-west and the south-east sides. The Y-tracery was restored in stone in 1949, based on fragments of window heads in Bethersden marble, or paludina limestone, once on show within the manor. These were recovered from an excavation at the eastern corner of the chapel. The north-west window has a hollow-chamfered rear arch, a window seat in Bethersden marble, and pegs for shutters but no shutter recesses. Some original stone flooring remains by this window. The brick of which the rest of the floor consists was probably laid in the sixteenth century. The south-east window has no evidence for a window seat but does have pointed recesses in which shutters could be folded back. Between the fireplace and the garderobe doorway is a window with a shouldered lintel. Renn suggests that it may have replaced an original arrowloop,[6] a companion to the arrowloop in the eastern corner.

The fireplace was not restored in 1949 for lack of evidence. The chimney breast is square and battered externally, as is the entire north-eastern wall. Part of the worked stone jamb and a small

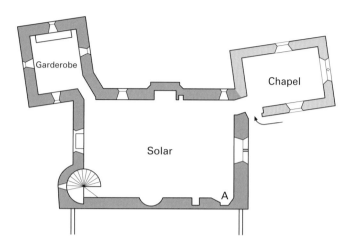

FIRST FLOOR

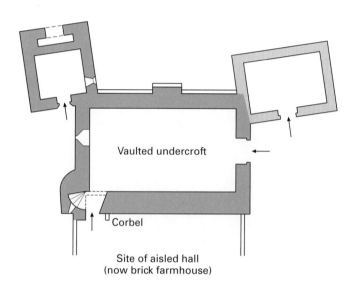

GROUND FLOOR

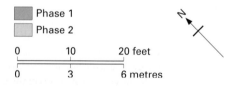

FIGURE 88 Old Soar Manor: floor plans

section of hearth kerb on the right-hand side of the opening have survived and beside them a small cupboard.

On the south-western wall at A is a blocked window, now obscured by the eighteenth-century farmhouse, but originally offering a view over the aisle of the hall. Close by is another small cupboard. Centrally on the wall is a roughly blocked opening. No worked stone is visible. It would have been a suitable position for a squint looking over the hall and may subsequently have been chosen as the point at which to breach the wall for a doorway when the hall was floored in the seventeenth century.

This imposing room retains its original three-bay, crown-post collar-purlin roof. The crown posts have moulded caps and bases, the braces are straight and square-sectioned and the lateral braces extend to soulaces. The crown struts at the gable ends rest on stone corbels.

The garderobe block undercroft is entered from the south-west. A wall separates the room from the wide privy shaft, which has an unusually large external arch to give access for cleaning out the shaft. In the south-east wall there is an arrowloop covering the base of the solar north-east wall. On the floor above there is an arrowloop in each wall, one of them being inconveniently above the privy shaft. The entrance from the solar is by a narrow passage skewed across the angle so awkwardly managed that it must be deliberate. The large cleaning arch and the big privy shaft make the garderobe vulnerable to entry at first-floor level. The narrow skewed entrance must therefore be defensive.[7]

The chapel undercroft has a doorway but no windows. The upper entry had an external staircase for which no evidence survives but which probably ran along the chapel wall, thus preserving the privacy of the solar. The chapel has three windows but no arrowloops. The breach in the wall between the solar and the chapel probably dates from the use of the solar as a grain store, when an agricultural door was made in the east window aperture (fig. 88). The south wall holds a piscina with cinquefoiled head and triangular canopy containing a lobed trefoil and crockets. The decoration of the piscina is more fourteenth than thirteenth century and is one of the reasons for suspecting that the chapel block is an addition to the rest of the house.[8] Other reasons are its alignment, which is east-south-east rather than east, and the lack of any defensive features. It has a collar-rafter roof with soulaces.

When the east window was unblocked in 1949 by removing the agricultural door, glazing bar grooves were found. As the lord of the manor must have felt life was reasonably secure to risk putting glass into such a large window, its scale is an additional reason for proposing a later date for the unfortified chapel block than for the fortified solar and garderobe projection. Attached to the left-hand jamb of the east window is an ornamented five-sided bracket for a candle or statue. Its shaping is different from the arcade corbel in the hall while the floreate carving is similar but not identical. The work appears to be by different hands and again may indicate a separate, later building programme.

Allowing the chapel to be of a later date confirms Derek Renn's survey of the defensive features. In addition to the arrowloops that survive on both floors, he suggests that others formerly existed on the sites of the shouldered-arched window, the breach between solar and chapel, and the window site overlooking the south aisle of the hall at A. With outlying arrowloops in the garderobe, this would give all-round coverage in the event of an attack.

There are nine remaining arrowloops. All, except the partially obscured one on the staircase, terminate in semi-circular base œillets, an uncommon feature in Britain at this date but found earlier in France.[9] They were commissioned at some cost by a man with an understanding of military features and they were meant to be used.

Early manor houses often consisted of a hall surrounded by detached buildings, which served the functions of upper and lower ends. Old Soar Manor represents an intermediate stage between this discrete collection of buildings and the contiguous grouping of elements under one roof. The solar is attached to the hall but the garderobe and chapel are only just attached to the solar, as Wood says, 'touching like playing cards at the corners'.[10] There is little that is comparable in Kent in date, or layout of defensive features,[11]

and the house should be compared nationally with Manorbier Castle, Charney Bassett Manor, and Little Wenham Hall.

NOTES

1 This entry has been contributed by Jayne Semple.
2 'Not far from 1300', Turner and Parker (1851) 175; c.1290, Wood (1950) 38; 1271–99, Pearson et al. (1994) 100; late thirteenth century, Renn (2001) 247.
3 Date inscribed on two bricks in the front wall of the farmhouse: GRK 1780, WMTK 1780. K refers to Knowles, the farmer at the time.
4 The defensive attributes of Old Soar Manor have been examined by Derek Renn in his recent paper (2001), and the discussion on defence owes much to him.
5 Turner and Parker (1851) show a doorway; Wadmore (1897) shows external and internal drawings of a window; Wood (1950) describes a window and shows it on her plan, but describes it as a doorway in her Ministry of Works guidebook (1950) although a window is still shown on the plan.
6 Renn (2001) 241.
7 In 1313 Christ Church Priory, Canterbury, built a hall with services and chamber end at their manor house, Court Lodge at Great Chart, with a diagonal projection that seems to have been a garderobe like that at Old Soar Manor. Still occupied, the shell of this hall building retains evidence of the two-light trefoil windows in the hall, a cross passage, the tripartite services division to a detached kitchen, and an external approach to the solar above the services. RCHM, *A Gazetteer of Medieval Houses in Kent* (1994) 66–7.
8 Wood (1950) 38 thought the sexfoil drain of the piscina might be earlier than the fourteenth-century date she proposed for the upper part but gave no reasons.
9 E.g. Loches Castle, 1204, Renn (2001) 243.
10 Wood (1950) 38.
11 Thirteenth-century houses in Kent include Luddesdown Court (early to mid-thirteenth century), Eynsford Castle, Temple Manor, Strood, Nettlestead Place, Stone Castle, Squerryes Lodge, Westerham (all mid-thirteenth century), Newbury Farmhouse, Tonge, and Nurstead Court (1314).

T. H. Turner and J. H. Parker, *Some Account of Domestic Architecture in England*, I (1851) 173

J. F. Wadmore, *Arch. Cant.* 22 (1897) 310–15

A. Oswald, *Country Houses of Kent* (1933) 13–14

M. Wood, *Thirteenth Century Domestic Architecture in England* (1950) 36–8

S. Pearson, P. S. Barnwell, and A. T. Adams, *A Gazetteer of Medieval Houses in Kent* (1994) 100–1

S. Pearson, *The Medieval Houses of Kent* (1994) 37–41, 50–3

P. S. Barnwell and A. T. Adams, *The House Within* (1994) 10–13, 59–60, 92–3

D. Renn, *Arch. Cant.* 121 (2001) 237–50

OLD WOKING MANOR AND OATLANDS, Surrey

Little remains of the medieval manor of Woking by the River Wey, held by the Despensers. An inventory of 1327, now lost,[1] shows that it was already a building of some size with a great hall, two chapels (one for the owner and his family and one for the household), two chambers, a pantry and buttery adjoining the hall, a kitchen, bakehouse, brewhouse, larder, and laundry. There were three lodgings for the treasurer and other officers and knights, and two further chambers elsewhere for knights and esquires. The residence was surrounded by a double moat with a gateway and drawbridge protecting the inner moat and a two-storeyed gate and dwelling defending the outer moat. The orchard was protected by its own moat with a drawbridge and gate. Outside were various farm buildings – barns, stables, cartsheds, and cowsheds.

The inventory was occasioned by Edward III's grant of Woking manor to his uncle, Edmund Holand, earl of Kent, after the execution of Lord Despenser in 1326. The property was held by the Holand family until 1416 when it was bequeathed to the Beauforts, dukes of Somerset. It was confiscated by Edward IV but Margaret Beaufort, Henry VII's mother, resumed occupation in 1485. She surrendered it to her son in 1503 in exchange for Hunsdon House in Hertfordshire. Henry VII promptly initiated building work and it became a favoured Tudor palace. It fell into decay after James I sold the property in 1620.

The site, at the end of Carters Lane half a mile east of the church, has never been thoroughly examined although a summary plan of undocumented excavations carried out in 1912 was published in 1986.[2] Apart from the moat and banks running to the River Wey, nothing stands of the early fourteenth-century residence. The two visible remains in a sea of grass and nettles are of early Tudor date. One is a plain oblong stone structure standing to first-floor level where the main apartment lay. The side walls are well faced with ashlar stone and internally support a stone-ribbed ceiling of six bays with brick infilling. There are three rectangular lights and two four-centred doorways of early sixteenth-century date. The much larger elongated brick building at right angles, now badly ruined, is later.[3]

Oatlands, another Tudor palace with earlier origins, lay 7 miles north-east of Woking. Excavations in 1968 revealed evidence of a substantial mid-fifteenth-century house pre-dating the more well-known Henrician palace totally destroyed in the mid-seventeenth century.

The earliest structure on the site was an early fifteenth-century timber-framed building. It was replaced by a more substantial brick house on the same alignment in the middle of the century. This was enlarged by the insertion of a gatehouse at an oblique angle to the range, which moulded brick jambs suggest was erected in *c*.1470.[4] A subsequent phase included the formation of a moat with a new revetment to the gatehouse, prior to Henry VIII's acquisition of the house in 1537 and its repair and considerable extension for royal occupation.

NOTES

1 Copied by Symmes, Brit. Lib., Add. MS 6167. *Surrey Arch. Coll.* 7 (1880) 46–7. Tolworth Manor (now part of Surbiton), another Despenser property surveyed at the same time, was moated with a gateway and drawbridge leading to two halls, six chambers, a chapel, kitchen and scullery, bakehouse and brewhouse. Again there were two barns, two ox houses, a stable, a garden, and a watermill outside the main occupational area. VCH, III (1911) 520.
2 *Surrey Arch. Coll.* 77 (1986) 240.
3 Authors refer in 1880 to the existence of 'massive foundations' and in 1911 to 'a brick gateway of the earlier fifteenth century, much dilapidated' leading to the stone and brick vaulted building. *Surrey Arch. Coll.* 7 (1880) 48; VCH, III (1911) 383.
4 Sir Bartholomew Reed died seized of land called Oatlands in 1505 and the remains seem to have been those of his family home. VCH, III (1911) 477.

Old Woking Manor
R. A. C. Godwin-Austen, *Surrey Arch. Coll.* 7 (1880) 44–9
VCH, *Surrey*, III (1911) 382–3

D. J. Haggard, *Surrey Arch. Coll.* 55 (1958) 124–6
H. M. Colvin *et al.* (eds.), *The History of the King's Works*, IV, pt 2 (1982) 344–8

Oatlands
A. Cook, *Surrey Arch. Coll.* 66 (1969) 1–9
H. M. Colvin *et al.* (eds.), *History of the King's Works*, IV, pt 2 (1982) 205–17
HBMC, *Excavations at Oatlands Palace* (forthcoming)

ORPINGTON 'PRIORY' and the houses of Christ Church, Canterbury

Originally in the countryside of west Kent, this house of the priors of Christ Church Cathedral Priory, Canterbury, is now a museum and garden attached to the library of Orpington town, an oasis in a sea of suburbia. King Cnut's chaplain gave the manor of Orpington to Christ Church in 1032, with the present building reflecting three primary building phases. The core of the hall and services block is late thirteenth century, showing that the house was always a substantial residence. A camera block was added in the late fourteenth

PLATE 159 Orpington 'Priory': camera and upper chamber blocks from the east

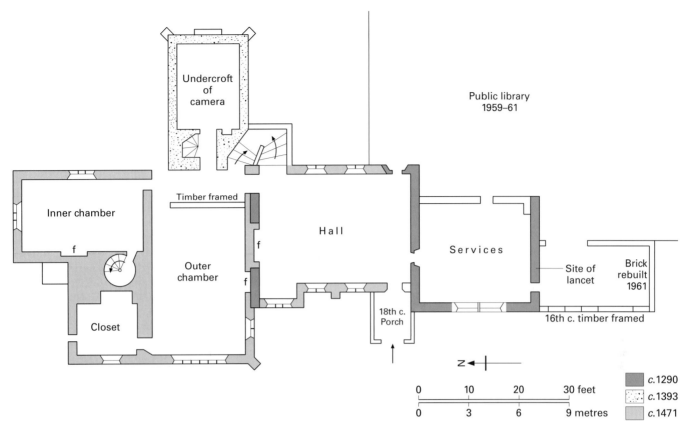

FIGURE 89 Orpington 'Priory': ground plan

century next to the upper chamber block that was rebuilt and extended in the later fifteenth century at the same time that the hall was renewed.

Built almost throughout of flint with ragstone dressings, part of the hall including the rear door of the cross passage and the single off-centre service door, and the blocked lancet in the services area, may be associated with the substantial building work undertaken by prior Eastry in 1290. It was noted at the time that a new hall and chapel were erected and two chambers of timber, one for the prior (with garderobe) next to the hall, and one for his knights.[1]

In 1393, prior Chillenden built a three-storeyed camera at right angles to the hall as an extension to the original framed chamber block.[2] The two diagonal buttresses are not bonded to the end wall and may be later. The undercroft, initially reached by an internal newel but subject to an enlarged doorway in the late fifteenth century, has three ribs supporting the ceiling and was probably used for storage. The residential first floor has renewed cinquefoil windows, and the second floor has renewed single- and twin-light trefoil windows with part of an original one traceable on the south side. The higher-level approach to the upper room arises from the late medieval rebuilding of the upper chamber block.

The hall was totally reconstructed by prior Sellinge in 1471, when it was given its present character.[3] Windows with uncusped four-centred lights were inserted in the upper half of the side walls at the same time that a bay window and end-wall fireplace were inserted. The apartment was beamed and ceiled but there is no evidence that attic rooms were created above it. The present roof is a rebuild of 1960 while the stair linking the hall with the first-floor

suite is a late nineteenth-century alteration of a Georgian structure.

The upper chamber block, built as a cross wing to the hall, replaced the earlier, timber-framed, and probably narrower structure. It was extended by a north wing to create an outer and inner chamber at ground- and first-floor level. The low north-west doorways in the outer chambers may have served garderobes, but as there is no building line in the outer wall they were probably the approach to contemporary closets. Both inner chambers were newel linked. The upper rooms are timber ceiled below crown-post roofs.

Prior Sellinge's work improved the scale and comfort of the house. Positioning the hall windows in the upper part of the side walls was popular during the second half of the fifteenth century and, like the dais window and end-wall fireplace, emulated the halls of the largest households. The two suites of private chambers at the rear of the hall with their fireplaces were similarly on a generous scale. All the uncusped windows of this phase have been harshly renewed, as has much of the outer walling and interior during its occupation as a private house between the mid-sixteenth and mid-twentieth centuries.[4]

Eastry (1285–1331) and Chillenden (1391–1411) were the prime rebuilding priors of Christ Church – in the cathedral,[5] the monastic precinct, and its country houses. Hardly anything survives of the prior's lodging at Canterbury apart from the porch added by prior Sellinge (1472–94) with his study built above the entrance. The precinct, though, retains the two-storeyed lodgings built by Chillenden for visitors (Archdeacon's House) and the more complete and lavish house 'Meist Homors' (now the King's School) for his guests.[6]

Apart from Orpington, the priory built houses at Chartham, Monkton, and Eastry in east Kent, with Caldecot in west Kent as a permanent retreat and holiday residence for the monks. Monkton Court has lost its extensive stone and timber-framed ranges since the late nineteenth century, leaving only a few late fifteenth-century fragments. A small anonymous flint building stands at Eastry Court, but considerably more at Chartham where the eighteenth-century frontage of the Deanery conceals prior Eastry's hall of 1303 and prior Chillenden's parlour and upper chamber of 1394. In about 1500, prior Goldstone II added a gatehouse and lodgings, now destroyed. The large chapel, believed to have abutted the solar wing, was pulled down in 1572. The site was enclosed by a moat which remains in part, and there was an inner garden and vineyard nearby.[7] As well as the prior and his visitors, monks staying there on holidays in the mid-fifteenth century were entertained in the hall by the minstrels of the earl of Exeter, the duke of Somerset's actors, and the harpist of Cardinal Beaufort.[8] Mersham Manor (1313) and Court Lodge, Great Chart (c.1325–40) were stone houses built by the priory for the managers of their estates.

NOTES

1 Obit of Eastry, Reg. 1 f.212ff. In 1333, the knights' chamber was dismantled and rebuilt on a new site.
2 Obit of Chillenden. *Anglia Sacra*, ed. H. Wharton, I (1691).
3 *Ibid.*, Obit of Sellinge.
4 The timber-framed extension to the services block is probably sixteenth century, an addition shortly before or after the Dissolution when the estate was broken up and the house purchased by the Hart Dyke family of Lullingstone.
5 R. Willis, *The Architectural History of Canterbury Cathedral* (1845); F. Woodman, *The Architectural History of Canterbury Cathedral* (1981).
6 R. Willis, *The History of the Monastery of Christ Church Canterbury* (1869). Though the reconstruction of the guest house was begun in 1376–7, it was remodelled for cardinal Beaufort in c.1444–5 with the principal chamber above the services. The open hall with the dais end lit by a pair of bay windows filled nearly two thirds of the building. It stood comparison with the best examples of contemporary domestic architecture. G. L. Harriss, *Cardinal Beaufort* (1988) 367. The hall was floored in the sixteenth century.
7 M. J. Sparks and E. W. Parking, *Arch. Cant.* 89 (1974) 169–82; RCHM, *A Gazetteer of Medieval Kent Houses* (1994) 28.
8 C. E. Woodruff, *Arch. Cant.* 53 (1940) 7.

P. E. W. Street, *The Priory, Orpington, Kent* (1934) (copy in library)
A. Baxter and Associates, *The Priory, Orpington: Conservation Plan* (2001) (copy in library)

PENSHURST PLACE, Kent

Like Knole, Penshurst is a house of extended development – almost of accretion – and like its neighbour, it seems to grow out of the landscape rather than be imposed upon it. Arthur Oswald commented that the Elizabethan and later work is not so much added as woven into the earlier, medieval fabric[1] and, as we shall see, there are some particular reasons for this. The present structure is the result of at least eight different building periods, but the finest of these is the mid-fourteenth-century grouping which has always

formed the centre of the house. Together with Haddon Hall, the heart of Penshurst Place is the outstanding survival of domestic architecture in England of its period.

SIR JOHN PULTENEY, 1338–49

The house is one of the earliest examples of the fully fledged medieval plan which formed the basis for all major residences for the next 200 years. The central hall, approached by a porch leading into a cross passage with opposing doors, was flanked by a two-storey cross wing at either end. This work was undertaken for Sir John Pulteney, who bought the manor of 4,000 acres in 1338 and died of the plague eleven years later. Of Sussex origins, Pulteney inherited lands in Warwickshire and Leicestershire from his grandfather and went into the rapidly developing cloth trade in London. His business prospered spectacularly, initially as a member of the Drapers' Company, then receiving crown patronage in the 1320s, and developing as a leading wool exporter in the 1330s. Business brought wealth and Pulteney first emerged as a financier in the 1320s, and was soon lending to the crown to the extent that he became one of the leading underwriters of Edward III during the opening phases of the war in France. He was particularly astute enough not to join the group of wool merchants who lent monies to the king which ended in their bankruptcy (1338–41), and he spread his activities into the wine trade and the practice of victualling the troops which has proved so profitable in succeeding centuries. Honours followed in succession, initially as alderman, then in 1331 as lord mayor – a post which he held on three further occasions before 1337 – followed by a knighthood in that year. He also undertook royal assignments, including negotiations in 1334 in Flanders on behalf of the king, for which he received several manors as a reward for his services. By 1334, Pulteney was the wealthiest man in Kent, and at the time of his death was one of the wealthiest in England. Had he lived longer, he may well have founded a dynasty as another successful merchant did a generation later, William de la Pole of Hull.

Externally, three notable features of the house immediately catch the eye. The first are the boldly decorated windows of the hall descending almost to the ground. The window tracery, partially replaced by sash windows in the mid-eighteenth century, has been reinstated to the original design and incorporates parts of the original workmanship, particularly the heads of ogee quatrefoils with small trefoils plugging the gaps to the hood moulds.[2] It is a particularly fine example of the recently evolved geometric tracery of the Kentish school of masons. The forward relieving arches between the buttresses supporting the embattled parapet were particularly necessary at Penshurst to carry the thrust of the steeply pitched hall roof. This dominates the house from every viewpoint. It was originally covered throughout with Horsham stone slates, but the weight of these gave cause for concern in the later nineteenth century so that the upper part was replaced with red tiles to lighten the load on the supporting timbers. Thirdly, the stonework of Penshurst is a joy. Like Hever Castle, it is built of golden-coloured sandstone streaked with brownish stains of iron. Cut in blocks of different colour and size, it creates a wonderfully warm texture that was also used by several later generations to create a harmonious structure belying its five centuries of development. As Marcus Binney has pointed out, the masonry work is seen at its finest in the arch over the north entrance porch where the voussoirs are cut so that the lines of the grain fan out from a single centre.[3]

PLATE 160 Penshurst Place: hall range from the outer court

The two-storeyed *porch* is a splendid survival, unaltered since its construction, buttressed and with a stair turret giving roof access. The window of the upper room is a prominent one under a depressed arch, with tracery comparable with but not the mirror image of that in the windows of the great hall. The porch has tierceron vaulting, crumbling foliage bosses, and inserted side benches. The inner arch with roll and sunken moulding has a bold band of quatrefoil decoration framing the original oak door (barred) with a wicket for daily use[4] (pl. 185).

The cross passage is flanked by a textbook example of linked doorways on one side opening into the offices and kitchen passage, and a later screen on the other side giving access to the hall. The south doorway is relatively plain (also barred), and initially lacked porch protection for the present structure is a late sixteenth-century addition, incorporating an original hall buttress and deliberately intended in materials and form to match the medieval work.

Like the porch, the *hall* stands virtually unaltered since the time of its construction. At 62 feet long and 39 feet wide, with the four-bay roof rising 58 feet from the ground, this magnificent apartment has no peer in fourteenth-century England. It was clearly designed to be an apartment of light, initially with three elongated windows in each of the side walls[5] and a group of windows in both gables. The side windows have broad splays while the end windows – a large four-light opening with elaborate quatrefoil heads below the collar beam and two smaller windows in the gable heads – also have the benefit of throwing light on to the massed timbers of a normally dark area. To span the hall's considerable width, tie beams were not considered practical. Crown posts were therefore carried on five collar beams supported on massive arched braces rising from heavily moulded wall plates. The ten life-sized wooden figures of men and women seem less structurally essential. Originally they would have presumably been supported on stone corbels but inexplicably these have been removed, and at the same time the feet of the figures abruptly cut off. Surprisingly, the roof is of chestnut rather than oak, and because it must have been designed by one of the foremost carpenters of the period has been attributed to William Hurley, the king's master-carpenter.[6]

The red floor tiles and central octagonal hearth are at least sixteenth century and may be earlier. In any case, the blackened crown posts are evidence of long use with the smoke escaping through a louvre. An eighteenth-century replacement louvre was taken down when the roof was restored a century later.[7] The screen may incorporate medieval elements, but the footings and pillars are late sixteenth century and the cusped heads of the panels are of plaster of later date. Between the windows are the shadows of wall paintings of knights in armour beneath canopies – ethereal figures today in place of their initial rich medieval colouring. Even so, they prominently alluded to Pulteney's knighthood, the first granted to a merchant. To complete this summary of the least-altered medieval hall in England, the two trestle tables are attributed stylistically to the late fifteenth century[8] and the fire dogs are late Tudor with the Sidney pheon or broad arrow (pl. 203).

In two respects, this hall is not free of criticism. There was originally a window above the north entry, its outline still traceable on the internal plaster. It either was never completed when the porch room was raised or else was blocked when that structure became a secondary addition associated with the construction of the services and chamber block. The unusual tracery of the courtyard-facing window supports the latter possibility. More critical is the character of the roof rafters and their braces, which are totally plain, lacking even a basic chamfer. They are crude in comparison with the mouldings of the main trusses.

A door from the dais gives access to the vaulted *undercroft* of four bays at a lower level to the rear of the hall, now partitioned into one large and some smaller rooms used for wine storage. The reveals of the windows under depressed heads indicate the position of original openings in the west wall, but the windows in the south wall are nineteenth-century reopenings. It has been suggested that this undercroft is a remnant of a late thirteenth-century house built by Sir Stephen Penchester (or Penshurst), builder of Allington Castle but buried in Penshurst church in 1299.[9] Externally, the masonry suggests that it is co-eval with the remainder of the mid-fourteenth-century work. Internally, the vaulting ribs die into the central pillar without any intervening capital, a feature common between the mid-thirteenth and the third quarter of the fourteenth century but which is repeated in the north porch and shares with it common masons' marks. The architectural evidence favours Pulteney's time rather than fifty years earlier, while setting out the whole site from this one feature would be a limitation at variance with the style and character of the remainder of Pulteney's work.

The original approach to the *upper residential block* was by a newel stair of which the upper flight still leads to the roof. This approach was altered to the present broader one in the second quarter of the fifteenth century as part of Bedford's expansion of the private apartments. The north window lighting the dais was blocked at the same time, when it was converted into a doorway leading to an added range, with its head reused to light the new broad stairs with plain vaulted bays.

The large first-floor room is still basically the mid-fourteenth-century withdrawing chamber but it was heavily altered 500 years later. Initially, it was lit on three sides, for lightness was a characteristic of Pulteney's house, more than is apparent today. This chamber illustrates the variety of window forms within the same apartment – a characteristic repeated in the hall and lower chamber block. The large window in the north wall with its two-centred head (converted into a doorway in the earlier fifteenth century) was similar to those in the hall, while the smaller window nearby with its depressed head is like those in the undercroft. The two openings in the west wall are quite different and have depressed arches and deep reveals, again blocked when the abutting apartments were

PLATE 161 Penshurst Place: stair to residential apartments

added in the second quarter of the fifteenth century. The large window in the south wall is mid-nineteenth century, as is the hooded fireplace although the jambs are original. The small opening looking into the hall may be a Victorian conceit or a recovered original feature, but the wall cupboard is genuine. The two-centred door in the south wall probably led to a garderobe, one of several located on this side of the house.[10]

At the lower end of the hall, the *services and chamber block* stands in fine condition. The three centrally positioned doorways, linked by their hoods, served the buttery, pantry, and kitchen passage respectively. The north room (buttery) overlooking the entrance court has a cupboard identical with that in the withdrawing chamber, a secondary doorway opening from the kitchen passage, and traces of a third doorway with a relieving arch above the later replacement fireplace formerly leading to an office in line with the courtyard façade. The south room (pantry) also has a secondary doorway, originally external but now opening from the later south porch. The kitchen passage was blocked in the early nineteenth century, for the kitchen and associated offices had fallen into decay by the late eighteenth century and the remains were pulled down by 1836. Their original form can be made out to some extent in Kip's view, with the octagonal louvre of the kitchen as a prominent feature.

The south tower projecting from the corner of the block is the

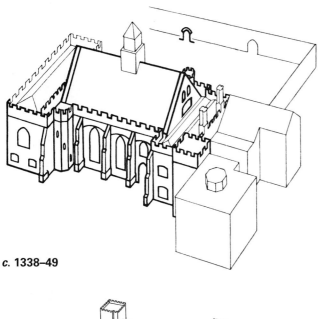

c. 1338–49

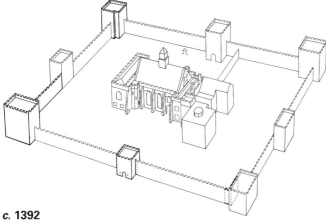

c. 1392

FIGURE 90 Penshurst Place: house development *c.*1338–49 and *c.*1392

one element of the overall design which does not conform to the standard plan, although it is integral with the remainder of Pulteney's work. It is related to the approach to the important apartments above the services and its almost windowless form suggests its purpose. It was usual for rooms in this position to be reached from a door in the cross passage, but at Penshurst the approach was from the originally external door beyond the south cross-passage door. It opened into a corridor partitioned out of the pantry area, leading to the base of the south tower with a stair rising to the upper floor. This was replaced by the present staircase during the nineteenth century but the upper landing retains two original window loops and two recesses for lamps. The further door on this landing may have been for a garderobe or more probably to the roofs of the subsidiary offices and kitchen. A squinch passage leads to the first of the upper rooms[11] (see fig. 91).

The area above the services may have been a single room of considerable size, though it was almost certainly partitioned initially, as it was until 1996. The larger outer room was heated, with its fireplace concealed behind the panelling, while the inner chamber was of greater privacy with garderobe access but a later inserted fire-

place. The window overlooking the entrance court, larger than its counterpart to the south and with elaborate tracery identical with that in the hall, made this room one of considerable style. There was a corner approach to the unheated porch chamber with cupboard, and there was access via a doorway with corbels above it to a passage over that to the kitchen. This was an important suite of rooms, probably for guests of the highest rank, with an independent approach leading to a heated outer chamber, and a high-quality inner chamber with a bedchamber or privy chamber above the north porch.[12]

Despite the size and extent of the existing buildings, they are by no means the sum of Pulteney's residence, which would have been supported by extensive lodgings, a chapel,[13] *offices, stables and outbuildings*. None of these has survived the later development of the house except for a fragment in the north court. The lower walling of the north range facing Pulteney's hall shows two blocked lights of early sixteenth-century date and an opening into the cellars with blind tracery similar to that in the withdrawing chamber. Although this range was built in brick in the later sixteenth century, this ashlar walling was retained although the fourteenth-century cellar opening was recut when the range was virtually rebuilt in the early nineteenth century.

Penshurst is not a naturally defensive site. It lies in the valley of the stripling Medway and everything that was built in Edward III's reign declares an openness totally alien to any defensive intent. Yet Pulteney was granted a licence to crenellate his house in October 1341.[14] No military features can be attributed to this period and in fact the licence does not mention such words as fortify, turret, or tower. It only says 'crenellate' and that simply meant the embattlement of the newly built walls, suggestive of pedigree and status. Had Pulteney even built an encircling wall, then it was replaced by the present defensive walling following the second licence granted fifty years later.

A more domestic note is glimpsed by a contemporary reference to the *gardens* near the house. The present gardens were restored by Lord de L'Isle and Dudley in the 1850s to the form shown in Kip's view of 1728, a layout confirmed by the recent discovery of a mid-eighteenth-century estate plan. They are possibly of Elizabethan origin but their medieval character would have been rather different. One of the earliest account rolls in the Penshurst muniments (1346–7) includes references to Curteys the gardener. He was essentially responsible for the kitchen garden which was stocked with root vegetables, madder for crimson dye, and teasels for the cloth industry. Apple and pear trees provided fruit for Pulteney's family, but the vines failed that particular year so that no wine could be made for the household.[15]

Any assessment of Pulteney's work recognises that it was on a regal scale, and not surprisingly, given his London connections. The contrast with the contemporary work at nearby Ightham Mote can be pushed too far, but here were two residences of common plan which illustrate not only the differences between a country house and a princely residence but the totally different realisation between provincial and London work. This is not so much a question of scale as of the quality of the design, the use of high-quality building materials, the delicacy of the decorative details, the variety of window forms even within the same apartment, and the panache that makes the Penshurst work so outstanding. Of course, most of this can be attributed to Pulteney's wealth, for as Parker pointed out in 1853,

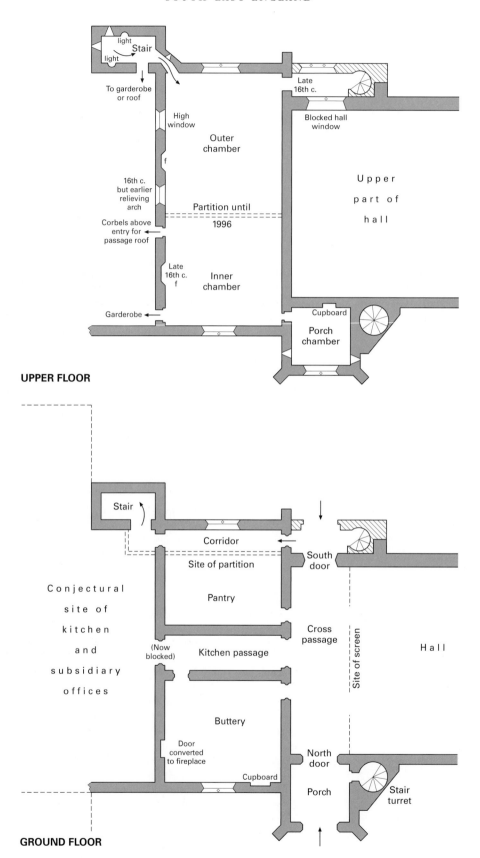

UPPER FLOOR

To garderobe or roof

High window

Outer chamber

Late 16th c.

Blocked hall window

Upper part of hall

16th c. but earlier relieving arch

Partition until 1996

Corbels above entry for passage roof

Late 16th c. f

Inner chamber

Garderobe

Cupboard

Porch chamber

Stair

light

light

GROUND FLOOR

Stair

Corridor

South door

Site of partition

Pantry

Conjectural site of kitchen and subsidiary offices

(Now blocked)

Kitchen passage

Cross passage

Site of screen

Hall

Buttery

Door converted to fireplace

North door

Cupboard

Porch

Stair turret

FIGURE 91 Penshurst Place: site plan of services and chamber block

390

Pulteney's work partakes 'more of the character of a palace than of an ordinary house'.[16] Small details such as the contrast between the relatively plain outer entry and elaborate inner doorway to the hall, the care taken to use the grain of the stone to deliberate effect, the enriched string course, embattled transoms, and the wealth of window tracery wholly Decorated in spirit, contribute to the quality of the building and reveal the hand of an outstanding master-mason. John Harvey has suggested that the consultant or designer could have been William Ramsey III (d.1349), the king's chief mason for all works south of the Trent.[17] Certainly, Pulteney was a friend of the king and an architectural patron who was likely to seek the services of the most highly regarded designer of the age.

Given the owner's origins, Pulteney's house is not overtly ostentatious. Its scale is certainly impressive, but only the hall would arouse the wonder of contemporaries. There was no double residential block for the family, abundance of turrets, or surfeit of decoration. In fact, all the elements of Penshurst are subordinate to a controlled framework of dignified splendour. Pulteney's residence stands out from almost all contemporary buildings not so much by its scale as by the quality of its workmanship, by the extent of its survival to the present day in a much extended house, and by its excellent state of preservation.

Sir John's architectural achievement needs to be seen as a reflection of mercantile ambition and success in the fourteenth century. Penshurst was the equal of the archbishop of Canterbury's residence at Lambeth or Mayfield, and was only surpassed by the royal houses and those of a handful of courtiers. For in Penshurst's subsequent development and expansion, it is easy to overlook the size and quality of Pulteney's country house. And it needs to be seen in that light – as a hunting and retirement residence – for Pulteney was too astute a businessman to leave London for very long when it was clearly the centre of all his activities. Princely though his country house may be, his London home was literally occupied by a prince. Nothing remains of that house for which he received a licence to crenellate in 1341, but it is said that it had forty rooms and it was certainly magnificent enough to become the home of the Black Prince until 1359. Pulteney's building patronage did not stop there. According to Stow, he also built a chantry chapel for three priests in Old St Paul's Cathedral (where he was buried), a college for a master, thirteen priests, and four choristers at St Laurence Poulteney (1336), and the parish church of Little All Hallows in Thames Street.[18] Outside London, he built the church of the Carmelite friars in Coventry (1342) in recognition of his antecedents and inheritance from Warwickshire, and crenellated a house at Cheveley in Cambridgeshire. This was also covered by the 1341 licence, but as Penshurst was neither moated nor towered, the square moated enclosure and the foundations of a round tower at Cheveley need further study before they can be attributed to the wealthiest London draper of his generation.

SIR JOHN DEVEREUX, 1382–93
Pulteney's widow married Sir Nicholas Lovayne, and the widow of their son married Sir John Devereux in 1382. During the early part of his life, he was a close friend and comrade-in-arms of the Black Prince in Aquitaine and Spain. Later in life, he was a colleague of Sir Simon Burley who was building up a substantial core of estates in Kent.[19] In September 1392, Devereux was granted a licence which permitted him 'to enclose his manor of Penshurst, Co. Kent,

with a wall of stone and lime, crenellate and turret the same, and hold the premises in fee'.[20] The earlier enclosure was encircled with an embattled wall defended by three-storeyed towers at the corner (and possibly marking the approach) and lesser towers in the middle of each side. This was the pattern that had been adopted at Westenhanger and Bodiam castles a little earlier and it confirms that any implementation of the earlier licence was limited in scope. All the towers and much of the linking wall survived until the first quarter of the eighteenth century and are shown most clearly in the valuable bird's-eye view of the house by Kip (1728). Nearly twenty years later, Vertue's view shows that the two intermediate towers on the eastern and western sides had been pulled down.

Today, only the isolated garden tower remains complete, two storeys high, featureless, and with a stump of walling on the east side showing that it connected with the south-east tower. The doorways are late sixteenth century and the fenestration is also post-medieval. The footings of the south-east tower survived a mid-nineteenth-century rebuilding, and portions of the walling on the east side of the courtyard were still visible in 1853.[21] The President's Tower and the Gallery Tower, on the line of the enclosure, seem to be original work too, for both are built of stone abutting later brick ranges.[22] Part of the linking wall has survived on the west side, incorporated in the outer wall of Bedford's range (see below) and the adjacent late Tudor Nether Gallery. Contrary to the circular form adopted at Scotney, Cooling, and Bodiam castles, these towers are rectangular like the slightly earlier ones at Hever.

Granted in the wake of attacks by French and Castilian marauders, the licence to crenellate was one of the last to be sought in Kent in response to the external dangers of Richard II's early years. The scale of this work was more extensive than it seems today, particularly the size of the corner towers which can be gauged by standing inside the ground- or first-floor end areas of the Gallery Tower. Such structures were more pertinent at the time of Devereux's acquisition of the property than ten years later. As in other contemporary instances such as Farleigh Hungerford and Cooling castles, it is possible that the licence applied to work already in hand and which had been virtually completed at the time of Sir John's death in the following year, particularly as the estate reverted to his wife and her daughter by her first husband rather than to Devereux's son.[23]

JOHN, DUKE OF BEDFORD, 1429–35
In 1429, Penshurst was sold to John, duke of Bedford (1389–1435), the brother of Henry V. He undertook the third of the major building campaigns at Penshurst by erecting the impressive range at right angles to Pulteney's work. It overlapped a corner of the earlier buildings to make use of Pulteney's withdrawing chamber, and extended as far as and incorporated Devereux's defensive wall.

Bedford's range was three-storeyed – a relatively low ground floor, a line of tall first-floor apartments, and a sequence of attic rooms. The ground-floor rooms with their generous square-headed two-light windows in both outer walls were for relatively high-status staff. The tall first-floor windows with their deep encircling splays betray a French influence, as does the probability that there was always a line of attic rooms. They would have been lit by large gable-headed windows in line with the parapet *à la française*, replaced by the present ones in 1575.[24]

The initial layout of this range is unclear. It may have consisted

The range was intended to provide an additional suite of rooms for Bedford and his family on a scale compatible with his position. His emblems, the falcon and the ibex, crown the roof gables. As with Pulteney's work, two- and four-centred arches are used in association with each other. Bedford also remodelled Pulteney's stair leading from the great hall to make the approach to his private apartments more broad and stately. This alteration is most obvious externally: the incorporation of an earlier hall buttress and the higher string course and battlements can be seen from the ground, while Pulteney's earlier spiral staircase can be identified from the roof.

Bedford also seems to have been responsible for creating a further range of apartments backing on to Pulteney's chamber block, approached from doors opening out of his new building lobby at ground- and first-floor levels. A secondary approach was created from the great hall by blocking the window lighting the dais and inserting a door in the former embrasure. Although the majority of the brick Lobby Tower at this point is early sixteenth-century work, it is built over an earlier stone base.

It is particularly disappointing that no records exist of Bedford's buildings prior to the mid-nineteenth-century reconstruction. The duke was mainly abroad from 1419 until his death in 1435, except for short periods in England during 1426–7 and 1433 when he was dealing with national problems and political quarrels.[26] He was responsible for substantial building activity in Rouen – the *palais*, the castle, and his manor of Joyeux Repos – and a pretty 'castle' made of stone and brick at Fulbroke in Warwickshire.[27] It looks as though Bedford intended to make Penshurst one of his major houses when he retired from the wars in France, and added the apartments and ranges to provide further accommodation at a time when private suites were becoming fashionable, and lodgings were required for senior staff. This and the French influence at Penshurst particularly befitted Bedford's status as regent of France and protector of the infant Henry VI.

PLATE 162 Penshurst Place: Bedford Range

of one large reception hall, or more probably two apartments and an end closet preceded by a lobby. This is still the layout at ground level, where the four rooms retain their original window frames and partition walls with original doorway openings. The broad lobby accessed Bedford's added apartments to the north opposite the newel serving all floors,[25] and a small polygonal projection at the foot of these stairs housing a still useful garderobe.

The two first-floor reception rooms were of equal size and of increasing privacy, an outer and inner chamber with end passage or closet. The outer room was formerly lit by a second south-facing window removed and infilled to take Devey's fireplace, while the blocked arch to the north, visible externally, may have been to a garderobe. Devey's second-chamber fireplace may have also been a window replacement. The present height of the two rooms suggests there was always an attic floor rather than uncomfortably tall apartments open to the roof. These roof rooms were refenestrated in 1574–5, but a more drastic restoration was carried out by the young George Devey in 1851. Photographs taken at the time show that he largely dismantled the building before rebuilding the roof, west end wall, ceilings, and present window tracery in place of the eighteenth-century sash windows.

LATER FIFTEENTH-CENTURY ADDITIONS

All further alterations for the next 150 years were relatively minor. Some modest work was put in hand by Bedford's younger brother, Humphrey duke of Gloucester (1391–1447), shortly after the estate was granted to him, for the accounts for 1435–9 record repairs to the porch, a corner tower, the chapel and other buildings.[28] Although no existing work can be ascribed to him, some of the buildings which formerly existed in the south-east angle of the enclosure and shown in Kip's view may date from his time, or that of the 2nd duke of Buckingham (1460–83), who is also known to have carried out some repairs[29] and entertained Edward IV here. In August 1519, the 3rd duke lavishly entertained Henry VIII and his court at the vast cost of £2,300, but it was not until some time after the advent of Sir Henry Sidney in 1554 that a sequence of major changes and additions were made between 1573 and 1585 which transformed the house. Interestingly, much of Sidney's work was deliberately old fashioned to harmonise with the medieval buildings. He used an out-of-date form of doorway, stone rather than brick for some of his structures to blend with the older work, and made additions in a deliberately sub-medieval style. Just as important, though, is that whereas some Elizabethan magnates were anxious to sweep away their old homes and build anew, Sidney and his wife refurbished the great hall and proudly used it and Pulteney's

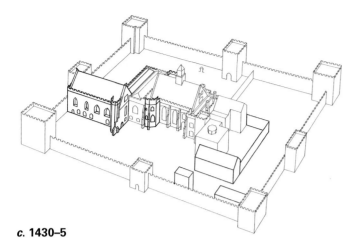

c. 1430–5

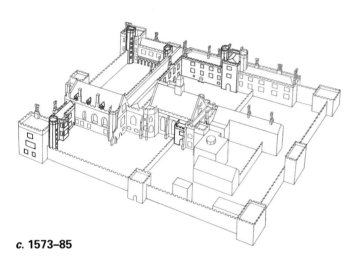

c. 1573–85

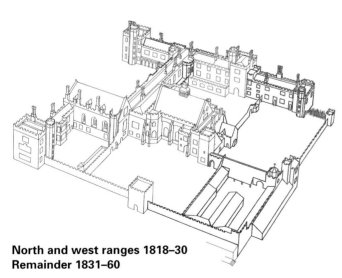

**North and west ranges 1818–30
Remainder 1831–60**

FIGURE 92 Penshurst Place: house development of *c.*1430–5, *c.*1573–85,
and *c.*1818–60

apartments well over 200 years after their construction. The Sidney alterations are shown on the accompanying elevations, together with two further development sequences during the nineteenth century of a property that still cries out for the detailed analysis and assessment that such a wonderful, stimulating, but perplexing house deserves.

NOTES

1 *Country Houses of Kent* (1933) 28.
2 This can be clearly seen in Neale's view of the north front (1828). Not all the hall's windows were glazed, for netting was purchased in 1470 to cover the windows of the hall and keep out the pigeons. L. F. Salzman, *Building in England* (1952) 174.
3 Binney and Emery (1973) 1.
4 The decoration of the doorway is another characteristic of the four-teenth-century Kentish school of decoration. J. H. Harvey in *Studies in Building History*, ed. E. M. Jope (1961) 161–3.
5 As will be mentioned later, the dais window was blocked to create the approach to a range added in the early fifteenth century, while that over the south door was necessarily limited to a smaller version, blocked when the south porch was added.
6 J. Harvey, *Eng. Med. Arch.* (1984) 155.
7 A fifteenth-century louvre exists at Gainsborough Hall, Lincolnshire, while the oak beams supporting the bell cage above the chapel roof of *c.*1285 at Eastbridge Hospital, Canterbury, give a broad indication of how one in the south-east might have been structured.
8 P. Eames, *Medieval Furniture* (1977) 221.
9 M. Wood, *The English Medieval House* (1965) 92–3. Turner and Parker (1853) 278–9 suggested this undercroft was even earlier.
10 The mid-nineteenth-century beam-supported ceiling is a George Devey replacement.
11 The tower is not bonded into the services block and was possibly height-ened at a later stage, perhaps in *c.*1392 with a head not unlike that of the tower incorporated at the end of Sydney's gallery.
12 Access was improved in the later sixteenth century when the south porch and wooden stair was erected and a new door into the outer chamber.
13 One existed in the 1430s and was subject to minor repairs in 1469–71. *Report on the Manuscripts of Lord de L'Isle*, ed. C. L. Kingsford, I (1925) 234, 236. Its existence from the 1340s is likely in view of Pulteney's other building projects.
14 *Cal. Pat. Rolls: 1340–43*, 331.
15 Felix Hull, *A Fourteenth Century Gardener's Account*, Cantium, 6, no. 3 (1974) 66–7.
16 Turner and Parker (1853) 278.
17 Harvey, *Eng. Med. Arch.* (1984) 244. Also J. Bony, *The English Decorated Style* (1979) 61.
18 J. Stow, *Survey of London* (1598), ed. C. L. Kingsford (3rd edn 1971).
19 *Arch. Cant.* 100 (1984) 221, 227. Burley lived for a time at Leybourne Castle, 15 miles from Penshurst.
20 *Cal. Pat. Rolls: 1391–96*, 164.
21 Turner and Parker (1853) 281.
22 Neither tower has any internal features earlier than the sixteenth century. The hipped roofs shown in a later seventeenth-century portrait of the 4th earl of Leicester had been removed by Kip's time.
23 John Newman (1969) 53, 437, attributed these defences on historical grounds to Bedford, but Marcus Binney (1972) confirmed their late fourteenth-century date.
24 The east gable retains an earlier relieving arch above the replacement Elizabethan window.
25 The underside of the stairs is curved to create a running line, a form copied by Sir Henry Sidney in the 1580s for his stairs at the upper end of the long gallery.
26 E. C. Williams, *My Lord of Bedford: 1389–1435* (1963).

27 Leland, *Itinerary*, II, 47. A. Emery, *Greater Med. Houses*, II (2000) 330.

28 *Report on the Manuscripts of Lord de L'Isle*, ed. C. L. Kingsford, I (1925) 234.

29 *Ibid.* 236–7. On Gloucester's death, Henry VI had granted the estate to Humphrey Stafford, 1st duke of Buckingham. A consequence of his litigious nature was an attack on his park at Penshurst in 1451 when a considerable quantity of game was stolen. C. Rawcliffe, *The Staffords, Earls of Stafford and Dukes of Buckingham* (1978) 178.

T. H. Turner and J. H. Parker, *Some Account of Domestic Architecture in England*, II (1853) 278–81

J. H. Parker, *Gentleman's Magazine*, July 1863

H. A. Tipping, *English Homes* Pd 1, I (1921) 166–88

J. Newman, *The Buildings of England: West Kent and the Weald* (1969) 436–40

M. Binney, *Country Life* (March/May 1972)

M. Binney and A. Emery, *The Architectural Development of Penshurst Place* (1973)

PORTCHESTER CASTLE, Hampshire

In 1396, Richard II made peace with France and married the seven-year-old daughter of the French king. As the threat of invasion had diminished, funding became available to update some of the royal residences and make them more comfortable. In addition to the redevelopment of Westminster Hall and a house at Sutton near Chiswick, Richard rebuilt the residential ranges within the inner court of Portchester Castle as a small palace-residence for occupation when hunting in the neighbouring forest of Bere, or waiting with his new wife to sail to France.

The initially important defensive structure at Portchester had become of little military significance by the fourteenth century, though it proved useful for mustering troops embarking on overseas expeditions during the earlier part of the Hundred Years' War, and subsequently became vulnerable to French attacks. For these reasons, the castle was maintained and garrisoned throughout the century. Edward II had spent over £1,100 on rebuilding the hall and west range in 1320–6, but this work was pulled down at the close of the century in favour of a programme encompassing a new hall, kitchen, and services, and a sequence of residential apartments round two and a half sides of the inner court between the earlier entrance and the Norman keep.[1]

Work under the master-mason Walter Walton and the master-carpenter Thomas Clevere was initiated in April 1396 and completed in August 1399, at the point of Richard's demise so that it is extremely unlikely he ever enjoyed his new accommodation. It was built in approximately the same position as the earlier ranges but essentially on new foundations, with the construction of the lower part of the hall preceding that of the west and north-west ranges, with the kitchen following as the last structure.[2]

Masons, carpenters, plumbers, and labourers were recruited early in 1396 and stone was brought from the Isle of Wight and Beer in east Devon for doorways, windows, and fireplaces. Oaks were felled in the king's woods or sought from ecclesiastical and lay lords such as the abbot of Titchfield and Thomas, duke of Surrey. Hearth tiles were made locally, white tiles for firebacks were shipped from Flanders, and paving tiles were brought from Southampton. In

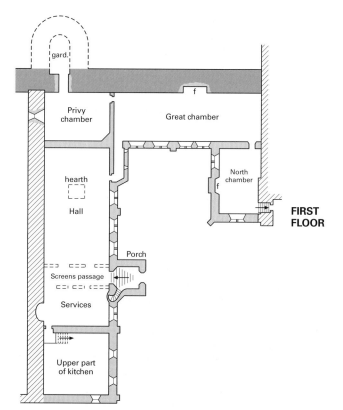

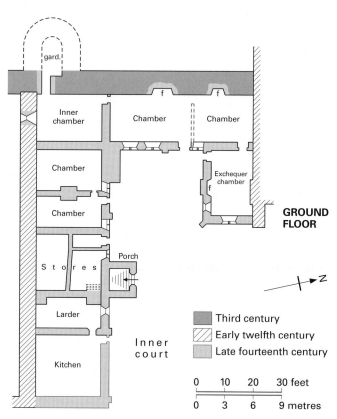

FIGURE 93 Portchester Castle: floor plans of Richard II's residence

1397 work was fully in progress on the hall range and advanced enough by 1398 for roofing to take place. Oil for preserving the hall timbers against sun and wind point to the existence of a wooden louvre, while a later entry shows that there was also one covered with lead over the kitchen called a 'fumerel'.[3] In 1399, roofs were leaded, and glass was made and painted with shields, badges, and borders for the windows of the hall, great chamber, chapel, and exchequer room and the high chamber adjoining it. Candles had been used at night to hasten speedy completion. £1,702 was spent in nearly four years, of which £1,595 19s. 11d. was incurred in building costs – over half on labour, a third on materials, and the remainder on transport.[4]

The plan was necessarily determined by the earlier defensive walls and restricted site, with almost all the windows courtyard-facing. Some of the services were positioned at ground level underneath the hall, but the location of the principal apartments at the upper level was dictated by the site as much as for status reasons. Only the shell remains of this residence with very little decorative evidence to clothe the skeletal walls. Room layout and descriptions are therefore brief, for the ranges are like a series of boxes, empty of contents.

The façades warrant attention before the individual rooms are explored. That of the south range is by no means regular, even though it is all of a single build. Though the kitchen and services to the east are three-storeyed, their windows are not in line. The hall is two-storeyed but with an awkward end two bays, partly through the passage projection to the west range with a small high window above, and partly through the lack of balance between the ground-level doorway and window with those in the neighbouring bay.

The raised hall was approached through a two-storey porch. The elegant two-centred outer arch with hollow-moulded jambs is set in a square frame with stops in the form of lantern holders. The entry bay has lost both its vault and the straight flight of steps into the hall, but it retains the inner arch with its deeper hollow-moulded jambs and higher rear arch common at this time. A spiral stair rises to the small room above the porch, the chamber over the services, and an octagonal roof turret depicted in 1733.[5]

The hall area, 64 feet by 23 feet internally between the dais and the kitchen walls, was divided by lost timber partitions into three – the screens passage, the hall proper, and a storeyed unit below the screens. The hall, 41 feet by 23 feet, was lit by three tall, courtyard-facing, twin-light transomed windows, set close together to ensure maximum light, for the opposite wall – unlike that in most halls – was blank, though no doubt lined with hangings. Because of the wall passage to the royal apartments, there was only room for a small window above, lighting the dais end. The short length of wall cornice on the south side and the lack of roof corbels point to a low-pitched tie-beam structure (with louvre) resting on wall plates.

Two entries from the inner court accessed the rooms below the hall serving as stores and chambers respectively. The two stores lay below the screens passage, the two chambers below the dais. The latter, courtyard lit, with the entry serving the outer from which the inner one was approached, were separated by a central thickened wall carrying the hall hearth above.

The three-floor area below the screens was multi-purposed. The ground floor was a larder with drain, entered from the kitchen. The first floor, opening from the screens passage, was for services. It had

a two-light window to the court, the door to the kitchen, and the steps to the ground-floor store. The fireplace is a later insertion. The chamber above the services was residential, with a two-light courtyard window and contemporary fireplace in the opposing wall. It also accessed any gallery over the screens passage.

The almost square ground-floor kitchen, 23 feet by 22 feet, rose the height of the range to an open roof. It was courtyard-approached with immediate access to the adjacent larder and a flight of steps opposite so that food could be carried to the first-floor services. As wall hearths are clearly absent, there was probably a central hearth and louvre. The two lines of windows in the upper walling were at half levels: three single lights below a single twin light.

The upper façade of the west range is more balanced than that of the hall range, but it still has the quirk of a conjoined window to one side of a ground-floor entry. The stone-roofed passage from the hall dais opened into the great chamber that filled most of the west range's upper floor. Eleven feet longer than the hall and possibly screened at the lower end, it was lit by four twin-light transomed windows to the courtyard with the last bay windowless, almost like that in the hall. The enormous fireplace in the outer wall was central to a room covered with a low-pitched roof.

A door at the lower end accessed the royal privy chamber behind the hall dais. There was no fireplace, and because of its vulnerable position at the corner of the enclosure, the room was lit by a single light making it a particularly cheerless apartment. The half-round tower of the Norman enclosure, destroyed in c.1790, held garde-robes at both levels.

Because the upper end of the great chamber abutted the keep, the third royal chamber was built at right angles. It was a more comfortable apartment than the privy chamber, with generous two-light windows, a fireplace with white tiles at the back, and stepped access to the chapel in the keep's forebuilding.

The ground floor of this west range repeated the upper plan with the area under the great chamber divided into two by a now lost partition. The windows were generous, and three of the four rooms had fireplaces which the fourth under the privy chamber lacked, though it had a garderobe facility. The lack of internal access between the two floors meant that the suites were independent of each other.

This royal accommodation was basically a rebuilding on the earlier plan, with the addition of an extension alongside the keep replacing demolished outer forebuildings. All ranges were of random flint and rubble with greensand and Beer stone dressings, though the external walls were initially rendered and whitewashed. The buttressed walls stand to their full height but have lost their embattled parapets and are in a raddled state. Most of the doors and windows were of standard form, the latter of different sizes. All windows had cinquefoiled lights, with those of the larger first-floor rooms of two lights with a small eyelet above and a transom, though virtually all tracery has been destroyed. Roofs were low pitched and lead covered. This accommodation was necessarily compact, but the keep was still in use and its ground floor was vaulted and given a new entry arch in 1396–8 at the same time that several new windows were inserted in the first-floor chambers.

This sequence of royal chambers was comfortable, but not spectacular like Gaunt's work at Kenilworth Castle. The layout was unfussy and not without some ingenuity in working within, and

PLATE 163 Portchester Castle: hall and residential range from inner court

maintaining, the defensive curtilage. Because of this, it was necessary to site some of the residential chambers at ground level instead of limiting them entirely to the first floor as at Windsor Castle's upper ward. To help achieve speedy completion, windows and door openings were of standard form in an austere early Perpendicular style. Unlike Westminster Hall, there was an absence of decorative sculpture except for the modest embellishment of the entry porch and the hall cornice. Even so, this work is important because of its structural clarity, relative completeness, and precise building documentation.

Richard II did not live to enjoy his splendid new residence and his successors made no use of the castle except for Henry V at the time of Agincourt. By Norton's day (1609) the buildings were still standing and leaded, but while Richard II's hall was 'very fayre and spacious', there were also some 'dark and malincolye roomes'. However, the castle's use as a Napoleonic prisoner-of-war camp shows that it was still not without some military value 200 years later, with the roofs of the royal apartments retiled for occupation, since removed to leave only the fourteenth-century masonry shell.

NOTES

1 A second hall against the north wall of the inner court had been rebuilt for the constable during the mid-fourteenth century. It was raised above

three earlier store rooms but only the unbroken (and earlier) outer wall survives and the guard room created at a higher level within the projecting Norman tower. The constable, Sir Robert Assheton (1376–81), added a four-storey tower to provide additional personal accommodation, though the only documentary record is for the final status of this named tower in the account roll for 1385. The earlier windowless ground-floor room held the cesspit to the latrine of the unlit room above. The second and third floors were two well-windowed heated chambers – a private suite of domestic character. Two features of the larger uppermost room warrant attention. The two-light window has a raised hood with a line of blind trefoil lights surmounted by a large rose – decorative elements that the subsequent royal work now lacks. Mindful of its defensive position, this room has keyhole-shaped gunports on two levels covering three outer faces – among the earliest in England providing all round gunfire.

2 Cunliffe and Munby (1985) 29–34.
3 VCH, III (1908) 156.
4 HKW, II (1963) 790–1; Cunliffe and Munby (1985) 128–31, 151–75.
5 Cunliffe and Munby (1985) pl. xv.

VCH, *Hampshire*, III (1908) 151–8

S. E. Rigold, *Portchester Castle: Handbook* (1965)

B. Cunliffe and J. Munby, *Excavations at Portchester Castle IV. Medieval, the Inner Bailey* (1985)

J. Goodall, *Portchester Castle: Handbook* (2003)

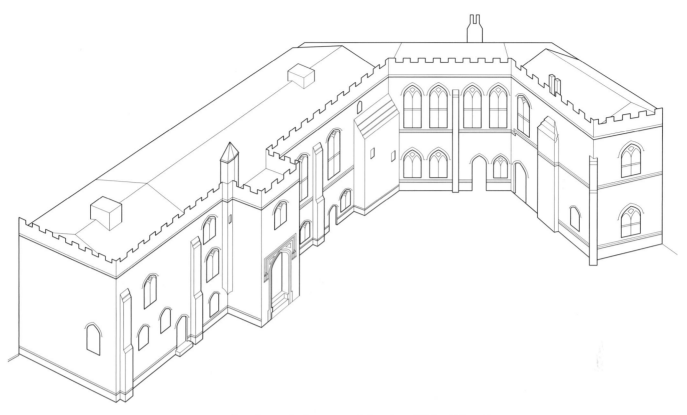

FIGURE 94 Portchester Castle: courtyard elevation of Richard II's residence

RYMANS, Sussex

Still slightly withdrawn from the modern world yet within sight of Chichester Cathedral, Rymans retains the greater part of its early fifteenth-century form in little-altered state. In 1410, the property was sold to William Ryman, a locally prominent lawyer and knight of the shire in parliament between 1420 and 1432, who died in 1443. The early fifteenth-century character and individual form of the house suggested that it was built in the years immediately following site purchase. L-shaped, the hall and services forming the greater length were replaced by a more modest two-storeyed flint and rubble structure in the later seventeenth century after the Ryman family had sold the property to a neighbour in 1654. However, the residential rooms at the angle and the short 'office' wing have survived complete. 'Office' is used here in its current sense as a work-room for Ryman seems to have carried on his professional activities from home. As the angle block is three-storeyed and the adjacent wing is two, it is usually referred to as a tower, but it served no defensive purpose for it was a residential unit in vertical rather than horizontal mode.

Nothing survives of the hall except the line of its roof and two doorways at ground- and first-floor level in the end wall leading to the chamber block.[1] The lower one could be anticipated but the upper one is unexpected and indicates there was an internal wooden stair at the upper end of the hall. It also gave immediate access to a straight mural stair leading to the uppermost chamber. Linking all three tiered chambers and the roof was a projecting newel on the opposite side allowing considerable internal freedom of movement.

The ground-floor chamber was relatively dark, with a single light (restored) adequate for storage or staff purposes. Two further doorways, another window, and a replacement fireplace were inserted in 1913 to facilitate residential occupation. The two upper rooms – withdrawing chamber and bedchamber – are well served by fireplaces (altered) and generous twin-light windows in two outer walls, formerly shuttered, with the taller second-floor chamber of particularly light and airy character. The first-floor chamber had a garderobe opening off the north-west corner.[2] The

PLATE 164 Rymans: from the south-east

397

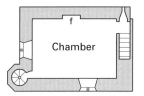

SECOND FLOOR

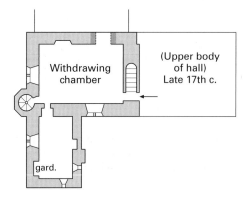

FIRST FLOOR

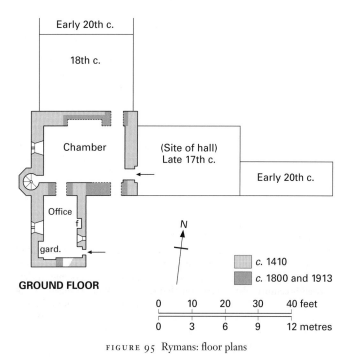

GROUND FLOOR

FIGURE 95 Rymans: floor plans

Ryman's self-contained office is as satisfactory as any similar office 600 years later. As the architect-owner Claude Phillimore pointed out in 1966, the three windows were always there 'so that this snug room catches the sun all day long. The little east window is clearly contrived so that light falls on one's books as one sits warming one's feet by the fire – a refinement typical of the thoughtful planning of this house.'[3] The upper chamber was an inner room to the first floor family room and again sported comparable fireplace, garderobe, and window facilities to the office below. The spacious plaster vault was made by Phillimore in 1951 to create the feeling of the original open timber roof.

The design qualities of this house are quietly striking. It was built of tightly mortared blocks of ashlar brought from Ventnor in the Isle of Wight. The chamber block, with walls 3 feet thick, is shaped by offsets at ground-floor and between the first- and second-floor levels, with an outward-facing moulding at roof level. The twin-light windows are liberal in scale, with crisp traceried heads inserted in recessed frames (as at Swanborough Manor), while those in the office wing are more modest. All mouldings are bold and well designed. Ornament is discreet, with plain chamfers to all internal doorways, one fireplace with leaf spandrels, and a gargoyle at roof level as an exuberant excess. Internal access is generous, leading to lofty chambers at both upper levels. Although it is close to the head of Chichester harbour and was built within a generation of French raids on the Sussex coast, Rymans has no defensive elements – moat, gateway, curtilage wall, or battlements[4] – but was a gentleman's residence which still retains a considerable amount of original and untouched work.

NOTES

1 W. D. Peckham, the owner of Rymans from 1922 to 1950, suggested that the hall may have existed on this site from the thirteenth century onwards ((1939) 157), but it could equally have been co-eval with the remainder of the structure.
2 Peckham (1939) 162, 163. The doorway is concealed by panelling.
3 Phillimore (1966) 6.
4 Phillimore (1966) 7, notes that the roof was originally protected by a plain stone parapet.

W. D. Peckham, *Sussex Arch. Coll.* 80 (1939) 149–64

VCH, *Sussex*, IV (1953) 138–9

C. Phillimore, *Rymans, Apuldram: A Description* (1966): notes held at the house

SALMESTONE GRANGE, Kent

Salmestone Grange and Minster Grange are two almost complete exemplars of a particular type of ecclesiastical residence, the latter dating from the mid to late twelfth century and the former from the later thirteenth and fourteenth centuries. They were both attached to the Benedictine abbey of St Augustine's at Canterbury and they are within 4 miles of each other. Salmestone was initially responsible for only 89 acres of arable land and was occupied by few monks, but it became a retreat by the early fourteenth century for the abbot and monks of St Augustine's and was significantly enlarged as a consequence.[1] The grange has never been totally abandoned and is still occupied, and now lies within the outskirts of Margate.

Salmestone is a particularly fine example of a monastic residence

pyramid roof, a seventeenth-century feature, was rebuilt after a fire in the 1950s.

The lower office wing has an independent ground-floor room, not linked internally until 1913. With its own external entry, small windows in the three outer walls (south enlarged), fireplace, and garderobe originally screened from the body of the room, William that is essentially secular in structure and development. However, it is not an easy one to appreciate through its complex development. No structure has been identified before the thirteenth century and at least five building phases can be traced during the next hundred years (fig. 96).

1. Mid-thirteenth century.

Within the heart of the grange is a chalk and flint undercroft with a three-bay barrel vault. Partially below ground, it was originally entered from the west and has been truncated at the east end. It is not known what it supported and its relationship to the other buildings is unclear.

2. Late thirteenth century.

During the fifty years between about 1270 and 1320, the grange was radically developed. Two parallel timber-framed structures were erected, one of them over the earlier undercroft. Embedded tie-beam braces at first-floor level above the curtailed end of the undercroft and the king-strut roof relate this phase to contemporary Canterbury structures. The parallel range and roof to the south is a post-medieval rebuilding, but the west-facing flint wall added at a slightly later date encompasses both parallel ranges and is not later than the early fourteenth century. The purpose of these ranges is not known but the upper rooms were probably chambers, externally approached.

3. *c.*1300–10.

A substantial two-storey range was thrust westwards at the beginning of the fourteenth century, consisting of a low ground floor with great chamber above. The characterless lower room with heavily restored windows was probably used for storage. The great chamber is still approached from an outside stair to the original doorway with fine head-stop. The room retains its early open character with a contemporary wall fireplace (renewed hood) and external stack, some original window tracery, heavily restored in the mid-1930s, and a four-bay crown-strut roof. South doorways at both levels (upper new window) communicated with the ruined two-storeyed block to the south-west, possibly intended for storage with a subsidiary chamber above.

4. *c.*1320–6.

The small but fine rectangular chapel of knapped flint can be closely dated by its consecration in 1326.[2] The two-light side windows and the three-light east window with ogee cusped quatrefoils have been competently restored. The chapel retains its high-quality piscina and sedilia while the striking stained glass windows of 1936–51 are by the Australian artist John Trinick. The well-made three-bay roof is of crown-post form with moulded tie beams and wall plates. The brick-built covered way replaces an original feature, marked by the flint spur next to the chapel entry.

5. Later fourteenth century.

The ground-floor hall is undoubtedly the 'new hall' recorded as the work of Thomas Ickham, sacristan of St Augustine's between 1370 and 1391, erected at a cost of £66 13s. 4d.[3] It was 46 feet by 23 feet, and consisted of three bays lit by tall transomed windows on both sides. The cross passage lay at the north end but the offices here were replaced in 1629 when the hall was converted into a two-storeyed house and extended northwards. The outer walls were retained, with a traceried window on the east side, outline evidence of the others, a south doorway to the res-

PLATE 165 Salmestone Grange: 'new' hall and covered way fronting phase two range

idential accommodation, and the roof of crown-post construction of noticeably poorer quality than that over the chapel. Smoke-blackened timbers point to a central hearth.

No further changes were made apart from a splendid fireplace in one of the bedrooms (now destroyed), for the abbey seems to have preferred using the grange at Minster as its favoured retreat where its buildings were updated in the early fifteenth century.[4]

Salmestone does not follow the conventional plan but was a house of accretion. One of the best-preserved granges in England, it holds four different roofs displaying a clear sequence of regional development as well as a great chamber and chapel in retained early condition. The two parallel ranges and the 'new hall' are still occupied, so that the house reflects a planning 'messiness' today that is probably less removed from monastic reality than architectural historians would like to think.

NOTES

1 Two barns, one thatched and one tiled in 1647, stood south of the house until the early nineteenth century. The monastic chronicler Thomas Thorne recorded in 1318 that the grange was occupied by two monks and their household, and was surrounded by fields and orchards. T. Thorne, *Chronicle of St Augustine's Abbey, Canterbury*, trans. A. H. Davis (1934).

2 Register of Archbishop Walter Reynolds.

3 C. Cotton, *Arch. Cant.* 37 (1925) 159.

4 Because Minster Grange was such an isolated community on the Isle of Thanet, it enjoyed the rare distinction of its own mid-twelfth-century church, excavated in 1929–30. The two residential ranges of mid and late twelfth-century date were refashioned by abbot Hunden of St Augustine's (1405–20) in *c.*1413. His initials are in the spandrels above the north doorway of the north range. Both sides of the west range were refenestrated with transomed and cusped twin lights. The north range was more elaborately but on the south side only, where two cusped lights on each floor were separated by twin quatrefoil panels with blank shields to create a more formal façade. The hall was given a new crown-post roof at the same time. *Arch. Jour.* 86 (1929) 213–23; *Trans. Anc. Mon. Soc.* 17 (1970) 39–50.

W. A. S. Robertson, *Arch. Cant.* 12 (1878) 360–5
E. Impey, *A Guide to Salmestone Grange* (1992)
S. Pearson, Supplement to *Arch. Jour.* 151 (1994) 43–6

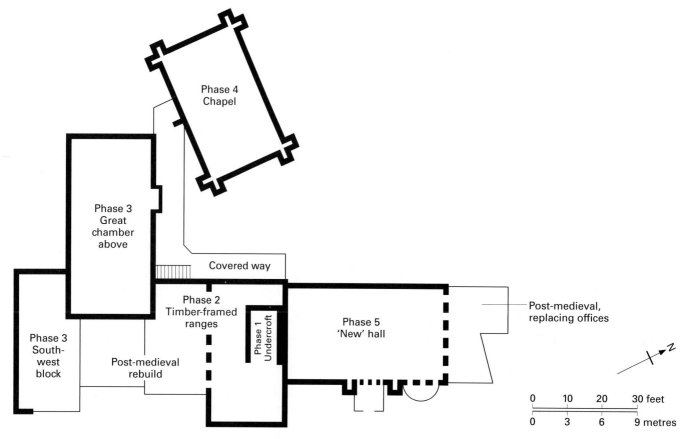

FIGURE 96 Salmestone Grange: site plan

SALTWOOD CASTLE, Kent

The manor of Saltwood was granted to the see of Canterbury in 1026. At the time of the Domesday Book, it was held by Lanfranc but in the keeping of Hugh de Montfort, a genuine companion of the Conqueror, to safeguard the Channel coastline; Hugh held as a tenant of the archbishop. His successor in the mid-twelfth century so disgraced himself on the field of battle that Henry II confiscated his estates in 1163, including Saltwood. The king's appointment of a belligerent castellan accelerated the tensions between Henry and his archbishop, and brought the castle into the mainstream of English history as the refuge for the murderers of Becket immediately before and after his martyrdom. Before the close of the century, Richard I had restored the property to the see of Canterbury, which held it until 1540 when it was conveyed to the crown, after which it declined into farm use with only the gatehouse sporadically inhabited.

Basically, Saltwood is an early ring work, subsequently strengthened by an encircling inner curtain broken by three simple rectangular towers of late twelfth-century date.[1] The entrance tower (fronted by the later gatehouse) lay astride the curtain but the others were built projecting inside the courtyard. At the same time, the timber-palisaded outer bailey was given the protection of a gateway. Considering its proximity to the coast, this castle was modest, almost crude. However, an important sequence of residen-

tial apartments was added during the fourteenth century, culminating in one of the major residential and defensive programmes of Richard II's reign.

The castle stands near Hythe on a promontory between two minor streams with the waters of the English Channel formerly closer than today. Like Leeds Castle, Saltwood was protected by water defences which were widened, probably in the later thirteenth century, into a lake on two sides. The courtyard's southern face overlooked this lake and was the obvious position for any major residential development[2] (fig. 97).

The earliest of these apartments is the single-storey hall, 59 feet by 32 feet, occupying the middle of the bailey wall which was essentially rebuilt. The deep porch with benches on either side and the tall gabled end wall indicate that it was an unaisled hall of good size and quality, but destruction means that little is known of its form or decorative character. The early form of the doorway at the upper end suggests that there was probably a contemporary upper chamber block, replaced in the late fourteenth century by the audience hall and the newly built accommodation facilities in the gatehouse. The relieving arch in this upper end wall could have supported a window in such a block looking into the hall, subsequently closed by Courtenay's work.

The contemporary lower chamber block is destroyed on three sides but door openings in the curtain wall indicate that it was three-storeyed and roofed at right angles to the hall. The cellar, now filled

PLATE 166 Saltwood Castle: engraving from the south-east by S. and N. Buck (1735)

but excavated in 1936, was approached independently from the courtyard. One corner of the ground-floor offices was partitioned off to provide access to the broad staircase in the south tower. Both floors above the offices consisted of a major residential apartment and tower-contained room (first floor with garderobe) and an independent mural passage to a further doorway. Destroyed walling makes the planning here unclear, but these first- and second-floor entries may have given lobby access to further rooms eastwards, rebuilt later in the century. The stairs also served a third-floor towered room with wall-walk approach.

This was a suite of apartments on the grandest scale, and can be paralleled with the three-storeyed end blocks at Chepstow and Ludlow castles (late thirteenth century) and the double block at Ludlow's upper end of early fourteenth-century date. The simple porch mouldings and door openings with two-centred heads could be late thirteenth century, but an unaisled hall and possible double chamber block point towards the early fourteenth century (fig. 98).

In the middle of the century, any second block was replaced by a grand two-storeyed extension – a low ground-floor chamber supporting an impressive reception room above with windows totally breaking the security of the outer wall which the earlier hall had respected. The ground-floor apartment was lit by three deep splayed and barred lights towards the courtyard, leaving the outer wall unbroken. The upper chamber, 56 feet by 22 feet, is lit by seven windows – three in the outer walls and one at the east end – each one of three cinquefoil traceried lights grooved for glass. Their heads continue across the intervening bays as wall arcading, stopping short of the destroyed west end possibly because of a balcony. The chamber was roofed with a timber structure of low pitch. With access principally from the broad mural passage in the adjacent three-storeyed block, this chamber was a grand reception room for honoured guests (without garderobe provision). As with the earlier work, there is no pertinent building documentation among the archiepiscopal records at Lambeth Palace, but on the evidence of similar window forms the reception chamber was built at about the same time as Etchingham church (1363) and Cobham College hall (c.1370).

A generation later, all buildings at the upper end of the hall were replaced by archbishop Courtenay (1381–96) to provide enhanced facilities appropriate to the primate of England. The grand staircase, principally approached from the courtyard but making use of the earlier door of the still-used hall, gave majestic access to this second hall and subsidiary access to its undercroft. Courtenay's audience hall was built at right angles to the earlier one and, in keeping with his concept of majesty, was raised like its contemporaries at Kenilworth and Portchester castles.

The undercroft, 53 feet by 20½ feet, is partially below the level of the courtyard and is approached by a broad doorway in the middle of the end wall. Its roof was carried on eight stone arches. Despite the four small light vents, this chamber would have been used for pages and staff in attendance on the lords above, with the steward's room at its far end.

The upper hall was restored by Philip Tilden for Lady Conway with 'particular freedom of expression' between 1936 and 1939.[3] Lord Clark who purchased Saltwood in 1953 told me that much of the walling had survived to battlement level but that the window tracery was totally by Tilden. Christopher Hussey also recorded that Tilden built his conjectural roof 6 feet lower than the original level to avoid a steeply pitched room obtruding above the silhouette of the existing ruins.[4] Yet Tilden's reconstruction was sympathetic to the spirit of the late fourteenth century, enhanced by a few medieval decorative elements collected by Sir Martin Conway.

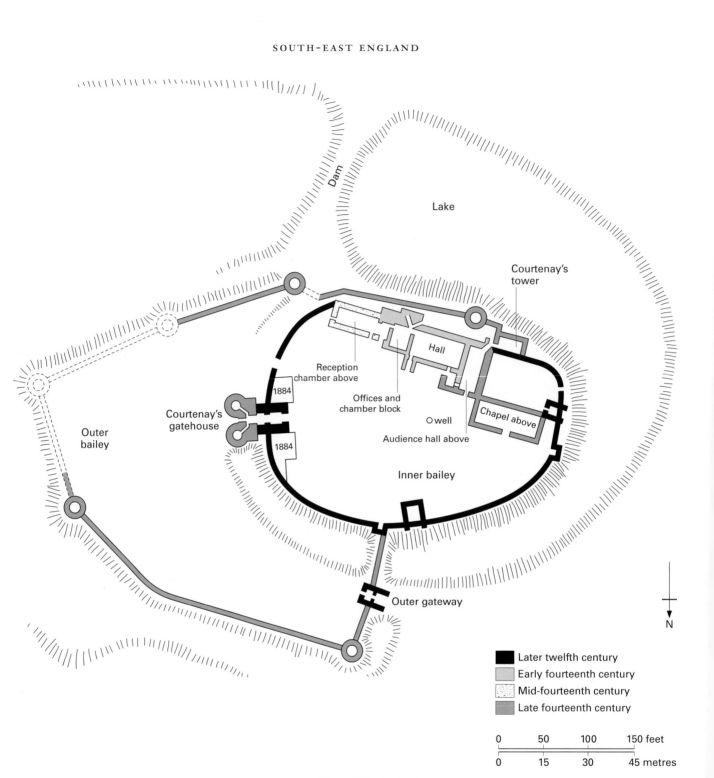

Key:
- ■ Later twelfth century
- ▨ Early fourteenth century
- ░ Mid-fourteenth century
- ▨ Late fourteenth century

FIGURE 97 Saltwood Castle: site plan

The hall, 54½ feet by 27 feet, is slightly larger than the undercroft. The dressed stonework of the doorway at the head of the stairs has been ripped out but the internal arch is of a simple two-centred form. The apartment is well lit by three two-light windows with transoms in the west wall and one of three lights with transoms in the north wall, all set within rear arches. Doorways at the upper end give access to a mural stair and wall-walk, maintained throughout all alterations, and a lobby to the principal room in the project-

ing tower. This contemporary addition, ruined at the time of the Conways' purchase, was restored for them by Tilden, who added the fireplaces, windows, and ceilings in both lobby and main chamber. This tower provided substantial residential accommodation on three floors – one for the steward, an ante-chamber and retiring room for Courtenay, and a room above reached from the wall-walk which may have been used as a treasury or security store.[5]

Courtenay's chapel at right angles to his hall was linked by a short

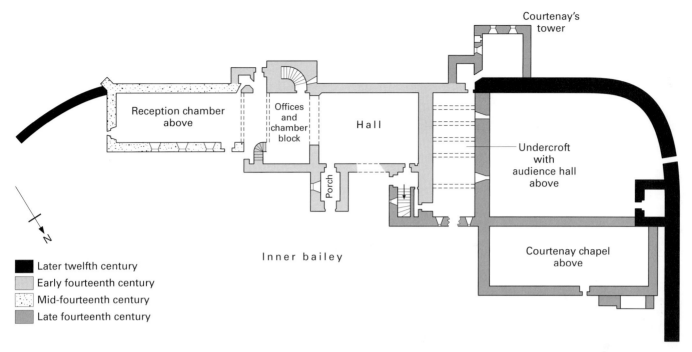

Courtenay's
tower

Reception chamber
above

Offices
and
chamber
block

Hall

Porch

Undercroft
with
audience hall
above

Inner bailey

Courtenay chapel
above

N

■ Later twelfth century
▨ Early fourteenth century
▧ Mid-fourteenth century
▦ Late fourteenth century

FIGURE 98 Saltwood Castle: ground plan of residential apartments

passage (restored) at first-floor level corbelled above their common junction. The chapel is a two-storeyed structure, 75 feet by 27 feet, built at the same time as the hall, more extended than it but sharing a common offset 3 feet from the ground. Two of its walls stand 12 and 14 feet high, with the entrance to the ground-floor room in the middle of the principal courtyard wall, but the openings in the opposite wall are later insertions. The large projection towards the west end marks the base of the stair to the generous first-floor chapel with its piscina close to the corbelled passage. It has been improved by Lady Conway, but a drawing of 1888 confirms its position at that time and makes it likely that this was the chapel consecrated by archbishop Arundel in 1401.

This imposing line of residential apartments would have been supported by offices, lodgings, and services which have failed to survive. The grass-covered footings close to the north-west curtain are evidence of such structures, while the kitchen may have been a detached building near the well, 55 feet deep, in the middle of the courtyard.

Courtenay's residential work was preceded by his updating Saltwood's defences in the light of the French and Castilian raids of 1377–80. Apart from the earlier gateway, the outer bailey has been attributed to a range of dates from the early thirteenth century[6] to the late fourteenth century.[7] No licence to crenellate was sought, but the rebuilding of the bailey with added concentric protection on the south side was possibly initiated by Sudbury[8] and completed by Courtenay.[9] The comparable outwork at Cooling Castle (1381–5), also capable of accommodating substantial armed forces, was defended by similar circular towers. The elongated loopholes with their short cross slots are comparable to those at Hever (c.1383) and Cooling castles, while the 'inverted keyhole' gunloops in the tower overlooking the dam can be dated to the decade 1380–90 by comparison with work at the West Gate, Canterbury,

Southampton, and Cooling. Even so, the crossbow slits are an anachronism.[10]

Dominating the whole site is Courtenay's extremely impressive gatehouse, in front of and incorporating the earlier inner entry. Externally formidable, with particularly tall drum towers placed fairly close together, machicoulis, portcullis, and drawbridge rebate with chain holes, this gatehouse thrusts forward boldly across the earlier moat like a self-contained tower-house. Courtenay's splendid architectural creation, bearing his arms and those of Courtenay impaling Canterbury, is in no way belittled by the sympathetic rear additions of 1884 by Beeston which restored its habitable splendour.

Four-storeyed with towers rising higher to nearly 80 feet, this gatehouse was well provided with heated chambers on all floors and garderobes (chutes grouped at rear). The two hexagonal guardrooms, the outer passage (only one bay original), and the principal first-floor chamber were all vaulted. Other original elements include fireplaces with four-centred heads, some doors, and a little medieval glazing.

Attributed with justification to Henry Yevele,[11] this gatehouse is an architectural masterpiece. Through its aspiring proportions, the careful positioning of the offsets and windows, the quality and clean lines of the stonework, the internal flight of steps within the vaulted entrance passage, and its total projection across the moat and in front of the earlier gateway and curtain wall to create a dominating effect, the Saltwood gatehouse is a fitting climax to one of the major building programmes of late fourteenth-century England. Defence and residence have rarely been in such harmony, not even in the tower-house at Warkworth Castle, and hardly ever within an architectural composition of such overwhelming nobility.

Saltwood is a complex but little-known castle displaying an impressive sequence of high-status reception rooms under the

PLATE 167 Saltwood Castle: gatehouse from the east

formidable protection of water and concentric defences. Its partial restoration in the 1880s and 1930s and occupation by two eminent art historians – Sir Martin Conway and Lord Clark – have imbued the site with qualities of respect and care that are a refreshing antidote to some of the overmanicured and overrestored properties in south-east England. Even so, Saltwood Castle awaits the detailed architectural, landscape, and documentary assessment that such a rewarding high-status residence richly deserves.

NOTES

1 Charles Coulson draws my attention to the enigmatic entries of a *turris* recorded in 1163 and the punitive destruction of 1175 costing 20s. in the Pipe Rolls after the reception of Becket's assassins.

2 Matthew Johnson draws attention to the major element of designed landscape here as at Ludgershall, Kenilworth, Fotheringhay, and Bodiam castles: *Behind the Castle Gate* (2002) 40–1.

3 P. Tilden, *True Remembrances* (1954) 165.

4 Hussey (1942).

5 Like the contemporary activity at Dartington Hall, the restoration of the grand stairs, audience hall, and tower rooms during the 1930s re-created a particularly important sequence of archiepiscopal work to something approaching its original grandeur. The fact that the hall was used by Sir Martin Conway to display some of his medieval tapestries and by Lord Clark as his working library enhanced the value of Tilden's work.

6 D. J. Cathcart King, *Castellarium Anglicanum*, I (1983) 237.

7 J. Newman, *The Buildings of England: North-East and East Kent* (1969) 425.

8 *Cal. Close Rolls: 1377–81*, 404.

9 In 1382, Courtenay sold materials from a house near Saltwood and other manor houses to defray his expenses, *Jour. Brit. Arch. Assoc.* 20 (1914) 198.

10 The earlier inner bailey wall may have been upgraded at the same time.

11 *Eng. Med. Arch.* (1984) 361–6. He is known to have been responsible for Cooling Castle with defensive characteristics similar to those at Saltwood, and to have advised Canterbury city on strengthening its walls, the crown on repairing the castle there, and Courtenay and the priory of Christ Church on the design of the new nave. The West Gate at Canterbury (*c.*1378–80), credited to Yevele on stylistic grounds, is a precursor of the Saltwood structure, a powerful composition albeit on a smaller scale.

F. Beeston, *An Archaeological Description of Saltwood Castle* (*c.*1890)
C. Hussey, *Country Life* (November/December 1942)

SCOTNEY CASTLE, Kent

On the edge of the Kent and Sussex border south of Lamberhurst, Roger Ashburnham's castle at Scotney lies in the unfrequented valley of the River Bewl. The castle was built on two islands within an encircling moat which was expanded on the south side to form a small lake.

Little medieval stonework survives. The rectangular outer ward, slightly smaller than the inner ward, retains its revetment but no internal structures other than two stumps of the outer gateway. The inner gateway was a passage flanked by four piers formerly supporting a chamber above.[1] The lower courses survive of the wall enclosing the rhomboid-shaped inner ward and the emplacement of the four circular angle towers. These were two storeys high and the south tower still stands to its machicolated parapet and pyramid-capped roof. The two rooms were courtyard-approached, the upper from an external stair. This tower and the associated south curtain with doorway illustrate the association of two- and four-centred arches so common in the late fourteenth century. As at Amberley Castle, a residential cross range bisected the ward and dominated it. Today, the hall range is a rebuild of *c.*1630 attached to a more cottage-like block of *c.*1580.[2]

The manor of Scotney existed by the early twelfth century, and a house within the next two centuries, but the castle was erected by Roger Ashburnham, probably in response to the invasion scare of the late 1370s. He had inherited the estate in 1358 and had become a prominent local administrator. As Conservator of the Peace for Kent and Sussex from about 1376 to 1380 (with Sir John Etchingham and Sir Edward Dalyngrigge of Bodiam), he recognised the need to protect his property from raiding forces, even though it lay nearly 20 miles from the sea. There is no documentary evidence for its construction, although the machicolated tower is similar to contemporary work at Cooling and Bodiam castles and the small triangular piers occur at Hever Castle. The site has never been excavated or subject to geophysical survey, but Christopher Hussey suggested that the outer ward was the site of an earlier house and that Ashburnham's work was the creation of the new inner ward at the same time that he diverted the River Bewl to create a wider moat and lake.[3] Ashburnham died in 1392.

Scotney was built of large blocks of locally quarried stone. It was a strongly fortified house, though the gateway was modest, the towers were low, and there were no gunports. The significance of this castle does not lie in its modest stone remains but in the water-developed site. Like Bodiam, the site of Ashburnham's residence was weak, overlooked by sharply rising ground to the west. The residence was therefore given extensive water protection as occurred at Bodiam, at Saltwood, and earlier at Leeds Castle. Even so, an incision in the embankment separating the river from the moat would have drained it, though the subsidiary stream and springs would have maintained it as a quagmire. The water defences were essentially to persuade marauders to move to easier targets elsewhere.

Yet the defensive motive can be overplayed. As at Nunney and Bodiam castles, the visual appearance and approach cannot be ignored. A visitor coming from the west towards the outer gate at the south end of the site made a processional approach of visual interest and surprise. We know of a considerable number of medieval élite-managed landscapes, many water-enhanced.[4] Unlike Bodiam, early nineteenth-century landscaping round the castle has disguised the line of the initial approach. Research may be able to identify this, but even without such information, it can be appreciated that the water defences at Scotney were those appropriate to a knight's or magnate's residence, although Ashburnham was only gentry. The moats and lakes were as much a reflection of the imagery and symbolism that Ashburnham sought as the display of technology and protection that had been initiated by defensive needs.

Today, the ruins are romantically reflected in the lily-filled moat, for Scotney is a classic example of the early nineteenth-century

PLATE 168 Scotney Castle: south tower

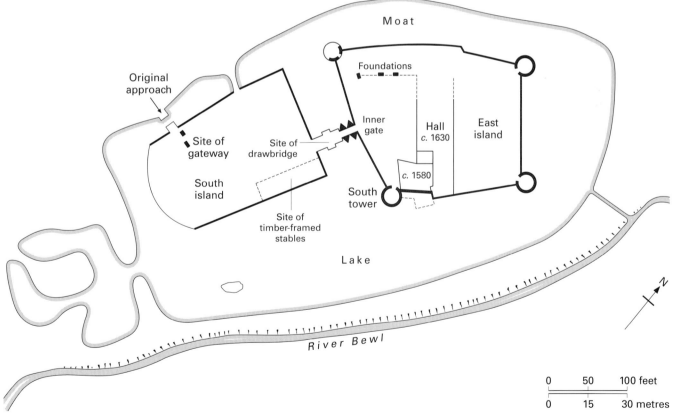

FIGURE 99 Scotney Castle: site plan

405

Picturesque movement of landscape gardening. Unlike Penshurst and the castles at Leeds and Hever, the medieval buildings at Scotney are now entirely subsidiary to the gardens and setting, although deservedly used as their exquisite focal point.

NOTES

1 Will of Thomas Darell, 1558. Hussey (1955) 5.
2 Well shown in F. Grose, Supplement to *Antiquities of England and Wales*, II (1787) 64.
3 Hussey (1955) 2, 5. The third small island to the south-west with a sculpture by Henry Moore has been modified substantially since the site plans made by Edward Hussey in *c*.1837. It may well have been created some time after Ashburnham's development of the site.
4 M. Johnson, *Behind the Castle Gate* (2002) 33–54.

E. Hussey, *Arch. Cant*. 17 (1887) 38–48
C. Hussey, *Country Life* (July 1920; September 1956; October 1969)
C. Hussey, *A History of Scotney Castle : Guide Book* (1955, reprinted 1979)

SOUTH CHARFORD MANOR, Hampshire

Dairy House Farm in the tiny settlement of South Charford, 2 miles west of Breamore, retains a highly unusual and little-known brick tower built by Sir John Popham during the mid fifteenth century.[1] Constructed by a professional soldier and veteran of the French wars, the manor house was moat-enclosed and the tower retains the platform of a substantially built timber-framed and jettied top storey.

Nothing else survives of the manor house apart from the tower, for it was replaced by Dairy House Farm in the seventeenth century, a two-storeyed, timber-framed building, brick clad and extended in the eighteenth century. The three-storeyed tower stands at one end of the house, crowned by a later pyramid roof. The tower is quite small, 17 feet by nearly 14 feet externally, with walls only 2 feet thick and lacking stone quoins above ground level. The bricks are an unusual pale biscuit colour, 9 in. by 4½ in. by about 1¼ to 2 in., laid in English bond, with ashlar dressings.

The ground floor retains the stone jambs of the original east entrance but not its arched head. The rear arch has a timber lintel. There is a single blocked light in the north wall, only 3 inches wide, with joint evidence of one opposite, and the chamfered sill of a third light (rebuilt brick jambs) in the west wall. The three ceiling joists seem to be original.

Of the two entrances to the occupied first floor, that on the south side was probably the original one and the other possibly a window. Both doorways have eighteenth-century moulded architraves. The second floor retains its chamfered entrance with steep four-centred head, and a recess in the south-west corner which may have been a garderobe. The narrow west window with square head, stanchion, and saddle-bars was grooved for glass and retains an original shutter. The floor was raised by 6 inches in the seventeenth century when the wooden entry door was replaced.

The third floor was a jettied timber structure that projected 1½ feet beyond the outer face of the tower. It is now represented by no more than its heavy platform under the present seventeenth-century roof after the framed walls were pulled down and the jetty cut back on two sides. The principal cross members, at least those on the east and south sides, were carried on substantial curved and

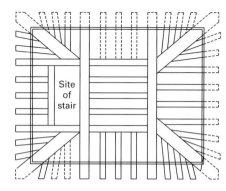

THIRD FLOOR PLATFORM

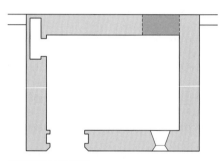

SECOND FLOOR

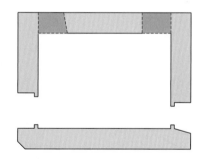

FIRST FLOOR

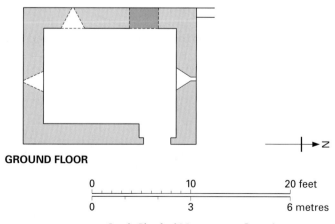

GROUND FLOOR

FIGURE 100 South Charford Manor: tower floor plans

chamfered brackets of which one survives, presumably resting on stone corbels. The dragon beams were similarly braced on corbels that remain. The upper face of the platform timbers were pared to carry the sill plate to the former top storey. An area to the south, now spanned by a narrow inserted timber, marks the position of the stair to this storey.[2]

The relative thinness of the walls and the lack of any defensive superstructure show that it was not a military tower. The small size of the rooms, only 13 feet by 10 feet internally, and the absence of fireplaces suggest that if this was a residential tower it was only in a supporting role to a larger structure. A lease of 23 March 1530 helps to clarify its context, for Anne Bulkeley and her son Robert granted John and Peter Trepoke of Breamore 'all the scite of the manor of Suthcharford with all the londes, medewes, pastures . . . except and reserved to the seid Anne and Robert . . . with all the mote and ponds, a lytell new enclosed orchard, the half garden, the grete hall and towre with the cross chamber, a kechyn, 2 chambers in the gate howse, a convenyant stable for the seid Anne and Robert . . . when [they] wull lye, inhabite, dwell or tarry upon the said manor'.[3]

All these buildings have disappeared without record, but it is likely that the tower adjoined the cross range, probably across the first- and second-floor doorways at the south-east angle, with the lack of abutting evidence pointing to a timber-framed structure. The ground floor was entered externally, while the jettied top storey, stair-approached internally, would have been a look-out with distant views across the flat land of the Avon valley.[4] The context of this structure is all the more interesting because there is little doubt that it was constructed by Sir John Popham and is the earliest known use of brick in Hampshire.

South Charford Manor was held by Oliver Zouche and his family during the first half of the fourteenth century but there is a gap in its ownership until it was acquired by Sir John Popham before 1428.[5] The Pophams had been established in Hampshire since the early twelfth century and had frequently represented the county in parliament during the fourteenth century. Sir John was a member of a cadet branch of the family, who is first recorded in 1418 when he was granted the custody of Southampton Castle that his father had held at the time of his death that year. Sir John held a third of a knights fee at South Charford in 1428 and a quarter of one at North Charford, and purchased or acquired a small and scattered group of manors during the next thirty years.[6] John fought under Edward, duke of York at Agincourt and under Henry V at the siege of Rouen, and remained in Normandy under Bedford, well rewarded for his military and administrative activities. He was chancellor of Anjou and Maine, but changed from military to diplomatic service during the mid-1430s, beginning with the Congress of Arras. After Bedford's death, Popham became a retainer of Richard, duke of York, and as their friendship burgeoned he was employed on diplomatic missions across Brittany and Normandy, held the treasurership of the royal household from 1437 to 1439, was elected member of parliament for Hampshire in 1439–40, and appointed to York's council. By the mid-1440s, he was past active employment in the field, and though his diplomatic standing was high,[7] he declined to be elected speaker of the Commons in 1449 on the grounds of age and poor health. There is no evidence that Popham married,[8] and he was buried in the London Charterhouse where he had endowed two chapels ten years previously.

The tower is clearly fifteenth century and may be reasonably attributed to a relatively wealthy owner who had served under three leaders notable for their interest in brick (Henry V at Sheen, Bedford at Fulbrooke, and York at Hunsdon) as well as a colleague of that circle of professional soldiers whose residences reflected the same taste (Sir John Fastolf, Sir Andrew Ogard, and Ralph, Lord Cromwell). Construction between about 1428 and 1463 can be narrowed to the probability of the 1440s and 1450s, making the use of brick in the region anticipatory by two generations before Bishop's Waltham Palace, Basing House, and Warblington 'Castle'. The wet moat still surrounds the house platform on the south and east sides – broad on the south, rechannelled on the east. The gatehouse possibly stood close to the present north-east entry across the dry ditch.

NOTES

1 It is not recorded in the county volume by Pevsner and Lloyd, and barely so in the relevant one by the VCH. It was discovered and surveyed by N. J. Moore in 1982.
2 The flue at this level marks the position of a removed west-facing stack serving eighteenth-century inserted first- and second-floor hearths, now blocked.
3 Hampshire Record Office IM53/1389.
4 The fifteenth-century brick stair turret at Riccall Manor House, Yorkshire, similarly terminated in a look-out chamber across the meadows of the River Ouse. A. Emery, *Greater Med. Houses*, I (1996) 187.
5 VCH, *Hampshire*, IV (1911) 562.
6 J. S. Roskell, *Proc. Hampshire F. C. and A. Soc.* 21 (1958) 40–1.
7 He was nominated for the Garter in 1447, though the king of Portugal was elected instead. For Popham's career, *ibid.* 38–52.
8 He settled South Charford Manor on Alice, the wife of William Herteshorn, *ibid.*

SOUTHFLEET RECTORY, Kent

Since the 1950s, this mid-fourteenth-century house between Dartford and Gravesend has been divided into two residences known as Friary Court and Old Friary. It is made up of a hall flanked by a two-storeyed upper cross wing and a replacement services end – an early example of the common late medieval house plan in southern England. The house was originally flint-faced, but it has been partly covered in cement.

The hall has been divided into two floors and so altered during the early nineteenth century that the principal survivals are the large two-light transomed windows in the side walls with ogee-headed lights with split cusps and a sexfoil head, under a square hood mould that is possibly later.[1] There are two on the entrance front, flanked by a small dais light, and one on the opposite side. This two-bay hall consisted of a cross passage marked by the remains of a spere truss opening into the body of the apartment, with a short upper bay. The hall is spanned centrally by a tie beam with crown-post truss but that over the dais bay, possibly supporting a canopy, has been removed. The roof retains louvred evidence.

The form and date of the services block is not known, for its replacement, now a staircase hall, is early nineteenth century. The upper chamber wing is a substantial one, a cross wing with a rear extension. It was divided into three principal rooms at both levels, a three-bay chamber, a one-bay inner chamber, and a garderobe block. The ground-floor rooms are lit by single cinquefoil lights and the upper floor by similar twin-headed lights. Both floors were independently approached, with no internal link. The upper floor seems to have been approached by an external stair to the doorway into the withdrawing chamber, now converted into a window. The chamber retains fireplace evidence and its crown-post roof. The garderobe may have been divided from the inner chamber by a timber-framed partition. The whole marks a development stage between the upper block of *c*.1290 at Old Soar Manor and the contemporary double solar development at Ightham Mote.

The house is usually attributed to Thomas Alkham, rector of Southfleet from 1323[2] and chancellor of Rochester diocese from 1327. He died in 1356 in a house architecturally attributable to the second quarter of the fourteenth century and probably to the 1340s.[3]

NOTES

1 RCHM (1994) 118.
2 Rigold (1967) 18–21.
3 A second but less well-preserved contemporary stone rectory with hall and solar block survives at Cliffe at Hoo. K. Gravett in *Collectanea Historica*, ed. A. Detsicas (1981) 187–91; RCHM (1994) 39–40.

S. E. Rigold, *Dartford District Antiquarian Society Newsletter* 4 (1967) 18–21
RCHM, *Gazetteer of Medieval Houses in Kent* (1994) 117–18

STARKEY 'CASTLE', Kent

The fortress appellation was probably first added to this manor house during the late eighteenth century. It is an almost complete fourteenth-century house standing exposed on the edge of the marshes of the River Medway 2 miles south-west of Rochester. It consists of a hall with services and chamber cross wing, and an added annex under a hipped roof at the south-west angle. The upper chamber block was pulled down during the early eighteenth century. The house is built of Kentish ragstone with chalk dressings. It was refurbished after sale in 1808 but sank to farmhouse status from which it was rescued in the late 1970s when it was stripped of most later accretions.

Access is by opposing doorways to the cross passage, both with two-centred heads with unbroken mouldings, although that on the east side is more elaborate. There were no protecting porches. The two-bay hall has been floored and partitioned, possibly in the mid-sixteenth century, although the upper floor was reopened to the roof as a single chamber in 1980. The upper end of the original hall was lit by a tall three-light window which dominates the entrance front and is now filled with Regency tracery of simplified fourteenth-century style. The barrel-shaped roof is supported on three heavily moulded arch-braced trusses carried on stone corbels of angel's heads and shields, with the thrust of the central truss

PLATE 169 Starkey 'Castle': from the east

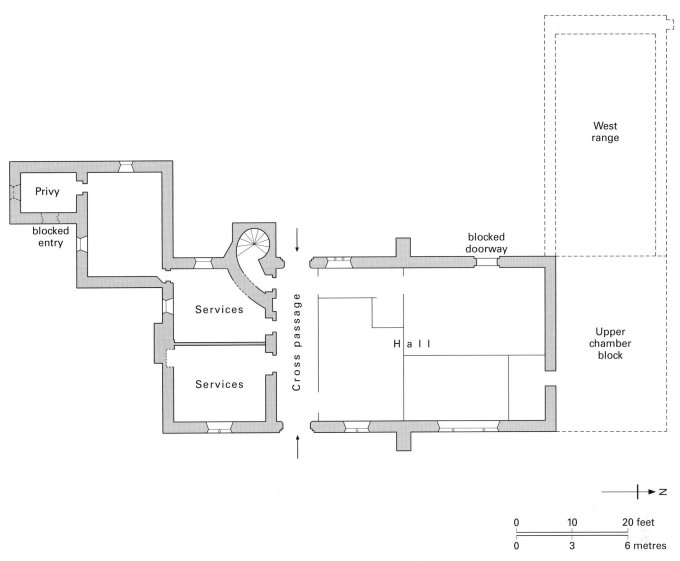

FIGURE 101 Starkey 'Castle': ground floor

carried on the only buttresses at Starkey. There was formerly much evidence, in the 1960s, of soot blackening from an open fire.[1]

Doorways with two-centred heads open from the screens passage into two chambers in the lower block separated by a timber-framed partition, while a third entry gives newel access in a projecting turret to the upper chamber. This imposing room has tall transverse gables supporting a roof comparable to that in the hall, again of two bays with three moulded trusses carried on stone corbels with blank shields. However, it differs from the larger roof in several respects for while the hall is a common rafter roof with no true principal trusses, the chamber roof has a steeper pitch, more substantial timbers, and moulded purlins and rafters. The two roofs are probably co-eval, though the possibility of a late fifteenth-century remodelling cannot be excluded. The chamber is lit by a substantial three-light window (and Regency tracery) in the east wall, with a later fifteenth-century fireplace replacing an earlier one. The added block at the south-west angle provides a larger outer and smaller inner chamber at both levels, a reflection of the earlier prac-

tice at Old Soar Manor. The smaller chamber was a garderobe with access facility in its south-east face.

The foundations have been traced of the upper chamber block, approached from a two-centred doorway in the west wall to a projecting stair. Two corbels and a rebate for the floor indicate that this cross wing was two-storeyed. The brick in the end wall of the hall was inserted during the early eighteenth century when the block was replaced by brick outbuildings demolished in 1980. Excavations for a 1990s extension west of this block revealed a fifteenth-century cellared range.[2]

The house is a relatively complete single build with two service chambers and no obvious kitchen facility, though a late sixteenth-century estate map shows a detached louvred building west of the house that may have served such a purpose.[3] The house has substantial pretensions to comfort. The doorway and window mouldings suggest that it was built during the second half of the fourteenth century, closer to the last quarter than the beginning of the third. If the simplified window tracery in the principal window was replaced by cusped lights, then it would not be unlike that adopted at Cobham College hall in *c*.1370. The chamfer above the foundations of the house continues round the secondary chamber block but at a slightly different height, and this, with the lower roof and fifteenth century window form throughout, suggests that it was built to provide additional accommodation a century after the construction of the house.[4]

The manor was owned by the bishop of Rochester in 1334 and there is documentary evidence of a house in the early fourteenth century, but the present structure is of later date.[5] Hasted mentions that the property was in the possession of Richard Bysets in the reign of Edward III and that it was purchased in the later fifteenth century by Sir Humphrey Starkey, chief baron of the Exchequer in 1484 (d.1493 without heirs). The house was probably erected by Bysets in *c*.1370 and modified by Starkey in the later fifteenth century, when he erected the north-east range at the same time that he divided the hall, and added the garderobe wing. Harris and Hasted attest to the former existence of 'a handsome chapel' while early estate maps indicate substantial but now lost outbuildings.[6]

NOTES

1 Swain (1966) 123.
2 Ward, Cross, and Bennett (1990). The site was covered by an extension in 1992, linked to the hall by a corridor and an uncomfortably designed wood-enclosed stair.
3 *Ibid*. 251.
4 Ward *et al*. (1990) prefer a single late fifteenth-century date for the whole house.
5 It was known as the manor of Lyttlyhall and Wouldham. E. Hasted, *History and Topographical Survey of Kent* (2nd edn 1798) IV, 403; J. Harris, *The History of Kent* (1719) 337.
6 Ward *et al*. (1990) 250–2.

E. R. Swain, *Arch. Cant.* 81 (1966) 118–25
E. Mercer, *NMRC Report* 39731
A. Ward, R. Cross and P. Bennett, *Arch. Cant.* 108 (1990) 244–52

STERBOROUGH CASTLE, Surrey and the Cobham family

The Cobham family acquired Sterborough in the late thirteenth century. A licence to crenellate the site was granted to Reginald Cobham in October 1341,[1] followed two years later by a licence to build a chapel.[2] By her will of 1369, Cobham's widow, eight years after her husband's death, was 'holding a little fort built like a castle with a very strong wall, and a hall, chambers, other buildings, and a new garden'.[3] At that time, the hall held a great dorser with the nine kings standing therein, while the castle briefly touched local fame through hosting the captive duke of Orléans after Agincourt.

The site is a low-lying one on the Surrey–Kent border, midway between Lingfield where the family are buried and the castle built a generation later by a branch of the Cobham family at Hever. The perimeter stone walls of Sterborough Castle rise 3 feet above the level of the moat, a particularly broad and extended barrier on its eastern side. The castle was quadrangular, with small round towers at each corner and broader rectangular projections on three sides, with that facing south forming the gatehouse. The plan lacked the crisp regularity of Bodiam and Cooling castles. Nothing else survives, for the castle was thoroughly destroyed in 1649 and any residual walls were removed when the interior was landscaped in the mid-eighteenth century. In 1754, a two-storeyed stone and embattled garden house was erected in the north-east corner on earlier foundations, and the remainder of the site was piled high with soil and planted with trees and paths. The whole site was landscaped again in 1986–9, when the moat retaining walls were capped with brick. No medieval structures were found during this activity, though any early foundations lie several feet below the present soil level.

Sterborough Castle is an incipient Bodiam design with its broad moat, circular angle towers, square projections between them, central courtyard, and enclosing two-storeyed residential ranges. It is even closer in form and date to Westenhanger Castle, crenellated in 1344, while the drawing made by Wenceslaus Hollar in about 1640 shows that it had an affinity with Hever Castle.[4] The corner towers were small, tall, and almost toy-like in appearance, the gatehouse had frontal buttress supports, and both sites have external triangular projections to support chimney flues. The largest unbroken side at Sterborough, opposite the gatehouse, would have been the site of the hall. The offices lay to its left with the oddly shaped corner tower containing the kitchen hearths, while Hollar's engraving shows that the buttressed eastern projection carried the chapel. The whole was moat-surrounded as an integral landscaping element rather than for defence.

THE COBHAM FAMILY

The Cobham family began as lawyers, had become local gentry before the mid-thirteenth century, and rose to the baronage within a hundred years. By the mid-fourteenth century, there were at least three branches of the family, and their many siblings created an extensive and confusing network of relationships which is only too apparent when contemplating the many brasses and tombs in Cobham and Lingfield churches. They lived not far from each other, close to the Medway and its tributary, the Eden. At the accession of Richard II, John 3rd Lord Cobham (late 1320s–1408) lived at Cobham and Cowling Castle near Rochester, and Reginald 2nd Lord Cobham (1361–1403) at Sterborough Castle near Lingfield. Between them lay the residences of Sir Thomas Cobham of Rundale (1343–94), who occupied Allington Castle near Maidstone, and his relation John Cobham who came from Devonshire and built Hever Castle.[5]

The family were used extensively in local government, parliament, and administration. The lords Cobham and Sir Thomas were commissioners of peace for their counties in 1381, but it is uncertain if the John Cobham who represented Kent in the parliaments of 1391, 1394, and 1397 was the Cobham of Hever or not.[6] John, 3rd Lord Cobham was first summoned to parliament in 1355, served in several expeditions to France between 1359 and 1376, and sufficiently impressed the court to be employed on at least three embassies. He lived at the manors of Cobham and Cooling, 6 miles to the north, and undertook a broad range of building activities throughout the middle years of his extraordinary long life. Nothing survives of his prime residence which stood on the site of the 1662 central block of the present Cobham Hall, although the wings of *c*.1582–1603 were an attempt to extend and update the medieval family home.[7] In 1362, Cobham initiated his foundation of a college of chantry priests at Cobham by enlarging the existing church. He

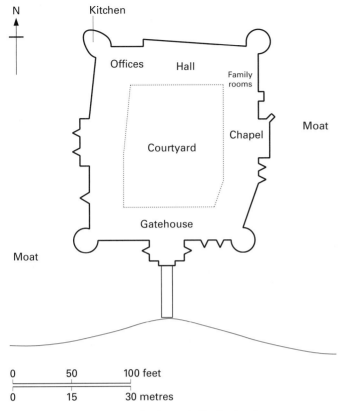

N

Kitchen

Offices   Hall

Family
rooms

Moat

Courtyard

Chapel

Gatehouse

Moat

| 0 | 50 | 100 feet |
| 0 | 15 | 30 metres |

FIGURE 102 Sterborough Castle: site plan

retained the thirteenth-century nave and choir, but built the west tower, refenestrated the nave and aisles, and added the sedilia and piscina. In 1370, construction began on the complementary hall, quadrangle, and chambers for a master and seven priests, originally linked to the church by a bridge. Work was nearing completion in 1383,[8] and since 1596 the castle has continued to serve a domestic purpose as an almshouse.[9]

French coastal attacks in the late 1370s endangered Cobham's manor at Cooling which had been in the hands of the family since the mid-thirteenth century. Richard II's appeal to defend the coastline was taken up by Cobham, who replaced the dilapidated house with the present castle between about 1379 and 1385, with the licence to crenellate granted in February 1381. As the copper panel in English on the outer gateway in the form of a charter proclaims, the work was constructed for the 'help of the cuntre' while Cobham called on the services of the royal mason, Henry Yevele, who oversaw a plan of the simplest design[10] (pl. 113). John Cobham had responded to the dangers of the late 1370s in a more private way by obtaining a licence to crenellate his residence at Hever. Towards the close of the fourteenth century, therefore, all four leading members of the family were living in defendable residences.

During these years, the 3rd Lord Cobham seems to have become uncomfortable with the policies of the young Richard II and was one of the members of the reforming commission in 1386 and an appellant who impeached several of the king's favourites in 1388. He suffered from the king's counter-attack at the Shrewsbury Parliament in 1398, was impeached, and was banished to Jersey until he was able to return following the accession of Henry IV in

1399. Cobham was well over eighty when he died in 1408 and it was because he had no heirs that his building activity was so extensive. Although buried at the Grey Friars in London, the contemporary brass of him at Cobham holding the church in his hands, together with the inscribed copper plate of purpose on the outer gate at Cooling Castle, proclaims the twin motivations of spiritual and civic concern that dominated his life. Six hundred years later, his work at Cobham still offers domestic and spiritual comfort, with the college, hidden behind the church, continuing to provide accommodation for pensioners in the tranquillity of the Kent countryside.

The inscription on the tomb of the 2nd Lord Cobham of Sterborough (d.1403) suggests that he was as distinguished for his military services and sage council as for his sumptuous hospitality. But although the Cobhams were of regional importance, most Kentish families were content with an essentially local influence – traditional rather than innovatory in outlook.

NOTES

1 *Cal. Pat. Rolls: 1340–43*, 304. The site was known at that time as Prinkham.
2 Manning and Bray (1809) 341.
3 *Cal. Inq. P.M.* 12 (1938) 327, and VCH, IV (1912) 305.
4 Manning and Bray (1809) 367.
5 Sir Thomas Cobham's father, John Cobham, held the manor of Hever at the time of his death in 1362. John Cobham was therefore related to the Rundale rather than the Sterborough or Cobham branch of the family. For the history of the family, see *Com. Peer.*, III (1913) 343–54; *Arch. Cant.* 9 (1877) 49–112; *Surrey Arch. Coll.* 2 (1864) 115–94; and Napier (1973) 373–425.
6 T. May, *Arch. Cant.* 82 (1967) 1–31.
7 The residence had been neglected in favour of Cooling since the early fifteenth century when the Lollard Sir John Oldcastle and his wife, Lord Cobham's granddaughter, lived there (and he only the most well known of her five husbands). Only one daughter was issue from all these marriages and it was her great grandson who was in occupation when Sir Thomas Wyatt of Allington Castle assaulted and captured the castle in 1554.
8 J. Harvey, *Eng. Med. Arch.* (1984) 231.
9 C. Hussey, *Country Life* (December 1943/February 1944). Sir Reginald Cobham of Sterborough continued the family tradition by founding a college at Lingfield in 1431 similar to that at Cobham but on a smaller scale. Nothing remains of the stone and timber-framed lodgings built at the west end of the churchyard round a small cloistered court with a hall and parlour for a master, six chaplains, and some clerks. Aubrey, *History of Surrey*, III (1911) 64. The parish church was made collegiate by Sir Reginald and his wife and largely rebuilt by them except the tower.
10 The relevant documents are transcribed in *Arch. Cant.* 2 (1859) 95–102, and are discussed in 9 (1877) 128–44. See also L. F. Salzman, *Building in England down to 1540* (1952) 461–2, and Harvey, *Eng. Med. Arch.* 361–2. Other works include, D. Knoop, G. P. Jones, and N. B. Lewis, *Ars Quatuor Coronatorum* (Trans. of Quatuor Coronati Lodge) 45 (*c*.1932) 48–53, and *Arch. Cant.* 46 (1934) 52–6. For a radical reappraisal of Cooling Castle, M. Johnson, *Behind the Castle Gate* (2002) xiii–xix. It is possible that the prestigious qualities of the college and church tower at Cobham were also the result of Yevele's involvement. John Harvey, *Henry Yevele* (1946) 30, 37. Lord Cobham certainly used him in 1381 for the new south aisle and porch at St Dunstans in the East in Tower Street (near Thames Street), where Cobham had his London house, and two years later Yevele designed a new stone bridge across the Medway at Rochester, part paid for by Cobham, who donated the bridge chapel. The church was destroyed in the Great Fire and the bridge was replaced by one 70 yards north in 1857.

O. Manning and W. Bray, *History of Surrey*, II (1809) 341–7

J. W. Flower, *Surrey Arch. Coll.* 2 (1864) 115–94

J. D. Mackenzie, *The Castles of England*, I (1897) 100–1

VCH, *Surrey*, IV (1912) 304–6

F. H. Napier, *Lingfield: The Story of a Surrey Parish* (1973): typescript copy in Lingfield library

SWANBOROUGH MANOR, Sussex

Swanborough Manor was built as a grange of Lewes Priory, the principal house of the Cluniac order in England. The origin of this particularly early structure was a single-storey hall range, 37 feet by 15½ feet, open to the roof. Of early thirteenth-century date, its origins are marked by an oculus in the end wall, a single lancet in the north wall, and the original entry evidence. Two doorways in the nearby end wall gave access to the services. This hall range was converted into a two-storeyed residence at the beginning of the fif-teenth century when a floor was inserted, the walls were raised, and a new roof was constructed at the higher level. New extensions were also developed at both ends. Shortly after the Dissolution, the body of the house was extended by a substantial timber-framed wing at right angles to it.

The division of the principal range shortly after 1400 necessi-tated refenestration at both levels. The new two-light windows have boldly cusped trefoil heads and strong hood moulds, similar to the

contemporary windows at Michelham Priory gatehouse and Rymans. The ground-floor chamber was ceiled with an embattled wall plate and moulded cross beams, and the upper chamber with a barrel roof closely divided by curved braces. The wall fireplaces, slightly off-centre, are fifteenth-century insertions with four-centred heads and cusped spandrels. The upper half of two screens of that time, now affixed to the end walls of the ground-floor chamber, are the same width as the range and probably served as partitions in it.

The two-storeyed gateway added at the lower end was simply a thickened wall with a two-centred archway at ground level. A spiral stair led to a passage above created in the thickness of the wall. It is now a columbarium, but with evidence of two-centred windows in the outer walls (and a cross arch) it must have led to a building on the west side, destroyed or replaced by the present farmhouse.[1] Even though the two-centred heads and simple chamfers of the gateway suggest fourteenth-century work, it must have been added at the same time that the range was divided, to which it was linked at both levels.[2]

A two-storeyed block was also added at the upper end.[3] New doorways in the middle of the party wall and at the adjacent angle led to the lower chamber, and to the upper one via an outer stair-case. Walter Godfrey suggested that this block was initially a ground-floor chapel open to the roof with the upper doorway serving a gallery, and that it was subsequently truncated and floored.[4] Although the roof may well be a reused structure, the

PLATE 170 Swanborough Manor: hall range from the north

412

angle quoins look original and the upper doorway could equally have been the approach to a private upper chamber with garderobe.

Less than 2 miles from the mother house, Swanborough was a profitable grange and not leased out until two years before the priory's dissolution in 1537.[5] Even so, it was often described in its later years as a manor, and with its conversion, virtually became a manor house usable by the prior of Lewes. He was certainly reluctant to part with it at the Dissolution, when it came into the hands of Thomas Cromwell.[6]

NOTES

1 The two fifteenth-century oak doorways inserted in the principal room of the sixteenth-century timber wing are further indications that the property was formerly more extensive at that time.
2 Contemporary doorways at the north-west angle of the main range led to a minor chamber north of the gateway and a first-floor garderobe rather than an external stair.
3 Platt attributed this chapel unit to the grange's original development: (1969) 20–1.
4 Godfrey (1936) 13.
5 Platt (1969) 68–70.
6 *Ibid.* 127–9. Five miles east of Swanborough stands Alciston Court, a valuable grange of Battle Abbey. The flint-built residence retains its two-bay hall (early fourteenth century), lower cross wing, partly timber-framed (mid? fourteenth century) and five-bay upper cross wing (fifteenth century). The fine barn 170 feet long is sixteenth century but the earlier dovecote is ruined. J. A. Brent, *Sussex Arch. Coll.* 106 (1968) 89–102 and 'Alciston Manor in the middle ages', MA thesis, Bristol University, 1965; R. T. Mason, *Sussex Arch. Coll.* 116 (1978) 159–62.

W. H. Godfrey, *Country Life* (November 1934)
W. H. Godfrey, *Sussex Arch. Coll.* 77 (1936) 3–14
VCH, *Sussex*, VII (1940) 52–3
C. Platt, *The Monastic Grange in Medieval England* (1969) 20–1, 68–71, 127–9, 237–8

TONFORD MANOR, Kent

The gateway and one remaining side of this fortified manor house are approached down a narrow cul-de-sac lane leading to the River Stour, less than 2 miles south-west of Canterbury. The house was built by Sir Thomas Browne, deputy treasurer to Henry VI, under a licence to crenellate granted in 1448.[1]

The site is approximately square and moated. The moat is sluggishly filled with water on the east side, dry on two further sides, and filled in for garden purposes on the north. Browne's manor was roughly square, with semi-circular towers at the angles and intermediate turrets on the west and possibly the other sides. The residential apartments lined at least two sides of the courtyard, with the hall facing the gateway.

The modest entry is set close to the south-west angle and forward of the enclosure. Built of knapped flint, the plain side walls of the passage are spanned by a tall four-centred arch with capitals reminiscent of the contemporary Daundelyon Court gatehouse at Garlinge. In this case, however, there was a chamber above the passageway but there were no angle turrets or even gate evidence.

The passage is linked by a short stretch of walling to the west curtain, the principal survival. Rising to two floors at the point

PLATE 171 Tonford Manor: post-medieval house between north towers

where it has been incorporated in an eighteenth-century residence, the curtain is marked by four half-round towers, two intermediate and two at the angles. They are built of a mixture of flint, brick, and ragstone, with one of the intermediate towers attractively decorated with chequerwork of brick infilled with flint. There is a mixture of single- and two-light windows under square heads in the walling marking a line of chambers against the curtain with a six-light window (restored) incorporated in the post-medieval house at the north end. This structure makes use of one of Browne's ranges, as it incorporates three hammer-beam trusses of chestnut indicating that the hall lay in this angle of the enclosure.

The trim lawn, rose-covered walls, and symmetrical façade with its early example of diapered brickwork cannot disguise the fact that Tonford Manor was designed to give the appearance of defence. A water-filled moat, gatehouse, and towers with battered bases helped to create the appearance of castellated nobility. And the reason for this lies in Browne's trajectory career. Initially a humble exchequer clerk, he was appointed a shire member of parliament (1445–6), under-treasurer (1447), speaker of the House of Commons (1453), and royal councillor (1453).[2] If the treasurers of England could build mansions like Wingfield Manor, Stourton House, and Herstmonceux Castle, then a deputy could at least aspire to a more modest version of the contemporary Sussex palace-like fortress. Browne was an *arriviste*, a strongly supportive Lancastrian, who took the opportunity in 1448 to obtain crenellation licences for four other sites, three centred on his landed interests across east Kent at which nothing survives, and Betchworth Castle in Surrey (q.v.) Yet the structure that Tonford Manor most closely resembles is the contemporary flint-built castle at Baconsthorpe in Norfolk. It was built in two phases, initiated in 1460 by John Heydon (d.1479) and extended by his son Henry by 1500. John was also a locally important Lancastrian supporter like Browne. His fortified house is similarly rectangular, with a line of four towers on the west side (half-round intermediate, square at the corners), a line of residential chambers against the curtain and the hall in the adjacent north-west angle. Almost concurrently with John Heydon's work, his son Henry (d.1504) was also developing the brick-built Wickham Court in Kent (q.v.).

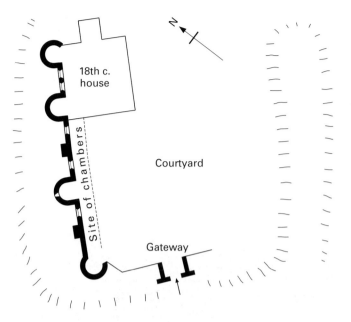

18th c. house

Courtyard

Site of chambers

Gateway

FIGURE 103 Tonford Manor: site plan

NOTES
1 *Cal. Charter Rolls* 6, 102.
2 For his career, J. C. Wedgwood, *History of Parliament: 1439–1509* (1936) 123–4; J. S. Roskell, *Nottingham Med. Studies* 7 (1963) 79–105.

WALTON MANOR, Surrey

The manor of Walton on the Hill was held by John Waleton during the second half of the thirteenth century and by John Droxford, bishop of Bath and Wells, from 1307 to 1329. The tenancy was in the hands of guardians of John de Braose for the next thirty years or so, before passing to the Arundel family until 1437.[1] The manor stands on the North Downs, opposite the church and within the bailey of a motte.

The buttressed stone-built hall and chapel block with the suggestion of further walling to the north indicate that this was a residence of some scale. It was modified in the seventeenth century and substantially extended in a Norman Shaw style in 1891. The property was partitioned into two residences in *c.*1980 but the medieval structure has been retained as a single family unit. Unfortunately, it had been badly bruised by successive owners so that only the shell survives, with inserted floors and partitions, patched and plastered walls (internally and externally), and windows punched all over the place.

The house was developed round a single-storey hall, 38 feet by 22 feet and therefore slightly larger than that at Ightham Mote, with the chapel opening off the south-east angle. The former was divided into two storeys in the early seventeenth century and the latter in about 1785.[2] Original features are scarce. In the hall, two of the three office archways survive, the central one higher than its fellows, and the inner facings of the tall north and east windows of the chapel.[3] These suggest that the house was built during the first half of the fourteenth century, but the ornate recess (rather than window) in the chapel at first-floor level is clearly of mid-

thirteenth-century date. Its position and that of the two adjacent fourteenth-century doorways, one with dagger spandrels, suggest that they are post-medieval insertions, brought from elsewhere when the house was reduced, divided, and partitioned. A stone house is a rarity in Surrey, and those parts that survive are closer to the early work at Ightham Mote than the present structure suggests. Both hall and chapel were built on a generous scale, with the windows of the chapel particularly so.[4]

NOTES
1 VCH, III (1911) 316.
2 Manning and Bray (1809) 813.
3 The head of the east window, but not its tracery, survives in the roof.
4 There are the remains of another fourteenth-century stone chapel in Surrey at Frensham Beale manor house.

O. Manning and W. Bray, *History of Surrey*, II (1809) 813
W. P. D. Stebbing, *Surrey Arch. Coll.* 23 (1910) 108–32
VCH, *Surrey*, III (1911) 316–18

WESTENHANGER CASTLE, Kent

Three miles north-west of Hythe, Westenhanger Castle is hemmed in between the Channel Tunnel railway and the grandstand of Folkstone racecourse. It is the same distance from Saltwood Castle, but whereas that early fortress was developed to the highest residential standards during the fourteenth century, culminating in the great gatehouse, Westenhanger was a modest fortified house initiated by Sir John Criol under a licence to crenellate in 1343.[1] The residence was described as a castle in October 1381 in a report of the attempted abduction from it of Sir John's widow,[2] so that construction can be ascribed to the third quarter of the century.

The castle stands close to the water meadows of the East Stour with a dam formerly holding water in the moat, now dry except on the south side. The oddly shaped quadrangular platform suggests that there may have been an earlier house, though excavated pottery cannot be more closely dated than the mid-fourteenth century.[3] The single courtyard is curtain-wall surrounded, with small round towers at three corners, a diagonal square tower at the fourth angle, and square mid towers on three sides with the gatehouse in the middle of the fourth. The base of the gatehouse is the earliest structure, pre-dating the curtain wall though probably not by many years. The entry was modest, a short forward projection from the bridge across the moat that opened into the slightly later passage flanked by a small unit either side the curtain, replaced during the early sixteenth century. The passage with polygonal responds was vaulted and portcullis protected in a structure not unlike a small version of the postern gate at Bodiam Castle.

The ragstone curtain wall rose direct from the moat as at Bodiam, but barely survives to any height outside the northern part of the site. It was nearly 20 feet above the moat, possibly higher on the residential east side, but only 3 feet thick throughout its length. The two tiny frontal towers hardly projected externally from their corners and were therefore not flanked by ranges. The two rear towers are larger, one round (north-east), one square (south-east), and projected into the moat. The two-storeyed north-east tower, converted into a dovecote in *c.*1575, is still in good shape and roofed.[4] It was next to the kitchen, as the similar tower is at Bodiam.

PLATE 172 Westenhanger Castle: from the north-east

Only the base of the south-east tower survives, its different shaping possibly a consequence of it being close to the high end of the hall. Two of the mid towers have been reduced to low levels but that in the middle of the north side stands almost to full height. It is three-storeyed above a low basement, with a single small room on each floor, lit by narrow loops, with alcove garderobe in two rooms.

The residential range lay opposite the gateway, but hardly any structures survived the later development of the site. The hall directly faced the gatehouse, with the jamb of a tall window traceable in the north curtain, evidence of a high-end partition to the south, and a first-floor cinquefoil light above the services to the north. There is no evidence of contemporary ranges against the north or south curtain.

Despite its name, Westenhanger was never a castle but a defendable house. The walls are weak, the towers are modest, and the moat was dam-held and therefore not a serious defence to a determined attacker. There are some external references to the far more formidable (and later) castle at Bodiam, but not internally where the single-range residence was relatively modest. Criol's house essentially proclaimed status and wealth at a time when the threat from France that marred Richard II's reign had not yet become manifest.

In 1501, Sir Edward Poynings acquired the structure and began to remodel the castle before his death in 1523, with the work completed by his son. The residential apartments were enlarged and extended round the courtyard, with work finalised by Henry VIII after 1540, so that there were separate suites for the king and queen four years later.[5] Little remains of the further activity undertaken during the late sixteenth century for the present red-brick house in the north-east angle was developed during the eighteenth century from farmhouse origins after the castle had been sold and largely demolished after 1701.

The castle's base court includes a late sixteenth-century barn[6] and a slightly earlier stone 'stable' block among the host of subsidiary farm buildings.

NOTES

1 *Cal. Pat. Rolls: 1343–45*, 106.
2 *Cal. Pat. Rolls: 1381–85*, 133, 319.
3 Martin and Martin (2001) 205. This paper supplants the earlier accounts, including H. Sands in *Memorials of Old Kent* (1907) 200–2, ed. P. H. Ditchfield and G. Clinch; G. Clinch in *Arch. Cant.* 31 (1915) 75–81, and *Arch. Jour.* (1929) 313–14.
4 *Vern. Arch.* 33 (2002) 109.

5 *HKW*, IV, pt. 2 (1982) 283–5.
6 *Vern. Arch.* 33 (2002) 109–10.

Archaeology South-East, Unpublished report on Westenhanger Castle, Stanford, Kent (2001)
D. and B. Martin, *Arch. Cant.* 121 (2001) 203–36

WICKHAM COURT, Kent

Wickham Court is a little-known and superficially complete house on the very edge of south London. A belt of playing fields and farmland hold back creeping suburbia so that Court and church, standing together on rising ground, still retain an element of independence. The house is currently used as a college of further education.

The manor of West Wickham was purchased by Sir Henry Heydon in October 1469 shortly after his marriage to Anne, the daughter of Sir Geoffrey Boleyn. His father had prospered as a private lawyer in Norfolk and had initiated Baconsthorpe Castle in the northern part of that county. The Heydons were minor gentry whose rapid rise in the social scale was fostered by Henry Heydon's marriage. The neighbouring Boleyn family of Salle had recently purchased Blickling as their new home in Norfolk, followed by Hever Castle in Kent in 1462, within reasonable riding distance of London where Sir Geoffrey had been lord mayor in the 1450s. Henry Heydon, though, decided not to stay in Norfolk but to move close to his wife's family in Kent by acquiring West Wickham and some adjacent properties 9 miles north of Hever.

No building records are known but Leland records that Sir Henry built 'a right fair Manor Place, and a fair Chirche', with work likely to have been initiated shortly after he acquired the estate. In contrast with the spreading plan of Baconsthorpe, Wickham was compact, an almost square block, 66 feet by 67 feet, built round a tiny courtyard with tall octagonal turrets at the angles. The present

PLATE 173 Wickham Court: from the north-west

entrance is extremely modest, now protected by a nineteenth-century porch. The building is so compact that it was essentially a continuous enfilade of rooms round a central light well, not unlike the earlier but much altered gloriette at Leeds Castle.

The house was built entirely of brick except for stone dressings. Each side is extensively pierced by two- and three-light transomed windows but all these are nineteenth-century insertions with the original window pattern difficult to discern. It is the bold angle turrets rising high above the roof that provide the principal element of articulation. They have a slight batter and an unaltered pattern of small single-light windows terminating in blind windows well above roof level. There would have been a forecourt – the modest entrance makes that certain – but there is no evidence of the moat, gateway, defensive windows, or machicolations imagined by a writer in 1963.[1] The battlements are relatively recent and decorative.

The entrance front is currently three-storeyed but this is the result of later changes to an otherwise two-storeyed house. The spandrels of the entrance doorway hold the arms and supporters of Henry Heydon on the left and those of Heydon impaling Boleyn on the right. The doorway opens into a narrow passage leading to the small timber-framed court, 18 feet by 20 feet, at a slightly higher level. Originally open to the sky, it was partially filled in the later sixteenth century with a grand staircase. The position of two or three former windows overlooking this courtyard can be traced.

The only apparently original interior is the single-storey apartment at the north-east angle with its heavy beamed ceiling and post and panel internal walls. The fireplace in the outer wall has H and A entwined by a lover's knot in the spandrels with dragons and monkeys. The three windows in the same wall are replacements, with sills higher than elsewhere. The larger window in the east wall is a Victorian alteration. These four windows contain later fifteenth-century glass with the arms of Heydon and associated families. It was brought to the Court from the church in the nineteenth century but it may have originated in the house. Unlike his father, Henry Heydon was a Yorkist. He was appointed controller of the household of Edward IV's mother, Cicely duchess of York, and was knighted in 1485. The arms in the hall windows reflect not only his marriage but his service to the crown. They therefore include those of Heydon with diagonal strips with the Heydon motto, the arms of Heydon impaling Willoughby following his daughter's marriage to Lord Willoughby of Eresby, as well as the royal arms, those of Cecily Neville, and those of her daughter, the duchess of Suffolk.[2]

The upper end of the room has been altered, with a flight of steps and an internal oriel window of markedly nineteenth-century character. The other two reception rooms are of early eighteenth- and mid-nineteenth-century form.

Access to the first floor was originally by stairs in the south-east and north-west corner turrets, with the other two turrets serving as closets. They all have a slight batter and are lit by single-light windows with brick headers (in most cases original). The original south-east stair survives. No early features remain at first-floor or roof level.

Henry Heydon had at least nine children. After the death of his father in 1480, he spent most of his time between the family estates centred on Baconsthorpe Castle in Norfolk and his West Wickham estates. Like his father, he had been trained in law, beginning his career as steward to the estates of Norwich Priory before his appointment as steward to Edward IV's mother. In addition to

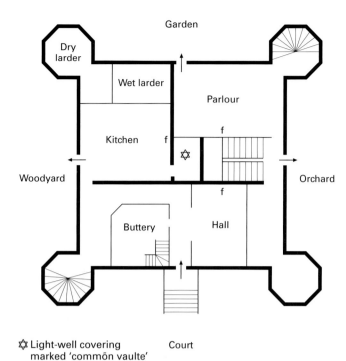

Garden

Dry larder

Wet larder

Parlour

Kitchen   f   f

Woodyard

Orchard

f

Buttery   Hall

✡ Light-well covering   Court
marked 'commōn vaulte'

FIGURE 104 Wickham Court: initial ground plan based on that by
John Thorpe c.1600

Wickham Court, Henry extended the courtyard at Baconsthorpe Castle and made substantial additions to West Wickham church in ragstone and brick, and the churches at Kelling and Salthouse in Norfolk. He died in 1504. The Heydons were not major landowners but gentry of standing, supported by the profitable sale of wool from Norfolk and timber from West Wickham. The family's fortunes declined in the second half of the sixteenth century and they sold West Wickham in 1580 to the Latham family. It was they who roofed the inner court and inserted the present staircase. During the nineteenth century, they thoroughly reorganised the interior, refenestrated the house in Tudor style, and added the two-storeyed porch with a first-floor window taken from the church during its restoration in 1847.

A copy of a nineteenth-century survey plan in Maidstone Record Office shows that the present layout bears little relationship to the original one. Even more relevant is one of the drawings in John Thorpe's book of drawings prepared between c.1596 and 1610 which Sir John Summerson identified as that of Wickham Court, again to quite a different layout.[3] The drawing shows the regular placement of two four-light windows in each outer face, separated by a centrally positioned doorway. The entrance, indistinguishable in size from the other doorways, was prefaced by steps. It opened direct into the screens passage of the hall. The offices and kitchen filled one side of the central light well, the hall and parlour the others. Internal walls were brick-built, with timber partitions separating the buttery and wet larder. The plan suggests that changes had already been made to the house, particularly the insertion of the grand stair between the hall and parlour. However, the two opposing newels were still in use – one for the family from the parlour and one for staff from the offices corridor. The absence of any compass on Thorpe's plan or any correlation between the present internal

walls and those on the drawing shows the comprehensive character of the internal development after the mid-sixteenth century. However, I have used the two stair positions to align the plan in a way that seems to match the brick footings in the cellars. This indicates that the present porch and entry are on the site of the original entry and that the hall, the parlour, and the room taken by the grand stair were on the south side of the house. This highly individual residence and its internal plan warrant a detail critical analysis between the documentary and structural evidence.

NOTES
1 M. Gregory, *Arch. Cant.* 78 (1963) 1–21.
2 D. I. Hill and C. R. Coucer, *Jour. British Society of Master Glass Painters* 11 no. 2 (1952–3) 94–104.
3 *The Book of Architecture of John Thorpe*, ed. J. Summerson (1966) 91 and plate 80. The volume is held in the Sir John Soane Museum. The West Wickham drawing is of the earliest building covered by the 149 domestic plans.

WILMINGTON PRIORY, Sussex

Founded before 1100, Wilmington was an outpost of the Benedictine abbey of St Mary of Grestain in Normandy, serving as the centre for their estates in England. As there was only the priory, two monks, and some servants, they made use of the adjacent parish church. Nor was there any claustral layout, for the priory was constructed and functioned more like a grange than a monastery. This is how it was treated in the fourteenth century, when several additions were made to the conventional thirteenth-century hall range that was subsequently replaced. Since the Dissolution, the property has been put to a number of uses so that it is a mixture of ruins and farmhouse-type accommodation today.

At the beginning of the fourteenth century, a generous two-storeyed porch was added to the earlier hall, essentially to create a roomy first-floor chamber rather than be in line with the triple-columned hall doorway below. The chamber has a three-light east window and crown-post roof. Later in the century, a new entrance with portcullis protection was added and quadripartite vaulting inserted in the passageway.

The contemporary chamber block constructed in the angle between the hall services and porch was a substantial work. This block, extending the original kitchen and services at ground level, provided a large first-floor chamber and thereby shifted the centre of Wilmington's residential accommodation from the upper to the lower end of the house.

At about the same time, the old hall was replaced by a new one above an undercroft immediately west of the porch. The southern façade stands to its full height, flanked by polygonal stair turrets between the remains of an original first-floor window with seats (altered in the late sixteenth century). There were formerly two further windows with seats in the short east wall, but it is not known how the opposite wall was windowed or the means of access from the ground-floor hall. The hall was 43 feet long and 25 feet wide internally, the extensive fenestration at the southern end suggesting that the apartment may have been divided into an outer and inner chamber, with a new doorway in the former to the porch chamber and the turret staircases in the latter leading to the ground floor and roof respectively.[1]

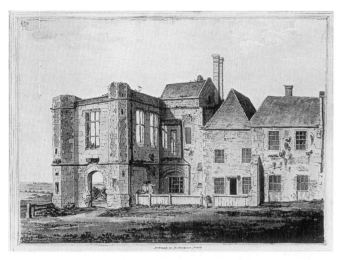

PLATE 174 Wilmington Priory: from a drawing by S. H. Grimm (1780)

Several elements in this 'monastic' context are relevant to contemporary residential architecture. The two-storeyed chamber block was particularly spacious, and because of its position provided luxurious accommodation for the prior at the lower end of the hall. Furthermore, it was elegantly designed, with the southern façade making contrasting use of greensand blocks (lower turrets, upper walling) and flint (upper turrets, lower walling). Godfrey reasonably suggested a date of 1360–70 for this work, when alien priories were taken into the king's hands on the renewal of hostilities during the second phase of the Hundred Years' War.[2] With an eighteenth-century stair, it is now used for accommodation by the Landmark Trust. In addition to the defensive entry, the priory was also protected by a three-storeyed drum tower at the north-west corner of the new chamber block. This was destroyed in the late eighteenth century but is mentioned in a schedule of 1393 and illustrated in a drawing by Richard Bugden in 1725.[3] The house, however, was not embattled but had plain parapets.

NOTES

1 Other fourteenth-century additions included a short north-east wing with vaulted cellar and dormitory over, an extension to the south-east range with chapel (?), and heightening the porch, but they did not materially affect the planning of the house.
2 Godfrey (1928) 20.
3 Martin and Martin (1988) 3, illus. 3 and 10.

W. H. Godfrey, *Sussex Arch. Coll.* 69 (1928) 1–28, 50–1
D. and B. Martin, *Wilmington Priory. Reports of Historic Architecture in Sussex*, 1046 (1988) 1–16 with numerous plans and diagrams

WINCHESTER COLLEGE, Hampshire

William Wykeham bought the site and founded his college in 1382 to raise the educational standard of the clergy through their schooling at Winchester, preparatory to a university education at his senior foundation of New College, Oxford.[1] The Winchester establishment was designed to accommodate ninety-six boys – seventy 'poor and needy' scholars, sixteen choristers, and ten commoners – overseen by a warden, headmaster, and ten fellows, assisted by three chaplains, an usher, and three choir clerks. All were accommodated within the college except for a number of commoners from wealthy families who were housed in the town. The conjunction of junior and senior foundations on this scale was unprecedented in Europe, as was the scale and quality of the buildings. New College, Oxford, was built first between 1380 and about 1386, followed by the work at Winchester between 1387 and 1401.

A well-watered site was chosen outside the city walls, beyond the jurisdiction of the mayor but under that of the bishop whose palace was close by.[2] The buildings were erected round two courts, an elongated rectangular outer court essentially for services, and a squarer inner court, both gatehouse-approached. Immediately beyond lay a cloister or cemetery. Though the planning similarity to New College is immediate, the scale, layout, and quality of the Winchester buildings established the yardstick for all schools seeking the highest standards between the fifteenth and twentieth centuries. The foundation stone was laid in March 1387, with the inner court completed and occupied in March 1394. Work was initiated on the outer court and cloister immediately afterwards and was completed within four years, followed by the exchequer tower between 1397 and 1400. All work was under the direction of William Wynford, bishop Wykeham's master-mason, and was completed three years before the bishop's death in 1404.[3]

Winchester College is an acknowledged pathfinder in the development of schools in England and Wales[4] but it also plays a significant if little recognised role in late medieval residential development. It shared the common facilities of a domestic environment – hall, kitchen, services, living and working accommodation, and entry gateway, organised round a central quadrangle. Though the founder's purpose determined the undue scale of the chapel, the buildings have altered minimally in appearance or function, and are as clear in layout today as in David Loggan's engraving of 1675. While the associated senior foundation at Oxford was limited by its construction within the city walls, the junior establishment enjoyed greater latitude by its development outside the walls of Winchester. And because the building of the school was secondary to that at Oxford under the common responsibility of Wykeham's master-mason, it was able to benefit from improvements in the layout and design of the parts common to both buildings.

Hall, chapel, and muniment tower are entirely of limestone from the Isle of Wight, but the remainder of Chamber Court is essentially flint-built, with ashlar limited to dressed stonework. Even greater use was made of flint after Wykeham began to concentrate on the cathedral and the college was left to its own devices, e.g. cloister, stables, and exchequer tower.

OUTER COURT

Outer Court was secondary in construction to Inner or Chamber Court but the two were a unitary conception. The initially austere street face was unbroken except by the greater height of the entry. The two-storey Outer Gate was erected in 1394–7, with the flanking ranges nearing completion by 1398. The broad four-centred entry arch with hollow and roll-moulding chamfer opens into a fine stellar-vaulted passage with bosses. Insecure foundations resulted in the dropped inner arch and the outer and inner buttresses added within a few years of construction. The extremely fine statue of the

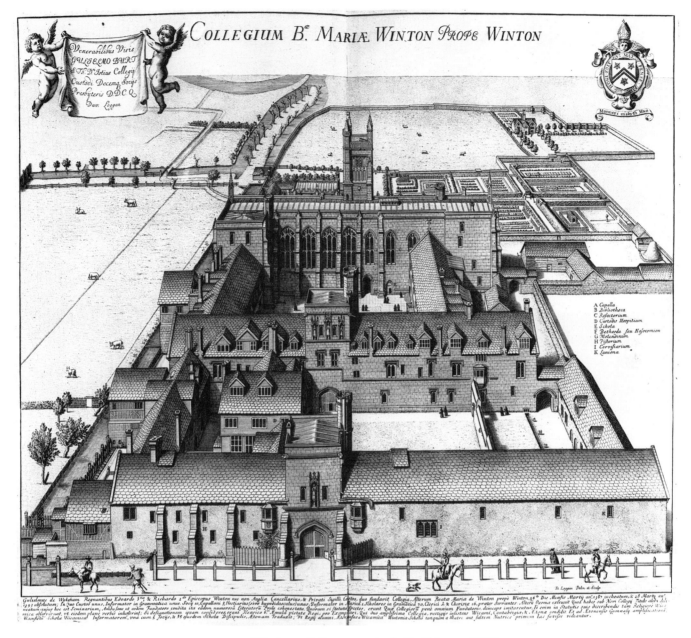

COLLEGIUM Bᵃᵉ MARIÆ WINTON PROPE WINTON

PLATE 175 Winchester College: engraving by David Loggan (1675)

Virgin and Child within the central canopied niche is original and shows slight traces of the colouring applied in 1466.[5]

The outer court was used essentially for domestic offices, with the steward of the college estates housed above the outer gate and the warden strategically positioned in the rooms above the gate to the inner court. With the advent of married wardens in place of celibate priests in the later sixteenth century, it was necessary to develop further accommodation in the eastern part of the court and into the bakehouse and granary in the north-east range by 1597. But the accommodation was still inadequate, and so the north-east street range was rebuilt for the warden in brick in 1730, reusing some of the earlier buttressed flint walling.[6] The east range (a mill and a laundry) was redeveloped and heightened in brick in the mid-

eighteenth century, and the east side of the court was infilled in 1832–3 with a knapped and squared flint frontage in Gothick style.

The few windows to the street were narrow, barred lights. As in any monastic precinct, this was not defensive but simply to limit external noise and distraction. The three bays next to the porter's lodge in the north-west range may have been a small hall with retained entry doorway and evidence of an arch-braced and tie-beam truss. The remainder was two-storeyed with single lights at both levels and an external stair to the upper floor (doorway converted to a window). The ground floor was initially the brewhouse and malthouse,[7] judiciously converted by Sir Herbert Baker into the college library in 1932–4 with enhanced fenestration.

Outer Court was originally intended to be the same length as the

419

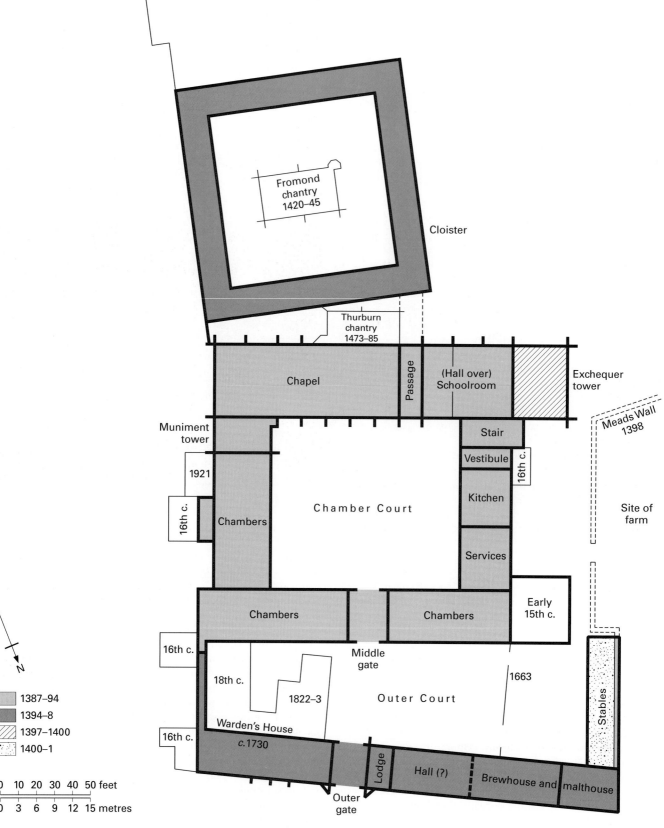

Fromond
chantry
1420–45

Cloister

Thurburn
chantry
1473–85

Chapel

Passage

(Hall over)
Schoolroom

Exchequer
tower

Muniment
tower

Meads Wall
1398

Stair

1921

Vestibule

16th c.

16th c.

Kitchen

Chamber Court

Site of
farm

Chambers

Services

Early
15th c.

Chambers

Chambers

16th c.

Middle
gate

18th c.

1663

1822–3

Outer Court

Stables

Warden's House

16th c.

c.1730

Lodge

Hall (?)

Brewhouse and malthouse

Outer
gate

N

1387–94
1394–8
1397–1400
1400–1

0 10 20 30 40 50 feet
0   3   6   9   12 15 metres

FIGURE 105 Winchester College: site plan

main court, stopping at the 1663 wall, but the acquisition of additional land to the west in 1393 enabled the court to be extended.[8] In 1398, the court was closed on the west side by a precinct wall, with a gateway leading to the college farm and meadows. The stables were built against this wall in 1400–1 at a lower height than the street range. The angle between the stables and the south chamber range was closed during the early fifteenth century by a two-storeyed residential block of unknown purpose (upper part Georgianised).

CHAMBER COURT

Middle Gate is a storey higher than Outer Gate, but with the same form of entry archways. The first-floor chamber was lit on both sides by two twin-light transomed windows, and the second floor by single lights flanked by three canopied niches. The central niche to the front retains the much decayed statues of the Virgin Mary flanked by the kneeling figure of bishop Wykeham, and a replacement angel of the Annunciation (original in museum). The three figures on the inner face are considerably more worn. The walls of the entry passage are plain – the lower part ashlar, the upper part Ventnor greensand – but crowned with a tierceron vault with a single central boss. The first-floor room was the warden's 'aula', that above was his bedchamber and oratory, and he had the use of the first-floor room to the east (pl. 103).

As at New College, Oxford, the hall and all-dominating chapel are in line, but this stone-built, heavily buttressed range faces the entrance rather than standing to one side of it. The assertive muniment tower acts as an end stop but the exchequer tower beyond the lower end of the hall is hidden from view. Neither tower is higher than the main range, for their octagonal stair turrets do not make any meaningful statements.

The room below the first-floor hall was the original schoolroom for scholars and commoners. Known as Seventh Chamber, it is lit by three two-light windows on the south side and originally had a central wooden pillar supporting the floor above.[9] The east end was partitioned in the nineteenth century and the lower part of a window converted into a door to create a passage to the free-standing school of 1683–7.

The flight of stone steps (replacing oak flitches) to the hall in the south-west corner of Chamber Court rises under a head dying into the wall, four-centred with wave and hollow moulding under a two-light open window. At the head of the stair is an original lantern holder. The hall, 63 feet by 30 feet and 40 feet high, is of four bays. The four south and three north bays are almost filled with tall two-light trefoiled windows with transoms and high window seats. The low-pitched roof of braced tie beams with open quatrefoil spandrels retains the original form, though it was completely renewed in 1819, when the open hearth and louvre were eliminated. An inventory of 1422 refers to six curtains and hangings that decorated the walls and to four great tables,[10] precursors of the present ones, and as in a domestic hall, the door could be barred.[11]

The screens passage is marked by three entries of unbroken moulded arches and higher rear arches, with the taller and broader entry next to the approach opening on to a now-destroyed stair to the kitchen. All three doorways retain their hatches. The smaller entry at the passage end with its original door of 1399 accesses the exchequer tower.

The kitchen range filling the west side of Chamber Court has

PLATE 176 Winchester College: hall range from Chamber Court

been altered by centuries of use. The kitchen vestibule formerly opened on to the kitchen stair parallel to the hall stair, destroyed in the eighteenth century. The kitchen, 25 feet by 20 feet and open to the roof, is lit at the upper level by two windows in both outer walls, now late Georgian to the Court. A wall fireplace replaced the central open fire in 1520. The louvre has also been removed but the original shaped roof retains its line of wind braces.

The four-storey exchequer tower, erected between 1397 and 1400, is flint-faced, with stone buttresses and single trefoil lights in its three outer faces. The ground floor is spanned by a four-part tierceron vault, majestically springing from a central octagonal pillar and grotesque figured wall corbels. The first floor retains its early divisional evidence in the now united buttery and pantry opening off the screens passage. The second floor, used for auditing the college estates and for exchequer or bursary purposes, is divided by a wooden screen into two rooms with animal-decorated tiled floors, wall fireplaces with square-headed lintels, and plain beamed ceilings.[12] The ill-lit third floor was used for storing cheeses from the early fifteenth to the early twentieth centuries.[13]

The chapel was originally entered from the passage beneath the hall dais, which also accessed the cloister to the south. It has been enclosed and converted into an ante-chapel. The chapel rises nearly

PLATE 177 Winchester College: Chamber Court with chambers, services, kitchen, and vestibule

60 feet, the full height of the south range. Both sides of its six bays are filled with tall three-light cinquefoiled windows with an east window of seven lights. The thin-ribbed but multi-cusped lierne vault is of wood, not stone. It is of quasi-fan design, one of the earliest essays of a form which characterised the Perpendicular style. Designed by Hugh Herland, the royal master-carpenter, it was repainted in 1952 following the scarlet and off-white colour scheme believed to be original. The east window incorporates some of the early glass, sent to Shrewsbury for repair in 1821 and returned instead with new glass copying the old! Some of the remainder was recovered in 1949 and placed in the west window of Thurburn's chantry.[14] The figures of the building staff beneath the head of Jesse – the mason William Wynford, the carpenter Hugh Herland, the clerk of works Simon Membury, and the glass painter Thomas Oxford – are noteworthy and support the documentary evidence that the same team of craftsmen were responsible for both of Wykeham's foundations.[15] The choir stalls with misericords are original work of c.1393–4, but the sedilia and reredos under the east window are additions of 1469–73. The latter, with evidence of colouring on the blank tracery of the north side, is of fifteen niches with crocketed and pinnacled canopies, restored by William Butterfield in 1874–5.[16]

The foundations of warden Thurburn's chantry chapel, opening from two bays on the south side, were laid immediately before his death in 1450. Construction began in earnest in 1473–4, and the bell tower above the western bay three years later with completion in 1485.[17] The two lierne vaults and forty-one bosses are of high-quality workmanship, possibly made at Oxford for they are comparable with William Orchard's work at the Divinity School there, and brought to Winchester for erection.[18] Apart from some of the glass of 1393–4 from the chapel's east window (with the kneeling figure of Richard II) reset in the chantry's west window, the chantry holds much glass of c.1502–3 by the glazier responsible for the contemporary windows in Great Malvern Priory church.[19]

The two-storey north and east ranges were devoted to pairs of chambers at both levels, each pair separated by a ground-floor passage holding a straight flight of steps to the upper floor. There were eight chambers in the north range, four each side of Middle Gate, and four more in the east range. These twelve chambers accommodated the fellows, scholars, choristers, and staff, but their separation was marked externally by a bold string course between the two levels (with the higher section of Middle Gate as a contemporary aesthetic modification), and by a window pattern identifying a difference in scale and layout between the ground and upper rooms. This can be most readily appreciated on the east side, less heavily altered internally than that on the north with its windows of

1812. The roof was destroyed by fire in 1815 but the block retains its original garderobe projection to the rear (now stair) with a new garderobe block added in 1541–2 over the stream, the Logie.[20]

Each chamber was between 30 and 35 feet long and 20 feet wide with rammed chalk floors. The pattern of single- and two-light windows indicates that the upper floor consisted of a chamber with opposing twin-light windows and end fireplace. There were two studies with single lights at the end further from the stair, and a third study partly over the stair. The ground-floor chambers were heated but had no partitioned studies. The six ground-floor chambers held the seventy scholars, with about thirteen in each chamber, whereas the upper floor was occupied by three fellows to a chamber, each enjoying his own study-cubicle.

The south end of the east range is closed by the three-storeyed muniment tower, made up of a single room on each floor, vaulted with bosses, and two-light windows with quatrefoil head in the east and west faces. The ground floor was and still is an ante-room or vestry to the chapel, with stair access to the upper floors and octagonal roof turret. Its doorway from Chamber Court is a Victorian insertion in the base of the window. The first and second floors with their heavily barred windows have always been used for storing the college muniments. The first-floor room is notable for the quality of its roof bosses and corbels, one a probable portrait of Wykeham, and for its green and yellow glazed floor tiles.[21] Some of the muniment chests are contemporary.[22]

Site restrictions south of the chapel determined that the cloister should lie at an angle rather than in line with it, though the entrance is almost opposite the chapel exit and was originally linked by a storeyed passage, pulled down in 1862. The cloister, 132 feet square, has entirely bare flint walls externally and four internal walks with barrel-shaped roofs. The broad three-light openings filling the nine buttressed bays facing the garth on each side have two-centred heads and cinquefoil lights. Initially intended as a cemetery, the cloister was for long used for teaching and study. The similarities to the cloister at New College are immediate, as is its isolation and detachment from the outside world.

In the centre of the garth is the free-standing chantry chapel of John Fromond, steward of the college manors, who died in 1420. Built of Ventnor greensand from the Isle of Wight, it was initiated in 1420, consecrated in 1437, and completed by 1445. The buttressed chapel with tall triple lights was limited to the ground floor, with the upper floor designed (and still used) as a library, stair-approached from the chapel interior. Hence the well-lit bays of two-transomed trefoiled lights (triple at each end) and the absence of any fireplace.[23] The chapel is highly decorated internally, with a line of blind tracery below the many windows, culminating in a multi-bossed vault.[24]

The four-stage bell tower that was an integral part of the cloister at New College was not erected here until seventy years after Wykeham's death. It was of an attractive slender design on a limited site, tall, well buttressed and with attractively decorated windows to the bell chamber.[25] It was more effectively integrated with the college buildings than the tower at Oxford.

ASSESSMENT

Wykeham's two educational foundations are key buildings of their period through their lordly scale in the newly developed Perpendicular style, but Winchester is particularly important

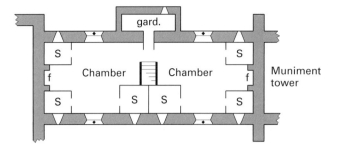

FIRST FLOOR

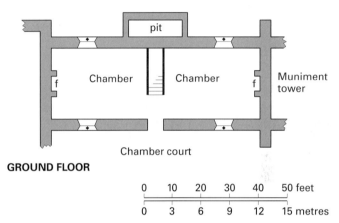

GROUND FLOOR

| 0 | 10 | 20 | 30 | 40 | 50 feet |
| 0 | 3 | 6 | 9 | 12 | 15 metres |

FIGURE 106 Winchester College: floor plans of east range

because of its spacious layout, logical design, and high standards. Overriding all these characteristics is that the college stands close to the architectural *grande idée* of its founder. Though the foundation has been subject to some modifications and many additional buildings in the course of six centuries, these – unlike in most country houses – have left the original concept relatively untouched. Although planned to reinvigorate English education for the church and state, Wykeham's concept owed no allegiance to monasticism. Its immediate models were recent university colleges and contemporary religious communities, but they, and Winchester in particular, were influenced by domestic architecture.

Built seven years after New College, the Winchester foundation benefited from some of the problems encountered at Oxford. The college was built on a smaller scale as befitted the junior foundation, but its construction on an unrestricted site outside the city walls gave Wynford greater scope to create a more spacious precinct. The main court was set back upon the site, allowing the outer court to be used for services and the inner court to be entirely residential. In adopting this double-courtyard layout, Wynford consolidated a domestic plan which had its origins in military architecture. Wynford formalised what had hitherto been only partially realised in contemporary buildings such as Dartington Hall, or limited by earlier structural and site restrictions as at Windsor Castle. Though the quadrangle was a basic tenet of contemporary multi-occupied buildings, such as the colleges of secular priests at Cobham (*c*.1370) and Arundel (1380) and charterhouses such as those in London (1371) and Coventry (1381), it was even more so in larger domestic residences.

Because of site freedom, the layout at Winchester scores over New College, enabling all the services, stables, brewhouse, granary, and slaughterhouse to be grouped round the outer court. This, in turn, allowed two gateways rather than a single one, and for both to be finely conceived in scale. Furthermore, Wynford aligned the outer gate with the middle gate, and that with the face of the dominant building – in this case, the chapel. And he built up the drama of approach by making the middle gate more structurally imposing and decoratively enhanced than the outer entrance. This was more obvious before the erection of the warden's range against it in 1822–3. Though the collegiate purpose had necessarily determined the prominence of the chapel, the greater planning latitude permitted Wynford to position the hall and chapel facing the inner gate, rather than lying to one side as at New College. Earlier defensive structures had determined a not dissimilar layout under Edward III at Windsor Castle's inner court, but the Winchester progression was deliberate, only needing the greater prominence of a hall in any domestic layout to create an alignment that became standard for greater houses throughout the fifteenth century.

Hall and chapel were in line as at Oxford, but in reverse at Winchester so that the chapel had a large east window. The administration was unified in a tower consisting of a beer cellar, the buttery and pantry, the exchequer and audit room, and a store room at the top, but there was no library until one was built after 1420 above Fromond's chantry chapel.

Both foundations adopted the first-floor hall, a feature chosen by the previous generation for buildings of the highest status as at Windsor and Kenilworth castles and several northern palace-fortresses, but Wykeham confirmed its suitability for communal foundations of standing as much as for more domestic environments. The warden's lodging was not distant from the hub of the establishment as in most monasteries, but positioned where he could survey the staff and servants in the outer court as much as the boys and fellows in the inner court. Though the same junior and senior division between ground- and upper-floor lodgings – between multiple and more individual occupation, between shared and privileged facilities – was practised at both New College and Winchester, the Winchester chambers were larger because of the need to house the greater number of boy scholars. Nor was there any lowering of design standards for the more junior foundation. Single lights were as broad as possible for maximum light with cinquefoil heads, while the narrower paired lights were given trefoil heads, both forms under square hoods with decorative stops. The relevance to domestic architecture is enhanced at Winchester by the use of cobbles and paving to the courtyards rather than the grass swards beloved of most Oxford and Cambridge colleges today.

As much care was given to design quality and variety as if the school had been an episcopal palace. The glass, or rather what remains of it, was among the best of its time, while the chapel roof (though significantly not the hall in this establishment) was of innovative design. Window heads were varied: two-centred (hall, chapel, muniment tower, stables), four-centred (outer and middle entries, school room, hall stair), and square-headed (chamber ranges and gateways). All except the chapel had hood stops, usually in the form of heads but occasionally animal figures.[26] Nor is the fenestration rhythm or character of Chamber Court broken by the kitchen and associated offices. The windows of the later buildings – the exchequer tower, stables, and brewhouse ranges – are plain,

without hoods and stops. Mouldings were modest, essentially limited to hollow and roll forms but markedly weaker in the chapel than those created for Wykeham in the cathedral. The several vaults were a generous and expensive enhancement, sometimes modest (Middle Gate) but usually not, and furnished with well-carved bosses such as Wykeham's arms (Outer Gate) and grotesque heads (beer cellar corbels). Buttresses were stepped and crowned with decorative and shaped heads, but confined to the chapel, hall, and muniment and exchequer towers in contrast with the plain-fronted ranges of both courts.[27] Though the stair turrets are a whispered reminiscence of military architecture, parapets are plain until the roofing of Fromond's chantry in the 1440s. Many windows retain their shutters and the walls their puttock holes, so often filled in contemporary buildings by overzealous nineteenth- and twentieth-century restorers.

Both of Wykeham's foundations were essentially inward-facing, with few windows to the outside world and a high enclosing wall elsewhere. But Winchester, far more than New College, Oxford, retains its original buildings in little-altered condition to give a classic example of late fourteenth-century intention and realisation. Here stands a substantial and coherent group of mainly domestic and corporate residential purpose, formerly ranged round two quadrangles to give possibly the earliest fully developed domestic double-courtyard plan in England. More than the Oxford foundation, Winchester College was the ordered template for the equally structured, functionally ordered, and stylish mansions of fifteenth-century England.

NOTES

1 The project had been maturing for some years beforehand, with a school-master appointed in 1373. G. H. Moberley, *Life of William of Wykeham* (1893) 121–2.

2 WCAS (1926) 51–2.

3 J. H. Harvey, *Eng. Med. Arch.* (1984) 353–6. Despite the work of several distinguished college archivists, a detailed analysis of the college's early architectural development is still awaited.

4 Henry VI paid several visits to Winchester College between 1441 and 1452 preparatory to drawing up his plans for Eton College and King's College, Cambridge. Harvey (1965) 122–5. Other comparable fifteenth-century foundations include those of archbishop Chichele at Higham Ferrers School and All Souls, Oxford, and bishop Waynflete at Wainfleet and Magdalen schools and Magdalen College, Oxford.

5 H. Chitty and S. Pitcher, *Medieval Sculptures at Winchester College* (1932).

6 Harvey (1965) 114. Its early form is shown in Loggan's engraving of *c.*1675 and an oil painting of the college of *c.*1692 in the warden's house. Hawkes (1933) 45.

7 Beer was served in hall until the 1830s.

8 WCAS (1926) 70.

9 A similar supportive pillar survives in the contemporary entrance range at Dartington Hall.

10 WCAS (1926) 89–90.

11 The hall was panelled in 1540 and the windows reglazed in 1931. The college retains a splendid collection of plate, including the founder's spoon (early fifteenth century), a Gothic looking Election Cup of *c.*1555, and three contemporary items, a silver and parcel gilt ewer and basin, a silver-gilt salt, and a silver standing bowl. C. Oman, *The Winchester College Plate* (1962), a revised reprint from *The Connoisseur* (January 1962) 24–33.

12 The exchequer room retains an early fifteenth-century oak hutch with two tiers of cupboards for documents.

13 Learnt in discussion with Dr John Harvey in 1963.

14 J. Harvey and D. King, *Archaeologia* 103 (1971) 149–77. The V and A Museum also holds three lights from two of the chapel windows.

15 Note 3 above and G. Jackson-Stops in *New College, Oxford*, ed. J. Buxton and P. Williams (1979) 159–64. In addition to the obvious planning factors common to both buildings, such as the hall and chapel built back-to-back, there are close stylistic similarities including almost identical window tracery and gateway statuary.

16 The two early sixteenth-century tapestries hung in the chancel are believed to have been woven to decorate the cathedral on the occasion of prince Arthur's christening in 1486.

17 H. Chitty and J. H. Harvey, *Antiq. Jour.* 42 (1962) 208–25. Initially there was a rood screen across the middle of the chapel so that the chantry enlarged the original ante-chapel to the west.

18 *Ibid.* 217–18.

19 Some of the glass from this chantry was transferred to the east window of Fromond's chantry in 1772.

20 The mid-sixteenth-century garderobe block serving the north-east range of chambers is also visible from the warden's garden. For the layout of the rooms round Chamber Court, WCAS (1926) 81–4.

21 The tiles in the room above are much more worn. For details of the tiles here and in the exchequer tower, E. C. Norton, *Proc. Hampshire F. C. and A. Soc.* 31 (1976) 23–42.

22 For the archives, J.H. Harvey, *Archives*, 5 (1962) 201–16.

23 The roof is a replacement of 1771–2.

24 For Fromond's chantry, H. Chitty, *Archaeologia* 75 (1926) 139–58.

25 For the tower, H. Chitty, *Proc. Hampshire F. C. and A. Soc.* 9 (1920) 37–80. The tower and Thurburn's chantry were rebuilt by Butterfield in 1862–3.

26 Of the seventy-two bosses in the chapel, forty-four have stylised leaves, twelve are human heads, eight are heads with leaves, and eight are miscellaneous.

27 Those of the cloister walks do not have a comparable aesthetic claim.

T. F. Kirby, *Annals of Winchester College* (1892)

A. F. Leach, *A History of Winchester College* (1899)

Winchester College Archaeological Society (WCAS), *Winchester, Its History, Buildings and People*, (1926; 3rd edn 1933)

C. Hawkes, *Winchester College: An Essay in Description and Appreciation* (1933)

J. D'E. Firth, *Winchester College* (1949)

J. H. Harvey, *Jour. Brit. Arch. Assoc.* 128 (1965) 107–28

WINCHESTER, HOSPITAL OF ST CROSS, Hampshire

The Hospital of St Cross is memorably sited by the open meadows of the River Itchen, a mile south of Winchester. It is the only one from medieval England that can vie in scale and architectural quality with those of France and Spain.[1] This foundation also enjoys several high-quality elements totally apposite to the study of domestic architecture – a hall undercroft of *c*.1300, the first-floor hall and kitchen wing of *c*.1385, and the more grandiose gatehouse of *c*.1430 and lodging ranges of *c*.1450. However, the building documentation is extremely lean, and this spectacular complex of medieval buildings, comparable with the finest contemporary domestic and ecclesiastical work, has yet to be subject to detailed architectural analysis.[2]

The foundation for thirteen poor men and a daily dinner for one hundred other poor men was established by bishop Blois, possibly in about 1136 but only certainly by 1151. The magnificent church,

built intermittently between *c*.1160 and *c*.1250, established the scale for all subsequent additions that have survived. They were initiated about the close of the thirteenth century with a low undercroft supporting a first-floor hall. Accessed under the porch steps, it was vaulted with plain-chamfered ribs dying into the facets of the columns. Apart from being a useful area for storing the hospital's beer and ale casks, the position of this structure helped to determine the enormous scale of the hospital's inner court a century and a half before the foundation was enlarged by bishop Beaufort (1404–47).

Like the similar and much-altered undercroft and hall at Merton College, Oxford, the undercroft at St Cross supported a contemporary hall whose flint walls were reused in the present structure. This was a consequence of the drastic repair programme of the master, John Campeden (1383–1410), to make good the negligence and depredations of his immediate predecessors, and particularly Roger Cloune (1370–4) who had turned out the brethren, pulled down some of the buildings, and allowed the hall roof to collapse. Appointed by bishop Wykeham, Campeden and his successors, Thomas Forest (*c*.1426–63) and William Westbury (1465–*c*.1474), reflected the architectural enthusiasm and standards of their episcopal patrons to make this hospital one of the significant residential complexes of late medieval England.

Leaving the porch to one side for the moment, the hall entry with continuous hollow moulding and high-quality head stops of a king and queen (Richard II and Anne?) opens, via an early wicket door, into the cross passage. The left-hand wall is solid, for the kitchen and services lie north of the passage, a practice subsequently adopted at Winchester College. The side sections of the simple screen are original, plain planks with a central cross member, flanking a central replacement with two openings. Above is a coved balcony frontage with projecting central section of late fourteenth-century date.

The hall, 45 feet by 24 feet internally and 32 feet high, is a splendid and little-touched example of its period. It is lit by three south-facing and two opposing windows (the services wing prevented a third) of two-transomed cinquefoiled lights with quatrefoil head. Originally shuttered, the heads of the south-facing windows retain mid-fifteenth-century glass, while the two dais windows were more extended to hold seats. The central hearth (with louvre evidence) stands on a replacement raised brick floor. The high collars of the four-bay side-purlin roof are supported on extended braces rising from stone angel corbels carrying coats of arms, except for those at the upper end which have St Christopher and foliage. Above the wall plate is a line of blind trefoiled panels[3] and three rows of curved wind braces. The late Decorated windows with their hint of early Perpendicular character, comparable with those of 1384–90 in the church tower, and the elegantly light form of the roof point to the later fourteenth century, though dendro dating is urgently needed. Before he initiated the nave vaulting in 1407, the master, John Campeden, is recorded as having spent £1,980 5s. 6d. on new buildings and repairs to the Hospital since 1383,[4] work that included eleven chambers for the thirteen poor brethren and almost certainly this hall. Less elaborate than that of 1387–94 by William Wynford at Winchester College, a mile to the north, it is attributable to the earlier years of Campeden's rule.[5]

The contemporary kitchen wing opening from the north end of the cross passage is divided into two – a short passage with buttery and pantry to one side, and an end kitchen. The buttery had direct

PLATE 178 Winchester: Hospital of St Cross: hall interior

access to the hall; the pantry had hatches to the kitchen. The two rooms above, now empty, are stair-approached from the kitchen passage and retain their crown-post roofs. The kitchen, 23 feet by 18 feet, rises through two floors like that at Bishop's Waltham Palace, though here with a tie-beam and crown-post roof. The opposing windows of two cinquefoiled lights with traceried heads have been renewed, as has the service door to the outer court. The large fireplace filling the end wall holds a mid-Georgian range, for meals continued to be prepared here until the close of the nineteenth century.

The kitchen served not only the hall for the master and thirteen poor men, but also the hundred indigent men who were served with a meal each day in their own hall in the outer court across from the kitchen. This fourteenth-century structure, attributed to c.1334, refenestrated in the fifteenth century and subsequently truncated, established the imbalance between a small outer court and the vast inner quadrangle consolidated by Beaufort's enhancement programme which was initiated with his rebuilding of the inner gate.

The three-storeyed gate tower, with a plain rather than an embattled parapet, tactfully blended into the earlier and lower hall and entry range. Inspired by and modelled on Wykeham's inner

gate-tower to Winchester College, Beaufort's stylish but dignified structure was in dressed stone instead of the flint rubble used for the earlier domestic work. The ground floor is filled with a broad entry arch of continuous mouldings and four-centred head, set in a square frame with the arms of Beaufort and England in the spandrels and a frieze of four heads separated by four-leaved flowers.[6] Above is a two-light cinquefoil and transomed window under a square hood, while the second floor has three elegantly canopied niches, one retaining the kneeling figure of Beaufort wearing his cardinal's hat. The whole frontage is framed by two-stepped buttresses set back from the corners. The inner face is more simple, with the same fenestration but a polygonal stair turret and a single slender niche with a Victorian replacement statue of the Virgin and Child. The now empty rooms above the tierceron-vaulted entry were an extension of the master's earlier chamber over the porter's lodge and retain their original floors and a fireplace at first-floor level with four-centred lintel head. The uppermost stage consists of two rooms, one above the other, with single cinquefoil lights on each side. The date of this work is not certain, but it occurred between 1427 when Beaufort was awarded a cardinal's hat and his refounding of the hospital in 1446. The years close to c.1430 are most probable.[7]

Beaufort made two modifications to the earlier hall. He added the single-storey entry porch with its two-centred entry arch, single-bay lierne vault with a central boss sculpted with the arms of Beaufort and his cardinal's hat, and a plain parapet. Its squat character contrasts unfavourably with the two-storeyed church porch on the opposite side of the court. Beaufort also erected the line of internal steps from the dais to his additional master's rooms in the gatetower.

Beaufort's intention to bring higher architectural standards of scale and design, already signalled by his magnificent gateway, culminated during the closing years of his life in his refounding and enlargement of the hospital on a most generous scale. It was redesigned to hold thirty-five brethren, three sisters, and two priests, with the brethren to include those who had retired from the cardinal's service. As with the collegiate foundations of Wykeham and Waynflete, the genesis of this project must have been in train for several years prior to 1446. In May 1439, Beaufort purchased lands for the hospital's endowment. He was granted a royal licence in 1443 to transfer properties to the master and brethren worth £500 per annum. Building activity seems to have been initiated in the early 1440s,[8] but Beaufort's endowment did not prove as long-lasting after his death in 1447 as he had planned and the project almost foundered forty years later when the hospital was reduced to two brothers and a priest (1486). Part of the reason for this lay in the lavish expansion of the hospital's accommodation by his successor, bishop Waynflete, who obtained a charter from Henry VI empowering him to carry out his predecessor's intentions for what was significantly described as the House of Noble Poverty. However, the fundamental reason lay in Beaufort's failure to secure the necessary charter of incorporation, so that the endowment income was usurped by his unscrupulous kinsfolk.[9]

Nothing survives of the pre-fifteenth-century accommodation for the brethren and staff that must have been an integral part of the hospital from the time of its foundation.[10] Whatever existed was replaced between c.1440 and c.1460 in the radical reorganisation and formal layout arising from the generously planned lodging ranges for the forty inmates of Beaufort's enlarged foundation.

PLATE 179 Winchester: Hospital of St Cross: inner court with gateway, hall, and lodging range

Twenty-four were accommodated in the range filling the west side of the inner court and sixteen divided equally between the shorter ranges to the north and south. These ranges are continuous with the tiled roof of the earlier hall, giving considerable unity to the whole development.

The six doorways with four-centred heads in the two-storey west range open on to a lobby with a straight stair accessing two ground- and two first-floor lodgings. Each unit is made up of three rooms, a heated chamber facing the courtyard and two rear rooms, one with a garderobe facility and double light, and one with a single light. Because of the stairs, the ground-floor front room, 14 feet by 13 feet, is smaller than that above, 17½ feet by 12 feet. The line of frontal chimney stacks topped with tall octagonal chimneys gives the range a dramatic rhythm: the projecting paired garderobes to the rear astride a stream create a more subdued one. All the windows have been modified, mainly with eighteenth-century frames, but many of the internal partitions seem to be original, retaining the three-room division to the present day. Their use is also possibly unchanged, from living chamber, bedchamber with garderobe, and store[11] to the present sitting room, bedroom, and kitchen. The upper lodgings were originally open to the existing crown-post roof structures (pl. 13).

The short lodging range closing the south side of the court and the church was pulled down in 1789.[12] The remaining units in the north range next to the hall were converted in the later seventeenth century into accommodation for the master in place of that in Beaufort's tower. In 1899, a new house was built for the master outside the precinct, enabling these rooms to be modified shortly afterwards to make good some of the lost lodgings and to provide administrative offices.[13]

The surviving lodging range is of considerable architectural significance, not only for its unaltered state but because its planning marks an important stage in the development of greater privacy in domestic accommodation. The chimney stacks, frontal instead of to the rear as hitherto, created a stylish architectural feature, and with an elaboration that denoted pride in their provision. More importantly, they enabled the range to be two rooms deep, with a large front chamber and rear rooms differentiated in size, fenestration, and facilities. Undoubtedly, such sumptuous accommodation arose from Beaufort's keenness to be generous to those retired employees who faced reduced circumstances, but this grand gesture, not dissimilar in scale to the domestic units in Carthusian monasteries, set a standard for lodging accommodation that was not matched until the royal residences at the close of the century. Not only did

427

Beaufort's intentions at St Cross bring the overall development and plan of the hospital much closer to the collegiate foundations of Wykeham, Waynflete, and the crown at Winchester, Oxford, and Eton, but he instilled the same high quality and determined architectural stamp on the hospital that the more well-known educational foundations have always enjoyed.

NOTES

1 Three books on this subject span the twentieth century: R. M. Clay, *The Medieval Hospitals of England* (1909); W. H. Godfrey, *The English Almshouse* (1955); E. Prescott, *The English Medieval Hospital c.1050–1640* (1992). B. Howson, *Houses of Noble Poverty* (1993) is a more popular survey.

2 The most succinct summary to date is by Richard Haslam (1989).

3 M. Wood notes a resemblance to the stone frieze above the contemporary nave arches in the cathedral: *The English Medieval House* (1965) 323.

4 A. M. Carr, 'The career of John de Campdene with specific reference to the hospital of St Cross, Winchester, 1383–1410', MA thesis, University of York (1960).

5 Wood alternates between *c.*1383 and the late fourteenth/early fifteenth century: *English Medieval House* 29, 325.

6 Said to represent Beaufort, his half-brother Henry IV, his father John of Gaunt, and his mother Katherine Swynford.

7 C. A. Hewitt claimed the years 1404–7 'according to that institution's records' (*English Historic Carpentry* (1980) 195, 287), but *c.*1427–40 is more likely, before the cardinal had completed his work at Bishop's Waltham and the major programme at Wolvesey in 1441–2. G. L. Harriss, *Cardinal Beaufort* (1988) 368–9.

8 There was building stone at the hospital in 1440–1, unused for Beaufort's addition at East Meon, while paving tiles and nails were brought from Southampton in 1444. J. N. Hare, *Hampshire F. C. and A. Soc. Newsletter* 16 (1991) 30.

9 G. Belfield, *Proc. Hampshire F. C. and A. Soc.* 38 (1982) 103–11; Harriss, *Cardinal Beaufort* 370–4.

10 The earlier pensioners' quarters are believed to have been attached to the south-east angle of the church round a small cloister, with other buildings for the domestic staff north of the church, including services and the master's chambers. C. Currie, *Hampshire F. C. and A. Soc. Newsletter* 23 (1995) 27–8.

11 Dr W. A. Pantin suggested bed-sitting room, store room, and buttery: *Med. Arch.* 3 (1959) 249.

12 Immediately south of this range and the church lay a small garden and a moated orchard, both of *c.*1400, a rare survival in the region. C. R. J. Currie, *Hampshire Gardens Trust Journal* 11 (1992) 19–22; *Med. Arch.* 37 (1993) 265; 38 (1994) 219; 39 (1995) 219.

13 There was a further mid-fifteenth-century lodging unit in the outer court as an extension of the kitchen wing, two-storeyed with three large self-contained chambers on each floor and with a projecting latrine turret at the east end rear. Each chamber had its own fireplace (though the stacks have been removed) with a single light on each side. A narrow internal corridor to the front on each floor accessed the lodgings and latrine turret. The roof is a crown-post structure, but the stair to the upper floor has been lost in the conversion to stables. Hare, *Hampshire F. C. and A. Soc. Newsletter* 16 (1991) 30–1.

VCH, *Hampshire*, V (1912) 66–9
P. Kidson and J. Harvey, *Arch. Jour.* 123 (1966) 216–17
P. Cave, *The History of the Hospital of St Cross* (1970)
Y. Kusaba, 'The architectural history of the hospital of the church of St Cross, Winchester', PhD thesis, University of Indiana (1983)
R. Haslam, *Country Life* (January 1989)
P. Hopewell, *St Cross* (1995)

WINCHESTER, THE DEANERY and the residences of St Swithun's Cathedral Priory

Cathedral priories were a peculiarly English institution, whereby the bishop was the titular abbot but the running of the monastery was carried out by the prior. There were eight such monasteries before the Dissolution and the prior was a considerable figure in his own right at each of them.[1] He was not only the head of a wealthy house, but also in charge of its estates and finances, and an important figure to the outside world. Not surprisingly, he occupied houses that were only second to those of the bishop in number, scale, hospitality, and distinguished visitors, but only two of St Swithun's survive – at Winchester and Michelmersh.

The Prior's House, now the Deanery, in Winchester's cathedral close, is Janus-like. The south-east corner of the former cloister area is dominated by the line of buttress-separated windows of the mid-fifteenth-century prior's hall. From the close, the mid-thirteenth-century open porch with its Tudor superstructure attracts the eye. The primary aspect from the dean's garden to the east is the late seventeenth-century long gallery, while the north face looks like the back of a suburban brick house with its eighteenth-century addition. The Deanery is a multi-period property, L-shaped and flint-built under the priors, but extended to the north and east in brick by the deans in 1660–8 and 1672–3, with further internal changes in the early nineteenth century.

Only two structures are relevant to this study, the porch and the prior's hall. The triple open-arched and four-bay vaulted porch of about 1250, with its early examples of shouldered lintels and Purbeck marble, was a status approach to a hall of unclear position but possibly to the north. It is probable that the floor above this imposing and extremely elaborate entry was a chapel, for encaustic tiles of contemporary date were found under the present floor in the late 1960s,[2] but a withdrawing chamber here cannot be ruled out. It was converted into two domestic rooms in the early sixteenth century when two further rooms were added above, lit by windows of uncusped lights. The fine clasped-purlin, queen-post roof also dates from this time.

The present approach to the first-floor hall is by a curved stair of 1808 from the end bay of the porch, but the original approach seems to have been from an external stair to an entry close to the south end of the hall. The base supporting the stair and part of the door head survives in the much-altered wall face. It was probably porch-protected, marked by the line of walling cut back to the face next to the blocked window.

The area below is divided into featureless service rooms and offices. The kitchen at the north end has a large hearth with a low head, while the room at the south end has two and a half bays of blind arcading of early to mid-thirteenth-century date, possibly part of the service rooms to the smaller hall that preceded the present one. The unusual angle of the first-floor hall of the Prior's House was probably determined by retained earlier buildings. This major apartment, 79 feet by 28 feet, was built in 1459, when three large oaks in the prior's manor of Manydown were cut down for its roof. The six-bay apartment was lit by five windows in the west wall and possibly by a further one in the end bay opposite the original entry point. The character of the end wall towards the close is not known, for it had suffered from seventeenth-century alterations

PLATE 180 Winchester, Prior's House: from the cathedral close

before it was rebuilt in 1808, but there was at least one more window in the second bay of the east wall. Each window was divided by a transom into four cinquefoiled lights under a hexafoil head and hood with badly damaged stops. These windows were originally shuttered and had seats, but even by 1649, the windows were still half-glazed, half-shuttered. An early drawing shows there was also a large window above the dais, destroyed when the house was extended towards the cathedral in the 1660s. At the same time, the hall was divided on the line of the second bay into a greater and a lesser room and ceiled at the level of the window heads to enable attic rooms to be inserted.

The six-bay roof was fully exposed in 1969 and is a magnificent example of its period. It is of arch-braced collar construction with raking struts above the collars, and the braces supported on stone corbels carved as heads but carrying an integral moulded stone foot to the braces. The spandrels are decorated with open quatrefoils with central flowers and pierced mouchettes, and there are three lines of wind braces, the uppermost reverse-curved. Between the fourth and fifth bays is the partial frame of a louvre, though no trace of any stone pillar has been found at ground level to carry the hearth. Though new attic rooms created in part of the roof in the

1960s and the seventeenth-century inserted floor inhibit full appreciation, this is a most imposing structure in pristine condition, appropriate to the elevated hall favoured by those of high status in the fifteenth century or who aspired to be so.

Winchester cathedral priory held about thirty manors, mainly in Hampshire and Wiltshire. Many of them had a home farm, similar to a monastic grange, but some of them also had a country house for the prior. Such houses were distinguished by their greater size, a private chamber for the prior, a chapel, additional rooms for guests or household officials, and sometimes a gatehouse. Such houses existed at Chilbolton, Crondall, Hurstbourne Priors, Michelmersh, Silstead, and Wootton St Lawrence, but hardly anything survives at any of these country retreats except at Michelmersh, and that was only identified in 1992.[3]

Eight miles west of Winchester, Manor Farm, Michelmersh, consists of four ranges of which three are medieval in a ⌐L shape. They include the outer wall of the hall, a single-storey passage-like unit at right angles, and the occupied two-storey solar block. A post-medieval farmhouse was attached to the last. The hall wall retains the lower part of two windows possibly of thirteenth-century date. Three sides of the passage-like block stand about 8 feet high, earlier than the fourteenth-century solar block which necessitated the addition of an upper storey as the only means of early access from the hall. The solar block is remarkably complete, with three ground-floor rooms and two upper chambers. The ground floor was stone-divided in a one third to two thirds ratio, with the larger room further divided into two by a lost wooden screen. The end room retains four single lights and traces of vine-scroll decoration betokening high-status occupation. The upper floor was divided into a larger and a smaller chamber by a now-missing framed division positioned above the stone one below. The larger room was lit by ogee-headed lights and retains the curved timbers of a barrel-type roof, dendro dated to 1321–2.[4] The smaller room has simple rectangular lights and a roof of straight timbers. The standard and quality of these features suggest that the upper floor was the prior's withdrawing chamber and inner chamber or closet, in a block which carries extensive evidence of its early fourteenth century date.

NOTES

1 Bath, Canterbury, Durham, Ely, Norwich, Rochester, Winchester, Worcester.
2 The tripartite open porch of Beaulieu Abbey gatehouse (early to mid-fourteenth century) was also surmounted by a chapel. Also M. Wood, *The English Medieval House* (1965) 230.
3 The manor of Hinton Ampner was a perquisite of the almoner but his house was destroyed by fire in the early sixteenth century and replaced by one destroyed in 1793.
4 E. Roberts, *Hampshire Houses 1250–1700* (2003) 237.

Winchester

J. Munby and J. Fletcher, *Medieval Art and Architecture at Winchester Cathedral: British Architectural Association Conference Transactions* (1982) 101–11
J. Crook, *Proc. Hampshire F. C. and A. Soc.* 43 (1987) 125–73
J. Crook (ed.), *Winchester Cathedral 1093–1993* (1993)

Michelmersh

E. Roberts, *Proc. Hampshire F. C. and A. Soc.* 48 (1992) 107–19

WOLVESEY, HIGHCLERE, and the residences of the bishops of Winchester

The episcopal centre of the see of Wessex was established initially at Dorchester upon Thames. It was moved to Winchester in 662 with the building of a cathedral church there. At first, the see covered the kingdom of Wessex and the greater part of the West Country, though it was gradually reduced in size as new bishoprics were established at Wells and then at Exeter. Much of the wealth and influence of the bishops of Winchester stemmed from the late Saxon era when the city was the capital of Wessex and, for a time, of England. By the beginning of the twelfth century, the see was limited to Surrey, Hampshire, and the Isle of Wight, but nevertheless, it continued to be the richest in the country and long retained that supremacy. It was only with the creation of the bishoprics of Guildford and Portsmouth in 1927 that the diocesan boundaries were substantially reduced.

The bishops were frequently among the leading statesmen of the middle ages, for the see was led by a remarkable number of highly competent administrators and politicians, some of them among the most powerful of their generation. During the middle ages, ten of them served as chancellors of England, four were treasurers, two were keepers of the privy seal, and one was chief justiciar. William Wykeham (1367–1404), Henry Beaufort (1405–47), and William Waynflete (1447–86) spanned nearly 120 years – a triumvirate almost as important for their architectural patronage as for their political activity.

At the beginning of the thirteenth century, the bishops held forty-three manors in the south of England. They were mainly within a 40 mile radius of Winchester, with Taunton (Somerset) and Witney (Oxfordshire) as important outliers. Large-scale arable farming was practised across this substantial body of highly organised estates. This continued to be so after the Black Death, though on a reduced scale until the 1430s when leasing to tenant farmers became common.

We know a great deal about the organisation, capacity, and key events of the estates of this bishopric because of the survival of the annual accounts for all the episcopal manors from 1208–9 to 1710–11. They do not survive for every year, and as they are summaries of more detailed accounts their information is necessarily selective. Even so, they give an unrivalled picture of medieval social and agrarian history, and are a rich source much used by historians.[1] More recently, their value to architectural historians has begun to be recognised, initially at Farnham and subsequently at Winchester and for the bishop's houses in Hampshire. The estate of Bishop's Waltham, for instance, is particularly well documented, with only six years missing for the eighty years of Wykeham's and Beaufort's rule. Even the absence of building references in the accounts does not preclude such projects: those for Esher give little indication of the residential development there in the 1460s and 1470s. Even so, the Winchester accounts provide more detailed information on the building activity on a single group of estates between the thirteenth and fourteenth centuries than exists for any other outside the royal patrimony.

The bishops had a broad spread of residences at nearly half their estates, encompassing castles, palaces, country houses, and hunting lodges. We are fortunate that several of them still stand, with Wolvesey in Winchester as the primary secular survival of the Romanesque period. By about 1000 it included a timber hall, chamber, and chapel, while excavations in the 1970s revealed a church-type structure in line with a range of timber buildings.[2] This was replaced by a sequence of stone structures during the first half of the twelfth century, one of several buildings which helped to make Winchester one of the leading centres of architectural patronage during the first half of the twelfth century. This work formed the heart of the palace throughout the middle ages, for Wolvesey was also an administrative and economic centre as well as the main residence of the bishops.

The extent and defence of the see were marked by four castles, essentially developed by bishop Henry of Blois (1129–71) and slighted by Henry II in 1155. Taunton had been established by bishop Giffard (1107–29) and strengthened by Blois.[3] Farnham Castle (q.v.), an already established resting place half-way between London and Winchester, was fortified during the 1130s. Downton and Merdon castles were closer to Winchester. Downton had been an episcopal manor since the later seventh century and Blois built a motte and bailey castle there, as he did within the Iron Age earthworks at Merdon. Taunton is now a museum; Farnham remained an episcopal residence until 1955 and is now an ecumenical centre. The earthworks at Downton were landscaped in the eighteenth century as garden terraces, while Merdon was abandoned in the fourteenth century, though a little stone walling survives.[4]

Witney and Bishop's Waltham seem to have been fortified houses rather than castles. The early twelfth-century keep-like tower discovered at Witney in 1984 within a perimeter enclosure was a strong solar tower – the personal rooms of the owner – similar to the early Norman tower at the Bishop's Palace, Norwich.[5] The same applies more clearly to the tower in a pivotal position between the mid to late twelfth-century hall and the contemporary residential range at Bishop's Waltham. This work became the core of Wykeham's extensive remodelling and enlargement campaigns two centuries later.

The bishops had ten houses in Hampshire by the beginning of the fourteenth century, though their occupation levels fluctuated. John Pointoise (d.1304) particularly favoured Wolvesey, whereas Edington (d.1366) preferred Bishop's Waltham and Highclere, as did Wykeham. It was Wykeham who redeveloped the earlier fortified house at Bishop's Waltham (q.v.) as a substantial country residence on a palace-like scale, while Highclere was not far behind in size or outlay. The house at East Meon (q.v.), the centre of one of the see's largest estates, was principally an accounting centre, only occasionally used by the bishops and their guests. It was a minor residence, similar to but far better preserved than those at Fareham, Hambledon, and Marwell.

The thick stone walling incorporated in the central block of the Elizabethan/Victorian Roche Court a mile north of Fareham is less meaningful than the evidence of the bishop's house at Hambledon. The three blocked doorways of c.1180–1200 in the south wing of the mainly Tudor Manor Farm presumably opened into the offices and kitchen passage with chamber above, while the second structure was possibly an inner room with garderobe on analogy with that at East Meon.[6] The present residence and court house at Overton is a sixteenth-century timber-framed successor to the earlier episcopal house next to the parish church.[7] The moat and chapel ruins of the bishop's house stand at Marwell but the more substantial survival is the much-altered Marwell Hall nearby, where

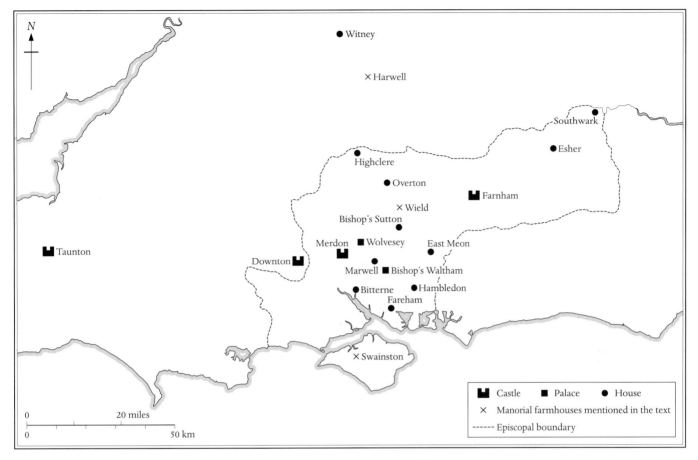

FIGURE 107 Residences of the bishops of Winchester

the central section retains the base-cruck roof of *c.*1315–25 above a nineteenth-century plaster roof of a three-bay hall built for a kinsman of the bishop of Winchester.[8] Manorial farmhouses such as Wield near Bishop's Sutton and Harwell in Berkshire were timber-framed, modest, and essentially for the farm bailiff.[9]

As the bishops frequently travelled to and from Westminster and London to participate in national affairs, they were among the first to establish a permanent residence nearby, on the south side of the Thames. Attributed to Blois, Winchester House in Southwark quickly developed into one of the largest episcopal properties in the London area (q.v.) and was an indispensable base for national as well as diocesan affairs. Apart from Farnham Castle, convenient stopping points were also established at Esher in 1245, where the gatehouse built by Waynflete by 1484 is still an occupied residence (q.v.) and at Bishop's Sutton in Hampshire.[10]

During the first half of the thirteenth century, the bishops concentrated on founding a number of new towns within the see, for the property rents and the tolls from markets and fairs proved a rich source of income. Three of the towns were entirely new developments in open countryside – Hindon near Tisbury (Wiltshire), Newtown in Burghclere (Hampshire), and Newtown (Isle of Wight). Three were established across a river from earlier settlements – Downton (Wiltshire), New Alresford, and Overton (Hampshire). New Alresford, 2 miles from the bishop's house at Bishop's Sutton, was established in 1200 at the point where bishop

Godfrey (d.1204) had built a great dam across the River Itchen to create a reservoir, one of the largest secular earthworks of medieval England.[11] The plantation became a leading wool market in the fourteenth century. Downton was established in about 1207, Overton in 1217, and Newtown in 1218 between the bishop's manors at Highclere and Burghclere, with its prosperity continuing until the late seventeenth century. Hindon, on the road from Winchester to Taunton, was established in 1219–20, and Newtown in 1256 near the bishop's house at Swainston built about seventy years earlier. Both were initially prosperous, but more commercial towns nearby prevented their long-term urban expansion.[12]

With the benefit of the wealthiest see in England, the bishops were among the great architectural patrons of their day, particularly during the later middle ages. Like Edward I and Edward III and magnates such as John of Gaunt and Thomas, 3rd earl of Warwick, William Wykeham was one of the outstanding building entrepreneurs of the later middle ages. His abilities were first displayed as clerk of the works at Windsor (1356–61) and other royal works such as Hadleigh (1359–61) and Queenborough castles (1361), and then as keeper of the privy seal (1363–7), but as soon as he was vested as bishop in 1367 and then chancellor (1367–71 and 1389–91), his rule encompassed a non-stop programme of building campaigns. He began in the 1370s by improving the more important episcopal houses – rebuilding at Highclere, refurbishing at Wolvesey and Farnham, and remodelling at Bishop's Waltham.[13]

More fundamental and distinguished projects followed: the establishment of Wykeham's educational and religious foundations of New College, Oxford (1380–7) and Winchester College (1387–94). At the same time, he continued with the conversion of Bishop's Waltham into a country palace for himself and his household (1387–96). Most of the Court House at East Meon was rebuilt between 1395–7 and the private accommodation at Farnham was improved in 1399, but the major work during the last ten years of his life was the reconstruction of the cathedral nave which his predecessor had initiated in the 1360s.

By the beginning of the fifteenth century, the episcopal residences – as elsewhere in England – were being reduced in numbers. They were essentially limited to Winchester and Southwark and the two stopping places between them – Farnham and Esher – with Bishop's Waltham as the prime country mansion. This was not because of any financial limitations, far from it, but because Henry Beaufort's activities were rarely diocesan. His priorities were to use his semi-royal position and ecclesiastical preferment to further his overwhelming political ambitions in England and to cut a major figure in the universal church abroad.[14] Created cardinal in 1427, he was equally desirous of amassing a fortune to further his power and political aggrandisement.[15] Not surprisingly, Beaufort's building activities were not as substantial as his predecessor's and were principally concentrated on improving accommodation standards. They included enhancing the private rooms and adding the cloister and great lodging range at Bishop's Waltham (1438–42), heightening and reroofing the east hall at Wolvesey (1441–2), and rebuilding the chapel there (c.1442–6). His most substantial development was the lodging accommodation at the Hospital of St Cross outside Winchester, where his work included not only new rooms for the warden but ranges for the retired retainers of his episcopal household.[16] Wykeham and Beaufort both sought to bring discipline to the earlier practice of irregularly planned buildings but placed less emphasis on the status language of the castle than most contemporary magnates. And while maintaining the continuous religious role in their works, they were anxious to enhance the aspect of lodging and privacy as much as those of comfort and luxury.

William Waynflete was less significant politically than Wykeham or Beaufort, but his building and educational patronage was as extensive and as important as Wykeham's.[17] Headmaster of Winchester College throughout the 1430s, Waynflete was appointed provost of Henry VI's school at Eton in 1441 and bishop of Winchester six years later as his reward for developing the royal foundation. An efficient and fair-minded administrator, Waynflete was more concerned with diocesan affairs than his immediate predecessors. A loyal Lancastrian supporter, he only stepped on to the political stage during the last four years of Henry VI's reign and became politically negligible under his Yorkist successor. Waynflete took the opportunity during these later years of his episcopate to implement his educational activities, which had been initiated with the foundation of Magdalen Hall in 1448 and its refounding as Magdalen College ten years later. The building of the college matured in 1468 and more particularly between 1474 and 1490, while the associated school next door was initiated in 1480. Whereas the work at Eton during his provostship had encompassed stone (chapel, hall) and brick (accommodation), his own Oxford foundations were in stone, though he used brick for his school at Wainfleet in Lincolnshire at the close of his life (1484–6).

Subsidiary building projects arose from his duties as the leading executor of the will of another Lincolnshire man, Ralph, Lord Cromwell (d.1454) and of that of Sir John Fastolf (d.1459). He was responsible for overseeing the building of Tattershall church (c.1469–82 in stone) and the chantry college and grammar school (1460s in brick), and diverted the funds intended for Fastolf's college of priests and poor men in the outer ward of Caister Castle to his Oxford foundation (1464). Finally, he improved the accommodation at Farnham Castle and Esher Place, in both cases with brick gatehouses. The imposing residential tower at Farnham was erected in 1470–5, and the more domestic one at Esher by 1484.[18]

An analysis of the episcopal registers of Wykeham and Waynflete (see table) indicates the number of visits and therefore the relative importance of their residences during the later fourteenth century[19] and the mid to late fifteenth century respectively.[20]

	William Wykeham	William Waynflete
Winchester House, Southwark	762	834
Bishop's Waltham	352	319
Esher	311	254
Farnham	274	66
Highclere	186	2
Wolvesey	120	170
Marwell	55	6
Bishop's Sutton	3	0
Merdon	3	0
East Meon	0	2
Hambledon	0	0
Fareham	0	0

Wolvesey has always been the prime residence of the bishops of Winchester. This Anglo-Norman palace of considerable complexity continued to be occupied, with only modest alterations and some remodelling, until abandoned in the 1680s in favour of an entirely new residence at the side which is the bishop's current home. The ruined palace stands as the largest secular survival of the twelfth century. William Giffard built a massive residential block (a series of chambers called the 'west hall') in about 1110, to which Henry of Blois added the ceremonial east hall with chambers in c.1135–8. The palace was given a defensive perimeter in 1138–41, followed by three fortifications on its circuit after the civil war of 1141, a keep-like kitchen, a massive garderobe tower (both 1141–54), and a new gatehouse facing the city (c.1158–71). It is essentially this ruined courtyard structure that stands today, the most substantial residence of Romanesque England. Martin Biddle has identified at least fourteen building periods, but the work of later bishops was essentially confined to remodelling the upper chambers, where neither roofs, refenestration, nor painted decoration survive. As at Bishop's Waltham and Winchester House in Southwark, there was a second court containing the stables, barns, offices, and a wool store, but this has been similarly swept away. Nor does much survive of the substantial changes undertaken by Wykeham which included widening the moat, rebuilding some of the curtain walls, and remodelling the bishop's apartments (1372–6), as well as repairing the precinct and city wall in anticipation of French attack in 1377.[21] His successor, bishop Beaufort, maintained the property in good state, reroofed the east hall in

1441, and was responsible for rebuilding the chapel at the south end of the west hall. Though there is no record for this, it probably occurred between 1442–3 and 1447 for the account rolls are missing for these years. The palace continued as a royal as much as an episcopal occupied residence throughout the fifteenth century and the first half of the sixteenth, but though it was maintained in fair condition for the next century, its inconvenience and old-fashioned character led to its abandonment in favour of a new baroque palace in the 1680s on the site of the second courtyard.

Built round three sides of a court immediately south of the Romanesque palace and on the axis of its entrance, the south and west ranges had been completed by 1684 and the east service range by 1717. This baroque residence was drastically reduced by pulling down the east and most of the south range, leaving the west range as the present residence of the bishops. The north end incorporated the mid-fifteenth-century chapel of the medieval palace, and this as much as the bishop's house was remodelled by W. D. Caroe in 1927–8, prior to episcopal reoccupation after a gap of 140 years spent at Farnham Castle.

The first-floor chapel lies at the south-east end of Giffard's residential range of c.1110 and is the only medieval part still roofed and in use. It stands on Norman foundations, either an extension by Giffard or an early addition by Blois, with the chapel at the same level as the principal Norman apartments. It was rebuilt in the mid-fifteenth century by cardinal Beaufort, but only the shell is original, for the interior was fundamentally remodelled by bishop Morley (1662–84) in 1670–1, and modified again by Caroe in 1928. The ground floor is currently inaccessible and it is not known whether it was an undercroft or a lower chapel, or even whether the area was vaulted or pillared. The interior of the three-bay chapel, 38 feet by 29½ feet, is essentially of the 1670s, when the south-facing windows were given horse-collar tracery, a stripped-down version of the clerestory windows in the cathedral but closer to the form adopted in c.1696–1704 at St Mary's, Warwick. Earlier structures against the north wall meant that it was unpierced, enabling Caroe to extend the two-storeyed services block against it. The east window is a Caroe modification, more medieval than its fellows, with glass of 1933. The marble floor, panelling, balcony and king-post roof (of reused medieval timbers) are by bishop Morley, and the ceiling by Caroe. The west entrance was also permanently closed by Caroe and replaced by the flight of steps on the south side. Despite its external appearance, this chapel is barely medieval in form or content.

The manor of Highclere, 4 miles south of Newbury, was part of the large estate of Clere which included the manors of Burghclere, Newtown, and East Woodhay. The bishop already had a residence at Highclere by the early thirteenth century, together with enclosed parkland for hunting and fishing (the fishponds subsequently transformed into Milford Lake). The house was gradually expanded, so that by the mid-fourteenth century there were two courtyards, an outer barton court and a gatehouse-approached residential inner court with the buildings in discrete units linked by covered ways as at Clarendon and Kennington palaces.[22] Bishop Edington (1346–66), who rebuilt Edington priory church (1351–61) and initiated the present nave of Winchester cathedral, also refurbished some of the structures at Highclere.[23] However, it was William Wykeham who redeveloped the inner court to convert it into a major episcopal residence where the nineteenth-century Highclere

PLATE 181 Wolvesey, Bishop's Chapel: from the south

'Castle' now stands. Episcopal visits sharply declined during the fifteenth century and the estate was farmed by local tenants until its sale in 1551.

The estate accounts for 1370–1 refer to the employment at one stage of 432 masons and labourers working under the supervision of Sir John Keton. Ninety-five men worked for a day digging the foundations, while 191 men were employed carting building materials from the quarries in Burghclere, Bentley, and Whitley. Unlike the extended redevelopment of Bishop's Waltham Palace, building work was spread over only a few years, often involving the mason John Spillesbury, who was at Highclere on many occasions between 1370 and 1397.[24] Wykeham continued Edington's work in the outer court but he concentrated on an entirely new core of residential apartments round the inner court. Between 1370–1 and 1375–6, he erected a new first-floor hall above a vaulted undercroft, with offices, high chamber, chapel, and other high-status rooms, but he made no attempt to create an integrated courtyard plan any more than he did at Bishop's Waltham.[25] In effect Highclere seems to have served as a prelude to Wykeham's more ambitious projects at Wolvesey Castle (1370s), Bishop's Waltham (1370s–80s), New College (1380s), and Winchester College (1390s), all with first-floor halls as at Highclere.

433

The estate passed through several families between 1551 and 1692, when it passed by marriage to the Herbert family who still own it. The site was thoroughly stripped for the mid-eighteenth-century classical house that was the precursor of the present Elizabethan-style mansion of 1839–42 by Sir Charles Barry for Henry Herbert, 3rd earl of Caernarvon.

NOTES

1 The rolls (account books after 1453–4) were transferred from the Public Records Office to Hampshire Record Office, Winchester in 1959.
2 Biddle (1986) 4.
3 C. A. R. Radford and A. B. Hallason, *Proc. Somerset Arch. and N. H. Soc.* 98 (1952) 55–98.
4 VCH, *Hampshire*, III (1908) 418; M. Thompson, *Arch. Jour.* 123 (1966) 221. In 1413 a 'logge' or hunting lodge was built in the park south of Merdon Castle, a little west of the present Hursley Park House. D. L. Peach, *The History of Hursley Park* (1974) 18.
5 B. Durham, *Witney Palace: Excavations at Mount House, Witney in 1984* (1985).
6 E. Roberts, *Hampshire F. C. and A. Soc. Newsletter* 19 (1993) 21–2; *Vern. Arch.* 30 (1999) 106. The east-wing roof is dendro dated to 1473–6.
7 E. Roberts, *Hampshire F. C. and A. Soc. Newsletter* 14 (1990) 30–1; *Hampshire Studies* 51 (1996) 89–106; Roberts (2003) 10–11, 243.
8 J. Crook, *Antiq. Jour.* 73 (1993) 37–68.
9 E. Roberts, *Arch. Jour.* 150 (1993) 476; J. M. Fletcher and C. R. J. Currie, *Arch. Jour.* 136 (1979) 151–72 and C. R. J. Currie, *Oxoniensia* 57 (1992) 137–42.
10 For the associated parks and fishponds to these and other episcopal properties, E. Roberts, *Proc. Hampshire F. C. and A. Soc.* 42 (1986) 123–38; 44 (1988) 67–85; 49 (1993) 229–31. See also the coverage and listing of secular and ecclesiastical older parks in Hampshire, *Hampshire Countryside Heritage*, V. *Historic Parks and Gardens* (1983) 3–6, 34–6.
11 E. Roberts, *Proc. Hampshire F. C. and A. Soc.* 41 (1985) 127–38.
12 M. Beresford, *Med. Arch.* 3 (1959) 187–215.
13 In c.1377–80, Wykeham purchased Broughton Castle, Oxfordshire, possibly as a base for overseeing the building of his new foundation at Oxford, for there was no other quality episcopal residence in the area. A more imposing approach to the private chapel at Broughton, the highly unusual loggia, and the enlargement of the gatehouse may be ascribed to him. The property passed in 1402 to Sir Thomas Wykeham, the bishop's great nephew, who obtained a licence to crenellate the property four years later.
14 G. L. Harriss, *Cardinal Beaufort* (1988).
15 His enormous loans to the crown, used to strengthen his control over people and situations, totalled over £210,000 over a thirty-year period.
16 Beaufort had as much love for Canterbury as Winchester. In return for being granted the house 'Meist Homors' within its precincts for life, he left the cathedral £1,000 towards its fabric fund. F. Woodman, *The Architectural History of Canterbury Cathedral* (1981) 194–5.
17 V. Davis, *William Waynflete: Bishop and Educationalist* (1993).
18 Waynflete was also responsible for the grisaille frescos on the walls of Eton College chapel, 1477–88, and was probably the patron of the great screen in Winchester Cathedral. P. G. Lindley, *Burlington Magazine* 131 (1989) 604–17; 135 (1993) 797–807.
19 Drawn from *Wykeham's Registers*, ed. T. F. Kirby (1899), and E. Roberts, *Arch. Jour.* 150 (1993) 477, which also records the visits of four previous fourteenth-century bishops to the eleven Hampshire properties.
20 Drawn from Davis, *William Waynflete* 159–74.
21 Biddle (1986) 18–19.
22 Phillpotts (2000) 116–17.
23 *Ibid.* 122–3.
24 J. Harvey, *Eng. Med. Arch.* (1984 edn) 279.
25 Phillpotts (2000) 124–8.

Wolvesey
M. Biddle, *Wolvesey: Handbook* (1986)
M. Biddle and H. Galine, *Wolvesey Palace.* Winchester Studies, 6, ii (in preparation)
J. Musson, *Country Life* (March 1997)

Highclere
VCH, *Hampshire*, IV (1911) 285–6
G. D. Dunlop, *Pages from the History of Highclere* (1940)
C. Phillpotts, 'Plague and reconstruction: bishops Edington and Wykeham at Highclere', in *Fourteenth Century England*, ed. N. Saul (2000) 115–32

Other properties
M. Thompson, *Medieval Bishops' Houses in England and Wales* (1998)
E. Roberts, *Hampshire Houses: 1250–1700* (2003) 200–4

WONSTON OLD HOUSE, Hampshire

The Old House lies close to the church at Wonston in the valley of the River Dever, a tributary of the Test. Externally, the balanced Georgian frontage and cottage-type extensions – late eighteenth- and late nineteenth-century work respectively – cloak the relatively complete framework of a substantial early fifteenth-century house. Mainly built of flint rubble with ashlar dressings, it consisted of a central hall, formerly open to the roof, with end cross wings. The services cross wing was originally timber-framed, as was the detached kitchen to the south, now encased in a more recent structure. The upper cross wing retains an unusual but contemporary storeyed extension (fig. 108).

The mid-Georgian façade of c.1767 with its centralising storeyed porch stands a few feet forward of the original frontage and in line with the lower cross-wing projections. The porch opens into a frontal corridor, with the first of two broad arches to the right marking the position of the original entrance. This has been lost, but the opposing entry at the far end of the cross passage retains a continuous chamfered arch with low four-centred head, base stops, and masons' marks. The cross passage, now 3 feet broader than originally, is lined with inserted sixteenth-century linenfold panelling.

The buttery and pantry are generously sized rooms, separated by the link passage to the formerly detached kitchen. This important three-bay timber-framed structure has been encased in a post-medieval brick face, but it still retains its arched open hearth in the end bay. The buttery (dining room), with an exposed internal face of flint nodules and stone quoins, retains its entry doorway with four-centred head and one of four ground-floor rectangular lights. Any early features in the pantry (sitting room) are concealed by the massively moulded walnut panelling of c.1700. The tripartite division of the rooms above the services, probably replacing a single chamber, lacks early features except for the four crown-post trusses above the ceilings. Timbers discovered within the brick walls of the present kitchen during remedial treatment in the 1990s suggest it is on the site of a rectangular predecessor, and though without clear evidence of its date, it could be a late medieval structure.

PLATE 182 Wonston Old House: from the south-west

The hall, originally about 23 feet by 20½ feet but now almost square, was ceiled with an inserted floor in the early eighteenth century. The room is entirely Georgian in character, including fenestration, fireplace, and cornice. To create its generous height and retain the original roof pitch, the upper corridor and two attic rooms were raised at a higher level than in the cross wings. The multi-raftered roof is a contemporary replacement.

The upper cross wing was divided at the beginning of the eighteenth century into a staircase hall and chamber at both levels. The ground-floor chamber with its Regency bay window has a single rectangular light, whereas the room above retains a single trefoiled light with sunk spandrels, depressed rear arch, and shutter rebate – the only decorated window in the house. The contemporary extension is more rewarding. The ground floor has a late Victorian bay window on the west side, but two rectangular lights, one with a timber head, and a door in the north-east angle with a remade two-centred head. The room above (now partitioned) has another single light in the west wall, a triple-divided light in the east wall, and a door immediately above the lower one, marginally wider, and with its original two-centred head. This room was formerly open to a three-bay roof, remodelled in the eighteenth century but incorporating at the south end two trusses of the original plain crown-post roof.

The Old House, held by the bishops of Winchester from before the Conquest until 1898, was possibly built by a leading tenant or an episcopal official, though it may have been a rectorial house since its inception.[1] It was an H-shaped house of considerable scale, and though lacking most of its detailing, the plan and walls are virtually complete. Hall, cross wings, and extension are contemporary, united by common crown-post roofs of plain construction. The hall would have been box-like in its proportions compared with the upper rooms of the cross wings, but the upper wing benefited from the extension, to have a two-roomed lodging on each floor – a larger outer chamber and smaller inner chamber with the latter equipped with a garderobe in a timber-framed (?) projection at both levels.[2] Post-medieval alterations have eradicated the evidence for the approach to the upper floor at each end of the house, though a line of revealed dressed stone indicates the west position of the first-floor doorway from the outer to the inner chamber.[3] The door and window evidence points to the years either side of 1400, but the discovery by the present owner of two cinquefoil window heads in the grounds of the house, probably removed during the early nineteenth-century remodelling, favours the early fifteenth century – the time of Beaufort rather than Wykeham.[4]

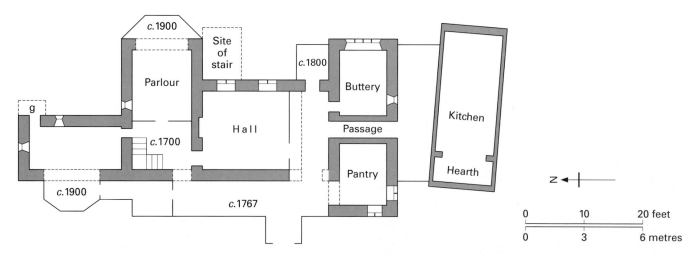

FIGURE 108 Wonston Old House: ground plan

NOTES

1 This was the case with the Manor House, Old Burghclere, a wealthy medieval rectory on an aristocratic scale. The two-bay aisled hall, 32 feet by 28 feet, with crown-post roof has been dendro dated to c.1328–9. Both cross wings are late medieval, the upper one of four bays. *Vern. Arch.* 28 (1997) 176–7; E. Roberts, *Hampshire Houses 1250–1700* (2003) 4–6, 230. The partly ruined chamber block of the wealthy medieval rectory at Odiham, now known as The Priory, stands with evidence of three first-floor chambers, dendro dated 1448–9. Roberts, *Hampshire Houses* 239.

2 This is far more likely than the intercommunicating stair proposed by the VCH, which would have broken the privacy of these rooms.

3 The cut-back joist in the buttery probably marks the position of the stair to the chamber above. That between the hall and upper cross wing was probably within the small projection at the north-east angle of the hall, removed in 1767, RCHM, *Report* (1997).

4 At this time, the rector of Wonston was John Forest who entered service under Henry Beaufort, bishop of Lincoln (1398–1404), followed his patron to Winchester in 1404, and held several offices including the mastership of the Hospital of St Cross and the position of Beaufort's vicar-general (1417–25). He was dean of Wells from 1425 to 1446.

VCH, *Hampshire*, III (1908) 453–4
RCHM, *Report: The Old House, Wonston* (1997) by N. Fradgley

WYE COLLEGE, Kent

John Kempe was born at Olantigh, a mile from Wye, in 1380. Successively bishop of Rochester (1419–21), London (1421–6), and York (1426–52), he was chancellor of England from 1426 to 1432 and a leading Lancastrian supporter. He obtained a licence in 1432 to establish a secular college of priests and a free school at Wye, to make amends for his preoccupation with state business, but building did not commence until 1447.[1] He was transferred to the see of Canterbury five years later and died in 1454. There are no building records, but as detailed college statutes were drawn up in 1447 and staff appointed in the following year, it is likely that building was initiated in the mid-1440s and was nearing completion by 1448. In that year, a master, six priests (including a chaplain, precentor, and music master), two clerks, two choristers, and a master of grammar were appointed.[2]

Excavations in the early 1950s showed that he enlarged the church to twice its present size to accommodate the college, by adding two transepts and a new chancel. This work was destroyed, in part by a collapsing steeple in 1572 and then by earth tremors in 1686, warranting a replacement short chancel in 1706. After the college had been dissolved in 1545, it was converted into a house, but became a charity school in the early 1700s until adapted by the University of London in 1892 as its centre of agricultural studies and countryside management.

The college was a small one, originally built round three sides of a small quadrangle with the fourth side closed by a wall facing the church. It was built of ragstone and rubble, with the wooden cloisters and timber-framed superstructure rebuilt in brick in 1735–9, when the sash windows were fitted. The original windows were square-headed, of one, two or three lights with cinquefoil heads. Some of the original timber framing survives internally.

The college buildings are almost complete, though modified from their initial function. They were originally approached from Wye High Street, with passage access in the south range to the kitchen and offices at the lower end of the hall and the parlour at the upper. There were two rooms over the kitchen and offices and one above the parlour. The master's lodging and dormitory or priests' lodgings lay on the north side of the quadrangle and the grammar master's rooms on the south. The hall, 43½ feet by 20 feet, stands complete with its cross-passage doorways and screen. The end walls are timber-framed, with that at the lower end retaining one of the service doorways. Stuart Rigold considered that the studding in the end walls was the earliest datable example in Kent. The screen of 1610, removed in 1895, was replaced by the present one in 1945. The hall is lit by two windows in both outer walls with twin transomed lights with cinquefoil heads, but there was initially a third window in each wall. That on the east, of unknown form, was replaced by a bay window in 1892. The head and sides of a matching window on the west side can be traced in the plaster above the fireplace and brick stack inserted in 1610. Because of the master's doorway opening off the hall dais, the windows were not regularly sited opposite each other. The hall, never ceiled or floored, retains a crown-post roof[3] and some fifteenth-century panelling against the north wall.[4]

PLATE 183 Wye College: hall range from Brick Court

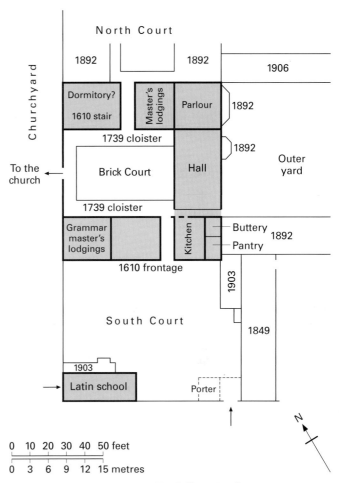

FIGURE 109 Wye College: site plan

The withdrawing chamber was approached by a door (now con-cealed) in the north-east corner of the dais. This much altered-room is essentially a Jacobean parlour with an 1892 bay window. The central beam may be original but the windows either side of the fireplace were concealed when the room was enlarged and pan-elled as part of Sir William Monyns' domestic improvements of *c*.1610. The chamber above has seventeenth-century panelling, while the cellar beneath the parlour is an original feature. The heavy oak staircase was inserted west of the passage in *c*.1610 but at its head is the crown post of the 1440s roof and evidence of the timber-framed courtyard wall.

Only the shell of the south range survives, retaining one-, two-, and three-light windows towards the street in the ground-floor flint walling. The timber framing above was brick-replaced in 1739. An early beam or two survives internally, but nothing else to indicate its original plan. The possibility that the west end was a chapel is conjectural.

The Latin School garden is lined with a wing (wheel room) that does not have medieval origins as a brewhouse, bakehouse, and stables as claimed, for it dates from 1849. The isolated building in the corner facing the street is the shell of Kempe's grammar school, with retained windows and churchyard entrance. It was formerly two-storeyed.

In 1362, Sir John Cobham (d.1365) had founded a chantry at Cobham for priests to say prayers for the souls of himself and his family. In 1370, a licence was granted for buildings to be erected to house the five chantry priests to the south of Cobham parish church. By the close of the fourteenth century, the material posses-sions and prosperity of the college had grown, as had the number of priests to nine. Lord Cobham reconstituted the abandoned college in 1597, after sixty years of decay, with its hall, kitchen, and individual rooms pressed into use as an almshouse for twenty persons, a function it still fulfils. Whereas the parish church at Cobham retained its independence of the nearby college (as did that at Higham Ferrers), the church at Maidstone was totally rebuilt by archbishop Courtenay in 1395 as an integrated part of his collegiate foundation (like those at Arundel, Fotheringhay, Manchester, and Tong). Wye College was similar in its constitution forty years after

that at Maidstone. Except for Fotheringhay and Tong, all these foundations retain their residential buildings to a lesser or greater degree. In the case of the three in Kent, the remains are of consid-erable scale and extent, with obvious similarities in layout to secular houses as well as to educational foundations.

NOTES

1 His plans were delayed by protracted negotiations with the abbot of Battle over the purchase of land adjoining the parish church.
2 G. H. Cook, *English Collegiate Churches of the Middle Ages* (1959) 4, 162–5.
3 The main tie beam is positioned not centrally but towards the lower end to avoid the direct heat from the open hearth.
4 A valuable survival lies opposite the college where a late medieval pil-grims' inn, since divided into houses, retains the canopy of its hall dais with bench-end chase and painted upper section. Attributed to the third quarter of the fifteenth century, it is one of three known canopies so far identified in Kent and the only one to survive in good condition.

C. S. Orwin and S. Williams, *History of Wye Church and Wye College* (1911)
E. W. Parkin, *Arch. Cant.* 145 (1985) 209–31
S. A. Richards, *Wye College and Its World* (1994)
J. D. Sykes, *Historic Wye College: A Visitor's Guide* (1994)

LONDON AND SOUTH-EAST ENGLAND CASTLES: RESIDENTIAL ADDITIONS

1336	Tower of London	Great hall heightened and reroofed, windows facing keep renewed	*HKW*, II (1963) 728
mid-fourteenth	Amberley, Sussex	Hall and apartments	see text
1361–6	Tower of London	Lodgings for constable	*HKW*, II (1963) 728
*c.*1360–76	Arundel, Sussex	Hall and apartments	see text
1367–70	Rochester, Kent	Hall and chambers rebuilt	*HKW*, II (1963) 811–12
1376–81	Portchester, Hants	Ashton's Tower remodelled	*HKW*, II (1963) 789–90
1381–96	Saltwood, Kent	Audience chamber and chapel	see text
1385–97	Carisbrooke, Hants	Residential block	*HKW*, II (1963) 594–5
1390–5	Winchester, Hants	Hall windows modified	*HKW*, II (1963) 863–4
1396–9	Portchester, Hants	Royal palace within inner court	*HKW*, II (1963) 789–92
1396–9	Tower of London	Lodgings for keeper or privy wardrobe	*HKW*, II (1963) 728
1470–5	Farnham, Surrey	Lodging tower in form of new hall entrance	see text
*c.*1471–83	Dover, Kent	A 'stately tower furnished with handsome apartments'	W. Darell, *History of Dover Castle* (1786) 26, 36–7, 60–1
*c.*1471–83	Dover, Kent	Keep refurbished for royal suite	*HKW*, II (1963) 641

PLATE 184 Mayfield Palace: hall porch (*c.*1330)

PLATE 185 Penshurst Place: hall porch (*c.*1340)

APPENDIX 4

LONDON AND SOUTH-EAST ENGLAND: RESIDENTIAL LICENCES TO CRENELLATE

STANDING			DESTROYED		
			1305	London, house by Temple Bar	Walter, bishop of Coventry and Lichfield
				London, tower by gate (Bucklersbury)	William Servant
			1307	Westbourne, Sussex	Matthew 'Monte Martini'
1308	Petworth, Sussex	Henry Percy (see also Yorkshire)	1308	Westminster, house at Eye	John Benstead
			1310	Bromley, Kent	William Blyburgh
			1311	London, house in Silver Street	John Pelham
				London, house in Distaff Lane	John Pelham
			1313	Colbridge, Kent	Fulk Payforer
			1314	London, house in Bread Street	John Wengrave
			1315	London, house in West Cheap	Robert Kelsey
			1318	Iden Moat, Sussex	Edmund Passelewe
			1322	Westbury, East Meon, Hants	Robert Lewer
			1329	Perching, Sussex	Robert Ardern
				Dedisham, Sussex	Thomas Tregoz
			1332	Mereworth, Kent	John Mereworth
				Cheriton, Kent	John Mereworth
			1337	London, house on Cornhill	John Coloygne
				London, house in Fleet Street	Robert, bishop of Salisbury
			1338	London, house in Baynards Ward	John Molyns
1339	Boughton Aluph, Kent	Thomas Aledon			
1341	Penshurst Place, Kent	Sir John Pulteney (see also Cambridgeshire)	1341	London, Pulteney's Inn	Sir John Pulteney
				Austin Lodge, Kent	Reginald Cobham
				Sterborough, Surrey	Reginald Cobham
			1342	Freshwater, Isle of Wight, Hants	Giles Beauchamp
1343	Westenhanger, Kent	John Kiriel			
			1347	Enfield, Middlesex	Humphrey, earl of Hereford (see also Essex)
			1363	Boughton Malherbe, Kent	Robert Corby
			1365	Fishhouse at Binstead, Isle of Wight	William, abbot of Quarr
1377	Amberley, Sussex	William, bishop of Chichester	1377	London, house in Fleet Street	Ralph, bishop of Salisbury (repeat)

STANDING

1383	Hever, Kent	John Cobham
1385	Bodiam, Sussex	Sir Edward Dalyngrigge
1392	Penshurst Place, Kent	Sir John Devereux
1441	Herstmonceux, Sussex	Sir Roger Fiennes
1448	Tonford, Kent	Thomas Browne
	Betchworth, Surrey	Thomas Browne
1479	Great Dixter, Sussex	Sir John Elrington

DESTROYED

1379	Betchworth, Surrey	John Arundell
1382	Shoford, Maidstone, Kent	William Topcliffe
1385	London, house in Carmelites, Fleet Street	Matilda Well
1433	Greenwich, Kent	Humphrey, duke of Gloucester
1437	Greenwich, Kent	Humphrey, duke of Gloucester (repeat)
1447	Aldingbourne, Sussex	Adam, bishop of Chichester
	Amberley, Sussex	Adam, bishop of Chichester
	Bexhill, Sussex	Adam, bishop of Chichester
	Broyle, Sussex	Adam, bishop of Chichester
	Cakeham, Sussex	Adam, bishop of Chichester
	Drungewick, Sussex	Adam, bishop of Chichester
	Ferring, Sussex	Adam, bishop of Chichester
	Preston, Sussex	Adam, bishop of Chichester
	Selsey, Sussex	Adam, bishop of Chichester
	Sidlesham, Sussex	Adam, bishop of Chichester
	Turzes, Sussex	Adam, bishop of Chichester
	West Wittering, Sussex	Adam, bishop of Chichester
1448	Eythorne, Kent	Thomas Browne
	Kingsnorth, Kent	Thomas Browne
	Tong, Kent	Thomas Browne
1474	Bridgecourt, Battersea, Surrey	Laurence, bishop of Durham
1479	Udimore, Sussex	Sir John Elrington
1487	Brockley, Kent	John Guldeford
	Halden, Kent	John Guldeford
	Hawkridge, Kent	John Guldeford
	Tenterden, Kent	John Guldeford
	Higham, Sussex	Sir Richard Guldeford
	Camber, Sussex	Sir Richard Guldeford

Part III
SOUTH-WEST
ENGLAND

14

SOUTH-WEST ENGLAND:
HISTORICAL BACKGROUND

DORSET AND WILTSHIRE

DORSET is a relatively self-contained county, less affected by twentieth-century commercial development or residential expansion than its neighbours, Wiltshire and Hampshire. Dorset is still primarily an agrarian county of rolling chalk downs, broken by the broad but shallow valleys of the Frome and the Stour and their tributaries. The inhospitable coastline has been little touched, while the county is bounded by the open expanse of the vale of Marshwood towards Devon, the broader Blackmore Vale towards Somerset, and Cranborne Chase towards Wiltshire. Only the residential onslaught from Poole towards the conurbation of Bournemouth introduces an alien note in this unhurried and quietly contained shire.

Two lines of chalk upland extend across Dorset from near Beaminster, one arching north-east to Cranborne Chase and Wiltshire (the Dorset Heights) and the second stretching in a belt to Dorchester, Lulworth, and the Purbeck Hills. For building purposes, Dorset also benefits from spasmodic outcrops of the limestone belt that sweeps from the Somerset border (Ham stone) and Sturminster Newton (Marnhull) to Yorkshire, with outcrops between Bridport and Weymouth and 'islands' at Portland and Purbeck. The golden Ham stone was used for high-quality buildings in the north-west, including the abbeys at Sherborne, Forde, and Cerne. The coarser, duller Coralline limestone from Marnhull was used more widely, as at Fiddleford Manor and Sturminster Newton Manor House, while the comparable local quarries near Abbotsbury provided the stone for Woodsford 'Castle' and Athelhampton Hall. Purbeck 'marble' was highly popular for decorative work from the later twelfth century, with a 'golden age' between c.1250 and 1350,[1] while roofing slates were quarried locally. Brick is unknown before its single occurrence at Witchampton in the time of Henry VIII, while thatch continues to be popular, even for larger houses since the seventeenth century such as Woodsford 'Castle' and Hammoon near Sturminster Newton.[2]

Medieval Dorset was not a wealthy region. The north was bounded by the forests of Blackmore and Gillingham and the open heath of Cranborne Chase.[3] In the south, there were the lesser forests of Bere, Powerstock, and Purbeck and the marshland edging Poole Harbour. The chalk downs that cover over half the county were not conducive to agriculture, until their value for sheep runs was exploited from the mid-fourteenth century to become the source of the county's prosperity until the nineteenth century. Towns were few, while settlements were small and limited to valley bottoms. There was little industry. Cloth manufacture was modest and confined to Dorchester, Wareham, and Sherborne. Bridport

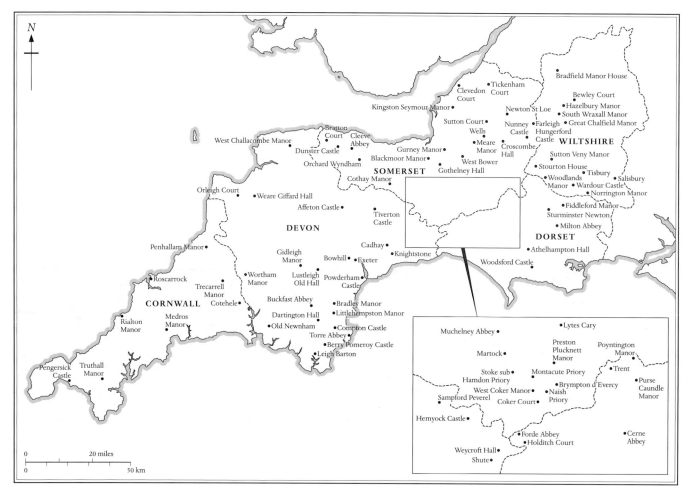

FIGURE 110 South-west England: residences described in text

was notable for rope making but coastal trade was local except from Poole towards the close of the middle ages, while the Portland quarries were not worked until the mid-seventeenth century.

The early twelfth-century bishop of Salisbury built a palace-fortress at Sherborne, while King John similarly developed major residences at Cranborne and within Corfe Castle. There was little subsequent royal, episcopal, or baronial development within the region. Unlike its neighbours, Dorset cannot boast a Wardour Castle, Dartington Hall, or Winchester College. For Dorset was essentially a region of gentry houses from the mid-thirteenth to the early seventeenth century, with some barely recorded. The principal seat of the Turbevilles, a leading family from the early four-teenth to the early eighteenth centuries, lay at Bere Regis, south-east of the church, with the last remains pulled down by the mid-nineteenth century. The great fifteenth-century kitchen at Canford is indicative of a major but otherwise virtually unknown house, while 'the goodly maner place . . . hard by the paroch chirch'[4] at East Lulworth, the family home of the Newburgh family from the late twelfth to the mid-sixteenth centuries, was supplanted in 1608–10 by Lulworth Castle, the 'hunting lodge' of the 3rd Lord Howard of Bindon. The 'fair maner place cauled Kingeston Haul' noted by Leland was replaced in the late seventeenth century by Sir John Bankes' mansion at Kingston Lacy. Held from 1229 by John Lacy, earl of Lincoln and by the duchy of Lancaster from 1349 to 1603, this double-courtyard house had been visited by John of Gaunt, Henry IV, and Henry V.[5] Those houses that have survived from the late medieval period tend to be not far from towns – Poyntington and Purse Caundle Manor House are near Sherborne, Fiddleford Manor and Sturminster Newton Manor are close to the town of that name, while Moigne Court, Woodsford Castle, Athelhampton Hall, and Wolfeton House are within reach of Dorchester. This certainly helped with access but was not axio-matic, as Witchampton Manor House and Childhay show.[6]

During the fifteenth century, three families initiated aggressive land expansion – the Martyns from Devonshire were the first, fol-lowed by the Trenchards from near Lymington in the middle of the century, and the Strangways at the close of that period. All partici-pated in the sheep-farming boom[7] and subsequently redeveloped their properties. The Martyns rebuilt Athelhampton Hall between 1485 and 1495, and the Trenchards during the first quarter of the sixteenth century, and the Strangways built Melbury in about 1540 and a house within Abbotsbury Abbey three years later. Not sur-prisingly, the leading monastic houses had been in the vanguard, particularly Cerne and Milton with their flocks of 6,629 and 7,329 sheep respectively in 1535[8] which had funded spectacular new dining halls for their abbots.

PLATE 186 Childhay Manor: hall porch

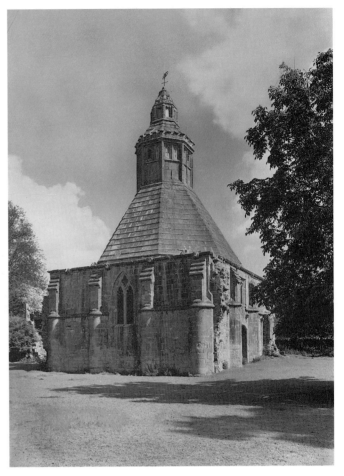

PLATE 187 Glastonbury Abbey: abbot's kitchen

Medieval Wiltshire mirrored the character of Dorset rather than Somerset, with its chalk downs, many forests, and widespread ecclesiastical landholding, though the downland had little appeal to medieval life outside the river valleys of the Salisbury and Bristol Avon. Forests formerly covered a large proportion of Wiltshire, with nine separate tracts during the thirteenth century including Chippenham and Selwood in the west and Savernake and Clarendon in the east.[9] The church held a grip on property across the shire, from the bishops of Salisbury and Winchester (at Downton) to nearly fifty ecclesiastical foundations, mainly clustered round Salisbury, Marlborough, and the River Avon.[10] In addition, there were the holdings of abbeys outside the region such as Shaftesbury (with granges at Bradford-on-Avon and Tisbury), Romsey Abbey (Steeple Ashton), Glastonbury Abbey,[11] and academic foundations including New College, Oxford (Colerne) and King's College, Cambridge (Alvediston). Apart from outsiders such as Sir John Fastolf, lord of Castle Combe, there were few lay magnates until the presence of Lord Lovel at Wardour in the late fourteenth century and Lord Stourton at Stourton in the following one. Locally prominent men during the fifteenth century included Thomas Calston of Bewley Court, the Longs of South Wraxall, the Pavelys of Brook Hall, and the long-living Thomas Tropnell of Great Chalfield, steward to Lord Hungerford and member of parliament for Bedwyn in 1429.

Fifteenth-century Wiltshire witnessed growing prosperity, with a change in the balance of lord and tenant relationship as gentlemen farmers and clothiers emerged.[12] For west Wiltshire became one of the leading cloth producing areas in the country from the late fourteenth century onwards, bringing labour and service benefits, the growth of villages (Castle Combe) as well as towns (Trowbridge, Salisbury), and widespread landscape changes from arable to pastoral farming. Only the recession between c.1450 and 1470 marred the remarkable prosperity of the region.[13] Talboys at Keevil, for example, was a mid-fifteenth-century merchant's house formerly called Brent Place after the clothier William Brent,[14] but it was not until after the Dissolution that the more wealthy clothiers, lawyers, and tradesmen were able to acquire some of the prime land of the county.

SOMERSET

The geographical character of Somerset differs markedly from Dorset and Wiltshire but the county's medieval holding, agrarian practices, and industry followed similar paths. However, in the case of Somerset, our understanding of them has been enriched by more extensive historical research (and even more so in Devon). With its varied coastline facing the Bristol Channel, the county is spanned by lines of modest hills separated by low-lying areas – the Somerset Levels. Attempts at drainage and flood defences began in Roman

PLATE 188 Wells, Bishop's Palace: Burnell's hall and chapel with Jocelin's range

times, were practised by the church from the thirteenth century, were mastered during the seventeenth century, but still demand constant maintenance.[15] The sequence of hills extends from the limestone Mendips and Polden Hills to the sandstone Quantocks, Brendon Hills, and the inhospitable moorland of Exmoor. Except for this last area, the diversity of soils, the fertile vales, and good-quality building stone have made Somerset agriculturally rich, relatively easy to traverse, and studded with a glorious range of noble buildings. In particular, the golden stone from Ham Hill was used extensively in the southern part of the county, and for doors and windows in more distant areas. Doulting stone was similarly popular towards the east, as was Bath stone from the tail of the Cotswolds. This high-quality limestone belt continued across west and north Wiltshire with the finest quarries at Box and Chilmark.[16]

Once again, the church was the largest landowner in the county, followed by the gentry, with the former holding more than a third of the region. The property of the bishop of Wells was spread widely, whereas the manors of the bishop of Winchester were centred on Taunton and the holdings of Glastonbury Abbey were within easy reach of that foundation. There were also numerous monastic foundations, including Bath, Bruton, Cleeve, Keynsham, Muchelney, and Woodspring, which not only controlled the surrounding countryside but were a powerful economic influence through their enormous sheep flocks and pioneering drainage schemes and land reclamation. Ecclesiastical prosperity was sig-

nalled not only by the Bishop's Palace and Vicar's Close at Wells but by the diversity of monastic buildings that have survived, including the abbot's kitchen and hall at Glastonbury, the abbots' lodgings at Cleeve and Muchelney, the gatehouse at Montacute, barns at Pilton and Doulting, and country houses at Meare and Chew Magna. Even two of the finest medieval inns in southern England – the George and Pilgrim at Glastonbury and the George at Norton St Philip – were originally monastic lodging houses.[17]

In such an agriculturally rich county, the lack of resident peers is surprising, particularly as many of the gentry developed a portfolio of profitable holdings as the shire developed sheep farming over the earlier mixed farming system. In 1791, Collinson printed a list identifying ninety gentry resident in the county in 1502.[18] Two centuries later, their status and places of residence were researched[19] and the careers of the more important members summarised. The listing points up the relatively small numbers of this class of society compared with the extensive number of parishes in the county (482). There was only one peer, Lord FitzWaring, who was resident at Tawstock Court in north Devon, and of the ten knights, four were resident in neighbouring counties. The most important include Sir Amias Poulett (d.1538) of Hinton St George, sheriff of Somerset in 1485 and member of parliament for the county in 1495, who rebuilt Hinton House after inheriting it in 1488; and Sir Walter Hungerford (d.1516), who lived as much at Heytesbury in Wiltshire as at Farleigh Hungerford Castle, just as Sir Hugh

Luttrell (d.1521) preferred to live at East Quantoxhead Manor rather than Dunster Castle as his successors do today. Of the higher gentry, Thomas Tremayle (later knighted) built himself the splendidly preserved Blackmoor Manor, while John Hymerford (d.1501) of East Coker was a royal servant who was the king's receiver and constable in Somerset. The majority were men of lesser means and influence, with locally significant legal and administrative interests, such as John Sydenham of Brympton d'Evercy and Nicholas Bluet of Greenham Barton (both with yearly incomes of £100), while more typical were John Sydenham of Orchard Wyndham (£66 6s 7d), and Nicholas Bratton of Bratton Court, Thomas Michell of Gurney Manor, and Nicholas St Loe of Sutton Court, all with annual incomes of £40.

Apart from Bristol, Somerset is not a county with large towns but one of numerous villages and hamlets except in the Mendips and Exmoor. South-east Somerset, in particular, is rich in ridge and furrow and lynchet evidence of dense medieval cultivation and habitation.[20] However, as in the neighbouring shires to the east and south-east, prosperity declined during the earlier fourteenth century, partly arising from the period of terrible weather from 1315 to 1318 that heralded poor harvests and grain yields, disease, and the abandonment of marginal lands. The consequences of the Black Death accelerated the situation, with falling rents, the commutation of labour services, and the growth in peasant holdings. In 1360, the men and women working outdoors on Chedzoy manor, for instance, withdrew their labour to increase the pressure on nearby demesne holdings and the prospect of letting them out to tenants.[21] This rise of a rental economy not only affected the pattern of landholding, but encouraged replacement of corn crops with grass for the ubiquitous sheep, and accelerated the demand for cloth. In 1395, Somerset was the only county to produce more than 10,000 cloths, followed by Wiltshire with between 5,000 and 10,000 and Dorset with below 1,000.[22] The valleys of the Frome and the Bristol Avon became increasingly important for their fulling mills, with Bristol as the developing distribution and exporting centre for this far from nascent industry. The widespread economic and settlement recovery from the 1460s was marked by the renewal of sheep farm enclosure, the growth of small holdings and vernacular houses, and the wonderful church towers – lofty and richly decorated – for which the region is famous.

Somerset has few grand mansions, but it holds a wealth of medium-sized residences, though few of the medieval period can be as firmly attributed to wool production or the cloth industry as many commentators have claimed. The legal profession was more often responsible, funding the construction of Gothelney Hall, Gurney Manor, Blackmoor Manor, and West Bower Manor. The same applies across the border, with a lawyer responsible for Great Chalfield Manor and, contrary to most texts, with no evidence that Robert Long of South Wraxall Manor was involved in the wool trade.[23]

DEVON AND CORNWALL

For Devon and Cornwall, the combination of three moorland bosses, an extended coastline with deep inlets to the north and south, the contrasting colours of the land from hard grey granite to warm red sandstone, and the absence of major industrial conurbations all help to give the south-west peninsula its distinctive character. The land never rises very high – only parts of Exmoor and Dartmoor exceed 1,300 feet – and is marked by a sequence of relatively short but swift-flowing rivers and south-facing wooded valleys.[24]

Devon is the third largest county in England after Yorkshire and Lincolnshire, and like Cornwall is still essentially rural. The barren and uninhabited granite masses of Dartmoor, Bodmin Moor, and West Penwith separate the undulating and populous southern lowlands from the rather monotonous and thinly populated central area and harsher northern coastline. Nearly a third of the region's population is concentrated in the three urban sprawls of Exeter, Torbay, and Plymouth. All other towns are relatively small, for Devon and Cornwall are marked by a pattern of several hundred parishes (over 450 in Devon, 210 in Cornwall) and a network of scattered settlements.

The south-west peninsula enjoys a wide range of building materials. Devon limestone is particularly durable, ranging from the light-coloured stone near Beer to the mid-grey/pink limestone of the Ashburton–Torbay–Plymouth region. It was used for Compton Castle and the bishop's houses at Chudleigh and Bishopsteignton. Beer stone is better for internal than external work, easy to cut and quick to harden on exposure to the air. Its benefits and limitations are exhibited inside and outside Exeter Cathedral. Fine-grained sandstone is found in the lower reaches of the Exe, Taw, and Torridge as at Bickleigh Castle, with the more rusty red-coloured breccia edging Torbay. It is of variable quality but was popular for churches. Slate was widely quarried in both counties for it was easy to work though not of high quality. It occurs in the Tavistock and South Hams area, with local quarries resourcing Dartington Hall and Leigh Barton. Delabole roofing slate from north Cornwall was prized for its lightness, workability, and durability, and can be found as far afield as south Wales and northern France. Granite was not considered a 'polite' building material before it was first used in Cornwall in the early sixteenth century at Bodmin church, Trecarrell Manor, and Cotehele. The other igneous rock, trap or basalt, is a pink to purple rock found in the Tiverton–Crediton area and used at Exeter Castle. Flint, common in Wiltshire and Dorset, creeps across the border to east Devon at Hemyock Castle and Shute. Cob, a long-lasting mixture of clay and chopped straw often used for farmhouses and cottages, occasionally occurs in larger houses such as Bowhill, while thatching has a remarkably extended history in Devon.[25] Brick was used no earlier than the 1620s at Ince 'Castle', but Leland records its occurrence a century earlier in Devon when the lawyer George Rolle used it to build 'a right faire house' in place of the medieval one at Stevenstone near Torrington.[26]

In 1225, Henry III granted the shrievalty of Cornwall and its tin workings to his younger brother Richard, and two years later made it an earldom. Richard already held Launceston Castle but he secured that at Tintagel in 1236, persuaded the heiress of the honour of Cardinham to part with Restormel Castle and Lostwithiel in 1268–9, and rounded off his acquisition policy by buying Trematon Castle and several linked estates two years later. He died in 1272 and was buried in the abbey he founded at Hailes in Gloucestershire rather than in Cornwall. His son Edmund (d.1300) redeveloped Restormel Castle and made Lostwithiel the capital of his earldom where he erected the buildings that house his officials, the so-called 'Duchy Palace'.[27] Edmund resided in the county but his successors did not, even though Edward III raised it

PLATE 189 Shute: from the site of the hall

to a duchy in 1337 and bestowed it on his eldest son in perpetuity. As ducal visits were nonexistent, there was much manoeuvring to gain its stewardship,[28] but the royal officials kept the duchy in touch with the wider world and brought a rare management efficiency and solvency compared with many estate blocks elsewhere in southern England.[29]

There were few magnate families in Devon during the later middle ages but it is surprising how many events revolved round their houses. The two largest honours during the thirteenth century, those of Okehampton and Plympton, were combined in 1335 in the hands of Hugh Courtenay at the same time as he was created earl of Devon. The redevelopment of the castles at Tiverton, Okehampton, and possibly Plympton was part of his self-aggrandisement programme, but the Courtenays always remained one of the poorest baronial families in England. Their pre-eminence was challenged twice. The first time was in the late fourteenth century by the king's half-brother. After John Holand, earl of Huntingdon, had purchased the manor of Dartington near Totnes, he rebuilt the Hall as a dynastic centre for his family, was created duke of Exeter in 1397, and built up a courtier's affinity that seriously threatened the Courtenays. Holand's execution in the first months of Lancastrian rule put an immediate end to this powerful invader but other magnates stepped into the gap that had been opened up. The Bonville family, centred on Shute close to the Dorset border and the Courtenays' home at Colcombe, was a longer-lasting threat, extending from the mid to the late fifteenth century when central and southern Devon suffered a more intense period of political instability than any other part of the country outside the north of England.[30]

The problems were already in train when Sir William Bonville attacked and pillaged Weycroft, the home of his neighbour Thomas Brooke in 1427 who promptly obtained a licence to crenellate his house with the explicit support of Humphrey, duke of Gloucester, two earls, and five knights. A year later, Edward Pomeroy and his family were expelled from their manor house at Berry Pomeroy next to the church by a rival family faction, but the heart of the problems in Devon lay in the long-simmering resentment between the earl of Devon and his enemies, the earl of Wiltshire and Lord Bonville of Shute. In 1451, Courtenay mobilised forces against Wiltshire and then Bonville at Taunton Castle, and though the duke

of York calmed the situation, it broke out again in 1455 when the earl and his son attacked Bonville and his supporters, murdered his lawyer in his house at Upcott Barton, commandeered Exeter, and besieged his kinsman and Bonville supporter at Powderham Castle for two months. The earl's subsequent success at the pitched battle at Clyst Bridge was followed by the thorough pillaging of Shute by the earl's men. However, Courtenay died shortly afterwards while Bonville trimmed his sails until his death in 1461.

The succeeding period of calm under Yorkist rule was broken several times. Initially it was by the fleeing earls of Warwick and Clarence from Dartmouth in March 1470, followed by the earl of Oxford's attack on St Michael's Mount in 1473. The western rebellion against Richard III towards the close of 1483, part of Buckingham's rebellion, was led by Thomas Grey, marquess of Dorset, Sir Thomas St Ledger of Dartington Hall, Sir Thomas Arundel of Lanherne, and Richard Edgcumbe of Cotehele. Their failure was followed by flight overseas, except for St Ledger who was executed. The Cornish rising of June 1497 and the march to London to protest against the royal taxes levied to pay for the war with Scotland was quelled at Blackheath.[31] Three months later, Perkin Warbeck's arrival near Land's End was soon supported by up to 8,000 men, but his failure to take Exeter not only was his death knell but closed more than half a century of turbulence in the region. Even so, much of Devon and Cornwall continued to be on a war footing until well into the sixteenth century, for the piratical attacks that had long plagued the southern coastline continued unabated.

Political misfortune did not necessarily mean a permanent setback. The Holands returned to Dartington during the second quarter of the fifteenth century, though their interests lay mainly at court and the family died out in 1475. The Bonville inheritance passed to the great granddaughter of Sir William Bonville who married Thomas Grey, marquess of Dorset in 1474 and initiated a new era in the fortunes of that Leicestershire family. Though the Courtenays had been attainted in 1461 and again ten years later, a distant cousin recovered their lands and honours in 1485 just as Sir Thomas Fulford recovered the lands his father lost after his execution in 1461, enabling his son to initiate the rebuilding of the ancestral home at Fulford during the early sixteenth century. Even so, the Courtenays no longer held a monopoly of aristocratic privilege and affinity, for several families such as the Bourchiers and Dinhams were now vying for power, with incomes almost equal to the reduced circumstances of the Courtenays.

The sharp decline in the number of knights between the mid-fourteenth and late fifteenth century seen across the country is similarly reflected in Devon, for the total of thirty-three knights recorded in 1324 (including six aged or decrepit) had fallen to eight in 1434 though they included Sir Philip Courtenay of Powderham, Sir Roger Champernowne of Bere Ferrers and Modbury, Sir Nicholas Carew of Mohuns Ottery, Sir Thomas Brooke of Holditch, and Sir John Dinham of Nutwell.[32] Below this relatively narrow band was a broad spread of minor gentry and freeholders with little differentiation initially. There were sometimes two or three such landholders in a parish across this extensive region, helped by the proportionately greater areas of waste and common land than anywhere else in England outside Northumbria.[33] Many of the locally important families of the late middle ages had already been established in their locality since the late twelfth century,

PLATE 190 Lostwithiel 'Palace': engraving from the south-east by S. and N. Buck (1734)

including Bonville of Shute, Champernowne of Modbury, Dennis of Orleigh, Dinham of Hartland and Nutwell, Fulford of Great Fulford, Giffard of Weare Giffard, Pomeroy of Berry Pomeroy, and Stucley of Affeton. Many of these also held land in Cornwall but the houses with which they are associated all date from the late middle ages.[34]

As elsewhere in the south-west, the opportunities offered by land availability after the Black Death meant the assimilation and extension of scattered holdings into large farms across the region and that movement of social climbing that marked the later middle ages.[35] Such estates rarely numbered more than twelve manors, though they could be extremely large, while those who held scattered properties leased out those furthest away to service their own household. Place Barton, Ashton, the home of Sir James Chudleigh, the four times married member of parliament, still retains the farm that was always part of this much-altered gentry courtyard house. The Fortescues of Weare Giffard and the Bluetts of Holcombe Rogus were also farmers with estates developed during the early and mid-fifteenth century, as were those of the Malherbe family of Payhembury, whose accounts survive though not their house. The practice of accumulation and the benefit of upward mobility was so widespread across the region that Hooker identified nearly 400 such families in Devon by the early seventeenth century.

The same story applies to Cornwall, though the total absence of magnates or higher gentry in Cornwall brought even more prominence to small landholders and social climbers. Their estates were modest – as were their houses – but they were fiercely proud of their antecedents and status. By the close of our period, the local gentry constituted a higher ratio to the number of parishes than in any other county in England.[36] Only then did families such as the Edgcumbes of Cotehele, Grenvilles of Stowe, Godolphins of Godolphin House, and the Treffry brothers of Place, Fowey – all well rewarded for their loyalty by Henry VII – develop houses of architectural pretension that reflected their higher standing.[37]

The only other landlord of significance in the south-west peninsula was the church, which held a sixth of Devon's acreage but far less in Cornwall. The bishop of Exeter possessed twenty-four manors in Devon, bringing in twice the income of the eleven in Cornwall supplemented by a small return from those near London. In 1535, the bishop's income was £1,600 a year, about two-thirds that of the earl of Devon. The dean and chapter of the cathedral had fourteen manors in Devon but the substantial income from tithes and manorial courts raised that to £1,072 a year, while the properties of the two leading monasteries of Tavistock and Plympton were not much less at £986 and £837 a year.[38] The estates of the other twenty-nine monasteries[39] were scattered and brought in less than £500 a year, led by Buckfast at £486 though the majority were considerably lower than this.[40] Even so, the Dissolution of the Monasteries coincided with the collapse of the Courtenay domain, so that the land transfers and sales made by the crown during the late 1530s were even more ground-shaking than elsewhere in southern England.

The Black Death seems to have impoverished the south-west peninsula far less than other parts of southern England, with a relatively speedy recovery by the late fourteenth century in agriculture as well as the three localised activities of tin mining in Cornwall and Dartmoor, the nascent cloth industry affecting Exeter, Tavistock, and South Molton, and shipping from the south coastal ports.[41] Despite the mid-century setback which permanently damaged the tin trade in favour of Cornwall,[42] nearly 95 per cent of the pre-Victorian churches in Devon date predominantly from the later Perpendicular period,[43] with eminent entrepreneurs adding personalised chapels such as those by wool merchants at Cullompton and Tiverton[44] and the splendid glass inserted in St Neots church between 1480 and 1530.[45]

The Hundred Years' War fostered the trade of the southern ports with the building of war vessels, transporting troops and supplies, and serving as contractors to the benefit of such people as Hawley

449

of Dartmouth and the Bonifaces and Michelstows of Fowey. Dartmouth and Plymouth were protected in Richard II's reign with walled and towered enclosures,[46] but the War also brought foreign raids and piracy which continued well into the sixteenth century.[47] A tower-house was built at Gomerock opposite Dartmouth Castle in the early fifteenth century[48] and a blockhouse at Fowey in c.1460, but it is the castle built by the citizens at Dartmouth between 1481 and 1495 that is seen as the first offensive artillery fortification in England.[49] It was followed by Kingswear Castle on the opposite bank of the Dart estuary between 1491 and 1502 and similar action by other south-western ports. Even the owners of Berry Pomeroy and Compton castles considered it essential to protect their residences near the coast with expensive but meaningful protection.

NOTES

1 G. D. Drury, *Proc. Dorset N. H. and A. Soc.* 70 (1949) 74–98; R. Leach, *An Investigation into the Use of Purbeck Marble in Medieval England* (1978).

2 M. Billett, *Thatched Buildings of Dorset* (1984).

3 A. Horsfall, *Proc. Dorset N. H. and A. Soc.* 119 (1997) 59–64. Cranborne Chase covered about 25,000 acres.

4 Leland, *Itinerary*, I, 253. Leland commented on the armorial glass windows in the parlour of this manor house, *ibid*. The Newburghs were buried at Bindon Abbey, 3 miles north of Lulworth, founded in 1172 by Roger of Newburgh.

5 A large archive of account rolls from 1295 to 1462 held at Kingston Lacy, supported by limited excavation in the mid-1990s, has revealed the form and layout of this substantial residence. By the fourteenth century, the gatehouse opened into an outer court holding the granary, storehouses, workshops, and sheds, while the inner court enclosed the house, and separate chapel, kitchen, and bakehouse. Some of the stone buildings were thatched and many of the lesser ones were either of cob or timber-framed, as was the case at Shute across the Devon border. The house included an 'old' hall (possibly twelfth or thirteenth century at first-floor level) as well as a 'great' hall, while the small excavation on the site revealed plain floor tiles, painted plasterwork, decorated stonework, and roof tiles. The house was in ruins by 1493. M. Papworth, *Proc. Dorset N. H. and A. Soc.* 120 (1998) 45–62.

6 The medieval deer parks, often associated with major houses, are surveyed in a sequence of seventeen papers by L. M. Cantor and J. D. Wilson, *Proc. Dorset N. H. and A. Soc.* 83–100 (1962–78). The small hunting lodge built at Pamphill in the early fifteenth century had a first-floor hall and solar. It is now a house within the Kingston Lacy estate. M. Papworth, *Jour. Brit. Arch. Assoc.* 147 (1994) 57–121.

7 As did Sir Roger Newburgh (d.1515) of East Lulworth. For details, A. Oswald, *Country Houses of Dorset* (1959) 16.

8 *Valor Ecclesiasticus*, I (1810) 227–92.

9 Over ninety deer parks have been identified in Wiltshire. K. Watts, *Wilts. Arch. and N. H. Mag.* 89 (1996) 88–98.

10 Detailed in VCH, *Wiltshire*, III (1956) 150–397.

11 Excavations in 1963–8 at Gomeldon, near Salisbury, revealed the abbey's sheep and arable holding with living accommodation from the late twelfth century and farm buildings of the thirteenth and fourteenth centuries. J. Musty and D. Algar, *Wilts. Arch. Mag.* 80 (1986) 127–69.

12 J. N. Hare, 'Land and tenant in Wiltshire c.1380–1520', PhD thesis, University of London (1976).

13 A. R. Bridbury, *Medieval English Clothmaking* (1982); E. M. Carus-Wilson in VCH, *Wiltshire*, IV (1959); J. N. Hare in *Conflict and Community in Southern England*, ed. B. Stapleton (1992) 25–30.

14 A rare timber-framed house for Wiltshire, the hall gallery carries the garter arms post 1432 of the lord of the manor, Arundel quartered with Maltravers.

15 M. Williams, *The Draining of the Somerset Levels* (1970); M. Havinden, *The Somerset Landscape* (1981) 109–12, 149–71.

16 For building materials, E. H. D. Williams, *Proc. Somerset Arch. and N. H. Soc.* 135 (1991) 123–34.

17 E. H. D. Williams, J. and J. Penoyre, and B. C. H. Hale, *Arch. Jour.* 144 (1987) 317–27. Also F. Mann and K. Rodwell, *The George Inn, Norton St. Philip* (1999).

18 *History and Antiquities of the County of Somerset*, I (1791) xxxix–xl.

19 M. Havinden, 'The resident gentry of Somerset in 1502', *Proc. Somerset Arch. and N. H. Soc.* 139 (1996) 1–15. Havinden makes some corrections to the original listing of 1502, including some with seats elsewhere, amending the total of resident gentry to ninety-eight.

20 Map in *Aspects of the Medieval Landscape of Somerset*, ed. M. Aston (1998) 86.

21 M. Siraut in *Somerset*, ed. T. Maybury and H. Binding (1999) 33.

22 R. A. Pelham in *An Historical Geography of England before 1800*, ed. H. C. Darby (1936) 250–2.

23 Over 105 deer parks have been identified in Somerset, mainly developed between the mid-thirteenth and mid-fourteenth centuries: J. Bond, *Somerset Parks and Gardens* (1998) 26. Episcopal and monastic holdings were numerous but the majority of parks were in secular hands, mainly greater and lesser gentry. Most of them were in south Somerset and averaged between 100 to 300 acres.

24 *The Geology of Devon*, ed. E. M. Durrance and D. J. C. Laming (1982); *The Geology of Cornwall*, ed. E. B. Selwood (1998); V. Cheshar in *Historical Atlas of South-West England* (1999) 35–40.

25 J. Cox and J. R. L. Thorp, *Devon Thatch* (2001).

26 *Itinerary*, I, 173. The house was rebuilt in 1869.

27 N. J. G. Pounds, *Arch. Jour.* 136 (1979) 203–17; L. M. Midgley, *Ministers' Accounts of the Earldom of Cornwall, 1296–97* (1942–5).

28 The dispute over this stewardship was the long-running cause of the armed conflict between the earl of Devon and Sir William Bonville which climaxed in 1455. A similar dispute over the deputy stewardship between Thomas Clemans and John Glyn culminated in Glyn's murder by Clemans' men.

29 Compare the assessment by J. Hatcher, *Rural Economy and Society in the Duchy of Cornwall 1300–1500* (1970) 257–9 with the sour one by L. E. Elliott-Binns, *Medieval Cornwall* (1955) 166–72.

30 N. Orme in *Historical Atlas of South-West England*, ed. R. Kain and W. Ravenhill (1999) 144–5.

31 W. J. Blake, *Jour. Roy. Inst. Cornwall* 20 pt 1 (1915) 49–86.

32 J. J. Alexander, *Trans. Devon Assoc.* 71 (1939) 289–300; 72 (1940) 283–304.

33 W. G. Hoskins, *Devon* (1954) 79.

34 The deer parks serving most of these houses are earlier. Nearly fifty have been identified in Devon, with the majority established during the thirteenth and fourteenth centuries, including those of the Courtenays at Chulmleigh, Colyton, Norton, Okehampton, and Tiverton, and of the bishops of Exeter at Crediton, Morchard Bishop, and Paignton. R. Iles in *Devon Gardens*, ed. S. Pugsley (1994) 21–7. Part of the stone boundary walls remain at Berry Pomeroy and Chagford, and at Dartington with the remains of a lodge in the middle of the park. A. Emery, *Dartington Hall* (1970) 19.

35 H. Fox in *The Agrarian History of England and Wales: 1348–1500*, ed. E. Miller (1991) 152–74, 303–23, 722–43, and in *Historical Atlas of South-West England* 273–9.

36 J. Cornwall, 'The early Tudor gentry', *Economic History Review* 3 (1965) 459–61.

37 L. E. Elliott-Binns (1955) 231–54, 356–62.

38 Hoskins, *Devon* 81.

39 There were nineteen in Devon, nine in Cornwall, and the collegiate foundation at Glasney near Penrhyn, established by bishop Bronescombe in 1265 to bring ecclesiastical reform to a remote part of his diocese but insufficiently endowed to flourish.

40 *Unity and Variety: A History of the Church in Devon and Cornwall*, ed. N. Orme (1991); C. Holdsworth in *Historical Atlas of South-West England* 206–11.

41 W. G. Hoskins in M. Finberg and W. G. Hoskins, *Devonshire Studies* (1952) 233–49; J. Hatcher, *Rural Economy and Society in the Duchy of Cornwall: 1300–1500* (1970) 35–6, 144–7, 149–51. This era of relative prosperity continued until the 1440s.

42 Several early buildings associated with each of these three industries can still be seen. The 'castle' at Lydford had been a purpose-built gaol for the Stanneries since its construction in 1195 and continued to be used as the prison for Devon offences until the eighteenth century. A. D. Saunders, *Med. Arch.* 24 (1980) 123–86. For a brief survey of the nearby area between 550 and 1550, P. White, *Medieval Dartmoor* (2001).

43 B. Cherry and N. Pevsner, *Devon* (1989) 42–3.

44 E. Carus-Wilson, *Med. Arch.* 1 (1957) 104–17.

45 This was essentially funded from the duchy profits of tin mining, supported by the earl of Devon and the local gentry. It is the only glazing survival in England that compares with the contemporary glass at Fairford. J. Mattingly, *Jour. Roy. Inst. Cornwall* 3 (2000) 9–55.

46 There was also the more personal reward granted to Richard Merton in 1340 of a licence to crenellate his house at Great Torrington 'in consideration of his goodwill in the war with France'. *Cal. Pat. Rolls: 1340–43*, 39, repeated seven years later.

47 As late as 1542, the people of Teignmouth complained to Leland about recent French raids. *Itinerary*, I, 225.

48 Possibly the consequence of the crenellation licence granted to John Corp, a prominent local merchant, in 1402. *Cal. Pat. Rolls: 1401–05*, 219. Gomerock was also the terminal of the Dartmouth boom chain, first recorded in 1462. *Med. Arch.* 43 (1999) 241.

49 B. H. St J. O'Neil, *Archaeologia* 85 (1936) 129–58; A. J. Saunders, *Dartmouth Castle: Handbook* (1983).

15

SOUTH-WEST ENGLAND: ARCHITECTURAL INTRODUCTION

DORSET is an appropriate introduction to the houses of south-west England, for with one key exception the early flourish of royal and episcopal castles in Wiltshire and Dorset was followed by almost total withdrawal from them. The ten stone castles in Wiltshire, led by the royal properties at Ludgershall, Marlborough, and Old Sarum and the episcopal fortresses within Old Sarum and at Devizes, Malmesbury and Downton were all in decay by 1350.[1] Of the six stone castles in Dorset, only the dramatically sited royal fortress at Corfe and the early twelfth-century episcopal palace-fortress at Sherborne continued to be occupied throughout the middle ages.[2] Building work at both sites had been completed before the close of the thirteenth century except for a tiered five-chamber tower added at Corfe Castle in 1377–8 which only survives at undercroft level,[3] and some contemporary modifications at Sherborne.[4]

DEFENDABLE HOUSES

Our interest in Corfe Castle lies in the extremely important royal house built within the inner ward for King John in about 1201. Though badly ruined, its plan is relatively clear, but the region is particularly fortunate in possessing a second house for the same king at Cranborne. Despite its wholesale remodelling in the early seventeenth century which has converted this manor house into one of the most beautiful residences in southern England, the structure of *c.*1207 stands remarkably complete. These two houses, far earlier than any others surveyed in this volume, are of outstanding importance not only because of their early date and royal status, but because of the relative completeness of their plan and form and their relevance to regional developments up to 150 years later.

Both residences were stimulated by the king's love of the hunt in the royal forest of Purbeck and across Cranborne Chase. The two-storeyed house built on the flattened peak of the castle hill at Corfe has been known as the 'Gloriette' (the glorious house) since at least 1280.[5] The principal ranges above vaulted undercrofts consisted of a first-floor hall with a presence chamber or chapel at its lower end, and an elongated *camera* at its upper end filling the south side of a small court, with the north side lined by a three-storeyed porch and stair approach. The building is entirely domestic, and even in its ruined state its austere but stylish decorative character is clearly of the highest architectural quality, 'representing a sophisticated and elegant mode of life'.[6] Slight evidence remains of a narrow west range that may have been used by the queen but nothing of the associated kitchen and services area. The contrast of this compact but distinguished house of 1201–4, built to replace or supplement the stark and uncompromisingly bare keep of *c.*1105 close by, speaks loudly of the massive development in residential architecture within a hundred years.

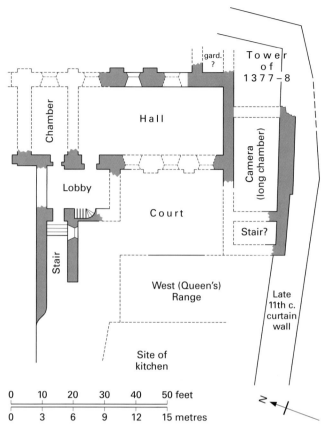

FIGURE 111 Corfe Castle: first-floor plan of King John's house

the projecting spiral stair in line with the massive internal division, still a prominent feature of the south façade of the manor house, which was also served by a garderobe turret at the south-east corner. This last feature was replaced in the early seventeenth century by a tower built to match the thirteenth-century three-storeyed tower at the south-west corner of the house, now raised a further storey at that time. The crenellated parapet was carried on a continuous line of decorative corbels, one of the many features that have survived over 800 years.

The many large Jacobean windows inserted in the thirteenth-century walls by the 1st earl of Salisbury, as well as the modified internal floor levels and fittings of *c*.1608–12, diminish the fortified character of this house which is far more apparent in Norden's elevation. It could be argued that this signal survival was not deliberately defensive and that the small ground-floor windows, vaulted undercrofts, and a dominant crenellated parapet were simply characteristic of the time and were repeated at Corfe. But while the latter was guarded by the curtilage of a fortress that made further

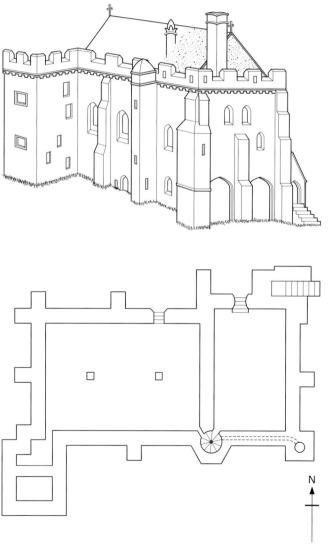

FIGURE 112 Cranborne Manor House: view from the south-east and ground plan, based on the survey made by John Norden, 1605

We are extremely fortunate that John Norden's survey of the manor of Cranborne, prepared for Robert Cecil, 1st earl of Salisbury in 1605, has survived, with an elevation and plan of the house on the title page giving a remarkably clear record of this early royal residence.[7] They can be compared with the visible evidence at Cranborne Manor House, for earlier assessments attributing this residence to the fourteenth century have been disproved after a detailed examination of the structure in 1971, confirming internal discoveries during restoration work in the 1960s.[8] Dating from the first decade of the thirteenth century,[9] this royal manor house survives to an extraordinary extent.

Norden's drawing shows a heavily buttressed and crenellated residence with the principal apartments raised above a larger and a smaller ground-floor undercroft separated by a thick wall. The principal apartment was a heated first-floor hall, probably open to the steeply pitched roof, above the two-pillared vaulted undercroft.[10] The eastern end was multi-storeyed, with the smaller vaulted undercroft incorporating a low mezzanine floor approached from the external covered stair shown in the drawing. This probably opened into an entry hall and guard lobby, apparently ill-lit. Above was the royal chapel, retaining its original lancet window and piscina, separated from the chaplain's chamber with a contemporary aumbrey. The uppermost floor with the two windows shown in the end wall was the royal chamber, with the fireplace (and that of the chaplain below) served by the two chimneys above. This sequence of rooms and the roof were reached by

PLATE 191 Chideok Castle: engraving of the gatehouse by S. and N. Buck (1733) shortly before its destruction

protection unnecessary, the height of Cranborne is notable, and the walls were 5 feet thick, while the recovery of a ground-level double-splayed loop in the 1960s indicates that the approaches to the house were deliberately covered in case of attack. The enclosing moat was filled in centuries ago during an early stage in the growth of the ravishing gardens that enhance this manor house, but the other defensive elements – the vaulted undercrofts, the raised apartments, the embattled parapet with arrowslits, and the projecting towers – occur again at Woodsford 'Castle' a century and a half later.

Before reaching that development, several other houses within a short distance of the coast had taken defensive steps. In 1267, William Moyne obtained a licence to crenellate his home at Owermoigne,[11] while Godlingston Manor with its end tower is a smaller version of Lympne Castle in Kent.[12] Only the quadrangular platform is obvious at Chideok Castle, built by Sir John Chidiok (d.1387) under licence in 1370, though Buck's engraving of 1733 shows that the gatehouse was four-square with octagonal corner turrets.[13] More remains at Holditch Castle, crenellated by Thomas Brook in 1397, including part of its towered enclosure and sixteenth-century gatehouse. This leaves Woodsford 'Castle' as the pre-eminent fortified house of the region and one of the most important fourteenth-century survivals in southern England. There is no visible evidence of the moat, the quadrangular layout, the west gateway, or the hall that are known to have been an integral part of this property. And the surviving residential range dates not from the licence to crenellate of 1335 but from a rebuilding of about thirty-five years later. This well-preserved range displays a highly individual plan of ground-floor service rooms below a line of first-floor residential apartments, arranged as a multi-unitary complex. Though its defensive character has been permanently softened by a replacement thatched roof, as well as the loss of the crenellated parapet and two interlocking towers, the range consists of at least two service and three residential units, the former tunnel

vaulted, well lit, and spacious, while the apartments above combined generous facilities with elegant workmanship. Built by Sir Guy Brian in about 1370, the range reflected the movement for household privacy and planning complexity that was a hallmark of the later fourteenth century.

During and after Sir Guy's time, Dorset gentry continued to maintain a wary eye on defensive possibilities, as the crenellation licences for Herringston and Hooke Court indicate.[14] The mid-fourteenth-century manor house south of the River Stour at Sturminster Newton had been built within the protective banks and ditches of a prehistoric fort, while the gatehouse at Wolfeton House is probably fifteenth century.[15] However, in its modified Tudor garb, it joins those early sixteenth-century domestic additions that add such charm to the houses at Bingham's Melcombe, Athelhampton, and Sandford Orcas (fig. 113).

The defendable houses in Wiltshire and Somerset were more numerous than formidable. The granting of a licence to crenellate did not necessarily mean implementation. The nine awarded to the bishop of Salisbury in 1337 for his houses in Wiltshire and elsewhere (and renewed forty years later) were precautionary, as were those in Wiltshire by the earl of Hereford in 1347. The bishop of Winchester continued to maintain Taunton Castle primarily as an administrative centre for his manor of Taunton Dene.[16] There were two other occupied castles in Somerset: Stogursey and Dunster. The mid-thirteenth-century defence at Stogursey was held and maintained by the FitzPayn family in the fourteenth century, and by the Lord Poynings for most of the fifteenth century, followed by the earls of Northumberland, who fitted out a new audit room in the 1490s before the house fell into decay by the mid-sixteenth century.[17] Even if Dunster Castle is essentially a Jacobean mansion clothed by Salvin in medieval dress during the late 1860s, the property had witnessed continuous occupation by the Mohun family before the Luttrells acquired it in 1376.

During the fourteenth century, several new men of influence in Somerset signalled their arrival by crenellating their houses. In the early part of the century, it was Simon Montague at Yarlington (1313), Adam Bret at Torweston (1316), and John Beauchamp at Stoke Sub Hamdon and Hatch Beauchamp (1333). Sir William Montague was pardoned for crenellating his residence without authority at Donyatt in 1329, but Edward II had been furious after Richard Bigot had perpetrated the same offence at Marston Bigot but had compounded his felony by insulting the royal messenger.[18] More modest capabilities extended from embattled walls (Clevedon Court, Sutton Court) or a tower (Merryfield, Ilton) to portcullis-protected entries (Clevedon Court) or simply a moat (Marston Magna).

The fortified houses at Nunney (1373), Farleigh Hungerford (1383), and Wardour (1393) are far more impressive demonstrations of conspicuous expenditure. Farleigh Hungerford incorporated an earlier house in a multi-courtyard residence with pepper-pot corner turrets, but was defensively weak. The lost range of family apartments was as impressive as the clearance of the village a generation later to create an outer court and appropriate the parish church as a private chapel. Nunney was built in a valley bottom, all outward show like a fierce dog but soft-bellied once approached. Like Wardour, Nunney is a highly idiosyncratic residence, exotically shaped, vertically challenging, and judiciously decorated. Both residences are single-phase structures but

PLATE 192 Woodsford 'Castle': from the inner court

Wardour is far more ingeniously planned, with interlocking levels and a clear demarcation between family apartments, staff and household rooms, lodgings, and service facilities. Wardour is a residence of great personality, planned to be the new dynastic centre of Lord Lovel's family by the leading master-mason of south-west England (fig. 114).

Like Dorset, Somerset is a region of fifteenth-century domestic gatehouses, ranging from the second one added by Sir Hugh Luttrell at Dunster Castle and those at Cleeve Abbey and Montacute Priory to the numerous modest examples that include Newton St Loe Manor, West Bower, Naish 'Priory', Chew Magna, and Cothay, where they gave status as well as high-quality accommodation.

As in Dorset and Somerset, the military purpose for erecting a castle in Devon or Cornwall was essentially short-lived, but their residential function sometimes ensured extended occupation.[19] Some early foundations, such as the royal castle at Exeter, and Totnes with its shell keep rebuilt by 1326,[20] continued in use, while others established for political purposes such as Okehampton and Tiverton were remodelled during the early fourteenth century with replacement apartments, hall, lodgings, and offices. Their earlier defences were not extended, so that Okehampton in particular lacked projecting towers or flanking fire capability. Tiverton Castle

became the *caput* of the Courtenay family, though the remains hardly do it justice, while Okehampton gradually came to be used as a hunting lodge, occasional residence, and administrative centre (as did Plympton Castle). Restormel had been rebuilt by the earl of Cornwall at the close of the thirteenth century as a comfortable residence and administrative centre close to the region's tin production,[21] with the earlier castles at Launceston, Trematon, and Tintagel maintained.[22] Berry Pomeroy Castle is an anomaly, a late fifteenth-century fortress long after the need for such structures had ceased but the consequence of a nervous reaction to the possibility of piratical raids. Dartmouth Castle with its blockhouse and artillery defences of 1481–95 has a history stretching back to 1336, when Edward III commissioned Hugh Courtenay to take measures to protect the town on account of rumours of attacks by the French,[23] but the later structures are more important for pointing the way to the purely functional purpose and defensive trend that Henry VIII's blockhouses exploited to the full.

One of the earliest fortified houses in the region was that built by the lord of Gidleigh, who emulated his Courtenay neighbour in expanding his modest tower-house of *c.*1300 with a solar block in the same way that the earlier keep had been enlarged at Okehampton Castle. Even less survives of Sir William Ferrers house at Bere Ferrers, crenellated in 1337,[24] but Sir William

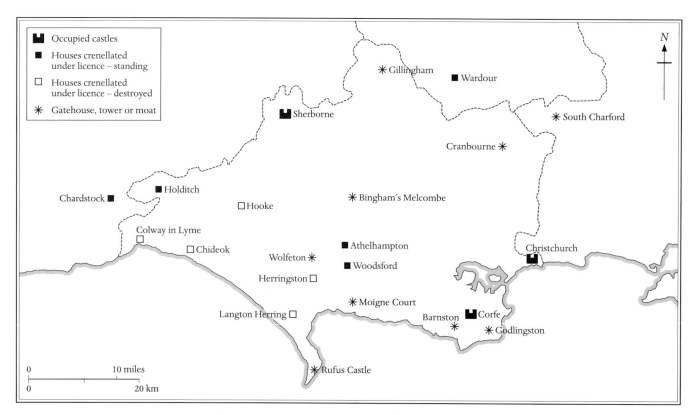

FIGURE II3 Dorset: defendable residences 1200–1500

PLATE 193 Nunney Castle: from the south

Asthorpe was more ambitious in developing a castle-like residence at Hemyock in 1380. It followed the conventional quadrangular plan with corner and intermediate towers, possibly rendered externally. Asthorpe was a fractious outsider, so that his castle was intended to afford physical protection as much as to declare his status, but his residence was essentially mutton dressed as lamb. Powderham Castle, by a junior branch of the Courtenay family ten years later, was far more substantial. The all-encompassing domestic range of *c*.1392–1406 essentially serves as the shell for the still-occupied Georgian and Victorian interiors. Yet this range had been modelled on the contemporary hall range at Dartington Hall, making the accommodation that the Courtenays had developed at Tiverton and Okehampton two or three generations earlier look extremely old-fashioned.

Devon and Cornwall reflect the same span of reasons and the same range of house defences as Dorset. New families applied for crenellation licences to build on or near abandoned castles at Bampton (1336) and Torrington (1340), and at Ruan Lanihorne, though no further licences were awarded in Cornwall after the creation of the duchy in 1337.[25] Gatehouses a century later were primarily domestic, as at Affeton and Bickleigh, both prefacing lost single courtyards. Rich monastic communities near the coast as at Torre and Tavistock sought the protection of strong walls and gatehouses (both with gunloops), as did the bishop of Exeter for his houses at Chudleigh (1379) and Paignton. Far more meaningful were the defensive frontages added between 1450 and 1480 to the earlier house at Compton. They were more functional than is usually accredited, and were necessary to protect a vulnerable residence for the same reasons as applied to the near-contemporary

456

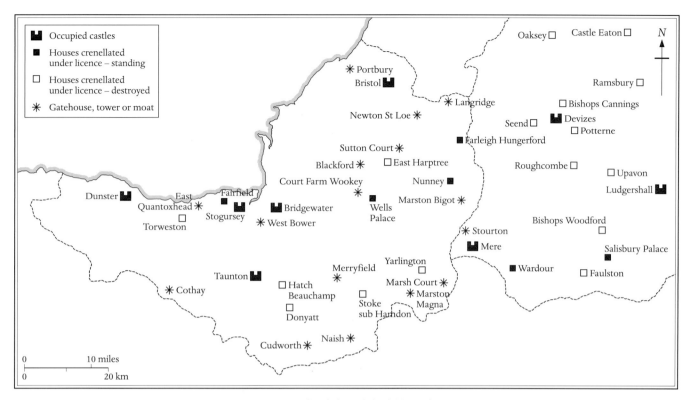

FIGURE 114 Somerset and Wiltshire: defendable residences 1300–1500

castle at Berry Pomeroy. Such defences were no longer the consequence of foreign invasion during the Hundred Years' War but of piratical attacks against the vulnerable south-west anchorages followed by swift inland raids. After an attack on Cornwall's principal port of Fowey in 1457, Leland records that the town's leading merchant Thomas Treffry 'buildid a right fair and stronge embatelid towr in his house: and embateling al the waulles of the house in a maner made it a Castelle: and onto this day it is the glorie of the town building in Faweye'.[26] Leland also reported that Glasney College at the head of Penrhyn Creek had been 'strong walled and castellated with three strong towers and guns',[27] but though a few stretches of walling survive, there is no documentary evidence for their dating. Even the solar tower that John Milliton added during the early sixteenth century to his house at Pengersick overlooking Mount's Bay was provided with gun ports and a defensive drop slot to protect his family from seafaring marauders[28] (fig. 115).

ARISTOCRATIC AND MANORIAL HOUSES

Devon

Except for Weare Giffard Hall and two contemporary mid-fifteenth-century manor houses in the north, all the primary secular residences in Devon lie in a crescent from Tiverton, Exeter, Buckfastleigh, and Tavistock to the sea – the most accessible, populous, and economically viable part of the county. Moreover, several of these properties have been fortunate in their rehabilitation during the twentieth century. The recovery and restoration of Dartington Hall in 1928–37 led the way, followed by Compton Castle in 1931–58, both of them private enterprises, followed by English Heritage at Bowhill and Leigh Barton between 1980 and 1996, the Landmark Trust at Wortham Manor during the same period, and the National Trust at West Challacombe in the 1990s, and private owners across the Cornish border at Trecarrell (1961) and Cullacott (1995).

Uplowman Court, not far from the Somerset border, is one of the earliest non-fortified houses in Devon, surveyed by John Thorpe but now only partially standing and attached to a post-medieval farmhouse. This early fourteenth-century structure does not conform to the standard plan but was Z-shaped, with a solar and chapel block that survives in part though the hall is missing. Compton Castle (early to mid-fourteenth century) displays the classic plan of hall with upper and lower cross wings but with the long-lost hall rebuilt in 1954–5.[29] The hall and upper cross wing of Lustleigh Old Hall of about the same date still stand in fine condition, even though the hall is now seen through Regency eyes. Yet it is still open to its highly rhythmic roof, with one of finer quality with lateral braces spanning the solar. Lustleigh promulgates that roofs were to be a major feature of Devon houses, more than any exterior element, and this was spectacularly confirmed at Dartington Hall between 1388 and 1400.

Built by John Holand, half-brother of the king, earl of Huntingdon and for a time duke of Exeter, Dartington is palace-like in scale and, significantly, totally undefended in character. It might be expected that the hall range would be substantial, but its magnificent hall was spanned not by a base-cruck structure as was usual in the region but, at the earl's insistence, by a highly impressive hammer-beam roof. Furthermore, the outer court was lined by two mammoth ranges of individual lodgings, only surpassed by

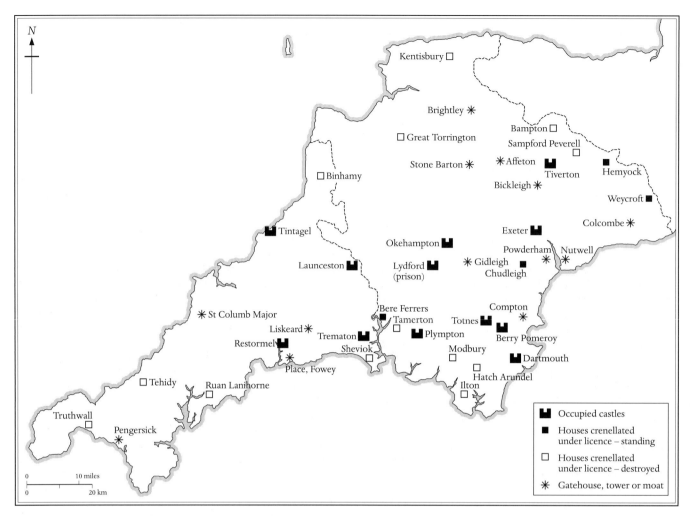

FIGURE 115 Devon and Cornwall: defendable residences 1300–1500

those a generation earlier at Windsor Castle, and by a less regular second court holding some of the private quarters of the earl and countess. So Dartington's innovations also encompassed the introduction of the double-courtyard form in south-west England. That form was adopted in Devon at Old Newnham (late fifteenth century), North Wyke (early sixteenth century), and Great Fulford,[30] complemented by the triple courts at Compton Castle, and more significantly by the four of Lord Bonville's mansion at Shute. The remnant of this non-fortified house of the 1430s was mainly built in stone but some of the offices and agricultural buildings were timber-framed.

Dartington Hall is notable for the absence of the one structure that might have been expected in a leading mansion of its time, an impressive gatehouse. What survives is an earlier entry block that was no doubt going to be replaced with a more imposing entry but was prevented by the earl of Huntingdon's execution in 1400. Gatehouses became architectural showpieces in Devon, with mid and late fourteenth-century examples at Tiverton and Torre Abbey and lost fifteenth-century examples at Compton Castle and Bradley Manor, a house built by a family who had been members of the earl of Huntingdon's affinity. The more relaxed approach – the status

signal – is exemplified at Bickleigh and Affeton, residences by a cadet branch of the Courtenay family and the head of the Stucley family respectively, with Affeton more architecturally showy. The gatehouses at Weare Giffard and Leigh Barton are on a more modest scale, with the practice continuing with the elaborate if late examples at Tawstock (1574), Shute (late sixteenth century), Bradstone Manor (c.1610–20), and Colleton Manor (c.1621).

No hall exceeded that at Dartington but the guest hall at Buckfast Abbey came close and puts the smaller one at Okehampton Castle into perspective. Fifteenth-century halls were relatively modest, as at Bradley, Bowhill, Orleigh, and Weare Giffard, though this last, like Dartington, is an alien house in a Devon environment – one from Somerset or west Wiltshire such as Great Chalfield Manor which it resembles in plan, scale, and decorative richness.

The family apartments at Okehampton are modest compared with those of similar date at Compton, but Compton is also an example where site restrictions by the late fifteenth century determined that such apartments should now extend beyond the lower end of the hall, hitherto an area generally limited to services and staff. This was a more extensive practice than is usually appreciated, and was particularly prevalent in Devon extending from the guest hall at Buckfast Abbey (an early example) to Wortham, Old Newnham, and Cotehele.[31] A further consequence was that the kitchen was now sited across the courtyard, as at Compton, Bowhill, Littlehempston, and possibly Weare Giffard Hall. Even the residential remnant of the 1430s at Shute has now been identified as the services and staff rooms round two sides of the kitchen court at the lower end of the hall. Yet the scale is substantial, hinting at the size of this multi-courtyard mansion. Equally impressive are the two lodging blocks at Leigh Barton, more complete than the still-occupied ranges at Dartington Hall. Though Leigh Barton is the house of minor gentry of farming class, similar lodging units can also be seen at Old Newnham and Morwell Barton.

The county retains a particularly large number of chapels and oratories, for Devon parishes were large, and houses were often isolated and churches difficult to reach in winter.[32] Sometimes permission was given to celebrate divine worship in a room in a house, as at Bindon,[33] but often a separate building was erected as in the fifteenth-century survivals at Ayshford, Bradley Manor, Compton Castle, or Fardel Manor.[34] They can also be found during the same century in less well-to-do households, as at Bury Barton, Lapford,[35] or Higher Alfardisworthy, near Bradworthy.

Until the close of the fourteenth century, the base-cruck form was usual for high-quality roofs throughout the region, as at Buckfast Abbey guest house and Bridford Barton, and can be seen in a hybrid form at Lustleigh Old Hall and above the entrance block at Dartington Hall.[36] Arch-braced trusses with heavy ridge pieces and two or three rows of curved wind braces was usual during the fifteenth century, as in the halls at Bradley Manor, Littlehempston, and Knightstone, and the upper chambers at Shute and Wortham. The mid to late fifteenth-century house at Wortham also marks a major change in house occupation, in this case the insertion of a floor in the hall during the first decade of the sixteenth century, with a contemporary roof over the newly created great chamber.

There were no immediate successors to the hammer-beam roof at Dartington Hall until the sequence beginning about fifty years later of 'false' hammer-beam roofs, where the arch braces rest on the hammer-beams, omitting the hammer posts altogether. Three such roofs survive in north Devon, all from the second half of the fifteenth century. That over the hall at Weare Giffard is among the most ornate in England and possibly the leading claimant for that title. It was certainly the precedent for its neighbour at Orleigh Court which emulates it less successfully, even to the line of wooden heraldic beasts sitting on the ends of the hammer beams. West Challacombe Manor spanned a slightly larger hall but lacks the decorative panache of its neighbours. The second group of grand, ornamental roofs, centred on Exeter, includes two of hammer-beam form at Cadhay and the Law Library, Exeter.[37] They have the distinctive features of cusped intermediate trusses, straight wind braces with curved feet, and a coved apex. This group also includes the Guildhall and Deanery at Exeter, and Bowhill. This last is a well-restored courtyard house built for an Exeter merchant in c.1500 that combines business facilities with comfortable residential chambers as well as good-quality craftsmanship and vernacular construction.

Unyielding Devon stone inhibited external decorative detailing, but there are finely carved entry doorways at Weare Giffard Hall and Orleigh Court. No chimneypiece excels the overblown example by bishop Courtenay at Exeter Palace, but several have rectangular lintels with quatrefoils or shields as at Exeter Deanery, Cadhay, and Knightstone. Mid to late fifteenth-century wall paintings survive in Littlehempston Manor hall and Berry Pomeroy Castle chapel (religious) and Bradley Manor (secular), and a splendid armorial tapestry of the Dinham family of Nutwell hangs in the Cloisters Museum of New York.

Wiltshire and Somerset

The halls of some of the greatest early houses in Wiltshire and Somerset were aisled, including those at the royal palaces of Cheddar and Clarendon, the royal castle at Ludgershall, the early twelfth-century episcopal palaces at Old Sarum and Devizes, and the mid to late thirteenth-century halls at Wells (nearly 60 feet) and at Exeter (48 feet) in neighbouring Devon. But this sequence of spectacular display was limited to the highest levels of society,[38] with Henry III developing Clarendon into one of the major royal palaces in England with tiled floors, brightly painted walls, stained glass, and high-quality sculpture. It needed constant maintenance under the first three Edwards, culminating in major building work under Edward III including remodelling the great hall in 1358–9, possibly by replacing its aisles with an imposing single-span roof. The palace declined under Richard II and was desultorily visited by Henry VI, until his last visit in 1453 culminated in the first of his mental disorder attacks. The more recently developed royal palaces nearer London – Windsor, Sheen, Eltham, and Greenwich – were preferred, so that the site decayed until the excavations of the 1930s and 1960s revealed some of the secrets of this still grass-covered site.[39]

Except for a glorious clutch of residences of Edward IV's time close to the Somerset border, Wiltshire is not notable for its late medieval houses. That palm is held by Somerset, where their range, social scale, and lack of standard plan is particularly rewarding in a region that retains more late medieval houses than any other in England or Wales. Bishop Jocelyn's residential range of 1230–40 at Wells is on the grandest scale (as was bishop Burnell's aisled hall of c.1280), while that at Martock a generation later reflects the comparable structure of the episcopal treasurer. The solar cross wing of 1250–70 with rare contemporary wall painting was never supplanted by a more up-to-date upper cross wing, though the hall was rebuilt in 1330–50 and given a new roof in the next century.[40] Bratton Court illustrates the stage during the early to mid-fourteenth century when the hall had two-storey units at each end, the upper one extended during the following century. Clevedon Court of c.1320 shows the same basic plan writ large, with sixteenth-century replacement chamber blocks but retaining the original two-storey porches, triple service doorways, hall window and stair bays, and a glorious chapel over the dais bay window. Clevedon also illustrates a particularly early example of a balanced façade.

Coker Court is an early fifteenth-century large-scale house by the Courtenay family, of which the generously proportioned hall is the principal evidence today, possibly influenced, like Courtenay's development of Powderham Castle, by the comparable imposing apartment at Dartington Hall. The balanced façade includes an early example of a dais bay window, a highly popular feature in the Dorset/Somerset region between the mid-fifteenth and mid-sixteenth centuries. There was another one in the hall at Stoke Sub Hamdon Priory, showing that this quasi-monastic foundation, rebuilt in c.1444, was architecturally up-to-date. On a smaller scale,

Cothay Manor (1485–90) similarly adopts the plan of hall with flanking wings but in an H-shape rather than round a courtyard. This is a markedly informal and picturesque manor house at a time when the stylistic vanguard favoured formality and symmetry, as at Great Chalfield Manor. But Cothay also retains many original features and fittings including extensive contemporary wall paintings. For a contemporary development on the most sumptuous scale, the north range added by Dean Gunthorpe (d.1498) to the Deanery at Wells was of the highest quality, emblazoned with his rebus and heraldic devices. Above his first-floor suite of ante-room, great chamber, and private inner chamber were three further rooms of similar scale, plus a turret room. Other internal changes and the new forecourt gateway were of a standard comparable to that of a magnate's residence.

A regionally important group of mid-Somerset houses led the development of reducing the importance of the hall in favour of a great chamber above it. The initiator was bishop Bekynton (1443–65) at his Wells palace, followed by Gothelney Hall in the 1460s/70s with its clearer display of a single-storey hall and substantial chamber over, with a thrilling roof structure. The development is even easier to appreciate at Blackmoor Manor of c.1475–1500, with the added benefit of three little-altered high-end chambers – parlour, ante-chapel, and chapel – with the high-quality rooms above open to the roof. Though Gurney Manor did not have a floor inserted in the hall until 200 years later, the significance of this house lies in its unitary development between about 1400 and 1460 as the Dodesham family became more prosperous, and in the survival of their tiny oratory and rare courtyard pentice. If the rapid sequence of fifteenth-century extensions at Gurney Manor illustrates the synergy of financial and physical expansion, Sir William Patton's house of c.1420 at Croscombe reminds us that knighthood and a large house were not necessarily synonymous.

A second regionally important group of houses developed shortly afterwards in the north-east, extending to neighbouring Wiltshire and Gloucestershire. They were all generous hall and end-unit houses with balanced frontages, erected or modified during Edward IV's reign. They included Tickenham Court and the lost house of Kingston Seymour (Somerset), South Wraxall Manor, Great Chalfield Manor, Bewley Court, and Hazelbury Manor (Wiltshire), and Little Sodbury Court (Gloucestershire). Bewley Court is the earliest, and South Wraxall developed in stages from the mid-fifteenth century, while Great Chalfield nearby is a single-phase structure of the late 1470s, glorious in its completeness and richness. In each case, the medium-sized hall includes a two-storey porch matched by a dais bay with closets over. The single bay at Kingston Seymour and Tickenham had two-centred heads while the other houses had four-centred heads opposite a second bay for the stair. Kingston Seymour and Tickenham had almost identical roof structures, Kingston Seymour, Great Chalfield and Little Sodbury had withdrawing chamber squints, while South Wraxall with its added gatehouse and to a lesser extent Great Chalfield retain their forecourt buildings. Great Chalfield also exhibits some innovative design features, richly detailed workmanship, and early furnishings.

Gatehouses often became lodging units. This is most readily appreciated in the mid-fourteenth-century example at Wells Palace and then at Dunster Castle, but can be seen on a modest scale at Cothay Manor and in Wiltshire at Tisbury and South Wraxall.

Porches developed in scale from two storeys at Coker Court, Greenham Barton, and Cothay, to three storeys at the Bishop's Palace, Salisbury, and four storeys at Birdcombe Court. The chapels at Woodlands Manor and Lytes Cary were separate buildings with quieter reticulated tracery than that of the internal chapel at Clevedon Court. The fine chapel at Blackmoor Manor was a high-end projection as at Compton Castle, while the oratory at Gurney Manor was on the most personal scale.

Roofs tend to be more modest than those in Devon.[41] Compared with south-east England, base-cruck roofs are rare for high-status buildings. The primary examples are those of the Old Deanery hall, Salisbury (1258–74) and the solar at North Cadbury Court (1286–1318), followed by the early to mid-fourteenth century examples at Bratton Court and the first hall at Orchard Wyndham.[42] The most elaborate of these structures was the seven-bay roof with higher braced collars and ball flower ornament of c.1320–5 spanning the refectory of Bradenstoke Priory in Wiltshire, until its reconstitution in 1927 at St Donat's Castle, Glamorganshire.[43] Arch-braced collar trusses span the second hall at Orchard Wyndham and this was the most common structure for high-status houses across Somerset and Wiltshire from the second quarter of the fifteenth century. Nearly all of them have wind braces arranged in tiers of curved or scalloped patterns. Those at Bewley Court are enriched with circles holding six-petalled flowers or tracery. Lighter intermediate trusses in the middle of each bay were frequently introduced to give a richer decorative effect. Two structurally similar but contrasting roofs span the halls at the Treasurer's House, Martock (c.1450) and Cleeve Abbey (probably 1450s) – the former relatively quiet with wide bay spacing and patterned wind braces, the latter elaborated with carved figures and intermediate trusses. The fifteenth-century roof at Whitestaunton Manor House (1446–78) has particularly elaborate wind braces and embryonic hammer beams. Hammer-beam roofs were too pretentious for Somerset but they were much favoured in Salisbury from an early date at 9 Queen Street (c.1306), Balle's Palace (1370–85), and Hall of John Halle (late fifteenth century), with the form spreading to Porch House, Potterne and South Wraxall Manor (both late fifteenth century).

Dorset

Dorset has already been identified as among the richest counties in England for houses of the thirteenth century, with their clear demonstration of impact and continuity on their immediate successors.[44] And it is the services and chamber unit that are the dominant survival from the fourteenth century. Sir Guy Brian's highly individual and well-preserved range of apartments above the services at Woodsford 'Castle' of c.1370 has already been considered. Attention must be drawn, though, to the quality and complexity of these apartments, lacking only one important element, the roof, which was replaced by a utilitarian one in the mid-seventeenth century. It is the contemporary roofs which are of value at the second property, Fiddleford Manor. Possibly built by the sheriff, William Latimer, during the third quarter of the century, the house's relatively small scale today belies its initial size and high standard. The roofs over the hall and chamber cross wing were retained in the face of Tudor remodelling: standard West of England structures of arch-braced collar-beam trusses strengthened by wind braces and further horizontal braces in the withdraw-

PLATE 194 Great Chalfield Manor: hall and solar block from the site of the inner court

ing chamber. This room also possesses a rare contemporary wall painting, part of an Annunciation reminding us that religious subjects, as at Cothay, were by no means uncommon in a secular environment. Fiddleford Manor is still roofed, whereas the slightly earlier offices and chamber block to the lost hall of the abbot of Glastonbury's house a mile away at Sturminster Newton is in ruins.

Fifteenth-century houses in Dorset tended to be medium-sized, gentry-owned properties, often loosely developed round a court with the fourth side enclosed by a wall as at Poyntington Manor, Purse Caundle Manor, and Bingham's Melcombe. They are attractive if not architecturally distinguished, though Athelhampton Hall struts with style. Built c.1490–5 by Sir William Martyn, a successful sheep farmer and local administrator, the house had an open approach that was distorted by a gatehouse and enclosing wall between the mid-sixteenth and mid-nineteenth centuries, though the angled parlour wing that replaced the original solar block by 1550 is as striking as the earlier hall it abuts. The full-height porch and polygonal bay window characterise Martyn's individuality, as does the turret terminating the service end, but the glory of the hall is its roof of arch-braced collar trusses enriched with extraordinary reverse-curved braces. The contrast between early medieval residences a century apart noted at Corfe applies over a similar time span between Woodsford 'Castle' and Athelhampton Hall.

Porches had become increasingly dominant and a source of outward display, like that at Childhay Manor fronting a rebuilt seventeenth-century hall block and kitchen wing (pl. 186). It is an uncouth late fifteenth-century structure with its embattled parapet of outsize merlons, top and bottom string courses, and a striking line of animated corbels.[45] It was only a short step to the slightly later and more sophisticated examples at Athelhampton, and Cerne and Forde abbeys. More imposing is the 80 foot long kitchen wing attached to the imposing Victorian mansion at Canford. Divided into a larger and smaller chamber, each with two massive hearths – one in a projecting stack and one back-to-back against the internal division – the scale is comparable with the kitchens at Dartington Hall and Wingfield Manor. Though the architectural features are fifteenth century, little is known about the substantial house this wing served. Its east wall is fourteenth century, and though there was a house here in 1221 owned by William, earl of Salisbury, its subsequent development and layout await further research.[46]

The late medieval houses of Dorset are notable for their enthusiasm and delight in decorative work. Like Wiltshire, Dorset quickly embraced the hammer-beam form as at Tyneham House (later fourteenth century), followed by that spanning the hall at Milton Abbey, the roof probably moved from the abbey to cover a barn at Winterborne Clenston, and the even plainer one now covering a barn next to the former nunnery at Tarrant Crawford. By

461

PLATE 195 Forde Abbey: porch tower

this time, decoration had also embraced the oriel at Purse Caundle, the hall screen of 1498 at Milton Abbey, and the low-pitched panelled ceiling of the abbot's hall at Forde Abbey. Early Renaissance decoration was welcomed at Forde and enhanced the windows at Wolfeton House, emphasising that there was no architectural differentiation between monastic lodgings and large domestic residences. Architectural invention continued well past the middle of the sixteenth century with the unusual belvedere tower at the heart of Giles Strangway's remarkable house of c.1540 at Melbury Sampford, while lozenge-shaped panels, finialed buttresses, and decorated gables and chimneys enhanced Athelhampton Hall, Bingham's Melcombe, Sandford Orcas, and Barrington Court across the Dorset–Somerset border.

Cornwall

Discussing Cornish houses last rests not on their physical placement in the far west but on the quality of the standing evidence. They begin well enough with the excavated foundations of the late twelfth- and thirteenth-century courtyard house at Penhallam which have been left exposed. This residence of the Cardingham family is particularly important for its early date, the clarity of its plan, and the development of an impressive group of stone buildings, and as a demonstration of the sophisticated standards of a wealthy family by the mid-thirteenth century. There is no immediate successor or worthy continuation until the early Tudor mansion

at Cotehele. The gap has to be filled by the fragmentary remains of the administrative buildings of c.1290–1300 of the duchy of Cornwall (pl. 190)[47] and three fourteenth-century chapels at Erth Barton, Inceworth, and Shillingham (ruined), all close to Plymouth Sound.[48]

The early part of the Edgcumbes' courtyard mansion at Cotehele survives to represent the leading families of the mid to late fifteenth century, for nothing stands of Sir Thomas Grenville's house at Stowe near Kilkhampton[49] or that of Sir Henry Bodrugan at Bodrugan near Mevagissey.[50] The Courtenays' house at Boconnoc was replaced in the eighteenth century,[51] and that of the Arundells at Lanherne a little earlier,[52] as was the house of the Penheales at Penheale.[53] Yet courtyard residences may not be quite the rarity they seem, for Penhallem is an early example (as is the residential shell keep of c.1280–90 at Restormel), before the thread is picked up two centuries later at Cotehele, Trecarrell (with another detached chapel in the outer court), and Roscarrock lower down the social scale.

Like the smaller houses of Devon, the several fifteenth-century houses that survive in Cornwall are of distinctive regional character – isolated, at the end of a narrow trackway or lane, and built of local stone and slate. They combine elements of 'polite' houses with those of vernacular character, though in Cornwall it is often the setting rather than the architecture that is most impressive.[54] These lesser gentry houses consist of a low-built single range, courtyard-protected as though shielding the occupants from the storms and gales that sweep across the peninsula. The range is uncomplicated, a hall open to the roof with a two-storey service and chamber block at the lower end as at Rialton, Roscarrock, Truthall, and Medros where the chamber extends over the cross passage. Medros, Rialton, and Roscarrock retain their courtyard enclosure, as does Truthall where the Beer stone traceried courtyard-facing windows contrast with the rubble rear wall and vernacular cross-passage doorway. Arch-braced collar roofs were usual, as were wall fireplaces in the halls – to the side at Truthall and Medros, in the gable end at Rialton. The kitchen was a separate building at Truthall but had become integrated with the services at Rialton and Medros. With the early sixteenth century, halls became more lofty as at Cotehele and Trecarrell, both with arch-braced collar trusses, to be followed by houses of more metropolitan character such as Godolphin (1530s), Arwennack (1530s), Mount Edgcumbe (1547–53), and Trerice (1570s).

MONASTIC FOUNDATIONS

South-west England retains the finest group of monastic residential units in England. Dining halls and abbatial lodgings predominate but they also include dormitories and kitchens. The former, in particular, were often subject to rebuilding programmes during the last century of monasticism. Yet the view that the monasteries had outrun their spiritual purpose and social value by the beginning of the sixteenth century and that their decline was compounded by an excessive rebuilding spree of essentially secular character needs to be reconsidered. The tendentious assessments of Cromwell's commissioners have determined the views of historians for far too long so that they have judged monastic worth during the 1530s on essentially single-source evidence. There was considerable building activity in the west of England between the mid-fifteenth and early sixteenth centuries which spanned all orders from the Augustinians at Bristol, Bradenstoke, and Woodspring and the Benedictines at Cerne Abbas, Glastonbury, Milton, and Muchelney, to the Cistercians at Cleeve and Forde, and the Cluniacs at Montacute. They all concentrated on the rebuilding of their domestic facilities. The long-established spiritual pattern of worship had not altered, nor had the physical context in which it took place. There was little need to modify the church, even though it was often too large for the number of participants. But their domestic needs had changed, with greater weight now given to privacy, comfort, and wider hospitality. It is not surprising that dining halls were rebuilt, lodgings were created, and abbatial quarters extended. Many monasteries were still efficiently run and functioning effectively, so that their heads – just like many secular households – were now prepared to spend their income on updating their facilities. There was no great wave of opprobrium at this activity, for even monastic heads needed to take account of the expectation and opinions of the outside world. The rebuilding at Forde, Cleeve, Muchelney, and Glastonbury should be seen not in a condemnatory light but as an ecclesiastical counterpart to the vibrant secular activity of the period.

The sequence opens with a rare survival. The early fourteenth-century guest hall in the outer court at Buckfast Abbey, only fully recognised in 1982, is one of the few standing examples of guest accommodation in southern England. A further wing had to be added in the fifteenth century to meet the demand for further visitor facilities. Sherborne Abbey retains two first-floor roofed halls at right angles to each other. One was the fifteenth-century guest hall above the thirteenth-century cellarer's range filling the west side of the cloister. Now used as the school library, it retains its opposing lines of high windows and contemporary collar-beam roof. The second hall with a possibly fifteenth-century roof that may have been converted into the abbot's hall is now the school chapel of entirely modern character.[55]

Abbot David Junyer led the vanguard of major developments in the south-west during his fifty-year rule of Cleeve Abbey (1437–87) which established the yardstick for greater comfort and privacy followed by other foundations. He divided the thirteenth-century dormitory into private chambers for the monks, built individual lodgings for the corrodians or senior monks, rebuilt the refectory with an intricately designed roof to serve primarily as his own hall, and redeveloped his private quarters. The result is the most splendid range of fifteenth-century roofed monastic apartments in the country, some retaining evidence of their original painted decoration. They could be – and were – transferred after the Dissolution to a secular environment for regular use without modification. The refectory and abbot's lodging at Muchelney Abbey are slightly later, and while the Muchelney refectory is ruined, the abbot's parlour still retains its sumptuous fireplace, oak settle, painted glass, and 1470s ceiling.

The prior's house of St Nicholas Priory in the middle of Exeter has been particularly well preserved through occupation after the Reformation as the town house of a West of England family. The early Norman west cloister range was sumptuously remodelled in about 1500 with a new entrance tower and kitchen, and upper-floor division into hall, prior's chamber, and guest accommodation spanned by new roofs. However, it is the three Dorset foundations that attract most attention, beginning with the hall of c.1498 at Milton, enveloped in Lord Milton's mansion of 1771–6. Externally,

the hall is unremarkable. Internally, the relatively plain lower walling was embellished with a moulded string course with copious heraldic insignia, and culminated in a roof of considerable ingenuity. Basically of hammer-beam form, it was elaborated and decorated to create a complex structure intended to bedazzle the beholder. The spere-like cross-passage screen, a rare survival, is equally impressive, built in three sections surmounted by a highly ornate cresting that owes as much to the eighteenth century as to original workmanship.

Only the hall porch stands at Cerne Abbey, built by abbot Sam in c.1505, but it is an appropriate link between those at Milton and Forde, combining the more restrained character of the former with the fan-vaulted porch and oriel of the latter. Abbot Chard's rebuilding activity at Forde between 1526 and 1539 was substantial and costly. It included the cloister and more, but the principal thrust of his expenditure was the total rebuilding of the hall and lodgings for himself on a scale that positions it among the most important domestic work of its time in the West of England. The tall entry porch is an outrageous display of elaboration, preceding a single-storey hall and a two-storey residential block terminating in a three-storey domestic tower. In contrast with the external face, the hall is a model of internal restraint. It has been foreshortened and now lacks its dais window, while the roof is not the elaborate trussed structure of Milton or Athelhampton or the planned stone vault, but a low-pitched panelled ceiling retaining its original red and green colour scheme. Chard's sequence of private apartments was totally remodelled in the 1650s and is essentially of that date, though the two-storey block retains its original roof above the lavish plaster ceilings of the Commonwealth period. Like Wolfeton House completed in 1534, Forde was in the vanguard of using decorative Renaissance motifs – putti, scrolls, bearded and winged monsters, mermen, and sphinxes – but in this instance cut short from further development by the guillotine of the Dissolution.

Since the guest hall and abbot's quarters of 1320–5 at Bradenstoke Priory were taken away in the late 1920s – after much public outcry – to St Donat's Castle, Wiltshire is bereft of residential remains outside Lacock.[56] Bristol and Glastonbury have lost their important residential structures, leaving only the gateway at Bristol and the striking fourteenth-century kitchen at Glastonbury as an indication (churches aside) of their wealth and standing. Few of the thirty-six houses in Devon and Cornwall were financially significant and they have left little standing evidence.[57] The post-medieval conversion of the abbot's hall at Torre Abbey into a dining room and then a Catholic chapel (1779) has debased its value, though the fifteenth-century towered approach is a precursor of those at Cerne Abbas and Forde Abbey. The refectory at St Germans Priory forms the frame for Soane's drawing room and saloon for the Eliot family[58] but the better-preserved refectory at St Michael's Mount, remodelled for the St Aubyn family, retains its original proportions, some windows and the late fifteenth-century replacement roof.[59]

Gatehouses are more common in Devon, with a complete one of c.1380–90 at Torre Abbey, a restored early fifteenth-century one at Canonsleigh, and a fine ruined one of the early sixteenth century at Cornworthy. Elements remain of two fourteenth-century gatehouses of Abbotsbury Abbey, the inner one converted into a house, and part of the precinct walls.[60] Far clearer are the same features at Cleeve Abbey. Two sides of the 28 acre precinct were enclosed by

PLATE 196 Wells, Bishop's Palace: Bishop Ralph's entry gate (*c*.1340)

PLATE 197 Dunster Castle: Sir Hugh Luttrell's inner gate (*c*.1420)

PLATE 198 Newton St Loe Manor: Lord Botreaux's entry gate (early fifteenth century)

PLATE 199 Cleeve Abbey: Abbot Dovell's upgrading of earlier inner gate (early sixteenth century)

wet moats, much of the precinct walling stands, and part of the frame of the outer gateway can be traced prefacing a court which terminates with the main gateway, of thirteenth-century origins, remodelled, plastered, and decorated by abbot Dovell in the early sixteenth century. Apart from Cornwall, barns are plentiful across the region, with fine examples erected by the abbeys at Glastonbury and Shaftesbury, notable for their scale and roofs, with the fifteenth-century example at Buckland substantially larger than the abbey church it served.[61]

These volumes consistently underline that there is little difference between monastic lodgings and country houses and their secular counterparts. The abbot's house at Meare exemplifies this in a property that has never been enlarged since its construction by the abbot of Glastonbury in about 1300. It shows an increasingly rare house form for its time – a first-floor hall and residential chamber with chapel wing – a southern version of Markenfield Hall. The hall was externally approached, while the chapel was virtually a glass cage, not unlike the bishop's chapel of c.1290 at Wells Palace. Morwell Barton in Devon was an equally ambitious but more up-to-date country residence for the abbots from Tavistock 3 miles away.[62] Rebuilt by abbot Dynyngton (1451–90) round a generous courtyard, it is approached through an embattled central gatehouse with rib-vaulted carriageway, with a heated and garderobe-provided chamber over. The hall lay opposite, now subdivided but retaining several smoke-blackened roof trusses. There were several lodging units with cinquefoil windows in the two-storey ranges, but the property, heavily altered in the nineteenth century, is still used for farm purposes, as is that at Meare. Ecclesiastical establishments could be just as mindful of comfort and high-quality workmanship as monastic foundations. The Rectory at Sampford Peverell was initially built by Henry VII's mother for her own use, while Stoke Sub Hamdon 'Priory' and Buckland Old Rectory (Gloucestershire) were essentially small-scale manor houses.

NOTES

1 O. H. Creighton, *Wilts. Arch. and N. H. Mag.* 93 (2000) 105–19 for a list of all early Wiltshire castles. The later fortress at Mere, developed by the earl of Cornwall under licence in 1253, had been abandoned by 1398 when some of its roofing lead was reused by Richard II at Portchester Castle, while Lord Zouche's Thames-side castle at Castle Eaton (1311) was in ruins by Leland's day, *Itinerary*, I, 127.

2 C. Pomeroy, *Castles and Forts: Dorset* (1998); RCHM, *Dorset*, 5 vols. (1952–75). A crenellation licence was awarded in 1257 to the bishop of Winchester and two years later to Richard, earl of Gloucester for a castle in the Isle of Portland, but the present cliff-top blockhouse with gun-ports and a lost machicolated parapet, known as Rufus Castle, is attributable to the late fifteenth century (RCHM, *Dorset*, II pt 2 (1970) 252–3), rather than to Richard, duke of York a generation earlier. *Proc. Dorset N. H. and A. Soc.* 69 (1948) 65–7.

3 RCHM, *Dorset*, II pt 1 (1970) 63, 77. Also S. Toy, *Archaeologia* 79 (1928) 85–102; W. Douglas Simpson, *Proc. Dorset N. H. and A. Soc.* 73 (1951) 77.

4 Bishop Wyvill of Salisbury had recently repurchased the property following two centuries of crown occupation. Excavations in the 1960s revealed the foundations of a group of fourteenth-century buildings west of the great tower of unclear character or purpose but possibly for prison usage by the crown. They were swept away in the late fourteenth century when the castle became an episcopal administrative centre with a new south range and later alterations to the great tower by bishop Langton (1485–87). P. White, *Arch. Jour.* 140 (1983) 63–70.

5 J. A. Ashbee, *Jour. Brit. Arch. Assoc.* 157 (2004) 23. The translation today might be 'garden or pleasure pavilion'.

6 RCHM, *Dorset*, II pt 1 (1970) 60. The ruins are described *ibid.* 74–7.

7 Hatfield House, Cecil Papers. Maps suppl. 18.

8 RCHM, *Dorset*, V (1975) 7–12; M. Binney, *Country Life* (May 1973). The tactful restoration of this house in 1863–5 by the 2nd marquis of Salisbury and by that family since 1929 can be compared with the similar sympathetic treatment accorded Haddon Hall in the 1920s. The dismissive earlier assessments of *HKW*, II (1963) 922 and M. Wood, *The English Medieval House* (1965) 13, stem from A. Oswald, *Country Houses of Dorset* (1933) 63 and (1959) 124.

9 King John hunted from Cranborne on at least fourteen occasions between 1200 and 1213 (T. D. Hardy, *Archaeologia* 22 (1829) 124–60), but the expenditure of £67 6s. 4d. in 1207–8 by Ralph Neville, the chief forester, on 'building the king's house of Cranborne' identifies its primary construction period. Pipe Roll, 10 John, 202. King John established a further fortified hunting lodge next to the River Lodden on the edge of Gillingham. Only its rectangular ditch and bank survive. *HKW*, II (1965) 944–6; RCHM, *Dorset*, IV (1972) 51–2. The early to mid-thirteenth-century house at Tollard Royal with its first-floor hall is much altered and cannot compare with that at Cranborne only a few miles away.

10 RCHM, *Dorset*, V (1975) 10 states that this undercroft was the kitchen. Norden's plan shows no hearths nor his elevation any related chimneys. Though the undercroft had become a kitchen area by the early seventeenth century, the original kitchen would have been a detached building as was the case at the royal house within Corfe Castle.

11 *Cal. Pat. Rolls*: 1267–70, 41. Moigne Court retains a striking line of plate-traceried windows lighting the first-floor hall and service range of c.1270–80. Though the fact is not immediately obvious, the house was formerly moat-surrounded, with further banked enclosures eastwards. RCHM, *Dorset*, II pt 1 (1970) 184–6; M. E. Wood, *Thirteenth Century Domestic Architecture in England* (1950) 16–18.

12 Overlooking Swanage Bay, the house consists of an oblong buttressed range, with a large ground-floor doorway with two-centred cusped head of c.1280–1300 opening into the former hall with service-end continuation. The three-quarter round tower at the upper end has a pronounced batter, tiny loops lighting the two upper floors, and a curtailed head with conical slate roof. RCHM, *Dorset*, II pt 1 (1970) 294–5; Wood, *Thirteenth Century Domestic Architecture* 14–15. The late thirteenth-century manor nearby at Barnston had an enclosed courtyard with a gatehouse until the mid-nineteenth century, but its date and defensive attributes are unclear. W. D. Filliter, *Proc. Dorset N. H. and A. Soc.* 22 (1901) lx–lxvi.

13 *Cal. Pat. Rolls*: 1367–70, 371. The licence was repeated ten years later, *ibid. 1377–81*, 491. It is less than a mile from the sea, and the moat enclosing the platform is particularly deep on two sides, but the stonework proved too readily available to the villagers of Chideok and local road builders after its Civil War slighting for any structures to survive. Like the slightly later castles at Donnington and Bywell, the gatehouse – pulled down in 1741 – was the dominant feature of this site.

14 Although the outer walls of the former courtyard house of Herringston may date from the licence to crenellate of 1336, no visible features are earlier than the late sixteenth century. A lease of 1441 refers to a gatehouse, but no such structure survives. RCHM, *Dorset*, II pt 2 (1970) 388. Hooke Court retains the large rectangular moat that surrounded the 'ancient manor house' noted by Leland. The fifteenth-century buttressed east wing (*ibid.* I (1952) 126), was pulled down in 1965. The Dominican monk John Siferwas (d. after 1421) who illuminated the Sherborne Abbey Missal between 1396–1407 and the Gospel Lectionary made for John, Lord Lovel of Wardour Castle as a gift to Salisbury Cathedral, was a member of the Siferwas family of Hooke whose forbear, Robert Siferwas, had been granted the licence to crenellate the house in 1344. The four-square character of The Chantry at Bridport frequently led to its attribution as an isolated tower-house (*ibid.* I (1952) xxxviii) but defence played no part in its development.

15 The conical-roofed drum towers at Wolfeton, immediately north-west

of Dorchester, are at least a century earlier than the central block of the 1530s. The towers are of unequal size and incorporated gunloops covering the entrance, but in its elegant remodelled form this gatehouse was built for effect rather than defence. The Trenchards inherited Wolfeton in 1480, and though nothing within this intriguing and highly individual house pre-dates Sir Thomas Trenchard (d.1550), work in the late 1490s is documented on a late medieval residence that was substantial enough to receive archduke Philip of Austria and Joanna of Castile in January 1506 after they were caught in a storm on their way to claim the throne of the Netherlands. RCHM, *Dorset*, III pt 1 (1970) 63–9; A. Oswald, *Country Life* (August 1953); J. Goodall, *Country Life* (August 2002).

16 Bishop Langdon (1493–1501) repaired the upper part of the inner gateway to serve as the exchequer room for his estates, marked by date plaques and his arms over the gate. R. J. E. Bush and M. Meek, in *The Archaeology of Taunton*, ed. P. Leach (1984) 11–16.

17 VCH, *Somerset*, VI (1962) 136–7.

18 J. Collinson, *History of Somerset*, II (1791) 213–14. The platform of this overgrown site, 122 feet by 109 feet, is surrounded by a moat 20 feet wide. The house had sunk to farmhouse status by Edward IV's reign. M. McGarvie, *Proc. Somerset Arch. and N. H. Soc.*, 118 (1974) 15–24. This and the fortified houses of the county are listed in R. Dunning, *Somerset Castles* (1995).

19 R. A. Higham, *Devon Arch. Soc.* 46 (1988) 142–9. Also his article in *Historical Atlas of South-West England* (1999) 136–43 and PhD thesis of 1979, University of Exeter.

20 S. E. Rigold, *Totnes Castle: Leaflet* (1979) 4; *Trans. Devon Assoc.* 86 (1954) 241–2.

21 N. Molyneux, *Restormel Castle: Handbook* (2001). Earl Edmund made his home at Restormel during the later years of his life, while the Black Prince stayed there during his three visits to Cornwall. The Leland-attributed 'castle' at Liskeard (*Itinerary*, I, 205) was a duchy-fortified manor house, built by the first earl. The hall, three chambers at each end of it, and the chapel were wall enclosed with a gateway in 1337. *HKW*, II (1963) 980.

22 A. D. Saunders, *Launceston Castle: Handbook* (1998), followed the major excavation programme of 1961–82. Also *HKW*, I (1963) 470–3; II (1963) 693–4, 804–5, 845–7. Tintagel Castle is now thought to have been non-military in purpose, developed by Richard, earl of Cornwall after 1233 as a prestigious symbol of the traditions of Cornish lordship which he inherited. R. A. Higham in *Historical Atlas of South-West England* (1999) 141, accepting O. Padel in C. Thomas, *A Provisional List of Imported Pottery in Post Roman Western Britain and Ireland* (1981) Appendix 2. The castle was built in traditional fashion even though defence was not its purpose. B. Davison, *Tintagel Castle: Handbook* (1999), noting the many changes in site interpretation since the 1930s. Tintagel is a classic Cornish combination of a spectacular setting with modest architectural interest.

23 B. H. St J. O'Neil, *Archaeologia* 85 (1936) 131.

24 *Cal. Pat. Rolls: 1334–38*, 558. The uppermost floor of the 'towre imbattayled', noted in Symond's Diary in 1644, now at the rear of the early eighteenth-century house of Bere Barton, was removed in the nineteenth century so that the structure with its stone newel and garderobe could be incorporated under a roof extension as a storeroom with bedroom above. The dining room may date from the fifteenth century, with evidence of blocked late medieval windows and part of the embattled enclosing wall, facing the junction of the rivers Tamar and Tavy. Sir William and his wife enlarged the nearby church (1333), which holds their attributed tomb.

25 Sir John Lercedekne's licence of 1335 was one of five awarded in Cornwall during the early 1330s. Leland noted that the property had an outer and inner court and seven towers, though these were assumed by Tomkin in 1730 to be only turrets and appendices to the round tower 50 feet high which was still standing in his day. Virtually all the remains had

been pulled down in 1718 to help build the nearby village. *Itinerary*, I, 199. For a detailed late eighteenth-century account by the rector, *Jour. Roy. Inst. Cornwall* 7 pt 2 (1974) 109–17; H. M. Whitley, *ibid.* 9 pt 3 (1988) 425–48.

26 *Itinerary*, I, 204. Unaltered until 1790, Place House at Fowey is essentially a Tudor display to an earlier house that was extensively remodelled by the early Victorians. J. Musson, *Country Life* (October 1998); J. Whetter, *Cornish People in the 15th Century* (1999) 57–71. The estuary at Fowey was protected at the same time by two blockhouses (one survives) with a chain stretched between them. Also A. D. Saunders, *Arch. Jour.* 130 (1973) 232–7.

27 *Itinerary*, I, 197.

28 The position of St Michael's Mount in the Bay meant that the monastery there needed to be fortified from an early date. By 1400, Syon Abbey was charged with its defensive maintenance and garrison provision, but in 1473 it was captured by the earl of Oxford and held for four months in the earl's desperate attempt to support the deposed Henry VI. The Arundell house of 1572–4 at Trerice seems to have incorporated the lower part of a three-storey solar tower next to a hall, revealed by excavation in 1954. Comparisons are usually made with that at Pengersick Castle. E. M. Jope, *Studies in Building History* (1961) 206–8. Arwenack Manor, Falmouth, probably built by the first John Killigrew *c.*Henry VIII, was built round three sides of a courtyard which a mid sixteenth-century map shows with a circular corner tower of defensive capability. D. Croghan, *Arwenack, Falmouth* (1973) 5. The castellated structure surmounting Carn Brea is essentially an eighteenth- and nineteenth-century folly but it retains some medieval elements. It was called a castle tower by William Worcester in 1478 (J. Harvey, *Itineraries* (1969) 21) and a castelet by Leland (*Itinerary*, I, 190), but it may have been the tower of a fortified house, a chapel, or a hermitage.

29 The classic plan was still practised well over a century later at Knightstone.

30 This isolated and little-known mansion is poorly documented, externally plain with rendered façades, and essentially of *c.*1560, 1689–1700 (including the now abandoned north range), and *c.*1800. Part of the service court to the rear has been pulled down and all of the outer court, though its foundations show when the grass is parched. H. A. Tipping, *Country Life* (August 1914).

31 The practice can be seen as far afield as Ashby de la Zouch Castle and Ightham Mote.

32 Bishop Brantyngham (1370–94) issued more than 130 licences in Devon alone, while bishop Stafford (1394–1421) was responsible for at least a hundred more. W. G. Hoskins, *Devon* (1954) 228.

33 The first-floor chapel with its Perpendicular window and fittings looks more 1500 than 1425 when Roger Wyke obtained a licence from bishop Lacy. This stone-rubble house a mile from Axmouth has an odd plan, with the north range hall floored in the early sixteenth century at the same time that several stone chimney pieces were added in the west block. The house was altered in the early seventeenth and mid-twentieth centuries when a single-storey extension was added.

34 Licensed in 1432, the chapel at Fardel is a large one, with arch-braced roof, aumbrey, piscina, sedilia, and a fine east window of two quatrefoils above three cinquefoil lights. The rubble-built range in extension, with upper and lower central doorways, was originally residential. This multi-period house of the Raleigh family from 1303 to 1613 is typical of many small manor houses in Devon with its span of fifteenth-century porch, late sixteenth-century inserted floor in the medieval hall, and upper cross wing with seventeenth-century plasterwork, eighteenth-century staircase, and original transomed end window with cinquefoil lights. Slade, 2 miles to the north-west, retains the elaborate late medieval five-bay hall roof that Fardel lacks. The wall plates and braces supporting the arched trusses are decorated on their undersides, the purlins are heavily moulded, and the three lines of wind braces are unrestrained and enhanced with sixty bosses at their intersections. This is a typical

example of a busy interior contrasting with a plain exterior as at Orleigh Court or Bowhill.

35 N. W. Alcock, *Trans. Devon. Assoc.* 98 (1966) 105–31. A classic example of a Devonshire farm complex with a hall range dendro dated to 1328–39. *Vern. Arch.* 28 (1997) 139.

36 Devon roofs are reviewed by J. Thorpe in *Regional Variation in Timber-Framed Building in England and Wales down to 1550*, ed. D. F. Stenning and D. D. Andrews (1998) 79–87.

37 The slightly later, highly decorated hammer-beam structure at Bradfield lies outside this local 'school'. Also H. A. Tipping, *Country Life* (December 1903).

38 The only other surviving aisled hall in Wiltshire is Old House, Market Lavington, an early fourteenth-century manor house of Edington Priory. *Wilts. Arch. Mag.* 80 (1986) 173. The hall of Greenham Barton in Somerset was also originally aisled.

39 T. B. James and A. M. Robinson (eds.), *Clarendon Palace: The History and Archaeology of a Medieval Palace and Hunting Lodge* (1988). Like the excavation report for the royal hunting palace at Ludgershall (2002), that for Clarendon Palace is more telling than the standing evidence. Also *HKW*, II (1963) 910–18 and *Med. Arch.* 44 (2000) 311 for the proposed park and site management plan.

40 Kilve Manor House of about 1280 displays the same T-shaped plan but has lost its hall and the solar wing is ruined.

41 J. Penoyre, *Proc. Somerset A. and N. H. Soc.* 141 (1998) 77–89; 142 (1999) 311–15.

42 A catalogue of over 300 cruck-roofed buildings, mainly in central and south Somerset and across all periods, has been established for the county. R. de Z. Hall *et al.*, *Proc. Somerset A. and N. H. Soc.* 114 (1970) 48–73; 117 (1973) 102–6; 121 (1976/7) 55–66; 123 (1978/9) 27–53; 125 (1980/1) 45–66. A similar number have been identified in Dorset, mainly towards the north.

43 RCAHM, *Glamorgan*, III pt 1b (2000) 315, 333–4; A. Emery, *Greater Med. Houses*, II (2000) 640 n.90.

44 Witchampton and Barnston reflect key planning changes between the middle and later years of the century. C. F. Wright, *Proc. Dorset N. H. and A. Soc.* 87 (1966) 255–64; RCHM, *Dorset*, V (1975) 105–6. RCHM, *Dorset*, II pt 1 (1970) 43–5 needs revision in the light of internal alterations in the early 1970s. Also R. Machin, *Arch. Jour.* 134 (1977) 297–302.

45 RCHM, *Dorset*, I (1952) 53–4. Childhay was the seat of the Crewkernes, who married into the Childhay family in the time of Edward III and held the property for nearly three centuries. A. Oswald, *Country Houses of Dorset* (1959) 57–8.

46 RCHM, *Dorset*, II pt 2 (1970) 209–11. The previous house on the site was built in the early seventeenth century. The plan given in J. Hutchins, *The History and Antiquities of the County of Dorset* (1774) is of its outbuildings only, destroyed in *c.*1765.

47 The misnamed 'duchy palace' was made up of a line of two-storey buildings serving as the administrative and tax centre, the county court and judicial centre, and the stannary court and assay base of the duchy. N. J. G. Pounds, *Arch. Jour.* 136 (1979) 203–17. The principal rooms above the undercrofts seem to have been two halls of almost equal size, with the southern one provided with gable-end garderobes above a stream. The most famous back-to-back apartments on this scale were Edward III's great hall and chapel at Windsor Castle seventy years later. There was a slightly narrower and separately built third hall, boldly buttressed, with single- rather than double-light first-floor windows. The remains are distressingly incorporated in eighteenth- and nineteenth-century structures.

48 Shillingham chapel is next to a contemporary chamber block, converted

into a farmhouse during the seventeenth century. It is described by K. Ray as a first-floor hall with end windows, mural fireplace, and evidence of side windows, above a divided undercroft. *Cornish Arch.* 33 (1994) 230–1. Also T. H. Turner and J. H. Parker, *Some Account of Domestic Architecture in England*, II (1853) 304–5; E. M. Jope, *Studies in Building History* (1961) 202.

49 It was replaced by an imposing red-brick mansion in 1679, illustrated by Edmund Prideaux in the 1730s before its demolition in 1739. A farmhouse stands on the site of the stables. W. R. Wilson-North, *Cornish Arch.* 32 (1993) 112–27.

50 A few early fifteenth-century fragments and a coat of arms have been incorporated in the late eighteenth-century house on the site. J. Whetter, *Cornish People in the 15th Century* (1999) 19–25, 39–47, 113–45; J. Whetter, *The Bodrugans: A Study of a Medieval Cornish Knightly Family* (1995).

51 Some late medieval windows and doorways survive in the outbuildings.

52 The present late seventeenth- and eighteenth-century house with early Tudor origins became a Carmelite convent in 1794. An account roll of the Arundell family by the steward of Lanherne survives for 1466–7. *Jour. Roy. Inst. Cornwall* 2 (1953) 25–32. Chideok Castle in Dorset became the family's second seat after the marriage of Sir John Arundell to Catherine, daughter of Sir John Chideok in 1451. Branches of the Arundell family had a seat at Trerice (rebuilt during 1570s) and an earlier and less imposing one at Ebbingford.

53 One medieval window survives in the early seventeenth-century replacement house by the Grenville family after they had purchased it in 1572.

54 The most well-known example is the small, vernacular manor house or possibly steward's house at Tintagel, commonly known as the Old Post Office. Often ascribed to the fourteenth century, it may be early fifteenth century in origin (V. M. and F. J. Chesher (1968) 27–9), but with considerable doubt as to how much primary structure still stands. S. Rigold, *Arch. Jour.* 130 (1973) 247–8; M. Binney, *Country Life* (July 2003). The county resurvey of listed buildings during the 1980s added very few further examples to V. M. and F. J. Chesher, *The Cornishman's House* (1968); *Cornish Arch.* 25 (1986) 150.

55 The much-altered block to the north-west is believed to have been the abbot's lodging, altered or rebuilt by abbot Ramsam (1475–1504). RCHM, *Dorset*, I (1952) 212–13; *Arch. Jour.* 140 (1983) 19. The so-called guest house at Cerne Abbas is small and an attribution only.

56 H. Brakspear, *Archaeologia* 73 (1923) 225–52, written shortly before the sale. The barn from the priory, shipped to the United States of America in 1928, was rediscovered in its crates in 1998.

57 Most of the foundations were in the less harsh landscapes south of the moors, with the earls of Cornwall mainly supporting houses outside the county. Reports on all the religious houses in Devon were prepared for Devon County Council and HBMC between 1980 and 2000. Also C. Holdsworth in *Historical Atlas of South-West England* (1999) 206–11.

58 C. Hussey, *Country Life* (October 1948); *Arch. Jour.* 130 (1973) 291–2.

59 J. R. Fletcher, *A Short History of St. Michael's Mount*, ed. J. Stephan (1951); P. Herring, *St. Michael's Mount: An Archaeological Assessment* (1992) summarised in *Cornish Arch.* 32 (1993) 153–9; J. Cornforth, *Country Life* (8 June and 9 September 1993).

60 RCHM, *Dorset*, I (1952) 4–8; L. Keen, *Arch. Jour.* 140 (1983) 22–4.

61 That at Abbotsbury of *c.*1400 is 272 feet long with twenty-three buttressed bays: RCHM, *Dorset*, I (1952) 4–8; Keen, *Arch. Jour.* 140 (1983) 22–4.

62 H. P. R. Finberg in W. G. Hoskins and H. P. R. Finberg, *Devonshire Studies* (1952) 154–71.

16

SECULAR ART, DECORATION, AND FURNISHING, 1300–1500

THE majority of medieval houses in England and Wales are still in private hands but their interiors essentially reflect the living circumstances of the last 200 years. One or two museums or publicly owned properties have tried to reinstate a medieval character through their furnishings (Leeds Castle, Gainsborough Old Hall), but I know of only one private residence in Shropshire that has made such an attempt. Medieval secular culture has to be drawn from a broad range of sources, though in the past this was essentially limited to documentary and manuscript illustrations. More recently, it has been appreciated that some houses are able to make a major contribution to the subject, together with a range of fittings and furnishings that have survived little-known in museums and institutions.

CULTURAL CHANGES DURING THE LATER MIDDLE AGES

Culture aspires to standards of taste in the arts, humanities, and behaviour. It is a reflection of a particular time and place, but whereas it changes with considerable rapidity today, the time span of change during the middle ages took rather longer. At the extreme, it took over a hundred years before the first manifestations of the Italian-based Renaissance reached England. Until the time of Edward I, the centralisation of the church and the powerful cultural forces coming from Europe throughout the twelfth and thirteenth centuries meant that English culture tended to be French-based, though there was also an Italian element in the first flowering of arts in England under Henry III. The change to a more nationalistic attitude was initiated by Edward I and then Edward III, the former with his conquests and unification plans for Wales and Scotland, and the latter with his military and political successes against France.

Culture reflects wealth and social relations. The bonds of society were loosened during the later middle ages, for though the church and government were more deeply conservative after the Black Death, economic and financial pressures hastened social mobility. The statute of labourers (1351) and its reissues, like the sumptuary legislation of the same period, was unable to stem an era of changing economic and personal relations. Social and cultural boundaries became more complex during the fifteenth century, and though the title 'gentleman' was first adopted early in that century, the connotations of birth and lifestyle that it implied had existed earlier. Prominent among the gentry were lawyers, a profession barely known before the rise of common law during the thirteenth century but who, as in all succeeding ages, have rarely been backward in social advancement or in adopting a comfortable lifestyle. But the route to gentrification also lay with service and patronage in relation to those of higher status, whether magnate or knight, one of the aspects of bastard feudalism which helped to move society from a landed to a moneyed structure. For new and rising families, living like a gentleman was a way of securing class recognition, while for those of higher standing, the difference had to be more overtly demonstrated by cultivated taste and ostentatious display.

Culture benefits from ease of movement, which England was well placed to provide. A relatively slender island with many ports and navigable rivers meant extensive trade within the country as well as to and from the continent. Culture, like trade, was a two-way traffic. It extended from masons travelling to distant parts of the land as the labour movement for constructing Edward I's Welsh castles has confirmed, to transporting materials considerable distances. A common religion across Europe not only encouraged a hierarchy of officials travelling to and from Rome or Avignon and between monastic mother houses, but pilgrims of all social rank travelling to and from Jerusalem, Santiago de Compostela, and Canterbury. Magnates such as the earls of Derby and Salisbury fought in Spain in 1342–44, Lord Clifford was slain in Germany (1389), Lord FitzWalter was taken prisoner in Tunis and died in Venice (1406), while the Scropes of Bolton and Masham were frequent crusaders. Edward I's master-mason and the family of bishop Grandisson of Exeter came from Savoy, while English craftsmen worked in Paris and Avignon. Booty from the French wars put many highly expensive and fashionable items into circulation across the country, while foreign artisans such as brickmakers and glaziers were welcomed during the fifteenth century.

The court was a leading cultural centre for much of the later middle ages but there was no distinctive court style, nor were the kings such lavish patrons as those of France.[1] London was a vigorous city of European scale which greatly impressed a Venetian visitor in 1498 overawed by its many goldsmiths, but there were several regional centres of creative activity. York, Norwich, Coventry, and Bristol enjoyed their own artistic hinterlands, while lesser centres such as Durham, Shrewsbury, Oxford, and Exeter were able to sustain their own regional cultures. For the majority of England was less insular and more culturally absorbent than might be imagined. The greater houses where people paid rent often provided service and were frequently visited by musicians and storytellers fostering a nationalistic culture, particularly in Wales. Towns and fairs were centres for the sale and purchase of goods, while the church and monasteries provided education as well as spiritual guidance. After the Black Death, the dominant architectural form was the grid-iron pattern of Perpendicular, distinctly English and applicable to house, church, and institutions, that allowed a flood of light to illuminate the cultural and artistic displays within.

In broad brushstrokes, English cultural activity during the later middle ages can be considered in four phases.[2]

1290–1360. After an initial phase of self-conscious Englishness under Edward I striking down Welsh and Scottish culture, the political uncertainties of Edward II's reign, the famine of 1315–17, and subsequent economic recession were followed by the horrors of the Black Death and recurrent outbreaks of the plague. Yet the exuberant Decorated style of architecture was as receptive to foreign influences as to cross-fertilisation between the different regional centres. The skill and quality of *opus anglicanum* was sought across the continent at the same time as scholars from Oxford were of European influence on theological, scientific, and intellectual life.

1350–1400. Overlying the last plague outbreaks of the 1360s was the ebullience from repeated successes on the battlefield in France and an outbreak of patriotism between the 1340s and 1370s. Propaganda encouraged a sense of national identity, so that England saw itself as the equal of France, exemplified by Edward III's claim to the French throne (1340), the foundation of the order of the garter (by 1348), the adoption of a national saint (St George replacing Edward the Confessor), and the use of the royal arms as those of the nation. Edward III's court, centred at Windsor, became the most splendid in Europe, with a cosmopolitan ambience and a magnetism that drew the admiration of his subjects in a manner without precedent since the Norman Conquest. Architecture quickly recovered after the plague, encouraged by royal projects such as those at St Stephen's Chapel and Windsor Castle, and though manuscript production suffered for at least a generation, figure sculpture did not decline but was, if anything, more vigorous.[3]

This period of conspicuous consumption, hardly stifled by attempts at sumptuary legislation, was maintained throughout Richard II's reign. Despite a new note of criticism, royal hospitality continued to be lavish. Richard read in French as well as in English, while several of his household knights were book owners and poets (Sir John Clanvowe, Sir John Montague). Tapestries were brought from Flanders; Gaunt recruited French musicians and developed a household that could vie with those of the French king's uncles. Richard's queen from Bohemia introduced a central European element linked to the court of her father Charles IV in Prague, while Richard shared his father's and grandfather's love of jewels and expensive clothes in emulation of the Valois court, though he was not a cultural leader and the achievements attributable to him have been fundamentally challenged.[4] Yet there was a balance between foreign and English craftsmanship, with the latter totally dominant in architecture, sculpture, and woodwork.

1400–70. The international Gothic style of elegant poses, sinuous drapery, patterns, and harmonious colours spanned the twenty years either side of the new century. It was a style associated with royal and aristocratic courts across Europe, and it extended in England from the glass in Wykeham's collegiate foundations to the illuminated manuscripts of the first decade of the fifteenth century by Herman Scheerre. Even so, the court lacked cultural vitality, for the interests of Henry IV and Henry V were dominated by political and military pressures. Both kings were literate and musical, as were Henry V's brothers, the dukes of Clarence (d.1420), Bedford, and Gloucester. More than under Richard II, the cultural palm passed to these and other leading courtiers. Clarence was noted for the music of his chapel; Bedford was determined that his court at Rouen and Paris should not give ground to the French dukes.[5] Bedford and Gloucester were bibliophiles, with Gloucester providing a link with the humanities of Italy through his Bodleian library foundation. Henry VI's interests lay in more spiritual matters and his twin foundations at Eton and Cambridge, so that the court was in a state of intellectual lassitude for most of this period, buffeted by economic recession, defeat in France, and dynastic strife thereafter.

1470–1510. The Yorkists and then the Tudor triumph fostered a more confident and culturally rich phase, helped by an authoritative royal household, a period of population growth, and quickening economic prosperity. Edward IV and Henry VII were aware of continental developments. Edward had strong links with the

PLATE 200 Eton College: north side of chapel, wall paintings showing St Elizabeth, the Miracle of the Jewess, a saint, the Story of the Knight, St Redegund, and the Story of the Knight's Wife Who Was Sold to the Devil

Burgundian court and lived for a short time in Bruges (1470–1). Flanders was the primary influence on English art throughout this period, ranging from the Eton College wall paintings to the fifty or so manuscripts acquired by Edward IV, the only major group to have survived, owned by a medieval English king. Henry Tudor spent his formative years in France and Brittany. The royal glazier Bernard Flower came from the Low Countries, while Pietro Torrigiano was a Florentine who reinvigorated English sculpture as well as introducing terracotta and putti to England. Domestic comfort was increasing, not only in the greater number of rooms in a house, now with fireplaces and window glass, but in furniture, furnishings, and possessions, particularly among the gentry and lesser ranks of society.

Spanning much of this era from the mid-fourteenth century onwards was the increased use and development of the English language and the spread of literacy. It was stimulated and encouraged by a new wave of grammarians after the plague as much as by pride in being English and dislike of speaking French. This spread of literacy stemmed from the vitality of regional culture, of which *Piers Plowman* (Shropshire/Malvern) and *Sir Gawain and the Green Knight* (south Cheshire area) are only the best-known examples, but extended across the middle and even the lower orders of society. The development of a commonly understood language at a time of conscious national identity was compounded by its acceptance as the language of government as well as for everyday transactions. It also came to be a language suitable for literary compositions by Langland, Chaucer, and Gower and encouraged the translation of the Scriptures into the vernacular. The introduction of print technology and the founding of a number of grammar schools during the fifteenth and early sixteenth centuries pointed up the widespread growth in literacy, education, and taste. This spread of literacy generated a demand for books, not expensive or high-quality manuscripts which became increasingly rare, but for practical and cheaply produced romances, histories, and ballads. Market expansion meant workshop production, stocked products, and lower

artistic standards. This is similarly reflected in alabaster carvings and brass effigies, products sought by a broader and increasingly affluent element of society, the lower gentry and merchants. By the close of the middle ages, culture was more widely diffused and far less the prerogative of the élite. Patronage had become a possibility for a broader spectrum of society.

English medieval culture did not exist in a vacuum but was subject to diverse continental influences. Twentieth-century scholarship emphasised the Englishness of English art, from Edward Prior and William Lethaby to Nikolaus Pevsner and John Harvey. Furthermore, there has long been an apology for English workmanship, so that high-quality artefacts such as the Wilton Diptych were attributed to foreign artists, usually French or in this case from the Netherlands or Bohemia. It therefore took some time before any correlation was made between the diptych and the quality of the contemporary wall painting in the Byward Tower of the Tower of London, discovered in 1953, and even longer for there to be broad agreement on the English provenance of the diptych and its date of about 1395.[6]

Changing attitudes to English art were stimulated by the Courtauld and Warburg institutes in the 1930s and the work of a generation of refugee scholars. The reassessment of English medieval art was furthered by two exhibitions, 'The Age of Chivalry: 1200–1400' in 1987 and 'Gothic: Art for England 1400–1537' in 2003.[7] These confirmed the widespread stimulation and influences of European activity, from that of Norway or Rome during Henry III's reign and the opening years of Edward I, to Italian influences on English manuscript painting during the first half of the fourteenth century[8] and Bohemian art in the later fourteenth century.[9] The windows in the chapel of New College, Oxford, and the fragments of its retable show that William Wykeham's patronage helped to encourage the International Style in England, as does the high quality of the Sutton Valence retable (c.1370–80). Its influence can also be seen in the Pepysian sketchbook, generally accepted as English work of the late fourteenth century, with figure and animal drawings that could be used for manuscript miniatures, embroideries, glasswork, and woodwork.[10] The tomb of Richard, earl of Warwick (1447–50) shows him wearing armour of the latest Italian design, but while a Netherlands influence on the Eton College chapel wall paintings (1477–87) has been much discussed, it is difficult to find close parallels to these paintings in contemporary northern Europe.

We have finally recognised the error of Ruskin's belief that English Gothic art was inferior to French art, and are slowly moving away from the assumption that the arts in England must follow those in France rather than precede or parallel them. The kings sculpted by Thomas Canon for Westminster Hall in the 1380s can be compared with contemporary statues in Vienna, and though sculpture and stained glass were devastated and dissipated by mid-sixteenth-century iconoclasm, the glass that remains at Wells, Tewkesbury, Warwick, and York is of remarkable quality and high artistic expression. Sometimes English work can be in the vanguard of artistic development, as in house and collegiate building during the second half of the fourteenth century.

Political and artistic boundaries did not necessarily coincide. The closest countries to England were France, the Netherlands, and Norway but political relations between them varied from friendly to hostile and were changeable from generation to generation. The question as to which is the dominant factor in a work of art, the artist's country of origin or his place of work, has yet to be resolved. Is the statue of *c*.1320 in the Musée de Cluny attributed to Guillaume de Nourriche English work from the Norwich area or French work by an English artist?[11] Is the work of Herman Scheerre, whose workshop was in London, English work or that of a German or Netherlands artist? Why was England famous across Europe for textiles, misericords, pewter, funeral brasses, and alabasters while the Ile de France was notable for ivories, manuscripts, and gilded work? And how do we differentiate late fifteenth-century Parisian gilding from that of late fifteenth-century London? English art was far more in the mainstream of European culture than was recognised in the past, giving as well as receiving input from abroad, such as the English design of the tomb of John XXII at Avignon (1335–45) or the Perpendicular-style abbey church at Batalha in Portugal (*c*.1400–38).

SECULAR ART AND FURNISHINGS

There was no difference in the medieval world between religious and secular art. This is most immediately apparent in wall painting, where religious depictions occur in the hall and family rooms at Fiddleford Manor, Littlehempston, and Cothay Manor. Again, it was common practice throughout the later middle ages for one or more horses of a knight or magnate to be given to the church where he was buried, together with his helm, crest, and surcoat of war for display over his tomb.[12] Gothic art was a single art form that could be expressed in different materials and forms. If pressed, an artist would probably say that ecclesiastical art was of a higher order because of its purpose to serve God, but artists worked in different materials and media and for a range of patrons whose only differentiation was in their promptness to pay. Artists rarely signed their names – signatures were not relevant as they became much later. It was the patron who mattered, usually identified by his heraldry rather than by name. Later in the fifteenth century, the role of the patron was made more explicit. The names of those who funded

Long Melford church were inscribed in the clerestory windows, arcades, and porch for all to read, while the donor's name in the stained glass of Merton College chapel was displayed in every window. By the close of the century, donors of diptychs and triptychs were not only named but depicted at the foot with their patron saints.

Art was not cheap, so that it could only be afforded by the wealthy. Apart from the church, that initially limited it to the royal family and the aristocracy, but even the crown was not without its problems. Once the era of royal castle construction was over by the beginning of the fourteenth century, royal building projects took generations to complete. The large-scale exceptions were Edward III's Windsor Castle rebuilding and Richard II's two modest apartment ranges at Portchester Castle. Political and financial misfortunes meant that Henry III's abbey church at Westminster, Edward I's chapel at Westminster Palace, Henry V's palace at Sheen, Henry VI's chapel at Cambridge, and Edward IV's chapel at Windsor had to be completed by later generations. English courtiers might work on a smaller scale (though quite a number did not, including Gaunt, Wykeham, and Lord Cromwell) but their houses were often completed and furnished within their lifetime, as at Bolton, Dartington, Herstmonceux, Stourton, Wardour, and Wingfield. Similarly, Wykeham at Winchester and New College and Waynflete at Magdalen oversaw the completion, furnishing, and occupation of their educational foundations within their lifetime. The same applied on a lesser scale to many knights throughout our period and to minor gentry, merchants, and lawyers during the fifteenth century, but high-quality art was still not yet readily available to the majority of the population.

Applied and figural art could be as powerful and as impressive in a secular environment as its religious counterpart. The epitaph on the tomb of the Black Prince in Canterbury Cathedral includes the lines 'On earth, I had great riches, which gave me great nobility/Lands, houses, great treasures, fine cloths, horses, silver and gold.' Houses made a statement of lineage, personal status, and wealth. They were as much a reflection of an owner's power as of his thirst for recognition. They were the vehicle which enabled an owner to display his standing and generosity to his friends and guests, as much as his wife's clothes reflected the providence of her husband. The greater houses might be private retreats but they were rarely sealed from the outside world. There would be streams of visitors, staff would change, while households included periodic members – administrators, reeves, auditors, and lawyers – with news and gossip from the outside world. Magnates would be employed on royal business at home and abroad, gentry would travel on regional matters, while marriage alliances brought integration with those of higher or lower estate leading to further intercommunication between houses, nearby as well as those further away.

Wealthy people today are reluctant to display their wealth overtly – it is considered vulgar. Those of a more assertive age such as the Victorians had no such qualms, nor did they during the later middle ages. There were no moral or social reservations or inverted snobbery about spending money lavishly and openly. The artistic patronage of the Beauchamp and Neville families in the mid-fifteenth century, as exemplified by Richard, earl of Warwick (d.1439) and Richard Neville, Warwick the Kingmaker (d.1471), reflected their immense wealth and closeness to the court. The money bags so conspicuously displayed by Treasurer Cromwell at Tattershall Castle and Wingfield Manor drew attention to the funding source of his properties and their contents. Purchases, particularly expensive ones, were as much an assertion of property and taste as of expense and craftsmanship. The more public rooms might be decorated with tapestries or wall paintings of a didactic nature such as battle scenes or representation of heroes. The more private rooms were intended to impress honoured guests with more informal tapestries and those with coats of arms and personal emblems, and choice *objets d'art*. Owners might not be able to read books they purchased, but they could admire their content and show off the quality of their illuminations just as we admire them today, for after buildings, manuscripts are the most extensive cultural survival of the middle ages. Such possessions were deployed as symbols by which to lay claim to or confirm status and to help underline social distinctions, for art was a permanent display of power.

Three questions need to be asked when considering the content and furnishings of an English or Welsh interior. Is the surviving evidence of a high or parochial aesthetic standard? How does it compare with contemporary standards in northern Europe? Is the relatively modest amount that survives representative of the country at that time or not? Wills, inquisitions, surveys, and letters provide a wealth of documentary information. They detail the range and sometimes the quality of household goods, but inquisitions and surveys only record the permanent furnishings in a property, not the portable and usually most expensive items that were carried from house to house. What they do show is that a very small percentage remains of the portable wealth of the upper echelon of society. Similarly, few interiors survive that have not been subject to continual redecoration or modification. Even if an apartment retains its walls, roof, and window tracery, as in the hall at Stokesay Castle or the private apartments at Bolton Castle, floors have been replaced, walls stripped of plaster, and recent glass inserted in the windows. Where medieval houses have survived in continuous occupation, they reflect the taste and changes of later generations, even where medieval interiors have been reinstated as at Much Wenlock Prior's House. There is no medieval ensemble equivalent to the Tudor apartments and furnishings at Hardwick Hall. It is a question of taking isolated survivals such as the candle holders at Bolton Castle, the stained glass at Ockwells, or the table and benches at Penshurst and using them as exemplars of items mentioned in documents. And when it comes to the more portable items – tapestries, books, silver, jewelry, and clothing – the evidence is just as limited. Yet quality can only be considered on the basis of what can be visibly assessed rather than purely from inventories and letters using phrases such as 'very rich' or 'ornate'. Such words are more likely to reflect pride of ownership than their monetary or artistic value.

Much has been written about the formal conduct and lifestyle of a medieval household – its rules,[13] etiquette,[14] food preparation, and consumption,[15] goods and chattels,[16] and the entertainment provided.[17] Less has been written about the furnishings of a house, with most of it drawn from inventories and other documentary sources. Thomas Calston, for instance, a member of a Wiltshire gentry family from near Calne with a legal and business background, developed his estate by buying land and property near Lacock and Bewley from 1386 onwards.[18] He acquired timber-framed Bewley Court soon after 1391 and extended it shortly afterwards. In 1396,

he was granted a licence to celebrate mass in any worthy house and in 1399 the bishop of Salisbury permitted him to celebrate mass 'in the oratory of his house in the parish of Lacock'.[19] Calston filled a number of important local offices such as member of parliament for Marlborough in 1390 and for the county in 1402 and 1406, and was sheriff of Wiltshire in 1415. The value of Thomas Calston's tenure stems from the inventory written in Latin after his death in 1418.[20] It reveals that his possessions included two Lancastrian livery collars, and much silver, and that Bewley Court was furnished as richly as a magnate's residence. The hall held three tables, a chair for Calston probably in front of the 'new hanging with side pieces', a bench with a 'worn' curtain with side pieces behind it for his family, and six stools. The parlour held a painted hanging and bench, two oak folding tables, and a cupboard. In the pantry were tablecloths, some embroidered, napkins, brass candlesticks, drinking vessels, and a bread bin. The chapel held silver communion vessels, an alabaster relief of the Virgin Mary, vestments and prayer books together with the chest that held them. Calston's red-curtained bed, coverlet, and six cushions were decorated with the arms of his second wife, three red circles on a white ground. A blue coverlet and tester decorated with rabbits and an armorial cover were stored in a small adjoining chamber which held Calston's deed chest 'well bound with iron'. The garderobe was filled with a hugger-mugger of items filling almost half the inventory. They ranged from beds, worn sheets, a chasuble, and portable breviary, to the hangings for a war tent, pack saddles, axes, crossbows, coats of mail, visors, and gloves. The total value of the goods in this store room was worth more than all the other items in the house. There were other furnishings listed in the chapel chamber and the chamber over the chapel, the kitchen with its bronze cooking pots holding from two to ten gallons, brewhouse, farrier's workshop, stable, and farm store. The inventory of silver and jewels is badly damaged and illegible, but it was substantial and came to £100 6s. 8d., as against the house contents valued at £60 1s. 9d. None of these items has been traced and the same is true of most late medieval inventories, though the relatively plain secular cup and cover of *c*.1430–50 from Lacock that was converted after the Reformation into a communion cup has a contemporary local provenance.[21]

Architecture is essentially a framework to enclose functional space. A Gothic cathedral was more than just a stunning architectural concept – it was an awe-inspiring space that was only complete when filled with images, sculpture, stained glass, paintings, and precious metals. Frame and purpose, though, were both focussed on a single function, the worship of God. Houses were similar in their totality. The framework included the basic components of hall, chamber, and services, but by the later middle ages most of the greater houses had become complex in their development. As important as the consideration of their form and technical development is the study of the space created and the use made of it. This flows from an appreciation of the organisation of a household, how the occupants lived, and how the demand for greater privacy was achieved through the planning function. Today, our medieval houses, like our churches, lack the original contents, the furnishings, the colour, and the artefacts that were an essential element of any residence during the middle ages. This quintet of ownership, setting, architectural form, purpose, and content should be the bedrock of medieval house studies.

Whereas most French cathedrals are of a single if extended style, nearly all English cathedrals display a range of architectural styles. English medieval houses are similar. A handful can claim a relatively short construction period, as mentioned earlier, but the majority are residences of accretion and development. The plainness of a Georgian house exterior was in deliberate contrast with the richness and elaboration of the interior. A similar contrast occurs in some late medieval 'castles' like Maxstoke, Nunney, and Bodiam, where the relatively plain and balanced façades gave little hint of internal richness. The use of brick at Herstmonceux was more explicit in this respect, but the majority of subsequent houses like Athelhampton Hall, Gainsborough Hall, or Wingfield Manor boasted an external elaboration designed to advertise the greater sumptuousness of the interiors, while others such as Hylton and Raglan castles prefaced entry with an armorial display of their owner's standing and 'lordship'.

What we lack in medieval houses today, as much as in our churches, is colour. A close examination and analysis of the west fronts of Wells and Exeter cathedrals in the 1990s revealed traces of the original paintwork. By a process of digitisation, it has been possible to prepare illustrations of the fronts showing their original brilliance. During restoration work to the east window of Fountains Abbey in 1992, the moulding rebates at its apex could be seen to retain the brilliant blue and silver of the medieval painting even though the stonework had been exposed to the elements for centuries. Stone, wooden, alabaster, and ivory carvings have rarely retained their polychrome decoration,[22] painted wood has darkened, tapestries have usually faded from a blaze of colour to a shadow of their original tones, while wall paintings are not often more than dusty shadows of their initial brilliance, though the high quality of the wall paintings uncovered in the late 1960s at Horsham St Faith Priory was a revelation.

The houses in these three volumes are bare in comparison with their original character, and although we have a few glimpses of what they may have been like, we lack the banners and hangings, the furnishings, the painted glass, the kitchen and chapel contents, and the personal items that gave them richness and individuality. Wooden roofs and corbels would often be brightly painted, while attendants would be wearing embroidered livery. The visual was a vital component of medieval life, but we tend to overlook it through concentrating on architectural form. We also need to read the images, though few enough have remained, particularly the sign language of heraldry that drew attention to marriage alliances, friends, and distinguished neighbours. Heraldic decoration would have been the principal motif of a late medieval house, displayed not only on tiles, glass, and banners but in wood carvings such as the heraldic beasts from Naworth Castle and those surmounting the roof posts of Weare Giffard Hall and Orleigh Court. We also need to know more about household management, etiquette, and ceremony at the levels of society below the crown and magnates, to help us interpret the structural and decorative evidence that has survived.[23]

INTERNAL FITTINGS AND DECORATION

External decoration

Heraldic display was a prime form of external as much as internal decoration. The tiers of shields that mark the gatehouses of Kirkham Priory (c.1300) and Butley Priory (1320–5) commemorated generous donors as did those on the later collegiate gatehouses at Cambridge. But most late medieval armorial displays were more personal. None of the heraldic pennants and banners that adorned castle and mansion walls have survived outside manuscript illustration, but many examples of high-quality carving have withstood centuries of weathering. They range from a single badge, the Percy lion at Warkworth or the letter b at Raby Castle to the arms of the builder's family as at Raglan Castle or Nevill Holt. There is less external sculpture in the Midlands and south than in northern England where more than twenty residences declare their pedigree. Bothal Castle is one of the earliest (1343–4) but splendid displays can be seen at Cawood, Danby, Harewood, Naworth, Sizergh, and Warkworth castles as well as at lesser houses such as Cockle Park Tower, Dalston New Hall, and Paull Holme. They were usually a feature of the entrance approach, with those at Hylton and Lumley castles as the most spectacular armorial display (both late fourteenth century), but heraldry was also an element of the corbel table of the gatehouse at Steeton Hall (c.1360). Such visual imagery was a reminder of where power resided when some northern families were more important to the locality than the distant crown. It was a visible statement of position, authority, and influence, frequently made more apparent by painting or gilding which have virtually always worn away.

Other external decoration included elaborate mouldings and window tracery, figurative gargoyles, and gable-surmounting heraldic beasts (Great Chalfield Manor, c.1480). Pinnacles were sometimes carved to support armorial weather vanes as at Athelhampton Hall (c.1495), an early stage in the development of the decorative motifs that mark many Tudor rooflines.

Ironwork

Most of the medieval ironwork in England and Wales is found in churches – doors, chests, and tombs – in the form of handles, hinges, or grilles.[24] Very little domestic evidence remains, though the scrollwork decorating the entry door to Merton College hall is a splendid late thirteenth-century survival. Some elaborate hinges are contemporary with the hall doors they hold, but they are usually utilitarian. Iron or bronze doorknockers and ventilation plates can occasionally be found (the latter at Dartington Hall), but more usually only their position indicates a domestic door.

Stained glass

Stained glass was the only medium discovered and fully developed during the middle ages. English artists were as skilled and as inventive as their colleagues in France but iconoclasm and fragility mean that only a modest amount of evidence has survived to prove it. This applies as much to domestic as to ecclesiastical environments, with the further limitation that the former has received even less detailed study.[25]

Windows in the most important rooms, particularly the hall, withdrawing chamber, and chapel in the larger houses, would be glazed, but often only in the upper lights: the lower ones would be barred with iron and shuttered for ventilation purposes. Glass was translucent rather than transparent but though stained glass became comparatively widespread in royal residences during the thirteenth century, it only extended to large-scale houses from the fourteenth century onwards. Figured glass was essentially limited to the chapel, with heraldic glass usual in the hall and private apartments, though most of the surviving evidence dates from the fifteenth century.

PLATE 201 Ockwells Manor: hall windows

Armorial designs were particularly popular because they highlighted family and neighbouring connections, as in the halls at Buckland Old Rectory (1470s) and at Athelhampton Hall (c.1485–95). Some of the most impressive examples were interspersed with family mottoes, as at Ockwells Manor (1450s). The twenty-nine religious panels in Leicester Museum from a local domestic glazing scheme of 1490–1500 include some winning details of contemporary interiors. Labours of the Month occur from the mid-fifteenth century, with Norbury Hall retaining six such roundels of c.1480, while the slightly later bay window in the hall of the Commandery, Worcester, is filled with animals, birds, and plants.

Much of the mid-fifteenth-century figured glass from the chapel of Hampton Court near Leominster was sold during the twentieth century and is in museums, but some smaller armorial panels survive *in situ*. The chapel at Haddon Hall retains a rare donor portrait (Sir Richard and Lady Vernon, 1427), but some churches retain similar figures who had built or extended their nearby manor house, as at Bere Ferrers (Sir William and Lady Ferrers) and Tewkesbury Abbey (Lord Despenser), both fourteenth-century, and Luton (Sir John Wenlock) and Gipping (Sir James Tyrell), both fifteenth-century examples.

Tiles

Early floors were either of beaten clay or of chalk, like the hall floor in the Old Deanery, Salisbury, or covered with a spread of mortar as in the late fourteenth-century hall floor at the Manor of the More, Rickmansworth. Flagged floors were laid where there was a local supply of suitable material. The use of hand-made tiles for flooring developed from the early thirteenth century for they were hard-wearing, easier to clean, and more attractive-looking than clay flooring. They quickly became a feature of churches and abbeys and it is there that most examples survive, as in the refectory at Cleeve Abbey (1271–2) and that at Denny Abbey (mid-fourteenth century). The simplest tiles were those that were plain but with alternating coloured glazes, often in different shapes, decoratively arranged. The most popular tiles were those with a surface decoration in a contrasting colour to the body of the tile, usually red and white to become the brown and yellow colours most frequently seen today. Decorated tiles were quickly adopted for a domestic environment, with heraldic designs predominating rather than foliage and geometrical patterns. Impressed and relief tiles were rare.

A considerable number of production centres and schools have been identified from the mid-thirteenth to the mid-sixteenth century, almost all stemming from ecclesiastical evidence, with the bulk of the literature following their development, distribution, elaboration, and variable quality.[26] Few secular pavements have remained in position, with those in the muniment rooms at Winchester College and New College, Oxford as an exception. One of the few complete domestic pavements is that from Canynges House, Bristol (*c*.1480–1515), now in the British Museum, while that at Clifton House, King's Lynn (*c*.1325), the oldest secular tiled floor discovered so far, has been left *in situ*. Among the most elaborate was the heraldic floor at Thornbury Castle, made for Edward Stafford, duke of Buckingham, shortly before his execution in 1521. Designed in groups of four tiles, they were given to the V & A Museum in 1890 but have been supplemented by some more found on site in 1982 and kept there.

Wainscot

Wainscot or wood panelling took over from the wall hangings as a feature of important apartments at the close of our period but little enough remains today. Wainscot was used as early as the thirteenth century in royal residences,[27] while the sides of the main rooms of the Percy residence at Wressle were 'ornamented with a great profusion of sculpture, finely executed in wood, exhibiting the ancient bearings, crests, badges, and devices of the Percy family, in a great variety of forms, set off with all the advantages of painting, gilding, and imagery'.[28] Unfortunately, the castle was gutted by fire in 1796 and abandoned. One of the few later fifteenth-century examples to survive is the flushed oak panelling in the Courtenay Chamber of Maidstone Palace. Within fifty years, a group of houses in the Thame area were enhanced with high-quality linenfold panelling by the same craftsmen, including Nether Winchendon House and the abbot's houses at Thame Park and Notley Abbey (now at Weston Manor), confirming that ecclesiastical and secular patronage had long been indistinguishable.

Wall decoration

Internal walls would have been plastered and whitewashed to lighten the rooms. High-quality chambers were often decorated with red lines imitating stonework (thirteenth century at Wells Palace) but secular wall paintings were more extensive than formerly believed.[29] Unfortunately, their discovery is very much a hit or miss affair, usually revealed during restoration. Those that have survived are often fragmentary and faded, like the red foliated scrollwork (mid?-fourteenth century) in the buttery of Stokesay Castle, but two outstanding survivals were revealed in the late 1940s and late 1960s. The end wall of the refectory of Horsham St Faith Priory includes a monumental Crucifixion (discovered in 1924) and a unique cycle of subsequently revealed narrative scenes illustrating the foundation of the priory. Created in *c*.1250 and still brilliantly coloured, they reveal that the artist made incised drawings on the dry plaster base and then added colour with a range of up to ten expensive pigments and media hitherto unknown in mural painting. White lead ground was used and colours were applied *a secco*, over which translucent oil glazes were laid. Moreover, some of the narrative scenes, that revealed fascinating details of contemporary life, were retouched in the first half of the fifteenth century, a rare enough practice though it also occurred at Westminster Palace.[30] The secular paintings in the great chamber at Longthorpe Tower found after the Second World War are one of the most complete schemes of domestic wall painting in northern Europe, attributable

PLATE 202 Muchelney Abbey: interior of abbot's parlour

to about 1330 and depicting biblical, didactic, and secular subjects. The quality is regional, as befits its patron, but what is surprising is the sophistication of the iconographic programme. Secular and religious subjects occur in a common context, all enriched with inscribed scrolls and Latin texts.

The mid-fourteenth-century mural paintings in St Stephen's Chapel, Westminster, were reduced by James Wyatt in 1800 to a few precious survivals that show they were among the most magnificent of the middle ages. The chapel was not large, 90 feet by 30 feet, so that the paintings were correspondingly small in scale but jewel-like in quality. Italian influences have been detected in the perspective architectural niches and more particularly Sienese influence in the brocade clothing and the wall angels. The loss of this outstanding work of art and the documented paintings in the other royal apartments has been slightly rectified by the recent discovery of two further scenes in a royal context. The better preserved is the total painted decoration of a private room and lobby for Edward III in the Rose Tower of Windsor Castle. Completed in 1365–6, it is an elaborate repetitive pattern of roses set in flowery borders against a crimson covered background. The Crucifixion scene in the Byward Tower of the Tower of London, attributed to *c*.1390–5, was painted in the International Style, with the display of sumptuous materials complemented by the delicacy of handling. The beautifully shaded figures are set against a background of gilt popinjays, fleur-de-lis, and lions arranged in a diaper pattern on an emerald ground.

The fifteenth century has few secular wall paintings of such high quality and they are lower down the social scale. This is mainly because of the growing desirability to have the latest status symbol – tapestries, or painted wall hangings. The windows in a hall were now inserted in the upper register to allow for such hangings to be installed below, with the hooks at Wingfield Manor still visible. Wall paintings were not so luxurious as hangings or capable of being draught-excluders, but they were cheaper and more durable and therefore continued to be favoured, particularly in lesser households. The hall walls at Belsay Castle, initially decorated with red vine scroll, were covered with a second scheme in two tiers during the mid-fifteenth century, a naval scene above a line of heraldic shields hung from trees against a floral and wooded background imitating millefleurs tapestries.[31] At Cothay Manor (late fifteenth century) the hall paintings include the hanging and funeral procession of Renard the Fox, while a private chamber was decorated with a local saint and possibly a heresy painting. Cothay illustrates the inclusion of religious subjects in a domestic context which also occurs at Fiddleford Manor, where the solar includes a late fourteenth-century Annunciation, at Rochford Tower near Boston with a similar subject (early sixteenth century), and at Littlehempston Manor, where the Resurrection was painted above the hall dais. The painting of the Virgin Mary and possibly St James of Compostela in the form of a fictive tapestry (c.1500) in the modest hall at Cullacott was painted over in the 1520s with the Tudor arms and St George and the Dragon. The knights painted between the windows in the hall at Penshurst Place and Farleigh Hungerford Castle hall and chapel had equally given way by the close of the fifteenth century to a detailed representation of the house's builder as at Great Chalfield Manor. These last examples, however, point up the modest or even the poor standards that were accepted at the time, though the painted verdure tapestries of c.1500–20 in the withdrawing chamber of Bramall Hall hint at the availability of quality workmanship. It is regrettable that we have no survivals from magnate houses for either the fourteenth or fifteenth centuries, but high-quality work was still being created towards the close of the era, influenced by Netherlandish art. The scheme of c.1470 discovered in 1970 in the prior's chapel at Durham Cathedral Priory and that of c.1490–1500 recovered a few years later in the gatehouse chapel at Berry Pomeroy Castle help the celebrated grisaille scenes in Eton College Chapel (1477–87), the finest late medieval mural paintings in northern Europe, to be judged in a national context. But it was the parlour of Haddon Hall that was the harbinger of the future, when its beamed ceiling was covered with painted decoration of compartmentalised badges and shields on a chequered ground (c.1490–4) and the room was panelled a few decades later.

FURNISHINGS

Furniture

Furniture and furnishings had symbolic as much as practical significance. Furniture, in particular, spoke of an owner's estate and standing. Certain pieces of furniture such as a cupboard or buffet were an adjunct of ceremony and helped to sustain the dignity of the household's social structure. Chairs filled a similar function. Furniture was rarely elaborate. It was intended to be practical, partly because it was usually covered with rich textiles, and partly because it was usually movable and taken from house to house. For that reason, an inventory rarely gives the full extent of a house's furnishings for they were limited to the permanent items that never moved, particularly the kitchen and offices used by the resident staff.[32]

Because of its durability, more stone furniture has survived than that constructed of wood. Stone window seats are common though unadorned. Like wooden chairs and benches, they were intended to be covered and softened with cushions and textiles. Stone benches occasionally survive as in the hall at Harewood Castle, but stone tables are rare. Fragments of a thirteenth-century marble table found in Westminster Hall, 19 feet long and 3 feet wide, were possibly from its dais table.[33] The window embrasures of the prior's hall and private chamber in his lodging range at Wenlock Priory are filled with stone tables instead of window seats. Contemporary with the remainder of

the prior's lodging of c.1430 and splendidly preserved, they are of half octagonal shape on moulded pillars. Stone built wall cupboards or lockers are frequently found in houses, sometimes with the slots for a shelf, but only a few ecclesiastical examples retain their original doors, such as those of c.1410 in the Zouche Chapel, York Minster.[34] Stone lavers or washing basins varied from the plain at Wingfield Manor, Raglan Castle, and Lyddington Palace (fifteenth century) to the more decorative examples at Battel Hall and Dacre Castle (fourteenth century). But buffets or sideboards were often more elaborate such as those serving the hall dais at Harewood Castle (mid fourteenth century) or the audience chamber of Lincoln Bishop's Palace (mid fifteenth century).

A few wooden cupboards, buffets, and tables have survived. What we call a cupboard was usually described as an aumbrey or armoire, that is a piece of furniture capable of being closed with a door. It could either be shelved or unshelved, free-standing or built into a recess. The free-standing tripartite cupboard in the muniment room of Westminster Abbey is more likely to be of the late fifteenth rather than the more usually ascribed late fourteenth century,[35] while the fixed one in the Vicars Choral exchequer at Wells is of c.1457. Special armoires were reserved for plate, or for textiles and clothing if in a bedchamber. A buffet or dresser was an open-shelved piece of furniture for displaying plate in the hall or chamber, or utensils in the kitchen, usually called a cupboard in early times. There would be a number of open shelves, sometimes stepped, on which pewter, silver, or gold plate could be displayed. It was often sited near the high table to add dignity to the upper end of the hall, for it was an item closely associated with social aspiration and behaviour. No stepped buffets have survived but the cupboard in the Museum of London is attributed to the late fifteenth or early sixteenth century while that associated with Marguerite of York after her marriage to Charles the Bold in the Musée Communal, Malines, is dated to c.1478–97.[36]

From earliest times, chairs were a symbol of authority. Kings were crowned in chairs of state while bishops dispensed judgments from thrones such as those in Norwich and Canterbury cathedrals. The royal chair of state in Westminster Abbey was made in 1299–1300, though Paul Binski has suggested that it was designed not as a coronation chair but as a ceremonial chair intended for Henry III's shrine area, subsequently used for the coronation service from Henry IV's reign onwards.[37] In major households the head had his own chair, and it was usually sited at the high table, with a second chair in his withdrawing chamber. The wide chair from Evesham Abbey (Almonry Museum) is made up of midfourteenth-century components, while the better-preserved guild chair in St Mary's Hall, Coventry, probably a double chair seating the mayor and the master of the guild, dates from the mid-fifteenth century.[38] Chairs were often made like folding stools for ease of transport, though the box type with panelled back and sides is little known before the early sixteenth century. Members of the household sat on benches, the most common form of seating during the middle ages. A long bench from Barningham Hall is possibly an early fifteenth-century example (V & A Museum). There is evidence of a fixed bench next to the fireplace in the hall of Great Chalfield Manor and a rare survival in situ in the form of a settle close to the fireplace in the abbot's parlour at Muchelney (c.1500) but much altered.

The privileged area of a hall would be identified by a table parallel with the upper end wall, often raised on a dais with a project-

PLATE 203 Penshurst Place: fifteenth-century trestle table in hall

ing canopy over the chair or chairs for the owner and his wife. Tables were usually heavy and plain. They were often made up of boards laid on trestles to facilitate movability. The only known trestle tables are the two in the hall at Penshurst Place, stylistically attributed to the late fifteenth century, while the slightly later altered one from the Deanery kitchen of Durham Cathedral Priory is now in the Burrell Collection.[39] The remarkable circular table in Winchester Castle hall has been dendro dated to the late thirteenth century, but it lost its legs in 1348 when it was hung up in the context of Edward III's chivalric emulation of King Arthur's round table.[40] From the fifteenth century, fixed or dormant tables became more common.

Chests would be found in a hall, withdrawing chamber, bedchamber, or garderobe. They were appropriate for storage and the safe-keeping of money or documents. Hence the several ecclesiastical survivals with the earliest extant dating from the thirteenth century. If chests had feet, they were furniture; handles indicate portability or luggage use. A plain iron-banded chest of the late fourteenth century stands in the muniment room of Winchester College,[41] while that associated with Richard Bury of Durham of c.1340, embellished with polychrome decoration on the inside of the lid, is in the Burrell Collection.[42] The majority of chests decorated with carved frontal panels are in churches but those with secular scenes such as that in Harty church, Kent, illustrating a tournament, may have had domestic origins.

The frame of a bed was of the simplest form but would be richly draped in any well-to-do house. Carved posts, rails, and wooden backs are unknown before the close of the middle ages. The canopy of a bed was a celure, usually of silk or damask, the tester or back of the bed was often decorated with heraldic embroidery, while the enclosing curtains were ring-suspended and voluminous. The hangings and cover would be as lavish as possible, for beds not only were found in withdrawing as well as bedchambers, but were items of dignity and expense. Owners spent more money on them during the middle ages than on any other type of furniture. The richest beds had drawn-up or conical canopies of velvet, silk, of even gold thread. We have to rely on documentary evidence, manuscript illustrations, and paintings for evidence of medieval beds as no genuine survivals are known, though the unique medieval cradle of buttress-supported box-form displayed in the Museum of London is reasonably attributed to the close of the fifteenth century. Children used truckle beds stored under the main bed, while staff slept on straw mattresses on the floor. (For kitchen utensils, see pages 161–2.)

Panel painting and portraiture

Charles V of France (1364–80) has been linked to the rise of portraiture in the modern sense of the word. Part of the ideology of the Valois kings, like those in England, was investment in royal statues, images, manuscripts, and paintings. Charles is recognisable by his bulbous nose, broad face, and slight double chin, and he ensured that representations of him were realistic.[43] His precept was followed in England. The painting of Richard II in Westminster Abbey is a monumental icon – an idealisation of kingship as much as the earliest formal portrait in England. It has never been subject to an extended study but was probably painted in the 1390s at about the same time as the contrasting small-scale Wilton Diptych.[44]

Panel painting developed during the fifteenth century, stimulated by artists of the 'Northern Renaissance' such as Jan Van Eyck (1390–1441), who took the Virgin out of an abstract gold background and placed her in a domestic setting. At the same time, Gothic art moved out of the flat two-dimensional form to a three-dimensional form. This replaced the concept of several stories or aspects of a story within a single frame, with a single subject in a fixed perspective. Netherlandish portrait painting was admired by the more wealthy in England from the second quarter of the fifteenth century. When cardinal Beaufort was in Flanders in 1432 or 1438, he sat for his portrait by Jan Van Eyck.[45] In 1446, Edmund Grimston, a Suffolk gentleman and minor diplomat sent to the Netherlands by Henry VI, took the opportunity to commission his portrait from Petrus Christus. In the 1470s, Sir John Donne commissioned a triptych from Hans Memling to serve as a portable altar for his house near Kidwelly,[46] while the provost of Trinity College church in Edinburgh commissioned a large-scale altarpiece from Hugo van der Goes depicting the provost, James III of Scotland and his family, and their patron saints. The chapel at Cotehele holds an early sixteenth-century Flemish Crucifixion as well as its original altar cloth of c.1500, but the panel painting of St Edward the Confessor and a pilgrim of c.1370 on the chapel altar at Forthampton Court is a rarity. It has been in the house since the Reformation, possibly brought there by the last abbot of Tewkesbury, though it may have always been in that house chapel.[47] Certainly, the panel portrait of c.1460 depicting an elderly person, possibly a Scudamore of Kentchurch Court with a reasonably accurate portrayal of that house in the background, is in its original location.[48]

Plate

A display of plate – silver, silver-gilt, or gold – was a statement of pride and wealth, as it still is at royal banquets. Yet no medieval royal plate survives apart from two coronation items held in the Tower of London, a late Romanesque anointing spoon and the ampulla in the shape of an eagle, probably of Henry IV's time.[49] For plate was regularly pawned or sometimes melted down, as that of the English crown was during the Commonwealth. Richard Whittington, the wealthy lord mayor of London (d.1423), owned a substantial collection of plate, of which only four spoons survive (Mercers' Company, London), so that the finest repositories of medieval plate are held by the colleges of Oxford and Cambridge, continuing institutions from the medieval world.

At Oxford, some of the finest contemporary plate is held by All Souls College, including a striking pair of silver-gilt wine flagons with swan handles and chained stoppers of *c*.1400–40 given by the college founder, archbishop Chichele.[50] They were designed as much for display as for practical use, as was Chichele's spectacular salt-cellar (1420–40) of a giant striding across a meadow supporting a rock crystal container on his head.[51] In addition, the college holds a fine group of mazers, including one given in 1448. Corpus Christi College holds an equally elaborate display piece, a silver-gilt salt cellar with pearls and originally with blue enamel behind the openwork panels (*c*.1494–1501).[52] This college also holds a pair of silver-gilt basins used for ceremonial washing before a banquet, one made in 1493 and the other a copy of 1514.[53] The elaborate and expensive plate given by Wykeham and his successors to his foundations at Oxford and Winchester is well known,[54] while Christ's College, Cambridge holds some of the silver-gilt secular plate given by Lady Margaret Beaufort to her foundation.[55] The equally precious Studley silver bowl and cover of *c*.1400, possibly used by a noble child to eat from, is among the earliest and finest pieces of English domestic plate (V & A Museum),[56] though the plain silver saucer discovered in 1986 in the ruins of Shrewsbury Abbey is a century earlier (Rowley House Museum, Shrewsbury).[57]

Sculpture

Stone sculpture played little part within a house except in the chapel. Roof corbels were rarely a display of craftsmanship and ingenuity for they were usually limited to angels or foliage, or left plain for painted coats of arms. The stone screen of *c*.1370–7 in the upper hall of Raby Castle decorated with lion heads, masks, branches, and leaves is a rare secular survival of high-quality workmanship more usually seen in an ecclesiastical setting. The furnishings of a chapel would be a combination of several crafts – masons, glaziers, sculptors, wood carvers, embroiderers, and illuminators.[58] It is rare to find these combined today but Wykeham's twin foundations and their records help us to redress the balance.

Wykeham was an outstanding patron of the arts and his chapel at New College, Oxford retains several eye-catching elements. There were no fewer than eighty, rather crowded standing saints in the main chapel windows, apart from the many figures in the altar reredos. There were further examples of figurework in the roof corbels and misericords, while the patron is known to have given the chapel twelve missals, now all lost. The college chapel at Winchester is of more simple design but was similarly richly fitted out. The ceiling is complex, while the stained glass is more free and less stiff than at Oxford. It was also more radical, with fully modelled figures and large architectural canopies. In addition, it depicts the artists involved, as well as figures of Richard II and Wykeham, showing the bishop's high regard for his artists. The college

received several missals at the same time, rich in design and expensive, though now lost.

The detailed rules of the colleges mention that the students should not jump down from the tables as that would disturb or move the alabasters, glass, paintings, and other sumptuous works. For Wykeham's patronage was intended to make an effect – not so much a didactic one as that of visual appearance and richness. It is probable that he brought this same approach to his first major project, as clerk of the works for the reconstruction of the royal apartments at Windsor Castle during the crucial period October 1356 to November 1361. Chroniclers record how beautiful they were, with the rooms in the Rose Tower giving a hint at what has been lost. But Wykeham advised Edward III to build in a beautiful and ostentatious way, with the buildings 'most sumptously refitted and refurbished throughout'. His success in this may have been more responsible for his rise to power than his administrative skills. Nor does it take too much imagination to extend this visual approach, encompassing glass, woodwork, embroideries, and books, to Wardour Castle, built by Wykeham's friend John, Lord Lovel, or to the standing ruins at Wingfield Manor or Sudeley Castle.

Little wood sculpture survives, though some examples were held until recently in Naworth Castle, Cumbria. The three oak figures of the 1470s representing retainers of the Dacre family – a knight in armour, a youthful squire, and a man-at-arms – are now in the V & A Museum. The 6 feet high standing beasts of *c*.1520 from the hall of the same castle – bull, dolphin, griffin, and ram holding banners – were heraldic representatives of members of the Dacre family.[59] They were commissioned by Thomas, Lord Dacre (d.1525) and are similarly in the V & A Museum. Smaller and less ornate beasts surmount the fifteenth-century hall roofs at Weare Giffard Hall and Orleigh Court nearby in north Devon, in both cases believed to be contemporary with the hammer-beam trusses they surmount.

Textiles

The loss of fabrics and textiles is one of the greatest gaps in our appreciation of medieval English life. The account rolls of the period show that the expenditure on such furnishings, particularly for beds, was huge, but hardly any examples survive. Textiles particularly suffer from usage, wear and tear, and changes in taste, so that the only secular English survival is that in the Musée de Cluny. This stunning early fourteenth-century remnant carrying the royal arms was possibly a horse trapper.[60] Its embroidery in gold thread gives an idea of its cost and visual splendour, prompting no change in the attitude of earlier monastic chroniclers and preachers like Peter of Blois (1135–1212), forever quick to criticise the nobility's vanity of empty display: 'They embroider their saddles and blazon their shields with scenes of battle and tourney, delighting in a certain imagination of those wars which in very deed, they dare not mingle in or behold'.

The only other evidence we have is in the religious embroideries, usually cut down or mutilated to serve a later function. *Opus Anglicanum* was one of the glories of medieval England, coveted throughout Europe. Most of the finest examples are religious copes, found today in France, Italy, and Germany. They were regarded as status symbols, sought after by cardinals and popes, with those in the Vatican retained since their initial purchase. The Bologna cope (early fourteenth century) in the Museo Civico, Bologna, survives unaltered[61] whereas the Jesse (1295–1315) and Butler-Bowden copes (1330–50) in the V & A Museum and the early fifteenth-century vestments from Whalley Abbey (Townley Hall Art Gallery and Museum) survive as remade fragments, cut up to meet changing taste and usage.[62]

Textiles enriched architectural settings by introducing colour and subject matter, with the added benefits of portability and enhancing comfort. We have to turn to illustrations, particularly French, for examples of their use. They are often shown as cloths of state behind important people, draped over thrones or furniture, or used as cushions. In addition to embroiderers, painters often worked in the Great Wardrobe of the royal household, mainly on decorative work such as emblazoning arms and crests on banners and preparing embellishments for tournaments, masquerades, and royal festivities.[63] Heraldic banners used appliqué needlework rather than paint to facilitate frequent reuse while the tents and pavilions used by the royal household in 1350–2 were ornamented with colourful needlework.[64]

Wall hangings

The development of medieval tapestries was initiated in the southern Netherlands during the second half of the fourteenth century and quickly became the most sought-after, expensive, and important of the luxury arts during the late middle ages in northern Europe.[65] Charles V of France had 200 tapestries at the time of his death in 1380. Designed to be used as wall hangings, they would be pushed aside if covering a door or pulled back to avoid a chimney breast. They were carried from house to house, partly because of their value and richness, and partly to provide warmer rooms and apartments, and create a sumptuous public or private setting. The subjects included stories from the Bible, classical epics, chivalric romances, arms and heraldic devices. Many were designed as a sequence to give a theme to an apartment. The most famous are still held as groups of tapestries – the Apocalypse of c.1373–80 for the duc d'Anjou at Angers Castle, the Nine Worthies (c.1400–10) and the Hunt of the Unicorn series (1495–1510) at the Cloisters Museum, New York, the Five Senses with Lady and the Unicorn at the Musée de Cluny, Paris, and the four hunting tapestries at the V & A Museum. The Arthurian legend and other worthies appealed to Edward III and his successors as the progenitors of English kings, popularised by Sir Thomas Malory's *Morte d'Arthur* in c.1470, and yoked by Henry VII to his dynastic claim. The tapestries making up the Lady and the Unicorn sequence for Jean le Viste of Lyons between 1484 and 1500 are among the most refined survivals of late medieval art. The hunting tapestries of c.1425–30, not a set but of similar date and style from the south Netherlands, show the participants in elaborate court dress. They may have been commissioned by John Talbot, 1st earl of Shrewsbury (d.1453), from whom they passed to the 6th earl (d.1590) to help furnish Hardwick Hall.[66]

Heraldic tapestries blazoned with the owner's arms and badges could be equally impressive. That with the royal arms in the hall at Haddon Hall with the lions of England quartered with the lilies of France, attributed to 1460–70, is reputed to have been held by the Vernon family since the mid-sixteenth century. Lord Dynham of Devonshire commissioned his Netherlands tapestry of 1488–1501 (Cloisters Museum) as part of a set for a particularly grand room (pl. 204).[67] A slightly later one is that with the arms of Henry VIII at Nether Winchendon House, but few tapestries in England can be ascribed to an English commission, though the fragments of fifteenth-century tapestries in York Minster came from the Masham branch of the Scrope family.[68] The millefleurs tapestry of a mounted knight of c.1481 with the arms of Jean Daillon, seigneur de Lude (Montacute House) is an example of the transfer of the Penshurst Place wall paintings to a later medium.[69] The repetitive thirty tapestries of c.1450 with the device and monogram of Chancellor Rolin and his second wife to enclose the beds of his hospital at Beaune show how tapestries could be used as expensive hangings almost like wall paper. But the only high-table tapestry still in the position for which it was designed is that of c.1500–10 in St Mary's Hall, Coventry.[70] Tapestries could also be used to cover beds, seat furniture, and tables, with some heraldic examples of c.1350–75 bearing the arms of Beaufort, Turenne, and Comminges in the Burrell Collection and elsewhere,[71] and a table example of c.1500 in the Cloisters Museum.[72]

Painted or 'stained' cloths preceded tapestries, with documented Flemish examples from about 1275, and were cheaper than tapestries. There is a fine early set of twenty-five cloths in the Musée des Beaux-Arts, Reims (1460–1520). Painted cloths were hung on the hall walls at New College, Oxford in 1453 and a contemporary ecclesiastical fragment is held by the Society of Antiquaries of London. The cloth of c.1470 at the Strangers' Hall Museum, Norwich of 1470, showing the arms and members of the Buxton family, confirms that they could be as detailed and as elaborate as tapestries.[73] Most of the surviving examples, though, are from the later sixteenth century (Coughton Court 1596, Yarde House, Kingsbridge) to the eighteenth century (Owlpen Manor 1715).[74]

GARDENS

It is being increasingly appreciated that gardens were as integral to the layout and display of a house as its approach, landscaping, and enclosing moat. No medieval garden survives, but the positions of several have been identified and some reconstructed after archaeological excavation.[75] For the recovery of original gardens and the plants they held as well as the broader field of landscape archaeology have become burgeoning disciplines. External landscaping during the fourteenth century has been established at Bodiam, Fotheringhay, and Saltwood castles and from the fifteenth century at Bronsil Castle and Lamphey Palace,[76] while fourteenth-century gardens within a castle's walls have been traced at Farleigh Hungerford and Whittington castles. That at Farleigh Hungerford was next to the hall and chamber block and the outer curtain, divided into two quadrants by a pitched stone path, while the outer court at Whittington incorporates the earliest viewing mount discovered so far, within an elaborate ditched water system.

When people lived close to plants throughout their lives, used them for medicinal purposes, and depended upon the seasonal growth of crops and vegetables, it is not surprising that carved leaves and flowers were more than just decorative, they were an essential part of life. They occur in houses on capitals and corbels, and sometimes on a larger scale on screens like that at Raby Castle (fourteenth century). They could be tinctured and bring colour to a room. Flowers and plants form the background of tapestries and hangings, and decorate the foot of the right-hand wing of the Wilton Diptych. A boxwood gittern in the British Museum of c.1300–30, probably used by a minstrel at the English court, had the sides densely carved with panels of vine, hawthorn, and oak and

PLATE 204 Late medieval tapestry: millefleurs armorial tapestry with arms of Lord Dynham (*c.*1487–1501)

with vignettes taken from the labours of the month.[77] Gardens sometimes decorated the walls of a room. They survive from Roman times but the most famous medieval example is the Chambre du Cerf in the Papal Palace, Avignon, painted in 1343, not as a landscape *per se* but illustrating the activities appropriate to the privileged in a forested landscape – hunting and fishing.

A RICHLY DIVERSE RESOURCE

This small selection of secular items, noted whilst I have been visiting museums and some of the houses covered in these volumes, gives a taste of the riches that were an essential and indispensable adjunct to the greater houses of England and Wales during the fourteenth and fifteenth centuries. Unfortunately, the lethal combination of the Reformation, changing taste, financial imperatives, and the many vagaries of survival of anything portable or fragile have all contributed to the limited reservoir of artefacts from the middle ages. But what is increasingly clear is that it is unnecessary to be apologetic about the standard of British medieval art. That of France has long been held up as the exemplar of artistry, but far more of it survives – secular as well as ecclesiastical. The relatively small amount surviving makes a very positive statement of British craftsmanship, creativity, and taste. Some of the art was insular and conservative but much was inventive, of outstanding quality, and rich in meaning. Nor should it be forgotten that British art was also a two-way market. England was markedly cosmopolitan, not only finding foreign markets for its own art as much as for its wool and cloth products, but employing in turn some of the finest craftsmen from north-west Europe, particularly France and the Netherlands. It is increasingly recognised that much of the high-quality art in this country throughout the period under review cannot be neatly parcelled into 'indigenous' and 'foreign' any more than it can in northern Europe. The factor common to all these countries was the similarity of styles, ethos, and execution, and that factor is called Gothic. Patrons simply sought the best craftsmen in a particular field within the limits of their purses, whether regional, national, or international. As a consequence, we are building up a national mosaic that is no longer elusive but one that is increasingly seen to be rich, diverse, and demonstrative of the high standards of secular patronage across late medieval society.

NOTES

1 English Court Culture in the Later Middle Ages, ed. V. J. Scattergood and J. W. Sherborne (1983) and G. Matthew, The Court of Richard II (1968). The Lancastrian Court, ed. J. Stratford (2003), questions the extent to which that court was a centre of cultural power.

2 J. Evans, English Art 1307–1461 (1949). The succeeding volume covering 1461 to 1553 of this eleven-part series was never written. See also the little-known two-volume work Medieval England, ed. A. L. Poole (1958). More recent essays include C. Richmond, 'The visual culture of fifteenth-century England', in The Wars of the Roses ed. A. J. Pollard (1995) 186–250; D. Gaimster and P. Stamper (eds.), The Age of Transition c.1400–1600 (1997), and the dense but valuable catalogue Gothic: Art for England 1400–1547, ed. R. Marks and P. Williamson (2003). Wales followed its own artistic path during the later middle ages, A. Emery Greater Med. Houses, II (2000) 688–91.

3 P. Lindley in The Black Death in England, ed. M. Ormrod and P. Lindley (1996) 125–46.

4 J. W. Sherborne in English Court Culture in the Later Middle Ages (1983) 6–7, 21, opposing J. Evans, English Art 1307–1461 (1949) 399.

5 The Bedford Inventories: The Worldly Goods of John, Duke of Bedford, Regent of France, 1389–1435, ed. J. Stratford (1993).

6 The Regal Image of Richard II and the Wilton Diptych, ed. D. Gordon, L. Monnas, and C. Elam (1997).

7 Two catalogues are primary research sources: Age of Chivalry, ed. J. Alexander and P. Binski (1987) and Gothic, ed. Marks and Williamson. They are frequently noted below.

8 O. Pacht, Journal of the Warburg and Courtauld Institutes 6 (1943) 51–70.

9 A. Simpson, The Connections between English and Bohemian Painting during the Second Half of the Fourteenth Century (1984).

10 Age of Chivalry, ed. Alexander and Binski 402.

11 Ibid. 418. See also The Cambridge Illuminations, ed. P. Binski (2005).

12 Those of the Black Prince still hang above his tomb but not the set of fine black hangings with ostrich feathers which he bequeathed at the

same time. Henry V's helm and shield were still hanging over his tomb in Westminster Abbey during the early eighteenth century.

13 The Household of Edward IV, ed. A. R. Myers (1959); The Regulations . . . of the Household of . . . the Fifth Earl of Northumberland, ed. T. Percy (1905).

14 Manners and Household Expenses in England in the 13th and 15th centuries, ed. B. Botfield (1841); A Fifteenth-Century Courtesy Book, ed. R. W. Chambers (1914).

15 Manners and Meals in Olden Time, ed. F. J. Furnivall (1868); Curye on Inglysch: English Culinary Manuscripts of the Fourteenth Century, ed. C. B. Hieatt and S. Butler (1985).

16 T. Amyot, 'Inventory of Sir John Fastolfe', Archaeologia 21 (1827) 232–80; Viscount Dillon and W. H. St John Hope, 'Inventory of Thomas, Duke of Gloucester: 1397', Arch. Jour. 54 (1897) 275–308; The Bedford Inventories, 1389–1435, ed. J. Stratford (1993).

17 C. Bullock-Davies, Menestrellorum multitudo: Minstrels at a Royal Feast (1978); G. R. Rastall, 'The minstrel court in medieval England', Proceedings of Leeds Philosophical and Literary Society 18 (1989).

18 B. and R. Harvey, Wilts. Arch. Mag. 81 (1987) 63–4.

19 Register of Richard Mitford, Wiltshire Record Office D1/2/6, f.4 and 140.

20 PRO, E.154/1/31. It is transcribed in Wilts. Arch. Mag. 81 (1987) 65–7.

21 Gothic, ed. Marks and Williamson, 316. Some secular items only survive because they were given to the church during the sixteenth century, such as this cup, the silver-gilt drinking bowl of c.1480–1510 held by St Michael's church, Bristol and the silver-gilt dish of c.1400 with an engraved knight and lady now at St Mary, Bermondsey.

22 Though S. Boldrick, D. Park and P. Williamson, Wonder: Painted Sculpture from Medieval England (2002), help to redress the balance.

23 J. Cherry, Medieval Decorative Art (1991) provides a useful introduction.

24 J. Geddes, Medieval Decorative Ironwork in England (1999).

25 R. Marks, Stained Glass in England during the Middle Ages (1993) 92–102, makes a welcome exception.

26 J. A Wight, Medieval Floor Tiles (1975); J. M. Lewis, Welsh Medieval Paving Tiles (1976); E. Eames, English Medieval Tiles (1985).

27 M. Wood, The English Mediaeval House (1965) 395–7.

28 J. Savage, History of the Castle and Parish of Wressle (1799).

29 T. Borenius and E. W. Tristram, English Medieval Painting (1927); E. W. Tristram, English Wall Painting of the Fourteenth Century (1955); A. Caiger-Smith, English Medieval Wallpainting (1963); Wood, Eng. Med. House, 394–402. D. Park is preparing a book on this subject.

30 This and the following wall paintings are discussed under the individual building entries, plus evidence at Martock (c.1260) and Bradley (c.1500).

31 C. Babington et al., Our Painted Past (1999) 70.

32 E. Mercer, Furniture 700–1700 (1969); P. Eames, 'Documentary evidence concerning the character of domestic furnishing in England in the fourteenth and fifteenth centuries', Furniture History 7 (1971) 41–60; P. Eames, Medieval Furniture (1977). A. C. Wright, Medieval Furniture (1976) is a little known Southend Museum publication with a useful corpus of drawings from a wide range of sources.

33 The remains together with a conjectural sketch of the table form, are displayed in the Jewel Tower, Westminster.

34 J. M. Fletcher and M. C. Tapper, Med. Arch. 28 (1984) 124, correcting Eames, Medieval Furniture, 15–17.

35 Eames, Medieval Furniture, 30–3.

36 Ibid. 65–70.

37 W. Palmer, The Coronation Chair (1953); P. Binski, Westminster Abbey and the Plantagenets (1995) 135–40.

38 The arms of a crown supported by two lions on the back of the chair suggest that it may date from Edward IV's reign: J. C. Lancaster, St. Mary Hall, Coventry (1980) 61. The late fourteenth-century oak stall from Much Hadham church, Hertfordshire, one of three conjoined sedilia, is like a secular chair of the period.

39 R. Edwards, The Shorter Dictionary of English Furniture (1964) 532; Gothic, ed. Marks and Williamson, 312.

40 The table top was painted between 1516 and 1522: M. Biddle, *King Arthur's Round Table* (2000). The fourteenth-century round table on a heavy architectural base in the chapter-house of Salisbury Cathedral is possibly a made-up piece.

41 After 1372, J. M. Fletcher and M. C. Tapper, *Med. Arch.* 28 (1984) 124. Their paper refers to several other chests, cupboards, and panel paintings.

42 *Age of Chivalry*, ed. Alexander and Binski, 426–7; Eames, *Medieval Furniture*, 108–80; Edwards, *The Shorter Dictionary of English Furniture*, 183–9.

43 He had life-size images of himself and his wife placed on one of the doorways of the Louvre, on the church of the Celestins, Paris (now in the Louvre Museum), on linen in the Parement de Narbonne (Louvre Museum), and on his portrait (Louvre Museum), small, informal, and probably part of a group.

44 J. Alexander in *The Regal Image of Richard II and the Wilton Diptych*, ed. Gordon *et al.*, 197–206. With this exception, the earliest panel portraits of English kings are late fifteenth century. The one of Henry V may be based on an earlier but lost profile portrait.

45 M. Vale, *Eng. Hist. Rev.* 105 (1990) 338–54.

46 Emery, *Greater Med. Houses*, II, 690. In the National Gallery, London, as is that of Grimston on loan from the earl of Verulam.

47 *Age of Chivalry*, ed. Alexander and Binski, 214–15.

48 Emery, *Greater Med. Houses*, II, 554. For an overall view of this subject, M. Rickert, *Painting in Britain: The Middle Ages* (1965).

49 Two crowns associated with the English monarchy survive in Europe, that taken by Henry IV's daughter Blanche to Germany in 1401 on her marriage to Prince Louis of Bavaria (Munich Residenz) (*Age of Chivalry*, ed. Alexander and Binski, 202–3), and the small crown of *c*.1461–74 that Margaret of York may have worn at her wedding to the duke of Burgundy in 1468, given to Aachen Cathedral in 1474 (*Gothic*, ed. Marks and Williamson, 154).

50 *Gothic*, ed. Marks and Williamson, 238–9.

51 *Ibid.* 312–13.

52 *Ibid.* 244.

53 *Ibid.* 242–3.

54 C. Oman, *Connoisseur* (January 1962); C. Oman in *New College, Oxford*, ed. J. Buxton and P. Williams (1979) 293–305. Two other schools, Eton College and Christ's Hospital, hold plate collections.

55 *Gothic*, ed. Marks and Williamson, 246–51.

56 *Age of Chivalry*, ed. Alexander and Binski, 525–6; *Gothic*, ed. Marks and Williamson, 315. C. Oman, *English Domestic Silver* (1959 edn).

57 This museum also holds a fourteenth-century pewter cruet found in Tong Castle in 1977, one of several examples found in castle excavations including Ashby de la Zouch, White Castle, Ludlow, and Weoley (all fourteenth century). *Age of Chivalry*, ed. Alexander and Binski, 238–9.

58 The glass, sculpture, and tomb in the Beauchamp chapel at Warwick show the high standards practised in the mid-fifteenth century, as do some of the alabaster altarpieces that survive (often abroad), but the stripping of altars has been particularly thorough in domestic chapels. The fine tabernacle with the head of St John the Baptist (1470–85), now in the Burrell Collection, represents a popular subject for private devotion, with this particular example possibly from Yorkshire: *Gothic*, ed. Marks and Williamson, 341.

59 Though displayed from 1840 to 1999 at Naworth, it is possible they were moved there from the Dacre family home at Kirkoswald Castle after it was dismantled in the early seventeenth century: *Gothic*, ed. Marks and Williamson, 292–3. The beasts were repainted after the fire at Naworth in 1844.

60 *Age of Chivalry*, ed. Alexander and Binski, 202.

61 *Ibid.* 456.

62 *Gothic*, ed. Marks and Williamson, 411. Also Arts Council, *Opus Anglicanum: English Medieval Embroidery* (1963); K. Staniland, *Embroiderers* (1991).

63 W. A. Shaw, *Burlington Magazine* 65 (1934) 171–84 for Gilbert Prince, the first painter to be named 'the king's painter' in 1377; J. H. Harvey, *Burlington Magazine* 89 (1947) 303–5 for Hugh St Albans.

64 K. Staniland in *England in the Fourteenth Century*, ed. W. M. Ormrod (1986) 236–46.

65 A. S. Cavallo, *Medieval Tapestries* (1993) 57–77.

66 L. Woolley, *Medieval Life and Leisure in the Devonshire Hunting Tapestries* (2002) 23. Two early sixteenth-century pieces preserved at Magdalen College, Oxford similarly show courtiers in magnificent garments. Some of the manuscripts also commissioned by the 1st earl of Shrewsbury from a Rouen *atelier* have been dubbed as work by the Talbot Master: *Gothic*, ed. Marks and Williamson, 182–3, 230–1.

67 B. Young, *Metropolitan Museum of Art Bulletin* 20 (1961–2) 309–16; Cavallo, *Medieval Tapestries*, 272–7.

68 *Yorkshire Archaeological Journal* 64 (1992). The sixteenth- and seventeenth-century tapestries in the audience chamber of Tattershall tower-house were brought in by Lord Curzon in 1914.

69 *Masterpieces of Tapestry from the 14th to 16th century*, ed. F. Salet and G. Souchal (1973) 119–21.

70 S. McKendrick, 'Tapestries from the Low Countries in England during the fifteenth century', in *England and the Low Countries in the Late Middle Ages*, ed. C. Barron and N. Saul (1995) 44.

71 W. Wells, *Treasures from the Burrell Collection* (1975) 22; A. S. Cavallo, *Tapestries of Europe in the Museum of Fine Arts, Boston* (1967) 29–30; and his *Medieval Tapestries*, 84–93.

72 Cavallo, *Medieval Tapestries*, 373–6.

73 *Gothic*, ed. Marks and Williamson, 291–2.

74 F. E. Matley Moore, *Trans. Worcs. Arch. Soc.* 8 (1982) 73–9; N. Mander, *Country Life* (September 2003).

75 J. H. Harvey, *Mediaeval Gardens* (1981); *Medieval Gardens*, ed. E. B. Macdougall (1986); E. Whittle, *The Historic Gardens of Wales* (1992).

76 M. Johnson, *Behind the Castle Gate* (2002) 19–54.

77 *Age of Chivalry*, ed. Alexander and Binski, 426.

SOUTH-WEST ENGLAND:
BIBLIOGRAPHY

DORSET

THE spectacular backbone of all Dorset studies is the Reverend John Hutchins' *The History and Antiquities of the County of Dorset*, first published in two volumes in 1774, the year after his death. Subsequent editions of this indispensable work with new material were issued in four volumes in 1796–1815, edited by R. Gough and J. B. Nichols, and again in 1861–73, edited by W. Shipp and J. W. Hodson (reprinted in 1973). All subsequent and present writers are still in his debt. In contrast, only two Victoria County History volumes have been published (1908, 1968), with neither of them covering individual parishes, and the earlier increasingly out of date. C. Taylor's *The Making of the English Landscape: Dorset* (1970) is one of the more perspicacious volumes in this national series, but the study of medieval Dorset awaits an author. The bibliography of the county up to 1960 is covered by R. Douch, *A Handbook of Local History: Dorset* (1952) with a supplement to 1960 (1962).

The buildings of Dorset have been well served. They are very capably described by A. Oswald, *Country Houses of Dorset* (1st edn 1935, followed by a judiciously extended 2nd edn in 1959), and by J. Newman and N. Pevsner, *Buildings of England: Dorset* (1972), one of the more eloquent volumes in this series. For a detailed illustrated inventory, the Royal Commission on Historical Monuments covered the county in five volumes (5 in 8) between 1952 and 1975, though this lacks a comprehensive index. Work on west Dorset had been initiated in 1938 and a third of the county had been completed before the Second World War, but there was a delay in publication through hostilities and confirmation in 1946 of the extension of the Commission's remit to include all monuments from 1714 to about 1850. Even so, the county could have been covered relatively swiftly in four volumes, whereas it took a further thirty years to complete in a sequence of volumes and parts, leading to questions being asked in the House of Commons about the Commissioners' efficiency and expenditure control. It was directly responsible for the Commissioners abandoning their foundation remit to publish any more county inventories. The goal of total comprehensiveness and lack of management control had allowed volume preparation and publication to become a monument to excess. Yet, Nikolaus Pevsner and his team had covered all the counties in his national Buildings of England series in forty-six volumes between 1951 and 1974, with the first volumes on Wales and Scotland following five years later.

The *Proceedings* of the Dorset Natural History and Archaeological Society is the leading archaeological journal, published since 1877. *Somerset and Dorset Notes and Queries* has continued to be issued since 1888, while the report of the Summer

Meeting of the Royal Archaeological Institute at Weymouth in 1983 was published in *Arch. Jour.* 140 (1983) 1–82.

WILTSHIRE

Three early county histories are still valuable, though patchy in the quality of their materials: John Aubrey, *Wiltshire Topographical Collections*, edited and enlarged by J. E. Jackson (1862), the Wiltshire section in volume XV of J. Britton and E.W. Brayley, *Beauties of England and Wales* (1814), and Sir Richard Colt Hoare, *The History of Modern Wiltshire*, 5 vols. (1822–7). H. Goddard, *Wiltshire Bibliography* (1929) covers the county to that time, followed by R. A. M. Green, *A Bibliography of Printed Works Relating to Wiltshire, 1920–60* (1975).

Wiltshire has advanced much further than most parts of England with the publication of the volumes of the Victoria County History during the later twentieth century, with seventeen volumes to date and five more to complete the project. In addition to the detailed parish surveys, volume IV (1959) includes essays on the county's agricultural background by R. Scott and on the cloth industry before 1550 by E. M. Carus-Wilson. The county's medieval history awaits an author, but J. N. Hare has contributed papers on the 1450 rising, in *Southern History*, 4 (1982) 13–32, and fifteenth-century lord and tenant relationships, in *Conflict and Community in Southern England*, ed. B. Stapleton (1992) 16–34. The active Wiltshire Record Society, founded in 1937, has published fifty-five volumes to date.

The local antiquaries' journal, *Wiltshire Archaeological and Natural History Magazine*, has been published since 1854. Renamed *Wiltshire Heritage Studies* in 2000, it is only since the 1960s that the essentially prehistoric content has been leavened with papers on medieval and later houses. However, the county has been better served than many through early works including S. J. Elyard, *Some Old Wiltshire Homes* (1894) and *Memorials of Old Wiltshire*, edited by A. Dryden (1906). Nikolaus Pevsner's *Wiltshire* (1963) in his Buildings of England series was one of the more detailed volumes, Pevsner having been a resident of the county and buried at Clyffe Pypard. More recently, Pamela Slocombe, *Medieval Houses of Wiltshire* (1992) has brought together a broad span of material drawn from the archives of the Wiltshire Building Record housed at Trowbridge's Library and Museum Service. Several properties are described in the Summer Meeting reports in the *Journal* of the Royal Archaeological Institute at Salisbury (1920, 1947) and Bath (1930) while John Chandler has embarked on a planned seven-part parish history of the county, *Wiltshire: a History of Its Landscape and People*, vol. I, *Marlborough and Eastern Wiltshire* (2001). The *Medieval Catalogue* of objects recovered from Salisbury, Clarendon Palace, Old Sarum, and other nationally significant sites held at Salisbury and South Wiltshire Museum warrants several volumes (1990 ongoing).

SOMERSET

The prime early source is John Collinson, *The History and Antiquities of the County of Somerset*, 3 vols. (1791), reprinted in one volume in 1983 ed. R. W. Dunning. Only one volume was published, covering the centre and south-east of the county, of W. Phelps, *The History and Antiquities of Somerset* (1836), while C. E. H. Chadwyck-Healey, *The History of Part of West Somerset* (1901) is necessarily limited in scope.

M. Havinden, *The Somerset Landscape* (1981), inaugurated a series of publications on the landscape and early history of the county, many of them with contributions by Michael Aston, including *The Archaeology of Somerset*, ed. M. Aston and I. Burrow (1982), its companion volume *The Archaeology of Avon*, ed. M. Aston and R. Iles (1989), and the broad-ranging *Aspects of the Medieval Landscape of Somerset*, ed. M. Aston (1988). Medieval Exmoor is surveyed in *The Field Archaeology of Exmoor*, ed. H. Riley and R. Wilson-North (2001). L. and R. Adkin, *A Field Guide to Somerset Archaeology* (1992), has some relevant entries but the *Proceedings of the Somerset Archaeological and Natural History Society* has been the primary source since 1851. Papers published in *Somerset Archaeology*, ed. C. J. Webster (2000), to mark 150 years of the Society, include valuable summaries on medieval rural settlements, monasteries, and the parks and gardens of the county.

The medieval history of the county has lagged behind landscape studies. Six volumes of the Victoria County History have been published to date but the four topographical volumes cover less than a third of the county. *Christianity in Somerset*, ed. R. W. Dunning (1976), has a useful opening chapter but T. J. Hunt and R. R. Sellman, *Aspects of Somerset History* (1973), hardly does justice to the many resources available. R. Dunning, *History of Somerset* (1983), gives a brief overview.

N. Pevsner's *The Buildings of England: South and West Somerset* (1958) and *North Somerset and Bristol* (1958) are the premier resource for the county. Individual buildings are covered in the Summer Meeting programmes of the Royal Archaeological Institute at Bath (1930), Taunton (1950), and Bristol (1977). Briefer entries occur in R. W. Dunning, *Somerset Castles* (1995), and on several medieval properties in his *Some Somerset Country Houses* (1991). Robert Cooke, *West Country Houses* (1957), illustrates some of the lesser houses of Somerset, Wiltshire, and Gloucestershire, with a wealth of privately obtained illustrations. J. Bond's *Somerset Parks and Gardens* (1998) is an equally richly illustrated volume as is J. Penoyre, *Traditional Houses of Somerset* (2005).

DEVON

The earliest topographical account of Devon is John Hooker's 'Synopsis Chorographical of Devonshire', written in 1599 by the chamberlain of Exeter but never published (Brit. Lib., Harl. 5827). Hooker was an early antiquarian of considerable standing, as was Sir William Pole (d.1635) whose scattered papers were published in 1791 as *Collections towards a Description of the County of Devon*. R. Polwhele, *History of Devonshire*, with two topographical volumes covering only part of the county (1793 and 1806), is more informative on buildings than many such surveys, and was followed by William White's better *History, Gazetteer, and Directory of Devon* (1850, 3rd edn 1890). Volume VI of Daniel Lysons' *Magna Britannia* (1822) was the most useful historical and topographical survey of Devon before W. G. Hoskins' panoramic survey *Devon* (1954) which set a standard not yet attained elsewhere in south-west England. It also includes a detailed bibliography which was updated in the revised edition of 1992. The county's development is more briefly covered in R. Stanes, *A History of Devon* (2nd edn 2000).

Three collections of early topographical illustrations are invaluable. Those by Edmund Prideaux of 1717–27 are mainly of his family's houses in Cornwall and Norfolk but with some properties in Devon. They are edited by J. Harris in *Arch. Hist.* 7 (1964)

17–108. The watercolours by John Swete illustrating his diaries of journeys through the county between 1789 and 1800 are handsomely reproduced in four volumes, *Travels in Georgian Devon*, ed. T. Gray and M. Rowe (1998). The illustrated diaries of Peter Orlando Hutchinson from 1846 to 1870 were edited by J. Butler, *Travels in Victorian Devon* (2000).

Unlike Cornwall, studies on medieval Devon are rare. W. G. Hoskins' essay, 'The wealth of medieval Devon' in W. G. Hoskins and H. P. R. Finberg, *Devonshire Studies* (1952) 212–49, is a rare excursion in this field. For economic history, see J. Youings in *Exeter and Its Region*, ed. F. Barlow (1969) 164–74 and for agriculture, H. Fox in *The Agrarian History of England and Wales: 1348–1500*, ed. E. Miller (1991), but the political and social analysis of the county during the later middle ages has yet to be written. Some of the essays are relevant in the *Historical Atlas of South-West England*, ed. R. Kain and W. Ravenhill (1999), a particularly impressive publication in layout and cartography, but as usual with such publications, marred by major subject gaps.

The *Transactions* of the Exeter Diocesan Society were initiated in 1847, followed by the *Transactions* of the Devonshire Association in 1862, 'for the intercourse of those who cultivate science, literature, or art in different parts of Devon'. Science has always been in the forefront of the Association but historical and archaeological studies gradually increased, supported by a considerable number of regional branches and specialised sections across the county. The *Transactions* of the Devon Archaeological Society was first published in 1929 in response to the increased interest in the subject and is now the leading journal in this field.

The most comprehensive architectural survey of the buildings of Devon is the labour of love by Bridget Cherry in preparing the 2nd edition of N. Pevsner's *The Buildings of England: Devon* (1989) which replaced his two volumes of 1952. It also has a detailed bibliography, and is supplemented by three books of essays edited by Peter Beacham, *Devon's Traditional Buildings* (1978), *The Archaeology of the Devon Landscape* (1980), and *Devon's Buildings* (1989). The accounts of the Summer meetings of the Royal Archaeological Institute at Exeter are reported in *Arch. Jour.* 70 (1913) 495–557; 104 (1957) 128–84; and the supplement to 147 (1990) 1–119. They supersede the report of the 1927 Exeter congress and papers in *Jour. Brit. Arch. Assoc.* 33 (1927) 3–180. The Summer meeting of the Institute at Bideford was reported in *Arch. Jour.* 157 (2000) 407–66.

Cornwall

Cornwall was well served from an early date with volumes that include Richard Carew, *The Survey of Cornwall* (1602), ed. Thomas Tomkin in 1811, William Borlase, *The Antiquities Historical and Monumental of Cornwall* (1754) (reprint of 2nd edn in 1973), and R. Polwhele, *The History of Cornwall* (1803). Regrettably, Charles Henderson's projected history of Cornwall never progressed beyond his assembly of myriad documents, deposited in the Royal Institution of Cornwall, Truro, and his *Essays in Cornish History*, ed. A. L. Rowse and M. I. Henderson (1935).

Medieval Cornwall has been far better served than medieval Devon. F. E. Halliday, *A History of Cornwall* (1959), gives a broad-based survey of the county from the Stone Age to the twentieth century, as does W. G. V. Balchin, *The Making of the English Landscape: Cornwall* (1954). More pertinent is L. E. Elliott-Binns, *Medieval Cornwall* (1955), though his research ceases at 1400. The more polished volume by A. L. Rowse, *Tudor Cornwall: Portrait of a Society* (1941), commences with the Wars of the Roses, though J. Whetter, *Cornish People in the Fifteenth Century* (1999), helps to fill the gap. J. Hatcher's *Rural Economy and Society in the Duchy of Cornwall* (1970) is a wide-ranging study that embraces more than the duchy's seventeen manors, while A. Preston-Jones and P. Rose, 'Medieval Cornwall' in *Cornish Archaeology* 25 (1986) 135–85, summarise archaeological research since the mid-twentieth century, including work on settlement patterns, long-houses, churches, towns, industry, and artefacts.

As with Devon, there are no relevant volumes of the Victoria County History or the Royal Commission on Historical Monuments. Nikolaus Pevsner's *The Buildings of England: Cornwall* (1951) was the earliest of his series and its summary descriptions reflect this, despite revisions by E. Radcliffe (1970). The best account of Cornwall's early houses is the essay by E. M. Jope, 'Cornish houses 1400–1700', in the volume he edited, *Studies in Building History* (1961) 192–222. It is supplemented by V. M. and F. J. Chesher, *The Cornishman's House* (1968), a wide-ranging survey of the smaller and vernacular houses of the region to the close of the eighteenth century. The Report on the Summer meeting of the Royal Archaeological Institute at Truro, *Arch. Jour.* 130 (1973) 223–95, spans a wide range of properties, as does the illustrated volume by D. E. Pett, *The Parks and Gardens of Cornwall* (1998).

The long-established *Journal* of the Royal Institution of Cornwall, founded in 1818, has few relevant medieval papers before 1970. In 1961, the West Cornwall Field Club, founded in 1933–5, became the Cornwall Archaeological Society, with the earlier *Proceedings* replaced by *Cornish Archaeology* from 1962 onwards. Since the 1980s Cornwall County Council has supported a highly active archaeological unit which publishes a particularly extensive range of regional, local, and site-specific surveys.

AFFETON CASTLE, Devon

LIKE Bickleigh 12 miles to the east, Affeton 'Castle' is a substantial fifteenth-century gatehouse to a fortified house of which little else remains. This remotely situated residence was built of local grey rubble with freestone dressings by the Stucley family, a cadet branch of the Stukelys of Great Stukely in Huntingdonshire who acquired the manor when Sir Hugh Stucley married Katherine Affeton in about 1434. Three centuries later Sarah Stucley married into the prosperous Bideford trading family of Buck, with the family dividing their time between Hartland Abbey, Daddon, and Affeton Castle. In 1859, George Buck took the title by licence of Sir George Stucley in preference to his patronymic name to establish himself as heir to the landed Stucleys rather than the mercantile Bucks. A year later, the gatehouse at Affeton was rehabilitated as a shooting lodge by David Mackintosh, who subsequently worked at the Stucley seat of Hartland Abbey.[1] Today, Affeton Castle is the centre of a substantial estate run in tandem with that at Hartland Abbey.

Proudly standing above the wooded valley of the Little Dart, a tributary of the River Taw, Affeton is the only significant late medieval secular residence in central Devon. Sacked three times during the Civil War, this two-storey gatehouse was described in 1859 as 'a ruin . . . with a turret at one corner and a battlement, and windows of late Gothic character'.[2] Approximately 60 feet by 22 feet, it has corner buttresses with roll-moulded offsets, and a garderobe projection at the south-east angle. The central passage, infilled in 1860, has an outer entry of three lines of roll moulding with capitals under a depressed four-centred head. The inner entry has lost its frame and has been converted into a window. As at Weare Giffard Hall, the windows are under relieving arches, giving some confidence to their position, though they were heavily restored by Mackintosh. They are of two cinquefoil lights under a rectangular hood with square stops, repeated above with the larger first-floor chamber marked by taller transomed windows. The inner face of this oblong gatehouse has a striking three-storeyed stair turret with canted sides rising extremely high above the embattled parapet to accommodate a further room and its own embattled head. Probably of mid-fifteenth-century date, the gatehouse was extended at the north end in 1860 when the interiors were totally remade for domestic habitation. The only original internal features are the stone newel within the stair turret and the first-floor doorway opening off it.

As at Bickleigh, the gatehouse at Affeton was a major, perhaps the predominant element of a strong house rather than a fortified one. It retains more of its early character than Bickleigh, though seen through Victorian eyes externally, and entirely so internally. Independent of the gatehouse is the post-medieval thatched domestic range marking the north and part of the east side of the former inner court. Nothing seems to pre-date the late sixteenth century in a building much altered in the late eighteenth century.

NOTES

1 M. Hall, *Country Life* (December 1993), though there is also a reference to work in progress at Affeton in 1868–9; R. Haslam, *Country Life* (September 1983).

2 T. H. Turner and J. H. Parker, *Some Account of Domestic Architecture in England*, III pt 2 (1859) 350 under the house's alternative name of Alston.

ATHELHAMPTON HALL, Dorset

The approach to this late medieval mansion, 5 miles north-east of Dorchester and beside the River Piddle, is one of the most charming in southern England. Immaculate lawns, a gravel drive, and a hint of the stunning garden offset the creamy stonework of a large but not overpowering house that stands with its angled wing like the embracing arms of a welcoming aunt. The hall, porch, and services range facing the visitor were built by Sir William Martyn during the closing years of the fifteenth century. The angled west wing and the destroyed gatehouse at right angles to it were completed by his heirs within two generations. The remainder of the house was rebuilt in two phases in the late 1890s and the early 1920s.

Athelhampton Hall is built of Oolitic limestone, as is Woodsford 'Castle' less than 3 miles to the south, but the contrast between the two could not be sharper, though both were proclamations of career success with little more than a hundred years between them. One was a fortified development of *c*.1370; the other is a multi-windowed mansion of *c*.1490–5. Woodsford has lost its hall and entry porch which is the glory of Athelhampton, while Woodsford's residential range is a large but more complex one than the Martyns' solar block or the mid-Tudor parlour wing that replaced it. Both houses were subject to licences to crenellate, but this documentation is misleading in both cases. That for Woodsford applied to structures now destroyed, while that for Athelhampton was entirely symbolic and irrelevant.[1]

The hall and two-storeyed porch are little touched, built of ashlar-faced limestone from Portesham near Abbotsbury, and with characteristic Dorset roofs of smaller tiles from the ridge giving way to large stone slates above the outer walls. The frontage is embellished with a continuous moulded string course to the plinth, and a further one supporting the bold embattled parapet. The porch demonstrates the individuality of the master-mason and his patron. It is six-sided instead of the usual square, with two canted sides and small half-circular shafts instead of diagonal buttresses rising to figures at parapet level. Those either side of the entrance represent the chained ape crest of the Martyn family and the Faringdon crest of Sir William's first wife. The two-centred entry arch has a continuous hollow chamfer and hood surmounted by the Martyn crest and worn end stops. The remainder of the porch is more plain – an unremarkable two-light window to the upper room, a more modest inner arch, benches, open quatrefoil windows in the side walls, and a totally blank ceiling above (not original).

The upper body of the hall exterior has a four-light window, outlined by roll moulding, hollow chamfers, and a square hood, centrally divided by a stepped buttress terminating in a lion finial at

PLATE 205 Athelhampton Hall: hall and porch from the west

parapet level. The bay window repeats the individuality of the porch, five-sided with shallow stepped buttresses at the angles, initially square but rising in triangular form to a grotesque head. Twin-light windows fill each face, divided by two transoms into six units, the lowest and uppermost with ogee-headed tracery with open spandrels and the middle tier with basic two-centred heads. All lights are plain, an early example in this region of the cuspless form. This commanding window is an immediate but secondary development to the original concept, astride the third and fourth bays of the hall rather than fully lighting the dais, and has a lower battlemented parapet and one which cuts into the continuous moulded string course of the hall parapet.

The lower part of the services range is contemporary, heightened, gabled, and refenestrated in the early seventeenth century, but terminating in the original six-sided turret. It retains the string course to the plinth and parapet of the hall and porch but the single lights are 1890s replacements. The east front is basically a continuation of the services, with the common lower string course as far as the east gable, to give an extended wing. The south turret dates from about 1895 when this range was remodelled and extended.

The solar block beyond the upper end of the hall continued to exist until the early nineteenth century for it (or a replacement) is shown in John Buckler's plan of 1828.[2] This much-altered block was rebuilt in the early twentieth century for the generously scaled mid-Tudor parlour wing had made the original structure almost redundant.[3] A short stub of Martyn's original work was retained at the north-west angle of the rebuilding. The inner court and north range are shown in Buckler's plan, but the latter was rebuilt (like the solar block) in 1920–1 in a lacklustre Tudor style.[4]

The four-bay hall, 38 feet by 21 feet by 50 feet high, is particularly well lit. Above the further doorway of the cross passage is a

PLATE 206 Athelhampton Hall: hall roof

two-light window set in a square frame, and there is a slightly later three-light window high in the gable end wall lacking any moulded jambs.[5] The upper part of the second and third bays is spanned by four-light windows, almost opposite each other, though only the buttress of the north window is in line with the central roof truss, while the bay window similarly sits astride the third and fourth bays.

The internal layout is unremarkable. The dais bay has always been warmed, though the fireplace has a renewed head and jambs. The panel-concealed door to its right is original, opening into an 1890s replacement of the solar undercroft. The dais archway to the 1920s stair is also original but with inserted capitals.[6] The linenfold panelling was added in the 1890s at the same time that the late fifteenth-century screen was introduced from a house in Devonshire.

The glory of this hall lies in two major features – the interior of the bay window and the timber roof – and two supplementary features, the entry doors and the heraldic glass. The oak doors at each end of the cross passage are decorated with blind tracery of four cusped lights and a multi-patterned head. The bay window, opening from a tall four-centred arch rising from slender wall shafts, has an interior lined with blind stone panelling of miniature buttresses. They rise to stone ribs, swelling midway into diamond shapes to form a vaulted head. The doorway to the parlour wing is original

(with renewed head), so that the solar block was initially wider, but was cut back in the mid-sixteenth century to give direct access to the new angled wing. Some of the heraldic glass, as in the other hall windows, is original, with good-quality Victorian additions.[7] The roof is an arch-braced, collar-beam structure of five principal trusses with two lines of cusped wind braces. The extremely deep upper purlins are decorated with two rows of formalised flower bosses. Each bay is divided by subsidiary principals, all rising from gadrooned replacement stone corbels.[8] What overwhelms this roof and dominates the hall are the extraordinary reverse-curved braces, marching army-like from the cross passage to the dais.

The interior of the services need not detain us. Two cross-passage doorways with four-centred heads remain in the hall end wall – one in the centre, and one further eastwards. It is assumed they opened into two service rooms, now united in a single parlour of modern character. No evidence has been found of a door nearer the entry, nor the stair approach to the upper floor. It is possible, therefore, that the centre doorway opened into a lobby to the two service rooms, and that the second doorway was the stair approach. The room above the services retains a square-headed fireplace with a spectacular frieze of six ogee-shaped panels rather than the usual circles enclosing quatrefoils with plain shields, alternating with dec-

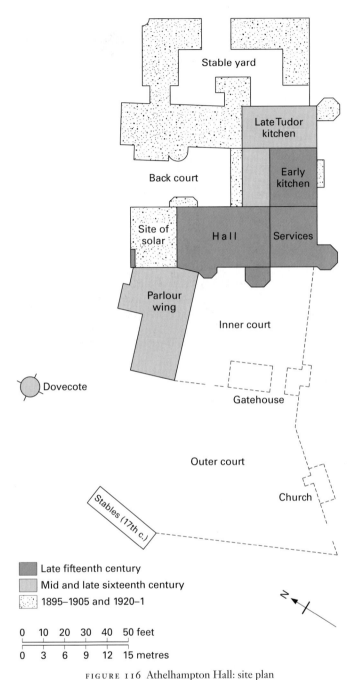

Stable yard

Late Tudor
kitchen

Back court

Early
kitchen

Site of
solar

Hall

Services

Parlour
wing

Inner court

Dovecote

Gatehouse

Outer court

Church

Stables (17th c.)

■ Late fifteenth century
░ Mid and late sixteenth century
· 1895–1905 and 1920–1

| 0 | 10 | 20 | 30 | 40 | 50 feet |
| 0 | 3 | 6 | 9 | 12 | 15 metres |

N

FIGURE 116 Athelhampton Hall: site plan

of the Skinners Company, sheriff of London in 1484, and lord mayor in 1492, and died in 1509.[9] William Martyn of Dorset, a leading local landowner and sheep farmer, began to hold local offices from 1470 onwards, was a collector of customs and subsidies at Poole in 1473 and 1476, and was a strong Yorkist supporter. A frequent commissioner of the peace, he inherited the manor of Athelhampton in 1485, and initiated building after that date when his first wife was still alive, and in 1495 when the licence to crenellate was awarded and permission given to enclose 160 acres for a deer park. Sir William died in 1504 and was buried in Puddletown church.[10] The Hall reflected his wealth and social status and was as much the *beau idéal* of the late medieval house to him as it is to us today. It is a house of considerable style, with its attractively shaped miniature buttresses, unusual window and fireplace tracery, and over-the-top hall roof. The battlements and service turret are probably as much conservatism as any social statement, for the expensive heraldic glass display of his marriage alliances made that point far more effectively.

NOTES

1 *Cal. Pat. Rolls: 1494–1509*, 43. The licence was 'to enclose and fortify [the] manor of Adlampston, co. Dorset, with walls of stone and lime, and to build towers within the said manor and crenellate the same'.

2 Brit. Lib., Add. MS 36361, f.128.

3 The highly decorative parlour wing is architecturally attributable to Robert Martyn, who succeeded in 1524 and died in 1550. It is stylistically similar to other contemporary houses in Dorset including Bingham's Melcombe, Melcombe Honey, and Sandford Orcas. This last retains its associated gatehouse whereas the contemporary three-storeyed one at Athelhampton, 17 yards in front of the porch, was pulled down in 1862. Like the parlour wing, it was built of the same Portesham stone as the hall, enhanced with golden Ham Hill stone dressings. Some of its stonework decoration survives in the grounds of the Hall, and the arms of Robert Martyn and his wife Elizabeth Kelway, formerly under the inner-facing oriel, is now preserved in the house. The gateway was linked to the house by an enclosing wall shown in Buckler's drawing of 1828, T. Garner and A. Stratton, *The Domestic Architecture of England During the Tudor Period*, I (1911) 122. The late Tudor kitchen block is an entirely utilitarian structure.

4 Athelhampton was among the earliest houses to be recorded for its visual and aesthetic interest. In 1828, John Buckler made a number of drawings, as did Benjamin Ferrey six years later, Edward Blore, and Joseph Nash. The photographic record extends as far back as 1853, while its internal restoration (particularly the service rooms and parlour wing) by A. C. de Lafontaine between 1895 and 1906 was lovingly recorded by *Country Life* in 1906 and again in 1984. George Cockrane was responsible for the replacement work of 1920–1. The magnificent architectural gardens were initiated by Lafontaine in 1891–9 and extended by Sir Robert Cooke between *c*.1960 and 1985.

5 It has been redundant since the seventeenth century when the attic storey was added above the services and kitchen wing.

6 Not shown in Nash's engraving of the interior: *Mansions of Olden Times* (1839) III, x.

7 The best is in the north-east window with the late fifteenth-century armorial achievements of Martyn, Faringdon, and their predecessors, the Pydeles. This glass is mentioned in the 1774 edition of Hutchins, *History of Dorset*.

8 The roof bears comparison with the almost contemporary one at Milton Abbey where the trusses spring from wall plates. This may well have been the case at Athelhampton, but decay meant that the bottom of the trusses had to be replaced in plaster painted to imitate wood, possibly in the eighteenth century.

orative devices, and five small figures below – two Martyn apes and three Faringdon unicorns. The corner turret retains a quadripartite vault, plaster covered. The remainder of the services range, now the dining room with bedrooms above, was probably the original kitchen.

The manor of Athelhampton had belonged to the Pydeles until its heiress married Sir Richard Martyn in the early fifteenth century, a member of the long-established Martyn family with estates in Pembrokeshire and Devon including Dartington. Sir Richard's grandson, William Martyn, has long been confused with the highly successful London merchant of the same name who became master

9 A. Colbourne, *Proc. Dorset N. H. and A. Soc.* 113 (1991) 192–3 for their respective careers.

10 His alabaster effigy within a canopied tomb shows Sir William in armour of *c.*1475 with a collar of Yorkist suns and roses, while his will of 1503 confirms that the tomb was prepared well before his death. He had been sheriff of Dorset and Somerset in 1489 and 1500 and knighted at about the turn of the century. The Martyn family died out in 1596 with the demise of Nicholas Martyn when his property was divided between his four daughters. W.G.W. Watson, *The House of Martin* (1906).

C. Latham, *In English Homes*, II (1907) 33–42
A. Oswald, *Country Houses of Dorset* (1959) 65–8
RCHM, *Dorset*, III pt 1 (1970) 9–13
C. Aslet, *Country Life* (May 1984)

BERRY POMEROY CASTLE, Devon

Without stumbling into semantics, one can describe Berry Pomeroy as that rare structure, a late fifteenth-century castle rather than a fortified house. When the Pomeroy family replaced their long-established manor house nearby, they gave their new homestead formidable protection. Of quadrangular plan, the castle stands on a limestone promontory overlooking the steep-sided Gatcombe valley so that only three sides of the enclosure needed to be defended. This was not simply an embattled enclosing wall but a severe defensive frontage of gatehouse, curtain walls, at least one and probably two mural towers, and a postern tower. Now bereft of its crenellated parapet, this frontage was protected by a deep rock-hewn ditch (now filled), the gatehouse by a bridge, portcullis, double doors, and machicolation between the towers, and the curtain wall by a backing rampart. The gatehouse and standing tower were amply furnished with gun ports designed with triple openings for use by a hand gun, a light breach-loading swivel gun, and a bed-stock cannon within the same enclosure. The roofs of the gatehouse and tower were also solidly built, capable of serving as ordnance platforms. Yet despite this bristling face, the site was inherently vulnerable, for it is commanded by rising ground on the south side, now the romantically wooded visitor approach.

Built of locally quarried slate, the gatehouse consists of two canted towers, three storeys high, separated by a first-floor chamber above the entrance passage. The ground-floor chambers were unheated, vaulted defensive rooms (not guardrooms) with a strong room or armoury to the rear, while the second-floor rooms combined guard occupation with windlass equipment. The reroofed residential hall between them had opposing windows, a fireplace, and a granite arcade to the front embracing the open tower rooms.

PLATE 207 Berry Pomeroy Castle: gatehouse and curtain wall enclosing Seymour house of 1560s

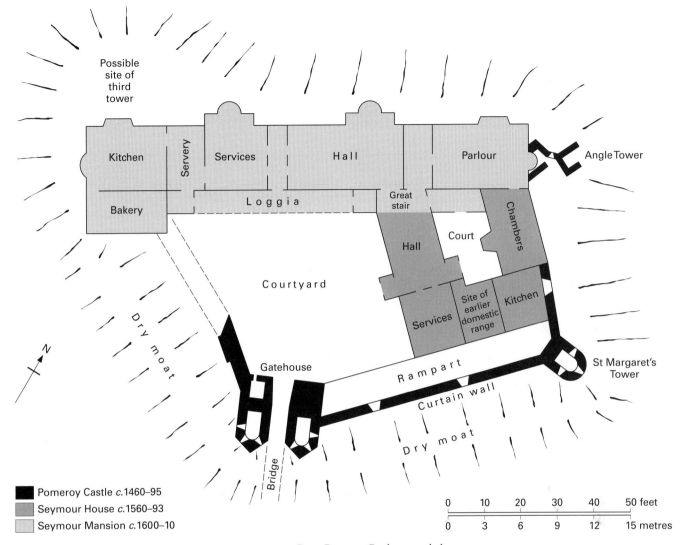

Kitchen · Servery · Services · Hall · Parlour · Angle Tower

Bakery · Loggia · Great stair · Court · Chambers

Possible site of third tower

Courtyard · Hall · Services · Site of earlier domestic range · Kitchen

Dry moat

Gatehouse · Rampart · St Margaret's Tower

Curtain wall

Dry moat

Bridge

N

■ Pomeroy Castle c.1460–95
▨ Seymour House c.1560–93
▢ Seymour Mansion c.1600–10

0   10   20   30   40   50 feet
0   3   6   9   12   15 metres

FIGURE 117 Berry Pomeroy Castle: ground plan

The easternmost bay was a screened oratory with a wall painting of the Adoration of the Magi. Based on fifteenth-century Flemish paintings, this soft-toned but fairly complete fresco above the altar was painted in about 1500.[1]

The south curtain and wall walk were built against an earth and rubble rampart which had been erected immediately beforehand, possibly to prevent any slippage into the newly dug dry moat but also to prevent mining.[2] The U-shaped mural tower, now three- but initially four-storeyed, is thrust well forward to cover the south and east faces of the castle. The utilitarian vaulted ground-floor room retains a storage cupboard, a lamp bracket, and a clean example of a triple gun port, while the upper floors with fireplaces and first-floor garderobe were residential. The rampart formerly continued against the east curtain, partially replaced by the Elizabethan house which looms over the remains of the buttressed postern tower with its guardroom and flight of steps to a rock spring below.

Little evidence was found during the extensive excavations and consolidation work between 1980 and 1996 of the late fifteenth-century hall, offices, or residential apartments. They seem to have

been grouped round a central courtyard, entirely replaced by the tower-like courtyard house of the 1560s built by Sir Edward Seymour at right angles to the outer wall. This was sumptuously extended by the palace-like hall and apartment range overlooking the Gatcombe valley developed by Sir Edward's son during the first decade of the seventeenth century.

Berry Pomeroy was one of the many estates in Devon granted to Ralf de Pomeroy very soon after the Norman Conquest. The Pomeroys became one of the most respected and long-established families in Devon and frequently held locally important offices, though they took no part in national affairs. There are no specific dates for the construction of Berry Pomeroy Castle, but it is a single-period structure attributable on architectural grounds to either the 10th Henry Pomeroy who held the estate from 1446 to 1487 or his son, Richard Pomeroy (d.1496). The reasons for such a defensive work lay in a localised regional problem, the various French raids along the coast during the 1460s–80s which also stimulated fortifications nearby at Dartmouth and Compton castles. The castle is therefore ascribed to between about 1460 and

1495 with the form of the gun ports strongly pointing towards the later date. The reference to the castle in a document of 1496, when the widow of Richard Pomeroy was assigned a third of both the capital messuage and the castle, shows that it had been completed by that time.[3] Henry Pomeroy was a commissioner of the peace for Devon during Edward IV's reign while his son was sheriff of Devon in 1473–4 and again in 1492–3.[4] Building responsibility is unclear, but rests between them during the later stages of the Wars of the Roses. Two centuries later, the castle was abandoned by the Seymour family and quickly became a romantic, ivy-clad ruin.

Berry Pomeroy was a private castle, of traditional quadrangular character like Tiverton and Hemyock castles but with innovative artillery defences. Whether the Pomeroys built a fortified house or a castle, is debatable, but the choice of this site is significant in preference to the family's long-held manor house close to Berry Pomeroy church. Though it is nearly 5 miles from the sea, the defences were as strong as those at Dartmouth Castle (1481–94) and rather more than might be considered necessary to ward off small-scale attacks. There was provision for a small garrison, with guardrooms, wall-walks, and sophisticated cannon openings which provided a continuous enfilade of fire spanning the line of the moat, and a gatehouse with canted or beaked towers like those at Raglan Castle (c.1458–69). Unlike Raglan, the Devon castle was not of strategic political significance. Nor would it have been able to withstand a major assault, any more than many earlier castles could have done. Yet the position and military display gave the family high-quality security as much as it emphasised their social standing. The document of 1496 refers to both Pomeroy residences: the thirteenth-century one by the church is referred to, as always, as the manor house, while the second one is distinguished from its inception as the castle – a term hitherto unknown in any of the extensive family records.[5] It immediately became the principal family seat, within the circuit of the thirteenth-century deer park,[6] until severe financial problems in 1547 forced Thomas Pomeroy to sell his most valuable asset through a third party to Edward Seymour, 1st duke of Somerset, 'Protector Somerset', prior to his execution in 1552.[7]

NOTES

1 The magi, one black, are shown bearing their gifts before Joseph (the missing figure on the left-hand side?). One of the magi is kneeling before the Virgin Mary and baby sheltered within an open timber-framed stable shown as a ruin. The base of the cradle survives. On the far right are what might be two heads (the donors?) with a castle in the background (Berry Pomeroy?).

2 The south-west curtain has an internal passage with mural latrine for sentry use at the foot of the stair to the wall-walk.

3 Brown (1996) 11, 205. No earlier occupational evidence was found on the site during the excavation programme covering the courtyard interior, ibid. 10.

4 E. B. Powley, The House of De La Pomerai (1944); Brown (1996) 204–5.

5 Brown (1996) 203–6. To consider Berry Pomeroy as a fortified house rather than a military defence (ibid. 1) underestimates the meaningfulness of the fortifications and the local worries of attack that had, in the different circumstances of a rival faction in 1428, previously forced the Pomeroys to flee their house. The defences were neither symbolic nor superficial as was usual in contemporary fortified houses, but of serious military intent, necessitating a high level of expenditure to excavate the rock ditch and erect fortifications with the latest artillery features.

6 First recorded in 1207, and covering 100 acres by 1305, ibid. 5. Its walls still stand in many places more than 10 feet high.

7 Between the early twelfth and early fifteenth centuries, the St Maur (later Seymour) family held Penhow Castle and other properties in Monmouthshire. A. Emery, Greater Med. Houses, II (2000) 635. During the fifteenth century, a junior line moved to Wiltshire and attained gentry status at Wolf Hall, Savernake. It was they who acquired Berry Pomeroy, and subsequently Maiden Bradley (1552) in south-west Wiltshire where the Seymour family still live.

S. Brown, *Proc. Devon Arch. Soc.* 54 (1996) 1–366
S. Brown, *Berry Pomeroy Castle: Handbook* (1997)

BEWLEY COURT and three Wiltshire manor houses

Bewley Court, Bradfield Manor House, Hazelbury Manor, and Sutton Veny Manor House retain their late medieval halls but little else of contemporary value. Unbroken occupation at all four properties has resulted in additions, destruction, and rebuilding between the seventeenth and twentieth centuries, with Hazelbury and Bewley displaying the best and worst of twentieth-century rehabilitation. Apart from the chapel block at Woodlands Manor, Wiltshire is not a county of Decorated-period houses, so that the hall at Sutton Veny Manor Houses serves as a counterpoint to the riches of the Perpendicular style that extend from Norrington Manor and Wardour Castle in the late fourteenth century to Great Chalfield and the less complete houses noted below a century later.

The stone-built hall at *Sutton Veny* is flanked today by an offices block of 1693 and an upper residential block of c.1830. The opposing fourteenth-century hall doorways with continuous moulded chamfer and two-centred head open into a cross passage with an early twentieth-century screen and two doorways with wave moulding to the former services. The hall, 37 feet by 23 feet, is divided into two and a half bays, lit by two generous Decorated windows in the side walls of tall twin-trefoil lights under a quatrefoil head.[1] The wooden shutters were made for and painted with Chaucerian scenes by Sir William Nicholson in the 1920s. The roof has arch-braced collar trusses supporting four-way posts. The end wall fireplace, 7½ feet long, is a late fifteenth- early sixteenth-century insertion. This hall is a graceless apartment with the close rafters contributing to a particularly dour structure. Though long used as the rectory until 1913, the house seems to have been a modest one by William Wauton (d.1350) or more probably the Hungerford family who held the manor from 1359 to 1685.[2]

The hall at *Bewley Court* was originally as modest as that at Sutton Veny but the fifteenth-century developments changed its character as fundamentally as those of the twentieth century. Situated above the meadows on the opposite bank of the River Avon from Lacock Abbey, Bewley Court initially consisted of a fourteenth-century timber-framed hall and high-end parlour block under a common roof ridge, with an offices and chamber cross wing at the lower end. During the fifteenth century, all three units were stone faced except for the jettied west-end parlour wall which was stone faced by Harold Brakspear in c.1912. The hall lost all side light in favour of two projecting bay windows at its upper end, with additions either side the parlour block plus a north-facing mural fireplace and a new south porch in line with the offices. These side additions to the hall and chamber block are reflected in the change of roof levels and the new embattled south façade (pl. 304).

In its remodelled form, the porch opened into a two-bay hall, 27 feet by 19 feet, solely lit by the opposing large square bay windows at its upper end. The south bay gave direct access to an enlarged parlour and a broad flight of stairs, in the opposite direction but parallel with the hall, rising over the porch to an oriel-lit withdrawing chamber above the services and most of the kitchen in the cross wing.[3] Originally four bays long, this room with main and intermediate trusses was truncated by the kitchen extension in the seventeenth century. The hall north bay was the approach to a similar flight of stairs leading to the great chamber above the parlour, but this addition was also destroyed in the seventeenth century.

The kitchen and offices wing was extended again in 1902 by Harold Brakspear prior to his more extensive restoration of Bewley Court in about 1912. This was not Brakspear's finest hour. He destroyed the fourteenth-century timber-framed partition between the hall and two-storey parlour block to create a grossly oversized apartment open to the roof. At the same time, he moved the fireplace from the north wall of the hall to the now-revealed end wall of the parlour to serve as the fireplace to the extended hall. Brakspear's work not only eradicated the generous parlour and great chamber over it but entirely destroyed the integrity of the house.[4] All subsequent occupiers have found this broken-backed residence an impractical one.

The later fifteenth-century remodelling[5] was a highly personal approach to the standard house form, with the tight planning adopted here followed elsewhere in this region, with the bay windows lighting the hall also providing lobby access to the other principal rooms. The hall bay arches are two-centred with hollow chamfer and the windows are trefoiled lights. The roof was standard – arch-braced collar trusses rising from high-set stone corbels, with two lines of curved wind braces decorated with small geometric carved roundels.[6] There was evidence of sooted timbers and traces of a hall louvre above a central hearth. Brakspear was of the opinion that the cross-passage screen was always of stone and he recreated its form based on fragments of moulding from the top panel. But an equally individual feature of the hall, and without parallel, is the decoration of the side walls in the absence of windows. A moulded string course divided the inner face into two halves, the lower with curved heads and a central string reaching to an embattled semi-octagonal corbel on blind conoid moulding, and the upper section rising square to the embattled wall plate.

Opposing hall bays occur at Great Chalfield and South Wraxall manors, but the two-centred form at Bewley is similar to the single bays at Tickenham Court and Kingston Seymour Manor. Porch and lower cross wing in line is repeated at all but South Wraxall Manor, while the first-floor oriel also occurs at Great Chalfield Manor. All four houses were built or remodelled in Edward IV's reign and Bewley Court is of that time. It is, however, more clumsily enlarged through retaining the earlier hall and parlour block, though the results were highly individual.

During the 1330s, the property was held by Nicholas Beuelegh when he was one of the two highest taxpayers in the parish. He was probably responsible for the original timber-framed house.[7] Towards the close of the century, Bewley (a derivation of Beverley) was purchased by Thomas Calston, who enlarged the earlier house and added a chapel, licensed by the bishop of Salisbury in 1399.[8] Calston was appointed high sheriff of Wiltshire in 1415, and the inventory made after his death in 1418 reveals the position of the

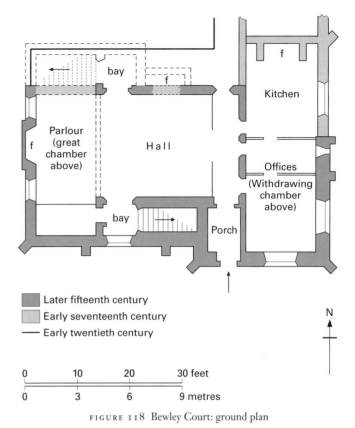

FIGURE 118 Bewley Court: ground plan

hall, parlour, great chamber, and parlour chamber, as well as other conjecturally positioned rooms as well furnished as those of a magnate (see page 472). His daughter Elizabeth (d.1464) married William Darrell of Littlecote, but the fundamental alterations to the property were probably by their son Sir George Darrell (d.1474), keeper of the king's wardrobe. Towards the close of the century, Sir Edward Darrell (d.1530) added the outer archway to the porch, altered the stair over it, and inserted the uncusped transomed window in the south bay in place of the earlier two-centred window, but Darrell chose to spend most of his life developing Littlecote rather than Bewley Court as the family home. His grandson therefore sold the property in 1543 to a neighbour, William Sharington, shortly after that Tudor courtier and entrepreneur had acquired Lacock Abbey.

Hazelbury Manor, 5 miles west of Bewley Court, was also rehabilitated and enlarged by Brakspear in 1920–5, but far more sympathetically, so that he considered it his most successful and satisfying restoration work. A multi-period courtyard house, the property is almost impossible to see from the nearby roads as it is sited in a shallow combe. Unlike Bewley Court, any earlier structure by the Croke family was all but swept away after the Croke heiress married John Bonham during the late fifteenth century.[9] His redevelopment of the property mirrored contemporary work at South Wraxall and Great Chalfield manors, both less than 3 miles away.

The earlier fourteenth-century hall was of stone, with the angle quoins unbroken from ground to eaves abutting a timber-framed lower wing. The core of this hall was retained, for Brakspear discovered the lower part of a two-light fourteenth-century window in its north wall, but the apartment was clothed anew. Bonham added

PLATE 208 Hazelbury Manor: from the south

a two-storey battlemented porch, a mural fireplace, and two upper end bays with panelled arches. That to the forecourt is a three-sided bay window, but the one opposite opened into a newel, replaced by a stair in the late sixteenth century, and in the early twentieth century by one from Shrewsbury.[10] Bonham's hall roof was of standard local form except for the angled struts above the arch-braced collar trusses, and three lines of wind braces.

The end ranges are also late fifteenth century, with the upper one of the same width as the hall, in line with it, and residential on both floors. The lower wing seems to have been like the two neighbouring manors, with a heated ground-floor parlour instead of the usual services and a high-quality chamber over, but that at Hazelbury had both oriel and garderobe projection, though only the oriel support survives. The kitchen was in an extension with end-wall fireplace.

According to Leland, the house 'was a thing of a simple building afore that old Mr. Boneham father did build there'.[11] The house was initially as commanding as Great Chalfield Manor, if less well detailed, with the battlemented porch and bay window as the most

prominent features until the wings were raised and refenestrated. As the early windows were uncusped, as at Chalfield, the work is unlikely to be earlier than the last years of the century. John Bonham, whose father had rebuilt the house, died in 1548. His son, Sir John Bonham (d.1554), initiated the enlargement that was completed by Sir John Yonge (d.1592) when the wings were raised and extended and a new range enclosed the north side of the courtyard. Further changes were made by the Speke family in the early seventeenth century, and again in about 1710 when the principal rooms were given large sash windows.[12]

Brakspear found evidence of a large embattled forecourt and the foundations of the gatehouse depicted on an estate map of 1626. Of considerably more interest is the highly individual garden layout retained at the rear of the house, made up of a battlemented north wall with broad rampart walk on its inner face, and embattled bastions at the north-west and north-east angles. The wall is interrupted by an inserted gateway surmounted by the arms of the Speke family (after 1610), but nearby is a wide corbelled projection, now a garden seat but similar to the garderobe projections surmounting the enclosing wall of the Louvre depicted in the October miniature of *Les Très Riches Heures* of the duc de Berry (c.1410). This garden structure is probably a late sixteenth-century evocation of an earlier age. It is not defensive but a decorative garden amenity of pseudo-military but romantic form. The gardens were restored in 1925–6 and redesigned by Ian Pollard during the 1980s.

Far less survives today of *Bradfield Manor House*, the last of these fifteenth-century Wiltshire homes, 9 miles north-east of Hazelbury and also with a lost forecourt and gatehouse. Of rubble construction with Cotswold tiled roof, the buttressed hall with end units is a single range under a common roof ridge. Continuous occupation and farm usage until the late 1990s has resulted in a thoroughly remodelled interior that scarcely does justice to the original scale of the house. The only early to mid-century evidence is the entry, the transomed hall windows, and the six-bay roof. The two-storey porch was pulled down before 1861, leaving only the cross-passage entry with double wave moulding (and a nineteenth-century hood) while the windows are of twin cinquefoil lights under a quatrefoil head and two-centred hood. The two on the south side are complete, and there is the upper half of one on the north side with a small light nearby to a former stair to the upper chamber. The hall was ceiled at eaves level in the early seventeenth century without destroying the six bays of soot-covered arch-braced collar trusses.

The end blocks were remodelled in the early seventeenth century when an imposing three-storey residential block was added at the north-east angle[13] followed by a further north-west wing. This substantial house was depleted of its south-west range, hall porch, two-storey gatehouse, and plain enclosing wall after John Aubrey's visit in 1670, though his drawing shows all these features.[14] Bradfield Manor was held by the Russell family from 1304 to 1466, when it passed from John Russell (d.1472) to his apparent heir, John Collingborne. It was held by William Collingborne from 1476 until 1484, when he was executed for rebelling against Richard III. Collingborne rose from a minor position in Edward IV's household to gentleman usher but he lost his position in local affairs after encouraging Henry Tudor to land in England and depose the king in 1483. He compounded his felony by pinning libellous ballads and rhymes on the doors of St Paul's Cathedral, including his famous and widely circulated jibe against the king's advisors: 'The Rat, the Cat, and Lovell our Dog rule all England under the Hog'.[15] The king sequestered Bradfield Manor which he gave to one of his chaplain's and trusted financial advisor, Thomas Chadderton, whose family retained it.

NOTES

1 Another similar window in the stable block is probably a remnant of the original upper chamber. The hall was heavily restored in 1921.

2 VCH, *Wiltshire*, VIII (1965) 63. Polebridge House, also in Sutton Veny, retains a substantial hall attributable to the second quarter of the fourteenth century with an arch-braced collar roof notable for its cusped braces, cusped wind braces, and infilled trefoil braces flanking an ogee quatrefoil in the end wall.

3 Harold Brakspear remade the oriel window based on one at Great Chalfield Manor but stonework discovered in the 1980s shows that it followed a different form. Harvey, Harvey and Slocombe (1987) 71.

4 Brakspear was also responsible for the single-storey replacement on the north side of the hall, carried out for George Palmer.

5 The attempt to link the house inventory of Thomas Calston in 1418 with

the architectural character adopted for the reconstruction of the hall, porch, and withdrawing chamber is not convincing. Harvey *et al.* (1987) 72–3.

6 The earlier great chamber roof has later wind braces matching those in the hall.

7 Until 1912, the timber-framed west wall held a two-light window with ogee heads, suggesting the years between c.1320 and 1350. Brakspear (1912) West Elevation.

8 Harvey *et al.* (1987) 63–4.

9 The Croke family had controlled the high-quality stone quarries at Box since the mid-twelfth century.

10 Porch and bay were reconstructed by Brakspear from foundations and recovered carved fragments. He also installed the timber screen from a house in Barnstaple and added the gallery above.

11 *Itinerary*, I, 134.

12 Three fifths of the gabled west range and the whole of the north side of the courtyard are a Brakspear rebuild on mid-sixteenth-century foundations. The work was carried out for George Kidston.

13 This may have replaced an earlier tower-like chamber block such as the fifteenth-century structure illustrated by John Buckler in 1808 at the Manor House, Stanton St Quinton, 2 miles south but long ago destroyed. VCH, XIV (1991) 215–16.

14 Reproduced in VCH, XIV (1991) 111.

15 R. Horrox, *Richard III: A Study in Service* (1989) 192–203. One of Collingborne's several Wiltshire associates involved in Buckingham's rebellion against Richard III was Sir Robert Willoughby, who escaped to Brittany until Henry Tudor's victory at Bosworth. Upon his return Willoughby, created Lord Willoughby de Broke in 1491, made Broke or Brook Hall his principal residence between 1485 and his death in 1502. R. J. Skinner, *Wilts. Arch. Mag.* 87 (1994) 116–22. Brook Hall near Heywood consists of a seventeenth-century farmhouse with Tudor elements and a late eighteenth-century Gothick façade, and a rear wing of c.1500 that was formerly a lodging range. Both were restored in 1990–1. The little-touched buttressed lodging range has three ground-floor entries, uncusped lights at both levels, separate upper-floor heated chambers with garderobes, and an eight-bay roof of arch-braced collar trusses.

Bewley Court
H. Brakspear, *Wilts. Arch. and N. H. Mag.* 37 (1912) 391–9
B. and R. Harvey and P. M. Slocombe, *Wilts. Arch. and N. H. Mag.* 81 (1987) 63–73

Hazelbury Manor
H. Brakspear, *Arch. Jour.* 87 (1930) 483–4
G. J. Kidston, *A History of the Manor of Hazelbury* (1936)
H. A. Tipping, *English Homes* Pds 1 & 2, II (1937) 91–104

Bradfield Manor House
VCH, *Wiltshire*, XIV (1991) 110–11

BLACKMOOR MANOR, Somerset

Like several smaller manor houses in Somerset such as Gothelney, Bratton, and Meare, Blackmoor is the centre of a working farm. This has helped to preserve its early character, for Blackmoor, as Pevsner noted, is a rare and fortunate survival kept externally in almost the state it was built.[1] More importantly, its internal condition is equally untouched. This Somerset house is an early example of the development of a great chamber surmounting a ground-floor hall as at Gothelney Hall, though not as large or as spectacular as its neighbour. More visually striking is the retained sequence of three unoccupied rooms – parlour, ante-chapel, and chapel – which have been little touched since the late fifteenth century. Above the parlour and chapel are two further spacious chambers creating a sequence of high-status apartments at odds with the initial paucity of accommodation at the lower end of the hall. This was rectified within a generation. The house was probably built by Sir Thomas Tremayle (d.1508), who had purchased the manor in 1476, with his son John (d.1534) adding the kitchen wing at the south end of the property. Even so, there is little architectural difference between the two phases, while subsequent modifications have been minimal.

Blackmoor Manor is a single-range house with reverse end wings, emphasising the forward position of the chapel at the upper end and the rear position of the kitchen at the lower. Two-storeyed throughout, it is built of local red sandstone rubble and characterised by two- or three-light windows with nipped ogee heads, as are the doorways. They suggest the last quarter of the fifteenth century.[2] The only exceptions to this are the chapel windows with debased trefoil lights and depressed four-centred heads.

The porch inner doorway with ogee head and roll and hollow moulding, more shallow than at Gurney Manor nearby, opens direct into the hall. There was no opposing cross-passage doorway. This ground-floor hall, 32 feet by 18 feet, is well lit by a three-light window to the forecourt and a pair of two-light transomed windows in the rear wall, one blocked. The original wall fireplace has a later chamfered lintel. The low-pitched, eight-panel ceiling is supported on moulded beams that are more massive than the visible portion suggests. The broad arch at the upper end is filled with two Georgian doors opening on to the chapel passage and a replacement stair to the upper floor blocking the passage windows.

The parlour retains its sixteenth-century state – rammed chalk floor, lime-washed walls, and a little wooden furniture. It is lit by a three-light window (plus a single blocked light), warmed by the end-wall fireplace with straight-headed lintel, and served by a ground-floor garderobe approached from a chamfered doorway with four-centred head. The plain ceiling was remade at a slightly higher level than originally when the badly fractured end wall was repaired in the late nineteenth century.

The passage opens into a room prefiguring the chapel, lit on both sides but unheated. Its purpose is not clear but it serves as the house entry to the domestic chapel and had an unglazed wooden window in the stone wall separating it from that area. There was an external entry to the chapel, so that it was used by outsiders as well as by the family and household. It stands as a little-touched example with a three-light east window, single-light side windows, highly decorated niches, a trefoil-headed piscina, and a balcony with sockets on an underside beam for the posts of a screen. The post-medieval alterations have been the insertion of a plain flat ceiling below the original trusses, the brick floor, and infilling the balcony face leaving the outline of its central opening.

The three doors at the head of the eighteenth-century replacement stair open into the great chamber over the hall, the lesser chamber over the parlour, and a further chamber over the ante-chapel. The roof spanning the lesser chamber, exposed in 1980, is of the standard Somerset type of arch-braced collar trusses with three lines of curved wind braces. The room repeats the end-wall fireplace and garderobe of the parlour underneath and is divided from the great chamber by a post and panel partition. The chamber over the hall is divided into a corridor and ceiled bedrooms but

PLATE 209 Blackmoor Manor: hall and chapel wing from the south-east

exploration in 1980 confirmed that the original roof trusses survive, of the same form as those exposed.

The room above the ante-chapel reflects alterations made in the later sixteenth century when the gallery was infilled, the fireplace inserted,[3] and the attic room above extended by incorporating the area above the added chapel ceiling, lit by the inserted gabled end window.

The limited scale of the offices at the lower end of the hall and the original newel-approached room above was soon expanded by the adjacent kitchen cross wing. The upper floor was a two-room lodging, the outer room with a blocked fireplace and the unheated rear room with a garderobe.[4] A slightly earlier pair of similar interconnecting rooms above the kitchen occurs at Gurney Manor. Although this wing is closely integrated with the body of the house and has similar windows, its secondary development is confirmed by the use of slightly cruder and less massive roof timbers.

Thomas Tremayle (later knighted) was a locally significant person who crowned his success as a lawyer and justice of the King's Bench (1489–1503) with a striking gentry residence of c.1486–1500.[5] Blackmoor Manor is one of an early and regionally important group of houses with a single-storey hall and great chamber over. Apart from the hall, the house has four high-status rooms, the parlour and the three upper rooms originally open to the roof, plus a well preserved chapel with ante-chamber. It is a generously planned residence, with the kitchen integrated with the body of the house, at least not long after its completion, and stairs at both ends. Though a continuous upper floor made the lower stair strictly unnecessary, it helped to emphasise the social distinction between owner and staff. The independent two-room lodging of the kitchen wing may have been for a lesser member of the family or a leading household official. The forecourt was probably enclosed, crossed by external access to the chapel, as still occurs at Great Chalfield Manor. The architectural detailing is poor and the roof structure is routine, but its little-modified condition helps to make Blackmoor Manor one of the best-preserved and interesting late medieval houses in southern England.

NOTES

1 *The Buildings of England: South and West Somerset* (1958) 90.
2 Ogee heads in fifteenth-century west of England residences include the George and Pilgrim Inn at Glastonbury (between 1456 and 1493), the

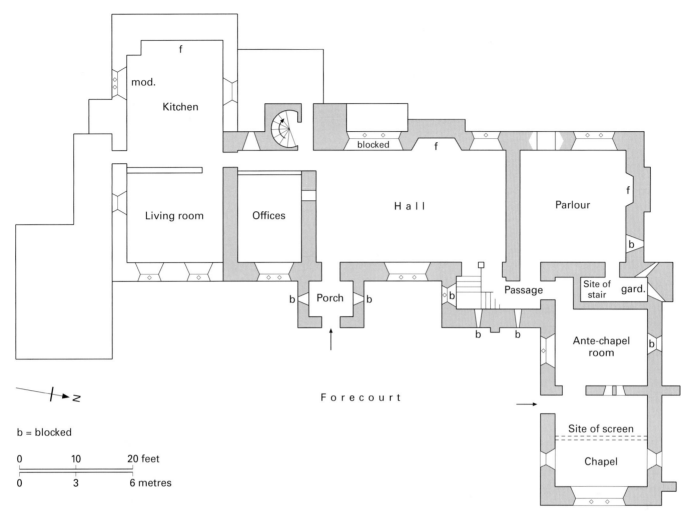

FIGURE 119 Blackmoor Manor: ground plan

b = blocked

0   10   20 feet

0   3   6 metres

solar wing at Tickenham Court (1470s), the hall bay at Athelhampton Hall (c.1485–1500), and the hall and chamber wing at Cotehele (c.1500–10).

3 It was possibly at this time that the garderobe entry was transferred to this chamber and a steep stair inserted opposite it, now blocked.

4 For the upper floor plan, N. Cooper, *Houses of the Gentry: 1480–1680* (1999) 71.

5 For a brief career summary, M. Havinden, *Proc. Somerset Arch. and N. H. Soc.* 139 (1996) 5–6. Dendro-dating, *Vern. Arch.* 35 (2004) 108.

E.H.D. Williams, *Proc. Somerset Arch. and N. H. Soc.* 118 (1973–4) 36–8
VCH, *Somerset*, VI (1992) 80

BOWHILL, Devon

Originally standing in the countryside on rising ground more than a mile south of Exeter, the manor house of Bowhill was enveloped by residential suburbs during the early twentieth century and now looks thoroughly incongruous in its surroundings. Painstaking restoration between 1980 and 1997 not only reversed its swiftly deteriorating condition but retrieved most of the house's original late fifteenth-century character. It was the home of three generations of

Hollands (unrelated to the Dartington Holands but a younger branch of the Hollands of Countesswear nearby), of whom the last named was Roger (c.1450–1506), the son of Thomas Holland (d.1472), a prominent citizen of Exeter. Roger traded in cloth and wine, was controller of the ports of Exeter, Dartmouth, and Plymouth, member of parliament for Totnes in 1491 and for Exeter in 1504, three times sheriff of Devon, and recorder of Exeter for the last eight years of his life. His daughter married John Carew of Antony in Cornwall and the Carews held the property until its sale at the end of the seventeenth century began three centuries of decline.

Bowhill is a quadrangular house with ranges now on two and a half but formerly round all sides of the inner courtyard. The hall was built of locally quarried grey and purple volcanic stone with dressings in Heavitree sandstone and Beer stone, but the rest of the house is of cob covered with a yellow ochre limewash.[1] It stands on the former Exeter to Okehampton road. A wide passage through the south range divides the house proper from the working area, for the Hollands' business activities were an important consideration in the planning of this house. Buck's inclusion of Bowhill in his engraving of the city of Exeter in 1726 indicates that the Carews added a residential range to the east, that the forecourt boundary

PLATE 210 Bowhill: hall range and parlour from the east

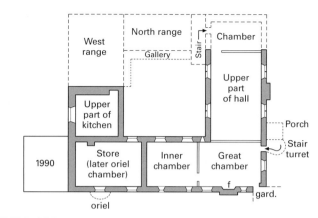

FIRST FLOOR

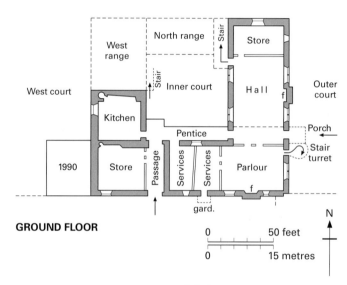

GROUND FLOOR

FIGURE 120 Bowhill: floor plans

wall was crenellated, and that the outbuildings to the west may have included a chapel (as well as a barn destroyed in 1972).

The hall, open to the roof and approached through a two-storeyed porch destroyed in the eighteenth century,[2] filled most of the east range, with a store room at the upper end, formerly with a chamber above. A parlour entered directly from the cross passage marks the beginning of the two-storeyed south range with two service rooms beyond, one unusually with a garderobe, and both linked to the hall via a 1992 rebuilt pentice between the kitchen and hall. Above was the great chamber and an unheated inner chamber. At this point, a massive cob wall separates the residential from the working and business accommodation. The two further rooms of the south range were initially for storage, with evidence of an opening in the ground-floor ceiling for hoisting sacks into the room above. Only half the west range survives, the kitchen with a vast end-wall fireplace, although it can be seen externally that the upper rooms of the long-burnt-down two-storeyed block to the north had gallery access. This working part of the house was subsequently converted into a separate dwelling at the close of the sixteenth or in the early seventeenth century, when the kitchen was ceiled to provide an additional upper room.

The late fifteenth-century hall is lit on both sides by tall square-headed transomed windows of two lights with cinquefoil heads above and below the transoms. Externally, the labels on the fore-court side terminate in carved heads, and internally the lower mullions are pierced for shutter fastenings. The hall has a mural fireplace (altered by the Carews), an earth floor, and a stud and plank upper end wall, but its glory is the spectacular roof. The four bays are spanned by heavily moulded arch-braced collar trusses with cusped intermediate trusses. Above each collar is a distinctive coved head while an equally unusual local feature is the line of straight wind braces with curved feet. The similarity to the nearby roofs at Cadhay and those in Exeter at the Guildhall, the Deanery and 8 The Close illustrates how local craftsmen developed a distinctive form from a common regional pattern (see pages 508–9).

Beyond the hall is a store room with two unglazed windows.[3] The chamber formerly above was reached by a lost stair from the doorway with a semi-circular head in the north-west corner of the hall. In 1958 there were traces of an arch-braced roof.[4]

Bowhill is unusual in the placement of a parlour instead of the offices at the lower end of the hall. This room is lit by a mutilated window of cinquefoil lights under a square label, heated by a plain mural fireplace, and retains its heavily moulded framed ceiling. The pair of doorways with four-centred heads from the cross passage and the service room suggest that this so-called parlour may have been partitioned and less spacious than today, with further traffic from the entry to the polygonal newel serving the great chamber above.[5] This stair turret at the side of the porch was pulled down in the eighteenth century.

Though the approach has been lost, the great chamber retains a corner doorway to a garderobe and a fireplace similar to that below. It is surmounted by a fine roof to a simplified design of that above the hall but retaining its original foliated bosses at the junction of the timbers. The unheated inner chamber may have been Holland's bedchamber.[6] A doorway has subsequently been cut through the thick cob cross wall, linking the two previously separated parts of the house. The upper store room was converted by the Carews into a large chamber with an inserted fireplace and oriel window, destroyed after Buck had illustrated it in 1736 and not reinstated during the 1980s.

Richard Holland (*c*.1385–*c*.1455), who represented Devon in parliament in 1430, had been granted a licence to celebrate mass at Bowhill in the previous year. The second quarter of the century is not incompatible with the form of the hall and parlour windows with their cinquefoil heads, the cross-passage doorways with two-centred heads, and other doorways with four-centred heads. However, it is now considered that the whole house dates from the final years of the fifteenth century after a fire had burnt down the rather smaller house on the site in the 1490s.[7] The parlour ceiling has been dendro dated to a probable felling range of 1491–1507[8] but it has not been possible to take satisfactory cores from the roofs of the hall or great chamber for dendrochronology purposes. On grounds of typology and comparative structures, they are late in the century, though the feet of the hall trusses sit uncomfortably on a band of cob rather than the stone walling below, indicating a raised and possibly secondary development phase.

Bowhill was a grandly appointed house combining formal design and high-quality craftsmanship with partial vernacular construction. The elaborately decorative roofs set it apart from most late medieval Devon houses, with that over the hall and great chamber among the finest surviving examples of the local school of carpentry that flowered during the early Tudor period. The fireplaces in the principal room (but not that inserted in the oriel chamber) are also of a distinctive local pattern. The placing of a store room beyond the hall is not unusual in Devon, while the kitchen follows a common regional pattern of being opposite the hall. The position of the parlour where the service rooms are normally located may have been determined by the business aspects of this house's development. It is not clear how the paired doorways which are a feature of Bowhill worked, but they may relate to a secondary development shortly after completion. The function of the lost ranges is not known, whether for guests, staff, warehousing, or business activities. Even so, Bowhill stands almost complete as a merchant's opulent country residence looking northwards to Exeter city and eastwards to the trading facilities of Exeter quay. It is a striking example of a marriage celebrated in about 1500 between a trading warehouse and the fashionable courtyard house of a highly successful businessman.

NOTES

1 Cob is a building material particularly associated with Devon. Made from straw with added water trampled into mud by oxen, the material was laid on stone foundations in layers up to 9 feet thick. The next layer was only added after the first had dried. Bumps were smoothed out and the wall plastered with wetter mud before a coat of limewash was applied. Provided the roofs overhang the wall to prevent rain penetration, a cob wall can last for centuries, as Bowhill demonstrates. Why cob was used here rather than stone has not been fully explained when financial resources were not an issue. The stone walls of the hall were also concealed by the limewash, probably over a plaster covering. See also R. Harrison, *The Conservation and Repair of Bowhill, Exeter* (1999).

2 Shown with the adjoining stair turret in Buck's engraving.

3 The windows, ceiling, doorways, and partition wall with the hall here are reconstructions of 1980–2 based on surviving evidence, as are the roof bosses in the hall.

4 Everett (1958) 205.

5 The view that this chamber was originally part of an early fifteenth-century structure burnt down by fire late in that century (Slade (1990) 93, 96) is no longer accepted, though evidence of this earlier building was found during site excavations in the 1980s.

6 No longer thought to have been divided originally as suggested by Slade (1990) 96.

7 Cinquefoil windows under square labels regularly occur at the turn of the century, as in the cloister of Magdalen College, Oxford, Henry VII's chapel at Westminster Abbey, and Gurney Manor, Somerset.

8 *Vern. Arch.* 30 (1999) 116.

A. W. Everett, *Arch. Jour.* 115 (1958) 203–7
H. G. Slade, *Arch. Jour.* 147 supplement (1990) 93–7
S. Blaylock, *Bowhill, Exeter, Devon: The Archaeological Study of a Building under Repair, 1977–1995* (2003)

BRADLEY MANOR, Devon

John Swete's painting of Bradley Manor in 1795 in his *Picturesque Views of Devon*[1] shows the house isolated at the foot of the wooded valley created by the River Lemon as it flows towards the open lowland before joining the Teign estuary. Much of the lowland is now covered by the expanding town of Newton Abbot, but the house quite remarkably preserves its solitude, still hidden in the woodland. Nor has the house changed much since the eighteenth century, except for the regrettable loss of its gatehouse for no good reason in 1842.

This early fifteenth-century gentry house is low built, almost crouching – the antithesis of the vertical form adopted by Sir Philip Courtenay only a few years earlier for his fortified house at Powderham nearby. Bradley is L-shaped, but for our purposes its significance centres mainly on the late medieval front range. The core of the south wing at right angles to it is a two-storeyed thirteenth-century stone-built house, possibly its chamber block, but little has survived continuous occupation and hardly any telling detail. Interest in this wing rests on its reroofing in the early fifteenth century and the subsequent internal decoration of two upper rooms.

In 1402, Richard Yarde of Yarde near Salcombe[2] married Joan Ferrers, a local heiress of Churston Ferrers near Brixham, who came into the ownership of Bradley three years later. Rather than live in the old house, this young couple built an entirely new one at right angles to the earlier property. It was made up of a central hall with storeyed porch, flanked by the parlour and services with chambers above, and a kitchen set back from the main frontage as at Dartington Hall and abutting the earlier property. The approach was completed by a gatehouse and wall enclosing a small forecourt. Within a few years of completion, a chapel was added in 1427 as an extension to the parlour. Richard Yarde (d.1467) was appointed a justice of the peace in 1434 and sheriff of Devon in 1442–3. He and his wife lived at Bradley for over sixty years, but it was their second son, Gilbert (d.1492), who infilled the front between the two wings with a gabled façade during the 1470s or 1480s. All subsequent work, mainly internal apart from the coach house wing of *c*.1700, has not overly damaged Bradley's late medieval character.

The buttressed and multi-gabled frontage maintains the modest height of the single-storey hall and chapel. This low line is even more obvious at the rear, where the roof sweeps the length of the range, scarcely interrupted by the solar dormer or the services gable. The house is built of locally quarried rubble limestone, with granite for the doorways and fireplaces and Beer stone for the

PLATE 211 Bradley Manor: from the east

windows. The exterior always seems to have been rough plastered and whitewashed.

The idiosyncratic refronting in the late fifteenth century adds much sparkle to the house, though the work must have been costly, necessitated destroying the hall bay window, and barely extends the accommodation within.[3] Apart from the gables, the façade is dominated by the two lines of windows. The principal ground-floor rooms have two-transomed lights of four cinquefoil heads under a square hood with end stops. One survives complete but the two windows nearby have lost their cusped heads and were foreshortened to create internal window seats. The first-floor windows are similar but in rectangular oriels, except for the central one with canted sides. They are surmounted by heavy early Victorian crenellations in place of slate roofs, introduced at the same time that the southernmost oriel and gable were added over the kitchen. All the fifteenth-century windows retain their iron bars, fragments of old glass, and dramatically carved external heads. Those north of the porch represent the beasts of the four evangelists and were originally painted red and green. Those of the central oriel are also original but the remainder are recent replacements. This strikingly fenestrated frontage is offset by two contrasting fifteenth-century windows, a single trefoil light above the entrance as a reminder of the absorbed porch, and the multi-traceried head of the three-light chapel east window. This frontage display of fifteenth-century exuberance is without parallel in south Devon since the administrative transfer of Forde Abbey to Dorset.

The granite porch doorway faces a similar inner entry with plain chamfered jambs and continuous two-centred head.[4] It opens into the cross passage with an opposing doorway of comparable character, both with still-used door bars. The hall, originally 37 feet by 17 feet, was curtailed by 5 feet at its upper end in the later sixteenth century to create a larger parlour with chamber above. The present screen is made up of seventeenth-century panelling. The wall fireplace retains its original stone lintel of granite slabs. The windows have been replaced, that in the west wall by a vast bay in the mid-nineteenth century. The east-facing bay was pulled down during the late fifteenth century when the frontage was extended, leaving a redundant archway with capitals and double-chamfered head, now filled with a screen incorporating early Renaissance panels of c.1534. The five-bay roof is spanned by modest arch-braced collar trusses with coats of arms which are unpainted and difficult to see, including those of the two families responsible for its construction. The trusses were formerly painted with red and yellow decoration.

The enlarged parlour and chamber above are essentially of late Tudor character, though the former retains the base of a newel (stair replaced) to the room above and the original east window left open after the chapel had been added against it. The upper room retains the doorway to a garderobe in the north-east corner.[5]

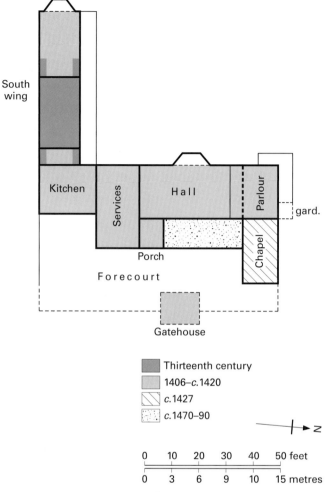

South
wing

Kitchen

Services

Hall

Parlour

gard.

Porch

Chapel

Forecourt

Gatehouse

■ Thirteenth century

▨ 1406–c.1420

▨ c.1427

▨ c.1470–90

← → N

0   10   20   30   40   50 feet

0   3   6   9   10   15 metres

FIGURE 121 Bradley Manor: site plan

south wing was given an arch-braced collar roof like that in the hall, with a single line of wind braces. The trusses were painted scarlet and the area was divided into two. The smaller room was panelled and plaster ceiled in the late seventeenth century, with the cornice enriched with swags and shells. The larger room, 40 feet long until it was divided in the early nineteenth century, retains part of a striking stencilled pattern of black fleur-de-lis on a white ground and a painted striped curtain next to the window, both attributable to the years close to 1500. The IHS monogram with the emblems of the Passion is no later than the mid-sixteenth century.[6]

The Victorian passion for pulling down gatehouses and courtyard-enclosing walls to open up vistas is understandable, but it deprives this house of some of its character as similarly occurred at Athelhampton Hall and Cochwillan. Like the contemporary survival at Leigh Barton, the Bradley gatehouse was two-storeyed, off-centre from the hall entry. The larger upper residential chamber enjoyed two-light transomed windows to the front and rear, a fireplace, and a garderobe, for gatehouses like this made a social not a defensive statement.[7]

Bradley is a relatively small manor house of conventional early fifteenth-century plan, but with the benefit of a contemporary chapel. It is possible that its development was influenced by that at Dartington Hall only 6 miles south. Some of the Yarde family had been members of the earl of Huntingdon's affinity,[8] and their house adopted Dartington's double-courtyard form and followed the same basic hall range plan. The generous accommodation included the remodelled wing of the earlier house and then an extra room behind the exuberant frontage added in the late fifteenth century. Bradley has a homely rather than a sophisticated character so that interest lies less in its structure than in its incidentals – the lost gatehouse, the frontal fenestration, the wall paintings, and the chapel interior. It has also managed to retain the seclusion that used to apply to so many medieval houses until the late nineteenth century but rarely does today.

NOTES

1 Manuscripts held in Devon Record Office, Exeter. Also John Swete, *Travels in Georgian Devon*, ed. T. Gray (1997).

2 Part of the fourteenth-century family home at Yarde is encased in the Tudor courtyard house with the front range rebuilt by the Dyer family as a separate house in 1680, remodelled in 1718. For the owners of Bradley between 1154 and 1500, J. J. Alexander, *Trans. Devon. Assoc.* 68 (1936) 187–95.

3 This frontage created two small rooms at each level. The lower ones have been made into a corridor. The upper rooms, one absorbing the porch chamber, are open to arch-braced collar roofs.

4 The services doorway from the porch was inserted in 1890 in place of a bench along the wall.

5 It is not clear whether the late sixteenth-century roof replaced a cross wing or one always in line with the hall roof.

6 The small shield near the door with the arms of Peniles seems to be part of an early fifteenth-century decorative scheme, while the red and black pattern of Renaissance-type decoration in the south-west corner is part of a mid to late sixteenth-century scheme that formerly extended the length of the room.

7 Illustrated in Woolner (1989) pl. 6. The stonework from the two windows is held in store.

8 A. Emery, *Dartington Hall* (1970) 43, 55.

D. Woolner, *Bradley: Handbook* (1989 edn)

RAI, *Arch. Jour.*, Summer Meeting Programme, 147 (1990) 97–101

The chapel, 21 feet by 11 feet, has been little altered since bishop Lacy of Exeter granted a licence in February 1428 for the celebration of mass. Well-lit by two south-facing and a striking east window, its retains its aumbrey with trefoil head, altar stone, two corbels for statues, part of the screen, and a fragment of the alabaster reredos. The close-set braced-collar roof of wagon-shaped character retains its contemporary bosses and wall plate carvings. The tiny gallery from the chamber over the parlour was reconstructed in 1993 from evidence discovered during the chapel's restoration during that year.

The services end of the hall has three doorways, two to the services and the taller one to the room above. The services have been united in a single room. The adjacent kitchen, as at Powderham Castle, retains its end-wall fireplace and massive granite lintel, with a roughly made inserted ceiling when the two floors above were added in c.1600 to help accommodate the heir and his wife and their nine children. At the same time, the barrel-shaped roof of the adjacent room over the services was plaster ceiled, the fireplace remade, and the plaster overmantel inserted. This chamber was formerly reached by a newel from the screens passage and lit at both ends, but the room was curtailed at its west end in the nineteenth century to create a corridor and facilitate stair access.

During the early fifteenth century, the upper floor of the earlier

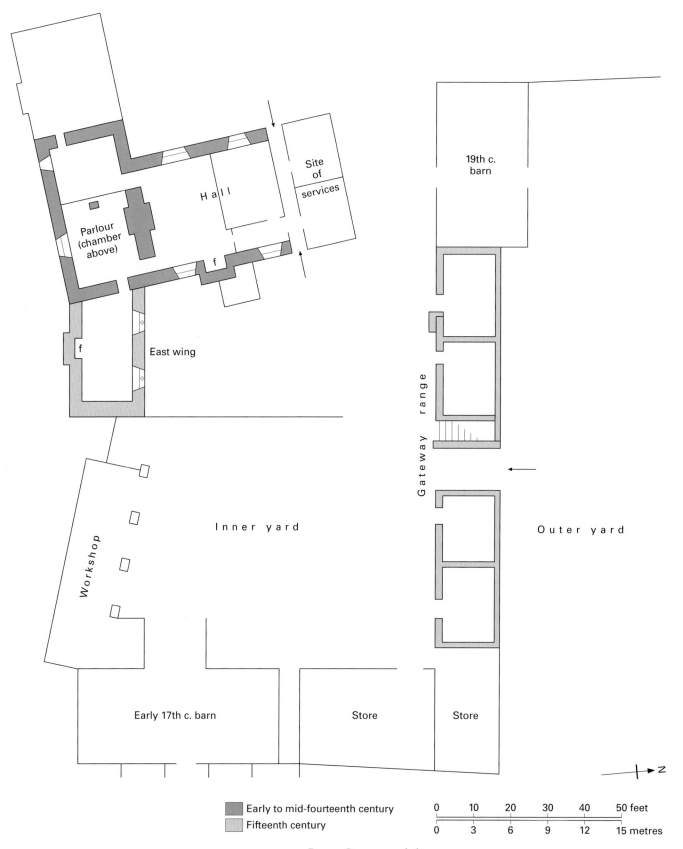

Parlour (chamber above)

f

East wing

Hall

Site of services

19th c. barn

Gateway range

Workshop

Inner yard

Outer yard

Early 17th c. barn

Store

Store

Early to mid-fourteenth century

Fifteenth century

N

0	10	20	30	40	50 feet
0	3	6	9	12	15 metres

FIGURE 122 Bratton Court: ground plan

502

BRATTON COURT, Somerset

Bratton Court does not seem to be one of the greater houses of medieval Somerset but it is architecturally important, though long occupied as a working farm. Standing alone on the side of a combe facing the sea at Minehead, the house is approached through a gateway range of farm units prefacing the forecourt of agricultural buildings with the house at a higher level on the fourth side.

Of early to mid-fourteenth-century date, the house of roughcast stone consists of a hall with two-storey end units of service with chamber over, and an extended parlour with chamber over. A fifteenth-century wing projects east from the parlour block, forming the most distinguished element of the ensemble. The whole farmhouse was heavily altered in Victorian times, including all the windows except for those in the east wing.

There was no porch to the cross passage of the two-bay hall, 37½ feet by 24½ feet, spanned by smoke-blackened arch-braced cruck trusses. It was ceiled in the seventeenth century when the fireplace and external stack were added, and divided into two rooms.

The services unit was thoroughly altered by the Victorians and is featureless. The parlour wing extended westwards beyond the line of the hall. The ground floor has a central braced post (like that in the entry block at Dartingon Hall) and may have been divided into two at this point. The six-bay upper chamber was originally undivided and open to the seven arch-braced collar trusses with clasped purlins and decorative wall plates. The west extension is a late rebuilding of a sub-medieval structure.

The east wing at a lower height has prominent fifteenth-century wooden-framed windows at both levels, of two cinquefoil lights, cusped above and below the transom. The upper floor with three modified windows of cusped lights has an external entry opening into an ante-room and chamber with fireplace spanned by four jointed crucks with wind braces. This may have been subsequently used as a manorial courtroom as at Preston Patrick Hall in Cumbria and Danby Castle in Yorkshire.

The house belonged to the Bracton family, whose most famous member was Henry Bracton (d.1268), the eminent jurist and author of the much-used treatise on the laws and constitution of England. In 1317, Robert Bracton was granted a licence for an oratory at Bratton Court, and the property subsequently passed through the Fry, King, and Lytton families. Like Blackmoor Manor, Gothelney Hall, and Meare Manor, Bratton Court is still the heart of an active

PLATE 212 Bratton Court: house from inner yard

farm, with a fifteenth-century gateway range with a tall central entry and superior two-bay room over. The barn at the north end of this range is nineteenth century but that at the south-east corner is late sixteenth/early seventeenth century with jointed cruck roof.

Despite extensive Victorian changes, this is one of the earliest still-occupied houses in Somerset, formerly with an open hall and a substantial contemporary parlour wing. It is part of a manor with outbuildings, all too frequently lost, and more closely resembles its late medieval state than many more sanitised ensembles.

E. H. Williams and R. G. Gilson, NMRC, no. 041845
E. H. D. Williams and R. G. Gilson, *Proc. Somerset Arch. and N. H. Soc.* 123 (1978–9) 40–7, 51–3

BRYMPTON D'EVERCY, Somerset

The view from the forecourt entrance is one of the most beautiful medieval ensembles in the West of England. With the attractive stable block on the immediate left-hand side, the extended forecourt towards the irregular house frontage is flanked on the right by an independent two-storeyed house and the church with its striking bell-cot, all built in golden Ham stone and set in a sloping wooded landscape. The name derives from the manor's ownership by the d'Evercy family in about 1220, but the earliest work is more than two centuries later.

The two-storeyed block towards the church is neither dower-house nor priest's dwelling but a short lodging range of mid-fifteenth-century date. The ground floor, in particular, has been subject to modification in a matching style as late as 1723 (datestone), which confuses the original plan.[1] The later doorways are distinguished by simpler external mouldings and the absence of ashlar rear arches, and the windows by plain two-centred almost semi-circular heads instead of cusped lights. If we ignore these features the range's early form becomes more clear.

The ground floor was divided into three lodgings, all approached from the courtyard though now lacking internal division. Room 1 was entered from the doorway adjacent to the stair turret, with continuous double hollow chamfer of slight depth and acute four-centred head. Room 2 was approached from the blocked doorway two-thirds along the frontage, and room 3 from the present entrance at the west end. Rooms 1 and 3 are about 18 feet square; room 2 was nearly twice that length. All the windows in the churchyard wall are late insertions and some of the others are replacements, but at least one in the centre of the courtyard face is original with its cusps hacked back. The two end chambers were furnished with garderobes in the churchyard wall, the entrance with an acute head in room 3 survives, but that in room 1 has been replaced by an inserted doorway when all external evidence of garderobe existence was removed, though shown in Knyff's early eighteenth-century engraving of the house. The central chamber has a fireplace in the courtyard wall with low four-centred head and plain lintel (chimney removed).

The majority of the windows lighting the upper floor are original, retaining their square-headed labels with stops and two-light cinquefoil heads in the churchyard and west gable wall, but with the cusps of the more extended transomed windows towards the courtyard hacked away. The possibly secondary semi-octagonal stair turret with embattled parapet gave access to the smaller of the

PLATE 213 Brympton D'Evercy: house from the west with lodging range

upper rooms retaining garderobe doorway and fireplace with decorated lintel.[2] The larger chamber with garderobe doorway and plain fireplace lintel was approached from the ground floor by a newel stair sculpted out of the courtyard wall thickness, lit by cross loops.

How did the range work? The lack of ground-floor partitions precludes certainty, but the entrances show that there were three lodgings, possibly independent of each other, though rooms 2 and 3 may have worked as a double lodging – the outer room with taller entrance and garderobe and the inner chamber with fireplace and subsidiary doorway. The first of the upper rooms with its broad stair approach and seventeenth-century plaster ceiling, was a self-contained unit like that below, with its own garderobe and fireplace. The remainder may have worked as a single chamber with ground-floor access and almost centrally positioned fireplace, for though the five bays of the roof over this section with cinquefoil wind braces show no partition evidence, an outer and inner division is far more likely. The present partitions seem to be later, when the roof above them was modified.

What is the date and purpose of the range? The hollow double chamfers, acute four-centred heads, and cinquefoil lights and wind braces are mid rather than late fifteenth-century features, but greater precision is difficult without the documentary evidence so markedly lacking at Brympton. In 1434, the manor was purchased by Sir John Stourton (d.1462), Lord Stourton after 1448, who already owned Preston Plucknett Manor House nearby and rebuilt Stourton House in Wiltshire. He gave Brympton in dowry to his daughter upon her marriage to John Sydenham in about 1448 and the house may have been developed by them before his death in 1464. Their son, who did not come of age until the year of Bosworth Field, would have been unlikely to build before the 1490s – too late for the stylistic evidence. It was he who cut back the window cusps in the 1520s to match his remodelled frontage of the

adjacent house and give the appearance that the range was contemporary work. Its courtyard position, external form, internal plan, and lack of any kitchen or service facilities make its lodging function clear. It was probably matched by a comparable range on the opposite side of the courtyard, linked by a wall with central entrance or gateway, but this and any outer court have been united in the present landscaped forecourt.

The house is composed of work of several periods replacing the early hall and two end units. The central block facing the approach was rebuilt in Elizabethan times as a two-storey structure with the new ground-floor hall given a contemporary plaster ceiling. What survives of the medieval hall is the gable-end walls and two end doorways with the same mouldings and acute four-centred heads as those in the lodging range. The outer wall of the three-storeyed service unit to the left has kept its original stepped corner buttress, in a block remodelled in the late 1520s when the stair turret and two-storeyed bay window with the royal coat of arms and plain window heads were inserted.[3] This unit was reserved by John Sydenham for himself and his wife when he made the house over to his son in 1534.[4]

The high-end unit with its buttressed and embattled south face has been stripped internally, but Tipping records that 'considerable remains of a large four-light Perpendicular window with cinquefoil headed lights has been found in the south face of this block at first-floor level', but it was probably an oriel.[5] A contemporary range extending eastwards overlapped the upper end of the hall and solar unit. It is defined by the present staircase wall and an extension of the buttressed solar wall as far as the kitchen wing. The wide cellar entrances with mouldings similar to those in the hall and lodging range give access to an extended area at half ground level with no other fifteenth-century evidence, but the six widely splayed two-light windows (possibly late sixteenth century) point to a residential rather than cellar purpose. It is now covered by Sir John

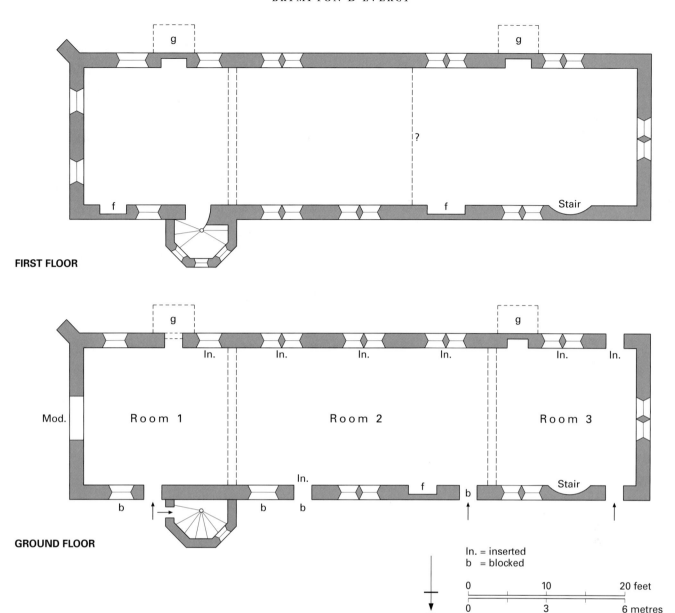

FIGURE 123 Brympton D'Evercy: floor plans of lodging range

Sydenham's dramatic range of the 1650s, built a few feet outside and beyond the line of the medieval south wall, just as the Elizabethan façade of the hall block was built forward of its original line.

Though the structural evidence is fragmentary, Brympton d'Evercy was one of the largest late medieval houses in Somerset, with a particularly extended hall range and family wing, and a forecourt with lodgings showing that the Sydenhams had a large household. Its development was even more complex than suggested here but fortunately it has been subject to few structural changes since it was sold by the Sydenhams in 1772.

north and east walls, implying that the turret was secondary and probably higher. The fireplace lintel may be a replacement brought from the house. A higher-quality first-floor lodging is repeated at Ewelme Manor (c.1420–50) for a high-status official. It retained this function at Brympton in Jacobean times.

3 Comparable work was being undertaken 7 miles away at Lytes Cary.
4 Gray (1965) 41.
5 Tipping (1937) 34. However, inside is a fifteenth-century archway with richly moulded jambs, the rear arch of an oriel window

H. A. Tipping, *English Homes*, Pds 1 and 2, II (1937) 31–50
J. D. Gray, *Proc. Somerset Arch. and N. H. Soc.* 109 (1965) 40–6

NOTES
1 Possibly a consequence of later use as a dower-house.
2 Andor Gomme has drawn my attention to the straight joint between the

BUCKFAST ABBEY GUEST HOUSE, Devon

The rebuilding of the Benedictine abbey at Buckfast between 1884 and 1938 was followed by the restoration of the abbey precinct in 1982–94. The former incorporated the one residential unit that had survived the Reformation, the tower of the abbot's lodging (see under Torre Abbey). The latter rescued and reconstructed the guest house and associated wing. A Benedictine monastery established nearby in 1018 by Aethelweard, ealdorman of Devon, was re-established on the present site as a Savignac foundation in 1136, and absorbed into the Cistercian order eleven years later. After the abbey's dissolution in 1539, the site remained unoccupied and ruinous until it was bought in 1800 by Samuel Berry, a local mill owner, who erected a Gothick house on part of the west cloister range. He levelled the rest of the site, allowing only some outer-court buildings to remain for farm purposes. Most of Berry's house of 1806 was incorporated in the rebuilding of the claustral ranges by French Benedictine monks in 1884, followed by the church in 1907–38, to become the only medieval monastery restored in England to enable a contemplative life to be followed.[1]

The inner wall and arch of the twelfth-century north gate, a range of domestic buildings facing the west front of the abbey, and the frame of the late medieval south gate, all in line, mark the extent of the abbey's outer court from the River Dart. Part of the domestic range was dismantled shortly after the Dissolution and the remainder was reordered into farm buildings used until the early twentieth century. It was when they were needed for visitor facilities that the buildings were surveyed, their original function as a guest hall and domestic wing identified, and the structures restored in 1990–2.[2]

The guest range, 125 feet by 44½ feet externally, consisted of a rectangular structure of a hall open to the roof with two-storey end blocks, both with garderobe extensions. A single-phase early fourteenth-century rebuilding on twelfth-century foundations, much of the structure had survived to about wall plate level, including most of the courtyard-facing wall with its entry door, the lower gable with two doorways to the services beyond, and the external gable of the upper block. The 1990 rebuilding incorporated these structures but for only half their width, with the western half left as a yard as it had been since the later sixteenth century.

The dressed stonework of the single hall entry has been reinstated, as well as the outline of one of the two three-light windows which would have been matched by two west-facing windows. Much of the original internal plaster has been preserved, as well as the washbasin by the entry, served by a spring from the nearby slope. The present utilitarian roof, covering only half the hall's original width, does not seek to follow the original structure, of which a substantial truss slot remains in the lower gable. It was probably of base-cruck construction like that proposed for the early fourteenth-century hall at Okehampton Castle.[3] Little survives apart from the frame of the upper-end block, probably sleeping accommodation but now used as a bookshop (ground) and store (above). This end unit was unusual in having an internal drain against the gable that may have served a line of garderobes at ground level as in a monastic rere dorter, with the upper chamber using the facilities in the projecting garderobe, now outlined externally. More remains of the services block, with two service doorways to the central kitchen passage and the larger of the two service

PLATE 214 Buckfast Abbey: south wing of guest house

rooms that flank it. The smaller service room could only be accessed from the passage. The single chamber above seems to have been approached from an external stair against the south wall also serving the adjacent garderobe extension. The windows have been stripped of all dressed stone, but the chases for the roof timbers are visible, and the lower walls of the garderobe. The kitchen was a detached building, its unexcavated position identified in 1982.[4]

The south wing was added during the late fourteenth or fifteenth century[5] to provide additional accommodation, though it was never linked with the guest hall and was significantly positioned at its lower end, as was beginning to become common in larger houses. It consisted of three low service or store rooms and a single upper chamber, inhabited as a farmhouse until the early twentieth century. Though the detail of doors, windows, roof, and internal partitions had been lost, sufficient evidence survived for the building to be restored to its original state. Entry was from the south side, where there were a pair of ground-floor doorways and a single one above, stair-approached and with a pent roof-landing like those to the west lodgings at Dartington Hall. With a third doorway to the east, the ground floor was made up of three independent rooms, each separately windowed to the north, with that closest to the guest hall linked to it by a forced doorway to serve, perhaps, as a supplementary buttery. The upper chamber was lit by two tall oblong windows in the north wall and a wider one at the upper end, with another facing it. The lower end of this room was poorly lit and probably partitioned from it. There was a substantial fireplace in the south wall with recovered evidence of a smoke hood (restored) and the scars of the trusses of a seven-bay roof which was reinstated, like the floor, with timber from the abbey's woods in 1992. The present arch-braced collar trusses follow a locally popular form so the original roof was probably similar. This hall's purpose is not certain. It was not linked to the guest hall and there was no garderobe, though there was a drain in the window sill opposite the entry, a mural fireplace, and a generously lit upper-end bay. It may have served multiple communal uses, possibly as a dining hall for visitors on business, abbey staff, or corrodians served by the nearby kitchen. Shortly

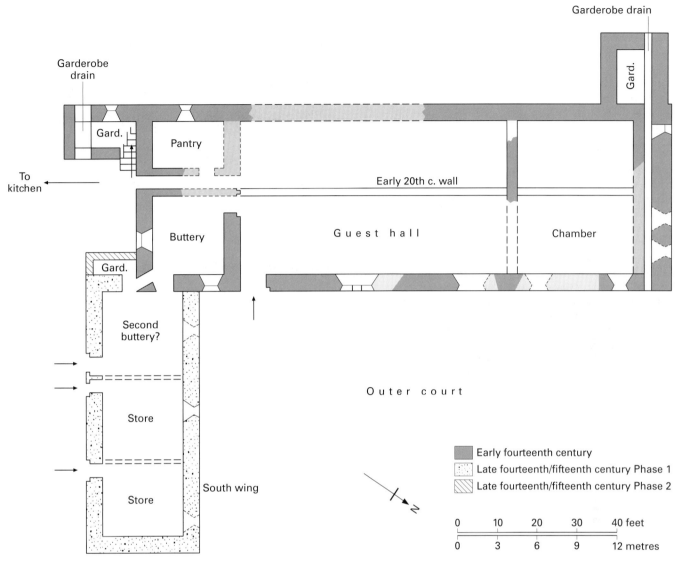

Garderobe drain

Garderobe drain

Gard.

Gard.

Pantry

To kitchen

Early 20th c. wall

Buttery

Gard.

Guest hall

Chamber

Second buttery?

Store

Store

South wing

Outer court

N

Early fourteenth century

Late fourteenth/fifteenth century Phase 1

Late fourteenth/fifteenth century Phase 2

0	10	20	30	40 feet
0	3	6	9	12 metres

FIGURE 124 Buckfast Abbey: guest house ground plan

after its construction, a garderobe was added at the north end, originally with a wall-enclosed shaft to the drain below.

The guest house at Buckfast Abbey was one of the most important in south-west England, for it was close to the crossing of the River Dart by the primary road from Exeter to Plymouth. It was, in effect, a self-contained house, barely differing from a secular residence in the region except through the scale of its hall, 62½ feet by 34 feet internally and among the largest known in Devon or Cornwall. Cistercian guest houses were usually sited in the outer court as at Kirkstall Abbey where its original and subsequent development has been traced in detail,[6] but few later examples have been as well preserved as that at Buckfast Abbey.[7] The fifteenth-century wing was added as an adjunct to the existing facilities to meet the pressure of community service on one of the wealthiest abbeys in the region, for by the close of the fourteenth century the abbey owned extensive sheep runs on Dartmoor, seventeen manors in central and south Devon, town houses in Exeter, fisheries on the

Dart and the Avon, and a country house for the abbot at Kingsbridge.[8]

NOTES

1 For the rebuilding of the abbey, F. A. Walters, *Arch. Jour.* (1923) 258–67.

2 For the excavation, recording, and assessment, Brown (1988) 13–89. For the two gates, *Med. Arch.* 36 (1992) 207–8.

3 *Proc. Devon Arch. Soc.* (1982) 67–70 and (1988) 72–5.

4 Brown (1988) 24.

5 Neither limited excavation nor structural analysis provided closer datable evidence, *ibid.* 65. Robin Clutterbuck attributes it to abbot Kyng: (1994) 16.

6 S. Wrathmell, *Kirkstall Abbey: The Guest House* (1987); Emery, *Greater Med. Houses*, I (1996) 376–7.

7 For a survey of known monastic guest houses in England and Wales, Brown (1988) 76–7. The so-called 'guesthouse' at Buckland Abbey was built as a farm building and not adapted for domestic use until after the Dissolution. C. G. Brown *et al.*, *Trans. Devon. Assoc.* 53 (1995) 44–60.

8 Stéphan (1970). This early fifteenth-century house, rebuilt by abbot Slade (d.1415), no longer stands though some wood panels from it have been incorporated in the abbot's throne inside the abbey church.

Dom. Stéphan, *A History of Buckfast Abbey* (1970)

S. W. Brown, *Proc. Devon Arch. Soc.* 46 (1988) 13–89

R. Clutterbuck, *Buckfast Abbey: A History* (1994)

CADHAY and a local carpentry school in Devon

Late medieval church and house roofs differed from each other in Devon, with wagon roofs common in ecclesiastical buildings and base-cruck and then hammer-beam roofs crowning the halls of several major secular buildings. Dartington Hall (*c.*1388–99) was the earliest to adopt the hammer-beam form, followed during the later fifteenth century by the halls at Weare Giffard, Orleigh Court, and West Challacombe Manor in north Devon and by the Law Library in Exeter and Cadhay in south Devon. These last two are products of a highly individual local school of carpentry centred on Exeter during the later fifteenth and early sixteenth centuries.

Six roofs can be attributed to this school – four in Exeter, at the Law Library, the Deanery, Palace Gate, and the Guildhall, and two not far from the city, at Bowhill and Cadhay. To determine the form and date of Cadhay, a manor house a mile north-west of Ottery St Mary, the roofs at the other properties need to be considered. Though the form of their main trusses differed, they are characterised by similar mouldings, distinctively shaped intermediate trusses, semi-circular coving above the collar level, and straight wind braces with curved feet, though not all elements are present in each design. These roofs are limited to secular buildings, though not necessarily to contemporary support walls, and their order of construction is unclear.

The building programme of *Exeter Guildhall* extended from 1466, when Hooker recorded the order to rebuild the hall, to 1469, when the building programme was in its final stages.[1] This elongated hall, 62½ feet by 24⅓ feet, is lit by three windows in both side walls and a larger altered one in the upper-end wall. The roof does not relate to them and the third bay from the end is abruptly cut by the window head, suggesting that the wall and roof design were not co-ordinated. The seven-bay roof consists of eight main arch-braced trusses and seven intermediate trusses with continuous ribbing above and below the upper purlins. The lower wind braces are almost straight, with curved feet. The roof is attributed to the late 1460s on the documentary evidence for the building, but the dendro dating is equivocal and could be *c.*1498, during the four years before 1500 for which no accounts survive.[2]

The first of the hall roofs within the cathedral close is the *Law Library* (8 The Close). The contemporary hall, 32 feet by 22 feet and cluttered by partitions, retains its cross-passage doorways and the traceable position of the side windows with fleuron heads. The three-bay roof with louvre is an impressive hammer-beam structure, a smaller version of that at Westminster Hall, repeating its arch-braced trusses and traceried infilling. It differs from the royal roof in having a coved section above the collar, lower straight wind braces with curved feet, and detailing similar to the Deanery roof, so that it may confirm the fifteenth-century rather than the suggested early sixteenth-century attributions.[3]

PLATE 215 Exeter, The Deanery: great chamber roof

The second cathedral close roof, only recently discovered at *Palace Gate*, has a base-cruck structure in contrast with the sophisticated hammer-beam form at the Law Library. The third roof is inside the *Deanery*, a rambling house subject to many additions and alterations throughout its history which make its development particularly difficult to unravel. Among the late medieval extensions added to the thirteenth-century ground floor hall was a parlour with great chamber over, approached by contemporary doors of fifteenth- rather than sixteenth-century character. The windows in the south front at both levels were flat-headed with hood moulds and square labels (upper windows remodelled in 1768), but no record was kept of the evidence for the windows in the north wall (or traces of wall painting) said to have been found in the early 1970s. The great chamber was initially of six bays, but one was cut off in the later seventeenth century. The roof has moulded arch braces springing from stone corbels with cusped intermediate trusses to short hammer beams and coved rafters. It is the plainest of this group of roofs, lacking wind braces or any other decorative features. It is usually dated by the initials J V for John Veysey, dean from 1509 to 1519 and bishop from 1519 to 1554, on the parlour fireplace jambs, with the preference to the earlier appointment. However, the floor timbers have been dendro dated to 1400–35, substantially earlier than the assumed date for this addition. Subsequent dendro dating of the roof confirms the probability to around 1420.[4]

The four-bay roof spanning the hall at *Bowhill* (see pages 497–9) has plain arch-braced collar trusses, with the distinctive cusped intermediate trusses, coved head above the collar, and a line of straight wind braces with curved feet. Though this roof sits awkwardly on the stone side walls, with the feet of the trusses set in cob, it is attributed to the house rebuilding of *c.*1498–1500 and is matched by a contemporary sister roof of plainer character in the great chamber.

Cadhay, an apparently mid-sixteenth-century house that may well be earlier, seems to be the last of these building projects. It is quadrangular in shape, and the north range has a central entry with the great hall to the left, now divided into two floors. The three-bay roof has gigantic arch-braced trusses of semi-circular form with applied mouldings and the distinctive coving above collar level.

PLATE 216   Bowhill: hall roof

There are characteristic intermediate trusses and straight wind braces with curving feet. The roof was mutilated in about 1737, when the first floor was inserted and the hammer-beam trusses including posts and central arch braces were removed.[5] The roof also seems to have been curtailed at the same time by one bay, for although the upper end wall is solid, that at the lower end is a partition wall inserted in about 1737 on the line of the screen to create an entry passage with chamber above and a projecting bay central to the range.

The house had been held by the de Cadehayes for over two centuries before it passed by marriage to John Haydon in 1527. The hall roof is a high-quality structure which has been dated towards the end of the fifteenth century,[6] and as late as 1545 when it was recorded that Haydon was in occupation at Cadhay.[7] This is extremely late for an open hall roof, and several architectural fragments of cusped heads with shields preserved in the house also point to the earlier period. They may be from fireplaces similar to that in the hall, plastered over, as were others in the 1730s, and revealed in 1910. Considered in isolation, the hall fireplace, not unlike those in the Deanery, would be ascribed to the last quarter of the fifteenth century or shortly after the turn of the century, yet the arms in quatrefoils above the fireplace and traceried frieze are those of Haydon's great nephew Robert Haydon and his relations, which precludes a date before Robert's ownership of the manor in 1587. The fireplace is certainly not as late as that, or even the 1540s, suggesting that the arms were a recutting of Robert Haydon (1587–after 1617). It is possible therefore that the hall was erected by the de Cadehayes a few years either side of 1500, with its framework, fireplace, and hammer-beam roof retained during the remodelling of the house a generation or two later.[8]

This distinctive group of grand and ornamental roofs by a local school of master-carpenters spans nearly a hundred years. The Deanery roof of *c*.1420 is the earliest, possibly followed rather later by the Law Library roof with some similar detailing. The Guildhall structure is attributable to the closing years of the century, followed by Bowhill of *c*.1500. The hammer-beam roof at Cadhay is probably the latest, but has such close similarities to that at the Law Library that a date about the turn of the century is more likely than the commonly ascribed one of about 1530 to 1540.

NOTES

1 L. Parry, *The History of the Exeter Guildhall and the Life Within* (1936); Blaylock (1990) esp. 129.
2 *Vern. Arch.* 33 (2002) 105.
3 Sir Cyril Fox, *Arch. Jour.* 114 (1957) 138–9; D. Portman, *Exeter Houses: 1400–1700* (1966) 67–8.
4 *Med. Arch.* 44 (2000) 259; *Vern. Arch.* 33 (2002) 104–5.
5 It is also possible that this roof had vertical tracery as in the Law Library. Coate, Baldwin, and Spittle (1957) 162.
6 Coate *et al.* (1957) 162.
7 Thorp (1990) 102 and 101, where it is noted that Risdon reported in 1620 in his *Survey of Devon* that John Haydon had built a 'fair new house'.
8 John Haydon (d.1587), an extremely successful lawyer, favoured an old-fashioned style as other parts of the house testify, as well as his tomb in the church at Ottery St Mary. His earliest work after acquiring Cadhay in 1527 was to enclose the earlier courtyard with the south range and its so-called 'long gallery', always attributed to the end of the sixteenth century though the four-centred arches, buttresses, and butt joints with the adjacent wings suggest the early 1530s. It was followed by his main programme attributed to the late 1540s on the evidence of thirteenth-century material included in the walls and chimneys acquired after the dissolution of the college of priests at Ottery St Mary in May 1545. If so, his only alteration to the retained earlier hall was the refenestration of its windows.

Cadhay
L. Weaver, *Country Life* (January 1913)
Mrs Whetham, *A Manor Book of Ottery St. Mary* (1913)
M. Coate, M. Baldwin, and D. Spittle, *Arch. Jour.* 114 (1957) 159–63
J. R. L. Thorp, Supplement to *Arch. Jour.* 147 (1990) 101–3
O. N. William-Powlett *Cadhay: Guide Booklet* (n.d., *c*.1982)

South Devon roofs
M. Wood, *The English Mediaeval House* (1965) 316–18
S. Blaylock, *Trans. Devon Arch. Soc.* 48 (1990) 123–78

CERNE ABBEY, Dorset

All that stands of the Benedictine abbey at Cerne is the mid-fourteenth-century tithe barn, the mid-fifteenth-century guest house, and the early sixteenth-century porch tower of the abbot's hall. The abbey had been among the more wealthy of the Dorset monasteries, with a substantial landholding in the county and extensive sheep runs on the surrounding hills, but its income had fallen during the later fifteenth and early sixteenth centuries as a consequence of leasing.[1]

A mid-eighteenth-century house stands at the head of Abbey Street, developed out of the abbey's south gatehouse, and behind it are the guest house and porch tower. Built by abbot Thomas Sam (1497–1509), the porch is essentially a pendant to that of 1498 at Milton Abbey and the tower of 1528 at Forde Abbey. It combines the restrained character of the two-storey entry at Milton with the ebulliently decorated three-storey tower at Forde. Built of Ham stone in about 1505, Sam's porch is impressive but less showy than that at Forde, though it follows the same form of diagonal angle buttresses, a single-bay entry passage, a two-storey oriel with canted sides, and an embattled parapet (mid-nineteenth-century rebuild). The outer entry arch is four-centred with dominant animal stops. The porch is fan-vaulted with a central shield carrying the rebus of

PLATE 217 Cerne Abbey: hall porch

abbot Sam. The oriel has two windows of five cinquefoil ogee lights with two lines of quatrefoil-enclosed shields – at the base and between the windows – with the arms of England, the duchy of Cornwall, and local families, and the rebus of abbot Sam.[2] The stair approach and heated porter's lodge (with heated room above) lay to one side of the entry passage. The stair accessed the two rooms tiered above the entry, both with plain side fireplaces. Abbot Charde's tower at Forde was essentially that at Cerne writ larger – in scale, in decoration, and in flamboyance.

A small portion remains of the contemporary hall of indeterminate size, against the rear face of the tower. The square-headed doorway in it is decorated with the arms of the abbey and the duchy of Cornwall in the spandrels. Above there are a decorated string course and two groups of wall shafts presumably supporting the roof trusses. The nearby window is late sixteenth century.[3]

NOTES
1 VCH, *Dorset*, II (1908) 53–8; M. P. Brown, *The Book of Cerne* (1996).
2 Oliver and Oliver (1938) 18–22.
3 The supposed guest house nearby was built in the mid-fifteenth century with alternating bands of stone and knapped flint. Of two storeys, 53 feet by 17 feet internally, it is in two parts with a stone divisional wall but lacks floors and has a modern roof. The eastern area has a first-floor oriel with transomed cinquefoil lights, relatively modest compared with the porch tower. A fireplace taken from here and now in the adjacent house is claimed to have the initials of abbot John Vanne (1458–70).

V. L. Oliver and V. F. M. Oliver, *Proc. Dorset N. H. and A. Soc.* 59 (1938) 15–25
RCHM, *Dorset*, I (1952) 77–9

CLEEVE ABBEY, Somerset

The abbey at Cleeve was a late Cistercian foundation established in 1198 by the earl of Lincoln as a colony of Revesby Abbey. It prospered, with a building sequence spanning the greater part of the thirteenth century, though its numbers declined during the fourteenth century, particularly after the Black Death, coinciding with a period of indiscipline and financial instability.[1] Matters were taken in hand during the fifty-year rule of abbot David Junyer (1437–87), so that there were fifteen monks and two corrodians when this locally well-loved house was dissolved in 1536. The church has been reduced to foundation level but the claustral ranges are as fine as any in England and Wales. The roofed south range, in particular, warrants inclusion in this volume, for it retains one of the most sumptuous halls of the mid-fifteenth century above two self-contained lodgings, with a further group of rooms that were probably the personal accommodation of the abbot.

The plan and character of this major Cistercian rebuild is best appreciated from the south side rather than from the cloister which retained the lower part of the original thirteenth-century structure. Its greater height than the adjacent ranges (dormitory and farmhouse) is immediate, as is the line of stepped buttresses on this side, for the range was rebuilt in two storeys with a three-storey residential end block. Apart from a through passage at the east end, the ground floor consists of a pair of spacious lodgings with their chimney flues concealed in two of the buttresses. Above are the great windows of the dining hall, with the pulpit stair projection in the penultimate bay converted into a post-medieval chimney stack. The smaller windows at the west end light the hall lobby and the abbot's private rooms. The whole is built of local stone with a twentieth-century replacement tiled roof. The range was built at right angles to the thirteenth-century refectory and sits astride its northern end. Its foundations have been exposed, as well as the spectacular tiled floor of *c*.1260, for this was a ground-floor hall, whereas abbot Junyer wanted a more fashionable first-floor hall next to his new lodgings. From the cloister court only the line of five hall windows makes a show, with the retained entry and lavabo next to it matching the simplicity of the adjacent thirteenth-century dormitory.

THE LODGINGS

The pair of ground-floor lodgings under the dining hall are similar in layout and particularly generous in scale. The cloister entry immediately accessed the spacious outer chamber, 22 feet by 15 feet, lit by a single shuttered light each side of the end-wall fireplace with straight-headed lintel. The adjacent doorway led to the narrower, unheated inner chamber with single light and window seats. The barrel-vaulted garderobe next to this doorway was flushed by an external drain. Both rooms have renewed beamed ceilings, and retain considerable plaster evidence, and a cobbled floor from seventeenth-century stable use.

If the first lodging was luxurious, the second one was even more superior. Its approach is angled, creating a small lobby with trefoil-

PLATE 218 Cleeve Abbey: dining hall with lodgings below from the cloister, dormitory range

decorated ceiling, possibly partitioned from the outer chamber to give it greater privacy and comfort. This heated room is slightly wider (16½ feet) and has two shuttered windows of two transomed lights with trefoil heads. It is linked to the inner room by a well-lit passage, flanked by the garderobe with storage space under the hall stair opposite. The unheated inner chamber has lost the dressed stonework of its two-light window, but retains the ceiling beams, plasterwork, and cobbled floor as before. It had access to the abbey kitchen next door.[2]

This fine pair of lodgings are as generous as any in a contemporary private mansion. They may have been occupied by senior monks in the abbey's hierarchy or by corrodians, wealthy outsiders who paid the abbey a lump sum of money to provide them with board and lodgings in their old age.[3]

DINING HALL

The mid-thirteenth-century entrance to the ground-floor refectory was retained to serve the new one built 200 years later, though now opening on to a flight of steps curving towards the multi-columned hall entry with depressed head. It opens into one of the finest and least-altered medieval halls in southern England. Smaller than its predecessor,[4] abbot Junyer's hall is flooded with light from both sides but particularly from the south. These larger windows of three cinquefoils lights and multi-cusped heads are transomed, with a line of glazed quatrefoils above the lower cinquefoil lights. The lower part of the five north-facing windows was always blank to clear the cloister roof. No stained glass survives.

The seventeenth-century fireplace destroyed the pulpit for meal-time readings but the doorway and stair leading to it survive. Traces

PLATE 219 Cleeve Abbey: dining hall range from the south

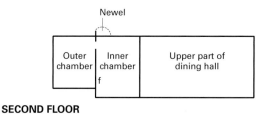

SECOND FLOOR

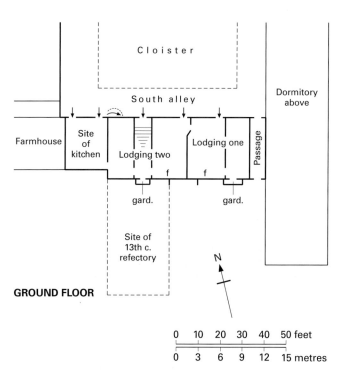

FIRST FLOOR

GROUND FLOOR

| 0 | 10 | 20 | 30 | 40 | 50 feet |

| 0 | 3 | 6 | 9 | 12 | 15 metres |

FIGURE 125 Cleeve Abbey: site plans of south range

of the end wall Crucifixion wall painting above the dais remained until the beginning of the twentieth century, but nothing survived by 1950 and the walls have been replastered and colour-washed throughout.

The glory of this hall is its roof, divided into ten bays by alternate principal and subsidiary arch-braced collar trusses rising from larger and smaller corbels of angels holding shields. The embattled wall plates are decorated with vine leaves, with a line of carved angels projecting from the feet of the trusses. The sides of the principal trusses are decorated with trefoil-shaped arches with fifty foliated bosses at the junction of the purlins. The chases remain for boarding the roof between the trusses to create a panelled wagon ceiling, but there is no evidence that this final stage was carried out. Nor is there any sign of a central hearth or louvre.

ABBOT'S LODGINGS

The sequence of four rooms at the lower end of the hall is prefaced by a lobby at the head of the dining hall stair. The first room is a painted chamber with access to the gallery opening from the hall to the second room, drastically modified for post-medieval farmhouse use. Above this pair of rooms and hall stair are two chambers open to the roof. These four rooms are divided between the end of the mid-fifteenth-century south range and the much lower seventeenth-century farmhouse, which was also set back from the earlier structure. However, the north wall of all four rooms is entirely fifteenth century, confirming that this end of the farmhouse is contemporary with the dining hall[5] even though the remainder is entirely post-medieval.

The waiting area with plastered walls at the head of the dining hall stair is well lit by a transomed two-light window, and has benches and a tiled floor (only the wood seating survives).

The painted chamber is a narrow room with a two-light window and a substantial fireplace. During the years close to 1500, the wall opposite was painted with an illustration of a legend from *Gesta Romanorum*, a book of moralising tales. Using mainly red and brown colours, a double-arched bridge was painted in outline, spanning a fish-filled river. An elderly man prays in the centre of the bridge, flanked by a lion and a dragon. St Catherine and St Margaret stand on either side of the bridge. The remainder of the room was also painted.

The 3½ foot wide gallery opening from the lower end of the hall is spanned by three stone arches marking the inner stone wall and the post and panel partition. Two of the arches have wall painting and graffiti evidence.

The entry and adjacent wall to the second room are contemporary but otherwise featureless, reflecting its post-medieval farmhouse use. However, an external building line and west-facing wooden-framed window internally indicate that the present farmhouse was a seventeenth-century addition abutting the earlier rebuild.

The room immediately above is equally plain and retains no fifteenth-century features outside the blank north wall and adjacent doorway to the spacious second room above the painted chamber, gallery, and hall stair. This was a high-status chamber with opposing twin-transomed lights with cinquefoil heads, shutter rebates, and pins in the opposing outer walls. It retains the fireplace, fragments of wall paintings, and a continuation in simplified form of the dining hall roof. A steep, narrow newel, now half-ruined, gave direct access to this chamber from the south cloister walk and nearby kitchen. It was never the prime approach to such an élite chamber but was primarily for service use.

This body of rooms divides into two groups. The hall lobby prefaces the heated painted chamber. This was a self-contained unit, for the secondary door to the gallery is a conversion from the original hatch. The window is also more modest than in the other group of rooms. It may have served as an office, an exchequer room, or the abbot's secretariat. It is unlikely to have been used for receiving guests or social entertainment, especially as the gallery provided a separate approach to the second group of rooms. The first one would have been a withdrawing chamber where the abbot could entertain visitors in some privacy. A modern replacement stair is the approach to his more private rooms above, with that over the painted chamber of considerable status. It is probable that these three rooms were occupied by the abbot but there is no conclusive evidence. They are smaller than the comparable lodgings at Muchelney and Forde, but their position in relation to the dining hall and kitchen as well as the high quality of the uppermost room make them an appropriate suite for the abbot to withdraw from the hall, entertain his guests in some privacy, and retire to a chamber comparable to his position in the abbey's hierarchy.

The last abbot, William Dovell (1507–36), made some changes to the earlier gatehouse (pl. 199),[6] but during the early 1530s he replaced the west range with a new glazed cloister walk and converted the former lay brothers' quarters into further accommodation for himself beyond Junyer's rooms.[7] It was this area of the abbey that was converted into a country house during the mid-sixteenth century, extending from the monastic dining hall to Junyer's and Dovell's apartments, now sumptuously appointed.[8]

OVERVIEW

The tranquil setting of Cleeve Abbey is one of its many special qualities, as are the spectacular late thirteenth-century tiled pavements and extensive wall paintings. Surmounting all are the high standard, extent, and remarkable roofed condition of the claustral ranges. They are among the most extensive and best preserved in England. They show how the early Cistercian ideal of architectural and domestic austerity became modified by later generations. For this abbey enjoyed a revival in its fortunes, in the numbers of its community as well as in financial terms between about 1430 and 1530 which was expressed architecturally in the wholehearted rebuilding of the south range.

The resurgence of building activity across the country after the lull of the early fifteenth century extended to monastic foundations just as much as to secular houses and parish churches.[9] Cleeve was the exemplar in the Somerset region, followed by Glastonbury and Montacute later in the century and by the abbatial houses at Muchelney and Forde under the early Tudors. The disappearance of lay brethren, the financial benefits of corrodian accommodation, the increasing desire for comfort, and the enhanced social position of the abbot were all factors in the fundamental restructuring at Cleeve. Though the Cistercians had developed the plan of south ranges with the dining hall on a north–south axis, the replacement was realigned on an east–west axis, and was smaller than its predecessor, given greater prominence by its raised position and elegant stair approach, and crowned with a spectacular roof with high-quality decorative elements that make it among the most satisfying of its period. This apartment could be used for a personal dining hall by the abbot in association with his own rooms as much as for the frater for the whole community. The two groups of lodgings provide a vivid contrast. The high standards and comfort of the lodgings for senior monks or for corrodians are comparable with any in a secular mansion, while the less well-preserved abbatial lodging is enhanced by the most important contemporary Cistercian painted decoration in England.

This work under the skilled capability of abbot Junyer may be

attributed to the middle years of the century. In the early 1450s, the chapel at Blue Anchor Bay was lost in a cliff fall. Junyer replaced it with one at Chapel Cleeve nearby, consecrated in 1455, together with a hospice for pilgrims south of it which has windows, a roof and a fireplace identical in character and detailing to the masonry and carpentry at the abbey.[10] Dendro dating in 2003 confirmed a felling date of 1430–59 for the dining hall roof timbers.[11] In sum, if it were not for the adjacent structures, the whole of the mid-fifteenth-century range at Cleeve Abbey – hall, private rooms, and lodgings – could be transferred to a secular environment for daily living without modification. It resembled 'more a comfortable country mansion than an establishment dedicated to spiritual progress through the denial of worldly comforts'.[12] This concern for creature comforts meant that hardly any changes were necessary a hundred years later, with even the Crucifixion above the hall dais retained throughout its Elizabethan and Jacobean use as a private dining room. As Cothay shows, none of the religious wall paintings in this part of the country would have been out of place in a late medieval secular context any more than they were subsequently.

NOTES
1 Gilyard-Beer (1960) 5.
2 Blocked in the eighteenth century when the cloister access was also forced through.
3 These rooms may have been occupied by the two corrodians recorded at the time of the Dissolution, John Mychell and Edward Walker, gentleman. The latter paid the large sum of £27 for his corrody. R. W. Dunning, 'The last days of Cleeve Abbey', in *The Church in Pre-Reformation Society*, ed. C. M. Barron and C. Harper-Bill (1985) 58–67.
4 51 feet by 22 feet compared with 71 feet by 26 feet.
5 The ground floor was originally the abbey kitchen, though nothing survives of its hearths except two bread ovens. The area above may have originally been the end part of the lay brothers' accommodation in the west range. The wall stubs visible from the cloister show that its roof was also much higher until the farmhouse modifications and extension. Farm use ceased by the close of the nineteenth century but the range continued to be inhabited until the 1940s.
6 This is basically a modest early thirteenth-century structure of outer lobby, originally with benches under the later infilled arches, a pair of central gates, and a vaulted rear passage with a single heated upper chamber. The porter's lodge was an east-facing extension with an almonry added on the west side during the fourteenth century, but both projections have been pulled down. During the early sixteenth century, Dovell upgraded the upper chamber with new windows, fireplace, and Somerset-type roof and at the same time added the external text and name panels under his gable niches and sculpture (rare survivals).
7 Kelly believes that the abbot's lodging probably replaced the lay brothers' accommodation in the west range from at least the fourteenth century: (2000) 450.
8 Kelly (2000).
9 D. Knowles, *The Religious Orders in England*, III (1959) 21–4.
10 Gilyard-Beer (1960) 8. The building has been converted into a house and was extended in 1913.
11 *Vern. Arch.* 34 (2003) 101.
12 J. H. Bettey, *Suppression of the Monasteries in the West Country* (1989) 15–16.

E. Buckle, *Proc. Somerset Arch. & N. H. Soc.* 35 (1889) 81–120
R. Gilyard-Beer, *Cleeve Abbey: Handbook* (1960)
S. Harrison, *Cleeve Abbey: Handbook* (2000)
F. Kelly, *Arch. Jour.* 157 (2000) 449–52

CLEVEDON COURT, Somerset

A mile from the shoreline of Clevedon, the Court is sited at the foot of a steep hill that is part of the 10 mile ridge from the Avon Gorge to its finger end near the sea. Facing the drained Somerset levels, the house is seen today against a heavily wooded backdrop, though the large oil painting of *c*.1720 in the house shows it in a bleaker landscape more akin to its late medieval setting.[1] The house was developed by three families. Its attribution to Sir John Clevedon in the years close to 1320 is based on architectural as much as documentary grounds. Sir John died in 1336, and after the death of his son forty years later, the property passed by marriage to the Wakes of Northampton by the mid-fifteenth century, and was held by them until 1630. In 1709, the house was purchased by the Bristol merchant Abraham Elton, whose successors still occupy it under the National Trust. Both families were responsible for two major development phases: the Wakes in the 1530s and late 1560s, and the Eltons in the 1730s and after a fire in 1882.

The layout of Sir John's house is immediately apparent – a hall and cross passage, flanked by chamber blocks at each end – but it is the scale that impresses. The cross passage is prefaced at both ends by two-storey porches while there are two further projections off the upper end of the hall. Much of this work survives in good state but the chamber blocks with their Tudor windows, finialed gables, and Renaissance elements are essentially the work of John Wake, completed by 1570.[2] The house, full of quirks and family stories, has yet to be subject to a detailed structural analysis so that the following account is provisional.

The fourteenth-century frontage was one of recessed planes, dominated by the two-storey porch and hall bay with contrasting-positioned buttresses, opposing angle newels extending to the roof, and plain pitched parapets. The entry porch, one of the largest of its period, has outer and inner moulded jambs, two-centred head, moulded hood with end stops and, surprisingly, a portcullis groove. The recessed hall wall is almost filled with an eighteen-light window under the relieving arch of its predecessor, for this is an early sixteenth-century insertion (with replacement head) whereas nearly all the other windows on this side of the house are a generation later. The exceptions are the single trefoil lights to the upper room of the porch, and the phantasmagorical chapel windows in the upper half of the assertive bay at the dais end of the hall. This bay is ashlar-built as against rubble stonework elsewhere. Furthermore, porch, hall, and bay all rise from a well-defined plinth, not carried across the end chamber blocks, for they are essentially Elizabethan rebuilds, the offices front crowned with a gable supporting the Wake emblem.

Turning to the rear, the porch at the further end of the cross passage is narrower but slightly longer than the principal entry. It has a modest version of the front doorway, a similar stone newel but only to the chamber over the porch, and repeats the portcullis facility. The two-storey bay at the north-west end of the hall is also diagonally buttressed, has a pitched plain parapet, and may have originally held the stair to the withdrawing chamber, though it has been more heavily altered than any other elements.

The front entry, a commanding arch with continuous double chamfer and hood terminating in damaged stops, opens into the cross passage. To the right is a classic example of triple service entries to the offices, with the slightly higher central one opening

PLATE 220 Clevedon Court: entry porch, hall, and chapel block

into a kitchen passage. With single continuous chamfers, they are grouped together under a continuous hood mould terminating in head stops, a feature repeated at Penshurst Place (*c*.1338) and more elaborately at Northborough Manor (early 1330s).

Even with its tall screen and inserted ceiling, the hall, 40 feet by 26 feet, still retains its original scale and dominating focal position of the house, externally and internally. This apartment reflects all the key phases in the house's development. The hall would have originally had a central hearth with the smoke escaping from a louvre, but the gables above the ceiling retain chimney shafts over the three-light trefoil windows with blocked evidence at the service end of a five-light window filling the lower part of the gable. However, an inspection by the National Trust's architect in 1994 concluded that these medieval windows and chimney shafts had been salvaged from the hall and withdrawing room. They were probably set up in the second Wake period as post-medieval light and ventilation improvements to the hall. They were not primary smoke-vents and there is no evidence for such a feature locally. The fireplace and windows are of *c*.1530 by Richard Wake (d.1558), followed by his son's overlarge lobby doorcase of *c*.1570. The plaster screen and coved ceiling were added in the 1730s, destroying the roof timbers of Sir John's hall, while the high 'spy' window is an 1883 insertion. The south bay, approached from the dais through a commanding archway similar to the inner entry of the front porch, retains a twin trefoil-light side window with an Elizabethan replacement window to the front.

Only the shadow remains of the upper chamber block, for it was virtually rebuilt in the late 1560s when the single room at each level was divided into a west lobby and library (ground) and stair landing and state bedroom (first). An attic floor was added at the same time.[3]

Rear court

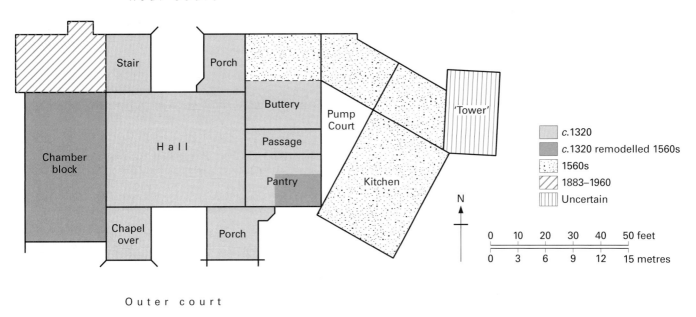

Outer court

FIGURE 126 Clevedon Court: site plan

Were it not for one feature, it might be thought that the whole structure was an Elizabethan rebuild. However, after the fire of 1882, a fourteenth-century doorway was revealed at first-floor level in the 3 foot thick north wall, with a single chamfer, two-centred head, and hood mould ending in better-preserved head stops of a man and woman than elsewhere. This was the entry to the withdrawing chamber from a stair presumably extending from the projection north of the hall dais on the site of the present mid-eighteenth-century stair, even though the approach to it from the hall is mean and unconvincing, particularly when compared with the great arch opposite.[4]

The withdrawing chamber is the sole approach to the chapel in the upper half of the hall bay. The entry is plain, with an adjacent recess and newel to the roof, but the room is overwhelmed by the two ogee reticulated windows, a network of cusped quatrefoils with half-quatrefoils round the edges.[5] The burnished glass was inserted in 1883, a few months after the trefoil-headed piscina with its broken bowl, the altar slab next to it, and the oblong east window above had been discovered; it had been blocked and plastered over until then. The fourth wall has a two-light trefoil window looking down into the hall for the benefit of staff assembled there to participate in services, for the parish church, 2 miles distant, was often inaccessible through flooding in the winter. The room retains its pitched roof with moulded wall plates and cross beams.

Only the framework of the offices and chamber block at the lower end of the hall is original. The pantry has been converted into a display room. The central passage is filled with a Victorian stair, though its exit jambs are traceable in the Pump Court. The buttery, shaded from the sun, originally extended only as far as a wall running from the north-west corner of the Pump Court, where its angle overrides the jamb of a Caernarvon arch (see below). However, part of the area was incorporated in the late 1560s extension and the remainder left as a narrow passage spanned by two

nineteenth-century medieval-style arches. The upper floor would have been approached from the front newel which also accesses the room over the porch with the blocked head of its original front window and roof of moulded wall plates and cross beam. The rooms above the offices and those at attic level are entirely 1560s and later.

The most puzzling architectural problems at Clevedon Court lie in the buildings round the small triangular Pump Court east of Sir John's house. His detached kitchen would have been here, facing the central passage exit and well. The present kitchen building, in use until 1957, is a large room at an oblique angle to the remainder of the Court, with no pre-Tudor evidence except for the entry and this seems to have been inserted from elsewhere during the drastic 1960 restoration by the National Trust for the Elton family. This high-ceilinged but much-altered building has Tudor and later windows and an end-wall fireplace, but the stack with its double chimneys is nineteenth century, as are the attic rooms. The structure is more probably a sixteenth-century replacement to the four-teenth-century kitchen, rather than fulfilling the claim that it is an earlier stone-built great hall.[6]

In the north-west corner of Pump Court is an early feature, a shoulder-arched doorway (one shoulder missing), possibly early fourteenth century but with its left jamb overridden by the offices block of c.1320.[7] An even earlier structure may be the four-storey 'tower', abutting the Tudor/Victorian range and a corner of the kitchen but unrelated to either of them. Tall but small, only 24 feet by 16 feet externally with 3 feet thick walls, it is rubble-built with dressed quoins of a local stone unused elsewhere in the house. It has a remade ground floor entry, an inserted chimney stack, no early woodwork, and a raked roof capping the walls. It lacks individuality outside the oblong loops lighting the upper floors, but though it has been attributed to the second half of the thirteenth century,[8] the loops are similar to those lighting Sir John's newels. Its date and purpose are enigmatic but it does not relate directly to Sir John's work.

OVERVIEW

The manor of Clevedon had been held by the family of that name since the late twelfth century, with Sir John as its holder by 1303. In 1323, bishop Drokensford of Wells inducted ten young men in the chapel of Sir John Clevedon while the latter's will of 1336 included the bequest of a chalice 'to the chapel of St Peter in my manor'.[9] A construction date of about 1320 is reasonable in a house that has since become one of modest taste and understated comfort, for the Elton family have never been given to elegance. What makes the Court special for the medievalist is the scale and quality of the house, with the different stonework suggesting phased development during the later years of Edward II's reign. There are two spaciously proportioned porches to the cross passage rather than one, indicative of a rear as well as an outer court no longer obvious today. The hall proportions are generous[10] and there is the uncommon feature of two deep projections at the dais end of the hall rather than the more usual one, with the secluded south projection possibly an inner sanctum for the owner and his family.[11] Similar large bays did not occur for another half-century, with those of Gaunt at Kenilworth and Hertford castles followed by regional examples at Coker Court, Tickenham Court, and Norrington Manor.

The accommodation is generous and breaks down into a number of self-contained units, particularly at the lower end where the upper porches were individually approached. Doorways, windows, and parapets were liberally scaled, workmanship was boldly conceived but with delicate touches such as the moulded plinth, hood stops, and stepped buttresses, but the explosion of reticulated tracery in the chapel is in total contrast with the sobriety displayed elsewhere.[12] There is no obvious explanation, any more than there is for the portcullises, an early example of a military element in a social context. Apart from its vulnerable position overlooked by rising ground at the rear, there is no evidence that the house was moated or in any other way defended. The oil painting of *c*.1720 tells us much about the outer walled court, and that it held a medieval barn. The embattled wall, like that still at Sutton Court, ran up the slope to a second, inner court wall immediately in front of the house. The barn appears to have been demolished and rebuilt *c*.1800 in a corresponding position well to the east, and the inner court wall was taken down. Similar flanking garden court walls to the rear of the house were also removed or reduced, and survive only in part. There is a less-altered section running north from the tower. This leaves the uncertain impression of secure porches as the disconnected elements of a formerly more secure enclave. Even so, were the portcullises protection against raiders or pirates, or were they a symbolic statement, a status symbol, or a theatrical gesture to be raised for an approaching guest or lowered each evening for house discipline?

NOTES

1 J. Harris, *The Artist and the Country House* (1979) 117.

2 The ground-floor chimney piece had the initials and arms of John Wake, while heraldic glass in the window was dated 1570. Sir Arthur Elton, *Proc. Somerset Arch. and N. H. Soc.* 27 (1881). Both were destroyed in the fire of 1882.

3 The west front is a 1960 rebuild after an unwanted twenty-room Victorian west range had been pulled down.

4 It is possible that a similar arch to the stair has been infilled and plastered over. All the literature refers to an outside approach to the first floor,

highly unlikely in an élite house by this date. Though the evidence for an internal newel by the west lobby arises from the Victorian curved recesses associated with the inserted 'spy' window and revealed stonework above, it may incorporate vestigial material of the original newel access to the withdrawing chamber.

5 Any thoughts that this ebullient tracery was a consequence of Victorian enthusiasm is dispelled by the oil painting of *c*.1720 where it is detailed.

6 The view of Sir Arthur Elton noted by Oswald (1955) 1673, and by Elton and Elton (1962) 6. The Trust's architect examined the finials of the kitchen gable from scaffolding and found intact sixteenth-century roughcast below some nineteenth/twentieth-century replica work in concrete. His view is that the kitchen block and adjoining wings are entirely Wake II period and represent the deliberate introduction of diagonal sixteenth-century planning to the orthogonal medieval house, effecting a pragmatic connection of servery to house via the Pump Court and making a ready link to a new use of the tower.

7 Shouldered arches occur as late as 1341 in the gatehouse of the Bishop's Palace, Wells.

8 See note 6.

9 Episcopal Register.

10 The slightly later hall at Haddon Hall (*c*.1330–50) was of a similar scale, 42 feet by 27 feet.

11 The similar projection at the contemporary but small-scale Abbot's Grange at Broadway had an independent ground-floor room below the chapel.

12 Because of this sharp contrast, the possibility needs to be explored whether these windows were a replacement by Sir Edmund Clevedon in *c*.1340. The work was probably carried out by a mason from Wells Cathedral, where the tracery is closer to the ogee form of the choir east window of *c*.1340 than the lady chapel windows of *c*.1320. Woodlands Manor (*c*.1330) also has a window with a similar reticulated head.

J. Collinson, *The History and Antiquities of Somerset*, III (1791) 166–9

Sir Ambrose Elton, *Proc. Somerset Arch. and N. H. Soc.* 45 (1899) 14–20

A. Oswald, *Country Life* (June/July 1955)

A. Elton and M. Elton, *Clevedon Court: Guidebook* (1962)

COKER COURT, Somerset

Pevsner's comment that Coker Court is 'an uncommonly interesting and rewarding house'[1] is particularly apposite, for it combines fifteenth-century splendour with eighteenth-century sobriety. It stands on a narrow terrace cut out of rising ground next to the parish church of East Coker overlooking the Yeo vale, with a landscaped approach that replaced the late medieval forecourt.

The manor of East and West Coker came into the hands of the Courtenay family in 1306. The property was divided in 1377 when Hugh Courtenay, earl of Devon, willed East Coker to his younger son, Sir Philip Courtenay of Powderham (d.1406).[2] Held by this younger branch of the family for over two centuries, the present hall and offices range of Coker Court was redeveloped during the early fifteenth century. Sold by the Courtenays in 1591, the manor house was purchased by archdeacon Helyar in 1616, who made a number of alterations and additions shortly afterwards. It was the mid-eighteenth-century successor who replaced the family apartments and rooms round one and a half sides of the earlier courtyard between 1766 and 1770 with a grand stair and suite of reception and private rooms under the direction of Joseph Dixon of London.[3] The remaining two halves of the west and north ranges were filled

PLATE 221 Coker Court: hall and porch from the north

an otherwise earlier hall. So does the contemporary columned frame and overmantel added against the earlier mural fireplace with its square-headed lintel.

The body of the hall is lit by tall two-light transomed windows essentially filling each bay, three on the east (entrance) side and two on the west (courtyard) side. They lack window seats but have bold trefoil lights below a pair of elongated quatrefoils under a hood mould. One of the courtyard-facing windows was blocked when the eighteenth-century staircase hall was erected, and the other was reinstated in the late nineteenth century, retaining the original sill. The entry door mouldings and bold trefoil heads of the hall windows suggest the first quarter of rather than the mid-fifteenth century.

The hall was totally Georgianised in the eighteenth century, with shuttered windows, classical door frames, a plain flat ceiling, and an enclosed balcony, all removed in the 1890s. The five-bay roof, now of uniform chocolate brown colour, seems to be the original one, subject to 'the alterations we did to the house [that included] renewing a good many of the oak beams that were rotten'.[4] The roof is of a common Somerset type, with plain wall plates, principal and intermediate trusses of arch-braced collars, and two lines of wind braces. However, it was enhanced with some decorative detailing, including trefoil cusping above the principal collars and an upper line of paired wind braces, but the corbels were hacked off when the Georgian ceiling was inserted so that the six main trusses look unsupported.

Opening off the dais end is a generously proportioned bay window, 17 feet by 11 feet, step-approached, with a plain high arch. Diagonally buttressed, it was lit on two sides by windows similar to those in the body of the hall though the slightly lower one was blocked in the eighteenth century and has lost its tracery. The panelled roof is supported on four almost square-headed trusses rising from foliated and crenellated corbels. Similar to the rear arches of the parlour windows in the abbot's lodging at Muchelney Abbey, this roof is probably a late fifteenth-century insertion when the chamber above was created (now bathroom).

This is a spacious, dignified apartment of excellent proportions, with an early example of a dais bay window and a four-light gable window lighting the roof over the dais area. The remade doorways at the upper end of the hall may reflect the original approach to the family apartments but they were totally destroyed in the mid-eighteenth century.[5] The replacement two-storey and attic south range with its plain symmetrical and pedimented seven-bay Georgian façade holds three handsome reception rooms with high-quality fireplaces and three comfortable bedrooms above, while the shorter west range is three-storeyed with attics. To the rear is a large classical staircase hall, entered from the medieval hall and overlapping its exterior face.

The ground-floor offices at the lower end of the hall were remodelled as a single room in the early seventeenth century[6] with early twentieth-century fireplace, window, and ceiling replacements when the hipped roof above was rebuilt as a vertical gable end. Yet it is not without interest. The three doorways in the cross passage consist of two identical single-chamfer entries with four-centred heads and a slightly taller third doorway. This last opened into a left-angled passage with original two-light courtyard-facing window, leading to the kitchen with its 11 feet wide hearth and four-centred lintel. The two spacious offices, now a panelled parlour, would have been entered by the adjacent doorways, with one of the

in 1900 by the Heneage family during their substantive restoration of the house. This essentially four-phase residence was divided into two in the 1970s when the medieval hall and Georgian range were converted into one living unit, and the offices block and late nineteenth-century infill were made into a second home.

The house is built of local Ham stone with an early twentieth-century replacement stone tile roof. The buttressed hall range is on a grand scale, a smaller version of that at Dartington Hall, with the hall similarly free of internal furnishings. The porch is plain, step-approached but lacking side benches, windows, or decorative ceiling. The outer entry arch has continuous double wave chamfer to two-centred head and hood: the inner arch is a little more elaborate with continuous double hollow chamfer, two-centred head, and foliated stops. The opposing cross-passage doorway is similar, but without the hood and stops, and was protected by a single rather than a double drawbar, though with the added rarity of a squint to the inner court.

The hall, 55 feet by 25 feet, is on a generous scale. The cross passage is separated from the body of the apartment by a fine early seventeenth-century screen with two studded openings separated by coupled Doric columns. Like those at Audley End and Stonor Park, this soberly detailed screen contributes a contrasting note to

PLATE 222 Coker Court: hall interior

offices retaining its hatch from the kitchen. However, there is no evidence how the generously proportioned upper chamber was reached.[7] It is possible that there was a fourth doorway in the cross passage close to the porch, now blank walling, which accessed a destroyed stair. Even so, this leaves the approach to the unheated but well-lit room above the porch unexplained[8] for any direct entry from the chamber over the offices was physically impossible. It is most likely that the original screen at Coker Court was a rare example of a ceiled one providing access to the porch room, replaced in the early seventeenth century by the present door in the middle of the end wall.

Coker Court displays a balanced late medieval façade with the porch projection mirrored by the dais bay, and tall windows flooding the hall with light. But what is most impressive about this house is its scale. The hall is larger than that of a knight at Haddon Hall, a magnate at Minster Lovell, or the Courtenay family at Powderham Castle. Not much smaller than the episcopal halls at Bishop's Waltham and Croydon palaces, it is generously proportioned, relatively complete, and little known. In 1473, the house was held by Sir William Courtenay of Powderham and Coker (d.1485), with his two sons at Muchelney Abbey, presumably for educational purposes.[9] The house was possibly developed by his grandfather, Sir

John Courtenay, about whom little is known. As his elder brother held the family seat at Powderham after the death of Sir Philip in 1406, Sir John Courtenay may have built Coker Court as his base immediately after his marriage, but his early death in 1415 before his brother, who had no heirs, meant that Sir John's son, Sir Philip (d.1463), became the head of this branch of the Courtenay family, bringing the Coker and Powderham estates together again. Possibly influenced by the hall range at Dartington (c.1388–1400), the family quarters at Coker Court would almost certainly have been as extensive as those of the offices and kitchen area but probably not so large as their eighteenth-century replacement.

Sir Philip's son, William, member of parliament for Somerset in 1455–6, was living at Coker in 1458 when he received a pardon for his Yorkist sympathies. In 1471–2, Sir William's bailiff made payments of 16d. for glazing the stair window and 2s. 6d. to the tiler for pointing the east side of Sir William's chamber.[10] There is little doubt that the Court was always a courtyard house, with the late nineteenth-century additions replacing older buildings. But in addition, Coker Court, like Brympton d'Evercy and Thame Park, enjoys that delightful contrast between a substantive late medieval range and an imposing classical structure of uniformity and restraint at a right-angle to it.

NOTES

1 *South and West Somerset* (1958) 162.
2 Sir Matthew Latham, *The Annals of West Coker* (1957) 135, 140.
3 Dunning (1991) 31–2.
4 Tipping (1909) 25.
5 The upper part of a window with cinquefoil lights and traceried head, now used as the back of a garden seat against the offices wall, may well have come from this range.
6 Opening from it is a scrumptious panelled and plaster-ceiled parlour of *c*.1620 by archdeacon Helyar (d.1645).
7 Now a featureless corridor and two bedrooms, one with a Jacobean fireplace. Late Victorian photographs show a two-light transomed window in the east (entrance) wall with a small window below lighting this side of the offices.
8 Formerly with windows on three sides. The archdeacon was responsible for inserting the Helyar arms in the lower lights of the front-facing window and the cross on the gable head.
9 Tipping (1909) 21.
10 Dunning (1991) 28. He also spent 33s. 4d. on the great garden and a close under the court in 1474–5 and 6s. 6d. on a bridge to the park in 1509–10, *ibid*.

H. A. Tipping, *Country Life* (January 1909)
R. Dunning, *Some Somerset Country Houses* (1991) 27–32

COMPTON CASTLE, Devon

Like the Hastings' residence at Ashby de la Zouch, the Gilberts' fourteenth-century house at Compton is a rare example of an undefended property converted well over a hundred years later into a fortified residence. Architecturally, the house divides into three building periods – an early to mid-fourteenth-century hall with upper and lower cross wings, mid-fifteenth-century replacement cross wings with major extensions, and the substantial defensive additions of a date and purpose that will be considered shortly.

Except for a 145-year gap, the house has been held by the Gilberts for nearly 700 years. The manor was in the hands of the Comptons from the early twelfth to the early fourteenth century when Joan, daughter and co-heir of William Compton, married Geoffrey Gilbert of Totnes. There was a break in the Gilbert holding between 1785 and 1930, when Commander Gilbert repurchased it and was responsible for its resuscitation during the following twenty-five years. This fundamental restoration paralleled that of the Elmhirsts at Dartington Hall nearby, on a smaller scale but similarly encompassing the reconstruction of the hall to restore the integrity of the building. Unlike John Holand's mansion, the interior of Compton Castle is not particularly revealing except as an example of mid twentieth-century 'historic-style' furnishing. Interest primarily centres on the architectural development of the house and its highly individual character.

Compton is built of limestone rubble with green schist and sandstone dressings, and Beer stone used internally. It initially consisted of a hall flanked by solar and service rooms but the hall was pulled down between 1750 and 1755 leaving the property broken-backed, with the later cross wings isolated. The hall was rebuilt for Commander Gilbert to plans prepared by F. A. Kay in 1954–5 using the original foundations and incorporating recovered elements of

stonework.[1] There was never any preliminary entry porch but parts of the cross-passage doorways are original, with continuous moulded jambs and two-centred heads under a plain hood. The hall, 42 feet by 31 feet internally, retains its original end walls. That at the lower end has a central pair of service doorways with hollow chamfer and two-centred head, with a third original one further south to a later newel. The hall windows consisted of a quatrefoil above two-transomed lights – the upper with ogee trefoil heads were glazed, and the lower with shouldered heads were shuttered. Their form was as determined from recovered stonework, as were the rear arches. The pitch and form of the four-bay roof of arch-braced collar trusses were determined by end-wall evidence, but the oak screen, panelling, and mural fireplace were reconstructions – the screen copied from an example in the V & A Museum and the fireplace almost certainly an addition to the room's original plan. On architectural grounds, the hall may be attributed to the early to mid-fourteenth century, most probably to the years following Joan Compton's marriage between 1311 and 1329 to Geoffrey Gilbert (d.1349), member of parliament for Totnes in 1326.

Part of the original doorway jamb with hollow chamfer and two-centred head survived at the upper end of the hall, opening on to the reconstructed stair turret to the upper chamber block. The ground floor is basically contemporary in scale with the hall and it is assumed there was originally a single chamber above, but the two upper floors are a rebuild of the early to mid-fifteenth century, when the chapel was added to the north and the chamber tower with second newel to the south-west. A similar tower had been an integral part of the upper residential block of Powderham Castle (*c*.1400). All the rooms have retained their doorways with two-centred heads and flat jambs, and fireplaces with plain lintels, except for the earlier one supported on half-octagonal jambs in the first-floor withdrawing chamber. Some of the higher windows retain their cinquefoil heads, but the timber-framed windows, floors, and roofs are mid-twentieth-century replacements.

Compton's early to mid-fifteenth century expansion encompassed both ends of the house, following the three-storey precept of Dartington Hall (*c*.1388–1400). It may have been the work of William Gilbert, who died in 1428, but was more probably undertaken by Otho Gilbert, who came of age in 1438 and died in 1494.[2] Not only did the redevelopment provide substantially more accommodation, but because of Compton's position in a hollow, the uppermost rooms were among the best lit. This unusually included one above the chapel with fireplace and cinquefoil lights.[3] The chapel was relatively modest, with identical east and north windows of four cinquefoil lights with moulded capitals and traceried heads, a plain vaulted ceiling, a two-light opening from the withdrawing chamber (and a squint in the room below), a cinquefoil piscina, two brackets and the remains of a Beer stone reredos. This chapel was similar in position, scale, and features to its near contemporary at Bradley Manor (1427) but is of higher architectural quality.[4]

The rebuilding of the services and kitchen at the lower end of the hall and their expansion as a three-storey residential range seems to have been a second phase of this mid-fifteenth-century activity. The two service rooms are now entirely modern, though fulfilling a similar function to the twentieth-century kitchen created in the otherwise featureless 'steward's room'. This was a frontal extension paralleling the chapel. A three-storey link block and kitchen were

PLATE 223 Compton Castle: defensive frontage

added at the rear – their construction in line with the services was physically impractical. Like the chapel, the kitchen rises through two storeys, with a barrel-vaulted ceiling and chamber over. Lit by a small barred window (like those at Cotehele) and a large seventeenth-century one, the far end is filled with a broad hearth with three flues and two side ovens. The ground floor of the link block is a passage with kitchen serving-hatch and a barrel-vaulted store under residential rooms. These and the remainder of the first- and second-floor apartments provide the present living accommodation for the Gilbert family, with nearly all the rooms lit by twentieth-century timber-framed windows (trefoil slits in the newel turret) but four with fifteenth-century Beer stone fireplaces with kerbs.

The third phase in the expansion of Compton Castle was equally expensive. It was a three-pronged programme of defensive measures – the addition of four towers to the main building, the erection of a defensive frontage, and the whole protected by a fortified enclosure.

The entry frontage was defended by two towers added at the further corners of the chapel and the 'steward's room' respectively, while further towers were added to the east side, one extending the store room and the other at the south-east corner of the kitchen. None of these towers is bonded to the building it abuts. They all project boldly, are broader at the base than the head, and are buttressed, machicolated, and four-storeyed, with pitched roofs so that they rise above the immediate landscape.[5] The frontal towers, 1 and 2, have ground-floor slits angled to the approach and are lit by narrow single lights. Those at second- and third-floor levels have replacement cinquefoil heads distorting the utilitarian character of these towers. Tower 3 shows their original form and placement. The three faces of towers 1 and 2 were provided with corbel-supported machicolated bays at second-floor level with a single light and sloping roof. Tower 3 was primarily a garderobe tower, but with well-preserved ground-floor gun loops with iron stays. Tower 4 is the least altered, with the ground- and first-floors barrel vaulted, and with three-barred rectangular windows and gun loops at ground level, and no fireplaces.

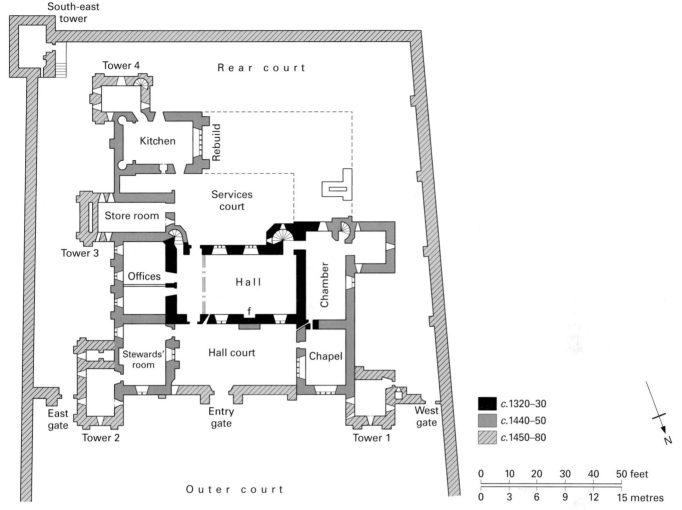

South-east tower

Tower 4

Rear court

Kitchen

Rebuild

Store room

Services court

Tower 3

Offices

Hall

f

Chamber

Stewards' room

Hall court

Chapel

East gate

Entry gate

West gate

Tower 2

Tower 1

Outer court

■ c.1320–30
▨ c.1440–50
▧ c.1450–80

0 10 20 30 40 50 feet
0   3   6   9   12 15 metres

N

FIGURE 127 Compton Castle: ground plan

A defendable frontage was added between the frontal towers 1 and 2, creating a small court protecting the windowed hall. The curtain wall was buttressed, with off-centre portcullis-protected entry, barred door, and corbel-supported windlass room above. Nearby is an oblong gun port and two corbel-supported machicolated bays, with two more over the chapel and services extension. The chapel window retains its heavy iron grille added for protection, but the transomed residential windows to the left of the entry are twentieth-century insertions replacing post-medieval enlargements.

The castle's frontage is extended on the left-hand side by a repetition of the portcullis abutment with a low-set gun port nearby, though the right-hand extension has merely a barred doorway. Because the castle is surrounded by higher ground on three sides, it was enclosed with a 24 feet high wall, in part buttressed on the inside. It is now capped but was presumably embattled originally. The line of putlog holes, 5 feet below the present head on the south and west sides, formerly carried the supports for a timber wall walk. The south-east angle was given the additional protection of a three-storey tower, with the two lower floors reached from the rear court.

Accounts of the house before the hall had been rebuilt reasonably attributed the defences to about 1420.[6] Since Everett's 1941 plan of the property in his 1956 account of the rebuilt hall, this extensive building programme has been attributed on unsupported evidence to about 1500, subsequently amended by him to about 1520.[7] Not surprisingly, John Gilbert's embattled façade has also been claimed as 'a record of intent . . . unsupported by genuine defences . . . a show-front only'.[8] The intensity and archaic character of the fortifications would be out of character for both attributions, though not if the additions were considerably earlier. Mid-Tudor doorways and windows would almost certainly have four-centred heads as at Cotehele or Holcombe Court, but those at Compton have two-centred heads and plain jambs, differing very little from the work attributed to Otho Gilbert of about 1440–50. All the added towers are ingeniously interlocked, with the adjacent accommodation with fireplace and garderobe facilities, so that a date not much later is architecturally likely and historically probable. The additions are particularly predisposed towards the east side of the castle. Three of the four towers were added here, the subsidiary entrance was portcullis-protected, the lookout slot near the principal entrance faced this way, while the south-east corner of the enclosing wall was given additional tower protection. Any attack was anticipated from the east and north-east rather than the west or south, i.e. from Torbay 3 miles away, not from inland.

Devon was noted for its lawlessness during the fifteenth century, extending from the expulsion of the Pomeroy family from their house at Berry Pomeroy (1428) to the Courtenays' murder of Nicholas Radford at Upcott in 1455, their occupation of Exeter and subsequent siege of Powderham Castle, and their skirmish with the Bonville family at Clyst Bridge that same year. However, the defences added at Compton seem more determined by French coastal raids. They had been responsible for the improvement of the defences at Plymouth from 1404 onwards, Southampton in about 1417–20, and Portsmouth in 1420–2. Blockhouses were erected at Fowey and Polruan after French raids in 1457. The castle at Berry Pomeroy was erected not long afterwards, possibly as early as the 1460s and not later than about 1490, while Dartmouth Castle was built in 1481–94, followed shortly afterwards by the Kingswear blockhouse.[9]

It was to meet these raids and piratical attacks that Compton Castle was fortified. The defensive additions are too extensive, too substantial, too purposeful, and too costly to be merely 'ostentatious rather than functional'.[10] The east portcullis, multiple machicolated bays, and gun ports capable of raking the base of the walls are carrying status too far. The Gilberts' fourteenth-century house was no more sited with defence in mind than Holand's mansion at Dartington. However, in the changed circumstances a century or more later, Compton's vulnerable position was obvious. It was to overcome this that the fortifications were added. They were not intended to withstand military attack but were competent enough to keep a raiding force at bay and protect the family within.

Compton Castle is a late fortified house *par excellence*. Like Bradley Manor, it has lost its gatehouse to the outer court, though its foundations have been located.[11] Much of the buildings round the rear court has also been lost, extending from the rebuilt west wall of the kitchen to the site of the south-west tower. Compton was an even more extensive and multi-courtyard house than today, though expansion brought the drawback of a more cramped property. Its vulnerable position and lack of any moat were responsible for the meaningful defences added between the 1450s and the 1480s and maintaining the earlier balanced façade of hall and cross wings. Symmetrical defensive frontages were characteristic of this period, as at Herstmonceux (*c*.1438–49), Baconsthorpe (1440s), Bronsil (1450s), and Kirby Muxloe Castle (1480–4). Building attributions at Compton Castle are tentative in the absence of documentary evidence or dendrochronology capacity, but this house has the considerable benefit that it stands as a roofed survival with few post-medieval alterations. It is a rare and little touched if idiosyncratic late medieval gem.

NOTES
1 Much dressed stonework was recovered by A. W. Everett who suggested the hall's early form: Everett (1956) 78–85; Haslam (Nov. 1981).
2 Everett attributed it to 1450 (1956) 76, followed by Gilbert (1979) 8.
3 Geoffrey Gilbert tells me that the window in this room above the chapel facing the approach was brought by his father from the rear of the house because of its sound condition. Was the original opening more defensive?
4 William Gilbert and his first wife were granted a chapel licence in 1398 and he and his second wife one for a portable altar in 1422. The chapel window tracery is less complex than that for Otho Gilbert's chantry of 1485 in Marldon church.

5 The kitchen tower has lost its uppermost floor. The absence of these defensive features confirms the earlier date and residential function of the south-west tower added to the upper chamber block. Nearby are the footings of the garderobe pit of another tower, but its date and function are unclear.
6 J. Parker, *Some Account of Domestic Architecture in England*, III pt 2 (1859) 352; A. H. Thompson, *Military Architecture in England during the Middle Ages* (1912) 358 and *Arch. Jour.* (1913) 544; S. Toy, *The Castles of Great Britain* (1953) 214. Hugh Watkin had opted for the decade 1460–70 in 1927: *Jour. Brit. Arch. Assoc.* 33 (1927) 148.
7 Everett (1956) 76; reproduced in Gilbert (1979) 4; *Arch. Jour.* 114 (1957) 171; B. Cherry and N. Pevsner, *Devon* (1989) 285. The plan in N. J. G. Pounds, *The Medieval Castle in England and Wales* (1990) 283, is at variance with the text, 266.
8 C. Platt, *The Architecture of Medieval England* (1990) 251, 287, followed by Cherry and Pevsner, *Devon* 285–6. Yet Cherry admits that the towers are to some extent genuine, while Platt had previously described the front as 'thoroughly medieval in flavour': *The Castle in Medieval England and Wales* (1982) 183.
9 R. Higham (ed.), *Security and Defence in South-West England before 1800* (1987) 40–6; 'Berry Pomeroy Castle', *Proc. Devon Arch. Soc.* 54 (1996) 156–8, 204.
10 Cherry and Pevsner, *Devon* 53.
11 Gilbert (1979) 13, 17.

G. M. Hills, *Jour. Brit. Arch. Assoc.* 19 (1863) 1–12
A. H. Thompson, *Arch. Jour.* 70 (1913) 544–6
A. W. Everett, *Trans. Devon. Assoc.* 71 (1939) 343–5
A. W. Everett, *Trans. Devon. Assoc.* 88 (1956) 75–85
Cdr W. R. Gilbert, *Compton Castle: Handbook* (1979) with many subsequent editions
R. Haslam, *Country Life* (November 1981)

COTEHELE, Cornwall

The centuries-old family home of the Edgcumbes has changed relatively little since its construction during the early years of Tudor rule. The house has long been known for its romantic position at the head of a combe overlooking the River Tamar, its evocative tapestry-hung interiors, and its isolation from the cut and thrust of modern living. Architecturally, Cotehele is a remarkably homogeneous building with all post-medieval additions – late sixteenth and mid-nineteenth century alike – markedly sympathetic to the original structure. The interior and its furnishings reflect two dominant periods – late medieval and late seventeenth century – and similarly offer a cogent and harmonious sequence of romantic, if formal, antiquarian rooms. Both aspects are more complex than they seem, for the early character of this house has exerted an overwhelming impact on its subsequent development. This has led to two architectural problems and hindered a third. The use of similar materials and form many years apart makes it difficult to distinguish between different building phases. A large number of two- and three-light windows inserted between the late sixteenth and mid-nineteenth centuries are almost indistinguishable from the original fenestration, as well as substantially altering the internal character of the rooms they serve.[1] No documentation relates to building activity before the mid-seventeenth century,[2] while the badly needed dendrochronology survey and detailed architectural analysis have only just been initiated.[3]

In the light of these considerations, undue attention has to be

Lodging units

Subsidiary approach

Entry gate

Retainers' Court

Dormitory lodging

West entry

Chapel

Guard room

Lodge

West range

Old dining room

1650

Punch room

Stair

Hall Court

Stair

Kitchen court

South range

Offices

Gateway

Hall

Kitchen

Oven

East range

(Library)

(Dining room)

(Stair hall)

Late fifteenth and sixteenth century

c.1860s

| 0 | 10 | 20 | 30 | 40 | 50 feet |
| 0 | 3 | 6 | 9 | 12 | 15 metres |

N

FIGURE 128 Cotehele: ground plan

given to the shaping of windows and door heads to help differentiate the various building phases. It will be suggested that nothing obviously pre-dates the second half of the fifteenth century. The north wall of the chapel is one of the earliest areas of surviving masonry and may be contemporary with the 1411 licence, but most of the development occurred in several phases betwen the late fif-

teenth and mid-sixteenth centuries when the house reached its present scale. A three-storey tower extended the family's apartments vertically in the late sixteenth century and was subsequently modified in the 1650s, while the east range was converted from household lodgings into a line of Victorian apartments in 1861–2 for the dowager countess of Mount Edgcumbe.

PLATE 224 Cotehele: entry range

The present approach to the house passes a late medieval barn towards the towered gateway in the middle of the south range with the Retainers' Court to the west.

RETAINERS' COURT

The west entrance range sets the tone for much of what follows – two-storey, rubble-built with dressed stone for the windows and doorways, and slate roofs. The large entry arch is two-centred, set in a square head with roughly carved spandrels. The windows lighting the room either side of the passageway are significant. One is an oblong opening, heavily barred, common to most of the ground-floor rooms but frequently replaced by a single light as on the left-hand side of the entry. The upper-floor windows were usually single lights towards the outer world, but one of them has been replaced by a two-light window under a square hood with stops as subsequently occurred elsewhere. What gives this initial approach an element of precaution is the combined loop and gun port, low set on the right hand side of the entrance, but this proves to be secondary, as is the entrance arch.

A door from the simple entry passage opened into the porter's lodge, while the opposing room with fireplace and gun port, only accessible from Hall Court, was more in the nature of a guard room. Hall Court reveals the internal face of this range, with single uncusped lights to both ground and upper floors. In the subsequent development phase commensurate with the hall range, the rooms at both levels were up-graded with two- and three-light windows, the latter separated by dressed granite blocks.

The west range is flanked by two additions. The nave part of the chapel with entrance and finialed bellcote projects into the Retainers' Court, leaving the altar wall flush with Hall Court. The south-facing block with its undecorated single light is set back from

and at an angle to the entrance range. The rear wall of this southern building, that is the part facing the Hall Court, is one of the earliest areas of masonry in the complex, similar in character to and possibly contemporary with the north wall of the chapel. The rest of this structure seems to be an eighteenth-century building.

Before entering the body of the house, the remainder of the Retainers' Court should be considered. Initially it would have been enclosed with an embattled wall and simple entry gateway, as Stuart Rigold suggested.[4] The wall was almost entirely replaced by two ranges of lodgings. That to the south, repeating the oblong barred openings and lights above to a wider room on both floors than elsewhere in the house, was possibly dormitory-type staff accommodation or an upstairs hall. That to the west has a pair of ground-floor entries and a further single entry to separate lodging units. The interiors have long been altered for domestic occupation.[5]

HALL COURT

The south and east ranges of Hall Court were originally single-storey, heightened in a subsequent phase to become two-storeyed lodging ranges. The outer faces were almost unbroken at ground level with single lights above, while the courtyard face had single lights subsequently amended to double-light windows. The three-storeyed gate-tower was inserted at the same time as the facing hall was rebuilt, while the east range was drastically remodelled in the early 1860s.

The exterior of the south range was forbidding, with only a few single lights placed high in the wall. This configuration was maintained when the embattled gate-tower was punched through the range. Built of dressed granite blocks, this tower is the key feature identifying the house on a schematic map of the estate of c.1550–60. The entrance doorway with four-centred head and carved spandrels, like that to the hall, is set within a higher arch and hood enclosing the family arms in the tympanum. The single-entry passage, enhanced with a transverse ribbed vault in granite, directly faces the hall entry. It was intended to give a heightened approach to the house, emphasised by its scale, a military-type parapet, and the use of dressed granite stone in a rubble-built wall. The stair accesses a first-floor lobby with a pair of facing doorways with carved spandrels (probably a Victorian assemblage) and a twin-light unglazed window. A stylish entry doorway with two-centred head opens into the first-floor room with fireplace and three-light courtyard-facing window, uncusped, with two-centred head and decorated spandrels. A mural stair leads to the second-floor room with similar fenestration, fireplace, and garderobe. This was an important two-room lodging, accentuated by the lobby approach and the original embattled parapet. The courtyard windows date from the same time as the gate-tower and were part of the upgrading of the range commensurate with the reorientated approach to the house. The gatehouse interior was refitted in the Victorian period and seems to have become offices during this time.

The east range initially consisted of oblong barred openings at ground level and single lights above to the outer world and is so shown in photographs taken in about 1850, a few years before the range was converted into living quarters for the widow of the third earl. The two courtyard doorways had square and semi-circular hoods respectively, but most of the windows are enhancements following the 1861–2 remodelling. Externally, this extended to refenestrating the valley-facing frontage and adding the large porch with bay window above. Internally, the range was remodelled as a library, stair hall, and dining room at ground level, with the drawing room, countess' bedroom and dressing room above. However, the restraint of the drawing room open roof of arch-braced collar trusses and three lines of wind braces suggests it may have followed the original form. Earlier retained features of this range include a garderobe projection, with another projection for a stairway rebuilt as a chimney stack.[6]

The hall is built of rubble stone with a head of square granite blocks which continue across the gable end of the contemporary residential block. The upper register of the hall's outer walls is pierced by three twin-light windows with a dominating four-light transomed window at the dais end. The courtyard-facing windows of the residential apartments are two adjacent sets of three-transomed lights. All are set in square heads, the larger with hoods and end stops, with decorated spandrels, concave mullions, and lights with nipped ogee heads. The hall entry repeats the form of the gateway entry with four-centred head but plain spandrels, and a heraldic shield in the tympanum that would have emphasised the family's standing. The hall and adjoining cross wing have a complex phasing and none of the present windows or doorways is contemporary with the wall. The upper windows and granite ashlar masonry of the hall are associated with a heightening of the walls, presumably to make the hall more grandiose and to fit in with the two-storey lodging range that adjoined it.

The hall entry opens unusually a third of the way into the body of the apartment, which has no evidence of a screens passage. This is a reflection of the earlier hall and services block in extension of it, both replaced by the present single apartment but retaining the same entry position. The hall, 42 feet by 22 feet, is given majestic scale by the height and decorative moulding of the seven-bay roof

of arch-braced trusses, their feet curving down the wall, and four lines of intersecting wind braces. The three doorways at the lower end promise the usual services beyond – again a reflection of the earlier hall but now to different purpose. One was the stair to the east range, one opens into the former offices (now Victorian dining room), and one leads via a passage to the kitchen. The well-lit upper end is marked by a lateral fireplace with four-centred granite head, the archway to the family apartments, and a brilliant stained glass display of early sixteenth-century heraldic panels of families associated with the Edgcumbes. The hall's early character is stimulated by the Tudor studded oak door, the uneven lime ash floor, the lime-washed plaster walls, and the evocative armorial display.[7]

The family residential range, Victorian-buttressed to the west, has generously scaled windows with decorated spandrels and nipped ogee heads, similar to those facing Hall Court. Originally, the range was a single room, a grand apartment 56 feet long, subsequently heightened to become two storeys, with a consequent revision of the window layout in the west wall and that overlooking Hall Court. The two floors were linked at the north-west corner by the recess remodelled in the eighteenth century to take wine bins. The upper apartment was open to a nine-bay roof, similar to that over the hall with arch-braced collars with moulded edges and three tiers of overlapping wind braces. The range was reroofed in 1872 (dendro dated). The ground floor was divided in 1650–1 into the Old Dining Room and the Punch Room, with the former retaining the original fireplace. The straight stair of timber steps to the upper rooms is a replacement of the same date by Piers Edgcumbe (d.1667) when the landing and two upper rooms were created and ceiled. Again, the fireplace in the further South Room is the original one. This also has a quatrefoil peep hole into the hall, probably original whereas the one in the lower end of the hall is Victorian. The room also accessed the private pew overlooking the chapel altar.

The chapel is divided by a contemporary screen into almost equally proportioned nave and chancel. Staff entry was from the Retainers' Court, with that from the family apartments forced through the chancel wall. The three-cinquefoil-light east window with double quatrefoil head (heavily restored c.1880) retains some of its original glass, including the figure of St John and the coats of arms of the Tremayne, Holland, and Durnford families, while the glass in the two-light south window is a little later, probably c.1520–30. Apart from the plaster and ribbed barrel-shaped roof with wooden roses at the rib intersections, other original items include the nave floor tiles, the earliest unaltered domestic clock in England, an early sixteenth-century Flemish painting of the Crucifixion, an altar triptych of 1589, and the crimson velvet altar cloth with twelve apostles *appliqué* and the arms of Sir Piers and his first wife (not on display).[8]

The kitchen and offices lay at the lower end of the hall in an unusual position north-east of it. The square kitchen, open to the roof, has a great hearth filling its north wall and a subsidiary one to the west. The room has lost its louvre, is top lit by post-medieval windows, and has nineteenth-century roof timbers.

BUILDING SEQUENCE

A branch of the Edgcumbe family from near Tavistock have held the Cotehele estate since 1353. Though the simple one-light windows suggested to early writers that some of the ranges were of

PLATE 225 Cotehele: Hall Court

the fourteenth or early fifteenth century,[9] no certain visible evidence pre-dates the third quarter of the fifteenth century at the earliest. The house which existed here by 1411 when its chapel was licensed by the bishop of Exeter may have been of courtyard form with some of its rubble walls incorporated in the present structure, but to all intents and purposes, Cotehele is an almost complete house of the Yorkist and early to mid-Tudor periods. In 1446–7, William Edgcumbe initiated the family's practice of representing Plymouth in nearly every parliament for over four centuries, but the rebuilding of Cotehele can be more confidently attributed to his grandson and great-grandson. They were the first members of the family to achieve more than local fame, but it was a case not of the younger completing the plans initiated by the elder but of an inchoate development and aggrandisement programme consequent on their rising political, financial, and social standing.

Building attributions are hindered by uncertainty as to the age of either Sir Richard or Sir Piers Edgcumbe. Richard seems to have been very young when he entered into his inheritance. He was not politically active until the late 1460s as member of parliament for Tavistock (1467–8), escheator for Devon and Cornwall (1467–88), and justice of the peace for Cornwall (1474–5). He was

a strong Lancastrian supporter, active during the re-adeption of Henry VI (1470–1) but pardoned by Edward IV two years later. He was similarly pardoned by Richard III for supporting Buckingham's failed rebellion in 1483, though he had already fled the country to join Henry Tudor in Brittany (November 1483). He became the future king's personal friend, supported him at Bosworth Field, and was rewarded with a knighthood, the office of controller of the king's household, several local offices and manors, and diplomatic assignments in Scotland and Ireland before his death in 1489.[10]

He was succeeded by his twenty-one-year-old son Piers,[11] who saw some military action at home and aboard,[12] was knighted in 1494 and made knight-banneret in 1513, and held a range of offices in Devon and Cornwall throughout his life, including the office of sheriff eight times.[13] Sir Piers had married Joan Durnford, a local heiress, in 1493 so that the presence of her arms in the hall windows before her death in 1520 rather than those of his second wife provides a *terminus ad quem* for the majority of Sir Piers' work.

The activity of these two members is marked by a change in building materials. Sir Richard used a brown and grey slatestone with ashlar dressings while Sir Piers used courses of cut granite blocks.

This should not be taken as a hard and fast rule, particularly as there has been much subsequent patching and modification. But cut granite was a sophisticated and expensive material, used for several local buildings attributable to the first decade of the sixteenth century. They include Place, Fowey, by Sir Piers' fellow-Lancastrian Sir John Treffry and Trecarrell Manor by Sir Henry Trecarrell (*c*.1500–11), and subsequently St Mary Magdalene, Launceston 1511–24, Wortham Manor by John Dinham (*c*.1500–15), the College of Week St Mary founded in 1506, and prior Vivian's additions at Rialton Manor (after 1508). The contemporary houses at Trecarrell and Wortham are particularly relevant, not only for their close proximity and common use of arch-braced roofs but for the distinctive architectural features of nipped ogee window heads and carved tympanum doorways, and the intersecting wind braces of the great chamber roof of Wortham.

Pending any further dendrochronology survey, the sequence of Cotehele's architectural development can be postulated as a series of closely related phases, initiated by the west range. This seems to hold the earliest masonry, including the lower part of the chapel north wall which would indicate that it was of similar length to the present structure. The south-west corner of Hall Court has an early return wall, but the alignments of the earlier walling suggest a much more irregular layout than shown in the surviving ranges. Hall Court seems to have been the first construction area, with the ranges creating a squarish court with the contemporary chapel projecting outside the court as at Bradley Manor (1428) and Compton Castle (1440–50). The hall on the north side was narrower than at present, with an entry accessing a blind screens passage which separated the services at the eastern end. At this stage, the relatively modest family apartments were possibly in line with the hall rather than in a cross wing as later.[14]

In phase two, the present west range was constructed, but without the passageway into the Retainers' Court. The present kitchen, which may have originated as a separate bakehouse, is likely to belong to this phase.

Phase three of *c*.1500–10 represents an expansion programme, with the widening of the hall and upgrading of the ranges enclosing the south and east side of Hall Court. The evidence for this is the squared and regularly coursed slate walling built upon a granite foundation plinth that is found in the chapel east wall and in the hall range, as well as in the east and south ranges. Widening the hall range seems to have occasioned the awkwardness at the corner where it meets the chapel. The hall is likely to have had a mural fireplace at this stage, and it has been confirmed that the roof timbers were felled in about 1500. Allowing for a few years to season, construction can be attributed to the later years of the first decade.[15] The development of the Retainers' Court was also initiated during this period.

Phase four of *c*.1520–30 was the most extensive and costly of all the work undertaken in the development of Cotehele. With the exception of the hall, the ranges round that court were made two-storey by heightening the walls and included the appropriate stair access. The hall walls were also raised with granite ashlar, its roof was raised (reusing the earlier timbers), and further windows were added in the form of a clerestory. The more important windows were emphasised by hoods ending in large square labels with simple leaf decoration, but they did not grace the less important high hall windows of the new three-storey extension below the hall that cut

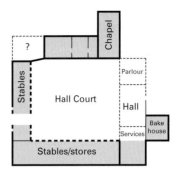

Phases 1 and 2 later fifteenth century

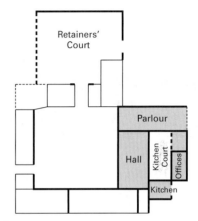

Phase 3 early sixteenth century

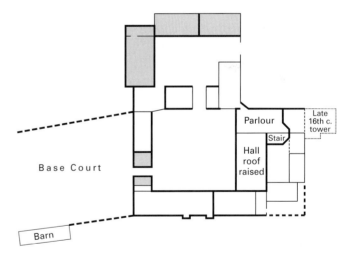

Phase 4 mid-sixteenth century

FIGURE 129 Cotehele: building sequence *c*.1450–1530

into the earlier east range. At the same time, the granite-towered entrance was inserted in the rubble-built south range to create an improved approach to the house.

The tower at the north end of the family apartments was the last major development phase, apparently towards the close of the sixteenth century, to provide superior and more private rooms for the family. It was remarkably conservative in form and detail, with the doorways, rectangular windows, and embattled parapet simulating the character of an earlier generation. This anachronistic solar tower, well over a century out of date, was an early example of anti-quarian taste and attitude to past values rather than any limitations of rising ground to the north. It was the first stage of a conservative movement that was fostered by Piers Edgcumbe's alterations in the early 1650s and by the family's long-term absence from the prop-erty after the close of the century.

Sir Piers' wife had brought the Mount Edgcumbe estate over-looking the mouth of the Tamar as part of her dowry in 1493, but it was her son Sir Richard (d.1560) who built the house there between 1547 and 1554 which became the family's principal seat in the late sixteenth century. This decision meant that Cotehele became a secondary property and was therefore relatively little altered thereafter. Yet it was never reduced to farmhouse status but maintained and occasionally used. Architecturally, Cotehele has stood still since this decision, just as a similar one at about the same period saved Haddon Hall from any further development. The feeling that time has little changed since then has been heightened at Cotehele by the gradual but deliberate policy during the mid-Georgian period of introducing furniture of the late sixteenth and seventeenth centuries, and a substantial number of tapestries from the second half of the seventeenth century, as well as chair and bed upholstery of a slightly later period to enhance the antiquarian character of the house for the family to show visitors.[16]

The final phase in Cotehele's development was the remodelling of the east range in the early 1860s, highly credible and restrained externally though less so internally. At the same time, the services at the north-east corner of the house, hitherto single-storey east of the kitchen, were extended and heightened for domestic staff atten-dant on the countess.

DESIGN ASSESSMENT

Thanks to extensive post-medieval window enhancement, Cotehele was originally very different externally from its present appearance. It was hardly a fortified house, but it shows the basic precautions of a lightly defended, inward-looking residence – a high enclosure wall, a gun-port-protected entry, barred ground-floor windows including the chapel west window, and narrow upper-floor lights. Furthermore, the exterior-facing walls, including the tower, bear much evidence of render, indicating that the early house was probably finished with limewash, so that it would have looked very different from its present stony character. This change from lime-wash to exposed masonry may have occurred in the eighteenth cen-tury or the Victorian period, as the 1860 alterations were built without render.

The house was initially modest, with a smaller hall than today, equally lacking any towered porch. Its expansion reflects the increasing wealth, growing confidence, and higher political and social standing of two members of the Edgcumbe family. As Sir Richard became more politically important after 1485, the house was enlarged to accommodate his expanding household. Within a few years of inheriting, Sir Piers undertook a substantial develop-ment programme that included rebuilding the hall and private apartments on a more showy, formal, and ambitious scale, addi-tional good-quality staff rooms below the hall, and a new group of offices serving the retained kitchen to facilitate access at the rear of the hall, heightening the separation of 'family' and 'service' in the day-to-day running of the mansion. The family apartments main-tained the scale of the hall, with equally handsome windows, large fireplaces, and a striking roof to the upper chamber. The ground floor was virtually a private hall with the upper room as a personal withdrawing chamber – both architecturally devalued by their later division. The new gateway in the mid-sixteenth century empha-sized the Edgcumbes' status and dramatised the approach to their hall, while the further lodging units round the outer court were nec-essary for his even larger household.

The significance of Cotehele lies in its clear demonstration of a late medieval and early to mid-Tudor house reflecting the political and social standing of a leading family in regional politics through more imposing and larger apartments, greater privacy for the family, and an increasing number of lodging ranges for guests and senior household officials. Despite the mid-Victorian remodelling of the east range, this accommodation span is broader, better pre-served, and more accessible than in any other contemporary mansion in southern England.

Missing today are the associated offices and services necessary to serve this expanding household. Only the buttressed barn survives from the services surrounding the new Base Court, though 'the remains of old farm buildings' were recorded in 1859.[17] Leaving aside the small kitchen court as a servant facility only, Cotehele is an example of a triple-courtyard house – a small-scale version of those well-known early sixteenth-century paradigms of status Thornbury Castle and Hampton Court. Yet by the time Sir Piers decided to enhance his father's house, his values were more towards the past than the future. If he had wished to be up-to-date, the hall would have been prefaced by a porch tower as at Wortham Manor, spanned by a hammer-beam roof as at Weare Giffard, and enhanced by a dais bay window as at Place, Fowey. If he had wished to be radical like some of his fellow courtiers, he would have pulled down his father's house in favour of an outward-looking single courtyard house as at Temple Newsam (possibly 1490–1505), Compton Wynyates (1510s), Sutton Place (1520s), and Cowdray (1520–30). He would have replaced the open-to-the-roof hall with a single storey one with a great chamber above, as was already being prac-tised locally at Wortham Manor and more grandly at Sutton Place and Kenninghall (1520s). But the backward-looking movement had already begun which later generations followed, so that Cotehele became a mellowed survival of late medieval England, as 'ancient, large, strong and fayre' today as it was in 1602.[18]

NOTES

1 The reuse and resiting of earlier windows was being practised as early as 1650–1, National Trust (1991) 20.

2 Most of the family archives were destroyed when the family seat at Mount Edgcumbe was bombed in 1941.

3 Carried out by the Historic Environment Services of Cornwall County Council for the National Trust following their receipt of an early draft of this assessment in 2001. The present text reflects the work of the Cornish Services unit.

4 Rigold (1973) 257. The present entry arch is slightly later.

5 The first-floor rear lights are original to the wall, contra Rigold (1973).

6 The hall possibly extended further east into what is now the northern end of the east range, and the present end of the hall is a blocking. The early doorway in the countess' bedroom was inserted from elsewhere in the 1860s.

7 Most of the arms and armour hung on the walls is mid-seventeenth century, with a few earlier items, all in the same position as J. C. Buckler's watercolour of 1821. The oak furniture is seventeenth century.

8 *Gothic: Art for England 1400–1547*, ed. R. Marks and P. Williamson (2003) 339.

9 T. Garner and A. Stratton, *The Domestic Architecture of England During the Tudor Period*, I (1911) 49–50; Tipping (1937) 76; N. Pevsner, *The Buildings of England: Cornwall* (1951) 45.

10 J. C. Wedgwood, *History of Parliament 1439–1509* (1936) 291–2.

11 His age is uncertain. Wedgwood states he was twelve years old in 1497 *ibid*. 292, but S. T. Bindoff ascribes his birth to 1468: *History of Parliament 1509–58*, II (1982) 81. As Piers was admitted to Lincoln's Inn in 1488 and married in 1493, his birth in 1468 is accepted.

12 He helped to rally the men of Devon and Cornwall against Perkin Warbeck (1497) and joined Henry VIII in France at the 'Battle of the Spurs' (1513).

13 Detailed by Bindoff, *History of Parliament* 81–2.

14 Whether the initial layout of Cotehele encompassed any protective measures is an open question. During the 1460s and 1470s the coast was subject to piratical attacks and the locality to bitter feuds. Towards the closing years of Edward IV's rule, Sir Richard was assaulted with murderous intent by his neighbour, the young Richard Willoughby, and thirty-four armed men, while on another occasion Willoughby's supporters stole some of the chattels from Cotehele and threatened to burn down the house. Richard Edgcumbe (d.1562) was still involved with suppressing piracy eighty years later.

15 *Vern. Arch.* 35 (2004) 84.

16 J. Cornforth, *Country Life* (February 1990); also C. Wainwright, *The Romantic Interior* (1989). The marvellously evocative set of seventeen lithographs by Nicholas Condy, *Cotehele on the Banks of the Tamar*, with a text by Rev. F. V. Arundell (*c*.1840) not only show the house and its interiors little changed from today, but their state by the third quarter of the eighteenth century.

17 Turner and Parker (1859) 358.

18 Richard Carew, *Survey of Cornwall* (1602).

T. H. Turner and J. H. Parker, *Some Account of Domestic Architecture in England*, III pt 2 (1859) 357–60
4th Earl of Mount Edgcumbe, *Records of the Edgcumbe Family* (1888)
H. A. Tipping, *English Homes*, Pds 1 and 2, II (1937) 69–90
S. Rigold, *Arch. Jour.* 130 (1973) 256–9
The National Trust, *Cotehele House: Handbook* (2005 edn)

COTHAY MANOR, Somerset

In its tranquil countryside setting, Cothay Manor stands as the archetypal late medieval Somerset manor house, not grand but homely. Situated within a network of narrow lanes between Wellington and the Devon border, this moated, gatehouse-protected hall and cross-wing house is built of local red sandstone, rubble-coursed with Ham stone dressings, though the hall and porch have been roughcast and colour washed. Internally, the house retains many original features, including considerable contemporary wall painting evidence.

The de Cotthehee family, first recorded here in the early thirteenth century, lived at Cothay until 1457, when John Cothay and his wife executed a series of deeds that transferred all their lands to John Bluett and his son in return for a life interest in the property. The Bluetts were a locally important family, members of parliament for Somerset during the fourteenth century, who developed homes at Kittisford and Almsworthy, and later at Greenham Barton and Holcombe Rogus.[1] John Bluett (d.1463) was succeeded by his son Walter (d.1481), who settled the manor of Cothay on his younger son Richard (d.1524) rather than his older brother so that Richard was

unable to enter the property until a family dispute had been settled in 1485. This branch of the Bluetts lived at Cothay until 1605, when they sold it to William Every (d.1652), sheriff of Somerset in 1638–9. Four generations of Every occupied the house until the close of the seventeenth century when it was let to tenants. It was not until the early twentieth century that the house's fortunes were reversed, first by Lt. Col. Reginald Cooper between 1925 and 1937 and then by Sir Francis Cook from 1937 to 1947.

The house reflects four primary development phases. It is essentially a house of the last quarter of the fifteenth century, developed by Walter or Richard Bluett in two phases, but it incorporates evidence of an earlier property on the site, including the moat as well as some fourteenth-century architectural elements. Shortly after acquiring the manor in 1605, William Every added the three-storeyed dining room block at the rear and altered some windows, but the sequence of tenants left little mark on the property until the gatehouse was restored in 1927–9 and a residential wing added in the 1930s.

Standing close to the east bank of the River Tone, the gatehouse range commands the site and obscures the front of the house. It consists of a heavily buttressed entry tower, originally embattled[2] with lower ranges on either side though the short one to the left has been pulled down. The outer arch of roll and hollow moulding and four-centred head opens into a plain entry passage with a broad inner arch to the forecourt. The single upper room with fireplace and garderobe is a rebuild to plans on a drawing-only basis by Sir Harold Brakspear (1926–7). The north lodging range was essentially two dormitories of differing status – the ground floor with small square windows, the upper floor with single and double lights, a fireplace, and garderobe facility. The greater width of this buttressed range overlapping the rear of the gatehouse suggests it was a secondary development. The moat formerly abutted this range, with the bridge across it raised by chains through the two square openings either side the outer entry. Even so, this gatehouse was built for show, not defence, with the arms of Richard Bluett and his wife Alice Verney above the outer arch proclaiming their status.

The small forecourt, now with a single modern wall to the south but probably enclosed on both sides, was formerly cobbled. The barn to the north-east next to the 1930s link block, retains five raised-jointed crucks with high collars. Originally with hipped end walls, it is probably no earlier than the late seventeenth century.[3]

The house follows the high-quality regional plan of a central hall with upper and lower cross wings projecting front and rear, surmounted by decorative gable heads. The symmetry of this frontage is not fully realised, for while the hall and upper cross wing are buttressed, the lower wing is not, and the porch jostles uncomfortably with it. This may be a consequence of its early seventeenth-century refacing, but a second cross wing is not common in Somerset, and it may have been added as an afterthought in a two-phase development. Most of the windows are original, the more important with twin-transomed lights of uncusped four-centred heads, blind spandrels, and no hood moulds except over the porch oratory window. The rear frontage was always less regular, with an extended lower cross wing, disguised by the early seventeenth-century three-storey extension covering the cross-passage exit. No evidence has been found of any second court buildings during nearly a century of gardening activity.

The porch entry of three moulded jambs to a column and capital

PLATE 226 Cothay Manor: from the forecourt

and two-centred head seems to have been retained from the fourteenth-century house on this site. The inner archway repeats the roll and hollow moulding and four-centred head of the gate-house entry. There are no side benches or porch windows and only a plain panelled ceiling, but the oak door (with drawbar) is original.

The opposing cross-passage doorway has a plain chamfer, and, like the porch entry, is not central to the markedly wide passage with its timber-framed end wall. It is possible that this wall is another retained element of the earlier home.

The hall, 34¾ feet by 19½ feet including the cross passage, stands open to the seven-bay roof. With stone side walls and framed end walls, this apartment has never been disfigured by an inserted floor. The cross passage, separated from the hall by the original plain post and panel screen with two openings, was formerly lit by a window above the outer doors. They existed until *c*.1605 when the gallery was inserted to facilitate access to the added bedrooms, about a foot lower than the rooms it served. The windows were converted into doorways, but the splay of the west window and jamb of the low window in the east wall reflecting light from the oratory were revealed during Lt. Col. Cooper's restoration.

The body of the hall is lit by twin-light windows deeply splayed in the upper walling, two to the forecourt and one by the fireplace, though there was a second one on the other side until covered by the dining room block in *c*.1605. The windows retain their shutter pins and bar sockets. The jambs and square-headed lintel of the 10 feet wide west-wall fireplace repeat the roll and hollow moulding characteristic of the house. The side walls retain wall painting evidence, not in good condition but unrestored, unlike the paintings elsewhere in the house. That near the middle of the forecourt wall shows scenes from the fable of Reynard the Fox, including the hanging by two geese on a gibbet, and running along the wall to the north is the fox's funeral procession. The large head near the dais is said to be that of St Christopher, the patron saint of travellers. The paintings are ascribed by E. W. Tristram to the later fifteenth century and by E. Croft-Murray to *c*.1500–10.[4] There was no recovered evidence for the slight rise in the floor paving created by Cooper to mark the dais position. The two doorways in the upper end wall are concealed by the early seventeenth-century panelling that formerly extended along part of the side walls.[5] The doorways have bold ogee-shaped door heads, a feature not found elsewhere in the house but occurring in a further earlier framed wall.[6] The roof is of standard Somerset character. Between the end walls, six arch-braced collar trusses rise from corbels of wooden figures carrying shields, now blank but originally tinctured. The three rows of wind braces create a distinctive pattern by arrangement in reverse pairs.

The upper cross-wing ground floor has always consisted of two rooms, both with beamed ceilings and early seventeenth-century

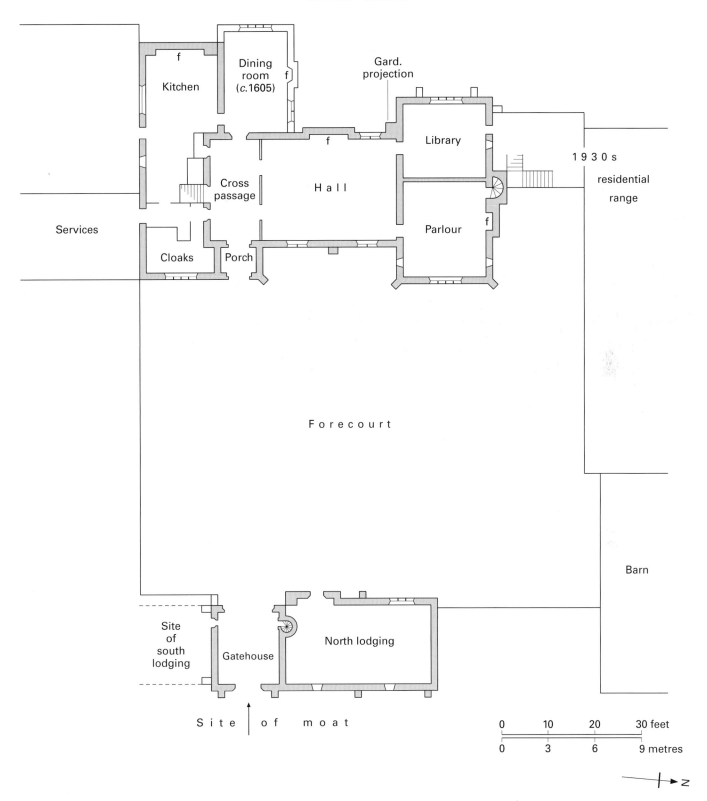

Kitchen

Dining room (*c.*1605)

Gard. projection

Library

1930s residential range

Cross passage

H a l l

Services

Parlour

Cloaks   Porch

F o r e c o u r t

Barn

Site of south lodging

Gatehouse

North lodging

S i t e   o f   m o a t

0   10   20   30 feet
0   3   6   9 metres

N

FIGURE 130 Cothay: ground plan

wooden-framed windows. The panelled parlour retains two original single lights, a fireplace with moulded jambs and lintel similar to that in the hall, and a four-panelled ceiling, each panel subdivided into four. Hardly anything remains of the frieze of men in early Tudor dress above the panelling of a century later which conceals better-preserved work. The original purpose of the slightly smaller west room is not known. It has no fireplace and a low ceiling, roughly remade with a crude cross beam during tenant occupation. Storage at the high-status end of the hall is unlikely but use as a Summer parlour is possible.

The upper chamber could only be reached by the projecting newel from the parlour. This single chamber, 35 feet by 16 feet, is principally lit by a two-light transomed window at each end, supplemented by three single lights. The oculus window with cusped wheel tracery in the west gable is another fourteenth-century retained feature.[7] The fireplace has a replaced lintel to the base of the original jamb, but the small framed opening into the hall nearly opposite is of very uncertain date.[8] The four-bay roof is of arch-braced collars and three lines of wind braces. The walls of the room have been given panache and unity by the painted decoration of flowers, leaves, and vegetables by Arabella Robb in 1997. Its original character would have been rather different, for the cross beam in the floor at three-quarters of its length suggests a partition position, but the lack of braces originally to the central truss (the present ones are additions) points more strongly to a central division. In any case, this area was initially planned as an outer chamber with fireplace, and a more private inner chamber with garderobe projection off its south-west corner, visible externally.

The three doorways in the framed wall at the lower end of the hall are irregularly positioned, both outer doorways with a lower four-centred head than the central arch. The immediate response is that the two lower doorways opened into the services, with the taller central archway giving corridor access to a detached kitchen, but the lack of any other approach to the upper floor and the scale of this cross wing show that the kitchen has always been integral to the house. The lower cross wing, unlike the upper wing, was built to a three-room plan at all levels. The service area (towards the forecourt) has been remodelled several times, but the present kitchen makes use of the original end-wall hearth.

The twentieth-century stair to the upper floor replaced an earlier steeper one to the blocked doorways with four-centred heads at the side of the present seventeenth-century bedroom entries. The original approach was by a newel (as in the upper cross wing) revealed under the floor boards in 1958. The Fresco Room overlooking the forecourt retains a fireplace with a plain chamfer and large flat lintel, windows of c.1605, and a four-panelled framed ceiling. The room is notable for the religious frescos. That near the oratory door depicts the Christ Child, fully formed, coming down in a beam of light from the Godhead, a lily, towards the Virgin Mary. This is a late medieval heresy denying the Virgin birth. Another to the right of the window includes a female saint with a person kneeling at her side, possibly the house owner at that time. The saint may be St Sidwell, a local saint who became a cult figure at Moorbath, 5 miles from Cothay.[9] At the side of the fireplace is a late Tudor costumed figure, perhaps representing a Bluett. The frieze all round the room with texts in Gothic lettering on ribboned scroll has been much restored, particularly on two walls. This bedroom was the only access to the

oratory over the porch, 8 feet square and lacking a piscina but retaining the hagioscope from the Fresco Room angled on the altar. The central roof truss is supported on winged angels in stone.[10]

The central (Gold) room with fireplace retains an overpainted mural of the Virgin and Child in a roundel, enclosed by a geometric border with two shields in the spandrels. The whole covers part of the wall beam as well as the plaster infill, but the drawing of the child is crude. The fragments of other frescos can be traced, including one painted above the fireplace lintel. The room above the kitchen lacked a fireplace until the twentieth century, when the windows were also replaced. The roof trusses of this wing have plain collars but the windows with shutter features similar to those in the hall suggest the three attic rooms were original to the house. They were approached from a central area above the Gold Room where two wooden stair baulks still survive behind a floor-height panel in the north-east corner.

ASSESSMENT

Cothay was an aspirational house. The Bluetts retained elements of the previous residence, particularly the moat, the entry doorway, and the framed end walls of the hall to give it occupational continuity and preterition, but otherwise they built anew. The window form indicates that it was not erected before about 1480, and as there was a four-year gap before its ownership was determined in Richard Bluett's favour, construction between about 1485 and 1490 is most likely, with the lower cross wing as a secondary development.[11]

The house is not particularly large, was built to a common southern England plan, and was backward- rather than forward-looking. The elevations are informal and picturesque at a time when the stylistic vanguard favoured formality and symmetry, as at Great Chalfield Manor. Some features are markedly old-fashioned, such as the newel from the parlour to the withdrawing chamber, repeating the practice of Tickenham Court (1471–6), rather than a more dominant stair approach from the hall within a rectangular projection. The roof trusses of that apartment are also closer and therefore more dense than might be expected for a hall of this comparatively modest scale.

Though Cothay is relatively plain and not in the vanguard of architectural fashion, it has retained its original character to a remarkable degree. It is distinguished by the retained clarity of plan, the unspoilt internal character, the survival of many original fittings, and an outstanding range of contemporary wall paintings of secular and religious character. The early seventeenth-century additions are in harmony with the earlier work, as was its sympathetic restoration during the 1920s and 1930s,[12] so that it continues to be 'one of the most characteristic and perfect fifteenth century manor houses in the country'.[13]

This is true enough, but it fails to take into account two further prestigious elements of architectural and social distinction. The gatehouse was one of the last to be erected in the region, a statement of standing achieved by the younger son of a local family.[14] The adjacent lodging range identifies the scale of Richard Bluett's household, providing accommodation for staff of lower and higher social rank in the same way as the ground-floor rooms did at either end of the hall. Cothay is not only 'one of the most perfect small English houses of the late fifteenth century',[15] but also a statement by a member of the local gentry that he had 'arrived'.

NOTES

1 Nothing survives at Kittisford or Almsworthy. Greenham Barton is essentially a single-range rubble-stone house with a commanding porch to the front and a substantial north-west kitchen wing to the rear. At the rear was an enclosed court, with a ruined gateway on its east side. The porch with cinquefoil upper windows, together with the cross-passage doorways, is later fourteenth century though possibly of *c*.1403 when John Bluett's wife came into her father's fortune. A. W. Vivian-Neal, *Proc. Somerset Arch. and N. H. Soc.* 80 (1934) 17–24. The earlier hall was that rarity in south-west England, an aisled structure, of which a single truss survives in the cross passage. The apartment was remodelled in about 1500 when the fireplace and five-light transomed windows were added. The upper-end doors in the same position as those at Cothay open into a single rear chamber with newel (rebuilt in 1920–1), though one of the dais doors probably accessed a lost stair to the upper room. The lower cross wing was rebuilt in the nineteenth century but the almost detached kitchen wing, overlapping one corner of the hall range, is fourteenth century. Cothay shows how such a kitchen unit, with its newel-approached upper floor, could be more closely integrated with the other services of the house by the late fifteenth century. In *c*.1430 John Bluett of Greenham married Maud Cheseldene of Holcombe Rogus. The Bluetts redeveloped Holcombe Court during the early sixteenth century as a courtyard house, with the hall range dominated by a four-storey porch tower. The house was substantially modified during the later sixteenth century and remained the principal residence of the Bluetts until 1856. NMRC, BF 078551; C. Hussey, *Country Life* (September 1933); E. M. Phillips, *Country Life* (January 1915). B. Cherry and N. Pevsner, *The Buildings of England: Devon* (1989) 487–90.

2 Brakspear's reasonable restoration was replaced by the present plain parapet during the 1970s.

3 The services and offices south-west of the house, remodelled in the 1930s, incorporate seventeenth-century outbuildings.

4 The subjects have been identified by Stephen Rickerby, Courtauld Institute. The dating is by Tipping (1937) 58–60; E. Croft-Murray, *Decorative Painting in England: 1537–1837* (1962) 15, 175.

5 It is believed further wall paintings survive behind this panelling which, like that in the parlour, was painted in the late seventeenth century to resemble walnut.

6 Tipping also noted that evidence of earlier windows was found in the walls of the present hall: (1937) 51.

7 The east gable has an air vent, visible externally.

8 An original opening, like that in the chapel, would have been in stone.

9 E. Duffy, *Voices of Moorbath* (2000) 73–7.

10 As the west entry was initially a window, it is possible that this porch room was an early seventeenth-century addition as at Gurney Manor. If so, the windows were reused and the squint was meaningless except to a recusant.

11 In the 1980s, Robin Bush, Taunton Archivist, found a survey of Richard Bluett's estate of March 1488 describing 'the site there enclosed and ditched around, within which all that messuage and building called the Court Place, pools, orchard and garden which the said Richard caused to be built and constructed with his own wealth'. *Country Life* (August 2002).

12 The stair of 1732 in Sir Francis Cook's wing is said to have been brought from a Somerset house.

13 N. Lloyd, *A History of the English House* (1951 edn) 196. Christopher Hussey waxed even more lyrical in his response to Lt. Col. Cooper's furnishing of the house. Tipping (1937) 56–7 and J. Musson, *The English Manor House* (1999) 77–80.

14 The arms of Richard Bluett and his wife, hitherto preserved in the house, were reset on the gatehouse during the 1926–7 restoration in what was thought to have been their original position. Tipping (1937) 52.

15 N. Pevsner, *The Buildings of England: South and West Somerset* (1958) 133.

T. Garner and A. Stratton, *The Domestic Architecture of England During the Tudor Period* (1929 edn only) 21–2

H. A. Tipping, *English Homes*, Pds 1 and 2, vol. II (1937) 51–68, repeating C. Hussey, *Country Life* (October 1927)

J. Goodall, *Country Life* (July 2004)

CROSCOMBE HALL, Somerset

Sir William Palton's house of *c*.1420 shows that knighthood and a large house were not necessarily synonymous. Positioned immediately north of the fine parish church, the house's survival is the consequence of its long use as a Baptist chapel until 1974 – hence the graveyard in front of the hall.

The house was a 50 foot long range of hall with offices and chamber block at the lower end under a common roof ridge. The addition of an upper block extended the hall range by 15 feet, but this second-phase development has long since been pulled down.

The hall has a plain entry with two-centred head, but the more elaborate opposing north entry indicates that the house was formerly approached from this side, with its hollow-moulded doorway set in a square ogee-moulded frame. Neither entry was porch-protected. The four-bay hall, 32 feet by 20 feet internally, was lit on both sides by two tall transomed windows with twin cinquefoil lights under a quatrefoil head and hood mould. There are now two on the north and one on the south side, for the second one here was subsequently converted into a bay window giving entry to both levels of the upper chamber block. The loss of these structures has left a blocked window. The hall was restored by the Landmark Trust in the 1980s to its original condition, with the rubble-built walls colour-washed and the chapel's 1860 ceiling removed to expose the five arch-braced trusses with ogee-curved struts above the collar and three rows of wind braces. The dais-end fireplace, a relatively early example, was reopened, the walls replastered internally, and

PLATE 227 Croscombe Hall: from the south

the lower window lights shuttered. The embattled stone shelf between the two south windows was cleaned to clarify the arms of Sir William and his wife, flanked by those of Palton with Botreaux and Palton with Wellington.

Sir William died in 1449 without heirs. It was a sixteenth-century successor who added the upper chamber block with ground- and upper-floor fireplaces, approached through the added bay window and lobby as at Fiddleford Manor and similarly pulled down.

Two of the doorways at the lower end of the hall opened into the centrally partitioned services, while the narrower one near the south door accessed the upper chamber. This two-storey unit has been modernised, but the beamed kitchen retains its end-wall hearth while the chamber above retains a cinquefoil light, a fire-place with ogee-moulded jambs and head, and a doorway to a former garderobe.

Croscombe Hall is a late example of a gentry house with chamber at the lower end of the hall. The form of this range has parallels with that fifty years later at Tickenham Court, particularly the layout of the offices and chamber block, as well as the four-bay hall, with a similar stone shelf and bay window to an added residential block.

DARTINGTON HALL, Devon

Like Haddon Hall, Wingfield Manor, and Raglan Castle, Dartington Hall is one of the pivotal houses of late medieval England. And like Wingfield Manor, it was almost entirely con-structed in under fifteen years, so that this Devon mansion by the king's half-brother has a rare unity of character and development of national significance. Dartington Hall was the only medieval house subject to a detailed monograph between those of the early twenti-eth century[1] and books marking the millennium.[2] In view of my detailed analysis in 1970,[3] the following only summarises the present structures before reconsidering significant aspects of this beautifully sited residence.

The manor of Dartington belonged to the Martin family from the early twelfth century to the mid-fourteenth century, and passed to the crown in 1386. Two years later, Richard II granted it to his half-brother John Holand, earl of Huntingdon, who had married John of Gaunt's second daughter. For a time, he was a leading magnate, but he spent much of his later years at Dartington rather than at court, and developed the present mansion until his execu-tion in 1400 for plotting to restore Richard II, following his depo-sition by Henry IV. The family retained Dartington until the line ended with the death of Henry Holand, duke of Exeter in 1475. Among successive owners and tenants, the most eminent were Margaret Beaufort, the mother of Henry VII (1487–1509), and Henry Courtenay, earl of Devon (1525–39). In 1559, the estate was acquired by Sir Arthur Champernowne, and it remained the seat of his descendants until they sold it to Leonard and Dorothy Elmhirst in 1925. The medieval buildings, by then much altered or derelict, were restored with meticulous craftsmanship by William Weir between 1926 and 1938[4] and have been held in trust since 1931.

What immediately strikes a visitor to Dartington Hall is the scale of this late fourteenth-century house. It only has to be compared with the earlier and contemporary buildings in the region – Tiverton and Powderham castles, the episcopal palace at Exeter, or Bradley Manor – to appreciate that Dartington is essentially a met-

PLATE 228 Dartington Hall: hall range and kitchen from North Court

ropolitan import. This is the grandest medieval house in the west of England, looking very much like an Oxford or Cambridge college in scale, enhanced by the lawns and landscaped grounds and colle-giate-like activities that are integral to the continuing function of the Hall. Dorothy and Leonard Elmhirst would be quietly content to see it so maintained at the beginning of the twenty-first century.[5]

DESCRIPTION

Though the Hall is sited on a low rise above the River Dart and can be breathtaking when viewed from the western terraces, the approach is misleading. Any evidence of an outer court has been destroyed by the tarmac road and car park, while the vernacular character of the entrance block and the extended low roof of the barn to its left hardly prepare the visitor for the scale of what is to follow.

The buildings are grouped round an exceptionally spacious courtyard, 265 feet by 164 feet. Beautifully landscaped by Beatrix Farrand in 1932–5, it is the largest house enclosure prior to the six-teenth century and was never spanned by any lost ranges.[6] The hall faces the entrance with its towered porch centred on the gateway, replacing any previous buildings. An inquisition of April 1388 states that 'the buildings and site of the manor and park are somewhat in ruin and decay through lack of repair',[7] suggesting that nothing was done after it had been vacated by the Martin family in 1359 when it was held as one of the many properties of Lord Audley (d.1386). Rebuilding began as soon as Huntingdon had acquired the estate in July 1388, for two months later the dean and chapter of Exeter Cathedral granted him 'slate from the quarry of their manor at Staverton for the roofing of the buildings of the said manor at Dartington'.[8] No further building documentation has been found,

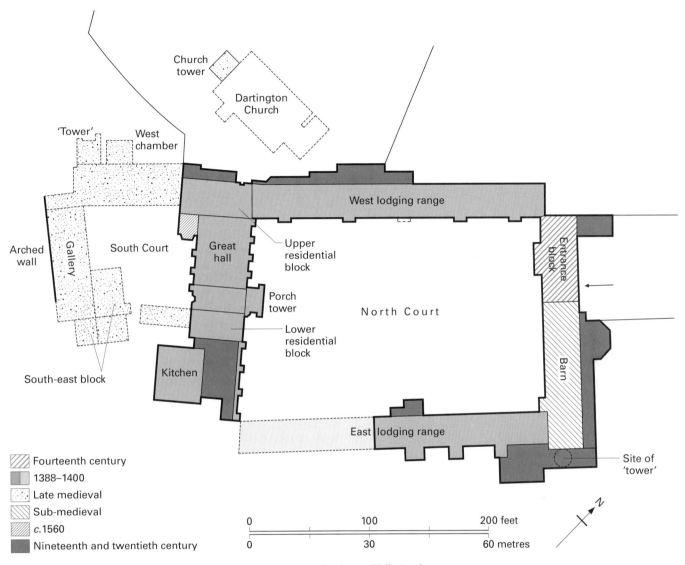

FIGURE 131 Dartington Hall: site plan

though the bosses of the porch tower vault enclose the wheat ears of John Holand and a Lancastrian rose, while the chained white hart of Richard II on the central boss limits its construction to between this badge's first occurrence in October 1390 and Richard's deposition in September 1399.[9]

The long two-storey ranges on the east and west sides of the north court, with contemporary features occasionally peeping out, were built within a few years of the hall. The date of the cruder north range with the entrance archway is more problematic, but the roof structure dates from the fourteenth century. Because of Holand's execution, it seems that he had not time to build the grand gatehouse that one might expect for an establishment on this scale. Private apartments, except for those at each end of the hall, are also lacking, but these may have been provided in the buildings formerly grouped around a smaller courtyard to the south which survived until the late seventeenth century.

Local dark grey limestone has been used throughout the building across all periods of construction. The irregular untrimmed

blocks were quarried nearby, with smaller pieces being used as infill between the larger. Selected stones were used at corners and slightly dressed, but otherwise with very little trimming. It is not possible to distinguish different building periods by the stone used or by the method of building.[10] Local slate was used for paving and probably for roofing in the late fourteenth century, while Beer stone was standard for all dressed work internally.

The two-storey *entrance block* is simply pierced by a large carriage arch on the axis of the hall porch. The archway is curiously crude, round headed, without dressed stone voussoirs. The door frame is original, with doors designed by Weir. There is no other datable masonry as the windows either have been renewed or are over-large insertions. Regrettably, twentieth-century roof lights have been inserted on the north side, creating a bad first impression.[11] Beyond the porter's lodge is a large ground-floor room with sturdy central octagonal post. It had long served as a stable and may always have been so used. The upper floor has always had an external approach of vernacular character to a landing large enough for twin doorways, opening into a heated room of four bays with garderobe access and a two-bay room over the entry passage and porter's lodge. The much-restored roof is a complex structure which has given rise to some discussion, for it may reflect two building phases. The trusses seem to be those of a base-cruck structure possibly of early fourteenth-century date, modified at the close of the century with crown-post features similar to the roof at the lower end of the hall range.[12] Only dendro analysis will resolve the problem, though the significance of this block to John Holand's rebuilding programme can be overplayed. More pertinent is that the excavation of 1962 revealed evidence of a late thirteenth-century structure close to the south court and presumed to be part of the Martin residence,[13] while this possibly early entrance range lay over a hundred yards from that Martin occupation area.

Though the ranges lining both sides of the north court look intriguing, it is preferable that a detailed examination of John Holand's buildings should begin with the hall range. The hall is approached through the three-storey *porch tower* with a handsome two-centred entry archway with wave-moulded outer order and shafts below the soffit. The windows above are Champernowne alterations of the later sixteenth century. Steps rise to the porch, emphasising the high-status approach. The porch has an eight-rib vault with a central boss of Richard II's white hart on a heraldic rose surrounded by the wheat ears of John Holand. Four subsidiary bosses repeat the pattern of the rose and wheat ears. The inner doorway with two more finely moulded continuous hollow chamfers leads into the cross passage. On the left is the classic medieval arrangement of three close-set doorways to the buttery, pantry, and kitchen passage, with a fourth door to the stair accessing the apartments over the porch and service rooms. The opposing cross-passage doorway to the second court is relatively plain but has a door bar socket.

The *great hall* is on the grandest scale (69 feet by 38 feet) and among the finest of its date in England. Of the original fabric, apart from the walls, there remain the moulded two-centred rear arches of the four opposing windows, the carved corbels for the roof timbers, the doorway with badly pitted mouldings in the south-west corner formerly leading to the solar block, and the 17 foot wide fireplace with moulded flattened arch and double flue. It is among the earliest examples of an end-wall fireplace, positioned directly at the rear of the dais and clearly not an insertion.

The nascent Gothick tracery of the windows is surprisingly sympathetic to the hall for its period, between 1734 when Buck's engraving shows square-headed Tudor windows (pl. 11) and the late eighteenth century when the present form is depicted in views of that time. William Weir's post and panel screen of 1932 was based on one nearby in the Church House Inn, Torbryan, although this is a vernacular rather than an aristocratic model. The abstract patterned banners, designed by Elizabeth Peacock (d.1969) during the 1930s, were introduced to restore an element of medieval furnishing at the same time as reducing resonance in the hall.

The impressive five-bay hammer-beam roof is entirely the work of William Weir between 1931 and 1933. It was inspired by the shadow of the medieval timbers remaining on the end wall after the old roof had been taken down in 1813 and the apartment left as a shell. Holand's original roof is now known from George Saunders' drawings of 1805, but they were only made available some years after Weir's structure had been completed.[14] The late fourteenth-century roof combined two structural techniques – the hammer-

beam and the crown-post system. The hammer-beam trusses supported cambered tie beams which carried crown posts with four-way struts. In addition, there were lateral braces from the hammer beams to square-set purlins, and subsidiary trusses in the form of thicker rafters between each of the hammer-beam trusses. Holand's roof was an experimental but important stage in the development of the hammer-beam roof and one which preceded Richard II's remarkable technical and aesthetic achievement at Westminster Hall by only a few years. Weir did not attempt to copy the earlier roof, for the plaster outline was indicative but not prescient of the early form. He chose a more conventional hammer-beam design, with a slightly wider span between the hammer posts for stability, and omitted the crown posts, as their existence was uncertain on the basis of the end-wall outline. He did not insert lateral braces, but added three tiers of wind braces, not in the original design, to strengthen the new structure.[15]

The two *service rooms* flanking the central passage to the kitchen serve entirely modern purposes but retain their early studded doors, one with air holes and a decorative metal plate. This group of arches and doors in the cross passage, in excellent condition, is a fine ensemble of late medieval workmanship. The fourth doorway (with door-bar sockets) opens onto a spiral stair giving access to a pair of apartments, a small room over the porch and a larger one over the buttery and pantry, both with original lightly moulded square-headed fireplaces.[16] The larger chamber was heavily altered by the Champernownes in the late sixteenth century when they inserted the decorative plasterwork in the north part of the room. Weir added the sixteenth-century panelling from Shepley, near Huddersfield, and plain solid beams. On the floor above is a similar suite of altered rooms, but the larger one has no fireplace.[17] The most important feature here is the east gable wall above the inserted ceiling, where the plaster reveals evidence of a crown-post roof supported on a cambered tie beam over this part of the hall range. This group of comfortable residential apartments *may* have been used by the family or senior members of Holand's household staff.

The large *kitchen* was originally free-standing with its own tiny court screened from the main court by a buttressed wall. The kitchen (now used as a dining hall) was linked in the 1930s to the body of the hall range, with the court infilled by a more modern kitchen. This imposing fourteenth-century apartment, 33 feet square, was a roofless ruin before its restoration by Weir. Fortunately, it retained the two massive fireplaces in adjoining walls, their arches rebuilt and with one supporting a reconstructed hood. The apartment is lit by six tall windows with shouldered heads set high up, the ones in the east and south walls original. Weir's roof is entirely conjectural but the whole was a particularly sensitive restoration.

The private house at the upper end of the hall range, ostensibly neo-Elizabethan, is the *upper residential block* of late fourteenth-century origin, with original outer walls and twin stack serving the principal first-floor room as well as the hall. The block, always of three storeys, retains the original ground-floor approach from the hall as at present, and the doorway in the south-west angle to a lost stair turret and approach to the first-floor chamber.

This block was much altered by the Champernownes internally and externally, with a rebuilt gabled top floor, and late Tudor extension on the south side. Some eighteenth-century alterations, including Venetian windows on the south side, were replaced when

PLATE 229 Dartington Hall: hall interior towards the screens

the house was Gothicised in 1846–51 according to proposals by archdeacon Froude (a trustee during a Champernowne minority). More elaborate restoration schemes by Pugin came to nothing. Much of the nineteenth-century work disappeared in 1928–30 when Weir renewed all the south and west windows. The interior today is largely Georgian, with a mid-eighteenth-century marble-paved hall, restrained plasterwork, and a fine staircase with twisted and fluted balusters. There is a special frisson in opening the dais door to move from a medieval to a Georgian interior. The stair leads to a suite of three early eighteenth-century panelled receptions rooms on the first floor of the adjoining west range with dentil cornices and fluted pilasters to the fireplaces.

The special interest of the *west range* is that it is nationally one of the most notable survivals of a range of medieval lodgings. It is not precisely aligned with the hall range, and on architectural grounds may be a few years later, probably *c.*1395–1400, but repeating the shouldered window heads already seen in the kitchen. Much of the detailing has been altered, but one can still recognise its division into five groups of lodgings, each group consisting of four rooms, two on each floor, reached from the projecting porches. The group at the north end is the best preserved, with its pair of four-centred doorways under the porch, external stair, and roofprotected landing to the upper doorways. Each chamber was a self-contained unit, 22 feet by 20 feet, with all the requirements for an individual lodging – a two-light transomed window with shouldered heads, a doorway opposite to a garderobe in a (now destroyed) wooden projection on stone foundations, and a rear fireplace (see the row of chimney stacks along the back wall). All walls were plastered, and each lodging was separated from its neighbour by a timber partition with the upper chambers open to a roof of arch-braced collar trusses.[18]

Of the remaining lodgings, the outer stairs have been taken down though the porches remain, except for the middle one, destroyed in the eighteenth century. The interiors have been much altered and most of the windows are eighteenth-century replacements, but an occasional four-centred doorway, fireplaces, and the head of a window or two show that the pattern was repeated throughout the range except for the last four-room unit. Its porch had only single entries, with the upper one enclosed by a later timber-framed structure with ogee-headed lights (renewed 1976). The doorway at each level accessed a larger end room next to the hall, with the standard lodging opening from it instead of the porch.

The south end of the *east range* was demolished in the early nineteenth century when the remainder was converted to coach house and stables. This section was restored to residential use in the 1930s but has been remodelled internally several times since as meeting rooms and bedrooms. However, Buck's engraving (pl. 11) and two late eighteenth-century drawings show that the range formerly consisted of a series of lodgings extending to the hall range and similarly patterned into groups of four rooms at two levels. Externally approached, each chamber again had a two-light window under a shouldered head[19] and rear-wall fireplace, but the garderobes were contained in stone-built projections (one with retained drain). The surviving details combined with the pictorial evidence indicate that the east range is slightly earlier than that opposite. The doorways have two-centred heads, the windows lack transoms, and the rear garderobes are larger and stone built, for this range is contemporary with the great hall.

These two extended ranges lining both sides of the courtyard provided ten pairs of lodgings on the west side, with two larger than the remainder, and probably fourteen pairs on the east, a total of forty-eight separate chambers. They not only are a rare survival but are built to a high standard of comfort to accommodate Holand's household officers and retinue.

The north court is completed to the east by a low barn of four-teen bays with upper and lower collar trusses. It was unbuttressed and may be of late or sub-medieval date. It was converted to a theatre in 1933–8 by Robert Hening and Walter Gropius when the polygonal nineteenth-century threshing house to the north became a foyer.

The hall cross-passage doorway and, more importantly, the original doorway in the south-west corner of the kitchen indicate there was always a further court south of the hall range, and this is confirmed by the isolated wall with its line of seven four-centred openings. Excavations in 1962 revealed that it was the outer wall of a late medieval gallery, 84 feet long, and was part of a complex linked by ranges to the rooms at each end of the hall. So here was a *second court*, not very large and irregularly planned, that included a two-roomed block south-east of the gallery and two projecting chambers from the west range (see fig. 131). This court was clearly constructed by a person of importance with a desire for privacy.

It has been attributed to the late fourteenth century[20] and to the late fifteenth or early sixteenth century.[21] However, further limited but detailed excavation during the 1990s has indicated that the structures are more complex and incorporate work from several periods.[22] As it stands, this late fourteenth-century mansion has insufficient accommodation for the family and guests of a leading magnate and close member of the royal family, particularly in view of the scale of the hall, the kitchen, and the lodging ranges. A second court was almost certainly planned and possibly initiated as an integral part of its development, holding the private quarters of John Holand and his successors and essential for the privacy, comfort, and lifestyle of a magnate of his wealth and standing.

The construction of Dartington Hall during the second half of Richard II's reign is of major significance in the development of the late medieval house. It is the only large-scale mansion of completely non-defensive form in an era of defendable residences. Furthermore, it retains several structures – a substantial hall with hammer-beam roof, lodging ranges, and possibly a second courtyard complex – of considerable architectural importance for the period. Any review of the Hall must begin with an appreciation of the person who was responsible for its development.

JOHN HOLAND, EARL OF HUNTINGDON

John Holand was the younger son of Sir Thomas Holand and Joan, the daughter of Edmund, earl of Kent. His date of birth is unrecorded, though it was probably in the mid-1350s, and little is known about his infancy or youth.[23] In 1360 Joan married Edward, the thirty-year-old prince of Wales, so that John and his older brother Thomas were brought up in the Black Prince's household under the supervision of his yeoman, John de la Haye. The early upbringing of the two Holand brothers must be set against the background of the second phase of the Hundred Years' War, initially with success during the mid-1360s in Aquitaine and Gascony where Joan gave birth to two boys – the short-lived Edward of Angoulême and Richard of Bordeaux – and subsequently witness to major setbacks at the hands of the rejuvenated French command and the decline of England's most chivalrous knight (d.1376).

John Holand was probably in his early twenties when his young half-brother, Richard of Bordeaux, succeeded to the throne in 1377. John participated in an attack on St Malo in the following year led by his soldier uncle, John of Gaunt, duke of Lancaster, was knighted in 1380, and held some minor offices such as justice of Chester (1381) and lieutenant of Ireland (1382). He led the interrogators involved in the murder of a Carmelite friar who accused Lancaster of plotting to murder Richard (1384), and in the following year killed Sir Ralph Stafford, a close friend of the king, in a brawl near York during preparations for the partially successful invasion of Scotland. The king swore vengeance on Holand, who was a marked outlaw until a royal reconciliation was engineered by John of Gaunt so that he could appoint Holand constable of the army that he was planning to lead to conquer Castile. The fleet left Plymouth in July 1386, but not before Gaunt had had to organise a shot-gun wedding between his second daughter, the twenty-two-year old Elizabeth, and his constable, and now son-in-law.[24]

Gaunt's Castilian campaign was a failure, with the army ravaged by disease and hampered by disagreement with his Portuguese ally, and with a temperamental constable who lacked military or administrative competence.[25] Holand returned to England early in 1388 to put the best gloss on the collapse of Gaunt's expedition, and he was rewarded by the Appellants – the opposition magnates now seeking appeasement – with the earldom of Huntingdon and a grant of land valued at £1,333 6s. 8d. per annum.[26] It is impossible to avoid the conclusion that the Castilian campaign wrought a fundamental change in Huntingdon and John of Gaunt. The disease which had ravaged the Lancastrian army may have physically weakened Huntingdon too. There was no repetition of his earlier violent outbursts, while Gaunt entered upon a period of co-operation with the king that marks the last ten years of his life. A great hunting party given by Gaunt at Leicester in 1390 for Richard and his queen, his brothers, son-in-law, and many lords, bishops, and ladies was symptomatic of the change in outlook and restoration of family unity.

For Richard's personal rule to succeed during the 1390s, he needed to build a new courtier nobility round him. His earlier distaste for his half-brother was replaced by royal favour and the bestowal of profitable offices, including admiral of the King's fleet from the Thames westward (1389), chamberlain of Richard's household for life (1390), and a series of land grants. But though Huntingdon was now a thoroughgoing loyalist and one of the king's confidants,[27] he was politically obedient rather than an instigator. He did not become an activist in parliament or in the council chamber until the last two years of Richard's reign, when he became a prime member of Richard's inner circle.

The rebuilding of Dartington Hall had begun immediately after Huntingdon had been raised to the earldom, and probably continued until the close of the century. It was intended that it should reflect his position and wealth as a major figure in the south-west and on a sufficient scale to accommodate his family, household, and retinue. Like Lord Scrope, who refused to take office under Richard II after 1382 and retired to the castle he was building at Bolton in Wensleydale, Huntingdon chose to build his new residence far from the court or important lines of communication. On the other hand, Devon was a large county where royal power was weak.

Huntingdon had initially chosen Dartington as his home some years before his peerage,[28] but the construction of a spectacular mansion here reflected not only on Huntingdon but also on the king who had made it possible and who now enjoyed a substantial outpost of Ricardian lordship. The badges of the two families in the hall porch symbolised and cemented this mutual association of gratitude and support. The Hall was intended to be not only the dynastic centre of this younger branch of a semi-royal family but also a hymn of gratitude to the monarch who had made it possible.[29]

Huntingdon was at the Hall in October 1393,[30] and he entertained several members of the Courtenay family there in April 1396.[31] His wife and children were in residence in March 1400 shortly after the inventory of goods and chattels had been drawn up testifying to the richness and extent of some of the furnishings in the Hall at that time.[32] The list is only partial, but the Hall was clearly furnished in a manner appropriate to Huntingdon's position. It includes nine beds, each with its own set of curtains, seventy-nine rugs and hangings, forty cushions, and eight carpets as well as a tapestry in the great hall. Books, armour, and kitchen equipment are also identified but tables, chairs, benches, and ornaments are not. The inventory confirms that the Hall contained a chapel, and though none of the items has survived the vicissitudes of six centuries, timber insertions for carrying tapestry hooks were found above the hall fireplace in 1933. Some fragments of contemporary stained glass have also been traced at Weare Giffard Hall, where four badges have been inserted in the hall windows showing Huntingdon's wheat ears enlaced with the gold letters I and E, the initials of John and Elizabeth Holand.

Huntingdon's presence in Devon challenged the established dominance of the Courtenay family in the county, heightened by Huntingdon's elevation to the dukedom of Exeter in 1397 and the further enhancement of his estate holding.[33] It was one of the examples at the close of Richard II's reign where entrenched territorial nobility and regional power were being upset by incomers.[34] Though Huntingdon avoided upsetting local interests, the threat of a new and potentially much wider sphere of influence than the Courtenays exerted was short-lived, for John Holand's regional pre-eminence was erased within two years.

In 1397, Huntingdon had toyed with helping to lead a crusade,[35] but this was quickly forgotten in the events that led to Richard II's and Huntingdon's unexpected and startling arrest of the five Appellants – the duke of Gloucester, the earls of Arundel, Warwick, and Nottingham, and the archbishop of Canterbury – and their exile or death. While Huntingdon was rewarded with the dukedom, success went to Richard's head. The capriciousness of his rule, the oaths of loyalty, forced loans, and arbitrary fines inexorably came to a head with the royal confiscation of the duchy of Lancaster's estates immediately after Gaunt's death (1399). Huntingdon was now numbered among the king's most active supporters at court and he accompanied Richard on his futile two-month Irish campaign (June–July 1399). They were both arrested by Gaunt's son, Henry Bolingbroke, shortly after their return to Pembrokeshire. Richard was captured and imprisoned, and abdicated, Bolingbroke was chosen as king, while Exeter was stripped of his dukedom. The attempt by the Holand family that winter to restore Richard to the throne through rebellion was an ignominious failure, concluding with the execution of Huntingdon at Pleshey Castle and the murder of Richard II at Pontefract Castle.

Though Huntingdon had been a capable exponent of jousting in his youth, he was also impetuous, flamboyant, quick-tempered, and extravagant. It is probable that the revenue from Huntingdon's estates at the beginning of 1397 was between £2,000 and £2,500 per annum, plus the fees from custodial castles and the valuable profits from feudal incidents. At the same time, his outgoings were equally substantial, including staff, household, and administrative costs, clothes and furnishings for his family and household, the many annuities and recorded gifts of jewels, clothes, silver, and plate, and the cost of his splendid new mansion in Devon. No wonder Richard II had to pardon his half-brother from all his debts due to the crown in May 1393 and again in April 1399.[36] The presence of Thomas Litlington, the king's painter, in his company during the Irish expedition is possibly indicative of artistic appreciation, while several books were discovered among his personal possessions at Dartington Hall in 1400, suggestive of literacy. The chronicle *Traison et Mort de Richard II*, possibly written by an unfriendly member of the countess of Huntingdon's household,[37] shows that he was not devoid of warmth or charm to his wife and children. Like the king, he was deeply conscious of his lineage, anxious to surround himself with the trappings of display, and imbued with an exalted sense of importance.[38] But Huntingdon was also a mediocrity, devoid of military ability or sagacious counsel, thrust into a position where he could do manifold disservice to himself and those close to him. To some extent, he was a typical product of late fourteenth-century chivalry – aggressive in temper and militant in taste – but in his case compounded by minimal ability and a wayward nature.

PLANNING AND DESIGN ASSESSMENT

A non-defensive site

In view of the foregoing background, the non-defensive character of Dartington Hall is all the more surprising. The last thirty years of the fourteenth century was a period of intensive military and defensive building activity across England by both magnates and élite gentry.[39] Some of the castles such as Queenborough, Cooling, and Scotney and the additions at Carisbrooke and Saltwood were built to defend the south-east from anticipated attacks from France. Earlier houses in the region such as Amberley and Halnaker were now given additional protective enclosures. Northern fortresses such as Bolton, Lumley, and Raby reflected baronial assertiveness, while Baginton, Wardour, and Warkworth castles adopted the fashionable tower-like form. Some residences were embellished with the trappings of defence for status reasons as at Donnington, Farleigh Hungerford, and Wingfield castles, but even the major residential ranges developed within Caldicot, Kenilworth, and Portchester castles avoided impairing the protection of the earlier fortifications. In contrast, Huntingdon's Devon mansion was totally lacking in any such defensive measures, and stands almost alone in this respect from its contemporaries.

The entrance is rather crude, simply a large carriage arch and passage within a two-storeyed unit. It lacks portcullis, wall-walk, or battlement protection, while the outer archway is without dressed voussoirs. There is no datable masonry, but the modest character of the block and its roof structure suggest that it was an earlier building on the site at the time of Huntingdon's acquisition. Even so, he surely cannot have intended to leave this block as the approach to the magnificent mansion he was building. His premature death when he was less than fifty years old probably precluded the fulfilment of any plans to replace it with the grand gatehouse that might be expected for an establishment on this scale which long continued to be an architectural showpiece in Devon.[40]

Despite the presence of springs and a brook a hundred yards south-west of the Hall, no traces have been found of any enclosing moat, wet or dry. Admittedly, as it stands on gently rising ground above the River Dart with a small dell to the south, neither feature would have afforded even minimal defence, while the churchyard and adjacent higher ground to the east increased the residence's vulnerability. Trenching in front of the entrance block on several occasions during the last seventy years has proved extremely difficult because of the rocky subsoil but has never revealed evidence of a drawbridge or ditch, while a drawing of the Hall of about 1540 shows the totally open character of the north side at that time.

Yet this drawing, part of an annotated pictorial review of the state of the coastal defences from Exeter to Land's End,[41] also shows the Hall with three towers (fig. 132). Caution must be shown in reading too much into this telescoped thumbnail sketch of the Hall, for although the accuracy of the map is accepted,[42] there is a conflict of opinion as to whether or not the detailed drawings of the coastal fortifications are reliable.[43]

The hall is shown rising above the east range of lodgings marked by three gables, possibly symbolically representing those still above the garderobe projections. The taller block at the south end is in the position of the kitchen and not unlike its present form. On the other hand, none of the buildings round the second court seems to be shown despite their presence at that time. The remaining elements of the illustration are three towers – one behind the great hall and one on either side of it. That to the left is surmounted by a substantial projection topped by a turret and that to the right, seemingly circular, has a tapering portion supporting a slender upper structure. Significantly, none of these towers is embattled, although the purpose of the map was to show all fortifications in the region.

Two tower-like structures exist today, the church tower and the porch tower, and evidence has been discovered of a third. Neither of the surviving towers is as tall as those shown in the drawing, but that behind the great hall is in the right position and shaped correctly for the church tower. Leaving aside the porch tower for the moment, part of the lower courses of a large circular tower was discovered in 1936 during preparations for an extension at the east end of the barn. No record was made of the discovery, which was recalled for me by Leonard Elmhirst in 1958 although he was uncertain about the thickness of the walling. It may have been a survival of the Martins' tenancy, or it may have been a late medieval addition like the adjacent barn – possibly a dovecote or a beacon tower. It does not have any obvious military significance, is awkwardly sited for such a purpose, and was not integrated into the adjacent ranges.

Equally enigmatic is the tower depicted to the left of the great hall. It is possible that the foundations discovered in 1962 and 1993–9 during excavations on the site of the second court were its footings,[44] but it was an added feature with varied wall thickness, making this a problematic development.[45] The drawing may even represent the porch tower, admittedly on the wrong side of the hall, but illustrating its projecting upper section and capped staircase

FIGURE 132 Dartington Hall: *c.*1540

turret. The ease with which it is possible to compare what looks like a strong tower with a much more modest survival shows that too much should not be read into the sketch, so that the question of accurate representation or otherwise is left open. Equally clearly, these towers do not convert the site into a defensive one. All the usual appurtenances of fortification – moat, drawbridge, portcullis, battlemented curtain wall, machicolations, wall-walk, and flanking towers – are totally absent. The battlements of the hall and chamber blocks are entirely decorative, for Dartington was an open site, totally different in concept from almost every other residence built by Huntingdon's fellow magnates during the late fourteenth century. It is also the first of a new type of late medieval mansion – the trophy house – characterised by almost total rebuilding, development round more than one courtyard, rapid completion, standing open to the world, and visibly reflecting the owner's achievements and status.[46]

The lodgings

The two ranges of lodgings filling the sides of the great courtyard are a survival of national importance. The west range stands complete, divided into five groups of chambers. Four of them are identical sets of four self-contained lodgings, externally approached. The block adjacent to the hall was built to a different plan, with two larger rooms and two standard chambers opening from them. Of this group, the former may have been communal rooms for junior staff, possibly a hall or dormitory as at Ewelme (1420s to 1450) and Bishop's Waltham Palace (1438–42).[47] Though part of the east range on the opposite side of the court was destroyed at the beginning of the nineteenth century, pictorial evidence confirms that it extended to the kitchen offices and was similarly patterned into groups of four rooms. Both ranges were 20 feet deep internally, but the east lodgings were built a few years earlier and were only 17 feet wide rather than the 22 feet opposite.[48] Together, they made a total of forty-six standard self-contained lodgings and two communal lodgings.

The development of lodging ranges in a domestic environment was a corollary of the growth of seigniorial households during the second and third quarters of the fourteenth century. A magnate's desire for more permanent residence in preference to periodic progressions, the growth of households with their greater division of staff duties, and the necessity to employ large numbers of retainers resulted in an architectural form reflecting this development in a nobleman's lifestyle. Rarely have staff lodgings survived on such a scale as those at Dartington, and few from such an early date. Later ranges were built with the lodgings approached from internal corridors in preference to individual entrances, but for their time, the Dartington lodgings were built to a remarkably high standard of domestic comfort, confirming contemporary documentary evidence that household members enjoyed relatively high living standards.

What is less clear is how many people occupied a lodging, or whether they were all permanently used. A magnate's household was essentially made up of two groups – the officials, staff, and domestic servants permanently employed by the lord and his wife, and the retainers who held the lord's livery and were periodically attached to him. Household numbers varied considerably, but it has been estimated that the household of the higher nobility during the second half of the fourteenth century consisted of between fifty and a hundred permanent staff while a baron would have between twenty and fifty staff.[49] In 1384–5, the earl of Devon distributed liveries to 135 staff, of whom at least sixty were permanent members of his household at Tiverton Castle.[50] Some of the forty-eight or so lodgings at Dartington may have housed Holand's most senior officials and retainers but there was probably no hard and fast rule. The principal officials might occupy an individual lodging but it was usual for staff to share. They might be in pairs, sleeping in a bed together,[51] with the essential proviso that no man should have to share with another of lower social standing than himself. It is also likely there were always a number of vacant lodgings at any one time. Retainers' attendance was intermittent, employees could be granted leave of absence for long periods, while the ten or more attendants of even a minor titled guest (never mind about a baron) had to be accommodated.

What is significant about the Dartington ranges is their occurrence in a mansion that, even without their presence, clearly reflected the close association between Huntingdon and the king during the period of construction. We have little indication of the size of Huntingdon's retinue, but the facts that the contingent accompanying him to Scotland in 1385 was the largest of any knight present, the hall at Dartington was almost the largest constructed during the last quarter of the fourteenth century, and the lodgings built for his household were particularly extensive suggest that Huntingdon supported a retinue of considerable size. We know the names of some of his household staff – his steward, chamberlain, chaplain, butler, and pantler – but there is evidence that Huntingdon rapidly expanded his retinue during the late 1390s at the same time that he became a far more active supporter of the king. Richard II was similarly developing a considerable retinue of liveried servants, notably the Cheshire *vigilia*,[52] but Huntingdon's

PLATE 230 Dartington Hall: longitudinal section and cross-section of dais end of hall by George Saunders (1805)

retinue was notoriously undisciplined. The many illegalities perpetrated by its members point to active encouragement rather than any lack of leadership on Huntingdon's part.[53] Two contracts survive for September 1399, when Huntingdon retained Thomas Proudfoot and John Trenarke for personal attendance on the earl and his family at an annual wage of £10.[54] Though these are haphazard survivals, Huntingdon was one of the leading magnates angrily accused in 1399 of having committed numerous oppressions 'under colour of ther Lordeshipes', bringing anti-livery legislation to a head. At the point that Huntingdon was deprived of his dukedom (November 1399), he was specifically forbidden 'to give liveries of sign or to have a greater retinue than necessary for his household'.[55] History and architecture are conjoined at Dartington in this spectacular courtyard development, without parallel since the destruction long ago of the similar lodging ranges built by Edward III round the upper ward of Windsor Castle.

The great hall roof

It might be anticipated that the hall roof of Huntingdon's new mansion would be a striking architectural display. It could have been a base-cruck structure such as that spanning the guest hall at Buckfast Abbey or formerly over the hall at Okehampton Castle (early fourteenth century). It might have been combined with a crown post supporting a collar purlin like those over the nave vault of Exeter Cathedral (early to mid-fourteenth century), or even a line of arch-braced collar trusses with two or three side purlins and wind braces. This last had been adopted for the markedly wide hall at Penshurst Place (c.1341–9) and was used in larger Devon houses during the following century, as at Bradley Manor (early fifteenth century), and Shute Barton and Littlehempston Manor (mid-fifteenth century). Such a structure could have been used to grand

effect in the great hall at Dartington, but the chosen form was a hammer-beam structure. Was there a particular reason for this?

The hammer-beam principle had already been in use for a century, initially for relatively modest structures.[56] It occurs in the kitchen at the Bishop's Palace, Chichester (c.1300), but the first extant hall adopting this form is the so-called Pilgrims' Hall in Winchester Cathedral close, part of a range that was possibly guest accommodation at St Swithun's Priory.[57] Though of a single constructional phase of c.1310–11, this range included trusses of raised aisle, base-cruck, and hammer-beam design – elements which all occur at Dartington Hall. Though we have no doubt lost other examples, the hammer-beam form also occurs in the hall of Upton Court in Berkshire (early 1320s) and probably as a mid-fourteenth-century insertion in the earlier hall at Tiptofts Manor in Essex.[58]

The first hammer-beam roof on the grandest scale was probably erected in c.1376 at Kenilworth Castle by William Wintringham for John of Gaunt, to span the widest secular unaisled hall in the country at the time of its construction.[59] From that point onwards, the form suddenly became fashionable and was adopted in court circles. At this time, Richard FitzAlan, 3rd earl of Arundel rebuilt the hall at his patronymic castle. It was destroyed in 1643–4 but was described as resembling those spanning the halls at Westminster and Eltham Palace, i.e. of hammer-beam form.[60] It was then chosen by Huntingdon for his Devon residence (c.1388–1400), followed almost immediately by Richard II at Westminster Hall (1393–9) for the most prestigious roof of the era.

The similar form chosen by a close group of court patrons cannot be coincidence, though there are structural and decorative differences between those of Gaunt and his nephews. Huntingdon's roof lacks the great arch ribs and decorative tracery of Westminster and the decorative stone tracery characteristic of the walls at Kenilworth that may have extended upwards in an imitative timber structure. Between these two there was also a close relationship between the leading craftsmen that is not reflected at Dartington.[61] Lynn Courtenay has also suggested that the origins of the Westminster roof lie as much in the arch-braced and collar form as with the hammer-beam bracket, and that its prototypes were the roofs at Windsor Castle, New College, Oxford, and Lambeth Palace rather than any identified hammer-beam structures.[62]

The master-carpenter employed by Huntingdon came from a different tradition of roof construction and one that may have stemmed from a Hampshire/Sussex school of carpentry that extended into Wiltshire and Devon. John Harvey traced such a link during the first half of the fourteenth century. Thomas of Witney who worked at Winchester Cathedral presbytery during the first years after 1300 had moved to Exeter Cathedral by 1316 and was employed there until his death soon after 1342. In addition to his masonry ability, he was exceptionally skilled in carpentry and may well have introduced the hammer-beam design into south-west England.[63] John Crook also adds that he may have been responsible for bringing the base-cruck form to Devon.[64] The link between Hampshire and Devon is strengthened by the hammer-beam roofs identified in Wiltshire, and more particularly at Balle's Place, Salisbury until its removal in 1962. This roof was similar to that of the Pilgrims' Hall, though with a flat rather than a cambered collar, and a crown post braced four ways, and lacking the carved heads on the hammer-beams ends. It was attributed to between 1370 and 1385[65] and was far more a precursor of the severely practical structure at Dartington than the highly decorative synthesis achieved by the royal carpenters at Westminster.

Yet what we see today is not the whole story. Saunders' drawings of Huntingdon's roof shortly before its destruction in c.1813 show there were small pendant projections at the ends of the hammer beams, while William White's *History, Gazetteer, and Directory of Devonshire*, published in 1850, states that the ceiling of the hall was embellished with the arms of Richard II and the duke of Exeter.[66] Apart from the fact that this might help to limit the hall roof to Holand's ducal years, i.e. 1397–9, White was probably recording evidence observed before the roof had been pulled down a generation earlier. A patron as prestige-conscious as Huntingdon would have wanted not only the most visually impressive and distinctive roof that could be achieved, but one that embraced his courtly rôle. The cultural and symbolic features of this roof reinforced what the porch bosses have already told us. In its form and decoration, it was as much a reflection of gratitude by Huntingdon for family support as a public display of his loyal affiliation to Ricardian authority.

The second court

As it stands today, the Hall is a truncated building. Excavations on my behalf over much of the lawn south of the great hall by Colin Platt in 1962 revealed considerable evidence of a second court, with further information provided by a resistivity survey by Anthony Clark in 1963 and training excavations in a small section of the west range by Christopher Currie in 1993–9.

This court was not large and was irregularly planned. It consisted of a two-storeyed gallery, 24 feet wide and 84 feet long internally, linked at each end by a range apparently extending to the upper and lower residential blocks respectively. A large staircase was recovered at the junction of the gallery to the west range, and the first of the two projections from this range has been excavated to some depth. Platt identified it as a tower, approximately 16 feet by 10 feet internally, with fireplace and garderobe channel to one side.[67] Currie has subsequently shown that it was at least two-storeyed with a basement, and was an added feature with a 5½ foot thick south wall and pronounced batter.[68] Next to it was the massive wall base to a second unit of about the same size, revealed by excavation and the resistivity survey.[69] The destruction of the remainder of this range towards the house seems to have been particularly thorough and a timber-framed structure on sleeper walls cannot be ruled out.

A small ante-chamber at the south end of the gallery led to a block of two rooms, the larger entered by a door from the internal court but otherwise lacking in distinctive features. The resistivity survey identified a detached narrower range extending to the lower residential block and in line with the first-floor doorway of that block. This may also have been timber-framed.

The site excavations as well as the irregular planning and position of the various buildings confirm there was more than one late medieval development phase. The presence of earlier buildings, with one identified astride the open court attributed to the later thirteenth century,[70] may have dictated the position of the subsequent structures. But what is now clear is that this second court was a multi-phased development, with the last stage occurring in 1700–20 when the buildings were demolished and the area wall-enclosed to create a formal quadrangular garden incorporating the row of arches still standing on the south side.

I have reconsidered my initial interpretation of the site since 1970 when I attributed much of its development to the late fourteenth century. The area has been shown to be more complex, with the latest assessment determined by the date of the standing arched wall. A measured survey has confirmed that it was part of a gallery, probably two-storeyed, erected between the mid-fifteenth and the early sixteenth centuries.[71] This is a wide time span, allowing an attribution to one of several owners of Dartington Hall. In the opinion of Currie and Rushton, the gallery may be as late as the 1540s but is pinpointed to c.1500 on the comparative basis of two-storeyed galleries in England. By a quantum leap, this attribution is then extended across all structures that make up the second court, eliminating any earlier activity by John Holand, earl of Huntingdon, or his immediate successors.[72] All conflicting evidence is overcome by ignoring it.

The sequence of ownership of the Hall between 1461, when Henry 4th duke of Exeter fled the country, and the advent of the Champernowne family in 1559 is clear, but occupation information is much more scarce. No expenditure on or visits to the Hall can be traced after 1483 by Margaret, countess of Richmond and Derby (1487–1509), by Henry Courtenay, earl of Devon (1525–39), or by the last two queens of Henry VIII (1539–48).[73] According to Leland, in the 1540s Sir Thomas St Ledger was the last person to have kept house at Dartington,[74] and in my opinion, it was he who had the means, the motive and the opportunity to build the gallery.

St Ledger had married the king's favourite sister Anne, shortly after she had divorced her first husband, the duke of Exeter, in 1472. For her part, Anne had been able to secure all of Exeter's estates after his attainder in 1461 and was able to settle them on her second husband upon her own death in 1476. St Ledger therefore had the financial resources, as well as the incentive, to build a gallery befitting the duchess of Exeter's semi-royal status and which would enhance a mansion that was beginning to look old-fashioned. Construction between 1472 and St Ledger's execution in 1483 for rebelling against Richard III not only meets the dating span of the standing wall but also sets it in the vanguard of a new form of architectural development. Galleries were becoming popular in larger houses well before the Tudor period. Apart from the fact that first-floor galleries over loggias were already a mid-century talking point (*vide* Much Wenlock, Herstmonceux, Eton College, Ockwells, Knole), one of the earliest comparable two-storeyed survivals is that at Croydon Palace, 75 feet long and 15 feet wide with windows on both sides, attributed to archbishop Bourchier (1454–86). If St Ledger wanted to impress his wife in the early 1470s or later status-conscious friends like Sir William Stonor's wife who visited the Hall in 1482, then what would be more natural than to erect the latest architectural feature?[75] If so, then the development of the second court can be attributed to the 1470s or early 1480s, with the opinion that the work was carried out between 1500 and 1540 during ownership of absentee royal proprietors[76] as tendentious.

Turning to the possible date for the development of the court and the different attributions, it is helpful to consider the planning, archaeological, architectural and documentary evidence in turn. The area is relatively small, with an irregular disposition of structures. Unfortunately, it has not yet been possible to give exact dates for the excavated medieval structures because the ground surface, more than 5 feet deep in places, was not reached by Platt or Currie.[77] Nor has the whole site been subject to excavation, so a phased development plan has not yet proved possible. Even so, the

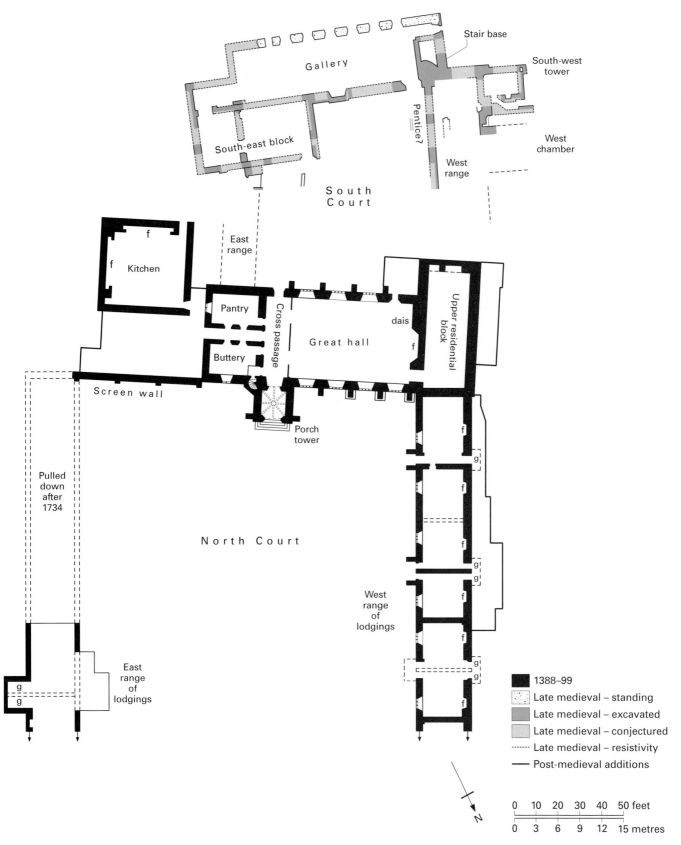

FIGURE 133 Dartington Hall: ground plan of hall range, north court lodgings, and south court excavations

structures seem to include a late thirteenth-century building attributed to the Martin family and the gallery that I ascribe to the years close to 1475. The date of the two excavated towers and other structures is still unclear. There is little doubt, though, that the overall development of the site was always limited by the sharply falling ground to the dell to the south.

Irregular planning was a feature of large-scale houses such as Penhallam (early thirteenth century), Clarendon Palace (mid-thirteenth century) and Kennington Palace (mid-fourteenth century). But the last was on the cusp of the more regular courtyard development expressed at Maxstoke, Bolton and Bodiam castles and was demonstrated at Dartington by the north court of c.1388–1400. The contrast between this and the irregular, smaller second court suggests to me that the latter preceded the large formal outer court rather than following it a century and a half later, *pace* Currie and Rushton. Furthermore, the Martin-attributed building and the area's subsequent development enjoin the view that this court may have been the original centre of the residence well before the late fourteenth century.

Finds were recovered from the west range during the 1990s that extend from the twelfth to the seventeenth centuries. The late fifteenth-century phase is the more immediately identifiable through the Hispano-Moresque plate, the traceried head of a window, and a pin of about 1500. The earlier pottery that has been recovered is less clearly attributable for it is essentially rough work, typical of the region. As Platt did not recover any pottery evidence clearly identifiable to the late fourteenth century, he rejected any buildings of that time, but he did not excavate enough on a heavily built-up site to find the fourteenth- to early fifteenth-century Totnes-type ware that Currie did.[78] These sherds were modest in number but relevant. Platt and Currie both recovered considerable quantities of glazed ridge tiles, clearly differentiated by their coarseness and better quality. John Hurst was of the opinion that the better-quality green-glazed tiles were of the late fourteenth or early fifteenth century, and that the poorer second type of hard sandy fabric and light incisions and decorative white paint were made in the second half of the fifteenth century.[79] Yet despite this considerable body of work, the site has far from yielded up all its secrets.

Holand's surviving personal accommodation is extremely limited, though his intention to extend it southwards is signalled architecturally by the late fourteenth-century cross-passage doorway to the second court, the first-floor doorway nearby, and the entry in the south-west corner of the kitchen.[80] The question is whether Holand was able to carry out his intention or not. Though the second-court excavations were only partial, they revealed much of the west range[81] while the resistivity survey of 1963 identified the east range in line with the lower residential block. Some of the buildings may have been timber-framed in part or whole, while Holand's sudden death when he was still in his late forties would have stopped any construction work in its tracks. Replacement or redevelopment a hundred years later is more likely than Currie and Rushton's suggested total initiation on a virgin site during the early sixteenth century. If the distinctive irregular planning of Dartington's second court suggests any particular period, it is that of piecemeal organic development during the fourteenth century, rather than the structured planning and regularity practised throughout the Tudor period.

The inventory of Holand's goods at Dartington Hall drawn up after his execution in 1400 identifies more personal goods than can be contained in the three family chambers of the upper residential block. Even if the two rooms above the services are included – highly unlikely to be used by a magnate so close to the services and kitchen[82] – the inventory stands short without the second court. Far more important is the inclusion of items referring to the private chapel, for which no structural evidence has yet been found. Such a chapel would have been close to the family apartments as in other contemporary magnate residences such as Bolton, Kenilworth and Raby castles. And the only position for such an important structure would have been as part of the second court.

To assess the claim that the double-courtyard plan was a post-1500 development rather than part of John Holand's concept,[83] the mansion needs to be put into a wider context. It is clear from leading contemporary residences such as Wardour, Warkworth and Bolton castles that they were planned with a sequence of spacious private apartments for the family. If the tower-like form preferred meant that their planning was necessarily complex, as in the examples given, the relative absence of such restrictions as at Woodsford, Kenilworth or Raby castles enabled a more generous spread of private apartments to be created. The concurrent royal lodgings on an extremely limited site at Portchester Castle (1396–99) included a great chamber, privy chamber, third royal chamber and chapel, plus the adjacent rooms in the earlier keep, while the contemporary family accommodation built by a knight nearby at Powderham Castle (1392–1406) is more extensive than the single solar block for the semi-royal family at Dartington Hall.

The planning regularity practised at this time is demonstrated by the outer court of 1388–1400 at Dartington, while the inchoate planning of the second court belongs to the earlier tradition. It extends as far back as the royal palaces at Kennington (1340–63), the Savoy (1350–7) and Rotherhithe (1353–6). Formal courtyard planning had become standard for elite residences by the early fifteenth century as at Winchester College (1387–1401 with two courts) and Sheen Palace (1414–22 initially with a single court), followed by double-courtyard residences such as Southwell Palace (c.1426–36), Minster Lovell Hall (c.1431–42), and Wingfield Manor (1439–56). This had become even more so for high-status houses on new sites later in the century, as at Sudeley Castle (1441–78), Knole (1456–86) and Cotehele (c.1470–1530). Where there are major early to mid-fifteenth-century additions at irregularly planned sites, it is because the position of the new work was determined by the earlier layout, as at Shute (1430s/40s), Croydon Palace (c.1445–1500), Orchard Wyndham (by c.1420), and even Acton Court as late as the 1530s. It is not unreasonable to see this occurring with the gallery at Dartington.

The obvious absence of several necessary chambers at Holand's residence essential to the lifestyle of a leading magnate in the late fourteenth century, such as his private suite, a chapel and accommodation for honoured guests, is only resolved if at least part of the second court was erected to provide them. Huntingdon's staff and retinue were generously housed in nearly fifty chambers built to a high standard of comfort. But are we to believe that the apartments of the king's half-brother, married to the duke of Lancaster's daughter, were simply two linked chambers in the upper residential block above an independent ground-floor room? Unless the initiation of a further court is postulated, the contrast between staff and seigniorial accommodation at Dartington would be undignified and inexplicable to any of Holand's contemporaries.

It is possible on historical grounds for John, 3rd duke of Exeter to have added the court in the late 1420s during a break in his thirty-year military career in France, but a recent survey of his finances has confirmed that the strain of raising his ransom at that time and his preference for court life whenever in England led to a total lack of interest in his south-west estates.[84] It is far more likely that his father's extensive building programme included the essential elements necessary to create a residence befitting his semi-royal status. The scale of the hall and north court which provided such extensive lodgings for members of Holand's household is totally at variance with the scale of his personal accommodation as it stands at present. The inventory made after Holand's death in 1400 confirms the existence of a number of richly furnished apartments, while recent work on late medieval households has underlined that it was the number, size, and quality of the apartments in a house as well as the size of the household that helped to determine a magnate's standing with his peers, his neighbours and his tenants.[85] Outward show rather than personal ability was all important in late medieval society, and without some of the private apartments round the second court Holand's impressive residence is missing an essential element. The excavations are far from conclusive, but the development of the site may have been initiated well before Holand's time, followed by his planned and probably executed activity that formed the basis for a major restructuring in the late fifteenth century.

Dartington Hall represents success as well as failure in Holand's eventful life. He was a pioneer in architectural planning in south-west England with a large-scale residence of metropolitan character that was entirely non-defensive, and encompassed an innovative roof for his ceremonial hall, multiple lodgings for his extended household, and a more private court for his family. He also intended that the Hall should be the dynastic centre of the younger branch of this semi-royal family but it did not become so. His execution and forfeiture in 1400 was swiftly followed by his wife's remarriage to Sir John Cornwall, and though she was assiduous in reassembling the forfeited estates, she did not share Holand's enthusiasm for south-west England. Dartington was subject to the long minority and military career abroad of Holand's thrice-married son John (d.1447) while his grandson's preference for politics and court life contributed to the forfeiture of all his estates in 1461 and death without heirs in 1475. The mansion was becoming old-fashioned until it was occupied by Edward IV's brother-in-law in 1476. Sir Thomas St Ledger is far more likely to have built the gallery than any non-attending royals who, we are asked to believe, were responsible for an irregularly planned and probably piecemeal-developed courtyard in a much later era when formality, visual regularity and symmetry had become essential for high-status mansions.[86]

CONCLUSION

If the Hall represents a failed dynastic centre by a member of the royal family, it also stands as one of the most spectacular domestic survivals of medieval England. It is a building of national importance, planned on a most generous scale, with several features contributing to the development of the late medieval house, including planning evidence of being the earliest non-collegiate double-courtyard residence in the country. Yet it has some parochial elements too, particularly in the form of the entrance block and hall roofs. It eschewed the decorative tracery and panelling of the court school, and was designed as a low, spreading residence rather than in the compact vertical mode adopted by Holand's peers at Wardour, Nunney, Bolton and Warkworth. What was certainly never anticipated was the order and setting that the Hall acquired

five centuries later, for the scale and grandeur of the buildings and their majestic sylvan setting create an atmosphere of quiet beauty and dignity that make a visit to Dartington one of marked pleasure.

NOTES

1 They include books by F. H. Cheetham on Haddon Hall (1904) and W. H. St John Hope on Cowdray (1919) and the castles at Belsay by Sir Arthur Middleton (1910), W. H. St John Hope on Windsor (1913), the Marquis Curzon of Kedleston on Bodiam (1926) and Curzon with H. A. Tipping on Tattershall (1929).
2 J. Heward and R. Taylor, *The Country Houses of Northamptonshire* (1996); *Ludlow Castle*, ed. R. Shoesmith and A. Johnson (2000); T. Tatton-Brown, *Lambeth Palace* (2000).
3 Emery (1970). It replaced short accounts in *Arch. Jour.* 30 (1873) 440–2 and 70 (1913) 553–7, and my assessment in *Arch. Jour.* 115 (1958) 184–202.
4 R. Snell, *William Weir and Dartington Hall* (1986). Weir died in 1950.
5 Dorothy Whitney of New York and Old Westbury (d.1968) and Leonard Elmhirst of Houndhill, Yorkshire (d.1974). M. Young, *The Elmhirsts of Dartington* (1982).
6 A. Clark in Emery (1970) 267.
7 *Cal. Inq. Misc.: 1387–93*, 4.
8 Exeter Cathedral Library, Chapter Act Book, MS 3550 f.45r.
9 Though Richard II had used the white hart as a personal ornament in the form of jewellery as early as 1379, he did not use or publicly distribute it as a badge before the Smithfield tournament in October 1390. M. V. Clarke, *Burlington Magazine* 58 (1931) 283ff; M. Campbell in *The Regal Image of Richard II and the Wilton Diptych*, ed. D. Gordon, L. Monnas and C. Elam (1997) 98–101.
10 Prof. Scott Simpson in Emery (1970) 268–72.
11 One of the more crass judgements of English Heritage was their decision in 1995 to prevent the reinstatement of roofing tiles as originally in place of these horrendous insertions on the grounds that they were early examples of Hope Crittal metal windows and reflected the 1930s developments. Academic exactitude and the shibboleth of 'preserve as found' was preferred to architectural integrity. On that basis, Leonard Elmhirst would never have been allowed to restore the ruined hall and kitchen during the 1930s if English Heritage had been in existence.
12 N. W. Alcock and M. W. Barley, *Antiq. Jour.* 52 (1972) 135–6; J. Crook, *Archaeologia* 109 (1991) 149–50. This assessment lies between the attribution to the early fourteenth century by early commentators such as T. H. Turner and J. H. Parker (1859) 353 and A. H. Thompson (1913) 553 and mine to c.1388–90 in 1970: 143–5. It is significant that the comparison made by Alcock with the barn roof at the bishop of Exeter's manor at Bishop Clyst hitherto ascribed that roof to the early fourteenth century, but it has now been dendro dated to 1387: *Vern. Arch.* 28 (1997) 164, 166.
13 Emery (1970) 264–6.
14 Devon Records Office: Z 15/38/1/7.
15 By making structural modifications such as using side purlins unrelated to the trusses and timbers that are aesthetically too light for the structure, Weir's work betrays its date. Holand's roof also has deviant elements which betray its experimental character, but this is not an isolated case. Other hammer-beam roofs have proved structurally experimental as at Giffords Hall, Suffolk (Emery, *Greater Med. Houses*, II (2000) 103), and at Westminster Hall where there is considerable disagreement about the forces acting within the roof: J. Weddell, *Arch. Hist.* 42 (1999) 47–67. Nor does the removal of the hammer-beam part of the roof at Cadhay seem to have weakened the structure. D. F. Stenning has suggested that as a roof based on the end wall 'shadow' would be impractical, the original structure must therefore have been of base-cruck form: *Vern. Arch.* 29 (1998) 93–9. This is theory based on supposition. Though Saunders made a series of detailed drawings of the hammer-beam roof while it was still *in situ*, Stenning dismisses this structure as 'inherently unworkable' even though he does not doubt its existence over several centuries. This

contradiction is never resolved, but is obscured by opinions based on Saunders' theoretical replacement of the 1810s and Weir's modified but achieved concept of the 1930s. Both started from totally different circumstances that are hardly the yardsticks to judge the viability of a regionally alien concept built 400 or more years earlier for a magnate whose views transcended local limitations.

16 Twentieth-century forced door to the balcony.

17 The peephole into the hall is a Victorian conceit.

18 Usage of the north-end block in 1995 meant partitioning one of the ground-floor rooms, converting the fireplace into a window, and uniting the two upper rooms into a single area with the two garderobe doorways modified as windows.

19 The complete 1934 example in a rear wall and the fragment of an original one from elsewhere were inserted by eager masons during Weir's absence. Elmhirst prevailed on him to allow them to stay *in situ*.

20 Emery (1970) 190–202.

21 C. Platt, *Arch. Jour.* 119 (1962) 216.

22 C. Currie, 5th Interim Report (1998) 8; 6th Interim Report (1998) 8.

23 John Holand has not yet found his biographer. In the meantime, the family is summarily covered in *Com. Peer.*, V (1926) 195–200, VI (1926) 653–4 and Emery (1970) 23–69 where all references for this text are given. Also M. M. N. Stansfield, 'The Holand family, Dukes of Exeter, Earls of Kent and Huntingdon 1352–1475', Oxford University, DPhil thesis (1987).

24 If the note by the early fifteenth-century copyist Shirley is to be believed in the manuscript of Chaucer's *Compleynt of Mars*, Trinity College Cambridge, Sir John Holand had already pursued the light-hearted Isabel, the duchess of Lancaster's sister, a few years earlier.

25 P. E. Russell, *English Intervention in Spain and Portugal in the Time of Edward III and Richard II* (1955).

26 *Cal. Pat. Rolls: 1385–89*, 494–5; *Rolls of Parliament*, 3, 250b–251b.

27 N. Saul, *Richard II* (1997) 244. His London residence was the Thames-side mansion Coldharbour: J. Schofield, *Medieval London Houses* (1995) 217–18.

28 He held the manor for the few months from December 1384 to April 1385. *Cal. Pat. Rolls: 1381–85*, 515–16.

29 The phrase is D. Starkey's in describing Sir Richard Clements' Ightham Mote in *The Later Middle Ages*, ed. S. Medcalf (1981) 273.

30 *Cal. Pat. Rolls: 1391–96*, 639.

31 PRO E 40/6964.

32 *Cal. Pat. Rolls: 1399–1401*, 241: PRO Chancery Inq. C145/278, no.26 transcribed in Emery (1970) 267–8.

33 For his relations with the Courtenays, M. Cherry, 'The crown and the political community in Devonshire 1377–1461', PhD thesis, University of Wales (1981) and *Southern History* 1 (1979) 90–3.

34 Saul, *Richard II* (1997) 442–3.

35 Huntingdon's own copy of Philippe de Mézières, *Abrégeance* of the Rules of his Order of the Passion that he established to encourage the European aristocracy to crusade against the Turks is in Bod. Lib., MS Ashmole 813.

36 Emery (1970) 260–3 for an analysis of Huntingdon's income.

37 *Ibid.* 263–4.

38 Saul, *Richard II* (1997) 438–42.

39 For an illustrated survey of major residential architecture during this period, Emery (1970) 103–37.

40 The practice of building gatehouses in Devon like those at Tiverton (mid-fourteenth century) and Hemyock (1380) castles was maintained at Berry Pomeroy Castle (*c.*1460–95), at the mid-fifteenth-century fortified houses at Bickleigh, Affeton, and Compton Castle (destroyed), and at the undefended residences at Bradley (by 1420, destroyed), Weare Giffard Hall (between 1454 and 1472) and Leigh Barton (*c.*1500), with Tawstock (mid-sixteenth century), Shute (late sixteenth century) and Colleton Manor (*c.*1621) as elaborate if late examples.

41 Brit. Lib., MS Cott. Aug Ii, art. 35–90.

42 J. R. Kenyon, *Arch. Jour.* 138 (1981) 218–19; *HKW*, IV (1982) 374, 594–5.

43 *Ibid.* 598 n.6; R. A. Higham *et al.*, *Proc. Devon Arch. Soc.* 43 (1985) 66.

44 C. Platt, *Arch. Jour.* 119 (1962) 209–10.

45 C. K. Currie, 6th Interim Report (1998) 9.

46 A. Emery, *Greater Med. Houses*, II (2000) 494–6.

47 M. Airs, *Arch. Jour.* 135 (1978) 277–80; J. N. Hare, *Arch. Jour.* 145 (1988) 236–7.

48 Emery (1970) 218.

49 C. Given-Wilson, *The English Nobility in the Later Middle Ages* (1987) 90.

50 M. Cherry, *Southern History* 1 (1979) 72–5.

51 A. R. Myers, *The Household of Edward IV* (1959) 116, 117, 128.

52 C. Given-Wilson, *The Royal Household and the King's Affinity* (1986) 222–3.

53 A. Goodman, *John of Gaunt* (1992) 334.

54 *Cal. Pat. Rolls: 1399–1401*, 244, 255.

55 *Rolls of Parliament*, 3, 451–2.

56 L. Courtenay in *Science and Technology in Medieval Society*, ed. P. Long (1985).

57 J. Crook, *Archaeologia* 109 (1991) 129–59.

58 Emery, *Greater Med. Houses*, II, 157–9.

59 *Ibid.* 403–4.

60 T. W. Horsfield, *History, Antiquities, and Topography of the County of Sussex* (1835) 126 quoting J. Cartwright, *History of the Western Division of Sussex* (1830).

61 *Vide* W. Wintringham and H. Herland in J. Harvey, *Eng. Med. Arch.* (1984) 337–8, 137–41. Also H. M. Colvin in *English Court Culture in the Later Middle Ages*, ed. V. J. Scattergood and J. W. Sherborne (1983) 137–8.

62 L. Courtenay, *Jour. Soc. Arch. Hist.* 43 (1984) 301–9. The form of Hugh Herland's roof for William Wykeham's chapel at New College, Oxford (*c.*1380–6) is arguable. Courtenay supports the view that it was possibly of hammer-beam form, while G. Jackson-Stops favours a tie-beam structure in *New College, Oxford*, ed. J. Buxton and P. Williams (1979) 171.

63 *The Medieval Architect* (1972) 134–6; *Eng. Med. Arch.* (1984) 338–41; R. K. Morris in *Medieval Art and Architecture at Exeter*, ed. F. Kelly (1991) 57–84.

64 *Archaeologia* 109 (1991) 50.

65 H. Bonney, *Wilts. Arch. Nat. Mag.* 59 (1964) 155–67; RCHM, *Salisbury*, I (1986) 135–6. The Commissioners also identified several other roofs in the city of possibly hammer-beam or false hammer-beam construction dating between the early fourteenth and early fifteenth centuries.

66 (1850) 518–19.

67 C. Platt, *Arch. Jour.* 119 (1962) 208–24. Platt is of the firm opinion that all the buildings of the second court were dated to *c.*1500, *ibid.* 219.

68 Currie, 6th Interim Report (1998) 3, 9. The thickness could have been for defensive reasons (though this is not supported by a west wall only 4 feet thick) or to counter site instability.

69 A. Clark in Emery (1970) 187, 266–8.

70 Platt, *Arch. Jour.* 119 (1962) 212; Emery (1970) 264–6.

71 As discussed on site with Currie in 1997 and by him in *Arch. Jour.* 161 (2004) 204–5.

72 C. Currie and N. Rushton, *Arch. Jour.* 161 (2004) 207–8.

73 M. K. Jones and M. G. Underwood could find no expenditure on Dartington by Margaret: *The King's Mother* (1992) 93–136. Platt attributed the development to the countess with the 'tower' and thought it was possibly a survival of the defensive traditions of bastard feudalism: *Arch. Jour.* 119 (1962) 218–19. Currie oscillates between the last five owners of the manor over the years 1476–1549 without further precision: *The Lie of the Land*, ed. R. Wilson-North (2003) 57. *Arch. Jour.* (2004) 206.

74 *Itinerary* I, 219.

75 Even though St Ledger's marriage to the king's sister was short-lived,

this loyal, royal servant was anxious to develop his patrimony in the West of England during the closing years of Edward IV's reign, *Cal. Pat. Rolls: 1477–83*, 91. Emulation at Dartington of the royal family's remodelling of Eltham Palace (by Edward IV) as well as Penrith and Sudeley castles (by Richard, duke of Gloucester) is not unreasonable, particularly as St Ledger's young daughter was declared heiress to all the duke of Exeter's estates in 1483: C. Rose, *Richard III* (1981) 109–11.

76 Currie and Rushton, *Arch. Jour.* 161 (2004). As abandoned artefacts are more usually associated with periods of decay rather than of construction, my attribution more closely harmonises with that of the early Tudor finds.

77 C. Currie, *6th Interim Report on Dartington Hall Gardens* (1998) 8 and his essay, 'Dartington Hall and Shilston Barton', in *The Lie of the Land*, ed. Wilson-North, 56–7.

78 John Allan in Currie and Rushton, *Arch. Jour.* 161 (2004) 208. His report on the pottery finds will be published in the *Proceedings of the Devon Arch. Soc.*

79 Emery (1970) 192–3.

80 The kitchen doorway would have led to an as yet unexplored service area.

81 Trenches by Platt in 1962 recorded structures extending across about three-fifths of the site. Those by Currie were essentially limited to part of the west range, a heavily reworked area with results that essentially confirmed Platt's earlier activity there.

82 The use of chambers for the owner's family above the services at the lower end of the hall was a late fifteenth-century development on restricted sites such as Ightham Mote and Cotehele.

83 Currie and Rushton, *Arch. Jour.* 161 (2004) 189.

84 M. Stansfield, 'John Holand, Duke of Exeter and Earl of Huntingdon (d.1447)', in *Profit, Piety, and the Professions in Later Medieval England*, ed. M. Hicks (1990) 103–15.

85 K. Mertes, *The English Noble Household* (1988) 102–3, 132–8; C. M. Woolgar, *The Great Household in Late Medieval England* (1999) 46–82.

86 N. Cooper, *Houses of the Gentry 1480–1680* (1999) 74–93; S. Thurley, *The Royal Palaces of Tudor England* (1993) 248–62.

Anonymous, *Arch. Jour.* 30 (1873) 440–2

A. H. Thompson, *Arch. Jour* 70 (1913) 553–7

C. Hussey, *Country Life* (August/September 1938)

A. Emery, *Arch. Jour.* 115 (1958) 184–202; reprinted with revisions in *Studies in Medieval Domestic Architecture*, ed. M. J. Swanton (1975) 134–52

A. Emery, *Dartington Hall* (1970)

EXETER, BISHOP'S PALACE and episcopal houses in Devon

In contrast with the honey-grey limestone of the cathedral, the Bishop's Palace immediately south of it is built in the vivid red sandstone from Heavitree. The aisled hall, service rooms, and chapel begun by bishop Brewer during the 1240s and completed by 1290 when a licence to crenellate was granted to bishop Quinil (1280–91) were retained with little alteration until the seventeenth century. Bishops during the late thirteenth and fourteenth centuries primarily concerned themselves with redeveloping the private apartments in place of the earlier solar block, so that by the close of the middle ages the palace extended from near the cathedral chapter-house to within a few yards of the city walls.

The palace has shrunk considerably since then. The service range towards the city walls was pulled down in two stages, 1695 and

PLATE 231 Exeter, Bishop's Palace: bishop Courtenay's fireplace

1812, leaving only the three glazed arches to the offices and kitchen passage looking out to the palace gardens. The extended west wing of private apartments was rebuilt in Tudor style by Edward Gribble in 1846–8 as part of his wholesale reconstruction of the palace. It is now used as the diocesan offices and library. As the bishop's chapel was incorporated into the cathedral as its vestry in the 1950s, the bishop's residence is concentrated today within the framework of the mid-thirteenth-century three-bay hall with wooden arcade posts, as subdivided in the 1660s and remodelled in 1762–77.

Four late medieval elements survive in this much-altered palace.[1] The entrance arch and some of the walling of the precinct gate-house are fourteenth century, though the upper walling has been renewed. A plain, single-storey south porch was added to the aisled hall in the early fourteenth century, and extended upwards in the early sixteenth century and again by Gribble in the 1840s. Bishop Grandisson (1327–69) added a three-storeyed extension to the west wing (*c.*1335–40, destroyed 1846), which included a first-floor parlour with a fine timber ceiling from which six carved bosses survive, five in the Victoria and Albert Museum (one with Grandisson's arms) and one in Exeter Museum.[2]

The most spectacular survival is the fireplace from Grandisson's parlour, added by bishop Courtenay (1478–87). It has been moved twice since then, most recently in 1952 to the bishop's drawing room. Standing 12 feet high, it is undeniably impressive, but it is

PLATE 232 Bishopsteignton, bishop Grandisson's chapel

also outrageously overdecorated above the square-headed opening, with flower bushes at the ends, three unduly large arms of the Courtenay family surmounted by the mitre, sword, and keys of the bishopric, and the whole crowned with the royal arms like some late Elizabethan tomb.[3]

Until 1877, the diocese of Exeter encompassed the whole of Devon and Cornwall, and was the fourth-largest diocese in England and the sixth in episcopal revenue above Lincoln and Norwich. But much of the see was difficult to travel and was considered by many, including bishop Grandisson, as being on the edge of the known world. In 1535, the bishop's net income was £1,600 a year, half of it from his Devon estates, a quarter from those in Cornwall, and the remainder from the properties in or near London and various fees.[4] He held twenty-four manors in Devon, with Bishop's Tawton, Crediton, and Paignton as the richest. There were houses at nine of these, though several were in poor condition by the time of bishop Redman (1495–1501), and one had been recently destroyed.[5]

There are modest house remains at five Devon properties but none at the five smaller and infrequently visited houses in Cornwall.[6] The episcopal house at *Bishop's Tawton* near Barnstaple was the only one in north Devon, a house that Leland records bishop Vesey (1519–54) had reduced in size but improved in appearance.[7] Today, the settlement is dominated by Tawstock Court, the mansion of the Bourchiers with its adjacent church, rather than Court Farm where the medieval-looking towers and battlements are a consequence of remodelling in *c*.1800. The remains of the country houses in south Devon are in a line south of Exeter – Chudleigh, Bishopsteignton, and Paignton – for the bishops were early appreciators of the 'English Riviera'. Little enough though stands at Bishop's Clyst, even though it was their principal country residence between the mid-fourteenth and mid-sixteenth centuries.

The scanty remains in the grounds of Palace Farm on the south side of *Chudleigh* are not overly rewarding. The most substantial element is the 10 foot high, ivy-covered wall enclosing the west side of the triangular site. It extends for nearly 400 feet, over rising ground, with four splayed loops and a broad open-backed rectangular projection of tower-like shape but relatively thin walling. The higher end of the wall terminates a little short of a square structure

made up of two parallel undercrofts, roughly vaulted, supporting long-lost rooms above. The broader undercroft retains blocked window evidence, a projecting angle stair turret, and what may have been the base of a broad stair to the upper rooms, while the narrower undercroft has a garderobe shaft. The outer wall of a separate building stands not far away. It has long been used as a building stone resource by Chudleigh town, and late eighteenth-century engravings show this unexcavated earthwork-covered site little different from today. Though bishop Bronescombe (1257–80) is recorded as having stayed here, the ruins have no datable features, while the documentary evidence is imprecise except for the award of the licence to crenellate granted to bishop Brantyngham (1370–94) in 1379, for a fortalice here or elsewhere within his bishopric on his own land.[8] Bishop Stapledon (1307–26) conducted ordinations in the chapel in 1321, a hall is referred to under bishop Brantyngham, and a privy chamber, parlour, and chapel under bishop Lacy (1420–55), and an arched gateway is recorded in the late eighteenth century.

Though bishop Bronescombe was also responsible in 1258 for initiating the country house on a hillside site half a mile north-east of *Bishopsteignton*, the present buildings were erected nearly a century later. In his will of 1369, bishop Grandisson claimed that he had erected 'convenient and sumptuous buildings . . . in the manor of Bishop's Teignton' though we cannot date the structures there more closely. The residence was a rectangular one of red sandstone, developed round four sides of a courtyard, including part of a chapel and several short runs of walling incorporated today in a group of farm sheds and byres. The farmyard entry includes the jambs of the original entrance, with a length of courtyard walling extending to the fourteenth-century chapel of which two walls stand full height. The buttressed south wall retains a line of high-set lancets with trefoil heads and a stoup, and the east gable has three lancets with a taller central one. Currently used as a cow shed, nave and chancel had their own entry doors from the south. There is garderobe and fireplace evidence of domestic buildings on the east side of the courtyard, with a considerable length of boundary wall further east.

Whereas Chudleigh and Bishopsteignton retain their rural setting, the bishop's house at *Paignton*, one of his richest manors, overlooks the street activity of a seaside resort. Standing immediately south of the parish church, the embattled sandstone wall 14 feet high encloses a substantial courtyard, 330 feet by 130 feet, built on falling ground that holds the vicarage of 1910 and the parish hall of 1951. Domestic foundations suggest that the bishop's accommodation lay at the south-west corner of the churchyard, though an occasional single light and a fireplace point to further accommodation against the precinct wall near the four-storey tower at its south-east corner. This 16 foot square tower is unbuttressed, but with full-height batter, ground-floor entry, and internal stair. The ground and first floors have narrow oblong lights but the two upper floors are generously provided with twin trefoil lights with ogee heads in all four faces. Attributed to bishop Grandisson (1327–69), these upper rooms provided him and his successors with a scenic view and a quiet retreat.

Bishop Bronescombe bought the manor of *Clyst*, 4 miles east of Exeter in 1265, but the present High Victorian Gothick house is an aggressive rebuilding of 1803 and 1863.[9] It incorporates two small ground-floor rooms with early sixteenth-century ceilings, though pictures of the house by John Swete in 1801 show its late medieval form.[10] Though Bronescombe presumably initiated the house, it was possibly remodelled by Brantyngham in the 1370s, who frequently resided here.[11] The account rolls from 1374 to 1525 and Swete's two illustrations indicate there was a moat, a gatehouse, and an enclosing wall. The house was built round three sides of an irregular court, dominated by the hall, the chapel wing, and possibly a tower at the north-west corner. The hall had two louvres while the bishop's apartments and his first-floor chapel were below the hall and not at its upper end. Today, the sole medieval survivals are the seven- (formerly nine-) bay barn with a base-cruck roof of 1387[12] and the early sixteenth-century stables, both outside the immediate curtilage of the house.[13]

Nothing remains of the small Cornish residences at Cudden Beke near St Germans, Lanner near St Allen, Lawhitton near Launceston, Pawton, or Penrhyn.[14] Bishop Stapleton initiated Exeter House, the substantial London residence on the north bank of the Thames,[15] while he and his colleagues used now-lost houses at West Horsley in Surrey and Farringdon in Hampshire whilst travelling between the West of England and the capital.[16]

NOTES

1 A fifth late medieval element, the bay window of *c*.1500 in the south front, was brought from a house near Broadgate, demolished in *c*.1840. It was three-storeyed, but that did not stop Gribble from reducing it to two to fit the palace elevation. It is filled with some early armorial glass and lights the dining room.

2 C. Tracy, *English Medieval Furniture and Woodwork* (1988) 31–4; *The Age of Chivalry*, ed. J. Alexander and P. Binski (1987) 464.

3 Illustrated in *Arch. Jour.* 147 (1990) 44; described by M. Wood, *The English Mediaeval House* (1965) 271.

4 *Valor Ecclesiasticus*, II, 298–91.

5 Crediton, Chudleigh, Bishop's Clyst, and Paignton were in fair condition, those at Bishop's Tawton and Bishopsteignton (Radway) were less so, Ashburton and Bishop's Nympton were almost destroyed, and Peterhayes (near Yarcombe) was 'utterly destroyed by the late bishop'. Westminster Abbey Muniments 3529 reported by H. Tapley-Soper, *Devon and Cornwall Notes and Queries* 22 (1942–6) 78–80.

6 For the episcopal manors in Cornwall, L. E. Elliott-Binns, *Medieval Cornwall* (1955) 302–5.

7 *Itinerary*, I, 171.

8 *Cal. Pat. Rolls: 1377–81*, 377.

9 Described and illustrated by C. Brooks, *Country Life* (February 1990).

10 *Travels in Georgian Devon*, 4 vols. ed. T. Gray and M. Rowe (2000).

11 Alcock (1966) 141.

12 *Vern. Arch.* 28 (1997) 164–6.

13 Seven miles south-east was Place Court at Colaton Raleigh, the country house of the deans of Exeter cathedral. It is undistinguished externally apart from the two-storey fourteenth-century porch with chapel over opening into the rebuilt hall and a cross wing with good arch-braced roof.

14 The only secular survival in Cornwall is the buttressed barn of the bishop's manor at Cargoll, west of Newlyn East, a fifteenth-century structure with arch-braced collar trusses, on a property acquired by bishop Bronescombe in 1269. E.M. Jope in *Studies in Building History* (1961) 200–2.

15 J. Schofield, *Medieval London Houses* (1994) 210.

16 N. Orme, *Exeter Cathedral 1050–1550* (1996) 32.

Exeter
J. F. Chanter, *The Bishop's Palace, Exeter, and Its Story* (1932)
S. Blaylock, Supplement to *Arch. Jour.* 147 (1990) 41–5
J. Musson, *Country Life* (March 1998)

Bishopsteighton
M. Laithwaite, S. R. Blaylock and K. A. Westcott, *Proc. Devon Arch. Soc.* 47 (1989) 53–69

Bishop's Clyst
N. Alcock, *Trans. Devon. Assoc.* 98 (1966) 132–53

EXETER PRIORY and monastic lodgings in Devon

Devon retains two substantial lodging ranges of monastic heads at Exeter and Torquay, with that hidden in the middle of Exeter among the best preserved in southern England. Much of Exeter Priory had been torn down within a few years of the Dissolution in 1536. The site of the Benedictine priory church lies beneath a Methodist chapel of 1812 and twentieth-century housing, while the chapter-house range is covered by a Catholic church of 1792. The badly bruised Norman and late medieval refectory range with its casement windows has been converted into flats with a conference room above,[1] leaving the twelfth-century cellarer's range as the principal survival. Most of this was transformed into the prior's house and guest hall of some scale and magnificence at the close of the fifteenth century. Its survival followed its adoption in the 1560s as the town house of a wealthy citizen, with Elizabethan modifications and plaster ceilings, and tenement changes after the mid-seventeenth century, but they were sufficiently minor for the structure to retain its essential character of a late medieval prior's house.[2]

The west cloister walk has long been used as a pedestrian passageway (Mint Lane) from which the Norman range directly opens. The original approach would, of course, have been from the west, where the impressive storeyed projection in Heavitree sandstone was added in about 1500. This opened into one of the earlier ground-floor rooms, possibly the cellarer's checker, subsequently converted into an entrance hall with a handsome Beer stone panelled four-centred arch opening from the added lobby and main stair.[3] The opportunity was also taken to rebuild the adjacent Norman kitchen with two generous hearths, capable of serving the prior's new hall as well as the rebuilt monks' refectory to the east. The kitchen rose through two floors, with the original attic room for staff removed in 1916 exposing the roof of *c*.1500.

The upper floor of the range was heightened in *c*.1500, when it was converted into a guest hall with bedchambers at each end, and crowned throughout with a good-quality roof with arch-braced trusses with curved ends and two tiers of wind braces. The new broad stair led into the hall, with a Tudor mural fireplace and side doors in the plank and muntin end wall. Beyond are two narrow chambers, one heated and one with a (screened) garderobe. They may have been used for guests, though the occupational function in such circumstances is usually guesswork. Steps at the lower end of the hall open into a large heated room that possibly served as the prior's chamber, with its own well-preserved garderobe turret, adjacent window, and fragments of pre-Reformation wall painting. An oak panelled screen, removed in 1881, formed a passage against its east side for service from the narrow kitchen stair to the guest hall. There is a small inner chamber over the main stair that could have served as the prior's private chapel open to the roof. The subsidiary wall stair from the hall leads to a room above, perhaps remodelled after the Dissolution from an upper pew for guests.

PLATE 233 Exeter, St Nicholas' Priory: guest hall

This residential range survives in roofed condition as one of Exeter's museums since 1913, simply furnished and little known. The priory was never a large foundation but it was reasonably wealthy, with a broad spread of endowments.[4] This residential range is less striking than the more flamboyant contemporary survivals at Forde and Muchelney abbeys, but it reflects the same purpose of enhanced dining and domestic facilities. It is in a better condition than those in most Benedictine monasteries, and comparable in scale and date with the similar changes made to the chapter-house range at the Cistercian abbey of Valle Crucis.

The abbot's hall and residential tower at *Torre Abbey* have similarly survived through post-medieval occupation, but the layout is more diffuse in this museum mansion on Torquay's sea front. Founded in 1196, Torre Abbey became the wealthiest monastery of the Premonstratensian order in England. In response to this situation, the upper floor of the late twelfth-century west cloister range was remodelled in the fifteenth century to provide a new guest hall and parlour for the abbot, and a four-storeyed tower was added at the side for his accommodation. Hall, parlour, and tower were retained by Thomas Ridgeway when he converted two of the cloister walks into a private residence in 1598 – the core of the present eighteenth-century mansion.

A new approach was created to these lodgings from the outer court next to the tower. The entry with depressed two-centred head opens on to a broad flight of steps with a modern roof but original two-light window with multi-traceried head. A right-angled turn opens via the original door into the first floor of the tower, an ante-room to the abbot's hall. It retains a particularly fine ogee-canopied lavabo, with the ogee form (and the same mason's marks) repeated over the doorway to the hall, though the two-light window nearby was remodelled in *c*.1875.

The hall continued to function as a dining room under the Ridgeways (1598–1654) and Carys (1662–1929), much as it had during the later middle ages. However, in 1779 George Cary converted the room into a Roman Catholic chapel when the present windows and apse were inserted into the original walls, though the barrel roof was retained, with plaster infilling between the ribs and bosses at the rib joins, doubled at the dais end. This roof still exists throughout the remainder of the range, above eighteenth-century plaster ceilings and rooms converted out of the abbot's parlour.

The four-storeyed tower, now with a harled façade, has a single room on each floor and rear newel projection. The ground floor opens into the lobby to the original undercroft of the west range. That above is the aforementioned ante-room to the hall. The two upper rooms were for the abbot's use. The second floor with its three-light window now has a ceiling, panelling, and fireplace of *c*.1875. The third floor has a single cinquefoil window in the side walls, a garderobe chute, and a modern clock within the frontal window frame. This tower is not unlike the more conventional porch towers to the abbot's halls at Cerne Abbas and Forde Abbey and was similar in function.

A not dissimilar tower stands at the south end of the former west range at *Buckfast Abbey*, three-storeyed, rubble-built, with a new plain parapet and a prominent polygonal stair turret with embattled head. The ground-floor doorway has moulded jambs and continuous two-centred head. The renewed windows of two cinquefoil lights of slight ogee form under a square hood are of increasing scale, with the uppermost transomed. They light a single room with fireplace and garderobe on each level. Erected during the fifteenth century, and possibly by abbot Kyng (1467–98) as guest extension to his lodgings, this tower can be compared with the towers at the bishop of Exeter's house at Paignton, as well as that at Torre Abbey.

Two other Devon foundations have left fragmentary evidence of residential lodgings. The prior's house at *Frithelstock* (Augustinian) is fourteenth century in origin, for the bishop's visitation of 1400 mentions the prior's room and hall.[5] The thick walls of the front range of the present L-shaped farmhouse may be those of the hall, but otherwise the structure is of the early and late seventeenth and the nineteenth centuries. Little more survives above ground of the domestic buildings of *Buckland Abbey*, not one of the richest Cistercian foundations despite holding estates in west Devon covering 20,000 acres. Interest centres on the bold conversion of the church into an Elizabethan mansion by the seafaring families of Grenville and Drake, but the small fifteenth-century tower and stair turret with a fleuron string course below the battlemented parapet and ogee-headed doorway internally may have been part of the detached abbot's lodging north of the abbey church.[6] Bull House next to the Benedictine priory of *Pilton*, now in a suburb of Barnstaple and at the head of its most attractive street, is believed to have been the prior's house, but confirmatory evidence is lacking. The former priory buildings seem to have lain north of the church,

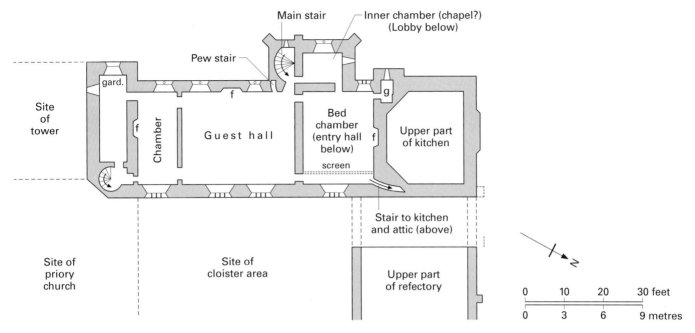

FIGURE 134 Exeter, St Nicholas Priory: first-floor plan of west range

though Bull House, with its fifteenth-century hall range, entry block, and early sixteenth-century solar wing, is one of the best-preserved late medieval town houses in Devon.[7]

NOTES

1 The tall refectory windows are blocked and floor divided, while the exposed arch-braced roof of *c*.1455 is markedly utilitarian. *Vern. Arch.* 33 (2002) 78.

2 The comparable range of about 1300 of St Katherine's Priory, a Benedictine nunnery at Polsloe, a mile north-east of Exeter, has survived far less well. It retains the carcase of the first-floor guest hall but lost its medieval roof in 1867. Externally approached, the hall retains its spere screen partition walls, the upper end opening into the prioress' room and the lower one with five doorways (now three) to the offices and the lost detached kitchen. Sandwiched between a 1930 housing estate and a railway line, this red sandstone range, long used as a farmhouse, was badly restored in 1980 as a community centre. *Med. Arch.* 23 (1979) 250–1.

3 This room retains the best of the lime-plaster ceilings of *c*.1580. The guest hall retains the best of the contemporary wall paintings.

4 G. Oliver, *Monasticon Dioecesis Exoniensis* (1846); R. Graham, *Jour. Brit. Arch. Assoc.* 33 (1927) 58–9.

5 C. A. Ralegh Radford, *Proc. Devon Arch. Exploration Soc.* 2 pt 1 (1933) 20–7. Also R. P. Chope, *Trans. Devon. Assoc.* 61 (1929–30) 167–91; M. Gillard, *Arch. Jour.* 157 (2000) 452–5.

6 G. W. Copeland, *Buckland Abbey: An Architectural Survey* (1963); C. G. Brown *et al.*, *Trans. Devon Arch. Soc.* 53 (1995) 25–82. The precinct wall dates from the licence to crenellate granted in 1337.

7 J. H. Rudd, *Arch. Rev.* (1925) 178–84; M. A. Reed, *Pilton, Its Past and Present* (1985) 151–9; M. L. Corney, *The Bull House, Pilton* (1985), privately printed.

Exeter Priory

H. Lloyd Parry and H. Brakspear, *St. Nicholas Priory, Exeter* (1921); revised edn by J. Youing (1960)

J. Allan, *St. Nicholas Priory, Exeter: Handbook* (1999)

Torre Abbey

D. Seymour, *Torre Abbey: An Account of Its History, Buildings, Cartularies and Lands* (1977)

M. Hall, *Country Life* (April 1991)

FARLEIGH HUNGERFORD CASTLE, Somerset

Like Wardour Castle, the site of Farleigh Hungerford Castle was chosen for its visual qualities. A position on higher ground to the south would have been more strategically sound, or one less close to the parish church, but Sir Thomas Hungerford preferred to adopt the earlier manor house overhanging the nascent River Frome and facing the undulating landscape of the Wiltshire Avon. This is also one of the contrasts with Sir John de la Mare's contemporary valley-bottom castle at Nunney, 9 miles distant. Both were developed during the 1370s by members of the same social class. Neither was a fortress and both were defensively weak, overlooked by higher ground, though given the external character of military pretension. Sir Thomas and Sir John both chose the same basic plan – a rectangle with round corner towers, but whereas the towers at Nunney were tightly drawn to the central residential block to create a compact tower-house, Hungerford preferred to spread his accommodation round several courtyards, prefaced by a central gatehouse. Both residences were crenellated, but while Nunney was water-surrounded, Farleigh Hungerford was dry-moated. To put it at its most basic, Nunney was innovative while Farleigh Hungerford was old-fashioned. Both castles were inhabited for over 300 years but are now ruined – the former with still-standing walls, the latter mainly reduced to foundation level. The importance of Farleigh lies in its adaptation of an earlier structure, and while the outer court at Nunney has disappeared, that at Farleigh Hungerford holds the primary standing buildings – the gatehouse and towered outer enclosure, the roofed parish church, and the adjacent priests' house.

PLATE 234   Farleigh Hungerford Castle: engraving from the north by S. and N. Buck (1733)

Farleigh Hungerford Castle is a three-period structure. Site idio-syncrasies, straight joints, and planning oddities suggest that Sir Thomas Hungerford (d.1398) took the earlier manor house and extended it with a castellated enclosure, for which he sought a pardon for crenellating without licence in 1383.[1] His residence was grouped round three principal courts separated by the pivotal great hall flanked by services and a residential block – a survival of the initial manor house. Sir Thomas' First Court was surrounded by household lodgings, the Garden Court abutted the family apart-ments, while the Kitchen Court enclosed the offices, kitchen, and amenity units. Sir Thomas' son, Sir Walter Hungerford (d.1449), added the outer court, taking in the earlier parish church which he converted into the family chapel after building a new church for the village half a mile away in c.1443.

Extending to no more than an acre but seeming larger, the site determined the position of the four corner towers, with those on the north slope immediately above the River Frome given thicker walls from a splayed base. Hungerford's centrally positioned gate-house had round-fronted towers flanking a central passage,[2] though only footings remain rising from a pronounced batter from the drawbridge-crossed dry moat.[3] The First Court lay to one side of the site. It was lined on three sides with ranges between 15 and 21 feet deep, probably lodging accommodation for household members and guests. The multi-occupied east range was separated by a narrow court from the family apartments, 12 feet away to ensure their privacy. The entrance range terminated in the small five-storey south-west tower with garderobe-provided rooms on each floor. As with the south-east tower, the several broken window frames of the uppermost floor give it the appearance of an embat-tled parapet. This could not be more inaccurate. A sketch made between 1650 and 1670 shows that, instead of a parapet, both towers were capped by conical roofs which covered the tops of the walling.[4] Such roofs survive in abundance in France, but as no castle in England or Wales retains its original pepper-pot roofs, this sketch is particularly valuable.

A broad paved path across the cobbled First Court led direct to the hall porch. The buttressed hall took advantage of the falling ground to be built above an undercroft, so that entry was by a flight of nearly twenty steps[5] to the first-floor apartment. Sir Thomas retained this earlier hall, even though raised halls had gone out of fashion at least a generation earlier except for the grandest houses. According to a mid-eighteenth-century account, 'the walls of the hall were covered with fresco paintings of men in armour and war-riors on horseback which remained until Mr Houlton pulled down the old mansion in 1730'.[6]

Only the foundations remain of the kitchen and offices to the left (west) and the immediate family apartments to the right (east), both survivors of the earlier manor house. The kitchen area was exca-vated in 1845, when 'many hundred cartloads of rubbish' were taken away and most of the foundations built up as low walls to facil-itate site interpretation. The remainder of the site was cleared between 1919 and 1927, when the methods of consolidating the standing structures aroused much local ire.[7] Neither of the excava-tion programmes was written up so that there is some doubt about how these foundations should be interpreted, hindered further by their incompleteness.[8]

The offices were grouped round supplementary courts or light wells, marked today by cobbles and turf with gravel identifying building interiors. Next to the hall porch and in line with it was the scullery, with a stone floor drain and sink, followed by the square kitchen and the bakehouse (hearth and two oven bases) built against the outer wall, still standing to almost full height. East of the bake-house is the main drain of the whole sloping site, which also cleared the two chutes from the garderobes next to the base of the stairs to the wall walk. The nearby residential north-west tower with garde-robe projection has been reduced to base level.

The site of the large chamber block at the upper end of the hall is marked out, but because of falling ground its undercroft would have been particularly tall. The private or family apartments added by Sir Thomas on the east side of the castle would have been a magnificent enfilade of rooms. Nineteen feet deep, they were approached from a large stair projecting into the Garden Court,

PLATE 235 Farleigh Hungerford Castle: hall site, south-east tower, and chapel from Kitchen Court

opening into an apartment 40 feet long.[9] According to the rebuilt walling, it was succeeded by three smaller rooms of slightly differing length, terminating in the full-height four-storey tower. The north end of this residential range is a confusing group of compartmentalised foundations (including some sixteenth-century work) with garderobe provision.

What these foundations supported can best be gleaned from Buck's invaluable engraving of the range made not long after its abandonment. The range was two-storeyed, with all the principal rooms on the upper floor lit by twin-transomed windows with traceried heads. The scale and high quality of these apartments are evident, even if their layout and detailing are lost. However, there is a significant mismatch between Buck's engraving of 1733 and the excavated foundations of this range as laid out today. Buck shows an irregular frontage with several forward projections with late fourteenth-century windows, whereas the foundations suggest a single line of rooms with an unbroken frontage. As the accuracy of Buck's work over a thirty-year period is singularly high (and can be checked here with his depiction of the still-standing building further south) while the mid-nineteenth- and early twentieth-century site clearance was decidedly shoddy, greater reliability should be placed on the former than the latter. The only standing evidence is the south-east tower, of which the first floor with its tall shuttered windows, fireplace, and semi-domed garderobe closet, the heated chamber above, and the multi-windowed top-floor

chamber suggest the calibre of this accommodation. The other recovered element indicative of the same quality is the generous rectangular garden between the hall and the north curtain, an adjunct to the family apartments and those in the destroyed north-west tower. A central cobbled path was recovered, but no planting evidence was identified or would have been recognised in the 1920s when garden archaeology was unknown.

It was not until the death of Sir Thomas Hungerford's widow, Joan, in 1412 that their son Sir Walter took control of the castle. At that time, the area immediately in front of the castle was occupied by the parish church and the hamlet that it served. Lord Milton sweeping away Milton Abbas in the 1780s to improve the landscaping of his mansion had a precedent 300 years earlier when Lord Hungerford similarly swept away the village houses, gated and wall-enclosed the area, and took over the parish church as his private chapel and family mausoleum. At the same time, he endowed two chantries and built a house for the chaplains immediately to the rear of the church. This work may be attributed to between 1425 and 1435.

The approach to this new outer court was marked by a modest enough east gateway: a two-storey square tower of passageway and heated chamber above. The entry was protected by a drawbridge and a double door with the Hungerford sickle badge above and the arms of Sir Edward Hungerford c.1520. Between this entry and the subsidiary square gateway opposite, the area was enclosed by a plain wall 15 feet high, much of it still standing to parapet level (rebuilt battlements), with two two-storey round towers with timber-framed frontages. The curtain wall also used to support stables and framed outbuildings erected against it.[10]

The modest single-cell church, erected in the mid-fourteenth century,[11] was extended on the north side in c.1380 by the Hungerford chapel to hold the tomb of Sir Thomas and his wife, now surrounded by a rare wrought iron grill of c.1450. Sir Thomas also inserted the east window, while his son enlarged the side windows of c.1440, all blocked after 1789 when the chapel was reroofed. The high-quality wall painting of St George slaying the dragon is a distinguished representation of a knight of c.1440, painted against a silver brocade background that now appears red. The hard-to-see fragments of a contemporary kneeling knight wearing the arms of Hungerford on his surcoat probably represent the 1st Lord Hungerford.[12] Their survival is particularly important in view of the similar wall paintings that decorated the hall of the castle.

The priests' house was erected in 1430 for the priests serving the chantry founded by Sir Walter in 1426, dedicated to his father, and the chantry established in 1443 for himself. The two priests lived in the house until the dissolution of all chantries in 1547, when it became a private dwelling, doubled in length during the seventeenth century. The southern half was the original house, 25 feet by 17 feet, divided by lost partitions into three rooms on both floors. Entry was at the north end (in the side wall), opening into a passage accessing a heated central room with flanking chambers, one with stair evidence and the other with a latrine (now with later fireplace).[13] Items recovered from the excavations are exhibited, including a thirteenth-century baluster jug, inlaid floors tiles, and post-medieval detritus.

The significance of this extensive but fragmentary mansion lies as much in its encapsulating the two-generation rise of the now

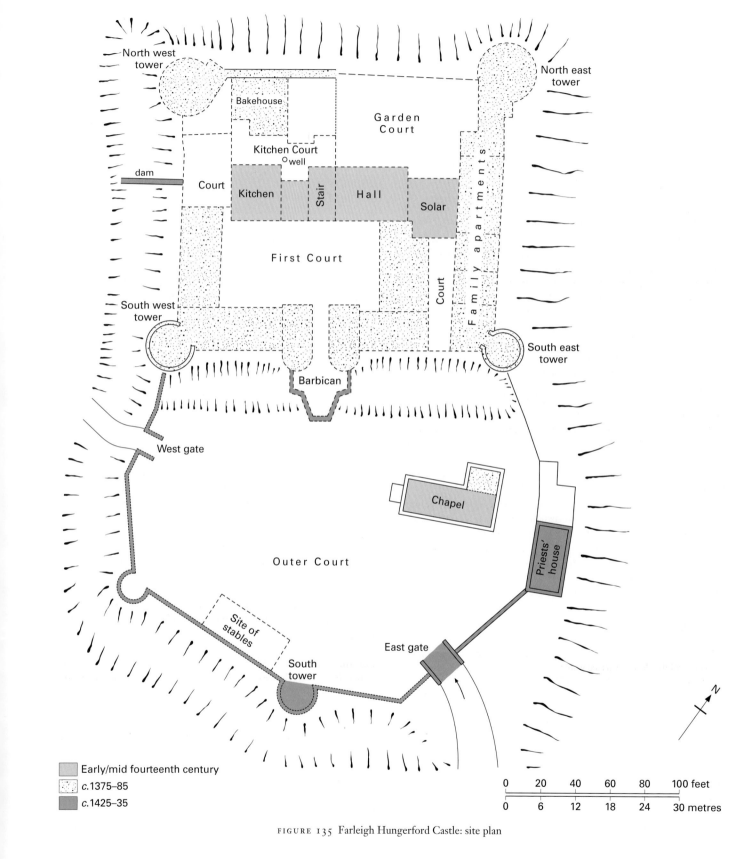

North west tower

North east tower

Bakehouse

Garden Court

Kitchen Court
○ well

dam

Court

Kitchen · Stair · Hall · Solar

First Court

Family apartments

South west tower

Court

South east tower

Barbican

West gate

Chapel

Outer Court

Priests' house

Site of stables

East gate

South tower

Early/mid fourteenth century
c.1375–85
c.1425–35

0 20 40 60 80 100 feet

0 6 12 18 24 30 metres

FIGURE 135 Farleigh Hungerford Castle: site plan

powerful Hungerford family as in reflecting the form and character of a residence befitting knighthood and ennoblement. The family came from Hungerford, Berkshire, via Heytesbury, Wiltshire.[14] By the second quarter of the fourteenth century, the family were already Wiltshire gentry, knighted, and steward of the earl of Lancaster's Wiltshire estates. Thomas Hungerford (d.1398) was the prime founder of the family fortunes. Citizen, merchant, and mayor of Salisbury in 1356, escheator and sheriff of Wiltshire, Thomas represented Wiltshire or Somerset thirteen times in parliament. As John of Gaunt's steward, his influence was significant and contributed to his appointment as the first recorded speaker of the House of Commons (1377). Sir Thomas had purchased the Farleigh estate from the Burghersh family in 1369, and there is little doubt that he had initiated his redevelopment of the earlier house by the mid to late 1370s, with completion by the time he was pardoned for crenellating without licence in 1383. At the same time, Sir Thomas built up his landholding in Wiltshire and Somerset, as his son did in the south-west through his two marriages.

Sir Walter Hungerford scaled even greater heights. He was sheriff of Wiltshire, served in several parliaments, became speaker of the House of Commons in 1414, fought in France, and was steward of the royal household under Henry V. He was a prominent council member during Henry VI's minority, created Lord Hungerford (1426) and Treasurer of England (1426–32). By the time he died in 1449, the family were in the middle ranks of the peerage.[15]

His sons and grandsons were impassioned Lancastrian supporters for which the 3rd Lord Hungerford suffered (executed 1464), as did his eldest son (executed 1469). The family recovered Farleigh, but they never matched their earlier eminence and this was not helped by land division and alienation. Two centuries later, Sir Edward Hungerford (d.1711) wasted his substantial inheritance, sold the castle in 1686 to help pay his debts, and died in poverty. When Sir Edward entered into his inheritance, Aubrey recorded that the castle was unchanged from early times,[16] but within a few years of its sale the property had been stripped of its furnishings and fixtures, and it was ruinous by 1701. A painting of the castle of c.1725–30 shows that two of the towers still retained their conical roofs,[17] but they had disappeared by 1733 when Buck visited the site.

NOTES
1 *Cal. Pat. Rolls: 1381–85*, 340.
2 Similar to the gatehouse of 1377 at Amberley Castle.
3 In about 1430, Sir Walter added a dam across the west arm of the moat to control the flow of surface water.
4 Bod. Lib., Oxford, MS Aubrey 3 f.187.
5 Recorded by Rev. J. E. Jackson (d.1891). Notes on Farleigh Hungerford Castle, bound volume I, 265, Devizes Museum.
6 *Ibid.* I, 260. The Houltons of Trowbridge owned the castle from 1730 to 1891.
7 H. A. Tipping, *Country Life* (November 1921) 692–6.
8 Even the English Heritage handbook admits that 'it is impossible to trace the plan from the existing remains' (1986 edn) 6.
9 The site as laid out shows a post-medieval central division and some minor internal wall footings.
10 R. Wilcox, *Proc. Somerset Arch. and N. H. Soc.* 124 (1980) 99. A barbican with a half-octagonal front was added at the same time, updating Sir Thomas' gatehouse to which it was joined by side walls.

11 Excavations in 1973–6 north of the church revealed the footings of a late twelfth-century church. R. Wilcox, *Proc. Somerset Arch. and N. H. Soc.*124 (1980) 91–4.
12 Best seen in the painting made in 1844 when much more detailing survived.
13 A. D. Saunders and T. J. Miles, *Med. Arch.* 19 (1975) 165–94.
14 Heytesbury House holds nothing of the Hungerford family except two armorial plaques from the house that the 1st (and last) Lord Hungerford of Heytesbury was building at the time of his execution in 1540. The present Heytesbury House was erected in 1782.
15 For the Hungerford family, J. L. Kirby, 'The Hungerford family in the later middle ages', PhD thesis, University of London (1936), with a summary in *Bull. Inst. Hist. Res.* 18 (1940); J. S. Roskell, *The Commons and Their Speakers in English Parliaments: 1376–1523* (1965) and M. A. Hicks, 'The Moleyns ransom and the Hungerford land sales 1453–87', *Southern History* 8 (1986) 11–35. For Leland's attribution of the castle's development through ransom money after Agincourt, see page 281.
16 Bod. Lib., Oxford, MS Aubrey 3 f.187.
17 Brit. Lib., Add. MS 18674.

Anonymous, *Picturesque Illustrations of the Antiquities of the Chapel of St. Anne within the castle of Farley Hungerford by a member of the Antiquarian family of Edinburgh* (c.1800)
J. E. Jackson, *A Guide to Farleigh Hungerford* (1879)
English Heritage, *Farleigh Hungerford Castle: Handbook* (1946 and many later editions)

FIDDLEFORD MANOR, Dorset

The modest character of the manor house at Fiddleford – a blank end wall, small windows, modern replacement roofs – belies its former scale. A closer examination reveals the ground-marked outline of a larger hall and upper-end block, while the almost concealed north face of the hall hints at its former importance. This is only revealed internally, with two spectacular fourteenth-century roofs above the hall and first-floor chamber, and a contemporary wall painting.

Standing next to the River Stour a mile east of Sturminster Newton, this house was built between the early and mid-fourteenth century. It may have been for William Latimer, who acquired the manor of Fiddleford through marriage in about 1355 and was appointed sheriff of Somerset in 1374 and of Dorset in 1380. The property was purchased in 1539 by Thomas White (d.1555) and his wife Ann, who remodelled and extended the residence. It remained in the hands of the White family until the mid-seventeenth century, when the older part of the house began to fall into decay. It was rescued by the predecessor of English Heritage in 1956, with the Pitt-Rivers family retaining the still-tenanted sixteenth-century north wing.

Built of rubble Greensand and Marnhull limestone, the exterior of this T-shaped house does not reveal its basic fourteenth-century structure, though its shaping hints at an early date. It consists of a single-storey hall with an offices and chamber cross wing, and independent roof structures. That over the hall is higher, but both roofs follow the Dorset practice of mainly clay tiles, with stone slates for the courses immediately over the side walls. All windows are mid-sixteenth century, using a higher standard of dressed stone, and this is the date of the marked-out footings of the hall extension and two-

PLATE 236 Fiddleford Manor: hall and chamber unit from the south

unit chamber block. These were pulled down in the late seventeenth century when the hall was truncated to its present shape.

By the mid-sixteenth century, the hall was porch-approached on both sides, but the north porch has been pulled down, while that to the south has been vernacularised. The much-maligned south face of the hall has a window of three uncusped lights under a square label, while the north face bespeaks the extent of the mid-Tudor remodelling. The wall has been faced with creamy Marnhull limestone, embellished with octagonal shafts with moulded bases and caps that are continued as a plinth and a string course to the label over two windows with three uncusped lights.

Both entry doors have continuous-moulded jambs and four-centred heads of a date more clearly apparent in the cross passage, where three elaborate doorways stand in the ashlar-faced wall – one is the inside of the entry from the south porch and the others open into the buttery and pantry. Restored in 1968 from a damaged state, each doorway has a multi-moulded base with shell cap, and a wave-moulded chamfer to the square frame enclosing a four-centred head with leaf spandrels. The end stops to the office entries have the initials T W and A W (interlaced on the south label), identifying the Whites' preference for the late Gothic style.

The cross passage 7 feet wide, with its early Jacobean panelled partition and balcony, opens into a hall almost 20 feet square, though originally about 7 feet longer. It is lit by the three aforementioned windows, and has plastered walls (renewed) and a reset sixteenth-century fireplace surround in the later end wall. The

glory of this hall is its fourteenth-century roof, now of three bays with the fourth bay truncated by the end wall. The collar-beam trusses are supported on moulded arch braces with central strut, and there are two tiers of wind braces. This is a standard West of England structure. However, all members above and including the collar are cusped to form two trefoils and a higher central quatrefoil. The inner faces of the wind braces are similarly decorated, the lower row with cinquefoil cusps and an open trefoil, the upper row elaborated into an oval shape. The third bay from the entry retains evidence of a smoke louvre to an open hearth.

All the windows of the cross wing are mid-sixteenth-century replacements. The partition separating the two low-ceiled service rooms was reinstated in 1970 to recreate their original volumes. Both rooms are of comparable size, but the sixteenth-century chamber stair projects into the buttery while the second room was formerly divided by a central partition (chases in cross beam), with a pantry next to the cross passage and a service unit with an original window converted into an external door. The Whites' kitchen was the adjacent room in the added north wing.

The broad flight of oak stairs of sixteenth-century construction[1] give access to the upper chamber with its Tudor inserted wall fireplace.[2] All else is of the later fourteenth century. Removal of plaster in the 1960s revealed the original end-wall window of two trefoiled lights with transom and ogee quatrefoil head, rear arch, and window seats. The contemporary wall painting at its side was discovered in 1990, part of an Annunciation with the Angel Gabriel on the left,

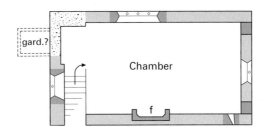

FIRST FLOOR

but missing the Virgin Mary on the right-hand side except for a corner of her robe.[3] The choice of a religious subject in a secular chamber was not uncommon, as the wall paintings in the Byward Tower at the Tower of London and those at Cothay Manor and Longthorpe Tower confirm. Jamb evidence at the opposite end of the room points to possible garderobe provision.[4] The three-bay roof shares many features with that in the hall, though it is even more elaborate. The four arch-braced collar trusses support cusped vertical struts to the ridge, with the principal rafters above the collar also ogee-cusped to create a decorative head as in the hall roof. This is multiplied by horizontal cusped braces from the top of the collars to the moulded purlins, and by four rows of highly decorative wind braces. This roof impresses as much today as it did originally, creating a spatially effective room which would have been enhanced by the brightly coloured walls.

Hall and cross wing seem to be contemporary, attributed to the second rather than of the third quarter of the fourteenth century, offering 'the most spectacular medieval manor house interior in Dorset'.[5] It is probable that the cross wing with its impressive first-floor chamber was originally a solar block at the dais end of the hall, with a matching offices wing at the east end.[6] White reversed the whole house, replacing the original offices with a new unitary solar block at the east end, and inserting the impressive doorways and all the other features relevant to the offices under the retained residential chamber. This practice was being repeated at about the same time at Purse Caundle Manor 7 miles away, where similar if less elaborate hall and cross-passage doorways were inserted at the dais end. If this was so, the position of the smoke vent in the third bay of the hall indicates that it was originally a five- or six-bay structure.

The fundamental changes to the hall by Thomas White in the mid-sixteenth century necessitated much wall rebuilding, but his work was of a comparable high quality. The earlier roof was retained and in part protected by the massive beams White inserted to support a flat moulded plaster ceiling, now above the staircase at Hinton St Mary Manor House. The Whites also extended the hall with two opposing projections at the upper end – an oriel and a stair or passage way (?), now marked on the ground, as is their two-unit solar block. Excavations have shown that the principal chamber had a richly decorated plaster ceiling, similar to that in the hall. This wing was demolished towards the close of the seventeenth century when the hall was shortened and the porches taken down. During the same period, a wing was built from the south-west corner of the house, demolished in 1956 to bring the Manor closer to its original state. Despite the vicissitudes of extension, demolition, and neglect, Fiddleford Manor stands with Woodsford 'Castle' as the finest Dorset houses of the fourteenth century, with the Manor as a fitting precursor of those a century later at Purse Caundle and Athelhampton.

NOTES

1 The ornamental stepping of the internal splay of the sixteenth-century window lighting these stairs is similar to the contemporary ones in the hall at Forde Abbey (c.1528).

2 The plaster overmantel with the initials of Thomas and Ann White is held in store.

3 A more complete Annunciation of the earlier fourteenth century survives in Tarrant Crawford church, 9 miles south-east and next to one of the richest nunneries of England.

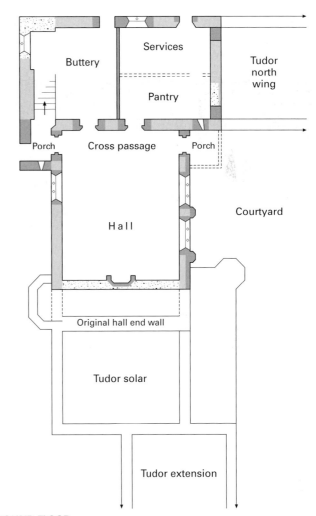

GROUND FLOOR

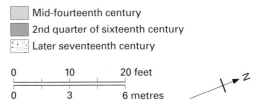

Mid-fourteenth century
2nd quarter of sixteenth century
Later seventeenth century

0   10   20 feet
0   3   6 metres

FIGURE 136 Fiddleford Manor: floor plans

4 RCHM, III (1970) 275 records that the nearby corner of the now destroyed seventeenth-century wing may have also been fourteenth-century work.

5 John Newman and N. Pevsner, *The Buildings of England: Dorset* (1972) 408. The dating needs clarification. The roofs were initially thought to date from William Latimer's ownership, but two solar timbers with felling dates of 1301–33 and 1324–56 suggest somewhat earlier. The hall timbers were not suitable for dendro work. *Vern. Arch.* 34 (2003) 91.

6 The excavation notes suggest there was evidence for a medieval cross wing at the east end of the hall, though the information is imprecise.

RCHM, *Dorset*, III pt 2 (1970) 271–6

FORDE ABBEY, Dorset

Standing in the landscaped gardens facing the magnificent south frontage of Forde, with its irregular line of linked buildings, different window forms, and common embattled parapet, it is difficult to conceive that this was an ensemble of monastic buildings, or that the well-tended lawn covers the site of the abbey church and cloister garth. The two-storeyed east range stretching northwards more befits its ecclesiastical origins, but the multi-gabled north side, viewed from the kitchen garden, betrays nothing older than continuous residential occupation. This mansion looks as though it was consistently domestic, assuredly of late medieval origin with added classical fenestration, but surely not monastic. The interior is totally different – revealing on the one hand a number of little-touched monastic rooms, and on the other hand a sequence of imposing baroque apartments. For the abbey at Forde is essentially a three-period property made up of claustral rooms of the twelfth and fifteenth centuries,[1] very extensive alterations and additions by abbot Chard during the early sixteenth century, and an equally striking refurbishment and updating by Edmund Prideaux in the

mid-seventeenth century. Since then, the house has been little touched, though occupation has been continuous.

This Cistercian abbey was established in 1141 on fertile land in the valley of the River Axe. Its income was derived from eight estates at Thornecombe and the nearby area of Dorset, supplemented by three properties in Devon, two in east Dorset, and a substantial one in Somerset, to give a middle-ranking return of £360 per annum at the time of the Dissolution. Richard Pollard purchased the abbey in 1539, and either he or his immediate successors were responsible for pulling down the abbey church and most of the cloister walks, and for modifying abbot Chard's lodgings. It was not until the property was purchased in 1649 by Edmund Prideaux, Cromwell's solicitor-general throughout the Protectorate, that the domestic buildings were dramatically remodelled, during the following ten years before his death, to create one of the finest sequences of baroque workmanship in the country, encompassing woodwork, panelling, fireplaces, fenestration, and plasterwork. The activity of Thomas Chard, abbot from January 1506 to 1539, had been equally substantial and of comparable workmanship, so that the association of these two contrasting styles, linked by the common use of local rubble stone and ashlar dressings, works surprisingly well.

Chard, born at Honiton, was educated at St Bernard's College, Oxford (now St John's) and was elected abbot of Forde before he had finished his disputations necessary to be awarded his doctorate in October 1507. He was one of the commissioners appointed in 1513 to reform the English Cistercian monasteries and held that post until at least 1527.[2] Chard was diligent, ambitious, and extremely capable, achieving an extensive rebuilding programme 'with incredible splendour and magnificence', though the common attribution of this phrase to Leland is fallacious. Chard was a reformer, anxious to update his monastery, and he did so on a mammoth scale. Much of his work lies outside the scope of this

PLATE 237 Forde Abbey: abbot's lodging, hall, porch, and saloon from the south

volume for it encompassed the first-floor refectory and its approach, private accommodation for the prior and some senior monks, reorganising the out-of-date lay brothers' dormitory as new guest accommodation, adding a chamber (described as a 'library') over the chapter-house, and rebuilding the entire cloister.[3] Most of this would have had to be completed before Chard could adapt the earlier guest building as his own improved hall and lodging. For while the latter is on such an extensive scale and so richly decorated that it is among the leading domestic developments of the early sixteenth century, the less obvious work affecting the claustral buildings was its essential prelude.

The three-storey entry porch immediately proclaims the scale of Chard's vision and the financial resources available to undertake it. Higher than any other south-facing element, this porch is among the most elaborate of its time (pl. 195). The sides are markedly plain except for the open ground-floor windows, but the frontage is a tiered proclamation of outrageous display. Even the diagonal stepped buttresses at the front angles change from plain facing to higher trefoiled panels (a not dissimilar change enhanced the earlier porch at Athelhampton Hall). The entry arch of two lines of hollow moulding is set in a square frame with end stops of shield-carrying angels, but the frame is pinnacled, the moulding is three-sided, and the stops are extremely low. A multi-moulded corbel above supports a two-storeyed rectangular oriel with the windows separated above and below by panelled friezes. The windows are of six cinquefoiled ogee lights, separated by mini buttresses at the corners from a further light on each side. Those to the front below the transom were replaced by plainer wooden ones in the mid-seventeenth century. The friezes consist of three frontal and two side panels of shields set in diamond-shaped frames. The lowest band has those of local families (Courtenay quartering Redvers with badges of the house of Courtenay), the middle band bears the initials and devices of Chard and the abbey, while the more extended upper band

repeats these, together with angels with musical instruments and a Latin inscription 'Made in the year of Our Lord, 1528 by Thomas Chard, Abbot'. Though the inner doorway repeats the character of the outer one in a more modest form, the side windows follow the complex head of the cloister windows (one partially blocked in the seventeenth century) and the porch is fan-vaulted with four conoids.

The hall frontage to the left is more calm. The walling is plain and uninterrupted between the low moulded plinth and the foot of the windows which fill the greater part of the wall. These are separated by stepped buttresses which do not extend to the ground but stop at the base of the windows. Each window, under a plain almost flattened arched head, is of four lights, cinquefoiled above and below the transom. Above the windows and below the seventeenth-century embattled parapet is a band of panels carved with Renaissance motifs (mermen, sphinxes, putti, winged monsters) divided into three by the buttressed heads.

The porch and the line of four magnificent windows serving what is clearly a single-storey five-bay hall are immediately followed by a fundamental architectural change, a classical two-storeyed frontage above a low basement. This is one of the many alterations made by Edmund Prideaux, though the roof line is continuous with that of the hall and was conceived with it as a single unit. It is followed by a taller three-storeyed tower above a basement, again subject to Prideaux's alterations but crowned with a low-pitched roof behind the seventeenth-century embattled parapet so that there is no change in the line of the roof ridge. Both classical frontages were refenestrated in the mid-eighteenth century with polygonal glazing bars, but that this taller block is undoubtedly by Chard is confirmed externally by the corner buttress and by the end wall repeating the early sixteenth-century window of four cinquefoiled ogee and transomed lights. The further high window of trefoil lights is part of the seventeenth-century additions. That this part of Chard's

PLATE 238 Forde Abbey: lodgings, hall range and saloon from the north

PLATE 239 Forde Abbey: hall interior

guest master's bedroom above retains a sixteenth-century fireplace and the original newel to the roof.

The hall interior is essentially that of *c.*1528 by Chard, quietly modified by Prideaux. It follows the same form as the slightly earlier abbot's hall at Milton Abbey of increasing complexity with greater height. The lower walling was initially blank (now covered with advanced mid-seventeenth-century panelling) with the windows in the upper two-thirds originally flooding the hall with light from both sides. They repeat the external splayed bases with a double rhythm and narrow panelled internal reveals, with the slender shafted walling between resting on carved angel heads. The north-facing windows were blocked at different times between the mid-sixteenth and mid-seventeenth centuries (as they had been in the hall at Knightstone, 16 miles south-west, during the 1560s), enabling a grand stair, a new chimney stack in place of that one bay to the west, and the family lobby and stair to be built against the north-facing wall during the 1650s.

The roof is not the elaborate trussed structure that might have been expected in the west of England and that had been displayed at Milton Abbey twenty years earlier. It is a low-pitched, almost flat ceiling with coved sides to the wall where it meets a quatrefoil frieze above the embattled wall plates. The ceiling is a seven-bay structure in a five-bay hall, each bay subdivided and spanned by nine subsidiary beams creating a total of 112 panels. The outer ones have rectangular cross ribs; the inner ones have diagonal ribs. The ceiling retains its retouched red and green colour scheme, with carved bosses at all intersections and gold stars in the middle of each panel.

The king-post roof above the ceiling is original and, like the hall ceiling, continues 30 feet further westwards above the first part of the abbot's lodging, though now concealed by the 1650s plaster ceiling immediately below it. This leads to two questions. Is the hall ceiling original or a seventeenth-century Prideaux reconstruction using original materials,[6] and is the 30 feet section further west part of the original hall, but sub-divided from it by Prideaux with a cross wall when this smaller section was made two-storey?[7] These are the commonly held views,[8] even though the present well-proportioned hall (55 feet by 28 feet) would become an apartment of excessive length with the further extension. My initial examination of the area suggested that this division had possibly existed since the time of abbot Chard, with the hall of no greater length than at present,[9] and that Chard's lodgings had been particularly expansive, with an outer chamber on two floors preceding the three-storeyed unit at the end of the range. The scale of such accommodation would have been much more appropriate (as well as being in proportion to the size of the hall) at a time when greater privacy and more generous facilities were becoming the norm.

Little of Chard's lodging is visible internally, for the comprehensive changes made by Prideaux in the mid-1650s to update these rooms with baroque panelling, fireplaces, and plaster ceilings for his personal occupation give them their essential character today. This remodelling was as wholehearted as that by Robert Cecil, 1st earl of Salisbury, fifty years previously of the large early thirteenth-century hunting lodge of King John at Cranborne.

However, I was unhappy with some aspects of my interpretation and asked Patric Morrisey to re-examine the abbot's lodging on my behalf. He has confirmed that Chard's hall was originally 84 feet long and was curtailed with the present west wall in the mid-seventeenth century. Moreover, the joists common to the newly created west

lodging was broader than the hall block is confirmed by the north-west face of the house, where the angle is clasped by a narrow three-storeyed extension, probably a garderobe. The area behind, between this and a second early Tudor extension to the east, is a mid-seventeenth century infilling, occasionally reusing early sixteenth-century windows and carved panels to create a thoroughly confusing ensemble. From the kitchen garden, the rear of the hall stands with its line of windows infilled and the mid-seventeenth-century chimney stack towering above the roof line.[4] So the sequence of abbot Chard's lodging is a single-storey hall, now followed by a two-storey block under a common roof ridge, terminating in a broad three-storey tower with garderobe projection at the rear. The two- and three-storey structures were raised over basement rooms, now partially concealed with windows raised in the late nineteenth century so that grass could be planted up to the frontage.[5]

Visitors arriving at the porch tower would be received by the guest master, and directed from his lodge served by the window now blocked by the seventeenth-century stair. This replacement stair leads to the well-furnished first-floor porch room with its locker, closet, and oriel window enabling the guest master to see who was entering the outer precinct or the church. An almost hidden west-facing window enabled him to keep an eye on the frontage of the newly built lodging, while the hall screens passage and the dais table were monitored from the two spy holes in the outer lobby. The

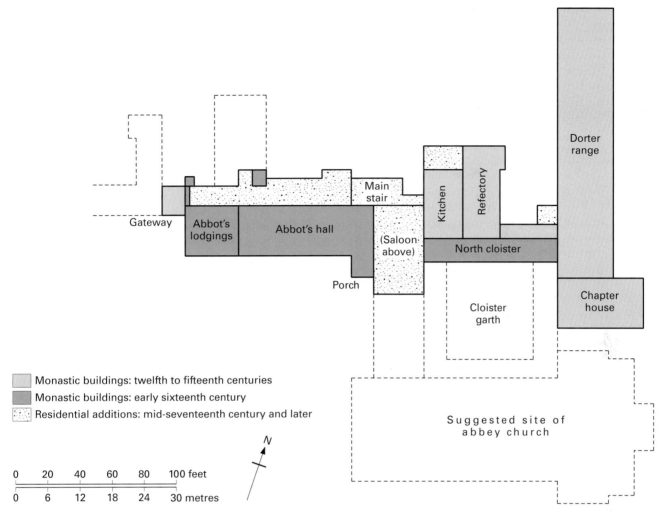

FIGURE 137 Forde Abbey: site plan

Monastic buildings: twelfth to fifteenth centuries
Monastic buildings: early sixteenth century
Residential additions: mid-seventeenth century and later

dining room ceiling and the floor of the bedchamber above are also of that time. The blocked windows on the north side of the hall, infilled after the dissolution of the abbey, extended for at least one more bay than at present, with the final north window visible in a present-day bathroom. The original painted wooden roof at the upper end of the abbot's hall survives above the second-floor bedroom, while the south wall of the basement under the west dining room incorporates one side of a bay window lighting the hall dais.

Chard's hall was extremely attenuated for its width, though flooded with light from both sides. The dais bay was marked by two features. There was initially a south-facing bay, evidenced in the basement and at roof level, almost as large as the porch, long since pulled down. However, the dais wall still retains a stone panel with the abbey arms, the initials of Thomas Chard, and two angel supporters, now visible in the inserted first-floor bedroom. Its low-set position suggests it may have been positioned above the original entrance to Chard's lodging. It is unclear what form of roof Chard envisaged. The marked narrowness of the hall would allow it to be covered with a stone vault and the abrupt curtailment of the pilasters between the windows suggests that such a structure was planned. As the buttresses do not extend to the ground, a wooden

vault was probably envisaged, painted to resemble stone, though the beginning of a stone vault was recently found in the roof space. In the event, this was abandoned and the present low-pitched, multi-panelled structure was chosen. This may have been on the grounds of cost, or more likely because Chard realised which way the political wind was blowing after the fall of Wolsey and the initial attacks on the church, and chose to complete the hall as swiftly and as economically as possible. The inclusion of instruments of the passion in its decoration point to completion before the suppression of the monastery, but the outside possibility that it was remade during the mid-seventeenth century from original materials has not yet been settled.

The basement under the abbot's lodging is earlier than the structure above, lit by windows that formerly extended much lower than today. The area has a number of fifteenth- and early sixteenth-century doorways suggesting north and west external entries, but the position of any internal access is unclear.[10] The abbot's more public apartments were on the ground floor and his more private rooms above, with the second floor reserved for privileged guests. The ground floor consisted of Chard's reception chamber, approached from the lost door in the hall dais wall. It is now the

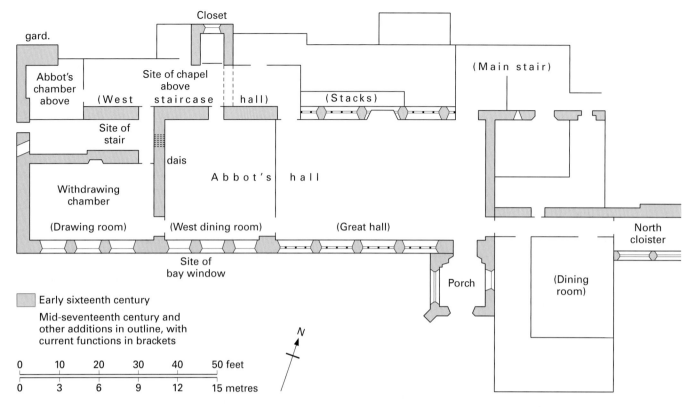

FIGURE 138 Forde Abbey: ground plan of abbot Chard's hall and lodgings

family's tapestry-hung drawing room and entirely mid-seventeenth century in character. The small room to the north-west terminating in the garderobe turret was used by the abbot's clerk.

Dr Morrisey has confirmed that the two substantial parallel walls (see plan) held the stair serving the upper floors with stone cross arches (one survives) and north-facing windows. One of these was reused by Prideaux when he expanded the stair area to create his grander western hall and staircase. Chard's more private first-floor room (above his withdrawing chamber) retains its west window of four cinquefoil ogee and transomed lights (lower blocked) within a square head and an early Renaissance carved panel above. Converted in the mid-seventeenth century into a bedroom with fireplace, it is now used as a divided playroom. North of it was Chard's bedchamber with corner garderobe, while his chapel lay eastwards with a projecting sacristy. The towered second floor for honoured guests followed a similar three-room plan of principal room, bedchamber with garderobe, and chapel with east-facing window. Several Cistercian foundations had two private chapels within the abbot's lodging, but that reserved for visitors at Forde had no need for a second sacristy.

ASSESSMENT

Forde was among the wealthiest monasteries in Dorset and it is frequently argued that Chard's residence is 'on a scale to justify the Reformation and the Dissolution'.[11] Chard's work is certainly on a princely scale, with a substantial hall, a porch of striking pretence, and an extensive suite of private apartments. In itself, that is no different from contemporary lodgings for the head of the abbeys at

Battle, Milton, or Thame. The decorative lavishness that worried so many late nineteenth- and twentieth-century commentators was no more than the fashionable practice of the time by crown, leading laymen, and educational institutions. Abbots such as Chard, Huby of Fountains, and Vyntoner of St Osyth and their predecessors saw themselves as much leaders of the church as the bishops and, not surprisingly, had followed the bishops in building separate lodgings with high standards of comfort. We do not castigate bishop Rotherham for building a tower-house at Buckden or archbishop Kempe for converting his house at Southwell into a palace-residence, but we speak with hindsight when it comes to monastic practice. Monastic heads were no different from wealthy laymen in following the fashion for thoroughgoing domestic rehabilitation. It was a reflection of their relative prosperity and wish to keep up with rising standards of living. It can be seen as much in Augustinian houses (Newstead, St Osyth) and Benedictine (Milton, Muchelney) as in Cluniac (Castle Acre, Wenlock) and Cistercian (Cleeve, Forde, Thame). And while the commissioners' report of 1536 castigated many houses for their failure to maintain their buildings, others were shown to be 'in marvellous good reparacion', 'newe builded', or 'in very good state'.[12]

Chard's extended development programme enhanced Forde Abbey's important pastoral rôle. Guests arriving on horseback would have their mounts taken through the existing archway to the stables in the rear yard. They would then proceed on foot towards the entrance tower prefacing the new guest hall, which may not have been completely finished at the time of the Dissolution. The hall filled the space between the front of the abbey church and the lay brothers' dormitory and an existing fifteenth-century building

564

which Chard expanded and encased in Ham stone as his own lodging unit. In some ways, Chard's work was backward-looking, particularly in the use of ogee revival forms, multi-cusping, and heavily moulded jambs at a time when Tudor domestic work favoured simplicity, with cuspless tracery and plain doorways as at Cothay Manor or Brympton d'Evercy. Towered lodgings had long been favoured by monastic heads, as at Repton, Hailes, and Norton, but the three-storey tower at Forde was combined with a more extensive residential complex, as was the case at Thame. In other ways, Chard's work was remarkably up-to-date. The hall was an extremely impressive reception area, initially intended to be crowned with a vault rather than the present comparatively restrained panelled ceiling after Chard chose to modify his elaborate plans in about 1530. The Renaissance decorative devices are among the earliest in England, similarly used at St Osyth Priory and Thame Abbey and equally mixed with structural members of the late Gothic form. This 85 foot long hall also supports the view that those developed in the largest houses during the early sixteenth century were on a grander scale than before. Chard's structure also supports the associated trend for such impressive apartments to become more narrow, emphasising the contrast between the lower and the higher ends of the apartment.[13] While Chard's suite of lodgings was not similarly excessive in scale, it seems to have followed the practice of voluptuous decoration externally and increasing privacy internally.

Attention should also be drawn to a remarkable aspect of Edmund Prideaux's transformation of the abbey buildings during the Commonwealth.[14] He not only created an ordered and relatively balanced façade but he ensured that his centrepiece, the projecting Saloon, was slightly lower than Chard's porch tower which remained the dominant feature of the whole frontage. Though he gave the lodgings a classical façade and shortened Chard's hall, he left that apartment untouched in form and purpose, while the added first-floor eastern range, bringing horizontal unity to the frontage, was raised above the unmasked cloister walk. Finally, all the disparate elements were united externally by that outmoded feature, the embattled parapet and internally by the late medieval hall that continued to serve as the pivot between Prideaux's family rooms and his formal apartments. Despite his deeply held Puritan beliefs, Prideaux clearly had considerable sympathy for the retained late Gothic buildings, as well as for a contemporary lavishness that makes his interiors the finest in England of the Commonwealth period.

NOTES

1 The abbey was laid out on the standard Cistercian plan, with all the monastic buildings north of the church. The site of the abbey church, consecrated in 1239 but much rebuilt between about 1350 and 1400, has never been excavated. Of the surviving monastic buildings, the mid-twelfth-century chapter-house (now private chapel) was built shortly after the abbey's foundation. The early thirteenth-century dormitory above a pillared undercroft was originally partitioned on each side into lancet-lit cubicles for the monks and open to the roof. Divided centrally in the early nineteenth century to form a broad corridor with a line of servants' bedrooms to one side, the late fourteenth- or fifteenth-century arch-braced collar roof survives above the mock-vaulted plaster ceiling. The early thirteenth-century refectory was shortened and surmounted by a grander one in the early sixteenth century that was converted into a library in the late nineteenth century. Its late medieval form is virtually complete with windows, reading recess, and a striking twelve-bay roof divided by arch-braced collar trusses. Tree-ring dated to between 1480 and 1524, the collars support alternate scissor and saltire struts and decorated spandrels, with the three central lines of wind braces repeating the saltire pattern. The early thirteenth-century kitchen, modified in the fifteenth century, was extended and ceiled in the mid-seventeenth century, though its fifteenth-century roof is exposed in the bedroom above. The saloon further west was created out of some heavily mauled first-floor rooms, probably the lay brothers' dormitory, modified by Chard as guest accommodation. Blocked medieval windows survive behind the Mortlake tapestries and a fourteenth-century arch-braced roof above the magnificent plaster ceiling.

2 Chard's career needs to be reassessed to correct R. G. Bartelot, *Notes and Queries for Somerset and Dorset* 20 (1930–2) 250–3; M. Allen, *History of Forde Abbey* (1846); J. S. Udal, *Proc. Dorset N. H. and A. F. C. Soc.* 9 (1888) 136–46; and J. H. Pring, *Memoirs of Thomas Chard* (1864) who confused the abbot of Forde with the prior of the same name at Montacute.

3 This work is to be the subject of a monograph by Dr Patric Morrisey, who suggested to me that Chard's architectural activity over nearly thirty years should not be considered piecemeal, but as part of his vision for a reformed Cistercian monastery incorporating the order's devotion to learning and scholarship as well as to hospitality and pastoral activities.

4 The fireplace and stack had initially been inserted in the next bay westwards in the mid/late sixteenth century until moved by Prideaux.

5 The most prominent evidence of earlier buildings here is the low two-storey fifteenth-century gateway of single passage with room over. It abuts the west end of Chard's block and is set well back from his frontage.

6 As stated by RCHM, I (1952) 245.

7 *Ibid.*

8 O. Hill and J. Cornforth, *English Country Houses: Caroline 1625–1685* (1966) 111; West (1983) 26.

9 The contemporary hall at Horham Hall (c.1505–25) with a similar low panelled ceiling had comparable proportions (46 feet by 24 feet), while the halls in mansions or institutions of relevant standing are similarly proportioned as at Fawsley Hall (c.1510: 52 feet by 24 feet), Corpus Christi College, Oxford (1512–17: 53 feet by 24 feet), and Cowdray (c.1520–30: 59 feet by 28 feet). Halls of great length were usually matched by comparable width as at Wingfield Manor (c.1440: 72 feet by 37 feet) and Hampton Court (1532–5: 97 feet by 40 feet).

10 Now approached from a low door in the present drawing room.

11 J. Newman and N. Pevsner, *Buildings of England: Dorset* (1972) 210.

12 D. Knowles, *The Religious Orders in England*, III (1959) 24.

13 J. Grenville, *Medieval Housing* (1997) 107–9.

14 Hill and Cornforth, *English Country Houses: Caroline 1625–1685*, 111–18. West suggests that Edward Carter was responsible for these alterations: (1983) 28.

RCHM, *Dorset*, I (1952) 240–6
J. Cornforth, *Country Life* (March/April 1963)
J. J. West, *Arch. Jour.* 140 (1983) 25–8

GIDLEIGH MANOR, Devon

Gidleigh, sheltering in the tree-covered folds of Dartmoor's eastern flank, is almost as remote today as it was 200 years ago. Well maintained in the grounds of a post-medieval house next to the parish church, the standing tower is a puzzle as it lacks the associated structures that were an integral part of this manorial residence of the Prouz family.

Misleadingly known since the seventeenth century as Gidleigh Castle, this two-storeyed tower is part of a substantial habitation

PLATE 240 Gidleigh Manor: solar tower from the east

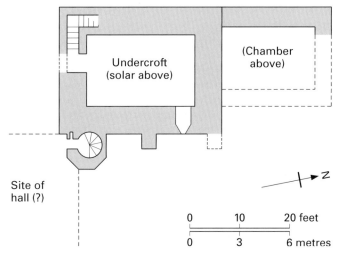

FIGURE 139 Gidleigh Manor: ground plan

occasionally revealed when the ground is hard dug, and marked by two culverts, one in line with the tower and one at right angles to it parallel with the later house. Built of roughly shaped granite blocks with 6½ feet thick walls, the tower consists of an undercroft with residential chamber above, approached from the half-octagonal stair turret, bonded not added at the south-east angle. Its position at the foot of a terraced slope points to the tower's essentially residential function rather than to any military purpose.

The ground floor with its east face supported by two half-buttresses is accessed today through a post-medieval forced entry. Originally, it could only be approached from the upper floor via the mural stair with single loops on the half and upper landing. The room, 22 feet by 13 feet, is vaulted, supported by three cross ribs, and lit by a single loop.

The upper floor retains its fireplace with a high straight lintel, flanked by windows of one and two lights respectively, the latter with window seats. There is a further window in the south wall, and the walls were originally plastered. Though there is a doorway in the north-west corner, the principal approach to this solar chamber was from the projecting newel with a drawbar slot at its foot and steps to the roof. It was complete until the 1920s when the upper section collapsed, though the stones of the cruciform loop in its face are preserved in the nearby house.[1] The solar has lost its pitched roof but there are traces of a wall-top parapet.

The tower functioned in association with other lost structures, though their form and function are not clear. Windows precluded any abutting structure on the south side, whereas the north wall is unbroken except for the first-floor doorway with drawbar socket to a lost building. Its lower walling is thinner, but continues the tower's west wall and is bonded to it, while projecting stones in the north face can be interpreted as supporting the bracing for a timber-fronted wall. However, the narrowness of this building 18 feet by 10 feet, and the barring of the first-floor doorway from within this lost apartment rather than from the tower side mitigates against it being the hall, but rather suggests it was an inner chamber. The prominent newel similarly opens from a lost structure, probably the hall, though the tower's fenestration shows that this can only have covered the south-east corner, and would have lain at right angles to it.

With its thick walls and first-floor habitation, the 'tower' at Gidleigh appears not dissimilar to the smaller tower-houses of Cumbria and Northumbria, functioning in association with a stone or timber-framed hall. But the Devon structure, poorly sited for defensive purposes, was not originally free-standing but the greater half of a residential block, attached at its south-east angle to a now lost hall. Though there is a lack of decorative material, a date either side of 1300 is most probable, with a preference towards the early fourteenth century. The manor, held by the Prouz family since the mid-twelfth century, became the centre of a substantial holding of eight manors by the time of Sir William Prouz (1280–1316), whose father had been sheriff of Devon (1269). The 'tower' was constructed about the same time as substantial work was undertaken at Okehampton Castle, 7 miles away, using the same Aplite stone for dressed work, a similar mortar composition, and a common decorative repertoire, e.g. doorstops.[2] The property seems to have stagnated after it passed to Sir William's daughter, who lived elsewhere following her marriage in 1323 to Sir Roger Moeles of North Cadbury.

NOTES
1 See the drawing of 1825 in Grumley-Grennan and Hardy (2000) 33.
2 Blaylock (1993) 3.

J. S. Amery and R. H. Worth, *Trans. Devon. Assoc.* 57 (1926) 267–72
S. R. Blaylock, *Gidleigh Castle: A Survey of the Standing Remains* (Exeter Mus. Arch. Fld. Unit, 1993) and *Med. Arch.* 37 (1992) 255–7
T. Grumley-Grennan and M. Hardy, *Gidleigh: A Dartmoor Village Past and Present* (2000)

GOTHELNEY HALL, Somerset

A house is recorded at Gothelney in about 1275[1] but the tower and south wing of the present Hall date from the fourteenth century. Whatever else existed was replaced during the second half of the fifteenth century with a highly unusual and distinctive tall structure that forms the body of the house today. It lies 4 miles west of Bridgwater and is built of local red sandstone with Ham stone dressings. The approach immediately reveals two unusual aspects, a markedly high central block fronted by a three-storey embattled tower. To its side is a nineteenth-century porch and two-storey corridor, for the Victorians modified and extended the property, thoroughly distorting its early character.

To appreciate its original form, it is best to begin with the well-preserved roof structure which reveals the plan, scale, and principal date of the house (fig. 140). It is an oblong range, 61 feet by 18 feet internally, divided by a wall 2½ feet thick into two units, 43½ and 15 feet long respectively. Both are spanned by a line of arch-braced collar trusses creating an eight-bay and a two-bay unit respectively. Alternate higher and lower corbels of shield-carrying angels mark five main and four intermediate trusses, all with moulded undersides, and there are three lines of cusped wind braces. The wall plates are embattled and decorated with rosettes.[2] In both side walls of the larger chamber are the straight heads of two blocked windows cutting across the roof bays rather than set within them, with the arched four-centred head of one of the east (forecourt-facing) windows having the hollow outer moulding set with fleurons, and panelled inside with spandrels to cinquefoil-headed panels. There is little doubt that these are the remains of a fine oriel. These windows are far too high to serve any hall, so that the plan revealed is a two-storey structure with a large well-furnished chamber open to the roof above what can only have been the hall of the house.

An external examination of the west (garden) frontage, less disturbed than that to the forecourt, reveals the first-floor string course separating the two principal units and details of both apartments. The later cross-passage porch adjoined a garderobe turret serving the rooms at the lower end of the main block. A broad semi-circular arch probably marks the position of a destroyed hall bay window. The three-light cinquefoiled windows of the upper chamber are more obvious than the projection of the west-wall fireplace, while the much-altered north-west extension may have originated as another garderobe turret to this room.

Post-medieval floor and partition insertions have created a confusing interior. The cross passage was not altered (rear entry with four-centred head) but was partitioned from the hall in the nineteenth century. Part of the 20 foot high hall has been retained, spanned by two massive cross beams, but the room is essentially Victorian – windows, doorways, fireplace, and coving. The upper end of the hall was divided into a ground-floor parlour with a late sixteenth-century fireplace and thin-ribbed seventeenth-century ceiling with a mezzanine bedroom above. The withdrawing chamber was divided into two bedrooms, both ceiled from the original roof and with nineteenth-century windows. The remains of a small north-west extension at this level point to a garderobe projection. The forecourt-facing corridor was added in an early Tudor style to provide access to these rooms, destroying the original windows in the process.

PLATE 241 Gothelney Hall: from the west

The end unit seems always to have been four-storeyed, with roof trusses each side of the stone partition wall. The uppermost room, approached from a mural stair at the head of the garderobe turret,[3] retains two gable lights, an early fireplace with hollow moulding and square-headed lintel, and its third tier of wind braces reversed. The chamber below has an early seventeenth-century fireplace. The ground and mezzanine rooms with garderobe facility retain doorways with chamfered jambs and two-centred heads, identifying the earlier fourteenth-century structure to the south. This extended end unit – now kitchen and offices with bedrooms above – retains two trefoil lights in opposing outer walls of the room above the kitchen. It is either basically fourteenth century or a sixteenth-century extension incorporating earlier features.

The tower opens from a broad fourteenth-century arch with continuous roll- and hollow-moulded jambs and two-centred head. As it opens from the nineteenth-century corridor, there must have been an early porch here, replaced by the present Victorian one nearby. The tower holds a Victorian wooden newel that is the main approach to the front-facing corridors. The original stone steps rise from the first floor to an upper room with an untouched three-light cinquefoil window with traceried head to the front and two-light cinquefoil side windows. A blocked window with three iron bars in the adjacent south wing shows that this floor was a later fifteenth-century addition to the earlier tower. The roof has had to be replaced, but not the six stone corbels of angels carrying shields. No link was broken through from the main range to this room, which may have been an oratory, though only the corbels are indicative of this. The newel continues to the embattled roof parapet.

Gothelney Hall is a fourteenth-century house of which the tower and probably the two-storey service and residential unit

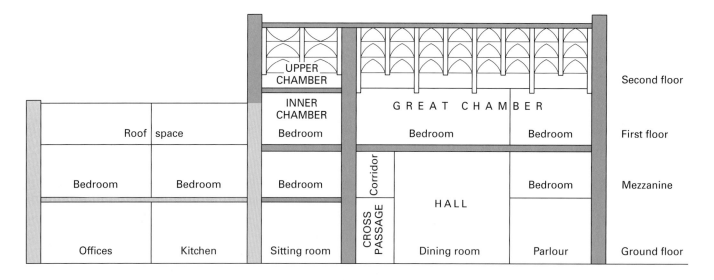

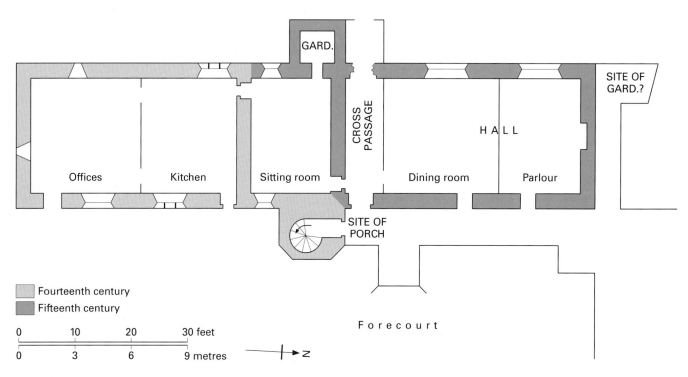

FIGURE 140 Gothelney Hall: ground plan and schematic cross-section

survive. The earlier hall was replaced in the fifteenth century by a ground-floor hall with great chamber above. The window form suggests the mid years, though this would be very early from a planning point of view. Downgrading the hall by inserting a great chamber above it had begun in East Anglia by about 1480 and in Wealden Kent by c.1510,[4] but the practice had been initiated in the West of England by bishop Bekynton at his palace at Wells (1443–65). As uncusped rather than cinquefoil window heads were already being adopted at Cothay by c.1485–90, Gothelney suggests that this fundamental planning change occurred during the years close to the 1470s, though only dendrochronology will clarify this.[5] The tower room was added at the same time. The lawyer Sir Alexander Hody (executed 1461) had acquired the manor in 1439, one of several he held in the area, as did his wife in her own right (see West Bower).[6] However, it is more likely that Hody's nephew was responsible for this forward-looking development that converted Gothelney into a high-status house of very considerable distinction.[7]

NOTES
1 VCH, VI (1992) 93.
2 Illustrated in M. R. Bismanis, *The Medieval English Domestic Timber Roof* (1987) 124.
3 It is crowned with a plain but high-quality barrel-shaped roof.
4 A. Emery, *Greater Med. Houses*, II (2000) 25.
5 Previous estimates have ranged from the early fifteenth century (W. A. Pantin, *Med. Arch.* 1 (1957) 141) to *c*.1500 (N. Pevsner, *The Buildings of England: South and West Somerset* (1958) 186).
6 VCH, VI (1992) 34. The family held this manor until 1622.
7 During his research into the family archives, Thomas Palmer (d.1734), the antiquarian owner of Fairfield House, 4 miles north-west of Gothelney, found a crenellation licence granted to William Verney in about 1473 to build a wall and seven round towers: VCH, VI (1992) 140 quoting Somerset Record Office D/P Stogs. 23/19. Palmer recorded that three towers still stood in his day on the boundary of a walled court to the east of the present house, while a map of 1610 shows that it was of courtyard plan at that time. The present E-shaped house is essentially late sixteenth and eighteenth century but retaining two finely carved timbers of the later fifteenth century spanning a first-floor chamber (like that at Gothelney Hall?) in the south-west wing, and a blocked arch of similar date in the cross passage. See also R. Dunning, *Some Somerset Country Houses* (1991) 55–9.

VCH, *Somerset*, VI (1992) 93–4
E. H. L. Williams and R. G. Gilson, NMRC, Archive no.41716 (1980)

GREAT CHALFIELD MANOR, Wiltshire

The fifteenth-century manor of Thomas Tropnell is one of the archetypal houses of late medieval England, a near-perfect example of its time still field-surrounded, moat-reflected, and linked by a forecourt to the little parish church of Great Chalfield. It is not immediately apparent that the house is neither of single build nor as extensive as originally, but the body of the residence wonderfully reflects its original layout and character, externally and internally, in an ensemble of rare beauty and calmness.

THE PERCY DWELLING

Situated 3 miles north-east of Bradford-on-Avon in agriculturally rich and champaign countryside, the Manor retains the isolation that has characterised the site since it was first developed by the Percy family. The William Perci recorded at Chalfield in 1199 was a branch of the more famous Yorkshire family of that name. William's successors held the property for six generations,[1] until the last one, Sir Henry Percy III who had succeeded by 1338, died at Cologne in 1356 during his pilgrimage to Jerusalem. He was survived by his second wife Constance, reputed to be the 'bedfelow and cosyne to maister Robert Wayvile, bisshoppe of Salisbury'.[2] She enjoyed three further husbands and had at least two children by the last, but also schemed to ensure that her grandchildren succeeded to the Chalfield estate rather than Sir Henry's daughter by his first wife. The long-living Constance continued to occupy Chalfield, until her death in 1419 prompted a raft of claims and counter-claims for ownership of the property.

Great Chalfield was initially a fortified house standing on the north side of a large moat-surrounded platform. The south side is bounded by a swift-flowing stream, but the water-filled moat remains on the east and north sides and can be traced on the west. The present forecourt and churchyard retain two half-round bastions, both reduced to a low level, the one 6 feet high in the north-east corner retaining three loops. The link walling of probable thirteenth-century date has been taken down, as has the remainder of the enclosure which may have extended as far as the sloping bank dividing the platform midway.[3] It is probable that the lost outer gatehouse opened into a first court of farm, stabling, and service units as it still does, marked by the replacement barn of 1752 with a medieval north end, and an inner entry replaced by the present end-range gateway. The church nave is also fourteenth-century Percy work[4] while the foundations of the circular tower south of the house may have been part of their residence otherwise obliterated by later rebuilding.

DOCUMENTATION

In total contrast with the contemporary manor house at South Wraxall nearby, Great Chalfield Manor is particularly rich in historical and architectural documentation.

The Tropnell Cartulary. The Tropnell family were of modest Wiltshire stock but the fortune of Thomas Tropnell was a consequence of his work as receiver-general of the 1st (1426–49) and 2nd Lord Hungerford (1449–59) and intimate supporter of this powerful family until the close of his life.[5] Born in *c*.1405 and probably a lawyer by profession, he was returned as a member of parliament for their county-held seat in 1429 and again in 1449. As a direct descendant of Sir William Percy (*fl*.1260) Tropnell soon cast his eyes on the desirable Chalfield estate.[6] For more than thirty years this Lancastrian supporter was embroiled in litigation, claims, and counter-claims between the several heirs of Sir Henry Percy's daughter Beatrice, and those of Constance and her husbands who resorted to planning an attack on the property to gain possession in July 1431. Tropnell purchased Neston Park in 1438 to be close to Chalfield[7] and was entangled in the battery of lawsuits that forms the basis of the Tropnell Cartulary, a record drawn up in 1464 and the following years of his protracted but successful fight for ownership. By 1452, Tropnell was the tenant of Great Chalfield manor. By 1467, he had obtained a release on any claims on the property from the direct heir of Beatrice (née Percy), and in 1482 obtained several legal opinions confirming his ownership.[8]

Like Ralph, Lord Cromwell's similar protracted manoeuvrings to obtain ownership of Wingfield Manor throughout the 1430s, success was followed by total rebuilding. Unfortunately Tropnell's substantial manuscript volume of the legal and administrative records of a careful man, preserved in the house today, includes no documentation referring to his building activity. Thomas died in 1488 and was succeeded by his son Christopher (d.1503) and grandson Giles (d.1553 without male heirs). The property passed through a sequence of families between the mid-sixteenth and early twentieth centuries, suffering from two sieges in 1645 when it was held by a parliamentary garrison (1644–6)[9] and from destruction of the ranges round the inner court during subsequent occupation.

The Buckler Portfolio. In August 1823, John Buckler prepared a portfolio of six watercolours – four exteriors (including the upper cross wing before its destruction), the interior of the hall, and a ground plan. The preparatory work for these beautifully detailed drawings, still held in the house, was completed in a single day.

The Walker Portfolio. In September 1836, the owner, Sir Harry Hurrard Neale of Walhampton, Hampshire, commissioned Thomas Walker to survey the Manor with a view to its restoration. The bound

PLATE 242 Great Chalfield Manor: entrance frontage from the forecourt

volume of forty-one pencil-drawn plans, elevations, cross-sections, and details (together with a further sixteen drawings of the church) by Walker, J. Prichard, and G. B. Wollaston is retained in the house. The majority of these drawings are among the twenty-eight plates and eleven pages of explanatory notes in Walker's published volume of May 1837.

The Brakspear Portfolio. In 1838, much of the east wing was demolished and the hall was floored and partitioned for tenant occupation. Further alterations considered at the close of the century were rejected in favour of more sympathetic proposals. Between 1905 and 1912, the Wiltshire architect Harold Brakspear carried out an extended restoration programme for Robert Fuller. The hall and lower cross wing were in a reasonable state but only the front wall survived of the upper cross wing and the rear wall of the timber-framed south wing. Brakspear's work was based on the drawings by Walker, with the retention of as much original work as possible. About 150 of his working drawings and plans are held in the house, together with the correspondence between owner and architect.

Though Brakspear's work was an extremely valuable reinstatement, he used a sharp yellowish stone – too hard-edged for comfort – unvariable woodwork, and occasional unnecessary window enlargement. Robert Fuller and his wife furnished the house for their occupation and developed the garden,[10] practices maintained by their successors and by the National Trust so that even the Edwardian character of the rooms has become a period statement in itself.

TROPNELL'S HOUSE

The plan of the house is simple, a central hall with end cross wings, with the two-storey porch offset by a similar projection at the upper

end of the hall. This was balanced by an opposing projection on the south side of the hall giving stair access to the principal withdrawing chamber. In place of the usual offices below the cross passage was a parlour with an equally important chamber above. The offices were located in a south wing forming one side of an inner court of which nothing else remains outside the foundations of the two enclosing ranges. The outer court of the Percys was retained by Tropnell for service and farm use.

The Manor is rubble-built with ashlar dressings and roofed with stone tiles from a quarry at Hazelbury 3 miles north. The walls were probably plaster-faced and colour-washed originally. The kitchen and offices wing was timber-framed though the present structure is a Brakspear rebuilding using the back wall, one original window, and some timber uprights. Apart from this restoration programme, the house has hardly changed since Edward IV's reign. The mid-sixteenth-century updating was modest, while there is little visible evidence of the farmhouse alterations of 1838–9. A house of such singular quality warrants analysis rather than description.

1. The frontage is a beautifully designed architectural composition of receding planes from the bold cross wings to the central hall. The wings are emphasised by first-floor oriels, though not identical ones. The adjacent two-storey projections are narrower, with lower gables but prominent diagonal buttresses. There is an ampleness of fenestration throughout the house, with the more important upper windows transomed and all of them emphasised by bold hoods with diamond-shaped stops. The front gables are crowned with spirited stone figures of a girded knight, a lion (with a well-sculpted mane), and two griffins holding Tropnell's arms, while armoured knights surmount the hall gables. The whole façade is a harmoniously balanced composition without being pedantically symmetrical. The fireplace stack is acceptable but the prominent chimney shaft jars, though it may have been heightened by a later generation. A Tudor lodging range and gateway on the west side, enclosing the forecourt, probably replaced an earlier range, but the west end of the little church with porch, window, bell-cot, and crocketed spire was a deliberate Tropnell addition to balance the ensemble.[11]

2. Form reflected function in a frontage that made a social statement. This would only have been apparent once the forecourt was entered from the outer yard, for the destruction of the front perimeter wall has given the house an 'openness' that it would not have had or wanted originally. The prominent porch invites hospitality. The hall fireplace stack suggests warmth, while the bay at the superior end indicates privacy.[12] The higher wings with their handsome oriels identify greater social importance, but with subtle distinctions highlighting the élite status of that at the upper end for Tropnell's use rather than for his guests. Similarly, the single lights below that oriel point to security storage areas, whereas the much larger window in place of the narrow lights for the buttery and pantry signify the importance of an area hitherto reserved for services. There is even a subtle extension of this frontal differentiation in the tiny stair projections to the rooms in the hall roof.

3. Though the basic plan of the house was common across southern England, Great Chalfield has several innovative planning features. There is no evidence that the hall had a dais, while both upper end projections were vaulted, pointing to a more formal and less frequent use of this apartment than hitherto.

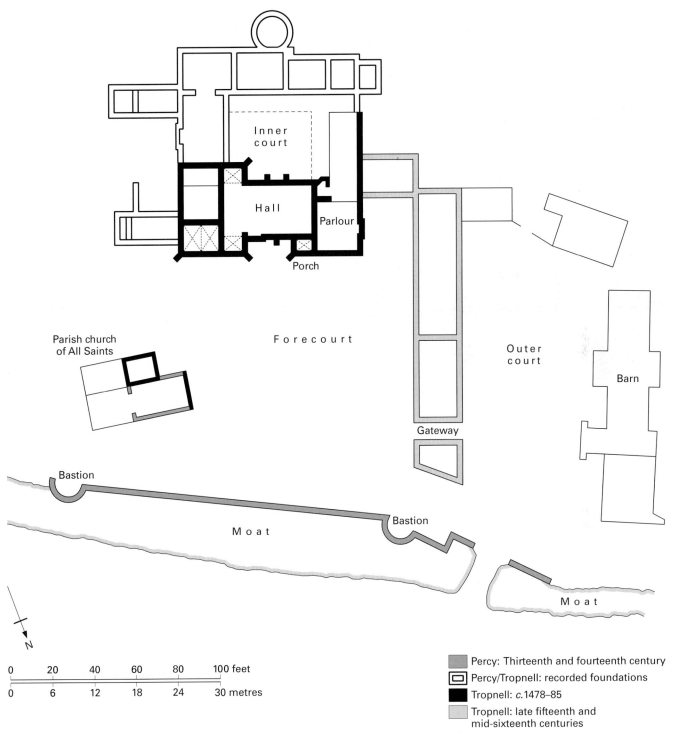

FIGURE 141 Great Chalfield Manor: site plan

Furthermore, the space between the hall ceiling and the high-pitched roof covering it seems to have been for staff occupation. This accommodation was certainly not as obvious or as important as the contemporary withdrawing chamber above the hall at Gothelney Manor or Blackmoor Manor, but the space was not left idle. There were windows in the gable ends and stairs from the closets over the porch and hall north bay, marked externally by corbelled and plain projections suggesting the roof area was divided for staff serving the owner and his guests at the upper and lower end of the hall respectively.

The ground floor of the upper cross wing was divided into two (now three including the rebuilt staircase), with the north room

571

PLATE 243 Great Chalfield Manor: hall interior by J. C. Buckler (1823)

octopartite-vaulted in two bays of single-chamfered ribs, and keystones recovered in 1905 from the garden. The window pattern suggests the area was partitioned into an ante-room and a larger inner room, possibly used as an exchequer and for document storage by a lawyer.[13] Security was important at Great Chalfield, with barred doors at all points of access.

Instead of the usual offices at the lower end of the hall, a cross-passage doorway opens into an important residential room with a fireplace, a sizeable front window (remade), and a shuttered squint to the porch. This was probably a parlour (now dining room with overmantel panelling and plaster ceiling of *c*.1560), with its early high status emphasised by the wall painting. The room above, usually a substantial apartment, was more so at Great Chalfield, with barred lobby and generously curved stair to a chamber with fireplace, original arch-braced collar roof, and oriel comparable to that lighting the withdrawing chamber at the high-status end of the hall. These developments were two-fold. They reflected the increasing gradation of ranks within a household and the need for more superior and private rooms. They also relegated the offices to a more subsidiary position than hitherto, no longer part of the hall development but

increasingly detached from it. In this house, the services were in a wing with the kitchen beyond, linked to the hall block by an open-sided corridor.

4. Great Chalfield exhibits some innovative design features. The two-light windows under four-centred heads have plain Y-tracery, totally uncusped and extremely early for a feature not used in stone buildings before *c*.1475.[14] As the hall was becoming a formal apartment, it was ceiled rather than left open to the roof.[15] It was a slightly cambered structure, divided by moulded cross beams into eight panelled areas. The coving above the wall plates was painted with Tropnell's motto *Le jong tyra belement* and his badge of a double ox yoke, with the central beam embellished with replacement bosses carved with the arms of Tropnell and his second wife and associated families (similarly carved in stone on the contemporary church screen). Bosses, beams, and coving were originally painted and gilded, most clearly visible today on the coving. But Buckler's interior view shows that each panel was subdivided by plaster ribs into nine sub-panels with sixteen varied bosses at the junctions. Details of these were illustrated by Walker after they had been taken to the bishop's palace at Wells, though one has since been returned to the house.

5. Tropnell's workmanship was richly detailed, extending to such minor elements as shaping the steps of the buttresses and the multi-ribbed jambs, head, and foliated spandrels of the hall fireplace. Both faces of the porch entry have roll, fillet, and hollow chamfers as well as shafts and capitals, with the outer face surmounted by a hood moulding with diamond-shaped stops matching those of the windows. The porch is enhanced with a high-quality tierceron vault with foliated bosses and two winged angels, one still carrying the arms of Tropnell.[16] The broad arches opening into the low bays at the upper end of the hall repeat the shafts and hollow chamfer of the outer entry, and have tierceron vaulting similar to the porch but with a single central boss with Tropnell's arms. The high standards are more obvious in the enriched oriels. That at the lower end is three-sided, rising from a scalloped base, whereas that at the upper end is slightly larger, half-round, with its base emphasised by a fleuron frieze above the scalloped base springing from two corbels of faces.[17] The transomed lights of both oriels rise above blind panels with cinquefoil cusping (the only example outside the hall screen), but whereas the lower head is embattled with Tropnell's arms and supporters above, that at the upper end is surmounted by a finely executed fleur de lis crown externally and a pendant fan vault internally. Only the three-part buttressed screen disappoints. The upper tier of blind cusped panels is embellished with a Perpendicular traceried head under a continuous moulded beam, but a spirited head rail would have been more in harmony with the work of the stone masons.[18]

6. The Manor retains several early furnishings. The entry door with its low wicket is original, as are the fragments of glass in the lower oriel of birds holding the message 'love God, drede shame, desire worship and kepe thy name'. More rare were the stone benches lining the side walls of the hall, shown in Buckler's view of 1823 but since removed, leaving only the scar of the shaped bench end next to the fireplace.[19] Whereas a few halls have genuine high-level squints (as at Little Sodbury Manor), this house has three. The two at the upper end, one with a mitred head and one with ass ears and a lost crown, may refer to the bishop of Salisbury and the cuckolded husband, and the one at the lower end with smiling face and curled hair to a contemporary observer.[20] Of outstanding interest is the wall painting in the parlour of the head and upper body of a corpulent man seated against a red and white striped background like a cloth of state. He wears an ermine-trimmed gown and carries what looks like a large money bag. It is usually claimed to be Thomas Tropnell, and though the painting is undoubtedly early, the figure seems to be crowned, or covered with a warm beaver hat.

CONSTRUCTION, SCALE, AND CONTEMPORARY DEVELOPMENT

Great Chalfield Manor was built between 1452 when Tropnell was first recorded as tenant of the property and his death in January 1488. Its development was long planned, for Tropnell purchased the quarry for building stone in June 1465,[21] but he was not in secure possession of the property until two years later. In the absence of any other documentary evidence, the lack of cusping to the window lights becomes particularly significant. This absence of cusps is not found before the late 1470s in churches such as St Helen, Bishopsgate, London (1475) and Tattershall (c.1475–82), in

residences such as Hatfield Palace (1479–86) and Kirby Muxloe Castle (1480–4), and in the school at Wainfleet All Saints (c.1484).[22] Its occurrence in Wiltshire can hardly be earlier, so that construction from about 1478 before Tropnell's second wife died to 1485 is most likely. The profusion of masons' marks at the upper end suggests there was anxiety to complete the work quickly. Even so, Tropnell was usually described as 'of Neston' rather than of Chalfield, and he was buried in the chapel he added to Corsham church 2 miles distant from Neston rather than in the one he added to the church within Chalfield's curtilage.

Some support for the likely date of the house is afforded by considering it in the context of contemporary gentry houses in the region – South Wraxall, Tickenham Court, and the lost but recorded manor house at Kingston Seymour. All four residences share the common plan of medium-sized halls with porch and upper bay projection, and cross wings creating multi-gabled front elevations. No two of the houses are identical. The hall windows at Kingston Seymour were full length but those at the other properties filled only the upper side walls. All windows were of cinquefoil lights below a quatrefoil head except at Great Chalfield. Tall two-centred arches prefaced the hall bays at Tickenham Court and Kingston Seymour, opening into a lobby and ground-floor withdrawing chamber, whereas the lower arches at Chalfield and South Wraxall were to less important rooms as they enjoyed a second bay opposite with direct stair approach to the principal withdrawing chamber. Three of the halls lack contemporary fireplaces or louvre evidence, while the mural fireplace at Great Chalfield was an afterthought.[23] The same three halls were spanned by principal and intermediate arch-braced collar trusses, with Tropnell's hall with its low-pitched ceiling as the exception. The position of the kitchen varied – directly approached from the cross passage at Kingston Seymour and Tickenham Court, in an extension in the Wiltshire houses with the offices replaced by a parlour. The chamber above was of superior quality in all four properties. Kingston Seymour, Tickenham Court, and Great Chalfield can be securely attributed to Edward IV's reign while South Wraxall may be reasonably ascribed to that period. Tickenham Court was a remodelling of an earlier house dendro dated to c.1471–6 while the others were new builds, with the architectural character of Chalfield indicating it was the last. Apart from their similarity of construction and minor differences of planning and design, what binds all four houses is their commonality of scale, layout, detailing, and social status.

Having said that, while Chalfield seems complete in itself, particularly since its restoration and subsequent occupation, Tropnell's residence was originally larger. South of the house lay a second court, of which only the foundations survive, destroyed well before any illustrated record. The offices wing was linked to one end of the south range, with the east range joining the upper cross wing of the present house. The recovery of these foundations in 1905 was not through formal archaeology, but the south range is clearly of two or more phases, while the east range is similar in scale to Tropnell's work, with a ground-floor mural fireplace and an upper-level door to the hall bay.[24] These foundations have been incorporated in the garden design of 1907–11 with the inner court as a paved area. (pl. 194). But there are also enigmatic east-facing projections from the upper end of the house, not necessarily by Tropnell, so that until site excavation is carried out the scale of Tropnell's residence and the possible incorporation of Percy structures remain unclear.[25]

Tropnell was a persistent, meticulous, and probably pedantic gentleman of considerable local standing. Just as the badges and arms at Tattershall Castle and Wingfield Manor made a statement of Ralph, Lord Cromwell's achievements as treasurer of England, the proud display of those at Great Chalfield Manor was an equally public testimony to Tropnell's success. A self-made member of the local squirearchy, he built up an estate of several Wiltshire properties to fund his legal and building activities, used his contacts gained through knowing the Hungerford family, and fought tenaciously for his right to a property which he so beautifully enhanced when in his seventies and near the closing years of his life.

SUBSEQUENT DEVELOPMENT

The short extension from the west face of the house was a secondary development with plain-chamfer doorways, and windows lacking Tropnell's distinctive hood moulds.

The extended west range and oblique entry gateway filling the west side of the forecourt were not linked to the body of the house before 1910. The line of four ground-floor doorways (some infilled) and regular single lights indicates a lodging range with windows lighting the stairs to the upper floor. South Wraxall Manor retains a similar but earlier forecourt lodging range, for this at Chalfield is of early to mid-sixteenth-century date. Prichard's elevation of 1836 shows it before the alterations which have totally modified the interior. No building line separates the end gateway block from the body of the range with its porter's lodge and independently approached room above, but its upper half was rebuilt in the later seventeenth century and surmounted by a pretty cupola.

In October 1823, John Buckler wrote to John Gage of Hengrave Hall, 'Great Chalfield I am bold to declare is one of the noblest remains of domestic architecture in England.' For us, the pleasure of the Manor lies not only in its charm and completeness but as a modest-sized house on the cutting-edge of developments during the next half-century.

NOTES

1 For the Percy succession, VCH, VII (1953) 60.
2 According to the Tropnell Cartulary, ed. J. Silvester Davies (1908) I, 276.
3 The forecourt was lowered in 1910 to improve the drainage of the house area.
4 The church is mentioned in 1349.
5 J. T. Driver, *Wilts. Arch. and N. H. Mag.* 93 (2000) 82–5.
6 VCH, VII (1953) 61.
7 The present house at Neston Park is a replacement of 1790, extended in 1840. By the time of his death, Tropnell had built up a substantial portfolio of properties in south-west Wiltshire, detailed in Davies (1908) xiv–xv.
8 Driver, *Wilts. Arch. and N. H. Mag.* 93 (2000) 85–9.
9 J. H. P. Pafford, *Account of Parliamentary Garrisons of Great Chalfield and Malmesbury* (1940).
10 J. Marshall, *Country Life* (June 1998).
11 Tropnell also added the south chapel with its fine stone screen and the wall paintings of the martyrdom of St Catherine.
12 Not until later would a visitor appreciate that the more important bay to the withdrawing chamber stair has two twin-light windows as against the one twin and one single light to the forecourt-facing bay.
13 Brakspear replaced the single east light with a twin-light window. It was Mr Fuller's opinion, 'surmised from traces of foundations', that the vaulting formerly extended further south, supported on central pillars. Tipping (1921) 331.

14 Cuspless windows were first used in brick buildings during the 1440s, e.g. Eton College, and Queens' College, Cambridge, and in a stone building at Tattershall church, c.1475.
15 Walker illustrates the structure above the ceiling with its three rows of purlins and central line of curved wind braces.
16 Gules, a fesse engrailed argent powdered ermine between three griffin heads of the same erased.
17 The pillar is shown by Buckler but surely such a crude support was never the original intention of the master-mason.
18 Brakspear copied the detailed drawings by Walker and Wollaston though he added the unhistorical open gallery.
19 Buckler failed to show that the hall fireplace had decorated spandrels though they were illustrated by Prichard. Not surprisingly, the stone paving in the hall was replaced by a sprung wooden floor nearly a century later.
20 Illustrated in T. H. Turner and J. H. Parker, *Some Account of Domestic Architecture in England*, III pt 1 (1859) 60 and opp.
21 Davies (1908) I, 350.
22 J. H. Harvey, *The Perpendicular Style* (1978) 200–2. Kirby Muxloe Castle and Tattershall church were the work of John Cowper, who may well have been responsible for bishop Waynflete's school in his home town. Cowper served his apprenticeship at Eton College during the 1440s. See note 14.
23 The insertion of the chimney stack upset the placement of the two adjacent hall windows, so that they are out of line with the correctly positioned windows opposite and their hoods are partly absorbed by the stack and porch respectively.
24 See Tipping (1921) 314.
25 The projection next to the upper block with its narrow end partition is the only structure in the house indicative of garderobe provision.

T. L. Walker, *History and Antiquities of the Manor House and Church at Great Chalfield, Wiltshire* (1837), suppl. to Pugin's *Examples of Gothic Architecture*, II (1837)
J. S. Davies, *Trans. Bristol and Glos. Arch. Soc.* 33 (1900) 193–261
J. S. Davies, *The Tropnell Cartulary*, 2 vols. (1908)
H. A. Tipping, *English Homes*, Pd 1, I (1921) 313–32
VCH, *Wiltshire*, VII (1953) 60–8
R. Floyd, *Great Chalfield Manor: Guide Book* (1980)

GURNEY MANOR, Somerset

Though a quarter of a mile from the small Somerset town of Cannington, Gurney Manor still faces open countryside on all sides, with the tower of Cannington church to the west and the bubbling waters of Cannington Brook close to its south façade. The house immediately reveals its periodic development like a series of building blocks around a small courtyard, but the exterior is given striking uniformity by flaxen colour-washed walls emphasising the darker dressed stonework of windows and doorways. This gives it a cohesion, emphasised by the standard tiled roofs of c.1890, at odds with its unitary development, though this was basically completed within the relatively short span of sixty years from about 1400 to 1460.

In plan, the hall range with its storeyed porch is flanked by projecting cross ranges, extended to the rear to form a small court closed by the kitchen and services block. For the medievalist, the house is an exercise in rapid expansion through business success, little affected by minor Tudor modifications. It was never a large manor house but retains most of the early structure, including carved gable heads, together with the extremely rare survival of a pentice between hall and kitchen. It declined to farm status in the mid-seventeenth century until divided into nine flats in the 1940s. It was restored as a single dwelling in the late 1980s so that its lime-plastered walls again stand brilliantly in the sunlight.

The house was initiated by a Gurney, but it was developed by two generations of Dodeshams, who acquired the property through marriage in about 1420 and held it until 1482 when it was bequeathed to the Michells, local gentry, who held it until the early seventeenth century.

EAST WING

The house developed in a sequence of phases, beginning with the east wing. This was originally a barn of some size, with traces of the cart entrance in the east wall and ventilation slits nearby and in both gable ends. It was a late conversion into a two-storey house with stone windows, though most of the openings are now metal framed in concrete settings of the 1940s. This barn, out of proportion to the rest of the manor, seems to be the earliest standing structure, possibly later fourteenth century, attached to a timber-framed building.

HALL RANGE

In about 1400, the early house was replaced with a three-bay hall range in stone – a two-bay hall open to the roof with a service room and chamber over at the lower end abutting the barn. This is still the core of the much-altered hall range today. The porch was initially single-storeyed, with slightly later four-centred outer and inner arches with diamond-shaped stops, the outer entry with shields. The upper chamber was added in the mid-seventeenth century.

The hall, 25 feet by 17½ feet, was not ceiled until the second half of the seventeenth century, when the upper bedrooms and corridor were created. The end-wall fireplace, like the four chamfered cross beams, is a relatively crude insertion of that time that clearly replaced an earlier hearth. The screens cross beam may be mid-fifteenth century but the Tudor-style windows at both levels are 1890 replacements.

The two-storey unit below the cross passage was remodelled in the 1530s as a parlour with fireplace, again with windows here and in the bedroom above of the 1890s.[1] The primary visible evidence for the early date of this range is the post and panel partition wall separating the hall from this end unit.

SOUTH RANGE

The early doorway at the upper end of the hall with hollow- and roll-moulded chamfer and four-centred arch opens into the lobby of the buttressed solar range. This was initiated in about 1420, shortly after the marriage of Jane Gurney to Roger Dodesham in about 1420, and was extended by their son about thirty years later. The range reflects this two-stage development at both levels. The larger ground-floor chambers, now a kitchen, have been totally altered, with low crude beams and a modern window. The smaller room a generation later with its taller panelled ceiling retains its two-light transomed window, the upper lights with cinquefoil heads, and original fireplace with hollow- and roll-moulded jambs. The west-facing five-light window with external dripstone was a 1530s replacement.

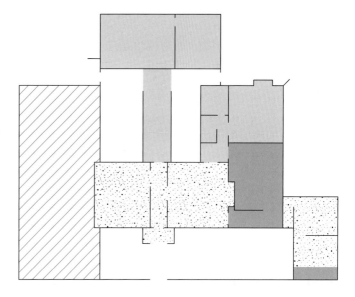

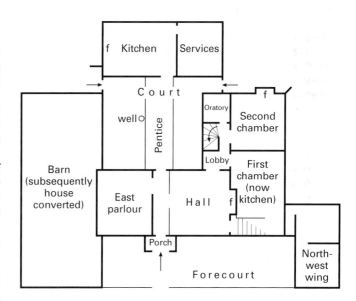

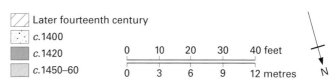

FIGURE 142 Gurney Manor: site plan and development phases

From the lobby, a stone newel rises to the upper floor but at its side is the minute oratory, only 8 feet square but a fifteenth-century gem. Despite all the alterations to the house, it retains the three-light east window with cinquefoil heads and altar recess, a further single light, and three unglazed slits to the adjacent chamber, stair, and courtyard passage. This oratory was so small that it could only hold the priest plus two or three participants: all other attendants had to worship outside. The fine piscina is embellished with a cinquefoil and crocketed gable between pinnacles and two blank

PLATE 244 Gurney Manor: from the south

shields. The four-square panelled ceiling is damaged but retains the IHS boss and part of a continuous fleuron frieze.

The newel ascends to the upper lobby. The front bedchamber is ceiled, and reduced by seventeenth-century panelling for a front corridor. The rear chamber, step-approached because of the higher ceiling below, is again the better-preserved room. It retains its fireplace and early window position (though with two- and four-light replacements of 1530) but is also open to the arch-braced collar trusses with two lines of wind braces.[2]

KITCHEN BLOCK

The mid-fifteenth-century kitchen block closes the fourth side of the almost square court. Again of two storeys, the ground floor is divided into the kitchen and services, both entered from simple doorways with four-centred heads and plain windows. The kitchen has an 11 feet wide hearth filling the end wall, and a hatch near the entry door. The smaller but well-lit second room with a three-light wooden-framed window was presumably for services.

The five-bay upper chamber, always part of the family accommodation, is approached from a short passage opening from the solar range. In comparison with the plain fenestration below, this well-furnished chamber has two twin-light transomed windows with cinquefoil upper lights under a square head. There is an end-wall fireplace, repeating the roll and hollow-chamfer moulding and square head, but with an embattled chimney cap. At the opposite end is a garderobe recess with chute. The whole is crowned with an open roof of arch-braced collar trusses. This room may have always been partitioned, though the present one is late sixteenth century when the fourth and sixth trusses were replaced.

COURT

The cobbled court, 31½ feet by 28 feet, could be entered from both sides of the kitchen block, making it a busy circulation area. It is also spanned centrally by a roofed pentice linking the hall cross passage with the kitchen entry and hatch. This exceedingly rare survival, particularly in a domestic context, is of three bays, with the horizontal roof-carrying beams locked into the hall and kitchen faces. The supports stand on low walls, except for the last bay which is open to give easy access to the two external entries. The pantile roof is of the 1890s but otherwise there is no reason why this single-

storey structure should not be contemporary with the kitchen block.

NORTH-WEST WING

This wing seems to be of two builds, of unclear origin though early enough to have been an isolated structure, possibly single-storeyed. The ground floor, lit by a single square opening, is used for storage and was possibly always so purposed. The single room above is essentially of late sixteenth-century character, including the arched approach from the side of the hall fireplace, windows, fireplace, and roof trusses.

THE FAMILIES

The Gurney family are recorded at Cannington during the thirteenth century, and by the early fourteenth century held the manor of this name created out of Cannington manor. Though at least ten building phases have been identified, all the key developments occurred during the fifteenth century. The first house, probably timber-framed, was replaced by the three-bay hall range in about 1400 by Hugh, the last of the Gurneys. In about 1420, Jane Gurney married Roger Dodesham (d.1450) from a rising local family, who probably initiated the solar cross wing. It adjoined the previously detached north-west wing, which was given an upper floor, externally approached on the west side, and rebuilt north end.[3]

Roger's son William (d.1482) became a prosperous lawyer who expanded the property to its present scale. He retained the open hall, updated with new doorways and possibly added the screen. He extended the solar range on both floors with its lobbies, stone newel, and oratory, and erected the kitchen block with its courtyard pentice to the hall.

William Dodesham bequeathed the manor to his niece Agnes Michell (d.1503), who was succeeded by her grandson Thomas (d.1539). It was he who was responsible for replacing some of the windows and fireplaces, and converting the former services next to the open hall into a parlour. These modest changes enhanced the comfort of the house, which otherwise continued unchanged. Towards the close of the century, Sir Bartholomew Michell (d.1616) inserted a floor (now gallery) into the second solar chamber, but the hall was not floored until the later seventeenth century for tenant occupation. Tenants occupied the house from 1616 until 1984, when it was returned over an eight-year period from multiple occupation to its original undivided state by the Landmark Trust.

This modest gentry house is an exceptionally clear demonstration of how a prime residence was developed during the fifteenth century in tune with the financial and business prosperity of its owners. The workmanship is competent but not of the highest quality, but the house is an excellent mirror of provincial standards. Beyond the hall, it was made up of a number of discrete units – a two-room lodging at the lower end of the hall, at least one chamber in the solar wing with two good-quality rooms above, and further units over the kitchen and services and in the north-west wing. The tiny oratory is a delightful survival, but rarest of all is the courtyard pentice.

NOTES
1 The internal stair to the upper chamber has long since been removed.
2 The newel was extended with oak treads and the balcony added in the end bay (formerly an inserted floor) during the 1580s. The stone head of

a king of *c*.1300 possibly came from Cannington Priory. It was found buried in the hearth in 1990.

3 The footings of the wall enclosing a tiny forecourt between the two wings are attributed to this period, but it may date from the house's farming days.

VCH, *Somerset*, VI (1992) 82–3
N. Cooper, *Houses of the Gentry: 1480–1680* (1999) 70–4

HEMYOCK CASTLE, Devon

If it were not for the licence granted to William and Margaret Asthorpe in November 1380 to crenellate their manor house at Hemyock,[1] few would suspect the date of the towers and enclosing walls of this fortified house. It is situated on the southern side of the Blackdown Hills and more particularly on a flat site in the middle of Hemyock village immediately west of the church. Archives and site artefacts show that this residence has thirteenth-century origins, though the only visible evidence is the spring-fed moat round the site.

Asthorpe's modest castle follows the conventional late fourteenth-century quadrangular plan of a twin-towered gateway in the middle of the east face with cylindrical corner and intermediate towers. The coarse rubble walling of local chert stone is characterless, but traces of rendering and limewash on the north-west tower indicate that all the walls and towers were originally so covered. The circular gateway towers, one almost to full height, span a vaulted passage with portcullis protection. The shells of two north towers stand 15 and 10 feet high, and where there are no footings the foundations of the other towers and curtain walling have been

PLATE 245 Hemyock Castle: remains of gateway

identified by limited excavation.[2] The short lengths of curtain traced from the two corner towers on the west side are not in line, and though an intermediate tower was identified, the two alignments may have been resolved by a second entrance at this point. The still-occupied house of knapped flint and rubble stone built overly close to the castle entrance has a fifteenth-century core,[3] but there are no remains of any contemporary courtyard buildings.

The Hemyock fortifications look more like an eighteenth-century sham than meaningful fourteenth-century defences, and this is close to reality. The 4½ foot thick walls and towers lack dressed stonework and there is a notable absence of windows. The gatehouse towers have no ground-floor access and could only be reached from above, while the portcullis chamber is functionally inadequate. The other towers have poor ground-floor entries and no habitable upper rooms. Sir William Asthorpe (d.1399) was a bastard who became *nouveau riche* through marrying into the locally wealthy Dynham family in 1362.[4] His 'castle' was all show and no substance. He became a member of parliament and sheriff of Devon (1375, 1384) but was always an outsider involved in several local frictions. One of these was an affray in 1384 when men supporting the abbot of Dunkeswell recovered cattle seized by Asthorpe, so that his fortified house served the dual purpose of giving him local security as well as demonstrating social advancement – an achievement at the cost of minimum expenditure. Even by Leland's day, the property had already been reduced to two or three towers.[5]

NOTES
1 *Cal. Pat. Rolls: 1377–81*, 552.
2 Plan in Blaylock (1992) 214.
3 Blaylock (1992) 212. The roof retains two arch-braced trusses and evidence of wind braces. The late medieval granite entrance doorway was brought from Cornwall in the mid-nineteenth century. Thirteenth-century pottery shards, green glazed ridge and louvre tiles and late medieval floor tiles were recovered from the site during the late twentieth century.
4 Margaret Dynham's grandfather was Sir Guy Brian of Woodsford 'Castle', Dorset.
5 *Itinerary*, IV, 74.

R. Sherwin, *Exeter Diocesan Archaeological and Architectural Society* 15 (1929) 46–53
S. R. Blaylock, *Med. Arch.* 36 (1992) 212–15
M. Sheppard, *Hemyock Castle* (1993)

HOLDITCH COURT, Dorset and WEYCROFT HALL, Devon

The Brooke family held two properties close to the Devon/Dorset border, both subject to crenellation licences and both now only a shadow of their former scale. Holditch Court, a mile south-west of Thorncombe, was the stronger. It was probably of rectangular character, though only a single rubble-built tower stands to full height, flanked by two short stretches of enclosing wall. Nearly square, with a projecting circular stair turret, the tower is marked by a high string course continuing along the flanking wall, with a second course marking the set-back of the top storey. The tower has two lights, with evidence of a larger window in the valley-facing curtain wall. The Court was well positioned above the Axe valley, with walls

4 feet thick, one standing nearly 30 feet high. It was a substantial residence, but as the greater part of the tower is ivy smothered and the remainder of the site is covered with farm buildings and slurry yards, the remains are not very eloquent.[1] The string courses in particular point towards the later fourteenth century, possibly to 1397 when Thomas Brooke was granted a licence to crenellate his house at Thorncombe.[2] The nearby farmhouse incorporates part of a sixteenth-century gatehouse.

Sir Thomas Brooke (d.1418) was MP for Somerset or Dorset on thirteen occasions between 1386 and 1413. Because of his administrative capabilities, he was one of the knights retained by Henry IV in 1405 to serve as a counter-balance to the dominating influence in the region of the earl of Devon.[3] His son and heir, also Sir Thomas Brooke (d.1439), was MP for Dorset in 1413 and served four times for Somerset between 1417 and 1427. Both father and son had Lollard associations, the son marrying Joan, the only daughter and heiress of Lady Cobham, the wife of the Lollard leader Sir John Oldcastle (Lord Cobham after his marriage in 1408), and he spent some time in the Tower of London for participating in his father-in-law's rebellion in 1414.[4] Possibly because of Sir Thomas' continuing Lollard sympathies after Oldcastle's execution in 1417,[5] his house at Weycroft, 2½ miles south-west, was attacked ten years later by his neighbour, William Bonville of Shute.[6] He broke into the property, assaulted the servants, and left a trail of damage. The consequence was that within three months Sir Thomas had applied for a licence to crenellate Weycroft, with the explicit support of Humphrey, duke of Gloucester, two earls, and five knights. Brooke could swiftly call on high-powered support when threatened and he received his licence in May 1427.[7]

Weycroft Hall, a mile north-east of Axminster, does not show any defensive features today.[8] The present stone-rubble house retains a tower porch (restored) from this period and a hall open to the roof with two-light transomed windows in both outer walls, the lower lights with cusped heads, the upper now with straight heads. The tie-beam roof (and end fireplace) are later. The east wing has been lost and the three-storey west wing with corner buttresses is now the same roof height as the hall. This is partly through its remodelling in the late sixteenth/early seventeenth century, as with the windows and chimney stack, but the lower wing retains an earlier window with reticulated tracery. Heavily restored in the late nineteenth century, its early fifteenth-century character is rather anonymous.

On his father's death, Sir Thomas' son Edward (d.1464) took the title Lord Cobham. Thirty years after Bonville's attack on Weycroft, the incident was subject to a striking replay, this time led by James Butler, earl of Wiltshire and Ormond. This staunch Lancastrian did 'gret wrongs, grev'nces and trespasses' to his Yorkist antagonist Lord Cobham. During the latter's stay at Holditch, the Court was attacked by '200 or mo men with force and arms arayd in manner of warre'. The siege lasted five hours and was beaten off only after the stables and outbuildings had been looted.[9] This incident, like the Bonville and Courtenay attacks on West Coker Manor and Powderham Castle at about the same time, highlights the widespread breakdown in law and order that marked the closing years of Henry VI's reign. Though differing in intensity between the regions, high politics was no respecter of property during these turbulent years, any more than during other partisan-

ship wars. Not surprisingly, the lords of Cobham moved from Dorset to their long-held house of that name in Kent, which the Brooke family subsequently rebuilt in the late sixteenth century.

NOTES
1 RCHM, *Dorset*, I (1952) 247 noted traces of a rectangular stone building 16 yards south-east of the tower and evidence of a bank and scarp.
2 *Cal. Pat. Rolls: 1396–99*, 85.
3 C. Given-Wilson, *The Royal Household and the King's Affinity* (1986) 233.
4 K. B. McFarlane, *Lancastrian Kings and Lollard Knights* (1972) 216.
5 J. A. F. Thomson, *The Later Lollards 1414–1520* (1965). Brooke was knighted between 1416 and 1421 and sometimes styled himself Lord of Cobham.
6 R. Higham in *Security and Defence in South-West England before 1800*, ed. Higham (1987) 41.
7 *Cal. Pat. Rolls: 1422–27*, 400. The earlier house was supported by a deer park of 800 acres granted under licence during the fourteenth century, and had a chapel from 1417 under licence from bishop Stafford.
8 Nor are any apparent in the watercolour of 1795 by John Swete in *Travels in Georgian Devon*, ed. T. Gray and M. Rowe, II (1998) 114.
9 Brit. Lib., Harl. Charters, 46 h.26 quoted by Sir Matthew Nathan, *The Annals of West Coker* (1957) 163.

KINGSTON SEYMOUR MANOR HOUSE, Somerset

Kingston Seymour lies on the coastal lowland edging the Bristol Channel south of Clevedon but the manor house was destroyed by fire in about 1850. Even so, it is pertinent to the development of Tickenham Court 5 miles north-east and to the Wiltshire manor houses at South Wraxall and Great Chalfield.

We are essentially dependent for an illustrated account of the house on *The Gentleman's Magazine* for 1835[1] and Garner and Stratton's description of 1911.[2] The drawing of the south front of the house by J. C. Buckler shows a stone-built fifteenth-century residence of a central hall recessed between storeyed projections abutting the cross wings. The porch opened into the broad cross passage of a modest hall, 26½ feet by 18 feet, open to the roof, independent of the cross wings, and gabled at both ends. The apartment was lit by a single transomed window in each side wall, but with a prominent bay window at the upper end with a tall, two-centred arch as at Tickenham Court. This was the sole access to the heated parlour, a single room filling the upper wing with a projecting stair at the far end to the withdrawing chamber above. The plan accompanying Garner and Stratton's text shows a single entry at the lower end of the hall direct into a 15 feet wide room, the kitchen, with access to a heated chamber beyond. A stair from the porch led to the important chamber over the services.

Windows were of two, three, or four cinquefoil lights, usually under square hoods with end stops though both upper-end chambers had traceried heads above the lights and two-centred hoods with stops like those to the hall windows at South Wraxall. Buckler's drawing of the hall roof[3] shows a five-bay structure of fairly plain arch-braced collars with substantial intermediate trusses and a single line of wind braces. It is uncannily similar to that at Tickenham Court. The apartment lacked a mural fireplace and there is no pictorial evidence for a louvre. The hall projections, both with closets over, were similar to the frontal ones at South Wraxall and Great Chalfield and repeat the prominent gables of the

PLATE 246 Kingston Seymour Manor House: south front by J. C. Buckler (*c*.1830)

latter. The withdrawing chamber squint overlooking the hall is a canopied opening,[4] rather than the masks that characterise the apertures at Great Chalfield.

Buckler's exterior view depicts a handsome residence of single build with a south-facing show front. As the south-west gable carried Edward IV's favourite *rose en soleil* badge, immediately adopted after his success at the battle of Mortimer's Cross (1461), the attribution of this house to his reign from 1461 to 1483 is reasonable. South Wraxall may have been built during the same period, as was Great Chalfield (*c*.1478–85), and like them Kingston Seymour was an entirely new residence; Tickenham Court was a remodelling by John Berkeley of an earlier house in *c*.1471–6. Kingston Seymour followed the general disposition of South Wraxall and Great Chalfield, though to a less generous plan, but was stylistically closer to the former than the more exuberant Tropnell house. But in its scale, plan, lack of hall fireplace or central hearth, almost identical hall bay and roof structure, kitchen position, beamed retiring chamber, and projecting newel to the withdrawing chamber above, Kingston Seymour has the closest syllogism with the remodelled Tickenham Court of 1471–5.[5]

By the early fourteenth century, the manor of Kingston Seymour was divided between the Wyke, Bourdon, and Kenn families. Throughout the fifteenth century, the Norton family of Bristol, the

Berkeley family of Stoke Giffard, and the locally important Kenn family each held a third of the manor. The Norton family were prominent Bristol merchants and it is possible that they were responsible for the erection of the manor house at Kingston Seymour. The aim of many aspiring Bristol merchants was to acquire a country seat, either by purchase or by marriage. The Kenn family were settled nearby at Kenn Court and were unlikely to need a second home so close. The estates of the Stoke Giffard branch of the Berkeley family were in Gloucestershire. They would have had little use for a house at Kingston Seymour when they held no other lands in Somerset.[6]

Even so, there are architectural parallels between this manor house and the contemporary development of Tickenham Court under the Berkeleys. As the side windows in the hall are not opposite at Kingston Seymour as they are at Tickenham, the former may be the slightly earlier building though the latter is known to have earlier origins. On the other hand, the slightly depressed curvature of the principal arch braces at Tickenham and their abrupt angular termination have been 'corrected' at Kingston Seymour. As Buckler's drawing of this hall roof also shows the intermediate trusses with collars and arch braces lacking at Tickenham, it is probable that Kingston Seymour was built subsequently during the later 1470s/early 1480s.

NOTES

1 October 1835, 370.

2 *The Domestic Architecture of England During the Tudor Period*, I (1911) 23–4.

3 Reproduced by J. T. Smith, *Arch. Jour.* 115 (1958) pl. XVII opp. 127.

4 *Ibid.*

5 The present house on the site, called 'The Old Manor', is a Victorian rectory to the front with a rear structure that may include part of the late medieval house. They are linked internally, but from above the roofs appear to be of different periods. The rear west wall of its 'parlour' incorporates a fireplace which may be the opening of that in the great parlour of the destroyed Kingston Seymour Manor House, though it lacks all decoration. There is no projecting chimney breast or newel in the 'parlour' of the Victorian rectory, though it is of the same width but 4½ feet longer. A rebuild on the western part of the medieval house incorporating some of its walling seems likely. I owe this examination of the Victorian property to Nicholas Deas.

6 I owe this paragraph and details of the manor's descent to Nicholas Deas. The Norton family continued to hold one third of the manor until the reign of Henry VIII; Richard Berkeley sold his share to Sir Thomas Trye in 1507–8, while Christopher Kenn (d.1593) was the last of the Kenn family to be involved in the manor's ownership.

KNIGHTSTONE, Devon

The architectural interest of Knightstone lies in its framework as a substantial fifteenth-century hall and storeyed cross-wing house with retained original roofs, remodelled in the late sixteenth and early seventeenth centuries. The aesthetic interest of Knightstone lies in its mid-twentieth-century rehabilitation, set in yew-hedged gardens of that time, in a still unspoilt rural setting. Situated just over a mile south-east of Ottery St Mary alongside a stream that runs through the garden, Knightstone is built of Beer rubble stone. With the exception of a small first-floor lancet, nothing externally suggests a date earlier than the years close to 1600 when the house was upgraded by the Shermans.[1] Gvilielmus (William) Sherman (d.1583), a wealthy Ottery St Mary merchant, had purchased the property in 1554 and was probably responsible for the two dominating rectangular hall windows, while his son John Sherman (d.1617) added the two-storeyed porch (1607 date stone) with its square-framed outer and inner doorways with link-decorated frames. The gable barge boards are early nineteenth century, the work of Dr Drury, headmaster of Harrow School, who bought Knightstone in 1805 and rescued it from a decayed state.

The cross passage, 9 feet wide, similarly exhibits the post-medieval changes with its two service doorways and panelled hall wall with single central entry (doorcase of *c*.1700). Excluding the cross passage, the hall retains its original volume, 29 feet by 21 feet and open to the roof, with three evident building phases. The alterations of 1567 include the two twelve-light rectangular windows in the west wall and the initialled and dated fireplace opposite with its quatrefoil-decorated lintel – old-fashioned for its time. The two contemporary three-light windows flanking the fireplace have been blocked, leaving external evidence only. The original three-bay roof structure is exposed, though most of the end bay was curtailed by the Shermans' cross-passage wall with room over, screened by plaster infill painted to look like timber. Two lightly moulded arch-braced collar trusses are visible, with half-bay collars and two lines of wind braces, all very plain. The third bay can be examined from

PLATE 247 Knightstone: from the west

the south cross wing, for the wall between the end braces is covered with extremely well-preserved wall paintings of *c*.1600 illustrating the Temptation of Adam and the Expulsion from Eden. At the same time, a plaster frieze was inserted with mermen and monsters, and figurative heads covering the feet of the trusses. It was possibly part of an inserted ceiling which has subsequently collapsed, leaving the original hall roof exposed.

The early nineteenth-century Tudor-style wooden door frames at the upper end of the hall open into the parlour and stair hall created in *c*.1820 in the upper cross wing. The Elizabethan window in the parlour end wall sits within the frame of a much larger opening, marked by outer jambs of similar character to the quoins, with the framing of a smaller window above. Was there a bay window or an extension here, curtailed in *c*.1820 (dated glass) when the present window was inserted? The east wall of the stair hall retains a sixteenth-century post and panel partition with evidence of a blocked door. The upper floor, now subdivided into three rooms, retains its arch-braced collar trusses, all but expunged by added ceilings. The principal bedchamber retains the single uncusped light visible externally and an Elizabethan fireplace with four-centred head.

The services in the lower cross wing were substantially altered in the late seventeenth century and twentieth century, but the kitchen in extension of the wing retains its shaped hearth beam. The upper floor retains three arch-braced collar trusses, plaster covered, whereas the cruder collar and wind braces above the kitchen are exposed.

The south extension, two-storeyed with attic, has a more vernacular look than the body of the house. It is set back from it, plaster-covered over stone and cob, with floors at a lower level than those in the south cross wing. The ground floor, less than 7 feet high, retains a wooden two-light trefoil window set in a square frame. The three-bay roof is exposed at attic level, with moulded arch-braced collar trusses and plain end collars.

Knightstone is a substantial late medieval house built by the Bittlesgate family, who held the property from 1371 to 1494, when it passed to the Bonvilles of Shute. The scale of this house is indicative of their standing among the local gentry, even though the angled position of the hall to both cross wings suggests at least a two-phased development. Similar roof forms throughout the

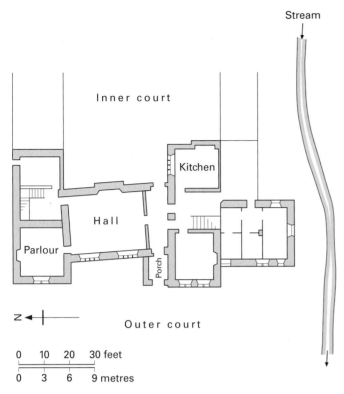

Inner court

Kitchen

Hall

Parlour

Porch

Outer court

Stream

z

| 0 | 10 | 20 | 30 feet |
| 0 | 3 | 6 | 9 metres |

FIGURE 143 Knightstone: ground plan

house, common to the fifteenth century, suggest relatively close phasing matching rising income. The roof is not unlike that of the mid-century at Shute, 9 miles east, and bought from the Bonvilles by William Sherman, but only dendro dating would bring greater precision. Even so, the medieval interest of Knightstone can be overplayed by positioning it higher in the pantheon of medieval houses than the evidence warrants, and by attempting to match the record of a chapel licensed by bishop Brantyngham in 1380 with the vernacular-type wing added below the services, in the least likely position for such a structure.[2] The restoration of this house by Colonel Jenner after 1941 was undoubtedly timely, but the architectural value of Knightstone lies more in its updating by the Shermans and the telling evidence they have left.

NOTES

1 Foundations 70 feet in front of the porch were dug up in 1941. Their form was unrecorded but they were said to be the outbuildings of a fore-court. Hussey (1950).
2 Hussey (1950). Hussey was a friend of Colonel Jenner who had restored the far more rewarding house at Cothay fifteen years earlier.

C. Hussey, *Country Life* (September 1950)

LEIGH BARTON, Devon

The deep narrow lane from Kingsbridge towards Loddiswell with its high hedges and steep incline is a fitting prelude to Leigh Barton, for the road approximates to the medieval level and the approach

imparts an air of mystery and surprise, with the gatehouse rising upon you without warning. This is part of the extensive additions made at the end of the fifteenth century to a typically small manor house of two or three generations earlier. The hall, originally open to the roof, with its two-storeyed parlour and service blocks under a single roof ridge, is all that can be seen upon entering the north court, but behind the house is a services and lodging extension of highly unusual design.

The problems posed by Leigh Barton have not been entirely resolved. They do not include the house, which is of the standard late medieval form in Devon, subject to the alterations of post-medieval habitation, and built of undressed rubble bonded with clays and earths. The cross passage opened into a single-storey hall, with what seems always to have been a two-storeyed parlour block at the upper end and a service and chamber block at the lower. The hall and upper block were entirely rebuilt in *c*.1620–5, but the cross passage and service block are two centuries older, early to mid-fifteenth century, with the internal stone stair and first-floor garde-robe as secondary but still late medieval insertions.[1]

It is the additions that are the mystery of Leigh Barton. South of the service block and projecting beyond its end wall on falling ground is an L-shaped structure consisting of a two-storeyed west range and a longer south range, of which only part survives. The west range is apparently stabling with chambers above; the south range is a kitchen with a chamber above, opening off an open gallery. The continuation of this range with one of greater width formerly helped to create a small court with a gap at its north-east corner for an entrance.

The quality and size of the accommodation is seemingly out of proportion to the house. The 'stabling' was approached from a wide doorway off the cobbled south court, with accommodation for twenty or more mules, a sloping floor and drain, and slit windows for ventilation.[2] Yet apart from one light, the windows were shuttered, which is unexpected if the area was simply stabling, but not if it was used in part or whole for storage or warehousing. The void (see below) could have served a hoist, but the accommodation, lacking the generous fireplace and garderobe provision elsewhere, was certainly not residential.

The adjacent kitchen is remarkably intact and well preserved. It is a large one, dominated by the fireplace totally filling the end wall with two bread ovens to the rear. It retains two wall cupboards and a serving hatch, while excavation revealed the post holes for wall tables or benches, and the floor drain. The well lies immediately north-west of the house but the water inlet and drainage holes in the south wall of the kitchen are original, the latter cleaning out the adjacent garderobe chute. Sockets were also found in the side walls for a box-like structure in front of the chimney breast that rose into the room above, an idiosyncratic feature that was reinstated in 1990 and interpreted as a smoke dispersal bay or food curing box.[3]

The planning of the upper rooms is extraordinary. The external stone steps and covered gallery with open timber arcade, contemporary with the remainder of the range,[4] gave access to two chambers, separated by a timber-framed partition ending in and dividing a paired garderobe within a common turret. The spacious south-west chamber was of a higher standing, with its shuttered windows in two outer walls, fireplace, and arch-braced roof, but the larger chamber with a less elaborate roof has the extremely rare feature of a heat box at the upper end – one bay of the room open to the

PLATE 248 Leigh Barton: from the west

kitchen hearth below and facing the stone flue. It helped to disperse the heat from the inadequately lit kitchen, and at the same time warmed the occupants of this chamber above. The room probably served a communal purpose.

From the external gallery, a galleried lobby along one side of the void, open to the stables below, led to a further chamber, again with two windows, fireplace, and garderobe with original doorway frame, and although this was the smallest of the lodgings it seems to have been of the highest status and furthest from the approach. Yet the south wall common with the lobby apparently extended only halfway up.

The destroyed extension of the south wing continued for at least 25 feet, marked by the stub of its outer wall until meeting the present farm buildings and by the excavated footings of its north wall. It had no upper gallery, for an internal stair against the kitchen wall gave access to the first floor, which was probably a dormitory rather than partitioned accommodation. It may have had a roof of six bays and was of more simple design than the surviving lodgings.[5]

Documentary evidence shows that the house was held by the Legh family as freeholders from at least the early fourteenth to the late sixteenth century, while the structure would accord with their occupational status at the close of the fifteenth century as aspiring members of the local gentry rather than as yeoman farmers.[6] Yet the purpose of the additions is a mystery. They are built of carefully dressed local Devonian slate blocks, far better than the house, with considerable care taken over the detailing. The upper windows are straight-headed with depressed or more generally cinquefoil lights,

and decorative hoods, were glazed, and were unusually large compared with other lodging units in the region. Doorways and fireplaces are generously proportioned if unshowy. Stairs are broad and the garderobes, limited to the upper floor, extended to the ground in neat rectangular projections. The service use of the ground floor is clear, as is the residential purpose of the upper chambers to different standards and numbers of occupants, but who were they? Was the accommodation solely for family use, was the property sub-let when it was developed for travellers or special visitors, or was the separate identity between house and lodgings maintained occupationally as well as structurally?

Part of the answer lies in the discovery during the 1990s of several other late medieval or sixteenth-century service and lodging ranges within a 25 mile radius of Leigh Barton of manorial or lesser status. They have been identified at Keynedon Barton, Sherford; Malston Barton, Sherford; Hatch Arundell, Loddiswell; Combe Barton, Bigbury; and Yarde, Malborough. They are similar in scale, layout (though with variations), position (across a courtyard to the rear of the original house), and social standing. The service and lodging range at Keynedon Barton is the best preserved, with a similar kitchen, upper gallery, and stone gateway.[7]

Yet these comparative houses do not totally resolve the problems of Leigh Barton, which cannot be divorced from the contemporary but partial enclosure of this residence with a non-defensive gatehouse and short lengths of walling on each side lining the lane. The latter never extended beyond their present lengths or enclosed the north court, unless wooden fencing was used. The gatehouse arch-

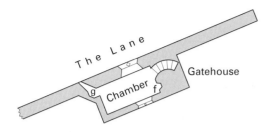

North court

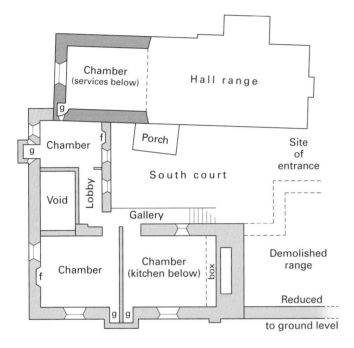

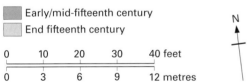

Early/mid-fifteenth century

End fifteenth century

| 0 | 10 | 20 | 30 | 40 feet |
| 0 | 3 | 6 | 9 | 12 metres |

N

FIGURE 144 Leigh Barton: first-floor plan

PLATE 249 Leigh Barton: gateway from the north

ways are very wide, with almost semi-circular heads to the front and rear. A broad stair on one side of the simple passage gave access to a further generous and well-lit upper chamber with fireplace, garderobe recess, and a concealed strong room above, approached by ladder. If this two-storeyed entrance was simply built for show – and this seems so – its size and the quality of the stonework, heavily tooled and beautifully laid front and back, are surprising and highly impressive.

The gatehouse and rear ranges were built at the same time, attributable on architectural grounds and dendrochronology to the period 1495–1514,[8] and most probably to Thomas Legh (d.1512) rather than to his son William Legh (d.1526). They may be interpreted as a reflection of the family's rising standards, aspirations, and household expansion leading to the construction of good-

quality units for family members, visitors, and guests rather than retainers or staff. It may have been the family's intention to replace the hall range in due course, but that was only achieved more than a century later, and hardly to the same striking quality or scale – a pattern repeated in some of the other manorial farmsteads in the area.

Sixteenth-century family records describe Leigh Barton as a 'mansion house'[9] but it is very much a child of its locality. The house is of a plan-form and development standard common in both larger and smaller houses in Devon. The high-quality masonry for the additions can be matched in nearby churches and grander houses: a smaller gateway existed at Bradley Manor, and there were kitchens across the courtyard at Kirkham House, Compton Castle, and Bowhill, lodging ranges at Okehampton Castle and Dartington Hall, and external galleries at Bowhill and Kirkham House. The infiltration of many of these features to smaller manor houses and farmsteads in the locality has been noted above. Yet Leigh Barton still retains a sense of isolation and completeness. Until the 1970s, it had been occupied for at least two centuries as a working farm. A great deal of internal restoration and renewal was necessary between 1978 and 1999 to reinstate this remarkable survival, but it was based on unequivocal evidence to revive a building of quixotic character in an area where it is assumed that remoteness negated high-quality building and generous planning standards. The survival of several lodgings in a better state than those at Dartington Hall and more clearly differentiated in their degrees of importance adds to the interest and rarity of this site.

NOTES

1 The cross-passage doorways retain evidence of their two-centred form, and the north doorway that of its drawbar. Part of the post and panel hall screen of late sixteenth-century workmanship survives with enriched moulding, partly concealed within the wall. It displays an elaboration by the Legh family commensurate with the lodging additions rather than the earlier small hall. The porch, initially two-storeyed, was added in c.1600. The hall roof was replaced when the upper end of the house was rebuilt in c.1620–5 and the upper floor extended throughout the building. Brown (1998) 15–39.

2 One of the windows was converted by a nineteenth-century farmer into a second doorway for his cattle.

3 Morley (1983) 89–91; Brown (1998) 65–6.

4 Brown (1998) 61.

5 Slade (1990) 114.

6 Morley (1983) 82–3, 99–100; Slade (1990) 112–13; Brown (1998) 11, 73–4. The seventeenth-century tradition that the house was a grange of Buckfast Abbey has no substance, nor was it a monastic retreat.

7 R. Waterhouse, 'Keynedon Barton, Sherford', *Proc. Devon Arch. Soc.* 58 (2000) 127–200. See also *Vern. Arch.* 31 (2000) 121. With late thirteenth/early fourteenth-century origins of a base-cruck hall and storeyed cross wing, this house of the Hals family was developed in *c*.1300 with an added chamber block and probable service extension. A first-floor chapel was created in the early fifteenth century followed by a lodging block later in the century. At the beginning of the sixteenth century, the quadrangular plan was created with gateway, with flamboyant crenellations added in the late sixteenth century.

8 Brown (1998) 93. The felling date range is 1494–1521, *Vern. Arch.* 30 (1999) 115–16.

9 Brown (1998) 11, 74.

A. W. Everett, *The Buckfast Chronicle* 7 no. 3 (1937) 148–57

B. M. Morley, *Proc. Devon Arch. Soc.* 41 (1983) 81–106

H. G. Slade, Supplement to *Arch. Jour.* 147 (1990) 112–14

S. Brown, *Proc. Devon Arch. Soc.* 56 (1998) 5–108

PLATE 250 Littlehempston Manor: hall range from the forecourt

LITTLEHEMPSTON MANOR, Devon

The manor at Littlehempston is a diminutive late medieval house, an isolated quadrangular residence, tightly encircling a small cobbled courtyard. Situated 3 miles north of Totnes, it stands below the brow of a small chine to the River Dart. Its early history is obscure. Henry I had granted the manor to Roger Arundell in the early twelfth century, and it was held by his successors until 1325 when it passed through marriage to the Stretch family. There is no architectural evidence to support the suggestion that it may have been built by Sir John Stretch of Littlehempston and Wolston during the second half of the fourteenth century.[1] Though the property had passed to the Cheyneys by the second half of the fifteenth century, it has been suggested that they granted it to the nuns of Canonsleigh Priory for use as a place of hospitality or made it over as a rectorial manor.[2] The house was used as the rectory to the scattered parish and distant church of Littlehempston from at least 1540 to 1921.

A narrow entrance in the nineteenth-century enclosing wall opens into a forecourt 45 feet square, with the hall range opposite, bounded by a thatched barn on the left and formerly by one opposite, marked on the tithe map of 1835.

The house entry, without porch protection, is a plain two-centred granite arch with single chamfer opening into the cross passage. The latter is separated from the body of the well-preserved hall by a primitive screen of alternate stiles and panels and twin openings. At a later date, the screen was continued upwards with plaster-filled vertical framing to enclose the end bay of the hall. Whereas the body of the house is two-storeyed, the small hall, 26 feet by 16 feet, is open to the roof. It is lit by an original twin-light window to the inner court with cinquefoil heads, but the two-light transomed window at the upper end is a 1920s insertion replacing an earlier one of which only the relieving arch survives. The right-hand jamb of a further window in the middle of the forecourt wall

was discovered in the 1920s, when the further jamb was added to create an extended slit window. The end-wall fireplace was inserted at the same time, for a central hearth was presumed in the absence of any previous means of heating. The four-bay roof is spanned by arch-braced collar trusses, with the upper part ceiled above the collar.

The walls are covered with the original plaster to within 4 feet of the floor, with extensive wall painting evidence. Much of the dais end wall is filled with a fine depiction of the Resurrection. Against a red background, Christ steps from a chest-like tomb, pointing to His wounds and raising His fingers in benediction. He is flanked on each side by an elegantly drawn angel swinging a censor. The elongated lozenge-shaped panel in yellow edged with a white band was not intended for a text but was a platform supporting the risen Christ and censing angels. The painting was dated by W. R. Lethaby to about 1450.[3] There are also traces of figures over the doorway to the parlour, and evidence of a vivid design of roses in lozenges of leaves over the remainder of the walls, the forecourt window jamb, and the screen. It used to be considered that the end-wall painting confirmed that the house had passed from secular to ecclesiastical ownership by the mid-fifteenth rather than the mid-sixteenth century,[4] but religious subject matter in a domestic environment was not uncommon, as the survivals at Cothay, Fiddleford Manor, and Cullacott demonstrate.[5]

The residential block lay north-west of the hall rather than to the rear of the dais. The parlour is approached from this end of the hall by a door with four-centred head and is lit by a replacement five-light courtyard-facing window. The jambs of the original fireplace opposite have heavy imposts, with the lower edges worked into a hollow chamfer. The bracket to the left is original. A diminutive, steep newel gives access to the withdrawing chamber above, approached by a plain wooden door frame with two-centred head. The room retains an original plain fireplace and garderobe recess in the corner, but the crude roof trusses are post-medieval and the two windows are later replacements.

So far, the planning of this house has been conservative, but the kitchen and offices lay on the further side to the tiny inner court to the hall. Now a single room filling most of the north range, it retains evidence of the partition that formerly divided it into two.

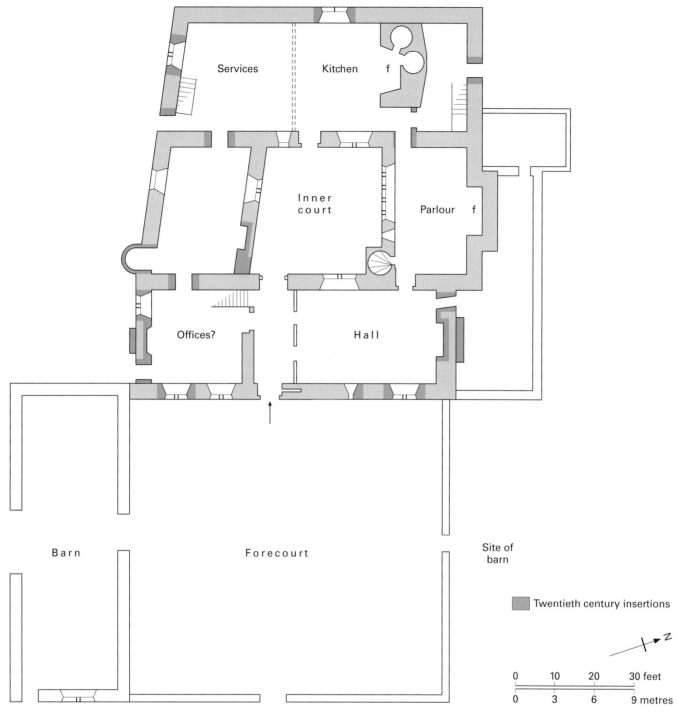

FIGURE 145 Littlehempston Manor: ground plan

The large end-wall hearth retains two ovens, with a circular pit in the lean-to behind that may have served the withdrawing chamber garderobe or was the remains of a curing chamber.[6]

From the hall cross passage, a large elliptical-headed doorway opens into a lower room which may have been used as offices but was not a parlour, as it was unheated until the 1970s. The adjacent room filling the south side of the court was originally smaller, pos-

sibly a store room, separated from the 'offices' by a passageway between the courtyard and the garden. The two were combined in the 1920s when the fireplace and new windows were inserted and the whole used as a drawing room.

Intercommunicating bedrooms of little character have been created in the south and west ranges with rough post-medieval roof trusses. The most important of these rooms was that above the 'offices', formerly approached by a straight stair from the cross-passage entry with two-centred head.[7] It retains further wall painting evidence. This room was subsequently extended when the end truss of the hall was repositioned and an inner room created above the cross passage, enclosing the wooden twin-light cinquefoil window that had formerly illuminated the cross passage.

Littlehempston Manor was built of local rubble stone and roofed with Cornish slates. Its position on a fairly steep slope enabled the water supply from above the property to flow down the hill in a box-shaped channel in a north-east/south-west direction under the hall and across the inner court. The house was developed in two primary phases. The hall and parlour ranges were a single build, using two- and four-centred heads but more particularly fifteenth-century windows with cinquefoil lights. This combination occurs as late as 1498 at Bowhill near Exeter but if the wall painting's ascription to the mid-century is correct, construction occurred earlier. The south and west ranges are post-medieval replacements of uncertain age – as early as the close of the sixteenth and as late as the early eighteenth century. The kitchen probably always lay on the west side, using previously wider foundations towards the northern end of the range. Neither range is bonded into the earlier ones and they have roofs at a slightly lower level. The whole was heavily restored in the 1920s, when many doorways were inserted and windows replaced or new-made.

This compact residence on a miniature scale is local work, untouched by the sophisticated design or decoration of Dartington Hall, the late fourteenth-century mansion of the earl of Huntingdon, on the opposite bank of the river. Littlehempston Manor is a well-preserved, relatively complete medieval house of quiet charm and seclusion, though never overcoming its crepuscular, inward-looking character.

NOTES
1 *Vide* Hussey (1933) 120.
2 Hussey (1933) 122; B. Cherry and N. Pevsner, *The Buildings of England: Devon* (1989) 538, with the alternative view by A. W. Everett to the author in 1960.
3 Hussey (1933); H. A. Tipping, *English Homes*, Pds 1 and 2, II (1937) xx.
4 Hussey (1933); W. G. Hoskins, *Devon* (1954) 408.
5 Cullacott, just across the Devon border with Cornwall on the side of the Otter valley 2 miles north of Launceston, is another modest house with splendid examples of late medieval wall paintings. It was part of Werrington manor, a holding of Tavistock Abbey until it was acquired by the Blyghte family in c.1525. Cullacott was possibly developed as a residence for the abbots rather than as a grange, but it was tenanted by Alice Colecote from at least 1495 to 1522 before occupation by the Blyghte family until about 1642. The house is in two primary parts. The hall, cross passage, service and chamber unit, built of cob on rubble footings, has been dendro dated to about 1475, slightly modifying *Vern. Arch.* 26 (1995) 60–2, while there is datestone evidence that the two-storey residential block at the upper end was added in 1579. Despite later additions and modifications through farm occupation until 1960, the major restoration of the early to mid-1990s revealed substantial evidence of two secular decorative schemes of c.1500–20. The hall, 26½ feet by 17 feet and over 35 feet high, is comparable in scale to that at Littlehempston, complete with jettied room over the cross passage, though the roof timbers are smoke blackened from an open hearth and the screen was replaced by a stone wall in the late nineteenth century. The upper end of the hall was painted in about 1500 with a fictive foliated tapestry hanging with diagonal bands of black letter text, lifted to

reveal the figures of Christ and the Virgin Mary. By about 1520, this was overlapped by the coat of arms of Henry VIII above. At the lower end of the hall, part of a high-quality scheme has been revealed depicting St George and the dragon, contemporary with the royal coat of arms. Both areas are nationally important decorative schemes giving a rare insight into the interior character of a lesser hall towards the close of the middle ages.
6 The latter was the opinion of A.W. Everett to the author.
7 The stair probably had open treads crossing the wide splayed light. The area is now a cupboard.

Anonymous, *Arch. Jour.* 70 (1913) 549–50
C. Hussey, *Country Life* (August 1933)

LUSTLEIGH OLD HALL, Devon

Lustleigh Old Hall is a testimony as much to the standing and financial resources of an early nineteenth-century curate as to that of any medieval owner. The initial view of the house is one of Regency Gothick, encompassing entry porch, stair hall, and gabled residential east block.[1] In the distance are the extensive stables and carriage house of Samuel Whiddon, the curate of Lustleigh, who restored and expanded the house between 1826 and 1838. Yet his work is wrapped round a substantial fourteenth-century hall and solar block, under multiple ownership since 1956. The hall was subject to drastic remodelling under the curate: the solar block was little touched by him.

The Old Hall lies half a mile above the village of Lustleigh on the eastern flank of Dartmoor. As it stands, the hall is 40 feet by 20 feet internally, buttressed on the west side which has the more obvious evidence of its early character than the approach side. Near the middle is a substantial granite doorway with single chamfer and two-centred head. Close by is a twin-trefoil-light window with quatrefoil head, a Victorian remake probably following the original form. During the insertion of the single light to the north in 1989, the relieving arch was uncovered of a second large window with evidence that it had been a bay window. Above the 1989 square-headed window is a wooden two-light trefoil window, brought from elsewhere during the nineteenth-century changes to light a galleried room. The east side has a Regency entry door, not in line with that opposite, and Gothick windows of the same date.

Internally, the hall is a single room, open to the four-bay roof but spanned by a close line of nine trusses. The principal trusses rise from short wooden pillars embedded in the walls with moulded capital and plain narrow band near the tapering base. Ogee trefoiled arch braces rise to the cranked collar with raked queen posts. The intermediate trusses are of similar form but lack the queen posts. The lower of the three sets of purlins have plain wind braces. The pronounced ogee shape of the trusses and their closeness give a dramatic rhythm to this dominating roof.

The problem with the hall is that it is not clear whether it was always a single apartment as it is today, or whether it has lost an internal partition that demarcated the services with chamber above at the south end. The position of the west doorway would be appropriate to a divided hall, but there is no evidence of partition chases in the relevant trusses. The Regency changes have smoothed out much of the hall's character, including any louvre evidence, so that the problem is unresolved.[2] Either the hall was a single apartment

PLATE 251 Lustleigh Old Hall: hall and solar wing from the west

as today which has lost its separate services block beyond the end wall and been subject to entry reorganisation in the early nineteenth century, or the entry is in the correct position in relation to the screens passage and the curate's changes have extended to eradicating the services within the frame of the hall. The position of the later bay window and the seventeenth-century chimney stack with fireplaces on both sides of hall and solar show that the services were never under the solar but always lay to the south.

The two-storey solar cross wing stands relatively unaltered except for the highly unfortunate decision in 1956 to partition it between two owners. One bay is linked to the hall; the further two bays are now in separate occupation. The ground floor, 33 feet by 15½ feet, has retained few features apart from the post-supported cross beam and the splay of a west window sufficiently large to have held two lights and pointing to its initial residential purpose. The splays and shape of a solar window above also survive, now with Regency tracery. No doubt there was a matching window in the east gable wall, obliterated by the Regency extension on that side. The hall stair may be on the site of the original approach to the chamber which probably had a fireplace in the north wall and a garderobe off the north-west corner.

The glory of this apartment is its roof. Arched braces rise from low-set half-round corbels to collars supporting king posts. What gives this structure its character is the use of trefoil shapes – for the braces and collars, the two tiers of wind braces, and the lateral bracing between the collars.[3] This stylish roof recalls that above the solar at Fiddleford Manor, a similar T-shaped house with hall and solar cross wing of comparable scale. Built by a sheriff of Dorset and also missing its early services block, it has retained both hall and solar roofs, attributable to the second quarter of the fourteenth century. Lustleigh Old Hall is probably of the mid-fourteenth century, with the possibility that it is a two-phased house with the solar enjoying a more accomplished trefoiled roof than the rather heavy-handed ogee structure of the hall. Both give the lie to the view that central Devon was necessarily a backward part of medieval England, though building responsibility is unclear.

The manor was held in the early fourteenth century by Sir William Prouz of Gidleigh (q.v.) and Chagford, who commissioned a mortuary chapel in Lustleigh church. He died in 1316 and his will

mentions a manor house in Lustleigh valued at 5s. a year. In that same year, his heiress daughter Alice married Roger Moels, whose elder brother, 4th Lord Moels, held the adjacent manor of Wreyland (the Wrey Brook flows through Lustleigh). This barony had been established by John, 1st Lord Moels (d.1310), who had at least four sons with the title passing in rapid succession to the first three of them until it fell into abeyance (1337). Roger Moels of Lustleigh (d.1323) was probably the youngest son whose eldest brother had married the earl of Devon's sister, and his elder niece (who held Wreyland) married Sir Thomas Courtenay. Lustleigh manor was therefore well connected with the Devon aristocracy during the first half of the fourteenth century, though the property must have passed after Alice Moels' death in 1335 to one of her three daughters by an earlier husband.[4] Alice had been responsible for ensuring that her father, who had died at Holbeton near Modbury, was reburied in Lustleigh church in 1329. She and her husband may have also been responsible for Old Hall, but such speculation awaits further documentary research and dendrochronology analysis.

NOTES

1 North-east by the compass but realigned for descriptive ease.
2 The galleries at each end of the hall are nineteenth- and twentieth-century insertions.
3 Bridget Cherry draws attention to the relative rarity of this local version of a crown-post structure. Laterally braced king posts also occur less than 8 miles north of Lustleigh at the Old Rectory, Cheriton Bishop, and at Clifford Barton, Dunsford. B. Cherry and N. Pevsner, *The Buildings of England: Devon* (1989) 256, 344, 546.
4 *Com. Peer.*, IX (1936) 5–8. The property was acquired by the Wadham family of Ilminster in 1403 who held it until the death of the last member, Nicholas, the founder of Wadham College, Oxford, in 1609. In that year, the Old Hall became Lustleigh rectory and continued to be so until 1927. The glebe terrier for 1679 states that the house consisted of a hall, a buttery, and seven other rooms plus a stable, shippen, hogsty, and three-roomed malthouse. The curate, Samuel Whiddon, failed in his attempt to acquire the living of Lustleigh, despite the considerable expenditure he incurred in renovating and expanding the ramshackle and partitioned rectory.

LYTES CARY, Somerset

Lytes Cary, lacking the epithet of manor, court, hall, or house, sits quietly hugging the fertile lowland of the River Cary. Built of local soft grey Lias stone with Ham stone dressings and partially tiled roofs, this manor house is a development of at least five phases that can be read on the south-west exteriors – the mid-fourteenth-century projecting chapel, and the mid-fifteenth-century hall recessed between an early sixteenth-century storeyed bay and porch when the earlier solar wing was replaced by an imposing residential range dominated by the embattled bay window. The offices were replaced by an aggressively pitched farmhouse between 1755 and 1770 and the inner court was closed on its fourth side by Sir Walter Jenner's family range of 1907–8. This is not an imposing house but one of gentle charm and subtle qualities.

The Lyte family are first recorded at the manor of Cary in 1286 with evidence of a house occupied by William Lyte (d.1316), but the earliest structure is the chapel of about 1340. Initially free-standing though abutting the house after the hall was erected a century later,

PLATE 252 Lytes Cary: hall range and chapel from the forecourt

this chapel is unusual in always being independent of the residence except for a domestic squint.[1] Its construction prompted Peter Lyte (d.1348), William's grandson, to transfer a chantry chaplain from Tuckers Cary to Lytes Cary in 1343. The chapel's scale and decorative character bespeak quality. The modest doorway moulding is enhanced by a bold hood with stops of inward-facing heads and a luscious finial of a nest of birds atop a leaf garland. The trefoil three-light east window with three quatrefoil heads is flanked by side windows using the same motifs in a totally different manner under a square head. The single west light retains some fifteenth-century glass though the sedilia has lost much of its cusping. The roof of thin arch-braced collar beams was renovated by Thomas Lyte (d.1638) in 1631 when the characteristic screen, box pew, and altar rails were added, as well as the armorial frieze of the Lytes and their relations.

The extremely plain porch and more elaborate hall bay with their handsome upper-floor oriels and capped gables are among the early Tudor additions to the mid-fifteenth-century hall, 37 feet by 21 feet internally. The primary medieval survival is the five-bay roof of high arch-braced collars springing from angel corbels holding shields with the Lyte arms. It is given distinction by the highly decorated wall plates of pierced quatrefoils linked by undercut tracery, and three tiers of cusped wind braces.[2] Possibly built by Thomas Lyte between taking up his inheritance in 1453 and his death sixteen years later, the hall was extensively modified in about 1530, when the four windows were enlarged from two to three lights by sharply

cutting back the earlier splays, and were given uncusped heads and contemporary armorial glass.[3] The fireplace was similarly enlarged, with jambs of the same character as the panelled arches to the added square bays flanking the dais. The east bay has an independent fireplace creating a personal inner room (possibly screened) while the west bay with its more refined panelled arch and stone newel accessed the family apartments.

Shortly after succeeding to the property in 1523, John Lyte (d.1568) undertook the major expansion of Lytes Cary in a phased programme with ranges round three sides of a central court. He replaced the earlier solar wing with a two-storey residential range against the earlier hall and parlour walls, but extending further westwards, with the commanding bay window dated 1533 and pierced quatrefoil parapet lighting the more important room on each floor. He similarly rebuilt the offices and north wing, but of this work only two late medieval service doorways and Lyte's basement windows survive, incorporated in the mid-eighteenth-century farmhouse. John Lyte's residential west range was destroyed before 1810 and left open until replaced in 1908 by the William and Mary style range with classical rooms.

Lytes Cary was the home of a single landowning gentry family from the late thirteenth to the mid-eighteenth century, with several members in the legal profession. They flourished most under the Tudors but never rose any higher socially. The workmanship of the medieval and Tudor phases is of good quality but sober rather than spectacular. Though of markedly differing periods, all roofs but the farmhouse one blend most agreeably. The property suffered badly during this phase between 1755 and 1907 until it was rescued and sensitively restored and furnished by Sir Walter Jenner (d.1948).

NOTES
1 In *c*.1450, the Hungerford family similarly built a replacement domestic chapel next to their manor house at Sheldon near Chippenham.
2 The first bay was rescreened and galleried in 1907.
3 Originally in Lyte's parlour and 'chapel' room but returned from a church near Taunton in 1908.

W. George, *Lytes Cary Manor House* (1879)
H. Maxwell-Lyte, *Proc. Somerset Arch. and N. H. Soc.* 38 (1892) 1–100 with a description of the house by E. Buckle, *ibid.* 101–10. Both reprinted as *The Lytes of Lytescary* (1895)
C. Hussey, *Country Life* (July/August 1947)
VCH, *Somerset*, III (1974) 100–1
R. Dunning, *Some Somerset Country Houses* (1991) 83–9
The National Trust, *Lytes Cary: Guidebook* (2001)

MARTOCK, TREASURER'S HOUSE, Somerset

The treasurer of Wells Cathedral chose one of the more wealthy livings of the diocese for his permanent residence, standing almost opposite the commanding fifteenth-century church of Martock. His T-shaped house, built in local Ham Hill sandstone, is made up of a mid-thirteenth-century cross wing at the lower end of the mid-fourteenth-century hall, with a rear projecting kitchen block of the later fifteenth century. The house has suffered from post-medieval additions, including a short late nineteenth-century extension to the cross wing, but it makes a valuable comparison with the fifteenth-century chantry college at Stoke Sub Hamdon, less than 2 miles away.

The outer walls of the still-tenanted chamber block are mid-thirteenth century, though only the upper-floor west window makes this immediately apparent. The ground floor has been subject to a number of changes, so that it is now divided by late Georgian partitions into a central passage flanked by a parlour to the west, and a stair, passage, and small room to the east. Only the parlour, created during the fifteenth century, warrants attention. From that time dates the single cross-passage doorway and rear doorway (now converted into a window), two windows of three cinquefoil lights each, the moulded ceiling beams, and the fireplace (now a seventeenth-century replacement).

The upper floor has also been subject to Georgian corridor and room division, but the unfurnished end room retains the primary features of this block. The mid-thirteenth-century gable window has two trefoiled lights with a quatrefoil above and a trefoiled rear arch. The window was glazed with painted glass[1] and shuttered. It is surrounded by a contemporary wall painting recovered in 1993–5, of outlined stonework with rosettes, a Crucifixion scene with Mary and St John in attendance above the window, and vine leaf decoration parallel with the line of the original roof pitch. Though the house was under ecclesiastical ownership, domestic wall paintings of *c*.1260 are nevertheless rare. The present single tie-beam and collar-braced roof with wind braces is probably fifteenth century. The blocked doorway in the south-west corner with its inward-facing chamfer is thought to have served a garderobe,

PLATE 253 Martock, Treasurer's House: hall and parlour wing from the forecourt

and though one might be expected in this position, the entry is particularly broad. It is more appropriate to a 10 feet wide inner chamber, destroyed when the kitchen was built but still marked by a vertical building line on the external wall.

The hall, 40 feet by 22 feet internally, was built at a slight angle to the cross wing. Entry is by opposing cross-passage doorways with continuous chamfer and two-centred heads. There is an unusually positioned but contemporary second door in the west wall, repeating the drawbar slot. A stone wall in place of any services screen was inserted in the seventeenth century to support a gallery chamber added above the cross passage. The hall is flooded with light from five windows, two in each side wall and one filling much of the end wall. Each window is of two transomed lights with cinquefoil head, set in broad splays with seats on the west side. They are under square heads externally and spanned internally by cinquefoil rear arches. The elongated end window is similar, but with the addition of a quatrefoil head almost touching the end roof truss.[2] The four-bay roof is spanned by moulded arch-braced collar trusses rising from an embattled wall plate. The three tiers of curved wind braces form a decorative pattern, with the lowest and uppermost arranged in pairs in each bay, contrasting with the central line of single spans to each bay. No fire evidence has been identified, neither hearth, louvre, nor sooted timbers.[3] It was roofed until the mid-nineteenth century with locally quarried slates and glazed ridge tiles, and the subsequent thatch covering was replaced with inappropriate clay tiles in the early twentieth century.

The Treasurers were rectors and patrons of Martock from 1226, when they acquired the priest's house, until 1849.[4] In 1262, Treasurer Hugh purchased a plot of land 80 feet by 40 feet on the east side of the property, so that it could be enlarged.[5] This would not be at variance with a date between about 1250 and 1270 for the cross wing. The ground floor, lit by small loops,[6] would have been for services with a fine-quality chamber above. Formerly with an east window identical with that still at the opposite end,[7] the upper floor was a single chamber[8] with an external approach abutting an earlier hall. This was either stone-built or possibly a timber-framed structure carried on a stone sill, 5 feet longer than the present hall following evidence of its greater length through excavation in 1993–5.[9] This earlier hall was replaced by a more imposing one during the second quarter of the fourteenth century, though the

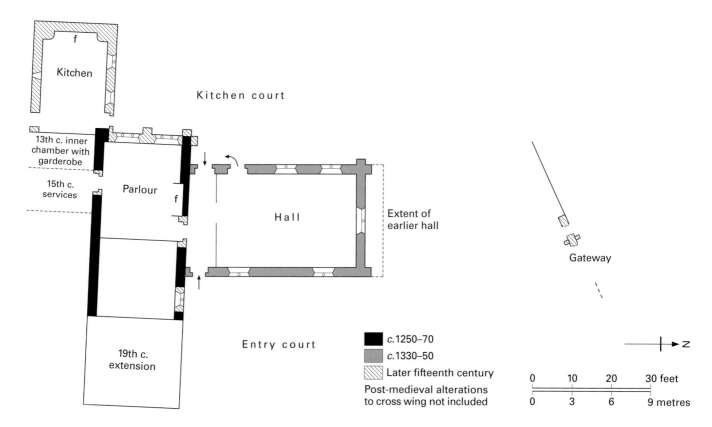

FIGURE 146 Martock, Treasurer's House: ground plan

roof seems to be fifteenth century. This was a hall for entertaining visitors and guests, well lit with attractively designed windows following the solar precedent of decorative rear arches. The hall lacked porches, but it has a simple but stylish roof, and has been restored internally, with colour-washed walls. The retention of a large end window above the high table confirms that the earlier retiring chamber was never supplanted by an upper cross wing as was so often the case, but the second door in the west wall may well have been the approach to an external stair rising over the cross-passage door to the solar.[10]

The original kitchen was replaced in the fifteenth century by one touching the south-west corner of the chamber block. This kitchen 21 feet by 15 feet and once again open to the roof after the removal of an inserted floor in the 1950s, has opposing entries with steeply pitched heads and a hearth 12 feet wide, almost filling the west wall. The services seem to have been moved to an abutting building when the parlour was created, now destroyed, but scarring the south face of the chamber block with a second vertical line.

The precinct was closed to the street in the fifteenth century by a gatehouse with side entry. A chamber over the chief gate of the house is mentioned in 1482,[11] but only the foot entry survives and the jamb of the larger arch for vehicles.

NOTES

1 Some of the fragments recovered during restoration in 1993–5 are illustrated in the National Trust leaflet (1998).
2 This window was unblocked in the 1950s after the seventeenth-century cottages against it had been removed.

3 Two well-carved late fifteenth-century wall brackets with quatrefoil frieze and embattled head supported on a coat of arms have been inserted in the hall at an unknown date, and one in the solar. They are similar to a bracket in the hall of Tickenham Court.
4 *Cal. of Manuscripts of the Dean and Chapter of Wells*, I (1907) 36–7, 51.
5 *Ibid.*
6 Uncovered in 1995 before internal replastering, but still visible from the kitchen court.
7 T. H. Turner and J. H. Parker, *Some Account of Domestic Architecture in England*, II (1853) 302. It was destroyed by the late Victorian extension.
8 The first-floor hall and solar plan proposed in the National Trust leaflet (1998) is a variant on Margaret Wood's suggestion of a first-floor hall that became a solar in the fourteenth century: (1950) 72. Neither is tenable, but see Wood's note 7 concerning a possible timber hall.
9 *Med. Arch.* 40 (1996) 278–9, where it is suggested that the hall was shortened and the gable rebuilt in the late medieval period.
10 The hall has been precisely dated to 1293–4 on the evidence of money spent that year on a new hall by the Treasurer, *Cal. of Manuscripts of the Dean and Chapter of Wells*, I (1907) 446. This refers not necessarily to the present hall, which has no late thirteenth-century features, but to its predecessor. Nor does it necessarily mean a rebuilding, *vide* VCH, IV (1978) 87.
11 Saunders (1935) 111.

Prebendary G. W. Saunders, *Notes on the History of Martock* (1935) 12–26

M. Wood, *Thirteenth Century Domestic Architecture in England* (1950) 72–4

VCH, *Somerset*, IV (1978) 87

The National Trust, *The Treasurer's House: Guide Leaflet* (1998)

MEARE MANOR FARM, Somerset and the houses of the abbots of Glastonbury

A walk round the exterior of this striking house next to Meare church, initially a manor house of the abbots of Glastonbury but long occupied as a working farm, immediately reveals that it has not been drastically altered since construction. A house was granted to abbot Amesbury upon his retirement in 1252,[1] but the present structure is essentially a single-period early fourteenth-century house, modified in the later sixteenth century. The house is L-shaped, with a projecting porch at the junction of the arms and with the further two sides enclosed by a high wall to create a rear court. The house is two-storeyed throughout: a low ground floor and taller upper floor of primary rooms. The ground floor was lit by single or paired trefoil lights under square heads, the upper floor by tall windows of two ogee-shaped cinquefoil lights under quatrefoil heads. All those on the entrance front were partially blocked, up to the relieving arch, with the lower half infilled with square-headed mullioned windows when the house was modified for farm occupation before 1600. The primary difference between the two arms is that the east wing is supported by stepped buttresses; the north wing is not.[2]

The entrance front is commanded by the two-storeyed porch with ogee-shaped gable, now surmounted by a top-heavy stone figure. Most of the ogee-headed lights of the porch have survived at both levels but the outer and inner entrances are later sixteenth-century replacements. The original inner doorway is probably that inserted in the farm outbuilding west of the house, with continuous hollow and roll moulding, two-centred head, and hood mould.[3]

The ground floor has long been partitioned for farmhouse occupation – the north wing is currently used as parlour, kitchen, and scullery, and the east wing as stair hall, sitting room, and unused end chamber. Internal divisions and habitation make it difficult to discern the original layout but some of the apparently stone walls shown on the plan by Turner and Parker no longer exist.[4] The ground-floor rooms have always been relatively low, with beamed ceilings, though the scullery was formerly vaulted. The present kitchen retains its fourteenth-century hearth with ogee-shaped lintel sides and short canted hood sharing its stack with the hall fireplace above. The present sitting room makes similar use of the east wing stack. The north-east doorway with internal-facing chamfer suggests stair access on this side of the wing to the hall above via the doorway shown in Turner and Parker's engraving and plan.

The upper floor apparently consisted of only two areas. Now approached internally by a tight Georgian stair, the upper level was initially entered from a pentice-covered external stair against the much-refaced west wall to the north-west doorway with continuous hollow and roll jambs, two-centred head, and four-centred rear arch. It opens into the north room, 61 feet by 23 feet, still little altered since abbatial vacation. It was lit by at least five windows with retained shutter pins and bar sockets, set behind attractive foliated rear arches. The two east-facing windows are complete but that in the west wall is blocked. The gable-end windows with taller transomed lights are off-centre to the gable. The west wall is dominated by the splendid original fireplace with corbel-supported lintel and a semi-octagonal and canted stone hood tapering to wall-plate level. Either side of the lintel is a decorative bracket with colouring evidence. The garderobe off the south-west corner has been destroyed but the narrow doorway is visible externally.[5] There is no doubt that this enormous room was partitioned not far from the fireplace and the doorway to the east wing, to create a hall with garderobe-provided inner chamber. Turner and Parker correctly mark such a division so that the fireplace heats the inner chamber.

PLATE 254 Meare Manor Farm: engraving of house from the north-east from Parker (1853)

The doorway opening into the east wing has a continuous hollow and roll chamfer and two-centred head with multi-moulded rear arch. Long partitioned into bedrooms and corridor, the east wing was originally a single room, flooded with light from the three tall windows in both side walls. They have all been blocked or reduced to smaller openings. Externally, there is a recut relieving arch spanning the gable-end wall, considerably larger than any others in the house, that may have supported a vast east window. The gable now carries a post-medieval corbel-supported chimney breast but the stack on the north side is original but enlarged. It now supports a later fifteenth/early sixteenth-century lintel of three blank shields in a multi-cusped panel, hinting at the room's subsequent and possibly original secular purpose.

None of the roofs survives, for both wings are covered with utilitarian trusses. On the basis of the contemporary 'Fish House' nearby,[6] they were probably of conventional Somerset type, i.e. arch-braced collar trusses with wind braces, but probably of highly decorative character.

Meare Manor Farm is built of local blue Lias which has not weathered well – hence the roughcast covered frontage and the poor state of the north wing with its refaced west and gable-end walls. Attributable on architectural grounds to the second quarter of the fourteenth century, this manor house was built by Adam Sodbury, abbot of Glastonbury (1323–34), abbot John Beynton (1334–42), or abbot Walter Monnington (1342–75).[7] All added to the residential facilities at Glastonbury Abbey but *The Chartulary of Glastonbury*, written by the monk John in about 1342, identifies Adam Sodbury as the builder.[8]

This 'fine old manor house'[9] is a major fourteenth-century domestic survival, a southern version of Markenfield Hall (c.1310–15). Both are L-shaped, essentially of single build, similarly planned at both levels, inhabited and with associated farm use, though the Yorkshire house has several vaulted ground-floor rooms and is moated. The Meare house has some unusual features. The ground floor has two substantial rooms with fireplaces, and if one was a small lower hall as at Markenfield, the other may have been a dormitory for staff attendant on the abbot.[10] There is a surprising lack of internal stair access – outside flights of steps were markedly old-fashioned by the second quarter of the fourteenth century. A first-floor hall was increasingly rare in southern England except in the grandest houses, while a framed rather than stone division between the hall and chamber is surprising. Fortunately, this north wing stands little touched. The small room over the porch was supplementary to the grand chamber filling the east wing, that *may* have started as a chapel but was subsequently secularised. Both wings were dominated by imposing two-light windows. Similar foliated rear arches to those of the north wing windows occur in the chapel at Berkeley Castle (1330s). The need to buttress the east wing indicates that the upper chamber was particularly impressive, with windows in all outer walls and spanned by a roof that was probably spectacular. It would have been like a glass cage and therefore needed buttress support. It was the monastic equivalent of the bishop's chapel of c.1290 at Wells Palace but not unlike the similar multi-windowed first-floor withdrawing chamber at Goxhill Hall, Lincolnshire, of c.1350–60.

The house stood in a courtyard, protected by a contemporary stone wall, possibly with the original kitchen and offices built against it. Two hundred years after construction, the house was

PLATE 255 Meare Manor Farm: engraving of first-floor hall window from Parker (1853)

described as 'having a fayre large hall, th'one halfe whereof is covered with leade and th'ither with slate, with viii fayre chambers, a proper chapell, with a kytchyn buttery and pantrye, and all other houses of office very necessary'.[11] A little earlier, a terrier of 1516 for abbot Richard Bere describes it as 'a very handsome and ample Manor-House, founded long ago and adorned by the present abbot with new chambers', possibly a west wing that no longer survives. Part of the manorial complex still retains abbot Sodbury's wall 'of great height and thickness, surrounding it strongly with stone enclosing within the said walls 3 acres and 1 perch'.[12]

Meare Manor Farm must be seen in context, for Glastonbury Abbey was the most prestigious monastery in the west of England. As a leading landowner in the region, the abbey's income at the time of the Dissolution was more than £4,000 a year – the same as that of Westminster Abbey. Most of the estates had been donated by the Saxon kings of Wessex, with the majority in Somerset and scattered holdings in Berkshire, Wiltshire, and Dorset. The abbey built at least eight houses for the abbot's use on its properties in Somerset, all within easy reach of the mother house, plus one in the three more distant counties. Only four are of substance today: the roofed properties at Meare, Norwood Park, and Ashbury, and the ruins at Sturminster Newton.

Pilton Manor House was initiated by abbot Michael Amesbury (1235–52), with additions by abbots Sodbury and Chinnock, but the present classical house is a rebuilding of about 1754 with an added Gothick wing that may incorporate some medieval elements.[13]

Among the sumptuous building projects that marked the last decades of the abbey's life were the four houses of abbot Selwood (1456–93). Ashbury Manor is not only a Somerset house transferred to a Berkshire landscape but a particularly early example of a house with a great chamber above the hall (see page 50). The central range of Norwood Park, a mile north of Glastonbury, is also by Selwood (carved panel with initials) but the extensions either side are essentially modern. Selwood's work is marked by paired window lights and buttressed gables with a prominent two-storey bay with embattled parapet in the middle of the east gable, but contemporary internal features are limited to beamed ceilings and a first-floor partition. The two short ranges that survive at Ivythorn Manor near Street were subdivided and extended by Selwood, who added the porch.[14] Nothing survives at East Brent Manor, north of Highbridge, though Selwood was responsible for a rather grand establishment with hall, parlour, chapel, large and lofty chambers, kitchen and services. Two stone figures of kings moved to the garden of Porch House, Wedmore, in the early eighteenth century are understood to have been brought from this manor before demolition.[15]

In addition to the extensive church enhancement carried out by abbot Bere (1493–1525), Leland records that he 'buildid the new lodging by the great chambre caullid the kinge's lodging in the galery' to accommodate Henry VII during his visit to Glastonbury in 1499.[16] Neither the abbot's house nor this royal extension survives. However, the foundations have been marked out of the fourteenth-century abbot's hall, 82½ feet by 55 feet, with rear withdrawing chamber. One corner of the hall stands in part, adjacent to the associated kitchen, a remarkable and fortuitous survival[17] (pl. 187). A prospect of the abbey prepared in 1712 and published by William Stukeley in *Itinerarium Curiosum* in 1726 shows a Tudor house some distance north of this kitchen. It was a three-storeyed residence with end wings, added to an earlier two-storeyed unit terminating in an octagonal turret. The property was in ruins in 1723 and it has been suggested that the early Tudor multi-light windows, doorways, and bay window fronting the Tribunal in the High Street of the town were taken from here for reuse between 1712 and 1723.[18] Bere also rebuilt Sharpham Park, drastically refashioned between the seventeenth and nineteenth centuries and now divided into two farm dwellings with little retained medieval character.

Nothing survives of the houses at Weston and Shapwick, or the more distant one at Damerham, 9 miles south-west of Salisbury, while the mid-fourteenth-century hall and chamber block at Sturminster Newton that was a favoured home of the last abbot is a forlorn ruin (see page 645).

More resonant evidence of the extent of Glastonbury's holdings is seen in the several barns that survive from the eleven recorded in Somerset in 1274–5. That at Glastonbury has been dendro dated to 1342–60.[19] Those at Pilton and Doulting are similar and attributed to *c.*1375–85, with West Bradley of the early fifteenth century. Doulting and West Bradley are still part of working farms, Glastonbury is a museum, while Pilton has been roofless since a fire in 1963.[20]

NOTES

1 H. Gray, *Proc. Som. Arch. and N. H. Soc.* 48 (1902) 41.

2 Turner and Parker (1853) show that the gable end was buttressed before the mid-nineteenth-century refacing, though not necessarily originally.

3 Jane Penoyre considers that the porch was an addition. Stephen Rippon suggests that the approach was possibly from the canalised River Brue north of the house, *Med. Arch.* 48 (2004) 103–5.

4 Turner and Parker (1853) opp. 297. It is surprising that such a rare survival has never been subject to a historical, architectural, or archaeological analysis since the mid-nineteenth century, despite the fact that English Heritage and many regional societies pay inordinate attention to the small contemporary dwelling a field away (see note 6).

5 Turner and Parker (1853) show a second garderobe in the opposite corner to the entrance doorway – a doubtful original position. The adjacent doorway may have been the service entry.

6 Standing alone a few hundred yards east of Manor Farm, this two-storeyed oblong dwelling was erected at the same time as the manor house and was originally plastered externally. It is traditionally believed to have been the home of the water bailiff on the edge of the extensive mere, that fluctuated between 3 and 5 miles in circumference, until drained in the mid-seventeenth century. The two floors were independent. The upper floor, approached by a destroyed external stair, consisted of two residential rooms – the much larger chamber with fireplace and two-light gable-end window, and a smaller end room with garderobe (destroyed). The present utilitarian roof replaced the original arch-braced collar trusses and two lines of wind braces, destroyed by fire in the mid-1880s. The three ground-floor rooms (one partitioned) lit by squared openings were for service use, said to be for the chief fisherman to dry, salt, and store fish, but the house is of markedly high standard for such an official, if he existed.

7 *John of Glastonbury, The Great Chartulary of Glastonbury*, ed. J. P. Carley (1985); J. P. Carley, *Glastonbury Abbey* (1996 edn) 40–7. I. Keil, 'The abbots of Glastonbury in the early fourteenth century', *Downside Review* 82 (1964) 327–48.

8 Dendro dated ground-floor beams from both ranges confirmed they were contemporary, felled between 1315 and 1343. *Vern. Arch.* 34 (2003) 93–4. Plan and elevation in J. Penoyre, *Traditional Houses of Somerset* (2005) 106.

9 Leland, *Itinerary*, I, 290.

10 As at Markenfield, there is an adjacent garderobe against the gable end, shown in Turner and Parker's plan before its rebuild.

11 W. Dugdale, *Monasticon Anglicanum*, I (1817–30 edn) 10; W. Phelps, *The History and Antiquities of Somerset*, I (1836) 569–71.

12 The wall is illustrated and marked on a plan of the village in Stephen Rippon's valuable article reconstructing the medieval landscape and the highly valued wetland resources centred on Meare that were held by Glastonbury Abbey, *Med. Arch.* 48 (2004) 91–130.

13 W. Dugdale, *Monasticon Anglicanum* I, 10–21, records that this manor house included eight chambers as well as the hall, chapel, eating room, kitchen, and services.

14 B. Little, *Somerset Countryman* (July 1958) 174–6. The wing added by Sir John Sydenham in the 1570s was destroyed after it had been drawn by Buckler in 1834.

15 Carley, *Glastonbury Abbey* 64.

16 *Itinerary*, I, 144. Leland also records that the abbot's great chamber was rebuilt by Nicholas Frome (1426–56).

17 No study on medieval houses can ignore this spectacular building, for apart from its structural qualities this kitchen is indicative of the facilities necessary to support the lifestyle and hospitality practised by a leading residential establishment during the later middle ages. The free-standing kitchen, 40 feet square externally but octagonal internally, is capped with a stone-slab pyramid roof rising to an octagonal lantern carrying a smaller one 72 feet high. To support this weighty structure, the walls are strengthened by half-round buttresses with a stepped polygonal upper stage. There are two opposing entries, with a third one on the east side, subsequently blocked. The room is lit by two windows of two cinquefoil lights with slight ogee moulding above, and smaller trefoil lights over the two entries. The fireplaces across each corner have massive two-centred arches and circular flues, now truncated at roof level. Eight low-set ribs rise from the corners to support a stone ring at the base of the larger octagon. This was essentially for ventilation, with fresh air entering through the louvres of the upper lantern and stale air escaping through those of the lower one. Responsibility for its construction is still uncertain with attributions ranging from the first quarter of the fourteenth century to the mid-fifteenth century, but as the window tracery is so similar to that at the Abbot's House and Fish House at Meare, construction during the 1330s is likely.

18 R. W. Dunning and J. and J. Penoyre, *Glastonbury Tribunal* (1997) 10. The 'tribunal' was a fifteenth-century merchant's house used for commercial purposes. Also R. W. Dunning in Abrams and Carley (1991) 89–93.

19 J. and J. Penoyre, *Proc. Somerset Arch. and N. H. Soc.* 142 (1999) 311.

20 C. J. Bond and J. B. Weller in Abrams and Carley (1991) 57–87.

Meare Manor Farm
H. Turner and J. Parker, *Some Account of Domestic Architecture in England*, II (1853) 297–300
Anonymous, *Trans. Somerset Arch. and N. H. Soc.* 9 (1859) 33–4

Glastonbury Abbey
N. Coldstream and P. Draper (eds.), *Medieval Art and Architecture at Wells and Glastonbury* (1981)
L. Abrams and J. P. Carley (eds.), *The Archaeology and History of Glastonbury Abbey* (1991)

MILTON ABBEY, Dorset

In their various stages of survival, the three Dorset abbeys at Milton, Cerne, and Forde offer a striking display of monastic building activity during the late middle ages – the imposing early fourteenth- and later fifteenth-century church at Milton replacing the one burnt down in 1309; the mid-fifteenth-century guest house at Cerne Abbas; and the early sixteenth-century cloister range at Forde – but their rebuilding programmes also encompassed the total redevelopment and upgrading of their abbatial lodgings. They survive in part at Milton and Cerne (both Benedictine) and are virtually complete at Forde (Cistercian). They span a forty-year period, between 1498 and 1538, and are among the last such works before the Dissolution of the Monasteries. They speak of the wealth and heady sense of display felt in Dorset, particularly by the monastic orders shortly before the cataclysm that swept them away.[1] The elaboration is primarily external at Cerne and Forde, essentially internal at Milton.

Milton is the earliest of the three, almost enveloped in the mansion built by Joseph Damer in 1771–6. An overbearing local

man who married the daughter of the 1st duke of Dorset, Damer was created Lord Milton in 1753 and earl of Dorchester forty years later, shortly before his death in 1798. Though John Vardy had submitted some preliminary plans which may have influenced the subsequent development, Sir William Chambers designed the quadrangular mansion in a style considered contemporary to the retained abbey church, though most of the interior decoration was by James Wyatt. The abbot's house and some of the adjacent buildings had been remodelled for secular occupation by Sir John Tregonwell in the mid-sixteenth century and they survived for two centuries until Damer bought the estate in 1752 and cleared most of them away in favour of his new mansion. Only the abbot's hall and entry porch were retained and incorporated in Chambers' design, as the reception hall to his principal suite of apartments on the west side of the mansion.

William Middleton, abbot from 1482 to 1525, seems to have brought his own finances as well as a thrusting personality to expand and enrich the abbey buildings. At the time of the Dissolution, the monastery was among the more wealthy in southern England, exceeded only by Sherborne and Shaftesbury in Dorset, though with most of its income achieved from farming out its lands. Middleton was probably a local man, and the combination of the abbey's financial standing and his own resources enabled him to initiate a major building programme. It encompassed the church[2] and his own quarters, including the still-standing porch and hall.[3] However, these structures are nearly as much a reflection of the late eighteenth century as of the late fifteenth century, though the changes introduced by Chambers and Wyatt have not been sufficiently identified.[4]

The original approach from the north was followed by Chambers when he used the porch and hall as the reception area to his new suite of apartments. Built of ashlar stone blocks, the two-storeyed porch has a two-centred entry arch set in a square frame. The arch has continuous roll and hollow mouldings, a hood terminating in weathered figures, and spandrels carved with a W and a crozier and the rebus of abbot Middleton. Above is a frieze of three coats of arms, of England, abbey, and founder, between blind quatrefoil and trefoil panels. The first-floor window has three ogee-headed lights of similar form to the treatment of the hall windows at Athelhampton (*c.*1490–5). The upper sides of the porch are plain, while the pierced parapet spanning the porch and hall is eighteenth century. The ground-floor corridors either side of the porch are obviously modern, but Buck's engraving of 1733 showing the west front of Middleton's house suggests that the porch was surmounted by the decorative finials favoured at this time in Dorset, as at Bingham's Melcombe. The floor between the porch and the room above was removed in the eighteenth century when the coffered wooden ceiling of multi-sunken panels was inserted.

The hall, 54 feet by 27 feet with its spectacular six-bay roof, retains its original proportions and volume. However, Chambers replaced the original ashlar facing blocks still visible on the courtyard side with alternating bands of flint and rubble stone on the church side to match the adjacent parts of his mansion. The entry doorways to the hall cross passage have continuous moulded jambs and four-centred head, but the vaulted kitchen to the east of the hall was pulled down in 1737 and the service doorways blocked.

Like the contemporary halls at Eltham Palace and Athelhampton, abbot Middleton's hall was an exercise in rising complexity and

Each section stands on a moulded base between multi-shafted diagonal pillars. Each one is divided horizontally by a shelf with shaped underside of quatrefoil and trefoil roundels, the middle section with the initials W and M and a blank shield. The panelling below this shelf has blind trefoil lights with blank shields at the base; the alternate panels are fielded. The same workmanship occurs in the panelling above the shelf, but with a mouchette frieze below and a ball-flower frieze above. In the central section are two canopied niches, one above the other. The screen is crowned with an elaborate cresting, ogee-shaped arches cusped and crocketed, between original finials surmounting the ends of each section. The cresting is wider above the two openings than the three sections where there are central busts of shield-bearing angels. The screen has been repaired, particularly the base, while the cresting looks almost Rococo. Possibly of earlier origin, it was added by Wyatt in the later eighteenth century, heightening the contrast between the discipline of the three sections and the overexuberant mid-Georgian flourish.

The amazing roof is basically a hammer-beam structure. The seven principal trusses rise from heavily moulded beams supported by decorated brackets springing from moulded stone shafts between the windows resting on angels carrying shields. The massive moulded braces rise in a broad two-centred curve to a collar carrying a head of open tracery. Intermediate trusses rise from unbracketed hammer beams to a subsidiary arch-braced and raised collar. The four tiers of wind braces between the three moulded purlins are cinquefoil cusped, arranged in four different paired patterns in each bay. This is an extremely elaborate and decorative roof in the contemporary West of England tradition. Apart from its structural complexity, it is enhanced with added decoration such as the music-playing figures and animals on the underside of the intermediate hammer beams, and pendants at the junction of the subsidiary braces, a quatrefoil frieze above the heavily moulded wall plate, and flat fleur-de-lis finials in the centre of each span of wind braces.[7]

The character and craftsmanship of this hall were intended to bedazzle the beholder. The lower walls have been painted or hung with painted cloths, while the many coats of arms and later sixteenth- and seventeenth-century stained glass still bring some colour to the gloomy spaces of the highly ornate roof. The character of increasing decoration with increasing height occurs as much in contemporary stonework (Sudeley Castle) as in interiors (Crosby Hall). The hall at Milton Abbey is no exception and it is all too easy to say that this heady sense of display personified the arrogance and wealth of a declining and self-centred institution. Yet it is very little different in form and style from the contemporary hall and entry porch of a local landowner at Athelhampton 5 miles south, while the screen can be paralleled at Wortham and the hall roof at Weare Giffard (q.v.) The richness and *joie de vivre* is redolent of the era and region, secular as much as monastic.

PLATE 256 Milton Abbey: hall towards the screen

embellishment: the lower part was relatively plain; the upper part was more ornate, culminating in a roof of considerable ingenuity. The bare lower walls are divided at a third of their height by a moulded string course with intermittent foliated bosses and coats of arms that extends from the screen, and at a higher level across the upper-end wall. Among the copious heraldry of local families, bishops, and abbeys is the rebus of abbot Middleton (bay window) and the date 1498 in Arabic numerals (west wall repeated on the screen). Above are uncusped triple-light transomed windows in the first three south-facing bays (two-light above the cross passage), and in the third to fifth bays on the north side, with plain four-centred heads set in square frames. The fireplace is a late seventeenth-century insertion by John Tregonwell (d.1680), while the vast rectangular bay window, usually considered original,[5] is too grandiose and ill-proportioned to be genuine. The four-centred approach arch is late fifteenth century but it is more likely to have opened into a smaller oblong or polygonal bay, half the size of the present deep structure, a miniature dining room with eighteenth-century ogee-headed lights and ceiling.[6]

Two original features give this hall its distinction. The screen enclosing the featureless cross passage is one of the most striking of its period. Two entrances are created between two side sections and a narrower central section, surmounted by a highly ornate frieze.

NOTES

1 These same attributes were responsible two centuries later for Joseph Damer's relocation of the small market town of Middleton to make room for his new landscaped park surrounding Milton Abbey. As the town lay south of the church and was moved half a mile away, one consequence was the creation of a valley setting within an amphitheatre of hills, of outstanding beauty for church and mansion.

2 His work included rebuilding the north transept, completing the central tower, vaulting the crossing and both transepts, and adding the stone reredos.

3 In the early eighteenth century, Hutchins recorded that the abbot's private apartments to the west included his dining room and a room with a panelled ceiling decorated with gold stars.

4 RCHM, III pt 2 (1970) 191–7.

5 *Ibid.* 195.

6 The majority of bay windows between the second half of the fifteenth century and the early sixteenth century were polygonal, but occasionally square or oblong bays occur (Eltham Palace hall *c*.1475–83; Bewley Court *c*.1490). It might be anticipated that the broad arch would open into a bay not unlike that at Hazelbury Manor (*c*.1500) or Lytes Cary (*c*.1525), but no bay windows throughout this period are so broad that they take up two bays of the hall. M. Wood, *The English Mediaeval House* (1965) 103–21. Incidentally, the bay plinth is chamfered whereas the original hall plinth is moulded, while the ceiling pendant with Middleton's rebus could have been readily brought from elsewhere.

7 A second and earlier hammer-beam roof, very probably from one of the abbey's domestic buildings, survives less than 3 miles away, over the downs at Winterborne Clenston, covering a barn within the curtilage of the Manor House of *c*.1530–40. The quality of the roof not only is totally alien to the function of a possibly mid-sixteenth-century building, but pre-dates it by at least a century. The deep but plain hammer beams are supported by curved and moulded braces resting on plain stone corbels. The ends of the hammer beams support verticals to the collar, with the additional support of large moulded braces. This seven-bay structure is a mixture of lavishly moulded reused timbers and plain additions to make good the many missing members. Relocation from the recently dissolved abbey nearby is very plausible, possibly from the frater. A. Oswald, *Country Life* (July 1962); RCHM, III pt 2 (1970) 295. A little to the east, a farm building at Tarrant Crawford associated with the lost (but extremely rich) nunnery there retains a late fifteenth-century roof of plain hammer-beam trusses. RCHM, *Dorset*, IV (1972) 88. A third, all-but-lost hammer-beam roof, and possibly the earliest, just about survives at Tyneham House, east of Lulworth. The village of Tyneham, commandeered by the army and forcibly evacuated, is in ruins and out of bounds. The south-west wing of Tyneham House, the late sixteenth-century home built by Henry Williams, was the service area and end bays of the hall built by the Russell family during the later fourteenth century, though the evidence can only be studied in records. RCHM, *Dorset*, II pt 2 (1970) 301–2; A. Oswald, *Country Houses of Dorset* (1959) 86–8. The surviving collar-beam truss of the hall was braced from short hammer beams, with multi-cusping to the braces and above the collar as at Fiddleford Manor. The partition wall between the hall and offices was entirely timber-framed, with the remains of two central service doorways and a taller stair entry to the chamber above.

A. Oswald, *Country Life* (June/July 1966)
RCHM, *Dorset*, III pt 2 (1970) 191–7
J. P. Traskey, *Milton Abbey: A Dorset Abbey in the Middle Ages* (1978)
H. G. Slade, *Arch. Jour.* 140 (1983) 61–5

MUCHELNEY ABBEY, Somerset

Glastonbury Abbey was superior to its Benedictine brother at Muchelney as an earlier foundation of considerably greater wealth and influence. Both have left few structures commensurate with their scale and regional importance, but Muchelney retains the late medieval abbot's lodging that the older foundation has lost. The church and most of the claustral buildings at Muchelney have been reduced to foundation level, but the lodging is incorporated in a conglomeration of buildings of the thirteenth to fifteenth centuries

south of the cloister. That they remain at all is entirely a consequence of their use as farm buildings from the mid-sixteenth to the early twentieth century. The district is still extensively farmed and subject to winter flooding that emphasises a still isolated community.[1]

From the abbey church site, the buildings look undistinguished, but from the south side they take on an entirely different aspect, with a boldly buttressed façade with large two-light windows, continuous string courses, and an embattled parapet with gable head behind. This small but complex site divides into three units in line. From the south, the visitor can identify the fourteenth-century kitchen block, the taller fifteenth-century abbot's lodging extending to rooms over the south cloister walk, and the contemporary but ruined ground-floor rectory.

The kitchen was initially almost square and was open to the roof. Much of the front facing the visitor is a farmhouse rebuild, with the nineteenth-century half reusing late medieval windows. Internally, the raised cruck roof is attributable to the early fourteenth century, as are the serving hatches and gable-end window.[2] Early in the fifteenth century,[3] the room was divided into two by a substantial stack with back-to-back hearths to create the east and west kitchens, the larger one serving the abbot's hall in the lost west range. A century later, a two-storey block of some aesthetic standing was added at the north-west angle.

Two sides survive of the ground-floor refectory, 55 feet by 23 feet, open to the sky. All the windows were in the destroyed south wall, with each of the four bays of the solid wall opposite backing on to the cloister walk filled with blind tracery panelling imitating the window pattern of five lights with cinquefoil heads above and below the transom.[4] Attributable to the years either side of 1500, the dais bay has been destroyed but the two doorways in the lower end wall are of different periods. One is fourteenth century, filled with reused material and a modern door: the other is *c*.1500 with panelled jambs, now blocked. They both open into the same large ground-floor chamber of the late fifteenth-century abbatial lodging.

The layout of the abbot's lodging is not immediately apparent, through the incorporation of earlier structures and post-medieval changes. The ground-floor room exemplifies the problem. It is lit by two end windows, a smaller and more damaged version of those lighting the chamber above, and spanned by a beamed ceiling divided into six panels. Apart from the refectory doors, there are four further entries – from the south cloister walk via an elaborately panelled archway (and the lavatorium nearby[5]), towards the stair accessing the abbot's parlour above, the multi-moulded doorway to the kitchen passage under that stair, and an entry from the west range (blocked). Six entries into what is now a single room mean partitioning, and in the absence of any obvious ceiling or wall evidence such screening remains speculative. It is reasonably certain that there was a division between the two refectory doors to create an outer lobby, principally approached from the cloister but perhaps from the (blocked) door opposite the first refectory entry.[6] It is possible that there was a further partition from the second refectory entry to the elaborate doorway opposite and the east kitchen via the angled passage under the stair. The outer lobby and possible kitchen passage would have taken up about two thirds of the chamber, leaving the remainder, unheated but with stylish windows, to serve as an ante-room for the abbot and his guests.

596

PLATE 257 Muchelney Abbey: abbot's lodging and refectory from the south

A comfortably wide flight of steps leads to the first-floor parlour, with an entry more elaborate than that immediately below to the kitchen passage. This famous room is lit by two twin-light windows with cinquefoil heads above and below the transom. The windows are set under square hoods externally and rear arches internally, with columned jambs extending to the sill. The upper heads and the four quatrefoils above retain their original blue and crimson glass with the initials of abbot Broke (1505–22). The sumptuous fireplace is in pristine condition, almost as fresh as the day it was cut but with the gentle weathering of age. The decoration above the square-headed lintel includes four quatrefoil panels with fleuron embellishment and two lines of grape and leaf decoration with the upper line extending over the outer columned jambs. Shafts rise to two wonderfully serene resting lions (inserted from elsewhere?) framing a formerly painted area. The beamed ceiling repeats the six-panel form of that below, with each panel divided into four. The oak settle under the windows with short returns is an extremely rare and well-preserved survival *in situ*. With upper and lower linenfold panels, pierced frieze, finials, and at least one locker, it is attributable to *c.*1500,[7] though its somewhat pristine condition suggests that it was 'improved' before its initial recording in the early nineteenth century (pl. 202).

A stair hacked through the wall accesses three small rooms over the cloister walk, taken over by the abbot for his own use. The middle room has a wagon roof, the end one has a collared roof with wind braces, and the third has an eighteenth-century ceiling. The wagon roof retains traces of painted pomegranate decoration while the middle and end rooms retain early sixteenth-century painted evidence of initiation wall hangings (middle room) and damask hangings below a vine-scroll frieze (east room).

The lodging and refectory were built of local blue Lias, with golden Ham stone for all detailing. Dendrochronology has given a felling date of *c.*1465–73 for the roof of the abbot's parlour.[8] This work, attributable to abbot Pipe (1463–89), was slightly later than the comparable development at Cleeve Abbey. It was similarly sited next to the monastic kitchen but smaller in scale, for this abbey's numbers were fewer. There were never more than twenty monks at Muchelney, and though this had fallen to thirteen in 1463 it had increased to fifteen in 1489.[9] There was no room for corrodian lodgings at Muchelney and the abbot's accommodation was more limited, but the tracery detailing was similar, as was the formalisation of the buttressed south frontage – an awareness of Renaissance concepts. In any case, both buildings were comparable in purpose, comfort, and scale with contemporary manor houses, and could be converted into desirable homes less than a century later with the minimum of expenditure.

597

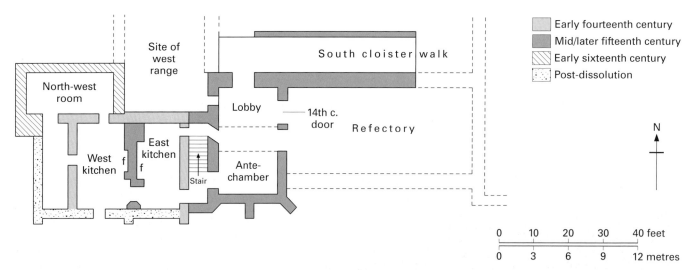

FIGURE 147 Muchelney Abbey: abbot's lodging, ground plan

NOTES

1 This modest settlement retains an important associated group of medie-val buildings including the parish church, the late fourteenth-century Priest's House with early Tudor alterations, the Almonry barn, and asso-ciated farm structures. For the Priest's House, see page 629.
2 Dendro dated to between 1312 and 1333. *Vern. Arch.* 34 (2003) 94.
3 Dendro dated to 1401, *ibid.*
4 A similar mirror scheme was followed in the cloister of Forde Abbey.
5 This identifies the refectory entry rather than that at the other (destroyed) end of the south cloister walk.
6 This may be a farmhouse insertion.
7 P. Eames, *Medieval Furniture* (1977) 213–14.
8 *Vern. Arch.* 34 (2003) 94.
9 VCH, *Somerset,* II (1911) 105–6.

T. Garner and A. Stratton, *The Domestic Architecture of England During the Tudor Period* (1911) 27–9
H. A. Tipping, *English Homes,* Pd II, vol. 1 (1924) 261–70 (from *Country Life,* April 1912)
J. Goodall and F. Kelly, *Muchelney Abbey: Guidebook* (2004)

NAISH 'PRIORY', Somerset

The monastic suffix given to Naish is a late nineteenth-century invention. The surviving parts of Naish Court, now uncomfort-ably close to the residential tentacles of Yeovil, are two adjacent units of a substantial early fifteenth-century house. A hundred years earlier, the property had been occupied by William atte Nasshe,[1] but like Coker Court and West Coker Manor nearby it soon came into the ownership of the Courtenay family. It was they who developed the present structure as a tenancy of their manor at East Coker and held it until the mid-sixteenth century.[2] There has been a considerable loss of essential buildings, so that by the beginning of the nineteenth century it had been reduced to two separate cottages, linked by a single-storey outbuilding.[3] As they stand in line no more than 18 feet apart, they were joined together in the late nineteenth century by an inserted unit, at the same time

as the substantial square stair projection was built. The Victorian work incorporated original windows, a number of corbels as hood moulds, and the octagonal chimneys and pinnacles which have given the house a unity totally different from its original form and layout.

Built of local rubble stone with dressed Ham stone and mainly stone tiled roofs, the two structures were a gatehouse and slightly taller residential unit. Both buildings were two-storeyed with windows of cinquefoil lights, single or in pairs, under square hoods. The single lights have plain hood stops: the paired lights have figured stops and ogee heads to lights flanked by spandrel mouch-ettes. The stair projection in particular is a convincing pastiche, with a reused triple-light transomed window and plain parapet with end pinnacles.

The gatehouse, now entirely domesticated, retains its entry arches. The outer one facing the lane in front of the house has con-tinuous wave moulding to a two-centred head and a hood with end stops (one lost). The door is of the same date with a central wicket and its upper part covered with applied tracery decoration which existed, though damaged, in 1857. Above is the spectacular oriel rising from two fan conoids to a line of quatrefoil panels with blank shields below the four cinquefoil lights. The embattled parapet is a late Victorian restoration with added crocketed pinnacles. The entry was flanked by two windows, one a nineteenth-century remake, but the entry arch and oriel springing from the door moulding are of single build. The rear arch, in contrast, has a line of blind trefoil panels between hollow chamfers, and no provision for a door.

The ground floor is divided into two rooms, both with nine-teenth-century fireplaces, windows mainly of the same period, and the larger room with a ceiling of (altered) moulded beams. There was initially a passage between the two arches, flanked by a room on either side, of which one passage wall has been taken down and the original entry to the other replaced.

The approach to the upper floor has been lost, but the Victorian stair replaced a newel of which the slight projection and first-floor 'squint' are evidence.[4] The upper floor – parlour, corridor, and

PLATE 258 Naish 'Priory': gatehouse from the north

ways, a narrow ground-floor entry with wave moulding and that above, discovered in the 1980s, with a plain chamfer. Both were external approaches into the west building rather than internal doorways. Furthermore, the lower part of the wall at the south-east angle is original, now with the blind head and hood of a Victorian doorway as shown in 1894,[7] since modified as a window. The short stem of original moulding in the angle and the corbel immediately above suggest there was a particularly imposing doorway here originally.

The west building was narrower than the gatehouse, 23 feet by 11 feet, with diagonal end buttresses, and had a single room at each level. The two ground-floor doorways are original, as is the south window. That opposite is Victorian, as are the beamed ceiling and fireplace. The end of the room is partitioned for a nineteenth-century stair, but the two half-landing lights suggest the position of a previous stair. The upper chamber, now ceiled, was originally open to the three-bay roof of plain collar beams and a single line of wind braces. This is a plain roof, lacking even chamfered principals. All the windows are original, with shutter rebates, including the trefoil light in the pinnacled gable end.

What are we to make of these separate units? Both structures were contemporary and, on the basis of the wave moulding and the horned headress of the window corbel, attributable to the first quarter of the fifteenth century. In 1979, R. G. Gilson put forward two alternative suggestions for the house layout. The first was that a hall and kitchen block filled the gap between the two units, extending southwards on the site of the present lawn, with a first-floor gallery to the 'chapel'.[8] The second was that a main range ran southwards from the south-west corner of the gatehouse, with its gable wall in line with the postulated 'chapel gallery'.[9] Apart from the uncomfortable proximity of a hall range next to the gatehouse, its external plinth precludes any substantive infilling between the two units, while the need for a chapel gallery is doubtful. The gatehouse was more probably a free-standing unit with a tight newel approach to the high-quality upper chamber. The function of the west building is unclear, but there was an extension from its south-east corner, with the destroyed ground-floor doorway opening into a corridor or elongated chamber with narrow entries into this building at both levels.

It is difficult to determine the original layout of Naish Court in the absence of any documentary or excavated evidence identifying the hall, solar block, or kitchen position, but this property of the Courtenay family was considerably larger than the present units indicate. In 1633, Thomas Gerard stated that it was 'an ancient gentleman's house', suggesting that it was still of some considerable scale at the time.[10] Just over 200 years later, the notebook of a local antiquary, James Fussell Moore of West Coker Hall, made up of hearsay and gossip in the later 1840s, records that one of the windows at West Coker Hall was 'of Nash, the part that falled down, time past'. The notebook also states that the gate passage opened into 'a sort of court' and that there were formerly buildings with 'fine great windows, fine carved windows . . . two great doorways, all gone, all gone'.[11] What is not in doubt is that the gatehouse was of particularly high quality with fine architectural detailing, while the lack of original fireplaces and the simple roof of the west building point to accommodation of lower status in a house with a layout yet to be determined.

bedroom – was originally a single chamber with two fine windows. The oriel has already been noted but there is a good-quality twin-light transomed window in the end wall with cinquefoil heads above and below the transom, a quatrefoil above, shutter hinges, and two particularly fine head stops of a bearded man with a crown and a woman with a horned headress. The bedroom and corridor are ceiled and characterless, but the parlour with its Victorian wagon-shaped roof is usually described as the chapel. This is on the evidence of the 'squint' and some ecclesiastical items recovered during the Victorian restoration, including an altar and the remains of a stone crucifix and screen fragment found under the floor.[5] However, there is no piscina, aumbrey, or other structural evidence, the altar was not identified as specifically from this room, while the site interpretation of the fragments is suspect.[6]

The Victorian link joined the two independent units, with a single room at both levels, without destroying material evidence. The west ground-floor door forced through the gatehouse broke the external plinth, indicating the absence of any abutting structure. The opposite wall of the west building retains two original door-

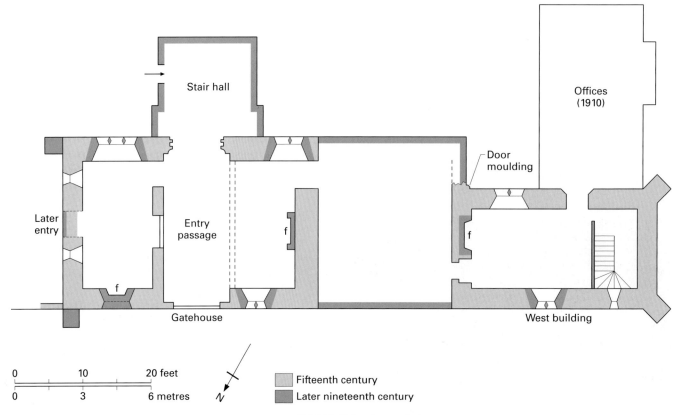

FIGURE 148 Naish 'Priory': ground plan

NOTES
1 Batten (1894) 175.
2 At the close of Henry VII's reign, Naish was held by James Courtenay, second son of Sir William Courtenay (d.1512). *Ibid*. 177.
3 *Ibid*. 174.
4 The side walls of this projection incorporated two stepped buttresses shown in W. W. Wheatley's engraving of 1849. They may well have been a late addition, with the east one incorporating part of this newel.
5 G. Troyte Chafyn-Grove, *Proc. Somerset Arch. and N. H. Soc.* 45 (1899) 51; 56 (1910) 33–5. The altar was removed to East Coker church.
6 The comments of G. T. Chafyn-Grove, the owner of Naish 'Priory', *ibid*. are applied to a conflation of deposited items. The stone crucifix was donated to Somerset County Museum by Rev. Penny in 1879. The wooden screen fragment was given by Chafyn-Grove twenty years later without details. The two large oak doors also mentioned by him covered with scriptural subjects in high relief as from Naish 'Priory' were probably the two carved oak panels deposited in Taunton Museum by George Bullock, *Proc. Somerset Arch. and N. H. Soc.* 24 (1873) 71. They seem to have been subsequently returned, according to a letter from the Museum Registrar to the author, July 2002. Chafyn-Grove also gave Naish Court its monastic origins, considered the west building to be a dormitory, and attributed its construction to the early fourteenth century.
7 Photograph in Batten (1894) opp. 174.
8 Report by Gilson (January 1979).
9 Report by Gilson (April 1979).
10 *Gerard's Description of Somerset*, 1633, ed. E. H. Bates, Somerset Record Society 15 (1900) 82.
11 Quoted by Sir R. de Z. Hall in *Proc. Somerset Arch. and N. H. Soc.* 106 (1962) 95. See also page 680, West Coker Manor.

J. Batten, *Historical Notes on Parts of South Somerset* (1894) 173–81
R. G. Gilson, Report on Naish Priory (January 1979), NMRC, Archive no.41794
R. G. Gilson, *Journal of the Yeovil Archaeological and Local History Society* 1 no.2 (April 1979)

NEWTON ST LOE MANOR and SUTTON COURT, Somerset

These two fortified houses, early fifteenth-century structures 4 and 11 miles west of Bath respectively, are both associated with the St Loe family. The defensive manor house within Newton Park stands a little distant from Stiff Leadbeter's mansion of the early 1760s for the Langton family. In the late 1940s, the mansion and manor house were taken over by Bath City Council for a teacher training college so that they are now surrounded by the many utilitarian buildings of Bath Spa University College.

Three elements remain of Newton St Loe, seen in reverse order of construction – a seventeenth-century outer gateway and stable block, an early fifteenth-century gatehouse, and a contemporary tower. More striking than the buildings is their position on a steep-sided spur above the Corston Brook, in a setting that was landscaped by Capability Brown and enhanced with an impressive lake. In creating this scenario, Brown demolished all the remains of the fortified house except the two standing structures, which he 'touched up'.

PLATE 259 Newton St Loe Manor: tower from the west

The mid-seventeenth-century gateway with its low archways opens into a plain rectangular court, formalised in the mid-eighteenth century. Opposite this outer entry stands the very early fifteenth-century gatehouse, with two eighteenth-century frontal piers supporting a turret at each end of a corbelled parapet of the same date (pl. 198). This two-storey entry retains a four-centred arch, a portcullis groove, a single circular gun port, and a pair of possibly original studded doors with wicket entry. It has the character but not the strength of defence. It opens into a two-bay vaulted passage with foliated bosses at the rib junctions and capitals, with chamber above. The porter's lodge and storeyed side block were refenestrated in the seventeenth century.

Though Leland noted that Newton St Loe was 'a faire maner place like a castelle building',[1] nothing survives of the inner court apart from the four-storey tower standing back from the promontory edge. The facing side is blank, broken midway by a half-round stair turret rising the height of the building, and the gable roof line of a supporting building. Moving round the tower, it is essentially seen to be of Elizabethan character, with the single room on each upper floor lit by large multi-light windows in the east and south faces, and with a contemporary Tudor projection on the north side. The parapet with its exaggerated crenellations and gargoyle heads is essentially eighteenth century, as is the rear porch.

The tower was built in the early fifteenth century. The ground floor has a four-centred doorway, a blocked loop in the east wall, and a garderobe nearby.[2] Higher blocked windows can be traced but only the tiny trefoil lights to the newel are untouched. The newel served all floors, a single room in each case, with the Elizabethan projection, possibly originally for garderobes, converted into a

modern stair serving the now characterless seminar rooms on the three upper floors.

The St Loe family held the manor until 1375, when it passed through marriage to William, Lord Botreaux (d.1395), whose successor was responsible for the present buildings. They were certainly completed before his granddaughter carried the manor to Robert, Lord Hungerford (d.1459).[3] Excavations between 1975 and 1985 revealed thirteenth-century artefacts and masonry buildings and an almost total rebuilding to a quadrangular plan attributed on broadly based grounds to the years either side of 1400.[4] The gatehouse was in the middle of the west range. The ground floors of the south and west ranges were used for stabling and storage, with residential apartments above including a tiled hall and a chapel close to the still-standing south-east tower. The north range was largely given over to services, which extended to the gatehouse.[5] Though the defensive site position had been long established, the excavators found no traces of a moat and the defensive elements were not formidable – loops instead of ground-floor windows, a crenellated parapet and wall-walk, and a mildly strong gatehouse. In terms of design, Dr Arnold places Newton St Loe Manor between the defensive Bolton Castle and the unfortified Dartington Hall.[6] It is not unlike a miniature version of Farleigh Hungerford Castle though there is no immediate parallel in the region. Unusually, the towers are square rather than the preferred round form of southern England.

Though *Sutton Court* at Stowey-Sutton was held by William Sutton during the early fourteenth century, the property had passed to Sir John St Loe by 1429, a cadet branch of the St Loes of Newton St Loe. Sir John's family held the property for well over a hundred years, before it passed in 1558 to Bess of Hardwick through her third husband, Sir William St Loe. Sutton Court is primarily a Victorian Tudor-style mansion by T. H. Wyatt (1858–60) and none the better for that. He retained the late medieval entry tower and Bess of Hardwick's adjacent residential block (dated 1558) but swamped or destroyed almost all earlier work.[7]

The rubble-built rectangular entry tower is three-storeyed but is dominated by the taller circular newel turret of diminishing height. Not unlike the south-east tower at Newton St Loe Manor, the entry doorway is set in a square frame, as are the two lights above, cinquefoil (first) and trefoil (second floor). This unremarkable structure, with renewed battlements, was probably the work of the first St Loe occupant.

The 11 foot high embattled wall enclosing two sides of the forecourt to the house is rarer, and the only element of potential defence. It is of the same red sandstone as the tower, and the present plain entry is an insertion, for the wall formerly extended round the whole site, though now replaced by terraces on the south side.[8] A similar embattled wall formerly enclosed Clevedon Court.

Leland seems to have made this 'old maner place' one of the bases for his Somerset tours,[9] for the detailed historical and architectural survey that the house warrants will surely reveal considerably more late medieval evidence under its Victorian garb. This may well prove more valuable than the remains of Newton St Loe Manor.

NOTES
1 *Itinerary*, V, 103.
2 The barrel vault is eighteenth century.
3 A. W. Vivian-Neal, *Proc. Somerset Arch. and N. H. Soc.* 94 (1948) 10–15;

D. W. Humphreys, *The History of the Manor of Newton St. Loe 1066–1945* (1967).

4 Arnold (2001) 87–9.

5 *Ibid*. 66.

6 *Ibid*. 112.

7 His Victorian hall incorporates the trefoil-panelled arch of an early Tudor bay window like that at Lytes Cary, and some late medieval roof timbers and angel corbels are known to exist. Sir Edward Strachey recalls the form of the house before it was overwhelmed by Wyatt's redevelopment programme: (1867) 86–7.

8 Strachey (1867) 83–4.

9 *Itinerary*, V, 103.

Sir Edward Strachey, *Proc. Somerset Arch. and N. H. Soc.* 14 (1867) 82–102

H. A. Tipping, *Country Life* (January 1910)

R. Cooke, *West Country Houses* (1957) 166–8

R. Dunning, *Some Somerset Country Houses* (1991) 105–9

C. J. Arnold, *Proc. Somerset Arch. and N. H. Soc.* 143 (2001) 57–115, replacing *ibid*. 124 (1980) 77–86

NORRINGTON MANOR, Wiltshire

Hidden in a downland valley on the edge of Cranborne Chase, this substantial but isolated late fourteenth-century house has lost some of its former glory. Hall and projecting cross wings were generously proportioned, and though the hall stands relatively complete, both end units have been rebuilt. Most of the upper residential block was redeveloped in the late sixteenth century, while the offices and chamber above were rebuilt during the following century. Unity was achieved by the common use of squared blocks of grey/white Chilmark stone. Yet despite these fundamental changes, Norrington Manor intrigues – its retained isolation for one thing, the atmospherically abandoned Elizabethan chamber block for another. Furthermore the hall is still regularly used by the family, the fifteenth-century porch makes a personal statement, while the existence of a large fourteenth-century vaulted undercroft surprises.

The construction of Norrington Manor can be attributed on architectural grounds to the early years of Richard II's reign, after the property had been sold to John Gawen in 1377. He or his son of the same name was sheriff of Wiltshire in 1399 and his family held the manor until 1659, when it was sold to Sir Wadham Wyndham, whose successors held it for a similar period until 1952.[1] The buttressed and soberly fenestrated hall, 43 feet by 23 feet internally, commands the approach. The stepped buttresses flank the dignified transomed windows of twin trefoil lights under a quatrefoil head with ogee-shaped tail. The three windows on the entry side and the two on the north side are under four-centred hoods with head stops, but there are no internal rear arches and window seats only on the sunny south side. Upper and lower lights were (and are) shuttered, with the window to the porch retaining the original arms of the Gawen family.

The entry is very modest – a plain continuous chamfer and two-centred head – with an inset sixteenth-century doorway. Both contrast with the two-storey fifteenth-century porch that brings a touch of bravura to the earlier restrained structure. Overlapping part of the hall wall, diagonally buttressed and with a plain parapet rising from a gargoyle-embellished string course, the decorative

qualities of this porch are underlined by the outer entry of three continuous hollow mouldings separated by fillets, set in a rectangular frame. The porch is vaulted, with thick chamfered ribs rising from head-supported capitals to meet at a cusped central circle with an animal's open mouth. This statement-making structure was possibly built by a mason who had previously worked on the mid-century additions for bishop Beauchamp at his Salisbury palace.

Though the hall framework is original, the screen wall, fireplace, roof, and withdrawing chamber entry are all later replacements. During the mid-fifteenth century, the approach to the upper residential block was enlarged with a tall arch with continuous roll and hollow moulding to a four-centred head.[2] In Elizabeth I's reign, the end-wall fireplace was inserted at the same time that the residential block behind was rebuilt, possibly by Thomas Gawen (d.1604). However, the head of the right-hand jamb is part of a four-centred arch suggesting that an end-wall fireplace may have been original to the hall, as it was at Dartington Hall. After an extended period of disrepair when the house was 'now almost in ruins',[3] the present flat ceiling was inserted in the early nineteenth century, resting on four rough beams leaving no evidence of the original structure.[4] The screen wall is a 1959 insertion to ceiling height, creating an unduly wide cross passage with chamber above.

The upper residential block and associated stair lobby are an Elizabethan rebuilding to upgrade the family accommodation. The ground-floor chamber was given an elongated south window, fireplace, and forced entry (blocked) from the hall. The generous upper chamber was provided with ten-light windows at each end and a fine chimneypiece in the party wall, but it has lost its plastered ceiling. Though roofed, both floors have been unoccupied since the eighteenth century and the staircase is destroyed.

The stair lobby is also the approach to the vaulted undercroft abutting the residential block which overrides it at the upper level. Divided into two bays 14 feet deep, single-chamfered ribs rise from low-set capitals to five foliated bosses in the first bay but only two in the second one. Each bay is lit by a single square light. On analogy with the similarly positioned undercroft at Ightham Mote, it is likely that the structure supported a chapel, particularly in a house nearly a mile distant from Alvediston church. On the other hand, comparison with the vaulted chamber at Great Chalfield Manor suggests it may have been for documents or valuables. As the Norrington undercroft stands at a lower level than the adjacent chamber, the possibility must be borne in mind that it may be earlier in the century than the body of the house.[5]

NOTES

1 VCH, XIII (1987) 10–11.

2 Not unlike the similar hall arch at South Wraxall Manor.

3 Colt Hoare (1829) 83.

4 The three lowest rows of roof tiles are stone (as in Dorset) but the whole roof was not necessarily similarly covered, for traces of thatch were found when the present clay tiles were laid in 1960. The house had been previously reroofed in the eighteenth century.

5 The house was landscaped in the eighteenth century, for the south-facing ground shows evidence of terracing when the young River Ebble was dammed to make an ornamental lake. VCH, XIII (1987) 11; Colt Hoare (1829) 82.

R. Colt Hoare, *A History of Modern Wiltshire*, IV (1829) 82–94

VCH, *Wiltshire*, XIII (1987) 10–11

PLATE 260 Norrington Manor: from the south

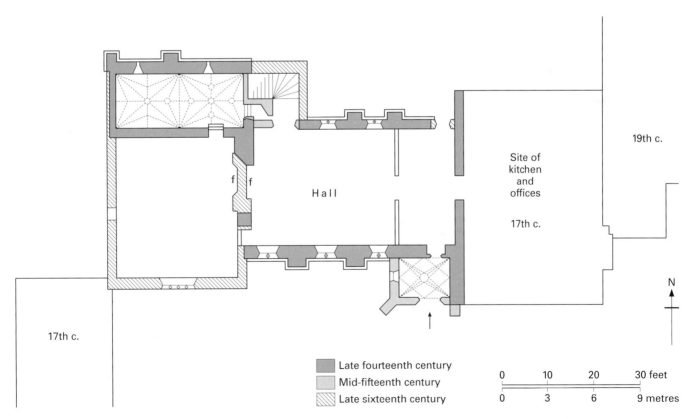

f f

Hall

Site of
kitchen
and
offices

17th c.

19th c.

17th c.

N

Late fourteenth century
Mid-fifteenth century
Late sixteenth century

0   10   20   30 feet

0   3   6   9 metres

FIGURE 149 Norrington Manor: ground plan

603

NUNNEY CASTLE, Somerset

'A rare French-style fourteenth century castle', proclaims the official English Heritage noticeboard at the approach to Nunney Castle, but only the date attribution is accurate. In November 1373, Sir John de la Mare obtained a licence 'to fortify and crenellate his manse at Nonny with a wall of stone and lime':[1] the compact tower-house with walls 8 feet thick and round corner towers was the consequence. The ground and first floors were lit by loops whereas the second and third floors were given single- and double-light windows. The whole was moat-protected, and crowned by a continuous machicolated gallery. The sole modifications in nearly three centuries of intermittent occupation were the enlargement of some of the loops into square-headed windows in the late sixteenth century and the insertion of a grand stair in the north-east tower. The castle was abandoned after a short siege in the Civil War which breached the north façade, though that front only collapsed in 1910.

In plan, the castle is made up of a four-storey central block with bold round towers at the angles, almost touching on the short east and west sides. The walls rise unbroken to the continuous machicolated wall-walk surmounting the edifice. A valuable sketch made in 1646 by a Royalist officer during the Civil War shows that the gallery was embattled, the smaller drum turrets were crowned with conical roofs, and the central block was covered with a single high-pitched roof.[2] The castle was built of local cream/grey oolite ashlar blocks in a well-constructed if somewhat weathered face rising from a low plinth. Most of the fallen masonry of the north front was carried away by the locals, before site clearance was undertaken during the 1930s which revealed that the roof had been covered with stone flags.

The moat initially washed the foot of the walls, for the terrace is a post-medieval addition, probably part of the Elizabethan modifications. The moat would have been crossed by a wooden bridge on the site of the present one, with the entry protected by a drawbridge with its chain drawn through the single vertical slit about 12 feet above the doorhead. The entry is outrageously modest, a doorway with single-chamfer jambs and four-centred head. It opens into a small lobby with decorated vaulted head and mural stair to the first floor. Only the framework of the castle stands, but the character of the north wall is shown in Buckler's drawing of 1822 before its collapse. No internal walls or partitions survive so that its layout is largely speculative, but it is clear that the principal rooms were in the central block with tower rooms opening directly from the angles on each of the four floors (pl. 193).

GROUND FLOOR

The great fireplace of the kitchen lay opposite the entrance, though it has lost its massive stone hood. The well and kitchen drain are in the nearby window, while the shaft rising from this and the next floor apparently extends to the roof.[3] The ground floor was not vaulted, and though the cobbles may be original, wall consolidation in the 1930s eliminated any internal layout evidence. The remainder of the floor would have been for services, with the south-east tower room for stores, aired by the single high loop. All loops are set in wide splays for light access, but none of those on this floor was shuttered: closure by movable frames is likely. The north-east tower was converted into a grand stair in Elizabethan times, with the outline of the treads on the inside wall.

PLATE 261 Nunney Castle: interior from the north-west

FIRST FLOOR

The mural stair opened into an upper lobby in the thickness of the north wall, almost opposite the fireplace. Like the windows either side of it, this fireplace is a late sixteenth-century insertion in a pinker stone than the original, but it may well have been a replacement as the windows were. The south-west and north-east tower rooms have garderobes, with the newel close to the north-east tower accessing the more private floor above.

SECOND FLOOR

The newel terminates in a ribbed and domed vault. The fireplace opposite is a late sixteenth-century insertion replacing the original lower one. Further along the south wall is a second fireplace, now blocked, but with its prominent relieving arch visible. So there were two heated rooms at this level, lit by good-quality two-light windows with retained tracery heads, moulded rear arches, and a window seat on one side. An external examination shows that the lower part of both windows has been built up, so that they were originally taller than today.

THIRD FLOOR

The stair approach is not clear, but it is probable that there were again two rooms rather than one vast chamber on this floor. The outer room was heated by a fireplace with an enriched lintel and both rooms repeated the two-light windows, smaller than but with

FIGURE 150 Nunney Castle: 1644

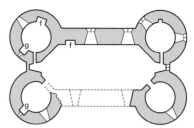

THIRD FLOOR

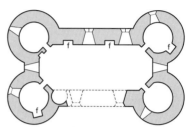

SECOND FLOOR

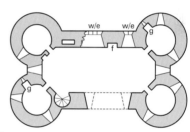

FIRST FLOOR

similar characteristics to those below. It might have been expected that these high-quality rooms would be open to the roof, but the line of plain corbels shows that they were ceiled – whether originally or in Elizabethan times can only be confirmed from scaffolding access. The two east-facing tower rooms have garderobes but the more important south-east tower room has window access and was heated. The south-west tower was an oratory, retaining its altar slab with moulded sill and five consecration crosses under the east window and canopied piscina nearby.[4] The four drum turrets at roof level provided supplementary accommodation.

What was the likely plan of this residence? Internal wall surveys by rectified photography or photogrammetry would help to clarify the evidence, but that at ground level is fairly clear. More than half of this floor was taken up by the kitchen, with the remainder devoted to two loop-lit service rooms. The two frontal tower rooms, with two and three loops respectively, may have been for staff accommodation.

It might be expected that the floor above, similarly with restricted light (until the late sixteenth century), would have been used for staff, with the well-lit hall on the floor above. This was the assessment of Stuart Rigold, who correctly pointed out that window size and external character were usually indicative of occupational status within.[5] Any alternative is equally speculative, but it was axiomatic of fourteenth-century planning that the kitchen and services should be as close to the hall as possible and not separated from it by a line of apartments, whether in horizontal or vertical mode. Furthermore, carrying food from the ground to the second floor via a mural stair, along a passage, and then by a tight newel would have been cumbersome. It is not unlikely that the mural stair opened directly into the heated hall, with the east end partitioned for service (possibly between the two shuttered loops, now blocked). Admittedly, the hall would have been dark, but so was that in the tower-house at Stafford Castle (1348–c.1368) with which Nunney has some affinity. This limitation was particularly noted by Leland in about 1545, when he also commented on the narrow stairs which the Elizabethan owners subsequently rectified.[6]

The second floor was divided into two good-quality chambers, roughly of equal size, an outer and an inner chamber, more lofty than those below, well lit, and heated. Functional titles become

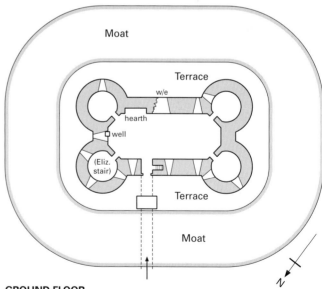

GROUND FLOOR

w/e late sixteenth century
window enlargement

0 10 20 30 40 50 feet
0   3   6   9 12 15 metres

FIGURE 151 Nunney Castle: floor plans

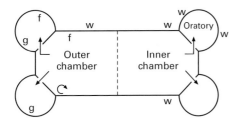

THIRD FLOOR

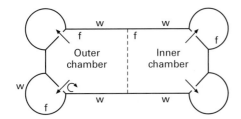

SECOND FLOOR

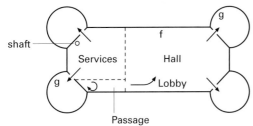

FIRST FLOOR

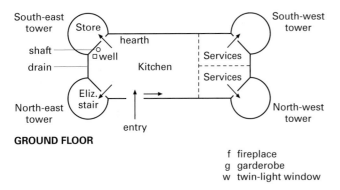

GROUND FLOOR

f fireplace
g garderobe
w twin-light window

FIGURE 152 Nunney Castle: suggested layout

guesswork but each chamber was supported by a heated tower room. The third floor was again divided into two, the heated outer room with two good-quality tower rooms leading off it, and the unheated inner room (bedchamber?) with the oratory opening off it. This floor would have been the most private accommodation for de la Mare and his family, with smaller windows than immediately below and a single light in the lost north wall because of the stair approach.

Writers commenting on this castle have hitherto been limited by military explanation and its 'French style'.[7] Superficially, Nunney looks defensive, with its moat, drawbridge, scaled windows, and imposing machicolated gallery.[8] On the other hand, it is built in a valley bottom, immediately overlooked by rising ground to the north, and encircled by a moat higher than the nearby stream and therefore swiftly drainable. The entrance is not protected by a portcullis or even a drawbar, while de la Mare is not known to have had any militant 'enemies'. What is increasingly apparent is that there was a landscaped approach to his residence. Though the towers and gallery always protruded over the village, announcing their presence as they do today, the approach was from the higher land to the north-west, where the castle would be only partially revealed – not only because of the outer court with its staff quarters and services marked by banks at the rear of the eighteenth-century house nearby but because the body of the castle was concealed on three sides by a 12 feet high wall that no longer stands.[9] Once a visitor had passed through this, only then would the full majesty of the castle be revealed, reflected in the broad moat-washed walls that rose from a fully exposed plinth.

But Nunney bespeaks a further issue, and that is power. Power usually needs to be visible and this is markedly so here. Born in about 1320, little is known about John de la Mare's early life so that it has been surmised that he must have fought in France, even though there is no supporting documentary evidence.[10] By the 1360s, he was a modest landowner, first appointed justice of the peace for Wiltshire in 1367, then sheriff of Wiltshire and of Somerset in 1377, and four times member of parliament. He was knighted in 1373, ten years before he died. It is no coincidence that his knighthood and the crenellation licence occurred at the same time. He had become a 'presence', a locally important person of standing who needed to assert his position clearly in the tenancy that his forebears had long held.

Nunney Castle was one of the several innovative and complex buildings marking the later fourteenth century that include Beverston Castle, Bolton Castle, Wardour Castle, and the Percy tower-house at Warkworth Castle. Externally, Nunney is notable for its disciplined design, almost classical in its formalism. Superficially, the gallery and conical turrets seem to give the castle a French 'character', but that is only because many more examples survive in France than in England, where both features were formerly more common. What they did give to the residence was an assertiveness, particularly when seen from afar. For Nunney was a reflection of its builder – formal, disciplined, and authoritative – while internally, moving upwards went hand-in-hand with moving from darker to lighter rooms and with increasing privacy in a building intended primarily for the de la Mare family and their guests.

The form of the castle has its precedents in central and northern England, most obviously in the keep at Dudley (c.1310–20) of almost identical plan though only two-storeyed, with the encircling wall (formerly present at Nunney) added a generation later. The tower-house at Stafford (1348–c.1368) followed the same concept, with corner towers but an elongated central block of elevated residential chambers. The form had been long established further north,[11] but it is most powerfully demonstrated by the four-storey tower-house at Langley (c.1346). The two-storey house of c.1260–80 at Haughton, though lacking the corner towers of

Langley, was doubled to a comparable height at the same time that de la Mare was making his bravura statement in Somerset. The possibility that Nunney Castle may have had architectural features found in France (and vice-versa, as with churches and monasteries) is not relevant to its significance on its own terms, for Nunney was essentially an English power-house. It was not a passive defence but an inhabited engine of authority – active and alive.

NOTES
1 *Cal. Pat. Rolls: 1370–74*, 367.
2 Brit. Lib., Add. MS 17062. The dormer window shown in the sketch may have been an Elizabethan insertion.
3 Rigold (1957) 11. Wardour Castle has similar internal rain-collection shafts.
4 E. Horne, *Proc. Somerset Arch. and N. H. Soc.* 75 (1929) 108.
5 Rigold (1957) 11–13.
6 *Itinerary*, V, 97.
7 The list extends throughout the twentieth century. French influence is suggested by A. H. Thompson, *Military Architecture in England* (1912) 325, compared to the Bastille as its model by Hugh Braun, *The English Castle* (1936) 107, and given the full panoply of Frenchness by Rigold (1957) 4, 9, and Colin Platt, *The Castle in Medieval England and Wales* (1982) 121–5. It is repeated in T. McNeill, *Castles* (1992) 127. W. Douglas Simpson, *Castles in England and Wales* (1969) 135, and D. J. Cathcart King, *The Castle in England and Wales* (1988) 157, were dissenting voices.
8 Its military capability has been assessed as 'strong and powerful' (D. J. Cathcart King, *Castellarium Anglicanum* (1983) 444) and as showing 'no lowering of the defensive guard' (R. Allen Brown, *English Castles* (1976) 134).
9 It is mentioned by Leland and the Royalist officer in 1644. The wall was unnecessary on the fourth side because of the stream. The only standing building of the outer court is the barn with diagonal buttresses to the two porches.
10 The claim that it was funded from the spoils of war in France was first made by J. Collinson, *History of Somerset*, II (1791) 218.
11 As in the later thirteenth-century castles at Dally, Tarset, and Edlingham. Emery, *Greater Medieval Houses*, I (1996). Matthew Johnson also draws attention to the smaller tower with four corner turrets and possibly machicolations at Mulgrave Castle: *Behind the Castle Gate* (2002) 110.

E. Green, *Proc. Somerset Arch. and N. H. Soc.* 22 (1876) 71–105
C. Hussey, *Country Life* (January/February 1943)
S. E. Rigold, *Nunney Castle: Guidebook* (1957)

OLD NEWNHAM, Devon

Half a mile north-east of the spreading suburbs of Plympton, Old Newnham is the early home of the Strode family before they moved to the much grander Newnham Park, built in about 1700. The late medieval house declined into farm use until rescued from poor condition in the early 1990s. Now in dual occupation with altered interiors, this L-shaped property consists of a two-storeyed manor house with an attenuated west wing, reflecting several building phases but dominated by the extremely tall solar block. It is possible that an east wing paralleled part of the surviving one, but the area is now covered by the converted agricultural buildings of the former farmyard.

This highly interesting house raises several problems which await a detailed architectural assessment. There were at least four

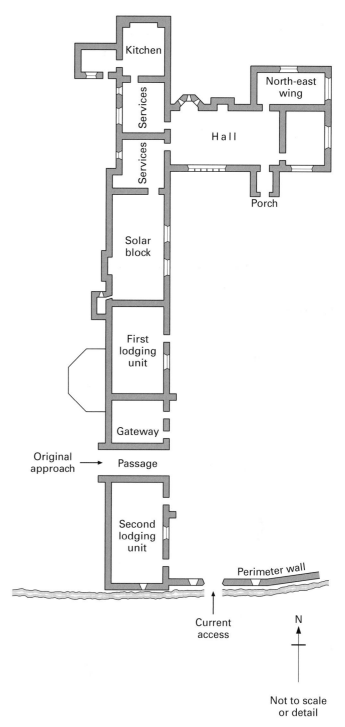

FIGURE 153 Old Newnham: site plan

primary development phases, immediately apparent in the different roof heights but unified by the common use of local grey granite rubble stone.[1] The heart of the house is the early fifteenth-century hall range to the north. The two-storey porch with an inner doorway of continuous wave moulding and two-centred head presupposes entry to the lower end of the hall, and this seems to be confirmed by the canted bay window at the west end, of two cusped lights and a transom to each face. However, this conflicts with the exposure of two doorways with two-centred heads in the west wall, opening into the services with the kitchen in a northwards arm. Either the services and kitchen initially lay in the heavily remodelled area east of the porch, or they were always at the west end and the entry door and bay window have been repositioned. On balance, the latter is rather more likely. The hall was of three bays, open to the roof of four arch-braced trusses. The upper floor of the north-east wing has trusses of similar character with wind braces, an apartment (now divided) associated with the family's personal accommodation. The services have been remodelled but the kitchen retains two original fireplaces, the principal one surmounted by an early sixteenth-century pinnacled vent. This hall range may have been built by John Strode after he had married a Newnham heiress in 1410. A chapel here was licensed by the bishop in 1432.

The original approach to the house was from the west, through the gatehouse block, but the present access lies across the small stream marking the south boundary. The enclosing wall overlook-ing it still stands 5 feet high in places, with low-set arrow slits and possibly a gun port next to the present entry. Part of this wall, with a further arrow slit (blocked), has been incorporated in the gable end of the adjacent range. This perimeter protection was possibly in response to local piratical attacks during the later fifteenth century, while the western side of the house has always presented a barely fenestrated face until farmhouse occupation.

Old Newnham was subject to a substantial early Tudor remodelling, when the orientation of the hall seems to have been reversed. The original fifteenth-century entry was moved to the former upper end of the hall and prefaced by the present two-storey porch, with four-centred outer arch with leaf spandrels. At the same time, the stone fireplace with upswept ogee head was inserted in the rear wall, the canted bay window moved nearby, and the large court-yard-facing window of six unarched transomed lights inserted opposite, between the former and present entries.

The imposing solar block was erected south-west of the newly created upper end of the hall. The ground- and first-floor rooms are lit by two pairs of three-light windows in square frames, the lower

PLATE 262

608

ones with nipped ogee heads (one altered) and those above with uncusped heads to the front and rear. The ground-floor room has high-quality moulded beams with foliage trails, the first floor has a framed ceiling with elaborate bosses, and the original roof is open to the attic floor. Both principal rooms were heated by fireplaces in the rear wall (the upper one like that in the hall), with the stack and stepped chimney terminating in a striking crenellated and pinnacled vent. The projecting garderobe, overlapping the adjacent block, served both floors.

At about the same time, the remainder of the west range took its present form of a 20 feet deep lodging unit, gateway block, and second lodging unit. The first unit with its altered windows has ground- and upper-floor entries with four-centred heads in square frames, the upper one with a wider door marking its higher social status. The outer arch of the gateway entry passage is plain, probably a rebuild, for the inner arch has a four-centred head with mouchette spandrels of similar form to the hall porch. Despite this, the entry block and end unit have pre-Tudor origins, for they incorporate part of the perimeter wall and doorways with single cham-

fers and two-centred heads. The upper doorways have depressed four-centred heads, almost touching the eaves of the lowered roof. The gable end has an extremely well-preserved first-floor garderobe overhanging the stream, retaining its decorative air vent.

The fourth development phase followed the abandonment of the house for the new mansion and its decline to farmhouse status. A floor was inserted in the hall, its roof was ceiled, and the windows were given casement frames. A west extension was added to the kitchen, the solar block was partitioned, unwanted structures were demolished, and the gateway and lodging units were degraded.

Old Newnham is a major fifteenth-century house of a locally important family with a yet unravelled building history. The various types of doorways and windows suggest different social occupational status which would have been emphasised by the forecourt's probable division into an outer and an inner court.

NOTES
1 The earlier work uses a lighter, softer stone for the two-centred doorways and hall bay window.

ıham: from the east

ORCHARD WYNDHAM, Somerset

Orchard Wyndham is a substantial medieval house of complex plan, made more confusing by an extended sequence of post-medieval developments. Over the centuries, it has grown into a figure of eight plan, with two courtyards and forecourt approach. The first court developed in two phases during the fourteenth century and the second in the late fifteenth century, each with its own hall, with the earlier one between the two courts and the later one facing the forecourt approach. This is the form of the house today, with the additions of outbuildings, stables, and coach houses, but it was even larger between the mid-sixteenth and early nineteenth centuries, with an L-shaped wing to the north-west shown in paintings of the house and its landscape in c.1750 by Robert Griffier.[1]

Continuous occupation has led to many alterations, with walls rebuilt or refenestrated, one of the courtyards roofed, internal walls added, and upper rooms ceiled. The greatest changes were made in the 1550s and the 1830s, but there were several lesser phases so that the structural evidence is difficult to interpret. From a medieval point of view, Orchard Wyndham is primarily a house of roofs and emasculated walls but of rare plan, though not helped by the lack of documentary evidence leaving 'historians near to bafflement'.[2]

Five braced-cruck trusses of a three and a half bay hall and end chamber of probable early to mid-fourteenth-century date are exposed in an upstairs corridor and bedrooms. With a span of 18 feet, the hall has been divided horizontally and vertically so that its detailing is concealed. Interestingly, the solar was an unstoreyed chamber with its truss smoke-blackened like those spanning the

hall, showing that both apartments had open hearths.[3] The range to the south-west, marked externally by Victorian gables, also has a jointed cruck roof – a second-stage development. The hall half-bay spanned the screens passage with a service room to the east. This was replaced in the late fifteenth century by the eastern cross range with an arch-braced collar-beam roof and two-light windows with two-centred heads (one survives in a cupboard). The ranges closing the south court also have jointed cruck roofs of fourteenth- or early fifteenth-century date. All the lower rooms were replanned as service rooms and offices by 1838–9, but the upper rooms have been consistently used by the family, some with early plaster ceilings from the sixteenth century onwards.

The most substantial survival is the north range of the second court of c.1490, consisting of a hall with a two-storeyed block at each end in local sandstone. This four-bay hall, 33 feet by 19 feet, is still the core of the house. The approach side was refenestrated in c.1550 and the entry has been destroyed, but early evidence peeps out among the many later changes, such as the lower jambs with hollow moulding of the opposing entry arch from the second court, infilled as a staircase hall in about 1720. A four-centred door has been exposed in the side wall of the buttery/pantry unit (now parlour with 1550s window), with the jamb of a contemporary door opposite. The withdrawing chamber (now library) retains an end-wall fireplace with depressed head and the side of a window, visible externally, with cinquefoil light and quatrefoil spandrel. The solar above (principal bedroom) retains a similar original fireplace behind the present one, the outline of an original window externally, and a door to the now destroyed mid-Tudor wing.

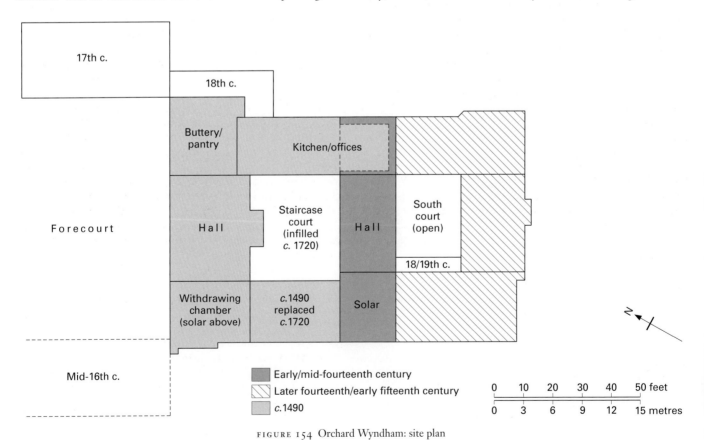

FIGURE 154 Orchard Wyndham: site plan

The plan of the range is clear, but the most striking remnant is the hall roof of collar-truss form with intermediate trusses. The lower braces and wall plate were hacked back when an intermediate floor was inserted in the eighteenth (?) century, removed in the 1950s to expose the original volume and proportions of this hall. The roof lacks wind braces, but the cusped and fleuron strut that fell through a false ceiling in the 1890s is claimed to be one, suggesting that the roof was initially more ornate. Wind braces do survive in the adjacent solar roof of arch-braced trusses, though concealed by the inserted ceiling. This is the most complete of the several medieval roofs, in an extended and complex house which would benefit from a detailed structural survey and a comparison between the roofs and the walling supporting them. It would also clarify the unusual plan of a second hall sited on the further side of an outer court which became the entrance approach.

Orchard Wyndham is close to the sea near Watchet and Cleeve Abbey, but not within sight of it. The house is hidden in a combe and moated, though only lawn depressions suggest this today. This house is particularly instructive as an example of rising standards of accommodation between the early to mid-fourteenth century and the late fifteenth century. The estate was owned by the Orchard family from at least 1287 until 1420, and passed by marriage in 1448 to the Sydenham family of Combe Sydenham. The mid-fourteenth-century work was probably carried out by John Orchard (d.1360), but the possibility that it was the work of his father Thomas Orchard (d.1310), the first of the family to make the house his principal residence, cannot be ruled out. The second hall range was built at the close of the fifteenth century by John Sydenham (d.1521), for Leland records that he 'buildid moste part or almost al the good building of Orchade'.[4] In 1528, the co-heir married Sir John Wyndham of Felbrigg Hall in Norfolk (d.1574), who set about enlarging the house, created the present hall elevation with its three deep recesses facing the entrance approach, and added the further north and west ranges.

The Elizabethan Sir John Wyndham II enlarged the estate and became the dominant local landowner, and inherited Felbrigg. As the family historian Thomas Palmer wrote in 1725 about his children, 'There are now more prosperous branches than there is (or perhaps ever was) of any other family in England, and all or the greater part of them raised by younger brothers born in this old house.' By the second half of the eighteenth century, the Wyndham properties include Petworth, Cockermouth Castle, Felbrigg, Orchard Wyndham, Norrington in Wiltshire, and Trent House in Dorset. Dinton in Wiltshire and Silverton in Devon became further houses of the Somerset branch of the family after Orchard Wyndham was detached from the Sussex group of estates in the early nineteenth century. In 1697 there were over sixty rooms at Orchard Wyndham, twenty-three of them service rooms, with more than forty beds, but the destruction of the added Tudor ranges by 1816 brought the house back to its former late medieval shape – except for the seventeenth-century wing added at the north-east angle.

NOTES
1 Three at Orchard Wyndham with further paintings at Petworth House and Taunton Museum.
2 Wyndham and Haslam (1985) 724. Dr Wyndham notes that a house of such significance over seven centuries can seldom have been accompanied by so little hard fact.

3 Report by K. A. Rodwell (1985–6), NMRC, no.44723.
4 *Itinerary*, I, 164. The work also included a chapel built under licence from the bishop of Bath and Wells in 1499. VCH, V (1985) 154.

VCH, *Somerset*, V (1985) 153–5
K. Wyndham and R. Haslam, *Country Life* (March 1985)
R. Dunning, *Some Somerset Country Houses* (1991) 126–8

ORLEIGH COURT, Devon

Orleigh Court, 4 miles south-west of Bideford, is an undistinguished house of substantial scale but disordered plan. Appreciation of its development is not helped by extensive remodelling during the 1870s and division into multi-occupation during the mid-1980s. However, the late medieval porch and hall have survived in splendid state, though best appreciated after visiting Weare Giffard Hall 3 miles away. Both houses are two-storeyed, built of local slate stone, with lofty halls of similar scale and hammer-beam roofs, but whereas Weare Giffard stands next to the village church, Orleigh lies at the end of a Victorian drive a mile north of the parish church at Buckland Brewer.[1]

The Dennis family held the manor from the thirteenth to the late seventeenth century and were responsible for the two-phase development of the medieval house which still forms the centre of the main front. The hall, 30 feet by 20 feet with walls 5 feet thick, dates from the early to mid-fourteenth century. This attribution rests on the two cross-passage doorways. That from the porch is two-centred with four lines of continuous wave moulding, not deep cut, while the opposing doorway to the inner court repeats the two-centred head but with a single hollow chamfer. The markedly thick walls extend to the upper residential block, though its interiors are entirely of *c.*1720 by the Davie family, prosperous Bideford merchants, altered in the 1870s by J. H. Hakewill for Thomas Rogers.[2]

The hall was remodelled during the later fifteenth century, clearly influenced by the recently completed work at Weare Giffard Hall and using the same mason for the outer arch of the two-storeyed porch. It repeats the two-centred head with outer jamb undercut with a continuous branch of vine trails and the inner jamb with fleurons, identical to the decoration of the two west porch arches at Weare Giffard. The 10 feet square porch at Orleigh is otherwise plain, as is the chamber above with its Victorian oriel, replacement single light, and ribbed ceiling. It was initially approached by a newel from the screens but is now reached from an angled stair.

The hall is a lofty open chamber, devoid of any screen or service doorways and with an eclectic mix of post-medieval elements. The single six-light transomed window in the south wall is a late Tudor or early Jacobean insertion, leaving no indication of the hall's original fenestration except for a relieving arch of a high north-facing window in a cupboard. The fireplace is an insertion of the Davie family who acquired the property in 1684, while the panelling is a mixture of Elizabethan and classical character brought from elsewhere in the house in the 1920s. The classical doorway at the north-east corner opening into the generous early eighteenth-century staircase hall to the upper residential block is on the site of the medieval approach.

PLATE 263 Orleigh Court: heraldic animals from the hall roof

The glory of this hall is its spirited four-bay hammer-beam roof. The trusses rise from stone corbels supported on busts, some of them angels holding shields, one of them with the Dennis arms of three battleaxes, and all with paint evidence. Large arched braces rise from the hammer beams to a high collar with open trefoil spandrels and crocketed pendants from the hammer beams. Intermediate arch-braced trusses and two lines of purlins divide each bay into six rectangular panels with straight wind braces in alternating patterns of diagonal and square crosses with central foliated bosses. The roof differs from that at Weare Giffard in having plain wall plates, no foliated cusping to the trusses, and alternative patterned wind braces. It shares with Weare Giffard the line of wooden heraldic animals sitting on the ends of the hammer beams at least until the mid-1980s, but rescued from potential sale and now standing on display above the fireplace. About 2 feet high, these ten supporters (one is a replacement) sit on their haunches with elongated legs and aggressive faces. They were not pegged into the hammer beams but are contemporary or near contemporary with the roof. They also confirm the lower quality of this roof compared with its neighbour, though it probably differs little in date. The Dennis family were never more than minor gentry, and

though they married into several locally important families, this roof marks the climax of their wider aspirations.

NOTES
1 It was this distance from the church that persuaded bishop Stafford of Exeter to grant a licence for an oratory at Orleigh in March 1416.
2 For his son's account of the families who occupied the hall, *Trans. Devon. Assoc.* 58 (1927) 185–92.

PENGERSICK CASTLE, Cornwall

This is not a castle but the only fortified manorial complex to have survived in Cornwall. It consisted of a single residential range of early Tudor date with a defendable solar tower, positioned between an outer and an inner courtyard to the west and east respectively. The original form and extent of Pengersick from the inner courtyard is shown in a mid-eighteenth-century drawing by William Borlase[1] copied from the later sixteenth-century depiction on the panelling in one of the tower rooms. Part of the (later?) inner courtyard wall and modest entry stands,

612

PLATE 264 Pengersick Castle: engraving from the main courtyard by S. and N. Buck (1734)

formerly with stables and services lining some of the walls. The initial approach was from the west, where fragments of the outer court survive with a nineteenth-century farmhouse, recently converted into holiday accommodation.

Borlase's drawing indicates that the embattled hall range was divided into two by an off-centre porch with chamber above. The part next to the solar tower was two-storeyed: that to the right of the porch was single-storeyed with one window to the inner court. This indicates that the hall, open to the roof and possibly with a dais window facing the outer court, was at the opposite end of the house to the solar tower which abutted the offices and retiring chamber above. This was the form and plan followed at Truthall (fifteenth century). The hall range was in ruins by 1790 and all but destroyed not long afterwards, though this action revealed two roof lines on the tower's north face indicative of at least one rebuilding phase.[2] The two-storey domestic unit added in 1920 incorporated short lengths of the outer walls, with the roof positioned to the lower of the two roof pitches.

The solar tower is the primary survival, facing inland rather than towards the sea half a mile away. With walls 6 feet thick, the tower is a dignified, lichen-covered structure with a square stair turret rising above its roof level. It consists of a single room on each of four floors, with the façade of the upper floors marked by rectangular windows of four lights with semi-circular heads under a common hood, a bold string course in line with the embattled parapet of the hall range, and well-proportioned battlements.

The ground-floor entry set in a higher four-centred arch[3] is protected by circular pistol loops, a mini machicolation, and an arched recess with a slot for scalding water and other unpleasant substances to deter attackers. The entry opens on to the spiral stair, lit by small square-headed loops, accessing all floors and the roof. The dark ground-floor chamber is notable for two dumb-bell gun ports in each of its three outer walls.[4] The doorway opening on to the stair at the first-floor level was the approach from the destroyed retiring

chamber over the services. Each of the three upper floors is a good-sized room with a large courtyard-facing window, a small one opposite, an original fireplace, and a garderobe. The uppermost room has windows on each side and the garderobe off the newel. This was a high-quality lodging tower, but all the interior woodwork and all but two ceiling beams were removed in 1920.

The Pengersick family was holding the manor at the close of the thirteenth century, with Henry Pengersick (d.1327) member of parliament for Helston in 1315–16 and 1327. In the mid-fourteenth century, the manor passed through the female line to John Bevill (d. after 1387) and before 1476 to John Millaton (d.1515).[5] The original residence may have been sited on the large platform north-east of the present house which was erected in an entirely new position. The hall range may be attributed to John Millaton, with the tower as secondary work, probably by his son John (d.1551). However, the duplicate lines of the hall range roof indicate that the tower preceded its reconstruction at some point in its development. The labels with the initial W on the top window of the tower may refer to John Millaton's son William, of c.1551–65, but possibly to refenestration rather than initial construction.

For the significance of Pengersick 'Castle' lies in this combination of hall and defendable tower which, if it were not for its position close to St Michael's Mount, could be readily mistaken for one of the many similar tower-houses in Northumberland or Cumbria erected between the mid-fourteenth and late sixteenth centuries. It adopted the same pattern of ground-floor entry, newel stair, and three or four floors, with the principal chamber on the first floor and more private retiring chambers above as at Halton (c.1390), Shortflatt (c.1400), and Hulne (1488) in Northumberland, or Branthwaite (late fourteenth-century) and Clifton (c.1500) in Cumbria, where evidence of an associated but not necessarily contemporary hall survives in all cases. The tower at Pengersick is an alien in the Cornish landscape but it seems to have been erected for the same reason, a mixture of necessary protection from sudden enemy raids, in this case piratical, and a statement of the owner's standing. Built during the early sixteenth century, Pengersick was initially like other houses of the late medieval gentry in Cornwall in showing little interest in defensive measures.[6] The kinsman to Pengersick's added defendable lodging tower is the late Tudor one at Cotehele, built essentially for privacy and prestige.

NOTES

1 Reproduced *Arch. Jour.* (1973) pl. VI opp. 270.
2 Illustrations of tower in *c.*1790 and *c.*1910 in *Studies in Building History*, ed. E. M. Jope (1961) pl. XXI opp. 20.
3 Similar to the south gateway entry at Cotehele (*c.*1495–1510) and the hall entry at Trecarrell (*c.*1500–10).
4 The dumb-bell gunloops are without parallel in south-west England.
5 Cornwall Archaeological Unit (1998) 8–11.
6 It is possible that Trerice consisted of a hall range and solar tower, built by Sir John Arundell (d.1471), though the only evidence today is the thickened walls and a half-cut window of the third storey when the tower was taken down in the 1570s to create a continuous roof line. E. M. Jope in *Studies in Building History* (1961) 206–7.

S. Schofield, *Arch. Jour.* 130 (1973) 264–5
Cornwall Archaeological Unit, *Pengersick, Breage* (1998)

PENHALLAM MANOR, Cornwall

The excavation of Penhallam Manor in 1968–73 revealed a highly sophisticated example of a thirteenth-century manor house. The site lies in a sheltered valley, reached by a pleasant ten-minute walk through woods from the Week St Mary/Poundstock road. The house stands at the junction of two streams, but when the site was stripped of scrub its layout was revealed with textbook clarity.[1] All the walls of local stone, 3 to 3½ feet thick, stood between 3 and 4 feet high, now turf-covered for preservation. The moat enclosing the site, about 20 feet wide but broader on the north side, was also cleaned out and is again water-filled.

The wooden bridge on the site of the original entrance leads via a wide passage to the rectangular courtyard, 55 feet by 60 feet, enclosed on all sides. Each range held an important structure – hall, camera, kitchen, and chapel – supported by associated rooms on a generous scale. The open hall lay opposite the entrance, with still-visible evidence of the lower-end entry and two service doorways, benches against both side walls, a dais with a fixed seat, and a hearth immediately in front of it. The two-storey camera, the earliest extant structure, was at right angles with no direct courtyard entry to ensure privacy. Its low undercroft was approached from the hall area by a short L-shaped corridor with a stair leading to the high-quality private room with mural fireplace on the upper floor. The two-storey extension at the lower end of the camera was a wardrobe with end-wall garderobe.

The kitchen in the middle of the opposite range was supported by a separate buttery, servery, and bakehouse to the north and backed by a pantry to the west. Above the buttery and servery was a high-quality chamber with garderobe, while there was a two-storey lodging with garderobe immediately south of the kitchen. The chapel next to the entrance on the south side of the courtyard similarly retains bench evidence against the side walls, the sanctuary step, and altar position. The gatehouse was at least two and pos-

PLATE 265 Penhallam Manor: foundations of hall range to camera block from the kitchen

sibly three storeys high, and the site was enclosed by a wooden fence round the inside edge of the moat circuit. There would have been outbuildings and stables, probably on the site of the post-medieval farmstead immediately to the south-west.

Penhallam Manor was a substantial house with a clearly laid out plan, and though now surrounded by trees it was originally an exposed site in the valley bottom. The moat and gatehouse suggest a defensive character, but apart from its vulnerable position the moat was only 4 feet deep in places, for these features were essentially for show rather than serious defence. The exterior walls were plastered and lime-washed so that the house would have made an arresting display to anyone passing through the valley on their way to Week St Mary.

The house stands within an early Norman ringwork with its inner bank utilised for the house platform. Building was initiated in *c.*1180–1200 by the lord's camera serving a hall subsequently rebuilt. The wardrobe was added to the camera at the beginning of the thirteenth century. Most of the buildings – gatehouse, hall, service rooms, and chapel – were erected between 1224 and 1236. The excavations revealed that the gatehouse had a counter-balanced drawbridge, replaced by a fixed bridge in the late thirteenth century. The hall had two-light windows with quatrefoil heads in both side walls, with the smoke from the hearth drawn away by a wattle and daub chimney hood. The last phase occurred in *c.*1300 when the kitchen and lodging unit were rebuilt.

Penhallam was one of the principal homes of the Cardinham family for 300 years.[2] Established by the mid-eleventh century, the family grew into one of considerable importance in the region, holding the largest honour in Cornwall. They seem to have used Penhallam only a few times a year, and when the family was not in residence it was maintained by a small permanent team of steward, porter, and maintenance staff. Most of the ranges were built by Andrew Cardinham (d.1256) during the second quarter of the thirteenth century, but as he had no male heirs the property passed through his daughter to the Devon family of Champernowne.[3] It was abandoned during the mid-fourteenth century and gradually fell into ruin. The house disappeared entirely, apart from the moat, until it was rediscovered in the mid-1960s.

Penhallam is a rare example of a thirteenth-century house in

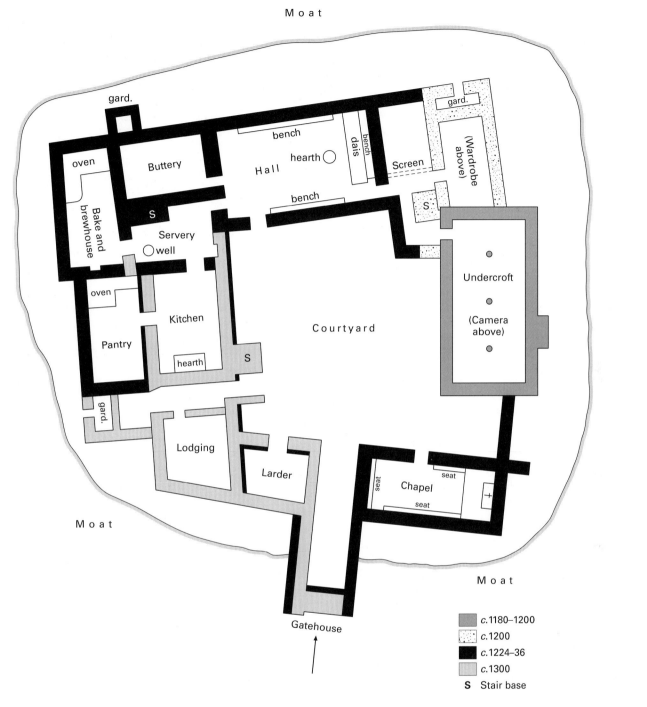

Moat

gard.

oven

Buttery

Bake and brewhouse

S

Servery

○ well

oven

Kitchen

Pantry

hearth

S

gard.

Lodging

Larder

bench

Hall

hearth ○

dais

bench

Screen

gard.

(Wardrobe above)

S

Undercroft

•

•

(Camera above)

•

Courtyard

seat

seat

Chapel

seat

+

Moat

Moat

Gatehouse

N

▬ *c.*1180–1200

▨ *c.*1200

■ *c.*1224–36

▤ *c.*1300

S Stair base

FIGURE 155 Penhallam Manor: ground plan

south-west England, with an outstanding clarity of plan and an absence of later additions. It was generously laid out, sophisticated in the context of the region, and with sufficient structural evidence and excavated finds to enable the purpose of nearly all the rooms to be identified. The garderobes and fireplaces in the family rooms and the spacious layout of the offices were highly developed for the period, and reflect the wealth as much as the importance of the Cardinham family.

NOTES

1 Beresford (1974).

2 The others were at Cardinham on the edge of Bodmin Moor and, from the twelfth century, at the more strategically sited Restormel Castle on a bluff above the River Fowey. Also I. Soulsby, *Med. Arch.* 20 (1976) 146–8.

3 In 1319, their tenant obtained a licence to have mass said in her oratory at Penhallam.

G. Beresford, *Med. Arch.* 18 (1974) 90–145

POWDERHAM CASTLE, Devon

In 1325, Hugh Courtenay, later 2nd earl of Devon, married Margaret Bohun, the daughter of Humphrey, earl of Hereford and Essex. Though her husband died in 1377 at the age of seventy-three after siring seventeen children, his strong-minded widow outlived him by fourteen years.[1] On her death in December 1391, she bequeathed her Powderham estate to her sixth son, Sir Philip Courtenay, who chose a low spur above the river foreland for his new house, situated 6 miles from Exeter on the west side of the Exe estuary. Whatever may have existed beforehand was swept away, and the replacement is attributed to him between 1392 and his death in 1406. There is no confirming documentation but this attribution agrees with the detailing of the surviving structure, which continues to be the spine and frame of Powderham Castle today. The alterations of 1539–40 have left little visible evidence, but the house was extended in a sequence of developments in 1710–27, 1754–6, 1766–70, and 1794–8, with equally extensive work in 1835–47. Yet the original shape and some of the character of Sir Philip's late fourteenth-century house surmounts all post-medieval additions, though it has also stopped all later architects from achieving a cohesive sequence of grand apartments.

In 1835, the 10th earl of Devon marked his succession to the peerage by commissioning the Devon-born architect Charles Fowler to restore and improve the family seat.[2] The 1995 discovery among the Courtenay archives at Powderham Castle of Fowler's papers and ground plan before he embarked on his alterations has clarified and amended earlier interpretations of the building.[3] His work included reversing the approach to the castle, so that it is now reached from Kenton through an operatic castellated forecourt of his making. Originally, the approach was from Starcross to the south, following the line of the estuary, and through the towered entry to the walled forecourt shown in Buck's engraving of 1734.

Superficially, Sir Philip Courtenay's plan is that of a late medieval Devon house – an elongated range made up of kitchen, services,

hall, and upper residential block in line, not unlike the earl of Huntingdon's contemporary range at Dartington Hall but with the kitchen attached to the services instead of isolated from them. The hall porch similarly dominated the frontage, but it is the east wing, north-west tower, and turrets projecting from the upper residential block that add considerable interest to an otherwise standard plan.

Sir Philip's house was markedly tall, seemingly of three-storey height throughout, for though it followed the earl of Huntingdon's hall range in principle, it was more compact (125 feet long rather than 150 feet) through adopting a smaller hall than at Dartington. However, the porch tower had to be four- rather than three-storeyed to rise above the roof line. It now sports what were described as 'improvements' in 1766, essentially a rebuilding in brick. The ground-floor vestibule opens into the hall, though it is difficult to visualise this room's original character since its division in the mid-eighteenth century to create the present marble hall and staircase hall, with a floor inserted above the former for a state bedroom.

The frame of Sir Philip's hall, originally 48 feet by 24 feet and about 50 feet high, survives, including both end walls, but the roof has been replaced and all windows have been blocked or lost. The three service doorways seem genuine enough, but Fowler's plan shows only the eastern one in use, with the other two marked by blocked recesses in the room beyond. Even if all three entries were originally genuine, with the taller central one serving the kitchen passage as at Dartington, their reinstatement and detailing is by Fowler. Nor is it certain there was a second cross door, for the present entry into the central west tower of 1798 is not in line with the medieval one opposite.[4] The square head and relieving arch of a blocked hall window survive immediately above the lead roof of Fowler's dining room. The lights had cinquefoil heads, of which an original single- (above services) and a two-light example (north-west tower) survive little touched, though the hall windows were probably transomed. There were three on the west side of the apartment, subsequently converted into rectangular mullioned and transomed windows in mid-Tudor times,[5] until one was blocked by

PLATE 266 Powderham Castle: engraving from the east by S. and N. Buck (1734)

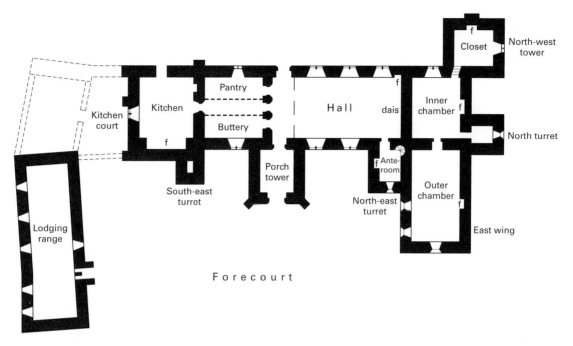

Kitchen court

Lodging range

Kitchen

Pantry

Buttery

South-east turret

Porch tower

Hall

dais

Inner chamber

Closet

f

North-west tower

f

North turret

Ante-room

North-east turret

Outer chamber

f

East wing

F o r e c o u r t

c. **1392–1406**

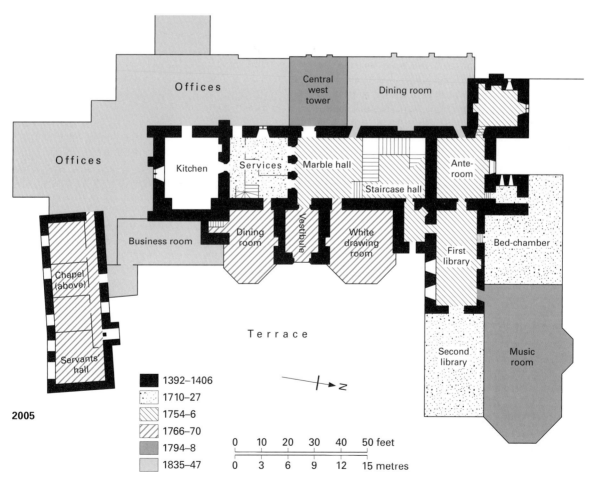

Offices

Central west tower

Dining room

Offices

Kitchen

Services

Marble hall

Staircase hall

Ante-room

First library

Bed-chamber

Business room

Dining room

Vestibule

White drawing room

Chapel (above)

Servants' hall

Second library

Music room

T e r r a c e

2005

■	1392–1406
�	1710–27
▨	1754–6
▨	1766–70
▨	1794–8
▨	1835–47

N

0	10	20	30	40	50 feet
0	3	6	9	12	15 metres

FIGURE 156 Powderham castle: ground plan, 1392–1406 and today

the added central west tower and the other two by Fowler when he modified the staircase hall.[6] In 2001, the chimney of Fowler's dining room fireplace was found to incorporate a second flue from a fireplace at the upper end of the hall, possibly from Sir Philip's time, heating the dais but walled-up when the staircase hall was created in 1754–6.

The relatively low position of the blocked hall window immediately above the roof of the single-storey dining room completed by 1847 raises the question whether the hall was initially open to the roof or always had a floor above it to create the seemingly common embattled roof line throughout the range. A hall of these proportions, as tall as it was long, is unusual but not unknown. A contemporary hall of similar proportions survives at Wardour Castle (c.1393–1400), while that at Minster Lovell (1431–40) is of almost identical proportions, 50 feet by 26 feet, with side walls 40 feet high so that the roof ridge was at a considerably higher level. This was probably the case at Powderham, though a floor may well have been inserted (possibly with heightened side walls and a replacement roof) at the same time as the mid-Tudor fenestration.

A doorway with double chamfer, two-centred head, and door pins opens from the former hall dais into an ante-room in the ground floor of the north-east turret. This accessed the east wing and the newel to the upper floor marked on Fowler's plan, though since converted into a china cupboard. Sir Philip's private apartments consisted of three rooms of increasing privacy – a large outer chamber, a smaller inner chamber, a closet in the north-west tower, and probably a garderobe in the north turret. The outer chamber was totally refurbished in the mid-eighteenth century to become the first library, but the quoins between this and the early eighteenth-century extension (the second library) were recorded in 1867.[7] Fowler's plan shows that the inner chamber had a west-facing window and a north-facing fireplace, until he converted the former into a doorway from his added dining room and ingeniously inserted a window above the latter. The rooms in the tower and turret are at a higher level for stability, with the larger one with an original fireplace and window, and the smaller with retained window frame and shutter pins.

The upper floor was a mirror of that below, but of greater privacy as befitted Sir Philip's personal use. The ante-chamber at the head of the newel has a recut two-light window. The outer chamber (gold room) is entirely mid-eighteenth century, but the inner chamber retains half its entry doorway and a mid-Tudor fireplace under an earlier relieving arch. The north tower has its original two-centred doorway, while the closet room in the larger tower retains an original cinquefoil window and newel to the roof within the corbelled angle.

The buttery and pantry beyond the screens would have been separated by partitions from the central passage, in line with the original kitchen entry of continuous double chamfer, four-centred head, and higher rear arch. The east wall of this kitchen, 26 feet by 20 feet wide internally, is almost entirely filled with a hearth 14 feet wide under a massive relieving arch. The inserted ceiling cuts off the heads of the high windows, one opposite the entry and narrower lights in the side walls.

The approach to the two floors above the services is unclear[8] but it is possible that there was a second-level floor above the kitchen, partly because of its height and partly because the south-east turret shown by Buck has no obvious function other than as a garderobe

PLATE 267 Powderham Castle: north-west tower from present entry court

to such a room. Fowler's plan also shows a small kitchen court bounded by a room on the south side with a markedly thickened west wall.

Fowler's remodelling of the forecourt terrace has obscured the fact that the south-east range is two-storeyed. He retained the superior roof of arch-braced collar trusses with two lines of wind braces, but converted the upper floor into a chapel with appropriate medieval-style windows. Buck shows a multi-gabled range, but the pair of entry doors with single moulding and four-centred heads suggest that this was originally a line of lodgings, 18 feet wide internally. This is strengthened by the discovery in 2000 of a chimney flue to a lost first-floor fireplace in the south wall. As the walls are thinner than those of the main body of the house and at an acute angle to it, this range is probably second-phase work.

Sir Philip's residence was a compact but generously provisioned fortified house, 'strongly built' as Leland noted in 1542.[9] Though gaunt, it lacks the obvious appurtenances of defence. Leland drew attention to a barbican or bulwark as sea defence, but this is likely to have been a late fifteenth-century response to local piratical attacks, as at Berry Pomeroy and Compton castles. Buck shows that the two-storeyed gatehouse was like the contemporary one remodelled by William Wykeham at Broughton Castle, essentially a

618

stylish but modest entry, while the forecourt wall was similarly lacking towers or turrets as in the Oxfordshire house. However, Powderham was protected on the south side by the creek of the River Ken and by marshland on all other sides. It was this that held the forces of the earl of Devon and his supporters at bay in November–December 1455 during their attempt to take the castle.[10] The gatehouse was pulled down in the 1760s at the same time that the estuarine meadows were drained to create the present parkland, though the creek is still liable to flood in winter.

Sir Philip's house was built in a local grey-white limestone in its rubble and dressed form, with slender buttressed walls, cinquefoil headed windows, and an extensive use of relieving arches in local red stone. The contemporary hall range at Dartington Hall was his model, with three-storeyed end blocks, a tall porch tower, and the common use of two- and four-centred doorheads. In his anxiety to build quickly at a time late in life, foundations were minimal, with the north-west tower built on gravel while the kitchen and the east wing were erected on gravel and rock outcrop. The south-west corner of the kitchen has had to be rebuilt in bands of red sandstone while Fowler underpinned the north-west tower to prevent collapse. All parts of the castle are united by a renewed embattled parapet that is as much Fowler as Georgian and medieval.

The similarities between Powderham Castle and Dartington Hall originated in the friendship between the earl of Huntingdon and the Courtenay family. Sir Philip had held the custody of the park at Dartington between March and May 1388, while he and his eldest brother, the earl of Devon, stayed with Huntingdon at Dartington in April 1396.[11] The nature of the three-storeyed upper residential block at Dartington bears on that at Powderham, for although the north-west tower was always three-storeyed[12] and the adjacent block was modified in the early eighteenth century by inserting the present arched windows at three levels, the overall height of Courtenay's structure as shown in Buck's engraving, makes three floors a distinct possibility from the late fourteenth century onwards. All this part of the castle was residential, with the ground-floor rooms beyond the dais possibly used by lesser members of the family. Sir Philip's own apartments were newel-approached from the lower to the upper ante-room leading to a sequence of three chambers of diminishing size with increased privacy. The further rooms above may have been used by guests. The rooms over the services at the lower end of the castle seem to have been on two upper floors, with the possibility of a substantial chamber above the kitchen as at Raglan and Ashby de la Zouch castles (1460s). Sir Philip was intent on outdoing his older Courtenay brothers at Tiverton and Okehampton castles, not only through being thoroughly up-to-date with a generous accommodation provision, but in showing how old-fashioned their residences had become, even though Tiverton had only been built a generation earlier and Okehampton remodelled a little before that.[13]

NOTES

1 *Com. Peer.*, IV (1916) 325–35. The castle has remained in the hands of Sir Philip's male successors to the present day. Two of Sir Philip's older brothers had issue, but as their lines died out in 1374 and 1556 respectively, the junior line became heirs to the earldom. This was not realised until 1831 when William, 3rd viscount Courtenay of Powderham successfully claimed it to become the 9th earl of Devon.

2 The forty-three-year-old architect had recently completed Adam's unfinished state rooms for the duke of Northumberland at Syon House

(1819–25) and the great conservatory there (1827–30). Also D. Presswell, *Charles Fowler at Powderham Castle* (privately printed 1997).

3 There is also a considerable body of Courtenay archives at Devon Record Office, Exeter.

4 In 1835, Fowler reported that the west tower was 'in a carcase state' with bare walls and exposed timbers. It had been left like that by Mr Jones, the builder. In origin, it was probably a mid-Tudor addition contemporary with the hall refenestration.

5 The relieving arch to one of these survives next to the late fourteenth-century evidence. A similar Tudor substitution for smaller late medieval windows in the hall occurred at Knightstone in 1567, at Blagdon Manor, Paignton, and at about the same time at Holcombe Court.

6 At the same time, Fowler made good the lighting of the stair by inserting the lantern above it in a mid-eighteenth-century style.

7 Harding (1867) 177. His claim that the outer chamber was added in about 1450 as a chapel was entirely speculative. The position of the chapel mentioned in bishop Lacy's Register for 1450 and 1455 is not known.

8 The first-floor door with four-centred head above the services is an insertion, probably to a mid-sixteenth-century gallery over the screens.

9 *Itinerary*, I, 232.

10 This siege was a consequence of the murder of Lord Bonville's respected lawyer at Upcott, near Tiverton, by Sir Thomas Courtenay, described as 'the most notorious private crime of the century'. The earl of Devon joined his sons to occupy Exeter, where they robbed and assaulted some of the citizens and ransacked the cathedral's treasure before advancing on Powderham Castle, because Sir Philip Courtenay was an ally of Lord Bonville through the marriage of his daughter to Sir Philip's son. R. L. Storey, *The End of the House of Lancaster* (1966) 165–75.

11 A. Emery, *Dartington Hall* (1970) 22, 98.

12 By Fowler's day, the uppermost floor had disappeared; the earl instructed him to open the two-light window and 'make an exact counterpart of the old one'.

13 The earl of Devon's enmity in the siege of 1455 was probably spurred by his failure to own Powderham through a common ancestor bequeathing it to the junior and not to the senior branch of the family. Storey, *The End of the House of Lancaster*, 171.

Lt. Col. Harding, *Trans. Devon. Assoc.* 1 (1867) 170–83
M. Girouard, *Country Life* (July 1963)

POYNTINGTON MANOR, Dorset

Like Purse Caundle Manor, also near Sherborne, Poyntington Manor is a medium-sized, mid to late fifteenth-century residence, located in a village, next to a stream, and built round three sides of a courtyard. It retains the gatehouse range that Purse Caundle lacks, but no more than the shadow of its hall on the opposite side of the courtyard. The three ranges were rubble-built with Ham stone dressings, with the east range substantially modified in the late sixteenth or early seventeenth century (as at Purse Caundle) when the large square-headed windows were inserted, a form followed again in the twentieth-century restoration.

The two-storey north or entrance range is original, with a high outer entry arch with double-wave-moulded jambs and four-centred head. Above is a two-light cinquefoil window under a square label with head stops, but the gable is a twentieth-century insertion. The inner arch has single-roll-moulded jambs, again with two-light window and added gable above, but the passage retains its original moulded ceiling beams. All the other windows are of *c.*1600

PLATE 268 Poyntington Manor: entrance range, residential range, and hall

except for the one of three uncusped lights in the west end wall above an original doorway with two-centred head.[1]

The hall across the courtyard always seems to have been relatively small, 25 feet by 19 feet. It retains a two-light cinquefoil-headed and transomed window, similar to those of the priest's house at Trent of the 1440s but without the label. Nearby is a deep buttress, next to a blocked doorway with two-centred head. The extension of this block has been remade with an ugly broad entry to the front and a window of four uncusped lights to the rear. The interior of the hall is almost entirely twentieth century – the six-light double-transomed east window, the fireplace, the flat ceiling and modern roof. It is possible that the apartment was always of modest size, with the west extension an adaptation of the services, but if so, it is not proportional to the remainder of the house.

The hall retains a door with two-centred head leading to the mid to late fifteenth-century stair projection accessing the east range. The stair has three twin-light windows with cinquefoil heads under a label leading to a suite of first-floor private rooms. Apart from a two-centred doorway in the entrance lobby, this range is entirely of c.1600, adapted for twentieth-century living.

The entrance block may be second-phase work to the hall and stair projection of c.1460, and though the offices may exist in outline, the kitchen, stables, and outbuildings probably completed the now open fourth side. Poyntington Manor is an example of a late Perpendicular courtyard house of some size and standing, but it was never intended to be a showy residence like Athelhampton Hall. It was a modest gentry house, modified in about 1600. It was subsequently let to tenants, truncated and used for farm purposes until rescued and adapted for a higher standard of occupation during the twentieth century.

The manor of Poyntington was held by the Cheyney family from the mid-thirteenth to the mid-fifteenth century, with all senior members knighted in turn.[2] The eldest daughter of Sir Edmund Cheyney (d.1430) married Sir John Coleshill (d.1484), and on her death in 1490 the estate passed to her nephew, Sir Robert Willoughby, soon Lord Willoughby of Broke (d.1502). It was held by that family until the early twentieth century, though let to tenants and tenant farmers after 1566. It is probable that the present house was developed by Sir John Coleshill and his wife Elizabeth Cheyney, with the early seventeenth-century alterations made by Sir Edward Parham and his wife when the property 'suffered many changes'.[3]

NOTES

1 The late medieval gateway to Bingham's Melcombe is similar to that at Poyntington, rubble-built and two-storeyed with a high-pitched four-centred entry arch with wave moulding. The side buttresses to the front are original but the windows are mid-eighteenth century. This gateway, originally freestanding, was also probably a few years either side of 1500. The remainder of the house, similarly round three sides of a courtyard, is essentially mid-sixteenth century. RCHM, *Dorset*, III pt 2 (1970) 165. The most imposing gatehouse in Dorset stands at the approach to Wolfeton House, a mile north-west of Dorchester. In its present form, the entrance is attributable to the early sixteenth century, but its two round towers with conical roofs (lower than in Hutchins' engraving of 1774) are thrust well forward of the gate passage and are structurally independent of it. Though the first-floor string course continues uninterrupted across the gatehouse block, it does not do so on the north and south sides. The two towers differ in size, their plinths are taller than those of the central block, and they retain gunloops covering the main entrance. Of late fourteenth-century shape rather than of 1500–10, these towers were probably retained from an earlier structure, protected by a moat with water from the nearby junction of the Cerne with the Frome. RCHM, *Dorset*, III pt 1 (1970) 65; A. Oswald, *Country Life* (August 1953); J. Goodall, *Country Life* (August 2002).
2 Lyte (1936) 204–12.
3 T. Gerard, *Description of Somerset*, ed. E. H. Bates (1900) 167.

M. Lyte, *Proc. Somerset Arch. and N. H. Soc.* 82 (1936) 203–16
RCHM, *Dorset*, I (1952) 187–9

PRESTON PLUCKNETT MANOR, Somerset

Like Naish 'Priory' nearby, Preston Plucknett 'Abbey' Manor has no monastic association. The imposing barn at right angles to the manor house seems to confirm the belief that the property was a grange of Bermondsey Abbey and this was perpetuated by a legal case during the 1840s.[1] In fact, shortly after the Norman Conquest, the district of Preston immediately west of Yeovil was divided into two. Part of the estate was granted to the Cluniac priory of Bermondsey, which held it until 1536. The other part of the estate was held by the Maltravers, FitzWalter, and Marshall families until it was bestowed on Alan Plugenet. Since then it has been known as Preston Plucknett, with the other manor identified as Preston Burmondsey. In about 1380, the Plucknett manor was sold to John Stourton, the head of a long-established Wiltshire family who had two sons, William and John. Sir William's immediate successor established the barony of Stourton[2] while John established the junior line at Preston Plucknett until the close of the fifteenth century. The manor had become a farm by 1664 and was subsequently held by a number of local families, including Edward Phelips of Montacute (1725–58) and the Ponsonby-Fanes of Brympton d'Evercy (1762–1920).[3] The land ceased to be farmed when the property was bought by a local building contractor in 1969.

The manor house was built by John Stourton the younger early

PLATE 269 Preston Plucknett Manor: offices, entry porch, and hall

in the fifteenth century, with documentary evidence of its existence by 1420. Nearly six centuries later, the residential tentacles of Yeovil had thoroughly enveloped Preston village, the farmland was developed as housing estates between 1979 and 1999, and the manor and barn are now occupied as the headquarters of a regional property company. These developments have wrought major site changes but the manor had already suffered from drastic modifications. The hall roof was lowered and the dais window shortened between 1841 and 1847 at the same time as rooms south-east of the hall were pulled down. A fire in the 1920s enabled the hall to be restored with a new roof, though retaining an inserted floor. German bombs damaged the building in 1940, with repairs eleven years later, while sequential office developments between 1971 and 2001 necessitated further internal alterations. The consequence is that the Manor looks relatively complete externally (and the barn even more so), but the internal changes have been so extensive that the plan and development of the house must essentially be read externally.

The barn dominates this manorial group with its double offset buttresses, central porch in the middle of the north and south sides, and lines of air vents: plain slits to the north and cruciform slits on the other three sides. The stone-tiled roof is supported by eleven raised cruck trusses with two lines of wind braces. The ten-bay interior, restored in 1972 with a mezzanine floor free of the side walls, is used for the storage of construction materials. This barn, at 104 feet long the largest in Somerset, is attributed to the

early fifteenth century and is probably contemporary with the house.

The Manor, built of local Ham stone, is made up of three units identified by a change in roof line, but only the hall and taller services range are medieval, marked by the octagonal gable chimneys.[4] The commanding two-storey porch is the least altered part of the house. Diagonally buttressed, the imposing square-headed entry, transomed two-light window above, and decorated gable head make a bold social statement. The continuous-chamfer and two-centred doorway of hollow, roll, and wave moulding is set in a square frame with blank shields and foliated spandrels. The early six-plank door opens into a deep, single-bay porch with stone benches and octopartite vault rising from low-set corbel faces. The inner doorway has single wave moulding, as does the opposing cross-passage doorway.

The three-bay hall, 46 feet by 22 feet internally, was less modest than its present divided state suggests. The first two bays on the west side have twin cinquefoil lights in the upper walling and a (restored) transomed dais window extending close to the ground, with cinquefoil lights above and below the transom and quatrefoil head. (The upper lights in the opposing wall are post-medieval, as is the mural fireplace.) The end wall has been rebuilt, eradicating the former fireplace[5] or possible entry evidence to a withdrawing suite of rooms. The striking doorway opposite the dais window, similar to the porch entry, has been brought from elsewhere, with its outer face towards the hall interior. The 1920s roof of arch-braced collars with crown post and three lines of wind braces may be a copy of the original structure.

The destruction of the family apartments in the mid-nineteenth century[6] emphasises the length of the services unit of two offices and kitchen in line. This part of the house is as wide as the hall and stands forward of it to overlap the porch, suggesting a co-eval but secondary development phase. Divided by a wall marked by the frontal buttress, the first of the offices was entered from the doorway near the porch, with an inner entry to the further office. The second cross-passage doorway is in line with the original kitchen entry at the end of a corridor (later converted into a staircase hall). All three rooms have late sixteenth- or early seventeenth-century square-headed windows and modernised interiors, though the kitchen retains its end-wall hearth (holding a safe) surmounted by the famous octagonal louvred chimney, with a second hearth in the east wall. The first room of the drastically altered upper floor retains a fine fifteenth-century square-headed fireplace with a three-part lintel of two blind trefoil lights flanked by quatrefoils with shields.

Stourton's house bespeaks his rising social standing. The porch is of superior workmanship to that of its contemporary at Coker Court, and the hall is an early example of the practice of high-placed side windows and elongated dais window, while the generously planned services gave more extensive accommodation facilities above than usual. Despite the business environment and adjacent residential and industrial development, Preston Plucknett Manor still retains its evocative fifteenth-century grouping of house, barn, grassed court, and buttressed boundary wall.[7]

NOTES

1 In 1841, the estate owner, Lady Georgina Fane, refused to pay tithes on the property as she was utterly convinced that it had once been in monastic ownership. She changed the name to Abbey Farm and took proceedings against the Tithe Commissioners to prove her point. Despite major expenditure on lawyers' fees, she lost her case five years later. The name Abbey Farm survived until 1979.
2 *Com. Peer.*, XII (1953) 296–304.
3 The history of the property was unravelled in 1969 by E. H. Silcox, a local schoolmaster. Copy of his notes held at the property.
4 The single-storey frontal projection is mid-nineteenth century, as is the end unit incorporating a medieval doorhead for a window.
5 Its octagonal chimney, reinstated in the 1920s to serve the inserted upper floor, is shown in a drawing of 1811. Garner and Stratton (1911) 25.
6 The site has never been excavated.
7 A short length of this south wall has been incorporated in a cottage.

T. Garner and E. Stratton, *The Domestic Architecture of England during the Tudor Period* (1911) 25–6
NMRC, no.45627 (2001)

PURSE CAUNDLE MANOR, Dorset

The manor house at the approach to the intriguingly named village of Purse Caundle is a relatively complete, medium-sized late fifteenth-century residence, but its architectural history is as unclear as the derivation of the village name. The house initially consisted of a single-storey hall with a two-storeyed offices and chamber block, and an outsize solar cross wing extending to the street with a contemporary first-floor oriel that immediately catches the eye. Seen from the street, the hall and offices block are in line, giving the house an apparent L-shaped core.[1] In the mid-sixteenth century, a double-gabled block was added in front of the hall façade, refaced in the early seventeenth century when the offices and chamber block was partially refenestrated to match. However, the primary development of this third phase of *c*.1600 was the extension of the solar cross wing, together with three broadly spaced south-facing projections to create a symmetrical E-shaped frontage – a formal façade in comparison with the earlier irregular one.

The manor of Purse Caundle was bought by Richard Long in 1428, but the present house was most probably built by his grandson, William Long (d.1524), who is buried under the canopied tomb in the nearby church.[2] In the mid-sixteenth century, the property passed to William Hannam (d.1576), who was responsible for the alterations at that time, while his grandson extended and formalised the south wing. The house is built of rubble stone with ashlar dressings, with better-quality ashlar used in the early seventeenth century, and all phases united with stone-slate roofs. Leaving the Jacobean addition to one side, the interest of Purse Caundle Manor lies in disentangling the mid-sixteenth-century work from that of seventy or eighty years earlier.

The conundrum of this house lies in two associated problems.[3] The first is that it is difficult to distinguish much of the work of the two early periods because of the adoption of a similar form of doorway with moulded jambs and four-centred head. It might be thought that one or two late fifteenth-century doorways were reset in the following century, and this certainly applies to the porch outer entry, but others seem to be of the later date and one of them has the initials W and H in the spandrels, identifying William Hannam's responsibility. A similar usage occurs in the mid-sixteenth-century alterations to the entrance and screen doorways of the hall at Fiddleford Manor, 7 miles away. There was clearly a preference at that time in this area for this old-fashioned style, possibly through employing the same mason. A close analysis of the slight variations in this doorway form is likely to clarify the details of Purse Caundle's early development.

The second problem arises from the present layout of the house, for the entrance, porch, and screens passage stand immediately adjacent to the impressive solar wing instead of the offices as might be expected, while the bay window at the upper end of the hall is next to little more than a small parlour. At some time, the house layout has been reversed, with the upper end of the hall becoming the lower, and as this is associated with several four-centred doorways to the screens, William Hannam's structural additions in the mid-sixteenth century included reversing the layout of his house.

Only the roof of the hall can be seen from the tight forecourt immediately in front of the house, but the apartment is more obvious from the west garden where there is a dominant five-light window with two transoms and cinquefoil lights. It is, however, an early twentieth-century reconstruction and not an accurate statement of what was previously there. Internally, the four-bay hall, 33 feet by 19½ feet including the screens passage, retains its late fifteenth-century roof, the mid-sixteenth-century reversed layout, and the seventeenth-century panelling inserted in the early nineteenth century after the cross-passage partition and gallery had been erected. The three mid-Tudor additions towards the forecourt – porch, chimney stack with rear closet, and hall bay – have already

PLATE 270 Purse Caundle Manor: from The Street

been noted externally but the employment of continuous moulded jambs and four-centred head extends from the fireplace to the adjacent closet doorway (with initials), and the plainer inner porch and pair of service entries. The stone panelled arch at the north end of the hall was intended to emphasise the new upper end of the apartment, and at the same time provide a dining recess with its own fireplace.[4] The hall roof consists of five arch-braced collar trusses with raking struts. Tie beams with a central vertical post were subsequently added underneath, with the beam ends inserted in the wall below the moulded plate. Above the wall plates is a quatrefoil frieze, and curved wind braces in pairs, cusped lozenge shape (lower) and plain two-centred arches (upper).

A single central entry accesses the former offices from the present upper end of the hall, now united in a single early seventeenth-century panelled room with original end-wall fireplace and later six-light window. The chimney breast is integral with the early rubble end wall, but it is unlikely to have served as the kitchen. It is possible that the wing extended further westwards (now covered by an early seventeenth-century extension) or eastwards parallel with the solar wing. If so, it was truncated in the mid-sixteenth century and reroofed in about 1600[5] when it was converted from a cross wing to an in-line structure with the hall and this apartment's roof strengthened with tie beams.

Apart from the hall roof, the most striking feature of this manor house is the late fifteenth-century solar wing. Both floors have square-headed two-light windows (restored) but the principal upper chamber terminates in the street-facing oriel. This striking three-sided, corbel-supported window has four cinquefoil lights above four blind quatrefoil panels with blank shields. To the south, the diagonal buttress is partly enveloped by an almost contemporary two-storey extension. The first floor retains its two-light uncusped window, but the remainder was modified in c.1600 to harmonise with the rest of the south frontage. Internally, the ground floor of the solar wing formerly consisted of two rooms, but the present accommodation reflects the post-medieval conversion into offices and kitchen.[6] The great chamber above retains its original five-bay wagon roof with carved bosses at the intersections and a highly striking leafy William Morris style wallpaper.

Purse Caundle Manor shares with Poyntington Manor the common characteristics of a medium-sized property, datable to the late fifteenth century, in a village situation, built round three sides of a rectangle with an enclosure wall on the fourth side (removed at Poyntington). Neither house is architecturally distinguished, but the mid-sixteenth-century and early seventeenth-century additions at Purse Caundle are highly conservative, giving the house a unity of materials and style. This helps to conceal its architectural history,

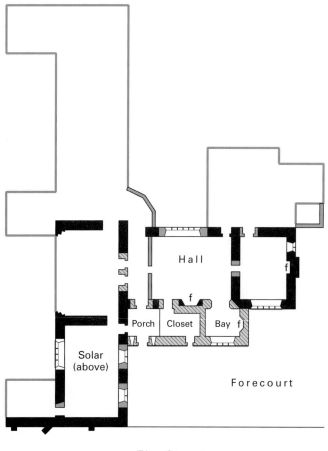

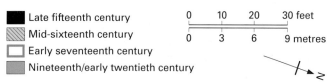

The Street

■ Late fifteenth century
▨ Mid-sixteenth century
□ Early seventeenth century
▦ Nineteenth/early twentieth century

0   10   20   30 feet

0   3   6   9 metres

N

FIGURE 157 Purse Caundle Manor: ground plan

and Antiquities . . . of Dorset (1815 edn) IV, 148, is usually thought to have been next to the hall fireplace, but it may well have been the approach to the great chamber and lain at the south-west corner of the hall. Its position is now marked by an early nineteenth-century angled passage.
7 Lord David Cecil, *Some Dorset Country Houses* (1985) 90.

A. Oswald, *Country Life* (November 1963)
RCHM, *Dorset*, III pt 2 (1970) 236–8

RIALTON MANOR, Cornwall

The manor is sited in a sheltered valley less than 3 miles from the Atlantic coast and the Victorian resort of Newquay. The unassuming rear façade, seen from a bend in the road, gives no indication of Rialton's quiet dignity, hidden behind its enclosing wall from the sprawling seaside resort nearby.

Domesday Book records that the manor was the largest held by Bodmin Priory, but it had been chosen as one of the prior's residences by 1283. There is no documentary evidence for the house's development. The low north range, built in the mid to late fifteenth century, consisted of a hall open to the roof, with a service and chamber block at the lower end. This was the same layout as at Truthall and Medros manors, but as at Medros the services room at Rialton was also the kitchen. During the early sixteenth century, prior Vyvyan (1508–33) added the imposing multi-windowed projection, the house's principal external feature, which overtops the lower roof line and was finished with an embattled parapet.[1] He was also probably responsible for the two wings which converted Rialton into a small courtyard residence. The hall was divided horizontally and vertically during the later sixteenth or early seventeenth century, and was subsequently used as a farmhouse. The wings were pulled down after the 1820s and all the windows replaced except for those in Vyvyan's porch.[2]

PLATE 271 Rialton Manor: prior Vyvyan's front projection

which was probably more complex than outlined here. But at the same time, this harmonious development by at least three generations more than a hundred years apart helps to make Purse Caundle Manor 'at once age-old and serene, mellowed not ravaged by time'.[7]

NOTES
1 The street is a minor road that was no doubt a track which formerly crossed the forecourt until it was curtailed to give the house greater privacy.
2 Richard Long was followed by his son John, who is mentioned in a deed of 1454, but their deaths are not recorded. The Longs may have been a collateral branch related to the Henry Long (d.1490) who probably initiated South Wraxall Manor, which has a gatehouse oriel not unlike that at Purse Caundle.
3 Ignored by RCHM, III pt 2 (1970) but recognised by John Newman, in J. Newman and N. Pevsner, *Buildings of England: Dorset* (1972) 354–5.
4 Similar dining recesses of this date occur at Bingham's Melcombe and Lytes Cary.
5 The first-floor room ceiling retains its fifteenth-century beams.
6 The stone stair leading out of the hall, noted by Hutchins, *The History*

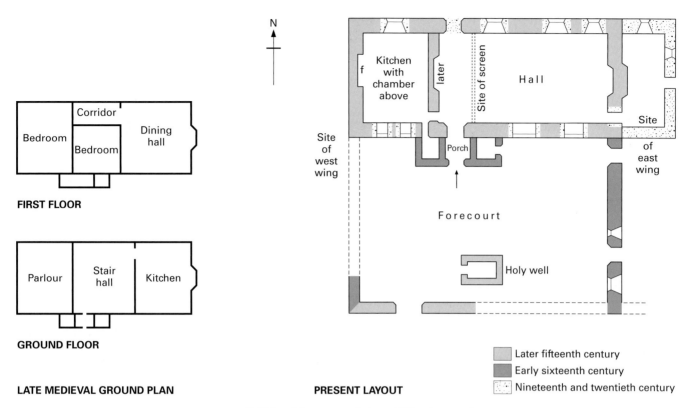

FIRST FLOOR

GROUND FLOOR

Bedroom

Corridor

Bedroom

Dining hall

Parlour

Stair hall

Kitchen

LATE MEDIEVAL GROUND PLAN

N

Kitchen with chamber above

later

Site of screen

Hall

Site of west wing

Porch

Site of east wing

Forecourt

Holy well

Later fifteenth century

Early sixteenth century

Nineteenth and twentieth century

PRESENT LAYOUT

FIGURE 158 Rialton Manor: ground plan, c.1530 and present layout

The small forecourt retains its late medieval entrance and some adjacent walling, though most of the present enclosure has been rebuilt on the line of the earlier walls. The holy well within the court, also late medieval, was no doubt the reason for this house's position.

The rib-vaulted entrance porch formerly opened into the cross passage at the lower end of the hall, from which it was presumably separated by a screen. The opposing doorway is now blocked. With the insertion of a floor within the frame of the hall, the ground-floor area was divided into an entrance and staircase hall, and kitchen. Neither room retains any original internal features. The initial proportions of the hall survive at first-floor level,[3] where the wagon roof has been restored to its original glory with revealed wall plates, ribbing, and wooden bosses.

The ground-floor kitchen with end-wall fireplace benefited from the small larder added as part of Vyvyan's porch. The original approach to the chamber above can no longer be traced, but the roof survives above the flat plaster ceiling renewed in the 1960s.

Prior Vyvyan converted the single-range accommodation into a much grander house. His most obvious addition is the two-storeyed frontal projection, a variation on the towered porch popular at the time. It consisted of the vaulted porch, flanked by the internally approached larder and the stair bay which rises to a first-floor lobby and study behind the three triple-light windows of the upper façade. The glazing of the two study windows with their rounded heads includes two roundels, one with the initials T V for Thomas Vyvyan and the other with the arms of Bodmin Priory, three silver salmon on a blue ground. But it was probably Vyvyan who also added the two-storeyed wings which, like the porch, overtopped the roof level

of the main block, as shown in the engraving of 1823 by J. Craig (from a drawing by F. W. Stockdale).[4] The east wing, with its two entries and two windows, is likely to have been a new kitchen and services to enable the original kitchen to be adapted for residential purposes, while the opposing wing would have been an extension of the prior's personal accommodation. Nothing survives of this structure, but A. L. Rowse recorded that two fine Perpendicular stone archways, removed from Rialton during the nineteenth century to a new farmhouse further up the valley, probably came from this wing. One had the words S Petrocus and the initials T V and the other Rialton and T V Prior Hoc Fecit, with the arms of England and the priory.[5]

Prior Thomas Vyvyan and his brother dominated early sixteenth-century Bodmin, one as head of the priory, the other (also Thomas) as vicar of Bodmin – an appointment of 1516 that he owed to his older brother. In the following year, prior Thomas was consecrated titular bishop of Megara to help out bishop Oldham of Exeter in Cornwall, so that it was not surprising that he became the most important churchman in Cornwall. Highly unpopular throughout Bodmin and its neighbourhood, this princely cleric, autocratic and avaricious, was a lesser Wolsey.[6]

NOTES

1 Trelowarren near Helston, the home of the Vyvyan family since 1427, looks medieval, particularly the west-wing chapel. However, recent research by Sir Ferrers Vyvyan has shown that though this consciously archaic E-shaped mansion may include some medieval elements, the core of the main block is early to mid-sixteenth century, the two wings are seventeenth century in origin, and the whole is a study in Georgian antiquarianism. J. M. Robinson, *Country Life* (July 1999) replacing

L. Weaver, *Country Life* (April 1916). Also T. H. Turner and J. H. Parker, *Some Account of Domestic Architecture in England*, III pt 2 (1859) 363.

2 A single square-headed granite window survives in the rear wall.

3 Currently used as a dining room with open stair access.

4 *Excursions through . . . Cornwall* (1824).

5 Rowse (1941) 585.

6 A. L. Rowse, *Tudor Cornwall* (1941). His sumptuous tomb of black Catacleuse stone and grey marble, part medieval, part Renaissance, was moved after the Dissolution from Bodmin priory to the parish church chancel.

A.L. Rowse, *Country Life* (September 1941)

ROSCARROCK, Cornwall

Like Rialton Manor, Roscarrock is a mile or two inland from the Cornish coast, hugging the side of a combe to shelter from the Atlantic gales. It is one of the few late medieval houses on the north side of the county, and until the late seventeenth century was the home of an important local family of the same name who provided an MP in 1347 and several county sheriffs during the fifteenth and sixteenth centuries.[1] Today, this small courtyard house commands a 730 acre farm extending to Port Quin and the sea, with the same acreage and field pattern that it held nearly 200 years ago.

The courtyard is range-enclosed on three sides, with the fourth side stopped by an original wall topped by battlements of cyclopean proportions, helping to keep out the vicious coastal storms. The east range is relatively recent, so that interest centres on the former hall range to the west and the entrance range to the south – the former no longer occupied and the latter serving as the present farmhouse.

The two-storeyed farmhouse range looks entirely early nineteenth century, externally and internally, with a slight change in roof level suggesting a two-period construction. Yet the twelve-bay roof running the length of the range is entirely of late medieval form, even though it reflects the phased development. The thick walls, no doubt original, retain no early features, but it is possible that the present ground-floor through-passage is on the line of the original entrance approach into the courtyard.

The hall range on the left-hand side of the small court has been downgraded to outbuildings but is still roofed, though no longer in use. The large cross-passage doorways, four-centred under square labels with fleuron stops and carved spandrels, are particularly impressive on the courtyard side. The single-storeyed hall was subsequently floored, its end wall removed, and a replacement seven-bay roof of sub-medieval form inserted, but it retains the original crenellated wall plates. The hall also has poor window survival. The cramped twin lights over the entrance doorways may well be reused material relating to the post-medieval division into two floors, while the patched courtyard walling hints at the position of the larger window that must have existed there. In the absence of any evidence of a wall fireplace, a central hearth is assumed.

The north end of the range below the cross passage is two-storeyed, with a low ground-floor room. On the analogy of Truthall, Medros, and Rialton manors, the ground floor was used for services and the upper floor as the withdrawing chamber. Approached from an altered external stair as at Truthall, this upper chamber retains its end-wall fireplace with large plain granite lintel with hollow chamfer, an original window with evidence of others

PLATE 272 Roscarrock: from the west coastal side

opposite, and the contemporary roof of four close-set bays spanned by arched collar trusses with substantial purlins, two lines of wind braces, and wall plates with half-octagonal columns marking the narrow bay divisions. The chamber was subsequently enhanced with a rectangular bay window (as at Medros) of six lights with rounded heads (1–4–1) and carved spandrels.

The hall and chamber range with continuous plinth and roof coping is of a single build. The chamber roof is not unlike that over the entrance range, but the latter is of an even higher quality, with moulded arched braces and purlins throughout but with the eight bays towards the hall enhanced by more dominant wind braces.[2] It is probable that the greater part of this south range at right angles to the hall was an expansion of the family accommodation in the more fashionable position beyond the upper end of the hall as at Medros rather than below it as at Truthall. Linked by a common plinth, both ranges are functionally and structurally related with a relatively short building span between the two phases.

The square-headed fireplace lintel, round-headed lights, and four-centred doorway heads are all forms common in Cornwall between the late fifteenth and seventeenth centuries. The difficulty of working granite makes most decoration stylised rather than particular, yet the roof structures strongly point towards the earlier period, and more particularly to two phases between the late fifteenth and mid-sixteenth centuries, although documentary and dendrochronology evidence will bring greater precision.[3] Roscarrock is a relatively complete gentry house of some considerable character. Its plan is relatively clear, the size and quality of the hall entrance still impress, as does the superior finish of the roofs, reflecting a peak in the fortunes of the Roscarrock family during their five centuries in the locality.

NOTES

1 An enamelled gold rosary of *c*.1500 in the V & A Museum, London, was discovered at Roscarrock.

2 None of the bays showed smoke evidence when the roof was repaired in 1985. The wind braces were concealed at the same time to reduce draughts.

3 The west range roof has been dendro dated 1510–40, *Vern. Arch.* 35 (2004) 85.

V. M. and F. J. Chesher, *The Cornishman's House* (1968) 34–6

SALISBURY PALACE and the residences of the bishops of Salisbury

Early in the tenth century, the large see of Winchester was divided into two, with Wiltshire and Berkshire centred on a new episcopal seat at Ramsbury. The bishops of Ramsbury were supported by the revenues from five large manors – Cannings, Old Sarum, Potterne, Ramsbury, and Sonning. These had been alienated to such an extent by the time of Edward the Confessor that the see had been united with that of Sherborne. As part of archbishop Lanfranc's policy of moving rural sees from villages to larger urban centres, Sherborne was moved in 1075 to Old Sarum, the first city and cathedral of Salisbury. During the middle ages, the bishops of this modestly wealthy see held at least five castles, a palace, six country houses, and a London residence, though not all were in their hands by the close of that period.

The castles at Devizes, Kidwelly, Malmesbury, Old Sarum, and Sherborne were all developed by bishop Roger (1107–39), Henry I's chancellor, justiciar, and powerhouse second only to the king.[1] Not surprisingly, this ostentatious builder aroused baronial jealousy and the ire of the king's successor. Devizes, probably founded by bishop Osmund (1078–99) and first mentioned in 1106, was so dramatically redeveloped by Roger by about 1138 that its strength and magnificence excited and impressed all who saw it.[2] It was seized by Stephen in 1139, played a prominent part in his ensuing war with the empress Matilda, and was retained by the crown until the sixteenth century. It was already in ruins at the beginning of that century, with the last vestiges vanishing under the mid-nineteenth-century monstrosity that covers the site today. Malmesbury was erected by Roger at the beginning of Stephen's reign in the monks' cemetery close to the west end of the abbey church, but its value was lost after the civil war and the monks were granted royal permission to demolish it in 1215.[3] Kidwelly was built to secure some of the newly conquered coastal lands in South Wales that Henry I granted to his minister in 1106, but the site has been subsumed under the present late-thirteenth-century fortress.[4] The ruins of Sherborne Castle stand as testimony to the high quality and palace-courtyard layout of Roger's work.[5] It was seized by Stephen at the same time as his other castles[6] and held in royal possession until 1331. By about 1130, Roger had also obtained custody from Henry I of the stone and earthwork fortress at Old Sarum and was responsible for adding the remarkable courtyard complex following the same form and scale as that at Sherborne, though only the foundations survive. Old Sarum was similarly surrendered to the crown, and though of declining value, held in royal hands until the sixteenth century.[7] Of all the castles, only one was regained by the see, and that in 1355, because Edward III had granted Sherborne to a private person twenty-four years earlier.[8] The magnificent 7½ feet high brass of bishop Wyville (d.1375) in Salisbury Cathedral with its unique representation of an episcopal fortress commemorates his tenurial achievement.[9]

The foundations of the aisled hall and a domestic wing excavated next to the Norman cathedral at Old Sarum in 1909–15 have been variously attributed, but they may be the work of bishop Osmund (1078–99). They were left to decay after the long-standing tensions between the castle garrison and the cathedral clergy came to a head early in Henry III's reign, resulting in bishop Poore (1217–28) moving his seat and church to the present valley site in 1219. Poore's new palace south-east of his cathedral consisted of an enor-

mous aisled hall and a two-storey residential block with short extension. Timber grants for hall and chamber were made in 1221, with completion by 1225. The hall, larger than the contemporary one at Winchester Castle, was replaced in the mid-fifteenth century, but the six-bay vaulted undercroft and upper chamber still stand though the latter was thoroughly converted into the bishop's drawing room in 1737.[10]

According to Leland, bishop Beauchamp (1450–81) updated the palace with a new great hall, parlour and chamber, probably between c.1457 and Edward IV's visit in 1466.[11] Beauchamp's replacement hall, 87½ feet by 37½ feet, was one of the largest built during the fifteenth century. It was destroyed shortly after the palace had been sold by the parliamentary authorities in 1648, but the handsomely designed three-storey porch still commands the palace approach. Though a floor was inserted within the original entrance in 1782, it retains the hollow-chamfered outer and inner arches with four-centred heads, two-light cinquefoil windows, and flamboyantly capped stair turret. The uppermost window retains some yellow and black stained glass and the vaulted stair head with its rib-divided compartments.

Part of the hall site was used in 1668–74 for a three-storey central block, but elements of Beauchamp's seven-bay apartment survive, including some of the outer walling, one of its many buttresses, the jambs of two windows, and the cross-passage rear doorway. As the lower gable end is now the end wall of the palace, nothing of the services block remains outside a double-hollow-chamfered doorway.

Beauchamp's two-storey parlour and chamber block at the upper end of the hall has been heavily altered. The external portal was added to the ground floor parlour by Sir Robert Taylor (1783–85) while the four-bay chamber above has long been used as a chapel, and continues to be so since the palace was converted to cathedral school use in 1947. However, the ground floor retains its hollow-chamfered windows with double-ogee-moulded rear arches and jambs, while those of the chamber above are roll moulded with trefoiled lights and traceried heads. The south-facing windows have been blocked while the mid-sixteenth-century rafter and tie-beam roof has later applied panels and carved bosses.[12]

Bishops never spent more than a few weeks each year in their palace[13] for when they were not attending the king, they were perambulating their diocese or staying in one of their country houses. Potterne was one of the most frequently used residences during the fourteenth century, as Ramsbury was during the later fifteenth and early sixteenth centuries.[14] But virtually nothing survives of any of the bishop's country houses, despite the fact that bishop Wyville was awarded a licence to crenellate his palace and all his houses in 1337 and that bishop Erghum renewed it in 1377.[15]

The risings in Wiltshire in the summer of 1450 in the wake of John Cade's rebellion were the most serious outside south-east England. They were focussed on William Ayscough, bishop of Salisbury, who was killed outside Edington priory church. Long-standing, deep-seated disputes between town and bishop were heightened by personal hostility towards one of the influential advisors to the incapable Henry VI. Salisbury Palace was attacked and his manor houses at Potterne, Ramsbury, and Woodford were sacked. But the rising was also a reaction to the recession that had struck the buoyant cloth-manufacturing industry in Salisbury, West Wiltshire, and Sherborne where the bishop had his estates.[16]

PLATE 273 Salisbury, Bishop's Palace: porch, replacement hall, parlour, and chamber block by J. C. Buckler (*c.*1830)

In Wiltshire, Woodford was noted as 'ruinous' in the early six-teenth century and was pulled down.[17] In 1860, traces of the rampart and ditch enclosing the house at Bishop's Cannings were said to be visible, though they can no longer be identified.[18] The episcopal house at Potterne was excavated in 1973[19] and though the village has the splendid timber-framed Porch House with central hall and gabled end wings dendro dated to 1468–99, the attribution of its construction to the bishop's steward has not yet been corrob-orated.[20] Ramsbury, next to the River Kennet, had a cloister in 1320 and was described by Leland as 'fair and old'. It was remodelled by the earl of Pembroke in the mid-sixteenth century but completely replaced by the fine brick mansion in the 1680s.[21] It is the impres-sive churches at Bishop's Cannings and Potterne which identify the episcopal presence today, rather than any domestic remains.

Further afield, the much-altered frame of Chardstock Court is basically late medieval,[22] but only a brick gateway stands at Sonning from a site that excavations revealed was extremely impressive (see pages 157–8). The bishop's London house south of Fleet Street is first mentioned in 1290 and the hall porch in 1401. Excavation on the site in 1986–7 revealed a mid-fourteenth-century wall protect-ing the site from the River Thames but the form and scale of the episcopal residence are not known.[23]

NOTES

1 E. J. Kealey, *Roger of Salisbury, Viceroy of England* (1972). For the castles, M. Thompson, *Medieval Bishops' Houses in England and Wales* (1998) 23, 85–90.

2 Its scale and character were extolled by the author of *Gesta Stephani*, William of Malmesbury, and Henry of Huntingdon. E. H. Stone, *Devizes Castle* (1920); *HKW*, II (1963) 626–8.

3 *HKW*, II (1963) 734; VCH, *Wiltshire*, XIV (1991) 132.

4 C. Fox and C. A. Ralegh Radford, *Archaeologia* 83 (1933) 93–123.

5 RCHM, *Dorset*, I (1952) 64.

6 He also appropriated Roger's enormous wealth on his death that year to fund his war against Matilda.

7 J. P. Bushe-Fox, *Old Sarum, Wiltshire* (1937); D. H. Montgomerie, *Arch. Jour.* 104 (1947) 129–43; *HKW*, II (1963) 824–8.

8 *Cal. Close Rolls: 1354–60*, 122. The crown had granted the property to William Montague, later earl of Salisbury, but the bishop already con-sidered it his by 1337 when he included it among the episcopal resi-dences that he sought to crenellate under licence.

9 The tiered castle shows the gatehouse guarded by a knight, the enclosed grassed bailey, the residential heart of the fortress presided over by the bishop, and the rear gate or postern at the head of the brass.

10 RCHM, *Salisbury: The Houses of the Close* (1993) 53–8. For an alternative view of its early development, Thompson, *Medieval Bishops' Houses*, 51–4.

11 *Itinerary*, I, 267. Beauchamp was the younger son of Sir Walter Beauchamp of Powicke whose home near Alcester no longer exists, though a little of the castle Richard Beauchamp remodelled at Bronsil stands in the shadow of the Malvern Hills. A. Emery, *Greater Med. Houses*, II (2000) 523–5. Bishop Beauchamp also supervised the first stage of the rebuilding of St George's Chapel, Windsor. J. M. J. Fletcher, *Wilts. Arch. and N. H. Mag.* 48 (1937) 161–73.

12 RCHM, *Salisbury: The Houses of the Close* 53–73; *Vern. Arch.* 31 (2000) 99–101. Also J. A. Reeve, *Wilts. Arch. and N. H. Mag.* 25 (1891) 181–91; C. Wordsworth, *Wilts. Arch. and N. H. Mag.* 25 (1891) 165–81; VCH, *Wiltshire*, VI (1962) 75.

13 K. Edwards, *English Secular Cathedrals in the Middle Ages* (1949) 104–5.

14 VCH, *Wiltshire*, VII (1953) 209; XII (1983) 19.

15 *Cal. Pat. Rolls: 1334–38*, 49; *ibid. 1377–81*, 9. The licence covers the five Wiltshire properties, Sherborne Castle and Chardstock in Dorset, Sonning in Berkshire, and the London house.

16 J. N. Hare, *Southern History* 4 (1982) 12–32; R. A. Griffiths, *The Reign of King Henry VI* (1981) 644–5.

17 VCH, *Wiltshire*, VI (1962) 223.

18 VCH, *Wiltshire*, VII (1953) 189. Naomi Payne has drawn my attention to the total lack of documentary evidence identifying any episcopal residence at Bishop's Cannings. Two documents in the register of Simon of Ghent (1297–1315) place the bishop there, but not necessarily in a residence at a manor which was next to Potterne where there was a much-valued episcopal house. Two adjacent houses with their ongoing maintenance costs were superfluous to a see which was relatively conservative in its residential provision.

19 N. D. McGlashan and R. E. Sandell, *Wilts. Arch. and N. H. Mag.* 69 (1974) 85–96.

20 *Vern. Arch.* 31 (2000) 88; VCH, *Wiltshire*, VII (1953) 207, 209.

21 VCH, *Wiltshire*, XII (1983) 19–22.

22 B. Cherry and N. Pevsner, *The Buildings of England: Devon* (1989) 253.

23 J. Schofield, *Medieval London Houses* (1995) 183.

SAMPFORD PEVERELL and priests' houses in south-west England

Few would argue on either scale or decorative qualities that priests' houses in south-west England can be numbered among the 'greater' medieval houses of England. However, several such houses survive, built between the fourteenth and early sixteenth centuries, retaining an extremely high standard of original condition, and in some cases revealing a surprisingly high-status origin.[1] In 1488, Lady Margaret Beaufort, Henry VII's mother, had a house built for her own use at her Devon manor of Sampford Peverell. She supervised work on diverting a watercourse to service a mill within her manor and at the same time, she contributed to the construction of the south aisle of the parish church, facing her new house which she subsequently donated to the rector for his own use.[2] This L-shaped residence was not large, but was comfortable with heated main rooms. The offices and cross passage serve a small ground-floor hall, for the parlour, the largest room in the house, fills the cross wing. It has a framed ceiling (as does the hall) and was surmounted by Lady Margaret's personal rooms, of an outer and a much larger inner chamber with a wagon roof.[3]

A considerable number of houses survive across the country, built for the parish clergy, rectors or vicars, ranging from the so-called vicar peles in Northumbria such as that at Corbridge, to the timber-framed priest's house at Alfriston in Sussex, the fine hall house at Buckland, and the stone houses at Congresbury and Muchelney in Somerset. Their scale and standards depended on the wealth and importance of the benefice, but by their nature such residences tended to be relatively small. Yet they could equal a manor house in scale, as at Marlow or Buckland, or be capable of aristocratic occupation as at Sampford Peverell. Moreover, their frequent occupation by the clergy until at least the nineteenth century has meant that they often retain considerable early structural evidence, often more so than gentry houses, and serve as a vital link between high-status and late medieval vernacular houses.

Of the several houses in Somerset, Muchelney and Congresbury are the outstanding examples. The late fourteenth-century single-range house at Muchelney is little touched except for the loss of the two rear stair turrets which accessed the storeyed end bays. The two-bay hall was open to the roof, with a service room below the passage and chamber over, and an unheated parlour with the priest's bedroom beyond the hall. The four-bay cruck roof with steep arch braces and rough wind braces carries the still thatched roof, while early Tudor improvements included larger windows and a fireplace in the hall.[4] The parallels with larger contemporary houses are immediate, and this applies to the grander one built about a century later at Congresbury by the executors of bishop Bekynton of Wells (d.1465).

Whereas one of the early nineteenth-century vicars of Muchelney thought of his house as 'only a small cottage' and went to live in another parish, the vicar of Congresbury built a new but severe four-square vicarage in 1824 in front of the substantial fifteenth-century house of previous incumbents. The latter is an oblong and buttressed two-storey house, plaster-faced, with a prominent off-centre ashlar-fronted porch. The pillared entry arch is surmounted by a continuous fleuron band under a hood with three shields supported by angels. The room above has a two-light transomed window, and a decorated panel in the gable with a figure of a scroll-carrying angel. All this decorative work survives in excellent condition. Internally, the chamber on the left-hand side is a three-bay hall with transomed cinquefoil-light windows with square hood and head stops, an end fireplace, and a beamed ceiling divided into rectangles. The lesser room on the right-hand side of the cross passage probably combined the kitchen with services. The three rooms above mirror those below, reached by newel from the hall. It opens into the principal room with untransomed cinquefoil lights, while the lesser chamber retains a contemporary fireplace. This spacious priest's house is an unspoilt example of *c.*1470, with highly decorated façade to a dwelling that adopted the up-to-date regional development of a ground-floor hall with primary chamber above. Sometimes smaller residences can be more articulate than their larger but more altered brethren.

Just as gentry houses differed in size and scale, so did those of the medieval parish clergy, reflecting the wealth or penury of the benefice. There were the richer holdings, often held by absentees or pluralists, the less wealthy benefices which might be combined with an office in a nearby town, and the unbeneficed clergy who were paid a salary for assisting an incumbent or deputising for a non-resident holder.[5] Their houses are likely to reflect the income and importance of the benefice, and possibly the standing of the patron.

■ Parish priests' houses
□ Chantry priests' houses

N

Buckland ■
Withington ■
Ashleworth ■
Elkstone ■
Syde □
Coln Rogers ■
North Cerney ■
Standish ■

Farleigh Hungerford □
Stanton Drew ■
Congresbury ■

Mere □

Walton ■

Winsford ■

Muchelney ■
Stoke Sub Hamdon □

Marnhull □
Lyscombe ■

Sampford Peverell ■
Ilminster □
Trent □

Kentisbeare ■
Combe Raleigh □
Wimborne Minster ■

Colyton ■
Bridport □

Dunchideok ■

0   10 miles
0   20 km

FIGURE 159 South-west England: medieval parish and chantry priests' houses

Rectors, who were entitled to all the revenues of the holding, were responsible for building and maintaining their houses. Vicars only enjoyed a limited proportion of the church's revenue, so that responsibility for building and maintaining their houses usually rested with the patron, lay or ecclesiastical. W. A. Pantin points out that the finest priests' houses in south-west England were those of ecclesiastical benefices, such as that at Muchelney appropriated by the nearby abbot, or the house at Congresbury, appropriated by the chapter of Wells Cathedral.[6] But rectories always held some glebe land, necessitating barns and agricultural outbuildings, so that they often took on the character of a small farmstead. The larger rectories and vicarages frequently needed assistant clergy – chaplains and clerks – as well as a servant or two, so that the house might resemble a family home, sometimes one large enough to include guest accommodation.[7]

There is no major difference architecturally between these houses and those built for chantry priests.[8] A chantry was founded by a person for mass to be celebrated in a church for the benefit of his or her soul and those of other enumerated persons. They became increasingly popular from the late thirteenth century

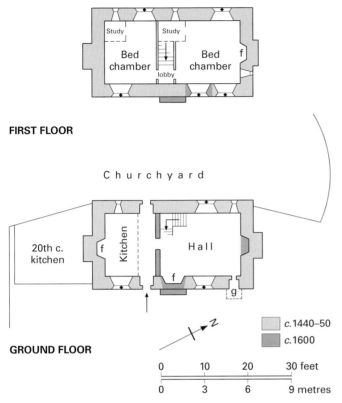

FIRST FLOOR

Churchyard

GROUND FLOOR

c.1440–50
c.1600

0   10   20   30 feet
0   3   6   9 metres

FIGURE 160 Trent, The Chantry: floor plans

PLATE 274 Trent, The Chantry: from the south

onwards, particularly with the gentry and wealthy townspeople, until their suppression in the mid-sixteenth century.[9] The foundation would be sourced by a permanent endowment, or through the property being held by an institution who would pay the priest a stipend. Chantry foundations varied in scale from substantial collegiate establishments to several chantries in a large town church, and from a single chantry in a parish church to a single obit said once a year. Similarly, the accommodation ranged from a small college such as that at Stoke Sub Hamdon and large houses for several priests as at The Chantry, Mere in Wiltshire, to a small residence for two priests as at Farleigh Hungerford Castle, or even a house for a single incumbent as at Trent. Houses specially built for chantry priests do not differ in scale or layout from those for parish priests and a number similarly survive in good state, little altered by subsequent generations.

Houses built to accommodate chantry priests living together follow the normal house plan of a hall with parlour at the upper end and offices and kitchen at the lower. The hall may be open to the roof as at The Chantry, Mere[10] or a ground-floor room as at The Chantry, Ilminster,[11] and Farleigh Hungerford Castle (page 555). They differ from a standard plan only in their first-floor accommodation, where there are individual rooms for each priest, sometimes with study evidence. They and all the other examples that survive in the south-west are stone-built, self-sufficient residences, and date from the fifteenth century. The largest of these communal establishments is that at Stoke Sub Hamdon, similar in scale to some of the colleges of secular canons noted previously in East Anglia[12] but with a layout that differed little from that of a mid-fifteenth century

Somerset manor house (pages 642–3). While many chantries have no residential evidence, as in the case of Bromham (Wiltshire), Chipping Sodbury (Gloucestershire), Porlock (Somerset), and Paignton (Devon), the patchy survival of parish priests' houses reflects as much intermittent research as standing structures.

The Chantry on the east side of the churchyard at Trent is an impressive stone-built rectangular house with a simple two-room plan, centrally divided at both levels. The exterior is dominated by its splendid windows, four to the front and three to the rear. They are of two transomed lights with cinquefoil heads under a square hood with end stops – two at each level to the front, and one at ground and two above at the rear. In addition, there are four low plain lights at the rear, of a very subsidiary nature. The other dominating feature is the frontal chimney stack, much rebuilt and terminating in a lofty octagonal chimney. The poor quality of construction and its close proximity to the entrance suggest it is an insertion, and this is more likely when the interior is examined, with fireplaces served by the original gable-end stacks.[13]

The front and rear entrances have lightly moulded jambs and two-centred heads, the former with a square label. They open into a narrow passage, screened by a later stone wall to the hall on the right and formerly by a wooden partition next to the kitchen on the left. The hall, 18½ feet by 15 feet, retains its original moulded ceiling beams, for it was always a ground-floor room, long before this became the standard practice in larger houses. It is generously lit by the two facing transomed windows, with a low window close to the upper end and facing an inner doorway which probably led to a garderobe. The present fireplace has a contemporary square-headed lintel decorated with three quatrefoils enclosing shields and a rosette. Yet this hearth's markedly awkward position suggests that it replaced one in the end wall, served by the chimney breast and blocked after the lintel had been removed for reuse.[14] Apart from the incorporation of the cross passage in the kitchen, this room is little altered. The stair within the hall is a replacement in the approximate position of the original one which ascended between two narrow partition walls. The north bedchamber above the hall seems to have been the more important of the two upper rooms, with an end-wall fireplace as well as two transomed windows. The low window probably served a small study unit over the stair. The slightly smaller south bedchamber has a similar light near the corner for a study, but in neither case do the partitions survive. Both rooms were formerly open to a roof spanned by arch-braced collar trusses, but they were ceiled in c.1600 when the attics were added.

The group of fifteenth-century stone houses in Trent reflect this village's late medieval prosperity. There were two manor houses, but they changed hands with a frequency that meant there was never an outstanding manorial lord. Both have been substantially modified[15] whereas The Chantry has been little altered, externally or internally, and is markedly luxurious for its occupant. John Franks, a native of Trent and Master of the Rolls in 1428, established a chantry in Trent church before his death in about 1438. It was to be combined with the creation of four fellowships at Oriel College, Oxford, to be held by students from Devon, Dorset, Somerset, and Wiltshire respectively. The chantry was confirmed by royal licence in January 1441, and the college paid £8 a year to the patron or rector for the support of the priest, who received £7 6s. 8d. for his salary, the upkeep of the house, and the ornaments of the chapel, and 13s. 4d. for the support of an annual obit for John Franks.[16] The construction of The Chantry may therefore be attributed to the 1440s. As there are two bedrooms, one may have been for visitors or for a curate. The upper floor, in particular, is very similar to contemporary lodging accommodation in academic foundations such as New College and All Souls, Oxford, with their large chamber windows and small study lights.

Miss Wood Legh's *A Small Household of the Fifteenth Century* (1955) is based on the household accounts kept by two chantry priests at Bridport between 1453 and 1460. They reveal, for instance, that workmen were frequently fed at their table and they took in lodgers to help cover their costs. Their stone-built house on the south side of the town began life as a late thirteenth-/early fourteenth-century municipal building associated with the harbour. It was taken over and converted into a house in the later fourteenth century, divided at the rear to create a heated parlour and kitchen to the frontal hall, with the principal first-floor room given an extension over the porch, a fireplace, and a corner garderobe. The two chantry priests occupied it with little change.[17]

NOTES
1 Capably surveyed by W. A. Pantin, *Med. Arch.* 1 (1957) 118–46.
2 M. K. Jones and M. G. Underwood, *The King's Mother* (1992) 104.

3 Pantin, *Med. Arch.* 1 (1957) 139–40. The house does not look its age externally, for the upper floor of the hall range was rebuilt in c.1850 when all the windows with their four-centred heads were given wooden frames.
4 R. Haslam, *Country Life* (September 1994).
5 A. H. Thompson, *The English Clergy and Their Organisation in the Later Middle Ages* (1947); W. A. Pantin, *The English Church in the Fourteenth Century* (1955); N. J. G. Pounds, *A History of the English Parish* (2000).
6 *Med. Arch.* 1 (1957) 120.
7 For the houses in Somerset and Devon, Pantin, *Med. Arch.* 1 (1957) 118–46, and *Med. Arch.* 17 (1973) 172–4. For those in Dorset, the RCHM volumes, and for Gloucestershire, D. Verey and A. Brooks, *The Buildings of England: Gloucestershire* I (1999) 67–9; II (2002) 64.
8 W. A. Pantin, *Med. Arch.* 3 (1959) 216–58, where he draws attention to analogous types of lodgings, including those at educational foundations, vicars choral, and secular household lodgings.
9 G. H. Cook, *Mediaeval Chantries and Chantry Chapels* (1947) and *English Collegiate Churches* (1959). Such collegiate foundations were not new, but permanent residence and a communal life in a purpose-built establishment was. Some were the consequence of an extremely wealthy patron such as Edward III at St George's Chapel, Windsor, Henry, duke of Lancaster at New College, Leicester, and Richard, duke of York at Fotheringhay. For less outlay, the practice developed of building a special chapel within a church solely intended for such masses, and they are among the glories of late medieval ecclesiastical architecture.
10 Pantin, *Med. Arch.* 3 (1959) 224–31.
11 *Ibid* 231–4.
12 A. Emery, *Greater Med. Houses*, II (2000) 134–6.
13 RCHM, *Dorset*, I (1952) 258; Pantin, *Med. Arch.* 3 (1959) 237–40. The RCHM considers the front stack original. However, the upper window of c.1600 next to this stack suggests its probable date, added at the same time as the cross-passage wall and attic storey.
14 If there had been no hearth in this position, the stack serving the hearth above would have been corbel-supported at that level.
15 The south-east front of the Manor House north of the church incorporates part of a fifteenth-century hall with seventeenth-century windows and an inserted floor. The north-east wing is dated 1706 while the later south-west wing has reset fifteenth-century features. The smaller manor house, now called Church Farm, retains three fifteenth-century service doorways, one with an original door. Dairy Farm opposite The Chantry retains a four-light window with one of two cinquefoil lights above under a deep label. Even the Rectory retains a fifteenth-century doorway with foliated spandrels. RCHM, *Dorset*, I (1952); A. Sandison, *Trent* (1969).
16 *The Survey and Rentals of the Chantries . . . in the county of Somerset . . . 1548*, ed. E. Green, II (1888) 146, 326.
17 K. A. Rodwell, *Med. Arch.* 34 (1990) 122–43, replacing RCHM, *Dorset*, I (1952) 48. In the late sixteenth or early seventeenth century, the hall and parlour were decorated with geometric and floral wall paintings, a wooden screen was erected between the kitchen and rear parlour, and an attic storey was added with a columbarium. The stair and casement frames (in earlier stone window frames) date from 1870.

SHUTE, Devon

The approach to Shute is heralded by a pair of late eighteenth-century gate piers each side of the public road, followed a little further by a spectacular Elizabethan gatehouse with flanking walls and end turrets astride a green. The central entry leads onwards to a late medieval house in a parkland setting. These are the three key periods in the architectural history of Shute – a mid fifteenth-century mansion, substantially modified and extended in the 1560s, and replaced by a Palladian residence in 1787 using some of the materials from the earlier mansion.

Shute stands 4 miles from the sea in the lower valley of the River Axe, though the earlier house faces its tributary, the River Coly. With the marriage of Hawyse des Schetes to Sir Nicholas Bonville in about 1292, the manor of Shute passed into the hands of the Bonvilles. During the fourteenth century, they were one of the respectable but not among the pre-eminent families of Devon, though several members were knighted and Sir Nicholas' grandson, Sir William Bonville (d.1408), 'enlarged his estate . . . and made his principal dwelling in this place'. A frequent member of parliament for Devon and Somerset (1366–1402), sheriff of Somerset in 1380 and of Devon in 1389, and a property holder in Devon, Cornwall, Wiltshire, and Somerset, Sir William's will of 1408 lists a 'hall, chamber, pantry, buttery, kitchen, and pastry house within his manor of Shute'.[1]

Sir William was succeeded by his fifteen-year-old grandson, also William, who served in France under Henry V and Clarence, was knighted there in 1417, and served under Bedford in 1424. He attended several parliaments during the 1420s and married prestigiously – initially to the daughter of Lord Grey of Ruthin, and by 1427 to the widow of Lord Harington and the aunt of the 13th earl of Devon. Bonville was favoured with several local government posts, including sheriff of Devon in 1423, justice of the peace in Devon, Somerset, and Cornwall in the 1430s, and steward of the duchy of Cornwall in 1437. It is not unlikely that the fierce antagonism between Thomas Courtenay, earl of Devon (d.1458) and Lord Bonville that marked the region's politics during the 1440s and early 1450s arose over disagreement about his wife's property, personal antipathy, and particularly Bonville's considerable influence in local administration and court circles which culminated in his elevation to the peerage in 1449.[2] The long-simmering dispute broke asunder in an armed rebellion against Bonville in 1451 at Taunton, and in the earl's alliance with the duke of York in a failed military demonstration against Henry VI's government at Blackheath in 1452 (hindered by Bonville at Sampford Peverell), with Courtenay's subsequent loss of control and influence over West Country society. His isolation and antagonism towards his neighbour vented itself in a searing attack against Bonville and his supporters over a two-month period in 1455, initiated by the murder of Bonville's lawyer at his home at Upcott Barton,[3] even though he had been godfather to one of the earl of Devon's sons. Within five days, the news had travelled to East Anglia and was being discussed in the Paston letters, until it was succeeded by the report that the earl had attacked and commandeered Exeter, and was besieging his kinsman and Bonville supporter at Powderham Castle. The earl's success against Bonville in the armed conflict at Clyst Bridge, 4 miles from Exeter, was followed by the thorough pillaging of Shute by the earl's men, who seized a great booty of household furnishings, food, and cattle.

The final chapter of Bonville's highly successful life was a depressing one. His son and grandson were killed at the battle of Wakefield supporting the duke of York (December 1460). Despite Henry VI's promise of safety, Bonville was executed on the orders of Queen Margaret and the new earl of Devon after a Lancastrian victory at the second battle of St Albans (February 1461). Within six weeks, in a total reversal of fortune, the crushing Yorkist victory at Towton resulted in the earl of Devon's death and the restoration

of the Bonville estates by the newly crowned Edward IV to the one-year-old Cicely Bonville.

When she was scarcely fourteen years old, Cicely became the second wife of the twenty-four-year-old Thomas Grey, 1st marquess of Dorset (d.1501), and she lived until 1530. The manor of Shute was held for six months by the 2nd marquess (d.1530) and forfeited to the crown in 1554 when the 3rd marquess was executed for attempting to put his daughter, Lady Jane Grey, on the throne. The property was held for a short time by Sir William Petre, who sold it to Sir William Pole in 1560, a family who had held land at Colyton since about 1300 and owned Colcombe 'Castle' nearby. A successor, Sir John William Pole, built the Palladian house on the south-facing slopes of the park, now divided into apartments.

The L-shaped medieval fragment that still stands at Shute, built of flint rubble with ashlar dressings, is crowned with a boldly embattled parapet supported on a continuous string course terminating in gargoyles at the corners. Now three-storeyed, it served as a farm or barton for 160 years, before its rehabilitation as a residence in the 1950s initiated an extended discussion as to its original function which centred on its incorporating the hall and solar of the early house.[4] Nicholas Cooper's discovery in 1996 of a detailed survey of the mansion in 1559 revealed that the structure fulfilled entirely different functions.[5] It was a two-storeyed kitchen and service building with staff rooms above, built round two sides of the kitchen court, with the kitchen gate from the outer court on the third side.[6]

Figure 161, drawn from the information provided in the survey of 1559, reflects the layout and condition of the mansion at the point when it was sold to Sir William Pole for £300. The outer gate accessed the Outer or Base Court, surrounded by several stables with staff lodgings above and a great barn. Two opposing entries led to the Inner Court and Kitchen Court respectively, the former with the hall and residential apartments beyond it, and the latter to the kitchen and services with chambers above. Shute, like many of the greater houses of the fifteenth century, followed a multiple court-yard layout, and one which extended uphill from west to east. The upper end of the hall and the great chamber block were sited at the higher level, enabling the ground floor of the latter (used in 1559 as a wine cellar) to be built partially below ground level. Furthermore, the residential tower projecting from the corner of this block, possibly an addition to the initial layout, was the height of fashion between c.1445 and 1500.[7] The residential ranges built in the early sixteenth century by Cicely Bonville's second husband brought the house closer to the parish church, clearly viewed at that time as a manorial chapel, but it was not until the 1560s that an entirely new northern approach was created with the construction of the still-imposing gatehouse and flanking turrets (fig. 162). This survey is supplemented by a drawing of 1781 held by the Carew-Pole family of Antony, Cornwall, showing that the late medieval embattled south front from the present kitchen to the lost east tower was totally refenestrated by Sir William Pole (d.1587).[8]

The house known today as Shute Barton was a tall, formerly two-storeyed building of the mid-fifteenth century, with a lower kitchen gateway added on the west side in about 1500, not long before some minor modifications were made to the adjacent block. The house was altered more drastically in the 1560s when the middle storey was inserted, considerable refenestration was undertaken, and a

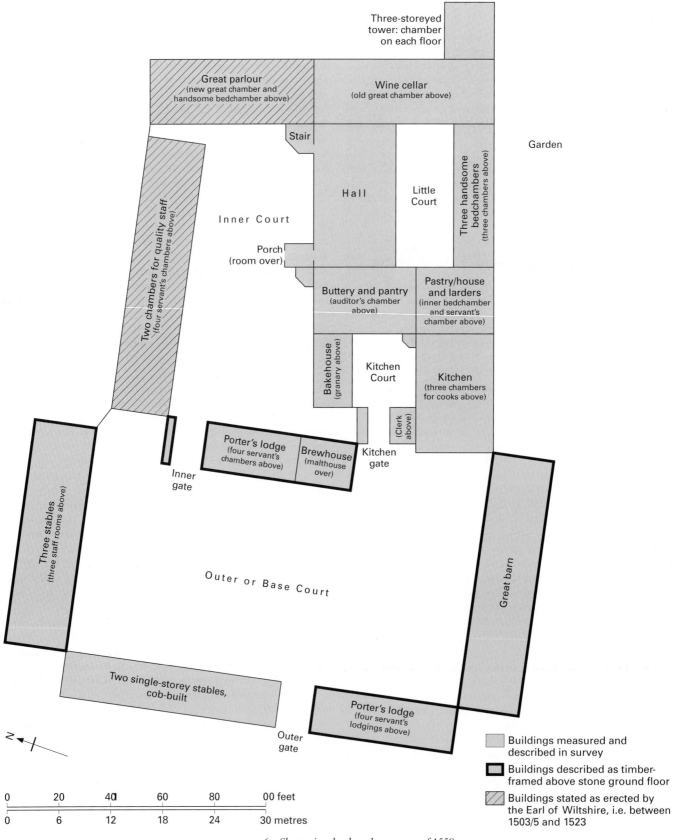

Three-storeyed tower: chamber on each floor

Great parlour
(new great chamber and handsome bedchamber above)

Wine cellar
(old great chamber above)

Garden

Stair

Hall

Little Court

Three handsome bedchambers
(three chambers above)

Inner Court

Two chambers for quality staff
(four servant's chambers above)

Porch
(room over)

Buttery and pantry
(auditor's chamber above)

Pastry/house and larders
(inner bedchamber and servant's chamber above)

Bakehouse
(granary above)

Kitchen Court

Kitchen
(three chambers for cooks above)

(Clerk above)

Inner gate

Porter's lodge
(four servant's chambers above)

Brewhouse
(malthouse over)

Kitchen gate

Three stables
(three staff rooms above)

Outer or Base Court

Great barn

Two single-storey stables, cob-built

Porter's lodge
(four servant's lodgings above)

Outer gate

N

Buildings measured and described in survey

Buildings described as timber-framed above stone ground floor

Buildings stated as erected by the Earl of Wiltshire, i.e. between 1503/5 and 1523

0   20   40   60   80   00 feet
0   6   12   18   24   30 metres

FIGURE 161 Shute: site plan based on survey of 1559

PLATE 275 Shute: Kitchen Court from the north with pastry house kitchen with chamber above, and Kitchen Court gateway

short three-storeyed extension was added on the south or garden side with decorated battlements. The house immediately displays the distinctive window form of these three primary periods – twin trefoiled lights set in square frames under a pointed relieving arch, twin uncusped lights, and flat-headed windows with bolection mouldings under square hoods with short end stops.

The present approach is from the north, in line with the showy gatehouse of about 1565 with its nineteenth-century replacement end turrets (fig. 162). Entry lies across the site of a bakehouse with granary above which made the Kitchen Court no wider than the kitchen gateway. This original approach was from the west (on the site of the present farmyard) and through the utilitarian entry passage with its flattened segmental entry arch with diamond stops and small side room. External steps lead to a single room above, with a two-light window overlooking the Outer Court, a single cinquefoil light to the Kitchen Court, a square-headed lintel to the fireplace (with quatrefoil light to the side) and arch-braced collar trusses. This 'ys a handsom chamber with a chimney leading upp by a vyce from the sayde lytle court. This chamber hath a closet adioyning unto yt And sved for the stuard or clerke of the kychens chamber.'[9]

Turning now to the main structure, this consists of two blocks, the kitchen on the south side of the court, and the services at a right angle on the east side. The 1559 survey reveals that the buttery and pantry lay to the north with the 'fayer' auditor's chamber over, and that the bakehouse and larder were in line with 'an ynner chaber or bed chaber [above] and another bed chaber for srvantes, and house of Offyce'. Thus the ground-floor services opened from the lower end of the hall, which was porch-approached. The octagonal turret opening from it with 'the vyce or stayer going to the sayd lodings' still stands at the north-east corner, next to the almost blank end wall of the hall supported by a line of late eighteenth-century buttresses. Beyond the hall lay a Little Court, from which the bakehouse and larder opened, marked today by the remainder of the

buttressed blank wall. The three-storeyed residential projection in extension of this block is not noted in the survey and therefore post-dates it (pl. 189).

The kitchen doorway with continuous-moulded jamb and two-centred head is flanked by two much-altered windows. Originally taller under a relieving arch, they were replaced in the mid-sixteenth century by lower windows (internal splays hacked back), square-headed frames and hollow chamfers, subsequently changed for casements similar to the present mid-twentieth-century replacements. An unaltered early window survives opposite, with two trefoil lights. The west wall of the kitchen is spanned by a spectacular hearth, 22 feet wide and 8 feet deep under a four-centred head. Buttress-supported externally, it is possibly the largest medieval hearth to survive in England and is a massive feat of masonry construction. The kitchen was originally much larger and taller, but a mid floor was inserted in the 1560s and the area was shortened with a post and panel screen to create an east-facing room at a slightly higher level, now a parlour.

The juxtaposition of kitchen and pastry house had occurred at Woodsford 'Castle' nearly a century earlier, and at Shute the hearth is 11½ feet wide with a plain low head. Yet there are some features here which suggest that the pastry house block was a secondary build, including the construction of the hearth against rather than within the kitchen wall, the different direction of the beams between the two service blocks, and the lower roof over the pastry house and larders.[10] The area now extends into the ground floor of the Elizabethan extension and is used as a dining room.

The jambs and relieving arch of the entry from the Kitchen Court to the former buttery and pantry survived a mid-sixteenth-century blocking and window conversion,[11] while the rooms have been remodelled for current occupation as a staircase hall, kitchen, and utility area. Just as the stair turret at the courtyard angle of the two blocks gave direct access (now filled) to the room above the kitchen, so the octagonal turret at the north-east corner was the approach to the chamber over the buttery and pantry. This last room is notable for the two-light trefoil transomed window facing north with shutter rebates. Though used by the auditor in the mid-sixteenth century, it would have been occupied initially by a higher member of the Bonville family, and open to the roof. This and the remainder of the block, subject to the inserted floor, is used for the deal stair, panelled withdrawing room, and featureless bedrooms, with further bedrooms immediately above the kitchen.

The original chamber high above the kitchen has been restored to its early condition. This four-bay room is lit by two pairs of trefoil-headed windows under a four-centred rear arch towards the Kitchen Court, and three twin-light windows with uncusped heads towards the garden. These were inserted shortly after 1500, and probably did not replace earlier ones as two of them undercut the ends of the roof trusses. Their insertion may have been in response to the creation of 'three chambers for the Cookes' mentioned in the 1559 survey. The head of the kitchen stack is so large that it not only fills the end wall but is of sufficient depth to allow a small closet to be inserted on each side – that to the south-east was a garderobe with its discharge slot some feet above the base of the stack. There seems to have been a fireplace in the middle of the opposite end wall, now marked by a diminutive hearth to one side. The wall plates and vertical timbers that carried the roof trusses were replaced by concrete ties in the 1950s, but the arch-braced collar

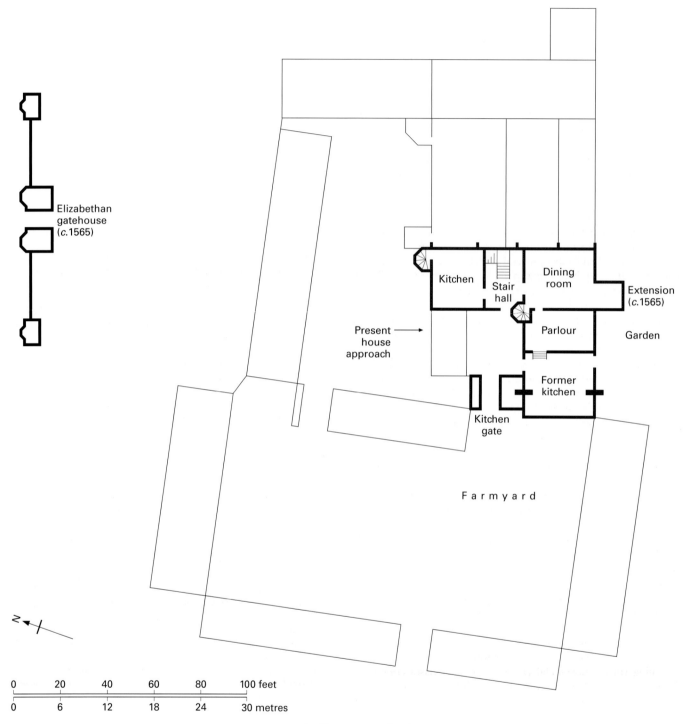

FIGURE 162 Shute: present site plan

trusses with hollow chamfers are in good condition, with two lines of plain wind braces.

Though the embattled parapet is contemporary with the earlier date of the house, there is no evidence that Shute was a fortified residence. Some of the ranges round the Outer Court were timber-framed above a stone ground floor, including the inner gatehouse. The present remnant has a marked verticality, and it is likely that it

extended to the earlier part of the mansion. The hall, 54 feet by 25 feet and 28 feet high, comparable in area and volume to that at Minster Lovell Hall (1431–40), 'hath an Ancient roof of Tymber'. It was as tall as the buttery and pantry block and may have been in line with it, while the octagonal newel turret at the side of the two-storeyed porch takes on the rôle of a look-out turret. At the upper end of the hall was a double-storeyed block of wine cellar with great chamber above, with 'a fayer tymber roofe seeled and painted wit dyvrs armes'. Higher still was a 'handsom lodging of one roome for a gentleman', 12 feet square, surmounted by a 'turreyy covred with leade'. Excavation of the site has never taken place though it would be likely to offer a valuable return.

Although it was formerly considered to be of the late fourteenth century, a date of c.1460 has been suggested for Shute, based on the ascriptions given in the survey of 1559.[12] The well-formed trefoil lights and two-centred arches suggest the former rather than the latter period, and this is not at variance with the associated four-centred forms. However, the survey states that 'the auntient house' was by Lord Bonville (d.1461), with additions by Cicely Bonville under her second husband and therefore between c.1505 and 1523. Bonville was one of the 'new men' of Henry VI's reign. Though of modest background, two financially rewarding marriages, personal energy, and political opportunism brought him rank and influence. He was a career soldier who fought in France in his youth and again in middle age, when he spent several years helping with the relief of Gascony as its seneschal and with a modest-sized army (1443–7). He was an extremely capable and energetic official in local government. In the 1430s and early 1440s,[13] he built up a power-base to challenge the long-held regional leadership of the earls of Devon, and forged political associations at court in the early 1450s that helped to topple the earls as the dominant power-centre in south-west England.[14]

Though Bonville's grandfather seems to have remodelled Shute during the last quarter of the fourteenth century, it was inadequate for Sir William's standing and his growing political position in the west of England. With the financial resources that marriage and offices brought, Bonville rebuilt Shute on a more expansive scale. The standing structure can be attributed to him, and probably the destroyed hall, chamber block, and associated lodgings for his family, friends, and staff. A date between his second marriage (1427) and his elevation to the peerage (1449) is most likely, with a weighting towards the 1430s when he was a thrusting young Turk making a statement about his political standing to his neighbours via an up-to-date house. It would have been before his extended absence abroad and the violent clashes thereafter with the earl of Devon. By the late 1450s, he was in his sixties and an old man, essentially retired from the tensions and polarisation of court politics, but the three-storeyed residential tower opening from the south-east angle of the great chamber may well have been a late addition.

Shute is a trophy house, one of a number built during the second quarter of the fifteenth century to reflect the spoils of war, success on the battlefield, or achievements as an officer of state or at court. A substantial number of such houses were initiated in the 1430s, including Minster Lovell Hall (1431–40), Caister Castle (1432–45), Hampton Court, Leominster (c.1434–c.1440), Wingfield Manor (1439–c.1450), Herstmonceux Castle (c.1438–c.1449), and Sudeley Castle (c.1441–58). Each one of these was built entirely anew on a site cleared of all previous buildings. They were essentially domestic in character, developed around two or more courtyards to provide adequate household as well as family and guest accommodation, were completed in the builder's lifetime, and reflected his achievements in war or at court. Though this may have applied to Shute, the irregular layout of the inner court could well have been determined by the position, if not the existence, of key structures of Sir William Bonville's late fourteenth-century residence.[15] The seal was set on Bonville's local supremacy and crown support when

Shute was visited by Henry VI on 14 July 1452, 'with a great train of noble gentlemen and others', during his extended progress to the west of England and the Welsh border.[16] It is reasonable to assume that Bonville, one of the fifteen lords accompanying the king, would want to show off his newly developed mansion that reflected his considerable standing in the region. A date for the construction of the surviving remnant in the 1430s/early 1440s mirroring Bonville's rising sphere of political influence and patronage, particularly with the upper ranks of local society, would not be at variance with the historical and architectural evidence, though dendrochronology would bring greater precision.

NOTES

1 *Exeter Register of Bishop Stafford: 1395–1419*, ed. F. C. Hingeston-Randolph (1906) 390.
2 R. L. Storey, *The End of the House of Lancaster* (1966) 85–6 and subsequently where he discusses Bonville's career at some length. This antagonism was exacerbated by two factors. Bonville had formed a warm friendship with Sir Philip Courtenay of Powderham Castle, a close kinsman but leading critic of the earl, while Henry VI made a serious blunder in 1440 when he bestowed the stewardship of the duchy of Cornwall estates on the earl as well as Bonville. R. A. Griffiths, *The Reign of King Henry VI* (1981) 574–6; J. R. Lander, 'Henry VI and the Duke of York's Second Protectorate 1455–6', *Bulletin of the John Rylands Library* 43 (1960–1) 44–69.
3 Most of this medieval house was rebuilt in the early seventeenth century.
4 Hussey (1951); National Trust (1996).
5 Devon Record Office 123/M/E99.
6 N. Cooper, *Houses of the Gentry: 1480–1680* (1999) 57.
7 A. Emery, *Greater Med. Houses* II (2000) 350–5.
8 Copy held in the house at Shute.
9 This and subsequent quotations are from the 1559 survey, see note 5.
10 I owe this suggestion to John McCormack.
11 It may have been the exit of a central passage between the services with a pentice to the kitchen, though an entry from the end of the hall cross passage into the Little Court, and thence along the south wall of the buttery and pantry to the fifteenth-century doorway opening from the staircase hall into the parlour (formerly the eastern half of the kitchen), is just as possible. The secondary addition of the pastry house and larders would not invalidate this approach.
12 Cooper, *Houses of the Gentry* 57.
13 During these years, Bonville was appointed constable of Lydford Castle and subsequently of Exeter Castle, and keeper of the western seas. While he subsequently undertook military service in Gascony, the earl of Devon refused to serve abroad in the hope that he might rebuild his position in the south-west during Bonville's absence. He failed, and briefly served abroad himself to try and influence government affairs, again unsuccessfully.
14 M. Cherry, 'The struggle for power in mid fifteenth century Devonshire', in *Patronage, the Crown, and the Provinces in Later Medieval England*, ed. R. A. Griffiths (1981) 123–44. The failure of the crown to resolve the long-standing quarrels between Devon and Bonville and equally those between Berkeley and Talbot, Neville and Percy, Norfolk and the Pastons during the mid-fifteenth century was symptomatic of the fundamental weakness of Henry VI's government and the collapsing authority of the crown.
15 This would still apply, even though two of the inner court ranges were rebuilt in the early sixteenth century.
16 B. Wolffe, *Henry VI* (1981) 259–61.

C. Hussey, *Country Life* (February 1951)
The National Trust, *Shute Barton: Leaflet* (1996)

SOUTH WRAXALL MANOR, Wiltshire

Two of the most important fifteenth-century houses in southern England lie within 3 miles of each other. The manor houses at South Wraxall and Great Chalfield were among the earliest to be subject to a detailed record in the late 1830s by Walker, and were accorded high praise during the early twentieth century,[1] but whereas Great Chalfield has always remained in the public eye, residential privacy has meant that South Wraxall withdrew from public notice. The latter was probably built during Edward IV's reign by a rising entrepreneur, and the former by a highly successful lawyer in c.1478–85, with both houses sharing common planning and design elements. However, South Wraxall was subject to a major development programme in c.1600, internal updating in c.1700, and extensive restoration shortly after 1900 when both houses were sympathetically handled, but whereas the medieval structure at Great Chalfield is compact and almost separate from the early twentieth-century work, the succession of development phases have made South Wraxall Manor a warren of a house.

This major residence lacks building documentation and has not yet been subject to a detailed architectural analysis, archaeological examination, or environmental survey. At least six primary building phases can be identified – three late medieval and three post-medieval – with evidence of secondary activity on several occasions. It is built throughout of local stone with Cotswold stone-tile roofs.

The imposing gateway at one end of an extended range of offices opens into a large courtyard, with a lodging range opposite and the hall and chamber complex to the right. The hall and cross wings were probably built in the years close to 1470, the gateway and first part of the lodging range at the end of the fifteenth century, and that range's extension and a lost one opposite next to the gateway by the next generation. All subsequent expansion occurred east and north of the hall core in a property notable for its late Elizabethan interiors and total dormancy throughout the Victorian period.

PHASE I : THIRD QUARTER OF FIFTEENTH CENTURY

There is no evidence that South Wraxall Manor was in any way defendable, lacking moat, defensive features, or even embattled parapets. In contrast with the later ashlar gateway, the hall range is rubble-built with ashlar dressings. The two-storey porch and bay window project forward of the hall, with the added chimney stack incorporating an original buttress. They and the overwhelming drawing room bay window give the courtyard a delightful if unplanned sequence of recessed planes. Porch, hall, and bay window are crowned with a continuous plain parapet with grotesque gargoyles.

Two features warrant particular attention. The window tracery is subtly varied. The twin cinquefoil lights of the porch window are surmounted by a lobed quatrefoil. The longer cinquefoil lights of the hall are below a two-light trefoil head, while the head above the three lights of the hall bay is of more pronounced Perpendicular character. All these windows are under four-centred hoods, but the head of the small two-light upper bay window differs again, under a square hood. Turning to the porch, it looks commanding with its diagonal buttresses, first-floor window, and bold entry arch with continuous roll and hollow chamfer and high-pitched four-centred head and hood. However, the inner entry is modest, with only a hollow chamfer, a flat ceiling, no side benches, and minimal area.

Post-medieval changes to the hall have not affected its initial character. The four-bay interior, 32½ feet by 20½ feet, is open to the roof, with opposing projections at the upper end opening from low arches repeating the roll and hollow chamfer of the outer entry. The apartment is lit by broad-splayed windows in the upper walling enhanced by four-centred rear arches rising from slender jamb shafts. There are two in the east wall and one in the west, subtly differing from the less deeply set three-light windows in both projecting bays.

The dark-painted roof is spanned by arch-braced collars with curved queen posts, with the heavy four-centred braces rising from extended wooden corbels of animals and angels carrying shields. These are supported in turn by short braced posts from stone corbels carrying more family shields – an incipient hammer-beam structure.[2] The heavily moulded wall plates and quatrefoil frieze might be expected but the usual rows of wall braces are replaced here by three lines of panels in each bay, separated by an intermediate truss. The panels are of elongated quatrefoil shape – the upper and lower row half-versions of the central row – enhanced with multi-traceried spandrels.

The post-medieval changes are not fundamental. The fireplace, stone chimneypiece, and stack were inserted in 1598. The screen was added at about the same time, with the forced entries to a balcony re-formed in the early twentieth century. It was at this time that the gable window was inserted to light the roof and the two-level corridor added against the east face giving close access to the upper windows. It incorporates an original window like those in the hall bays but was brought from elsewhere.

The layout of this hall with its upper bays was followed at Great Chalfield Manor, though with a much more modest roof. That at South Wraxall was highly decorative, and would have been even more impressive when the timbers were new cut and of light colour instead of the present dark staining, and the extensive decorative work was heightened by brilliant colours of which traces were found in the corbels during cleaning in 2001. There is no evidence of a louvre or original fireplace, so that this hall was unheated as at Tickenham Court, while the similar absence of a dais suggests that this apartment had now become a formal one for occasional use only.

The two hall bays opened into the ground floor of the upper chamber block, a totally altered structure at both levels. The left-hand bay serves the disappointing ground-floor facilities of entirely late twentieth-century character – two store rooms flanked by corridors. No medieval features survive, though the area, built against rising ground, was always low and ill-lit so that its function was never a primary one. It also incorporates a solid block of walling that supports a comparable bulk above.

The second hall bay opens on to an early eighteenth-century flight of stairs replacing the medieval one leading to the withdrawing chamber. This is one of the most spectacular late Elizabethan rooms in England and entirely of that era.[3] Four features vie for attention – the vast windows at each end, the magnificent stone carved fireplace and chimneypiece, the coved and decorated plaster ceiling, and the curious five-niche intrusion with contemporary panelling opposite the fireplace. All this is the work of Sir Walter Long, who created this apartment by enlarging the earlier chamber on two sides. The west and north walls were built 8 and 5 feet forward of the original outer walls and given the thirty-three- and

PLATE 276 South Wraxall Manor: hall range from inner court

thirty-light windows that now fill much of them. This expansion is indicated on the ceiling, where it changes from the curved shape that covered most of the fifteenth-century room to the flat section of the north extension where the plasterwork was discretely signed and dated J. Sweetman 1611.[4] By that time, the room had been enlarged from 31 feet by 19 feet internally to 36 feet by 22 feet internally. The intrusive bulk is explained by an examination of the roof structure above the ceiling, where there is a marked change in the trusses between those covering the original structure and those added by Sir Walter. Their juncture occurs above the intrusion which supported the enlarged roof area and ensured stability.

The cross-passage entries were identical with those next to them opening into the lower chamber block. One led via the steep newel to the well-lit room over the porch and the other formerly accessed the chamber over the offices by a stair shown in Walker's ground- and first-floor plans of 1838. The third opening is a 1900 enlargement of an original entry to what may have been the buttery and pantry, now a stair hall and study. However, the thinness of the internal partitions before 1900 (see Walker's plan), the lack of a ground-floor high-quality chamber opening from the hall bays, and the presence of a ground-floor parlour below the cross passage at Great Chalfield suggest the possibility that there was a comparable plan here. The single upper chamber has been replaced by the stair continuation and landing next to a panelled room with a fireplace of c.1600 with Long-initialled spandrels.

The kitchen was sited in an extension to the chamber block, as at Great Chalfield, and would have been open to the roof. The present structure of arch-braced collar trusses and three lines of curved wind braces is early but not necessarily original. Separated from the adjacent chamber block by a substantial internal wall and slightly higher roof, the kitchen was floored and given a new hearth by the later sixteenth century. I suspect that this was when the original structure was replaced and I have so indicated on the plans, but this much altered range awaits further analysis. By this time, the approach from the cross passage was pentice-protected (see roof lip), though the present corridor with framed upper storey is a 1900 replacement.

This is the extent of the original residence attributable to the Long family, whose name first occurs in the area in the early fifteenth century. The initial development is usually credited to Robert Long (d.1447) who had a house at South Wraxall in 1429 and is called Robert Long of Wraxall in 1448, the year after his probable death.[5] Leland states that Robert's advancement came through the patronage of the Hungerford family nearby, facilitating several property purchases in the area.[6] Robert represented the county in parliament in 1433 and was a commissioner of the peace in 1436. Yet there is nothing specific that determines Robert's responsibility for the present structure, while the closest parallels of both layout and detailing are with the gentry houses at Kingston Seymour, Tickenham Court, and Great Chalfield. All three can be

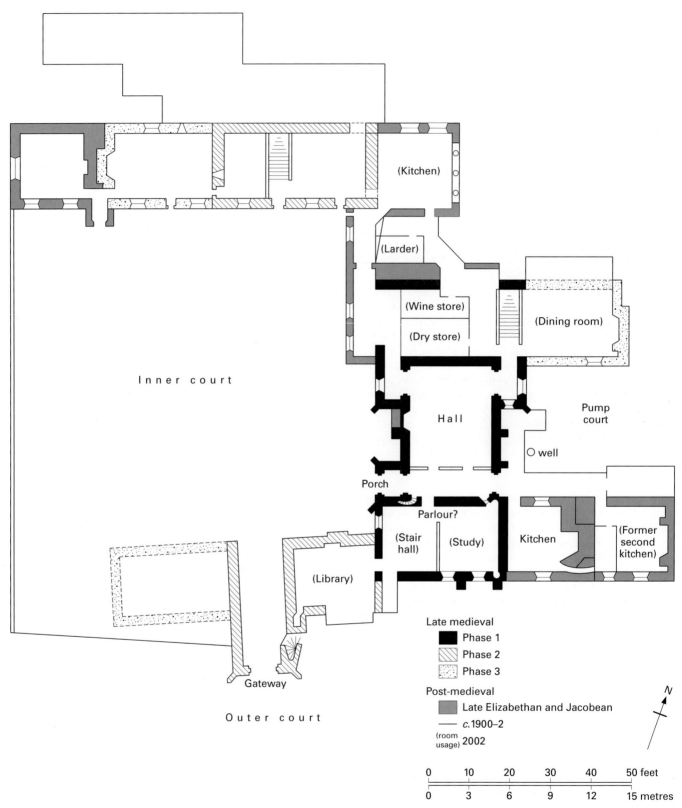

FIGURE 163 South Wraxall Manor: ground plan

reasonably attributed to Edward IV's reign, with Tickenham Court more precisely to 1471–6 and Great Chalfield to c.1478–85. South Wraxall and Great Chalfield both have an essentially formal hall but a surprisingly low non-residential area immediately behind, offset by the spacious withdrawing chamber over. They may well have had an innovative dining room or parlour below the cross passage, with the kitchen projecting outside the body of the house. However, the window detailing and roof form at South Wraxall are closer to those at Tickenham Court and Kingston Seymour, as is the lack of a mural fireplace in the hall. Until dendrochronology brings an element of precision, it is more probable that Robert's son, Henry Long (d.1490), was responsible for the present structure rather than his father.

PHASE 2 : LATE FIFTEENTH CENTURY

The second development phase was undertaken by Henry's heir and nephew Sir Thomas Long (d.1508), whose badge occurs on the gateway. This structure stands 15 feet proud of the attached range and was ashlar-built (pl. 302). One of the end stops of the square-headed entry arch is carved with a fetterlock, the badge adopted by Sir Thomas after he became lord of the Wiltshire manor of Draycote Cerne. The arch opens into a broad but plain passageway with low timbered ceiling and a 1900 replacement exit arch. The garderobe-provided lodging above, unusually reached by an external stair,[7] is notable for the three-sided oriel with modest corbelled base bearing the Long arms of a lion rampant, two rows of cinquefoil lights, and an embattled head. The parallel with one of the oriels at Great Chalfield Manor is even more obvious internally, as it repeats the same steps to the panelled base, and flat ceiling.

The gateway is joined to the body of the house by a two-storey block, now with 1900 bay windows to the front but retaining a garderobe in the angle, courtyard-facing cinquefoil lights, and early trusses above the plaster ceiling.

On the opposite side of the courtyard is a two-period lodging range, distinguished by a change in the character of the windows – the earlier opposite the gateway block with cinquefoil lights and the later with uncusped heads. Their junction is marked internally by the thickened central wall with a retained external light and side entry to the ground-floor lodging. The broader of the two early courtyard doors opened on to the stair serving the upper rooms. Each lodging was 15 feet deep, with rear windows but no garderobe evidence.[8] This range lay detached from the upper chamber block until it was linked with it at the beginning of the early seventeenth century.

The west end of the lodging range is in line with the west side of the gateway, suggesting that the outer court, initially enclosed by a wall linking the two, created a court half the size of the present one. There would also have been an outer court with stables and service units, making the external entry to the gateway lodging less exposed.

PHASE 3 : EARLY SIXTEENTH CENTURY

The three extensions of this phase enhanced both family and staff facilities. The two-storey extension east of the upper chamber block provided a handsome room at both levels, each opening from the original stair. Both rooms now have floor to ceiling stone chimney-pieces of c.1600, windows and panelling of c.1700, and plain ceilings, but the roof structure suggests earlier origins.

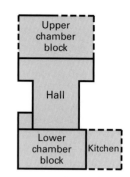

PHASE 1

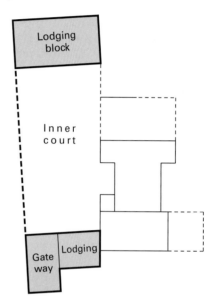

PHASE 2

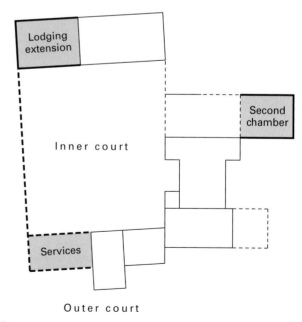

PHASE 3

FIGURE 164 South Wraxall Manor: late medieval development phases

The services were extended on both sides of the inner court – the lodging block to its present length with a similar range opposite next to the gateway. Nothing survives of this buttressed south range, shown in Buckler's drawing of 1808 but destroyed by the time of Walker's plans thirty years later. The inner court would have been extended, but only reached its present scale in the early seventeenth century, subject to landscaping three centuries later.

Sir Thomas Long, 'skilled in legal matters',[9] was succeeded by his son, Sir Henry, who died in 1556. It was he who was probably responsible for these additions but it was his grandson, Sir Walter Long (d.1610) who initiated the changes for which South Wraxall Manor is most famous.

LATER PHASES : c.1600–c.1900

At the close of Elizabeth I's reign, Sir Walter enlarged and remodelled the great chamber, added a stunning series of elaborately carved stone chimneypieces, inserted the screen and a since-removed plaster ceiling in the hall, and extended the house by two east-facing wings. The north one was for family use and the south one for services with rooms over, creating the extended buttress façade and varied roof line that fronts the house approach today. The hall fireplace is dated 1598 and the withdrawing chamber ceiling is signed and dated 1611.

About a century later, some of the family rooms were refenestrated and panelled, probably by Hope Long (d.1715) who held the house for sixty-three years. They introduced a note of calm harmony compared with Robert Long's busy hall roof and Sir Walter's ostentatious interiors.

South Wraxall Manor was not built by a clothier, but later branches of the Long family who settled in the Trowbridge/Bradford-on-Avon area made a rich living from the wool trade during the late sixteenth and seventeenth centuries.[10] The heirs of Thomas Long, an early eighteenth-century clothier of Melksham, inherited the Wraxall estate a century later. The Long family continued to hold the property until 1966 but they had long given up occupation. After short-lived use as a school in 1820–6, the house was closed and caretaker-maintained until 1900, when a new tenant, Richardson Cox, undertook a major restoration programme under A. C. Martin (1900–2). His judicious restoration of the Manor, untouched for two centuries, with extensive periodmatching work, brought the house to a state of comfort which has been maintained to the present day.

NOTES

1 E.g. C. Latham, *In English Homes*, I (1904) 217; *Country Life* (1904–5); Garner and Stratton (1911).

2 Illustrated in M. R. Bismanis, *The Medieval English Domestic Timber Roof* (1987) 201–3.

3 It was at this point in time that the closet above the hall west bay, initially reached from this chamber, was sealed off.

4 First observed during cleaning in 2001.

5 VCH, VII (1953) 22. Robert Long married a Popham whose arms, together with those of Long, are recorded in the hall by Aubrey. K. H. Rogers has confirmed that there is no evidence that Robert Long had any connection with the wool industry. Nor did he pay for the tower of Steeple Ashton church as is usually claimed.

6 *Itinerary*, I, 134–5, where Leland describes it as 'a little maner'. Great Chalfield was similarly linked to the powerful Hungerford family, as its builder Thomas Tropnell was steward to Robert, Lord Hungerford.

7 The internal entry was forced in 1900.

8 According to Garner and Stratton, 'the original roof with moulded principals and wind braces with pierced cuspings still remain above the modern ceiling': (1911) 42.

9 Leland, *Itinerary*, I, 135.

10 K. H. Rogers mentions Thomas Long of Trowbridge (c.1562) and Henry Long of Whaddon (c.1584) in *Warp and Weft* (1986) 28, 40, 43.

T. L. Walker, Supplement to Pugin's *Examples of Gothic Architecture*, III (1838) 1–18

T. H. Turner and J. H. Parker, *Some Account of Domestic Architecture in England*, III pt 2 (1859) 332–5

C. E. Ponting, *The Reliquary*, II pt 2 (1888) 95–9

E. Garner and A. Stratton, *The Domestic Architecture of England During the Tudor Period*, I (1911) 42–3

Anonymous, *Country Life* (March 1904; January 1905)

VCH, *Wiltshire*, VII (1953) 21–3

STOKE SUB HAMDON PRIORY, Somerset

Like Preston Plucknett 'Abbey' Manor and Naish 'Priory', Stoke Sub Hamdon 'Priory' is another Victorian misnomer in south Somerset. The property is not a monastic foundation but a chantry house, relevant to this study because of the completeness of the entire group of buildings.

During the thirteenth century, the local family of Beauchamp of Hatch held the manor of Stoke, living in the manor house they had built as a secondary home about a quarter of a mile north-east of the Priory.[1] John Beauchamp, knighted in 1306 but summoned to parliament and held to become 1st Lord Beauchamp in 1299, founded a chantry in the parish church in 1304 to be serviced by a provost and four chaplains.[2] The buildings under study were erected to house these priests and to serve as the centre of the farm that was their endowment and income. The barony was short-lived, for the direct line of Somerset Beauchamps fell into abeyance in 1361, with the property divided between female co-heirs. By the early fifteenth century, their relatives had left Stoke and the manor house fell into decay. The chantry continued to function through its independent endowment, but with only three priests by 1444. After the suppression of the chantry in 1548, the house continued in agricultural occupation until 1946, serving a farm that was the largest in the parish throughout the nineteenth century.

This community of priests was too small to warrant a quadrangular college but the house initially built here was almost ruinous by 1444 when bishop Bekynton of Wells ordered it to be repaired. The opportunity was taken to rebuild the property, reusing some of the ogee-shaped heads from the earlier building. What stands today is a mid-fifteenth-century house, extended to the rear during the seventeenth century when the opportunity was taken to upgrade the earlier windows, leaving only two trefoil lights untouched (porch and chapel). The forecourt retains several agricultural buildings, also built of the local golden stone, sufficient to support Leland's description of the property being 'large'.[3]

The forecourt is screened from the village street by a buttressed wall broken by an extremely tall arched entrance for carts and a smaller side entry (blocked) for pedestrians. The outer court is irregularly surrounded by a number of farm buildings of medieval

PLATE 277 Stoke Sub Hamdon Priory: hall range from the forecourt

origin. Against the street wall are thatched stables, built as two units, with attic hay lofts. Opposite is a thatched barn with central porch, a smaller version of that at Preston Plucknett Manor but in a similar relation to the house. Closing the third side of the court is a nineteenth-century open cattle shed. Behind the barn is a second yard, with the walls of three ruined buildings, a cart shed and granary, a barn opposite,[4] and a late medieval dovecote against its south gable holding about 500 nesting boxes. This grouping of barns, stables, dovecote, and enclosure was similar to the forecourt of many lesser manor houses which have all too often lost such utilitarian structures as a consequence of nineteenth-century 'tidying up'.

The compact fifteenth-century house, at right angles to the street, is made up of hall with porch and dais bay, offices with chamber over, and first-floor chapel. There was a separate unit to the rear that was probably the kitchen, built against and linked to the house by the contemporary buttressed wall. The accommodation was extended from this service unit in both directions along the street during the seventeenth century.

The two-storey porch with diagonal buttresses has similar outer and inner entry arches of continuous wave-moulded jambs and two-centred head. The windowless porch opens into the cross passage, with two central service doorways with pronounced ogee heads, one hacked away. An inserted stone wall replaces the former screen.[5] The hall, 36 feet by 18 feet, is once more open to the roof, though the roughness of the walls testifies to extended farm occupation, emphasised through stripping out the seventeenth-century inserted floor and internal divisions in the 1960s. Despite its external charm, the value of this hall is not immediate. The much-damaged four-bay roof of arch-braced collar trusses with raked struts and two rows of wind braces was routine rather than distinguished. The six-light window is early sixteenth century and the others are seventeenth century, when the mural fireplace was inserted. However, this was in the position of a fifteenth-century window of which the right jamb is partially visible. Next to it, a tall arch formerly opened from the dais into the south bay, open to the roof, with a tall south window and possibly a garderobe in the small west projection. This generous bay, very similar to that at Coker Court, gave the hall considerable style. Unfortunately, the arch was blocked in the seventeenth century, when the bay was floored to create two rooms, refenestrated, and given fireplaces.[6] At the same time, the end wall of the hall and its north return wall were rebuilt, removing any evidence as to whether there was a further chamber beyond the dais or not.

The room opening from the right-hand cross-passage door may have been used for services, but as the chimney stack (seventeenth-century fireplace) is original, it was more probably used as a parlour. The left-hand door served the stair to the first-floor chamber,[7] probably the chaplains' corporate bedchamber as enjoined in their statutes, with access to the porch room and chapel. The two-storey chapel projection with its bell-cot has an external entry to the ground-floor room of unknown purpose. The small chapel above retains its north trefoil light, ogee-headed piscina, and squint from the bedchamber.

The value of Stoke Sub Hamdon Priory is twofold. From the forecourt, this group of medieval buildings – the house with its street entrance and yard-enclosed agricultural buildings – still wears the character invested here in about 1450.[8] And though the domestic function of this small corporate residence was overlain with a quasi-monastic purpose, there was no architectural difference between this house and any other contemporary secular dwelling. In fact, the dais bay showed that it was in the forefront of up-to-date comfort.

NOTES
1 For the family, J. Batten, *Proc. Somerset Arch. and N. H. Soc.* 36 (1891) 20–59. Their house at Stoke Sub Hamdon was in existence by 1283 when John Beauchamp was buried in its chapel in October 1283. The house was crenellated under licence in 1333 at the same time that John 1st Lord Beauchamp (d.1336) obtained one for Hatch Beauchamp, 12 miles away, *Cal. Pat. Rolls: 1330–34*, 494. Two blocked gateways and some walling survive. The site was examined by W. W. Walter, *Proc. Somerset Arch. and N. H. Soc.* 35 (1889) 129–37, and again in 1976, P. J. Leach, *Proc. Somerset Arch. and N. H. Soc.* 124 (1980) 61–76. Nothing survives at Hatch Beauchamp earlier than the house of 1755 (Hatch Court).
2 Peters and Ireland (1979) 10.
3 *Itinerary*, I, 158–9. At the same time, Leland observed that the village held the very noble ruins of the great manor or castle of the Beauchamps.
4 The cartshed extension towards the house was elaborated with a mullioned window above a reused fourteenth-century lancet, solely for show as it was visible from the forecourt approach.
5 The two opposed openings in the hall next to the screen seem to be a cupboard and door, but neither function is clear.
6 During the 1960s, the left-hand jamb of the dais arch and the external jambs of the south window were exposed.
7 An original truss was found in the 1960s like those in the hall, embedded in the eighteenth-century ceiling.
8 The post-medieval additions extending southwards as a two-storey house add to the value of the streetscape and do not intrude into the late medieval scene.

W. A. Pantin, *Med. Arch.* 3 (1959) 219–24
VCH, *Somerset*, III (1974) 239–41
J. E. C. Peters and P. M. Ireland, *The Priory, Stoke-Sub-Hamdon: National Trust Leaflet* (1979)

STOURTON HOUSE, Wiltshire

Nothing survives of Stourton House, but this mid-fifteenth-century mansion was among the more important in southern England. In 1448, Sir John Stourton was granted a licence to

PLATE 278 Stourton House: sketch of house from the south by John Aubrey (1685)

enclose a thousand acres of pasture, meadow, and woodland[1] and though no licence to crenellate was sought, the association between house construction and emparking was a common one and was probably so here. Leland gives an unduly detailed description: 'The Lorde Stourton's place stondith on a meane hille, the soyle therof beyng stony. This maner place hathe 2 courtes; the fronte of the ynner courte is magnificent, and high embatelid castelle lyke . . . The goodly gate howse and fronte of the Lorde Stourton's howse in Stourton was buyldyd *ex spoliis Gallorum*.'[2] Visiting the house 150 years later, John Aubrey recorded that it was very large and very old, but 'little considerable as to architecture'.[3] He noted, however, the great open-roofed hall and an extraordinary large and high open-to-the-roof kitchen. He also added a sketch which shows that the house was two-storeyed, with ranges round three sides of the inner court with a plain wall closing off the fourth. Angle turrets rose high above the roof at each end of the principal range, but he does not show any other dominant feature.

The affluent banker Henry Hoare purchased the property in 1717 and quickly demolished it preparatory to erecting a Palladian villa nearby which he renamed Stourhead. The site of Stourton House lay almost opposite but a little south-east of the present mansion, near the east end of the stable yard. According to Sir Richard Colt Hoare in 1822, 'some of the subterraneous vaults of stone are still known and some aged Spanish chestnut trees mark the approach to it from the village of Stourton'.[4] In March 1799, Colt Hoare pulled down the outer gateway with two embattled towers leading from the village to his stable yard, and immediately rebuilt it to the same plan at the foot of the hill where it still stands, as do the Spanish chestnut trees. Two or three of the estate lodges also have deep-cut trefoil-light windows, possibly reproducing the late medieval form adopted by Lord Stourton for Stourton House.

The manor of Stourton was held by the family of that name since at least the twelfth century. There was a house here before the mid-fifteenth century[5] but it is likely that John, Lord Stourton (d.1462) built the house anew, as so many of his associates did at this time.[6] Though Leland attributed its funding to the spoils of the Hundred Years' War, funding was more probably the consequences of Henry VI's generosity towards a trusted friend and favoured member of the royal circle. Born in about 1399 and holder of several local offices during his late twenties, Stourton was knighted in 1432 and already richer four years later than several minor peers.[7] He was a minor rather than influential member of the Privy Council after his appointment in 1437, and one of the many custodians of the duke of Orléans (1438–9), but he was treasurer of the royal household from 1446 to 1453, and ennobled in 1448, the years that Stourton was emparked.[8] Nor did his rewards abate. He was made surveyor of all the parks and forests in Wiltshire (1447), granted the castles of Old Sarum and Mere (1454), and appointed joint guardian of Calais (1450–5).[9]

Stourton remained in the family for three centuries, with some minor additions to the house by the 2nd and 3rd Lord Stourton. Colt Hoare noted that he had identified 'an old chimney piece (of good Gothic taste) carved in stone with the arms of Stourton with those of Chidiok' and Berkeley of Beverston, the wife of the 2nd Lord Stourton (d.1477) and the wife of the 3rd Lord Stourton (d.1484) respectively.[10]

The fortunes of the Stourton family declined from the mid-sixteenth century onwards, leading to straitened circumstances. The house was attacked by parliamentary troops in 1644 and rendered uninhabitable, while the retained Catholic faith of the family meant exclusion from office, impoverishment, encumbered estates, and debt. There was no money to restore the family home, which was probably derelict by the early eighteenth century. As soon as the property had been sold to Henry Hoare, he signalled his intention to replace it with a 'modern edifice' by Colin Campbell,[11] on more elevated ground than its predecessor. Henry died in 1724 and was succeeded by his son of the same name (d.1789), who transformed the grounds during the mid-eighteenth century into the landscape for which Stourhead has ever since been world famous.

NOTES
1 K. Woodbridge, *The Stourhead Landscape* (1982) 5.
2 *Itinerary*, V, 105, 223.
3 *Topographical Collections of Wiltshire*, ed. J. E. Jackson and J. Britton (1862).
4 Colt Hoare (1822) 42.
5 There is a mutilated effigy of a lady of *c*.1400 in the fourteenth-century parish church. By the later fourteenth century, the family was already among the more wealthy gentry of Wiltshire and Somerset, with Stourton straddling the county border.
6 A. Emery, *Greater Med. Houses*, II (2000) 494–6.
7 H. L. Gray, *Eng. Hist. Rev.* 59 (1934) 607–39. By 1459, Stourton was lending substantial sums to the crown. R. A. Griffiths, *The Reign of Henry VI* (1981) 788 and n.114. Sir John also funded the restoration of the church and cloister of Stavordale Priory, 3 miles away, in 1439–43. The church is now a two-storey private house restored in 1905. G. Sweetman, *The History of Stavordale Priory* (1908); R. Haslam, *Country Life* (May 1992); *Med. Arch.* 37 (1993) 280–1.
8 His commendation identified personal probity, impeccable origins, and service to both Henry V and Henry VI. Stourton was probably a close associate of cardinal Beaufort. J. Watts, *Henry VI and the Politics of Kingship* (1996) 187. Other building treasurers of the royal household include Sir Walter Hungerford (Farleigh Hungerford Castle) and Sir Roger Fiennes (Herstmonceux Castle) while building treasurers of

England under Henry VI include Ralph, Lord Cromwell (Tattershall Castle, Wingfield Manor), Sir Ralph Boteler (Sudeley Castle), and Sir James Fiennes (Knole).

9 *Com. Peer.*, XII pt 1 (1953) 300–2.
10 Colt Hoare (1822) 42.
11 *Ibid.* 63.

Sir Richard Colt Hoare, *The History of Modern Wiltshire*, I pt 1 (1822) 42
Charles, Lord Mowbray, Segrave, and Stourton, *The History of the Noble House of Stourton* (1899)
D. Dodd, *Stourhead: National Trust Guidebook* (1981)

STURMINSTER NEWTON MANOR HOUSE,
Dorset

The south approach to Sturminster Newton is marked by a bridge of *c.*1500 across the River Stour and the earthworks of the 'castle' that formerly commanded it. The banks and ditches are probably the defences of a prehistoric fort rather than any medieval castle, for the property was the manor of Newton, held by Glastonbury Abbey from 968 to 1539.[1] The stone ruins within the embanked triangular spur are those of a fourteenth-century manor house, or more accurately the remains of the offices and chamber block to a destroyed hall.

It was a manor house of some quality, with the hall and storeyed block built in line. The latter stands to full height on three sides, though the gable high-end wall is not bonded to the side walls. All that remains of the hall are its two entries, relatively plain, with double-chamfered jambs and two-centred heads. One stands complete, but the east entry has lost its head. As the hall was 25½ feet wide internally, analogous structures suggest it extended between 35 and 42 feet towards the river, but the walls have been destroyed and the site has not been excavated.

Part of the common wall between the hall and chamber block stands, with two cross-passage doorways with two-centred heads, and the footings of two further doorways can be traced. These four doorways identify the standard plan of the offices, separated by a central kitchen passage, with the taller fourth doorway leading to the first-floor chamber.

The offices and chamber block is not large, 15 feet by 25½ feet internally, buttressed on the east side. The buttery and pantry were of low height. The east-facing room was lit by a single rectangular light. The west room, surprisingly, has no obvious light source but a low fireplace with a head identical with that in the chamber above. The door in the middle of the end wall, in line with the kitchen passage, is similar to the hall entries with a single continuous chamfer and segmental rear arch.

The first floor was a single chamber with a large window in both side walls, clearer on the east side and retaining its traceried head until vandalised in the 1960s. There was a small recessed rectangular light in the south-east corner, and a centrally positioned fireplace with depressed four-centred head in the gable wall. The doorway in the south-west corner with two-centred head was to a garderobe retaining a little of its projecting side wall. The chamber walls retain some of their plaster facing, with the gable wall marked by the beam holes for the trusses of a three-bay roof structure.

PLATE 279 Sturminster Newton Manor House: from the west

Leland refers to the 'faire maner place of an hille made stepe rounde by mannes hand caullid yn olde writings Newton Castelle . . . The castelle syns clerely decayed, and the abbates of Glessenbyri made ther a fair maner place, and usid to resorte onto yt.'[2] In the late thirteenth century, abbot Robert Petherton (1261–74) enclosed '*forinseca ballia quondam castelli*',[3] but the architectural character of this single-phase building points to an early to mid-fourteenth-century date, a little earlier than the solar block at Fiddleford Manor less than a mile away. At Sturminster Newton, the chamber block was built in line with the hall instead of as a cross wing, and with the solar above the offices instead of an undercroft (later converted to offices) as at Fiddleford. Because of the earthen banks and the steep drop to the river, this manor house was probably restricted to a hall and single end block, unless a second one lay at a right angle to the river-facing end of the hall. Built of rubble stone, the remains are marked by relieving arches above all openings and fireplaces, while the site abounds with fallen masonry, including the dressed stones of several cinquefoil window heads.

NOTES
1 *The Great Chartulary of Glastonbury*, ed. A. Watkin, I (1952) 60.
2 *Itinerary*, V, 107.
3 Adam de Downham, *Historia de rebus gestis Glastoniensibus*, ed. T. Hearne, II (1727) 535.

RCHM, *Dorset*, III pt 2 (1970) 282–3

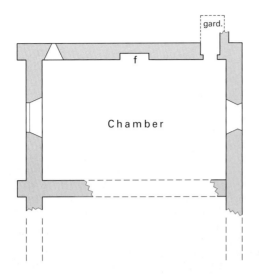

FIRST FLOOR

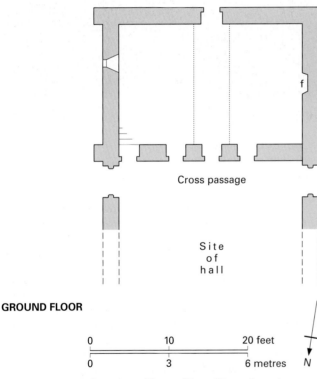

Cross passage

Site of hall

GROUND FLOOR

| 0 | 10 | 20 feet |
| 0 | 3 | 6 metres |

FIGURE 165 Sturminster Newton Manor House: floor plans

TICKENHAM COURT, Somerset

The Court stands immediately to the rear of Tickenham church on a low limestone ridge overlooking Kenn Moor, part of the north Somerset Levels. On initial examination the Court looks of single-period build, the third quarter of the fifteenth century, with a late Tudor extension, and this is how it has been assessed by the RCHM

survey.[1] However, it is a two-phased house, with part of the earlier structure retained during its redevelopment in the early 1470s.

The manor of Tickenham was held by the Basset family between the mid and the late fourteenth century, by which time it had passed by marriage to Sir Edmund Seymour (d. before 1422) and his wife.[2] Seymour's heir was his granddaughter Elizabeth, the wife of Thomas Berkeley (d.1444/5), a younger son of Sir Maurice Berkeley of Beverston (d.1460). Thomas' son John held the manor of Tickenham until his death in 1479. He had no issue and was apparently a tenant of Sir Maurice's grandson, Sir William Berkeley of Beverston (d.1485), who had held the manor since 1468. The property was subsequently occupied by the Asshe family as sub-tenants of the Berkeleys.[3]

The Court reflects the work of three periods, the mid to late fourteenth century under the Bassets or Seymour, the third quarter of the fifteenth century under the Berkeleys, and modifications by the last of the Asshes (d.1581). The property passed through a succession of owners and farm tenants from the mid-seventeenth century to the mid-twentieth century. It is this last factor that accounts for the almost complete preservation of the property, with the unpartitioned hall used as a cider apple store with a small hay loft, until 1946 when an extended programme of restoration was initiated.

The house is T-shaped, with the hall and offices forming the stem and the residential range its head. It is rubble-built of local lime-stone, but the original stone tiles were replaced in the late nine-teenth century with red clay tiles. The walls of both hall and range retain some of the original plaster facing. Its reinstatement and colour wash as at Gurney Manor or Birdcombe Court is greatly to be desired.[4] The original approach is not clear, but there is little doubt that it was from the south-east, possibly marked by the boundary wall used in part as the irregular rear wall of an eighteenth-century barn. A right-angle approach across a broad grassed area brings the visitor to the site of the hall porch. This forecourt has not yet been subject to a geophysical survey but pipe trenching indicates the presence of considerable building material.[5]

The hall has lost its porch and dais bay projections, the former rising to wall plate level with wall scars marking both their positions. The hall doorway and windows are a mixture of two- and four-centred heads, and this has led to considerable dating uncertainty.[6] Both cross-passage entries have four-centred heads with continuous roll and fillet mouldings and low four-centred rear arches. The three doorways in the lower end wall of the hall are of similar form but the tall arch of the dais bay (now glazed) in the angle between hall and residential range is two-centred with inner and outer hollow chamfers. The windows high in the side walls of the hall combine both features. They are of two cinquefoil ogee lights below a quatrefoil head under a two-centred hood externally and a four-centred rear arch internally.

The hall entries were drawbar protected, and the infilled sockets can be traced that carried the head rail of the timber-framed screen. The plain timber ceiling is a 1959 insertion concealing the original four-bay roof of principal and intermediate arch-braced collar trusses with three lines of lost wind braces, the lowest curved between the five principals, and those above prettily curved between all trusses, with the highest cusp shaped next to the roof ridge. The intermediate trusses are rudimentary but chamfered and

PLATE 280 Tickenham Court: hall and parlour wing from the east

stopped.[7] The roof is dendro dated to the summer of 1471,[8] and revealing it would add immeasurably to the value of this hall, as would the reinstatement of the plaster facing of the inner walls as in the refectory of Cleeve Abbey.

There is no sign of any mural fireplace or chimney stack, sooted timbers from a central hearth, or roof structure evidence for a louvre.[9] Heating may have been by braziers. The two facing decorative shelves in the side walls, a line of quatrefoils above a fleuron frieze, seem to have been inserted from elsewhere.[10] The bay window is a substantial one, approximately 8½ feet square, which not only accessed the residential range by a relatively modest entry identical with the cross-passage doorways, but may have held a fireplace as well as the large window lighting the dais area. It is likely there was a small chamber above, reached via internal steps from the residential range.

This hall, 37 feet by 20 feet, is a mixture of plainness and sophistication. Doorway mouldings were modest; the walls lack an ashlar plinth, and were plaster-faced. On the other hand, the position of the hall windows followed contemporary practice though they were off-centre to the principal roof trusses, and the bay window was spacious and imposing, while the hall roof was a highly decorative one for the region.

The question arises whether this hall is of the later fourteenth century with windows of that period, subject to some remodelling in the 1470s when the roof was replaced, or whether the reconstruction was more wholesale. The walls are of the earlier period. John Winstone has pointed out to me that the west gable wall shows the slight shadow of an earlier ridge and pitch line internally and the cut end of an axial post at ceiling level. Furthermore, there is substantial evidence that the side walls were raised 5 feet to the eaves level. Though the lower parts of the windows are formed of separate internal and external jamb stones, the heads sit on large single jamb stones the full depth of the reveals. The four windows had originally been set in gables with two-centred heads and rear arches, altered to their present form when the roof was raised in the 1470s. The projecting bay window with its two-centred head, almost identical with that at Kingston Seymour Manor (*temp.* Edward IV), and the porch were added at the same time. The earlier approach to the solar block had been by the door in the north-west corner of the hall (now seventeenth century) accessing the solar via a stair.[11] Whether the remodelling at Tickenham Court was undertaken by the tenant John Berkeley, or his overlord Sir William Berkeley, is unclear.

The residential range is made up of two units, linked by a half-octagonal stair turret but with the second unit marked by a lower roofline and internal floor level. The outer chamber is a generously lit room with transomed four-light window facing east, an equally large one to the south (blocked), and a pair of two-light transomed

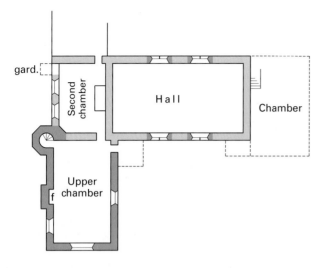

FIRST FLOOR

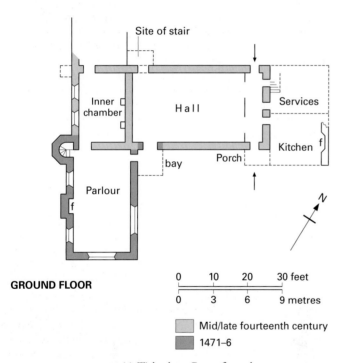

GROUND FLOOR

```
0        10        20        30 feet
0         3         6         9 metres
```

☐ Mid/late fourteenth century
■ 1471–6

FIGURE 166 Tickenham Court: floor plans

inserted hearth and stack, and a modified hood and shortened pair of cinquefoil lights. The engraving in Parker's 1859 volume shows this window in its original form, with similar windows at the upper level.[12]

The projecting stone newel, loop and quatrefoil lit, opens directly into the upper chamber. This was always a heated but more modestly lit room than below, with two twin-light windows and a larger gable-end window with two-centred head, now lacking its tracery and with a 1960s lowered sill.[13] It is open to a four-bay roof of arch-braced collars, plain-moulded wall plates, and three lines of wind braces. The doorway to the inner room has a slightly different form (two continuous roll mouldings) and steps to a lower floor level. It repeats the Tudor-style replacement windows of the lower room and retains the garderobe entry of late Tudor date, not revealed at the time of Parker's engraving. The two bays of roof trusses are of similar form and date to those in the adjacent room, though the timbers are more crude and most of the two lines of curved wind braces have been replaced.

This second unit to the rear of the hall and in line with it appears to be of the same date as its neighbour, particularly so in Parker's engraving with windows of common form throughout, and this seems to be confirmed by roof timbers in both chambers dendro dated to 1476.[14] However, the siting and height of this unit leave little doubt that it is earlier, of unclear date but of the fourteenth century, and retained at the same time as the original hall of the Berkeleys when the residential unit was extended. The stair turret cuts across the end truss of the second unit, while doors were forced through at both levels necessitating the upper steps still in place. The opportunity was also taken to refenestrate and reroof the second unit, though without raising the roof to the same height to create a continuous roof line. The earlier wall continuation on the west side was embraced by the northwards extension of 1570–5,[15] originally open to the roof.

The offices and lower chamber block has long since been pulled down and the site has not been excavated, but sufficient evidence survives for its cross-wing form to be established. A central timber-framed partition separated the services from the kitchen, approached from the two mid-cross-passage doorways, with the kitchen as the larger area through bringing its south wall in line with the south porch. The remains of the kitchen hearth and stack of uncertain date survive 16 feet from the cross passage. The doorway close to the north entry opened on to a flight of steps, loop lit, rising to the upper chamber of which part of the doorway head and door rebate survive in the hall wall. Any fireplace is likely to have been in the lost opposing wall, but the door jamb remains to the chamber over the porch.

Tickenham Court is a gratifying survival, an extremely well-preserved gentry house remodelled over a five-year period from 1471 to 1476, reusing the earlier hall and solar block, with the possibility that the lower end block was also remodelled rather than built anew. The absence of any heating in the hall and the siting of the parlour suggest that the former had already become a formal reception apartment in the 1470s redevelopment. The position of the side windows indicates that its lower walls were panelled or covered with tapestry-like hangings, while the generous hall bay, if heated, may have been a separate eating area.[16] The prominent position and scale of the added residential unit points to its growing importance, with transomed windows to take advantage of the

windows either side the original fireplace to the west. All windows have two-centred heads to the lights below the transom and cinquefoil ogee heads to the upper lights under a square hood and depressed four-centred rear arch. The wide fireplace has a four-centred head and plain lintel. Moulded cross beams divide the ceiling into eight panels, quartered by light mouldings with foliated tracery at the corners. This is a well-lit and comfortable chamber with newel access to the upper floor and nearby door to the inner chamber, both with the mouldings seen in the hall. The inner chamber reflects post-medieval farmhouse occupation with nineteenth-century Tudor-style windows, crude ceiling beams, parlour's ceiling height and a generous chamber above. The rooms of the earlier solar unit were converted into subsidiary or inner chambers. A similar development has been attributed to Birdcombe Court nearby.[17] However, it is possible that the Tickenham builder overstretched himself in the multi-windowed parlour, necessitating blocking the large church-facing window for stability reasons as similarly occurred in the mid-1530s range at Iron Acton Court.

NOTES

1 Fradgley and Burgess (1992–3) 1, 5.
2 J. Smyth, *The Lives of the Berkeleys*, ed. Sir J. Maclean, II (1883) 15; *Feudal Aids 1284–1431*, 4, 51.
3 *British Library Harleian Manuscript 433*, ed. R. Horrox and P. W. Hammond I (1979) 174. I owe the resolution of this property's complex ownership to the researches of Nicholas Deas.
4 For Gurney Manor, see page 574. A little earlier, a parlour cross wing, dendro dated to 1441–2, was added at the lower end of the earlier hall at Birdcombe Court, less than 2 miles east of Tickenham on the edge of the same limestone ridge. Possibly dating from the late thirteenth century, the hall was upgraded at the same time with a stone-vaulted porch under a four-storey tower. Only the tower and cross wing survived the mid-eighteenth- and early nineteenth-century Gothick redevelopments. M. R. Bismanis, *Arch. Jour.* 134 (1977) 303–6; *Vern. Arch.* 30 (1999) 111.
5 It is possible that this material and the earthworks relate to an unlicensed castle of the Stephen and Matilda era. The rubble stone could have been the resource used for the house. Buckler shows that there was a north porch approach from the church through the barton.
6 M. E. Wood, *The English Mediaeval House* (1965) 59, 104, 355, 366 followed by Plant (1977) 338. Also Fradgley and Burgess (1992–3) 2, 5.
7 J. T. Smith, *Arch. Jour.* 115 (1958) 131.
8 *Vern. Arch.* 25 (1994) 28–9.
9 Fradgley and Burgess noted some slight footings of a possible stack on the north side between the windows, but the walling does not suggest wholesale rebuilding. Near the north entry are some low courses of ashlar masonry, possibly reused earlier material. For an inadequate record of the restoration between 1946 and 1974, appendix 3 in Forrest (1975) 103–7.
10 There is a similar but better-preserved decorated stone shelf at Croscombe Hall, see page 534.
11 The door stop is up one step, set on rubble, with the seventeenth-century west extension wall running on part of the former projection.
12 Turner and Parker (1859) opp. 345. The drawings were by A. Nesbitt.
13 Buckler's drawing of 1828 shows the tracery of the upper window and suggests that the lower one was not yet blocked. There are also traces of a further window over the bay projection but this needs further investigation.
14 *Vern. Arch.* 25 (1994) 28–9. Even timber from the same tree was used in both units. Fradgley and Burgess (1992–3) 5, and appendix.
15 *Ibid.* John Winstone tells me that there is some evidence that the original solar in the cross wing was contracted when the parlour block was added.
16 The straight joint to the dais bay visible in the parlour is not a construction joint but confirmation that the dais initially stood alone and preceded the construction of the added solar wing.
17 *Arch. Jour.* 134 (1977) 306.

T. H. Turner and J. H. Parker, *Some Account of Domestic Architecture in England*, III pt 2 (1859) 345
J. Byrchmore, *Collections for a Parochial History of Tickenham* (1900)
D. Forrest, *The Making of a Manor: The Story of Tickenham Court* (1975)
R. Plant, *Arch. Jour.* 134 (1977) 338–9
N. Fradgley and R. Burgess, NMRC, no.BF 043630 (1992–3)

TISBURY, PLACE FARM, Wiltshire

Shaftesbury Abbey had held Tisbury manor since the tenth century and developed it as a grange for their nearby estates during the twelfth century. After the property had been leased out to tenants towards the close of the middle ages, the house was retained by the abbess for her own use. The tenant had to live in a house outside the precinct.[1] The property was called Manor Place in 1579, and though it has continued as an agricultural holding, it ceased to be a working farm in 2002. The house has been let, and the farm buildings are to be converted into offices and dwellings.

Like the abbey's grange at Bradford-on-Avon, Tisbury was also built outside the village, and this has helped to preserve this remarkable group of buildings. The outer gatehouse led into the forecourt with the byres and barn to one side. An inner gatehouse calmed the approach to the inner court with the abbess' house lining its east side. The west side of each court was protected by stream and marshland. The outer gatehouse was erected during the early to mid-fourteenth century; the inner gatehouse, house, and barn were built during the fifteenth century. Some time after the Dissolution, the agricultural buildings were separated from the forecourt by a wall, with new access to them further east to give Place Farm a less salubrious and more orderly approach.

The outer gatehouse is multi-buttressed to the front, with a broad carriage entry and modest pedestrian entry at its side, though with a bolder inner arch to the forecourt. Both passages have beamed ceilings. External stairs accessed the upper chamber, with two-light uncusped windows in both outer faces. Nothing survives of the two-storey wings added each side of this gateway during the late fifteenth or early sixteenth century except the buttressed south faces.

The inner gatehouse, on the opposite side of the elongated forecourt, is a more modest version of the outer gate. It repeats the two-

PLATE 281 Tisbury, Place Farm: outer gate from the street

storey form but did not need the wagon passage – only a pedestrian entry (shallow mouldings to entry arch) and a porter's lodge were necessary. This building originally seems to have extended further west, necessitating another more recent external stair to the room above.

The abbess' house at the side was a single range, heavily modified during the nineteenth century when the rear extension with gabled bay window was added. It had an open hall, with the kitchen north of it under a common roof ridge. During the early sixteenth century, both rooms were floored, though the kitchen retains its large end-wall fireplace and octagonal chimney. The house was always two-storeyed south of the hall, with the upper chamber retaining its roof of cusped arch braces. In the fifteenth century, the buildings incorporated two chapels, one adjoining the abbess' chamber.[2]

The farm buildings lay outside the two courts. The imposing barn is the principal medieval survival, low-buttressed on both sides with central transeptal porches and narrow air slits in side and end walls. The thirteen-bay cruck roof of corbel-supported arch braces and two tiers of collars was crudely made, but this barn still retains its thatched cover, remade by five men in 1971 at a cost of £18,000. The Tisbury barn lacks the grace of those at Great Coxwell or Bradford-on-Avon.[3] Place Farm not only reflects the double-courtyard layout of a much larger dwelling but, more clearly than most, reflects the busy activity of the outer court with stables, offices, and agricultural buildings, and the greater privacy of the residential inner court. The buildings are robust rather than architecturally distinguished, but none the worse for that in a highly attractive ensemble.

NOTES
1 VCH, XIII (1987) 198.
2 *Ibid.*
3 The most recent assessment of these barns is F. W. B. Charles, *The Great Barn of Bredon: Its Fire and Reconstruction* (1997).

A. R. Dufty, *Arch. Jour.* 104 (1948) 168–9
VCH, *Wiltshire*, XIII (1987) 198

TIVERTON CASTLE, Devon and the Courtenay family

The Courtenay family dominated the politics of late medieval Devon until their unremitting loyalty to the house of Lancaster and Tudor vengeance brought about their downfall. They were a close-knit family of regional though not national importance who came to England in the train of Eleanor of Aquitaine upon her marriage to Henry II. They were granted the manor of Sutton Courtenay in Berkshire, but Okehampton Castle became the centre of their holding through the marriage of Reginald Courtenay in 1173 to Hawisia, the heiress of the castle's founding family. The local influence of the Courtenay family, already considerable by the time of Hugh Courtenay's succession in 1292,[1] was substantially enhanced four years later when he became sole collateral heir to a second inheritance (as a consequence of an earlier Courtenay's marriage), to most of the Redvers estates in the West Country including the manors and castles of Plympton and Tiverton. The young Hugh Courtenay entered into his property in 1297 to practise the twin policy of expanding his property base through the accumulation of

manors, and by marrying his many children into the most important local or regionally significant families.[2]

Okehampton, perched above the valley of the West Okement, is a motte and bailey castle of late eleventh-century origin, drastically remodelled by Hugh Courtenay during the first half of the fourteenth century as a comfortable residence within the curtilage of the defensive courtyard. The ruins were subject to a detailed structural survey and excavation programme between 1972 and 1980.[3] The hall and services were a single structure under a common roof, the hall open to a roof of base-cruck trusses, while the services at the lower end were surmounted by a solar chamber. Lit mainly by two courtyard-facing windows, the hall had a dais with a large hearth immediately in front of it. The heated chamber above the services, lit by end windows, was approached by an external stair. The kitchen was a detached square structure. On the opposite side of the narrow courtyard lay the chapel and a line of two-storey lodgings with projecting garderobes. The parallels with other Devon buildings are clear – the common-roofed hall and services with Lustleigh Old Hall, the detached kitchen and lodgings with Dartington Hall, the residential addition to the earlier keep with Gidleigh – and though much of this work is attributable to the early fourteenth century,[4] the lodgings and kitchen were not erected until the close of that century.[5]

Despite this extensive building programme, Hugh Courtenay made the more accessible Tiverton Castle the residential heart of his estates. Like Okehampton Castle, Tiverton seems to have been a motte and bailey structure, with the motte flattened well over 200 years ago. Surmounting a cliff 60 feet high above the River Exe, the site is roughly quadrangular with two small round towers at the opposing south-east and north-west corners, the former standing to full height and the latter reduced to foundation level. These and the scanty curtain walling show that the defensive structures were always relatively modest. They can be attributed to the Redvers family, earls of Devon, who held the castle from 1106 to 1293, when it passed to the seventeen-year-old Hugh Courtenay. Unlike Okehampton Castle, Tiverton has not been subject to a detailed structural or archaeological study, for part of the site is still occupied, the remainder of the courtyard is covered by a landscaped garden, and the wide moat that gave protection on three sides has been infilled and partially built over. It is possible that the motte was abandoned by the time of the Courtenays, emphasising the castle's quadrangular shape and residential development.[6]

The still-occupied gatehouse facing the street was built of rubble sandstone quarried from near Exeter. It is in two conjoined parts. The later outer gatehouse is spanned by a multi-moulded and fleuron-decorated archway with two-centred head opening into a single-vaulted bay. The quadripartite ribbed vault in Beer stone rests on three-quarter corner pillars repeating the fleuron design on the capitals. The earlier inner gateway is narrow, with two lower vaulted bays with central bosses. Standing in line with the castle's east front of the same early to mid-fourteenth-century date, the rib-vaulted bays rise from pillars with round capitals but the inner and central arches have depressed four-centred heads from the late sixteenth-century alterations. The doorways to the guard rooms either side of the gateway have two-centred heads. That with a plain chamfer opens into a featureless room, and that of higher status with hollow chamfer is the approach to a late seventeenth-century stair. The upper floor was refenestrated in 1588 (datestone)

PLATE 282 Tiverton Castle: engraving from the south-east by S. and N. Buck (1734)

and converted into a gallery shortly after Roger Giffard of Chittlehampton had purchased the castle.[7] The first-floor heated room above the outer gateway with newel and garderobe on opposing sides is now open to the roof. Buck's engraving of 1734 shows that the gateway was formerly three-storeyed, with two well-lit upper rooms and a machicolated parapet, reduced in the nineteenth century to a single upper room with one three-light window and a rebuilt parapet. However, the retained roof of this outer gateway has been dendro dated to 1356.[8]

The north side of the castle courtyard is filled with a double-pile house of about 1700, substantially extended at the rear, and by a parallel battlemented street range built during the nineteenth century in a pseudo-Tudor style.[9]

The principal residential range lines the south side of the castle, terminating in a rectangular solar tower. This is the most complete survival of the Courtenay period. The earlier round towers were constructed of better-quality sandstone, but this rubble-built tower is thrust boldly forward of the curtain wall. Two-storeyed with a low ground-floor room (now with 3 feet ground-fill), it has two oblong and two rectangular openings. The upper chamber has a large two-light transomed window: the lower openings with shouldered head were shuttered, the upper cinquefoil lights were glazed with a quatrefoil above. There were two single lights with ogee heads in the south and west walls, one next to the fireplace. The inner wall retains plaster evidence below the corbels supporting a single-slope roof.

A corner thickening with newel evidence points to an approach from the now ruined south range. The interpretation uncertainties of the castle begin here. The hall may have stood against the south wall, marked today by a large gap in the curtain, with its lower end wall identified by a rebate at an angle to the curtain suggesting the incorporation of an earlier structure. Yet such a restricted site, barely 40 feet long internally (Okehampton hall is 47 feet long), throws up the question whether the hall lay parallel with the west curtain overlooking the River Exe, with the offices in line to the north. The square tower on this west side, now reduced to founda-

tion level, has drains and a garderobe chute discharging towards the river. Excavation is sorely needed to clarify this.

Nor is the remainder of the south range any clearer. The low undercrofts, lit by narrow slits in the curtain,[10] are separated by a partition wall 1½ feet thick. The tall upper floor has a double cinquefoil light with large quatrefoil head, a lancet to the east, and the frame of a window to the west with a single cinquefoil light. This could have been two service rooms in line under an important retiring room, possibly partitioned, with an external stair like the solar block at Okehampton Castle. However, the end room is a further problem. The blocked piscina in the outer wall suggests it was a chapel with the frame of a large window in the west wall,[11] but there is no evidence of any altar-facing window in the original east wall, now incorporated in three coach houses created in the 1860s when the outer wall was rebuilt outside the line of the curtain.[12] A chapel in this position only makes sense if it incorporates the area to the west, but such an apartment would never have been built above the offices serving a nearby kitchen in the courtyard.

Taking the solar tower as a starting point, it is most likely that the hall lay against the west curtain, with the services and kitchen to the north. East of the tower was a further majestic withdrawing chamber, now a gap in the south wall, with access to an extended chapel against the curtain above a line of undercrofts. All this is speculation awaiting the clarification of excavation.

The north and north-west sides of the castle have been pulled down, so that a substantial element of its layout is missing. Even so, it is possible to suggest a four-phase development before the close of the middle ages, beginning with the castle's foundation in the early twelfth century. The small south-east tower with two-centred ground-floor entry and loop to the side and two heated upper rooms may be later thirteenth century, with added buttresses, Elizabethan windows, and a 1969 roof. It is possible there was a further round tower at the north-east as well as the revealed base of the north-west tower, for one in the area covered by the Victorian wing is mentioned in an account of the Civil War siege of 1645.[13]

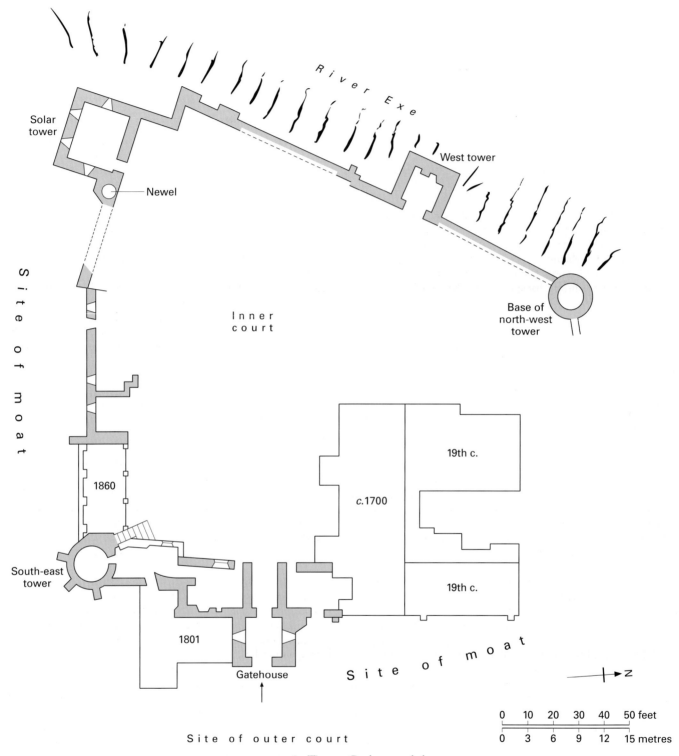

Solar
tower

Newel

River Exe

West tower

Base of
north-west
tower

Inner
court

Site of moat

19th c.

c.1700

1860

19th c.

South-east
tower

1801

Gatehouse

Site of moat

Site of outer court

N

0   10   20   30   40   50 feet

0   3   6   9   12   15 metres

FIGURE 167 Tiverton Castle: ground plan

The inner gateway, two rectangular towers, and the south range may be attributed on architectural grounds to the first half of the fourteenth century, the work of Hugh Courtenay (d.1340) but probably later than the £128 2s. 11d. spent on 'the new hall and chamber' recorded in 1308/9.[14] The outer gateway was an addition by his son Hugh Courtenay II (d.1377).

As at Okehampton, Tiverton Castle retained its defences throughout the later middle ages, primarily as an instrument and symbol of the power of the Courtenay family. The fourteenth-century additions were intended not to make the castle more defensive but to provide generous accommodation and domestic facilities and to enhance the approach to the castle's residential enclosure.

Underlying this was the creation of a residence befitting Courtenay's political ambitions and position as a leading landowner and his effort to obtain the earldom of Devon. In its present state, the fortress-mansion at Tiverton hardly conveys the dignity and standing of the family it served. The moat has been filled and its outer court totally destroyed.[15] There was no portcullis-protected entry, and the walls towards the church and town were interrupted by large windows. The lying-in-state of the princess Katherine, Edward IV's sixth daughter and wife of William, 9th earl of Devon (d.1511) in the castle's chapel in 1527, with the impressive entertainment after her burial in the church nearby, gives some indication of the splendour of the castle at the time.[16] Tiverton was no Raby or Alnwick Castle, the *caputs* of other earldoms, for the earl of Devon was numbered among the poorest members,[17] but it was the prime aristocratic residence in the region, updated by the Courtenays to be a suitable centre for their lavish lifestyle and one that became their favourite home. Its military origins are less obvious than at Okehampton which became an opulent hunting lodge, for Tiverton's domination of the town and church was all embracing, a more fitting background to their noble household before disintegration during the second half of the fifteenth century.

THE COURTENAY FAMILY

The family suffered from a rancorous feud with the Bonvilles and by attainder in 1461 and again in 1471 for their fervent support of the Lancastrian cause. A distant relative, Edward Courtenay (d.1509), was restored to the honours and earldom as its eighth holder by Henry VII (1485), and his son, Sir William Courtenay, married Katherine, Edward IV's daughter. William and Katherine's heir, Henry 10th earl, initially stood high in royal favour and was created marquis of Exeter (1525). He was rarely at Tiverton, spending most of his time at court or at his principal residence at Horsley in Surrey. But as the king's cousin, he was uncomfortably close to the throne, so when he drifted into supporting a West of England rebellion, he was speedily condemned, beheaded, and his estates forfeited (1539). His son, briefly restored to the earldom by Queen Mary, was similarly implicated in rebellion and died in exile, unmarried, in 1556. The senior Courtenay line was no more.

The foundations for the family's regional importance between the early fourteenth and early sixteenth centuries were laid by Hugh Courtenay I.[18] Though his tenurial success was crowned by the bestowal of the earldom of Devon in 1335,[19] five years before his death, the family never held any major offices of state, took little part in court politics, and were often financially strapped. Hugh II (d.1377) increased the family's holding from twenty to thirty-five manors,[20] but the Courtenays never acquired sufficient substance to expand their influence beyond regional politics. The family had more than its fair share of misfortune. Four sons of Hugh II died before their father, while the long life and the blindness that afflicted the later years of Edward, 3rd earl (d.1419) and the prior death of his four sons slowed the pace of the family's expansion. Later in the fifteenth century, their Lancastrian fervour brought execution, battlefield death, and the abeyance of the earldom (1461–85). Even so, the Courtenays had developed a powerful affinity by the mid-fourteenth century, dominated Devonshire politics for the next hundred years, and retained a social cachet long after their power-base had waned.

The Courtenays were *rentiers* and absentees, and among the earliest to adopt the practice of leasing out their demesne.[21] They

never cut a figure in national politics though they were pre-eminent in the county for two centuries, supported by their affinity and widespread collateral branches. When Henry Courtenay, marquess of Exeter, was attainted in 1536, he was the most important (though not the wealthiest) landowner in south-west England, based on his castle at Tiverton, his houses at Colcombe and Columbjohn, his hunting residence at Okehampton Castle, thirty-six manors, and overlordship of six boroughs. Less obvious was the influence his family's supporters had long wielded as sheriffs, justices of the peace, and commissioners, so that despite the earl's absence or minority, his affinity continued to dominate the county.

Tiverton Castle was the social and local administrative centre of their estates, capable of holding a substantial household of officials and staff. Its scale may be gleaned from the 1384–5 roll of the twenty-seven-year-old Edward Courtenay, 3rd earl, detailing the livery given to the body of men dependent on him. Apart from the earl and five male Courtenays, it names seven knights including Bonville and Prideaux, forty esquires drawn from well-known local families such as Champernowne, Clifford, and Ferrers, fifty-two yeomen, four minstrels, eight chaplains, three ladies-in-waiting, six pages, and fourteen lawyers, three of them the earl's stewards. The lawyers, and probably most of the knights and some of the esquires, were retained supporters rather than permanent household staff, but the roll suggests that possibly more than half of the 134 people identified were employed at Tiverton Castle, plus the grooms who were not eligible for this roll – a total of between eighty and ninety staff.[22]

The early years of the 3rd earl marked the peak of the family's influence. Edward was appointed admiral of the western fleet in 1383 and earl marshall two years later. At the same time, his three uncles also held high office – William Courtenay as archbishop of Canterbury (1381–96), Sir Philip Courtenay as Lord Lieutenant of Ireland (1383–5), and Sir Peter Courtenay as Richard II's chamberlain in 1388. Part of the Courtenay policy was to establish younger sons within the county and the adjacent areas of Somerset and Dorset, and to keep them there supported by manors drawn from the family's holding in order that their pervasive influence would be as wide and as continuous as possible.[23] It has been argued that this network of interrelationships helped the earl and his affinity to dominate the political life of the county to an extraordinary degree, giving direction to the aspirations of the gentry, and their pivotal role in the region left the government with no alternative but to deal with them.[24] Though the earls were nearly always resident in the region and the 3rd earl was markedly powerful during Richard II's reign when he had significant connections with court,[25] the pervasiveness of their hegemony and the family's ability to subordinate gentry politics to their will has been questioned.[26] Their local pre-eminence was suddenly rocked by the arrival of John Holand, earl of Huntingdon and Richard II's half-brother at Dartington Hall during the last twelve years of the fourteenth century. In any case, other sources of patronage arose during the early fifteenth century parallel with the 3rd earl's blindness, and exacerbated by the brief life of his grandson (1419–22) and the eleven-year minority of his heir (1422–33). The views of major figures at court such as Lord Hungerford and Lord Botreaux with West Country interests prevailed, while two emergent families, Sir William Bonville of Shute (page 633), and the Powderham branch of the Courtenays (page 619) became powerful political players. By the mid-fifteenth century, earl Thomas (d.1458) was fighting a rearguard action that culminated in the private war with Lord Bonville in 1455, with its siege of Powderham Castle and desperate skirmish at Clyst Bridge near Exeter. Eighty years later, Henry Courtenay, now marquess of Exeter, held thirty-six manors and eighty farms bringing in an annual rental of £2,100, plus the fees from six boroughs and various offices.[27] Though he was among the wealthiest landowners in the south-west, the Courtenays had long lost their stranglehold on the social structure of the county.

The span of the Courtenay properties across south Devon is still impressive. The powerful motte and bailey castle at Plympton had come to them as part of the Redvers estate. It had a twelfth-century shell keep with a later inner tower like that at Launceston Castle that may have been added by Hugh.[28] Tiverton was strategically sited astride the main route from Taunton to Exeter, as Okehampton guarded the approach from central Devon to Cornwall. Powderham Castle, the fortified house initiated by the blind earl's second son between c.1392 and 1406, was developed into an eighteenth- and nineteenth-century mansion to become the seat of the present earls of Devon (page 616). A fifteenth-century gatehouse stands at Bickleigh, a rubble-built wall of the manor house at Colcombe near Colyton, and the foundations of a walled enclosure with gatehouse next to Stone Barton Farm at Chulmleigh.[29] However, virtually all the branches of the family outside that at Powderham failed to take root, and their houses were returned to the head of the family and dispersed, as Bickleigh was in about 1510, or built over, like that at Exminster.

The enigmatic survival next to the farm buildings at Colcombe is the outer wall of a two-storey late medieval residential range with fireplace, fifteenth-century windows, and later mullioned replacements.[30] The gatehouse at Bickleigh promises much more, standing close to a crossing of the River Exe with a small Norman chapel in the outer court (pl. 300). Filling the east side of a quadrangular moated site, this sandstone-built gateway is three-storeyed to the front with projecting garderobe and stair turrets,[31] though now stripped of its embattled parapet. The central passage, with two bays of sexpartite vaults that seem to have been an afterthought, is the most telling survival, for the interiors are disappointing, stripped down during a heavy restoration in 1925.[32] The flanking guard rooms are featureless, while the upper chamber, approached by a stair of c.1600 and lit by contemporary windows in both outer faces, has been converted into a single broad chamber. The uppermost floor has been lost to the rear and absorbed to the front, while the original approach from a large newel stair at the south-west corner is ruined.

Built by a junior branch of the Powderham Courtenays who acquired the property in c.1410, this fortified house is closer in character to Bywell Castle with its combination of imposing entrance and residence, a truly gated house (though not portcullis-protected). In both cases, depressions indicate that the courtyard held domestic ranges.[33] With Bywell built by Ralph Neville, 1st earl of Westmorland in about 1420, the chamfered entry arch and cinquefoil lights at Bickleigh Castle similarly suggest an early to mid-fifteenth-century date. For other Courtenay houses, see the entries for Sutton Courtenay 'Abbey' and the south-west Somerset group of Coker Court, Naish 'Priory' and West Coker Manor.

NOTES

1 Detailed by G. A. Holmes, *The Estates of the Higher Nobility in Fourteenth Century England* (1957) 32–5.

2 *Ibid.*

3 R. A. Higham *et al.*, *Proc. Devon Arch. Soc.* 35 (1977) 3–42; 40 (1982) 19–151; R. A. Highham, *Okehampton Castle: Official Handbook* (1984) but modified by further work: *Med. Arch.* 36 (1992) 215–17.

4 Based on architectural and artefactual, not documentary evidence, R. A. Higham, *Proc. Devon Arch. Soc.* 40 (1982).

5 Confirmed in *Med. Arch.* 36 (1992) 217. Also 44 (2000) 259–60.

6 The possible site of the motte lay on built-over land north of the castle's present boundary. This would make the original castle considerably larger than today. The area opposite the main entrance, covered by two rows of houses, is still known as 'The Works', i.e. the outworks or outer court.

7 The early door at the north end, now opening from the stair projection, may have been the approach from an external stair. *Med. Arch.* 33 (1989) 175 suggests the windows in the east range and gate-tower were probably inserted during Katherine Courtenay's residence up to 1527.

8 The outer gatehouse would normally be attributed on architectural grounds to the later fourteenth or early fifteenth century, necessitating the reuse of earlier timbers, but a mid-century date is not unreasonable.

9 Attributed by B. Cherry and N. Pevsner, *The Buildings of England: Devon* (1989) 812, to the late sixteenth century, but it superseded the small end unit that Buck shows was still in existence in 1734.

10 The two doorways (one now a window) in the outer wall are post-medieval.

11 The piscina or laver does not look inserted. Any west partition standing on the narrow ground-floor wall would have been a light division or screen.

12 Buck's engraving of 1734 shows the lower part of a square projection forward of the curtain at this point, possibly part of another tower.

13 And noted in Dunsford's *Historical Memoirs of Tiverton* (1790).

14 Devon Record Office, CR 490.

15 The scale of these outworks is suggested in the account of the castle's siege of 1645, summarised by J. D. Mackenzie, *The Castles of England*, II (1897) 41.

16 Dunsford, *Historical Memoirs of Tiverton*.

17 K. B. McFarlane estimated that Edward Courtenay's income in 1382 was about £1,350 per annum, excluding a third of the estates held in dower until 1391: *The Nobility of Later Medieval England* (1973) 111. M. Cherry's estimate for 1374–5 or £1,500 per annum included the properties held in dower, *Southern History* 1 (1979) 75.

18 The family have not found a family recorder since E. Cleaveland, *A Genealogical History of the . . . Family of Courtenay* (1735). In the meantime, see *Com. Peer.*, IV (1916) 323–38; two important articles by M. Cherry, 'The Courtenay earls of Devon: the formation and disintegration of a late medieval aristocratic affinity', *Southern History* 1 (1979) 71–9, and 'The struggle for power in mid fifteenth century Devonshire', in *The Crown and Provinces*, ed. R. A. Griffiths (1981) 123–44. Both are based on his unpublished PhD thesis, 'The Courtenays, Bonvilles and political society in Devon 1377–1461', University of Exeter. Also J. A. F. Thomson, 'The Courtenays in the Yorkist period', *Bull. Inst. Hist. Res.* 45 (1972) 230–46, and M. Westmacott, 'The estates of the earls of Devon 1425–1538', MA thesis, University of Exeter (1955).

19 Though a substantial part of the inheritance of Isabel Redvers, countess of Devon in her own right, came to Hugh Courtenay in 1297 (with the rest mulcted by Edward I), he had to wait nearly forty years before the king allowed him Isabel's lapsed earldom.

20 Mapped by C. Given-Wilson, *The English Nobility in the Late Middle Ages* (1987) xiv.

21 J. Youings in *Exeter and Its Region* (1969) 166–71. She also draws attention to the family's debilitating effect on the prosperity of Exeter and Tiverton.

22 Brit. Lib., Add. Charter 64.320; Cherry, 'The Courtenay earls' 72–90. Also McFarlane, *The Nobility of Late Medieval England* 111 and Given-Wilson, *The English Nobility in the Late Middle Ages* 88–9.

23 As the Courtenays were leading patrons of Exeter Cathedral, they sometimes sought ecclesiastical preferment for their younger sons. D. N. Lepine, *Trans. Devon. Assoc.* 124 (1992) 44–58.

24 Cherry, 'The Courtenay earls' 71, 97.

25 *Ibid.* 75–6.

26 Given-Wilson, *The English Nobility in the Late Middle Ages* 75–6.

27 *Cal. Inq. P.M.* on the attainder of Henry, marquess of Exeter in 1539.

28 R. A. Higham *et al.*, *Proc. Devon Arch. Soc.* 43 (1985) 59–75; Cherry and Pevsner, *Devon* 683. For other building fabric donations by the 1st earl, R. A. Higham, *Trans. Devon. Assoc.* 121 (1989) 153–8.

29 The family also held Boconnoc near Lostwithiel in Cornwall between the fifteenth and early sixteenth centuries, sometimes occupied by the heir. A few windows and doorways of that time survive in the outbuildings to the early Georgian house.

30 Colcombe has been attributed to Hugh Courtenay who died there in 1291 and whose successors occupied the property throughout the fourteenth and fifteenth centuries. Lady Radford, *Trans. Devon. Assoc.* 67 (1935) 291–4. Its condition in 1795 when more of the house survived is depicted in two views by John Swete, *Travels in Georgian Devon*, ed. T. Gray and M. Rowe, II (1998) 110–11.

31 The stair extension from the first to the ground floor is a forced one of the 1920s.

32 C. Hussey, *Country Life* (April 1939); Cherry and Pevsner, *Devon* 170–2.

33 The lost south range was probably linked to the ruined newel, but the farmhouse-type range opposite is post-medieval.

G. A. Paterson, *Jour. Brit. Arch. Assoc.* 18 (1862) 237–46

R. Higham, 'The castles of medieval Devon', PhD thesis, University of Exeter (1979)

PLATE 283 Torre Abbey: inner gate

TORRE ABBEY and monastic gatehouses in Devon

Devon retains several examples of monastic gatehouses, from the twelfth-century north entry at Buckfast Abbey to the isolated early sixteenth-century example at Cornworthy. That at Torre Abbey is the best preserved and is still roofed. The Premonstratensian abbey facing the sea at Torquay was the order's richest foundation in England, and though the monastic church has been pulled down, two of the cloister ranges were converted into a private residence by the Ridgeway family in 1598, extended by the Cary family in the early eighteenth century. The gatehouse touching the junction of these two ranges was retained and partially occupied.

Built in *c*.1380–90 of local dark stone with contrasting red sandstone dressings, this was one of the three 'fair gate houses' noted by Leland.[1] From its position, it seems to have been an inner gate, with embattled parapet and polygonal turrets at each corner broadening towards the base. One of these rear turrets holds the stair, but the other was removed in the eighteenth century to facilitate access between the house and the upper chamber of the gatehouse. These turrets are notable for the inclusion of cannon loops, for the position of this monastery close to the sea warranted elementary precautions against possible foreign attacks during the first half of Richard II's reign.

The central block has tall carriage and lower pedestrian entries with semi-circular heads to front and rear. Both passages are of two bays, with simple ribbed vaults with the arms of the abbey and the Mohun family of Dunster Castle, the lords of the manor.[2] The taller entry passage rises through two floors, with a mezzanine level over the porter's lodge and pedestrian entry. The upper floor spanning the width of the gatehouse was a comfortable lodging, originally partitioned into two chambers. The outer one has single lights in both faces and a turret room. The inner chamber has two-light transomed windows in both faces, a fireplace, and a garderobe off one of the two turret rooms.

The gatehouse to the late twelfth-century Augustinian priory at Canonsleigh, refounded as a nunnery by Maud, countess of Devon in 1282, was ruined until its restoration and reroofing in 1998. Probably built during the mid-fifteenth century, it is of simple form, with two parallel open bays and a single room above with central image niche and crenellated parapet. The two barrel-vaulted bays for carts and pedestrians were of similar size, the former with a moulded mid arch with carved fleurons and the latter closed with a low arch and the newel to the upper floor. The upper chamber was lit by several twin ogee-headed lights under square heads, heated by a fireplace in the south wall, with a garderobe and retained seat in the south-east corner.[3]

Whereas Torre Abbey gatehouse stands complete but surrounded by the town, that at Cornworthy is ruined and quite alone in its greenfield site (pl. 303). This substantial survivor was an early sixteenth-century rebuilding to a lost priory of Augustinian nuns, founded in the mid-thirteenth century.[4] As at Torre Abbey, the ground floor consists of a tall vehicular entry (with an image niche above) and separate but lower pedestrian access. The wide vehicular entry with four-centred granite head at each end was spanned by a mid arch to create a two-bay passage with vaulted roof of rectangular ribbed panels. The subsidiary passage with plain end arches was similarly divided, but with octapartite vaults with central and side bosses. A single-storey building with high peep-through abutted the north wall, possibly a porter's lodge. To the rear, a barred doorway in a square frame accesses the projecting newel to the single upper chamber with one frontal and two rear windows, fireplace, and garderobe with chute evidence.

The manor of Cornworthy was granted by Henry VII to Sir Richard Edgcumbe of Cotehele shortly before his death in 1489. The towered entry to that house was built by his son in the first decade of the sixteenth century with the entry passage panelled with granite ribs not unlike that at the Cornworthy gatehouse. Though its upper walling and roof have gone, this substantial monastic entry is a high-quality late medieval survival, no different from the approach to a substantial secular residence.[5]

NOTES

1 *Itinerary*, I, 223.
2 The gatehouse has some similarity to the three-storeyed entry of 1419–21 at Dunster Castle.
3 *Med. Arch.* 37 (1993) 251–2.
4 The site was partially excavated in 1920, *Devon and Cornwall Notes and Queries* 2 pt 2 (1921).
5 The early sixteenth-century flint and stone gatehouse of the Cistercian abbey at Dunkeswell, equally as remote as Cornworthy and 7 miles south-east of Canonsleigh, is badly damaged. It retains part of the carriageway and the room south of it, but the north building is ruined and little remains of the upper floor. P. J. Weddell, *Dunkeswell: Devon Religious Houses Survey*, II (1986); *Med. Arch.* 35 (1991) 139–40. Two gatehouses survive of the Benedictine abbey at Tavistock, but like the abbot's hall, they have essentially been converted into stage scenery to the duke of Bedford's remodelling of the town in the early and mid-nineteenth century. The Abbey Gate is late twelfth century with fifteenth-century additions, fitted up as a library in the 1820s. 'Betsy Grimbal's Tower' is the relatively substantial if battered west entrance to the abbey precinct with polygonal turrets and a low central passageway. Between these two units is a late medieval hall, possibly part of the infirmary, used since 1691 as a nonconformist chapel and which may retain its original roof under the coved plaster ceiling. For a conjectural site plan of the abbey, *Med. Arch.* 48 (2004) 256. Finally, on the south-east edge of Tavistock is an isolated early sixteenth-century secular gatehouse. It was the crenellated approach to Fitzford, the seat of the Fitz family from the fifteenth to the early seventeenth century, demolished in the mid-nineteenth century. Three-storeyed with a granite ashlar front and the remainder in local stone, this gatehouse was totally rebuilt as a dwelling in 1871 when the top stage was reduced in height.

H. P. R. Finberg, *Tavistock Abbey* (1951)
D. Seymour, *Torre Abbey: An Account of Its History, Buildings, Cartularies, and Lands* (1977)
M. Freeman and J. Wans, *Trans. Devon. Assoc.* 128 (1996) 17–34

TRECARRELL MANOR, Cornwall

The granite-built hall of Trecarrell Manor is a remnant of what promised to be a fine late medieval courtyard house, 4 miles south of Launceston. The manor had been held by the Trecarrell family since the mid-twelfth century[1] but the earliest structure is the occupied farmhouse range with an arch-braced collar-truss roof with wind braces of *c*.1450. It was followed shortly afterwards by the chapel, an independent building on higher ground 80 feet south-east of the house rather than an extension to the earlier residence as at Bradley Manor, Compton Castle, and Cotehele. Reusing previ-

PLATE 284 Trecarrell Manor: hall from the south

ous foundations, this lofty rectangular chapel with three windows of three cinquefoil lights with quatrefoil heads retains two piscinas, statue pedestals either side the east window, evidence of a mid screen, and part of the decorative wall plate supporting the plain wagon roof. Because the chapel was some distance from the house, its west end held a small upper room with fireplace and garderobe for the chaplain.

The young Henry Trecarrell succeeded to the estate on the death of his father in about 1486, but it was some years before he began redeveloping the house. He completed the hall and part of the residential block filling the south side of the courtyard, and laid the outer wall foundations of the west range opposite the earlier and still-standing east range. Work was abandoned at this point, apparently because of the death of his young son in 1511.[2] Carved but unused granite blocks were left lying round the site, as similarly occurred at Berry Pomeroy Castle, for Henry now devoted all his energy and finances to rebuilding St Mary Magdalene church in Launceston (1511–24) with its well-known granite sculptured façades.

The hall is rubble-built but faced with massive close-set granite blocks to create stylish façades. Now 41 feet by 20 feet, the lower end wall is roughly built, a replacement for the original wall 2 feet further east, with a moulded jamb at the north-east corner marking the position of one of the doors to the kitchen and services. The barred entry doorways have four-centred heads in square frames, and the grander south door has the granite-cut arms of Trecarrell impaling those of his wife (d.1552) in a tympanum.

After centuries of farm use,[3] the original character of the hall was reinstated in 1961–3 with the removal of an inserted floor. It is lit by two windows in the upper register of both side walls, of three ogee-nipped lights below a sexfoil, and by a tall south-facing four-light transomed window with multi-decorated head rising 5 feet from the floor to near wall-plate level. None of the windows was grooved for glass but they have iron bars with transoms to which glass would have been fixed by twisted leading.[4] Richard Symonds noted in his diary for 1644 that the glazing was of coats of arms, including those of Trecarrell and his wife Margaret Kelway.[5] The roof consists of a line of eleven arch-braced collars with three rows of purlins above the wall plate, dividing it into a sequence of rectangular panels. These are decorated with cross timbers and carved wooden leaves. Those in the end bay were replaced in 1963 to show the original form, with the removed fragments mounted in a wall case. The granite fireplace with ogee-nipped moulding on lintel and jambs was sited at the upper end, close to the door to the upper residential block. The external tusks at the side of the courtyard doors from the hall dais and residential block supported a covered walk terminating in a stair to the upper chamber.

This two-storey end block was never completed, but left fireplace evidence at both levels in the rear face of the dais wall and a high peep-slit into the hall.

Sir Henry Trecarrell, a benefactor of Launceston and its church, was a man of considerable wealth and position. He held some duchy appointments, was mayor of Launceston in 1536 and 1543, and died in 1544 without male issue. His hall is reached from the north via the farmhouse, but the approach was originally from the south, with the chapel in the outer court and the hall entered by the armorial doorway. The abandoned inner court would have held the family apartments, with the likelihood that the farmhouse range would have been replaced in due course. Had it been completed, Trecarrell's house might have been similar in scale and quality to that of Sir Piers Edgcumbe at Cotehele, 9 miles away, for the parallels are close. The halls are almost identical in size, and they employed the same granite building stone – hitherto not used for high-quality houses – and possibly the same workmen with a common repertoire of nipped-ogee window heads, hall entries with the family arms in the tympanum, and armorial glass in the windows.

NOTES

1 P. Hull and R. Sharpe, *Jour. Inst. Cornish Studies* 13 (1985) 49–50.
2 W. Lake, *Parochial History of Cornwall*, III (1872) 153–4. There is no contemporary evidence for this. Also *Arch. Jour.* 130 (1973) 255.
3 For a vivid description and illustration of the site in July 1943 by John Piper before the restoration of the hall and chapel, R. Ingrams and J. Piper, *Piper's Places* (1983) 96–7, with the text reproduced in the introduction to this volume.
4 Jope (1961) 204. The windows were reglazed in 1963. The four-light south window is a seventeenth-century addition after the floor had been inserted.
5 *The Diary of Richard Symonds* (1859) 45.

T. H. Turner and J. H. Parker, *Some Account of Domestic Architecture in England*, III pt 2 (1859) 362–3
E. M. Jope, *Studies in Building History* (1961) 202–4

TRUTHALL and MEDROS MANORS, Cornwall

Three generations are responsible for Truthall Manor, each one contributing a range to enclose a small central court, with that of the late nineteenth century overshadowing that of the mid-seventeenth century, which in turn was larger than that of the fifteenth century. The fourth side of the court with its imposing gate piers has always been open. The late medieval hall range of this still isolated manor, 1½ miles north-west of Helston, is best viewed from the north farmyard, where the frontage is least altered, and this was the original approach to the house.

The range is a low one with walls 3 feet thick and standing little

PLATE 285 Truthall Manor: from the north

more than 10 feet high, now with a 1960s replacement roof of Cornish slates. It consists of three units in line – a hall open to the roof, a wide cross passage, and a service room with chamber over. Built of rubble granite with dressed stone for windows and doorways, the range is now used for farm purposes, with the hall stacked with bales of hay.

The north entry is of some style with its chamfered four-centred head, blind spandrels, and square hood. The opposing cross-passage entry has the four-centred head, but with joists holes above for a covered porch. The 8 feet wide passage has a stone wall to the services and a post and panel screen to the hall, both with single central entries. The hall, 26 feet by 16½ feet, retains two windows to the forecourt of two-transomed lights with cinquefoil heads, square hoods, and glass grooves. The window in the opposite wall is an insertion, but the nearby fireplace 8 feet wide is original, with its square-headed granite lintel with hollow chamfer. This four-bay hall is spanned by arch-braced collar-beam trusses to square-set purlins with no evidence of wind braces.[1]

The low end of the range consists of a service room with a three-light window to the forecourt and an inserted framed window in the end wall. As there is no fireplace, the kitchen lay elsewhere, not far from the south-west door. The chamber above, 19 feet by 17 feet, was probably always externally approached, as it is today by the stair to the 1642 range and a now blocked doorway.[2] The window is nineteenth century, the fireplace and side window are plaster-covered, and the roof is ceiled, so that the corbel-supported chimney stack and nearby light in the gable end are only visible externally. The narrow room created over the cross passage is a secondary development, made wide enough by projecting a foot into the hall, supported on a thin stone wall that probably replaced a timber screen. The window in this room is recent and the roof truss is a replacement.

Truthall Manor retains the principal range of a late medieval gentry house – relatively small in comparison with those in southern England but substantial in the context of Cornwall. From the forecourt the house looks stylish, with traceried windows of Beer stone and an imposing entrance doorway. It was intended to impress, but from the rear the hall was blank and the rear doorway was plain. Both chambers below the cross passage are low, the service room

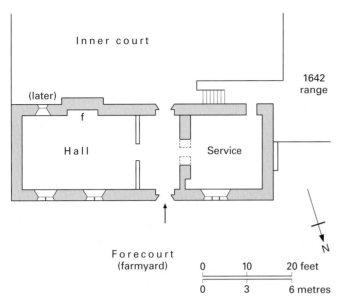

Inner court

(later)

f

Hall

Service

1642 range

Forecourt
(farmyard)

0   10   20 feet

0   3   6 metres

N

FIGURE 168 Truthall Manor: ground plan

particularly so, but as there is no evidence of rooms beyond the high end of the hall,[3] the upper room was the withdrawing chamber. It was at this end of the house that residential expansion took place in 1642, replacing some of the service units, while later farm buildings have replaced the forecourt walls. Truthall Manor was erected during the fifteenth century by a member of the Nance family who held it until it was acquired by a branch of the Arundell family during the earlier seventeenth century.[4]

Medros[5] followed a similar layout to Truthall, and can be more readily appreciated after visiting the Nance house first. Similarly isolated but further north-east in the Luxulyan valley a mile from the Eden Project, Medros is also granite-built with a recent replacement roof of Cornish slates. Whereas Truthall has been extended round three sides of a court, Medros has two ranges: a tall mid-seventeenth-century block at right angles to the earlier lower hall and chamber range. It follows the same form of hall open to the roof, cross passage, and service room with chamber above, all under a common roof ridge. Interest therefore lies in the differences from Truthall. Medros is still occupied and retains its high forecourt wall, with an entry 6 feet wide, with four-centred head. Its double doors were not barred.

The hall is marked by an added bay window and adjacent chimney stack, in dressed stone as against the rubble walling of the remainder of the range. The cross-passage entry has been hacked about, but the opposing one is complete, with hollow and roll moulding, high stops, and square-headed frame. The cross passage is 5 feet wide, with a stone wall 3 feet thick to the services with central door, and a timber-framed partition to the hall.

The two-period hall, only 19 feet by 16 feet, is of two bays with arch-braced collar trusses. There is a blocked window in the east wall, with the bay window and contemporary fireplace almost filling the courtyard side of the hall. The fireplace has a single stone lintel with central ogee head copying a Cotehele feature. The bay window has four tall lights with square heads, three in line and one at an angle. The third side encloses a doorway with four-centred head leading to the west wing.[6]

The entry to the lower chamber retains its two-centred head in wood. This room, 16 feet square, is now used as a parlour, with end-wall fireplace with stone lintel and a modern stair to the chamber above. This end unit differs from Truthall, as the service room was also the kitchen and the upper chamber extends over the cross passage and 3 feet into the hall.

Medros is probably an early sixteenth-century gentry house. Though the two-centred doorway and slightly smaller scale suggest it may be a little earlier than Truthall, the lower-end layout points to a transitional stage from the late medieval to the mid-Tudor period. It also differs from Truthall in its hall improvements, earlier added wing, and continued occupation.[7]

NOTES

1 The roof trusses were reinforced with tie beams in the 1960s.

2 An alternative approach is an internal stair from the north end of the cross passage, with the south-west doorway accessing a garderobe.

3 The upper gable end has a narrow air and light slit.

4 Rosewarne Wollas (formerly Rosewarne Manor), 200 yards from the Duchy College on the north side of Camborne, has been described as 'rare to find [a house] with so much obvious fifteenth century work on quite this scale'. Charles Thomas, *Arch. Jour.* 130 (1973) 262. This is to overindulge the modest evidence in a much-altered house. The hall is a little smaller than at Truthall and has been floored and refenestrated, while the service and chamber end is at an oblique angle with a two-light rear window of c.1520. The interest of Rosewarne lies in two added units – a sub-medieval chamber block at the upper end of the hall, and a storeyed block at right angles below the services.

5 Until recently, known as Methrose.

6 This and the other entry to the late wing are blocked as it is in separate occupation. Charles Henderson attributed this addition to Nicholas Kendall between 1622 and 1649.

7 Golden Manor near Probus, midway between Truthall and Medros, was the home of the locally noted Wolvedon family until the early sixteenth century when it passed to the Tregians. The two-storeyed buttressed structure that survives, with a small block at right angles to it, was essentially rebuilt as a barn in the late nineteenth century. It incorporates two late medieval windows with two-centred heads in the east gable wall, an early Tudor lintel used as a doorway head, and some corbels and decorative elements. The roof is a 1970 structure in place of the earlier upper cruck trusses. Though there is a small newel turret in the angle between the barn and the projecting unit, too little untouched work remains to make any meaningful assessment of the building's origins.

E. M. Jope, *Studies in Building History* (1961) 198–202
V. M. and F. J. Chesher, *The Cornishman's House* (1968) 29–31
F. Chesher, *Arch. Jour.* 130 (1973) 266–7 (Truthall)

WARDOUR CASTLE, Wiltshire

John 5th Lord Lovel was as susceptible to aesthetic considerations in choosing the site for his new residence at the close of the fourteenth century as Lord Arundell was for his new mansion nearby almost 300 years later. Wardour Castle, 3 miles from Tisbury, was positioned on a low spur projecting from a horseshoe of higher ground leaving the fourth prospect open to the valley of the Don Brook extending towards Donhead and Shaftesbury. Capability Brown's wooded landscape has got out of hand, so that the site is now tree-enclosed rather than nestling below open downland.

Nor is the castle complete. The towered residence is a tightly planned hexagon round a central court of similar shape, with the entrance front widened and brought forward to include two tall towers at the side. This highly unusual plan was mirrored by a parallel embattled outer wall, nearly 200 feet or more distant, to create a vast hexagonal outer court. Much of the present perimeter wall is an Elizabethan rebuild but it follows the line of the original enclosure. The approach was from the north, so that a visitor crossed the downland to look down on to the castle. The outer ditch and gatehouse on the widened north front have gone, though they probably lay to the rear of the eighteenth-century grotto and hopefully will be recovered from the present dense woodland. The central residence that confronted the visitor stood on rising ground,[1] but it was neither moat-mirrored nor ditch-surrounded. It would have seemed a totally idiosyncratic structure, exotically shaped, vertically challenging, judiciously decorated, and dominated by the high-set hall windows. The breathtaking panache of the residence has been somewhat lost through Elizabethan modifications, Civil War destruction, and eighteenth-century landscaping, but to a medieval newcomer, Wardour Castle would have been as novel and as exciting as the Great Exhibition was to a Victorian visitor.

SITE DEVELOPMENT

Wardour Castle is a two-phase residence, late fourteenth and later sixteenth century, but four periods have left their mark on the site. Lord Lovel acquired the manor of Wardour in about 1390 and was granted a licence to crenellate his house there in 1393.[2] The whole castle – and this is part of its significance – is a single-phase building completed by about 1400, eight years before Lord Lovel's death, with his wife surviving him until 1423.

As the family supported the house of Lancaster during the early years of the Wars of the Roses, the Lovel estates were confiscated by the Yorkist victor in 1461. Wardour passed through several hands before its acquisition in 1570 by Sir Matthew Arundell, a scion of the Arundells of Lanherne, Cornwall. He retained Lovel's residence, but refashioned and enriched it by 1578 in a modest classical-inspired style, possibly with the advice of Robert Smythson who was working nearby at Longleat.[3] Even so, he left the windows of the hall and kitchen, and adopted a routine sub-medieval form elsewhere in preference to the vast mullioned and transomed windows favoured, for example, by the earl of Leicester at Kenilworth Castle (1570–5).

An inventory of 1605 shows that Arundell's furnishing of the castle was almost as splendid as that at Hardwick Hall, including a long gallery (created out of the two second-floor family rooms) with a spectacular display of 192 pictures.[4] Because the Arundells were staunch Royalists, their house was subject to sieges in 1643, and again in the following year when mining brought down the southeast segment of the castle (pl. 287), leading to its permanent abandonment as a residence.

For a time, the family rented Breamore House in Hampshire but they also developed a small residence immediately outside the curtain wall at Wardour. The latter was enlarged during the late 1720s, with the ruins developed as the centrepiece of a formal garden shown in Buck's engraving of 1732. A generation later, Richard Woods drew up ambitious plans for landscaping the medieval park (1764–72), though in practice his work was limited to the area round the later mansion and that near the castle, including enlarging the castle lake,[5] tree planting, and the creation of the yew-lined panoramic drive, comparable to the contemporary terrace overlooking Rievaulx Abbey. Marriage to a rich heiress in 1763 restored the Arundell family fortunes, with James Paine commissioned to build a new mansion between 1769 and 1776. During the early 1780s, Capability Brown was commissioned to refashion the landscape, with the castle ruins as a prominent feature, enhanced by a girdle of subsidiary structures including a Gothick banqueting house (1773–4), a grotto, and a 'prehistoric' stone circle (both probably 1792).[6] By the 1820s, visitors were already beginning to visit and admire the ruins as well as the new mansion house nearby.[7]

DESCRIPTION

The castle is bereft of all outbuildings, so that the sward-like outer court gives a false impression compared with the stables and services that would have marked the original approach to the centrally positioned towered residence. Sir Matthew Arundell's alterations equally distort the castle's outer face, for though the hall windows were retained as was the corbelled gallery above, all other doors and windows (except those of the principal kitchen) were replaced by 1570s versions, at the same time that the front plinth was hacked back[8] and niches added. Arundell's internal alterations are primarily confined to classical doors and plain windows with curved heads, leaving Lovel's basic structure little affected.[9] Wardour Castle was an ingeniously planned residence of interlocking levels, with some segments five floors high but others of four, three, or even only two levels from ground to turreted roof level. Yet it was a cohesive structure, over 60 feet high, with only the window positions signalling the complexity of the house's internal plan. All ground-floor windows were single loops, with those lighting the upper rooms probably of increasing size, though now distorted by Arundell's standard replacement pattern of two or three lights. The base of the castle was enhanced by a deep batter, string courses, and a scalloped plinth, its head by four bartisans at the corners, and a deep-set fleuron cornice. The roof was a viewing platform and there were at least two observation positions – the corbel-supported gallery above the entrance, and the Great Chamber balcony overlooking the central court. It is the combination of a novel plan, a compact internal layout, and a high standard of workmanship that makes the suggestion of William Wynford's responsibility as the master-mason a reasonable one.[10]

The single entry to the central residence for family, visitors, and staff alike was through a low passage 30 feet long, protected at each end by a double door and a portcullis. Flares probably illuminated the three bays of fan vaulting, an early secular example, possibly highlighted with paint and gilding. The passage opened into a small hexagonal court, with the central well probably surmounted by an elaborate stone and painted superstructure. From this area, family, staff, and guests would disperse through some of the eleven doorways opening from the court, all with two-centred heads. The most prominent today is the twelfth, the taller entry arch with wave moulding characteristic of West of England workmanship in the late fourteenth century as at Dartington Hall, though it would have been surpassed by the stepped approach to the hall subsequently replaced by Arundell's classical doorway.

Family rooms

The initial curving flight of steps to the first-floor hall straightened under a vaulted bay with central foliated boss, to open into the

PLATE 286 Wardour Castle: entry frontage from the north

screens passage. This hall, 43 feet by 25 feet, is essentially a stripped-out vertical box rising the full height of the building, but now lacking screen, dais, wall plaster, and roof. It retains the two tall windows in the upper side walls with twin cinquefoil lights, transoms, traceried head, and slender columns supporting the rear arch, and totally rather than partially glass filled. Immediately below is a fleuron-decorated cornice circling the apartment, rising higher over the dais to allow for the platform and canopy of state. The lowest part of the side walls retains the fireplace in the court-yard wall (altered in the 1570s) and the entries to the windlass chambers built in the wall thickness. Curtains or wall hangings would have normally concealed their presence. The low-pitched four-bay roof was supported on slender triple shafts but the form of the trusses is guesswork.

Three doorways opened from the dais bay – one for staff housed at ground-floor level but capable of servicing the family rooms above, one to the lobby and family retiring chambers, and one to the second-floor lobby and more private higher chambers.

The first-floor family rooms were approached via the unheated lobby or ante-chamber (1570 added fireplace) with a fine west-facing window. The great chamber was a spacious well-lit room,

two windows looking towards the fishponds and park and a higher one opposite with a door below (blocked) to a balcony overlooking the inner court. The chamber was furnished with a side-wall fire-place, with access to the heated inner chamber in the now destroyed west segment. At the upper end of this chamber is an angled lobby with a corridor-approached garderobe, a second entry to the inner chamber, and newel access to the more private rooms above. This second-floor suite followed the same plan of ante-room, outer chamber, and inner chamber and had comparable facilities, but these rooms were open to the roof and with taller windows, the principal ones overlooking the park and the vale beyond. All the rooms were plastered internally, like most of those in the castle, though little enough evidence survives today, while these two suites in particular would have been very fashionably and expensively fur-nished.

Service rooms

The service rooms filled more than half the ground floor and the eastern segment above. The porter's lodge opening from the entry passage was unheated and lit by a single high window but was garderobe-provided. Immediately to the rear of the lodge and

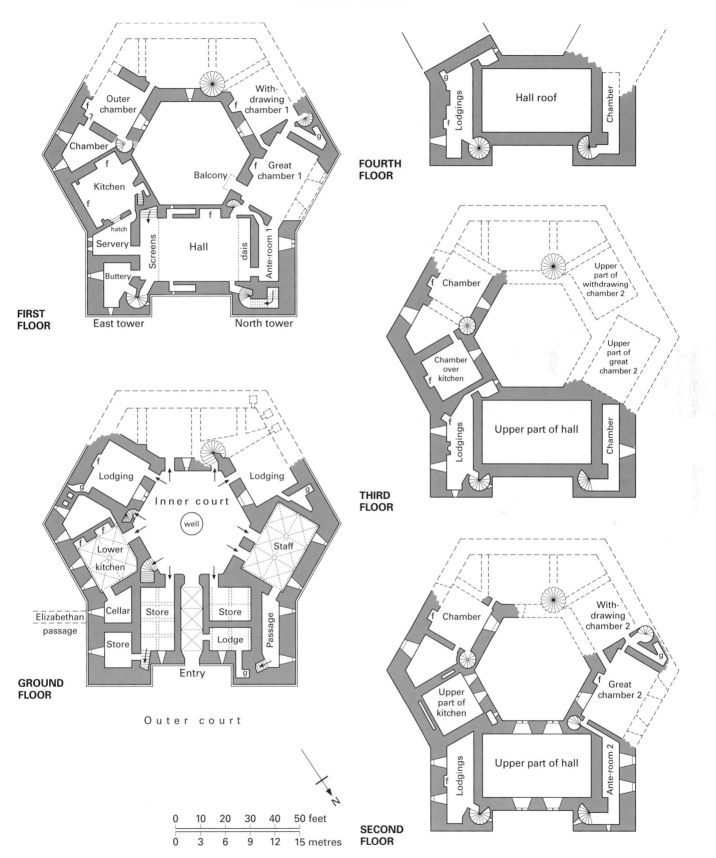

FIRST FLOOR

Outer chamber
f
?
Chamber
f
Kitchen
f
hatch
Servery
Screens
Buttery
Hall
dais
Ante-room 1
East tower
North tower
Withdrawing chamber 1
f
Balcony
f Great chamber 1
g
f

FOURTH FLOOR

g
Lodgings
f
Hall roof
Chamber

THIRD FLOOR

f Chamber
Chamber over kitchen
f
f Lodgings
Upper part of hall
Upper part of withdrawing chamber 2
Upper part of great chamber 2
Chamber

GROUND FLOOR

Lodging
f
g
Lodging
g
Inner court
well
Lower kitchen
Staff
Elizabethan passage
Cellar
Store
Store
Passage
Store
Lodge
f
Entry
g
Outer court

SECOND FLOOR

f Chamber
Upper part of kitchen
Lodgings
f
Upper part of hall
Withdrawing chamber 2
g
f Great chamber 2
Ante-room 2

0   10   20   30   40   50 feet
0   3   6   9   12   15 metres

N

FIGURE 169 Wardour Castle: floor plans

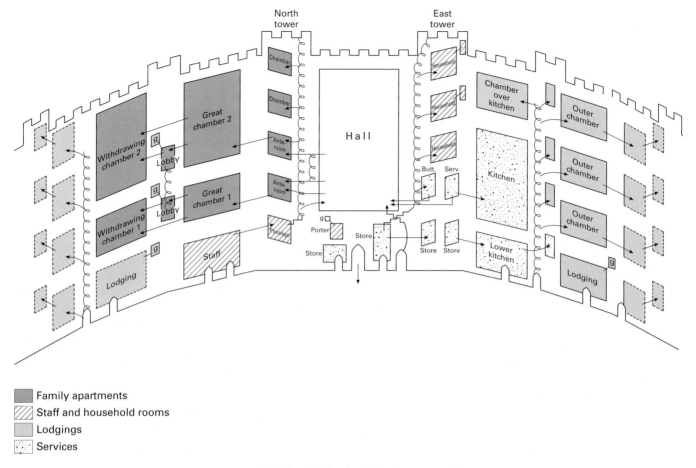

FIGURE 170 Wardour Castle: planning and movement diagram

opposite to it were two vaulted store rooms, both unlit, but with the larger one probably used for storing beer as it has service stair access to the buttery above.

Wardour has two kitchens – a ground-floor one for daily use and a first-floor kitchen directly above for special occasions or when the castle was fully occupied. The ground-floor kitchen was vaulted and retains two fireplaces, badly damaged but with their flues visible in the internal wall thickness. Opposite were two deeply recessed store rooms, the outer one with entry to a 1570 underground passage.

The buttery and servery were approached, as usual, from the screens passage, repeating the single-chamfered doorways common throughout the castle. The buttery with its three wall cupboards retains some of its wall plaster but the windows are 1570s enlargements. The servery light has been blocked but it retains the serving hatch from the kitchen next to that room's sole entry.

The first-floor kitchen was not open to the roof but was ceiled with a supporting central beam to allow for a chamber above. As its sole light came from two tall single windows in the courtyard wall, this room must have been hot and noisy when in use. The outer wall is filled with a massive fireplace but lacks the stone hood and supportive canopy. The chute at the side carrying rainwater from the roof to the cellar cistern has been exposed, as has the similarly positioned rain chute at Nunney Castle. There was a second fireplace with twin stacks in the party wall, now with a later

doorway forced through it to the room beyond, destroying the integrity of this group of service rooms which terminated with this kitchen.

There is one further staff room. Opposite the ground-floor kitchen is a three-bay vaulted room of some scale with two entries (one blocked in 1570) suggesting internal partitioning or at least proscribed entry and exit doors. For this was a page and junior staff room with extended passage[11] and newel access to the dais for attendance on the lord and his family. A comparable room and approach can be seen at Wingfield Manor (c.1439–46).

Household rooms

At the further end of the screens passage, a newel leads to three floors of chambers for household staff above the buttery and servery, and access to the roof. Although the rooms were of similar shape, they differed in their facilities. The second-floor room has a fireplace and two wall cupboards but no garderobe. The room above has a recess between the windows, possibly for a close stool, and a corner fireplace suggesting division into an outer and inner chamber with rebate evidence for a timber partition. From the heated inner room, a small bedchamber opened, overlooking the courtyard. This three-room lodging now has 1570s windows. The roofless fourth-floor lodging repeats the three-room form but with a garderobe and retained original window.

Guest rooms

Whereas the family chambers were on the upper two or three floors, the rooms in the south-eastern segment were on four floors. It is probable but by no means certain that they were used as guest chambers since friends and visitors needed to be well accommodated, though this accommodation – particularly at the lower level – may have also extended to senior household officials. Unfortunately, nearly all this segment of the castle was destroyed during the Civil War, leaving only one unit standing the full four storeys.

There were four individual entries to the ground-floor rooms, with evidence that two of them were heated chambers with garderobes.[12] The courtyard-approached newel served all three upper floors, with the immediate rooms with fireplaces in the outer walls and courtyard-facing cinquefoil-light windows, blocked and replaced by Arundell.[13] As the remainder of this segment has been destroyed to ground level, its plan, the approach to the rooms, and the range of facilities becomes speculative, but several paired lodgings are likely. It is possible that there were six such lodgings, made up of a larger outer and a smaller inner room with two more at ground level.[14] But this would depend on whether the chapel was also here, perhaps with separate household access and a gallery from the family apartments.

The chapel is among the forty rooms listed in the detailed inventory of the castle taken on 10 August 1605.[15] It itemises the extremely rich furnishings in eight reception rooms (including hall, great chamber, gallery, wardrobe, and chapel), four service rooms (kitchen, pantry, porcelain or china room, and linen room), and twenty-eight chambers with beds (including the withdrawing chamber). In addition, there were eleven tiny staff rooms over the stable and in the brewhouse and garden chamber, all of which may have been outside the main building. There may be a fair chance of establishing the original layout of the castle from this inventory, using the known position of some of the rooms. It is unlikely to have been altered very much since Lovel's day though the Smythson alteration may have led to some changes.

ASSESSMENT

At present, an assessment of Wardour Castle rests entirely on its surviving residential heart. In the absence of any geophysical analysis or archaeological surveys, it is assumed that the walled outer court was occupied by storehouses or services but it is an area that awaits research, as does the environment and landscape without. In this instance, however, the outer ward is enormous, nearly three times as large as that at Farleigh Hungerford Castle, suggesting that its purpose was far more than for service buildings. Was part of it a garden? Was it a fourteenth-century designed landscape within the curtain wall as well as without? The contrived setting of the central residence suggests so. The contemporary deer park beyond, mentioned in the licence to crenellate, has been recently identified on the ground and through an early eighteenth-century plan copying an older original. This shows the park symmetrically round the castle, divided into areas for fallow deer and red deer, separated by a still traceable ditch.[16] What landscaping element occurred within the outer court?

The castellate appellation is regrettable but understandable. The two frontal towers, portcullises, embattled parapet, and bartisans convey the external character of a fortress, even though it was no more than skin deep. Such measures were part of the repertoire of a grand mansion during the late fourteenth century and would have been adjudged as such. The two towers at the front are particularly striking and convey an impression that would have been belied by the other more generously windowed frontages. The single entry also emphasised the castle's military character, at the risk of inconvenience which Sir Thomas Arundell was quick to make good in 1570 by inserting an additional ground-floor entry and an underground passage for bringing in food supplies.

Once within, two factors predominated – social differentiation and domestic comfort. The former was immediately apparent, with separate entries for junior staff, household staff, officials, family, and guests. In addition to the three principal stairs for family (north tower), staff and officials (east tower), and guests (south courtyard), there were two subsidiary newels for the family's use (each end of Great Chamber), and possibly one between the guest rooms in the destroyed south-west segment where there is wall thickening at the courtyard angle. Domestic comfort would only have been apparent with room allocation revealing the number of individual chambers in this castle. Despite the ruinous state, the abundance of single and paired lodgings is immediate, as is the generous provision of fireplaces and garderobes which even extends to some of the ground-floor rooms. Chute evidence and the extensive drainage system show that considerable thought had been given to waste disposal. It is also axiomatic of medieval accommodation that the higher such rooms, the more privileged the occupant. This can be seen in the three tiers of household rooms with their differing facilities. Greater privacy with greater height also applied to the two suites of family apartments and even to the two kitchens – a rare feature in any residence, though repeated at Bolton Castle.

Decorative stonework was used with discrimination. Externally, it was limited to the beautifully detailed bartisans, the fleuron cornice under the parapet, the fan vaulting of the entry passage, and the tracery head of the hall windows. Internally, there were the hall cornice and rear arch shafts, elegantly vaulted stair heads, and the open roofs of the most important apartments. Even so, the emphasis at Wardour was on high-quality stonework, using blocks of Tisbury greensand with Chilmark limestone for decorative features. Doorways and fireplace lintels were plain, but not too much should be read into this. The total absence of wall hangings, painted walls, stained glass, floor tiles, furnishings, and plate means that the rooms have lost the sumptuous decoration that made the castle a miniature version of the royal court.

Wardour was a public statement of status and wealth, but more than that, the castle reflects the man who built it. Initially a minor baron, John Lovel's marriage in 1372 to Maud Holand, the heiress granddaughter of Robert, Lord Holand, brought him wealth and family links with Richard II, and the earls of Huntingdon and Kent. Lovel was never a member of the king's inner circle like his Holand cousins, but he initially benefited from royal grants and perquisites such as keeper of Devizes Castle in 1382 and he was a regular trier of petitions in parliament.[17] He was expelled from court by the appellants in 1388 but had staged a comeback by the mid-1390s and became actively involved in government again at local and national level.[18] Wardour symbolised his rise in standing, his political ambitions, and his right to be considered among the leading families of the land. The family had long held properties in Norfolk and Suffolk, Wiltshire, Oxfordshire, and Northamptonshire. The

PLATE 287 Wardour Castle: from the south-west

ancestral home at Minster Lovell in Oxfordshire was old-fashioned, while a second home at Titchmarsh in Northamptonshire was in ruin at this time.[19] As the fifty-year-old Lovel wanted to make his mark in an entirely different place, he acquired the manor of Wardour by about 1390 and chose a virgin site for the residence that came to mark his political ascendancy and royal favour.

One of the unusual features at Wardour is the choice of a hexagonal plan encompassing residence, internal court, and outer curtain wall. The claim that the castle was inspired by the small hexagonal castle built by the duc de Berry at Concressault near Bourges can be dismissed.[20] The multi-angular castle at Montaner (1374–80) is a closer parallel in France, as is the pentagonal castle at Holt (1282–1311) on the Welsh border. The circular multi-towered rotunda with enclosing circular curtain at Queenborough Castle (1361–75) has also been cited as an influence,[21] as have the twin towers fronting Westminster Hall and the decorative cornice within.[22] But the game of precedents and influences can be played endlessly and to little purpose when the source of its design lies far more assuredly with two men – the master-mason and the client he was serving.

We are fortunate that a rare early portrait of John Lovel survives, showing him receiving an illuminated lectionary from John Siferwas which Lovel subsequently donated to Salisbury Cathedral.[23] Siferwas was one of the more gifted artists patronised by the king, and this illustration and incident point to Lovel's similar patronage and aesthetic taste. He wanted a sophisticated and ground-breaking design that would be seen to be innovative, individual, and aspirational. Wardour was to be the new dynastic centre for his family rather than Minster Lovell.

Major houses during the late fourteenth century were either multi-courtyard residences such as Farleigh Hungerford Castle nearby, or Dartington Hall by Lovel's Holand cousin, or striking towered complexes like Bolton Castle or the tower-house at Warkworth Castle. Wardour was to be of the latter mould and necessarily demanded a leading master-mason. If John Lewyn was dominant in the north of England and Henry Yevele pre-eminent at court, William Wynford was the leading exponent in the south-west. Though there is no documentary evidence that Wynford was responsible, what is not in doubt is that this multi-level layout was

the work of an outstanding master-mason. Inspiration can be stimulated by contemporary developments, but while architectural genius rarely follows a direct trajectory, it is often the response to complex issues and seeming imponderables. The master-mason at Wardour responded to the issues set by Lovel, and thereby created an unusually shaped residence with a towered front of interlocking ingenuity to meet the different social and occupational levels of a magnate's household. It was a house like no other in England – *haute couture* rather than *outré*. The client obtained a stunning architectural concept that was noble in scale, intriguing in layout, and exquisite in detail. The fact that the castle also became Lovel's prime residence, the centre of his household, the hub of his estates, and a lavish entertainment base almost seems a secondary consideration.

NOTES

1 During the 1570s, the ground was built up by just over a foot on the approach side of the outer court, and by 8 feet to the south-west. There was further levelling during the eighteenth century.

2 *Cal. Pat. Rolls: 1391–96*, 261.

3 Girouard (1991) 46–8.

4 *Ibid.* A similar Elizabethan-created gallery in a castle still exists at Powis Castle.

5 It is possible that this was a major feature mirroring the castle like those at Kenilworth or Bodiam castles.

6 B. Williamson, *Lord Arundell's Park at Wardour* (1997). For the massive expenditure, debts, and the creation of a white elephant on a small estate, B. Williamson, *Wilts. Arch. and N. H. Mag.* 94 (2001) 56–67.

7 J. Rutter, *An Historical and Descriptive Sketch of Wardour Castle and Demesne* (1822). The historical account in VCH, *Wiltshire*, XIII (1987) 222 is all too brief.

8 L. Keen, *Wilts. Arch. and N. H. Mag.* 62 (1967) 70–1.

9 Some of Arundell's blocking of earlier windows and doorways was skilfully accomplished, particularly in the central court.

10 First put forward by John Harvey, *Eng. Med. Arch.* (1984) 354, who pointed out that Lovel had dined with bishop William Wykeham at Winchester in 1393 just as Wynford was completing Winchester College for the bishop (1382–c.1394).

11 Ignore the 1570 forced doorway in its outer wall.

12 This castle was well provisioned with garderobes, with several drains joining the main kitchen drain extending from the south-west and sloping towards the lake.

13 Unblocking has revealed an original ground-floor twin-light window.

14 B. Morley in *Collectanea Historica*, ed. A. Detsicas (1981) 111–12.

15 Wiltshire Record Office, Trowbridge, no. 2667/239. Mark Girouard kindly gave me a copy of his transcript of this inventory.

16 R. Haslam, *Country Life* (February 1993).

17 *Com. Peerage*, VIII (1932) 219–21.

18 N. Saul, *Richard II* (1997) 247–8.

19 Titchmarsh had been crenellated under licence in 1304 but an inquiry of 1361 declared it 'ruinous and destroyed'. For Minster Lovell, totally rebuilt by Lovel's grandson in the 1430s, see page 117. Wardour influenced the form of its hall.

20 Keen, *Wilts. Arch. and N. H. Mag.* 62 (1967) 67; Pugh and Saunders (1968) 12; B. K. Davison, *Wardour Castle: Handbook* (1999) 24; and C. Platt, *The Castle in Medieval England and Wales* (1982) 124–5, where 'it displays the very clear influence of France'. In any case, Concressault was not begun before 1402.

21 Girouard (1991) 44, 46.

22 Goodall (2005) 98, 99.

23 Brit. Lib., Harl. MS 7026 f.4 verso. Also M. Rickert, *Painting in Britain: The Middle Ages* (1954) 178–85; K. L. Scott, *Later Gothic Manuscripts 1390–1490* (1996) no.10; J. Backhouse, *The Sherborne Missal* (1999) 53.

H. F. Chettle, *Wilts. Arch. and N. H. Mag.* 50 (1944) 452–8
R. B. Pugh and A. D. Saunders, *Old Wardour Castle: Guidebook* (1968)
M. Girouard, *Country Life* (February 1991)
J. Goodall. *Country Life* (April 2005).

WEARE GIFFARD HALL, Devon

The Fortescues were originally a south Devon family from near Modbury, who rose to prominence during the mid-fifteenth century through the fortune made by practising at the bar. Sir John Fortescue (d.c.1477), a young chief justice in 1442, was an independent but perceptive assessor to both the Lancastrian and the Yorkist houses.[1] A hard-working judge, he declined to be influenced by the crown in several prominent cases in the 1450s even though he was a stalwart member of the court party. He followed the royal family to Scotland and Flanders after Edward IV's accession in 1461, was captured at the battle of Tewkesbury ten years later, and was pardoned and made a member of Edward's council. His several tracts were pragmatic and reasoned. They included a defence of the house of Lancaster and a disavowal of it in 1471. His *De laudibus legum Angliae* was composed in exile during the late 1460s for the young Prince Edward (d.1471), while his *On the Governance of the Kingdom of England* was written very shortly after his return, to explain the collapse of Henry VI's government and that fiscal supremacy was the basis for royal power. Sir John purchased Ebrington Manor near Chipping Campden, where he died and his descendants still live.

As with so many rising families, younger sons often married wealthy heiresses and founded new branches. In 1454, Sir John's second son Martin married Elizabeth Denzill, a descendant of the Giffard family, and so acquired Filleigh, Buckland Filleigh, and Weare Giffard in north Devon.[2] They built the present Hall at the last named, attributable to them on the grounds of architectural detailing and the inclusion of their arms, with completion before Martin's death in 1472.

The house was updated internally by Hugh Fortescue at the end of the sixteenth century, but a century later the Fortescues rebuilt Filleigh (now called Castle Hill) near South Molton and made it their principal seat, leaving Weare Giffard to an extended period of neglect. It was rescued by a younger son, George Matthew Fortescue, who restored, remodelled, and extended the house between about 1830 and 1832 so that it combines three development phases – 1460s, 1590s, and 1830s – with the first and third predominant and the house little touched since then.

Built of local rubble slatestone, Weare Giffard Hall stands above the meadows of the River Torridge 3 miles south-east of Bideford. It is the most imposing late medieval house in north Devon, approximately E-shaped to the front though substantially extended to the rear in the 1830s with kitchen, offices, staff quarters, and bedrooms, making it a two-build house though with its core little altered. The house displays two unusual characteristics. It stands close to the edge of the meadow bank with the hall range facing the river. Consequently, the gatehouse does not face the hall range but was positioned at the corner of the site, with a sharp drop immediately to the south and an approach facing what was usually the services wing and passing the end of it to reach the forecourt and hall entry. Secondly, the house has an abundance of architectural rich-

PLATE 288 Weare Giffard Hall: hall from the south court

ness, characterised externally by all window heads and several doorways (with visible relieving arches over both) and internally by the highly elaborate hall roof, imported woodwork, and stained glass.

The contemporary gatehouse, 23 feet by 17 feet externally, stands only 40 feet from the house, now isolated from the embattled wall that enclosed the site until the Civil War. It is a rare survival for the region, three-storeyed, battlemented, and with the arms of Robert Fortescue (d.1661) and his two wives flanking the frontal window (pl. 301). It is not defensive but a high-status entry, like the Elizabethan one at Tawstock Court near Barnstaple. The entry passage, 13 feet wide, has a semi-circular arch of sixteenth-century form at each end. Above is a two-unit lodging, both floors with two-light cinquefoil windows with a first-floor fireplace (later insertion above) and space for a ground-floor garderobe with slit window and river-facing discharge next to the 1980s repaired stair.

The present entry to the Hall is directly into the east wing and staircase hall created in the 1830s. However, for descriptive purposes it is assumed that a visitor has preceded past this wing to the hall doorway. This is an impressive entry with two-centred head under a hood mould terminating with carved heads, continuous mouldings, and the inner chamfer exquisitely carved with a tree branch with leaves scrolling around it. There is no evidence of a porch or indication of an adequate opposing cross-passage entry.

The hall, 33 feet by 19 feet internally, was lit from both sides by two-light windows in the upper walling, two to the south and four to the north. The latter were blocked in the 1830s because of the corridor added on that side, though the window over the screens passage was retained. All the windows were set internally under an acute four-centred head, except for the tall transomed window lighting the dais and reaching almost to the ground. This, like all the hall windows, has an elaborate head with twin cinquefoil ogee lights with quatrefoil spandrels, all under a square hood terminating in head stops.[3] The fireplace stack is not bonded to the outer

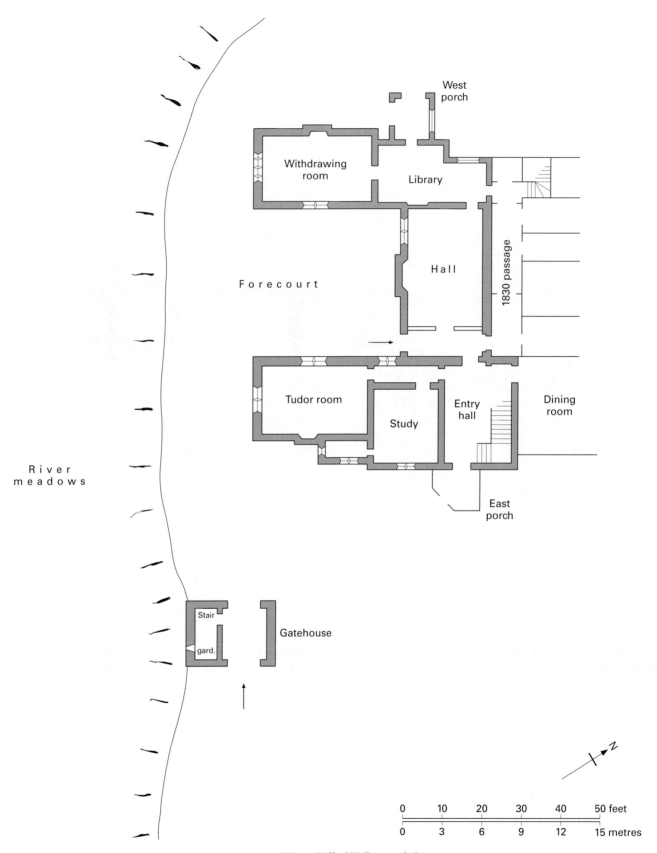

West porch

Withdrawing room

Library

Hall

1830 passage

Forecourt

Tudor room

Study

Entry hall

Dining room

East porch

River meadows

Stair

gard.

Gatehouse

N

0	10	20	30	40	50 feet
0	3	6	9	12	15 metres

FIGURE 171 Weare Giffard Hall: ground plan

PLATE 289 Weare Giffard Hall: hall roof

wall, but whether it is contemporary or not is unclear. The lintel has a four-centred head with the Fortescue arms of interlinked fishes and a rose in the spandrels, but there is a flatness above the central carving that is worrying.

The four-bay roof of hammer-beam trusses in this relatively small hall is spectacular beyond belief. Five braces rising from stone corbels, two with blank shields, support hammer beams from which arched braces rise to a high collar. The lower and upper arches are elaborately embellished with foliated cusping, four pendants (two in the middle with pinnacles), and quatrefoils in the spandrels. The intermediate trusses are more simply moulded and barely visible, but the two lines of wall plates are richly decorated, the lower with a running pattern of foliage and grapes, and the upper with continuous foliated cresting. Each bay is filled with straight wind braces, diagonally positioned between the moulded purlins. This creates a pattern of six squares per bay, each square with the decorative cusping emphasised by the lighter-coloured replacement panelling behind of 1832.[4] Virtuoso roofs with richly moulded trusses, extensive cusping, and pendants are a feature of Edward IV's reign, as at Crosby Hall, Eltham Palace, and the Oxford Divinity Schools. The inappropriately named 'false' hammer-beam roof at Weare Giffard is not out of place in such company, but this roof is embellished with

a line of wooden heraldic beasts sitting on the ends of the hammer beams. They include a greyhound and a dragon, the supporters of Henry VII, and therefore the structure is usually attributed to John Fortescue (d.1503).[5] However, as the similar line of wooden beasts on the hammer beams of the near contemporary roof at Orleigh Court nearby have never been pegged into the beams, their addition at Weare Giffard as at Orleigh Court is quite possible. Furthermore, the third hammer-beam roof in north Devon, at West Challacombe Manor, which features the heavy double ridges of two timbers repeated at Weare Giffard, has been dendro dated to the third quarter of the fifteenth century.

The hall is enhanced with a kaleidoscope of plaster, wood, and glass. In 1599, Hugh Fortescue added three large coats of arms in relief on the upper end wall, a further one above the fireplace, and smaller plaster ornaments on the side walls. The lower walls have linenfold panelling surmounted by Renaissance medallion panels[6] but the screen is a made-up ensemble of sub-medieval character with robust cylindrical uprights.[7] The heads of the windows, as elsewhere in the house, are filled with fragments of medieval and later stained glass, some of it original to the house, with the most complete ensemble filling the internal window over the screen.[8]

The two wings are similar in character – two-storeyed with a two-room layout at both levels and stripped of original features internally. Several of the courtyard-facing windows are genuine, with cinquefoil lights under rectangular hoods with stops, but some are 1830 replacements. The ground-floor end window of the west wing, for instance, succeeded the Venetian-style window shown in one of the 1803 watercolours of the house by Robert Smith, whereas the first-floor window above is genuine. The same watercolour also suggests that the 'west porch' projecting from the middle of the wing was formerly at the south-west corner of the terrace. The porch has obviously been made up and moved to its present position with brick backing in 1832, but it consists of two highly decorative fifteenth-century arches. The jamb of one, though badly damaged, is undercut with the foliage and grape trail already seen on the lower wall plate of the hall roof, with the arms of Fortescue with Joan Weare who married Richard Denzill I (c.1425) and Anne Courtenay, second wife of Richard Denzill 2 (c.1450), in the spandrels under a square hood with figured stops. The jamb of the second arch is lined with more conventional fleuron decoration under a two-centred hood with end stops.[9] Both arches are contemporary with the house but of unknown original location, though one may have been removed from the cross-passage entry to the inner court. The same mason combined the two decorative patterns in the hall porch entry at Orleigh Court.[10] Internally, the west wing is of stripped Regency Gothick character – two rooms at both levels with brought-in Jacobean overmantels and a replacement roof.

The east wing retains more original courtyard-facing windows, including a transomed one next to the hall entry with the lower lights of elongated cinquefoil character as in the hall dais window. The lights of the adjacent window were modified in the late sixteenth century, as were those in the end wall and east face, for they reflect the internal character of the rooms – with a panelled and plaster ceilinged ground-floor parlour and a plaster-decorated overmantel and frieze in the bedchamber above. The remainder of the wing is essentially the entrance and staircase hall of 1830–2, with fireplace, sixteenth-century Flemish carved panels, and a jumble of woodwork.[11]

Weare Giffard Hall has the plan and decorative richness of a fifteenth-century house of south Somerset rather than any Devon precedent. The wings are more elongated than usual, and this highlights the first of the house's problems. One wonders why the approach to the hall was so restricted by siting the property close to the edge of the river bank instead of setting it further back, and why it faced north/south rather than east/west to enable the gatehouse and hall entry to be in line. This implies that the gatehouse faced the kitchen and services in a standard layout. But it is probable that the layout of the Hall did not follow the usual pattern, and this is supported by the scale of the windows in the east wing. This part of the house seems to have been a second-stage development, awkwardly cutting into the side of the hall doorway and with both floors designed for family occupation. As Elizabeth Fortescue survived her husband by several years, this development may reflect two-family occupation between herself and her married son and his children. This, in turn, raises the double question of the original entry into the house and the position of the kitchen. There is some evidence for a services courtyard to the north of the hall[12] but the area has been subsequently overbuilt and the earlier layout is unknown.

The resolution of these problems lies in looking beyond south Somerset to south Wiltshire, and more particularly to the house that Thomas Tropnell erected at Great Chalfield between c.1478 and 1485. Tropnell was following in the steps of the Long family, whose nearby contemporary house at South Wraxall bears similar elements of gateway and house layout. But Great Chalfield Manor repeats the primary characteristics of Weare Giffard Hall. The gatehouse is at right angles to the house, forward from it, and leading into a forecourt limited by the front-facing moat. The hall is high-windowed with both flanking wings for family use. The services were round an inner court and have similarly been pulled down. Great Chalfield, like Weare Giffard, was a forward-looking house melding long-established features with new ideas. Martin Fortescue's house, like Dartington Hall in the south of the county, was an alien development in Devon, following metropolitan rather than established local traditions.

Fortescue's intriguing house has never benefited from the thorough analysis it warrants. What is not in doubt is its demonstration of mid-fifteenth-century exuberance – rare in the region and by no means matched by the contemporary frontage added at Bradley Manor in south Devon or the group of slightly later roofs near Exeter. The hall roof is without peer in the south-west, though it has attracted a range of opinions from 'remarkable' and 'virtuosic' to 'over-rated'.[13] The extensive 1830–2 embellishments of the Hon. George Fortescue have far from spoilt the Hall, though Avray Tipping's criticism was unrelenting. The Hall had been 'transformed into a confused pot-pourri of collector's fragments; a bewildering *omnium gatherum* of building materials; an unconvincing assemblage of structural and decorative parts, brought together from all quarters . . . [which] tells no sympathetic tale, teaches no consecutive lesson, satisfies no intelligent enquiry'.[14] Tipping's strictures, though understandable, are too harsh, for he ignored the fact that Fortescue had 'redeemed [the house] . . . from a state of ruin and neglect'[15] or that his work has enabled it to be comfortably habitable ever since. Yet nearly two centuries later, this house still holds several secrets awaiting disclosure to the diligent enquirer.

NOTES

1 For Fortescue's life, S. B. Chrimes' introduction to his edition of *De laudibus legum Angliae* (1942).

2 The eldest son, Sir Henry Fortescue, became the lord chief justice in Ireland, married a lesser heiress, and acquired Fallapit in East Allington, rebuilt in the nineteenth century. Buckland Filleigh, rebuilt in the early Georgian period, was sold in the 1840s. Filleigh was rebuilt in 1684–94 and 1730–40 and modified in the mid-nineteenth and mid-twentieth centuries. It is the only estate held by the Fortescues in the county, though they have been one of the most widespread and prominent families in Devon with thirty-one as members of parliament between 1382 and 1702, a barony in 1746, and an earldom in 1792. Earl Fortescue, *A Chronicle of Castle Hill 1454–1918* (1929). Nothing survives of the houses of the other branches of the family at Whympston near Modbury or Spriddlestone near Brixton by Plymouth.

3 Martin and his wife were also responsible for adding the south aisle to the church nearby. Four of the five lights to its east window have ogee heads with a quatrefoil above while the side windows have interlocking depressed heads. They were also responsible for the Jesse east window (now fragmentary).

4 Copies of Edward Ashworth's detailed drawings of the roof illustrating his brief paper of 1858 (published in 1861) are held in the house. See also T. Garner and A. Stratton, *The Domestic Architecture of England During the Tudor Period*, II (1909) 219, pl.CLVI.

5 Following Tipping (1924) 358–9.
6 Similar insertions were made in the Tudor hall at Great Fulford, probably when it was remodelled in the late seventeenth century.
7 A more untouched secular screen from north Devon is held in the V & A Museum, London, associated with a branch of the Giffard family. The moated site of their house at Brightleigh near Chittlehampton survives with its medieval retaining walls. The seventeenth-century house within the platform incorporates the fifteenth-century porch of the Giffards' home, while the V & A holds the three-bay hall screen of *c*.1500 with carved jambs, traceried heads above linenfold panels, and three coats of arms in the central bay. C. Tracy, *English Medieval Furniture and Woodwork* (1988) 161.
8 A. W. B. Messenger, *Trans. Devon. Assoc.* 75 (1943) 171–210, describes the plaster and glass heraldry and the associated pedigrees. The many glass fragments, interspersed with early nineteenth-century elements, were brought together by George Matthew Fortescue. Tipping thought that the sheaf of wheat tied with a knot between the letters I and E in the screen window stood for John Fortescue (d.1509) whereas it is the late fourteenth-century badge of John and Elizabeth Holand of Dartington Hall. The arms of Martin Fortescue are above.
9 The third side of the porch holds a contemporary panelled arched frame, converted into a window.
10 The ground-floor doorway of the three-storey fifteenth-century porch tower of Yeo Vale, Alwington seems to have been similarly decorated. It was pulled down in 1972. R. A. Lauder, *Vanished Houses of North Devon* (1981) 45–57.
11 For the importation of church furniture in a secular setting during the early nineteenth century, C. Tracy, *Jour. Brit. Arch. Assoc.* 152 (1999) 114–15. The two fifteenth-century lights without framing or hood inserted above the staircase window have also been brought from elsewhere.
12 Tipping refers to an office court with wings longer than those to the forecourt: (1924) 354.
13 M. Wood, *The English Mediaeval House* (1965) 319; B. Cherry and N. Pevsner, *The Buildings of England: Devon* (1989) 892; F. H. Crossley, *Timber Building in England* (1951) 140.
14 *Country Life* (January 1915) republished in Tipping (1924) 351–2.
15 Ashworth (1861) 152.

E. Ashworth, *Transactions of the Exeter Diocesan Architectural Society* 6 (1861) 151–7
H. A. Tipping, *English Homes*, Pd 2, I (1924) 351–60

WELLS, BISHOP'S PALACE and episcopal houses in Somerset

Without doubt, this Bishop's Palace is the most memorable of all those in England, combining high architectural interest with exquisite beauty of setting.[1] As one enters the moated precinct, its layout and development is immediately spelled out. Within a broad landscaped sward, four linked buildings sweep in an irregular curve from the embattled north wall. Their construction similarly spans four phases by four bishops. During the early thirteenth century, bishop Jocelin built the set-back storeyed range. Late in that century, bishop Burnell developed the chapel and hall to the forward right, almost reaching the south side of the site (pl. 188). During the mid-fourteenth century, bishop Ralph protected the precinct with an embattled gatehouse and towered walls, while a century later bishop Bekynton erected a more domestic-looking house backing on to the north precinct wall. The post-medieval

alterations, not immediately obvious externally, are mainly confined to early Victorian modification to bishop Jocelin's range.

As the palace has been described several times since John Parker's account of 1862, only a summary of the earlier buildings is necessary.

SITE

The palace site was determined by the forceful springs or wells that give the city its name. Still freely flowing, they provided fresh drinking water and water protection from the earliest times. Though there had been bishops of Wells from 909 who would have had quarters here, the first reference to a *palatium* is under the first Norman bishop, Giso of Lorraine (1061–88).[2] His immediate successor transferred the cathedral to Bath, but bishop Jocelin Trotman (1206–42) restored Wells as the centre of the diocese, now under a combined title. In 1207 King John granted Jocelin land south of the cathedral to form a park, and there is no doubt that the present precinct area dates from this time, possibly first enclosed by a palisaded fence. Of course, the interior was not the present manicured landscape of lawns and spreading trees but a mixture of courtyards, cobbles, clutter, and outbuildings, though evidence has been recovered of a medieval garden to the rear of Jocelin's range. There were also buildings that have been lost, such as bishop Burnell's kitchen and Bekynton's towered inner gateway and cloister walk dividing the area into two courts, but detailed research is in hand to identify the many changes during the past eight centuries.

JOCELIN'S RANGE

The front of the two-storey range built by bishop Jocelin Trotman, one of the most important survivals of its time, has been damaged by the Victorian inserted attic floor and gables. It is better to examine the rear face first, which retains the original levels. This oblong range of *c*.1230–40, helped by Henry III's gift of thirty oaks in 1233, consists of a vaulted ground floor, with the apartments above open to the roof (as in the thirteenth-century palaces at Worcester and Salisbury). The double pitched roof reflects the unusual internal plan at both levels, of a single-bay gallery to the front prefacing a double-bay area, divided by a cross wall into a larger and a smaller room – the bishop's hall and chamber at the upper level. A short contemporary wing of a small room with end garderobe projects from the north-east angle. Range and wing are marked by buttresses with close-stepped set-offs, a feature repeated from bishop Burnell's hall turrets for they are Victorian additions not present in Buck's engraving of 1733. The ground-floor rooms were originally lit by lancets on all sides (Victorian enlarged to the front) and the upper floor by twin trefoil lights with a quatrefoil in plate tracery, more elaborate in the end-wall windows.

The central Victorian porch protecting the original entrance, moved from one bay to the north by the late eighteenth century, opens into a ground-floor gallery with quadripartite vaulting. This was probably divided by two cross walls into rooms of 1–3–3 bays (see vault) and now has a late fifteenth-century fireplace. Opposite the original outer entrance position is the inner entry to the vaulted undercroft, with its central line of local grey/blue Lias stone piers. The two bays at the north end were partitioned, with access to the short wing. The first-floor apartments were originally approached by a stone newel at each end of the gallery. The principal one at the

PLATE 290 Wells, Bishop's Palace: engraving from the south by S. and N. Buck (1733)

south end survives, but the more private one was replaced by the far more convenient Jacobean stair of bishop Montague (1608–16). In 1845–54, Benjamin Ferrey stripped out the upper floor, embellished the earlier windows with their foliated rear arches, inserted the gabled attic floor, and added a new roof. His work for bishop Bagot (1845–54) was well intentioned but arrogant. His long gallery fronts a line of three reception rooms with fussy plaster ceilings by an upholsterer from Bath. In 1978, restoration work revealed that the plastered walls had been painted in the thirteenth century with ochre lime-wash and masonry patterns.

BURNELL'S HALL BLOCK AND CHAPEL

Only two sides stand of the great hall and chamber block built by bishop Burnell (1275–92) but his work of c.1290 was on the grandest scale. It was a buttressed parallelogram with an embattled parapet and octagonal turrets at the corners, two of them with roof-level closets. The hall was aisled, with the offices at the lower end flanking a kitchen passage, spanned by a single chamber above as wide as the hall.

The two-storey porch with corner turrets was pulled down after its depiction by Buck in 1733, leaving only its roof scar and that over the side stair to the first-floor chamber. The hall, 115 feet by 60 feet, had two-centred cross-passage doorways, a roof supported on two arcades, and three spectacular windows in the standing north wall reaching almost from the ground to wall plate level. There were formerly four on the opposite side, for Buck's engraving shows that the last bay was blank walling, for the existing shortened dais window and doorway have been inserted since 1733. The scale and quality of Burnell's work is outstanding. It is one of the largest halls in England, only surpassed by the early Norman palace halls at Westminster and Canterbury and the later one at Norwich (1318–25), almost matched by that at Winchester Castle (1222–35), but not surpassed by the halls at Eltham (1479–80), Christ Church, Oxford (1525–9), or Hampton Court (c.1530). Burnell deliberately contrasted the red and yellow sandstone rubble walling with ashlar-faced buttresses, and enhanced the corner turrets with multi-stepped buttresses. His windows are among the tallest in a medieval hall, with remarkably delicate tracery, shuttered below, glazed above. Excavations have shown that the floor was tiled, the roof was lead covered, while the embattled parapet is an early example of its use as a decorative feature.

The wall between the hall and the chamber block has been destroyed, so that only a partial skeleton survives of the offices with small lancets and the passage doorway to the lost kitchen, but there is considerably greater evidence of the retiring chamber. The windows retain more tracery than those in the hall, with Buck showing a further window in the lost south wall. The scar of the hooded fireplace is flanked by a mural passage and stair from the adjacent window to a turret garderobe, while the south-east turret retains a small vaulted closet with alternative lower and higher lancets.

Considering it was built towards the close of the thirteenth century, the siting of the withdrawing chamber at the lower end of the hall was increasingly archaic. This was not the case with Burnell's personal (not diocesan) residence at Acton Burnell (c.1284),[3] so that the Wells apartment probably served as a guest chamber with the bishop continuing to use Jocelin's range. Burnell's work at Wells not only contrasts with his Shropshire home but is equally a symbol of the power and wealth of a royal servant, Edward I's loyal chancellor, as well as one of the most powerful bishops of that era. It needs little imagination to visualise the setting for banquets like those during Edward III's visit over Christmas in 1331, when the bishop had to retreat to his house at Banwell, or that for two royal commissioners in 1337. On that occasion, 672 loaves, 86 pipes of wine, 349 pipes of ale, and many fish dishes of pike, eel, salmon, hake, plaice, and bream were consumed, followed by meat dishes of lamb, beef, duck, and chicken for 268 guests at a cost to bishop Ralph of £6 10s. 7½d.[4] The hall was stripped of its lead for Edward VI's treasury in 1552, while bishop Law (1824–45) destroyed the east and south walls shortly after his arrival to make the ruin 'more picturesque'. His offsetting contribution was to landscape the grounds.

It is arguable whether Burnell's scrumptious three-bay chapel preceded or followed his great hall. It abuts the hall's stair turret, but architectural analysis is supporting Parker's view that there was initially a two-storey chapel here at right angles to Jocelin's range and contemporary with it, linked by the newel between the two buildings. Bishop Burnell retained the earlier foundations and some of the lower elements such as the west doorway, but remade the greater part of the building. He created a glass box, window-filled on each side, with differing curvilinear tracery, local grey/blue Lias columns, and a high tierceron-vaulted roof with naturalistic foliated bosses rising from figure corbels of mixed date supporting stone shafts. Though it has lost all of its painted glass, for the medieval fragments of Rouen-area glass in the east window were 1830 insertions, this is a well-proportioned building of quiet simplicity and great beauty.[5] Taken together, Burnell's hall block and chapel were as highly confident and as accomplished as any contemporary royal work, military or domestic.

RALPH'S GATEHOUSE AND PRECINCT WALLS

Looking out from the terrace walk on the south side of the precinct, the visitor still obtains a little-altered vision of medieval England encompassing palace, cathedral, city, and countryside, for the fields, now farmed by the Church Commissioners, were part of the deer park granted by King John to bishop Jocelin. Immediately below, the landscaped moat was always broad, currently between 40 and 50 feet, but never more than a foot or two deep. It retains a narrow berm on the south and part of the east side, possibly through extending the watercourse in the mid-fourteenth century.

The three-storey embattled gatehouse of bishop Ralph (1329–63) is an oblong block recessed between broader, higher towers – polygonal to the front, flat-faced to the rear. The drawbridge (last raised in 1831 as a consequence of the parliamentary reform riots in Bristol), portcullis, double doors with wicket, and cross slits look meaningful but the building lacks a machicolated parapet or rear doors. The broad passage has a single plain quadripartite vault springing from head corbels. There are an ogee trefoil light behind the portcullis and two paired lights in the side walls (one ground, one first floor) but most of the windows are sixteenth-century enlargements. The building is still partially occupied (pl. 196).

Despite its martial face, this gatehouse is primarily a lodging block, divided into seven independent units of scaled accommodation (see sketch plan). The grading of the rooms by their position, window size, fireplace, and garderobe facilities determined the social level of their occupants. Immediately inside the wicket was lodging 1, a room of some quality and style. It had a vaulted ceiling, ribbed at the polygonal end above windows with shouldered rear arches. It has a large fireplace and a loop towards the drawbridge, within a cubbyhole that only a child could have manned. This was a combined porter's lodge and reception room. To the rear of the gatehouse, a separate entry and passage led to the newel with lamp bracket, rising to the first-floor lobby. The adjacent doorways have differentiated heads – two-centred and four-centred. Lodging 3 was a good-quality room with garderobe and retained original window. Lodging 4 over the entry passage had a fireplace with an octagonal chimney between two large windows, reduced in size for their sixteenth-century replacements. The newel continued to the upper

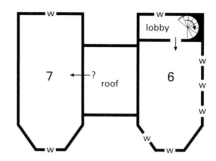

SECOND FLOOR

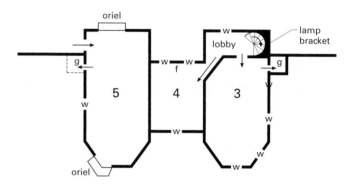

FIRST FLOOR

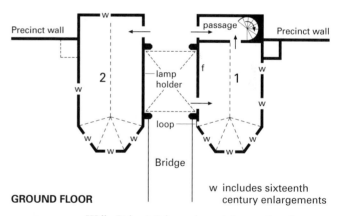

GROUND FLOOR

w includes sixteenth century enlargements

FIGURE 172 Wells, Bishop's Palace: schematic layout of gatehouse

lobby prefacing lodging 6 where the door opened on to the stair. The newel continued to the roof but there was no link between the east and west sides of the gatehouse. Lodging 2 repeated the vaulted ceiling and shouldered rear arches of the opposite unit but has lost its frontal ribs. The approach to lodging 5 seems to have been from the wall-walk where there is a blocked doorway. The room has sixteenth-century oriels at each end but has lost the garderobe projection shown in Buck's engraving. Lodging 7, now inaccessible, could only have been reached from the roof.

The walls enclosing the palace stand about 12 feet high, topped by an embattled parapet with occasional cross slits. There are five low circular towers boldly projecting from the angles of this pentagonal site, with a half-tower in the middle of the longest side facing the open country. The north-west tower is the most complete, with a lodging at both levels, the ground floor with fireplace, garderobe, and two cupboards, the upper room with none of these facilities.[6]

In March 1286, bishop Burnell had obtained a crenellation licence which covered the cathedral close, the palace precinct, and the adjacent residential complex of canons who were to be provided 'with sufficient gates and posterns to be opened at dawn'.[7] A little over fifty years later, the licence was repeated in March 1340 for bishop Ralph, for the palace and the security and quiet of the canons.[8] The gated, walled, and towered enclosure was the consequence of this second licence in a single building programme, but was it a meaningful defence? The nearest parallel is the similar precinct enclosure at Ewenni Priory (1150–1300). In my opinion, this was a serious defence to protect the monastery from the hostility of the Welsh.[9] Others have argued that it was primarily for prestige, and though it is recognised that the defences were of a costly and consistent military capability over a 125 year span, they are considered to be symbolic on the grounds that the site was too extended for serious defence.[10] Similarly, it has been considered that the Wells fortifications were built at a time of political unrest and social tension between the religious and civic authorities.[11] The latter undoubtedly resented this episcopal assertion, for their own crenellation licence of July 1341 was quickly revoked.[12] The gatehouse displays some military elements but was primarily a multi-residential block. The precinct lacks mid towers facing the town, and the 4 feet thick walls carry a 2½ feet wide wall-walk – hardly a fighting platform – while the moat is shallow. The east wall is built on the foundations of an earlier structure, possibly Burnell's, so that Ralph's building activity was replacement rather than initiation. In part, the Wells fortifications are an assertion of power and authority by a leading member of the clergy and political figure. But there is also a pictorial and landscaping element in their development, an increasingly important factor in fourteenth-century projects at Kenilworth, Westenhanger, Bodiam, and Saltwood castles. It is also possible that the bank and raised walk against the south wall overlooking the bishop's deer park was contemporary landscaping of the spoil displaced through moat excavation.

BEKYNTON'S WING

This is a relatively modest self-contained house forsaking the grandeur of the earlier ranges. Currently, it is a muddle in architectural terms and internal layout. Basically, bishop Bekynton (1443–65) erected a buttressed hall and withdrawing chamber above, with the upper end flanked by a three-storey tower on one side and a two-storey retiring wing on the other. All three units stopped a few feet short of the embattled precinct wall but at a diminishing angle to it, subsequently infilled. The kitchen wing, parallel to the retiring wing, faces Burnell's chapel. The house was drastically altered in the late eighteenth or early nineteenth century[13] when the hall and chamber unit were converted from two to three storeys, the rooms over the kitchen were modified, and the courtyard between the two wings was infilled. In the mid-nineteenth century, Ferrey rebranded the house with his thirteenth-century-style windows and replaced the roofs, while the twentieth century divided the property into flats and offices facilitated by a 1950s staircase.

PLATE 291 Wells, Bishop's Palace: bishop Bekynton's wing from the north

The primary interest of this house can be read on its east face, for the interior holds little of architectural interest. Bekynton's ground-floor hall was lit by three transomed cinquefoil-light windows under a square head. When the hall and chamber were made three-storey, the hall ceiling was lowered, the chamber windows were blocked, and casement windows were inserted at the new upper levels, now under reused drip moulds. The tower windows, though blocked on the south side, indicate the original levels.

The porch was added in 1556 in front of Bekynton's fleuron-decorated entrance carrying his arms and pinnacles. The hall would have been screened to separate the kitchen and offices approach on one side from the probable stair to the upper floor on the other.[14] The apartment originally extended to the early example of a three-light window behind the dais, remade in the early twentieth century when the room was divided into two and the composite screen inserted with Jacobean elements. The tower room is less altered, with its ground-floor garderobe (Tudor-enlarged with a small bay window) next to the stone newel rising to the upper floors and roof.[15] The chamber over the hall and its associated inner or retiring chamber were both given stylish oriels by bishop King (1495–1503) emulating those of Gunthorpe in the Deanery. Both open from four-centred rear arches and carry King's shield on an angel boss. The eight-sided chamber oriel is rib-vaulted and has two different window forms – plain segmental and ogee – with the quatrefoil frieze under them opened up and glazed to light two bathrooms below! The slightly more modest second oriel is panel vaulted and has the same window forms reversed.[16]

Bekynton was a prolific builder in Wells, whose work included the two monumental gateways to the market place, the 'Bishop's Eye' of c.1451 and the Penniless Porch, the houses on its north side facing the cathedral green of c.1453, the formerly decorated Brown's Gate, the Chain Gate linking cathedral and close of 1459, and the roofs and chimneys of the houses in the Vicars' Close in 1466.[17] Bekynton's palace work is the earliest example I know that reduces the importance of the hall in favour of the withdrawing chamber over. This mid-fifteenth-century example, possibly the initiator, was shortly followed at Gothelney Hall and Blackmoor Manor. Of further interest is that Bekynton's house turned its back on the earlier palace buildings in favour of the cathedral and its spring-fed grounds. Finally, Buck's invaluable engraving of 1733 shows a tall, polygonal turreted gate-tower at the corner of Bekynton's kitchen wing. Since destroyed but similar to that bishop's gateway approach from the market place, it was part of a cloister walk extending in front of the chapel to the hall dais to create an outer and much smaller inner court.[18]

EPISCOPAL HOUSES

The see, one of the smallest in England and Wales, was almost coterminous with the boundaries of Somerset. Since the main seat of the bishop was transferred from Bath to Wells in the early thirteenth century, the palace has always been the heart of the bishop's estate. Like his colleague at Exeter, the bishop of Wells held no episcopal castles as his neighbours did at Worcester, Salisbury, and Winchester. And less survives of his country houses than those of his fellow bishops.

During the later middle ages, Wells held nine houses in Somerset, one in Hampshire, and a fine residence in London. It lost most of them to the crown in the mid-sixteenth century.[19] Nothing survives at Blackford, Cheddar, Claverton, Evercreech, or Dogmersfield near Odiham on the road to Westminster. The precinct of the Norman palace at Bath has been traced well south of the Tudor abbey church and Norman cathedral site, with one end of the Norman hall revealed by excavation in 1984–5 and evidence that the site had been downgraded during the fourteenth century.[20] Part of the bishop's London house between the Strand and the Thames has been similarly excavated, though this early thirteenth-century site developed into a multi-courtyard house that achieved fame in the early seventeenth century for the earl of Arundel's collection of antique figures.[21]

Four sites retain modest remains. Court Farm, Wookey is the earliest, with hall and solar evidence including part of a fine doorway and window of c.1230 in a moated residence extended to courtyard form by Bekynton in c.1461–2 before post-medieval downgrading to a farmhouse.[22] The former royal palace at Cheddar was transferred to the bishop in the early thirteenth century, who rebuilt the hall in stone and the now ruined chapel late in that century.[23] Bishop Drokensford (1302–29) developed Wiveliscombe but only the sandstone entry arch of the gateway stands, minus the upper storey and with rebuilt side units. Banwell Court was rebuilt by bishop Bekynton in the mid-fifteenth century and retains his chapel amid the eighteenth- and late nineteenth-century expansion programmes.[24] The early Tudor gateway at Chew Magna is complete but routine, next to a fourteenth-century window incorporated in the late Elizabethan house that replaced the bishop's residence. Though only the moat survives at Blackford near

Wedmore, site excavations confirmed its use from the twelfth to the fourteenth centuries before bishop John Harewell (1369–86) demolished it. Judging by the character of the artefacts, the house may have been timber-framed, roofed with brown and green glazed tiles.[25]

NOTES

1 Pevsner (1958) 313. Apart from the episcopal castles at Durham and Farnham, only Bishop Auckland Palace and the ruined palace at Lincoln offer comparable architectural qualities.
2 Dunning (1982) 228.
3 A. Emery, *Greater Med. Houses*, II (2000) 502–4.
4 J. Armitage Robinson, *Somerset Rec. Soc.* 39 (1924) 72–81, 85–157. For two fifteenth-century diners at the palace, see F. A. Gasquet, *Downside Review* 15 (1896) 209–22, and for the furnishings of the palace apartments in 1399, see *Somerset Medieval Wills 1501–30*, ed. F. W. Weaver (1930) 294–7.
5 The parapet was raised by Ferrey to keep the chapel in scale with his heightening of Jocelin's range. There are additional fragments of the Rouen glass in the stair lobby of Bekynton's wing.
6 The interiors of the other two-storey towers are disappointing. The north tower is open on the inside, the north-east tower retains a drain outlet, the east tower has been remodelled, and the south tower is blocked by the landscaped bank against the inner face of the south wall.
7 *Cal. Pat. Rolls: 1291–92*, 229.
8 *Cal. Pat. Rolls: 1338–40*, 466.
9 Emery, *Greater Med. Houses*, II (2000) 692–3.
10 RCAHM, *Glamorgan*, III pt 1b (2000) 15, 125, 129. Protection for local families at times of attack and their support in defending the extended site are not considered, nor is the conflict resolved between the depletion of the priory's revenues after 1215 and substantial expenditure on meaningful defence seventy-five years later solely to 'impress'.
11 Dunning (1982) 234–5.
12 *Cal. Charter Rolls*, 5, 6–7.
13 Parker attributed it to bishop Beadon in c.1810: (1861–2) 152.
14 The stair would have been against the several feet of blank walling. Apart from some blocked courtyard doorways, the kitchen wing has been stripped of all early character to make twentieth-century offices, with the eighteenth-century rooms above converted into a flat in 2002.
15 The second-floor and most private room in Bekynton's house is also the tallest.
16 Part of the wall painting showing a fashionably dressed lady of c.1470–85, possibly Mary Magdalene or part of a narrative sequence such as Susannah and the Elders, was discovered during alterations in 2003.
17 William Worcester, *Itineraries*, ed. J. H. Harvey (1969) 295–7; *Register of Thomas Bekynton 1443–65*, ed. H. C. Maxwell-Lyte and M. C. Dawes, *Somerset Rec. Soc.* 44 (1934); A. F. Judd, *Life of Thomas Bekynton* (1961); *Proc. Somerset Arch. and N. H. Soc.* 142 (1999) 314–15. In discussions with the author in 1988, L. S. Colchester amended the Chain Gate attribution to the 1420s with the dog-leg bend added a generation later. Coterminous with his extensive building activity, Bekynton built up a household composed of local but intellectually capable men. R. W. Dunning, *Proc. Somerset Arch. and N. H. Soc.* 110 (1966) 24–39.
18 William Worcester also noted that Bekynton had erected chambers for visiting lords and a large kitchen, while the secretary of bishop Peirs (1632–70) recorded in the 1630s that the middle tower was marked by Bekynton's arms and rebus. H. E. Reynolds, *Wells Cathedral* (1881) 1i.
19 For their alienation and occasional recovery during the later sixteenth century, Dunning (1982) 239.
20 P. Davenport, *Archaeology in Bath 1976–85* (1991) 40–103; M. Chapman, P. Davenport, and E. Holland, *Arch. Jour.* 152 (1995) 95–108.
21 J. Schofield, *Medieval London Houses* (1995) 210–12; and page 231 of this volume.

22 J. Winstone, *Proc. Somerset Arch. and N. H. Soc.* 141 (1998) 91–101, has replaced much of J. Hasler and B. Luker, *ibid.* 137 (1994) 111–22. Also *Med. Arch.* 45 (2001) 318.

23 The Saxon and medieval palaces were excavated in 1960–2 in advance of construction of the Kings of Wessex School. The postholes of the west and east halls are marked by concrete blocks in a grassed area. *HKW,* II (1963) 907–9; P. Ratz, *The Saxon and Medieval Palaces at Cheddar* (1979). During her PhD research (Bristol University) into these episcopal houses, Naomi Payne has raised doubts about the use of Cheddar as a diocesan residence.

24 Usefully illustrated in R. Dunning, *Some Somerset Country Houses* (1991) 8.

25 I. M. Rendell, *Proc. Somerset Arch. and N. H. Soc.* 107 (1963) 71–8.

T. H. Turner and J. H. Parker, *Some Account of Domestic Architecture in England,* II (1859) 165–7

J. H. Parker, 'The Bishop's Palace at Wells', *Proc. Somerset Arch. and N. H. Soc.* 11 (1861–2) 143–57, reprinted separately in 1866

J. H. Parker, *The Architectural Antiquities of the City of Wells* (1866)

E. Buckle, *Proc. Somerset Arch. and N. H. Soc.* 34 (1888) 54–97

M. E. Wood, *Thirteenth Century Domestic Architecture. Arch. Jour.* Supplement (1950) 74–6

M. E. Wood, *Arch. Jour.* 107 (1950) 108–10 (with ground plan)

N. Pevsner, *The Buildings of England: North Somerset and Bristol* (1958) 312–16

R. W. Dunning, 'The Bishop's Palace', in *Wells Cathedral: A History,* ed. L. S. Colchester (1982) 227–47

L. S. Colchester, *Wells Cathedral* (1987) 159–80.

WELLS, THE DEANERY, Somerset

The contrast between the imposing scale and sprawling development of the Bishop's Palace and the compactness of the Deanery nearby points up the respective rôles of a leading political and episcopal figure and the executive head of a medieval cathedral of secular clergy – between national and regional importance. The Deanery was not a major structure until the appointment of dean Gunthorpe (1472–98), when the earlier buildings were refashioned and extended with a spectacular three-storey range, still little altered. This does not apply to the remainder of this quadrangular residence, seemingly compact externally but mightily confusing internally.

Positioned on the north side of the magnificent grass sward that helps to make Wells such a joy to visit, the Deanery is prefaced by an enclosed forecourt, with most of the higher-status rooms of this courtyard residence at the upper level. The house was occupied by the deans of Wells and their families until 1962, when the partial use of the property by the diocesan office since 1947 became a total one.

FORECOURT

The outer court is approached by a commanding gateway, ashlar-built to the front, linked to the Deanery by an embattled rubble wall. The ground floor has separate vehicle and pedestrian entrances, while the upper floor is a single lodging with transomed cinquefoil windows to the front flanking a central chimney stack. The fireplace was replaced in the seventeenth century, but the late fifteenth-century embattled head of its predecessor projects above it. The room has a corner garderobe, original entry door from the wall terrace, and projecting newel to the roof.[1] Though the rear window has ogee-headed lights, the gateway is contemporary with Gunthorpe's aggrandisement elsewhere. This gateway, entirely non-defensive and with expansive front windows, simply gave dignity to the Deanery approach, though it was modest enough when compared with the bishop's portentous palace gatehouse.

It is joined to the residence by a broad terrace rather than a wall-walk, 10 to 14 feet wide, with outer and inner embattled walls, entirely earth-filled. The most immediate parallel is the contemporary terrace at Berry Pomeroy Castle, providing a delightful promenade here overlooking the cathedral green.[2] Much closer is the comparable raised walk against the south precinct wall of the Bishop's Palace overlooking the deer park. The forecourt, divided in the eighteenth century by an embattled wall screening the dean's stables, faces a two-storey early to mid-fifteenth-century house, rubble-built and initially free-standing.

EXTERIOR

The fundamental development of this house can be read on its exterior face. The Deanery developed round a central court, reduced in size in the later nineteenth century and again in the later twentieth century. Whatever early form it took, the Deanery had developed round three sides of the court by the later fifteenth century. The entrance frontage reflects its closure in the early seventeenth century (ground-floor mullioned and transomed windows with late seventeenth-century replacement windows above). The buttressed south frontage towards the Close shows three development phases. The original wall was initially supported by low buttresses, enveloped by the taller ones of the late fifteenth century when the range was remodelled, faced with Chilcote stone, and surmounted by the embattled parapet. The string course was embellished with gargoyles, the merlons were decorated with blank (originally painted) shields and Tudor roses, and the pyramid turrets at each end were prettily panelled and ogee capped. The range was lit by two-light windows at ground level and the more important rooms above by four-light windows under square labels. But the range was totally refenestrated in the late seventeenth century by dean Bathurst (1670–1704), as was the west range with which it shared common levels. The clear building line between the two-storey west range and the three-storey north range shows that the former preceded the later fifteenth-century development.

Dean Gunthorpe's north range has a spectacular fenestrated frontage, elaborately lighting the three floors and mezzanine rooms at the west end. The ground floor was given single and twin lights, now with mid-Victorian additions. The upper floors had windows with cinquefoil lights, the more important transomed. One was developed as a slightly projecting oriel of four lights rising through two floors to the embattled parapet, and one as a first-floor bay with shield-decorated panels above and below the lights. This frontage is essentially shown in its present state in a late eighteenth-century engraving during dean Seymour's time (1790s), and though some eighteenth-century 'retouching' cannot be ruled out,[3] the façade is basically original. The range is spanned by a low-pitched roof, most apparent at the ends where the parapet follows its line, surmounted by a square turret at the south-west corner.

PLATE 292 Wells, The Deanery: from the cathedral close

The exterior reveals a basic five-period development.

Thirteenth century:	the low-buttressed south range. This development probably included the west range to form an L shaped house.[4]
Later fifteenth century:	dean Gunthorpe remodelled the south and west ranges and added the three-storey north range.
Early seventeenth century:	the central court was enclosed by the east range with its entry porch.
Late seventeenth century:	dean Bathurst refenestrated much of the house and remodelled the interior.
Late nineteenth century:	in 1888, dean Plumptree (1881–91) received a loan of £1,430 from Queen Anne's Bounty to pay for improvements to the building.

The Deanery awaits a thorough historical analysis and architectural and social survey, but a limited internal examination makes it clear that its development was a complex one, with several subsidiary building phases.

INTERIOR

The embattled parapet maintains the earlier form, but the entry range is primarily early seventeenth century, with an asymmetrical porch of the same date. It opens into a cross passage preparatory to the ground-floor hall in the usual position, with heated bedchambers above (now corridor and three offices), and a late seventeenth-century stair hall at its south end. Apart from the unadorned rectangular hall windows, several features point to its late Tudor date, including the low four-centred head of the outer entry (remade), less steeply pitched and without the hollow chamfer of the gatehouse entry. A glazed two-light window of the late fifteenth-century north range was blocked by the insertion of the cross passage (a development mirrored on the floor above), while

the upper end of the hall incorporates part of the earlier south range. The oblong hall with early seventeenth-century panelling incorporates an over-the-top late fifteenth-century pillared fireplace, similar to one in the Bishop's Palace, with trefoil panelled jambs and shaped mantel with quatrefoil and foliated decoration. It is possible that the hall replaced an earlier one open to the roof, heated by this fireplace, but the present range was probably the work of dean Haydon (1602–7), who found the property 'very ruinous and ready to fall downe' and spent 1,000 livres on repairs, with further work carried out by his successor.[5]

The south range is essentially of about 1690–1700, prefaced by the plain but dignified staircase to a large room on both floors. Most of the ground floor is taken up by the dining room with its high-quality marble fireplace, but with an earlier beamed ceiling, plaster-faced. The smaller end room (small sitting room) is undistinguished.

The upper stair lobby opens into the finest panelled room in the house, with an ornate plaster ceiling and frieze, coupled pilasters, and elaborate fireplace, 'much like a combination room in a college'.[6] The corner office beyond is again undistinguished.

The shorter west range holds a single room on each floor. The ground-floor drawing room retains seventeenth-century panelling and fireplace, and a late nineteenth-century frieze, while the single heated room above was divided in 1990 into a corridor and three offices. At that time, the door and associated wall at the junction with the north range was revealed, indicating the access created by Gunthorpe at this level between the two ranges.

The north range is the most substantial medieval survival, relatively unaltered. The courtyard-facing wall is marked by a plinth and two boldly shaped string courses of reverse curves, one above the other. The two doorways in this wall and that at the west end, all with steeply pitched heads, are original and possibly protected by a pentice. The ground-floor rooms were remodelled in 1987–90 as a kitchen, cloakroom, and entry hall with a new stair rising through three floors.

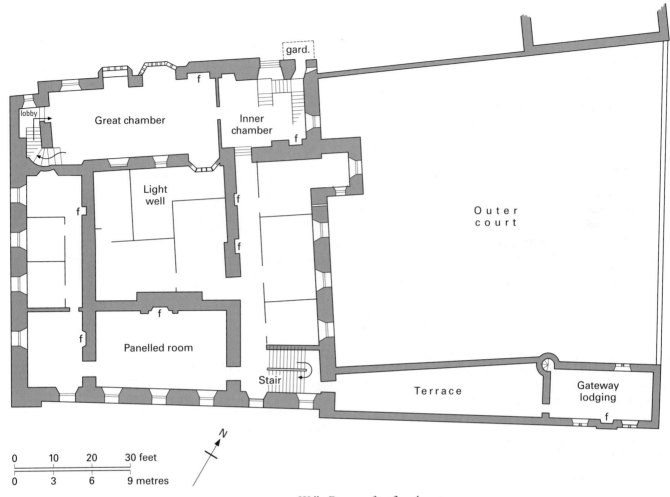

FIGURE 173 Wells, Deanery: first-floor layout

The original approach to the upper rooms was at the west end, via a straight stair with a line of rising chamfered arches above to the first-floor lobby. This retains a two-light window, a recess made from blocking a second one, and entry to the great chamber. This is an extraordinary late fifteenth-century room. The lower end is spanned by a bold stone arch supporting wall thickening above, with a canopied wash basin next to the entry. It may be helpful to articulate the layout of this room.

The first of the four bays has a two-light transomed window and newel access to the floor above (and the west range), but has lost most of its ceiling joists when this part of the room was formerly partitioned off. The second bay has a two-light courtyard-facing window (blocked) and the oriel opposite with multi-traceried window head, panelled sides, and decorative arched head. The third bay has a modern window to the courtyard, and the five-sided bay window opposite with cinquefoil transomed lights and fan and pendant head. The fourth bay has another five-sided oriel towards the inner court, with fan-vaulted head and episcopal shields, with Gunthorpe's rising sun on a shield outside. The fireplace is opposite, with steeply pitched head and Tudor roses in the spandrels. A plain post and panel partition separates this room from the 1987–90 staircase hall, though there is considerable doubt about its original position.[7]

The further or inner chamber, now filled with the 1987–90 stair, retains another four-light window with decorated panelled head, as well as two blocked windows, corner fireplace, ceiling beams, and garderobe doorway in the north-east corner.

Was the great chamber a single room or divided? The moulded ceiling beams show no evidence of partitioning while the mezzanine windows (see below) have little purpose unless there was unrestricted vision the length of the room. On the other hand, the lavabo and stair to the upper floor suggest an ante-room, possibly one bay deep, screened from the great chamber, and this would accord with the increasing movement towards privacy in a high-status range – ante-room, great chamber, and private inner chamber.

The second floor was prefaced by a low mezzanine room opening off the newel with canopied niche, fireplace, two windows, one with a Gunthorpe panelled head, and three tiny windows looking into the great chamber, two glazed and one with open lights. There were three good-quality chambers at this uppermost level of similar scale, separated by post and panels partitions, with windows in both outer walls, fireplaces, and a common low-pitched roof.[8] The east-end chamber was garderobe provided. There was a further room at the higher mezzanine level, now characterless, with a turret room above, 8½ feet by 7½ feet, with original beamed ceiling and arched stepped access to the roof.

This range was of the highest quality, emblazoned wherever possible by dean Gunthorpe's rebus and heraldic devices, and with different-styled panelled heads to the windows.[9] The first floor with its straight stair rather than newel approach probably consisted of an ante-room before Gunthorpe's great chamber with personal inner chamber beyond. Above were three high-quality chambers in line, with the last as the most important. The mezzanine rooms could have been for staff, with the lower one for senior staff attendant on the dean listening for commands from the open window.

Initially, the Deanery seems to have been L-shaped, enclosed on the north side in the late fifteenth century to create an [-shaped house. It is possible that Gunthorpe also closed the central court with a hall, replaced by the present range a century and a quarter later. This would have been not only commensurate with his aggrandisement programme, but in tune with the position of his kitchen and ground-floor offices at the lower end of the later hall. His withdrawing room and retiring room were probably at the upper level in his remodelled south and west ranges, with first-floor access to the self-contained suite of great chamber and high-quality lodgings in his sumptuous north range. Gunthorpe's work, prefaced by a new gateway and outer court, was of a scale and standard little seen outside contemporary royal and leading baronial houses. Gunthorpe basked in extensive patronage from Edward IV, and was the king's almoner from 1478, and keeper of the privy seal in 1480.[10] The Deanery was developed as a badged testimony to Gunthorpe's privileged position and standing in royal favour.[11]

NOTES

1 The present internal stair is a seventeenth-century addition.

2 At the west end are the remains of a newel to the Deanery roof.

3 Although the bay is not shown in Buck's engraving of 1736, the base seems original and the whole is remarkably competent for an eighteenth-century pastiche.

4 The office of dean of Wells was initiated in the mid-twelfth century but the earliest reference to his house occurs in bishop Jocelin's charter of 1236 in which he granted dean Merton the house and site which his predecessor had held. D. S. Bailey, *The Canonical Houses of Wells* (1982) 102–3.

5 Bailey, *Canonical Houses* 106–7.

6 Pevsner (1958) 318.

7 At the time of dean Robinson (early twentieth century), this undistinguished oak partition was in the centre of the room. He moved it towards the lower end until it was used again to replace the relatively solid wall in 1988, overly close to the fireplace and oriel. It was not keyed to the relevant ceiling beam 2 feet further east.

8 It was covered rather than replaced by a higher nineteenth-century roof.

9 C. Woodforde, 'John Gunthorpe, Dean of Wells. His coats of arms, badges, motto, and monogram', *Journal of the British Society of Master Glass-Painters* 9 (1943–6) 8–14.

10 The belief that this range was built to accommodate Henry VII in 1497 when he visited Wells to deal with the sudden insurrection of Perkin Warbeck does not accord with the architectural character of a substantial building of earlier date which is far more a paean of praise to the dean than to the king.

11 In a cathedral city with an *embarras de richesses*, attention must be drawn to the mid-fourteenth-century hall and associated buildings at the entrance end of the Vicars' Close. The two terraces of forty-two individually built houses lining the street are fascinating enough, particularly No. 22 restored by J. H. Parker in *c.*1863, but the first-floor dining hall

by bishop Ralph (1329–63) over the entrance gate to the Close stands little altered, though it was formerly divided by screens into hall proper, entry bay, and offices. Usually attributed to *c.*1347–8 but ascribed by L. S. Colchester in personal discussion to Edward Joy in *c.*1363, this hall retains several two-light Decorated windows, some with original glass, two wooden figures of the same date, and the original barrel roof. The fireplace and stone pulpit are attributed to treasurer Hugh Sugar (d.1489) and the three oriels to Richard Pomeroy (*c.*1500), and the benches are also late medieval. The kitchen to the west over a vaulted store room retains its stone floor and sink. The initial straight stair to the hall was rebuilt in the early fifteenth century as a towered stair with three rooms over a vault inserted in 1448, while the more decorative bridge from the cathedral was built in 1459 by bishop Bekynton. The offices include the treasury with its ten cupboards, the chequer with fireplace, lavabo, shutters, and wind-braced roof, and the muniment room with its series of rare deed boxes. This is a remarkably complete and well-preserved group of buildings, retaining a substantial quantity of original domestic fittings and furniture.

J. H. Parker, *The Architectural Antiquities of the City of Wells* (1860) 17–20

J. A. Robinson, *Country Life* (August 1913)

W. H. Godfrey, *Arch. Jour.* 107 (1950) 110–12

N. Pevsner, *The Buildings of England: North Somerset and Bristol* (1958) 317–19

WEST BOWER MANOR and the gatehouses at DUNSTER CASTLE and MONTACUTE PRIORY, Somerset

The gatehouses at West Bower Manor, Dunster Castle, and Montacute Priory reflect the form developed between 1420 and 1520 as the approaches to three totally different precincts in the same county – of leading secular, defensive, and monastic houses respectively.

Little early work survives of the spectacularly sited fortress at Dunster beyond the lower part of the mid-thirteenth-century gatehouse, three other circuit towers, and some walling of the contemporary lodging range incorporated in the early seventeenth-century mansion that is the centrepiece of Dunster Castle today.[1] In 1404, Sir Hugh Luttrell (d.1428) enforced the reversion of the castle to himself that his mother had purchased from the Mohun family thirty years earlier. Within a year of his appointment in 1418 as Henry V's first seneschal in Normandy, Sir Hugh had initiated a three-storey gateway across the castle's earlier ditch and at right angles to the much earlier gatehouse (pl. 197).[2]

The ground floor of this new outer entrance was divided by a tunnel-vaulted passage separating a room on each side, one with an internal newel and one with a rear-facing stair turret. Because of the steep approach, the northern half of the gateway with the entry passage was taller than the southern half. A transverse wall separated the two parts internally, preventing intercommunication at all levels so that the six rooms were all self-contained lodgings with their own fireplaces and garderobes. The northern rooms were totally independent: two of the southern rooms could only be approached from the internal newel. After Henry Luttrell raised the level of the lower ward in 1764–5, polygonal turrets were added against the south face of the gateway like stage scenery and a reused fifteenth-century doorway was inserted between them, opening into the top room. Salvin remodelled the interior of this uppermost room, removed the internal division, and heightened the roof to create a common embattled skyline in 1871–2.[3]

Built between 1419 and 1421, this commanding structure created a small yard in front of the retained thirteenth-century gateway. The relieving arches over the windows show they were enlarged from single lights about a hundred years later,[4] but the lack of any obvious portcullis, drawbridge, or machicolation evidence points to an absence of serious defensive intent.[5] This gateway was essentially a number of independent lodgings, grouped in two vertical units, in the form of an up-to-date ceremonial approach to the castle that Sir Hugh Luttrell had acquired only fifteen years earlier.

A generation later, the Coker family updated the earlier entry to their house at West Bower Manor rather than build a new gateway. Only a single range survives of this manorial property held by two wealthy Somerset families, the Cokers between 1335 and 1489 and the Seymours until 1552. Richard Coker, the head of the Bridgwater branch of the Cokers of West Coker and a member of parliament in 1335, had built up a substantial estate in the area and was licensed to have an oratory at West Bower in 1339.[6] Between 1461 and 1489, the property was held by Margaret Coker, who had married the Lancastrian lawyer Sir Alexander Hody (see Gothelney Hall). Within twelve months of his execution, in the same year that his wife succeeded to the property, she had married Sir Reynold Stourton. On her death, West Bower passed to her cousin and heir John Seymour, the grandfather of Henry VIII's third wife, and Edward duke of Somerset (d.1552).

West Bower is 2 miles west of Bridgwater and on the edge of Durleigh reservoir since 1938. The approach to the house is undistinguished. The two-storey gatehouse range was long used for farm purposes and its plain north façade with nineteenth-century casement windows reflects this phase of its history, which included some wall rebuilding. In its initial stage, possibly fourteenth century, this two-storey rectangular block was not a gatehouse. The central passage was inserted in a second phase of unclear date.[7] By the mid-fifteenth century, the south façade had been given felicitous elegance by the addition of polygonal turrets flanking a new central entry arch with a line of five machicolation corbels above.[8] These pyramid-capped turrets are crowned by miniature lanterns of two-light trefoil and transomed windows under a continuous head round all five upper faces. The head of each window is not pierced but holds a shield or flower ornament, while the string course immediately above is decorated with gargoyles.

The interior of this gatehouse has been subject to extensive post-medieval remodelling, including entry-passage closure and a lower ceiling in the late sixteenth century. The northern outer arch disappeared in the rebuilding while the rooms on either side are undistinguished. The left-hand turret holds a stone newel while the right-hand one may have been an oratory, screened from the adjacent family chamber, with the stone decorated windows retaining glass painted with flowering plants and the initials A and M, possibly identifying Alexander and Margaret Hody.

The gatehouse is flanked by a nineteenth-century farmhouse wing, creating two sides of a courtyard with evidence of a long rectilinear structure located opposite and traces of a moat north of the present buildings.[9] The house, never a large one, extended southwards towards the now-expanded Durleigh Brook. In 1540, it was

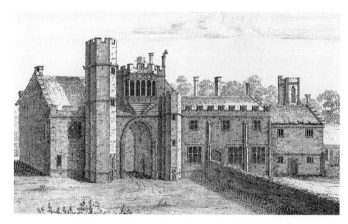

PLATE 293 Montacute Priory: engraving of the gatehouse by S. and N. Buck (1733)

described as in two parts, covered in lead and slate respectively,[10] while aerial photographs of the reservoir have revealed submerged evidence of a trackway, fishpond, and millrace associated with this manor house.[11]

The third gatehouse is the largest and most distinguished of the three, more appropriate to a mansion than to a Cluniac monastic precinct. Built by prior Thomas Chard (1514–32),[12] Montacute Priory gatehouse consists of a two-storey residential range interrupted off-centre by a tower-like entry block. The elaborate garden-facing frontage has polygonal stair turrets either side of the gate passage, the larger one rising a stage higher than the embattled parapet. Between the turrets, a multi-moulded base supports a substantial six-light oriel with blind quatrefoil panels above and below the lights. The windows of the short and longer wing flanking the entry are of two or three lights under square heads, with those to the right elaborated with transoms. It is built of honey-coloured Ham stone from the nearby hill, and the high-quality workmanship is evident from the stepped buttresses and stone-tiled roof to the man-size battlements, with those on the right-hand side repeating the quatrefoil decoration of the oriel. But there are also more subtle touches such as the top of the buttresses terminating in an arrow head touching the upper string course, figures surmounting the oriel, and its central merlon decorated with a bishop's mitre and the base of a sundial.

The village-facing façade is relatively plain – unadorned windows, chimney stacks, and garderobe projections. Only the entry has a note of distinction with its mirror-image oriel, the heads of the two buttresses with diamond-shaped columns surmounted by animals, and a centre merlon with the initials TC under a portcullis and mitre.

The modest entry arches contrast with the elaborate two-bay fan-vaulted passage, now domesticated. The range, of single-room thickness, was divided into five units marked by the four doors – two units at ground-floor level, two at first-floor level approached by the respective stone newels, with the larger one accessing the fifth unit over the entry passage and the roof. All these rooms have been subject to five centuries of ongoing occupation and their interiors are disappointing except for the fireplace in the oriel-windowed chamber.

The priory became the third richest house of the Cluniac order in England. The church and precinct seem to have lain under the fields to the south-east, but the site was comprehensively stripped to the benefit of the villagers and has never been excavated. It is natural to assume that the elaborate frontage was the abbey's face to the outer world but this would mean a contorted approach to avoid the adjacent rising ground and immediate access to all its residential chambers. The approach was, in fact, towards the relatively plain front as at present, so that only after entering the precinct did the wow factor strike home.

These late medieval buildings show how gatehouses had long ceased to have any military function and had often become substantial lodging units. Their frontages were relatively undistinguished, but in all three examples the inner faces were far more striking – through decorative qualities at West Bower Manor and Montacute Priory and by the sudden confrontation with the earlier gatehouse at Dunster Castle. Of the three, that at Montacute was the largest and most dominant, often the case with late medieval monastic gatehouses as though determined to surpass their secular equals.[13]

NOTES

1 Gibb (1981) 1.
2 H. Maxwell Lyte, *History of Dunster*, II (1909) 358–60.
3 At the same time, the ground floor of the thirteenth-century gatehouse towers was earth-filled and the tops lowered.
4 Probably by Sir Hugh Luttrell (d.1521) who set up the heraldic panel over the entrance.
5 The entry was closed by iron-plated doors but Gibb argues that its original character may have been more formidable: (1981) 13–14.
6 Sir Matthew Nathan, *The Annals of West Coker* (1957) 485–6; VCH, VI (1992) 211.
7 Jessop (1996) 50.
8 A square turret was also added at the north-west angle, probably a garderobe.
9 O. M. Jessop, University of Durham, Department of Archaeology Monograph (1995).
10 VCH, VI (1992) 211.
11 *Med. Arch.* 39 (1995) 238; Jessop (1997) 53–60.
12 Garner and Stratton (1911) 32–3.
13 A comparison between the Montacute gatehouse and that of the wealthy abbey at Glastonbury is instructive. Built nearly a century and a half earlier, the Benedictine gateway consisted of no more than a lodging at the side of the pedestrian passage and tall vehicular entry. The two-storey lodging is now dominated by an embattled storeyed bay window, a refronting appropriate to post-Dissolution use as an inn. Internally, it retains fragments of a painted screen and some decorative carving.

Dunster Castle
H. C. Maxwell, *A History of Dunster*, 2 vols. (1909)
J. H. P. Gibb, *Proc. Somerset Arch. and N. H. Soc.* 125 (1981) 1–15
The National Trust, *Dunster Castle: Guide Book* (1979)

West Bower Manor
VCH, *Somerset*, VI (1992) 210–11
R. W. McDowall, NMRC, no. 32472 (1957)
O. Jessop, Department of Archaeology Monograph 20, University of Durham and Newcastle upon Tyne (1996) 49–51
O. Jessop, *Proc. Somerset Arch. and N. H. Soc.* 140 (1997) 53–60

Montacute Priory
E. Garner and A. Stratton, *The Domestic Architecture of England During the Tudor Period* I (1911) 32–3
VCH, *Somerset*, II (1911) 111–15; III (1974) 214

WEST CHALLACOMBE MANOR, Devon

This white-washed house with rendered walls and Georgian framed windows on the south slope of Little Hangman Hill looks like an archetypal Devon farmhouse rather than a medieval manor house. It has been both, but its true character was only revealed during its restoration in 1993–9. The spectacular view from the house across the roofs of Combe Martin to Berry Down and the indented north Devon coastline has long been appreciated, but the discovery of the equally spectacular hammer-beam roof inside the house was a revelation.

The property consists of a substantial hall with a projecting cross wing at the lower end and evidence of one at the upper end, replaced in the early nineteenth century by a single-storey kitchen. The cross wings seem to have been erected in the late fourteenth or early fifteenth century, with the hall between them rebuilt during the third quarter of the fifteenth century and crowned with the now exposed hammer-beam roof. The storeyed porch was added during the later sixteenth century. All subsequent changes have been made within this framework – the insertion of a floor in the hall and its refenestration in the seventeenth century, cutting away part of the hall roof for a bedroom ceiling in the early eighteenth century when two families occupied the house, replacing the windows with casements in the early nineteenth century, and clearing away the hall bedrooms in the late twentieth century.

John Challacombe was one of five taxpayers in Combe Martin in 1332 and his family are still resident there today.[1] However, it has not yet been established that the Challacombes built the present house, for it was owned by the Orchards during the fourteenth

PLATE 294 West Challacombe Manor: hall roof

century and passed to the Prouz family in about 1475 through the marriage of Joan Orchard to John Prouz of Chagford. The coat of arms over the porch entry is probably that of its builder, John Prouz, who inherited the property in 1550. Most subsequent alterations by owners and tenants alike have been retained to facilitate continued occupation.

The initial build of West Challacombe Manor consisted of the lower cross wing and original hall, with the upper cross wing of different construction style added a little later. A single doorway opens from the screens into the ground floor of the west wing, originally offices served by an independent kitchen further west. The upper floor retains an unglazed wooden window of three trefoil lights (rear wall) and a wooden doorway with two-centred head in the front corner, possibly to a garderobe. The only evidence of the upper wing is the wall common to it and the hall.

The ceiling timbers of the lower cross wing have been dendro dated to 1453, raising the possibility that it was subject to modification if not rebuilding at that time.[2] Shortly afterwards, the earlier hall was pulled down and replaced by the present structure, 38 feet by 18 feet, with walls 4 feet thick. The entry inside the porch has a typical fifteenth-century two-centred head with continuous hollow chamfer and high stops. The position of the tall windows to the front was revealed when the render was removed in 1996, but the hall was enhanced with a large bay at its upper end (incorporated in the later pantry) with evidence of a large window in its north face. Wall thickening nearby suggests there may have been a mural fireplace. The glory of this hall is its roof, revealed in 1996 when the upper floor was cleared of all partitions to restore the area to its original dimensions. It is divided by a line of five primary and four subsidiary trusses, all of false hammer-beam type, creating a structure of eight narrow bays. The braces that helped to support the hammer beams have been hacked away. Large arched braces rise to the collars, with no crown posts above but a double line of ridge purlins. Above the embattled wall plate with double hollow mouldings rise three tiers of arched wind braces with foliated cusps, separated by well-moulded purlins. Though damaged by eighteenth-century modifications, this roof makes a splendid display, with its timbers felled between 1449 and 1474.[3]

This house belies its original scale. The hall was slightly larger than its near contemporaries at Weare Giffard Hall and Orleigh Court, and boasted a roof of comparable structural ingenuity if lacking their decorative panache.[4] In the absence of dendro dating for the false hammer-beam roof at Weare Giffard Hall, consideration as to whether that at West Challacombe was influenced by the Fortescues is speculative, but the closeness of the Challacombe trusses and the quite different bay patterning suggest the reverse is not unlikely. The loss of the upper wing has been compounded by replacing it with an eighteenth-century kitchen and offices that have reversed the layout of the house, and the plan has been further disguised by construction of the rectangular courtyard of byres and stables immediately in front of this élite end of the house.

NOTES
1 Combe Martin Local History Group, *Out of the World and Into Combe Martin* (1989) 68.
2 *Vern. Arch.* 30 (1999) 116.
3 *Ibid.*
4 The hall at Youlston Park, one of the few major houses in the region, pre-dates West Challacombe by about seventy years. This multi-period

residence was developed by the Chichester family round a core of *c.*1400 when the property was owned by the Beaumonts. The hall of that date, 31½ feet by 21½ feet, retains the relieving arches of the windows (courtyard side) and a base-cruck roof with crown posts, not unlike that over the entrance block at Dartington Hall. Five trusses survive with louvre evidence, all hidden by a replacement twentieth-century coved ceiling with late seventeenth-century frieze when this externally plain house was extended and sumptuously remodelled internally. C. Hussey, *Country Life* (May 1961).

WEST COKER MANOR, Somerset

An account of 1308–9 by William Curteys, bailiff of West Coker Manor, refers to cutting the timber and making the frame for a room with a camera above, reached by steps, four doors to the same, and a gate to the barton at a total cost of 23s. 6d.,[1] but nothing in the present manor house is earlier than the last third of the fifteenth century. West and East Coker, both held by the Courtenay family from 1306 to 1556, were divided between two lines of the family in 1377 by the will of Hugh Courtenay, earl of Devon, with East Coker and its manor house following the younger line of the family (see pages 516–19). West Coker continued in the hands of the earls of Devon, with the house occupied by George Middleton, possibly the earl's bailiff, in the mid-fifteenth century when it was caught up in the bitter quarrel between the Courtenay and Bonville families (see page 633). The manor house was burnt down in September 1457 by an armed mob led by the anti-Courtenay rector.[2] It is probable that the property was rebuilt shortly afterwards, and certainly well before the close of the century.[3]

West Coker Manor was purchased in 1591 by John Portman, a Devon entrepreneur knighted in 1605, who made some additions, with his family retaining it until 1829. A farmhouse phase followed until 1866, when it was bought by Dr John Moore. As he died shortly afterwards, the house was restored over a twenty-year period by his two sons. In 1908, the property was acquired by Sir Matthew Nathan, a diplomat and governor of Hong Kong, Natal, and Queensland, who employed Maurice Webb (Sir Aston Webb's son) in 1910–11 to extend the offices wing and convert it into a spectacular library. This multi-phase restoration over a forty-five-year period was extended and costly, with the consequence noted by the young Christopher Hussey in 1922 that 'everything is so spick-and-span that it might be a clever reproduction of a late medieval building rather than the thing itself'.[4] This is still so eighty years later, particularly as a consequence of the spectacular fireplaces in the house.

Today, West Coker Manor is accessed from the rear rather than the front, with its two wings thrust out from the central hall range in a welcoming approach, heightened by the common use of warm Ham stone. Yet its development is more complex than is immediately apparent, for though the hall range is of the closing decades of the fifteenth century with short south-east and north-west extensions, the north wing is of *c.*1600 while the south-east extension in late medieval style is of 1910–11.[5]

The original approach into the small west forecourt faces the single-storey porch, a delightful classical addition of 1600,[6] with the recut Portman arms contrasting with the late medieval entry with continuous hollow and roll moulding, original door, and drawbar. The screen separating the cross passage from the hall is a late

PLATE 295 West Coker Manor: from the east

Victorian insertion replacing the original post and panel screen moved to the present kitchen just over a hundred years later. The six-bay hall, 30 feet by 19 feet, is lit by three tall two-light transomed windows with cinquefoil heads above and below the transom, and a two-light east-facing window above the screen. The roof of arch-braced collar trusses has two lines of wind braces, the upper with short reverse returns and the lower of quatrefoils within circles. As these are at variance with those in the adjacent rooms and the quatrefoils are markedly thin, they are a later embellishment, in tune with other Victorian work such as the anomalous marble floor.

It is apposite to turn to the striking end-wall fireplace with its heavily decorated lintel divided into four with multi-cusped quatrefoils, the inner two with blank shields and the other two foliated. All the fireplaces in the principal rooms are in pristine condition. They are in period, but look new-cut, unaffected by age or farmhouse use, particularly when compared with contemporary examples such as that in the parlour at Muchelney Abbey. It is probable that they are late nineteenth-century insertions, extremely well done for the time,[7] but in some cases somewhat overlarge for their position though making use of original hearths and stacks with broad internal flues.

The doorways either side of the hall fireplace led to the parlour area and stair respectively. The rôle of the parlour and kitchen at the opposite ends of the hall had been reversed by the later nineteenth century. At the same time, major changes were made to the hall bay now holding the stone newel to the upper floor. Yet the window lighting the stair is of the same scale and character as those in the hall. This is appropriate to a bay window off the hall dais as at Coker Court but grossly out of scale to its function at West Coker Manor.[8] The bay may be a remodelling of one like that at the Court, with the Manor stair opening from it further north, but if so, a window that faces the porch is oddly positioned. In any case, the head of the newel terminates in an overtheatrical double-arched lobby – another element in the late nineteenth-century remodelling of this house.

The passage at the foot and head of the stair accesses the northwest extension, a single chamber on both floors with spectacular end-wall fireplaces flanked by a garderobe (trefoil lit) and a closet. Both fireplaces have large lintels with markedly crisp decoration but the ground-floor chamber also has an overly large stone buffet with a base of unmedieval shape. The upper room formerly extended over the stair lobby, from which it was probably divided by a wooden screen or light partition. The three-bay roof of arch-braced collar trusses is embellished with two lines of wind braces, decoratively arranged above a wall plate of three differing panels in each bay based on blind multi-quatrefoil patterns. The more decorative character of this roof compared with those of the hall range suggests that this short wing may have been a secondary development, subject to the Moores' drastic remodelling.

The other doors at the head of the stair access a small wall-thick chamber with a trefoil-headed squint overlooking the hall,[9] a garderobe projection, and the chamber over the parlour. This last was ceiled in 1600 when the plaster frieze was added and the mantelpiece with the Portman arms inserted above an earlier stone lintel. The original trusses survive above the ceiling, identical with those in the hall though now lacking the wind braces.

The original kitchen (now sitting room) opens from the single door in the cross passage. The south wall is filled by a massive hearth 14 feet wide with four-centred head and bread oven. As at Preston Plucknett Manor, where the kitchen hearth is similarly positioned, the chimney is capped with a splendid octagonal head with open trefoil lights. The original approach to the chamber above has been lost and it is now reached by a gallery stair or a stone one beyond the kitchen. This comfortable chamber has twin cinquefoil windows, that facing west with later square-headed lights but retaining the earlier drip mould with head stops. It repeats the end-wall garderobe and closet with the mural fireplace nearby enjoying a sharply detailed lintel of quatrefoils and mouchettes. The roof is similar to that spanning the hall, and though the end wall between the two apartments is timber-framed above a stone base, this does not suggest the incorporation of an earlier structure as it does at Cothay Manor.

The south-east wing seems originally to have been used as offices with chamber over but was modified to take a stone stair which terminates, very surprisingly, in a dovecote. This rare internal example for several hundred birds seems to have been an early seventeenth-century Portman insertion with an external door for the pigeoner and projecting stones for alighting birds. The remainder of the wing is Maurice Webb's extension to create a library for Sir Matthew Nathan (d.1939) rising through both floors, with a north-facing balcony, now lit by a 1980s medieval-style window. Webb's end wall with side windows and chimney stack is a reproduction of the former end wall of the short east wing that he removed.[10] Late Victorian photos show that this had the tusks of pulled-down walls, while plans prepared in 1910 indicate that Webb found the foundations of an earlier extension of the same length as today. The opposite wing was added by Sir John Portman (d.1612), making use of trefoil lights to the upper garderobe and closet.

What are we to make of this 'exquisitely beautiful small manor house'?[11] It is instructive to compare it with Coker Court, another fifteenth-century house of the Courtenays only 2 miles away. Both were developed by members of the leading baronial family in the region within fifty years of each other, but with a marked difference

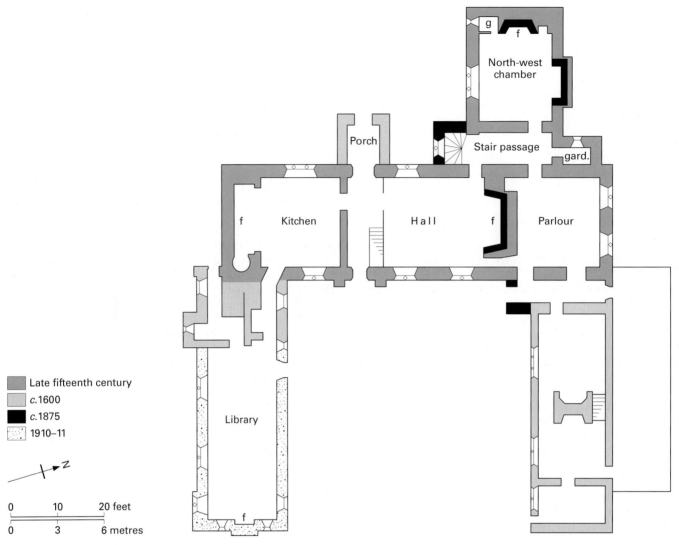

FIGURE 174 West Coker Manor: ground plan

of scale. Coker Court was a high-status house while West Coker Manor was a medium-sized gentry property. The Court was the main house of the Courtenay family for a manor that incorporated all three Coker villages (East, West, and North), with West Coker Manor treated more as a dower-house. The Court was a courtyard property while the Manor was essentially a single range with an extension at each end. Both retain halls open to the roof, though that at the Court is more than twice the size of the junior house. Both had generous family apartments but the kitchen and offices were reversed at the Manor, bringing the kitchen into the body of the house. Both properties were subject to additions in the early seventeenth century and to extensive late Victorian remodelling, 'for much of the present medievalism is recent replacement of a more or less conjectural kind'.[12] The most obvious elements are the fireplace lintels (and the buffet even more so), stylistically acceptable if slightly overlarge, in fantastically pristine condition, and suspiciously too good to be true to the house. They do not detract from its charm: they merely heighten it, as does the dramatic stair bay off the hall.

NOTES

1 Nathan (1957) 94–100, 462–6. The account is in private hands; a copy is held at the Manor.
2 Nathan (1957) 160–3, 484.
3 The attribution by Nathan to '"rebuilding" during the quiet years after 1471', *ibid*. 167, is an uncorroborated opinion.
4 Hussey (1922) 472.
5 Any entry gateway or forecourt buildings, as well as the bakehouse, brew-house, and farm buildings known to have existed at the rear, have all been swept away and the area landscaped.
6 Date formerly discernible on the weather-eroded gable panel.
7 Similar sympathetic work had been carried out a generation earlier by John Hicks when he restored Woodsford 'Castle', Dorset, in 1850–1. Hussey finally considered all the fireplaces genuine, though probably brought from elsewhere: (1922) 473–4.
8 The hood mould and head of this window are original, even if reused. The parapet concealing the bay roof does not occur elsewhere. In commenting on this 'oriel', Margaret Wood noted the use of contemporary material from elsewhere during a restoration attributed to 1830–40, *pace* Hussey, though she considered the hall fireplace (and others by implication) original to the house. *The English Mediaeval House* (1965) 59, 132, 270.

9 A similarly positioned feature occurs at Minster Lovell Hall.

10 From a practical point of view, a fireplace in the middle of the south wall would have been preferable to Webb's reflected exactitude.

11 N. Pevsner, *The Buildings of England: South and West Somerset* (1958) 338.

12 Hussey (1922) 471. Dr John Moore of Yeovil was an antiquarian who became an architect. He was responsible for building West Coker Hall in 1839–42 which incorporated brought-in medieval and Tudor features. As he died shortly after purchasing West Coker Manor, its restoration was initially carried out by his elder son John, followed by his younger son James (d.1893), though work had not been completed by 1889. Sir R. de Z. Hall, 'A West Coker antiquary of 1848', *Proc. Somerset Arch. and N. H. Soc.* 106 (1962) 88–97.

C. Hussey, *Country Life* (October 1922)
Anonymous, *Proc. Somerset Arch. and N. H. Soc.* 76 (1930) liv–lvi
Sir Matthew Nathan, *The Annals of West Coker* (1957)

WOODLANDS MANOR, Wiltshire

Quietly situated a mile south of Mere and the rolling downland of south-west Wiltshire, Woodlands Manor is an oddly developed house. From the approach, it seems to conform to the southern England plan of a hall with end cross wings, though the lower cross wing is unduly modest in comparison with the hall. The upper cross wing has been destroyed and replaced by an overly meek twentieth-century extension. It conceals the most important structure at Woodlands, a commanding two-storey chapel block parallel with the hall. It dominates the rear of the house, particularly in comparison with the services and kitchen wing.

The hall and projecting porch are early to mid-fifteenth century but the chapel block was erected during the second quarter of the fourteenth century. It is a survival of the house built by the Guphaye family who had already held the manor for some time. In *c*.1380, Jane Guphaye married Thomas Doddington, whose successors held the property until 1705. Work of all periods is in a grey/white limestone rubble, with the 1888 tiled roof replacing the early stone slabs.

The fourteenth-century chapel block is a tall, apparently independent unit since the destruction of the upper cross wing. External interest centres on the north face between the diagonal corner buttresses. The ground-floor windows are sixteenth-century insertions and the doorway is relatively recent. Above is a central entrance with two-centred head, the original external approach to the chapel from a lost stair. The trefoiled three-light window to the left has a reticulated head of ogee character under a deep square hood, not unlike that above the chapel altar at Clevedon Court (*c*.1320). The two-light transomed window to the right of the entrance and the east window of three trefoiled lights and Perpendicular traceried head are fifteenth-century replacements. Internally, nothing remains to indicate the purpose of the ground-floor room. Storage is often mentioned in such circumstances, but its position at the high end of the hall throws some doubt on this superficial characterisation. The internal approach to the first-floor chapel was at the west end, from the principal family room that formerly abutted it. The piscina is original, the medieval tiles are 1920 insertions from Stavordale Priory, while the wagon roof is part of a fifteenth-century refurbishment with the central beam a 1920 structural precaution.

PLATE 296 Woodlands Manor: from the south

The chapel block was secularised in about 1560–70. The ground-floor room was remodelled as a living room, leaving no evidence of its early character. The end window was replaced and new side ones inserted. An intricately patterned thin-ribbed plaster ceiling and effete vine frieze were added, and an imposing stone fireplace with Ionic columns inserted in the end wall supporting the Doddington coat of arms flanked by Corinthian columns and emaciated volutes (comparable with contemporary work at Longleat). An end-wall fireplace of more modest character was inserted in the chapel, which has also served as a bedroom until its recent refurbishment more appropriate to its original character.

The two-storey hall porch has a double-chamfered arch dying to the imposts, a framed ceiling, and a more simple inner entry to the cross passage. The buttressed hall is lit by two high-positioned windows of twin cinquefoil lights under a square hood with end stops externally, set in deep internal splays. Most of the light comes from a high-end cinquefoil window extending close to the ground, transomed with plain lower lights.[1] This is a small hall, 32 feet by 21 feet, with a contemporary end-wall fireplace 9 feet wide with segmental lintel. There was no dais. The nearby arch of continuous roll and hollow moulding is the approach to the short passage to the chapel undercroft and ground-floor utility rooms of the replacement cross wing. The three-bay roof is spanned by arch-braced collar beams supporting reverse struts with more modest intermediate trusses. There are two lines of cusped wind braces in reverse pattern, divided by the intermediate trusses.

The house was rescued from farm use by Meyrick-Jones in 1920–4, who removed the inserted floor in the hall, and added the stone flags, the solid cross-passage wall, and the wide balcony projecting well into the hall with its linenfold panels taken from three doors.[2] The balcony accesses the room over the porch with its close-trussed roof, though the original approach is unclear.

Nothing survives of the family rooms immediately behind the high end of the hall outside the first floor fireplace position, nor of

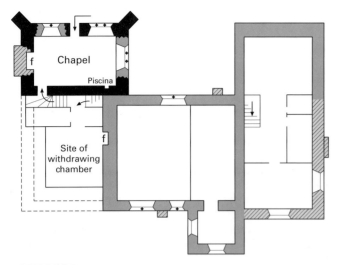

FIRST FLOOR

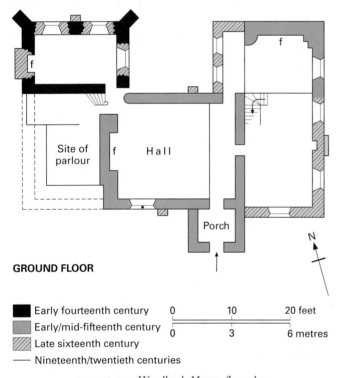

GROUND FLOOR

■ Early fourteenth century
▨ Early/mid-fifteenth century
▧ Late sixteenth century
— Nineteenth/twentieth centuries

0   10   20 feet
0   3   6 metres

FIGURE 175 Woodlands Manor: floor plans

the original stair leading to the upper chamber with chapel access.[3] The unit occupying the original parlour and chamber above was domesticated in 1948 without written record.

The services wing is essentially a late sixteenth-century rebuilding incorporating the fifteenth-century kitchen at its north end. This probably accounts for its modest, almost apologetic scale in relation to the hall. Internally, it has been thoroughly modified, with 1920s replacement windows, stairs, and partitions at both levels. The kitchen, projecting entirely beyond the line of the hall, retains its hearth with a beamed lintel filling the entire north wall.

Woodlands Manor was a gentry house that shows at least five development phases. It was built on clay, with retained moated evidence on the north and west sides. The chapel block was erected in about 1330 and is an important survival. Unlike the contemporary first-floor chapels at Clevedon Court and Ightham Mote, the Wiltshire structure was originally open to outsiders as well as serving the Guphaye family. The contemporary hall was replaced by the present one that is relatively modest in scale but well windowed, roofed, and heated. The high placement of the side windows and the post-Dartington Hall position of the fireplace suggest an early to mid-fifteenth-century date, as does the lack of a dais bay window favoured later in the century, but dendrochronology will bring greater precision. Twentieth-century owners have treated the house with care, but the cross-passage wall and the 'abnormally large' balcony are clumsy insertions, while the rooms on the site of the upper cross wing are too self-effacing for their position.

NOTES

1 Leigh Holman told me in 1958 that he remade the sill in 1946 and extended the iron bars.
2 His description of the restoration programme is more detailed than usual in *Country Life*, 10 and 17 May 1924.
3 The engraving of the house in *c*.1822 by P. Crocker shows the hall and chapel entries, fireplace, and stair lobby before the farmhouse addition by 1859. Colt Hoare (1822) 22; T. H. Turner and J. H. Parker, *Some Account of Domestic Architecture in England*, III pt 2 (1859) 332–3.

R. Colt Hoare, *The History of Modern Wiltshire*, I pt 1 (1822) 22–5
F. Meyrick-Jones, *Country Life* (May 1924); rewritten by H. A. Tipping, *English Homes*, Pds 1 & 2, II (1937) 17–30

WOODSFORD 'CASTLE', Dorset

Though usually known as Woodsford 'Castle', the appellation 'Manor' describes its form and development more precisely.[1] What survives is only a single, although the most important, range of a quadrangular fourteenth-century residence, crowned since the mid-seventeenth century by a softening thatched roof. It lacks two of its three rear towers, and its original roof timbers, tiling, and embattled parapet. Even so, it is a stunning survival, remarkable for its completeness, planning clarity, good condition, and relatively unaltered state.

Many late medieval houses retain pivotal evidence of the hall. Some retain a gatehouse, part of an enclosing wall or a moat. None of these remain at Woodsford. What stands is the owner's complex and innovative – or at least unusually planned – residential range, for Woodsford is among the most architecturally significant fourteenth-century houses in southern England.

The range stands close to a ford spanning the middle reaches of the River Frome, 4 miles east of Dorchester. It was part of a defendable house that had lost its associated components by the seventeenth century. The survivor, built of locally quarried oolitic limestone, was originally two-storeyed with three towers to the rear, the position of two of them marked by scarred walling with the surviving one indicative of their character and form. Despite superficial appearances to the contrary, this long rectangular range is fundamentally of single build, initially with a much lower-pitched roof running the length of the property. It was converted into a farmhouse in the mid-seventeenth century, when the greater part was raised by an attic storey with rectangular windows, new gables and chimneys, and the whole was reroofed. A short kitchen and bedroom wing was added by a prosperous tenant in about 1790 beyond the north-west corner of the frontage.[2] Some of the early character of the house, particularly the windows, was reinstated in a sympathetic restoration by John Hicks of Dorchester in 1850–1, and the property was subject to a further substantive restoration by the Landmark Trust in 1987–92. Continued occupation of this well-tended range is maintained without compromising its highly individual plan.

Over 110 feet long and 25 feet wide externally, the range seems to be of two components, marked by the change in roof level, but there is no break in the walling at that point and the architectural character is common throughout. The original roof of single length and slight pitch rose behind an embattled parapet which could still be made out in the mid-nineteenth century, though not towards the south end where the walling had been slightly lowered in the mid-seventeenth century.[3] The footings of the east and south-east towers could be seen in 1861, the east tower slightly shallower than its neighbour and incorporating garderobes.[4] The large framed panel on the north face of the north-east tower would have enclosed the arms of the builder.

The internal layout of the range is not immediately apparent. The principal living rooms are in line at first-floor level above a similar sequence of vaulted service rooms, except at the south end. There are four external doors to the seven ground-floor rooms, and two flights of steps (plus two internal approaches) to the six upper rooms. The latter divide into two suites consisting of a large outer and at least one inner room at each end, separating a third suite in the middle made up of two associated chambers with inner rooms. A corbel-supported pentice formerly ran across the frontage, protecting the several entrances (figs. 176–8).

GROUND FLOOR

Starting at the south end, the first doorway – like those throughout the ground floor – has a four-centred head, single plain chamfer and base stops. It opens into a room A on figure 177 with a single window, common to all rooms at this level, that is a rectangular loop, 35 inches by 10 inches, with plain chamfer. Unlike all the other ground-floor rooms, this first room was not vaulted but retains the corbels to support the timber floor of the room above, replaced in the seventeenth century by a crude one 3 feet higher, now with a ladder approach. The room was unheated. The two entries at the south end (now blocked) opened into a room (Ai) in the destroyed south-east tower, and by a short flight of steps to the newel stair to the front. Its solid but broken-down base is exposed externally, as is the curved inner face next to the upper doorway, with the stair probably continuing to the roof and south wall-walk.[5] Room A was the only ground-floor room directly linked with that above. It was also independent of room C: the present access between them is an eighteenth-century breakthrough (pl. 192).

The second doorway opens into room B with its plain barrel-vaulted ceiling supported on a continuous stone corbel along both side walls, common to all the rooms throughout the remainder of the range at this level. Room B has a single frontal light next to a small fireplace with corbelled head. Both face the massive hearth

that fills the east wall, with an almost straight-headed lintel and two inner ovens. There was no access to the ground floor of the destroyed east tower, and the north doorway is another eighteenth-century insertion, though that to room C is original. C is a narrow vaulted room, always internally approached, with a shuttered light at each end.

The third doorway accesses D, a room with a taller vault than its neighbours, and an end wall filled with a bifurcated hearth spanned by a segmental-headed arch with keystone. This kitchen has three wall recesses and a seventeenth-century four-light window inserted when this part of the courtyard wall was rebuilt. The internal approach to rooms E and F was reinstated in 1990. Room E has a single courtyard light next to the unbroken internal projection enclosing the courtyard approach to the upper floor. This prevented the three internal doorways from being in line. There was a second light in the east wall, converted into a doorway (now blocked) in the eighteenth century. Room F has two single lights in each end wall.[6]

Room G is now approached by a contemporary entry from the post-medieval kitchen wing, but it almost certainly replaced an original one from the courtyard or from a room on the courtyard side. The lack of a window in this wall may point to the latter. There are two single lights in the north wall with an enlarged door nearby (one jamb original) to room Gi in the north-east tower. The single lights in its two side walls are narrower than those elsewhere.[7] None of the ground-floor rooms holds garderobe facilities.

FIRST FLOOR

Starting again at the south end with room 1, the eighteenth-century floor has distorted the character of this important room for it cuts across the lower half of the fireplace and the newel approach in the courtyard-facing wall. The fireplace has a rectangular-headed lintel. The high-quality window nearby is of two transomed lights with trefoil heads, pintles for shutters, and a low four-centred rear arch. This window, like most of the double lights at Woodsford, was renewed by Hicks in 1850–1, but his mouldings and tracery seem to have been accurate when compared with those of the chapel east window discovered in 1990. The frame of a smaller twin-light window survives in the gable end wall. The doorway in the south-east corner opened into an inner room in the now-destroyed south-east tower. It was probably furnished with a garderobe for such an important chamber, as is the case with the tower room at the opposite end of the range. It is probable but unclear whether there was a second-floor chamber to the tower.[8]

The half newel projecting into the courtyard accesses rooms 2 and 3 from a common landing. Room 2 has a single trefoil light next to a small fireplace with a square head in the courtyard wall. At the further end is an original doorway in the party wall opening on to a short angled passage to the east tower. This is shared with room 3 which mirrors the single window, fireplace, and entry in the courtyard wall. Room 3, however, has a second entry at a raised level to the east tower. The multi-access to this tower suggests a shared chamber, probably with garderobe at first floor level, and a further chamber above, possibly at mezzanine level solely for room 3. Originally there was no communication in the party wall central to the range, which was as solid as that below. The present doorway to room 6 with pointed head and curved jambs, markedly different from those elsewhere, is a fifteenth-century insertion.[9]

PLATE 297 Woodsford 'Castle': residential range from the west

The remainder of the range is a single unit, approached from the short flight of courtyard steps that continue internally to a small lobby. Victorian partitions creating a lobby and ante-room distort the initial layout here, but there would always have been a division – probably an open wooden screen as the chapel lay directly ahead – on the line of the present solid partition. The doorway to the left opened into the principal chamber (room 4) and the flight of steps led to the chamber on the right (room 6).

This group of rooms is approached today from the north end of the range but they are described here in their original sequence. The lobby reflects the mid-seventeenth-century rebuilding and division, the refenestration of the courtyard wall, and the late twentieth-century replacement stair to the attic. Room 5, now used as a bedroom, was the chapel. The ogee-shaped piscina with trefoil head and shelf had long identified this use, but restoration in 1998 revealed much of the east window that had been supplanted by the present casement in the eighteenth century. The jambs, the head rising above the inserted ceiling, and half of the two side lights with cinquefoil heads were recovered. It is a telling comment on restoration attitudes between the mid-nineteenth and late twentieth century that, whereas Hicks would have remade the window on the basis of the revealed evidence, the Landmark Trust left the conflict unresolved between the damaged medieval structure and the wretched casement.[10]

Because of the higher vaulting to the ground-floor kitchen immediately below, room 6 has to be entered from steps. The two-light transomed and trefoiled window in the courtyard wall, with the lower lights shuttered, points to the relative importance of this room. As elsewhere, the fireplace is nearby, with square-headed lintel. The room has a splayed squint so that the occupant could partake in chapel services. The small door in the east wall opens on to an angled passage and probably to a mural stair in the east tower wall ascending to the uppermost floor (room 6a) with garderobe.

Room 4 is the largest room in the range, with windows in all three outer walls. Two of them are copies by Hicks of twin transomed lights with pierced spandrels in a square frame with four-centred rear arch – the upper lights with cinquefoil ogee heads, the lower with shouldered heads. The courtyard-facing window is seventeenth century in the rebuilt wall which included the fireplace restored by Hicks. Near the east window is a long sink set in a recess with four-centred head. The low-pitched beamed ceiling was reinstated in 1990 at its original height using the original beam sockets and corbel table. The two rooms in the north-east tower open from the same entry. Room 4a has two trefoil lights and a sink with drain and moulded base. At its side is the excellently preserved garderobe, stone screened, with trefoil light, replacement wood seat, and original pit below. The room above, 4b, approached by a mural stair, repeats the same layout with trefoil light (south) and lancet (east), but the garderobe was separated by a lost wooden screen.

The doorway in the north-west corner of room 4 (the present approach from the post-medieval kitchen wing) opened from the lost north range, as did the fourteenth-century doorway above it. This is reached by the adjacent newel at the side of the high-positioned semi-circular window, now blocked but bonded with the doorway. The newel, lit by a curiously shaped lancet and gunport,[11] rises from a solid base to the roof. The roof timbers throughout the range are 1979 replacements, but whether the early doorway led to further rooms or to the north wall-walk is unresolved.

PLATE 298 Woodsford 'Castle': residential range from the north

DESIGN ASSESSMENT

The manor of Woodsford was held by the Belets, followed by the Whitfields before the close of the thirteenth century. In October 1335, William Whitfield obtained a licence to crenellate his house,[12] but this does not apply to the present range which is at least a generation later. Architecturally, it dates from the second half of the fourteenth century, with the form of the piscina and the larger windows pointing to the years between about 1360 and 1380. In 1367, Sir John Whitfield sold the manor to Sir Guy Brian, who held it until his death in 1390. The property was subsequently owned by the Stafford and Strangways families, who let it out to tenants. It was between 1650 and 1660 that the range was adapted as a farmhouse, and it continued to be so for the next three centuries until sold by the Ilchester estates.[13]

In 1774, John Hutchins suggested that the house had originally been quadrangular. At that time, quite substantial ruins existed of a north range as well as the present range to the east, but he completed the two further sides in outline only.[14] A resistivity survey of 1990 identified evidence of an enclosure on the north and south sides of the site, and more clearly on the west side with a gap which may have marked the position of a gatehouse. A second outer enclosure was detected further west, repeating the likelihood of an entry in line with the principal one.

The documentary and geophysical evidence points to a quadrangular house with the entry opposite the surviving range, flanked at right angles by at least one and possibly two ranges. That on the north side may have held the hall but it did not abut the east range for there was a storeyed structure here, marked by the three tiered doorways. And if the range reflected the classic plan of kitchen and

offices, hall, and chamber block in line, then the inclusion of the kitchen and services in the standing range is markedly unusual. Whether there were further lodgings or an enclosing wall on the south side becomes more speculative, as does the possibility of towers at the angles. The outer court, not necessarily stone-enclosed, would have held stables and offices. A probable moat was identified in the eighteenth century, significantly on the side with the garderobe discharges.

Whitfield's licence of 1335 may well have authorised the gatehouse and his embattlement of the earlier house, which Brian replaced in part with the present residential range.[15] The Brians came from Torbryan in Devon and held land in Dorset, Somerset, and Pembrokeshire centred on Laugharne Castle. Sir Guy was initially a soldier who became a seasoned lieutenant, a diplomat, and counsellor and friend of Edward III. He fought in Scotland, Flanders, and France and bore the king's standard at Calais (1394–50). Though Brian was a member of parliament from 1350 to 1389, he was also an itinerant civil servant and administrator, holding several prestigious appointments that included stewardship of the royal household, leading an embassy to the papal court in 1361, admiral of the west in 1369, and ennoblement and garter holder in 1370. Like Reginald Cobham of Sterborough (q.v.), Brian was one of the 'new' men of the later fourteenth century rather than coming from one of the older established families, and he would have been considered a 'banneret' rather than a baron of the realm. He was sixty years old when he purchased Woodsford[16] and clearly developed the property for the comfort of his old age, though his elevation to the peerage may have been the immediate spur to his plans.

His east range was a multi-unitary development of at least two

SECOND FLOOR

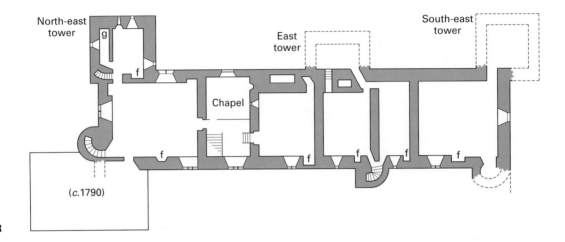

FIRST FLOOR

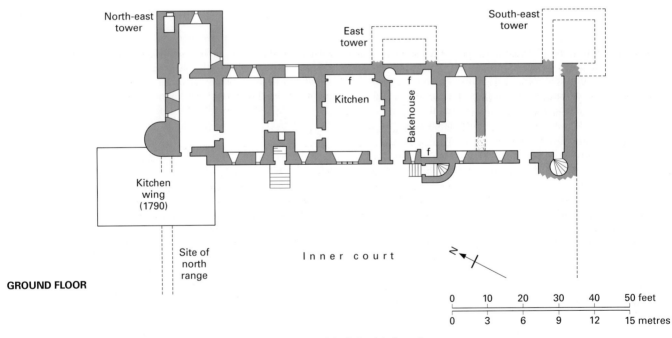

GROUND FLOOR

FIGURE 176 Woodsford 'Castle': floor plans

service and three residential units. With one exception, the ground-floor rooms were devoted to services, with the kitchen and 'pastry' or bakehouse next to each other. They were separated by a solid stone wall to limit the danger from fire but, as in the later house at Shute, they were associated offices, not two kitchens serving separate household units. The bakehouse has a single linked room next to it, and this may initially have been the case for the kitchen,

though it has three linked rooms today.[17] The service rooms were well lit and spacious, while the upper floor displays generous facilities and workmanship of considerable refinement.

None of the three residential units included a hall. That lay elsewhere. The principal suite lay at the north end with its own private chapel as well as several inner chambers. The lesser suite was at the south end in vertical mode. The third unit between them was two

688

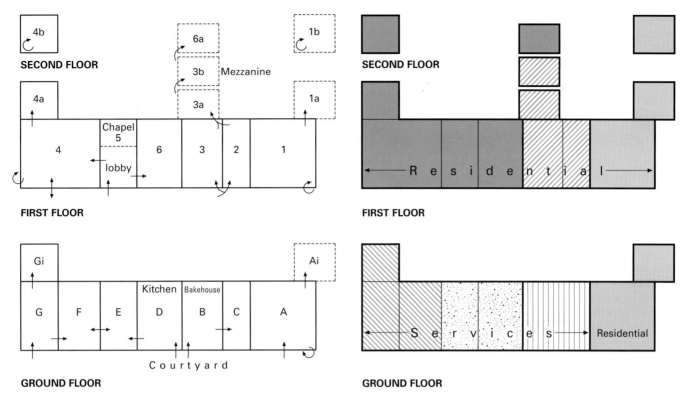

FIGURE 177 Woodsford 'Castle': room and entry identification

FIGURE 178 Woodsford 'Castle': unitary diagram of linked rooms

linked lodgings. This unusual division was probably a reflection of Lord Brian's personal circumstances in about 1370. As his second wife had died in 1359 after a ten-year marriage, the range was redeveloped for himself, his son, and his grandchildren.[18] The north suite would have been Brian's personal quarters, with the south suite possibly occupied by his son and family. The lodgings between may have been used for honoured guests, household officials, or others worthy of high-quality accommodation. What is not in doubt is that the range was built with considerable panache in response to highly individual circumstances. It reflects the growing need for household privacy and that movement towards planning complexity that marks the later fourteenth century. The presence of towers, brattices, and battlements in a range added to an already fortified site shows that continued defensibility was a factor in Brian's development – a consequence of his wartime experiences and the deteriorating situation with France. But overriding this is the more affirmative consideration that Brian's range at Woodsford reflected his spectacular rise from modest circumstances to diplomatic service, friendship with the king, and the honour of a peerage of the realm.

NOTES

1 Leland refers to Woodsford as a castle, but describes Chideok Castle as a 'manor house'. *Itinerary*, I, 249; IV, 108.

2 For descriptive purposes, the range is taken as lying north–south, with the courtyard frontage facing west and the towers projecting eastwards.

3 The widely spaced triple corbels on the north and east walls were probably for brattices rather than machicolated parapets.

4 The 1861 edition of Hutchins, *History and Antiquities of the County of Dorset*, ed. W. Shipp and J. W. Hodgson, I, 449.

5 Hutchins, *ibid.*, shows a tower at this point but this is highly unlikely, though more may have remained of the stair turret stump and curtain wall to give him that impression.

6 The internal steps against the courtyard wall were to a seventeenth-century opening breaking on to the stair to the upper floor with a line of four-centred heads.

7 The south light, shown on the RCHM plan as an insertion, is original.

8 There was no communication with room 2 until the narrow high-level one was punched through in the eighteenth century.

9 The RCHM suggest seventeenth century.

10 This lack of resolution is as demeaning to the integrity of the room as it is irrelevant to the primary or secondary development of the house.

11 Can this copy really be contemporary with the house or even genuine?

12 *Cal. Pat. Rolls: 1334–38*, 221.

13 Thomas Hardy, who trained in Hicks' Dorchester office in 1856 before working under Blomfield in London, based one of his more benighted poems on this 'castle'. Thomas Hardy, *Late Lyrics and Earlier* (1922).

14 *History and Antiquities of Dorset* (1861 edn) I, 449.

15 Hicks did not find any evidence of earlier work during his repairs to the range in 1850, nor were any identified in 1987–92.

16 It was one of the considerable number of properties he acquired in the West of England. For Brian's career, see R. G. F. Stanes, *Trans. Devon. Assoc.* 92 (1960) 248–78. For Brian's value to Gaunt, A. Goodman, *John of Gaunt* (1992) 292–3. Also R. Avent, *Laugharne Castle* (1995) 9–11.

17 This third unit was associated with the destroyed north range.

18 As his eldest son, Sir Guy Brian, died in 1386 without male issue, the barony fell into abeyance in 1390 and the estate was divided between his two young granddaughters. *Com. Peer.* II (1912) 361–2; H. J. Yallop, *Trans. Devon. Assoc.* 98 (1966) 386–97. In 1372, Brian founded a chantry at Slapton in Devon where the Brian family had long held the manor house. Only a tall tower survives of the chantry college and a few fragments incorporated into a house nearby. Brian was buried in Tewkesbury

Abbey where his striking canopied tomb lies opposite the more magnificent double tomb of his wife (d.1359) and her previous husband Lord Despenser (d.1349). Brian's tomb seems to have been suggested by the slightly earlier double monument opposite and stylistically was prepared well before his death in 1390.

A. Oswald, *Country Houses of Dorset* (1959 edn) 50–3
RCHM, *Dorset*, II, pt 2 (1970) 397–400

WORTHAM MANOR, Devon

Like the nearby houses at Cotehele and Trecarrell across the Cornish border with which it shares common architectural detailing, Wortham Manor was developed in three phases spanning the years close to 1500. As with the residences of Sir Piers Edgcumbe and Sir Henry Trecarrell, precise dating is absent, but Wortham differs fundamentally from them by developing into a far more forward-looking house. It is not a courtyard residence but one with a ground-floor hall with great chamber above – a prime example of its period in relatively complete condition, with quality fittings including doors, hall screen, and fine ceilings.

The property was held at the close of the fourteenth century by William Wortham, who had six daughters. Agnes, the fourth one, married Otto Dynham, a younger member of the Dynhams of Hartwell whose most distinguished member was the last of the senior line John, Lord Dynham.[1] The family name was maintained at Wortham until the mid-seventeenth century through six generations, including Otto's son Nicholas (d.1506) and his grandson John (d.1553) who had declined a knighthood twenty years earlier.

Wortham looks across the valley of the river Carey near its junction with the river Tamar three miles north-east of Launceston. L-shaped, the house is two-storeyed except for the accents of a second-floor chamber over the porch and the corbelled head of the rear stair turret. It was built of local sandstone with granite dressings and slate roofs, with multiple straight joints identifying separate building activity. Yet the house has an apparent unity of form and detailing that conceals a more complex story.

Edmund Prideaux's drawing of 1716 of the north front shows the forecourt wall enclosed, with the hall surmounted by an embattled parapet.[2] There was also evidence of a moated enclosure on the west side until the mid-twentieth century.[3] None of this has survived, though the porch retains two gunports, decorative rather than defensive. This very grand porch has a well-moulded granite entry with four-centred head set in a square frame surmounted by a decorative tympanum, a feature shared with the hall entries at Cotehele and Trecarrell, and the school at Week St Mary (1506).[4] The earlier inner entry is more modest and off-centre.

The ground-floor hall, 32 feet by 18 feet, has a splendid example of a three-section screen of linenfold panels, each section surmounted at the ends by crocketed pinnacles touching the cross beam. A contemporary cousin to that in the hall at Milton Abbey (1498), the screen was discovered elsewhere in the house by the architect Philip Tilden in 1943 when he recorded it, before becoming the house's owner two years later. Whether it was original to the property or not is an open question, but it is an outstanding example of its type and certainly enhances the character of the hall. The extremely thick north-facing wall with deep-set light, lateral fireplace (Tilden replacement), and upper-end window in line betrays two building phases, the original inner wall having been thickened

PLATE 299 *Wortham Manor: from the south*

with the outer section when the four-light window was added. The framed ceiling is spanned by three elaborately moulded cross beams and lines of moulded joists with all junctions enhanced by carved leaves and clusters of grapes. The two doorways in the upper-end wall are eighteenth-century forced entries, for the principal one is the granite doorway in the angle, similar to the cross-passage entries.

The stair to the upper chamber is a 1975 replacement to a landing with two-light cinquefoil window, formerly unglazed and shuttered. Originally 33 feet by 19 feet, the great chamber is slightly larger than the hall. It has an upper-end fireplace with four-centred lintel head, a recessed four-light window nearby, and a room over the porch at the lower end, now missing its partition wall.[5] The glory of this chamber is the five-bay roof of arch-braced collars rising from the lower of the two wall plates with three lines of moulded wind braces, intersecting to create a simple but effective pattern as with the hall and withdrawing chamber roofs at Cotehele. The lower-end division of this chamber with a post and panel partition occurred at a relatively early stage, together with the insertion of a second fireplace to heat the new room.

The lower parlour wing was a secondary development to the hall though it shares with it the same form of windows of two or four uncusped lights with ogee nips under rectangular hoods with square end stops. The single four-centred arch from the cross passage opens into a lobby with canted access to the ground-floor parlour with its cross-wall fireplace, four-light window, boarded and panelled ceiling with decorative cross ribs and knops at the intersections, and early seventeenth-century panelling and overmantel. The small end chamber has been divided and is featureless. The polygonal stair turret to the upper floor is clearly an addition cutting across the head of the earlier cross-passage doorway to the hall. The upper lobby with its wooden doorways with four-centred heads and roughly carved spandrels provided supplementary access to the great chamber as well as to the bedchamber above the parlour with original fireplace, a smaller version of that in the great chamber, and an inserted ceiling.[6]

That the upper end of the house was a cross wing is much more obvious in the Prideaux drawing of 1716 than in the present hipped roof. It now holds the kitchen, in a position that would not have been tenable originally. Its relocation here is identified by the eighteenth-century hearth, the adaptation of an earlier fireplace to farmhouse use, and the considerable enlargement of the end window subsequent to the Prideaux drawing. The chamber above formerly embraced the adjacent bathroom with its three cinquefoil-light window. It retains part of a much repaired arch-braced collar roof and a pair of reinstated wind braces.

The further parlour block is a later extension with its own entry, crude cross beams, and an early nineteenth-century Greek-style fireplace, but the windows of the chamber above repeat the nipped ogee head and fireplace form seen elsewhere.

Wortham's plan of medium-sized rooms on both floors comfortably opening out of each other fits well with present-day living practice, but it was only the conclusion of a four-stage development which must take account of fifteenth-century cinquefoil lights, early sixteenth-century ogee window heads, finer-quality walling to the front than the rear, an outstandingly early example of a ground-floor hall with chamber above, and the absence of contemporary services and kitchen in the body of the house.

Resolution starts with the hall, which seems to have begun as a

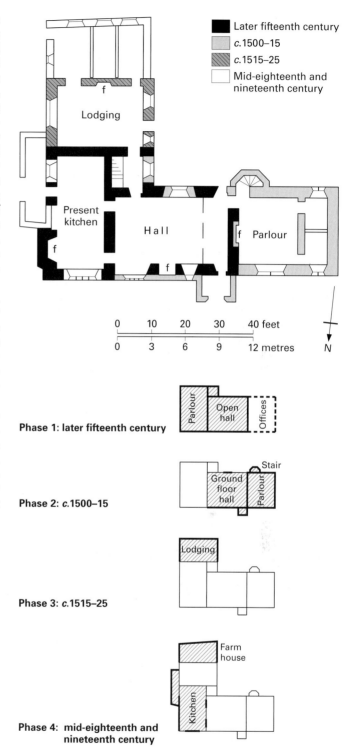

FIGURE 179 Wortham Manor: ground plan and development phases

mid to late fifteenth-century structure open to the roof. The upper cross wing is contemporary, with ground-floor parlour and solar over with cinquefoil-light windows and a roof of slightly earlier character than elsewhere. The offices were probably in their usual position below the hall, perhaps in a matching cross wing.

The development of Wortham reflects the major changes of the first decade of the sixteenth century at Cotehele, particularly the reconstruction of the storeyed family apartments as two great chambers and the use of common architectural details.[7] The remodelling at Wortham was particularly elaborate, displays high-quality craftsmanship, and is remarkably well preserved. The north wall of the early hall was thickened to carry the weight of the inserted floor and new roof over the newly created great chamber. The added frontage was built in superior masonry, regularly coursed, now with mullioned windows at both levels with hood moulds and carved stops, and an imposing porch with a tympanum-type entry and a cinquefoil-light window reused from the earlier hall.[8] The lower cross wing was replaced by the present extension to the hall range, creating a unified two-storey frontage. Coarser stone was used for the rear walls and the added stair turret, allowing the offices and kitchen to be resited southwards away from the body of the much-enhanced house.[9]

Very shortly afterwards, the cross wing was extended with a second unit with its own entry and chamber over. This was an independent lodging, possibly added for William Dynham, who was married, more than fifty years old, and still living at Wortham when his father died in 1553.[10]

The last development phase from the mid-eighteenth to the mid-twentieth century was initiated by adopting the high-quality parlour as a farmhouse kitchen with an outhouse nearby, and then by a further extension to the south wing. It was in this state that the house was rescued by Philip Tilden in 1945, who brought it back to its exceptionally well-preserved early Tudor condition,[11] still secluded, and sensitively maintained by the Landmark Trust.

NOTES

1 The Dynhams were a gentry family of local importance from the twelfth to the early sixteenth century, initially at Hartland in north Devon, where they founded the abbey, and from the later thirteenth century at Nutwell on the opposite side of the Exe estuary from Powderham Castle. John Dynham (1433–1501) was the outstanding member of the family, whose career developed from youthful esquire to elder statesman. An enthusiastic twenty-six-year-old Yorkist supporter, he helped Edmund, earl of March and the earls of Warwick and Salisbury to escape after their failure at Ludford Bridge via Devonshire and Guernsey to Calais (1459), and he followed this up with leading an expedition from Calais to Sandwich where he captured Lord Rivers and his son in their beds. After Edward's accession to the throne, Sir John was richly rewarded, becoming sheriff of Devon (1460–1), keeper of all the duchy of Cornwall manors in Devon (1467), and 1st Lord Dynham (1467). He benefited territorially from the execution of Lord Hungerford in 1464, but only became regionally significant as the king's chief supporter in the south-west after the death of the earl of Devon (1469). When Edward IV planned his French invasion, Dynham was appointed commander of all

armed forces at sea (1475) and a royal counsellor in the same year. Governor of Calais and steward of the duchy of Cornwall during Richard III's rule, he was sufficiently trusted by Henry VII to be appointed treasurer of the exchequer (1486). Dynham died holding that office in 1501, and his property was divided between four co-heiresses. Nothing remains of the medieval Nutwell Court, now a mansion of 1802 with an earlier stone first-floor chapel that may be on the site of that licensed in 1370. Hooker in his Synopsis Chorographical of Devonshire (1599) says that it was 'sometimes a castle of defence', in other words a fortified house. Dynham's will itemises his considerable amount of silver and gold plate and refers to his textiles, of which one still survives. Discovered in Appleby Castle in the mid-nineteenth century, his spectacular armorial tapestry, 12 feet square, is preserved in the Cloisters Museum, New York. Of wool and silk, this Tournai hanging centres on Dynham's large coat of arms with supporters, on a millefleurs background scattered with Dynham's badge of the top castle of a ship flying a St George's pennon, a reference to his seafaring exploits (pl. 204). As the arms are garter enclosed, this imposing tapestry is attributable to between about 1487 and 1501, with the likelihood that it was commissioned shortly after Dynham's garter appointment by 1488. B. Young, *Metropolitan Museum of Art Bulletin* 20 (June 1960). Also R. P. Chope, *Trans. Devon. Assoc.* 50 (1918) 431–92; *Com. Peer.*, IV (1916) 369–82.

2 *Arch. Hist.* 7 (1963) 108.

3 Oswald (1956) 1176.

4 John Dynham was responsible for overseeing the building of this grammar school 12 miles away, founded by his cousin Thomasine Bonaventure who was born at Week St Mary and became wealthy through marrying three London merchants in turn. As the school was also founded as a chantry, it was dissolved in 1548 and is now an occupied house with a forecourt enclosure.

5 The porch room has a cinquefoil three-light window and a steep stair to the attic above.

6 The fireplace in the small end room is twentieth century.

7 The distinctive window heads and arch-braced roof trusses were also used by Sir Henry Trecarrell at Trecarrell c.1500–11. The rear range of 10–11 The Close, Exeter, is also two-storeyed with arch-braced roof to the upper chamber, attributable to the first years of the sixteenth century.

8 Oswald (1956) 1176 suggests that the porch with its loopholes was an original component of the house, possibly of mid-fifteenth-century date. However, the poor alignment between the outer and inner entries and the character of the outer entry, rather than the straight joints, suggest that it was an addition.

9 Oswald noted in 1956 that there was evidence of a south wing running back from this west end which was finished off in makeshift fashion before Tilden repaired it: *ibid.* 1175.

10 William Dynham and his father had written letters to Thomas Cromwell from this house in 1536 over the payment of tithes for the school at Week St Mary.

11 P. Tilden, *True Remembrances* (1954) 169.

A. Oswald, *Country Life* (May 1956)

APPENDIX 5
CASTLES OF SOUTH-WEST ENGLAND: RESIDENTIAL ADDITIONS

Early to mid-fourteenth century	Tiverton, Devon	Hugh Courtenay, later earl of Devon	Hall, chambers, services	See text
Early to mid-fourteenth century	Okehampton, Devon	Hugh Courtenay, later earl of Devon	Hall, kitchen, chapel, lodgings	*Proc. Devon Arch. Soc.* 40 (1982) 19–151
1341–5	Launceston, Cornwall	Edward, the Black Prince	Hall reroofed and chamber built	*HKW*, II (1963) 693–4
*c.*1341–5	Tintagel, Cornwall	Edward, the Black Prince	Hall, kitchen and services rebuilt	*HKW*, II (1963) 846
1341–3 and 1355	Ludgershall, Wiltshire	Edward III	Repairs to residence	*HKW*, II (1963) 731
1377–8	Corfe, Dorset	Richard II	Gloriette Tower of five chambers	RCHM, *Dorset*, II pt 1 (1970) 63, 77

PLATE 300 Bickleigh Castle: gatehouse (early/mid-fifteenth century)

PLATE 301 Weare Giffard Hall: gatehouse (mid-fifteenth century)

1391	Bridgwater, Somerset	Roger Mortimer, earl of March	Repairs to hall roof and gatehouse	Dilks, *Somerset Arch. Soc.* 86 (1940) 96–105 VCH, *Somerset*, VI (1992) 206–7
1419–24	Dunster, Somerset	Sir Hugh Luttrell	New gatehouse and lodging	M. Lyte, *History of Dunster*, II (1909) 358–60
1460–95	Berry Pomeroy, Devon	10th Henry Pomeroy (d.1487) and Richard Pomeroy (d.1496)	Hall, chambers, offices	S. Brown, *Proc. Devon Arch. Soc.* 54 (1996) 1–366
1493–8	Taunton, Somerset	Bishop Langdon of Winchester	Inner gatehouse refitted	Dated plaques and arms of Langdon over entry
1490s	Stogursey, Somerset	Henry, earl of Northumberland	New audit room	VCH, *Somerset*, VI (1962) 136–7

PLATE 302 South Wraxall Manor: gatehouse (late fifteenth century)

PLATE 303 Cornworthy Priory: gatehouse (early sixteenth century)

SOUTH-WEST ENGLAND: RESIDENTIAL LICENCES TO CRENELLATE

STANDING			DESTROYED		
			1311	Castle Eaton, Wiltshire	Nicholas Seymour
			1313	Yarlington, Somerset	Simon Montague
			1316	Torweston, Somerset	Adam Bret
			1327	Roughcombe, Wiltshire	Thomas West
			1328	Torrington, Devon	Richard Merton (application)
			1329	Donyatt, Somerset	William Montague (pardon)
			1330	Tehidy, Cornwall	William Bassett
			1333	Stoke Sub Hamdon, Somerset	John Beauchamp
				Hatch Beauchamp, Somerset	John Beauchamp
			1334	Modbury, Devon	Richard Champernowne
1335	Woodsford, Dorset	William Whitfield	1335	Colway in Lyme, Dorset	Ralph Bloyou
				Ilton, Devon	John Chevreston
				Tamerton (Foliot), Devon	John Ocle
				Binhamy, Stratton, Cornwall	Ralph Whitchurch
				Ruan Lanihorne, Cornwall	Sir John Lercedekne
				Truthall, Cornwall	Ralph Bloyou
			1336	Sheviock, Cornwall	John Dauney
				Bampton, Devon	Richard Cogan
				Langton Herring, Dorset	Walter Heryng
				Winterborne Herringston, Dorset	Walter Heryng
1337	Bere Ferrers, Devon	Matilda, widow of William Ferrers	1337	Sampford Peverell, Devon	Oliver Denham
	Salisbury Palace, Wiltshire	Robert, bp. of Salisbury		Bishop's Cannings, Wiltshire	Robert, bp of Salisbury
	Sherborne, Dorset	Robert, bp of Salisbury		Ramsbury, Wiltshire	Robert, bp of Salisbury
	Chardstock, Dorset	Robert, bp of Salisbury		Potterne, Wiltshire	Robert, bp of Salisbury
				Bishop's Woodford, Wiltshire	Robert, bp of Salisbury
			1339	Sampford Peverell, Devon	Oliver Denham (repeat of 1337)
1340	Bere Ferrers, Devon	John Ferrers (repeat of 1337)	1340	Torrington, Devon	Richard Merton (applied in 1328)
	Wells Palace, Somerset	Ralph, bp of Wells			
			1343	East Harptree, Somerset	Thomas Gurney
			1344	Hooke, Dorset	Robert Sifrewast
			1347	Oaksey, Wiltshire	Humphrey, earl of Hereford
				Seend, Wiltshire	Humphrey, earl of Hereford
				Upavon, Wiltshire	Humphrey, earl of Hereford
				Torrington, Devon	Richard Merton (repeat of 1340)
			1370	Chideok, Dorset	Sir John Chidiok
1373	Nunney, Somerset	Sir John de la Mare	1376	Faulston, Wiltshire	Nicholas Benton

STANDING

1377	Salisbury Palace, Wiltshire	Robert, bp of Salisbury
	Sherborne, Dorset	Robert, bp of Salisbury
	Chardstock, Dorset	Robert, bp of Salisbury
		(all repeat of 1337)
1379	Chudleigh, Devon	Thomas, bp of Exeter
1380	Hemyock, Devon	Sir William Asthorpe and wife
1383	Farleigh Hungerford, Somerset	Thomas Hungerford (pardon)
1393	Wardour, Wiltshire	John, Lord Lovell
1397	Thorncombe, (Holditch) Dorset	Thomas Brook
1427	Wycroft, Devon	Thomas Brook and others
1451	Wells Palace, Somerset	Thomas, bp of Wells (repeat of 1340)
(1473	Fairfield House, Somerset	William Verney, see page 569)
1495	Athelhampton, Dorset	Sir William Martyn

DESTROYED

1377	Bishop's Cannings, Wiltshire	Robert, bp of Salisbury
	Ramsbury, Wiltshire	Robert, bp of Salisbury
	Potterne, Wiltshire	Robert, bp of Salisbury
	Bishop's Woodford, Wiltshire	Robert, bp of Salisbury
		(all repeat of 1337)
1380	Chideok, Dorset	Sir John Chidiok (repeat of 1370)
1457	Kentisbury, Devon	John Wolf and heirs
1462	Hatch Arundell, Devon	Thomas Gille
1515	Stonehouse, Devon	Sir Peter Edgcumbe

PLATE 304 Bewley Court: from the south-west

APPENDIX 7

THE ARCHITECTURAL VALUE OF JOHN LELAND AND THE BUCK BROTHERS

Throughout these volumes, constant reference has been made to the work of two primary topographical sources for late medieval England and Wales – the mid-sixteenth-century recorder John Leland and the mid-eighteenth-century artists Samuel and Nathaniel Buck. The former pioneered the practice of observation and direct inquiry in a sequence of travels across the Tudor countryside, while the latter made a pictorial record of over 400 medieval buildings at the point when their antiquarian value was being appreciated as much as their stimulation to romantic and picturesque sensibilities. Their architectural import, and in the case of the Buck brothers their accuracy, have been undervalued.

JOHN LELAND

John Leland (*c*.1503–52) was a youthful polymath – poet, antiquarian archivist, royal chaplain, librarian, and humanist – before he was thirty years old, when he received his royal commission to 'search after England's Antiquities, and peruse the libraries' of monasteries, cathedrals, and colleges for manuscripts of value (1533). The result is his *Itinerary*, a topographical compendium describing five journeys made between about 1539 and 1545, plus jottings and notes, most of them drawn up during his earlier visits to monastic libraries but some subsequent to his extended travels.[1] The publication drawn from the manuscripts now held in the Bodleian Library, Oxford[2] was initially edited by Thomas Hearne and published in 1710–12, with his notes following in 1715. The five-volume edition scrupulously prepared by Lucy Toulin Smith (1906–10) is the one invariably used today. It was reprinted with a preface by Sir Thomas Kendrick in 1964, and was turned into current English and rearranged by counties (excluding Wales) by John Chandler in 1993.

Leland's work was not a measured survey through England, and even less so Wales which was haphazardly covered between 1536 and 1539. Several counties, particularly Yorkshire and those of the Midlands and south-west England, were visited several times, while only scattered notes exist for those of south-east England, with East Anglia hardly covered at all.[3] Though Leland had gathered sufficient material by the close of 1545 to initiate writing the first of several planned works, he suffered a mental breakdown during 1547 that rendered him incapable of further work before his death five years later.

The value of Leland's *Itinerary* is manifold. It not only has topographical breadth and painstaking detail, but is a highly individual account by an eye-witness and insatiable researcher. Leland was not the earliest English topographical surveyor, for that honour falls to William Worcestre (1415–*c*.1485),[4] but the mammoth scale of Leland's enterprise far outstripped that of any previous traveller attempting to write a comprehensive description of England and Wales. His range was catholic – from archaeological sites to landscape, from newly extended churches to attractive gardens, from local industries to folklore. Leland's acute observation, indefatigable inquiry, and persistent research made him an ideal recorder.

Leland's mission was prompted by the Dissolution of the Monasteries, but in carrying out his assignment he built up a unique record of England and Wales at the point when the medieval way of life was being swept away by modernising forces.[5] He was not an easy or pleasant man, but by enjoying the hospitality of the aristocracy and gentry, this so-called 'king's antiquary' frequently pumped them for information. In Yorkshire, he talked to Sir Arthur Hopton of Swillington, Sir James Metcalfe of Nappa Hall, and Lord Scrope at Bolton Castle. He stayed with the earl of Westmorland at Brancepeth Castle and Lord Bergavenny at Raby in County Durham, and with Sir William Leyland at Morleys Hall in Lancashire. His host in Devon was Sir George Carew of Mohuns Ottery, and he enjoyed the Cornish hospitality of Sir John Arundell at Gwarnick, Sir William Godolphin at Breage, and Thomas Treffry at Fowey.

For the architectural historian, his work is peerless. For students of domestic architecture, he is our guide to the state of countless residences of late medieval England and Wales before they were modified, extended, or pulled down.[6] He frequently lists and describes the castles and their condition, notes the finest houses together with their parkland, identifies manor houses and their ownership, comments on recently built houses (particularly those of brick), and draws attention to monasteries newly adapted to secular use. Many residences are simply noted in passing, but others are pithily characterised from a fairly limited repertoire of adjectives. Those for Devon range from 'old' (Tawton Manor) and 'strong' (Powderham Castle) to 'fine' (Bishop's Clyst), 'very large' (Dartington Hall), 'excellent' (Tawstock Court) and 'with an embattled front' (Exminster Manor).[7] Occasional expansion proves particularly rewarding. At Tawton, 'Bishop Vesey had recently reduced the size of the house but made it more handsome.' At Dartington Hall, Leland's statement that after Sir Thomas St Ledger married the duchess of Exeter (1472) he set up home in that large manor house clarifies our interpretation of the excavations of the second courtyard.[8] His observation that 'George Rolls has built a very fine house of brick' at St Giles in the Wood near Torrington records the use of that material in Devon a hundred years earlier than any standing evidence.

Some of the largest residences are described in detail, such as the castles at Raby, Rockingham, Wressle, Thornbury, and Sudeley ('now falling into ruin, mores the pity'), the palaces at Scrooby and Bishop Auckland, and the fortified house at Harringworth. His description of Brancepeth Castle has enabled us to resolve the enigmatic layout of that much-altered fortress,[9] just as it facilitated the reconstruction of Edward IV's royal lodging range excavated at Nottingham Castle in the 1970s.[10] This inveterate traveller described the recent building expansion at Bishop's Waltham Palace and Grimsthorpe, and the recently completed houses at Belvoir, Groby, Melbury, Sugwas, and The Vyne.

A single word or phrase can characterise a house in a way that few official records do. South Wraxall Manor is 'small' while Berkeley Castle 'is no great thing' and was summarily dismissed. Sonning Palace was 'a good old stone built house', Chenies had been transformed to such an extent by Lord Russell 'that little or nothing remains unrestored', while Sir William Stanley transformed Ridley Hall 'from an old poor house into the finest gentleman's residence in the whole of Cheshire'. Leland is fascinated by the wall chimneys in the window heads of the hall at Bolton Castle extracting smoke from the central hearth, and finds great joy in the elaborate reading desk in the towered library at Wressle Castle.

Like any good recorder, Leland is frequently doubtful of the veracity of his informants. He disagrees with Lord Stourton by suggesting that the hillfort with double ditch in Stourton park was a manor house or castle, and thinks that the foundations in a garden at Castleford are those of a manor house and not of the castle as claimed by his informant. He could be critical. Seamer manor house 'is large but architecturally barren'; Sheffield Castle 'is far surpassed by Wingfield in Derbyshire even though it is only a manor house'. But occasionally his enthusiasm was uncontained. He 'saw no house in the north so much like the palace of a prince' as Sheriff Hutton Castle, while Wressle Castle bowled him over. 'In my opinion, this house is one of the most perfect beyond the river Trent and looks as though it is newly made . . . The castle wardrobe was exceptionally fine and so were the gardens inside the moat and the orchards outside it.'

He noted and sometimes described buildings now lost such as Henderskelfe (the precursor of Castle Howard), the 'fine stone house' at Plompton in Yorkshire, the strongly fortified monastery at Penrhyn in Cornwall, and a number of episcopal manor houses. He is sometimes the sole authority for historically important works such as Richard III's massive tower-house at Warwick Castle, the layout and character of the archbishop of York's manor house at Scrooby, and the form of the duke of Bedford's 'castle' at Fulford and its subsequent use as a building resource in the development of Compton Wynyates. He is also responsible for ascribing the construction of three houses and five castles to the spoils of the Hundred Years' War, identifying his source for four of them – Lord Stourton of Stourton, Sir William Berkeley of Beverston, Mr Hakluyt of Eyton, and Mr Tracy of Toddington for nearby Sudeley Castle – and is rightly sceptical of such ascriptions to the castles at Ampthill and Farleigh Hungerford. Long valued by antiquarians and topographers, John Leland's travels are an equally cogent resource for architectural scholars – ecclesiastical as much as secular – a careful eye-witness assessing a broad span of buildings on the cusp of that age of transition between late medieval and early modern England.

SAMUEL AND NATHANIEL BUCK

Landscape painting initially developed as vignettes to larger pictures in Flanders during the fifteenth century, with individual buildings first depicted in the accurate painted views of French palaces and castles in *Les Très Riches Heures du Duc de Berri* (c.1415). The convincing depiction of Kentchurch Court in the background portrait of 'Jack of Kentchurch' of c.1460 is a unique document in this country.[11] The practice became a subject in its own right in Italy during the later sixteenth century, where estate portraiture – the painting of country houses, gardens, and estates – is exemplified by Giusto Utens' prospects of the Medici villas (c.1599).

The first topographical artists in England were therefore foreigners, beginning with Wenceslaus Hollar (1606–77), who was born in Prague and came to England with Lord Arundel in 1636. His influence was wide because he was a master-etcher as well as a watercolour artist and he etched views for Dugdale's *Warwickshire* (1656) and Ashmole's *Windsor Castle* (c.1659). The Restoration encouraged a number of Flemish painters, including Jacob Knyff (d.1681) and Jan Siberechts (c.1700) who were the most important in developing the practice of bird's-eye views of houses, together with their gardens and estates. Knyff's views of Berkeley Castle and Siberechts' of Longleat exemplify their approach.

The early eighteenth century opened with two books developing the style of bird's-eye prospects, Leonard Knyff's eighty illustrations in *Britannia Illustrata* (1707) and those by Johannes Kip in Atkyns' *Gloucestershire* (1712). Their views were an accurate topographical record reflecting an owner's pride of possession, and it was this aspect which encouraged Samuel Buck, who dedicated his engraved views to the owners of the properties at that time, a practice which frequently complimented their long-held interest in county histories. The Buck brothers were to castles and abbeys what Knyff and Kip had been to country estates a generation earlier.[12]

Samuel Buck (1696–1779) was the pre-eminent eighteenth-century topographical recorder of medieval England and Wales. In 1721, this twenty-five-year-old artist set out to depict 'all the views of the most remarkable ruins of abbeys and castles now remaining'. His earliest work was of his home county, Yorkshire (1721–2), followed by Lincolnshire and Nottinghamshire. All the counties of England were covered during the next fifteen years, concluding with South Wales in 1740–41 and North Wales in 1742. Samuel was initially a draughtsman and engraver, who issued the first of a series of county volumes of twenty-four views of medieval ruins after he moved to London in the mid-1720s. He was assisted between 1727 and about 1754 by his brother Nathaniel, who died well before Samuel. It has not been possible to identify their respective responsibilities during their work together, though Samuel was the instigator.

Their practice was to obtain subscriptions from leading magnates and gentry within a clearly defined area a year in advance of publication. They would sketch the buildings during the summer months, work the material to finished drawings and engrave them during the winter months, and publish them in the following spring.[13] They specialised in views of medieval buildings but also undertook more than sixty panoramas of cities and towns, with a further twenty panoramas drawn and engraved between 1743 and 1753.[14]

Samuel retired from printmaking in 1754 and became a drawing master. Five years before his death, Robert Sayer issued all the engravings by the brothers in three volumes. The title page is the summation of their enterprise. 'Buck's Antiquities or venerable remains of above four hundred Castles, Monasteries, Palaces, etc. in England and Wales, with near one hundred views of Cities and

Chief Towns, by Messrs. Samuel and Nathaniel Buck who were employed upwards of thirty two years in the undertaking. In 3 volumes, volume 1 and 2 castles, monasteries, palaces etc. volume 3 of cities and chief towns. London, 1774.'

With few exceptions, all 428 buildings were medieval, with post-Reformation additions shown where monasteries had been converted to residential use (Chicksands Priory, Warden Monastery, Hinchingbroke Priory). In all, 240 castles were depicted, 150 monasteries, thirteen palaces, and twenty-five miscellaneous buildings. The last included some named houses (Drayton House, Scrivelsby Hall, Torksey Hall) plus a few mis-described (Camp's Castle, Dartington Temple, Minster Lovel Priory), and a number of late medieval castles. In all, over 120 residences detailed in these three volumes on greater medieval houses are illustrated in Buck's 'Antiquities'.

Buck was influenced by the panoramic approach of earlier Dutch artists working in England. A standard size, 14 ins. by 6 ins. was chosen for all 428 individual buildings, except for four country seats of later date.[15] An elevated viewpoint was used, sometimes low-set (Dartington Hall, Portchester Castle), sometimes bird's-eye (Whalley Abbey). The building was nearly always centrally positioned, outlined in pen and ink and then shaded, often with the addition of a grey wash to give further depth. The perspective was wide, usually over 200 degrees, and might include structures not visible from the chosen viewpoint (the gatehouse at Kenilworth Castle, the chapel at Sudeley Castle) to ensure maximum client interest. Occasionally Buck's bird's-eye view leads to foreshortening, so that Cockermouth Castle towers over the adjacent town, as Lord Cromwell's tower-house does over the ruined courtyard ranges at Tattershall Castle. The setting was often included (the River Wye at Chepstow Castle) and sometimes becomes the dominant feature (Abbotsbury Abbey, Belvoir Castle, Carisbroke Castle, Dinas Bran, though not at nearby Valle Crucis Abbey).

Nearly 90 per cent of the buildings engraved still survive in a state not too dissimilar to their earlier condition. A number have disappeared (Burstall Priory in Yorkshire, Chideok Castle in Dorset, Little Billing Priory in Northamptonshire, Horton and Widdrington castles in Northumberland). Some have become more fragmentary since Buck's day (Richmond Palace, and the castles at Kirkoswald, Pencelli, and Sheriff Hutton). Others have lost major structures such as the detached house at Scrivelsby Hall,[16] or have been drastically remodelled as at Powderham and Picton castles, Ewelme Manor, or Elton Hall – this last being one of the houses not included in the 1774 volumes. We are reliant on Buck for our appreciation of buildings now lost, such as the family apartments at Farleigh Hungerford Castle, the inner gatehouse at the Bishop's Palace, Wells, the gatehouse at Owston Abbey, and 'John of Gaunt's' Palace, Lincoln.

Though some commentators have disparaged them, the engravings by the Buck brothers are extremely reliable. Their work was painstaking and depended for its value on its accuracy. A poor representation of a building would be of little interest to their clients and their reputation would quickly suffer. Some of the earliest views (Sheriff Hutton Castle, Thornton Abbey gatehouse) show less precision than became standard, but the work was as true as possible in its detailing (Netley and Milton abbey churches). Its accuracy can be checked at a number of sites where there has been little change between the year of the engraving and the present day (Ashby de la

Zouch, Maxstoke, and Newport castles, Forde Abbey), or where alternative contemporary illustrative material exists (Berkeley and Warwick castles, Drayton House). This gives confidence to the validity of their work for structures subsequently destroyed.

Samuel and Nathaniel Buck were extremely capable draughtsmen, and were observant and hard-working. They could sometimes be pedestrian. Ranges can be too generalised (the upper ward at Windsor Castle, the courtyard at Belvoir Castle), while window tracery is not always shown with the precision we would wish (Ludlow Castle), but these barely disturb the incomparable value of this collection of engravings as a whole. Its value is immense for historical, architectural, and archaeological reasons. It is an outstanding cornucopia of information, particularly for properties lost or drastically altered since the mid-eighteenth century. This priceless resource, sometimes the only source of information, is without parallel for the next hundred years until the publication of T. Hudson Turner and John Parker's three volumes *Some Account of Domestic Architecture in England of the Middle Ages*.

NOTES

1 For Leland's career, *DNB*, XXXIII (1893) 13–17; T. D. Kendrick, *British Antiquity* (1950); T. S. Dorsch, 'Two English antiquaries: John Leland and John Stow', in *Essays and Studies* 12 (1959) 18–35; and the introductions to the editions by L. T. Smith, T. D. Kendrick and J. Chandler.

2 MS Top. Gen. e 8–15 for the itineraries; MS Top. Gen. c 3 for the *collectanea* with most of his notes.

3 There is little doubt that some of the gaps arise from manuscript losses after Leland's death, including a probable itinerary for East Anglia.

4 Leaving aside the summary description of England by the Chester monk Ranulph Higden in his *Polycronicon* of the 1340s, William Worcestre was the earliest architectural recorder in England. A member of Sir John Fastolf's household by 1438 and one of Fastolf's administrators after his death in 1459, Worcestre undertook two journeys to south-west England in 1478 and 1480 and one to East Anglia in 1479. His travels, written in Latin, include several descriptions and measurements of notable buildings. He accurately observed and noted his sources, a worthy exemplar to John Leland two generations later. William Worcestre, *Itineraries*, ed. J. H. Harvey (1969) and an essay by K. B. McFarlane in *Studies Presented to Sir Hilary Jenkinson*, ed. J. C. Davies (1957).

5 E. G. R. Taylor, 'Leland's England', in *An Historical Geography of England before AD 1800*, ed. H. C. Darby (1936) 330–53; M. McKisack, *Medieval History in the Tudor Age* (1971).

6 Unused, however, by Parker and Turner, Margaret Wood, or Maurice Barley in their books on medieval houses.

7 He pays particular attention to the houses of Cornwall, Cheshire, and Yorkshire where his epithets become warmer and more generous.

8 Page 544.

9 A. Emery, *Greater Med. Houses*, I (1996) 59.

10 C. Drage, *Trans. Thoroton Soc.* 93 (1989) 54–60.

11 *Greater Med. Houses*, II (2000) 554.

12 J. Harris, *The Artist and the Country House* (1979) 155.

13 *Samuel Buck's Yorkshire Sketchbook*, ed. I. Hall (1979). The sketchbooks are held in the Bodleian Library, Oxford, Gough Maps 3. They include properties not among those in the three volumes of 1774 such as Horston Castle, Derbyshire, and Sedbury Hall, Yorkshire.

14 *A Prospect of Britain: The Town Panoramas of S. & N. Buck*, ed. R. Hyde (1994).

15 Aston Hall, Melton Constable, Powderham Castle (part medieval), Worksop Manor (1744–5).

16 Buck shaded the gatehouse façade in the foreground to highlight the house behind, destroyed in 1956.

PLATES

ACKNOWLEDGEMENTS

The majority of photographs were taken by the author, but 82 and 83 were specially taken for this volume by The Royal Collection © 2004 Her Majesty Queen Elizabeth II. The following have been drawn from the collection of the National Monuments Record, Swindon: 1 5, 22, 23, 37, 38, 39, 43, 49, 56, 58, 59, 62, 63, 64, 68, 70, 75, 77, 101, 107, 119, 120, 128, 129, 130, 131, 132, 137, 146, 150, 151, 152, 155, 156, 157, 164, 165, 170, 171, 172, 183, 195, 201, 206, 215, 231, 239, 256, 268, 272. The author is also grateful for permission to reproduce their illustrations: Bath Archaeological Trust 17; Samuel Courtauld 89; the earl of Devon 267; Exeter City Museums 233; London, Guildhall Library 86; London, Museum of London, by Maggie Cox 95; London, Victoria and Albert Museum 142, 143; New York, Metropolitan Museum of Art 204; Jayne Semple 158; P.S. Stokes 42, 69, 76, 81; The National Trust 223; Wiltshire Archaeological and Natural History Society 273. The plans of Berkeley Castle are from the *Archaeological Journal* 122, and the drawings of Penshurst Place are taken from Marcus Binney and Anthony Emery, *The Architectural Development of Penshurst Place* (1973).

FIGURES

LIST OF FIGURES

INDEX

Detailed descriptions are given in bold type. Readers should also check for additional references on any given page.

INDEX OF HOUSES DESCRIBED IN VOLUMES I, II, AND III

Bold type identifies a detailed survey of the property. Light type identifies a brief description. For supplementary and passing references, see the individual indexes to each volume.